YOU WON'T FIND THESE
STATS IN ANY BOX SCORE

Get a whole new perspective on the game with the amazingly easy-to-understand TOPRs* and TPERs**. Unlike the standard individual records found in other books and in newspapers, these formulas take into account *everything* a player and his team do to help or hurt their run production. Little things like advancing the runner, getting batters to hit into double-plays, pickoffs, or taking the extra base loom large in who's really helping the club win games. Do these formulas work? You better believe it!

◇ In 1991, Seattle mistakenly traded away Bill Swift. Didn't they know he had the second best TPER in the league?

◇ Through 1992, Dwight Gooden's average TPER shows that his abilities have fallen to that of a third or fourth starter.

◇ Barry Bond's 1992 TOPR was the best offensive year in the big leagues in decades. Would he repeat?

◇ The Philadelphia Phillies' 1992 team TOPR/TPER revealed a little better pitching could project them right to the top of their division.

What will the '93 TOPRs and TPERs say about the 1994 season?

NORM HITZGES is a radio talk-show host in Dallas and a TV announcer for the Texas Rangers. He is the first analyst since Howard Cosell to hold a network analyst's job (ESPN) without having played the game, and is the author of *The Historical Sports Almanac,* a highly acclaimed book on the bizarre happenings in sports history. **DAVE LAWSON** is an unusual combination of baseball fanatic, numbers cruncher, career marketing man, and Alabama farmer. He developed the Hitzges-Lawson statistical method of player and team analysis.

---

*TOPR: (TOE-per) Total Offensive Production Rating
**TPER: (TEE-per) Total Pitching Effectiveness Rating

ESSENTIAL BASEBALL 1994

A REVOLUTIONARY
NEW METHOD FOR EVALUATING
MAJOR LEAGUE TEAMS,
PLAYERS, AND MANAGERS

NORM HITZGES AND DAVE LAWSON

A PLUME BOOK

PLUME
Published by the Penguin Group
Penguin Books USA Inc., 375 Hudson Street,
New York, New York 10014, U.S.A.
Penguin Books Ltd, 27 Wrights Lane,
London W8 5TZ, England
Penguin Books Australia Ltd, Ringwood,
Victoria, Australia
Penguin Books Canada Ltd, 10 Alcorn Avenue,
Toronto, Ontario, Canada M4V 3B2
Penguin Books (N.Z.) Ltd, 182-190 Wairau Road,
Auckland 10, New Zealand

Penguin Books Ltd, Registered Offices:
Harmondsworth, Middlesex, England

First published by Plume, an imprint of Dutton Signet, a division of Penguin Books USA Inc.

First Printing, March, 1994
10 9 8 7 6 5 4 3 2 1

Copyright © RATIOnal Baseball, Inc., 1994
All rights reserved

Printed in the United States of America
Designed by Folio Graphics Co. Inc.

Acknowledgments

With unending thanks to my first baseball broadcast partner, Merle Harmon, who deserves a spot in the announcer's wing of baseball's Hall of Fame and who already secured a place of honor in the "human Hall of Fame."

Many thanks to the Texas Rangers' Vice President of Public Relations, John Blake, and his staff, John Ralph, Taunee Paur and Michelle Salisbury, for the cheery way they always went about satisfying our endless stream of requests for information.

Thanks to Houston Astros Public Relations men Rob Matwick and Tyler Barnes for going far out of their way to send valuable information during the time when the writing crunch was the worst.

NORM HITZGES

◆

Thanks go to the following, without whom this book never would have happened:

STATS Inc. provided the current major league statistics reported herein, as well as the raw data employed in the TOPR and TPER formulas. Steve Moyer and Art Ashley get credit for translating our sometimes obscure requests for data. Thanks, fellas.

Howe Sportsdata International, the official statmonger to the minor leagues, delivered all of the minor league statistics as reported and included in the formulas. The applause belongs to Jay Virshbo.

Jake Lawson conducted all of the data processing, designed and produced every one of the graphics in the text, and offered welcome editorial comment. All this in his spare time, plus moral support and assistance above and beyond the call of sonship. This book, and his dad's life, would be awfully empty without him.

Paul Chung, who believed in the book's concept from the outset. As a consequence, all the baseball fans in the Lantz Harris Literary Agency joined the team and set about finding the book's best publisher—all "in the best interests of baseball."

Deb Brody, an editor blessed with great insight and patience, who still saw that we got it done, and done right. If not on time, it was close, nearly. Maybe. We'll be better next year, Deb, we promise.

DAVE LAWSON

CONTENTS

Baseball's plentiful database, coupled with the capabilities of the computer, have given us a welter of new statistics. Some of them are meaningful . . . many are not. In this statistical grab bag, it's not easy to determine which is which.

Worse, though, is the fact that this statistical flood has distracted our attention from the "forest" to the "trees" . . . the "underbrush" even. Now, we're told things like who was the league's best batter with a runner on 3rd, the count 3-and-2 with less than two outs in the 7th inning or later. And, if we wanted to know who led this category in road games only, well, somebody's got the answer to that too.

But do we *really* care? *Should* we care? Aren't we more interested in who the best player was, the best 2nd baseman, the best relief corps? How our team stood, what was right, what was wrong, what was needed, what wasn't? Who "won" a trade?

Of course, we're more interested in answers to these questions because *these questions are more important!*

This book concerns itself with these questions. We believe that the TOPR and TPER concept we've devised are a way to answer them intelligently, objectively and clearly. And, by golly, once we get out of the briers and brambles of its statistical "underbrush," the baseball "forest" is a beautiful sight indeed.

Consider, for example, what we found out about runs and where they come from. Runs are the glossy "finished product" that's assembled from the drab "raw material" of bases. Seems simple enough. But how much of this raw material does it take to produce a run? Turns out it takes right about *four* bases to make a run. That's the kind of delicate symmetry we found in our baseball "forest."

Just as no two snowflakes are identical, there is a seemingly infinite variation in the methods of manufacturing a run—from the majestic 450-foot home run to the sublime walk + swipe + bunt + blooper. But, no matter the method, over the course of a long season the number of runs a team scores will have an average constitution of about *four* bases—just as each and every one of those singular snowflakes has six sides. "Power" team or "speed" team, it makes no difference. No kidding! The "natural" laws of baseball, it seems, are no less unrelenting than the laws of nature.

When these baseball "laws" are flouted by teams and managers, when they waste a portion of their immutable 27 outs or grant their opponent an extra out or an unearned base, they pay the price. Like nature, baseball rewards the thrifty, and unerringly punishes the profligate.

Given this new and clear perspective on the game provided by TOPR and TPER, we are better able to appreciate that every base is valuable, each baserunner is precious and all outs are ugly—but only from one side.

Let's take a closer look.

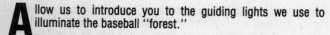

TOPR AND TPER EXPLAINED

Allow us to introduce you to the guiding lights we use to illuminate the baseball "forest."

◆ TOPR stands for Total Offensive Production Rating. It consolidates and quantifies all of the measurable areas of a given player's offensive accomplishments in a *single number*. We pronounce it TOE-per.
◆ TPER is Total Pitching Effectiveness Rating. It does the same thing for pitchers, directly opposing their performance to the batter's performance. Just like real life. It's pronounced TEE-per.

TOPR and TPER are tools that, for the first time ever, allow the measurement of everybody who plays the game—be he hitter or pitcher—by a single authoritative yardstick. Who contributed more to his team—the leadoff hitter who scored 120 runs or the cleanup man who drove in 120 runs? The .320 hitter or the 20-game winner? Or was it the manager? Conventional statistics provide ammunition for a good argument. TOPR and TPER provide the insight for an informed judgment.

TOPR and TPER are derived from a formula, of course. We'll get to that in awhile. First, it's important to understand the concept behind them.

The TOPR Concept

Let's start at the beginning.

What is a hitter's *job*?

Is it to produce wins? Well, we would hope that a hitter, finding himself in a game-winning situation, would respond with a game-winning hit. This was even an official statistic for awhile, remember? But the stat's vacuity was apparent and it was quickly dropped from baseball's ledgers. Basing a hitter's job description on "wins" would be equally vacuous.

Is it to produce runs? Runs are, after all, the stuff wins are made of. This has become a popular answer and most would now define the hitter's job in these terms. As in: A hitter's job is to generate *runs*.

But how does an individual hitter do this? What is the *only* way a hitter can generate a run single-handedly? The home run, of course. Yet home runs, by themselves, account for only 19% of all runs scored.

It follows that the vast bulk of all runs scored, over 80%, are the fruits of cooperation, a *team* accomplishment. Even the vaunted 3-run homer requires the cooperation of at least two teammates.

It is thus very difficult to assign a responsibility for "runs" to an individual hitter's job description, except in a remote way (runs scored or driven in) or in a theoretical fashion (runs "created"). But judging an individual's job performance on remote factors over which he has little or no control can be misleading. Any employee in the nation's workforce can tell you this. Similarly, judging how well a hitter's doing his job "in theory" has obvious problems, no matter how sound the theory.

What, then, *is* a hitter's job? What is it that you want from him that he can provide on his own and that he can then be judged by? The answer is obvious! An individual hitter's job is to produce *bases*—the stuff that runs are made of. It is the *team's* job to convert these bases into runs.

This particular insight is the starting point for TOPR.

We can readily measure a player's production of bases but, if we're serious about this thing, we have to measure something else too, don't we? We have to measure his "cost of production": how many outs did he "spend" to deliver his bases?

Outs are, in essence, a baseball team's "capital." Every baseball team enters every game with the same amount of limited "capital." Each team is allotted 27 outs, practically speaking, to achieve their desired result. How they spend these outs, and what they get for them, will determine the outcome. Thus, we need to be concerned with a hitter's "productivity."

In business, productivity is measured as "output per unit of cost"—as in "widgets per dollar." In baseball it's the same thing—only "output per unit of cost" translates to "bases per out." A hitter who produces *more* than his share of the output while consuming *less* than his share of the team's capital is, by definition, a productive hitter.

The hitter's job description is thereby modified to read:

◆ A hitter's job is to produce bases *and* minimize outs.

Accordingly, his job performance, his productivity, is measured by bases produced per out committed. This is the measurement that TOPR yields. We have only to calculate the results. We'll get into the precise method we use shortly.

The TPER Concept

If the hitter's job is to produce bases and avoid making an out, then what is the pitcher's job? It *must* be the exact opposite of the hitters job, mustn't it? So we arrive at this job description for the pitcher.

◆ A pitcher's job is to generate outs, and to minimize bases.

A pitcher's productivity is thus measured by the same formula as a hitter's. Only this time it's expressed as bases *allowed* per out *generated*. We call this measurement TPER and it's calculated just like TOPR, utilizing the identical elements.

If all of this seems absurdly simple to you, it's because it *is* that simple. The TOPR and TPER concepts are fundamentally sound, amazingly free of complexity and crystal clear: Productivity in baseball is measured by bases vs. outs, *all* bases and *all* outs, output relative to cost.

The "forest" is beginning to emerge from the statistical mists.

The TOPR and TPER Formulas

The TOPR formula provides a straightforward calculation of Net Bases Earned (NBE) by a player relative to his Gross Outs Committed (GOC). TPER is TOPR's mirror image, Net Bases Allowed (NBA) relative to Gross Outs Earned (GOE). In actuality, there is only one formula, the difference being the term in which the result is expressed.

Note our introduction of "gross" and "net" into the discussion, for they have an important bearing on the results. Take double plays for example. Doesn't a hitter who grounds into a DP *cost* his team a base that was previously earned by a teammate? Does he not also cost his team one *more* out than will be recorded in his batting statistics? The TOPR/TPER formula accommodates these broader results. All base-running events are treated in this "double-edged" fashion, as any outs that may occur simultaneously erase previously earned bases.

The Formula:

TOPR/TPER

Players:

$$\frac{\text{Net Bases Earned (NBE)}}{\text{Gross Outs Committed (GOC)}} =$$

Pitchers:

$$\frac{\text{Net Bases Allowed (NBA)}}{\text{Gross Outs Earned (GOE)}} =$$

$$\frac{H+BB+HP+XB+SH+SF+SB-(CS+GDP)}{(AB-H)+SH+SF+CS+GDP}$$

In Which:

H = Hits
BB = Bases on Balls
HP = Hit by Pitch
XB = Extra Bases
SH = Sacrifice Hits

SF = Sacrifice Flies
SB = Stolen Bases
CS = Caught Stealing
GDP = Grounded into Double Play
AB = At Bats

You'll note the following about the TOPR/TPER formula:

1. Every one of the elements employed are more or less common and generally available statistics. There's nothing obscure in the equation.
2. There are no statistician's abstractions or value judgments. The formula is composed solely of certifiable facts.
3. The formula's construction exactly reproduces each event in terms of its actual impact on bases and outs. The sac hits, for example, produce a base (in the numerator) and an out (in the denominator) just as they do on the field.
4. The formula, with its ten separate elements, is an *extremely* complete accounting of a player's entire offensive output and the outs which he committed or was responsible for. Similarly, for a pitcher, it's a complete record of the output he allowed and outs generated.

In sum, the TOPR/TPER formula is a complete and precise record of what a player or pitcher accomplished. It is what actually happened, not what somebody thinks may have happened.

The Unified Number

There's one more step to get to the single number that is TOPR and TPER.

What the above formula generates is a ratio of Net Bases to Gross Outs (e.g., NBE/GOC for a player, NBA/GOE for a pitcher). TOPR and TPER express this ratio in relationship to all the other players and pitchers in the league. This technique is called "indexing" and it's easy enough to do and to understand. We simply calcuate the NBE/GOC ratio for the league and make that equivalent to a TOPR (or TPER) of 100. Then we compare the individual player's NBE/GOC ratio to the league's ratio and express the difference relative to the 100 base. Like this:

TOPR/TPER Calculation:

	Net Bases (NBE or NBA)	Gross Outs (GOC or GOE)	Net Base/Gross Out Ratio	League Ratio	TOPR or TPER
1993 National League	39684	61294	.647	.647	100
1993 Barry Bonds	506	388	1.304	.647	201
1993 Greg Maddux	387	810	.478	.647	74

The average NL player in '93 produced .647 net bases for every gross out he consumed. This ratio also represents the output allowed by the average NL pitcher (league TOPR and TPER are always the same). The league's MVP, Barry Bonds, produced an astounding 1.304 net bases for every gross out, so that he was +101% more productive than the average player. He thus earns a TOPR of 201 which, let us assure you, is about as big as they come in TOPRdom.

The league's Cy Young winner, Greg Maddux, yielded only .478 net bases per gross out. This being −26% below the league average, it earns him a 74 TPER. With a number like that, there's no question he's an "ace."

That's it. TOPR and TPER are one *single* number that quantifies an individual player's or pitcher's complete performance package and, at the same time, rates him relative to his peers.

How good was Barry Bonds? A 201 TOPR says volumes.

A Demonstration Ride

Let's give the formula a test drive. How did the season records of American League Championship Series opponents Roberto Alomar and Jack McDowell stack up in TOPR and TPER terms?

TOPR/TPER Demonstration:

Line	TOPR Element	Symbol	1993 AL	1993 R. Alomar	1993 McDowell	Symbol	TPER Element
1.	At Bats	AB	77505	589	981	AB	At Bats
2.	Hits	H	20661	192	261	H	Hits Allowed
3.	Walks	BB	8006	80	69	BB	Walks Allowed
4.	Hit by Pitch	HP	633	5	3	HP	Hit with Pitch
5.	Extra Bases	XB	10937	98	111	XB	Extra Bases Allowed
6.	Total Batter Bases	TBB	40237	375	444	TBB	Total Batter Bases
7.	Total Batter Outs (AB-H)	TBO	56844	397	720	TBO	Total Batter Outs
8.	Batter Ratio	Ratio	.708	.945	.617	Ratio	Batter Ratio
9.	Sacrifice Hits	SH	702	4	8	SH	Sacrifice Hits Against
10.	Sacrifice Flies	SF	729	5	6	SF	Sacrifice Flies Against
11.	Stolen Bases	SB	1549	55	10	SB	Stolen Bases Against
12.	Caught Stealing	CS	-871	-15	-15	CS	Caught Stealing Against
13.	Grounded into DP	GDP	-1874	-13	-19	GDP	Ground DP Induced
14.	Net Baserunner Bases	BRB	325	36	(10)	BRB	Net Baserunner Outs
15.	Gross Baserunner Outs	BRO	4086	37	48	BRO	Gross Baserunner Outs
16.	Baserunner Utilization	Ratio	.080	.973	-.208	Ratio	Baserunner Control
17.	Net Bases Earned	NBE	40562	411	434	NBA	Net Bases Allowed
18.	Gross Outs Committed	GOC	60930	434	768	GOE	Gross Outs Earned
19.	NBE/GOC Ratio	Ratio	.666	.947	.565	Ratio	NBA/GOE Ratio
20.	Total Offensive Production Rating	TOPR	100	142	85	TPER	Total Pitching Effectiveness Rating

Normally, we display TOPR/TPER lines horizontally. This demonstration is arranged vertically so as to make the basic math easier to follow. The TOPR and TPER elements are arranged in two sub-sets:

a. The Batter Sub-set—which consolidates the bases and outs as a *hitter*. This result is summarized on lines #6 and #7 as Total Batter Bases (TBB) and Total Batter Outs (TBO) with their resultant Batter Ratio on line #8.

b. The Baserunner Sub-set—which consolidates *net* bases and *gross* outs recorded as a baserunner, or in concert with another baserunner. This result appears on lines #14 and #15 as Baserunner Bases (BRB) and Baserunner Outs (BRO). BRB is the net of sac hits + sac flies + stolen bases less caught stealing and double plays. BRO is the gross of sac hits + sac flies + caught stealing + double plays. The resultant Baserunner Utilization (or Control) ratio appears on line #16.

It's apparent from the demonstration that we're dealing with two highly productive and multiskilled talents here. Alomar hit for average (.326 BA), drew walks, slugged extra bases (.492 SLG) and ran the bases exceptionally well (55 SB in 70 attempts). Strong in every area of performance, he earned almost one base for every out he committed and produced a 142 TOPR—one of the ten best figures in the league. Note that, comparatively, his strongest suit was the Baserunner Sub-set, where the league average ratio was a pathetic .080 net bases/gross outs and Alomar's ratio was an eye-popping .973.

McDowell's performance was, from a pitcher's viewpoint, equally impressive. He gave up an average number of hits (.266 BA). But his opponents didn't walk (.314 OBP) nor hit for power (.379 SLG) and failed miserably on the basepaths (10 SB in 25 attempts). McDowell allowed only .565 net bases for every gross out he earned, good for an 85 TPER—one of the best marks in the league. Like Alomar, McDowell's Baserunner Sub-set reveals a strength. His utter control of baserunners not only created outs for his team, he was actually taking bases *away* from the opposition. It's not generally appreciated, but there is a wide variation among pitchers in this respect (as wide as it is among hitters, in fact) and it can make a crucial difference in their relative success.

The Case for TOPR and TPER

Now that you know what these TOPR and TPER critters are and how they're calculated, your next question is "How well do they work?"

For one thing, how do TOPR and TPER, which are predicated on bases, relate to runs? When you reach the Teams section, you'll find that the relationship of TOPR to runs scored and TPER to runs allowed is very, very close. You could even say *intimate*. Further, in '93 it took the AL 3.80 net bases to score a run while the NL used 3.89 net bases to put a mark on the board. In other words, around four bases per run. Somehow, that sounds about right.

Do TOPR and TPER have anything to do with winning? Just about everything, it seems.

When you view the '93 W–L standings, you'll find that the TOPR and TPER "standings" are almost precisely parallel. By applying TOPR and TPER to previous seasons, we've found that this result is the rule rather than the exception.

We also applied the concept to all 2,268 major league games played in '93. The team with the highest TOPR won 2,064 of them, or 91%. TOPR's record in one-run games was, in its own way, even more impressive: a winning percentage of .771 which will cop a pennant in any league.

TOPR + TPER = RPER

While it took the average team in the AL 3.80 net bases to plate a run (3.89 in the NL), some of the individual teams took a little more, others a little less. While the TOPR/TPER "standings" are *almost* precisely parallel to the actual league standings, they aren't *precisely* parallel. While the team with the highest TOPR won 2,064 games, what happened to the other 204?

TOPR's and TPER's extraordinary level of accuracy as a rule, caused us to believe that the few exceptions might be subject to yet another "law of baseball." Indeed they are, and we call it RPER (REE-per) for Run Production Efficiency Ratio. It has both an offensive and a defensive face to it, and it's a corollary of TOPR and TPER.

We established earlier that the individual player's and pitcher's job was concerned with bases. Runs, however, are the *team's* affair. The "team," importantly, includes the manager, whose impact on a team's performance may be considerably greater than we've been led to believe.

Some teams are curiously more efficient in converting their "raw material"—bases—into "finished product"—runs. Some teams impede their opponent's conversion process to a greater degree than others do. These differences tend to be minute, but they are nonetheless detectable by TOPR and TPER, and can make for a critical margin in the "W" column. Further, the differences trace to various sources—besides defense, of course, there is lineup constitution, staff construction, team "chemistry" and overall game management. These areas generally lie in the manager's realm and RPER is thus not only a team statistic, it is a manager's statistic.

TOPR and TPER vs. Conventional Statistics

TOPR and TPER don't so much replace conventional statistics as gather them into a single comprehensive number that expresses the whole of a player's or pitcher's productivity.

Each of the conventional individual hitting statistics find their way into TOPR and each is placed in its proper perspective. Batting average is represented by the inclusion of both hits and at bats, extra bases covers the slugging stats, walks and hit by pitch detail the on-base factor. Similarly, all of the factors relating to baserunning and advancing (or erasing) other baserunners are incorporated.

A couple of comments in this regard:

◆ On-Base Percentage (OBP) emerges as, by far, the most *powerful* of the conventional stats included in TOPR. This is because on-base ability is reflected on both sides of the TOPR equation: when a player reaches base he has, at the same time, *avoided an out*. The ability to reach base is revealed to be the single most valuable offensive ability and every one of the top TOPR players have it.

◆ Runs and RBIs play no role in the calculations of TOPR, nor should they. They are "team dependent" statistics, where an individual's total is largely reliant on those teammates batting behind or in front of the player in question. A player with a high on-base component in his TOPR is certainly in a position to score runs, but will he? Similarly, a player with a high power component is capable of driving in scads of runs—but *only* if there are teammates on base in front of him. Thus, OBP and Slugging Percentage (SLG) are better measures of the player's *capability* than are the raw totals he may be credited with.

The major benefit of TOPR, as a tool, is its all-inclusive nature. It conclusively identifies a player's overall offensive value and places him in a league-wide perspective. TOPR not only resolves the ongoing argument about who is the "best hitter" in baseball, for example, it also tells you by how much and why. Hint: '93 "best hitter" played on the West Coast, was +12% more productive than the runner-up, excelled in every category of offensive performance and had a daddy who could play some ball, too.

TPER resolves the same argument for pitchers, which is an even bigger step forward. Heretofore, rating the relative value of pitchers has been fraught with confusion. Until quite recently, starters were largely judged by their W–L record. The problem with this stat is that it is *highly* team dependent. A starter with the benefit of strong offensive support and a bulletproof bullpen is going to produce "wins" at a much higher rate than an equivalent pitcher laboring without this kind of team context (see Bob Welch, Oakland '90). There is a recognition now that ERA may be more indicative of a pitcher's performance and, without doubt, it is. Durability and dependability belong somewhere in our consideration, as well.

When it come to relievers, though, we're at sea again. The save count seems to dominate the discussion. But, yet, saves are like wins—highly dependent on team context and opportunity. A reliever's ERA has a place in this discussion too, but is rightly perceived to be of marginal importance. After all, one bad outing can "spoil" a reliever's ERA after twenty good outings. Plus a low ERA for a reliever doesn't necessarily mean that the reliever didn't "spoil" the starter's ERA by allowing inherited runners to score.

Finally, where do middle relievers fit in the picture? They have only the vapid "hold" statistic going for them and what does that mean, really?

In general, though, there seems to be a settled opinion gathering around ERA as being the most meaningful of a pitcher's stats, for all its recognized faults.

But, wait! TPER defines the pitcher's job as being "to generate outs and suppress bases." Runs, earned or otherwise, are the product of those bases, but the team shares importantly in the responsibility for the runs which may ensue.

Errors that cost outs and/or bases are one factor. The "earned" aspect of ERA gives only *partial* credit to the pitcher in this circumstance; the resultant run isn't charged to him. But neither does he get credit for the additional ⅓ of an inning he had to pitch as a result. TPER corrects this understatement of his effectiveness. What about misplays, a missed cutoff man resulting in an extra base on a throw or a botched fielder's choice which failed to produce the out that should have been there? ERA takes a "tough luck" position. TPER gives credit where credit is due. What about the bullpen? A pitcher's ERA is charged for runs that occurred while he was lathering up in the shower. Didn't the reliever at least *share* in the responsibility for these runs? TPER says he did. Finally, what about the pitcher who is unsettled by an untimely error and proceeds to get whacked, at no cost to his ERA? TPER credits him for the missing out, while it continues to hold him responsible for his subsequent failure.

Individually, these are minor calibrations. Cumulatively, they can loom large. ERA may have been the most meaningful pitcher's statistic in the past. But TPER surpasses it. TPER is the one statistic that amasses all of his debits and credits and gauges his performance strictly by what *he* did when *he* was on the mound. That's a breakthrough.

Moreover, TPER allows us to compare vastly different pitchers, Randy Johnson vs. Bill Swift, for example, and arrive at a solid conclusion as to their relative effectiveness. Or, alternately, cast the performance of a middle reliever (say, Mike Perez) against a closer (say, Lee Smith) and determine who's doing the better job.

TOPR and TPER Applications

The beauty of TOPR and TPER is that, as we work with them, we keep finding new applications—revealing more and more of the baseball "forest." Some examples that you'll see in other sections of this book:

◆ Team TOPR/TPER. A team is the composite of its individuals. Thus, teams have TOPRs and TPERs of their own, TOPRs and TPERs that rather precisely describe their performance and the reason(s) for their success and failures. We'll explore this issue in the Team section, including an assessment of exactly what it takes to win a championship.

◆ Batting and Baserunning Sub-sets. These segments of TOPR and TPER yield useful insights on certain players and pitchers. But the Baserunning sub-set really comes into its own when it's viewed on a team or league basis. You'll find more about this in the Team section and a study of the "NL Game."

◆ Park TOPR. We've calculated a value for each major league park in terms of the effect it has on offense. This becomes a *giant* issue when we discuss the Colorado Rockies.

◆ TOPR and TPER Trendlines. There is a distinct pattern in the year-to-year performance of individual players and pitchers. Their careers will tend to follow a generally well-defined curve from their rookie season to their retirement year. In this sense, their future TOPR and TPER performance becomes semi-predictable. You'll see considerable use of this application in the Free Agent Market section.

◆ TOPR and TPER Profiles. It turns out there are four, not three, basic offensive skills. Just "hitting for average, hitting for power

and running the bases" isn't good enough. TOPR and TPER profiles, for players, pitchers and teams, reveal a fourth—strike zone judgment (or command, if you're a pitcher).

◆ Prospect TOPR and TPER. It turns out that TOPR and TPER are equally applicable to the minor leagues. A rookie's true ability need no longer be an unfathomable mystery. The Farm section deals with this.

◆ Game TOPR. The TOPR concept, when applied to individual games, yielded highly positive results, as we mentioned earlier. TOPR is, in fact, a whole new way to "keep score." In most instances, it highlights exactly how a given game was won (or lost). We'll discuss this further at an appropriate point.

◆ Historical TOPR and TPER. Just because TOPR and TPER are children of the '90s doesn't mean they can't look backward. We'll take a peek in one of our essays.

◆ Projection TOPR and TPER. If the TOPR and TPER trendlines for the players and pitchers are "semi-predictable," might not the composite team composed of these individuals be "semi-predictable"? We tried it prior to the '93 season and the results are reported in the closing essay.

TOPR and TPER are a whole new way to look at our grand ol' game. Paradoxically, it seems that the best way to get a fresh, inside look at the game was, first, to get *outside* . . . away from the "underbrush" and stifling statistical mists, into the open spaces.

The view from there is *terrific*. The game once again becomes what it is: an elemental children's game of bases and outs, chock-full of both powerful drama and delicate nuance. An absolute delight, enjoyable at every level of understanding.

Here's hoping that TOPR and TPER contribute to your understanding. Now, let's set about ending some old arguments . . . and starting some new ones.

THE PLAYERS

SEE HOW THEY RANK

Ranking systems have become the rage of baseball analysis. But that shouldn't be terribly surprising. After all, it now seems as if baseball statistics record every player's every move from first appearance to farewell. What is more natural than to try to employ these statistics to somehow rank the players, either out of curiosity (if you're a fan) or out of professional interest (if you're an organization or a member of the media).

This quite natural inclination has led to as many ranking systems as there are opinions—and you know how many of *those* there are. Some are valid. Some are absolutely opaque. Some are just weird.

Herewith, our contribution to this mélange: The TOPR Rankings, our attempt to clarify the whole issue in one authoritative and conclusive stroke. After reading the first chapter, you know how we do it: the player's productivity, as determined by production (Net Bases Earned or NBE) vs. cost (Gross Outs Committed or GOC), expressed as a single number relative to the entire league's average productivity.

To start with—drum roll, please—let's present TOPR's Top 10 for both major leagues in 1993. Our "Ten Most Offensive":

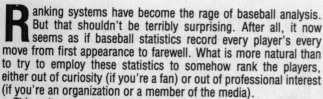

TOPR presents:

the Ten Most Offensive 1993

American League			National League	
1. John Olerud	179		1. Barry Bonds	201
2. Frank Thomas	170		2. Lenny Dykstra	152
3. Rickey Henderson	162		3. Andres Galarraga	151
4. Ken Griffey, Jr.	161		4. Darren Daulton	149
5. Chris Hoiles	157		5. John Kruk	147
6. Juan Gonzalez	150		6. Rick Wilkins	145
7. Rafael Palmeiro	146		7. Gregg Jefferies	141
8. Roberto Alomar	142		8. Fred McGriff	140
9. Tim Salmon	141		9. Mike Piazza	138
10. Paul Molitor	139		10. Larry Walker	136

First, let it be known that we do *not* purport that these lists represent the "Ten Best Players" in the AL or NL. Such a list would have to take into account—among other things—defensive talents and leadership ability and we aren't measuring these things. We *do* purport, however, that these ten players had the most productive offensive seasons in their respective leagues in 1993. This we *are* measuring—with absolute precision.

A few comments:

◆ Bonds' TOPR of 201 represents the fact that he was *twice* as productive as the average NL player. We've been accumulating TOPRs from 1980 forward; Bonds' 1993 performance is unprecedented—except for his own 1992 season, which was even *better* (217). His past two seasons are worth special treatment which you'll find later in the book.
◆ It was a vintage year for catchers. Four made the combined Top Tens of the two leagues, and Mike Stanley ranked #11 in the AL.
◆ It was a good year for the Jays and the Phillies, too. When three or four of a team's players make TOPR's Top 10, they *should* be in the World Series.
◆ One rookie made the Top 10 in each league. That made choosing TOPR Rookies-of-the-Year pretty easy, didn't it?

◆ Middle infielders and hitters from outside the middle-of-the-order are hard to find in the Top 10 of TOPRdom. That's understandable. Their job definitions tend to emphasize qualities other than "massive offensive output." We should, therefore, extend special respect to Messrs. Alomar, Henderson and Dykstra—all of whom did more, much more, than their spots in the field and/or the batting order called for.

How about the rest of the players? How did they rank?

Organization of the Rankings

In the following pages, we rank every major league player who reached 200 Total Plate Appearances (TPA)—along with a few who didn't, but we thought you'd be interested in them nonetheless. They're ranked by position, based on where they played the most games or, in some cases, where they clearly "belong." They are assigned to the league in which they finished the season. Each position is broken into three subcategories:

◆ *Regulars*—Guys who made over 400 TPA, plus the ones you'd immediately recognize as "regular" if he hadn't been hurt part of the season.
◆ *Others*—Guys who made over 200 TPA, but you wouldn't call them regulars (except in platoon roles).
◆ *Of Note*—Guys who made 100–199 TPA, but should be of interest to somebody outside their immediate family.

We did something else, too, that we hope you appreciate. We created a new position—IMPs, for Impact Multiple Position players. Where else would you have us classify Tony Phillips? As a utility player, you suggest? No! Tony Phillips is emphatically *not* a utility player as we understand the term. Besides, we have a separate ranking for utility players, all their own. Overlooked by other annual guides, we thought IMPs deserved better.

Symbols

We have footnotes on each of the ranking tables. But to save you from eyestrain, here's what they mean:

( ) A parenthesis around somebody's TOPR number means that he had less than 200 TPA. Our experience leads us to believe that, below 200 TPA, TOPR may not have enough data to chew on and can become a little less definitive. Directionally, though, it still seems a fair indicator of whether a player is going to be a fizzle, a titan or merely average.

* An asterisk means under 100 TPA. While we're not statisticians, we recognize that a TOPR number based on such a small sample isn't worth squat. So, we don't report the results, except in cases of announced retirement, where the TOPR number won't be the subject of anybody's judgment. Nor did we include such meaningless fragments in anybody's average.

– The dash simply means the player didn't appear in the majors that particular year. He could have been anywhere else (e.g., in the minors, college or Japan).

† The dagger indicates that the player accumulated at least part of his TOPR in the other major league that particular year. We rigorously keep AL and NL league data separate for reasons which shall become obvious.

TOPR Trendline Format

Here's an example of what you'll be seeing in the ranking section.

			7/1/94		.	TOPR Trendline		.	1993
Rank	Player	Team	Age	B	_1990_	_1991_	_1992_	3 yr Avg.	TOPR
1.	Chris Hoiles	BAL	29	R	*	86	140	111	**157**

Most of this is self-explanatory. Chris Hoiles was the #1 TOPR catcher in the American League. BAL is, of course, Baltimore. We've used the more-or-less standard three-letter code for major league teams throughout.

The player's age is expressed as "baseball age," i.e., as of July 1 for the coming 1994 season. Age is an _extremely_ important consideration in understanding a player's past performance and projecting his future, as is coming to be generally realized. It has been demonstrated by others that most players "peak" in their late twenties, 27 being the most likely single year, and darned if TOPR doesn't confirm exactly that. There is a distinct TOPR "curve" that reveals this pattern clearly.

The TOPR Trendline gives you the player's performance for the previous three seasons (1990–1992). You'll note that a clear trend is generally evident and is summed up in the three-year average (which is technically a "weighted" average, taking into account the player's number of appearances and the league norms for each year in the average). Note also that if there is a parenthesis, an asterisk or a dash in somebody's trendline, and we had a 1989 major league TOPR to fall back on, we used it to help bolster the reported 1990–1992 average. The "3 year average" should be considered the player's _established level of ability_, going into 1993—when, for better or for worse, he shed even more light on his talent.

Now, you can view Hoiles' 1993 performance in perspective. He broke in with a September trial in 1990, which didn't amount to much, in terms of opportunity or performance. In his '91 rookie season, he struggled some, managing to be, for a catcher, barely adequate offensively. In '92, at the age of 27 we might add, he _exploded_ as an offensive force to be reckoned with. He confirmed this performance in '93, becoming even more potent with the bat. 1994? We'll find out in good time, won't we? But he looks like an all-star-to-be.

Positional Norms

As is evidenced by the composition of TOPR's Top 10, you don't normally expect a shortstop or a catcher, say, to carry your offense. A separate and different standard must be applied. So, we've developed positional norms for both leagues that will allow you to evaluate a given player's offense, not only against the average player in the league (100), but against his immediate peers—those playing the same position he plays. These norms are based on the _regulars_ at those positions, not every Tom, Dick or Roberto who happened to find his way onto the field in the second game of a late season doubleheader. The norms won't necessarily be the average of the players listed as regulars at those positions either because, for this calculation, we used a) both sides of a platoon combination, even if only one made the "regular" list, and b) the relevant league data for players who changed leagues during the course of the season. For your edification, the positional norms of both leagues:

AL Positional Norms

Catcher	100
First Base	125
Second Base	100
Third Base	102
Shortstop	85
Left Field	121
Center Field	106
Right Field	105
Designated Hitter	105

40   100

NL Positional Norms

Catcher	102
First Base	116
Second Base	103
Third Base	107
Shortstop	100
Left Field	121
Center Field	108
Right Field	117
Pitcher	53

40   100

Interesting, don't you think? The NL gets more offense out of their right fielders and shortstops than the AL does. On the other hand, AL 1st basemen are a tower of strength (guys like Olerud, Thomas and Palmeiro make pretty good foundations for a tower). The AL's DH position is, compared to what should be legitimately expected, pitiful.

We promised you something on the distinction between the two leagues. See that 53 TOPR bringing up the rear of the NL lineup? That's the reason. NL players will tend to have slightly inflated TOPRs (compared to the AL) because the league average they're being ranked against includes the "pitcher-as-hitter" (which he obviously is not). If we take this inoffensive creature out of the mix, we find that the "Players Only" NBE/GOC ratio in the NL is .673 (or a 104 TOPR). _Technically_, NL players should be ranked on this baseline instead of the total league average. We thought all of this a tad confusing and unnecessary. The only application, after all, is when a player changes leagues. It's easy enough to remember that a player going from the NL to the AL should be slightly discounted (divide his TOPR by 1.04) and one going the other way should be theoretically reevaluated upward (multiply by 1.04). The NL "Players Only" TOPR has been a consistent 104 for as long as we've been pulling TOPRs, so you can consider it a constant.

Now, let's get to work—changing your impressions about some players, reconfirming them about others.

AMERICAN LEAGUE CATCHERS

			7/1/94		TOPR Trendline				1993
Rank	Player	Team	Age	B	1990	1991	1992	3 yr Avg.	TOPR
Regulars:									
1.	Chris Hoiles	BAL	29	R	*	86	140	111	**157**
2.	Mike Stanley	NYY	31	R	101	118	119	113	**137**
3.	Chad Kreuter	DET	29	B	*	*	81	81	**126**
4.	Mike Macfarlane	KCR	30	R	93	124	106	105	**122**
5.	Dave Valle	SEA	33	R	90	69	92	83	**99**
6.	Brian Harper	MIN	34	R	96	100	99	98	**96**
7.	Sandy Alomar, Jr.	CLE	28	R	102	(57)	75	84	**96**
8.	Ron Karkovice	CWS	30	R	107	(105)	102	104	**92**
9.	Terry Steinbach	OAK	32	R	84	87	97	90	**91**
10.	Pudge Rodriguez	TEX	22	R	-	68	81	76	**89**
11.	Dave Nilsson	MIL	24	L	-	-	(92)	(92)	**89**
12.	Greg Myers	CAL	28	L	74	89	*	82	**79**
13.	Pat Borders	TOR	31	R	104	77	90	91	**74**
14.	Tony Peña	BOS	37	R	80	72	73	75	**57**
Other Qualifiers (200+ TPA):									
-	Scott Hemond	OAK	28	R	*	*	*	*	**117**
-	Matt Nokes	NYY	30	L	87	111	98	99	**96**
-	Brent Mayne	KCR	26	L	*	79	58	69	**79**
-	Junior Ortiz	CLE	34	R	(96)	(62)	63	72	**58**
Of Note (under 200 TPA):									
-	Mike LaValliere	CWS	33	L	99	98	96	98	**(67)**
-	Carlton Fisk	CWS	46	R	126	89	91	103	**56***

* Under 100 TPA-not included in average. ( ) 100-199 TPA. † Includes NL TOPR, unadjusted to AL.

CHRIS HOILES

A star is being born . . . 1993's #1 offensive catcher in all of baseball . . . His home-runs-per-at-bat ratio of one every 14.4 trips to the plate was fourth best in the AL behind only the big thumpers Gonzalez, Griffey Jr. and Thomas . . . If only he could stay fully healthy for an entire season his numbers in HRs and RBIs would be eye-popping. A bad back in '93, a broken wrist in '92 and a torn shoulder muscle in '90 have set back his emergence . . . Underrated thrower whose effectiveness got much better as the season wore on and the wrist broken in '92 returned to full strength . . . Hard to believe Detroit tossed this guy into a trade package in 1988 so they could acquire Fred Lynn.

MIKE STANLEY

Check out those TOPR numbers leading up to '93 and you find this former handyman's always been a solid offensive player . . . Signed to a minor league contract in January of '92 after being dumped by the Rangers where he'd caught Nolan Ryan's seventh and final no-hitter. Even named his son after the Ryan Express . . . But his TOPR isn't what got him the starting job in May. Yankee pitchers, unhappy with the work of Matt Nokes, began a silent campaign for Stanley, a much superior catcher, thrower and pitch caller. Many feel his big numbers were just a mirage and that he'll backslide in '94. But if you look at his career TOPRs they suggest a player who'll always provide real pop in the lineup.

CHAD KREUTER

Would you believe another ex-Ranger catcher with a huge year? Also note that Pirate backstop Don Slaught, Baltimore spare part Mark Parent and Seattle catcher-utilityman Bill Haselman are former Ranger backstops playing elsewhere. At one point this season, all five started behind the plate on the same day . . . Had horrible TOPRs coming into '93. Perhaps just hanging around with all those big Detroit boppers rubbed off. But if that's the case why didn't he hit in Texas? . . . Should the Tigers take a chance his TOPR development's for real and deal Mickey Tettleton for pitching? Or was '93 a mirage for a player who once went three straight Aprils in Texas without a base hit? . . . Very good defensively and threw out 38.5% of opponent base stealers.

MIKE MACFARLANE

Vastly underrated . . . Another steady TOPR year marked by 20 homers and 27 doubles in less than 400 official at bats . . . A "plate diver" who tends to get hit by pitches regularly (16 in '93 and 15 the year before) . . . Much-improved thrower from early in his career when thumb and shoulder injuries gave him the reputation of a catcher that stealers could take advantage of.

DAVE VALLE

Put up his best-ever TOPR numbers in his free-agent-to-be season with career highs in games, homers, RBIs, doubles, walks and batting average. All this from a guy whose average in 1991 was so low that a Seattle-area bar named Swannies offered Tuesday night specials where drinks that evening were priced based on Valle's puny average. "Scotch and soda, sir? That'll be the Dave Valle special of the evening for only one-fifty-four" . . . Is his TOPR improvement real or a product of his pending free agency? How much will you pay to find out? . . . Plays very hard resulting in career trips to the disabled list for a lacerated right hand, dislocated ring finger, sprained left wrist, fractured ribs, torn knee ligaments in his right knee (twice), bone-bruised left hand and a hip pointer . . . Threw out 42.2% of would-be base stealers (#2 in AL).

BRIAN HARPER

If you crave consistency you'll love him. The steadiest TOPR numbers of any major league catcher . . . Fourth .300-batting-average season in the last five seasons . . . The ultimate contact hitter with 29 strikeouts and 29 walks in 573 plate appearances . . . In the last 40 years only four other receivers have put three .300 seasons back-to-back-to-back—Ted Simmons, Thurman Munson, Manny Sanguillen and Smokey Burgess . . . Not bad for a fellow who blew out his shoulder so badly in the early '80s that he couldn't even catch anymore and was passed from California to Pittsburgh to St. Louis to Detroit to Oakland to Minnesota in a six-year period.

SANDY ALOMAR

He's *baaaack* (hopefully) . . . A series of miseries limited him to less than 500 official at bats in the '91 and '92 seasons combined. But remember, from '90 to '92 he was the AL's starting all-star catcher—the first Indian to be a three-peat all-star starter since Ken Keltner in the middle '40s . . . Finally returned in August having lost the nearly 20 pounds he'd picked up during all that idle time and seemed to get stronger by the day . . . Can he stay healthy? A multimillion-dollar question in Cleveland.

RON KARKOVICE

With all apologies to Texas fans of Pudge Rodriguez, Karko's the best-throwing catcher in baseball. Nailed a major-league-best 50% in 1993 (48 of 96). But that was the only thing keeping him in the majors early in his career. Now he's a real offensive contributor. Actually slipped a bit TOPR-wise in '93 . . . Finally started to display the power he'd shown in the minors hitting 20 HRs. Had hit only 14 total in '89, '90 and '91. If he'd make better contact at the plate (29 BB and 126 K) his TOPR would put him up there with the "star" catchers.

TERRY STEINBACH

Has a reputation for being an "offensive" player that his TOPRs do not support . . . Injuries limited him to just 104 games but his numbers looked very much the same as in previous years . . . On the DL four of the last six years . . . Former All-Star game MVP ('88) and two-time starter . . . Doesn't walk much and a groundball hitter who tends to hit into a high number of double plays (48 the last 3 years). That combination tends to bring his TOPR rating down.

PUDGE RODRIGUEZ

Vastly overrated defensively at this point . . . A wonderful arm, but his percentage of runners thrown out dropped from 49% in '92 to 38% last season . . . Still poor at handling pitchers and blocking balls in the dirt. How in the world did he get the gold glove? Coming off his best TOPR season by far. Showing signs that he could be a real factor offensively after his first double-figure home run season and a Texas Ranger record 66 RBIs for a catcher . . . Still extremely young. Do you realize he's not even eligible for arbitration yet? . . . If he gets his defensive act together and the TOPR keeps rising the sky's the limit. But, like Steinbach, few BBs and lots of DPs.

DAVE NILSSON

Still has never hit even close to what his minor league numbers suggested he would (hit .418 in El Paso in '91 and .317 in Denver in '92). Those TOPRs projected him as an offensive force. But this Australian-born backstop continues to show very little extra base power (31 extra base hits and 83 singles in two years) . . . Off those minor league numbers he looked like a 129 TOPR in the bigs. In other words—a stud. Does a struggling Brewer franchise have the patience to wait for him to show that kind of number? Will he ever show it?

GREG MYERS

Has the look of a backup catcher . . . But a lefthanded-hitting, pretty solid backstop who can hit with some occasional power will always have a job in the majors . . . Staff ERA rose dramatically with him behind the plate thus increasing the speculation that the Angels will rush Chris Turner to the majors next season to take over the regular job.

PAT BORDERS

Note the negative TOPR trend for Borders since his solid 1990 season . . . Walk totals are incredibly low—96 free passes in six years in the majors! . . . A groundball hitter and that means high double-play totals (32 in the last two seasons) . . . With super prospect Carlos Delgado almost ready, would the Jays use this former World Series MVP as trade bait?

TONY PENA

Classy and aging veteran who was the worst offensive regular in the AL last season . . . This five-time-all-star and four-time Gold Glover hasn't hit above .263 or had more than 10 homers in seven years . . . Draws few walks and has hit into 203 double plays the last 12 years . . . Is his 13-year career over?

SCOTT HEMOND

The next Mike Stanley? . . . His 1993 TOPR should open some eyes and ought to get him more playing time somewhere. But then, his minor league TOPR of 122 (just like Stanley) suggested he would hit big league pitching . . . Can play multiple positions. One of those guys you like to have on your bench.

BRENT MAYNE

A perfect #2 catcher behind Macfarlane . . . Solid receiver and thrower . . . TOPR indicates you won't get much in the way of offense from him. But his minor league numbers (TOPR projection: 107) indicate that he's another who might start increasing his production . . . Like Nilsson, must show more extra-base pop (33 extra-base hits and 128 singles in nearly 700 official at bats).

MATT NOKES

Another whose reputation isn't matched by reality. Thought of as a solid offensive player. But check this year's TOPR and for that Matt-er the last few years. Yankees said Stanley took his job away because of defensive reasons when all along Stanley was also the better *offensive* player . . . Does have terrific home run power but, and here's a weird one, has fewer doubles than homers four years in a row (46 doubles, 67 homers)! . . . Very, very nice left-handed bat to have on the bench but definitely belongs behind Stanley.

JUNIOR ORTIZ

Had to play regularly for four months until Alomar returned and the wear and tear showed up in his TOPR numbers . . . This man, who named his son after himself, Adalberto Ortiz Jr. or Junior Ortiz Junior (making him Junior Ortiz Senior), has the profile of the ultimate backup catcher. Solid receiver. Terrific plus in the clubhouse. Knows the game. Works pitchers very well. Little power . . . Will take a walk only at gunpoint—11 last year and 116 in 11 years in the bigs.

MIKE LA VALLIERE

Looks like the Pirates did the right thing in releasing him. His TOPR numbers took a startling drop . . . Would being in better shape reverse that trend? . . . Probably a backup the rest of his career at this point.

CARLTON FISK

Even with LaValliere's poor season, the TOPRs suggest Chicago did the right thing in dumping this future Hall-of-Famer . . . Note the decline in numbers starting after his terrific 1990 campaign. Those are the figures to remember about Fisk, not the last couple of sliding, complaint-filled years.

AMERICAN LEAGUE 1ST BASEMEN

Rank	Player	Team	7/1/94 Age	B	TOPR Trendline				1993
					1990	*1991*	*1992*	3 yr Avg.	**TOPR**
Regulars:									
1.	John Olerud	TOR	25	L	122	117	123	120	**179**
2.	Frank Thomas	CWS	26	R	168	166	162	165	**170**
3.	Rafael Palmeiro	TEX	29	L	111	138	117	122	**146**
4.	Mo Vaughn	BOS	26	L	-	96	103	101	**136**
5.	Wally Joyner	KCR	32	L	105	124	96	109	**120**
6.	Kent Hrbek	MIN	34	L	128	119	115	121	**119**
7.	Cecil Fielder	DET	30	R	155	127	115	132	**115**
8.	Tino Martinez	SEA	26	L	*	(81)	93	90	**110**
9.	Paul Sorrento	CLE	28	L	(90)	*	109	105	**108**
10.	Don Mattingly	NYY	33	L	79	95	102	94	**107**
11.	John Jaha	MIL	28	R	-	-	(101)	(101)	**104**
12.	J.T. Snow	CAL	26	B	-	-	*	*	**103**
13.	David Segui	BAL	27	B	(66)	77	79	75	**98**
Other Qualifiers (200+ TPA):									
-	Randy Milligan	CIN/CLE	32	R	143	104	114	118	**136†**
-	Mike Aldrete	OAK	33	L	111†	98†	-	99†	**108**
-	Dan Pasqua	CWS	32	L	130	122	93	117	**91**
-	Carlos Quintana	BOS	28	R	96	109	DNP	102	**66**
Of Note (under 200 TPA):									
-	Mark McGwire	OAK	30	R	140	106	161	135	**(215)**
-	Glenn Davis	BAL/-	33	R	141†	(119)	105	121†	**(51)**

* Under 100 TPA-not included in average. ( ) 100-199 TPA. † Includes NL TOPR, unadjusted to AL.

JOHN OLERUD

A breakthrough season for a player seemingly destined for superstardom . . . Never spent a day in the minors and debuted as a TOPR player in the 120 range . . . "The Natural" got an American League record tying 33 intentional walks . . . Great numbers everywhere: 54 doubles, 114 bases on balls, 109 runs scored and 107 driven in. Hard to believe he actually "slumped" the last month of the year. At mid-season was flirting with a TOPR of above 200 . . . If he could run (one stolen base in his career) he'd challenge the all-time upper limits of TOPR-ism.

FRANK THOMAS

Rated behind Olerud? That's right. But check out those remarkable TOPRs for the last four years. The best four-year TOPR average in the American League . . . But then "The Big Hurt" figured to be this kind of star off his minor league TOPRs. They projected him right on the button to be a 170 TOPR in the majors . . . Remarkable patience at the plate—372 walks the last three years . . . A tight end at Auburn during Bo Jackson's senior year. Can you believe that in the first round of the 1989 draft Texas, picking fifth, decided to take a football player and convert him to baseball and chose instead Texas Tech defensive back Donald Harris leaving Thomas for the Pale Hose at pick #7? For just a moment, imagine the Texas lineup with Thomas in the middle of it. Awesome!

RAFAEL PALMEIRO

And speaking of the middle of the Rangers order, Palmeiro comes off his all-time best TOPR year. Another posting huge numbers on the brink of free agency . . . Hard to believe he was hitting .183 when May began . . . An incredible July with a TOPR far over 200 for that month in which he had 11 HRs, 34 RBIs, 13 doubles, a gaudy .852 slugging percentage and hit .426 . . . Want more ammunition? Finished the season with a consecutive games errorless streak of 113 games . . . The complete package. Even stole 22 of 25 bases. But if he stays in the AL will never likely make

an all-star team even as a backup given the presence of young superstars Olerud and Thomas.

MO VAUGHN

Another who broke through in '93. Minor league TOPRs suggested he'd be a 130 as a major leaguer. But those levels of accomplishment were far away indeed his first couple of seasons . . . First Red Sox player to hit 20 homers since Mike Greenwell did so in '88 and the first to drive in 100 runs in four years . . . Dropped nearly 30 pounds a couple years ago in an attempt to regain the stroke that made him the Big East Player-of-the-Decade at Seton Hall where his teammates called him "Hit Dog" . . . How good might his numbers become if Boston found a power threat to hit behind him in the lineup thus forcing pitchers to come to "Hit Dog" "mo" often?

WALLY JOYNER

Joyner's up-down TOPR trend continued. Little things contributed to Wally's World getting better in '93. A career high in walks (66) and a career low in double plays hit into (6) . . . If only KC had more true middle-of-the-lineup hitters, they could bat him where he truly belongs—in the second or sixth slots of the order where his 65 RBIs wouldn't seem like such a low total . . . Good, consistent player who drove in 217 runs his first two seasons but has averaged just 72 per year since.

KENT HRBEK

As the Twins fell apart hardly anyone noticed the kind of year Hrbie was putting together before elbow problems and the illness of his child cut short his season . . . Don't be deceived by that .242 batting average . . . The Twins "big man," who's displayed a fondness for beer and ice cream eaten together at times in the past, slammed 25 homers and drew 71 walks in about two-thirds of a season . . . Note the remarkable consistency of those TOPR numbers and, given his reputation and appearance as some free-swinging oaf, do you realize Hrbie's walked more than he's fanned for seven straight years?

CECIL FIELDER

What's this? "The Big Man" behind both Joyner and Hrbek in TOPRs? Not only is that correct but Fielder's TOPR trendline points straight downward off that high in 1990 . . . Homers down for the third straight year. . . . Double plays up to a career high of 22 . . . But, at just 30 years old, still an awesome presence in the middle of the order . . . In 1994 will probably celebrate the 10th anniversary of his last stolen base which came while Fielder played for Kinston in 1984. And, yes, that includes his 1989 year in Japan with Hanshin.

TINO MARTINEZ

Despite a year-ending left knee injury that required surgery, Tino's TOPR topped out at a career high 110. But that's still far away from his minor league numbers that suggested a player who'd eventually be a big time threat with a projected TOPR of 132. This former cleanup hitter for the 1988 U.S. Olympic team is showing signs of a breakthrough though. Homers and walks were up in '93, strikeouts slipped and double plays fell from an ugly 24 to only 7. . . . Maybe next year he'll step up near the level of the first baseman who proceeded him at Tampa, Florida's Jefferson High—Fred McGriff.

PAUL SORRENTO

Another solid, underpublicized season for a player the Twins simply dumped on the Indians in the spring of '92 . . . Two straight 18-homer, 60-plus RBI seasons and for a second straight year third on the club in those categories behind Belle and Baerga . . . Everyone in Cleveland seems to be waiting for prospect Reggie Jefferson to take his job. That might never happen.

DON MATTINGLY

His best TOPR year of the '90s and even that was only the 10th best at his position last season . . . This fellow put up TOPR years of 141 and 142 back in the middle '80s. But since then the power part of his game's slipped badly: 119 homers from '84–'87 compared with only 45 long balls in the '90's . . . Still a solid player but you must question whether or not the Yanks should continue to bat him somewhere in the middle of the lineup.

JOHN JAHA

Started so miserably, there was mid-season talk of shipping him back to the minors where his numbers had suggested he'd be a star. But he came on so well late in the year (always something to be a bit wary of) that the talent-shy Brew Crew must hope he'll continue to blossom next year while they direct their efforts to plugging other holes . . . Surprising speed leading to 13 SBs and only 6 double plays . . . When you're sitting in the cellar you pray people like this develop.

J. T. SNOW

What a weird season . . . first California was hit by an early Snow (.343 in April). Then Snow melted in May. Eventually Snow's fall became so pronounced that the Angels sent him back to the minors where he regrouped, returned and finished on an up note

. . . So which player will California see next season–the hot or the cold Snow? . . . Adding to the bizarre nature of Snow's season was his homer total of 16—more than he'd ever hit in his four minor league years . . . Wacky! But then what would you expect from a guy named Snow in California?

DAVID SEGUI

Simply unacceptable TOPRs for the position . . . Look up the chart to see just how much Baltimore gives away offensively at 1B. Every other regular AL 1B hit at least 5 more homers than Segui's 10. The average HR total of the 12 above him was 24. While the numbers did rise this year, there's still a high double-play total (18), little speed and that lack of extra-base power (only 65 in just under 1,000 major league at bats) . . . Might the O's switch him to his other positon—outfield? His TOPRs would be below average there also.

RANDY MILLIGAN

Why does this guy keep getting passed around? For reasons known only to God and cauliflower, Baltimore couldn't live with those solid TOPR numbers and sent him packing to Cincinnati. The Reds then shipped him to Cleveland during the summer of '93 and "Moose" simply kept putting numbers on the board . . . True, he's a bit of an odd first baseman whose power is to right center and who seems to prefer walking to swinging, but there's no doubting those TOPR numbers. Just ask the Orioles, who'd have loved to have had his contributions at that position last year.

MIKE ALDRETE

Might have resurrected his career thanks to the chance he got to play in Oakland when McGwire got hurt . . . How far had he fallen? He wasn't even included in the nearly 600-page 1993 Sporting News Baseball Register that included players like Ryan Hawblitzel, Norberto Martin and Jose Musset. Displayed a little pop (10 HRs), can play first or the outfield and hits lefthanded. Could parlay all that into a place on somebody's bench in '94.

MARK McGWIRE

How much did the A's miss McGwire? Check out the kind of monster start he'd gotten off to . . . Left with the heel injury May 14 and a month later was still leading the club in homers with 9 . . . In that month-plus after MM left, the A's tried six other cleanup hitters—Aldrete, Rubern Sierra, Kevin Seitzer, Troy Neel, Dave Henderson and Dale Sveum. They combined to hit .193 in 135 at bats as the season disintegrated . . . More effects of Big Mac's loss? Sierra hit .297 hitting in front of him. McGwire headed for the tub and Sierra's season average tumbled to .233 . . . If he and that giant TOPR return healthy in '93 so does much of the A's attack.

GLENN DAVIS

What happened to this man? Check out that gaudy 141 TOPR in 1990 before the blight of injuries hit . . . Is his career finished? Maybe. Maybe not. Remember Andres Galarraga's career seemed on the brink of disappearing before '93. If Davis gets healthy he's still in his early 30s. But does the player who put that 141 TOPR on the board in '90, the player who hit 122 homers and drove in 382 runs from 1986 to 1989 in the spacious Astrodome, still exist?

AMERICAN LEAGUE 2ND BASEMEN

Rank	Player	Team	7/1/94 Age	B	TOPR Trendline				1993 TOPR
					1990	1991	1992	3 yr Avg.	
Regulars:									
1.	Roberto Alomar	TOR	26	B	100†	128	143	123	142
2.	Lou Whitaker	DET	37	L	113	146	134	131	134
3.	Carlos Baerga	CLE	25	B	94	101	116	106	115
4.	Scott Fletcher	BOS	35	R	81	67	99	84	100
5.	Brent Gates	OAK	24	B	-	-	-	-	98
6.	Rich Amaral	SEA	32	R	-	*	(69)	(69)	96
7.	Chuck Knoblauch	MIN	25	R	-	103	117	110	96
8.	Joey Cora	CWS	29	B	(82)†	80	(117)	90	96
9.	Harold Reynolds	BAL	33	B	100	99	85	96	93
10.	Pat Kelly	NYY	26	R	-	87	96	92	89
11.	Doug Strange	TEX	30	B	-	*	(60)†	(60)	86
12.	Bill Spiers	MIL	28	L	71	102	*	88	73
13.	Jose Lind	KCR	30	R	81†	79†	66†	76	65
Other Qualifiers (200+ TPA):									
-	Damion Easley	CAL	24	R	-	-	(82)	(82)	108
-	Bret Boone	SEA	25	R	-	-	(62)	(62)	97
Of Note (under 200 TPA):									
-	Bill Doran	MIL	36	B	143†	109†	104†	119	65*
-	Jeff Frye	TEX	27	R			89	89	DNP

* Under 100 TPA-not included in average. ( ) 100-199 TPA. † Includes NL TOPR, unadjusted to AL.

ROBERTO ALOMAR

One of baseball's most complete players. Hits, hits with power, runs very well, fields exceptionally and throws well . . . Back-to-back TOPRs in the 140s puts him right up there with Sandberg who strung together three straight such seasons before '93 injuries struck . . . RBIs up for a sixth consecutive season . . . His 17 homers nearly doubled his previous career high . . . His 15-year veteran father Sandy Sr. knew early on his son would be a player: "When I had to punish him all I had to do was take his bat and glove away. I never had to spank him." Perhaps the scariest thought of all is that at 26 years old he's just approaching his prime.

LOU WHITAKER

Is he the most long-term underrated player in the game? The answer is almost certainly "Yes!" . . . If you average the last three TOPR years, he's the best 2B offensively in the game. Over four years just slightly behind Sandberg. Why? He's got the "perfect game." Hits, hits with power, steals a very high percentage, hardly ever hits into DPs and walks a lot . . . Career total of 997 RBIs. When he reaches 1,000 he'll be just the ninth second baseman to ever attain that total. The other eight are in the Hall of Fame . . . One tiny concession to age in '93. Played only 119 games, the second lowest non-strike year total of his sixteen-year career.

CARLOS BAERGA

No wonder the Tribe insisted he be part of the huge trade that sent Joe Carter to San Diego in December of 1989 . . . Just missed the Triple Crown for second basemen leading all at his position in HRs and RBIs but nipped for the 2B batting title by Alomar . . . Like Alomar, still a couple years away from the start of what should be his "prime" years. Second consecutive year he's had 200 hits, 20 HRs and 100 RBIs while hitting .300. Only one other second baseman in the game's history has had such a season. Rogers

Hornsby did it five times! A few more walks would move his TOPR up to the "SAW" level—Sandberg, Alomar, Whitaker.

SCOTT FLETCHER

An example of a player who does all the little things to win games . . . Underappreciated "Scooter" wasn't even supposed to be a starter in Boston before injuries forced the Sox to play him virtually every day. Same story in Milwaukee the year before. No homer power but tons of doubles . . . Is he getting faster as he gets older or just smarter? Has stolen 17 and 16 back-to-back, the two best SB years of his career.

BRENT GATES

An outstanding young player . . . Rushed to the majors when Lance Blankenship and Jerry Browne got injured. Unless the sky starts falling or fish start flying the job's his for years to come . . . Barely missed erasing Phil Garner's record for RBIs by an A's second baseman of 74 set in 1976. Gates drove in 69 and wasn't even called to the majors until May . . . What's his potential three or four years down the line? His 98 TOPR is about the same as Alomar's four years ago and a bit better than Baerga's in that same 1990 season . . . Might Gates be that good an offensive player eventually? His minor league TOPRs say "definitely" projecting him to eventually be a terrific 128!

CHUCK KNOBLAUCH

Slipped just a tad but still a very solid three-year-average TOPR of 105 . . . Total lack of power (5 HRs in 3 years) affects his TOPR. But the rest of the game of this former AL Rookie-of-the-Year remains rock solid . . . From 1976, when Rod Carew switched from 2B to 1B, through the arrival of "Knobber" in '91, no Twin ever held the starting second-base job as many as three years in a row. Remember John Randall, Rob Wilfong, Tim Teufel, John

"Clams" Castino, Steve Lombardozzi, Tommy Herr, Wally Back-man, Al Newman, Fred Manrique and Nelson Liriano? All tried. None lasted three years.

JOEY CORA

When Steve Sax and Craig Grebeck couldn't hold the job, Cora seized the opportunity. But then that terrific 117 TOPR as a part-part-time player in '92 suggested he might be a good choice . . . Finally playing near his minor league TOPRs which projected him as an above-average offensive player (TOPR 112) . . . Another guy San Diego got rid of at 2B (Alomar and Baerga) which is now a Padre weak spot (29-year-old rookie Jeff Gardner posted a 93 TOPR in '93) . . . This 5-foot-8 (honest, that's how tall the Sox guide says he is) pepperpot's finally emerging as a "power threat" hitting his first two homers ever in '93 . . . Drove in 51 runs. His CAREER total for parts of 5 seasons coming into '93 had been 43 . . . With his TOPR increasing only his glove might cost him the job—19 errors. UGH!

RICH AMARAL

"Amaral, better than he has to be." Finally got a big league job in '93 when touted rookie Bret Boone fell flat on his face early in the season . . . Spent 10 years riding buses and calling places like Geneva, Davenport, Winston-Salem, Pittsfield, Birmingham, Cal-gary and Vancouver home. With Boone traded away he might inherit the job full time or become a handy, handyman . . . 19 steals, 24 doubles in about two-thirds of a year's work . . . Plays several positions and after all those years in the minors just very happy to be here.

HAROLD REYNOLDS

His declining TOPRs suggest his better years are behind him . . . Stolen base percentage dropping badly (12 of 23 in '93, 15 for 27 the season before) and with his little power he must be a speed player to contribute . . . Extremely poor year hitting from the right side . . . But this former-star wide receiver from Corvallis remains a locker-room leader and could have a few solid seasons left if his running game can be revitalized.

PAT KELLY

About the same TOPR player three straight years . . . For a player with so little power (17 homers in just over 1,000 official at bats), he absolutely must increase his "walk power." Has only drawn 64 free passes in his career . . . Has a career walks-to-strikeouts ratio (64 BB to 208 K) like a HR hitter but without the pop . . . Led Yanks in steals but that's nothing to brag about. Had 14 while being throw out 11 times. No one else in double figures in New York where it must be against the law to steal.

DOUG STRANGE

That 86 TOPR may not look like much but the Rangers loved it! Injuries wiped out Franco, Frye, Huson and Ripken forcing Strange to play a strange position for him (he's actually a 3B) . . . TOPR numbers tumbled late in the year when Texas simply didn't have enough healthy bodies to give him any rest and forced him to play on a knee in need of post-season medical work . . . Figured he was headed for Japan before Texas extended him a "no promises" spring invitation. Made the team by telling them he could be their emergency third catcher. The catch was he'd never caught in a pro game in his life. Hey, when you're desperate for a big league job you lie a little!

BILL SPIERS

The best thing that can be said about Spiers year is that he was healthy enough to play in 113 games. Former first-round pick after starring at Clemson who's been bothered by various ailments. Started '90 on the DL recovering from shoulder surgery. Ended the year needing toe surgery. Missed virtually all of '92 after having two back surgeries, the second to correct a small leakage of spinal fluid caused by the first surgery . . . Virtually no power (but he did hit 8 in '91 before all the back surgery), few walks and not much of a running game (that was once better too) . . . Will he ever get back to that 102 TOPR of 1991? Perhaps only his surgeons know.

JOSE LIND

Barely beaten out by Tony Pena for the uncoveted title of the worse offensive regular player in the league . . . And as you can tell by his career TOPR trendline, it wasn't all that bad a season historically. No power (just 15 extra-base hits), no speed (3 steals) and no walks (would you believe 13?). In other words absolutely no offense . . . How long can anyone stay with those numbers at 2B just because the guy's an absolutely spectacular fielder (4 errors and a bajillion unbelievable plays)? Kansas City—could we have your answer please?

DAMION EASLEY

Ultra-skinny former 30th rounder thought by many to be too frail to ever be a full-time starter. Was erasing those doubts thoroughly when chronic shinsplints ended his season after 73 games . . . Slap-and-run hitter with decent walks totals and decent "doubles power" . . . Must improve his stolen base numbers and percentage . . . This former shortstop showed more than enough to warrant being given the job in '94. But that nagging question persists: can he survive the grind of 162 games? The Angels will try to find out.

BRET BOONE

Figured to be the M's starting 2B. Instead, a miserable .206 spring caused by trying to pull everything thrown to him resulted in his being the starter for Calgary. And he stayed there awhile as Rich Amaral did a splendid fill-in job . . . Returned a better player by mid-year with a TOPR several other clubs would happily live with at the position . . . That's what encouraged the Reds to deal for him to plug their 2B hole. Already the second-best TOPR player in Boone family history. Daddy Bob was a light-hitting 80–90 type most of his life. Granddaddy Ray was a 110–120 TOPR-type as a slugging third baseman . . . Surprisingly good power like granddad. But doesn't draw walks like his dad did. Like both—doesn't run much.

BILL DORAN

Is his career over? . . . Once a really terrific player. Check that gaudy 143 TOPR in 1990, just a tick behind Sandberg that season . . . But back problems have sadly cut into what could have been a marvelous run. If his body permits he might still make somebody a fine part-time player given that as little as two years back he was a three-figure TOPR player.

JEFF FRYE

Missed the entire year in Texas after blowing out his knee while jogging . . . A pesky hitter who must, like Kelly, learn to walk more . . . Never a great minor league base stealer, never much power, but could develop into a "Fletcher-type."

AMERICAN LEAGUE 3RD BASEMEN

Rank	Player	Team	7/1/94 Age	B	TOPR Trendline				1993 TOPR
					1990	1991	1992	3 yr Avg.	
Regulars:									
1.	Travis Fryman	DET	25	R	117	105	104	106	129
2.	Dean Palmer	TEX	25	R	-	96	108	104	118
3.	Robin Ventura	CWS	26	L	89	115	120	109	115
4.	Mike Pagliarulo	MIN/BAL	34	L	91†	89	(52)	85	110
5.	Mike Blowers	SEA	29	R	(76)	*	*	(76)	109
6.	Scott Cooper	BOS	26	L	*	*	103	103	104
7.	Wade Boggs	NYY	36	L	120	132	102	118	101
8.	Gary Gaetti	CAL/KCR	35	R	83	88	78	83	99
9.	B. J. Surhoff	MIL	29	L	102	81	87	90	91
10.	Leo Gomez	BAL	28	R	*	98	114	107	90
11.	Ed Sprague	TOR	26	R	-	(104)	*	(104)	82
12.	Craig Paquette	OAK	25	R	-	-	-		76
Other Qualifiers (200+ TPA):									
-	Jeff Treadway	CLE	31	L	95†	110†	(67)†	96	93
-	Scott Livingstone	DET	28	L	-	(103)	88	92	85
-	Alvaro Espinoza	CLE	32	R	61	77	-	72	81
-	Phil Hiatt	KCR	25	R	-	-	-	-	81
Of Note (under 200 TPA):									
-	Edgar Martinez	SEA	31	R	123	125	148	132	(106)
-	Keith Miller	KCR	31	R	97†	120†	113	111	(47)
-	Kelly Gruber	CAL/-	32	R	129	107	77	106	*

* Under 100 TPA-not included in average. ( ) 100-199 TPA. † Includes NL TOPR, unadjusted to AL.

TRAVIS FRYMAN

The best third base TOPR in the majors in '93 just ahead of Matt Williams and Gary Sheffield . . . His advantages include enough speed to steal a handful of bases and stay out of double plays (only 8 last year) and a walk total that rose from 45 in '92 to 77 last year . . . And walks may be the key to unlocking superstardom. Still strikes out too much but with the increased walks came a drop on K totals. If that continues, look out . . . In all at bats last year in which Fryman did not strike out he reached base over 48% of the time . . . Detroit's decided he's a 3B and will not convert him to SS.

DEAN PALMER

Same age as Fryman with an almost identical game: tons of power, runs enough to swipe 11 and stays out of double plays (5). But far too many strikeouts (154) and not enough walks (53) . . . Bothered by little nicks the last few seasons, especially hand and wrist problems . . . Many scouts feel he has enough bat speed to join teammate Gonzalez atop the homer standings if he figures out how to make more contact . . . Like Fryman, still makes too many silly errors (29) . . . Seems to get better every year which should worry the next generation of AL pitchers.

ROBIN VENTURA

Nolan Ryan's first and last knockout victim . . . Incredibly steady TOPR numbers three straight seasons . . . Walk totals have risen every year to a terrific 112 last season without affecting HR and RBI bottom lines . . . TOPR would have been much better except for that ugly 1-for-7 stolen base line and 18 double plays . . . But the biggest question about this former collegiate player-of-the-year, who had an Oklahoma State batting streak two games longer than the major league mark of 56 by Joe Dimaggio, revolves around whether or not he should be a cleanup hitter. He bats there because Frank Thomas is "incomfortable" in the 4-spot. Ventura's totals suggest he'd be much more suited to hitting second, fifth or sixth.

MIKE PAGLIARULO

Do not rub your eyes! Pags was the fourth best offensive third baseman in the league last year and a shrewd late season pickup by the Orioles . . . People disappointed in Pags keep waiting for the return of the power stroke that resulted in 60 homers with the '86–'87 Yanks. And while that stroke's not back, he has refined other parts of his game hitting .300 for the first time in his career . . . Key has been decreasing strikeouts. Just 49 last season after once fanning more than 100 times three straight campaigns in the middle '80s . . . With his TOPR back up and Leo Gomez's down, which direction should the O's go at hot corner next year? How about a platoon?

MIKE BLOWERS

And the surprises just keep coming at third base . . . Like Pagliarulo, another ex-Yank finding happiness elsewhere . . . Those who want you to cry crocodile tears over the Mariners' loss of Edgar Martinez haven't taken a good look at Blowers' TOPR totals . . . Manager Piniella remembered him from his days when both were in NY and gave him a chance. Blowers, a career .200 hitter with 7 homers in 290 at bats, responded with a .290/15 HR/57 RBI season . . . Sure, he's no E. Martinez (though he is TOPR-wise a T. Martinez) but '93 assures him of a bench/platoon spot somewhere even if Edgar returns healthy to the hot corner.

SCOTT COOPER

Decided not to keep Wade Boggs, moved the 10-years-younger and millions-cheaper Cooper into Boggs spot and got, well, Boggs-type numbers. While Boggs out-hit Cooper (.302 vs .279), Cooper had 7 more HRs and 4 more RBIs. Like Boggs, Cooper walks a lot (58), doesn't run much (5 steals) and avoids high double-play totals. Check how remarkably close they came out in TOPR . . . The obvious upside for Cooper is his age and potential to improve . . . One more Boggs-alike: Cooper came into '93 hitting .326 at Fenway and .260 on the road and last season proceeded to hit .325 at home and .236 away.

WADE BOGGS

Switch from friendly Fenway to Yankee Stadium didn't affect TOPR at all. But then those TOPR figures are down from the 120–130 range Boggs regularly lived in while leading the league in batting five times and on-base percentage six times . . . Worked with his father/hitting instructor Winn in the off-season to pull the ball more to take advantage of the short shot to right field in Yankee Stadium but hit just one HR there. His game's virtually the same except for the tumble (all the way down to .302!) in batting average which explains TOPR drop . . . Still draws tons of walks, hits for little power and almost never runs . . . At 36 years old might still have a few identical years left.

GARY GAETTI

Welcome back. Or at least part of the way back. When the Angels simply dumped him early in '93 it appeared his career was over. Once a feared power hitter, Gaetti's HR totals had fallen six years in a row from 31 with the '87 Twins to a dozen in '92. Had no HRs and 4 RBIs in 20 Angels games when the pink slip arrived . . . But KC was having a devil of a time keeping anyone healthy (Miller, Wilkerson) or productive (Hiatt) at 3B and they gambled on Gaetti . . . Gave them 14 HRs and 46 RBIs in half a year. TOPR in KC in the 110 area which would have put him around fourth among all AL third basemen . . . Is he truly back? It's your answer KC.

B. J. SURHOFF

Converted catcher moved to 3B where his TOPR numbers are below the positional norms making him ninth best at the position. Oddly, same TOPR would have made him #9 amongst AL catchers . . . Same old story: started slow and finished fast . . . Poor power totals for the position—7 HRs and that was a career-tying high . . . 79 RBIs easily a personal best . . . Will steal a few bases and gets tons of doubles (38) but power shortage stands out at this position where only Boggs of the 12 regulars listed at this position hit fewer dingers.

LEO GOMEZ

Still not producing anywhere near his minor league promise which projected him to eventually have Fryman-like TOPRs . . . Seemed to be coming up to a big year, given the way his TOPR had jumped in '92, but he backslid to unacceptable levels . . . Still produced 10 long balls. But a .197 average? And that 68-point drop came in a year when offensive totals generally leaped in the game . . . Absolutely no speed but oddly hit into just two double plays . . . What a tumble for a man who led all major league rookies with 16 HRs in '91.

ED SPRAGUE

Given the full-time job after the Jays found an Angel team to dump Kelly Gruber on . . . OK power figures of 12 HRs and 73 RBIs but woeful in some other areas that resulted in a tumbling TOPR . . . Drew only 32 walks and almost totally negated that small total by hitting into a league-leading 23 double plays. Toss in just one steal and his TOPR drops beneath players you'd think he'd rank ahead of . . . But he's still young and, at 26 next season, will again be the starting third baseman for baseball's two-time defending champs.

CRAIG PAQUETTE

Another of the youngsters rushed to the big leagues by the A's and this one's numbers suffered. Was ticketed for Tacoma. Then Kevin Seitzer failed to be the replacement for retired Carney Lansford, injuries struck other candidates and Paquette got the call. His 14 walks and 108 strikeouts tell you how overmatched he was at times . . . But there were some signs of life: 20 doubles, a dozen long flies and 46 RBIs in about two-thirds of a season's work . . . One thing must change—his number. He wears #3. Wrong! Wrong! Wrong! Anybody with the name "Paquette" should wear #6. "Six Paquette."

ALVARO ESPINOZA

Handyman who got into 129 games in various roles including sometimes-starter at 3B . . . Has the "Devil's Triangle" TOPR numbers—no speed, no power and no walks. In 283 plate appearances his SB/HR/BB combined total was 14! In order: 2 SB, 4 HR, 8 BB. But he's NOT an easy out as evidenced by that .278 average. But hard to believe the Yanks lived with this kind of TOPR from him as their everyday shortstop from '89–'91.

PHIL HIATT

KC wanted to give him the job based on his 27-homer year in '92 at Memphis. That total looked wonderful to the power-starved Royals. But they should have looked closer at his .244 BA that same season in Tennessee . . . Simply couldn't handle major league pitching early on so the Royals eventually turned to Gaetti . . . The problem? No contact! Struck out 82 times in 238 at bats thus leading to a strikeout average of .344 as opposed to a batting average of .218 . . . Also made an unsightly 16 errors in that limited time . . . Is he still a prospect? It's your answer KC.

SCOTT LIVINGSTONE

Now firmly stuck behind Fryman and in Detroit there's absolutely no way he gets DH at bats . . . Former Texas Aggie star who set Southwest Conference records for HRs and doubles but has shown almost none of that power in the minors or majors . . . Walks very little and is no threat to steal . . . Could be a player who'd blossom with playing time but probably needs a change of scenery to get it.

JEFF TREADAWAY

Another part of the Indians 3B platoon keeping the job warm until superb prospect Jim Thome arrived . . . Just as in his past, put up solid TOPR numbers for a spare part . . . Not much pop but, hey, this guy's now hit over .300 in three different major league seasons after being a .314 career minor league hitter . . . Nice, versatile player to have around even though his glove remains the weakest part of his game.

KEITH MILLER

Will he ever stay healthy? . . . Check those solid TOPRs coming into '93 and you can imagine why the Royals were so hurt by another Miller hurt that limited him to just 37 games . . . But that's the story of his career: '87—surgery to repair torn finger ligaments, '90—disabling hamstring pull, '91—disabling ankle bruise and '92—disabled twice with a back injury and a fractured tibial plateau (huh?) . . . Will he ever stay healthy enough to produce those nice TOPR numbers? It's your call KC.

KELLY GRUBER

His career appears over . . . Once projected as a brilliant player (check that 129 TOPR in 1990). But injuries and (some say) malingering has him on the unemployment line . . . But he's still young and, if fit and if he wants to, this former winner of the Superstars competition just might show up in somebody's camp.

EDGAR MARTINEZ

What a sad season for the defending batting champ. Pulled a hamstring in an exhibition game very late in spring training on a poor field in Vancouver and then repulled it less than two months after returning . . . Should heal and bounce right back to those eye-popping TOPRs that put him at the very top of AL third basemen.

AMERICAN LEAGUE SHORTSTOPS

Rank	Player	Team	7/1/94 Age	B	TOPR Trendline				1993 TOPR
					1990	*1991*	*1992*	3 yr Avg.	
Regulars:									
1.	Alan Trammell	DET	36	R	*122*	*99*	*(99)*	111	**125**
2.	John Valentin	BOS	27	R	*-*	*-*	*111*	111	**109**
3.	Tony Fernandez	NYM/TOR	31	B	*106*	*100†*	*99†*	102	**98†**
4.	Cal Ripken, Jr.	BAL	33	R	*113*	*141*	*95*	116	**97**
5.	Greg Gagne	KCR	32	R	*85*	*88*	*77*	83	**91**
6.	Mike Bordick	OAK	28	R	***	*70*	*103*	92	**84**
7.	Pat Listach	MIL	26	R	*-*	*-*	*109*	109	**83**
8.	Ozzie Guillen	CWS	30	L	*82*	*77*	***	78	**82**
9.	Omar Vizquel	SEA	27	B	*77*	*80*	*85*	81	**75**
10.	Spike Owen	NYY	33	B	*99†*	*92†*	*110†*	100	**75**
11.	Manny Lee	TEX	28	B	*80*	*69*	*93*	80	**71**
12.	Felix Fermin	CLE	30	R	*73*	*70*	*84*	74	**69**
13.	Gary Disarcina	CAL	26	R	***	***	*67*	67	**63**
14.	Pat Meares	MIN	25	R	*-*	*-*	*-*	-	**59**
Of Note (under 200 TPA):									
-	Dick Schofield	TOR	31	R	*99*	*78*	*89†*	88	**(75)**
-	Scott Leius	MIN	28	R	***	*115*	*78*	90	*****

* Under 100 TPA-not included in average. ( ) 100-199 TPA. † Includes NL TOPR, unadjusted to AL.

ALAN TRAMMELL

Bounced back to once again be a standout offensive player at a position marked by woefully weak performers . . . Free of injury, Tram returned to make nearly 450 plate appearances and display the kind of all-around game that begets solid TOPRs (12 homers, 25 doubles, a .329 batting average and a dozen steals) . . . Anyone at the Hall of Fame keeping track of this fellow's bottom line? He's closing in on 200 HRs and 1,000 RBIs. He's already well over 1,100 runs scored and 200 SBs. Just under a career .290 hitter with more career walks than strikeouts. Looking at what else is out there at shortstop makes this 16-year vet leap out at you.

JOHN VALENTIN

The find of the season in Beantown . . . Started late because of injury. But came on to give Boston real pop at an offenseless position. Missed by only 6 RBIs of being second on the team in that category to Mo Vaughn . . . Became the first Red Sox SS to homer twice in a game since 1970 when he went deep a couple of times against the Angels. Last one to do it? Rico Petrocelli . . . Has "Fenway swing" giving him enormous "doubles power" (40 in '93). This Seton Hall college teammate of Vaughn and high school basketball starting guard in a backcourt with future Notre Dame star David Rivers must reduce error count of 20 before respect will grow greatly.

TONY FERNANDEZ

Went from the outhouse to the penthouse when dealt from baseball's worst team, the Mets, to the best, Toronto. Strangely, his TOPR did the same . . . Was limping along with a TOPR in the 80s range in New York when traded. Suddenly exploded with a three-figure TOPR that lifted him to third overall in the AL and right back to the level he's played at so consistently for years now . . . When he hits .300 with a TOPR in the hundreds added to his slickness afield (still the best-rated fielder in major league shortstop history) he's one of the more valuable players in the game. Not bad for a kid that as a teenager was so poor he couldn't afford a glove and showed up for a Toronto tryout with a homemade mitt fashioned of string and a milk carton.

CAL RIPKEN

Those who believe that Ripken's quest to pass Lou Gehrig's mark for consecutive games played has resulted in him generally wearing down, will get fuel for their argument from a second straight below-100 TOPR season for a player who didn't have a TOPR below triple digits from '82 to '88 . . . What's caused the numerical decline the last few years? Let's start with a batting average that's been in the .250s now four of the last five seasons. Just 53 extra-base hits. Note that Boston's Valentin had 54 in 179 less plate appearances . . . But still a very solid contributor and at age 33 might play hundreds of games past the Gehrig total.

GREG GAGNE

TOPR rose to the highest level of the 90s thanks to spacious Ewing Kauffman Stadium that's a doubles paradise for him (32 a career high) . . . But that TOPR climbed basically because he became a better hitter. Did getting out of a "hitter's park" perhaps help him as a hitter? Hmmmm . . . Walks leaped to a career high of 33. That's right, in nine complete season's that's his *best* walk total. But he almost never hits into double plays (7) and gobbles up everything hit to him . . . Running game a minus getting thrown out 12 of 22 steal attempts. Give him the "stop" sign.

MIKE BORDICK

Limped away to a horrible start and slowly dragged his TOPR back into the 80s by year's end. You don't even want to know where it once was. (Tony-Pena-and-Jose-Lind-land.) . . . Very little power—just 21 two-baggers in a huge park that can yield many . . . Basically a singles hitter who runs a bit (10 for 20 SBs) . . . So which Bordick's the real TOPR Bordick—the 103 in '92 or the 84 last season? His minor league projections suggested he's a "high 80s type."

PAT LISTACH

Another whose TOPR dropped dramatically. But a hamstring pull and a viral infection were just part of a misery-filled season that limited him to 98 games . . . '92 Rookie-of-the-Year never regained form, especially on the base paths where his steals crashed from 54 to 18 . . . Despite his speed, has never shown a tendency to being any kind of an extra-base hitter and that will keep his TOPRs out of the elite level . . . But, with health, should return to '92 levels which his minor league numbers perfectly projected him as an eventual 108 major leaguer . . . But will he be a shortstop next season? A second baseman? A center fielder?

OZZIE GUILLEN

Came all the way back from major knee surgery that wiped out all of '92. But time on the shelf did nothing to alter a serious case of "baseonballsophobia"—the abject fear of drawing walks. Set an all-time White Sox record low by "working" opposing pitchers for just 10 free passes all season. Previous team record had been 11 set by Guillen in '91. The mark before that? Uh, 12, done twice—in '85 by Guillen and again in '86 by, uh, well by now you can guess who . . . Lack of freebies combined with very little power and stolen base figures reduced by the surgery kept him at a low TOPR point despite a career high .280 batting average . . . Fun to watch, unless you're a White Sox manager desperately in need of a base runner.

SPIKE OWEN

A horrible year given the kind of solid TOPRs he'd put up in the other league . . . Never had much power or stealing ability. Walks dropped and so did batting average. Made 14 errors in about two-thirds of a season and range has never been his strong suit . . . Was this an off-season and will the man whose real given first name is actually "Spike" bounce back to pre-'93 TOPRs? The Yankees must answer that question correctly as they prepare for a season in which they picture themselves major contenders.

OMAR VIZQUEL

Seemed to backslide a bit in '93 after a solid '92 in which he was robbed of the Gold Glove after committing just 7 errors. More than doubled that error total last season along with a 39-point drop in batting average . . . So, with that large a skid in BA, why did his TOPR not fall off more? Walks! A career high 50 . . . Should reconsider using him in the running game. A woeful 12 for 26 in steals after an almost-as-bad 15 for 28 the year before. That's simply unacceptable. So why keep flashing the steal sign? . . . Absolutely no pop with a mere 14 doubles (a drop of 8). Even with as brilliant as he can be in the field, he simply must become a better offensive player.

MANUEL LEE

Thank God for September. Was on a path to be the major league's worst TOPR until a late season run, in which he hit over .300 for the last five weeks, "vaulted" him all the way up to a 71! Would you believe he was in the 40s approaching the stretch run? . . . Injuries contributed to his terrible beginning. But then, they always do. Has never started more than 123 games in a season, and only once in six years as a regular has he made it to 400 official at bats . . . After committing just 7 errors the year before, made

10 in what amounted to about one-third of a season . . . 5 extra-base hits in 239 appearances? Just 14 the season before in over 450 PA? Can Texas win with him at short? Toronto did—with and without him.

FELIX FERMIN

The hardest man to strike out in the league by a mile. Fanned only 14 times—once every 36.7 at bats. Minnesota's Brian Harper next toughest at one K every 19.8 at bats . . . But Fermin also doesn't walk—just 24 of those. No power and almost no stealing speed combined to drag TOPR to the lowest of the decade for him . . . Also made 23 errors . . . Cleveland wants Mark Lewis to take his job turning him into a valuable spare part . . . But they've been hoping that for two years. For their sake it better happen in '94.

GARY DISARCINA

The most underrated fielder in the league. Made 14 errors but probably got to 50 balls many other shortstops wouldn't have even touched . . . But can a team carry even a gloveman this slick with sick TOPRs? When your total of walks and steals (20) is the same as your total of double plays and caught stealings, and there's no power (3 HRs), you're in big offensive trouble . . . To be fair he did slump late in the year dragging his TOPR down. And his minor league numbers suggest an eventual 86 TOPR which would be acceptable given how fabulous he can be afield.

PAT MEARES

Ticketed to be a Triple A middle infielder in '92 when starter Scott Leius went down immediately. Forced to play at least one level over his head and the TOPR showed it . . . Must learn to work pitchers. Seven walks in 361 plate appearances? He's the non-Latin version of Ozzie Guillen . . . If you're a Twins fan, understand he was rushed, forgive those horrible numbers, send him back to Triple A for the one season he might still need and hope he's ready again very soon . . . Minor league TOPRs offer big hope projecting him at around a 100. Stay tuned.

DICK SCHOFIELD

Like father like son. Dick, the son of Ducky, never was much of a hitter but appeared to have landed in an ideal spot starting with the Jays in '93. He'd provide the leather and they'd not need much "wood work" from him . . . But he broke an arm, Toronto dealt for Fernandez, and now phenom Alex Gonzalez appears about ready to take over the job leaving Schofield either as a backup or job hunting . . . Father Ducky a .227 lifetime hitter in parts or all of 19 major league seasons. Son Dick now at .228 in 11 years. This acorn truly didn't fall far from the tree.

SCOTT LEIUS

Played 10 games before rotator cuff surgery ended his season . . . So which player comes back from the DL? The Leius of 1991—a sparkling 115 TOPR that would put him right at the top at this position? Or the 78 of '92? It's anyone's guess.

AMERICAN LEAGUE LEFT FIELDERS

| | | | 7/1/94 | | TOPR Trendline | | | | 1993 |
Rank	Player	Team	Age	B	1990	1991	1992	3 yr Avg.	TOPR
Regulars:									
1.	Rickey Henderson	OAK/TOR	35	R	192	143	167	167	**162**
2.	Juan Gonzalez	TEX	24	R	*	113	118	116	**150**
3.	Tim Raines	CWS	34	B	125	111	135	123	**136**
4.	Albert Belle	CLE	27	R	*	114	113	113	**136**
5.	Greg Vaughn	MIL	28	R	100	115	103	107	**128**
6.	Brady Anderson	BAL	30	L	103	105	143	125	**119**
7.	Mike Greenwell	BOS	30	L	111	109	66	104	**116**
8.	Luis Polonia	CAL	29	L	106	102	89	98	**89**
Other Qualifiers (200+ TPA):									
-	Dion James	NYY	31	L	98	-	(111)	101	**121**
-	Kevin McReynolds	KCR	34	R	126†	107†	124	118	**98**
-	Chris Gwynn	KCR	29	L	(98)†	(98)†	*	98	**93**
-	Dan Gladden	DET	36	R	90	86	88	88	**91**
-	Pedro Muñoz	MIN	25	R	*	(125)	83	93	**86**
-	Mike Felder	SEA	32	B	108	100†	109†	105	**67**
-	David McCarty	MIN	24	R	-	-	-		**53**

* Under 100 TPA-not included in average. ( ) 100-199 TPA. † Includes NL TOPR, unadjusted to AL.

RICKEY HENDERSON

Can still do it! No matter what you think of his constant money complaints, his all-around game continues to have dramatic affects on the outcome of games . . . Probably will never again reach that gaudy 192 TOPR of 1990 but still hits, hits with power and steals remarkable percentages (53 of 61) . . . An incredible 120 walks, or almost exactly one free pass every five plate appearances meaning he walked at about a .200 average last year . . . Is he getting better on the bases? Eight caught stealings is the second lowest annual total of his career . . . At 35 years old might be impacting games for at least another five years. Then five more years and he enters the Hall.

JUAN GONZALEZ

An emerging superstar. First man with back-to-back AL homer titles since Jim Rice with Boston in '77–'78. Most likely to hit a homer in the majors last year—one every 11.7 at bats. Next best in the AL was Griffey at 1:12.9 . . . At age 23 had his first 80-extra-base-hit season. How rare are those? See the Seattle essay on Ken Griffey Jr. So why's "Igor" rated behind Henderson in TOPR? Incredibly low walk total of 30 unintentional free passes despite the fact that many pitchers *wanted* to pitch around him. Also, doesn't run at all and, because he hits the ball so hard, will pile up his fair share of DPs—12 last season and 16 the year before . . . Almost unbelievable to say about a player who has back-to-back 40-homer seasons but he's still very raw and some nights still doesn't seem to be able to figure it all out. The scariest thought of all? What if he keeps getting better?

ALBERT BELLE

A real banger. Had TOPR numbers very similar to Gonzalez before '93 and like Gonzalez took a major step forward last season . . . Seems to have fully overcome alcohol and behavior problems that held him back earlier . . . Topped the majors in RBIs with 129 and the AL in sac flies with 14. (Would you believe Gonzalez had only one?) . . . Very bright man who loves crossword puzzles and chess and keeps a daily log of what each pitcher throws him suggesting that those TOPR figures may continue to rise as Belle better learns the art of hitting . . . Walk totals jumped from 25 in

'91 to 52 in '92 to 76 last season. Steals leaped from 8 to 23 . . . A player of enormous ability who may just be starting to reach his prime on a team just approaching prime time.

TIM RAINES

What's this? Tim Raines and Albert Belle tied at a 136 TOPR? . . . His '93 may have been baseball's best-kept secret. But then, check out his '92 TOPR . . . The consummate leadoff hitter. Nearly twice as may walks as strikeouts, a 75% stealing figure, surprising power (16 HRs) and very few double plays (7). In short (for a player who's short) this guy can flat out play. And how about NO errors in '93? . . . Has succeeded in steals more than 85% of the time in his career trailing only Eric Davis among active players . . . If Chicago lets "Rock" Raines get away to free agency it'll be a real rock.

GREG VAUGHN

Both "Vaughns" broke through in '92. Unfortunately for Greg he did so in the midst of the Brew Crew's horrible season so hardly anyone noticed . . . On a powerless team that had a woeful total of 390 extra-base hits, he collected 60 of them. Eleven more HRs and 27 more RBIs than any other Brewer . . . Consider what he might have accomplished had pitchers feared anyone behind him in the lineup and not been able to pitch around him so often (89 walks), or work him especially tough realizing other Brewers weren't nearly the threat to hurt them as he was . . . Quietly emerging as a big-time player.

BRADY ANDERSON

Slipped a bit from his terrific TOPR of '92, but remained a solid contributor . . . Hard to believe now that for parts of four seasons ('88–'91) he was platooned because he was considered such a poor offensive player. Note that his TOPRs for the early '90s didn't agree with that assessment even before he broke through with that huge 143 in '92 . . . Tons of walks, 24-of-36 stealing and more than acceptable power make him, like Raines and Henderson, blueprints for the leadoff spot . . . And forget trying to double him up. In the last two years in 1,413 plate appearances has hit into only 6 DPs!

MIKE GREENWELL

Back from a series of injuries to his form and TOPRs of the late 80s and 1990 . . . What keeps him just below the elite level of AL LFs is a combination of moderate power (13 HRs), bunches of double plays (17), an average walk total of 54 and just 5 steals in 9 attempts. Knee and ankle injuries have robbed him of the quickness that once made him a mid-teens stealing threat . . . But does anyone realize that Greenie's been in the bigs for parts of all of nine seasons and has hit at least .300 in seven of them?

LUIS POLONIA

Is it any wonder the Angels say they're looking for a LF this off-season? Note how far beneath other AL regular LFs Polonia's numbers fall . . . A pesky hitter who will take a walk (48). But absolutely no pop—1 HR, giving him 7 in the last five years . . . Back-to-back 50-steal seasons but thrown out 24 times trying to steal . . . Could be a valuable spare part for lots of teams. But surely a starting player on the "All Most Quotable" team. After being dealt away by the Yanks, told the press: "The Yankees are interested in only one thing and I don't know what it is." When told once he'd been criticized by one of the team's pitchers for his legendary poor fielding, Polonia replied: "If I have anything to say I won't say it."

DION JAMES

A fabulous season that began with him buried deep on the NY bench and ended with him as a semi-regular . . . Was it a mirage or is he simply a late bloomer? Or did manager Showalter simply use him correctly? . . . Never even attempted a steal. Odd for a player who once swiped 45 in a single minor league season. Once the Brewers team rookie-of-the-year before tearing up a shoulder and wandering through Atlanta and Cleveland . . . Of all AL pinch hitters who appeared more than 15 times in that role was second in on-base percentage with a .480. First? How about Chip Hale of the Twins?

KEVIN McREYNOLDS

What happened to this player? . . . TOPRs and just about everything else keep declining. Batting average down for a fifth straight year to .245. Steals likewise down a fifth consecutive time (21 five years ago to 2 last season). But the biggest reason his TOPR keeps plummeting remains the power shortage. Seven years ago he hit 29 for the Mets. Every campaign since, that total's slipped to a career low of 11 in '93 . . . KC absolutely doesn't want him. But can't find anyone to take his $3,666,667 salary . . . Will his game ever stop declining? Would you pay to find out?

CHRIS GWYNN

Same round shape as brother Tony but doesn't TOPR like him . . . In a strange way very similar to the KC team he played for last year—little power, no speed and low base-on-balls totals . . . But a dependable pinch hitter (6 for 16) and players like him who come off the bench swinging (especially left-handed) will always have a home.

DAN GLADDEN

His TOPRs around 90 simply don't fit in the same lineup with the big boppers from Detroit . . . Injuries limited him to 91 games, by far his lowest total since reaching the majors full time in '85 . . . Game has really never changed—average power, low walk totals, decent speed and lots of DPs . . . Will be part of somebody's bench or platoon in '94.

PEDRO MUNOZ

Twins were hoping for more. Average dropped 37 points but occasional power kept TOPR from similar slide . . . Ignores walks and not a stealing threat . . . Terrific throwing arm and minor league and early career stats suggested he'd develop into a player who'd put up TOPRs over 100 . . . Twins are still waiting. Might be a career platoon/bench player.

MIKE FELDER

Spray hitter with speed whose game fell apart last season . . . Very nice TOPRs for the seasons before. But when a slap hitter's average falls to barely above .200 there's little else in his game to save him. Deprived of getting on base robs him of the steal totals that make his game effective . . . Doubled up only six times the last four years . . . Could still make someone a decent bench player.

DAVID McCARTY

Arrived with much fanfare. Ended with the lowest TOPR of anyone with over 200 plate appearances in all of baseball . . . Twins complained about his failure to adjust as a big league hitter and manager Tom Kelly quickly grew weary of his helmet-tossing episodes . . . But minor league figures suggest that he'll grow into a star . . . 1991 college player-of-the-year at Stanford. Fans yelped when he hit .333 in spring training but the club still shipped him to the minors. Turns out the club was right . . . TOPR math: 2 HRs + 2 SBs + just 19 BBs + .214 average = UGH!

AMERICAN LEAGUE CENTER FIELDERS

| | | | 7/1/94 | | TOPR Trendline | | | | 1993 |
Rank	Player	Team	Age	B	1990	1991	1992	3 yr Avg.	TOPR
Regulars:									
1.	Ken Griffey, Jr.	SEA	24	L	125	148	132	135	**161**
2.	Kenny Lofton	CLE	27	L	-	*	121	121	**134**
3.	Devon White	TOR	31	B	95	122	107	109	**120**
4.	Eric Davis	LAD/DET	32	R	135	127	104	124	**110†**
5.	Lance Johnson	CWS	30	L	89	81	91	87	**104**
6.	Shane Mack	MIN	30	R	130	129	134	132	**99**
7.	Chad Curtis	CAL	25	R	-	-	107	107	**99**
8.	Brian McRae	KCR	26	B	(94)	84	82	84	**98**
9.	Dave Henderson	OAK	35	R	119	117	*	110	**96**
10.	Billy Hatcher	BOS	33	R	104†	89†	74†	90	**94**
11.	Robin Yount	MIL	38	R	124	97	104	108	**94**
12.	David Hulse	TEX	26	L	-	-	*	*	**93**
13.	Bernie Williams	NYY	25	B	-	101	106	103	**91**
14.	Mike Devereaux	BAL	31	R	88	102	110	102	**89**
Other Qualifiers (200+ TPA):									
-	Milt Cuyler	DET	25	B	*	106	76	94	**83**

* Under 100 TPA-not included in average. ( ) 100-199 TPA. † Includes NL TOPR, unadjusted to AL.

KEN GRIFFEY JR.

The #1 base producer in the AL with 462 meaning he generates nearly three bases per game. Bonds had 506. TOPRs already in the stratosphere and he's three years away from the start of what is generally regarded as the prime period of a ball player's career . . . TOPR explosion upward due to two significant improvements. Everyone recognizes one of them—his leap from 27 HRs to 45. Less noticed, but perhaps the key to his elevating offensive game, was the even more dramatic rise in walks—from 44 to 96. Here's a 45-homer guy who actually walked more than he struck out! Most young power hitters for some reason think being a lot more selective at the plate will *decrease* HR totals. It's just the opposite as Griffey showed . . . Only complaint with him centers around the fact that he sometimes doesn't hustle, acting a bit bored with the game. Lord, what might his numbers be if he pays attention all the time . . . So good he's already had a candy bar named after him. One problem—he's allergic to chocolate!

KENNY LOFTON

Led the "American" League in hitting at .325. Uh, that's if you don't count the three guys from the Canadian team—Olerud, Molitor and Alomar . . . The blueprint for a leadoff hitter—blazing speed and smarts on the bases, walks keep going up, few DPs and nice extra-base pop . . . His 70 SBs set a club record . . . Former starting point guard on Arizona's pre-season #1 ranked basketball team now has 136 swipes in just two seasons. Are Henderson's records safe? . . . One additional huge plus—his throwing arm. Totaled 11 assists last season and 14 the year before. A star who may never start an AL all-star game because of Griffey.

DEVON WHITE

Everyone referred to '93 as Devo's best season ever. Not true. A slightly better TOPR in '91 . . . Hardest man to double up in the league—one DP every 199.3 at bats! . . . Most folks, dazzled by his speed (34 of 38 in steals) and that leather wizardry that's brought four Gold Gloves, overlook the surprising clout that's produced an average of 15 HRs a year since '87 . . . Would put up superstar TOPRs if he converted some of those Ks (127) into BBs (57) . . . Did Toronto really get this guy from California for a package whose key player going to the Angels was Junior Felix?

ERIC DAVIS

Found new life in Detroit which moved quickly after the season to get him re-signed for '94 and avoid him going to free agency . . . The game's leading active percentage base stealer—over 86% . . . Injuries robbed him of the kind of extraordinary numbers he put up in Cincy but still an exciting and vital lineup part IF he stays healthy . . . Didn't play 90 games in either '91 or '92 but got into 131 last season . . . Are there still TOPRs in the 130s left in that body? The Tigers paid $3 million in belief there were.

LANCE JOHNSON

"One Dog" put up the best TOPR of his career thanks to a more than 30-point jump in his batting average . . . In the city where the Bulls "three-peated," Johnson three-peated in threes leading the league in triples for a third straight season. Only others who can say that in history? Elmer Flick of the Indians, Sam Crawford of the Tigers, Zoilo Versalles of the Twins and Garry Templeton in San Diego . . . Oddly, gets very few doubles (18) when you consider all the threes he records (14) . . . Sensational stealing percentage again—83%, right around his career figure . . . How's this for an odd couple? Rail-thin Johnson was a Triton Junior College teammate of Kirby Puckett! Bet they never got their uniforms mixed up.

SHANE MACK

At first glance it appears Mack suffered a drastic TOPR drop. But look inside the numbers with us. Separated his right shoulder in spring training, tried to come back too soon and reinjured it. Gutted it out, tried to play through the pain and his game caved in. On June 28 had an ugly 89 TOPR and was dragging around a .224 average. But from that point on, once the shoulder had healed, put up Mack-like figures—a 121 TOPR and a .315 average . . . Badly overlooked player who's played in the rather ample shadow of Puckett for years . . . If you like safe bets take Mack to hit .300 with a TOPR back in the 120–130 range again in '94 . . . Did the Padres really think so little of this guy they left him exposed to the draft after '89 and got only $50,000 for him?

CHAD CURTIS

A little pest of a player . . . TOPRs solid for a second-year player and should improve significantly as Curtis (and the Angels) pick better spots for him to run. Had 48 steals but was thrown out an unacceptable 24 times . . . Also hit into 16 DPs contributing to a lowered TOPR . . . Not bad for a player drafted in the 45th round and told that the organization felt he might eventually be good enough to play on a Triple A level.

BRIAN McRAE

Many will be shocked to find McRae so low a TOPR player. But look closer at his game. He's a leadoff hitter who hardly ever walks (37 in just under 700 plate appearances). A poor steals ratio: 23 for 37. Surprisingly high DP totals (18 in the last two years) for someone with his speed . . . Did make a significant climb in batting average of nearly 50 points and makes some brilliant plays in CF . . . But must get far more selective at the plate and put the ball in play much more often rather than striking out 105 times. Fortunately he's got a father hanging around who can give him some awfully good advice on hitting . . . Can you imagine KC almost traded him for Darrin Jackson of the Padres early in '93? Sometimes the best trades you make are the ones you didn't make.

DAVE HENDERSON

Are the days that "Hendu Can Do" over? Leg injuries totally wiped out his '92 season and the start of '93. But by the end of last season the player that manager Tony La Russa once called "The least-publicized great player in our league" was again showing some of his old power (20 HRs in just over 400 plate appearances) . . . But for Hendu to get back to those 120-area TOPRs he must change that walks-to-strikeouts ratio of 1:3½ . . . Annually leads the league in smiles and has a terrific reputation as a player you like to have in your clubhouse. That should insure his place in the majors for another handful of years.

ROBIN YOUNT

Probably a DH next season . . . Last season's 94 TOPR the lowest of his career but not out of line with the kind of numbers he's put up the last three seasons . . . It's now been four years since he hit over .265 and now has put back-to-back seasons of a career low 8 HRs . . . His place in history's assured as the third youngest to ever reach 3,000 career hits behind only a couple of fair hitters named Cobb and Aaron.

BILLY HATCHER

Usable player who may be better when spot-played. Bounced back from two down seasons to put together decent numbers in '93 crediting the help from Red Sox hitting coach Mike Easler . . . Some encouraging signs of life in his game—9 HRs after hitting just 7 the two previous seasons combined and 14 steals after swiping a total of 15 in '91–'92 . . . Not in the defensive class of several of the CFs rated above him offensively. Has the look of a solid #4 outfielder.

DAVID HULSE

A surprisingly good rookie season for a player on the verge of being sent back to the minors several times early in the season . . . But to settle in as a long-term starter absolutely must draw more walks. Had only 29 as a leadoff hitter. Given that he'll never have any power (1 HR in over 500 major league at bats) he must get on base and use stealing speed (29 for 38) to impact the game . . . Figures might have been higher except for hamstring troubles that interrupted his last six weeks . . . Odd extra-base hit line: had as many triples (10) as he did doubles and homers combined (9 + 1).

BERNIE WILLIAMS

A tools-player that the Yankees keep waiting to explode and play to his minor league TOPR projections in the 130 area. But the Bronx Bombers can't wait much longer when their CF is TOPR-rated 13th among 14 starters . . . Decent power (31 doubles and 12 HRs) but a negative running game (9 steals, 9 throw outs) and extremely high DP totals (17) . . . Actually slipped from the TOPRs he put up his first two years. Are the Yanks patient enough to wait for him to bloom? George Steinbrenner's been called lots of things. But "patient" has never been one of them.

MIKE DEVEREAUX

His '91–'92 TOPR upswing seemed to suggest he'd break through to the mini-star level in '93. Instead he cratered and the O's dropped loads of hints they'd spend this off-season seeking CF help . . . A spectacular athlete who still holds the state of Wyoming high schools records in the 100-, 200- and 400-meter dashes and in the high jump, his acrobatic catches have become a regular part of the highlights on "This Week in Baseball." But to remain a regular anywhere he's got to reverse some of last season's drops—fell 26 average points, 16 extra-base hits, 32 RBIs and 7 steals . . . Part of what might have been the best college outfield ever at Arizona State along with Barry Bonds and former Texas #1 draft pick Oddibe McDowell.

MILT CUYLER

It appears Detroit's gotten very tired of waiting for him to develop . . . Leg injuries gutted his last two seasons after that respectable 106 TOPR his rookie year in '91 . . . Even with his high speed gets very few extra-base hits . . . Still stole 13 of 15 bases and swiped 41 of 47 in '91 . . . Only 25 years old and, with health, could still become a productive player. Look for somebody to try to get him away from Detroit in a minor deal and hope he makes major improvement.

AMERICAN LEAGUE RIGHT FIELDERS

Rank	Player	Team	7/1/94 Age	B	1990	1991	1992	3 yr Avg.	1993 TOPR
Regulars:									
1.	Tim Salmon	CAL	25	R	-	-	*	*	**141**
2.	Jay Buhner	SEA	29	R	(118)	124	108	115	**125**
3.	Paul O'Neill	NYY	31	L	105†	130†	112†	116	**118**
4.	Joe Carter	TOR	34	R	97†	126	118	114	**113**
5.	Kirby Puckett	MIN	33	R	125	105	126	117	**110**
6.	Ellis Burks	CWS	29	R	114	99	107	107	**107**
7.	Darryl Hamilton	MIL	29	L	(96)	102	114	107	**103**
8.	Jose Canseco	TEX	29	R	147	145	114	136	**97**
9.	Rob Deer	DET/BOS	33	R	117	108	137	120	**96**
10.	Wayne Kirby	CLE	30	L	-	*	*	*	**94**
11.	Ruben Sierra	OAK	28	B	108	126	111	115	**91**
12.	Mark McLemore	BAL	29	B	*	*	85	85	**90**
13.	Felix Jose	KCR	29	B	93†	117†	118†	110	**86**
Other Qualifiers (200+ TPA):									
-	Gary Redus	TEX	37	R	122†	123†	(110)†	119	**112**
-	Candy Maldonado	CUB/CLE	33	R	109	113	120	114	**82†**
-	Tom Brunansky	MIL	33	R	106†	97	117	106	**71**
-	Ivan Calderon	BOS/CWS	32	R	99	136†	(105)†	113	**59**
Of Note (under 200 TPA):									
-	Hubie Brooks	KCR	37	R	98†	110†	67	93	**(83)**

* Under 100 TPA-not included in average. ( ) 100-199 TPA. † Includes NL TOPR, unadjusted to AL.

TIM SALMON

Wow! A sensational season for the Rookie-of-the-Year and best TOPR RF in the league . . . Led the league's first-year men in BA, HRs, and RBIs. The first to win the Triple Crown for rookies since 1968 when Reggie Jackson did it . . . Already does some things like a veteran. Will accept walks—82 of them. Despite only average speed, hit into just a half dozen double plays . . . A monster throwing arm . . . Broken ring finger cost him the final three weeks of the season and an almost certain 100–RBI year . . . Will the pitchers figure him out and "smoke" Salmon next season? On the other hand, if, with the year's experience, he gets better he could be one of the biggest fishes in the major league pond for years.

JAY BUHNER

Another solid year for a player who might never get recognition playing next to Griffey Jr . . . Like Griffey his walk total leaped to its highest point ever (100 BBs) without affecting his power . . . First Mariner to ever have three consecutive 25+ HR seasons . . . From the Weird Dept.: plays in the homer-happy Kingdome but over the last two years has hit 30 of his 52 HRs on the road . . . Tends to blow very hot and very cold. Once went 118 at bats without a HR. A month earlier in that '91 season he'd homered in four straight games and a couple weeks later hit four in three games . . . If he cuts down tendency to fan (144), will move to the verge of stardom. Will anyone in Seattle notice?

PAUL O'NEILL

Many shook their heads when the Yanks dealt Roberto "Bobby" Kelly for O'Neill but he provided exactly what NY needed—an everyday left-handed bat in a stadium that favors lefties. Hit .345 at home . . . Only negatives revolve around lack of foot speed leading to relatively high DP count of 13 and non-involvement in running game . . . TOPR would have been substantially higher had his walk total not tumbled from 76 to 44 . . . Average had dropped three straight seasons entering '93 and extra-base hits had fallen off sharply. But that bleeding's stopped and it appears the Yanks RF spot's plugged for a few years to come . . . Weird: Kelly and

O'Neill, traded for each other, each recorded identical 118 TOPRs in '93.

JOE CARTER

Would you believe the weakest TOPR in the top five hitters in the Jays lineup! But when 113's your lowest you've got some kind of offense . . . Streaky hitter whose hot runs tend to carry a team. For example: didn't homer from June 28 through July 24. But still managed 33 for '93. The last time he didn't drive in 100 runs for the season Ronald Reagan was in the White House ('88) . . . Won't run much any more (his 8 steals were easily the lowest full-season total of his career in which he once swiped 87 bases in a three-year run in the mid-'80s) . . . Has 893 RBIs the last eight years—best in the majors. Even studs like Aaron, Robinson, Mantle and McCovey can't claim an "eight pack" like that. But still far from Ruth's best eight seasons from 1926 through '33 when he batted in an astronomical 1,161 runs. That fat man could play! So can Carter!

KIRBY PUCKETT

Another solid TOPR season despite not hitting .300 for only the second time since 1986 . . . Still leads the majors in hits and batting average since 1988 . . . With health his career numbers are starting to reach the point where you can at least ask if he's "Hall" material. In the first week of the '94 season he'll get hit #2,000. During the year sometime should get his 600th extra-base hit, 900th RBI and will finish the coming season close to 1,000 runs scored . . . Not bad for a player who wasn't even drafted out of high school because scouts who saw him then thought he was too weak and skinny to ever make it.

ELLIS BURKS

He's baaaaack! From '81 to '90 Burks averaged .291, 18 HRs and 75 RBIs. Then back problems greased the skids of his career to the point where this once budding superstar had to accept a $500,000 base salary and a contract laden with incentives just for a chance to play. What a bargain for the Sox! He returned to almost the identical numbers he'd put up before the back trouble. 1993: .275, 17 HRs, 74 RBIs . . . TOPRs still not quite back to that period though and probably never will be because Burks' diminished running game (just 6 for 15 in steals) . . . The only question for the Sox now is whether they're sufficiently satisfied that his hurts are behind him enough to offer a long-term contract.

DARRYL HAMILTON

Another one of those "good parts of a bad team" who seldom gets noticed . . . This whippet's hit .305 in the '90s . . . Starting to show a moderate power (a professional one-season high of 9 HRs) . . . TOPR would have been much higher had his running game not declined dramatically getting thrown out in 13 of 34 steal attempts . . . Needs to move walk totals out of the 40 range . . . what "Hambone" needs most is a good PR person so fans might begin to understand how good he's become.

JOSE CANSECO

His TOPRs suggest Oakland did the right thing when they dealt him to Texas. Note the decline from '91 to '92 and the steep drop when he blew out his elbow in an ill-advised inning of relief pitching. Wasn't drawing nearly the number of walks as he had earlier in his career and the bottom's fallen out of his running game. Remember when he stole 40 bases in '88? The last TWO seasons he's 12 for 25 . . . Defense had deteriorated to the point where that elbow injury'll probably turn him into a DH—a blessing for the Rangers . . . At age 29 (yes, he's only 29!) can he regain the form that made him one of the game's very best? Texas will pay over $10 million in salary the next two years to find out.

ROB DEER

Full name: Robert George Deer. Unbelievable that his name doesn't have a "K" in it . . . Led the league in striking out for the fourth time in his career. Strange thing about that awful note is that it enables Deer to join an elite group who can say that including Jimmie Foxx (7), Reggie Jackson (5), Babe Ruth (5), Mickey Mantle (4) and Pat Seerey (4). Actually it enabled Deer to join Seerey as the two who'll say they did it and didn't make the Hall of Fame . . . Reached 1,000 Ks faster than any player in history fanning for the 1,000th time in game #868, easily wiping out Dave Kingman who took 950 games to get a thousand whiffs . . . But Deer will always fan. The danger signs for his career revolve around his drop to an eight-year low of 21 homers. If Deer doesn't swat about 30 a year the rest of his game won't keep him in the game.

WAYNE KIRBY

A breakthrough year for the Kirby brothers. Younger bro Terry starred as rookie runner for the Miami Dolphins . . . After a decade in the bus leagues Kirby got his chance. With Whiten traded, Hill flunking again and Howard unable to seize the RF job on an everyday basis, Kirby gave the Tribe decent numbers though not the power associated with many of the others who play RF . . . Despite solid speed gets few extra-base hits and not many walks. A career-long infielder who, if one of the Indians intriguing prospects develops to take over RF, could turn into an impact multiple position player (IMP) . . . Forget trying to run on his arm. Oh, he might be a former infielder, but he posted a league high 19 assists.

RUBEN SIERRA

The #1 "out-maker" in the entire big leagues with 515, 25 more than NL leader Terry Pendleton . . . Note the major TOPR decline from his 126 in '91 . . . Imagine the size of the decline had his running game not returned? Successful in 25 of 30 steal attempts, and . . . Scouts point to his bulked-up body as the reason for his power slump. Hit 82 long balls from '87–'89. But has only 70 total the last *FOUR* years . . . Hurt badly when injuries took the presence of McGwire out of the lineup behind him. Sierra hitting .297 with

Big Mac back there, finished at .233 . . . Average trailed off in the second half of the season for the fourth straight year . . . Once seemed like a future Hall of Famer. Now, at 28, his career has question marks all over it.

MARK McLEMORE

A non-roster player in spring training who wound up playing 148 games in the outfield, a position he'd never been a regular at . . . TOPRs not in line with the position. But, should star prospect Hammonds return to take over this spot, might, like Kirby, be turned into a fine IMP . . . Numbers would have been higher except for 15 CS. Even harder to figure, for a guy with his speed and the fact that well over 70% of his at bats came from the left side, is that huge DP total—21 . . . Extremely handy player but with him in RF the O's give away lots of offense to their opponents.

FELIX JOSÉ

Totally forgive the '93 season. Injured his left shoulder so badly the Royals totally stopped using him as a RH hitter (a mere 30 plate appearances with two singles and no walks) . . . Hurt so he actually batted left-handed against rugged lefties like Jimmy Key . . . With the injury repaired he should return to those solid '91–'92 St. Louis TOPRs and provide some of the power KC desperately needs . . . Note 31 SBs. If those 40 double/14 homer totals he put up with the Cards reappear, he's in the top five at his position.

GARY REDUS

Oh, for a pair of good knees . . . Check out those wonderful TOPRs . . . A clubhouse leader with the kind of bench numbers managers crave . . . Says '94 will be his final year . . . Must be kept off artificial surface to keep the tendinitis from flaring up . . . If he wants to stay in the game after retiring all he has to do is say so and his phone will ring off the hook.

CANDY MALDONADO

TOPR fell through the floor after a succession of solid seasons . . . Indians, with an eye to what they wanted on their '94 bench, grabbed him when the Cubs tired of waiting for him to produce the figures of his past . . . Another like Redus who'll give you good part-time numbers as long as that woeful '93 TOPR doesn't indicate a declining career . . . Indians encouraged by his 5 HRs in just 92 PAs. Maybe that .186 batting average and 3 HRs through four months in Wrigley Field was nothing more than a bad dream.

TOM BRUNANSKY

Seems too young to be finished, but Bruno was Brutal last season . . . Hit further below his listed weight (.183 vs. 220 pounds) than anyone in the league . . . No power of any kind (16 extra-base hits) for a player who'd had between 40 and 59 extra basers every season of his 11-year career coming into '93 . . . Is he finished? Right now you can get him awfully cheap. And if '93 was simply a mistake you might get a real bargain.

IVAN CALDERON

How can a player drop in a free fall from a 136 TOPR two years ago to that dismal 59? One HR? For a fellow who once hit 28? Maybe all those trips to the injured list (nine disabled list moves since '84) finally ruined his career . . . Like Bruno, you won't have to pay much to find out if he's finished at age 32.

HUBIE BROOKS

The BA looks terrific—.286. But the rest of the numbers are totally empty: 1 HR, 0 SB, 11 BB . . . Once had 8 consecutive double-figure HR years but that power seemed non-existent last season . . . Is there a job waiting on somebody's bench or is he Japan-bound? . . . Has played the most games of any current major leaguer without playing in a post-season contest—1,611.

AMERICAN LEAGUE DESIGNATED HITTERS

Rank	Player	Team	7/1/94 Age	B	TOPR Trendline				1993 TOPR
					_1990_	_1991_	_1992_	3 yr Avg.	
Regulars:									
1.	Paul Molitor	TOR	37	R	*124*	*137*	*136*	133	**139**
2.	Danny Tartabull	NYY	31	R	*117*	*159*	*151*	145	**132**
3.	Harold Baines	BAL	35	L	*117*	*128*	*101*	115	**128**
4.	Troy Neel	OAK	28	L	-	-	*	*	**117**
5.	Kirk Gibson	DET	37	L	*125†*	*114*	*	117	**113**
6.	Julio Franco	TEX	35	R	*121*	*139*	*(93)*	126	**109**
7.	Chili Davis	CAL	34	B	*106*	*140*	*125*	125	**102**
8.	Dave Winfield	MIN	42	R	*111*	*110*	*134*	118	**98**
9.	George Brett	KCR	41	L	*135*	*97*	*95*	108	**93**
10.	Andre Dawson	BOS	39	R	*138†*	*113†*	*112†*	121	**90**
11.	Kevin Reimer	MIL	30	L	*(102)*	*113*	*109*	110	**86**
12.	Reggie Jefferson	CLE	25	B	-	*(65)†*	*	(65)	**85**
13.	George Bell	CWS	34	R	*98*	*113†*	*88*	99	**70**
Other Qualifiers (200+ TPA):									
-	Lonnie Smith	PIT/BAL	38	R	*131*	*123*	*(129)*	128	**145†**
-	Bo Jackson	CWS	31	R	*130*	*	*DNP*	122	**93**
-	Pete O'Brien	SEA/-	36	L	*82*	*93*	*92*	90	**93**
Of Note (under 200 TPA):									
-	Kevin Maas	NYY	29	L	*146*	*111*	*105*	118	**(104)**

* Under 100 TPA-not included in average. ( ) 100-199 TPA. † Includes NL TOPR, unadjusted to AL.

PAUL MOLITOR

Aging like fine wine. Three best TOPRs of his life are his last three . . . Became the oldest member ever of the 20 HR-20 SB club (22-22). Second oldest ever to pull that trick? It was the 37-year-old Molitor's 34-year-old teammate Rickey Henderson . . . Missed well over two total years of playing time due to eight trips to the DL from '80–'90. But hasn't been injured in any of the last three years, the longest healthy string of his career (476 games played) . . . Only man in history to have played at least 50 games at every infield and outfield position and DH . . . If you sat down at a drawing board and designed the perfect DH wouldn't you name it "Paul Molitor"?

DANNY TARTABULL

Just can't seem to play an injury-free season and, because of that, like Molitor, might be advised to remain a career DH . . . For some reason doesn't get the kind of respect those boxcar-TOPRs should bring. Averaging 29 doubles and 29 HRs the last three seasons despite playing just 131 games a year. TOPR decline the result of his lowest single season batting average of his career (.250). Terrific "opposite field" power . . . But is he really the son of Jose? Dad hit 2 HRs in a nine-year career. Danny blasted 4 his first week in the majors and 3 in one 1991 game.

HAROLD BAINES

The right kind of year to have when you're about to be a free agent . . . Highest batting average ever (.313) and solid power totals (20 HRs) given that he played in only 118 games . . . Aching knees preclude his ever being a part of the running game and tend to inflate DP totals (14) . . . Age and physical problems aside, can the O's afford to *not* sign the second best TOPR in their entire lineup?

TROY NEEL

Another player, like Brent Gates, who emerged when injuries and the A's horrible season forced them to give playing time to kids

. . . Former Texas Aggie scholarship football player who finished three homers behind Sierra for the club lead despite more than 200 fewer PA's . . . Another who might benefit from the return of McGwire to the lineup . . . Did Oakland really get this guy in a trade from Cleveland by sending the Tribe Larry Arndt?

KIRK GIBSON

Shocked those who felt the years of injuries had ended his career with the Pirates release in May of 1992. Sat out the rest of that season, got healthy, the fire to compete returned and his old Tiger team gave him a spring training shot. What a bargain they got! . . . Even into his later thirties can still run well enough to swipe 15 of 21 and grounded into just two double plays . . . With as hard as he plays why wouldn't you want him to keep coming back? . . . With all due respect to Bo Jackson's inspiring comeback from hip replacement, why didn't Gibson get more Comeback-Player-of-the-Year votes?

JULIO FRANCO

TOPR's a bit deceiving. Bothered by aching knees, Franco's numbers almost got him released in late June. Ranger manager Kevin Kennedy issued a play-and-play-hard-or-be-released edict and Franco kicked it into gear . . . TOPR for the final half of the year in the 120s . . . Knees felt good enough by late season for him to again steal occasionally (9 of 12). But 16 double plays dragged TOPR down . . . Insists his knees will be sound enough to allow him to return to playing in the field in '94. Regardless of whether he can or can't do that, this former batting champ and oh-so-tough out should be in the middle of somebody's batting order.

CHILI DAVIS

Set Angels franchise DH record with 27 HRs/112 RBIs . . . Weird: A .243 hitter who managed to hit well over .300 when hitting with runners in scoring position . . . Lowered BA and 18 double plays pulled TOPR down . . . Wildly varying power numbers: 22 HRs in '89, dipped to 12 in '90, then up to 29, back down to 12 and last year up to 27 again. Does that mean he hits 12 in '94? . . . Anybody out there realize that there's a chance Chili gets his 250th HR and 1,000th RBI next year?

DAVE WINFIELD

A huge TOPR plummet during a season in which Winnie got his 3,000th career hit . . . 76 RBIs marked his lowest non-strike season total since '76 . . . Every major number fell from the year before—HR, RBI, BB, BA and doubles. ONLY DPs increased. All that adds up to that massive 36 point TOPR fall . . . But there's no talk of retiring from this man born on the same day the NY Giants Bobby Thompson hit the "Shot Heard 'Round the World" to beat the Dodgers in the 1951 playoffs . . . Enters '94 already in the top 20 all-time in HRs, hits, RBIs and extra bases.

GEORGE BRETT

It turns out Brett's 1990 batting-title year marked his last hurrah. TOPR dropped nearly 40 points the next season and he remained a below-average offensive player his last three years . . . But Brett's wind-down should take nothing away from a glorious two decades. Only three men in baseball history can say they've accumulated 3,000 hits, 300 HRs and 200 SBs. The other two are named Aaron and Mays . . . And while Brett's place in history is assured, what does KC do to replace his bat and his presence? The last few years may not have been "Brett quality," but he still led the Royals in RBIs and doubles and finished second in HRs . . . Looking at those leveled-off-in-the-90s TOPRs suggests he did the right thing in retiring.

ANDRE DAWSON

Certainly not what the Red Sox wanted in terms of offensive input . . . The theory had been to make him a DH, save wear and tear on his aching knees and get more quality playing time out of him. But those balky knees and a broken right wrist bone idled him for more than 40 games . . . Even more discouraging was the 13 HRs, a career low . . . This once brilliant base thief (more than 300 in his career) hardly runs at all anymore and the double play totals keep mounting (18) . . . Can he bounce back to those career-long solid TOPRs? After his sixth knee surgery prior to 1990 everyone said no and check that year's TOPR. But in mid-July he turns 40 years old—and his knees are at least 80.

KEVIN REIMER

Former hockey player perfect for the DH because he truly doesn't have a defensive position. In fact, can sometimes look like a hockey player when in the outfield . . . Put up nice spare part/DH TOPRs in Texas but fell off dramatically in Brewtown. Batting average the lowest of his career (.249). That, combined with his typical moderate walk totals and high DP figures, caused that TOPR turndown . . . Nice bat to have around. Can he be a full-time DH? If Yount returns at that spot it limits his opportunities even more.

REGGIE JEFFERSON

After back-to-back minor league seasons hitting over .300 and a sparkling (though brief) late '92 season trial where he hit .337, the Indians believed he might have finally arrived. Wrong! . . . Solid enough as a lefty hitter but woeful from the right side (.196 with 1 HR in 120 PA) . . . Three Ks for every BB, a non-factor in the running game and only fair power. Some of these numbers must change or he soon goes from prospect to suspect.

GEORGE BELL

His release shocked many. But not to those who check his TOPR trendline. A below-average offensive player three of the last four seasons . . . Never walked much, hit into large amounts of DPs and never a stealing threat. Thus, when HR totals tumbled, so did Bell's TOPR . . . Observers of the game will be stunned to find that his supposedly good '92 season (25 HRs, 112 RBIs) didn't even net him a three-figure TOPR. But realize that the three players who hit in front of him (Raines, Ventura and Thomas) were on base 768 times that season. Subtract the times he drove himself in with those 25 dingers and Bell delivered *only* 87 more RBIs. Ruined 29 rallies with DPs . . . The White Sox noticed, and when his power outage appeared in '93, they quickly dumped him . . . Could those "big numbers" he put up in recent seasons still get him a job in Japan?

LONNIE SMITH

This guy gets absolutely no respect. People still giggle at the horrible fielder he once was—so bad he got the nickname "Skates" for the shaky way he played the outfield. But one glance at his TOPRs should stop the laughing. As good a spare part TOPRs as you'll find in the game in the '90s . . . Besides he's somewhat of a "good luck charm." Five of the teams he's been part of have made the World Series . . . Will he turn up in the league again next year at 38? If someone's smart he will. As this DH TOPR list confirms—you don't find many 145 TOPRs just hanging around.

BO JACKSON

If he'd only stuck with baseball. Note that 1990 TOPR—130. That was Bo before hip replacement surgery. That was Bo at age 27 with a chance to blossom into one of the game's more feared power hitters . . . Deserves all the credit imaginable for his remarkable comeback but you still tend to look at him and wonder "What if?" This post-surgery Bo still has some power. But how weird is hitting 16 HRs and only 9 doubles? Still doesn't draw walks and the player who once stole 27 bases didn't get any last year . . . Courageous as they come and still a major drawing card. But what are the chances his below-par TOPR rises substantially?

PETE O'BRIEN

Retired in mid-season after an 11-year career . . . Struggled with TOPRs in the low 90s in the '90s—unacceptable for either 1B or DH . . . Never returned to the 120-ish TOPR of his '86 season in Texas that seemed to mark him as a future star . . . Batting average, never below .260 from '84–'89, was never above that figure in the '90s.

KEVIN MAAS

Given the weak TOPRs of many of the other AL DHs, it seems odd Maas got sent to the minors for non-production . . . True, he only hit .205, but with his usual high-homer percentage and about one walk every 7 PA. Pitchers seemed to find a "hole" in his swing on the outer half of the plate after that fantastic 146 TOPR in his 1990 rookie season (actually half season would be more proper) . . . Truly weird career stat: he's hit 64 HRs but batted in only 164 runs in four years. One more weird one? How does one hit 64 HRs and only 39 doubles?

THE PLAYERS

AMERICAN LEAGUE IMPS

Rank	Player	Team	7/1/94 Age	B	TOPR Trendline 1990	1991	1992	3 yr Avg.	1993 TOPR
Regulars:									
1.	Mickey Tettleton	DET	33	B	122	138	139	133	**132**
2.	Tony Phillips	DET	35	B	110	123	118	117	**130**
3.	Dave Magadan	FLA/SEA	31	L	138†	117†	115†	124	**104†**
4.	Mike Gallego	NYY	33	R	70	100	96	88	**102**
5.	Kevin Seitzer	OAK/MIL	32	R	100	100	94	98	**92**
6.	Rene Gonzales	CAL	33	R	(76)	(69)	101	89	**82**
Other Qualifiers (200+ TPA):									
-	Jim Leyritz	NYY	30	R	87	*	(118)	97	**133**
-	Randy Velarde	NYY	31	R	78	85	98	89	**103**
-	Lance Blankenship	OAK	30	R	(74)	106	120	106	**93**
-	Jerry Browne	OAK	28	B	107	72	107	98	**76**

* Under 100 TPA-not included in average.   ( ) 100-199 TPA.   † Includes NL TOPR, unadjusted to AL.

MICKEY TETTLETON

The biggest TOPR in a lineup filled with big boppers . . . The prototype for a "pounder." Hits loads of homers and draws tons of walks (109 last season and 438 in the '90s). Hits with power from both sides of the plate making him platoon-proof. But best and perhaps weirdest of all, this moose of a man, who's just slightly faster than the great northern glacier, hardly ever hits into double plays. The three toughest to double in the AL last year were all "flyers"—Devon White, Brady Anderson and Harold Reynolds. Tettleton was fourth with 5 DPs in 637 PAs. And that's not a mirage. Hit into only 5 the year before also . . . 95 HRs the last three seasons. Quite a turnaround for a player who, in parts or all of eight minor league seasons, TOTALED 30 HRs and who once went on the disabled list in Oakland with a foot infection thought to have been caused by his tying his shoelaces too tight.

TONY PHILLIPS

Mr. IMP! . . . Had his first ever .300 season and best TOPR of his career. Led the majors in walks (132). Reached base safely 313 times (H/BB/HBP) in 149 starts or 2.1 times per game. Philadelphia's Lenny Dykstra, hailed for his remarkable season and second in NL MVP balloting, averaged 2.03 times on base per start . . . In '91 became the first player to ever start at least 10 games at 5 different positions. Did it again in '92 . . . The point man of the Tigers awesome offense. But then you'd expect that from a former star point guard at New Mexico Military where he paired in the backcourt with future NBAer Lewis Lloyd. After 5 seasons knocking around Oakland's minor league system, Phillips seriously considered leaving baseball to take a basketball scholarship to Clemson in 1982. Good decision not to, Tony.

DAVE MAGADAN

Something in Seattle certainly disagreed with him . . . Came over in late June from the Marlins in a trade bringing with him his usual fine assortment of batting skills that included an excellent BA along with terrific strike-zone judgment leading to a high walk total. It all added up to a Florida TOPR of 122. But that's not unusual if you check his standout TOPR trendline that shows his performance this decade makes him one of the game's most underrated line drive hitters (TOPRs of 138-118-121 leading into '93). So, what happened in Seattle? That glittering TOPR dropped like a rock plummeting to a woeful 88. This .286 Florida hitter with a smattering of HRs became a mediocre slap hitter (.259), with but one HR despite switching to a park far more conducive to extra base hits

. . . Was it "family pressure?" He is, after all, the cousin of Mariners manager Lou Pinella . . . Seemed a perfect IMP for an AL team in that he can play 1B and 3B competently and be a solid DH . . . But following the season the M's decided he wouldn't be sleeping in Seattle anymore and shipped him right back to the NL where, hopefully, the sparkling TOPRs of this slasher will return.

MIKE GALLEGO

Had the best TOPR of his life in '93 topping his previous career best put up in 1991 when he was about to become a free agent . . . Can have almost shocking power at times for such a small man (5'8", 175 pounds). Hit 10 long balls in '93 and 12 two seasons before that . . . TOPR would have been substantially higher were he not so DP-prone (16) . . . TOPR becomes even more impressive when you realize he plays most of his games at middle infield positions. Triple-figure TOPRs for middle infielders are more the exception than the rule.

KEVIN SEITZER

May have resurrected his career with his return performance in Milwaukee. After Oakland dumped him he seemed headed for the "journeyman scrapheap." Hit .290 for the Brew Crew and TOPRed in the 110 area which, on that woeful offensive team, qualified him as a star . . . Lack of major power, fairly high DP totals and moderate stealing figures (caught 47 times in 117 career SB attempts) will keep him right around the 100 area. But a very usable player whose Milwaukee BA last season was identical to his career BA entering the year.

RENE GONZALES

No relation to Juan by either birth or baseball ability . . . Seemed to be breaking through with that 100 TOPR in '92 but backslid last season . . . No power (15 HRs in over 1,500 major league PAs) and little stealing speed (21 SBs in his career) . . . Of late has drastically improved his walks drawn versus his number of strikeouts . . . A kind of baseball "Renaissance Man" who's bungee jumped, traveled to Australia to surf and coach baseball and took #88 when he arrived at Baltimore in '87 because the guy wearing the #8 he wanted didn't figure to give it up anytime soon (Cal Ripken Jr.).

JIM LEYRITZ

Captain of the Yankee "Goon Squad." That was the nickname coach Frank Howard hung on the Bombers' bench players extraordinaire—Leyritz, Mike Stanley and Dion James. By year's end Leyritz was the only one of the three who hadn't forced his way into the everyday lineup. But it certainly wasn't for lack of performance . . . TOPR numbers like Tettleton's came out of the blue if you check his career TOPRline . . . Like Tettleton, can catch, play the outfield or first base and just three years ago started 67 games at 3B . . . Another of those strike-it-rich stories about a player totally overlooked by scouts and undrafted coming out of the University of Kentucky (truly a player who came "out of the blue" so to speak).

RANDY VELARDE

Yet another of the keys to Yankee success. Like Gallego, check that three-figure TOPR for a fellow who plays a lot at shortstop. Can literally play any of the seven positions behind the pitcher . . . Surprisingly good power at times but very few walks and steals . . . A player other teams have tried to deal for because of the solid performance he can give at any one of the number of positions . . . Very, very high DP totals for a part-timer (25 in the last two years) . . . On this ever-changing roster only he and Mattingly have appeared in Yankee contests in each of the last seven seasons.

LANCE BLANKENSHIP

Blankenship shot "blanks" in '93 due to injuries limiting him to about a half season . . . Given his two previous seasons you'd expect him to bounce back to a role of prominence. But with the emergence of youngsters like Gates and Neel his role might be more limited . . . Remarkable TOPR in light of the fact he hit just .190. But an enormous walk total (67) and solid steal numbers (13 of 18) suggest he remains the kind of player whose quiet contributions could be part of a major bounce-back in Oakland.

JERRY BROWNE

Another of Oakland's injured IMPs. In fact, it was the A's use of Tony Phillips as an IMP a few years ago that led to the "creation" of such a player category . . . Suffered a broken hand early in the year and struggled very badly upon his return. But by year's end he'd dragged the BA up to .250 and the TOPR "up" to 76 (in August he was in Lind-and-Pena country) . . . Given the up-down nature of his career TOPR trendline it looks like the A's can expect him to pop right back up to 107 this year, the TOPR he's had in each of the two even-numbered years this decade.

AMERICAN LEAGUE UTILITY PLAYERS

Rank	Player	Team	7/1/94 Age	B	TOPR Trendline				1993 TOPR
					1990	1991	1992	3 yr Avg.	
Infielders (200+ TPA):									
1.	Chip Hale	MIN	30	L	*	-	-	*	119
2.	Tim Hulett	BAL	34	R	(98)	77	(89)	87	95
3.	Jeff Reboulet	MIN	30	R	-	-	(93)	(93)	85
4.	Torey Lovullo	CAL	28	B	-	*	-	*	84
5.	Dickie Thon	MIL	36	R	84†	84†	100	87	83
6.	Juan Bell	MIL	26	B	*	57	(88)†	69	82†
7.	Carlos Martinez	CLE	29	R	63	86	82	76	78
8.	Kurt Stillwell	SDO/CAL	29	B	87	89	79†	85	76†
9.	Craig Grebeck	CWS	29	R	(63)	129	103	103	67
Outfielders (200+ TPA):									
1.	Stan Javier	CAL	30	B	115†	(80)†	102†	102	109
2.	Darnell Coles	TOR	32	R	66	*	(123)†	86	91
3.	Scott Brosius	OAK	27	R	-	*	*	*	90
4.	Bob Zupcic	BOS	27	R	-	*	90	90	88
5.	Mackey Sasser	SEA	31	L	102†	93†	(72)†	92	68
Of Note (under 200 TPA):									
-	Jack Voight	BAL	28	R	-	-	*	*	(135)
-	Greg Litton	SEA	29	R	74†	(69)†	(88)†	76	(107)
-	Steve Sax	CWS	34	R	93	105	81	81	93
-	Turner Ward	TOR	29	B	*	(80)	*	(80)	(75)

* Under 100 TPA-not included in average. ( ) 100-199 TPA. † Includes NL TOPR, unadjusted to AL.

CHIP HALE

1993 was not a total loss for the Twins. They found Chip Hale! Huh? . . . That's right, the most hearty utility player TOPR in either league belonged to Hale, a career bus-leaguer who'd had a couple of "cups of coffee" with the Twins (no refills though) in '89 and '90 . . . Very little power and speed and an iron glove had apparently doomed him to a life in the minors before his bat forced his way on to the '93 roster. Of the 77 major league pinch hitters who appeared in more than 20 games in that role, Hale had the best BA (.412) and on-base percentage (.524) . . . Would you believe his 3 HRs were the most of any Twins middle infielder?

TIM HULETT

Everybody whose last name began with an "H" hit .300 for the Orioles last year—Hoiles, Hammonds and steady Tim Hulett . . . Arguably the best season ever for a player who's spent parts or all of 10 seasons in the bigs . . . Can play any infield spot but SS . . . There's always room on a big league bench for such consistency.

JEFF REBOULET

Another of the Twins powerless middlemen who, like Hale, kicked around the minors for 7 years before finally spending a full season in the majors in '93 . . . Classic good-glove-light-hitting player whose TOPR still looks respectable because he'll take a walk and steal an occasional base . . . On base percentage of .356 not bad at all, just one one-thousandth behind Hrbek and Gene Larkin for the club lead.

TOREY LOVULLO

Remember when Tiger skipper Sparky Anderson thought he'd be part of the Detroit infield for years to come? Now it appears he'll be a solid part of somebody's bench for a while . . . Good "doubles power" and patient enough to work for some walks . . . Switch-hitting adds to his value . . . Once part of a terrific UCLA team with Shane Mack and Todd Zeile.

DICKIE THON

Baseball version of the Everyready cat. Just when you think he's run out of "major league lives" he finds another one . . . TOPR decline from that 100 the year before in Texas attributable to one factor—decreased extra-base power. Just one HR and 12 extra basers, down from 22 in approximately the same number of PAs . . . But, oh what might have been. Has truly never recovered form since his horrible beaning by Mike Torrez April 8, 1984. The year before he'd hit 20 HRs, driven in 79 and stolen 34 while hitting .286. His highs in the 9 years since? 15 HRs, 60 RBIs, 19 SBs and last year's .269 BA . . . Awful coincidence: in November of 1977 during an off-season game Thon's younger brother Frankie, a terrific prospect in the Giants chain, was also struck in the head by a throw. Like Dickie, he experienced years of double vision which eventually ended his career.

JUAN BELL

How odd! At year's end Juan had a job and his much more famous and accomplished brother George didn't . . . This Bell's had all the tools for years. But his teams (Dodgers, Orioles, Phils and Brewers) keep waiting for him to put it all together. Will he ever? For a player with very little pop (though he did hit a career high 5 dingers in '93) he makes contact far too little—about a strikeout every four official ABs . . . Shaky glove. Not a base stealer . . . Still young but the clock's ticking on his career.

CARLOS MARTINEZ

Ugly TOPRs for a player who plays 1B and 3B . . . Career indicates he thinks walks are a social disease—about one free pass every 24 official ABs . . . Out of a job at season's end and maybe when next season begins too.

KURT STILLWELL

You look at those TOPRs in the '90s and it's hard to remember that this was once the second player taken in the entire amateur draft in June of 1983. Or that he was an AL all-star in '88 . . . His game remains essentially unchanged from those days when he was KC's regular shortstop from '88–'91. Very little power, not a base stealing threat and hasn't ever drawn 50 walks in a single season in his career . . . Used to get lots of doubles but those totals have fallen off . . . Never much of a glove whiz . . . What's his future? Stillwell's still young. That may be his biggest plus.

CRAIG GREBECK

What happened? Started the year as the ChiSox starter at 2B. Ended it buried deep on their bench . . . TOPRs continued their wild variance. Which one's the real Grebeck? That eye-popping 129 of two years ago or the 60s TOPRs of '90 and '93? . . . Never had much stealing speed, but complete loss of power in '93 led to TOPR free fall.

STAN JAVIER

Decent spare part who's now belonged to four teams in four years. Why does he get passed around so much? Solid TOPRs for a part-timer . . . Very little power. Last year's 3 HRs tied a career high. But good stealing numbers (12 of 14) and the best walks-to-strikeouts ratio of his career (27:33) . . . His .291 average helped him close in on father Julian who hit .257 for 13 seasons. Stan's up to .251 after parts of 9.

DARNELL COLES

Allied Van Lines loves this guy. Toronto was his sixth team in six years . . . Another of those "great athlete" types who knocked scouts' eyes out as Southern California's High School Athlete-of-the-Year leading to him being the sixth player taken in the 1980 draft . . . Never hit with enough power to be a DH. Never fielded well enough to find a defensive position. No functional stealing speed. Can fill in at 1B, 3B and OF. In other words, a career utility man.

SCOTT BROSIUS

Is Oakland turning him into another of their famous IMPs? In a late season series at Texas, he started four consecutive games at four different defensive positions . . . Has some pop—6 HRs. But more may be forthcoming. Hit as many as 23 in a single minor league season . . . Has enough speed to swipe six SBs without being thrown out . . . La Russa seems to know just how to get the best out of players like this. And there may be some talent in here to develop.

BOB ZUPCIC

Alphabetically the last player listed in the Baseball Register last season. Also finished last one other place—all-star balloting. Of the 224 players listed on the fan ballot he got the least votes—91,358. Florida's Scott Pose, sent to the minors in May, drew 12,000

more . . . Unusual number of doubles (24 in less than 300 official ABs) but no HR power in Fenway, few walks and no steals. Unless something in there changes his TOPRs will remain right where they've been for his two big league seasons.

MACKEY SASSER

His TOPRs have written "decline" all over him . . . Stop if you've read this before: No power, no walks and no speed . . . Did steal the first base of his six-year major league career . . . Inability to catch and throw makes him less valuable, especially with those tumbling TOPRs . . . Once viewed as the Mets catcher of the future. But his offense makes you wonder if he has a future.

JACK VOIGHT

Why didn't this guy play more? Orioles had a starting RF McLemore with a TOPR of 90, 1B Segui put up a 98 and 3B Gomez had a sad TOPR of 90. Voight played all those positions in the minors . . . Decent power. Double figure HRs in five of his six minor league seasons . . . Will draw walks . . . TOPR seems to be saying "Put me in coach, I'm ready to play."

GREG LITTON

The player once nicknamed "Microwave" in San Francisco because he heated up so quickly (was ready to play at a moment's notice), bounced back with the kind of year that made him so valuable in those NL years . . . Once of the few players who can say he's played every position in his career. Yes, he pitched an inning with the Giants in '91 . . . Still young enough to be around for years and probably will be . . . Like Sasser, will enter '94 looking for his second career steal.

STEVE SAX

Suddenly this five-time all star's a bit part player . . . After hitting .280 or better in six of his first 10 seasons, Sax has put up a .236 and .235 back-to-back . . . Leap in 2B error totals the year before cost him that starting job . . . White Sox applauded his attitude for not complaining about his disuse after playing in at least 135 games every year for the previous 11 . . . If, as the TOPRs indicate, his skills are deteriorating, he'll be on these "utility" lists for good. But $2 million a year is one huge "utility bill."

TURNER WARD

Pretty decent defensive outfielder. But his entire pro career's been "power-free." Used to steal bunches in the minors but that talent hasn't surfaced at all in the bigs . . . At least, the Jays thought, they had a contact hitter who'd put up a solid average. Wrong! A horrid .192 after hitting over .300 in very brief trials in three of his four previous seasons . . . Unless his speed surfaces, three-figure TOPRs seem out of the question.

NATIONAL LEAGUE CATCHERS

Rank	Player	Team	7/1/94 Age	B	TOPR Trendline 1990	1991	1992	3 yr Avg.	1993 TOPR
Regulars:									
1.	Darren Daulton	PHI	32	L	123	106	165	134	149
2.	Rick Wilkins	CUB	27	L	-	97	109	103	145
3.	Mike Piazza	LAD	25	R	-	-	*	*	138
4.	Don Slaught	PIT	35	R	129	110	132	124	106
5.	Joe Girardi	COL	29	R	79	*	74	79	99
6.	Darrin Fletcher	MON	27	L	*	(68)	78	74	95
7.	Benito Santiago	FLA	29	R	105	87	83	91	88
8.	Kirt Manwaring	SFO	28	R	*	(74)	86	82	87
9.	Tom Pagnozzi	STL	31	R	97	87	82	87	85
10.	Joe Oliver	CIN	28	R	92	79	98	91	83
11.	Todd Hundley	NYM	25	B	*	*	78	78	77
Other Qualifiers (200+ TPA):									
-	Scott Servais	HOU	27	R	-	*	72	72	100
-	Erik Pappas	STL	28	R	-	*	-	*	93
-	Charlie O'Brien	NYM	34	R	70†	(66)	(85)	73	90
-	Eddie Taubensee	HOU	25	L	-	*	89	89	88
-	Damon Berryhill	ATL	30	B	*	(75)	92	83	87
-	Danny Sheaffer	COL	32	R	-	-	-	-	79
-	Greg Olson	ATL	33	R	95	90	90	91	74
-	Kevin Higgins	SDO	27	L	-	-	-	-	62

* Under 100 TPA-not included in average. ( ) 100-199 TPA. † Includes AL TOPR, unadjusted to NL.

DARREN DAULTON

Funny how a World Series will make fans notice a star. In truth Daulton broke through to stardom last season. How good is he for his position? The TOPR norm for NL catchers is 102. That means he's nearly 50% better offensively than the others who wear the tools of ignorance . . . An example that you don't have to be fantastic at every phase of the game to put up terrific TOPRs. Hit just .257. But had 63 extra-base hits and drew 117 walks. Teammate Lenny Dykstra led the league with 129, Bonds came next with 126 and then DD . . . Hardest of all to fathom is that he was the hardest man to double up in all of baseball. Hit into just two twin killings in 637 PAs. And remember, he's had seven operations on his left knee alone . . . You look at him now and wonder who that "other" Darren Daulton was that posted batting averages of .204, .225, .208, .194 and .201 from '85–'89 and so frustrated Philly fans that they booed his son at the team's annual father-son game.

RICK WILKINS

After years of searching for a rugged, everyday receiver, the Cubs found Wilkins . . . Strangely, like Daulton, difficult to double up (just 6) . . . For those who might pooh-pooh his numbers as a result of his playing in the "friendly confines" of Wrigley Field realize he hit .356 on the road with an away slugging percentage of .712, tops in the entire league . . . Is he a mirage? Never hit higher than .277 in any of six minor league seasons before his .33 of '93 . . . If this former Furman Paladin turns a few more of his 99 Ks into walks (50 BBs) his TOPRs will reach the catcher's stratosphere . . . One more huge plus—nailed a league high 43% of opposing base stealers.

MIKE PIAZZA

Baseball people thought so much of him when he came out of Miami-Dade North Community College that they made him a 62nd-round draft choice. Not the 62nd player taken mind you, the 62nd round! So why'd LA take a shot at him? His dad Vincent was Tommy Lasorda's closest friend. Hey, in round 62 you've got time to make "courtesy picks." How many players were picked before

the '93 NL Rookie-of-the-Year in the 1988 draft? Try 1, 388! . . . Game looks almost identical to Wilkins' except for double digit DPs . . . Will pitchers find holes in his swing the second time around? Maybe. But his minor league TOPRs from '91 and '92 suggested he'd be a far above-average catcher in the 120 + area.

DON SLAUGHT

"Sluggo" just wanders along putting up extremely solid TOPR years without anyone noticing—except the Pirates. While other free-agents-to-be have been allowed to leave, the Buccos, knowing what they had, nailed him down with a contract extension . . . Hit .300 for the fourth time in his 11-year career and HRs jumped into double figures for only the second time as a big leaguer. So, why'd his TOPR decline? Little things like 13 DPs and a walk total of only 29 . . . Used to be a poor thrower but even that's improved significantly for this former UCLA star who caught a college pitching staff that included Matt Young, Tim Leary and former solid major league reliever Dave Schmidt. That team which also included veteran Yankee infielder Mike Gallego, never even made it to Omaha for the finals of the College World Series. But four of those five have gone on to play in baseball's World Series.

JOE GIRARDI

One of the many catchers the Cubs tried before finding Wilkins. But is his heightened TOPR a sign of improvement or just that he played in the park most conducive to offense? If it's the latter, you tend to wonder what kind of TOPRs Daulton, Wilkins or Piazza would have posted had they spent the summer in and with the Rockies . . . BA jumped to a career high .290 but still displayed very little power (3 HRs matching his career total coming into '93) . . . But no matter how you view his TOPR rise he was, of the 20 catcher's listed, #6 overall and lots of teams would happily live with that.

DARRIN FLETCHER

Thank heavens he got traded to Montreal because he wouldn't see any playing time these days with the two teams who previously owned him—the Phillies and Dodgers . . . Started to show some power with 9 long balls and 20 doubles. Especially encouraging was his plate patience—34 walks and only 40 strikeouts . . . The Expos have had six different opening day catchers since Gary Carter left after the '84 season. With Fletcher's TOPR improvement added to his already solid reputation behind the plate, he may be settling into this job.

BENITO SANTIAGO

Perhaps the Marlins biggest disappointment. They'd hoped he'd resurrect his once-promising career in Florida. Instead, the slide continued . . . A career low .230 BA and a third straight season with TOPRs in the 80s . . . One might be able to accept those figures were he some kind of gold glover. But the Marlins had 85 wild pitches and 29 passed balls, both major league leading totals. Opponents stole at a 70% rate and he had 11 errors . . . HRs did jump back into double digits as did steals . . . But numbers like these are not what you're looking for when paying $3.4 million to a former four-time NL all-star . . . In truth, he's now a below-average player.

KURT MANWARING

TOPR figures like Santiago's, but an extremely solid defensive catcher . . . Thanks to him hardly anyone ran on the Giants. Threw out 44 of 104 attempted stealers. That 42.3% put him barely behind Wilkins for tops in the NL and third overall behind Karkovice . . . TOPR would have been significantly higher were it not for 14 DPs . . . BA is OK but only 21 extra-base hits . . . With as fine a receiver as he has always been, Giants must be happy with his .275 BA, 44 points above his career average.

TOM PAGNOZZI

After years as a backup, has settled in as the Cards regular . . . TOPRs reflect the kind of player he's been and will likely remain. Small amount of power, very few walks and no stealing speed . . . Will sometimes shock you how far he can drive the ball as in his 436-foot HR last summer . . . Can he hold off the challenge to his job from three-years-younger backup Pappas? Check the TOPRs. Pappas would seem to have a higher possible topside. But can he catch like Pags who led the NL in fielding percentage in '92?

JOE OLIVER

A big, strong receiver the Reds keep waiting to breakthrough offensively. But with his .239 BA he's now hit under .240 three of the four years this decade . . . Does have some pop with 28 doubles and 14 HRs, both career highs . . . Extremely low walk totals (27), not even a stolen base attempt and 13 doubles-ups combined to again drag TOPR into the lower 80s . . . Reds traded prospect Wilson so the job's all his. But how long can a club live with a catcher whose figures put him in the lower third of all NL catchers offensively, without his having the kind of defensive ability as several of those who TOPR above him?

TODD HUNDLEY

The Mets continue to look on him as their catcher of the future. TOPRs in the 70s should make them question that right now . . . Does have some power—11 HRs, all as a left-handed hitter . . . But only 23 walks in 448 PAs, double figure DPs and no threat to run . . . Mets opponents ran at will stealing at a 72% rate . . . Mets must simply hope for improvement from Hundley whose minor league TOPRs did project him eventually into the 90's on a big league level.

SCOTT SERVAIS

Where'd those 11 HRs come from? Hadn't hit any in 242 official ABs coming into '93 and had *totaled* 10 in three minor league seasons . . . Only the departed Chris James homered at a better rate than his one every 23.5 at bats . . . Tailed off after the all-star

break hitting .200 in July, .147 in August and .188 in September . . . Makes a nice right-handed compliment to lefty starter Taubensee, especially if that 100 TOPR's a sign of seasons to come.

ERIK PAPPAS

A late developer? Former first-round pick of the Angels who's been property of California, the Cubs, Kansas City, the White Sox and now the Cards in 10 pro seasons . . . Shows absolutely no power on the major league level though he did hit 16 HRs in back-to-back seasons in the minors . . . TOPR helped greatly by 35 BBs in just over 250 PAs . . . if that minor league power emerges, he's valuable at least as a part-timer. That's a far cry from what he was last spring—a non-roster player who'd been picked up by Louisville as a six-year minor league free agent.

CHARLIE O'BRIEN

TOPR surge attributable to career high .255 average . . . For such a light hitter (.205 career into '93) strikes out very little and will coax an occasional walk . . . One of those journeyman types who manages to find a spot on someone's roster because he's a solid receiver and good in the clubhouse . . . If last year's TOPR's not a one-year thing he'll be around for a few more seasons.

EDDIE TAUBENSEE

Has put decent TOPR years back-to-back. Remember, though, that the 'Stros dealt star CF Lofton to Cleveland to get him . . . before you dismiss him as just another light-TOPRing platoon catcher, realize he's at the very same stage of his career and with fairly similar numbers to Daulton and Wilkins who broke through as prominent players . . . Started very slowly but hit .270 with 7 of his 9 HRs from late May to the finish . . . Positive sign: strikeout ratio reduced significantly last year from one K every 3.8 at bats in '92 to one every 6.5 in '93 . . . Before making any judgments perhaps it's best to wait and see about Taubensee.

DAMON BERRYHILL

Given his total lack of foot speed and career-long inability to draw walks, this is probably about the TOPR range he'll settle into for his career . . . Will display brief moments of power but he and platoon partner Olson may just be keeping this job warm until prospect Lopez is deemed ready.

DANNY SHEAFFER

Had look-sees with the Red Sox and Indians in the late 80s before expansion created a major league job for him. If only his combined BA in those stops had been his TOPR—.110! . . . Much better than expected .278 average but with the usual lack of power, absence of walks and speed . . . Decent veteran receiver who'll be in a job hunt every year.

GREG OLSON

After three years in the 90s his TOPR bottomed out in '93 . . . Worst average of his career—.225 . . . The usual handful of HRs and good walks-to-strikeouts numbers (29–27) . . . But that broken ankle suffered in late '92 slowed him down even more leading to 11 DPs . . . Like Berryhill, he hears the footsteps of the approaching prospect Lopez.

KEVIN HIGGINS

The immediate tendency is to ignore someone who's TOPR looks this hideous. Be careful . . . Oh, there are a bunch of ugly numbers. Only 5 of his 40 hits were for extra bases and none over the wall. Very high DP total of 7 considering he batted just 202 times . . . But he can catch and play OF-1B-2B-3B making him a possible future IMP . . . And his minor league numbers suggest there's a chance of "major" improvement. Three times hit over .300 and walked more than he struck out at all six bus league stops.

NATIONAL LEAGUE 1ST BASEMEN

Rank	Player	Team	7/1/94 Age	B	1990	1991	1992	3 yr Avg.	1993 TOPR
								TOPR Trendline	
Regulars:									
1.	Andres Galarraga	COL	33	R	99	77	91	90	**151**
2.	John Kruk	PHI	33	L	122	136	145	135	**147**
3.	Gregg Jefferies	STL	26	B	110	106	95†	104	**141**
4.	Fred McGriff	SDO/ATL	30	L	154†	148	159	154	**140**
5.	Jeff Bagwell	HOU	26	R	-	130	129	129	**131**
6.	Mark Grace	CUB	30	L	116	107	127	116	**120**
7.	Will Clark	SFO	30	L	123	144	145	137	**116**
8.	Hal Morris	CIN	29	L	124	132	103	120	**111**
9.	Eddie Murray	NYM	38	B	142	103	114	119	**102**
10.	Orestes Destrade	FLA	32	B	-	-	-	-	**96**
11.	Eric Karros	LAD	26	R	-	*	101	101	**87**
12.	Kevin Young	PIT	25	R	-	-	*	*	**86**
Other Qualifiers (200+ TPA):									
-	Sid Bream	ATL	33	L	122	101	124	117	**104**
-	John Vanderwal	MON	28	L	-	*	102	102	**96**
-	Frank Bolick	MON/-	28	B	-	-	-	-	**85**
Of Note (under 200 TPA):									
-	Todd Benzinger	SFO	31	B	83	84	80	83	**111**

* Under 100 TPA-not included in average. ( ) 100-199 TPA. † Includes AL TOPR, unadjusted to NL.

ANDRES GALARRAGA

Reunited with ex-mentor Baylor and, playing in the rarified air of the Rockies, Galarraga's numbers reached "rarified TOPR air." Third behind only Bonds and Dykstra . . . Only the second player ever to hit as high as .370 to win the batting title while walking as few as 24 times. Nap Lajoie did it in 1902 . . . By the by, Galarraga didn't want "all those walks." A dozen of the 24 were intentional . . . Leap from TOPR in 90s to his 151 was *not* totally out of left field. In the final half of the '92 season in St. Louis he hit .296 and TOPRed around 110 . . . Even if you factor out of his numbers the incredible park effect, Galarraga still TOPRed at 125 . . . What every team must ask itself, however, when considering Galarraga as a free agent is whether last season means he's all the way back and if those TOPRs will remain in this neighborhood if Galarraga changes neighborhoods.

JOHN KRUK

A star. He may not look like a star. But then neither did Jackie Gleason . . . A sensational 1990s TOPR average of 139! . . . Has now hit at least .291 every year this decade. Walks leaped from a previous career best of 92 up to 111 in '93 . . . What may be most shocking is the half dozen steals in eight attempts. Would you believe he once swiped 18 with the Padres . . . Did the Phillies really get him and utility man Randy Ready from San Diego for OF Chris James?

GREGG JEFFRIES

The Mets knew he could hit but dealt him because he didn't seem to have a position he could play defensively. K.C. saw him hit .295 with 49 extra-base hits and swapped him because they couldn't hide him defensively (a league leading 26 errors). St. Louis got him, put him at 1B, sat back and watched him post the best TOPRs of his life. Jeffries admits that not worrying about his "D" helped his "O" . . . Like so many others whose TOPRs rose remarkably, the betterment was traceable to walks. Drew 62 after never having reached the 50s in his career . . . Doesn't seem to

have terrific speed but a superb stealer (46 of 55) nearly doubling his previous career best (meaning he turned many of those extra walks into "doubles" with a steal) . . . 15 DPs kept him from being right there with Gallaraga and Kruk . . . Once a tantrum-prone, helmet-throwing terror. Now, simply a TOPR terror.

FRED McGRIFF

What's this? The man who finished third in MVP balloting wound up *fourth* among first base TOPRs? Would you believe the "Crime Dog" actually had his worst TOPR year this decade? But, hey, there's nothing wrong with a 140! . . . Slight decline due to minor decreases in walks and steals and 14 DPs . . . But for the '90s his average TOPR of 150 is second only to Bonds who, as you well know, belongs in the next league higher up anyway . . . Has now hit 208 HRs the last six years, tops in the majors. Who's second? Joe Carter with 186 . . . The only weak point of his game? Like Michael Jackson he wears a glove on one hand for no apparent reason—17 errors.

JEFF BAGWELL

Mr. Consistency! Beginning to look like we can pencil "Bags" in at a 130 TOPR every year . . . Average, HRs and steals went up. So why didn't his TOPR? DPs—20 of them. But that's the price you pay for hitting the ball very hard on the ground with men on base . . . Strange stat: his HBPs dropped from 12 to 3. Is he getting better at getting out of the way? But oddly, his season ended 20 games early (he'd played in every game until then) when a Ben Rivera pitch broke a bone in his left hand . . . Did Boston really give him up for reliever Larry Anderson and then two years later trade Phil Plantier for reliever Jose Melendez?

MARK GRACE

The first Cubs 1B to hit at least .320 (.325) since Bill Buckner did it in 1980 . . . So, with the jump in BA and rise to a career high 14 HRs, why did that TOPR slip? Again the answer's spelled "D-P" A league leading 25 rally killers. Weird when you consider that two years ago he hit into only 6 and had 14 in '92 . . . Truly ''Graceful'' around the bag. And how about that fantastic walks-to-strikeouts stat (71–32)!

WILL CLARK

For now ''The Thrill is Gone'' from the top of the TOPRs . . . His slipping attributable to a drop of 14 extra-base hits, a BA fall of 17 points, a tumble from 12 steals to 2 and 10 less walks. Fall would have been far more pronounced had he not had a terrific last five weeks hitting well over .300 . . . Strange thing about his free agency is that the teams that showed interest in him also had major interest in another left-handed-hitting 1B who was Clark's teammate at Mississippi State—Rafael Palmeiro . . . Homered on the first pitch ever thrown him in pro ball at Fresno in 1984. The next season homered in his first major league at bat—against Nolan Ryan!

HAL MORRIS

A portrait of what injuries can do to a TOPR. When injury free in '90–'91 put up a pair of terrific numbers. But a hamstring pull and a fractured hand limited him to 115 games in '92. Shoulder troubles reduced him to a 101-game season last year . . . Remember, this is the same player who was one hit away from winning the NL batting title on the final game of the season in '91 . . . Despite hurts hit .317 last year, only a point lower than what he hit in '91 . . . But power totals have dropped (not unusual for players having had hand and shoulder problems) and his tendency to have more walks than strikeouts mysteriously reversed itself. Never before had he had a pro season in which he fanned more than walked until his 51 K/34 BB 1993 . . . If he's healthy he's a very fine player at a position loaded with them.

EDDIE MURRAY

Doesn't have the best of ''clubhouse reputations'' but continues to put up reasonable numbers for a player of his age . . . TOPR would have been higher except for 24 DPs, just one behind co-league leaders Charlie Hayes and Grace . . . His first 100-RBI season since 1985 which had been the fourth year in a row he'd driven in triple figures . . . Walk total (40) lowest since '81. HR output of 27 highest since '85 . . . He and brother Rich now third on list of homering brothers with 445. Rich had 4. Eddie has 441. With his next HR ties Dave Kingman for 20th all-time . . . His 100 RBIs last year enabled him to pass Jake Beckley, Kaline, Killebrew, Hornsby, Schmidt, Lajoie, Goslin, Banks and Perez on the all-time list to move to #17 . . . The Mets say they no longer want him. Someone will.

ORESTES DESTRADE

Would like to provide you his TOPR history but don't have all the statistical information necessary from his previous career stop—four years with the Seibu Lions in Japan . . . Signed with Florida after bashing 154 HRs in four Japanese seasons. Responded with a team high 20. Even more encouraging was the fact that he hit most of them after the all-star break . . . Had the usual TOPR killers—17 DPs, no steals and a comparatively low walk total of 58 considering that he fanned 130 times . . . Can we expect improvement his second time around? Remember he turns 32 in May.

ERIC KARROS

Quite a slide for '92 NL Rookie-of-the-Year. But then, when you look at the barely-over-100 TOPR of that first season, it's not all

that much of a drop . . . HRs crept up. But his BA fell 10 points to .247, hit into 17 DPs, didn't steal a base and still rarely walks—especially for a player with his power (only 71 walks the last *two* seasons) . . . Minor league figures suggest he'll get better. All four of his seasons in the minors he hit over .300 with double-figure HRs and much better walks-to-strikeouts ratios. But then we've been fooled by Dodger minor league numbers before, haven't we?

KEVIN YOUNG

One of three Pirate everyday rookies along with Carlos Garcia and Al Martin. Considered the best prospect of the three but had by far the worst TOPR of that trio . . . Seemed to get into the bad habit of lunging, especially at off-speed pitches . . . Minor league figures suggest a big time improvement's ahead. Coming into '93 he'd hit .306 with 22 HRs and 158 RBIs combined in three seasons. Also swiped 18 bases in Triple A, but only two last season . . . Nicknamed ''Kevinski.'' But he sure doesn't look Polish.

SID BREAM

A platoon player who turned into a bit-part performer when McGriff arrived by trade . . . Lots of teams wouldn't have thought twice about sticking with a 1B who'd had a 117 average TOPR coming into '93. Not the title hungry Braves . . . TOPRs of late slipping because the multiple knee problems have robbed him of the speed that once enabled him to steal 13 bases. That reduction in foot speed also means ''doubles'' become singles and force outs become DPs . . . Still a steady, heady player with an outstanding glove. But with all those spectacular Braves prospects panting to get into the bigs, the Braves won't ask him back.

JOHN VANDERWAL

Has the look of a spare part . . . Occasional power. A little speed. Can play 1B-LF-RF . . . Manager Alou loves to use him as a pinch hitter. Over the last two seasons has batted 82 times in that role with 13 hits and an eye-popping 17 walks! Like everyone else he wants to make it big in baseball. But isn't it carrying it just a bit far to *marry* someone named Rawlings? Wife's maiden name—Neb Rawlings!

FRANK BOLICK

This switch hitter off the bench platooned with Vanderwal from the left side. But he didn't produce nearly as well hitting just .212 as a pinch hitter . . . In double digits in HRs in five of his six minor league seasons including a total of 27 at two stops in '92. But didn't show that kind of pop in his first season in the bigs . . . Had the look of a late bloomer coming into '93. But the Expos simply gave up on him at year's end.

TODD BENZINGER

Finally TOPRed back to his figures of the late '80s when he appeared to be an emerging offensive player . . . Gave the Giants solid and important offense when Clark went down to injuries. In fact, Benzinger played so well that even after Clark returned he got some starts while ''The Thrill'' sat the bench, something previously considered impossible by the Bay . . . Power reappeared. Remember, he hit 17 as the Reds regular 1B in '89 . . . Giants noticed his bounceback and quickly re-signed him after the season. He becomes much more important if Clark flees to free agency.

NATIONAL LEAGUE 2ND BASEMEN

Rank	Player	Team	7/1/94 Age	B	TOPR Trendline 1990	1991	1992	3 yr Avg.	1993 TOPR
Regulars:									
1.	Robby Thompson	SFO	32	R	98	128	110	112	**131**
2.	Delino DeShields	MTL	25	L	113	111	122	115	**124**
3.	Craig Biggio	HOU	28	R	96	113	125	111	**122**
4.	Luis Alicea	STL	28	B		*	101	101	**107**
5.	Ryne Sandberg	CUB	34	R	145	144	142	144	**105**
6.	Jeff Kent	NYY	26	R	-	-	108†	108	**103**
7.	Eric Young	COL	27	R	-	-	(82)	(82)	**103**
8.	Carlos Garcia	PIT	26	R	*	*	*	*	**96**
9.	Bret Barberie	FLA	26	B	-	(157)	100	117	**95**
10.	Mickey Morandini	PHI	28	L	*	92	92	92	**93**
11.	Jeff Gardner	SDO	30	L	-	*	*	*	**93**
12.	Mark Lemke	ATL	28	B	74	81	85	81	**86**
13.	Jody Reed	LAD	31	R	106†	98†	82†	95	**83**
Other Qualifiers (200+ TPA):									
-	Geronimo Peña	STL	27	B	*	122	145	134	**109**
-	Roberto Mejia	COL	22	R	-	-	-	-	**94**
-	Juan Samuel	CIN	33	R	102	107	96†	103	**86**

* Under 100 TPA-not included in average. ( ) 100-199 TPA. † Includes AL TOPR, unadjusted to NL.

ROBBY THOMPSON

A huge year, but if you check that '91 season, not an unexpected TOPR . . . Especially impressive when you combine the #1 TOPR at a position with his Glove Glove. But then the Giants actually had *three* players like that—Thompson, Matt Williams at 3B and OF Barry Bonds . . . Career highs in doubles, HRs and RBIs. Still strikes out great deal (97). But those whiffs also help keep his DP total down (7) . . . Despite persistent career-long back problems can still run selectively and effectively (10 for 14) . . . Weird: Was caught stealing 4 times last year. That matches the number of times he got nailed on June 27, 1986, when he set the major league record by getting caught 4 times in one game! . . . Steady and solid. No wonder San Francisco hurried to get his signature on a free agent contract right after the year ended.

DELINO DeSHIELDS

Made the right choice selecting baseball over a chance to play big time college basketball point guard at Villanova where he'd been offered a scholarship . . . "Bop" as he's called seems to be settling in as a star given that he's still years away from baseball "prime time" . . . Only thing that keeps him out of TOPR-superstardom remains puzzling lack of extra-base hits. Not that he'll ever hit many HRs. But you'd think a player with this kind of blazing speed (43 steals last year, 46 the year before and 56 in '91) would get more than 17 doubles and 7 triples. But that may happen as he develops. And he *is* still developing. Note that his strikeouts dropped from 151 in '91 to 108 and down to 64 last season when he actually walked more times than he fanned.

CRAIG BIGGIO

Kudos to the Astros for realizing they had to get him out from behind home plate to extend the career of this terrific offensive player . . . His 21 HRs were the most ever by an Astro middle infielder . . . In the top 10 in the league in hits, doubles, total bases and hit by pitch (ouch!). So why'd his TOPR slip instead of skyrocket? Created 17 outs by getting caught stealing—the fourth highest total in the league. His swipe total of 15 was his lowest in five seasons. The season before was 38 for 53. That's a huge skid

in running efficiency. Are those years of catching subtly taking their toll on his legs even though he's now a second baseman? . . . Clearly a premier offensive player at a position not noted for offense in the NL.

LUIS ALICEA

Finally got to see solid playing time and posted a nice TOPR . . . Like many Latin middle infielders, has almost no power. Three HRs matched his career total for parts of three seasons. But unlike many *will* accept a base on balls (47 in 411 PAs) . . . Also seems to be developing as a thief (11 of 12) after coming into the season with just three career steals . . . Rushed to the bigs in '88, disappointed the club badly and drifted back to the minors for three seasons before returning . . . Persistent rumors the Cards have wanted to deal him. Maybe it's that continuing high error total—11 . . . A career .224 hitter who suddenly jumped to .279. Is he a late offensive bloomer?

RYNE SANDBERG

Broke his left hand and missed the first month. Then fractured a finger and missed the last three weeks. Those injuries combined to help wreck his TOPR and drag him all the way down to the point where his figure looks "mortal" instead of the god-like numbers he'd been putting up . . . Only 9 dingers after nine straight years in double figures topped by 40 in 1990 . . . Just 9 steals from a player who once swiped 54 in a single year. And while you can say the decreased playing time caused that drop, he still hit into a dozen DPs . . . But injuries can have effects on all parts of a player's game. Should return to TOPR stratosphere next season with health . . . Needs 32 HRs to become the highest homer-hitting second baseman in the history of the game displacing Joe Morgan who hit 266 . . . All in all not a bad career for a guy who started by going one for his first 32 at bats.

JEFF KENT

Yes, there were some pleasant surprises in the midst of that sewer of a season in Flushing Meadows. Here's one of them . . . 21 HRs? 80 RBIs? Does anyone realize those numbers led all NL

2Bs? TOPR would have been right there with the biggies at this position except for an extremely low walk total (30) and, like the rest of his Mets mates except for Vince Coleman, a non-existent running game (4 steals for 8 attempts) . . . But if Thompson got the Gold Glove, Kent should get an iron one—22 errors. Ugh! . . . Don't be shocked if power total holds up. After all he did hit 11 the season before in just over 300 official at bats.

ERIC YOUNG

Another shocking TOPR leap by a player who landed in Colorado. But before you quickly discount his year because of that Mile High park effect realize that his game's not the kind generally helped enormously by the rarified air . . . Exploded with a 42-steal season. But then he did swipe 70 one year in AA and 76 in A-ball . . . No power to take advantage of the Colorado ''situation'' but a fantastic 63 BB 41 K year . . . You look at his TOPR and the one put up by the older and much more highly paid Dodger 2B Jody Reed and you wonder why in the world LA exposed him to the expansion draft . . . A keeper.

CARLOS GARCIA

First Bucco second baseman to reach double figures in HRs since Bill Mazeroski hit 16 in 1966 . . . Walks very little but, oddly, gets hit a lot—a team high 9 HBP . . . TOPR should rise with the minor adjustments all younger players begin to make in their game (walk a bit more, steal at a higher rate than 18 for 29, etc.) . . . Only 9 DPs, 11 errors and 25 doubles are all solid numbers for a first full season.

BRET BARBERIE

A Florida disappointment after being the third player the Fish hooked in the first round of the expansion draft . . . You can see from his past TOPRs why Florida bit on him . . . Barberie floundered at times but did have a pair of disabling injuries missing 10 weeks with an elbow strain and a knee ligament problem . . . Minor league TOPRs and early career numbers suggested a player that might eventually be 30 or more points up stream from last season's 95 . . . Perhaps, like Sandberg, we might simply suggest that, in evaluating him, you throw last season back and hope he catches an injury-free '94.

MICKEY MORANDINI

If you like consistency you've got to love a player whose three-year TOPR line reads 92–92–93 . . . Extra-base hits, walks and steals went up but the average tumbled leaving him in the same TOPR-land he's always lived . . . For a team that has fielding problems he's a major plus finishing second among all NL 2Bs in fielding percentage with a .990 . . . Why doesn't he run more with a fantastic 37-for-44 lifetime record as a thief?

JEFF GARDNER

Finally won a major league job as a 29-year-old rookie and performed basically the same on a major league level as he did down below. To wit: absolutely no power with one HR, the fourth of his nine-year professional career. Stole successfully just twice in 8 attempts . . . But a pesky hitter who wheedles a decent number of walks, avoids the DP fabulously (3) and has enough pop to put up 21 doubles and 7 triples (more than DeShields, for instance) . . . May not be the long-time answer as a starter at the position but a player who could be around a while as a solid spare part.

MARK LEMKE

First full season as the Braves regular 2B and responded with a TOPR almost identical to his career trendline . . . Despite a nice jump in extra-base hits, his TOPR stayed in the lower region for one overriding reason—a lack of speed. One steal (his second in four full seasons) and 21 DPs, fourth most in the entire league and tied for sixth most in all of baseball . . . Walked more than he fanned for a third straight year.

JODY REED

TOPR trendline in an uncomfortably steady downward direction . . . TOPRs in Boston were higher because of his remarkable doubles totals. Would you believe 129 two-baggers in a three-year period from '89–'91? Also hit in the .280s all three of those seasons. But popped only 21 doubles and a mere 25 extra-base hits in '93 as his TOPR fell to a career low . . . Never a speed player, but one steal and 16 DPs remain another cause for concern . . . Want more trouble? How about walks topping out at 38 when he'd drawn at least 60 each of his last four seasons . . . Average OK but the rest of the numbers look very, very empty . . . Will he return to form in '94? Dodgers must guess during the off-season.

GERONIMO PENA

Started fast, slipped toward the finish . . . Check out those impressive TOPRs entering '93. Will hit some long balls and a solid steal threat (13 of 18) . . . Most worrisome stat concerns his having by far the worst walks-to-strikeouts ratio of his career (25 to 71) . . . Basically platooned with Alicea and they're virtually the same player. Alicea: a 107 TOPR with 11 errors. Pena: a 109 with 12 errors. Alicea's a year older. Both switch-hit. But each is a far superior right-handed hitter thus making a platoon out of the question. Which one do you keep? Or do you keep both? Or neither?

ROBERTO MEJIA

Don't be at all deceived by that 94 TOPR. While it's OK (better than four ''regulars'' at 2B) it represents the first offering from a player who might blossom into something special . . . That 94 was compiled in the last half of '93 after being recalled from AAA. Last season was the first time this 21-year-old had played above A-ball . . . Terrific extra-base potential (had 24 extra-basers in less than half a season) . . . Like so many young hitters swings at the first thing he sees and can look lost at times. But he WAS just 21 and hit 14 HRs with a .299 average the first half year in AAA. Expect major improvement in the next year or two.

JUAN SAMUEL

Once a formidable offensive player whose game continued to decline in '93. A career low .230 BA. Used to run well enough to steal 72 bases in a big league season. In '93? Swiped 9 in 16 tries . . . As usual, very few walks and a high error total . . . He's been with five teams in five years. A candidate to make that six in six in '94.

NATIONAL LEAGUE 3RD BASEMEN

Rank	Player	Team	7/1/94 Age	B	TOPR Trendline				1993 TOPR
					1990	1991	1992	3 yr Avg.	
Regulars:									
1.	Matt Williams	SFO	28	R	114	116	91	108	**125**
2.	Gary Sheffield	SDO/FLA	25	R	114†	82†	150	123	**124**
3.	Charlie Hayes	COL	29	R	79	80	97†	85	**119**
4.	Dave Hollins	PHI	28	B	(79)	(143)	131	125	**118**
5.	Howard Johnson	NYM	33	B	119	147	109	127	**109**
6.	Todd Zeile	STL	28	R	112	114	117	114	**109**
7.	Steve Buechele	CUB	32	R	90†	102†	102	101	**108**
8.	Chris Sabo	CIN	32	R	126	133	99	122	**105**
9.	Jeff King	PIT	29	R	89	(104)	89	90	**102**
10.	Terry Pendleton	ATL	33	B	74	134	120	111	**92**
11.	Ken Caminiti	HOU	31	B	77	92	117	94	**92**
12.	Tim Wallach	LAD	36	R	112	84	89	95	**78**
Other Qualifiers (200+ TPA):									
-	Sean Berry	MON	28	R	*	*	*	*	**129**
-	Archi Cianfrocco	MON/SDO	27	R	-	-	91	91	**92**
Of Note (under 200 TPA):									
-	Dave Hansen	LAD	25	L	*	*	75	75	**(166)**

* Under 100 TPA-not included in average. ( ) 100-199 TPA. † Includes AL TOPR, unadjusted to NL.

MATT WILLIAMS

As if on cue Williams arrived at the age that supposedly starts a player's "prime" and recorded his best year . . . He'd always hit HRs in bunches (33 in '90, 34 the next year and 38 last season), still hardly ever walks (a decade *low* total of 27) and will never be any part of a club's running game. But the leap to his TOPR topper can be traced to one simple element—he made far better contact than he'd ever made before. His BA zoomed to a career best .294, up 67 points from the season prior. That led to, among other things, a whopping 75 extra-base hits, second only to Bonds in the NL . . . His 38 dingers wiped out the old Giants' franchise record for HRs by a third baseman set in 1938 by someone you don't think of as a third sacker. That '38 campaign, in which Hall of Famer Mel Ott swatted 36, was the only season he ever spent at the hot corner . . . Throw in a Gold Glove and the season became complete.

GARY SHEFFIELD

Has probably spent his last year at 3B. Injuries and a woeful glove (would you believe 34 errors?) have him ticketed for a future in the outfield . . . A shoulder injury limited him to 10 HRs and 37 RBIs in 72 games as a Marlin, a shadow of the Triple Crown contender he'd been the season before . . . Likewise, the TOPR tumbled. But imagine how good a hitter one must be to take a 27-point TOPR drop, struggle with injuries and still barely miss posting the best TOPR at your position in the entire big leagues! One remarkably intriguing part of a year when most of his figures fell was his reemergence as a stealing threat. In '90 he'd stolen 25. Then swiped just 5 each of the next two seasons. If healthy and the other numbers bounce back his '93 17-for-22 stealing numbers, could push his TOPRs toward the sky (the "sky" of course being Barry Bonds) . . . The only question about this ultra-talented athlete remains his commitment to the game. Has forced his way out of two other franchises in three years and occasionally makes statements about how much longer he'll play (he's not even reached "prime time" yet). But when focused and sound he's some player!

CHARLIE HAYES

The "Mile High" park effect drove his TOPR mile high. Had he not hit into an ugly major-league-leading 25 DPs he would have had the best TOPR at 3B in the bigs . . . Number-one doubles man in the NL with 45. That total, along with 175 hits and 98 RBIs, all set major league records for a first-year expansion player . . . A .250 career hitter who jumped to .305 . . . Ran more (11 steals) but not more effectively being thrown out six times . . . Coaxed just 43 walks but that was good enough for second on the walkless Rockies . . . Is not triskadekaphobic (fear of the number 13). Hit a game-winning three-run HR of Houston's Doug Jones on Friday the 13th . . . Are his numbers "real" or was it the park? Went from a three-year TOPR average of being 15 points below average as an offensive player to 19 points above. Our advice? Buy a home in Colorado, Charlie.

DAVE HOLLINS

A "throwback" type of player. When doctors told him he'd miss 4–6 weeks after surgery for a fractured hamate bone, he returned in 17 days . . . Has no speed but scored 100 runs for a second straight year . . . How much do the Phils like to walk? Hollins' excellent total of 85 freebies ranked him sixth in the NL but just fourth on the Phillies behind Dykstra, Daulton and Kruk . . . TOPR number actually declined significantly due to a falloff of 9 HRs and 7 SBs and his 15 DPs . . . Had terrific minor league TOPRs suggesting a player of this possible magnitude. So why did the Padres not even protect him on their 40-man roster after the '89 season allowing the Phils to steal him for the 50-grand draft price? . . . Had a horrid year afield—27 errors. And would you believe, with him at third the club went the entire '93 campaign without ever turning a 5–4–3 double play?

HOWARD JOHNSON

Injuries wrecked a second straight season for this once outstanding and versatile player. Has batted only 575 times the last two seasons—roughly the equivalent of one full year . . . His .238 BA isn't terribly far, though, from what he'd been doing—a .252 hitter for eight seasons with the Mets. Still drew lots of walks, showed some pop and stayed out of DPs (3) helping to prevent a TOPR free fall . . . How much can he bounce back to his old numbers if healthy in '94? Some team will have to "guess-timate" that in the free agent market this year . . . Can it be just seven years ago when, in 1987, "Hojo" and Darryl Strawberry became the first teammates to ever have 30–30 seasons (HRs and SBs) in the same year. My how things have changed!

TODD ZEILE

Most heralded his '93 season as a breakthrough. But his TOPR didn't. Yes, he did establish new personal highs for HRs (17), doubles (36) and walks (70). Terrific RBI total of 103, also his best ever. But remember—offense was up all over the NL and that eats away at individual TOPR rises . . . Also rapped into 15 DPs and steals, which had gotten as high as 17 two years ago, fell to 5 . . . What happened afield? He appeared to have made a smooth transition from catcher to 3B committing only 13 errors there in '92, his second season at third. But that number shockingly leaped to 33 last year . . . Has developed into a solid offensive player but what position will he call home?

STEVE BEUCHELE

TOPR numbers moved up slightly again. And with his steady and often spectacular fielding (had just 8 errors—how did Williams get the Gold Glove?) has moved into the class of the better 3Bs of the game . . . BA reached a career high .272 and a personal best 27 doubles. TOPR would have been even higher except for a terrible start (hit .178 the first two weeks) and achilles tendon problems that dogged him the final three months of the season . . . This former Stanford roommate of John Elway has had four seasons where he's committed less than 10 errors. So why's he never gotten that Gold Glove?

CHRIS SABO

This often-hurt player somehow avoided the terrible injury blight that struck the rest of his Reds teammates to post a club-high 148 games played, the second highest of his career . . . But free agent shoppers won't be impressed by back-to-back huge dropoffs from those glittering TOPRs of the early '90s . . . Has hit .244 and .259 consecutively, the lowest BAs of his six-season career . . . Used to run regularly (25 steals in '90) but with his 6 swipes last season now has just 10 total the past two years . . . Still solid afield and at 32 conceivably has several good seasons left.

JEFF KING

Roller-coaster TOPRs continue. Back up into triple figures after the big dip of 1992 . . . This career .230 hitter's BA exploded to .290. So why wasn't the TOPR much more impressive? HRs dropped from 14 to 9. And 17 DPs and just 8-for-14 stealing hurt . . . But the Buccos must be thrilled that this player who always fanned far more than he walked suddenly reversed that trend (59 BB, 54 K) . . . 18 errors far too many for a team that hasn't got enough overall talent to allow for "giving away" games . . . But the TOPR improvement may signal his development into the kind of player that made him the first player taken in the entire 1986 amateur draft.

TERRY PENDLETON

If King's TOPRs ride the roller coaster, Pendleton's must be on the giant one at Coney Island. Check his incredible variance. A horrid year approaching free agency in '90 with the Cards. Atlanta signed him and reaped the benefits with MVP-type numbers in '91

and an extremely solid '92. But the bottom fell out last year . . . BA slipped 39 points. That triggered the logical decline in extra-base hits and RBIs. DPs up to 18. Errors stayed fairly high at 19 . . . But his overall season and TOPR especially wouldn't look nearly so bad if you could just throw out the first month of '93. Hit a miserable .144 with 2 HRs and 7 RBIs. From there on was solid and durable as usual (.299 BA) . . . But his free-agent-to-be season looms. Will he bounce back or crater again like he did in St. Looie?

KEN CAMINITI

Another of the NL's incredible hot-cold third sackers. Will the real Ken Caminiti please stand up? If you look closely at that gaudy 117 TOPR of '92 you wonder if it was just a mirage. Otherwise he's a player into his 30s putting up well below-average TOPRs for his position . . . HRs (13) and doubles (31) identical to the season before. But his BA fell 32 points. Killed 15 rallies with DPs and committed an unacceptable 24 errors, the highest number in his career. But it's also the fourth time he's had more than 20 in a season . . . Can he hold off the challenge of super-prospect Phil Nevin?

TIM WALLACH

TOPRs keep falling. At 36, does it mark the end of a solid career? . . . Average in the .220s for a third straight season. A career-low 32 extra-base hits (Williams, for example, had 75) . . . Simply doesn't seem to drive pitches he used to pound . . . A far cry from the player who made five all-star teams, won a pair of Gold Gloves and used to bat cleanup in the middle of a terrific Montreal lineup.

SEAN BERRY

Hmmmmm. Turned 27 and seemed to step up several notches. There's that prime age factor again . . . A truly intriguing player given his numbers from a half season in '93: 14 HRs, 49 RBIs, 41 BBs, 12 of 14 SBs . . . Wouldn't you be inclined to find out if he can play every day? That's the Expos' problem. There's talk they'll shift Wil Cordero to 3B to make everyday room for the equally intriguing Mike Lansing at SS. If that happens, what becomes of Berry's playing time? If he's back at third he must bring a better glove—15 errors in half a year!

ARCHI CIANFROCCO

Packed off to San Diego when Berry and Lansing made the Expos infield scene a crowded one . . . Put together roughly the same kind of season in '93 as he did the year before . . . Does have surprising power including a couple dingers well over 400 feet . . . Must change that 17 BB-to-69 K ratio . . . Can also play 1B and the OF making him a possible IMP (Impact Multiple Position player).

DAVE HANSEN

Pinch hitter extraordinaire who might not be used much in that capacity next season because he could be the heir to Wallach's 3B job . . . Bounced back from that awful '92 (.214 BA with no power and no speed) to post that unbelievable TOPR. Still didn't show much pop (4 HRs). But, hey, when you're hitting .362 who nitpicks? . . . Walked more than he fanned and perhaps the most remarkable of all, didn't hit into a single DP? This from a player who has a four-year career total of one stolen base? Is all this a dream? But if you were LA wouldn't you consider finding out if his ability as a spare part last year might not translate into full-time solid numbers?.

NATIONAL LEAGUE SHORTSTOPS

Rank	Player	Team	7/1/94 Age	B	1990	1991	1992	3 yr Avg.	1993 TOPR
						TOPR Trendline			
Regulars:									
1.	Jeff Blauser	ATL	28	R	105	119	133	118	**128**
2.	Barry Larkin	CIN	30	R	111	148	133	128	**125**
3.	Jay Bell	PIT	28	R	100	111	104	105	**119**
4.	Andujar Cedeño	HOU	24	R	*	95	72	84	**99**
5.	Walt Weiss	FLA	30	B	93	(80)	74	84	**98**
6.	Jose Offerman	LAD	25	R	*	(78)	96	93	**97**
7.	Ozzie Smith	STL	39	B	97	122	114	111	**93**
8.	Wil Cordero	MON	22	R	-	-	(105)	(105)	**93**
9.	Ricky Gutierrez	SDO	24	R	-	-	-	-	**89**
10.	Royce Clayton	SFO	24	R	-	*	76	76	**88**
Other Qualifiers (200+ TPA):									
-	Kevin Stocker	PHI	24	B	-	-	-	-	**122**
-	Tim Bogar	NYM	27	R	-	-	-	-	**85**
-	Vinny Castilla	COL	26	R	-	*	*	*	**82**
-	Rey Sanchez	CUB	26	R	DNP	*	82	82	**77**
Of Note (under 200 TPA):									
-	Shawon Dunston	CUB	31	R	101	103	*	102	*
-	Jose Oquendo	STL	30	B	97	100	*	104	*

* Under 100 TPA-not included in average. ( ) 100-199 TPA. † Includes AL TOPR, unadjusted to NL.

JEFF BLAUSER

The best offensive shortstop in the bigs. That answer would probably win you a few bar bets. But, if you peek at the TOPR trendline, he's been at or near the top of the SS rankings for years now . . . Has one of the most unnoticed all-around games in the majors. Terrific power, especially for the position. Very high walk total (85). Solid stealing numbers (16 for 22). His 13 DPs are more than offset by a league high 16 HBPs . . . How do you figure the HBP list? You'd think pitchers would throw at the big dudes. Wrong! The '93 NL HBP leaders included Blauser, Derek Bell, Luis Gonzalez, Craig Biggio and Jerald Clark. Where are the big boppers? None of the NL's top 10 HR hitters showed up on the top 10 HBP list . . . Blauser's the first Braves SS to hit over .300 since Alvin Dark in 1948 . . . So, when will people start recognizing this guy's a star?

BARRY LARKIN

Another year—another injury. In '93 it was a thumb problem. The year before—a knee sprain. In '91, elbow, back and achilles troubles . . . But through them all he just hits and hits and hits. A .315 BA, the fifth straight year he's batted over .300 . . . TOPR has slipped slightly over these three hurting seasons because HRs have fallen and DPs jumped (13 in just 100 games) . . . Last Reds player to hit .300 at least five seasons in a row? Pete Rose who did it every year in Cincy from '65–'73 . . . A return of health should return his TOPRs to the upper echelon, especially with his fantastic 51 BB-to-33 K ratio and 14 of 15 steals . . . The complete player when completely healed.

JAY BELL

What a year for the ex-shortstops of Gonzalez–Tate High in Pensacola, Florida. Bell held down that high school's position. And when he graduated he turned it over to a player three years behind him in school—Travis Fryman. This year they played opposite each other in the All-Star Game . . . Bell's an accomplished player of "little ball." Led the league in sac bunts in '90 and '91. But his 13 last seasons represented a decade low. There was, however, a

reason the Pirates didn't ask Bell to bunt as often—they wanted him to hit. Career highs in BA (.310), walks (77) and SBs (16) . . . Has "double" written all over his stat sheet—32 doubles and 16 double plays . . . Those 32 two-baggers give him an even 100 the last three years . . . Factor in a Gold Glove, ending Ozzie reign as the NL's fielding wizard, and Bell joins Blauser and Larkin as the three star SSs in the NL. And please note how far ahead of the rest this trio ranks.

ANDUJAR CEDENO

One of those players whose "most noticed" numbers looked good—average up to .283, emerging as a hitter with moderate power (24 doubles and 11 HRs) and an encouraging jump to 48 walks. But still hits into a huge number of DPs (17) especially for someone who hits near the bottom of the order . . . Running game actually a negative (9 for 16) . . . Worrisome: was hitting .319 at the all-star break and tailed off considerably . . . While his TOPR figures don't belong anywhere near the top three SSs in this league, realize he's only 24.

WALT WEISS

Finally, a year without a visit to the DL. Last time he could say that Ronald Reagan was living in the White House ('88). Played 158 games after averaging only 91 a season the previous four seasons . . . Second only to Bell in SS fielding percentage . . . Steady, unspectacular player who offers very little power (just 17 extra-base hits, 14 of them doubles). Seven steals a career high . . . Walt Weiss Fan Club members should be extremely encouraged by a leap to 79 walks, 33 more than his previous single-season high . . . Fifth hardest in the entire NL to double—5 in 591 PAs . . . Don't forget this guy started at SS for four Oakland teams that won the AL West.

JOSE OFFERMAN

Will he ever develop into a solid player? Seems like LA's been waiting on him for years. But he's still just 25 . . . Led the majors with 25 sac bunts. Teammate Jody Reed #2 with 17 and LA CF

Brett Butler third with 14 (Butler topped the NL in '92 with 24 snapping Jay Bell's hold on the title of the league's top sacrificer) . . . There are detectable signs of improvement. Walks and strikeouts nearly balanced out (71–75)—always a positive sign in a young hitter. Steals rose to 30 but was still thrown out 13 times . . . One more very positive development—drove in 62 runs after totaling just 30 the season before indicating he's becoming a much tougher out in tough situations . . . But he's still one of the league's worst fielders—37 errors. UGH!

OZZIE SMITH

Is this fantastic career finally winding down? TOPRs say "yes" . . . Average stayed up (.288) and was the league's hardest to fan—once every 33.5 at bats . . . But walks fell to the lowest total in his 12-year Cardinal career. Stole 21, but that was also his least ever as a Redbird . . . Thus, the TOPR drop to the smallest in a decade . . . Perhaps most disturbing of all? Try 19 errors. Smith made only 18 miscues *combined* the two seasons before . . . But what a spectacular career it's been for a player who was unwanted out of LA's Locke High School where he played with Eddie Murray. Had to walk on at Cal State Poly–San Luis Obispo. Five years after he retires he'll "walk in" to Cooperstown.

WIL CORDERO

Might be something very special someday. Has wonderful power for someone so young at this position (32 doubles and 10 HRs) . . . Like many young Latin players, swings at everything, leading to a walk total that reached just 34 . . . Already solid stealing numbers (12 of 15). But that positive phase of his game erased by a dozen DPs . . . But 36 errors? Montreal believes he'll smooth out on the big league level. That's what LA was saying about Offerman three years ago and it hasn't happened. Is his eventual position gonna be SS or perhaps 3B? Has the kind of game that might eventually develop into 3B TOPR numbers . . . Expect TOPR numbers to move toward the very top of this positional list very soon. But his glove could make him a liability.

RICKY GUTIERREZ

Started the year as a spare part and ended as a regular . . . Doesn't have nearly the pop of a Cordero but already does many of the little things that pull his TOPR into the same area. Will walk—50. Hardly ever ruins rallies with DPs—7 . . . Odd: after hitting one homer total in his previous three minor league seasons, he belted 5 in his rookie big league season . . . Lucky to have gotten out of the Orioles organization by trade in September of 1992. There's still very little future for young Bird shortstops with that fellow Ripken still hanging around . . . One more bonus—only 14 errors.

ROYCE CLAYTON

Another of the slender, young emerging shortstops this league seems to be full of . . . Very solid BA—.282. But evidences the same deficiencies that plague others at this position. Walked only 38 times, a poor 11-of-21 stealing mark and 16 twin killings. All those combined to drag his TOPR to the bottom of the SS regulars . . . Like so many of the others here also had an ugly 27 errors. That represented 27% of all the flubs the entire Giants team made last season. Had four straight minor league seasons of 30 errors or more . . . Will his game mature? Will his obvious talent develop into star status? The Giants will take the time to find out as the Expos are doing with Cordero, LA with Offerman, Houston with Cedeno, etc.

KEVIN STOCKER

Literally burst on the scene at mid-year when Philly, feeling they already had enough offense, brought him to the majors for his glove work. So what happens? His goes TOPR-crazy and puts up a 122, far out of line from any reasonable expectation. After all, he'd hit .253 in three minor league stops before clubbing major league pitching at a .324 pace over the season's last half . . . No power but solid minor league stealing figures and hardly ever fans . . . Why'd pitchers hit him so often? Eight times to lead the team and finish 9th in the NL . . . Funniest part of Stocker's weird year? He didn't play well defensively at all which was the reason the Phils called him up in the first place—14 errors . . . Don't be surprised if this TOPR tumbles. Minor league TOPRs suggest 100 as a much more realistic area.

TIM BOGAR

Has the look of a utility player, which is what he was in the Mets minor league system starting at various times at all four infield spots . . . Has almost no power, no speed and has never shown a tendency to draw many walks . . . Must do better than 9 errors in such limited playing time.

VINNY CASTILLA

Where would his TOPR have been except for getting to play half his games at home where he batted .305? . . . A weird extra base set of 9–7–9 (9 doubles, 7 triples and 9 HRs) . . . Has an almost "Guillen-like" disdain for walks (13 in 357 PAs) . . . Absolutely no factor in the running game with 2 steals and was doubled up 10 times . . . Through July had 18 RBIs—all of them at home! After August 1, 11 of his 12 RBIs came on the road . . . Terrific at home and against left-handers (.305 and .333). Drops dramatically on the road and against righties (.206 and .228) . . . Unless walks and steals suddenly become part of his game he looks like a spare part. But minor league numbers indicate that improvement's a longshot.

REY SANCHEZ

The Cubs spent a good deal of the season crowing about the job Sanchez and Jose Vizcaino did filling in for Dunston at SS. But TOPR asks what all the commotion was about? Sanchez ended up with a meager 77. Vizcaino, listed under IMPs, put up a 93. And between them they committed 32 errors . . . Sanchez game basically has three drawbacks—no power, no speed and no walks. The terrible Trifecta of TOPR. Adding all three of those columns together last year gave him the number 16—and 15 of those were free passes. And realize he really didn't want to walk that many times—7 of the 15 were intentional . . . Was batting .324 through the first half and tailed off badly. But forgive that drop off to some degree as he was bothered by strains of the hip flexor and left knee.

SHAWON DUNSTON

He played just 25 games the last *two years*. Had back surgery May 13, 1992, and still isn't "back" . . . Did make a few token September appearances after a pulled hamstring set back his rehab even more during the '93 season . . . His '90–'91 TOPRs would put him at the top of the middle echelon of NL SSs. But does that player still exist? Cubs will find out. He has two seasons of a guaranteed contract left and last year the Cubbies paid $3,375,000 for those 10 at bats.

JOSE OQUENDO

Had fallen into disuse as a deep bench player before disappearing totally because of a heel injury in August, the second straight year a heel problem wiped him out . . . Solid, versatile, handyman when well. But how much of that versatility has been robbed by injury? . . . Once played in all 163 games of the '89 season with SL hitting .291. But you tend to ask the same question about him as the Cubbies ask about Dunston—does that player still exist inside what's become an injury-battered body? But like Dunston he's still young enough to write a happy ending to his career.

NATIONAL LEAGUE LEFT FIELDERS

Rank	Player	Team	7/1/94 Age	B	TOPR Trendline 1990	1991	1992	3 yr Avg.	1993 TOPR
Regulars:									
1.	Barry Bonds	SFO	29	L	173	169	217	185	**201**
2.	Kevin Mitchell	CIN	32	R	136	133	113†	129	**141**
3.	Ron Gant	ATL	29	R	138	136	115	130	**128**
4.	Phil Plantier	SDO	25	L	-	(176)†	95†	117	**128**
5.	Moises Alou	MON	27	R	*	DNP	127	127	**121**
6.	Luis Gonzalez	HOU	26	L	*	110	93	102	**121**
7.	Al Martin	PIT	26	L	-	-	*	*	**119**
8.	Bernand Gilkey	STL	27	R	*	83	121	107	**119**
9.	Vince Coleman	NYM	32	B	123	88	119	112	**101**
10.	Jeff Conine	FLA	28	R	*	-	*	*	**101**
11.	Jerald Clark	COL	30	R	(104)	89	89	90	**100**
12.	Derrick May	CUB	25	L	*	*	88	88	**99**
Other Qualifiers (200+ TPA):									
-	Pete Incaviglia	PHI	30	R	96†	85†	109	97	**120**
-	Milt Thompson	PHI	35	L	97	123	119	110	**94**

* Under 100 TPA-not included in average. ( ) 100-199 TPA. † Includes AL TOPR, unadjusted to NL.

BARRY BONDS

The finest offensive player in the majors and by a wide margin . . . If you sat down at a computer and designed the "perfect" player, you'd name him Barry Bonds . . . Hits for a high average and with outstanding power. (For the significance of his 88 extra-base hits, see the Seattle essay on Griffey.) Incredibly disciplined (126 walks) and turns many free passes into "doubles" with 29 steals . . . Also mix in a fourth consecutive Gold Glove . . . Just how good was his .336/46 HRs/123 RBI season? It would have won the NL Triple Crown in five of the last seven years ('92, '91, '90, '87 and '86) . . . Just missed the all-time mark for intentional bases on balls with 43. Ex-Giants slugger Willie McCovey drew 45 in 1969 . . . His season combined the very best traits of "little ball"—he led the league in on-base percentage—and "big ball"—he topped the NL in slugging percentage . . . Homered every 11.7 at bats and drove in a run every 4.4, both tops in the league . . . If he hits another 202 HRs in his career he and father Bobby will combine to catch Hank Aaron. The father-son team, baseball's all-time homering best, now has 554 (Bobby 332 and Barry 222) . . . What more can you say about him? Lots! See his essay in the closing section.

KEVIN MITCHELL

An enigma . . . When in the lineup his TOPRs tell you all you need to know about his impact. But his life's almost a day-to-day soap opera . . . In this decade alone has missed time with bone chips in the wrist, sore left knee, groin pull, another sore wrist, rib cage strain, fractured left foot, ear trouble, a sore foot and a bad shoulder. Number of games played has declined four consecutive seasons to a career low of 93 in '93 . . . His high TOPR based on his ability to simply bash the beejeebers out of the baseball—43 extra-base hits in just a bit over a half year . . . The extra weight he carries takes him totally out of any running game and contributes to an extremely high DP total (14) . . . But when he comes to play he's a star. It's just that you're never quite sure day-to-day if he will.

RON GANT

Another terrific season marked by career highs in HRs and RBIs (36 and 117). Average rose as did his walk total. So why the slight

TOPR slip? Tiny things like 14 DPs, a slight decrease in running game effectiveness, etc. . . . Third time in four years as a 30–20 man (HR–SB) . . . In the '90s has averaged 29 HRs, 97 RBIs, 99 runs and 31 SBs a season. So how's he only made it to one All-Star Game? One of those players who, for some reason, always seems to wind up in someone else's shadow and whose name keeps coming up in trade talks.

PHIL PLANTIER

Blossomed in San Diego . . . Boston got tired of waiting for him to duplicate his outstanding minor league TOPRs, dealt him away and spent the entire '93 campaign searching for a solid hitter to play in right field in Boston . . . How good was Plantier? His one-RBI-every-4.6-at-bats ratio was second in the NL only to a guy named Bonds . . . His HR-every-13.6-at-bats also #2 to (is this getting old, or what?) Bonds . . . Third hardest to double in the league behind the league's "Double Darrens"—SF's Lewis and Philly's Daulton . . . If his .240 BA ever rises to near his minor league numbers (hit over .300 three times) his TOPR will skyrocket towards Bondsland.

MOISES ALOU

As long as the dislocated and broken ankle he suffered late in the year mends, he'll be the best of Alous in major league history (Felipe, Matty and Jesus). Those three played 48 seasons and only Felipe's 92 RBIs in '62 for the Giants bettered Moises' 85 last season . . . Approaching the age where TOPRs often take a significant step upward (note that Bonds went from a 169 to an astronomical 217 the year he turned 27) . . . A few more walks would help the TOPR, especially since he's such a high percentage stealer (33 of 41 the last two seasons combined) . . . Holder of one of the more obscure major league records—"Most hits, all home runs, consecutive games." In a four-game span from July 6–9 he had six hits, all of them dingers.

LUIS GONZALEZ

The "other left fielder in Texas named Gonzalez" . . . Put up the best numbers of his career and that TOPR leap's easily understandable with a 57-point rise in batting average, reaching .300 with a hit in his final at bat October 3 . . . Doubles jumped from 19 to 34.

HRs up from 10 to 15. Thievery on the rise too (had 7 steals in '92, 20 in '93) . . . But maybe it's all traceable to a decided increase in patience at the plate. His walk total nearly doubled (24 to 47) . . . Finished especially strong hitting .327 after the all-star break . . . Another showing signs of TOPR stardom as his "prime time" approaches.

AL MARTIN

A late bloomer who spent seven seasons in the Atlanta chain without giving any hint he'd ever be major league material. But what a minor league free agent find for the Buccos . . . First rookie to lead the Pirates in HRs since Ralph Kiner drilled 23 in 1946. Also wiped out Kiner's rookie strikeout record of 109 with 122 whiffs. But all those Ks reduced his DPs to a microscopic 5 . . . Had never hit over 12 long balls in any of his seven Braves bus league seasons. But smacked 18 last year . . . Must elevate his walk total from last year's 42. Stole 16 and note that he once swiped 40 in a minor league year . . . Was '93 a mirage? Or will his TOPR rise even more as he nears that magic age of 27? . . . Piazza the only NL rookie with more HRs . . . Weird: didn't steal a base until July 3 and still wound up with 16.

BERNARD GILKEY

How about the strength of LF in the NL? Gilkey's very solid 119 TOPR gets him just eighth best at the position . . . How many Cardinal fans know that he was their club's leader in extra-base hits with 61? . . . Where'd those 16 HRs come from? He'd never hit more than 7 in any of his previous eight professional seasons . . . TOPR would have been much higher except for a mysterious leap from 5 DPs to 16 . . . For a player with significant speed, his steal numbers don't suggest that running him is a very good strategy. While he's swiped 33 the last two seasons combined, he's been thrown out an unacceptable 22 times making him just a 60% stealer, far below the percentage necessary to be considered effective . . . Tied for the major league lead with 19 outfield assists . . . Yet another NL LF approaching the TOPR upswing season of 27 years old.

VINCE COLEMAN

Unfortunately this once explosive offensive talent made on the field headlines in '93 for being "explosive" off of it . . . Off-field troubles coincided with on-field difficulties . . . Walk totals keep dwindling (just 21 last year) . . . 38 steals would be considered terrific for some players. But *this* player pilfered over 100 three times in his career . . . A perfectly balanced switch hitter: as a RH batted .279 with 1 HR and as LH batted .279 with 1 HR . . . How much didn't the Mets want him back after his problem-plagued '93? Despite the fact that he's signed through the '94 season, their post-season guide *did not* detail his career and most recent season. That same guide did include free-agents-to-be Fernandez, Murray, Johnson, O'Brien and Orsulak . . . With his one huge asset shrinking (just 99 steals the last three seasons combined) who will want him?

JEFF CONINE

The NL ironman. Became the first player ever to appear in all 162 games for an expansion team. Only he and Cal Ripken Jr.

reported for work every day last season . . . Decent power (12 HRs and 24 doubles). No factor in a running game and was double-dipped 14 times . . . KC exposed him to the expansion draft hoping Kevin McReynolds would refind his stroke and fill the LF job. TOPRs say KC made a mistake and should have kept this converted first baseman . . . His .292 BA second to Piazza among all NL rookies . . . Former pitcher at UCLA drafted in round 58 . . . He and wife Cindy reached the semifinals of the U.S. Racquetball Mixed Doubles Championships last October.

JERALD CLARK

TOPR reached triple figures for the first time. But, in Mile High, that improvement was to be expected . . . Nice pop with 45 extra-base hits. But a mere 20 walks really hurts a TOPR. Oddly, he was hit half as many times as he walked (10) . . . Average took a nice 40-point jump . . . Good versatility starting 29 games at 1B for the injured Galarraga and 15 in RF when Bichette got hurt . . . At 30, don't expect much in the way of TOPR improvement.

DERRICK MAY

Most fans will be shocked by this low TOPR ranking. But remember, TOPR measures the total impact, positively and negatively, of a player . . . Yes, he hit .295 with 25 doubles. But only 10 HRs. Of all the other LFs we've already listed, only the powerless Coleman had fewer . . . Must almost be forced to accept a walk—25 unintentional passes . . . Tends to hit the ball hard on the ground—thus 15 DPs . . . Has never shown any inclination at any level to wait out walks so hoping that number will rise is probably fruitless . . . His power stroke does seem to be emerging though . . . Still very young. But there are some very good, very young players above him at this well-stocked NL position . . . One small excuse for him? Pulled a hamstring on August 30 and went just 3 for 25 the rest of the season . . . Weird: Hit .102 against the Florida Marlins and .467 against the NL champion Phils.

PETE INCAVIGLIA

Resurrected his career in '93 after drifting through three other organizations in three years . . . Hit a career high .274. Best HRs-per-at-bat ratio of his eight seasons in the bigs . . . Despite starting just 86 games also posted a career best 89 RBIs . . . Led the Phils in HR ratio, RBI ratio and slugging percentage . . . Hardly ever walks. Doesn't run much. But all those strikeouts keep him out of DPs . . . Seemed to take to platooning in Philly like it was meant for him. Why didn't it work that way in Detroit or Houston?

MILT THOMPSON

The Phils other LF . . . TOPR dropped to a decade low 94. Average shrunk to .262 from .293 the year before and .307 in '91. Don't blame platooning. He was platooned in those better years also . . . Running game faltered badly. Just 9 steals for a player who as recently as 1990 stole 25 and in '87 swiped 46 . . . Solid pinch-hitting numbers (8 for 25) . . . Probably has years left as a part-timer. But that TOPR-speed drop has to be worrisome.

NATIONAL LEAGUE CENTER FIELDERS

Rank	Player	Team	7/1/94 Age	B	TOPR Trendline 1990	1991	1992	3 yr Avg.	1993 TOPR
Regulars:									
1.	Lenny Dykstra	PHI	31	L	147	149	140	146	**152**
2.	Marquis Grissom	MON	27	R	106	111	126	116	**122**
3.	Bobby Kelly	CIN	29	R	108†	114†	98†	106	**118**
4.	Brett Butler	LAD	37	L	129	113	137	126	**115**
5.	Sammy Sosa	CUB	25	R	97†	76†	108	93	**114**
6.	Andy Van Slyke	PIT	33	L	131	132	146	137	**109**
7.	Derek Bell	SDO	25	R	-	*	(95)†	(95)	**104**
8.	Ray Lankford	STL	27	L	(128)	105	131	119	**104**
9.	Otis Nixon	ATL	35	B	116	121	106	114	**101**
10.	Chuck Carr	FLA	26	B	*	*	*	*	**96**
11.	Steve Finley	HOU	29	L	87†	108	125	108	**93**
12.	Alex Cole	COL	28	L	134†	105†	92†	108	**91**
13.	Darren Lewis	SFO	26	R	*	108	91	94	**90**
Other Qualifiers (200+ TPA):									
-	Brian Jordan	STL	27	R	-	-	85	85	**123**
-	Deion Sanders	ATL	26	L	(76)†	(100)	135	111	**113**
-	Ryan Thompson	NYM	26	R	-	-	(92)	(92)	**96**
-	Willie Wilson	CUB	38	B	113	78	93	94	**87**
Of Note (under 200 TPA):									
-	Darrin Jackson	TOR/NYM	31	R	(91)	119	92	101	**59†**

* Under 100 TPA-not included in average. ( ) 100-199 TPA. † Includes AL TOPR, unadjusted to NL.

LENNY DYKSTRA

Just missed erasing the record for most times reaching base by a hit or walk this century. "Nails" totaled 323 Hs and BBs. Lefty O'Doul set the mark of 330 in 1929 . . . His 143 runs scored the most in the NL since Chuck Klein touched home 152 times in 1932 . . . The 129 walks broke the Phils team record of 128 set by Mike Schmidt . . . But those who know TOPRs weren't surprised. He's been this kind of player since he's been in Philly. But last year the team was so good that finally *everybody* noticed Dykstra . . . In the history of baseball only 38 players had reached base safely 300 times in a season. In '93 Dykstra became #39. Toronto's John Olerud became #40 and Detroit's Tony Phillips was #41.

MARQUIS GRISSOM

Dramatically changed his previous career reputation as "only a speed player" . . . Expos decided to move him into the critical #3 spot in the batting order and he responded with 19 HRs (he'd hit only 23 in the three previous seasons combined) and 95 RBIs—23 more than any other NL CF . . . His running game slipped just a bit because of his place in the lineup. But 53 steals in 63 attempts still rates him as one of the game's premier thieves . . . Walk totals remain moderate though increasing slightly every season . . . First Expo to score more than 100 runs since Mitch Webster and Tim Raines in 1987 . . . An emerging star just approaching his prime.

ROBERTO "BOBBY" KELLY

Whichever first name he prefers these days, what a shame that a separated shoulder wrecked the wonderful season he was having. On July 2, when he got hurt Kelly led the NL in hits (102). He appeared headed for a 60 extra-base hit-40 steal season . . . If he'd only walk more, just 17 freebies. . . . With his stealing speed those BBs would help him make even more of an impact . . . Asked the media to call him Bobby instead of Roberto on April 17. Good move! Hit .227 as Roberto and .333 as Bobby. But for some reason, after the season, asked to switch back to Roberto. Stay tuned.

BRETT BUTLER

Should open a "singles" club. Had 149 one-base hits edging the Cards' Jefferies for the league lead by 6. It's the fourth straight year he's led the NL in singles. No one's done that before . . . TOPR decline attributable to very slight drops in many areas (11 points in BA, a few less walks, etc.) . . . If only he'd made it to the majors sooner than age 26 he might have had more of a shot at the Hall. As it is, sometime next season he'll get his 2,000th hit, 250th double, 1,000th walk, 500th steal and score his 1,200th run.

SAMMY SOSA

Had the first 30HR/30SB season ever in Cubs history but still barely raised his TOPR . . . The little things still put his number down. Only 38 walks in 641 PAs. And that total was easily a career high! . . . Oddly, had more HRs than doubles and triples combined (33–30) . . . Had 14 DPs and would have had more except for those 135 strikeouts . . . But understand that next season he'll still be only 25 and may boost his TOPR again . . . His 17 outfield assists were the most by a Cub in 30 years (Lou Brock had 17 in '63). . . . To understand how truly rare Sosa's 30–30 season realize that in the entire history of this proud franchise they've only had three 20–20 guys! Frank Schulte (1911), Leon "Bull" Durham (1983) and Ryne Sandberg (three times).

ANDY VAN SLYKE

Another whose year was gutted by injury—a broken collarbone costing him 66 games on the DL. That led to his first "off" TOPR season of the decade . . . Was putting up a TOPR similar to that three-year rolling average of 137 before getting hurt. But in the 23 games after returning he hit just .272 with 2 HRs. Had been hitting .322 at the time of the injury . . . Rate of walks declined and hit into an unusually high total of 13 DPs . . . But next season at 33, given a return to health, he should bounce back to the status that's made him a three-time all-star and five time Gold Glover.

DEREK BELL

Very good power (21 HRs) and excellent speed (26 of 31 stealing) . . . Padres "stole" him from Toronto for the disappointing Darrin Jackson. Where would the Pads be had they not pulled off this deal and the one that brought the only other player on the club to hit more HRs and drive in more runs—Plantier? . . . But Bell's TOPR's never gonna ring big bells until he becomes more patient, drawing only 18 unintentional walks . . . But he's only 25. And just two years ago had a 63-walk minor league season. If that part of his game matures he's got some very good tools.

RAY LANKFORD

Started '93 being touted as a possible MVP. Ended it tied with Whiten for the third best outfielder's TOPR on his own club. What a skid! . . . What went wrong? Everything! Shoulder injuries early and late and a wrist injury that wiped out a couple weeks in mid-season combined to prevent him from ever finding his hitter's rhythm . . . Except for a team high 81 walks, you can pick a number off his '93 stat sheet and it declined from the season before . . . The average fell 55 points. A man who'd hit 20 HRs wound up with 7. Shouldn't have even bothered trying to run. The year before he swiped 42. In '93 he was an ugly 14 for 28 . . . Given the remarkable potential, just write off last season as a mistake.

OTIS NIXON

Headed for free agency off his worst season of the '90s . . . Average and steals declined. And basically that's Nixon's game. Will never provide any extra-base power—just 16 extra-base hits in '93 and an almost mind-boggling low total of 52 in the '90s . . . Walks up for a second straight season to a career-tying-best of 61 . . . Still an extremely dangerous thief (47 of 60) . . . Like his extra-base totals, Nixon's RBI numbers look like a mistake—24 last year. And that was his second best year in the decade, a period in which he's driven in just 92 runs in four years! . . . He's appeared in all or part of 11 major league seasons and has 147 RBIs. Bonds has more than that in his last eight months of play.

CHUCK CARR

Led the league in steals with 58 and in getting caught with 22 . . . Only Tommy Harper's 73 steals for the Seattle Pilots ranks above Carr in expansion history . . . That total of 58 was the lowest to lead the NL since Bobby Tolan did it with just 57 in 1970. . . . Given his speed game he must make a major increase from his total of 49 walks if his TOPR's to make any dramatic rise . . . The Reds, Mariners, Mets and Cards all drooled over his speed but tired of waiting for him to figure out how to get to first base so he could use it. Carr may be figuring it out—bunted for 17 hits last season. Want one more encouraging sign? Those 49 walks might not seem like many—but they're a professional career high for his 8 seasons.

STEVE FINLEY

A horrible '93 for a player who seemed on the verge of stardom . . . Most folks will point to .266 BA that plummeted 26 points. But more distressing to TOPR was a fall from 58 walks to a meager 28 and a huge drop from 44 steals to 19 . . . But he had legit excuses. Began the year fighting Bell's palsy and numbness from the viral infection that left him unable to close his left eye. Then a hairline fracture of his right wrist put him out past mid-May. Returned to hit .278 from then on. But that still does little to explain the drastic decrease in the walk-steal totals . . . Led the NL in triples with 13 despite not getting his first until the team's 41st game.

ALEX COLE

Job hunting again after being released by the Rockies after the season despite being their second best base stealer with 30 . . . That's always been the vital part of this part-timer's game. But the TOPR fell again to its lowest point in years. Never known as much defensively so his TOPR's his path to employment . . . A .283 career hitter who came in 27 points beneath that . . . As usual, absolutely no extra-base power and only a moderate number of walks (43) . . . Hey, when you move through the expansion draft to Colorado and your offensive numbers DROP, that's a bad sign!

DARREN LEWIS

Another whose low ranking might surprise some . . . But his '93 TOPR is certainly in keeping with his established career parameters . . . The Giants made him their leadoff hitter on May 16 and kept him there despite a .253 average and an inability to draw walks (just 30) . . . Swiped 46 to lead the club . . . Has never made an error in 316 big league games spanning 770 chances—both all-time marks. On May 10, 1994, will celebrate the third anniversary of his last error while playing for Phoenix against Albuquerque.

BRIAN JORDAN

Appears to have made the right choice in selecting baseball over being the starting free safety for the NFL Falcons . . . Could be a decent power hitter after belting 10 in just 223 official ABs. Add that to his .309 BA and you've got the makings of a very fine hitter . . . If only he walked more—12 last season and just 22 in 450 career PAs. But then, football players always want to "hit something." . . . Started '93 as the regular LF but got off to a horrid start. SL optioned him to Louisville. From his 6/25 recall to the season's end he hit .337 with all 10 of his HRs and 43 of his 44 RBIs and TOPRed in the 140 area . . . That binge should make him a regular come '94. But who gets bumped to make room for him?

DEION SANDERS

Will he ever choose between football and baseball? Or, sadly, like Bo Jackson, will fate make choices for him? . . . In what amounts to less than half a season he collected 30 extra-base hits and 19 steals . . . His outstanding speed virtually assures him of low DP totals (3) . . . With more walks (16) that speed would become an even greater weapon . . . All this despite basically going AWOL for three weeks in late April because of unhappiness with his limited role . . . TOPRs say he could be "Neon Deion" in this sport for at least another decade. But what does Deion want?

RYAN THOMPSON

The second half of what may prove to be one of the finest trades the Mets ever made. Got him and promising 2B Jeff Kent from Toronto for the late season rental of free-agent-to-be David Cone . . . Tall, athletic, graceful CF who must make more contact to be an everyday player (19 BB–81 K) . . . Appears to have terrific speed but doesn't steal bases (4 in 110 major league games) . . . Like Jordan, began the year in the bigs, disappointed, spent three months at Triple A and returned with strong finish.

WILLIE WILSON

Nearing the end of a solid 16-year career . . . Swiped 7 bases to move to 13th on the all-time list with 667 (Joe Morgan's next up the ladder with 689) . . . Added three triples to move his career total to 145, highest among all active players . . . Failed to steal at least 20 for the first time in his career. That streak of 15 years ties him for second with Lou Brock and Ozzie Smith behind Honus Wagner's 18 straight seasons with 20 or more steals . . . All in all not a bad career for a player who nearly opted to play running back at Maryland after accepting a football scholarship there in 1974.

DARRIN JACKSON

What's happened to him? . . . Appeared to have a nice career ahead of him a couple years ago after posting that 119 TOPR in '91 . . . His tour of Canadian duty lasted all of 46 games before the Mets actually sent Tony Fernandez to the Jays for his rights . . . He arrived in NY and got worse. Two extra-base hits and 2 walks in 31 games . . . This player, who stole 14 bases in '92 didn't even attempt one last year . . . Every number he put up looked sick. And that's exactly what he was—sick. With hyperthyroidism. It disabled him for six weeks and basically ruined '93.

NATIONAL LEAGUE RIGHT FIELDERS

| Rank | Player | Team | 7/1/94 Age | B | TOPR Trendline | | | | 1993 TOPR |
					1990	1991	1992	3 yr Avg.	
Regulars:									
1.	Larry Walker	MON	27	L	116	122	138	126	**136**
2.	Bobby Bonilla	NYM	31	B	124	140	120	129	**130**
3.	David Justice	ATL	28	L	148	144	135	142	**130**
4.	Orlando Merced	PIT	27	B	*	121	110	115	**129**
5.	Tony Gwynn	SDO	34	L	107	109	111	109	**128**
6.	Dante Bichette	COL	30	R	97†	87†	95†	92	**127**
7.	Reggie Sanders	CIN	26	R	-	*	132	132	**116**
8.	Mark Whiten	STL	27	B	*	88†	99†	94	**104**
9.	Eric Anthony	HOU	26	L	96	(63)	103	95	**95**
10.	Willie McGee	SFO	35	B	115†	108	98	108	**94**
Other Qualifiers (200+ TPA):									
-	Jeromy Burnitz	NYM	25	L	-	-	-	-	**119**
-	Jim Eisenreich	PHI	35	L	98†	93†	85†	93	**115**
-	Wes Chamberlain	PHI	28	R	*	102	99	101	**112**
-	Junior Felix	FLA	26	B	114†	87†	86†	97	**83**
-	Darrell Whitmore	FLA	25	L	-	-	-		**63**
Of Note (under 200 TPA):									
-	Darryl Strawberry	LAD	32	L	140	136	(110)	134	**(89)**

* Under 100 TPA-not included in average. ( ) 100-199 TPA. † Includes AL TOPR, unadjusted to NL.

LARRY WALKER

Oh, Canada, what a glorious young player! . . . Became the first Canadian-born player to ever put up a 20–20 season (22 HRs and 29 SBs). The Expos franchise had had five previous 20–20 seasons—all by Andre Dawson . . . Average dropped 35 points but the TOPR stayed virtually the same because of one incredibly encouraging sign. His walks-to-strikeouts ratio changed in one year from 41–97 in '92 to 80–76 last season . . . A remarkable power-speed combo with those 29 steals in just 36 attempts . . . total of 80 HRs ranks him fifth among all Canadians to play in the bigs with Jeff Heath's 194 the tops . . . Look out for a huge year. He learned the strike zone last season and is entering baseball's prime age—27.

BOBBY BONILLA

Despite all the caterwauling in the Big Apple, the Mets did get what they paid for a couple of years ago—one extremely steady producer. Check the rest of baseball—there just aren't many players putting up strings of 130 TOPR seasons . . . Missed the final 23 games with a ruptured shoulder ligament and still posted a career best 34 HRs . . . Fourth best HR ratio in the NL: one every 14.8 ABs . . . TOPR will return to the 140s of 1991 if the BA (.265) jumps back to that .302 level . . . With Hojo and Murray gone, the Mets say they're thinking of using him at 1B or 3B. Be careful! He's error-prone and mounting fielding problems can sometimes have a negative effect on TOPRs, especially in the "Boo Apple."

DAVID JUSTICE

Check the remarkable consistency of his TOPRs this decade—all at 130 or above . . . Only the fourth player in Atlanta history with a 40 HR–100 RBI season. The others were Aaron, Dale Murphy and Jeff Burroughs (who's now become more famous as the father of Little League World Series star-hurler Sean Burroughs) . . . #3 in the NL in HR ratio; one every 14.6 ABs . . . But finished with one of the weirdest stat lines in recent history. Can you believe a player with 40 HRs didn't reach 60 extra-base hits? Had only 15 doubles and four three-baggers . . . Should forget trying to steal with him (3 for 8) . . . Right in the heart of his career so expect this David to keep putting up "Goliath" numbers.

ORLANDO MERCED

Surprised? Don't be! His previous two-year TOPRs should have tipped us that his number could be headed for the tops at his position . . . Began the season as a switch-hitter before junking the right side May 9. Good move! Hit .302 batting lefty against lefties . . . Was TOPRing the 145–150 area before an ice cold finish (.213 his last 40 games) dropped him from the NL batting lead which he held as late as August 10 . . . Walks exploded to a pro high of 77 . . . A line-drive hitter whose power totals might jump dramatically some year as he learns which pitches he can "turn on" and attempt to drive out of the park . . . Grew up across the street from the Clemente family in Rio Piedras, Puerto Rico, and now plays the same position on the same team as his idol Roberto.

TONY GWYNN

You'll find his TOPR trendline odd, indeed. His leap to 128 orchestrated by an average that skyrocketed to .358, second only to batting champ Galarraga . . . Gwynn richly deserves his acclaim as one of the finest "hitters" in the game. But TOPR measures offense, not just hitting. Provides only sporadic power (7 HRs) though he collects bushels of doubles (41). That was good enough for fourth in the league even though injuries limited him to 122 games . . . But the fact that he makes such solid contact EVERY at bat actually can work against him. He draws only a moderate amount of walks (36) and builds up enormous DP totals (18) . . . And you look at that "round" physique and don't tend to think "run." But run he can, pilfering 14 of 15 . . . Is he a "natural" hitter? Think again! He's man-made. Made by Gwynn himself. "Captain Video" tapes each and every at bat and often carries tapes with him on road trips of all the pitchers he might face—to study during free time. One wonders how good many other fine hitters might become if they showed that kind of dedication.

DANTE BICHETTE

Hello Colorado! Hello blossoming TOPR! . . . Should immediately buy a cemetery plot at this stadium so he can be buried here. That's what was happening to his career—it was being buried—until Colorado dealt for him . . . Had always been a decent hitter

(.254 career) but never a .310 hitter. Always had fair power but never a 21-HR man. Always had decent extra-base pop. But 43 doubles? Never! . . . Also kept up his undernoticed running game swiping 14 though he was tossed out 8 times . . . What kind of "Colorado High" did he experience? Hit .373 at home—.252 away with 45 of his 69 extra-base hits being "homers" . . . Would you deal for him off those numbers? Absolutely not! Were the numbers a fluke of the park effects? Who cares, if he never leaves Colorado?

REGGIE SANDERS

Stardom may be just around the corner. Yes, his TOPR slipped a bit, but it's not unusual in developing players to see their charts waver a bit . . . Did anyone notice he became a 20–20 player (20HRs and 27 SBs)? . . . Numbers might have been higher had he not at times played with a sprained ankle and bruised elbow . . . An intriguing combo of speed and power that's missing just one factor—plate patience. A player with his remarkable stealing ability should draw more than 51 walks (118 Ks). Three times in the minors walked more than he struck out. If that starts happening in the bigs, look out! . . . Yet another entering the prime years of his career.

MARK WHITEN

Everyone got all excited about his remarkable power display in "Busch Canyon." Homered 4 times in the second game of a doubleheader against Cincy September 7. Weird notes about that outburst: a) Whiten hadn't gone deep in any game since August 11 before that quartet of taters, and b) the entire Cardinal team hadn't hit 4 in a game in over two years spanning 333 games . . . But for all the clamor, his TOPR hardly moved an inch even though his 25 HRs represented 5 more than he'd hit in his three-year career entering '93. Why? Doubles fell. That's right, he actually had a higher percentage of extra-base blows the year before. But everyone got all caught up in the glitz of his long ones . . . His running game efficiency dipped a bit and walks fell off measurably. In other words, his HRs went up everything else stayed the same or came down and his TOPR hardly budged . . . Possesses a fantastic arm which NL runners quickly decided not to challenge.

ERIC ANTHONY

TOPR numbers remain unacceptable for the position though he's still young enough for there to be a breakthrough season on his horizon . . . Power numbers are OK (15 HRs) considering the way the Astrodome works against power hitters. And he did lead three of his minor leagues in HRs . . . But that .249 season, a career best, raised his overall average in the bigs to a measly .223. This player simply must hit better. A pair of .300 seasons late in his minor league resumé suggest he will. But the Astros are waiting . . . Walking more and fanning less . . . Won't ever be a stealing threat . . . So his TOPR rise is probably totally dependent on him becoming more like a NASA countdown: "3 . . . 2 . . . 1 . . . we have contact!" More hits and Anthony's TOPR career will "lift off."

WILLIE McGEE

Former batting champ whose TOPRs have been on a slow, steady decline as he reaches his mid-30s . . . Hit .300 for a fourth time. But the rest of the numbers were pretty empty. Just 4 HRs, but then he never did possess much long-ball power. Doubles and walks up slightly. Successful in just 10 of 19 steals and had his usual high DP total of 12. Remember, he once led the NL with a 24-DP season . . . Still a serviceable player whose TOPR returns to triple figures if his running game rebounds . . . Weird: Led off for SF the first 17 games of the year without ever scoring a run.

JEROMY BURNITZ

Welcome to the bigs! Debuted with the second best TOPR on the team next to Bonilla . . . Might be a real star *very* soon. TOPR held down because of his ineffective running game (just 3 for 9). But minor league steal numbers (he had 31 in Double A league and 30 at Triple A in '91 and '92) suggest he'll become much more of a factor in this area quickly . . . Terrific power potential with 29 extra-base hits in half a rookie season . . . Already seems to know the strike zone with 38 walks in that half year . . . Will always be able to tell his kids he got his first homer off Ryan. Uh, Ryan Bowen that is . . . Only question may be a psychological one—can he stand the pressure of being the "Pheenom" in the Big Apple?

JIM EISENREICH

Has made a remarkable comeback after overcoming the neurological movement disorder known as Tourette's syndrome . . . The affliction forced him out of the game in the mid-'80s before medical help enabled him to control it . . . Posted a career high .318 average and 28 extra-base hits which, for a platoon player, is very good . . . Will walk, steal a base once in a while and generally stays out of the DP all contributing to the finest TOPR year in a while . . . Even at 35 a real plus bench player who the Phils moved quickly to re-sign right after the season ended . . . A vastly underappreciated fielder with just one error his last 228 games afield.

WES CHAMBERLAIN

Yet one more part of the four-man Phils OF platoon with Eisenreich, Incaviglia and Thompson. And, like the first two, experienced a solid TOPR rise . . . Also like Eisenreich, standout extra-base numbers (20 doubles, 4 triples, 12 HRs) in about a half year. Add these two platooners together and they gave the Phils 37–6–19 and a BA of just over .300. Hey, players can scream all they want about being "regulars." Some just perform better as "half-regulars" . . . Just one error in his last 107 games . . . Won't walk or run much but would probably be a 20-HR guy if he played every day. But why tinker with success?

JUNIOR FELIX

What a waste of talent! How can a player who had 15 HRs, 45 extra-base hits, 13 SBs and TOPRing at 114 at age 23 with the Blue Jays have sunk so far as to have been simply released in mid-season by the expansion Marlins? Just how much trouble must he be? . . . BA at .238 when the pink slip arrived . . . Had 10 BBs and 50 Ks. Ugh! . . . Remains one of the game's worst fielders . . . But this player actually led the Angels in extra-base hits in '92 and by late '93 was baseball's nowhere man! We'll ask again—just how much trouble must he be?

DARRELL WHITMORE

One look at his numbers and it appears he was "rushed" to the bigs to quickly. Was putting up fabulous numbers at Triple A Edmonton before Florida called. (Would they have summoned him if Felix hadn't been such a bust?) But his .355 with 35 extra-base hits in Canada turned into .204 with 12 in sunny Florida . . . One more indication of how overmatched he was, comes from a 10 BB-to-72 K ratio . . . Totally throw out '93 and hope the lack of success didn't discourage him. He's a player with big-time tools.

DARRYL STRAWBERRY

How the once mighty have fallen! . . . Now a huge question mark at the very point of his career that people are supposed to be asking if he's "Hall" material . . . Back problems that limited him to 43 games in '92 shut him down after just 32 last year. His recent on-and-off field difficulties tend to make you forget that he drilled 174 HRs in just a five-year period ('87–'91) before the back gave way. Lost in the pile of all his recent woes is that 39 HR—36 SB season in '87. Yes, there was TOPR greatness in him. Is it still there? . . . At 32 there's still lots of time to come back. But is there the will?

NATIONAL LEAGUE IMPS

Rank	Player	Team	7/1/94 Age	B	TOPR Trendline				1993 TOPR
					1990	1991	1992	3 yr Avg.	
Regulars:									
1.	Cory Snyder	LAD	31	R	86†	(55)†	106	87	100
2.	Mike Lansing	MON	26	R	-	-	-	-	99
3.	Bip Roberts	CIN	30	B	130	101	138	124	98
4.	Joe Orsulak	NYM	32	L	103†	88†	101†	96	96
5.	Jose Vizcaino	CUB	26	B	*	(75)	75	75	93
6.	Mariano Duncan	PHI	31	R	116	102	96	104	88
7.	Jeff Branson	CIN	27	L	-	-	(86)	(86)	75
Other Qualifiers (200+ TPA):									
-	Dwight Smith	CUB	30	L	96	(82)	100	94	124
-	Phil Clark	SDO	26	R	-	-	*	*	123
-	Jacob Brumfield	CIN	29	R	-	-	*	*	110
-	Daryl Boston	COL	31	L	111†	119	122	116	105
-	Tim Teufel	SDO	35	R	(109)	105	92	102	101
-	Dave Martinez	SFO	29	L	98	112	100	103	91
-	Chico Walker	NYM	36	B	-	95	116	103	84
Of Note (under 200 TPA):									
-	Nelson Liriano	COL	30	B	84†	*	-	91	(107)

* Under 100 TPA-not included in average; ( ) 100-199 TPA. † Includes AL TOPR, unadjusted to NL.

CORY SNYDER

An IMP who may have found a home in RF though his TOPR would put him well below that of an average NL RF . . . Career seemed much like Lazarus a couple years ago—dead. But he's arisen from a string of horrible seasons (a 1991 TOPR of 55?) to prove he belongs in the bigs. But unlike Lazarus who was commanded to rise and walk, Snyder doesn't walk. If only he did! Just 47 BBs and 147 Ks . . . Still has occasional power but nothing like the belter he was when he arrived with Cleveland in the late '80s (59 HRs in '87–'88) . . . Some will blame the hitting theories of White Sox instructor Walk Hriniak for messing him up. But in truth Snyder's decline was already at full speed when he arrived in the Windy City and made it windier (one "fan" every 3 at bats) . . . But still has a remarkable throwing arm and can play several spots afield . . . The kind of player you love as a "tenth man."

MIKE LANSING

Thank heavens for the chicken pox! Expos star 2B Delino De-Shields came down with them forcing the club to use Lansing to open the season. Promptly had the first five-hit game by an Expos rookie since Warren Cromartie in 1977 . . . Started 15 at 2B, 74 at 3B and 34 at SS . . . Much of the Expos' off-season maneuvering aimed at getting him into the '94 everyday lineup . . . TOPR would have been much higher except for 16 DPs . . . Terrific stealing percentage (23 for 28), excellent doubles power (29) and makes solid contact . . . If he's to play regularly next season his error total must dip from last season's 16 . . . Score another one for the Montreal scouting dept. The club bought his contract from the independent Miami Miracle team and two years later he's viewed as a crucial piece of this contending team's lineup.

BIP ROBERTS

Once a dynamic IMP whose season got blown away by injuries. Right out of the gate he injured his right shoulder and then sprained his right wrist four days later. Sprained his left thumb in June, an injury that would eventually require season-ending surgery . . . Average skidded from .323 to .240. TOPR would have slipped even further had not Roberts' running game remained outstanding (26 for 32). Speed also keeps him almost totally out of DPs . . . Can play any of the OF or INF positions (except 1B) but probably best at 2B or LF . . . Down year might make his price decline sharply as a free agent thereby making him a possible big-time bargain as long as he's healthy. And when he's well there are a pair of 130 TOPR seasons this decade to attract possible buyers.

JOE ORSULAK

OF-1B type who'll give you solid and often spectacular play afield and, as his career TOPR trendline indicates, steady offensive production . . . Did we say steady? Has hit between .269 and .288 six years in a row and, are you ready for this, was walked exactly 28 times each of the last three seasons . . . Doesn't strikeout or run much. Will spray the ball around with enough power so that pitchers simply can't put it right down the middle . . . Played on a platoon basis last season because he'd hit righties far better than lefties over the previous six seasons. Surprise! Bashed LHPs to the tune of .357 in '93 . . . Extremely solid and valuable fourth-outfielder type with a dynamite arm (set the Orioles' club record with 22 assists in '91).

JOSE VIZCAINO

Once thought of as a "no-hit-good-field" type, Vizcaino reversed himself in '93 to become a "pretty-good-hit-only-fair afield" player . . . TOPR jumped from mid-70s to mid-90s thanks to a torrid .347 April and .372 May and what amounted to, for him, a huge power season with 4 HRs. Entering '93 he'd drilled exactly 4 in his 6 pro seasons spanning 1,784 at bats . . . Swiped 13 but was caught 9 times and also hit into 9 DPs. Walks leaped to 46 indicating a new found patience at the plate. That'll sometimes happen with players getting their first real chance to play regularly—they don't feel as much pressure to "do something right now" to stay in the lineup . . . Slumped somewhat after the all-star break (.258) but his overall .287 must have thrilled the Cubs. Since 1980 Sandberg had been the only Cub regular middle infielder to hit over .280.

MARIANO DUNCAN

Bounced back and forth in the Phils middle infield making 48 SS starts and 62 at 2B . . . Intriguingly, the Phils were 70–40 when he started and 27–25 when he didn't. Hmmmmm, sounds like they'd best find a regular spot for this IMP . . . Surprising power (26 doubles and 11 HRs). In fact, he's averaged 10 HRs a year this decade . . . But his TOPR fell and has suffered career long from his "walkophobia." Batted 518 times and drew the grand total of 12 free passes! Had the same season's total in '91 in Cincy and 8 in '89! . . . Major TOPR truth—when your DPs exceed your walk totals as his did in '93 (13 to 12) your TOPR heads for intensive care . . . TOPRs must stay up because his glove (21 E) won't keep him in the lineup.

JEFF BRANSON

A spare part when the season began who wound up appearing in 125 games because of the Reds blight of injuries . . . Started at every infield position with the most at SS (48) and 2B (36) . . . Was hitting .417 on June 1. Then regular playing time arrived and he skidded to .241 at year's end . . . Will never have much pop so his 19 BB-to-73 K ratio must change . . . Also has little stealing speed but hits the ball in the air a lot so he stays out of DPs (4) . . . Handy to have around and a terrific pinch hitter: 6 for 17 last season and 19 for 51 in his career (.373) . . . As other Reds fell to various woes Branson wound up playing the fourth most games on the team all the while wearing a brace to protect a left knee that had been totally reconstructed following the '92 season.

DWIGHT SMITH

Started in all three outfield positions and contributed greatly as a 9-for-24 pinch hitter with 5 RBIs . . . Got a hit in the season's finale against the Padres to raise his BA to an even .300 . . . TOPR leap attributable to that BA jump and a sudden discovery of power (11 HRs after 21 his last 4 seasons combined) . . . Will steal a few and stays out of DPs (just 3). Numbers might have been even more attractive had a broken hand not cost him approximately five weeks of the season . . . Probably will never be a full-timer but 124 TOPRs are wonderful to have hanging around.

PHIL CLARK

Out-TOPRed his Colorado brother Jerald 123 to 100 . . . With that high TOPR he's got a chance to be a real steal for the Pads who got him from Detroit for the waiver price . . . Started games at RF, LF, 1B, 3B and C. In this day and age where flexibility's a major plus for a manager, Clark's got an opportunity to stick around a long time . . . Toss in his 13-for-37 pinch-hitting mark and he moves up another notch . . . Finally showed the kind of stroke (.313 BA) that encouraged Detroit to make him a #1 draft pick in June of '86 . . . Comes off the bench swinging (just 8 BBs) and won't participate in any running game but hit into just two twin killings . . . Approaching the age where players break through. Might he be a very late bloomer?

JACOB BRUMFIELD

Notice how many IMPs the Reds had? When everyone gets hurt, everyone else winds up playing everywhere . . . Primarily a CF (56 starts) but also opened up at the other two OF positions and started a pair at 2B . . . Has just the kind of versatility and offensive game you want from an IMP. Enough power to keep pitchers honest (26 extra-base hits in about a half season's play) and excellent speed

(20-for-28 stealing). And *ONE* DP! . . . Once a 7th-round draft pick of the Cubs with high promise until a severe shoulder injury that required surgery knocked him out of baseball for two full seasons ('84–'85) . . . In the midst of all their injuries it appears the Reds have found a kind of "poor man's Bip Roberts" should that former IMP-star leave to free agency.

DARYL BOSTON

Why doesn't this guy get more respect as a solid contributor? Check those TOPRs in the '90s. Now averaging a 114 TOPR for the decade . . . TOPR slipped primarily because his running game diminished. Just 6 steals after years of 19–15–12 in the '90s . . . His 14 HRs mark the fifth time he's been in double figures in the bigs . . . Few walks but also few DPs and errors . . . Don't be deceived by his 124 games played. A dozen times he was announced as a pinch hitter only to have the opposing team change pitchers after which he was then hit for . . . In 1990 *Woman* magazine named him one of the six sexiest men in baseball. Well, at least somebody noticed him!

TIM TEUFEL

Has been IMPing now for years playing wherever needed in the infield . . . For the year had 50 hits—5 of them on one night, April 14 vs. the Pirates . . . TOPR would have been much higher except for a horrible pinch-hitting season (3 for 32)! . . . Drew an impressive total of 37 walks in just 200 official at bats . . . One of those good guys to have around whose TOPRs indicate he'll stick around for awhile longer.

DAVE MARTINEZ

Began the year as the platoon CF with Darren Lewis. Landed on the DL in late April with a hamstring pull and by the time he returned Lewis had claimed that job full time . . . Capable of playing any OF spot or 1B . . . Hit a career-low .241. Hamstring kept him from being the kind of force he's usually been in a running game. Swiped only 6 after averaging 17 a season from '87–'92 . . . If his legs return in '94 he should again be a valuable spare part . . . Realize he's starting his eighth full year in the bigs and won't turn 30 until late September.

CHICO WALKER

An ugly TOPR season for a player whose bat must produce to keep the checks rolling in . . . Had hit .308 for the '92 Mets before plummeting to .225 last year . . . Switch-hits, played RF, LF, 3B and 2B last year. An underrated thief swiping all 7 he tried and now has 35 the last three years . . . Batted a mind-boggling 65 times as a pinch hitter with 15 hits. Only the Cards Gerald Perry and the Rockies Jim Tatum had more PH at bats . . . The Mets dumped him after the season. At 36, but with sound legs and versatility, look for him to show up in somebody's camp come spring.

NELSON LIRIANO

One of those vagabond players who keeps turning up in the bigs . . . Broke a foot in the Rockies first-ever exhibition . . . Closed the year on a tear—hitting .346 for September/October with 10 extra-base hits and 22 runs scored in 81 at bats . . . Will occasionally draw a free pass and swipe a base. Can play anywhere around the infield . . . And that .305 batting average, even for just a part of '93, will earn him a chance to make the Rockies his fourth team this decade.

NATIONAL LEAGUE UTILITY PLAYERS

Rank	Player	Team	7/1/94 Age	B	TOPR Trendline 1990	1991	1992	3 yr Avg.	1993 TOPR
Infielders:									
1.	Freddie Benavides	COL	28	R	-	*	(77)	(77)	89
2.	Alex Arias	FLA	26	R	-	-	(100)	(100)	88
3.	Tom Foley	PIT	34	L	(58)	(79)	(57)	65	84
4.	Craig Shipley	SDO	31	R	-	*	(66)	(66)	81
5.	Rich Renteria	FLA	32	R	-	-	-	-	76
Outfielders:									
1.	Glenallen Hill	CLE/CUB	29	R	101†	101†	95†	98	116†
2.	Dave Clark	PIT	31	L	(99)	*	*	92	112
3.	Kevin Bass	HOU	34	B	93	92	102	96	111
4.	Lou Frazier	MON	29	B	-	-	-	-	106
5.	Dave Gallagher	NYM	33	R	(75)†	94†	86	87	105
6.	Chris Jones	COL	28	R	-	*	*	*	100
7.	Thomas Howard	CLE/CIN	29	B	*	92	88†	90	86†
8.	Henry Cotto	SEA/FLA	33	R	91†	(119)†	100†	100	81†
9.	Lloyd McClendon	PIT	35	R	(68)	(129)	102	102	80
10.	Greg Briley	FLA	29	L	100	84	94	92	67
Of Note (under 200 TPA):									
-	Mark Carreon	SFO	30	R	118	71	80†	86	(126)
-	Kim Batiste	PHI	26	R	-	*	(51)	(51)	(91)
-	Lenny Harris	LAD	29	L	94	96	84	92	(80)
-	Mitch Webster	LAD	35	B	103†	83†	124	104	(77)

* Under 100 TPA-not included in average. ( ) 100-199 TPA. † Includes AL TOPR, unadjusted to NL.

FREDDIE BENAVIDES

Twice caught his spikes causing major injuries that interrupted his campaign missing a month and a half to knee surgery and the closing four weeks to an ankle sprain . . . TOPR will not rise much unless he learns to coax a few walks. Has the look of a ''younger Mariano Duncan'' with just 6 BBs in 223 PAs . . . Will never be a stealing threat. Thus offensive (TOPR) improvement totally dependent on getting on base more. And with a .286 BA there's not a huge amount of room for betterment there. Thus, the path to a big league regular job seems to rest with his ''taking a walk.''

ALEX ARIAS

Absolutely powerless hitter who started at least 13 games at 2B, SS, and 3B. A mere 8 hits for extra bases in 283 PAs . . . Also no threat to run stealing just once. What's odd about that though is that he swiped double figures in each of his 6 minor league seasons with a high of 41 . . . But unlike so many of these powder-puff hitting infielders, he'll work pitchers for walks thus keeping TOPR respectability . . . If his running game returns his TOPR will press triple figures and he'll always have a job.

TIM FOLEY

Some players develop into stars. Some develop an enviable ability to carve out a niche for themselves. 1994 will be his 12th major league season . . . TOPRs remain incredibly low. But the number he's worked on for years has been his pension size which will be terrific for a player of his limited talents . . . Started at every infield position . . . Homered for the first time in nearly four years. But he picked a notable hurler to take downtown—Atlanta ace John Smoltz. His previous tater? Dinged another good one—Rick Sutcliffe in '89. Followed up the Smoltz HR with a long ball off Frisco's fantastic closer Rod Beck. (So why can't he go deep against any ''easy meat'' types?) . . . Perhaps his eventual athletic claim to fame will be his career at Miami's Palmetto High where he played shortstop on the baseball team throwing right-handed and quarter-backed the football team throwing left-handed.

CRAIG SHIPLEY

Started at four different positions including a career first in CF . . . Average has dropped from .275 in '91 to .248 to last season's .235. Why, then, has the TOPR risen? . . . Displayed the first power of his career hitting 4 long balls. Also added a speed dimension with 12-of-15 stealing. Where'd that come from? Had stolen 9 bases total the last five years . . . In '86 became the first Aussie to play in the majors since the unforgettable Joe Quinn (TOPR not available) in 1901. Now, there are two native Australians on the same Brewer team—Lloyd and Nilsson.

RICH RENTERIA

Returned to the majors for the first time since playing with the Mariners in '88 . . . Mixed in some LF playing time with stops around the infield . . . That .255's a deceiving BA. Was the Marlins Mr. Clutch batting a whopping .347 (26 for 75) with men in scoring position . . . At 32 he can now say he's had a four-hit game and homered in the bigs (it was a ''Black Day'' for SF lefty Bud Black who surrendered Renteria's career #1). Never figures to be much of a TOPRer but only two errors for all the moving around he did suggests there may be a spot waiting on somebody's deep bench.

GLENALLEN HILL

''Spiderman'' joined the Cubs August 20 and immediately opened some eyes with terrific numbers: .345 BA, 10 HRs, 22 RBIs and an unbelievable .770 slugging percentage (194 TOPR). What happened in Cleveland where he'd limped along at .224 with just 5 HRs through the first three quarters of the season (85 TOPR)? . . . One of those players that Toronto and then the Indians waited and waited to develop . . . Always showed some offensive potential as TOPRs indicate . . . Got his nickname because he's deathly afraid of spiders. Besides his arachnophobia he appears to have a moderate case of ''baseonballsophobia'' walking just 17 times last season . . . Was his late season a fluke? Cubs are anxious to find out.

DAVE CLARK

Posted the best TOPR of his career with his fourth team in five seasons . . . Set careers highs in almost every category including 11 dingers in just 277 official ABs, the best power ratio numbers on the Bucs . . . TOPR would have been even more impressive but for 10 DPs . . . Drew 38 walks and probably assured himself of a job for '94 . . . Hard to remember now that he was a highly touted first-round pick of the Indians in '83.

KEVIN BASS

Once a very fine everyday player who appeared in 157 games three straight years in the late '80s for the 'Stros before a broken leg started him on a string of leg injuries that reduced him to being a vagabond OF . . . Returned to Houston and posted his best BA (.284) since hitting .300 in '89 . . . One of those players you feel for because he seemed on the verge of stardom back in '86 (at age 27 by the way) when he hit .311 with 20 HRs and 22 steals TOPRing well above 120 that year . . . Switch-hitter with a solid reputation for being a positive clubhouse influence.

LOU FRAZIER

Finally made it to the majors at 28 and put in a solid season . . . Originally drafted as a middle infielder but started games at 1B, LF, and RF . . . No power at all. But sensational running numbers (17 for 19) with 16 BBs and just 3 DPs tugged TOPR upward . . . Tied for ninth in the NL with 12 pinch hits . . . Seemed to have no shot at making an Expo team deep in OF players. But this bespectacled, six-year minor league free agent who'd been a driver for UPS simply shoved his way onto the squad. Now, is it all "ups" from here?

DAVE GALLAGHER

Very good defensive outfielder who's been with five teams in seven years and will begin with a sixth next season in Atlanta . . . A half dozen dingers marked a career best. Walked more than he fanned . . . Started at all three OF spots and at 1B all without making an error . . . May not be the majors best hitter but knows what it's all about. Invented the Stride-Tutor, a device that prevents hitters from overstriding . . . Combine that TOPR rise with his often brilliant glove work and he's a valuable guy to have around.

CHRIS JONES

Minor league free agent who'd had cups of coffee with Cincy and Houston in two years prior (one cup was "hot"—.292 at Cincy—and one was "cold"—.190 at Houston) . . . Has some power (21 extra-base hits) but seldom walks (10), fans too often (48) and will mix in an occasional steal . . . Minor league numbers suggest he'd be exactly this type of player, so what you saw in '93 figures to be what you'll get from him.

THOMAS HOWARD

TOPRs never seem to budge from right around 90 and that's simply not enough to assure him of continued employment at this level . . . A former Padres #1 draft pick who's hit over .300 at six different minor league stops but whose major league game remains virtually the same year-to-year: very little extra-base power, an average in the .260–.270 area, few walks and double figure steals . . . One of those players whose tools don't combine to produce much of a TOPR.

HENRY COTTO

A highly regarded fourth-outfielder type whose TOPR dropped off the face of the earth in a year he moved from Seattle to Florida, which is, by the way, the longest possible move geographically in the majors . . . Actually, he was fine as a Marlin, hitting .296 and stealing 11 of 12. As a Mariner he disintegrated: .190 BA with 3 extra-base hits and 2 walks in more than 100 PAs . . . Absolutely refuses to walk—would you believe 5 last season raising his career total to 107 in more than seven years of major league service . . .

His 16-for-21 stealing year continues his pattern of fantastic percentages having now stolen 130 lifetime while being caught just 26 times. That 83.3% ranks fifth among all active stealers with more than 100 swipes behind only Eric Davis, Tim Raines, Marquis Grissom and Kenny Lofton . . . Throw out that dismal start in Seattle and he's one of the best utility OFs in the game.

LLOYD McCLENDON

Another whose TOPR cratered. But unlike Cotto, McClendon's wheels and glove won't keep him in the bigs. That's solely the job of his bat. And his bat went ice cold . . . BA had tumbled from .288 to .253 the year before and dipped another 32 points last season. Powerful-looking player who displays little true power. Walked more than he fanned for the second time in three years . . . But at 35 those descending TOPRs spell trouble.

GREG BRILEY

The player they call "Pee Wee" is putting up TOPRs that can be called "pee wee." Bottom dropped out of his BA skidding 81 points down to .190. That, of course, impacts the key part of his game—an ability to make things happen on the bases. Stole only 6 after having 23 just two seasons ago . . . Had 13 hits and 7 walks as a pinch hitter, each number ranking in the league's top 10 . . . Released at season's end by the Fish. Will he hook on at just 29 with someone else?

MARK CARREON

Back in the NL after a washout year in Detroit and had the best year of his career . . . Average leaped to a career high .327. Returned to his place as one of the league's feared pinch hitters (10 for 35 with a HR and 8 RBIs). Now hitting .301 in that role over 73 at bats since 1991 . . . Started games in LF, CF, RF and 1B and produced everywhere . . . What did it cost the Giants to get a valuable spare piece like this? The price of a plane ticket. Carreon had been dumped by the Tigers and came to SF camp as a non-roster invitee. Sometimes decent players do fall through the cracks in the majors.

KIM BATISTE

In a battle to the finish edged Duncan as the Philly least likely to walk—3 freebies in 161 PAs. Two more walks in '94 and he'll barge into double figures in a career that now spans 133 games . . . Why don't younger players like this understand the importance of walks to a team and their own careers? With no measurable power he'll either make it or not on his ability to get on base. Why not walk? . . . Glove work suspect (10 errors) as the post-season underscored . . . Otherwise a nice contact hitter (.282) and a tough out in tough situations (.311 with runners in scoring position).

LENNY HARRIS

Low TOPRs finally cost this former LA starter his job and eventually moved him out of LA entirely . . . BA tumbled to a decade low .238. Stole just 3 after three straight seasons in double figures. Never had any power—thus a TOPR at 80 . . . Has walked more than he's fanned this decade but his game never seems to translate into runs . . . Batted in only 97 runs in three years as an LA regular ('90–'92), just 11 in 160 at bats last season and a woeful one RBI in 45 pinch-hit ABs . . . Will get an opportunity to make the Reds as a spare part.

MITCH WEBSTER

Where'd his TOPR go? This nine-year vet's game disappeared overnight . . . Average dipped to .244, the second worst ever. Just 2 HRs and 4-of-10 stealing for a player who, in better years, reached 15 and 33 in those categories . . . Just 6-of-30 pinch-hitting, which had been another of his specialties . . . Will he rebound in '94 like he did from that horrid 83 TOPR in '91 to post a wonderful 124 in '92? Or is the end of his career near?

THE
PITCHERS

SOMETHING NEW

Though player rankings may be kind of old hat to baseball fans, a coherent system of pitcher rankings—one that rationally achieves a sane result—qualifies as something new. In a sense, TOPR is evolutionary and TPER has a revolutionary aspect.

As you by now know, TPER is the mirror-image of TOPR. It gauges how effectively pitchers kept the hitters from doing *their* job. Face it, that's what pitching is all about: inhibiting offense, not "creating" defense. There's a parallel from high school physics that's apt. Scientifically, there is no such thing as hot *and* cold. Instead, heat is the only measured quantity and "cold" is the relative absence of heat. In the same sense, offense is the only quantity we're measuring. A *low* TPER reflects the relative absence of offense. Thus, a pitcher with a 75 TPER "freezes" the offense. Conversely, a pitcher with a 125 TPER is allowing the offense to "come to a boil."

You'll find that pitchers work within a much narrower range than hitters do. Indeed, a TPER below 90 is outstanding and worthy of all kinds of awards and financial consideration. Conversely, a TPER of 110 puts a pitcher on the edge of the cliff, awaiting release or a ticket to Triple A. Or it could mean he's hurting, just a little bit. The pitcher's margin between accolades and abject failure is numerically slender. It's the difference between turning opposing lineups into Darren Lewises (90) or Todd Zeiles (109).

So, who did the best job of keeping the guys with the lumber from laying the wood to it in 1993?.

TPER presents:
the *Kings of the Hill*
1993

American League			National League	
Starters:				
1. Kevin Appier	69		1. Bill Swift	70
2. Mark Langston	78		2. Greg Maddux	74
3. Jimmy Key	80		3. Jose Rijo	80
4. Alex Fernandez	82		4. John Burkett	80
5. Randy Johnson	83		5. Steve Avery	81
Relievers:				
1. Duane Ward	62		1. Greg McMichael	63
2. Jesse Orosco	71		2. Bryan Harvey	69
3. Roberto Hernandez	72		3. Jay Howell	72
4. Jeff Montgomery	73		4. Rod Beck	75
5. Tom Henke	74		5. Kevin Rogers	75

Unlike TOPR's Ten Most Offensive, TPER's Kings of the Hill need no disclaimer. Pitchers are paid to do one job and one job only: get the other guys *out*. Nothing else counts. You can quibble with our mix of starters and relievers. You *can't* quibble, though, with the fact that these were *the most effective pitchers* in their respective roles over the past season.

We need to say something about Montreal's Jeff Fassero in this connection. Fassero delivered a marvelous 75 TPER under difficult circumstances, converting from the setup role to rotation starter in mid-season. He didn't make TPER's list of starters, though, for the same reason he didn't win the league ERA crown. While starting 15 games he only accumulated 149.2 innings. We used the same measure as the league to determine our champion starters—162 innings—so he fell short of qualifying as a starter. He appeared 41 times in relief, facing a combined total of 616 batters, so he had no problem qualifying for the relief category. Alas, though, Kevin Rogers' TPER figured out to 75.3 and Jeff's to 75.4. So, he just misses being "crowned" again. Special mention is nonetheless due and, now, he has it.

Three things you'll spot about our Kings of the Hill:

1. We've got a bone to pick with the Cy Young Awards! Kevin Appier and Bill Swift, then, are hereby coronated as Kings Kevin I and Bill I of their respective realms. Congratulations, guys. Better that from us, than nothing from nobody. Cy Young winner Jack McDowell, it turns out, didn't even turn in the best TPER in the White Sox rotation!
2. *Four* Giant pitchers made the NL list. No, the Giants' success wasn't all Barry Bonds.
3. Middle relievers aren't unrepresented: Four of TPER's choices spent all or most of the season in this underappreciated role (Orosco, Howell, Rogers and McMichael, plus Fassero).

Organization of the Rankings

We ranked pitchers in three categories—starters, closers and in-betweeners. Rotation starters needed 20+ starts. We all know who the closers were. In-betweeners are the pitchers who neither started nor closed with any frequency.

We ranked "part-time" starters (under 20 starts) separately, making a distinction between those who were part time due to injury and those who filled this role by design (which is where Fassero fits in our scheme). "Debut" pitchers were also ranked separately. This category consisted of the in-season call-ups among starters and all rookie relievers. We figured you'd want to view these new arrivals in isolation to better figure what they've got going for them, if anything.

As with TOPR, TPER requires a minimum of 200 Total Batters Faced (TBF) to be considered reliable. This standard is our cutoff for all starters. We went to 30 appearances for relievers, though, to help you get a handle on the so-called "specialists." Consequently, you'll see a lot of ( ) in the 'tweeners rankings. Take the numbers contained therein with the prescribed grain of salt.

Symbols

Same as for hitters.

( ) Fewer than 200 TBF.
* Fewer than 100 TBF.
– Wasn't in the show.
† Contains data from the opposite league.

TPER Trendlines

The TPER Trendlines are constructed the same as TOPR Trendlines. We show 1990 through 1992 major league TPER with a 3-year weighted average (which may include his 1989 year, in the event of a dash or an asterisk). Here's Kevin Appier's, to give you a sample.

Rank	Pitcher	Team	7/1/94 Age	T	1990	1991	1992	3 yr Avg.	1993 TPER
1.	Kevin Appier	KCR	26	R	85	88	82	85	69

Pitchers' trendlines don't seem quite as indicative as hitters' trendlines. We suspect that incessant injuries and frequent role changes have something to do with this. Further, the relationship of age to performance isn't quite as clear as it is with hitters. Complete historical TPER data are limited, going back only through 1989 (when our friends at STATS, Inc. started accumulating all the necessary data with their customary thoroughness). We're not in a position, then, to generalize on the subject of the TPER Curve. We're beginning to think it might have a different shape, though, than the TOPR Curve, aside from the fact that it's ''upside-down.'' For one thing, it seems to consist of sudden ''plateaus.'' These new and strikingly different levels of ability, either better or worse than before, can then be maintained for several years. If this is indeed the case, AL hitters are going to suffer some extended grief at young Mr. Appier's hands.

Role Norms

We've expressed the norms for pitchers by role: Starters, Closers and In-Betweeners. We used ranges for starters and 'tweeners, both categories numbering 50 to 60 pitchers in each league. Think of it this way: The top stratum represents ''aces'' and other #1-type starters, along with top flight set-up men. The middle strata scale down from #2 quality starters and competent middlemen. The remainder are #5 starters or bullpen fringe denizens, at best. At worst, they've already pitched their way out of the majors.

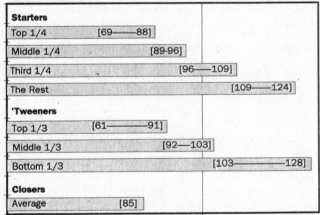

AL Role Norms

Starters	
Top 1/4	[69——88]
Middle 1/4	[89-96]
Third 1/4	[96——109]
The Rest	[109——124]
'Tweeners	
Top 1/3	[61——91]
Middle 1/3	[92—103]
Bottom 1/3	[103——128]
Closers	
Average	[85]

50   100

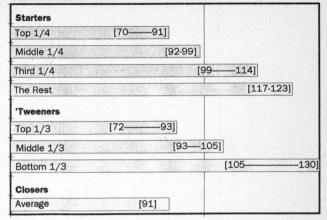

NL Role Norms

Starters	
Top 1/4	[70——91]
Middle 1/4	[92-99]
Third 1/4	[99——114]
The Rest	[117-123]
'Tweeners	
Top 1/3	[72——93]
Middle 1/3	[93—105]
Bottom 1/3	[105——130]
Closers	
Average	[91]

50   100

What does this tell us?

For one thing, the ranges for rotation starters and 'tweeners are nearly identical, in both leagues. You can think of a 'tweener, then, as very much like a starter. He is, in fact, an *extension* of the starter and similar effectiveness should be expected, but for fewer innings. It is patently not necessary, nor is it accurate, to think of middle relievers as the dregs of the staff. A little respect, please. You *need* them and you need them to be as good as your starters.

The TPER differential between AL and NL closers seems rather large, particularly as there is no significant difference between leagues in the ranges for the other categories. Are NL closers, as a group, somehow inferior to AL closers? Be aware that NL closers can easily go through an entire season without ever facing an opposing ''pitcher-as-hitter'' and that dreadful 53 TOPR at the bottom of the NL batting order. The quality of an NL closer's offensive opposition is thus far superior to an NL starters'. Facing pinch-hitters instead of ''pitchers-as-hitters'' justifiably causes the NL closers' ranking to slide a little bit mathematically. This fact would account for most of the difference versus the AL. Any that might be left isn't enough to worry about.

Incidentally, unlike hitters, TPERs for pitchers moving from league to league don't have to be adjusted to reflect the NLs ''Players Only'' bias. But you might want to spot an NL *closer* moving to the AL a couple of points—he might improve his TPER since he'll be facing the same batting order as the rest of the staff.

Back to work . . .

AMERICAN LEAGUE ROTATION STARTERS

Top Quarter:

Rank	Pitcher	Team	7/1/94 Age	T	TPER Trendline				1993 TPER
					1990	*1991*	*1992*	3 yr Avg.	
1.	Kevin Appier	KCR	26	R	85	88	82	85	**69**
2.	Mark Langston	CAL	33	L	101	86	86	91	**78**
3.	Jimmy Key	NYY	33	L	97	82	95	91	**80**
4.	Alex Fernandez	CWS	24	R	95	103	102	101	**82**
5.	Randy Johnson	SEA	30	L	102	103	104	103	**83**
6.	Chris Bosio	SEA	31	R	100	83	84	87	**84**
7.	Jamie Moyer	BAL	31	L	108	(158)	-	119	**84**
8.	Ben McDonald	BAL	26	R	83	104	106	99	**84**
9.	Jack McDowell	CWS	28	R	100	88	96	94	**85**
10.	Kevin Brown	TEX	29	R	88	97	79	87	**85**
11.	Jason Bere	CWS	23	R	-	-	-	-	**85**
12.	Chuck Finley	CAL	31	L	85	97	108	96	**88**
13.	Danny Darwin	BOS	38	R	79†	123	101	96	**88**

* Under 100 TBF-not included in average. ( ) 100-199 TBF. † Includes NL TPER, unadjusted to AL.

KEVIN APPIER

Essential Baseball's AL Cy Young award winner. Hands down! . . . Of the many phenomenal numbers "Ape" recorded in '93, the most imposing had to be his microscopic 8 HRs allowed! In 238 innings! That's a dinger every 30 innings! Next lowest among the starters? Texas' Kevin Brown permitted just 14—nearly double Appir's total . . . Had every sparkling number you'd want besides that: under 3 walks per 9 IP, just 11-of-19 stealers made it, threw 18 DP balls and opponents not only didn't take him out of the park, they simply didn't hit him (.212) . . . Only four times in 34 starts did he allow more than 4 runs . . . Six of his eight losses came when he permitted 3 runs or less. . . . Finished 39 points lower than the runnerup for the ERA title. No one had led his league in ERA by more than 34 points and NOT received the Cy Young since Nolan Ryan lost to Fernando Valenzuela in 1981 . . . Two years ago KC dealt Bret Saberhagen to the Mets. KC tried and tried to get the Mets to take the four-years-younger Appier instead. The Mets stood firm. No Saberhagen—no deal and "no" to Appier. Hmmmmm.

MARK LANGSTON

The best left-handed starter TPER in the majors . . . His 16–11 record for a team 20 games under .500 looks good in itself. But oh what might have been! His bullpen "blew" five wins. And he lost five straight games in September when the Angels could get him just seven runs total. In his 11 losses Cal scored a meager 17 runs . . . TPER drop to his all-time low attributable to his fantastic control of runners. Threw 22 DP balls and just 10-of-22 stealers succeeded . . . Has now had five seasons of 15 or more victories . . . Weird: Hit Robin Yount with a pitch in the fourth inning of the season opener. Pitched 252 more innings without hitting anyone.

JIMMY KEY

The free agent pitching buy of the year . . . Almost anonymous hurling star who, since moving into Toronto's rotation in '85, has had just one losing season in nine years (13–14 in '89) . . . TPER stays consistently in the 80s and 90s because he simply will not walk anyone—43 BB in 236 innings. That's 1.6 per 9 IP, the best in the AL . . . Also throws tons of DPs (25) . . . Will give up the long ball (26) but, with his exquisite control, that's to be expected . . . A sign his stuff's better than ever comes from 173 Ks, the highest of his career . . . Only pitcher in the majors with at least a dozen wins nine straight seasons. Topped 200 IP for the seventh time in those nine seasons. So why didn't Toronto try harder to sign him? . . . For as wonderful as that 18–6 record was, it would have been much better were it not for the Yankees "arson squad" of a bullpen that six times blew leads he turned over to them.

ALEX FERNANDEZ

Finally "arrived" . . . The Sox had been waiting for him to put his enormous ability all together and '93 became his breakout season . . . TPER (82) fourth best among all AL starters after a string of OK debut years (95–103–102) . . . The league hit just .240, could draw only about 2½ walks per 9 IP, and couldn't steal (only 5 for 16). In tight spots he produced a whopping 24 double play balls . . . Yes, he did allow 27 HRs, but that'll happen when you're working with leads and trying to throw strikes . . . Part of the credit for his emergence he attributes to his ability to shrug off HRs. "I learned that from guys like Jack McDowell and Tom Seaver. So now my philosophy [after a homer] is 'OK, it's done. Just give me a new ball and lets go' " . . . When in trouble, used to just rare back and fire. Now he employs all four pitches in his assortment . . . Since being demoted to Vancouver for a month in mid-'92 (something he still resents) he's 23–13 with an ERA just over 3 . . . At just 24 he's got a chance to star in hitters' nightmares for years.

RANDY JOHNSON

"The Big Unit" finally made a big splash! . . . Fifth best TPER in the AL . . . Toughest to hit in the majors—a .203 opponent's BA . . . Threw one of eight one-hitters in the league and had one of the three eight-game win streaks (with Wickman and Key, both of the Yanks) . . . In the entire big leagues last year there were eight games in which a pitcher fanned 14 or more—five by Johnson! . . . First to fan 300 in a season since 1989 and the first lefty to do so since Steve Carlton in '72 . . . But Johnson had always had stuff. What he'd never had was the ability to wiggle out of jams with a minimum of damage and to throw strikes at critical points, thus TPERs just over a hundred . . . But walks fell from an ugly 6¼ per game in '92 to an acceptable 3.6 per nine innings. That's a huge drop—nearly three runners per game. And his TPER dropped accordingly into "ace" territory . . . Did allow 22 HRs but that'll happen when you throw more strikes . . . Hit 16 men and allowed a strange-for-a-lefty 28 stolen bases. But also coaxed 16 DPs, a high total for such a strikeout pitcher . . . Was nearly the key to a *Yankee* championship. New York almost acquired him in late July for a multi-prospect package. Right after that fell through Johnson began his eight-game win streak. If he'd been in a Yankee uniform at the time, Toronto's Joe Carter might never have had the chance to be a World Series hero.

CHRIS BOSIO

Steady as they go. Three straight seasons right at 83–84 TPERs . . . But this one may have been the most remarkable considering his injury troubles. Broke his left collarbone colliding with Cleveland's Jeff Treadaway April 27. Doctors said he'd miss two months. One month later he returned. On June 6 he aggravated the injury during a beanball brawl in Baltimore costing him nearly another three weeks . . . Walks jumped abnormally by more than one per 9 IP but otherwise the same old Bosio . . . Allowed just eight SBs while throwing 13 DP balls . . . Fifth toughest to hit in the AL (.229) . . . Would have had better than a 9–9 record had the normally solid Seattle defense not deserted him. The M's, with the best "D" in the majors, leaked 12 unearned runs behind him. No other Seattle pitcher had more than 9 and in the entire year Seattle allowed only 53 UER . . . Threw the second no-hitter in M's history versus Boston on April 22.

JAMIE MOYER

1993's "needle in a haystack" . . . Had passed through four other organizations and seven years of his life since his last winning big league season before suddenly turning into the TPER ace of the O's staff . . . Lost his first three starts and his last three. In between went 12–3 . . . A hittable pitcher. But that's his *ONLY* TPER fault. Though the league batted .265 against him, they took him deep just 11 times . . . Excellent control—2.25 BB-per-9 IP . . . very good control of runners giving up just 5 SBs (6 CSs) and inducing 13 DPs . . . Lowest road ERA in the AL—2.44 . . . Allowed two earned runs or less in 17 of his 25 starts including his last 9 in a row . . . Beat fellow TPER aces McDowell (1–0), Finley (1–0) and Viola (2–1) . . . That first victory of the year over Viola on June 10 snapped an 0–11 streak dating back to September of 1990 when he won in relief while pitching for Texas . . . The secret of success for this son-in-law of former Notre Dame basketball coach Digger Phelps? Get the first batter out. Did that in 126 of 167 chances, the second best ratio in the league behind TPER King-of-the-Hill Appier.

BEN McDONALD

Oh, if he'd only skipped his final outing. Got bombed for 8 ER in 1.2 IP raising his ERA from 4th in the league to 12th (3.39) and dropping him out of the top five TPERs in the league . . . Allowed 3 ER or less in 28 of 34 outings . . . His 13–14 record would have been much better had he not gotten the worst offensive AND defensive support of any Oriole starter. O's hitters got him only 4 runs per game. The normally solid O's defense leaked 9 unearned runs behind him, 3 more than any other starter. As an example of the impact of the combination of those two downers, Big Mac allowed 2 ER or less 20 times but won only 9 of those games . . . Fourth toughest to hit in the AL (.228). . . HRs allowed shrink from 32 to 17 . . . Pitchers often experience big TPER jumps or drops and then stay at that new plateau for a while. If that's the case here, he's just arrived in "Ace-land."

JACK McDOWELL

The only man in baseball history with a Cy Young Award and a 12-string Rickenbacker (that's a guitar "Black Jack" plays in his rock band) . . . Now 81–49 for his career. That 62.3% puts him second to Lefty Williams in fanchise history (64.8%) and third among all active pitchers with at least 100 decisions behind Clemens (65.5%) and Gooden (65.5%) . . . Finished 22–10 but, oh, what might have been had he gotten better support. Chicago scored only 15 runs in those 10 defeats . . . Has now won 12 straight April starts and 15 of 16 in the opening month . . . What critics he has point to 20 HRs and a rather mediocre .266 opponent BA. But McDowell shuns numbers except for the numbers of wins. Often appears to "coast" when given a big lead . . . Forget running on him (10 of 25). But if you stay at first he throws lots of DPs (19) . . . Spent the off-season working on a followup album to his first release "Extendagenda" . . . What's your favorite baseball tune? "Take Me out to the Ballgame?" For Black Jack it's "Where's That Hit?" by the Hoodoo Gurus . . . Whatever else you think about him

or his choice of music, give him his due as an extraordinary winner. He's the '90s winningest pitcher—73–39, 65.2%!

KEVIN BROWN

What an odd way to get to an 85 TPER, 10th best among starters . . . Remarkably erratic, opening with a dazzling 4–1, 1.27 ERA for his first six starts and finishing with a sizzling 5–0, 1.74 ERA in September. But in between he was fortunate to be 6–10 given an ERA in the middle 5s for 21 starts . . . But the bottom line was his third-year under-90 TPER this decade . . . Must solve his continuing first inning troubles that saw opponents bat .312 for the season. Conversely, he's almost impossible to beat once he finds his groove limiting hitters to a .198 average from the seventh inning on . . . Low TPER the result of his ability to throw strikes (less than 3 walks per 9 IP), be stingy with HRs (allowed just 14, second best ratio in the AL to KC's Appier), freeze runners (stealers just 10 for 20) and use his heavy sinker to get 15 DPs . . . Recorded 65.8% of his outs on grounders, third best in the league. Not afraid to pitch inside as evidenced by 15 dinged batters, 2nd in the AL . . . Forget all the other pitchers in history known as "Yankee Killers." He's it! His 11–2 career vs. the Bronx Bombers make his win percentage the best of all time for those with at least 10 decisions against NY.

JASON BERE

The White Sox system churned out another ace. His 85 TPER made him the AL's 11th best starter . . . League hitters struggled mightily posting a terrible .210 BA against him . . . His only problem concerns his control (81 BB in 142 + innings) . . . But once on base runners can't take liberties with this baby-faced righty (9 of 17) . . . Think he might be a "flash-in-the-pan" that the league will figure out his second time around? Think again. In his "second time around" last year he proved even more devastating, winning his last 7 starts and posting a 1.95 ERA over his final 11 outings . . . Averaged 8.1 Ks per 9 IP, third behind Seattle's Johnson and New York's Perez . . . Grew up idolizing Boston's Clemens and used to carry around a Clemens baseball card. If he keeps pitching like this, Clemens'll have to carry around a Bere card.

CHUCK FINLEY

The answer to why his TPER took that giant step down from 108 to 88 can be found under the column with the heading "BB." Walks dropped from 4.3 per 9 IP in '92 to 2.9. That's a huge move when you pitch a career high 251 innings . . . Strangely easy to run on considering he's a lefty (21 of 30) . . . Fastball moves low in the strike zone creating 21 DPs . . . Hit 16 or more wins for the fourth time in the last five years . . . Led the AL in CGs with 13 . . . Like teammate Langston, suffered from a terrible lack of support at times, getting only 26 total runs in his 14 losses . . . Defense also hurt. Of Cal's 80 unearned runs allowed in '93, 20 came with him on the mound . . . Not a bad career going considering he once "chucked it all" as a youngster and headed home from college to work in the family's nursery farm business.

DANNY DARWIN

The "Bonham Bullet" set new career highs in starts (34), IP (229) and victories (15) at the ripe old age of 37 and easily led the Red Sox staff in all three categories . . . TPER has jumped all over the place this decade with years as good as 79 and as poor as 123 . . . Fantastic control—49 BB or 1.92 per 9 IP . . . Third most HRs in the AL (31) kept TPER from being in the Cy Young contender zone . . . Record's actually much better than it looks (and it looks very good) given that he had one of the most dismal Aprils in the majors (0–4, 8.20 ERA) . . . Earned the nickname "Dr. Death" because of the way he pitches inside to RHH. But he plunked only three of them all year. On the other hand, those RHHs managed only a .204 BA . . . Remarkably versatile and sturdy vet who's pitched in the majors the last 14 years in a variety of roles and only once in that time has had his ERA finish above 3.96.

AMERICAN LEAGUE ROTATION STARTERS

Second Quarter:

			7/1/94			TPER Trendline			1993
Rank	Pitcher	Team	Age	T	1990	1991	1992	3 yr Avg.	TPER
14.	Wilson Alvarez	CWS	24	L	-	93	116	108	89
15.	John Doherty	DET	27	R	-	-	75	75	90
16.	Eric Hanson	SEA	29	R	82	99	101	93	90
17.	Roger Clemens	BOS	31	R	74	76	73	74	91
18.	Mike Mussina	BAL	25	R	-	77	80	79	91
19.	Frank Viola	BOS	34	L	88†	102†	85	88	91
20.	David Wells	DET	31	L	87	92	122	97	91
21.	David Cone	KCR	31	R	91†	91†	102†	95	92
22.	Tim Belcher	CIN/CWS	32	R	92†	92†	97†	94	92†
23.	Jim Abbott	NYY	26	L	103	79	86	89	93
24.	Hipolito Pichardo	KCR	24	R	-	-	97	97	94
25.	Kenny Rogers	TEX	29	L	103	120	98	109	95
26.	Scott Kamieniecki	NYY	30	R	-	113	100	104	95
27.	Juan Guzman	TOR	27	R	-	78	80	79	96
28.	Bobby Witt	OAK	30	R	97	124	106	105	96

* Under 100 TBF-not included in average. ( ) 100-199 TBF. † Includes NL TPER, unadjusted to AL.

WILSON ALVAREZ

Dipped to a new low TPER plateau (89) after 93 and 116 debut seasons . . . Broke through at the same age as teammate Fernandez and in similar fashion . . . TPER plummet the result of becoming much, much more difficult to hit (.272 in '92 down to .230 in '93) . . . Superb control of the running game limiting opposing stealers to 21 of 38 while throwing 24 DPs . . . Walked 122 in 207 innings, most in the AL. A scary thought—what if he solves this problem? . . . His 15–8 record made him the first native Venezuelan to ever win more than 13 games in the bigs. (Luis Leal won 13 twice with the Blue Jays) . . . Why'd he suddenly emerge? Maybe because he got serious about being in shape. Often appeared fat and lazy before last season. But arrived in camp 15 pounds lighter, seemed more intent on doing his job and then went out and spent the year making opponents' averages "lighter."

JOHN DOHERTY

Best full season TPER on the Tigers in his first season as a full-time starter . . . His TPER jumped 15 points from his '92 figure because of a giant leap in HRs. He allowed just 4 in 116 IP in '92 before being nailed for 19 in 184+ last season . . . Outstanding control walking just over two men per nine innings and, at one point, making it through 112 hitters without a free pass . . . The key to his success? Perhaps the most remarkable control of runners of any RHP in the league. Only 7-of-19 stealers succeeded and he threw 25 DP balls! . . . Tiger scouts found him at tiny Concordia College in Bronxville, NY, . . . Grew up in an apartment building across the street from the outfield of Yankee Stadium.

ERIC HANSON

A roller-coaster year . . . Had the hottest TPER in the league in mid-May when he was unbeaten in five decisions. . . . Suddenly disintegrated losing six straight! . . . Settled back down to put up the second best TPER of his career. Did yield 17 dingers. But also did a solid job of controlling factors within his grasp: Runners succeeded in only 15 of 28 SB tries. Threw 19 DP balls. His already low walk total fell again to 2¼ per 9 IP . . . Seemed to refind his fastball last year after falling in love with a huge slow curveball that he threw constantly in '92 when he led the AL in losses . . . A solid #2 or #3 starter.

ROGER CLEMENS

For anyone else a TPER of 91 would mean a solid season. But when you're the "Rocket Man" and you've spent your TPER-life in the 70s, a 91 is tantamount to a disastrous year . . . His first ever sub-.500 season (11–14) . . . Combination of a strained groin in mid-season and a late year elbow problem caused him to miss the 30-start and 200-inning level for the first time since '85 . . . But, even when healthy, he didn't pitch anywhere near his career standards. ERA leaped 1.66 runs above his career mark. Opponents' BA shot up 20 points and HRs jumped from 11 to 17 despite pitching 55 fewer innings than the year before. Walk ratio up. Strikeout ratio down . . . Did throw 17 DPs or the damage might have been worse . . . Was '93 simply a fluke, injury-riddled year? Maybe. Maybe not. Some umpires whispered that his control wasn't anywhere near his old level . . . But even with all those negatives he's still in the top one-third TPER-wise of all starters. Not bad for a pitcher who, coming out of high school, was considered too frail by scouts and wasn't even drafted, forcing him to go the junior college route to begin his career.

MIKE MUSSINA

A victim of "base-brawl" . . . Injured his neck and back in a June 6 brouhaha with Seattle. Continued to pitch contending nothing was wrong. Wrong! . . . Mussina's year can be broken into BB (before brawl) and AB (after brawl). BB: 12 starts, ERA 2.86, 8–2. AB: 13 starts, ERA 6.37, 4–7, and a month on the DL. Did the brawl cost the Birds a pennant? . . . Still had solid control, superb at holding runners (stealers only 3 of 9) . . . Tended to give up the long one (20). That's a jump of 4 HRs over '92 in 74 less innings and that accounted for a lion's share of the TPER rise from 80 to 91 . . . Of all active ML pitchers with 50 or more decisions, his .692 winning percentage trails only Toronto's Guzman (.784) . . . His record after 50 starts in the bigs was 26–11. Clemens was 22–9, Gooden 29–12 and Hershiser 23–9. That's fancy company.

FRANK VIOLA

Yet one more solid season from one of the most consistent hurlers around . . . But injuries caused him to miss starts for the first time in his 11-year career . . . Made *just* 29 starts snapping a string of 10 straight seasons where he'd made at least 34. Had he done it again last year he'd have been able to say he was the only man this century to do so 11 years in a row . . . Did all the little things right to keep the TPER down: Stealers ran at only 50% (11 for 22), tossed 15 DP balls and yielded just a dozen dingers (less than one every 15 innings) . . . The last two seasons his strike-outs-to-walks ratio has declined substantially but his overall pitching efficiency hasn't seemed to be affected.

DAVID WELLS

A wild season that began with him being cut by the Blue Jays, the culmination of a long period of strife between him and Toronto manager Gaston. Loads of teams called to sign him. He selected Detroit because they'd give him an immediate rotation spot . . . Exploded at the start going 9–1 with a 2.68 ERA his first 15 starts. Then he collapsed over his last 15 starts going 2–8 with his ERA floating ever-upward to a final 4.19 . . . The "second half fall-off" also occurred his last two seasons with the Jays. Might a lack of conditioning be the problem? . . . Was bothered in August by an elbow problem that landed him on the DL . . . Runners swiped just 14 of 24. Had excellent control walking 2¼ men per 9 IP . . . Became extremely HR prone allowing 26 roundtrippers . . . But his 91 TPER still ranked him #20 among all AL starters and represents the third time in four years he's TPERed right around 90.

DAVID CONE

Another workhorse season and outstanding TPER but a disappointing record due to the ineptness of the Royals attack . . . Never pitched less than five innings in any of his 34 starts . . . Just like teammate Appier, permitted opponents more than four runs only four times . . . Royals managed a measly 101 runs in those starts, just a tick *under* three runs per game. KC scored 18 runs in his 14 losses. If Cone and his hitters were married he'd have ample grounds for divorce . . . Devastating pitch totals also continued. The man, who led all of baseball in pitches thrown in '92, had only four starts all season in which he threw less than 110 pitches. Seventeen of 125 or higher. TPER would have been even better had he not allowed 32 SBs with just 13 CSs and 13 DPs . . . Is there early evidence that all the abuse his arm's suffered has begun to surface? Strikeouts dropped more than two per inning to the lowest rate of his six full seasons and his walk total's inching up.

TIM BELCHER

Just how good must a staff be when a pitcher like Belcher is the "weak link" and gets shuffled to the bullpen come playoff time? . . . You like consistency? How about TPERs in the 90's of 92–92–97–92? . . . A solid all-around game with opposing hitters managing less than a .250 BA. . . . Coming to the Windy City really helped one part of his game—runner control. In Cincy stealers succeeded in 11 of 14. But in Chicago, with Karkovice behind the plate, they got shutout in five tries . . . He's now averaged 30 starts and 204 innings a year for six years without a single losing season.

JIM ABBOTT

When the Yanks turned over three prospects to the Angels they expected more than 11–14, 4.37 ERA and a 93 TPER (23rd in the AL) . . . Strikeouts have fallen significantly the last two seasons (from 158 in '91 down to 130 and down again to just 95). HRs leaped from 12 to 22. Uh-oh, that sounds like his stuff's weakening . . . Want more evidence? Opponent BA has risen each of the last two seasons also . . . Yanks averaged 4.7 runs per start. But that's deceiving. They got him 36 runs in three starts and just 3.9 the other 29. But that's a windfall compared to the lack of support given him in '92 when Cal got him only 2.55 runs per game. That woeful figure represented the "Big Bad Trifecta" for a pitcher—the lowest in the entire majors, the lowest in Angels' history and the lowest for any pitcher since the inception of the DH . . . TPER's risen from 79 to 86 to 93 of late. It stayed as low as it has because he induces a fabulous number of DPs (29) . . . Hasn't allowed a LHH to homer his last 64 starts covering 449+ innings.

HIPOLITO PICHARDO

A second consecutive solid and encouraging TPER year. There are major pluses popping up—like a Royals team high 17 DPs and just eight SBs vs. 7 CS. . . . A mere 10 HRs in 165 innings also looks terrific . . . Must develop more of an out-pitch against LHH who tattooed him at a .303 rate . . . Lacks a strikeout pitch (less

than 4 Ks per 9 IP) and that can hurt in tight situations where he needs to fan someone . . . But he's only 24 with extremely impressive TPERs and trends for one that age.

KENNY ROGERS

"The Gambler" gambled big time in the spring of '93. He'd carved out a nice career as a rubber-armed set-up man. But he understood that nobody pays to keep million-dollar set-up men around. So, he reasoned, if he was to remain a highly paid performer, he'd have to take on a more important role. He asked to start and he made it big . . . TPER of 95—best of the decade . . . While he was hittable at times (.263), he had fabulous control of runners (stealers were 4 of 15!). Mix in 12 pickoffs and you get the picture . . . His 16 wins are a one-season Texas franchise record for a lefty topping the 15 of Jon Matlack and Frank Tanana . . . Rogers got clobbered in a couple of isolated games inflating his ERA to 4.10. But overall, a very steady year holding opponents to three or fewer runs in 23 of 33 starts including 10 of his last 12.

SCOTT KAMIENIECKI

"Home Boy" continued his intriguing home-road dichotomy. Went 8–2 in Yankee Stadium with a 3.84 ERA. On the road slumped to 2–5 and the ERA rose to 4.56. The year before went 6–4 at home and 0–10 away . . . TPER shrunk again from 113 in '91 to 100 and then to 95 last season . . . Improvement due to his ability to control runners. Only 7-of-17 stealers succeeded and he tossed 22 DP balls . . . quietly becoming a solid #3 or #4 type . . . Solid pitcher at the University of Michigan but not the school's star. That designation went to his road roommate—Jim Abbott. That team also included future major league stars Hal Morris, Barry Larkin and Chris Sabo. So, why didn't they win the college title?

JUAN GUZMAN

How good is he? In a 28-game stretch beginning with the end of the '92 season and continuing into '93 he lost once! . . . But while the records of those last two years are very similar (16–5 in '92 and 14–3 last year), the pitching wasn't. Guzman's TPER jumped from exceptional to just better than average last year. His ERA rose 1⅓ runs per game. Walks rose significantly. Opposing batters hit 45 points better against him in '93 . . . So why'd his won–lost mark remain so glittering? Toronto's offense! . . . He made 10 starts last year in which he allowed five runs or more. His record in those "poor" outings? Just 2–2 with six no-decisions because his attack kept taking him off the hook . . . The Jays, who've been criticized in the past for overworking him, allowed him to throw 120 pitches or more in 12 starts including seven of his first 13 . . . Has remarkable natural stuff. For example: Orioles 2B Harold Reynolds marveled at the sinking action on his forkball. One problem. Guzman insists he doesn't throw one. "I just do different things and let it fly" . . . Did the Dodgers really give this guy to Toronto for Mike Sharperson? And is it true that the Jays really wanted SS Jose Offerman but LA insisted they take Guzman?

BOBBY WITT

Are the days of him being the "Wild, Wild Witt" over? Had averaged a woeful 6.16 walks per 9 IP during his stay in Texas. But pitching coach Dave Duncan found something to change because Witt made huge improvement in his control allowing only 3.73 BB per 9 in '93. That accounted for the lion's share of his TPER drop to 96, the best of his career . . . Just 16 HRs in 220 IP or .65 HRs per 9 . . . Threw 26 DPs but still has difficulty controlling runners (19 for 28 in steals) . . . Had a streaky season in which he lost six in a row and won five straight . . . His 14 wins were five more than the next highest A's winner . . . His record: 14–13. In his other six starts Oakland went 0–6 which tells you something about the A's pen. In April alone they blew three saves for him when he left with the lead . . . Witt quote for '93: "If I can throw them a strike on the first pitch, then I can get them to put it in play and we have a chance for an out." Wow, has he changed!

AMERICAN LEAGUE ROTATION STARTERS

Third Quarter:

Rank	Pitcher	Team	7/1/94 Age	T	1990	1991	1992	3 yr Avg.	1993 TPER
						TPER Trendline			
29.	Jose Mesa	CLE	28	R	90	126	105	111	96
30.	Roger Pavlik	TEX	26	R	-	-	102	102	96
31.	Cal Eldred	MIL	26	R	-	*	53	53	98
32.	Pat Hentgen	TOR	25	R	-	*	124	124	99
33.	Dave Stewart	TOR	37	R	82	116	101	99	100
34.	Fernando Valenzuela	BAL	33?	L	110†	*	-	110	100
35.	Dave Fleming	SEA	24	L	-	*	88	88	101
36.	Kevin Tapani	MIN	30	R	90	88	99	92	101
37.	Willie Banks	MIN	25	R	-	*	126	126	102
38.	Frank Tanana	NYM/NYY	40	L	113	102	111	108	106†
39.	John Dopson	BOS	30	R	*	*	105	105	107
40.	Chris Haney	KCR	25	L	-	116†	114†	115	107
41.	Joe Magrane	STL/CAL	29	L	93	DNP	(118)	96	107†
42.	Melido Perez	NYY	28	R	93	90	84	89	108
43.	Charlie Leibrandt	TEX	37	L	95†	98†	93†	96	108
44.	Scott Erickson	MIN	26	R	98	86	95	92	109

* Under 100 TBF-not included in average. ( ) 100-199 TBF. † Includes NL TPER, unadjusted to AL.

JOSE MESA

His 96 TPER's his best in three full seasons in the majors . . . Very hittable (.286) and 21 of those hits went a long way . . . TPER dropped though because he's gaining control, walking less than 3-per-9 IP. That's by far the best ratio of his career . . . Also did an outstanding job controlling runners throwing 18 DPs and only 12-of-26 runners succeeded, easily the best figure on the club . . . Hard to believe he'll just be 28 next season, his 13th in professional ball. Toronto originally signed him at age 15.

ROGER PAVLIK

Terrific stuff. Some nights can't throw a pitch "straight." But had, before '93, a career dotted with injuries that greatly slowed his progress . . . Seemed to be slipping more into the "suspect" category after a wretched spring cost him a spot in the rotation and got him sent to Triple A. Pulled his game together, returned and posted a very good year . . . Threw 19 DP balls, higher even than sinkerball specialist and staff ace Kevin Brown . . . Still battled control problems at times and threw a few too many "fat ones" (18). But extremely tough in tight spots. Opponents hit just .223 with men in scoring position . . . Number six in the league with 7.09 Ks per nine innings . . . Carries a six-game win streak into '94 and Texas didn't lose any of his final 10 starts.

CAL ELDRED

If ever a pitcher fit the term "workhorse" he's the one. Threw an AL high 258 innings, second only to Atlanta's Greg Maddux in the majors . . . That workload's a subject of some controversy. Had seven starts where he threw at least 137 pitches. History suggests it's simply unwise to ask a pitcher to "shoulder" such a load . . . His 98 TPER's nice but it pales when compared to his dazzling 53 for half of '92 . . . TPER shot up when his pitches started flying over fences. 32 HRs left him behind only Detroit's Mike Moore as the league's #1 "tater" grower . . . Control also worsened by about one-walk-per-9 IP . . . 21-of-30 stealers succeeded. Faced 1,087 hitters this season—the most in the bigs . . . Now that he's developed into a terrific pitcher, you wonder how teams feel that passed on him in the first round of the '86 draft. The three players taken just before him were Greg Blosser, Kiki Jones and Steve Hosey (Who?). Four pitchers were selected before Eldred: Ben McDonald, Roger Salkeld, Kyle Abbott and Jones.

PAT HENTGEN

TPER would have been much more attractive than 99 had he not allowed a team-high 27 HR . . . Can be run on (16 for 22) but countered that by throwing a club-high 18 DP balls . . . Can be hit (.258 opponent BA) but much tougher in tight spots (just .219 with runners in scoring position) . . . 12 of his 19 wins came on the road . . . Steady control (3 BB per 9 IP) and walked as many as five just once . . . Development of a sharp curve keyed his emergence . . . How odd that just as Hentgen was arriving, his idol—Jack Morris, now a teammate—saw his career departing.

DAVE STEWART

Has the reputation of a staff ace but has now TPERed in triple figures three consecutive years . . . Only a terrific finish lowered his number to an even 100 last season (permitted more than one run just once in his last six starts) . . . Tough to run on (13 SB, 12 CS). But his strikeouts-to-walks ratio declined to its lowest point ever and his HRs per inning rose to its highest ever. Both are warning signals for a pitcher who'll be 37 next year . . . But '93 was also his eighth consecutive non-losing season. And foes still managed to hit just .242 against him, the lowest figure of all Jays' starters . . . Hard to remember that he began his career as a catcher in the Dodger organization until one day somebody noticed the "catcher" was throwing the ball back to the mound harder than the pitcher was throwing to the hitter.

FERNANDO VALENZUELA

If only the season ended in July, his would have been one of the wonderful comeback stories of the year . . . Through his first 19 games he stood 10th in the league in ERA (3.34) and sixth in lowest opponent BA (.226). Then the roof caved in. His last 13 starts brought an ERA of 8.24 and opponents ripped him at a .317 rate . . . All that added up to a TPER of an even 100 . . . The good parts of his game? Only 10-of-24 stealers made it. Threw a remarkable 20 DP balls . . . The bad parts? Allowed 18 long ones and incredibly walked more than he fanned (79–78) . . . Only pitcher to shut out the champion Blue Jays . . . If you saw him the first half you'd have sworn he was back. If you saw him the second half you'd be wondering if he'll be back.

DAVE FLEMING

If you think baseball games are too long, go see him pitch. One of the fastest workers in the game at one point last year delivered a pitch to the plate just nine seconds after getting the return throw from his catcher . . . Began '93 on the DL with an inflamed elbow . . . Came off to make 26 starts with a deceiving 12–5 record. Deceiving because Fleming didn't TPER nearly as well last year as he did the season before in going 17–10 . . . Walks rose nearly one per 9 IP . . . Was taken downtown 15 times, two more than the season before when he threw 62 more innings. And his opponents BA leaped from .257 to .290. All that added up to a TPER jump of some 13 points to a mediocre 101 . . . So, how in the world did he win all those games? Little things. You can't run on him (8 for 20). Throws DPs (16). And a little luck—just three unearned runs allowed all season.

KEVIN TAPANI

Continued a disturbing pattern of slow starts and fast finishes that has marked virtually his entire career . . . Bombarded for the first three months (3–11, ERA 5.79, TPER astronomical) but totally different after the all-star break (9–4, ERA 3.12, TPER in the 80s). He's now 27–28, ERA 4.14 pre-All-Star game and 31–17, ERA 3.48 after the break for his career . . . It all added up to a 101 TPER, the first below-average season in his four-year Twins career . . . He absolutely must improve his ability to hold runners who ran wild stealing 42 times with only 13 CSs. That's flat out terrible! . . . Excellent control with the usual fairly high HR totals that often accompany very good control stats (21 HRs) . . . Made at least 34 starts and threw over 220 innings for the third consecutive season.

WILLIE BANKS

First full major league season resulted in an OK 102 TPER . . . A "fragile" type of pitcher who appeared to lose his stuff in the middle innings resulting in 30 starts without a CG. In fact, he's not finished any of his 45 starts in the bigs . . . Like the little girl with the curl, he can be very, very good (ERA of 2.07 in his 11 wins) or very, very bad (ERA 5.92 in his 12 defeats) . . . Very hittable (.280 opponent BA) and his control's still shaky 4.1 walks per 9 IP . . . Does a superb job on stopping runners. Threw 19 DP balls and runners succeeded in just 6 of 12 attempts . . . Minnesota considered him the best pitching prospect in America when they made him the third overall pick in the '87 draft.

FRANK TANANA

Baseball's version of the Energizer Bunny. He keeps going . . . and going . . . and going . . . Now has 20 years in the pension fund . . . TPER again hovered just over 100 with his usual components—lots of long balls (28) and outstanding control (55 BBs in 202+ IP). That's right, this soon-to-be-40 lefty topped 200 innings and has now done so 13 times . . . Moderately difficult to run on despite getting it to home plate at only about 75 MPH (15 steals) . . . You see him now and can hardly remember the flame thrower with the huge, nasty curve who fanned 530 men in two early seasons in California ('75–'76) . . . With Ryan retired and Blyleven gone, he trails only Jack Morris on the list of winningest active pitchers (244 to 240). Will Morris be active? Tanana will— somewhere. Lefties that can pitch 200 innings and get it over the plate always have a job waiting for them—even if they're 40.

JOHN DOPSON

The weakest link in an otherwise stout Red Sox rotation . . . Missed two full seasons recovering from elbow surgery before now putting in almost identical back-to-back years. Finished 7–11 both seasons with TPERs of 105 and 107 . . . At the all-star break qualified as one of the club's bright spots with a 7–5 record. But didn't win a game after July 8 posting an ERA roughly the same as his height—6'4" . . . Victimized by the long ball (16). The most hittable of all the season-long Sox staffers (.281) . . . Seems to tire or lose effectiveness his third time through the lineup . . . LHH especially hurt him (.302) . . . Free at season's end. Potential

investors will be attracted by that solid 12–9 season with an above average TPER in '89. But that was BS (before surgery).

CHRIS HANEY

"Mr. Haney" got banged around . . . This soft-toss lefty barely struck out more than he walked and permitted 13 HRs in 124 IP. That's especially poor for one who's supposed to be a ground-ball pitcher . . . Many nights his stuff simply doesn't fool hitters (.286 opponent BA) . . . As you'd expect from a lefty, runners don't succeed much . . . Now has posted three consecutive seasons TPERing well over 100. In KC, where pitching's emphasized and runs can be scarce, that can cost you a job.

JOE MAGRANE

A strange season for the pitcher that hitters once referred to as "Joe Migraine" . . . Began the year in the Cards rotation having made it all the way back after two injury-riddled seasons . . . Won five straight starts in June. But by mid-August was history, released by St. Louis after a string of ineffective appearances . . . Lots of clubs called. But Cal could offer an immediate starting slot . . . By September he had a modest three-game win streak as an Angel . . . TPERed at 107 for the season. . . . Is he getting closer to again being that pitcher who put up 18 wins for the '89 Cards? The Angels must think so. Right after the season they re-signed him to a multi-year, seven-figure, guaranteed contract.

MELIDO PEREZ

Entering '93, NY gave him a four-year deal worth more than $10 million. He promptly gave them 6–14, a 5.19 ERA, a bum shoulder and easily his worst TPER of the decade (108—42nd among AL starters) . . . The league drilled him for 22 HRs in just 163 IP. Tater total's risen three straight seasons . . . And how about that DP total—4? In 163 innings? . . . Still showed outstanding stuff at times fanning 8.2 per 9 IP, the second-best ratio in the league. So, how'd he get hit for a .267 average? And a 5.19 ERA? . . . Never won two in a row all season . . . Note the number of questions asked during this assessment. That's what Perez has become in NY—a multimillion-dollar question mark.

CHARLIE LEIBRANDT

Just like that his career's in jeopardy. Entered '93 off back-to-back 15 victory seasons and averaging more than 200 innings a year for the past eight years. Seemed on the way to similar numbers at the all-star break with nine victories and 118 innings. But his shoulder gave out and he didn't win a second half game . . . Until then he was the same old Charlie. A mere 2.7 walks per 9 IP. Ten pickoffs. But when runners did figure out his move he became simple to run on (19 for 24) . . . Second half struggles inflated TPER to 108, easily the highest of the decade . . . Texas bought out his contract at year's end . . . But if he's healthy in '94 someone'll get a truly professional pitcher.

SCOTT ERICKSON

Hit the skids in '93 . . . AL hitters torched him (.305) . . . Runners took off with abandon stealing an outrageous 28 of 32 attempts . . . Those steal totals become even more important to a pitcher who gets a wonderful number of DPs (26). But if the runner at first swipes second, there goes the DP . . . Two years ago TPERed like an ace—86, one of the 10 best starters in the league. Still an acceptable 95 in '92. But his 109 last season made him just the 44th best starter of the 54 we graded . . . Has not won back-to-back since mid-August of '92, a span of 36 starts . . . Allowed the most hits and most runs of any pitcher in the majors and that led to his suffering the most defeats . . . These numbers might seem discouraging. But here's a tip to GMs. If your team plays on grass, consider dealing for him. His "heavy sinker" has made him a career 18–12 with a 2.90 on the lawn but only 31–31 and 4.21 on plastic which happens to be the surface he calls home.

AMERICAN LEAGUE ROTATION STARTERS

The Rest:

Rank	Pitcher	Team	7/1/94 Age	I	TPER Trendline				1993 TPER
					1990	1991	1992	3 yr Avg.	
45.	Tim Leary	SEA	35	R	98	135	119	114	109
46.	Ron Darling	OAK	33	R	126†	120†	93	112	109
47.	Ricky Bones	MIL	25	R	-	96†	104	102	111
48.	Todd Stottlemyre	TOR	29	R	107	96	110	104	111
49.	Jaime Navarro	MIL	27	R	102	94	85	92	112
50.	Mike Moore	DET	34	R	103	87	105	99	112
51.	Bob Welch	OAK	37	R	93	102	88	95	113
52.	Jack Morris	TOR	39	R	102	91	92	95	116
53.	Bill Gullickson	DET	35	R	111†	100	106	106	119
54.	Rick Sutcliffe	BAL	38	R	*	113†	102	105	124
Injured:									
1.	Nolan Ryan	TEX	47	R	87	81	102	89	100
2.	Bill Wegman	MIL	31	R	(125)	81	91	89	107
3.	Charles Nagy	CLE	27	R	-	101	76	88	115
4.	Mark Gardner	KCR	32	R	96†	95†	114†	102	117
5.	Bob Ojeda	CLE	36	L	101†	102†	106†	103	(119)
6.	Mike Bielecki	CLE	34	R	117†	107†	97†	108	120
7.	Arthur Rhodes	BAL	24	L	-	(142)	95	108	127
8.	John Farrell	CAL	31	R	111	DNP	DNP	111	147
9.	Teddy Higuera	MIL	35	L	96	(92)	DNP	95	(162)

* Under 100 TBF-not included in average. ( ) 100-199 TBF. † Includes NL TPER, unadjusted to AL.

TIM LEARY

For a fifth starter you could do worse . . . And Leary had done a lot worse in the two previous years racking up horrible 135 and 119 TPERs . . . Still has some unattractive numbers like an opponent's BA of .300! How about a HR every eight innings! . . . Survived because he didn't beat himself. Stealers made it just 10 of 19 times. Threw a team high 21 DPs. Walked less than three per 9 IP. Hey, when the other guys are whacking you at a .300 clip you must do these things!

RON DARLING

Got a new contract and then got drilled . . . A career low five victories and a career high 5.16 ERA . . . A horrible beginning going 10 starts before win #1 on June 6. Won three times in July, again on August 18 and that was it . . . Had awful first inning troubles getting battered for a .312 BA and allowing 27 runs in 29 starts in inning #1 . . . Over the last four years he's averaged a 112 TPER. That's downright ugly. He's become more hittable and his strikeouts-to-walks ratio's declined. These are not good signs.

RICKY BONES

Supposed to be the club's #4 starter but he wound up with the #2 TPER. But his 111 made him just the 47th best AL starter, a real comment on the Brewers' rotation . . . Excellent control but had a real homer problem (28 in 203 IP) . . . Allowing 20 out of 25 stealers hurt . . . His 16 DPs helped . . . Got absolutely ripped in April (ERA 6.57) . . . Like Dracula, this guy died in the daylight: opponents banged away at a .343 clip in 10 day starts. At night? Opposing BA dropped to .250.

TODD STOTTLEMYRE

A second straight poor TPER year . . . The league hit a resounding .292 against him . . . He did manage to cut his HRs allowed significantly. But that plus was negated by stealers succeeding 24 of 31 times and his allowing 45 doubles, sixth most in the AL . . . Now a game under .500 for his six seasons in Toronto—a team that's 116 games over .500 for that same period.

JAIME NAVARRO

After his 17-win '92 seemed on the verge of becoming a dominating pitcher. Instead, he got his head handed to him . . . TPER skied from a sparkling 85 to a smelly 112. ERA leaped nearly *two full runs a game!* . . . Everything went wrong. Hitters bashed him at an even .300 rate. Walks rose nearly one per game. Runners ran wild (23 of 29). Yes, he did throw 19 DP balls but you're gonna get double dips when there's always somebody on . . . Appeared to have found it, reeling off five straight victories from mid-May through mid-June. But his effectiveness disappeared never to return . . . Given his three solid and improving TPER years that began this decade, the Brewers must simply cross their fingers.

MIKE MOORE

A season of weird contradictions for the veteran free agent signee . . . Won the "chuck-and-duck" derby allowing a league high 35 HRs. So how, then, did he also throw three shutouts? . . . Very, very hittable (opponents BA .271). So how did he wind up throwing two one-hitters and a two-hitter? . . . Strikeouts-to-walks ratio, that once reached as high as 3–1 in Oakland, slipped back to exactly even (89–89). Uh-oh, that can be a warning signal for veteran pitchers . . . Continued as one of the game's true workhorses making a team high 36 starts—the 10th consecutive season he's made 32 or more starts. . . . Add homer problems to 23 steals in 31 attempts and his "hittability" and you have a TPER rising to its highest point of the '90s (112) . . . Again, bugged by wild pitches (9). Now has 75 over the last five seasons . . . When Seattle chose him #1 in the entire '81 draft he became the first RHP ever picked first in the first round of the draft.

BOB WELCH

The lowest victory total (7) and highest ERA (5.29) in his 16-year major league career . . . It's almost unthinkable that the league hit .312 against him . . . Very high HR total of 25 in a mere 166+ innings or one every 6½ innings pitched . . . TPERed at 113, easily the worst of his life. And it might have been even uglier had he not done a superb job of stifling runners. Only 8-of-20 stealers made it and he induced 19 DPs. . . . His 14.6 runners per

9 IP made him the second easiest pitcher in the league to reach base against (Sutcliffe 15.8) . . . His next win will be #209 tying him at that figure with Milt Pappas, Don Drysdale and Vida Blue.

JACK MORRIS

Hard to watch this grizzled, old veteran struggle last year . . . Plagued by tendinitis early and shut down for good September 9 . . . Is that ugly 116 TPER a product of the injuries or a sign that the end has come? . . . None of his numbers looked "Jack Morris-like" . . . The league hit .302 against him and .329 with runners in scoring position. That's the most disturbing of all because of how unbelievably tough he'd been in such situations most of his career . . . His 244 wins second only to Ryan among pitchers active last year . . . Toronto bought out his contract. Will he be back? Given his competitiveness, don't bet against it.

BILL GULLICKSON

Veteran righty's TPER skied to 119, its highest point of the decade. But, thanks to his high-scoring Tiger teammates, the won–lost record didn't reflect his declining efficiency (13–9) . . . Got a late start because of arthroscopic knee and shoulder surgery in January and tried to pitch his way into shape putting up some ugly early numbers . . . By August he'd found his groove and ripped off six straight wins to be AL pitcher of the month . . . The league torched him for a .291 average and 28 homers in just 159 IP . . . Gets very, very few DPs (6). But his history of excellent control continued (thank heavens) . . . TPER has climbed from 100 to 106 to 119 in three years. His corresponding ERA rise has been from 3.90 to 4.34 to 5.37. But he continues to win. Has now posted a 47–31 record over those three seasons.

RICK SUTCLIFFE

A disaster of a season . . . TPER of 124 the lowest rated of the 54 AL regular rotation pitchers graded in '93 . . . Horrid numbers everywhere . . . Opponent's BA of .314! . . . Taken deep 23 times or once every 7⅓ IP . . . Walk ratio rose noticeably . . . Can't blame his offense which got him five runs per start . . . Might be able to blame a sore left knee however. Tried to keep pitching with it while Mussina spent time on the DL. Finally got it repaired and missed a month . . . Record reached .500 or better for the 11th time in 15 big league seasons . . . Had terrible first inning problems (34 runs in 28 starts) . . . Allowed 15.8 runners per nine innings—highest in the AL . . . Is he finished at 38 or was it the knee?

NOLAN RYAN

About the only thing left to say about the career of "Big Tex" is that the ending could have been better . . . Four major injuries and three stints on the DL . . . At age 46 and with his body breaking down, AL hitters could still only manage a .220 average against him . . . His 324 victories tie him with Don Sutton for #11 all-time . . . Finished with 5,714 strikeouts and 2,795 walks in his record 27 years. Both figures are all-time baseball bests. Here's another way to look at those totals: Ryan faced 8,509 hitters who either walked or fanned. In the course of a full season an ace will face around 1,000 hitters. Thus, some 8½ years' worth of hitters in Ryan's career didn't put the ball in play! . . . Trivia answer: his last strikeout victim was Angel catcher Greg Myers.

BILL WEGMAN

After two excellent seasons (TPERs of 81 and 91) it all came apart at the seams . . . Lost 14 games and basically pitched only half the year (18 starts) . . . Had his usual outstanding control but gave up 13 homers, one every nine innings . . . Opponents hit a robust .292 . . . And right in the middle of this messy season he headed for the DL with a stomach disorder and forearm strain . . . Fate could have treated him much better. The Brew Crew scored just 2.4 runs a game in his 14 losses . . . If health returns in '94, so should those TPERs in the 90 area.

CHARLES NAGY

A lost season . . . Bothered by shingles in spring training. Then needed shoulder surgery ending his year after just nine starts . . . Forget those ugly, abbreviated numbers. . . . The year before he threw 252 innings and won 17 while losing 10 for a team that finished 10 games below .500 . . . In '92 had that dandy-daily-double combo for a pitcher—very low walks (less than 2 per 9 IP) and few HRs (only 11—one every 23 innings) . . . If he's well, he's one of the league's best.

MARK GARDNER

Ripped for a second straight season . . . Can't keep the ball in the park with 17 HRs in 91 IP. UGH! And when you play in a stadium the size of the Grand Canyon like the Royals do, that's an even larger indictment . . . Can't run on him (just 8 for 19). But why try when he's giving up a HR for every 16 outs he gets . . . Once a big-time minor league strikeout king who now fans only about 5 per 9 IP pitched—a sign his stuff's deteriorating.

BOB OJEDA

Probably lucky to be alive and, given what he went through in '93, it's best to simply ignore his numbers. But, to his unending credit, he returned from those grave injuries suffered in the boating accident that killed two teammates . . . So despondent in the long days following the tragedy that he admits he contemplated suicide . . . Had three "around average" TPER seasons to begin the '90s . . . If he comes back he'll have all the game cheering for him.

MIKE BIELECKI

Injury-troubled veteran whose career hangs by a slender thread . . . Hammered for a 120 TPER in half a season which got him released . . . The league pounded him for a .310 BA . . . 14-of-15 stealers succeeded . . . Had that one huge season in '89 going 18–7 for the Cubs . . . Since then he's 27–31 with an ERA in the mid-fours and with a major elbow surgery.

ARTHUR RHODES

The season opened with such high hopes coming off that encouraging 95 TPER in '92. Then, everything went wrong. In truth, everything went *out*! Walloped for 16 taters in just 85 innings. And this is a guy who entered the season having not allowed a homer in his last 53 innings! Weird! . . . Seems to lose his stuff all of a sudden in the fifth and sixth innings . . . His walks-to-strikeouts ratio, that had been 2–1 in '92, fell to 1–1 last year (49 BB, 49 K) . . . Only Texas' Craig Lefferts and Cal's John Farrell allowed more HRs-per-IP than his 1.68 and they each got released . . . So, will he ever develop or has the backslide started? He's only 24, but contenders are notoriously impatient.

JOHN FARRELL

Got bombed. Then got dumped . . . Enormous 147 TPER mainly the result of the enormous distance most of the hits he allowed traveled. Gave up 22 HRs in just 90 IP. Wow! . . . Want more bad numbers? Try 44 BB and 45 K. How about opponents batting .301? Or maybe stealers going 14 for 17 . . . Has worked extremely hard to overcome major elbow damage that wiped out the '91 and '92 seasons. His '93 tells you there's lots of work left to do for a pitcher who once won 14 games with lowly Cleveland in '88.

TED HIGUERA

Continues his struggle to overcome back and shoulder problems that have dogged him since 1989. That TPER of 162, albeit in just 30 innings, tells you the battle's not going very well . . . Has thrown just 66 innings in the majors in the last three years . . . The Brewers keep waiting and hoping. They have to. He's signed to a long-term contract and made $3,250,000 last year—the highest salary on the club . . . But now he's approaching 36 and it's nine years since he won Rookie-Pitcher-of-the-Year ('85). Eight years since he had that 20-win season. Hey, he once won 69 games over just a four-year stretch. Does that pitcher still exist?

AMERICAN LEAGUE UTILITY PITCHERS

Starters/Relievers (5+ Starts)

			7/1/94		TPER Trendline				1993
Rank	Pitcher	Team	Age	T	1990	1991	1992	3 yr Avg.	TPER
1.	Al Leiter	TOR	28	L	*	*	*	*	86
2.	Tom Gordon	KCR	26	R	102	99	98	100	89
3.	Bill Krueger	DET	36	L	109	99	105†	104	97
4.	Mark Clark	CLE	26	R	-	*	113†	113	98
5.	Tom Bolton	DET	32	L	86	122	121†	107	100
6.	Paul Quantrill	BOS	25	R	-	-	91	91	101
7.	Joe Hesketh	BOS	35	L	114†	96	114	106	103
8.	Kirk McCaskill	CWS	33	R	82	106	94	94	105
9.	Brian Bohanon	TEX	25	L	(122)	106	122	115	108
10.	Bob Wickman	NYY	25	R	-	-	102	102	108
11.	Kelly Downs	OAK	33	R	90†	106†	105†	102	108
12.	Mark Leiter	DET	31	R	(139)	100	104	105	109
13.	Tom Kramer	CLE	26	R	-	*	-	*	112
14.	Matt Young	CLE	35	L	88	97	115	95	112
15.	Jeff Mutis	CLE	27	L	-	*	*	*	115
16.	Mike Trombley	MIN	27	R	-	-	(100)	(100)	115
17.	Dennis Cook	CLE	31	L	109†	*	110	110	118
18.	Julio Valera	CAL	25	R	*	*	99	99	123
19.	Shawn Hillegas	OAK	29	R	*	98	131	114	131

* Under 100 TBF-not included in average. ( ) 100-199 TBF. † Includes NL TPER, unadjusted to AL.

AL LEITER

Finally started to experience some of the success that had been predicted for him. His 86 TPER ranked as the best of the utility class. Had never been healthy enough to appear in more than 14 major league games in a year until '93 . . . Spent parts of '88, '89, '90, and '91 on the DL. Oddly, his brother Mark of the Tigers spent all of '86, '87 and '88 on the hurt list and part of '92 and '93. The Leiters may have talent but they are brittle . . . Al made his annual visit to the DL early in '93 for blister problems. But otherwise enjoyed a pain-free season . . . High number of walks (56 in 105 IP) about the only factor keeping his TPER from being spectacular . . . The league could manage just a .240 BA against him. Runners tried just a dozen steals and only seven made it . . . At 28, is he finally arriving or will he break again?

TOM GORDON

First he was "Flash" Gordon. Then "flash-in-the-pan." Now "Flash" has returned . . . Manager McRae thought he got too keyed up between starts and was best-suited to relief. But circumstances dictated his return to the rotation in mid-season and Gordon "flashed" the form that made him AL Rookie-Pitcher-of-the-Year in '89 . . . Opponents managed just a .223 BA and 11 HRs in 155 innings. But then, it's hard to take a pitcher long when he's buckled your knees with a snapping curve . . . His big-time "Uncle Charlie" also cost him, however—17 wild pitches, . . . At 26 and with his best TPER since that splashy '89 year, even Gordon now understands the need to continually progress: "A lot of guys may have great stuff and they do great things early in their career but, after that, you have to adjust and determine what it takes to stay in this league." 1993 represented a "flashy" adjustment.

BILL KRUEGER

Veteran's TPERs continues to hang around 100 as he pitches in a variety of roles . . . The league hit him at a .285 rate but, unlike most of his Tiger mates, the long ball didn't bother him—just 6 in 82+ innings . . . Getting 11 DPs also helped keep TPER down . . . There'll always be a place in somebody's pen for a lefty who stays healthy and offers versatility. Has now pitched for seven teams in seven seasons with at least one in every division, every time zone and every country possible in today's major leagues.

MARK CLARK

Indians found a flaw in his motion, which, when corrected, made a huge late-season difference (see Cleveland team write-up) . . . In just 109 IP he threw 11 DP balls. Only 8-of-18 stealers made it . . . So, given that he's already got terrific control, why wasn't his TPER far more spectacular? Homers. Lots of HRs—18! That's one every six innings . . . But the vast majority of those came before the change in his motion that added 5 MPH to his fastball . . . One of those pitchers who might come "out of nowhere" next year.

TOM BOLTON

Restored some stability to his floundering TPERs (122 and 121 the previous two seasons) with an even 100. . . . would have been much better except for one horrendous streak. Pitched exceptionally well from the beginning and had a 1.35 ERA the morning of May 5. But relieved against the Twins and failed to retire any of the five batters he faced. Three days later he came in against the Yanks. Same story, faced five and didn't get anyone out. The next day three more Yanks reached against him. At that point 13 straight had gotten on base and 12 of them scored raising that ERA to a whopping 8.10! . . . By season's end, TPER back down to 100 and ERA to 4.47 . . . He did some seriously good pitching after that horrible run. Usable swing man who started 8 and made 35 relief appearances going at least five innings four times.

PAUL QUANTRILL

Played virtually every role possible in his first full season in the bigs except closer . . . Terrific sinking action accounted for 16 DPs in only 138 innings . . . Must control runners better (stealers 12 for 13) . . . Poor record (6–12) could have been much better considering his TPER and 3.91 ERA. But like many Sox hurlers he got no support from his offense.

JOE HESKETH

Veteran lefty's season ended with elbow surgery . . . His 103 TPER might have been sky-high had it not been for an almost unfathomable 11 DPs in just 53 innings. Also permitted just four steals and four HRs . . . But the league hit him hard (.294) and he walked 4.9 per 9 IP . . . Coming off surgery and with several Red Sox youngsters knocking at the door, can he hold on to his job?

KIRK McCASKILL

Moved to the bullpen after coming off the DL in late June . . . TPER of 105 achieved with a strange mix of elements. Extremely hittable (.313) and 12 of those hits left the yard in 113 innings . . . But solid control, good against runners (8 of 17) and threw as many DPs as he did HRs . . . Seemed to take to relief very well though he'd had little experience with it (3.05 ERA in 62 IP) . . . Imagine the strength of a staff when they can take a pitcher like this (TPER average 97 this decade) and shuffle him into the pen because he's simply not good enough for their five-man rotation? Heck, in Detroit he nearly qualifies as their ace.

BRIAN BOHANON

Texas' frustrations with this former #1 draft pick finally bubbled over when they released him in October . . . Note the string of unimpressive career TPERs . . . Never gained command of his pitches walking 46 in 92 IP and with a poor .296 opponent BA that included 8 HRs . . . By season's end manager Kennedy wouldn't use him in any critical situation . . . Never seemed to make any progress in seven years in the organization. But he's young and left-handed so you know he's not through yet.

BOB WICKMAN

Led a "charmed life" for a second straight season. When he's on the hill the Yankees seem to score runs in waves. How else to explain a 14–4 record with a 4.63 ERA and 108 TPER? . . . Same story last year: 6–1, 4.11 ERA, TPER 102 . . . AL hitters banged him around for a .284 average and he walked 69 in 140 innings. Also has trouble with runners (20-of-29 stealing) . . . But the hard-sinking action on his fastball produced 18 DPs. That action's the by-product of a farm accident that cut the tip off his right index finger. The "stubbier finger" seems to give him unusual movement low in the strike zone . . . Won his first 8 of '93 giving him a 14–1 record at the start of his career. Only one other pitcher's had so brilliant a mark to begin a career—Yankee lefty and Hall of Famer Whitey Ford.

KELLY DOWNS

Downs' TPERs have a case of the "ups" rising from 90 in '90 to 106 and 105, and then to last season's 108. Three straight such years suggests that's his current level of ability. And that makes him a far-end-of-the-staff type . . . His TPER suffers from being very hittable (.287) with lots of HRs (14 in 119 IP) and a high walk total of 4½ per 9 IP . . . Very versatile type who can swing back and forth from longman to starter . . . Pretty easy to run on (13 of 17) but Downs keeps it "down" getting 15 DPs . . . He's at the stage where he'll have to fight for a roster spot each spring.

MARK LEITER

Had his season cut short by more shoulder surgery costing him virtually the last two months . . . Again played the swing man role making 13 starts and 14 relief appearances . . . Like many Tiger hurlers, bugged by the long ball—17 HRs in just 106 IP or about a dinger every six innings! . . . Runners don't try much (8 of 12). But he threw just 4 DP balls . . . Has now TPERed right at or just over 100 three years in a row. . . . Was really rolling when the shoulder started aching. Had a five-game win streak and his ERA down to 3.12 in June when the pains came . . . That he's pitching at all remains a minor miracle. Missed three total seasons ('86–'88) with right shoulder miseries. Confesses he often thought about giving up but his wife Allison wouldn't hear of it. During rehab

worked as a corrections officer in New Jersey and admits he had to step between jail inmates to stop fights. Attention hitters: This may not be the type of guy you want to charge on the mound.

TOM KRAMER

Third in innings pitched by a rookie behind Chicago's Bere and Boston's Quantrill. Second in rookie wins (7) to only Bere (12) . . . Elbow problems idled him twice . . . Like many of Cleveland's young hurlers, he's surprisingly adept at freezing runners (only 6 steals in 126 IP) . . . Has a nasty combination of a high number of walks allowed and a very high HR total (19) . . . Oddly, his control's gotten worse as he's progressed through the minors . . . Given that Cleveland had him ticketed for a year at Triple A before all their pitching problems surfaced, his 112 TPER doesn't look all that bad.

MATT YOUNG

This cat's running out of major league lives . . . His 1–6 '93 record brings his career bottom line to 55–95. Ugh! . . . His June 12 triumph in Texas snapped a more than two-year victory drought. Since his previous win, on May 20, 1991, Young had gone 0–14 in 47 appearances . . . Horrible control (57 walks in 74 IP) . . . Remains perhaps the poorest fielding pitcher in the majors.

JEFF MUTIS

Has had three trials with the Tribe the last three years producing ERAs of 11.68, 9.53 and last season's 5.78, and 115 TPER . . . Has never translated his minor league success (48–27) to the major league level . . . Decent control but 33 BBs compared to just 29 strikeouts seems to make a comment on his "stuff." So does that HR total of 14 in just 81 innings.

MIKE TROMBLEY

Spent his first full season in the bigs as a spot starter and middleman with a 115 TPER . . . unable to keep the ball in the yard, allowed 15 HRs in a mere 110 innings . . . Erratic stuff as he fans a high number (85) but also gets hit hard (.290) . . . Outstanding starter's numbers in the minors where he never had a losing season and never saw his ERA float above 3.65 . . . Hitters from the ACC must wonder how in the world he ever made it to the majors after posting a career 6–22 record with Duke. Holds the NCAA record for hitting 20 batters in the '89 season. Dinged just three in the bigs last year . . . With the year under his belt and that nice minor league background, he still rates as a decent prospect.

DENNIS COOK

Another less than spectacular TPER season for this lefty . . . Has had a couple of chances to carve a niche in the Indians rotation and failed to pin down a job . . . On July 20 the Tribe optioned him to the minors and he never returned . . . League banged him around at a .295 rate. High HR and extra-base-hit totals helped inflate TPER to 118 . . . Any future lies in some other organization.

JULIO VALERA

His career's in jeopardy after having to undergo elbow ligament reconstruction ("Tommy John surgery") on June 29. The prognosis suggests that he might not be back at all in '94 . . . Originally penciled in as Cal's #3 starter. But the elbow aches began before spring training had ended . . . We suggest ignoring his 123 TPER in light of the injury and remember instead that 99 he put up in 28 rookie starts two years ago . . . his future is up to the doc.

SHAWN HILLEGAS

Second dismal year in a row for a pitcher who's had chances with five organizations in six years and never really impressed . . . The league tattooed him for a .317 average and he walked more than he fanned . . . Now 24–38 in parts of seven seasons with an ERA in the 4½ area . . . Shipped to Tacoma July 20 to never return. When will he finally run out of chances? Or has he already?

AMERICAN LEAGUE CLOSERS

| | | | 7/1/94 | | TPER Trendline | | | | 1993 |
Rank	Pitcher	Team	Age	T	1990	1991	1992	3 yr Avg.	TPER
1.	Duane Ward	TOR	30	R	79	66	81	76	64
2.	Jeff Russell	BOS	32	R	(117)	86	79	88	(71)
3.	Roberto Hernandez	CWS	29	R	-	*	69	69	72
4.	Jeff Montgomery	KCR	32	R	95	90	73	86	73
5.	Norm Charlton	SEA	31	L	89†	87†	111†	93†	(74)
6.	Tom Henke	TEX	36	R	86	67	81	79	74
7.	Gregg Olson	BAL	27	R	82	92	78	84	(76)
8.	Gerry Dipoto	CLE	26	R	-	-	-	-	82
9.	Rick Aguilera	MIN	32	R	78	77	85	80	82
10.	Mike Henneman	DET	32	R	85	88	88	87	92
11.	Dennis Eckersley	OAK	39	R	42	84	73	67	98
12.	Lee Smith	STL/NYY	36	R	88†	91†	93†	90†	112†
13.	Steve Farr	NYY	37	R	80	72	74	76	127
14.	Doug Henry	MIL	30	R	-	(57)	103	87	128

* Under 100 TBF-not included in average. ( ) 100-199 TBF. † Includes NL TPER, unadjusted to AL.

DUANE WARD

His '93 was like the James Bond theme song "Nobody does it better" . . . Top TPER of all the closers—64 . . . The average hitter scratched out a .193 BA against him . . . Fantastic stuff and control (25 BBs and 97 Ks in 71 IP) . . . Threw 7 DPs while permitting only 3 SBs . . . Did allow 4 homers snapping a string of 171 games he pitched without allowing a long ball . . . How about that 12.18 Ks per 9 IP? . . . Entered the game needing to pitch just the ninth inning to get a save 36 times and was 36-for-36. Only blown saves (6) came when the club asked him to come in before the ninth.

JEFF RUSSELL

You name a category and "Russ" has wonderful numbers in it. In 46 innings, how about a 45 K-to-14 BB ratio? How about one, that's right, one HR? But then, that's also how many stolen bases he permitted—ONE! . . . Pitched so terribly in the spring Boston considered releasing him. Then burst from the gate saving his first 18 in a row . . . As a group AL RHHs didn't hit their average weight against him (.177) . . . Sadly, his only HR allowed and one of his four blown saves (he saved 33) knocked Boston out of first for the final time July 26 when Milwaukee's Tom Brunansky took him out with two outs in the bottom of the ninth . . . Three excellent declining TPER seasons in a row with 93 total saves in those years.

ROBERTO HERNANDEZ

Took total control of the Sox closer job in '93 after being given the job at the '92 all-star break . . . This guy's nasty. In '92 AL hitters managed just a .180 BA against him. Last season that rose "all the way up" to .228 . . . But his control sharpened a bit allowing a meager 20 walks in 78+ innings . . . Did surrender six dingers. But permitted just two steals all year . . . Actually had some early season rough spots. Then got downright stingy posting a 1.74 ERA with 26 saves in his last 42 games . . . Not bad for a fellow who won a varsity letter at the University of Connecticut in 1985 *as a catcher*! . . . If the Sox are lucky to have snatched him up in a very minor deal with the Angels in '89, he's lucky to be alive. Underwent delicate surgery in '91 to transfer veins from his inner thigh to his forearm alleviating a blood-clotting problem that doctors feared not only would threaten his career but also his life . . . Now he's back throwing 95 MPH heat with that repaired forearm. Ah, the miracles of modern medicine.

JEFF MONTGOMERY

The Rolaids Relief Award winner and rightly so . . . The league batted a meager .206 against him, up from .205 in '92! Just three homers in 87 innings . . . Not a huge strikeout pitcher or a DP machine (only three) but someone who simply gets the job done over and over and over . . . Much more sturdy than most closers. Able to go as much as three innings at times and has pitched at least 82 innings each of the last five seasons . . . Recorded 24 consecutive saves at one point, the third longest streak in ML history . . . Hard to believe now that just a few years ago KC had him in a support role for closers Steve Farr and Mark Davis . . . Does KC getting him from Cincy in '88 in return for OF Van Snider remind you of that Chevy Chase movie entitled "Deal of the Century"?

NORM CHARLTON

At 31 his career's at a crossroads because of a blown out elbow that required the so-called "Tommy John surgery" . . . Was rebounding splendidly from his awful '92 (TPER 111) when the elbow blew out in early August . . . The league hit him at a meager .179 clip. Runners hardly even tried to run and the walk-strikeout ratio had returned to a healthy 3-to-1 rate . . . But all that's history now. The M's released him at season's end because doctors don't figure him to be ready until mid-'94 at the earliest.

TOM HENKE

Ho hum, another outstanding season for the bespectacled "Terminator" . . . Again fanned more than a hitter an inning bringing his career average to 10.57 Ks per 9 IP, the best ratio in the history of the AL for pitchers who've thrown at least 400 innings . . . Will occasionally give up the long ball (7) . . . Had his fifth 30-save season. Only Lee Smith (8), Jeff Reardon (7) and Dennis Eckersley (6) have more . . . Number seven on the all-time saves list with 275 but four of the six ahead of him were still active at the end of '93 (Smith, Reardon, Rich Gossage and Eckersley) . . . His 66 appearances were his second most ever (72 in '87) . . . Opponents hit .205. Just one pitcher better in the entire league—the guy who replaced him as Toronto's closer, Duane Ward . . . Gave up George Brett's last hit and the last hit ever in the Rangers' old Arlington Stadium.

GREGG OLSON

Suddenly a future that looked incredibly bright has been clouded by injury. A torn elbow ligament ended his season in August and immediately began the period of worrying . . . Was having his best TPER season yet (76) when the elbow snapped . . . At 27 he's already 14th all-time in saves with 160. That's easily the best all-time at that age. Bobby Thigpen comes next with 131 when he turned 27 . . . But his terrific numbers did include some downers. First batters hit .341 against him (fourth highest in the league) and that led to 15 of 31 inherited runners scoring (very high for a closer) . . . Saved 29 in 35 opportunities including at least one save for all 11 O's pitchers who recorded a victory in '93 . . . Weird: The first batter he faced in '93, Texas' Doug Strange, homered. Didn't allow another dinger all year.

JERRY DI POTO

The club's closer of the future who had to arrive sooner than expected because of the death of Olin . . . One stat literally leaps out at you off his sheet: NO HRS ALLOWED IN 56 INNINGS! . . . Former third rounder out of Virginia Commonwealth U. who's progressed quickly and successfully through the Tribe system . . . One more thing to love about him—stealers didn't even bother to try. Would you believe just one attempt in 56 innings? Mix in 9 DPs over the same period and you've got the makings of a potential bullpen ace. Hey, he's already an 82 TPER and last year that rated him above people like Aguilera, Eckersley and Henneman. Pretty fancy company for a rookie.

RICK AGUILERA

A slight TPER slippage the last couple of seasons from those consecutive sparkling 70s to begin the decade, but still a first-rate closer . . . HR balls bothered him greatly in '93 allowing 9 in just 72 innings . . . Otherwise his numbers remained substantially the same. Fantastic control (less than one unintentional walk every six innings!) . . . Threw a "perfect game" in June retiring 27 consecutive batters at one stretch . . . Save totals would have been even more impressive than his 34 had the Twins given him anything to save. Just 10 opportunities the last 60 games . . . Weird: Has never allowed Toronto a run in 16 innings of regular season work and 3.1 in post-season. And those guys can hit!

MIKE HENNEMAN

His 63 appearances marked the sixth straight year he's pitched between 60 and 69 games out of the Tiger pen . . . Saved a career-tying high of 24, the fifth time he's topped 20 in six years . . . TPER rose slightly but his consistency in the '90s is admirable: 85–88–88–92 . . . How good is he at holding runners and delivering quickly to the plate? Pitched in 71+ innings and NO ONE EVEN TRIED TO STEAL! . . . Broke John Hiller's all-time franchise record for career saves (125) and starts '94 at 128 . . . Most closers usually get lots of saves but few victories. He's the exception. Has now won 56 games and lost only 30 in his seven seasons in the Motor City.

DENNIS ECKERSLEY

It had almost gotten to the point where you'd begun to think of him as the "God of the Bullpen." Then '93 arrived . . . His TPER leaped to 98. The league, which had hit .211 against him in '92, jumped up 50 points accounting for a major portion of the rise for

'92 when he TPERed 73 and won both the Cy Young and MVP . . . Blew 10 saves. From '88–'92 he'd blown only 27 total while racking up 220 saves, 43 more than the next highest total over that five-year period (Thigpen's 177) . . . Walked just 13 in 67 innings but that marked his *highest* total since '87 when he issued 17 freebies . . . Most of his '93 troubles could be traced to a sudden inability to handle LHHs. They touched him for a .323 BA and 5 HRs. The previous five years they'd hit just .215 against him . . . Remains the only pitcher in history with more than 100 complete games and 100 saves . . . Looking more and more like he'll miss being baseball's first "200–200" man. He's already well past 200 saves (275) but has just 183 victories . . . Wanna feel old? The AL named him Rookie-Pitcher-of-the-Year when Gerald Ford called the White House home (1975).

LEE SMITH

The Yanks acquired him August 31 from St. Louis to shore up their pen during the pennant chase. Wasn't much help because the Yanks didn't give him many chances. NY went 13–16 after his arrival. He saved all three games he had opportunities . . . But that season-long combined TPER of 112 represents the worst offering of his 13-year career . . . All of a sudden he began throwing long balls. At St. Louis he faced 195 batters and 11 took him out. Ouch! . . . If you get on base, go! Stealers swiped 12 of 13 . . . In 63 games covering 58 innings he got just one twin killing. That's the curse of being a high fastball pitcher . . . Reached 400 saves as a Yankee September 17. The all-time saves leader with 401 and now has eight straight 30 save seasons . . . His 58 innings marked the second lowest full season total of his career. ERA the highest ever for him. Has his stuff begun to desert him or was '93 nothing more than a bump in the long road of his wonderful career?

STEVE FARR

An absolutely wretched season! . . . TPER went through the roof even though the league hit only .253 against him. But he surrendered lots of "Farr ones"—8 HRs in 47 IP. His control totally deserted him—28 BBs . . . Post-all-star slump (6.19 ERA) caused NY to deal for Lee Smith . . . Seeing him last year made you wonder what happened to the superb reliever that had started the decade with TPERs of 80–72–74 . . . He's 37. The Yanks certainly didn't want him back at season's end . . . He's free coming off this awful year. What becomes of him? . . . But he's now put in over nine years in the bigs and has 33 wins and 118 saves since Kansas City fished him out of the minors in '87. He'd virtually given up hope of ever pitching in the bigs again and had taken a job as a welder when the Royals called offering a job in the bus leagues. He took it and has made about a bajillion dollars since (much better than welder wages).

DOUG HENRY

A "closer" whose awful season may have closed the door on any chance he ever had to again be the Milwaukee closer . . . That 128 TPER ranked as the worst of all 28 major league stoppers other than injured NL relievers John Franco and Rob Dibble . . . Literally everything went wrong. Hitters pounded him for a .300 average. Allowed 7 long balls and threw just 3 DPs . . . Had 16 saves at the all-star break but with a 4.58 ERA. Things only got worse with his second half ERA ballooning to 7.32 . . . What happened to the Doug Henry who permitted just 16 hits in 36 innings during the second half of '91 and TPERed at 57?

AMERICAN LEAGUE IN-BETWEENERS

Top Third:

Rank	Pitcher	Team	7/1/94 Age	T	TPER Trendline 1990	1991	1992	3 yr Avg.	1993 TPER
1.	Jim Poole	BAL	28	L	*	(68)	*	(68)	(61)
2.	Jesse Orosco	MIL	37	L	114	108	(86)	105	71
3.	Jim Austin	MIL	30	R	-	*	73	73	(81)
4.	Rick Honeycutt	OAK	42	L	72	(115)	(99)	91	(82)
5.	Danny Cox	TOR	34	R	-	113†	117†	115	82
6.	Larry Casian	MIN	28	L	*	*	*	*	82
7.	Scott Radinsky	CWS	28	L	99	75	99	89	83
8.	Mike Fetters	MIL	29	R	103	115	76	97	84
9.	Matt Whiteside	TEX	26	R	-	-	(85)	(85)	85
10.	Tony Castillo	TOR	31	L	109	(121)	-	112	87
11.	Jeff Schwarz	CWS	33	R	-	-	-	-	89
12.	Carl Willis	MIN	33	R	-	71	73	72	89
13.	Steve Frey	CAL	30	L	96†	(108)†	102	101	90
14.	Mark Eichhorn	TOR	33	R	94	64	88	82	90
15.	Todd Frohwirth	BAL	31	R	*	63	85	74	90
16.	Paul Assenmacher	CUB/NYY	33	L	87	93	121	97	91†
17.	Eric Plunk	CLE	30	R	96	140	92	115	91
18.	Greg A. Harris	BOS	38	R	103	89	88	94	91

* Under 100 TBF-not included in average. ( ) 100-199 TBF. † Includes NL TPER, unadjusted to AL.

JIM POOLE

The lowest TPER of any pitcher in the big leagues last year! . . . What sensational numbers! Allowed just 50 baserunners in 50.1 innings . . . Only two hitters took him deep all season. And only two others stole on him . . . O's tended to use him as a "spot pitcher" against lefties. Why? He got everybody out. LHH batted .177. RHH hit .174 . . . Why other Oriole pitchers sent him Christmas presents—he stranded 51 inherited runners, the most in the AL . . . Of his 55 appearances, 33 were hitless and 45 scoreless . . . Did Texas really waive this guy on Memorial Day 1991?

JESSE OROSCO

Like Old Man River, he just keeps rollin' along . . . After a couple shaky years to start the decade, he's bounced back with two superb seasons . . . Spectacular at the two things a reliever must do: a) don't walk anyone (17 BBs in 57 IP) and b) keep the ball in the park (just 2 HRs!) . . . Add to that the fact that runners hardly even bother to try to steal on him anymore (2 for 6) . . . Where'd all that "gas" suddenly come from? He fanned 67 men, over 10 per 9 innings . . . At some point next season he'll appear in his 750th major league game and his TPERs tell you the end's nowhere in sight.

JIM AUSTIN

One of the league's better-kept bullpen secrets . . . After toiling for six seasons in the Brewers' minors, he emerged with that 73 TPER in '92 and followed it up with a solid 81 in 31 games last year . . . Only fair control but opposing hitters just can't seem to figure him out—.191 in '92 and .230 in '93 . . . What we can't figure out is why Milwaukee suddenly shipped him to the minors in late July and they released him right after the season.

RICK HONEYCUTT

"Dr. Groundball" has returned . . . Over-40 sinker-slider specialist has bounced back from '91 shoulder surgery to regain his place among the very best of baseball's set-up types . . . Can't run on him (2 for 5) and can hardly ever take him out of the yard (2 HRs) . . . Missed 36 games after suffering a broken pitching

wrist covering 1B. But came back pitching like nothing had ever happened . . . Opposing hitters managed just a .182 BA with runners in scoring position . . . In his last 15 games he did not allow an earned run and hitters scratched for a .136 BA! . . . Completed the sixth year of his "second career." Started for 10 years. Has now relieved for 6. Looks like he could pitch till he's 50.

DANNY COX

Score one for the Jays' scouts. Their reports indicated that, while pitching out of the Pirates' pen late in '92, he appeared to have regained the kind of stuff that had made him a valuable Cardinals pitcher in the mid-'80s (18–9 in '85). They were right . . . Signed as a free agent, Cox TPERed at 82, fifth best of AL in-betweeners and second best of all the righties . . . Averaged a strikeout per inning, allowed only a .230 opponent BA and did a decent job of stifling runners . . . Led all AL relievers in first batter efficiency retiring 38 of 44. That's 86.4%!

LARRY CASIAN

The Twins pitching "find" of the year . . . Had a May-June streak of 17 consecutive appearances without allowing a run . . . Followed that up with a second stretch where he went untouched in 19 straight! . . . Gave up just one HR and that marked the first he'd ever given to an LHH in 80 major league games. Who hit it? Griffey Jr., of course . . . You simply can't run on him. One steal *attempt* in 54 games . . . One of Minnesota's few truly bright spots in '93.

SCOTT RADINSKY

Another quality set-up season in which he made a career-high 73 appearances . . . His four-year average for the decade is 68 games a season and always with TPERs in double digits . . . Has the three outstanding qualities you want from a bullpener—solid control, low HR total (3 in 54+ innings) and can get the strikeout when needed (44) . . . Runners only tried to steal twice all year . . . Now has 22 wins and 31 saves in four years out of the Sox pen and in that time has yielded just 11 HRs in 237 innings . . . Former drummer in teammate Jack McDowell's band.

MIKE FETTERS

Bounced back from elbow surgery to post his second consecutive solid TPER. Though he remained pretty hittable (.278), the ball seldom left the yard (4 HRs) and he did an outstanding job of controlling runners: 13 DPs and 6-of-13 stealers . . . But he seemed to have trouble with first batters and that led to his allowing 21 of the 46 runners he inherited to score . . . Former first-round pick of the Angels who seems to have found a home in the pen after being a starter in Cal's minor league system.

MATT WHITESIDE

Fast start helped him post that 85 TPER, identical to the TPER of his partial '92 season. Appeared in 21 of the club's first 49 games. But at that point his TPER began to rise amid talk that he'd been overused and had a tired arm . . . Pretty soon Texas got tired of watching him get hammered and shipped him to Oklahoma City for three weeks. But he wasn't any better after his return . . . Walked only 23 in 73 IP. Runners had no luck swiping, just 4 of 10. That helped him toss an impressive 11 DPs, one of the highest ratios of DPs-to-IP in the AL . . . Could use another pitch to keep hitters off balance.

TONY CASTILLO

A "garage sale" find . . . Picked up as a minor league free agent and he responded with an 87 TPER, tenth best among the 61 AL tweeners we graded . . . Like teammate Cox, outstanding against first batters faced, retiring 35 of 46 (76.1%) . . . A spot pitcher who's especially tough on LHH holding them to a .213 average . . . Threw seven DPs and permitted only four steals—OK numbers for a "hold 'em" type of pitcher.

JEFF SCHWARZ

Suddenly this 29-year-old career minor leaguer who'd spent 11 years in professional ball without ever throwing so much as a single pitch in the majors, broke through with a terrific 89 TPER as a right-handed spot pitcher . . . Spectacular against first batters (BA .176) . . . What made the difference between the guy who'd ridden buses for eleven years and the effective rookie out of the Sox pen in '93? Strikes! He began throwing more of them in the minors earning him a promotion. But he's still troubled by horrible stretches of poor control at times (38 walks in 51 innings) . . . But the league couldn't touch him (.201 BA) and only Lou Whitaker can say he's homered off him . . . Was '93 a mirage? Will he awaken from his dream and be riding a bus again soon? Who knows? But last season sure must have been fun.

CARL WILLIS

Yet another solid season for a pitcher the Twins grabbed off of baseball's "junk heap" three years ago . . . Now has TPERed 71–73–89 in those seasons. That's a 78 average, the best of any AL middleman whose been in the league the last three seasons . . . Became a lot more hittable last year (.259) accounting for his TPER rise . . . But walks remained low, runners managed only four steals and he threw only 2 HR balls . . . And all this from a man so despondent about his career that, after receiving a degree in physical therapy in the late '80s, he seriously considered quitting to work in a retirement home. With numbers like the one's he's been putting up, retirement's a long way away.

STEVE FREY

Emerged as the Angels' saves leader after spending life as a set-up man . . . TPER drop to a career low 90, the result of his getting awfully stingy with the long ball—just one . . . But control problems continued to plague him as they have throughout his career (26 BB in 48 IP) . . . More BBs than Ks, unusual for an "effective" reliever . . . Allowed just three steals . . . Much tougher to hit with runners on (.198) than with the bases empty (.278). Wore down after the all-star break with a 4.82 ERA in 20 games.

MARK EICHHORN

Vastly underappreciated "sidewinder" unless you follow TPERs. Here he's a star. Fourth straight good-to-very-good TPER year . . . Does two things you must have from a bullpener—throws strikes (only 22 walks in 73 IP) and keeps it in the park (3 HRs) . . . Would have an even more outstanding year except for early season difficulties that saw him allow 16 runs in his first 15 games. Given his side-arm delivery he's much tougher on RHH (.224) than LHH (.326).

TODD FROHWIRTH

Another solid season (TPER 90) though not nearly as flashy as his previous two (63 and 85) . . . Sixth in the league in appearances (70) and fourth in relief innings (96.1) . . . Over the last three seasons he's thrown more relief innings than anyone in the AL (298.2) . . . His "down under" style gets him tons of DPs (16) but makes it extremely difficult to hold runners (16 out of 20) . . . TPER rise attributable to a whole slew of small increases in everything from opponents' BA to walks to HRs allowed . . . Spent seven years with the Phillies organization before they gave up on him.

PAUL ASSENMACHER

Bounced back after a horrid '92 (TPER 121) with a very solid season (TPER 91) . . . Seemed to thrive in his new AL surroundings. Was TPERing over 100 with the Cubbies but after arriving in NY posted an absolutely spectacular 67! . . . In the Big Apple, hitters could manage only a .175 BA and no roundtrippers in 26 appearances (with Chicago: .288 and 5 HRs) . . . Has now made 291 appearances the last four seasons . . . Very versatile and useful pen-man. The type that's only noticed on a staff when the team's missing his particular ability to get critical outs in certain spots.

ERIC PLUNK

Another workmanlike 91 TPER . . . Seems to have been around forever but is still only 30 years old after eight seasons in the majors . . . Control, once an enormous problem, has gotten better. Last year had 30 BBs and 77 Ks in 71 innings, so you know he still has some very serious heat . . . Permitted only 5 HRs . . . Runners have a good chance of succeeding and his stuff gets him very few DPs (3) or he'd TPER even better. But as it is he's put up three TPERs in the 90s in the last four years.

GREG A. HARRIS

The workhorse of the AL with 80 appearances . . . Vastly underrated veteran has now TPERed in the high 80–low 90 area three consecutive seasons . . . Big breaking curve brought 103 Ks in 112 innings . . . Other TPER aids included 11 DPs, just 5-of-9 stealers and only 7 HRs . . . TPER would have challenged the upper class of the rankings (he was #18 in tweeners) but for 10 HBP and 14 intentional walks, which must be charged to his record . . . Remains hopeful of being able to throw left-handed in a game sometime. Already has a glove that converts so he could "switch pitch" and his LH fastball clocks at around 80–85 MPH. Question: Why would you want to try that when lefties hit only .253 to begin with? . . . Was TPERing in the fantastic high 70s until his final 8 appearances when he obviously wore down (0–3, ERA 28.69). Note: 28.69 is *not* a misprint.

AMERICAN LEAGUE IN-BETWEENERS

Middle Third:

Rank	Pitcher	Team	7/1/94 Age	T	TPER Trendline				1993 TPER
					1990	1991	1992	3 yr Avg.	
19.	Tony Fossas	BOS	36	L	(136)	88	(128)	109	(92)
20.	Gene Nelson	CAL/TEX	33	R	67	156	128	110	92
21.	Derek Lilliquist	CLE	28	L	115†	*	78	103	93
22.	Heathcliff Slocumb	CUB/CLE	28	R	-	111	(139)	121	93†
23.	Scott Bankhead	BOS	30	R	*	124	100†	111	94
24.	Jose DeLeon	PHI/CWS	33	R	104†	99†	108†	103	95†
25.	Mike Butcher	CAL	29	R	-	-	(109)	(109)	(95)
26.	Joe Grahe	CAL	26	R	118	110	86	101	95
27.	Stan Belinda	PIT/KCR	27	R	99†	100†	114†	104	96†
28.	Mark Williamson	BAL	34	R	86	113	*	98	96
29.	Alan Mills	BAL	27	R	143	*	89	105	96
30.	Jeremy Hernandez	CLE	27	R	-	*	(124)	97	97
31.	Cris Carpenter	FLA/TEX	29	R	*	90†	100†	96	97†
32.	Dennis Powell	SEA	30	L	140	-	99	117	(98)
33.	Steve Howe	NYY	36	L	-	61	*	61	100
34.	Ken Patterson	CAL	29	L	103	91	(147)	109	100
35.	Joe Boever	OAK/DET	33	R	105†	119†	92†	105	101
36.	Vince Horsman	OAK	27	L	-	*	(98)	(98)	(102)
37.	Ted Power	CLE/SEA	39	R	95	104	90	97	103

* Under 100 TBF-not included in average. ( ) 100-199 TBF. † Includes NL TPER, unadjusted to AL.

TONY FOSSAS

"The Mechanic" makes a living "fixing" LHH . . . Made 71 appearances. But threw just 40 total innings. He's a one- and two-out pitcher whose job consists of getting lefty hitters out in a critical situation. How well does he do his job? LHH batted .130 against him and struck out 21 times in 69 ABs . . . Inherited 60 runners and only 11 scored (81.7% efficiency) . . . Be careful though. TPER trendline suggests he's in a good-year-horrible-year pattern.

GENE NELSON

Had a blazing start with the Angels, hit a patch of ineffectiveness and Cal promptly dumped him. Texas scooped him up quickly and with good reason—92 TPERs don't show up on your doorstep every day . . . Once a part of the feared Oakland pen as the right-handed set-up man to "The Eck." Had that fantastic 67 TPER in '90 then struggled through '91 and got hurt in '92 at which point the A's released him . . . But at 33 next season he stands every chance of regaining his former stature.

DEREK LILLIQUIST

His conversion to a reliever turned him from a decent starter into a bullpen beast . . . Followed up his sparkling '92 TPER of 78 with a solid 93 . . . Forget running on him. Just 2 attempts in 64 innings . . . Excellent control. Only 5 HRs allowed. But that TPER rise attributable to a major leap in the opponents' BA. From a scintillating .187 in '92 to .269 last year . . . Inherited 42 runners, 23 of them in scoring position. Only eight eventually made it home . . . Combine his two-year totals in Cleveland and you get a 9–7 record with 16 saves and a 2.01 ERA in 127 games. That's stout!

HEATHCLIFF SLOCUMB

A strange season . . . Shuffled to the minors by the Cubs. Recalled, made 10 decent appearances and then dealt to the Indians. Started very strong in Cleveland. Through June had a 2.66 ERA in 20 innings. Then made two poor relief jobs the first week of July and that got him sent to the minors for more than two months . . . Too many walks (16 in 27 Cleveland innings) . . . But, before getting too excited about that 93 TPER realize it's his first real success of any kind on a major league level.

SCOTT BANKHEAD

Former first-round pick of KC with a long history of major arm problems . . . But when healthy and handled correctly he provides nice middleman work as he's done for two seasons now . . . Tended to give up the dinger last year (7 in 64 IP) but also tossed 7 DPs and permitted only three steals . . . Because of past arm miseries (shoulder surgeries in '87 and '90), his workload must be closely monitored. Made just 40 appearances in '93. But, oh, what might have been had the arm not given way. Went 14–6 for the '89 Mariners in 210 innings as the ace of the staff at age 26.

JOSE DeLEON

Keeps getting chance after chance based on his incredibly live arm . . . Now has nine years in the pension plan and still just 33 . . . But he may have, at last, found a role he can succeed in—middle relief. Flunked badly as a starter with but two winning seasons from '84 through '92. But the Phils and then White Sox spotted him in the less pressurized world of middleman and he seemed more comfortable . . . Has learned to hold runners (just 5-of-13 stealers made it) . . . But just one DP in 57+ innings? . . . Still bothered by wildness at times. But maybe he's found a home in the middle.

MIKE BUTCHER

Surprising work from a pitcher who began the year on the (oh, no) 60-day disabled list with major shoulder problems. He'd had surgery in November of '92. Those types sometimes *never* come back, much less in the same season . . . Returned to Cal by late June and managed eight saves . . . Is he a longshot closer possibility? Strikes out lots of people. Permitted just 4 of 17 inherited runners to score and none of the 23 first batters he faced got a hit (20 outs and 3 walks). Allowed only two HRs . . . Hmmmmm. Interesting. If his walk total comes down that TPER (95) will get awfully attractive.

JOE GRAHE

The master plan had him taking over the closer role from the departed star Harvey. The plan did not have him landing on the DL for five weeks in mid-season with shoulder tendinitis . . . Strange choice for the closer role since he's hardly ever fanned many more than he's walked . . . Did allow just 5 HRs. But perhaps his slight TPER rise from that impressive 85 in '92 (when he also saved 21) should be dismissed because of the shoulder . . . Just 26 and ability suggests he'll play an important role somewhere on the Cal staff.

STAN BELINDA

Former Pirates closer acquired in mid-year so that Montgomery might become a one-inning type of stopper . . . TPERs don't remind you of the kind of numbers true closers put up; hanging right around the "average pitcher" point . . . Gives up HRs—14 in 140 IP over the last two seasons . . . Does not control runners at all. All 13 stealers who tried against him in Pittsburgh this season made it. . . . Looks very good, though, in the role KC has designed for him. And remember, when closer Montgomery can't go, this guy did have 19 saves for the Pirates in four months.

MARK WILLIAMSON

Bounced back from elbow surgery that wiped out '92 to post seven wins in relief, second only to Chicago's Radinsky (8) . . . TPERed below 100 despite allowing opponents to hit .304 . . . What kept that TPER deflated? A) terrific control (25 BB in 88 IP), B) tough to take out of the park (5 HRs), C) difficult to run on (3 for 7), D) often gets two for one (10 DPs) . . . Opted for free agency after the season. If you erase that injury year in '92 he's posted a 30–17 record with 14 saves, 227 appearances and 360 IP in the other four seasons from '89–'93. Somebody'll give him a chance off those credentials.

ALAN MILLS

Exceptionally durable middleman who, for a short time, shifted to the role of closer with Olson out . . . His 100.1 IP trailed only Boston's Harris and Detroit-Oakland's Boever in terms of workload . . . Opponent BA terrific—.225. Even tougher with men on base— an AL low .187 . . . TPER would have been special had he not suddenly developed a case of "longballitis" allowing 14 roundtrippers. He'd been dinged just five times the year before . . . 13 DPs and only six steals allowed . . . In two years with the Birds since the Yanks dumped him he's 15–8 with a 2.92 ERA and a 92 TPER.

JEREMY HERNANDEZ

June 1 became "Hernandez Day" in Cleveland. On that date they made a pair of deals involving three guys named "Hernandez." They acquired Jeremy and got rid of Jose and Fernando . . . Full-year TPER of 97 . . . Allowed just 4 of 10 stealers to succeed and threw ten DPs along with decent control . . . But he had huge difficulties keeping the ball in play. Allowed 14 HRs in 112 innings . . . But consider that workload. That's 112 innings of bullpen work and 70 appearances. That's a gigantic amount of pitching . . . With more careful handling might the ball stay in the park more?

CRIS CARPENTER

Former All-SEC Georgia punter put together an overall acceptable 97 TPER but disappointed Texas after they dealt for him. Breaking out just his Texas stint he TPERed at 111 . . . Had a pair of OK Cardinal bullpen years before heading to Florida in the expansion draft where he burned up the NL. In 29 games he allowed just 29 hits in 37 IP with a 2–1 ratio of strikeouts to walks . . . But in Texas he couldn't seem to get through innings unscathed and had a couple of other ugly numbers: scored 10 of 31 inherited runners and first batters hit .300 . . . But a young, sturdy set-up man who's been generally effective for his three big league seasons.

DENNIS POWELL

The best of a shaky group of Mariner in-betweeners and set-up men with his 98 TPER ranking him 32nd among that large group of such pitchers . . . Seven HRs in just 47 innings and more than 4½ BBs per 9 IP are the negatives that jump out at you from a pitcher who's always had control troubles . . . Second straight year TPERing just under 100. But, with as sorry as the M's bullpen was last year, why'd they pick this guy to dump at season's end?

STEVE HOWE

The Yanks gave him a two-year contract worth $2.1 million-a-year entering '93. He gave them a 3–5 record, a 4.97 ERA and a 100 TPER (had a fantastic 61 the year before) . . . Yielded 7 HRs in 50+ innings while allowing hitters to motor along with a .297 BA. (In '92 they hit .122—that's right, .122!) . . . TPER stayed down because he retained super control (only six unintentional walks), threw eight DP balls and stealers simply have stopped trying (1 for 2) . . . Will he be worth that large contract in '94? The better question is why NY gave it to him in the first place. After all, he'd appeared just 20 times in '92 had only one year with more than 24 outings from '86–'92 because of his continuing drug troubles. Isn't this fellow the last one you'd give a multi-year contract to?

KEN PATTERSON

Journeyman lefty's been with four teams in three years . . . Decent performance (TPER 100) that would have been much better had he not walked 35 in just 59 innings . . . Much better after the all-star break limiting opponents to a .194 BA in 23 games with but one HR . . . If anyone was still watching, that last three months should get him a shot at making someone's pen. And, except for an ugly '92 season he's been a pretty usable pitcher. Evidence a record of 13–5 in four years pitching out of the White Sox pen ('88–'91) where teammates nicknamed him "Genius."

JOE BOEVER

Will the "real Joe Boever" please stand up? Was forgettable in Oakland (TPER 106) but fantastic his last two months in Detroit (85) . . . The differences were downright remarkable. In Oakland the league knocked him around for a .280 average with eight HRs. In Tigertown those numbers dropped to .179 and one HR . . . Adding the two stops together made him the second hardest working reliever in the entire league with 102 IP (Boston's Harris had 112) . . . Hard to run on (4 of 7) but bothered by wildness . . . Tigers liked what they saw and quickly re-signed him . . . What a workhorse! Since '89, with stops in Atlanta, Philly, Houston, Oakland and Detroit, he's pitched in 343 games and totaled 482 innings. That's an average of 69 games and 96 innings a season!

VINCE HORSMAN

The ultimate "spot" pitcher appearing in 40 games but pitching just 25 total innings . . . Usually brought in to get lefties out. Why? LHHs nailed him for a .297 average. RHHs could manage just a .216 BA . . . Allowed just 2 HRs in 25 innings. But both were three-run shots . . . Just 17 Ks to go with 15 BBs and only one DP ball. Hmmmmm. TPER of 102 made him a "star" in this pen though finishing behind only Honeycutt and Eckersley of all Oakland relievers . . . With Honeycutt gone can he set-up Eck?

TED POWER

Started the season as part of the emotionally shocked bullpen in Cleveland that lost friends Steve Olin and Tim Crews to that training camp boating accident . . . Got clobbered early (7.20 ERA in 20 games) leading to his Indians July 23 release . . . Signed in Seattle and almost immediately inherited the closer role when Charlton's elbow exploded . . . Finished with 13 saves, equaling the 15th highest total ever by an AL pitcher over 37 . . . While the overall TPER says 103, realize that his final two months in Seattle were a gaudy 78! No wonder the M's quickly re-signed him for '94 . . . When you see him trundle in during the '94 season check his belt. It's the leather one his friend Steve Olin used to wear in Cleveland.

THE PITCHERS

AMERICAN LEAGUE IN-BETWEENERS

Bottom Third:

Rank	Pitcher	Team	7/1/94 Age	T	TPER Trendline 1990	1991	1992	3 yr Avg.	1993 TPER
38.	Bob Patterson	TEX	35	L	87†	84†	101†	90	103
39.	Mark Gubicza	KCR	31	R	107	110	92	103	104
40.	John Habyan	NYY/KCR	31	R	*	71	104	86	104
41.	Storm Davis	OAK/DET	32	R	102	109	89	101	105
42.	Edwin Nuñez	OAK	31	R	85	(143)	112	104	105
43.	Mark Gardiner	MTL/DET	28	R	*	107	99	103	107†
44.	Greg Cadaret	CIN/KCR	32	L	96	94	127	104	108†
45.	Jeff Nelson	SEA	27	R	-	-	105	105	108
46.	Rich DeLucia	SEA	29	R	(77)	113	129	113	110
47.	Mike Hartley	MIN	32	R	92†	122†	119†	110	111
48.	Mike Timlin	TOR	28	R		84	88	85	113
49.	Bob MacDonald	DET	29	L	*	98	115	106	114
50.	Rich Monteleone	NYY	31	R	*	94	86	88	114
51.	Craig Lefferts	TEX	36	L	86†	105†	105†	100	120
52.	Rich Gossage	OAK	42	R	-	(93)	(102)	100	120
53.	Kurt Knudsen	DET	27	R	-	-	119	119	(124)
54.	Dwayne Henry	CIN/SEA	32	R	(116)	110	97	106	128†

Of Note (less than 30 Appearances):

-	Rusty Meacham	KCR	26	R	-	(132)	76	87	(123)
-	Mark Guthrie	MIN	28	L	90	114	92	96	*
-	Jose Melendez	BOS	28	R	*	88†	91†	89	*

* Under 100 TBF-not included in average.   ( ) 100-199 TBF.   † Includes NL TPER, unadjusted to AL.

BOB PATTERSON

After a couple of very solid TPER years in the pen of the division winning Pirates (back-to-back 87 and 84), he had his second successive mediocre campaign . . . Still had remarkable control (11 BBs in 46 IP) but gave up 8 HRs and proved fairly hittable all year (.282) . . . Same problems as Ranger teammate Carpenter: 12 of 29 inherited runners scored and first batters thumped him (.320 BA) . . . Had a stretch of solid pitching (at one point allowed one run in 13 appearances) and still gets lots of strikeouts (46 in 53 IP) . . . It wasn't enough to keep the Rangers from asking "Cowboy Bob" to ride off into the sunset when the season ended.

MARK GUBICZA

One time "ace type" who's never returned to his fantastic form from shoulder surgery . . . TPER over 100 for the third time in four years . . . KC tried him in a handful of starts early and he got hammered (29 runs in 31 IP). But switched to the pen and found a home (3.61 ERA in 43 games). Thus, that 104 TPER's more than a bit deceiving. Strictly as a middleman he TPERed in the 90 area— very sound pitching . . . The good news—only two HRs allowed in 104 innings! Wow! . . . The bad news—opponents hit a whopping .307 and stole 11 of 13 . . . Had five consecutive winning seasons from '85–'89 including 20–8 in '88. Will that pitcher ever return?

JOHN HABYAN

Another mid-season addition to shore up the Royals tweener corps . . . Fantastic 71 TPER in '91 but has been slightly worse than average now two straight years . . . Another "average pitcher" profile consisting of OK control, pretty hittable (.272) and about a HR every 9 IP . . . Seven tried to steal and all made it . . . Weird: At KC this righty held LHH to a .182 while RHH banged away at a .313 clip . . . Durable middleman who, in 12 seasons as a pro, has never been on a DL. How many pitchers can say that?

STORM DAVIS

Like teammate Boever, got roughed up and then released in Oakland but then threw so well in Detroit the Tigers opted to keep him around for '94 . . . Former star starter in Baltimore who's now used as a spot-starter-longman . . . Poor control (48 BB in 98 IP) led to TPER rise for the year to 105. But erratic as he's been at times, he's still pitched decently this decade TPERing at a 102 average . . . Has now made six stops in seven years.

ED NUÑEZ

Only Eckersley appeared more out of the A's pen than did this non-roster invitee to spring training (56 G) . . . The league nailed him for a .298 BA. But they seldom took his "high forkball" out of the yard (2 HR in 75 innings) . . . Finished strong allowing just 11 hits and one run his final 13 innings pulling his TPER down to 105 . . . That's certainly not earth shattering but it's his best in three years . . . Yes, he'll be "just" thirty-one next season. Signed at age fifteen with Seattle and was a minor league starting pitcher at sixteen . . . Can still "bring it" as evidenced by 58 Ks in 75 innings.

MIKE GARDINER

Picked up when the Expos dumped him. . . . Often brilliant minor league control hasn't surfaced in the majors (walked more than he fanned last year) . . . For his career he's now 15–25 with an ERA over 5. May find chances harder and harder to come by. But scouts wonder what happened to the pitcher they saw at Williamsport in '90 whose ERA knocked their eyes out (1.90), with other league bests in innings pitched (179) and strikeouts (149) while walking just 29. Where'd he go?

GREG CADARET

One of three vets KC picked up in mid-year to flesh out their pen . . . Those mid-90 TPERs in '90 and '91 now fading into his past as he's put a couple of forgettable years back-to-back . . . His problem? Try 30 walks in 40 IP. Figure in the fact that NL hitters raked him at a .305 rate and you know why the Reds dumped him Weird "crossed" tendencies. This lefty snuffed out AL RHH (.185) but LHH tore him to pieces (.346). That's not the kind of trend you want when you're a LHP brought in to get one LHH out.

JEFF NELSON

Big (6'8"), hard thrower who some nights just seems to over-power hitters. But by season's end you wonder how in the world his TPER could be 105+ . . . Failed miserably when given the chance to be Charlton's replacement . . . Walked nearly 5 per 9 IP. Stealers successful in 10-of-11 attempts . . . Can be dazzling (appeared in 11 games in 18 days early in the year allowing just one run in that span). But he can also be frustrating (ERAs of 8.68 in August and 5.19 in September) . . . Durable—137 appearances in two years . . . One of those guys you tend to hang with (and get hanged by) because he appears to have the tools.

RICK DeLUCIA

Spent the last two months at Calgary after disappointing as a RH set-up man . . . Third straight poor TPER with the usual problems . . . Gives up lots of HRs and still yields a high number of walks (23 in 42 innings), thus turning some of those roundtrippers into three-run jobs . . . Opponents' BA tend to be high (last year .272) . . . But just when you're about to give up on him you realize he did fan 48 in just 42 innings so he has more than ordinary stuff . . . Hard to remember that just three years ago he was a member of the all-rookie team after winning a dozen games in '91.

MIKE HARTLEY

Veteran "staff filler" type who's never duplicated the 92 TPER he put up while working as a utility pitcher for LA in '90 . . . Like most of last year's Twins' hurlers, his problems revolved around his hittability (an opponent BA of .281). Combine that with 36 BBs in just 81 IP and you have the picture of a pitcher working almost constantly with runners on base. And 11-of-15 stealers also succeeded . . . Add up such numbers and you get a 111 TPER.

MIKE TIMLIN

Has never quite regained his '91 form when he posted that eye-popping 84 TPER in 63 outings . . . Injuries cut his '92 in half and he never got it going in '93. The league hit him at a .284 clip and succeeded in all nine steal attempts . . . Seven HRs in just 55 IP also helped inflate the TPER . . . But inside these full year numbers there's hope. Posted a 2.95 ERA after the break as opposed to a 5.54 before. If he's returning to form, the Jays bullpen's got a chance to be really nasty in '94.

BOB MACDONALD

Jays fans howled when Toronto simply gave him away to fellow AL East contender Detroit. But he pitched woefully (TPER 114 after a 115 the year before in Canada) . . . Eight HRs and 33 walks in 65 innings . . . Gets few DPs (3) . . . Tigers gave him every chance, actually making him a co-closer with Henneman early. And he started beautifully. Won 3 and saved 3 and had his ERA under 3 until mid-June. Then he began throwing bombs and eventually the ERA rose all the way to 5.35 . . . Made 68 appearances. But durable's not an asset unless you're pitching well.

RICH MONTELEONE

Former first-round draft pick of the Tigers in '82 who's now "hung around" bullpens in Seattle, California and NY without making much of a ripple . . . Did have two pretty decent seasons leading up to '93 (TPERs of 94 and 86), but tailed off badly last season (114) . . . Opponents' BA jumped 27 points to .262 . . . But, by far, his biggest problem (and one that afflicted most of the Yankees' relievers) concerned his tendencies to give up the long ball—14. Or, an outrageous one every 6 IP! . . . He's free so there'll be another new uniform next season.

CRAIG LEFFERTS

What happened? . . . Though never a TPER all-star, he had some decent years before his figure ballooned to 120 in '93 . . . Had a horrible time keeping the ball in the park—17 HRs in a mere 83 innings of pitching—most of them coming during an ineffective stretch early in the season when he started eight games . . . The league hit .304 against him and .367 with men on base. Ouch! . . . By year's end Texas had seen enough.

RICH GOSSAGE

Will that awful 120 TPER be a soggy exclamation point to an otherwise terrific career? . . . Bad numbers last year the result of the combination of high walk totals, lots of extra-base hits, increased hittability and stealers succeeding in 6-of-7 attempts . . . But forgive him. On July 18, with Oakland's staff hurting, they had to leave him on the mound to take a horrid beating (7 runs in two-thirds of an inning). Given how little bullpeners pitch (he had 47+ innings), that kind of outing can taint an entire season . . . How old is this Goose? When he debuted Nixon was in his first term and the major league average salary was $17,000 a year. Yeah, he's seen a whole lot happen . . . He's only 34 games short of 1,000 in his career and his ERA's still under 3 (2.98)!

KURT KNUDSEN

Second season of getting blown away out of the Tiger pen . . . Has all the wrong combinations: hittable (.281), walks far too many (57 now in 108 major league innings) and serves up way too many fat ones (9 HRs or one every *four* innings!) . . . Had terrific minor league numbers, has yet to show *anything* in the bigs.

DWAYNE HENRY

His 128 TPER's the worst of the 54 'tweeners we graded . . . His usual high-walk total (35 in only 54 IP) . . . Threw six HR balls and just three DPs . . . Terrific radar gun readings for his fastball but it's straight as the proverbial string leading to high opponent BA (.273) . . . Declining TPERs into '93 gave hope that he'd finally begun harnessing the talent that many scouts felt he had . . . Seattle was his fifth organization in six years. And there'll be another in '94. Seattle waived him at season's end.

RUSTY MEACHAM

Sore shoulder muscles limited him to 21 innings. That this ultra-skinny righty even has muscles might surprise some. Maybe the major's thinnest man and certainly one of the game's fastest workers . . . Had a fantastic '92 (TPER 76) so his loss truly damaged the KC staff . . . If he's healthy in '94, the Royals' bullpen figures as one of the strongest in the game. That's *if* he's healthy.

MARK GUTHRIE

Cross your fingers that he'll be able to return from delicate major surgery. Doctors discovered that a blood-clotting problem he'd been experiencing had been caused by pressure from a rib that had impinged a vein. Had the rib removed in late August . . . Probably best to throw out his pain-filled, limited work for the year that produced that shaky 4.71 ERA . . . He'd posted a pair of TPERs in the low 90s in two of the previous three seasons when Minnesota used this versatile pitcher in roles ranging from spot starter to middleman to emergency closer . . . The type of pitcher you don't really miss until he's gone.

JOSE MELENDEZ

The season became a total washout. Started the year on the DL with a sprained thumb. Made it back to throw in just nine games before an inflamed cervical nerve root in his neck put him down for the year . . . Put up two marvelous TPER years (88 and 91) in San Diego causing Boston to deal for him. But, oh the cost. To get him the Sox sent Phil Plantier to the Padres where he blossomed into a monster (34 HRs and 100 RBIs) . . . If he can get right by '94 Boston should have an extremely usable set-up man . . . But it'll take a bunch of beautiful pitching to make the Beantown faithful forget that he came at the cost of Plantier.

THE PITCHERS

AMERICAN LEAGUE DEBUT PITCHERS

Starters & Relievers

Rank	Pitcher	Team	7/1/94 Age	T	1993 Statistics				1993 TPER
					GS	GR	IP	ERA	
Starters:									
1.	Phil Leftwich	CAL	25	R	12	0	80.2	3.79	89
2.	Aaron Sele	BOS	24	R	18	0	111.2	2.74	90
3.	Angel Miranda	MIL	24	L	17	5	120.0	3.30	91
4.	Steve Karsay	OAK	22	R	8	0	49	4.04	96
5.	John Cummings	SEA	25	L	8	2	46.1	6.02	104
6.	Albie Lopez	CLE	22	R	9	0	49.2	5.98	111
7.	Todd Van Poppel	OAK	22	R	16	0	84.0	5.04	113
8.	Hilly Hathaway	CAL	24	L	11	0	57.1	5.02	117
9.	Greg Brummett	SFO/MIN	27	R	13	0	72.2	5.08	119
10.	Eddie Guardado	MIN	23	L	16	3	94.2	6.18	133
Utility:									
1.	Rafael Novoa	MIL	26	L	7	8	56.0	4.50	110
2.	Russ Springer	CAL	25	R	9	5	60.0	7.20	132
Relievers:									
1.	Graeme Lloyd	MIL	27	L	0	56	63.2	2.83	81
2.	Bill Wertz	CLE	27	R	0	34	59.2	3.62	94
3.	Billy Brewer	KCR	26	L	0	46	39.0	3.46	(95)
4.	Ken Ryan	BOS	25	R	0	47	50.0	3.60	97
5.	Bobby Munoz	NYY	26	R	0	38	45.2	5.32	106
6.	George Tsamis	MIN	27	L	0	41	68.1	6.19	113
7.	Mike Mohler	OAK	25	L	9	33	64.1	5.60	115
8.	Brad Pennington	BAL	25	L	0	34	33.0	6.55	(140)

* Under 100 TBF-not included in average.   ( ) 100-199 TBF.   † Includes NL TPER, unadjusted to AL.

PHIL LEFTWICH

Former second-round draft choice who wasn't even invited to spring training and wound up as perhaps the most pleasant pitching surprise of the season . . . "Experts" would be astounded to find he TPERed better than Boston phenom Sele . . . Allowed just 5 HRs in 80 innings . . . Didn't allow a long ball in his last 11 starts in AAA . . . Walk totals reasonably low as they've been throughout his minor league career . . . Runners swiped just 4 of 8 . . . Minor league projections tabbed him as the best of the Angels' starting prospects and he pitched like it when opportunity knocked.

AARON SELE

An amazing debut season . . . Started 18 times and never allowed more than three runs. Would have had an even gaudier record than 7–2 but his pen blew four games he left with the lead. . . . Remarkable poise for a player in just his third year and summoned from the minors to replace the injured Clemens in the rotation. But rotation's what got Sele here—fantastic rotation on his curve ball that often appears to drop two feet or more on its way home . . . Hardly ever "hangs one"—just 5 HRs in 111 innings . . . Control could use some sharpening. Must stop runners a bit better (8 for 9). But those criticisms amount to nit-picking.

ANGEL MIRANDA

Promising debut for a skinny lefty who's been a pro for seven seasons now but is still just 24 . . . Prepped in the minors mainly as a reliever but thrust into the Brewer rotation when Boddicker retired in early July . . . Put up some intriguing numbers: Opponents hit just .226 against him and he averaged 6.6 strikeouts per 9 IP . . . Homer and walk totals a bit high but that's the norm with youngsters . . . Began the year on the DL with a shoulder strain. By mid-season the strength had returned and radar gun operators all over the league wondered how such a slender kid could consistently throw in the 90s . . . Looks like a comer.

STEVE KARSAY

Acquired for Rickey H. in the Toronto trade and TPERed well in eight late-season starts (96). . . . Oakland should be encouraged by just 16 BBs in 49 IP and only 4 HRs. . . . Skipped his final scheduled start to stop at 49 innings, one inning short of the cutoff point for 1994 Rookie-of-the-Year candidates . . . Still only 22 so there's lots of time for this former high draft pick who once skipped a minor league start to head home and attend a high school prom with his girlfriend.

JOHN CUMMINGS

Made eight emergency starts when injuries in the opening weeks hit the rotation. Didn't pitch nearly as badly as his 0–6 record indicates though the league did tattoo him for a .316 average . . . Decent control. Runners just 2-of-6 stealing and 7 DPs in 46 IP . . . Forgive his numbers since he was trying to make the jump from Class A ball (16–6 at Peninsula in '92) to the majors in '93.

ALBIE LOPEZ

Got a mid-season look-see after putting up encouraging numbers in AA . . . His good minor league strikeouts-to-walks ratio turned around when he hit the bigs (32 BB and 25 K) . . . Tended to give up the long ball . . . Went to Triple A after being demoted and pitched well . . . But his minor league pitching profile reflects the same problems he experienced on the major league level—too many walks and a well-above average number of long ones.

TODD VAN POPPEL

The Phenom arrived and, after the usual period of adjustment, acquitted himself well. Got hammered in his first four starts (ERA 7.47). But by year's end the record had evened out at 6–6 and the ERA came down to 5.04 . . . His TPER settled at 113. But it's not gonna get drastically lower if he doesn't start throwing some strikes. Walked 62 in 84 innings and 23 of them scored. They represented 46% of all runs he allowed in his 16 starts . . . You know he has the "stuff" from the league's low .243 BA against him. So, if he gets that stuff over at a much better rate he'll be nasty. And his minor league profile suggests that's his only real problem . . . But it is a *real* problem.

HILLY HATHAWAY

Young lefty got hit hard in his first trip around the major league block surrendering a .326 opponent BA . . . But the wildest and most worrisome numbers were his BB-to-K ratio. How about 26 walks and only 11 strikeouts? Sadly, that's the picture his minor league projections painted . . . Survived thanks to 11 DPs . . . Did have some arm trouble that lost him three weeks on the DL . . . If his future performance is as regal as his full name (Houston Hillary Hathaway III), Cal will be overjoyed.

GREG BRUMMETT

That 119 TPER's not much of an encouragement. But his minor league numbers are . . . AL and NL hitters combined to bat over .300 against him . . . Gets decent movement low in the strike zone leading to 11 DPs in just 73 innings . . . But must hold runners better. Permitted 12 steals (1 CS) . . . Minor league profile suggests he's a pitcher with well above average control who won't be bothered by HRs . . . College World Series MVP with Wichita State in '89.

EDDIE GUARDADO

Chunky lefty jumped from Double A to the majors and often didn't appear ready for such a sizable step-up in class . . . Hitters feasted on him (BA .319, plus 13 HRs in just 95 innings) . . . That's the stuff terrible TPERs are made of and his was terrible—133 . . . But ignore these ugly numbers (if you can) and check out those he posted down below. From mid-'92 through early '93 he'd won 11 straight decisions in 17 starts with an ERA in the 1.5 area. Minor league profile has all the right elements: high in Ks and low in hits, BBs and HRs . . . He's just 23 and you tend to excuse '93 as nothing more than a year in which the pitching-starved Twins rushed him to the bigs.

RAFAEL NOVOA

The Giants simply gave up on him after an injury-interrupted '91 season. Milwaukee grabbed him, sent him to their minors and maybe, just maybe, found something . . . Poor strikeouts-to-walks numbers (17 Ks and 22 BBs). But the year before at Triple A he fanned nearly three for everyone he walked so maybe his '93 was just rookie nerves . . . In '90, during his second pro season, SF called him to Phoenix to pitch against the parent Giants in an exhibition. He fanned seven in five innings including Will Clark, Kevin Mitchell and Matt Williams in order in the third inning . . . So, why'd they dump this supposedly hot prospect a year later?

RUSS SPRINGER

A major disappointment . . . Began the year as a rotation possibility. Pitched his way back to the minors with a woeful spring ERA of 6.75. . . . Made it back by June 3, but the numbers got no better. That 132 TPER's the result of many factors like 32 walks and 11 HRs in just 60 innings . . . Stealers ran at will (11 of 12) . . . Opponents batted a robust .303 . . . Season ended August 2 with a cracked facet joint in the lower back . . . Cal hopes that injury's the reason for the poor showing of this "key" player in the deal that sent Jim Abbott packing off to the Big Apple.

GRAEME LLOYD

A real find! Burst into the Brewers' pen setting a club record for rookie appearances—55 . . . Didn't allow an earned run over a 22.2 inning stretch from April 25 to June 4 . . . Did allow 5 HRs, but three of them came in his first eight innings of work. Just two in his last 55 . . . Remarkable control, especially for a young, string bean (6'7") lefty, walking a mere 13 hitters in those 63 innings (three were intentional!) . . . Only two runners even attempted steals! . . . Landed on the DL late in the season with a tired arm . . . By then AL hitters had become tired of him and his 81 TPER.

BILL WERTZ

Former 31st rounder who's put up terrific minor league numbers the last three years. His pitching profile down below showed excellent control, and well above average tendencies in all other areas . . . Debuted with a very nice 94 TPER for 34 appearances . . . Just one attempted steal against him! . . . Yielded only 5 HRs in 59 innings and the league could muster just a .238 BA against him . . . All in all, an exceptional beginning for a hurler who'd never thrown a pitch above the AA level when the year began.

BILLY BREWER

Forced his way on to the Royals staff in the spring after being scooped out of the Expos' system in the Rule 5 draft . . . A spot lefty who's truly devastating against LHH. They managed a mere .183 average against him (11 for 60) . . . Other Royals pitchers loved him as he allowed just 4 of 35 inherited runners to score . . . Threw 7 DPs in just 39 innings . . . TPER would have dropped into the terrific area but for 20 walks and 6 HRs in 39 innings . . . Given how little he cost, he qualifies as a minor steal.

KEN RYAN

Another Ryan with an "express" . . . Throws high heat—95 MPH plus. That brought him a strikeout per inning . . . As you might expect, control's a bit shaky at times. . . . Yielded only a pair of HRs in 50 IP . . . Some envision him as the Sox closer-of-the-future. Other scouts claim his fastball, though very fast, lacks the necessary movement . . . But this kind of arm doesn't come along very often, especially when you consider no one drafted him out of high school and Boston signed him as an amateur free agent.

BOBBY MUNOZ

Looks like an NBA power forward—6'7" and (at least) 237 pounds . . . Yanks switched him from starting to relieving in the minors to begin last season . . . was "yanked" up to the big leagues in late May . . . His 106 TPER would become much better if he'd throw strikes (26 walks in 45+ IP) . . . Stealers a perfect 6 for 6 . . . But he does keep the ball in the yard—only one HR . . . No question his arm's big time. So's his control problem.

GEORGE TSAMIS

Mediocre to poor numbers across the board in his debut season . . . A .317 opponent BA, 9 HRs in just 68 IP, a 27 BB to 30 K ratio . . . TPERed at 113. But that number would have exploded if were not for his extraordinary control of runners: Threw 10 DP balls and stealers were shutout (0 for 4) . . . Stuff looked very ordinary at times from this former Little League World Series star who pitched against Taiwan at Williamsport in 1979. (So, he at least should know how to get "older hitters" out.)

MIKE MOHLER

Young lefty who worked his way from a 42nd round pick in '89 to the Oakland pen in '93 . . . Batters had trouble hitting him (.241). But he had awful control (44 BB in 64 IP) and threw far too many "fat ones" allowing 10 taters . . . Especially effective against LHH (.183 BA) and maybe that's a clue to his future bullpen role . . . Had shoulder surgery after the season . . . But he's young and left-handed and, if healthy, you know he'll get his chances.

BRAD PENNINGTON

The ultimate "live arm." But often he hasn't the foggiest idea of where it's going when he turns it loose . . . Extremely high walk totals have plagued him at every level and accompanied him to the majors for his debut season in '93 . . . When behind in the count he appeared to "let up" a bit thereby making him unusually hittable (for him) at .266. And seven of those hits cleared the fence in just 33 IP . . . But the radar gun loves him and, if he ever learns to get it over the plate, hitters'll hate him.

NATIONAL LEAGUE ROTATION STARTERS

Top Quarter:

Rank	Pitcher	Team	7/1/94 Age	T	1990	1991	1992	3 yr Avg.	1993 TPER
						TPER Trendline			
1.	Billy Swift	SFO	32	R	81†	57†	73	72	70
2.	Greg Maddux	ATL	28	R	87	88	75	83	74
3.	Jose Rijo	CIN	29	R	84	77	82	81	80
4.	John Burkett	SFO	29	R	94	100	99	98	80
5.	Steve Avery	ATL	24	L	122	93	94	99	81
6.	Terry Mulholland	PHI	31	L	89	89	85	88	83
7.	Mark Portugal	HOU	31	R	96	102	86	96	84
8.	Pete Harnisch	HOU	27	R	106†	92	103	100	86
9.	Pedro Astacio	LAD	24	R	-	-	74	74	87
10	Tommie Greene	PHI	27	R	114	96	131	106	88
11.	Ken Hill	MTL	28	R	113	93	97	98	89
12.	Tom Candiotti	LAD	36	R	96†	86†	97	93	90
13.	Darryl Kile	HOU	25	R	-	118	115	117	90
14.	Dwight Gooden	NYM	29	R	97	95	98	97	91
15.	Curt Schilling	PHI	27	R	83†	106	73	81	91
16.	Rene Arocha	STL	28	R	-	-	-	-	91

* Under 100 TBF-not included in average. ( ) 100-199 TBF. † Includes AL TPER, unadjusted to NL.

BILLY SWIFT

The question had never been whether he could be an effective starter but rather how long it would be before he broke down. The durability question that dogged him in Seattle and San Francisco seemed to be resurfacing when he went into a seven-start slump in mid-August. But he emerged from it to post the league's best starter TPER . . . No surprise to TPER followers given he'd had an almost identical '92 and an unbelievable '91 out of the Seattle pen . . . Shuts hitters down on every TPER front . . . Allowed just 18 HRs, one every 11⅔ innings. Held opposing hitters to a measly .226 BA, fifth best in the NL. Outstanding control—a mere 55 BBs in 232.2 IP. Ground-ball pitcher whose sinker induces plenty of DPs (27). In short, if you drew up the ideal starter, he'd be it . . . Also, a member of the rare NL pitchers 20–20 club—21 wins and 21 hits.

GREG MADDUX

Another season in TPER heaven . . . First pitcher to ever win the Cy Young back-to-back with different teams . . . Winningest pitcher in the majors the last six years with 107 victories. Clemens next at 103 . . . First Brave to lead in ERA (2.36) since Buzz Capra in 1974 (2.28) . . . In his 10 losses Atlanta scored a total of 15 runs . . . Unlike Swift, durability's his calling card—six consecutive seasons of 230+ innings . . . Control has reached the unbelievable stage— about 1¾ BBs per 9 IP. Despite throwing all those strikes he seldom gets taken downtown—1 HR every 19 IP. Stretch run ERA of 1.85 in last 17 starts makes him the probable choice of the pitcher you'd name if your job depended on winning one game . . . Victory total might have been higher had the Atlanta defense not leaked mysteriously behind him—15 of the 85 runs he allowed were unearned.

JOSE RIJO

No wonder he broke down and cried after one particularly frustrating game late in the year. Managed only 14 wins despite posting another banner TPER season that brings his TPER average for the decade dead even with Maddux as the league's two premier starters over that four-year period . . . Five times the Cincy bullpen blew ninth-inning leads that cost him victories . . . #2 in the majors in Ks, #3 in ERA and innings pitched . . . In his nine losses the Reds scored just eight runs total . . . His 7.9 Ks per 9 IP the best of the league. His 2.2 BBs per 9 was ninth best . . . Once went 12 consecutive starts without allowing more than two runs . . . Did allow 19 HRs but an astounding 18 of them were solos . . . Defensively did not commit an error and *offensively* had an eight-game hit streak! . . . Last Red to lead the NL in Ks? Ewell "The Whip" Blackwell in 1947 . . . Has now posted six consecutive winning seasons, the longest string of any active pitcher.

JOHN BURKETT

His 22 Ws were the most by a Giants, pitcher since Ron "Teddy Bear" Bryant's 24 in 1973 . . . Utterly incredible control—40 walks in 231 innings. Didn't walk a single man in 13 of his 34 starts including one string of 124 batters without issuing a freebie . . . Struggled through seven minor league seasons getting just a cup of coffee with the Giants late in the '87 season and seemed doomed to a life of being a Triple A starter when Giants pitchers began dropping like flies in 1990. The call went out for Burkett and the rest, as they say, is history. Led major league rookie hurlers that year with 14 wins. Now has 61 the last four seasons, behind only Maddux and Glavine in the NL . . . Also a bowling star who's rolled four perfect games, entered several pro tournaments and averaged as high as 215 in league bowling . . . But of these, the accomplishment he might be proudest of concerns his hitting. Once a certain out (1 for 55 in '92), he literally exploded with a 9-hit season.

STEVE AVERY

The four pitchers who posted TPERs superior to Avery's are all righties and all from four to eight years older . . . Seldom does one so young reach ace status so quickly. And check his TPER trendline. What if the improvement he's shown every year continues. How low can he go? . . . Braves finished 28–7 in games he started including a stretch from May 2 through September 2 in which they went an unreal 21–2 . . . Walks reached a career low. Led the NL with 15 pickoffs . . . Now has 50 wins at age 23. Koufax had 20. Carlton had 14. Spahn had none. Ryan had 19. Seaver had 32.

TERRY MULHOLLAND

Those who check our TPER trends won't be shocked by high standing. Has pitched well all four of his Phillie seasons. It's just that the rest of the team was so miserable nobody noticed . . .

Suddenly the Phils got hot and Mulholland started the All-Star game . . . Now 50–43 the last four seasons for a team that's four games under .500 for that period . . . Ground-ball pitcher with terrific control (under 2 BBs per 9 IP) who's impossible to run on.

MARK PORTUGAL

Put up huge numbers in his free agent season, something to be leery of if you're the purchaser of his services for '94 . . . Won his last 12 decisions, the majors longest win streak of '93 . . . Remarkably consistent permitting three earned runs or less in 29 of 33 starts . . . But why'd he suddenly go 18–4 after being 27–25 the previous three seasons? His walks declined and he kept the ball in the yard. . . . Also threw 17 DP balls while permitting just 14 SBs, outstanding control of runners . . . Will he duplicate his numbers for his new employers? See the free agent notes.

PETE HARNISCH

Toughest to hit in the NL. Opposing hitters "banged him around" to the tune of .214 . . . Two near misses with no-hitters broken up by the Cubs' Mark Grace and the Padres' Jarvis Brown . . . Like teammate Portugal, got on a real roll after the All-Star break: 8–3, 2.11 ERA in 14 starts . . . TPER seems to be falling into a good-year-bad-year pattern. But he's just 27 and eligible to start putting good seasons back-to-back—a pattern many of those listed above him on the TPER list exhibited . . . What a steal Houston made when they got him, starting CF Steve Finley and now star Philly pitcher Curt Schilling all for Glenn Davis whose career may be over.

PEDRO ASTACIO

At 24 he's already the ace of the staff . . . Burst on the scene in '92 with that remarkable 74 TPER fueled by four shutouts in 11 starts . . . Finished '93 with a rush winning six of his last seven and at one point being scored on in only two of 42 innings during the streak . . . Tremendous poise for one so young. Already has excellent control and command of an off-speed pitch . . . Has now permitted just 15 HRs in 268 IP in the majors . . . You look at numbers like these and then at his age and wonder what he'll be like if he keeps improving.

TOMMIE GREENE

Literally unbeatable at home: 10–0 during the regular season . . . TPER's dramatic drop attributable to one specific improvement. Walks dropped from over 4½ per 9 IP to under 3. That's a monster move for a pitcher and often signals his "arrival" as a big timer . . . Opposing hitters managed just a .233 average and a mere 12 dingers. Began the year 8–0. Last Philly to do that was "Lefty" (Steve Carlton) in '81 . . . Actually left spring training as the team's #5 starter. But those days are over . . . If you think Atlanta's staff with Avery, Maddux, Glavine and Smoltz scares you, consider they tossed Greene into a deal with the Phils in 1990 that brought only Jeff Parrett and two spare parts in return.

KEN HILL

Was putting together a phenomenal season before a groin pull, May 21, complicated the last four months. Was 5–0 at the time. Tried to keep pitching with the injury but eventually landed on the DL and then posted just a 3–7 mark after the All-Star break . . . TPER drop traces to his total of just seven HRs allowed. In his first 18 starts he permitted just three HRs in 123 IP. All were solo shots. And all hit by the Mets the night of May 16 . . . As long as the groin pull's healed, Hill's numbers should continue to improve.

TOM CANDIOTTI

Yet another terrific year for one of the least noticed star hurlers in the majors . . . With 32 starts he's now made at least 29 every year since 1986 and pitched more than 200 innings for an eighth straight year . . . Excellent control for a knuckleballer (precisely one walk every three IP) . . . But terrible run support and a shaky defense that permitted a dozen unearned runs behind him doomed him to 8–10 record, leaving him at 103–103 despite a career ERA of 3.41 and TPERs that keep suggesting he should win more . . . But that's a heckuva run for a player considered so undertalented that he wasn't drafted coming out of St. Mary's (California) in 1979 . . . Has the strangest "assortment" in the majors, mixing knucklers and a big breaking slow curve.

DARRYL KILE

A breakthrough season. Again it's partially traceable to walks. Lowered his BBs per 9 IP nearly a full walk . . . Like many other star pitchers he was stingy with the long ball—just 11 . . . But for one so young Kile's ability to control runners stands out. Stealers, what there were of them, managed just 9 of 14. And that helped him coax 16 DPs. When your DPs exceed your SBs allowed you're doing one fine job . . . No-hit the Mets with only a walk to Jeff McKnight spoiling the perfecto . . . Kile's gem was the club's ninth since 1962—the most by any team during that period. The Dodgers and Angels teams have had eight. Nolan Ryan had seven . . . Note that while the Atlanta and SF staffs got most of the attention, the Astros had three of the top 13 TPERs in the NL.

DWIGHT GOODEN

The Doctor Is In! Back in! . . . After three mediocre TPER seasons, Gooden hinted he might be returning to prominence . . . Oh, the old Gooden's probably gone for good—the one that simply blew hitters away with a riding fastball and a knee-buckling curve . . . But at 29, with 154 victories and more than 2,100 innings behind him, he's now got the advantage of experience to blend with his still considerable stuff . . . Career-high 15 losses leave his lifetime record at 154–81, a percentage of 65.9. Slightly ahead of Clemens who broke in the same year (1984) and is 163–86 (65.5%) . . . That still leaves Doc #9 on the all-time list for best career winning percentage. (By the way the leader is Dave "Scissors" Foutz who won 69% in a career that stretched from 1884 to 1894.)

CURT SCHILLING

A third Philly pitcher in the top 15 and, like Greene, he's just approaching "prime time" . . . Solid season but as his TPER history suggests nowhere near as well as he pitched in '92 . . . ERA jumped 1⅔ runs per game but his record actually improved significantly from 14–11 to 16–7. Such can be the advantages of pitching for a suddenly-much-better team. But TPER measures pitching efficiency only—how well a hurler did his job. And this season Schilling fell off. Still very solid. But 23 HRs allowed led the Phils, and way up from 11 the season before . . . But all in all another very solid season for a man who has a dog named "Slider." Says Schilling: "I can't throw one so I bought one."

RENE AROCHA

Went from a spring non-roster player to the top TPER starter on the Redbirds . . . Had just 25 minor league starts under his belt after defecting from Cuba to the US in July of '91 . . . Opponents hit a robust .271 against him with 20 HRs. But what they got off him they earned. He gave the opposition a scant 31 walks—1.48 per 9 IP, second best in the league to teammate Tewksbury . . . Had a string of 25.2 innings without a walk at one point . . . Don't think of him as an inexperienced pitcher though. Recorded 100 wins pitching in Cuba before "escaping" to America.

NATIONAL LEAGUE ROTATION STARTERS

Second Quarter:

Rank	Pitcher	Team	7/1/94 Age	T	TPER Trendline 1990	1991	1992	3 yr Avg.	1993 TPER
17.	Tom Glavine	ATL	28	L	104	79	80	87	92
18.	Orel Hershiser	LAD	35	R	*	89	99	96	92
19.	Mike Morgan	CUB	34	R	94	76	87	84	92
20.	Andy Benes	SDO	26	R	87	87	97	94	94
21.	John Smoltz	ATL	27	R	95	90	89	91	94
22.	Doug Drabek	HOU	31	R	79	99	79	85	94
23.	Danny Jackson	PHI	32	L	100	136	102	107	96
24.	Donovan Osborne	STL	25	L	-	-	101	101	96
25.	Chris Hammond	FLA	28	L	*	93	106	100	96
26.	Bob Tewksbury	STL	33	R	86	99	77	87	97
27.	Chris Nabholz	MTL	27	L	83	83	96	89	97
28.	Greg Hibbard	CUB	29	L	83	89	101	91	98
29.	Eric Hillman	NYM	28	L	-	-	121	121	98
30.	Jim Deshaies	MIN/SFO	34	L	107	114	91	106	98†
31.	Ramon Martinez	LAD	26	R	86	89	108	93	98
32.	Kevin Gross	LAD	33	R	109	110	96	104	99

* Under 100 TBF-not included in average. ( ) 100-199 TBF. † Includes AL TPER, unadjusted to NL.

TOM GLAVINE

Just keeps winning—a third consecutive 20-win season. Last NLer to do that was Fergie Jenkins who had six straight 20-win seasons '67–'72 . . . TPER actually rose last season . . . ERA up nearly a half run. Walks rose also . . . Former fourth-round draft pick of the NHL LA Kings who does a terrific job of "checking" runners allowing just 9-of-14 steals . . . Got off to his usual fast start—13–4 through July bringing his record in those months since '91 to 43–12. But also did the unusual for him—finishing fast (9–2).

OREL HERSHISER

The only man in baseball to have wonderful TPER *and* TOPR seasons . . . Rang up his third solid season since recovering from major shoulder surgery that wiped out the '90 season and forced him to learn how to pitch all over again . . . Slowly but, it appears, surely, his strikeout pitch is returning. Walking a few more than he used to though . . . Would have been better than 12–14 had the horrible Dodger defense not leaked 20 unearned runs behind him. Ugh! . . . Meanwhile, put aside Hershiser the pitcher for a moment and turn to him as a hitter. Would you believe a .356 average? Only a 103 TOPR, though (no power) . . . But the best news of all is still that he made 33 starts for a second consecutive year. Not bad for a pitcher that many felt was finished three seasons ago.

MIKE MORGAN

What a long, strange road it's been. If it seems like he's been around forever it's because he has! Stepped out of Las Vegas' Valley High and right into Charlie Finley's Oakland circus in '78 at age 18 . . . Never had a winning major league season until his 14–10 with LA in '91 with that borderline spectacular 76 TPER . . . Has now strung together four decent seasons this decade averaging 33 starts and 224 innings a year but just three more wins than losses . . . ERA leaped a run-and-a-half mainly because he became more hittable. Opponent BA rose from .234 to .262 . . . A durable, dependable third-starter type. Just one problem with that. Note he's the first Cub listed. Like it or not, he was their ace.

ANDY BENES

Outstanding stuff and much pursued in the trade market. But somehow his TPERs never quite leap to the upper echelon . . . ERA rose to its highest in his 5-year career though a still very respectable 3.78 . . . Strikeouts-to-walks ratio changed negatively from nearly 3–1 in '92 down to 2–1 last season . . . Can be run on: stealers succeeded 21 of 28 . . . Taken deep 23 times . . . None of the previous numbers are awful. But together they paint a picture of a talented and still very young pitcher who's only a notch or two away from stardom. Maybe a change of scenery's what he needs.

JOHN SMOLTZ

Second in the league in IP (243+) and Ks (208) . . . The only starters harder to hit than his .230 were Harnisch, Swift and Rijo. That's right, Smoltz was the hardest to hit of this hard to hit rotation . . . TPER stayed above the others because of his control more than a walk per 9 IP higher than Avery or Maddux . . . His 15–11 record could have been better. He didn't seem to benefit much from the Braves' last half flood of runs. In 10 of his losses the club tallied just 16 total runs . . . Death to RHH—.199 BA . . . But despite his remarkable stuff he gives up a higher number of taters than you'd think (23) . . . The '87 deal that brought him turned into one of those clichéd "trades that helped both teams." Detroit got Doyle Alexander and a division title that year. Atlanta's now won the West three times with Smoltz approaching ace-level.

DOUG DRABEK

The Astros paid big money for the TPERs he posted in '90 and '92 (79 and 79). Instead they got the Drabek of '91 (99) . . . Nine wins represented the fewest in his eight-season career. His 18 losses mark his most ever and the most in the NL . . . Deserved a better fate as the 'Stros could manage but 30 total runs in those 18 defeats including being shutout three times and getting a single run six times . . . But he chipped in with his own set of negative numbers. Opponent BA leaped 36 points to .267 . . . Runners swiped 28 of 35 . . . And 12 wild pitches? From a "control artist"? That big, snapping curve can cost you a base at times when it bounces . . . Has now thrown at least 219 innings every year since '88.

DANNY JACKSON

Finally got his TPER beneath 100 for the first time this decade . . . Allowed just 12 HRs. But only 6 left the yard in '92. Excellent totals for a guy who's thrown over 200 innings each year . . . Opposing teams' BA dropped a bit. Threw 15 DPs. . . . Won his 10th on August 24 becoming the fifth of the Phils five-man rotation to reach double figures in wins . . . Remember that spectacular '88 season in which he went 23–8 with a 2.73 ERA and 15 CGs for the Reds? Since them he's 33–46 with only last year's TPER dipping below 100.

DONOVAN OSBORNE

Young lefty making strides as he approaches his mid-20s . . . TPER dipped from his rookie 101 to 96 . . . Solid control (what else do you expect for a Cardinals pitcher?) which also leads to being a bit homer-prone (18 in 155 IP) . . . Outstanding at stifling the running game. Just four steals in nine attempts (remember, in 155 IP) with 13 DPs . . . Won six in a row in mid-season but sat out the last month with shoulder tendinitis . . . Tough on LHH (.205 BA with but 2 HRs) . . . His 3.76 ERA the best in the rotation . . . One worry. In both the minors and majors his profile suggests he's very hittable, especially by RHH. Does he need an extra pitch to use against them? If he finds one watch out.

CHRIS HAMMOND

A club-leading 11 wins to go with a solid 96 TPER . . . Included in that 11-victory season was an eight-game win streak . . . Then he immediately lost seven straight . . . Superb command of runners allowing just 5-of-11 stealers to succeed and inducing a terrific 20 DPs . . . For a soft-toss lefty doesn't 10 wild pitches seem a bit odd? . . . Surrendered 18 HRs but 11 of those came in his first 64 IP. Only 7 over his final 126+ innings.

BOB TEWKSBURY

You'll never see him doing commercials trying to sell you a "Walkman" . . . Nearly became the first man to ever win more than he walked in the history of starting pitchers (17 wins—20 BBs). And he'd have done it had he not encountered a streak of uncharacteristic "wildness" walking an outrageous 14 batters in his last 13 starts. (For him that constitutes being "all over the place.") . . . Had walkless streaks of 55.1 and 35 innings . . . Fanned 97 to lead the Cards, the lowest staff-leading total (other than a strike year) since the '51 Cards . . . Allowed an NL high 258 hits (opponent BA .303) . . . Excellent all-around player fielding 65 times without an error and getting 14 hits as a batter. Drove in the game winner for himself twice . . . His 33 wins over the last two years trail only Glavine (42) and Maddux (40) in the NL.

CHRIS NABHOLZ

His fourth consecutive below-100 TPER (97) . . . If only his control were better. In '91 he passed just over 3 per 9 IP. By last season that figure had grown to more than 4½ per 9. That accounts for his rising TPER . . . Remains very difficult to hit (.236) with but 9 HRs in 161+ innings . . . Decent command of opposing runners and induced a dozen DPs . . . Add to those 63 walks, 8 HBP and 7 WPs. His erratic performances got him a ticket to Ottawa in late May . . . Aching forearm cost him six weeks late in the year . . . Weird: Since opening day '92, when he's started for the Expos following a Montreal win, he's 3–14 . . . Has completed only four of 88 major league starts, but he's an inch away from acedom.

GREG HIBBARD

His 15 victories represented the most by a Cubs lefty since Ken Holtzman won 17 in 1970 . . . TPER remained under 100 (98) because of his fantastic command of opposing runners. He threw an amazing 24 DP balls. In 191+ innings only *two* runners managed to steal out of the 12 who tried. Adding those two areas together gave him 34 outs after an opponent reached base. That can make a huge difference over the course of a season . . . He

remained very hittable (.286) . . . But his exceptional control further stifled opposing attacks (just 47 walks or 2.2 per 9 IP) . . . Eventually totaled nine starts in which he walked no one . . . His 15–11 season should be a lesson to younger pitchers. If you consistently throw strikes, work hard on holding runners and keeping the ball down so it stays in the park and there's a chance to get two for one—you can give up hits and still win. It's often not what a batter earns that beats a pitcher, it's what the pitcher gives for free that beats him.

ERIC HILLMAN

His 98 TPER's a testament to his control. While the league battered him for a .299 average he walked only 24 in 145+ innings. Went 38.2 innings without passing anyone over a seven-week period . . . Boasts a sparkling career 1.55 BBs per 9 IP . . . Did a decent job of keeping the ball in play (only 12 HRs) . . . Mets' "defense" really hurt him (19 of his 83 runs allowed unearned) . . . Hadn't won in 12 starts before beating St. Louis in his season finale . . . Joins Seattle's Randy Johnson as the two tallest pitchers in baseball history at 6' 10".

JIM DESHAIES

Veteran lefty who keeps turning up in rotations because he's durable and dependable. Made 31 starts between Minnesota and the Giants, stretch drive, the seventh time in his eight years he'd made at least 26 starts in a season . . . Combined TPER of 98 based on a remarkable ability to completely erase the opponents' running game. Of the 26 who attempted to steal, a meager 8 succeeded. That's 18 outs he got after a runner had reached base. Threw 18 DPs. There's 18 more. That's a total of 12 full innings, worth of outs he recorded once someone had reached base. That's sensational! . . . That also helped control big innings because he's homer-prone yielding 26 of them . . . Spring will arrive and someone will have found a rotation spot for him.

RAMON MARTINEZ

After wonderful TPERs of 86 and 89 to begin the decade, he's had the look of a pretty average pitcher the last couple years . . . A case of "tennis elbow" could be blamed in '92 . . . In '93 point a finger at wildness . . . Led the NL with 104 walks . . . Pretty middle-of-the-road numbers across the rest of his stat board . . . But there's a larger question about him. Did LA overuse him in '90–'91 when, as a 22/23-year old, he threw 455 innings? Check what's happened since those heavy workloads at his young age. After going 20–6 and 17–13 he's dipped to 8–11 and 10–12. The two worst ERAs of his five years have come back-to-back the last two seasons. Such numbers can still be affected by things somewhat out of a pitcher's control. But the strikeouts-to-walks ratio is all his own doing and his should put some furrows in LA brows. In '90 it was a dazzling 3.3 to 1. In '91 it slipped to 2.2 to 1. The descent continued in '92 to 1.5 to 1. Last year? 1.2 to 1. Are these totals telling us something? Maybe it's nothing more than the ups and downs of a young pitcher's career . . . Hopefully . . . Maybe.

KEVIN GROSS

Won his final four starts to get even (13–13) for the year, his highest win total since his career-high 15 with the '85 Phils. That by the way, also happens to be the last winning record he's had. Since '85 he's 84–103 . . . Extremely hittable veteran (.282). But relatively acceptable totals everywhere else including 14 DPs and 10 runners caught stealing . . . Over 200 innings pitched for the seventh time in nine years . . . His 12–1 triumph over SF on the final day eliminated the Giants. It marked the 21st time in his 32 starts that the normally subdued LA offense had gotten him four or more runs . . . Wags will point out he hasn't had a winning season since the NL suspended him in '87 for using sandpaper.

NATIONAL LEAGUE ROTATION STARTERS

Third Quarter:

Rank	Pitcher	Team	7/1/94 Age	T	1990	1991	1992	3 yr Avg.	1993 TPER
33.	Charlie Hough	FLA	46	R	107†	100†	96†	102	99
34.	Scott Sanderson	CAL/SFO	37	R	109	88	117	104	102†
35.	Rheal Cormier	STL	27	L	-	90	98	95	102
36.	Dennis Martinez	MTL	39	R	80	81	76	79	104
37.	Ryan Bowen	FLA	26	R	-	115	(189)	139	104
38.	Steve Cooke	PIT	24	L	-	-	*	*	104
39.	Greg Swindell	HOU	29	L	102†	83†	90	92	106
40.	Mike Harkey	CUB	27	R	90	*	110	94	107
41.	Armando Reynoso	COL	28	R	-	(151)	*	(151)	107
42.	Jose Guzman	CUB	31	R	DNP	90†	98†	94	108
43.	Greg W. Harris	SDO/COL	30	R	90	90	107	95	113
44.	Bob Walk	PIT	37	R	103	94	103	100	113
45.	Tim Pugh	CIN	27	R	-	-	(97)	(97)	114
46.	Ben Rivera	PHI	25	R	-	-	100	100	114
47.	Frank Castillo	CUB	25	R	-	91	100	97	114
48.	Doug Brocail	SDO	27	R	-	-	*	*	114

* Under 100 TBF-not included in average. ( ) 100-199 TBF. † Includes AL TPER, unadjusted to NL.

CHARLIE HOUGH

This old geezer just keeps punching his time clock reporting for work. And work he did—a staff leading 204+ innings at age 45 . . . His 9–16 record's more than a bit deceiving. The Marlins gave him two or fewer runs in 16 of his 34 starts . . . Became the first major league pitcher to ever have 400 starts and 400 relief appearances in a career . . . He's now reached 200 innings nine times, yet he didn't even become a starter until he turned 34 . . . His 99 TPER featured solid-across-the-board numbers including a .259 opponent BA, 19 steals against but also 14 caught stealings and only 3.1 walks per 9 IP—very low for a knuckleballer . . . Singled on June 4. His last hit also a single—came on June 4, 1980. He's only the 13th player to get a hit after his 45th birthday. . . . Next season will be his 25th in the majors. Two more and he ties former Texas teammate Nolan Ryan for the all-time record . . . How old is he? Since he turned pro there've been seven different presidents.

SCOTT SANDERSON

Another vet who's begun bouncing around the bigs . . . four stops so far this decade . . . TPER of 102 accomplished despite horrible problems with HRs (27 including 12 in just 48 SF innings) . . . That his TPER stayed below *four figures* with that kind of "long-ball-itis" tells you that he continues to have outstanding control (a mere 34 walks in 183 innings)! . . . Induced 13 DPs while yielding just 7 SBs in 13 attempts . . . Came flying out of the gate with a 7–2 mark in California. Hit the skids losing 9 straight before being waived and grabbed by Frisco. How many would guess he's won 67 games the last five years. Or that he's now a 154-game winner for his career?

RHEAL CORMIER

"Un-Rheal" ability to get the DP inducing 16 of them. Runners have given up even thinking about running on him—only five attempts in 145+ innings. Control of baserunners helped lower his TPER to 102 . . . But the league batted a solid .284 against him (with 18 HR) . . . Like most of the Cards' staff, refused to give in and walk anyone (27) . . . Overall, TPER has slowly moved in the wrong direction in his three seasons (90–98–102) . . . For the second straight year he struggled early and finished fast . . . '93 troubles might be traced to an aching shoulder that disabled him for 25 days . . . How'd the Expos miss drafting this native of Moncton, New Brunswick?

DENNIS MARTINEZ

The league literally stole him blind last season. Until '93 he'd been decent at holding runners. In '90 stealers went 19 for 28. Then next season they swiped 22 of 30. In '92 to run against him was counterproductive (22 of 42). What happened last season? Stealers succeeded at the unthinkable rate of 49 for 55. THIS IS NOT A MISPRINT! . . . Opponent BA leaped 35 points to .246 . . . Gopher-ball rate skyrocketed. In '92 he'd allowed 12. Last year—27 . . . All this added up to a TPER leap from a glittering 76 to a mediocre 104 . . . This type of move should be a red flag to any prospective buyer in the free agent market. When a veteran (39 years old) experiences this kind of dramatic drop-off, it often signals he's moved to a new and far less attractive level of performance . . . Won his 100th NL game on September 28 joining Cy Young, Nolan Ryan, Gaylord Perry, Fergie Jenkins, Jim Bunning and Al Orth as the only ones to ever win at least 100 in each league . . . Now stands 35 behind Juan Marichal on the list of all-time winningest Latin pitchers . . . His next win draws him even on the all-time list at 209 with Don Drysdale, Vida Blue and Milt Pappas.

RYAN BOWEN

All in all, a decent first full year in the bigs (TPER 104) . . . Had been pounded in parts of two seasons with the Astros . . . Like many youngsters, when he's good he can be very, very good. In his 8 victories he allowed just 8 ER over 56+ innings (an ERA of 1.27!). But when he's bad he can be horrid—the rest of the time he ERAed at 6.21! . . . Stifled power hitters (11 HRs). Allowed 15 steals but also threw 15 DP balls . . . But his control will limit his horizons if not repaired. Walked 87 in 156+ innings. That's nearly five per 9 IP. He will not win consistently with that kind of stat . . . Was 4–9 at the All-Star break. Used the mini-vacation to get married and went 4–3 in the second half. Hmmmmmm.

STEVE COOKE

Led all major league rookies in starts (32), innings (210+) and strikeouts (132) . . . Only two pitchers went the route against the champion Phils—him and teammate Tim Wakefield . . . TPER of 104 would have been substantially lower except for opponents' booming bats (22 HRs) and flying feet (22-of-31 stealing). . . . Encouraging control allowing only 2.5 BBs per 9 IP . . . The Bucs appear to have a real comer in this 24-year-old. So, given how good he looks, how'd he last until the 35th round in the '89 draft?

GREG SWINDELL

A native Houstonian who had an awful time pitching at home. In the Astrodome he went 3–9 with a 4.97 ERA. Away: 9–4, 3.59 . . . TPER leaped from 90 to 106 because he became very hittable (.283) . . . Terrific control with only 1.6 BBs per 9 IP, sixth best in the league. Ability to stay around the plate also resulted in balls leaving the park (24) . . . Hit the DL with a shoulder strain at All-Star time and, when healthy again, pitched better . . . For the last five years he's averaged 31 starts a season but only 11½ wins a year.

MIKE HARKEY

Once highly touted prospect continues his struggle to overcome constant shoulder problems . . . All of '91 and most of '92 wiped out by injury. Managed a 28-start season despite opening the year on the DL with—you guessed it—more shoulder difficulties . . . Simply didn't fool 'em allowing a sky-high .305 opponent BA . . . Outstanding control walking 2 or fewer hitters in 24 starts. Runners didn't take any liberties swiping just 7 of 13 and he coaxed 17 DP balls . . . But the strikeout column gives yet another indication of his decline. Just 67 Ks in 157+ innings. . . . Hits allowed rising. Strikeouts falling. Shoulder still worrisome. Once the fourth player taken in the first round of the draft. Now?

ARMANDO REYNOSO

The "ace" of the staff with his 107 TPER. Adjust that for the enormous positive effect his home park had on offense (and its corresponding negative effect on pitching) he actually pitched very well . . . Surrendered 22 HRs but 19 came with nobody on base . . . Solid control but hit 9 men (you've got to pitch inside to survive in Colorado) . . . Coaxed 18 DPs while yielding 11 SBs in 16 attempts . . . 12 victories fell one short of the all-time record for wins by an expansion pitcher . . . Picked off 8 men, an extremely high total for a right-hander. In fact, it led the NL RHPs . . . Rockies went 19–11 in his 30 starts, a pretty nice workload since he didn't make start #1 until April 30 . . . Lucky enough to make only 11 starts at home. But he seemed to enjoy being "Mile High" posting a 7–3 record there . . . One small positive note for pitchers in Colorado—it makes them better "hitters" too. He drilled a pair of HRs.

JOSÉ GUZMAN

One of the game's good guys who's made a stunning comeback from severe shoulder troubles that ripped well over two years out of his baseball life . . . But funny thing's are happening as that major problem drifts deeper into his background. He's fanning more than ever before—7.7 per 9 IP last season. But his ERA's climbing, reaching 4.34 last season. There's been a corresponding TPER rise from 90 to 98 to 108 . . . Last season's culprits were HRs (25) and walks (74 in 191 IP). While that BB stat certainly doesn't make him "wild," realize that he walked one less the year before in 33 more innings. Add that extra control problem to 19 steals allowed and only 10 DPs . . . One more worry. Given his history of shoulder trouble you know it makes the Cubs nervous that he couldn't pitch the last four weeks with shoulder tendinitis.

GREG W. HARRIS

The gopher king of the NL with 33. Almost certainly wouldn't have won that "honor" except for the mid-season deal that sent him to Colorado where he surrendered a ghastly 15 roundtrippers in 73 innings. . . . Considering that horrible tendency to give up the HR his 113 TPER's not all that terrible . . . The league batted .271 against him but he exhibited very good control (69 BBs in 225+ innings). Runners took every opportunity to run (22 of 31) . . . Really seemed "psyched" by the stadium effect. Arrived in Colorado carrying a 10–9 record and sporting a 3.67 ERA. In 13 rocky Rockies starts he went 1–8 with a 6.50 ERA . . . Formerly an outstanding set-up man, the Padres decided to switch him to starting in '91. He TPERed at a fine 90 that season but has slipped since (107–113). But pitching in Colorado would have caused Cy Young to "slip."

BOB WALK

Forced into the "ace" role last year by a series of injuries and ineffectiveness that struck other staffers . . . Logged over 185 innings for only the third time in his career and the strain showed in his TPER (113). His last season with such poor numbers came in '89 when he also threw lots of frames (196) . . . His TPER would have gone through the roof but for a whopping total of 24 DPs. That helped offset a .294 opponent BA that included 22 roundtrippers . . . His 5.68 ERA rates as the worst of his long career by nearly a run per game . . . At 37 is he winding down or does he simply need a less demanding role to snap back to usefulness?

TIM PUGH

Rode the roller coaster his first full season in the majors . . . His elevated 114 TPER results from a weakness in baseball's most basic area—he can be hit (.303) . . . Tends to give up the long ball (19) and can be run on (19 of 26) . . . But every night's an adventure. You might see him come within a whisker of a no-hitter as he did September 29 when SD's Billy Bean singled with one out in the ninth to break it up. Or, you might see him get ripped—in six of his 15 losses the opposition scored at least nine runs . . . When he was on he looked terrific—in his 10 wins he went at least seven innings in every game with a combined 2.02 ERA. But when he was off he got shelled—in his 14 losses as a starter the ERA skyrocketed to 9.28 . . . In other words, consistently inconsistent.

BEN RIVERA

Thank the good Lord for the Phils' phantastic offense . . . Big Ben (some say "Too Big Ben") won 13 games. Here are the run totals the Phils posted in his "lucky 13" victories: 9–10–15–5–5–7–8–13–8–10–10–7–and 6. That's an *AVERAGE* of 8.7 runs a game! That's how you win 13 games with an ERA of 5.02 and a TPER of 114 . . . The league whacked him at a .273 rate. He walked over 4½ men per 9 IP. Baserunners stole at will (15 of 18) . . . Virtually every number in his packet rose from the previous season leading to that 14-point TPER leap . . . How long can he keep a rotation spot if his numbers don't improve dramatically?

FRANK CASTILLO

Another Cubbie whose TPER's headed in a very wrong direction. After a solid debut season in '91, he's moved up to 100 and then up again to an unacceptable 114 . . . The last of his 5 wins came on July 30. Made only 7 more starts and 10 appearances after that . . . Thank heavens he does a marvelous job of freezing runners (stealers only 7 for 19) and has superb control (39 BBs in 141+ IP) or his TPER might have gone through the roof . . . The league knocked him around for a .293 BA with lots of "Waveland Avenue" shots (20) . . . Still young enough to be considered a prospect (25) but last season represented a major step backward.

DOUG BROCAIL

Spent 7½ years in the Padres' system before finally joining their rotation June 1 . . . His 114 debut TPER resulted from a mixture of decent control with high hitability (.283 with 16 HRs in 128+ innings) . . . Had one special five-start stretch starting in late August where he allowed just six earned runs in 28 innings but had only a 1–2 record to show for it . . . Allowed 10-of-14 stealers to succeed. . . . Weird: Allowed a pitcher to homer against him in three straight starts (Chris Hammond, Kevin Gross and Mark Portugal).

THE PITCHERS

NATIONAL LEAGUE ROTATION STARTERS

The Rest:

Rank	Pitcher	Team	7/1/94 Age	I	TPER Trendline 1990	1991	1992	3 yr Avg.	1993 TPER
49.	Tom Browning	CIN	34	L	100	108	131	108	117
50.	Jack Armstrong	FLA	29	R	94	133	113†	112	117
51.	Kent Bottenfield	MTL/COL	25	R	-	-	(85)	(85)	126
52.	Tim Wakefield	PIT	27	R	-	-	81	81	127
53.	Andy Ashby	COL/SDO	26	R	-	(120)	(143)	130	136
Injured:									
1.	Bret Saberhagen	NYM	30	R	90†	76†	90	84	81
2.	Sid Fernandez	NYM	31	L	92	(84)	98	94	82
3.	Trevor Wilson	SFO	28	L	78	86	109	92	90
4.	Bud Black	SFO	37	L	86†	97	102	94	97
5.	Wally Whitehurst	SDO	30	R	76	97	103	94	97
6.	Zane Smith	PIT	33	L	80	85	84	93	103
7.	Randy Tomlin	PIT	28	L	71	87	97	89	112
8.	John Smiley	CIN	29	L	103	90	87†	92	112
9.	Pete Smith	ATL	28	R	101	130	87	102	114
10.	Dave Nied	COL	25	R	-	-	*	*	123
11.	Bruce Hurst	SDO/COL	37	L	84	83	101	89	*

* Under 100 TBF-not included in average.   ( ) 100-199 TBF.   † Includes AL TPER, unadjusted to NL.

TOM BROWNING

Veteran followed up a struggling, injury-plagued '92 with a struggling, injury-plagued '93 . . . Starting with his last good season in 1990 (15–9 with an even 100 TPER) his number's taken a dramatic turn for the worse. His last three TPER seasons now read 108–138–117 . . . Made only 20 starts before fracturing a finger on his pitching hand and exiting for good in early August. The season before a ruptured knee ligament wiped out the final three months . . . League hitters were downright sorry to see him go (BA a whopping .333) with 15 gopher balls in 114+ innings . . . Had his usual impeccable control (a miniscule 20 BBs) and runners posted a negative trend against him (5 for 12) . . . He's now #10 on the Reds' list of all-time winningest pitchers having passed Johnny Vander Meer this season. Seven more victories and he'll ease by the immortal Frank "Noodles" Hahn . . . But this now-34-year old battler's clearly at a crossroads in his career.

JACK ARMSTRONG

TPERs remain among the ugliest in the entire game with the last three coming in at (gulp) 133–113–117 (double gulp) . . . But teams keep remembering that solid 94 TPER in 1990 when he went 12–9 for the Reds and started the All-Star game . . . Since that "star start" he's gone 23–51 with an ERA of 4.92 . . . Has the terrible combination of shaky control and homer-itis leading to a few "three-run shots." Walked 78 in 196 innings and allowed 29 dingers (second in the NL to Colorado's Greg Harris) . . . Also doesn't hold runners (stealers went 18 for 21) . . . But maybe there's a silver lining here. In 22 career relief appearances—where he can do without his hanging curve ball—he's 4-0 with a 1.74 ERA.

KENT BOTTENFIELD

Acquired in mid-season from Montreal where they were handing his head to him. Got to the Rockies and got treated the same . . . That hideous 126 TPER results from a variety of ills including a .294 opponent BA, 24 HRs in 159+ innings and a high walk total of 71 (with only 63 strikeouts. Ugh!) . . . Arrived at Colorado and immediately reflected the tutoring of pitching coach Larry Bearnarth who taught him a sound pickoff move (he nailed 6 after having none with the Expos) . . . That move helped him control runners much better. In Montreal 9-of-10 stealers succeeded. That ratio shrunk to 7-of-12 after working with Bearnarth.

TIM WAKEFIELD

The sensation of '92 turned into the stumble bum of '93. But maybe he's about to turn back again . . . The knuckler that had mystified NL hitters in '93 became his worst enemy last year (.291 opponent BA) . . . Also had horrendous control problems walking 75 with only 59 Ks in 128 innings (hey, when a knuckler deserts you, it goes far away!) . . . Threw a major league high 172 pitches in a single game against Atlanta. Right after that start he went 0–5 with a 7.59 ERA. Surprise, surprise, surprise. The moral of the tiny sad story is that exhausted pitchers, even knuckleballers, can't be abused without paying a price . . . The Pirates finally ran out of patience shipping him to Carolina where he fared no better (3–5 with a 6.99 ERA). Called back only to be bombed again in three straight outings. Then, out of the blue, that dancing pitch returned from wherever it had been vacationing and he threw back-to-back shutouts to close the season . . . TPER leaped from 81 to 127. But at least the ending was a happy one.

ANDY ASHBY

You want mega-ugly TPERs? He's got 'em. Got lit up in Philly the last two seasons (120 and 143). Expansion took him to Colorado and then San Diego where the shelling continued (TPER of 136, the worst of the rotation regulars we measured) . . . Would you believe the league hit .333 against anyone? A high walk total of 56 in 123 IP. . . . Pounded for 19 HRs. Now, you might excuse that enormous total (one every 6½ innings) on the basis of him pitching in Colorado most of the year. But most of the damage (14 HRs in 69 IP) was done in San Diego!

BRET SABERHAGEN

The season became a mess on AND off the field . . . Missed a start with acute bronchitis. Missed another with a stomach virus. An elbow spur idled him for 11 days. Left a start with back cramps. Season ended when he injured his left knee while warming up in the bullpen wiping out the last two months . . . Through it all, when he did pitch, he pitched extremely well . . . TPER of 81 would have tied him with Atlanta's Avery for fifth best in the NL had he made enough appearances . . . Was just hitting stride (four straight wins) when the year ended . . . TPER had lots of solid numbers and one outstanding one—fantastic control (17 walks in 139 IP). That's almost "Tewksbury-land" . . . Two years ago the Mets gave him a huge contract at more than $4 million a year. So far they've gotten a total of 34 starts and a 10–12 record over two years.

SID FERNANDEZ

More injury troubles . . . For the second time in three years "El Sid" spent major time on the DL. A torn knee cartilage cut 11 weeks out of the middle of the season . . . As usual, when he pitched he did well TPERing at 82. NL hitters again simply couldn't hit him (.192). But here's a truly weird stat—while he permitted just 82 hits in 119+ innings, an incredible 17 of them went over the fence or 21% . . . Perhaps the most deceiving stat of the season, though, was the Mets listing him at 215 pounds. What? Most observers figured that was about 30–50 pounds low . . . One Mets official anonymously worried about him saying "he's got 50-year-old knees" . . . Wonderfully effective pitcher who, for various reasons, never has become a big winner. In nine-plus seasons he's got only 98 victories despite a terrific 3.15 career ERA.

TREVOR WILSON

While his teammates battled the Braves he fought a string of injuries which disabled him three different times . . . Through it all managed to post a sparkling 90 TPER, his third 90-or-better beauty this decade though he's only won more than eight games once in that four-year stretch . . . His forte? DPs! He threw 19 twin killings last season . . . Also surrendered a very low 8 HRs in his 110 IP . . . Those abilities allow you to survive when the league hits .275 against you and your control's only average.

BUD BLACK

Like teammate Wilson, he visited the DL three times costing him three months. Through all the elbow problems he still managed an 8–2 record and a decent 97 TPER . . . Bothered by HRs (13 in 93 IP) . . . Injuries have now interrupted four of his last six seasons . . . With one year left on his SF contract, '94 becomes an important year for him to stay healthy. Otherwise, a life of being a vagabond awaits.

WALLY WHITEHURST

Bounced back from off-season elbow surgery to TPER at 97. For the decade he's averaged a very respectable 93 in a variety of roles . . . Had one exceptional string of nine starts leading into the All-Star break in which he allowed two runs or less in eight of the games. Won just three times however due to (here's a surprise) poor Padres support . . . Does a dynamite job of controlling runners once they've reached base. Only 3-of-10 stealers made it in 105 innings and he induced 11 DPs . . . His second half interrupted twice by pains in the rotator cuff area (uh-oh). But doctors claim they resulted from an ache and not a tear. Oh.

ZANE SMITH

Began and ended the season on the DL. He'd had off-season elbow surgery thus delaying his start. Arm trouble flared up after just 14 starts and he exited . . . Had strung together three very solid seasons TPERing at 90–95–94 in the '90s (so to speak) before his partial in '93 rose to 103. The entirety of the rise attributable to the opponents' BA jumping from .261 to .298 . . . Forgive that based on all the arm miseries and hope he's well for '94 . . . That'll be the final year of his Bucco pact so a comeback's important from a future-earnings standpoint.

RANDY TOMLIN

Another veteran Pirate lefty whose season disintegrated due to injury . . . Tendinitis tore six weeks out of the middle of the year. Elbow spur surgery wiped out the last six weeks . . . In and around all the pain his TPER leaped to an unattractive 112 . . . Hitters simply feasted on him (.291). That included 11 HRs in 98+ IP. The healthy year before he allowed 11 in 208+ IP! Now there's a reason for a TPER leap . . . But, like Zane Smith, ignore these numbers from '93 and hope he's well in '94. In the background you can hear the Pirates praying for both of them . . . Made it to the bigs out of tiny Liberty University which has also produced 1B Sid Bream, P Lee Guetterman and Steelers TE Eric Green.

JOHN SMILEY

A bone spur ruined the first season of his multi-year, high-dollar contract with the Reds with surgery wiping out the final three months . . . TPER of 112 with the usual elements of bad TPERism: opposing hitters enjoyed facing him (.286 with 15 HRs in 105+ innings) and stealers took advantage of his soft assortment to swipe 13 of 17 . . . Had won 70 games in the five seasons leading up to '93 with correspondingly attractive TPERs. Doctors who cut on him feel nothing physical should prevent him from regaining that form . . . If you're the opposing team, load up that lineup with RH power hitters . . . for his career he's allowed 98 HRs to RHHs and 12 to LHHs.

PETE SMITH

Simply no room in the rotation for him . . . Had a spectacular '92 (7–0 with an 87 TPER) but tendinitis and poor results got him bumped from the early season rotation in '93 . . . Also suffered from "homer-itis" allowing a disturbing 15 roundtrippers in only 90+ innings . . . After that outstanding partial season in '92 everyone wanted him, thinking he had no future in the Braves' talented pitching picture. Now he probably needs that change of scenery. Anyone still interested? He's still just 28.

DAVID NIED

The expected ace of the staff after the Rockies made him the top selection in the expansion draft . . . He'd progressed through the pitching-rich Atlanta system who simply had too much talent to protect him even though he had a string of glossy minor league credentials . . . Pitched and lost Colorado's first-ever season opener. Then won three straight before losing six in a row and tearing up an elbow ligament. That injury and the resultant three months off left him with an abbreviated season of 16 starts, 87 innings and that ugly 123 TPER . . . The league knocked him around for a .296 BA. But opposing hitters were not his worst enemy—he was! Walked 42 while fanning just 46. And when those runners reached first base they took off swiping 16 of 18 . . . Obviously Nied's game "needs" work. But first things first—make sure he's healthy.

BRUCE HURST

Threw only 13 innings while recovering from shoulder surgery performed in October of '92 so it's best to simply ignore any numbers flowing from his abbreviated season and concentrate on what he'd done earlier in his career. And what a career! . . . His idle '93 snapped a string of 10 consecutive seasons in which he'd won at least 11 games, the last seven of which had all been winning years (101–64 combined) . . . In nine of those previous 10 he'd thrown at least 211 innings and in seven of them posted ERAs below 4.00 . . . If he's well, who ever pays him next year has a solid addition to their rotation. *IF* he's well.

NATIONAL LEAGUE UTILITY PITCHERS

Starters/Relievers (5+ Starts)

Rank	Pitcher	Team	7/1/94 Age	T	1990	1991	1992	3 yr Avg.	1993 TPER
					\.		TPER Trendline	\.	
1.	Denis Boucher	MTL	26	L	-	144	(126)	135	(69)
2.	Jeff Fassero	MTL	31	L	-	72	99	88	75
3.	Kent Mercker	ATL	26	L	105	96	97	99	82
4.	Anthony Young	NYM	28	R	-	93	109	104	97
5.	Luis Aquino	FLA	30	R	92†	93†	99†	94	97
6.	Paul Wagner	PIT	26	R	-	-	*	*	98
7.	Bruce Ruffin	COL	30	L	120	98	129†	114	100
8.	Jeff Ballard	PIT	30	L	116†	110†	-	113	102
9.	Gil Heredia	MTL	28	R	-	(85)	(105)	97	102
10.	Bryan Hickerson	SFO	30	L	-	93	85	88	103
11.	Jeff Brantley	SFO	30	R	78	110	96	95	111
12.	Brian Barnes	MTL	27	L	(84)	106	84	96	113
13.	Omar Olivares	STL	26	R	81	93	100	95	115
14.	Willie Blair	COL	28	R	105	(138)	96	107	119
15.	Dave Otto	PIT	29	L	*	95†	128†	110	120
16.	Butch Henry	COL/MTL	25	L	-	-	115	115	120
17.	Frank Seminara	SDO	27	R	-	-	97	97	121
18.	Pete Schourek	NYM	25	L	-	123	103	110	128

* Under 100 TBF-not included in average.   ( ) 100-199 TBF.   † Includes AL TPER, unadjusted to NL.

DENIS BOUCHER

This native Canadian made five solid starts after being acquired from the Padres . . . Four came at home where the hometown hero made the turnstiles whirl. . . . Has now belonged to five organizations in three years . . . His partial TPERs with Toronto and Cleveland the two previous seasons hold little promise. Colorado grabbed him in the expansion draft and quickly dumped him on the Padres who never recalled him despite their well-documented pitching problems . . . But then he came home and everything fell into place . . . Was that late season cameo a mirage? The Expos, who badly need all the attendance they can get, fervently hope not.

JEFF FASSERO

Mr. Versatility! . . . Went from a set-up man to a rotation regular seemingly without any need for a period of adjustment . . . Which suited him better? Neither! Check the records—Starter: 7–4 ERA 2.29; Reliever: 5–1, ERA 2.28. . . . While his sparkling 75 TPER made him the majors' best "combo-man," it should come as no surprise when you check his TPER history and find that terrific 72 TPER he posted in '91 . . . Has all the proper elements for an outstanding pitcher except a slight softness regarding stealers (12 of 16). But otherwise, he's a portrait of effectiveness (.216 BA, just 7 HRs in 149+ innings and solid control) . . . Led all NL LHPs with 140 strikeouts . . . So why did the Expos shove him into the pen to begin with? Montreal manager Felipe Alou wondered the same thing: "After watching him pitch the last two months I'm sure a lot of people want to know whose decision it was in the minor leagues to make a relief pitcher out of him." Who indeed!

KENT MERCKER

Other teams salivate at the thought of having him as their closer. Still others yearn to acquire him and slide him right into their rotation. Pitching-rich Atlanta has the luxury of simply having him waiting in the wings . . . TPER reached a new personal best of 82 as his ability to keep the ball in the park improved (just 2 HRs) . . . Just what kind of stuff does he have? The last three years of opponents' BA should tell you—.211, .207 and .214. Wow!

ANTHONY YOUNG

Poor Anthony . . . His record losing streak reached a mind-boggling 27 straight before he won his only game of the season in relief on July 28. You'd expect a loser of 27 in a row to be a sub-marginal hurler. Not him. He TPERed at a better-than-average 97 and has a three-year average of right at 100 . . . Stingy with HRs (8) and induced 13 DPs . . . Stealers did take liberties swiping 15 of 17 . . . But overall he's more unlucky than anything else. During those 27 straight he did post 16 saves. Appeared in 81 games between wins and his ERA of 4.39 wasn't all that bad . . . The Mets leaky "D" totally undermined him. He gave up 62 runs and 20 were unearned! . . . Oddly, in the game that snapped his streak, an unearned run in the top of the ninth put him behind before the Mets rallied for two to win it . . . May need a rabbit's foot.

LUIS AQUINO

Versatile RHP, whom the Royals simply sold to Florida at the end of spring training despite his being an above-average pitcher for his entire stay in KC (TPERs of 92–93–99 leading up to '93) . . . Gave the Fish yet another workmanlike season (TPER 97) making 13 starts and 25 relief appearances despite missing a month with shoulder tendinitis . . . Keeps the ball in the yard allowing just 6 HRs. . . . Perhaps KC gave up on him because he tends to be a bit fragile with a trip to the DL in four of the last five seasons . . . But, as his TPERs suggest, he's a valuable, flexible staffer who, when healthy, gives a solid accounting of himself.

PAUL WAGNER

Rookie began the year in the bullpen and finished right in the middle of 1994 rotation plans . . . Made 27 relief appearances and 17 starts totaling 141+ innings . . . Solid 98 TPER built around outstanding control (only 42 BBs or 2.7 per 9 IP). Note his terrific strikeouts-to-walks ratio of 2.7-1 indicating he's got some mustard . . . Needs work holding runners (stealers went 18 for 25) . . . Threw a team high, and fifth most in the NL, 12 wild pitches . . . The Buccos got him in round 13 in 1989 and later got fellow rookie standout Steve Cooke in round 35. Now that's a good draft.

BRUCE RUFFIN

Entering '93 his career seemed more like a funeral procession nearing the graveyard until he popped up pitching very well in, of all places, the graveyard for pitchers—Colorado . . . To TPER 100 when half your games come in such an "unfriendly park" amounts to a real accomplishment . . . His 6–5 record snapped a string of six consecutive losing seasons in which he had a combined record of 34–60 . . . All of a sudden he posted 126 strikeouts in 139 IP and just 10 HRs allowed . . . Threw 14 DPs while runners made it just 14-of-23 attempts . . . Opened the season in the rotation but soon pitched his way into the pen where he suddenly became effective . . . The true turning point came when a line drive off the bat of his former Philly catcher and teammate Darren Daulton fractured a toe on his left foot. After suffering the injury he posted a 1.25 ERA in 36 innings allowing just 22 hits and only one HR while walking 13 and fanning 43!

JEFF BALLARD

Veteran finally made it back to the bigs in '93, . . . Was leading the American Association in ERA (2.29) when the Buccos called . . . His OK TPER of 102 aided greatly by an almost astounding 13 DP balls in but 53+ innings. Wow! . . . But he needed everyone of them. The league pounded him for a .332 average. But only three left the yard . . . And he did his normally efficient job of stalling runners (2 for 3) . . . Looked like he had the world on a string after going 18–8 for the '89 Orioles at age 25. But since then he's 12–24 . . . But maybe, just maybe, there's a bit of light at the end of the tunnel for this former Stanford graduate in geophysics.

GIL HEREDIA

Former Giants draftee and starting prospect who spot started and relieved in two stints with the '93 Expos . . . Excellent control (14 BBs in 57 IP to go with 40 Ks) . . . Kept it in the park (only 4 HRs. But the league hit him freely (.293). And runners swiped 7-for-7 . . . Has had some sparkling minor league campaigns . . . Age (28) puts pressure on him to deliver in an organization that's packed with pitching options.

BRYAN HICKERSON

Began the year in middle relief, moved into the rotation, returned to the pen and finally came back as a starter down the stretch. That versatility helped an injury-plagued Giants staff . . . TPERed at 103 after two very good years (93 and 85) both while being used in a variety of roles . . . TPER rise happened because some of the fly balls he gave up just continued to rise up, up and away. Gave up 14 HRs in 120 innings . . . The league hit a robust .291 against him but he got 11 DPs and only 4-of-10 stealers succeeded . . . So, what will he do next year? Start? Relieve? Yes!

JEFF BRANTLEY

Haunted by homers. Gave up a whopping 19 in 113 innings. The year before only 8 left the yard. That accounted for his TPER jump from an acceptable 96 to a discouraging 111 . . . By the end of the year this one-time closer and one-time rotation regular was being used only in mop-up situations . . . His control, never an asset, continued to bother him walking 46 and hitting 7 . . . But you can simply forget trying to run on him (1 of 6) . . . Any perspective employer for '94 might be wise to look beyond his struggling '93 to the pitcher who, from '90–'92, appeared in at least 55 games of relief each year, threw at least 86 innings each season, has never had a losing season and has never had an ERA above 2.95.

BRIAN BARNES

Montreal thought they had something special when he marched through their system leaving a trail of overmatched hitters. He made five minor league stops from '90 through '92 with his highest ERA being 2.77 . . . Fragments of '90 and '92 in the majors (TPERs of 84 and 84) further whetted the club's appetite . . . But after his 113 TPER of '93 they might simply be wondering just what they have here . . . Poor control (48 BB in 100 IP) . . . The league hit him for a .274 average but only took him out of the yard nine times . . . Perhaps blame that shaky TPER on his ever-changing role.

Began the season as the LH middleman. Moved into the rotation for 8 starts. Then bumped back into the pen as a set-up man . . . So, what's his future in the pitching-packed Expos? Starter? Middleman? Set-up? Or maybe, somewhere else?

OMAR OLIVARES

Attention: outgoing TPER being launched . . . Trendline's extremely discouraging, from 81 in '90 up to 93 and 100 and then last year's 115 when he allowed 14.3 base runners per 9 IP . . . The league banged at a .288 clip and he walked 54 in 118+ innings. Didn't stop the running game (stealers went 12 for 17). Threw 11 DPs but, considering the runners on base, that might have been "unavoidable" . . . Once a rising star and rotation member. Now he'll have to fight just for a staff spot in the spring.

WILLIE BLAIR

Opened the year with 20 relief appearances. Then made 18 consecutive starting assignments . . . Finished 4–10 as a starter but suffered from unusually bad support with the Rockies getting him a miniscule 14 runs in his 10 defeats . . . His inflated 119 TPER had the usual "Colorado" elements: high opponent BA of .306, lots of HRs (20) . . . Slight elbow injury forced him back into the pen at year's end . . . In the four years this decade, he's now pitched for four different major league teams.

DAVE OTTO

Veteran lefty whose once promising career has been dragged down by knee problems (both legs) . . . Made 8 starts and 20 relief appearances TPERing at an awful 120 before drawing his release . . . What would that TPER have ballooned to had he not thrown 14 DPs? The league whacked him for a .317 BA with 9 HRs in just 68 innings . . . Once a highly regarded draft pick, now at the point where he'll gladly report if some one will just call.

BUTCH HENRY

Clobbered again! Had been banged around as an Astro starter in '92. Drafted by the expansion Rockies and then dealt in midsummer to Montreal. Realizing that his numbers might be skewed more than a bit by his making 15 starts for Colorado, many of them in that distinctly hitter's park in Denver, slightly explains his ugly 120 TPER . . . But unattractive numbers turn up all over his stat sheet. Numbers like a .317 opponent BA, 15 HRs in 103 IP and 9-of-13 stealing . . . But he's only 25 and maybe the Expos' late season experiment with him in the pen may prove successful.

FRANK SEMINARA

As a Columbia graduate he's smart enough to know TPERs of 127 won't keep you in the majors. Began the season in the rotation but soon headed for Vegas after being bombed. Came back up, went back down, returned in September . . . San Diego had had high hopes for him after a solid 9–4 debut season with a nice 97 TPER in '92. But opposing hitters figured him out with their BA rising from .258 to .294. . . . Got three wins out of the pen the last four weeks. Did the Padres stumble on his eventual role?

PETE SCHOUREK

Ugh! TPERs of 123, 103 and last year's 128 don't suggest he's got much of a future . . . Opposing hitters ripped him for a .319 BA. Gave up 13 dingers and 10-of-14 steals in 128+ innings . . . His 5.96 ERA set a new Mets record as the highest in team history for anyone throwing at least 100 innings . . . A former third-rounder with fabulous minor league numbers every time he drops to that level. But, so far, he's not fooling anybody in the bigs.

NATIONAL LEAGUE CLOSERS

Rank	Pitcher	Team	7/1/94 Age	I	TPER Trendline 1990	1991	1992	3 yr Avg.	1993 TPER
1.	Greg McMichael	ATL	27	R	-	-	-	-	63
2.	Bryan Harvey	FLA	31	R	85†	70†	(94)†	79	69
3.	Rod Beck	SFO	25	R	-	100	63	78	75
4.	Jim Gott	LAD	33	R	103	92	85	92	78
5.	John Wetteland	MTL	27	R	118	*	97	104	79
6.	Darren Holmes	COL	28	R	*	108	80	98	80
7.	Randy Myers	CUB	31	L	74	98	113	95	84
8.	Doug Jones	HOU	37	R	72†	125†	78	88	104
9.	Gene Harris	SDO	29	R	(127)†	*	(97)†	113	104
10.	Mitch Williams	PHI	29	L	124	102	126	117	106
11.	Mike Stanton	ATL	27	L	*	71	91	80	109
12.	Todd Worrell	LAD	34	R	-	-	103	103	(127)
13.	John Franco	NYM	33	L	89	93	(67)	86	(136)
14.	Rob Dibble	CIN	30	R	74	92	70	79	(147)
Of Note:									
-	Mark Dewey	PIT	29	R	(96)	-	(88)	91	(77)
-	Alejandro Peña	PIT	34	R	94	87	(107)	94	DNP

* Under 100 TBF-not included in average. ( ) 100-199 TBF. † Includes AL TPER, unadjusted to NL.

GREG McMICHAEL

Where'd he come from? Dumped by the Indians' organization early in '91 and signed for the price of a bus ticket by the Braves. Did decent though unspectacular work over two minor league seasons before forcing his way onto this talented staff last spring . . . Pitched wonderfully in mop-up and set-up situations through three months before Manager Cox decided he should close instead of Mike Stanton. Ripped off 15 straight saves to start his career in that role, an all-time record . . . Just eight runs allowed his last 55 innings . . . Opponents struggled to solve him (BA .206). . . . Fantastic HR prevention—just three, or one every 92 outs! . . . Threw 10 DPs . . . Add it all up and he's the most effective pitcher in the NL with a 63 TPER.

BRYAN HARVEY

California exposed this high-salaried, former star closer to the expansion draft because they feared his arm problems might be career and/or effectiveness threatening. NOT! . . . Involved in 71.8% of the Marlins' 64 wins by either winning or saving. That percentage set a new all-time major league record . . . Notched 45 saves becoming the first man to ever save at least 45 in each league . . . Has radar-like control walking just 13 men in 69 innings and throwing no wild pitches. Only 4 HRs allowed . . . But he must do something about opposing runners who swiped 15 straight against him . . . The average hitter batted .186 against him. Ouch!

ROD BECK

Broke the existing NL record for saves in a season with 48 only to have Chicago's Myers ring up 53 the same season . . . Erased the old Giants record of 30 saves (held by Greg "Moon Man" Minton) on August 1 . . . ERAed at 2.16 and TPERed at 75 despite being homer-prone (11 in 79 + IP) . . . Want another weird note? How about only one attempted steal all season? . . . Took over the closer's role late in '92 and has now recorded 65 saves in about 1⅓ seasons . . . Set an NL record by saving 24 in a row . . . Especially tough on LHHs who've now batted .178 and .180 against him the last two seasons . . . Oakland drafted him but dealt him to the Giants in a minor deal before the '88 season because they'd become convinced he had a weight problem caused by a drinking problem. Beck admits he weighed 250 or more. Denies that he ever struggled with alcoholism. Says being "big" runs in his family with one 340-pound brother and another right at 300.

JIM GOTT

Jim's "Gott" it back . . . Once fire-balling Pirate reliever blew out his elbow in '89. Came back in '90 to spend three seasons as a set-up man with his TPERs telling us all loud and clear that his arm power was gradually returning (103–92–85 and then last year's 78) . . . Those 25 saves rank as the second-best single-season LA total ever (Jay Howell had 28 in '89) . . . Began the season with 19 + scoreless innings spanning five weeks . . . Think he's "Gott" some stuff? How about nearly four strikeouts for every walk! That's spectacular . . . Only six steal attempts in 77 innings along with 8 DPs indicating excellent job of stopping runners . . . Entered the bigs as a full-time starter with the Jays in the early '80s. Credit Pittsburgh for converting him to a pen man. Credit whoever repaired his arm back in '89 for doing a wonderful job.

JOHN WETTELAND

May have arrived as one of the game's dominant closers . . . Would you believe 113 Ks in just 85 IP? That's 11.92 Ks per 9 IP. Second best in baseball to the "other Canadian closer" Duane Ward who averaged 12.18 . . . Missed the first three weeks of the season after suffering a fractured toe during spring training . . . TPER of 79—unhittable (.188) and only 3 HRs in 85 innings. Just one obvious weakness—controlling runners who swiped 13 of 15. And in '93 he never did get a DP. Not one! But then, how could he when he was striking out everyone? . . . Nine wins and 43 saves along with a microscopic 1.37 ERA. You know your ERA's low when there's a decent chance you've got a higher IQ.

DARREN HOLMES

His emergence as their closer of the future qualifies as one of the most significant discoveries of the Rockies' first season . . . Colorado scouts loved his arm and that 80 TPER he'd posted in '92 with the Brewers so the club grabbed him with the #3 pick in the expansion draft with plans of making him their bullpen ace . . . He immediately flunked, leaving for the minors on May 9 with a horrendous 17.19 ERA in nine appearances . . . Stayed in the minors just two weeks and returned a "new man." Over his final 53 games he posted a sparkling 2.43 ERA with 23 saves over 59 + innings . . . His 80 TPER, in Colorado and given his terrible start, tells you just how well he pitched the final four months . . . Permitted just 3 SBs, 6 HRs and 20 BBs for the year. The league scratched out a puny .222 BA . . . Kudos to the Rockies' scouts for finding perhaps the best emerging pitcher in the entire draft.

RANDY MYERS

Simply an incredible season! . . . An NL record 53 saves including 14 for 14 in September. Also had stretches of 13 and 12 consecutive saves. No Cub ever before saved more than 11 straight . . . Pitched in 73 games finishing 69 of them . . . In 75+ IP he permitted just one steal! . . . Did allow 7 HRs but only touched for a .230 opponent BA . . . Most of the time simply strolled in and blew hitters away fanning 86 . . . 38% of all his outs came by strikeout . . . As superb as his '93 was realize he TPERed 10 points lower in '90 as part of Cincy's famed "Nasty Boys" bullpen. How dominating must he have been then? . . . Now the only reliever in history to save at least 30 games for four different franchises.

DOUG JONES

He stopped foolin' 'em . . . How about a closer getting hit for a .298 opponent BA including seven HRs? . . . Maintained his usual outstanding control. . . . Perhaps the ugliest number came from the situation he's supposed to handle best. The NL batted .350 with runners on with a .497 slugging percentage. Ouch! . . . Will he rebound at age 37? If he keeps to his pattern he will. Had a wonderful '90, a rotten '91, a terrific '92 and a terrible '93. Hmmmmmm.

GENE HARRIS

A closer with two distinct flaws—very, very poor control (37 walks in 59 innings). That's not the kind of stat you want strolling in from the pen with the bases loaded in the ninth inning. And runners just take off on him (10-for-10 stealing) . . . Does an outstanding job of HR prevention (3) . . . Had spent parts of the last four seasons in the bigs but '93 represented the first complete major league campaign for this now 29-year-old. Career set back some when he quit the Mariners hoping to become an NFL defensive back at age 26. He'd been a standout DB (that's football lingo) at Tulane . . . Started strong, slumped in mid-season and finished fast. Still has a decent arm but a 37 BB-to-39 K ratio certainly doesn't look like a closer's numbers.

MITCH WILLIAMS

Welcome to life on the brink . . . TPERs continue to stay well above 100 but he keeps his closer's job . . . Very tough to take downtown yielding but three HRs. Opponents could manage just a .245 BA . . . The flipside of these solid numbers reveals a continuing battle with control problems. (44 BBs in 62 IP) and a total inability to stop runners (all nine who tried to steal made it) . . . But that's been his pattern throughout a career in which he's now saved 29 or more games in five of the last six seasons . . . But two other factors should worry his employer this off-season. Can he rebound mentally from that horrible shock of giving away two Philly victories in the World Series? Even for a free spirit like Williams that's a major emotional hurdle . . . Even more disconcerting are the scouts' whispers that on some late season nights "The Wild Thing's" heater only reached the low 80s on the radar gun.

MIKE STANTON

By late July he'd already saved 27, within three of the Braves' franchise record held by the bearded and twirling Gene Garber. But the Atlanta braintrust correctly read the fact that he'd piled up those saves despite pitching poorly and handed the job to McMichael . . . Became little more than a spot pitcher after that throwing just 24 innings over his last 31 appearances . . . Nearly five walks per 9 IP certainly not the control you want in critical situations . . . Durable as they come with 202 games the last three years.

TODD WORRELL

LA signed him to a megabucks contract allegedly without giving

him a physical despite major arm problems in recent seasons. What they got for their millions was a very pricey mop-up man who again had a pair of visits to the DL . . . We'll start with the bad news. The league pounded him for a .313 BA. Six HRs in 38+ innings. Runners stole him blind (9 of 10). Todd's TPER hit skid row (127) . . . Now the good news. After horrible early-season appearances and those trips to the DL, he showed some signs of life . . . Over his last 21 games, fanned 22 in 25 innings with a 3.60 ERA. . . . Still not a closer-level ERA. . . . But, when you entered this stretch ERAing in the sevens and eights, that string looked glorious. Can he bounce back? Jim Gott did. With what LA's invested they better hope they've "got" another "Gott."

JOHN FRANCO

Brooklyn native who began the year with a surgically repaired elbow and had his season interrupted by elbow, rib cage and thumb problems . . . In between all this discomfort, the league pounded him for a .313 average. The year before they'd hit .209 against him . . . Six HRs in just 36+ innings after just one in 33 in '92 . . . Even his trusty control faltered walking 19 . . . A totally lost season in which his TPER *more than doubled*! (67 up to 136.) Yuck! . . . Tenth on the all-time list of save leaders with 236. But he's had only 25 over the last two injury-troubled seasons after racking up six straight years of 29 or more . . . If he's healthy again in '94 the Mets' pen all of a sudden looks respectable. If . . .

ROB DIBBLE

Looked like a walking MASH unit in '93. A perforated eardrum gave him all kinds of trouble early on. In late April, he fractured his left forearm on a play at home plate requiring surgery to insert a plate in the arm. Also sprained an ankle on that play. Returned to post a scoreless July (7-for-7 saves in 8.2 IP). But back on the DL to close the season with what doctors called weakness in each shoulder . . . For the season, horrid 147 TPER isn't *all* bad numbers as you might expect. Opponents still hit just .225 against him and he did fan 49 in 41+ innings . . . BUT—more than one walk per inning? Ugh! Eight HRs? Yuck! And 13-of-15 stealers succeeded? Geez! . . . The corps of doctors who treated him don't feel there's anything seriously wrong with him long term . . . speculating he changed the motion with his injured arm causing him to "open up" dramatically, putting more strain on his shoulder. But many have worried about what damage his violent motion might someday cause . . . Stay tuned. With this fellow there's never a dull moment.

MARK DEWEY

Continued his "waiver tour" of the NL. The Mets, who'd claimed him from the Giants on waivers in '91, put him on the wire in May and the Pirates grabbed him. At Buffalo he sparkled, at one point going 18 appearances and 22 games without allowing an earned run . . . That kind of pitching got him called up July 31 and he responded with two rousing months of excellent work (TPER 77) . . . Had a win, four saves and a 1.59 ERA in 12 August appearances . . . Did wind up blowing five save opportunities, a concern if that's the job the Buccos want him to do. But the league could muster only a microscopic .157 BA against him without a homer. . . . Showed enough to make the Buccos very interested.

ALEJANDRO PENA

The Buccos gave him a one-year, seven-figure contract . . . never threw a pitch because a blown-out pitching arm landed him on the DL March 22 . . . The Bucs and their fans got awfully hot, believing they'd paid good money for bad merchandise. (His '92 season had been shortened by more elbow problems.) So Pena and his agent worked out an extension whereby he still belonged to the club through '94 . . . When he's right, as in '90–'91, he puts up solid TPERs (94–87). Will he show up "right" in '94? The Buccos would like to see at least one pitch for their bucks.

NATIONAL LEAGUE IN-BETWEENERS

Top Third:

Rank	Pitcher	Team	7/1/94 Age	I	1990	1991	1992	3 yr Avg.	1993 TPER
1.	Jay Howell	ATL	38	R	92	86	92	90	72
2.	Kevin Rogers	SFO	25	L	-	-	(103)	(103)	75
3.	Xavier Hernandez	HOU	28	R	121	111	80	99	77
4.	Mike Jackson	SFO	29	R	109†	82†	104	98	79
5.	Steve Bedrosian	ATL	36	R	103	110†	DNP	106	81
6.	Pedro J. Martinez	LAD	22	R	-	-	*	*	82
7.	Larry Andersen	PHI	41	R	77†	76	78	78	82
8.	Lee Guetterman	STL	35	L	83†	90†	143†	101	83
9.	Don Pall	CWS/PHI	32	R	88†	76†	106†	91	83†
10.	Mark Wohlers	ATL	24	R	-	*	(79)	(79)	(84)
11.	Ricky Trlicek	LAD	25	R	-	-	*	*	86
12.	Mike Perez	STL	29	R	*	*	79	79	87
13.	David West	PHI	29	L	117	115	(128)	118	87
14.	Joel Johnston	PIT	27	R	-	*	*	*	87
15.	Roger Mason	SDO/PHI	35	R	-	(67)	110	99	92
16.	Jose Bautista	CUB	29	R	(116)	*	-	(116)	92
17.	Les Lancaster	STL	32	R	108	98	127†	108	93

* Under 100 TBF-not included in average. ( ) 100-199 TBF. † Includes AL TPER, unadjusted to NL.

JAY HOWELL

The best "tweener" in the NL with his 72 TPER . . . Want a picture of a terrific set-up man? Take a snapshot of him: in 58+ IP permitted just 3 HRs, 5 steals (with 5 CSs) and walked only 16. Can get the strikeout (37) . . . If you could change anything about him it would be his fragility. Visited the DL in '83, '86, '88, '90, '91 and '92 missing a total of 13 months of action . . . Down the stretch, as Atlanta played one crucial game after another, he allowed one run in his final 20 games over a span of 22 innings . . . Has the added ability to close if necessary having saved 153 games in his career including seasons of 29 (Oakland) and 28 (Dodgers) . . . Braves gave him a one-year contract looking for just the type of season he gave them . . . Who'll snatch him up now?

KEVIN ROGERS

The best LH set-up man in the league (TPER 75) and at only age 25! . . . Aren't young lefties supposed to be wild? He had only 23 unintentional BBs in 80+ innings . . . Yielded only three long balls and threw 9 DPs . . . Had been exclusively a starter through five minor league seasons before manager Baker converted him to the pen and gave him the pressure-filled job of pitching just in front of closer Beck . . . In the minors had the superstition of eating a baked potato the night before he was scheduled to start and spaghetti on his game day. So, what does he do now that he's being used in relief and pitched 64 times last year?

XAVIER HERNANDEZ

Seventh in appearances with 72 and that makes 149 over the last two years for this rubber-armed set-up man . . . Opponents batted a mere .212 and he fanned more than one per inning so you know his reputation for having one of the nastiest forkballs in the game comes well deserved . . . Season ERA 2.61 but just 1.79 over his last 55 innings . . . Needs work holding runners who got him for 9-of-11 steals . . . Imagine how much tougher that Toronto pen would be had they not let this guy get away through the minor league draft four years ago.

MIKE JACKSON

Pitched in a league-high 81 games . . . Total of 230 appearances and 248 innings over the last three seasons . . . TPERed at a career-best 79 due to much improved control and his toughness to

hit (.204) . . . Righties managed only a .171 BA . . . Just how good was the Giants' pen with Jackson and Rogers setting up Beck? Good enough so that SF posted a 92–0 record when leading after eight innings . . . Has now led his team in appearances the last five seasons . . . Stealers were 1 for 1 last year. One steal in 81 games?

STEVE BEDROSIAN

One of the most heartwarming comeback stories in years. Missed the entire '92 season because of his child's illness and his own injuries. Returned pitching better than he had in years (TPER 81) . . . Gave Atlanta a dynamite season. (5–2, ERA 1.63) . . . Walked just 14 in 49 innings while giving up four long balls. The rest brought back his exceptional stuff (Opponent BA—.194) . . . One negative—17 of 37 inherited runners scored . . . Will this former Cy Young winner be back to try it again? Why not?

PEDRO J. MARTINEZ

A special debut season with all the right numbers on his chart except control . . . Even with 57 walks in just 107 innings he still TPERed a flashy 82, so you know the rest of his makeup had to be outstanding. Held the league's hitters to a microscopic .201 BA with only 5 HRs. RHHs stood no chance (.163) . . . How outrageous must his stuff be to record 119 Ks in 107 IP? . . . His 65 games set a franchise record for rookie appearances . . . Inherited 33 runners and just 7 scored . . . Only 6 successful steals in 10 tries . . . May now possess the best arm of the pitching Martinez brothers. In a few years maybe that honor will go to the youngest of the Martinezes, baby brother Jesus who's averaging a strikeout per inning in the LA minors . . . The Dodgers also have another (unrelated) Martinez pitching down on the farm (Fili) and three infielders named "Martinez".

LARRY ANDERSEN

At age 40 he had the Phils' best strikeouts-to-IP ratio (67 in 61.2 IP) so you know his pitches still had real movement . . . TPERs remain borderline spectacular this decade (77–76–77–82) making him THE most effective NL tweener this decade . . . As you'd expect, he does almost everything well. For example, in his 61+ innings he allowed just 21 BBs, 4 SBs and 4 HRs . . . Has had just one ERA above 2.94 in his last seven years . . . How about some respect for one of the game's elder and unheralded stars?

LEE GUETTERMAN

Aging lefty put together his third very good year of the decade with an 83 TPER. Unfortunately his one bad year (an outrageous 143 TPER in '92) was a real doozy. And that meant he began '93 at AAA Louisville . . . Solid control (only 11 unintentional BBs in 46 IP) mixed with remarkable ability to keep his soft tosses from leaving the yard (1 HR) make him an ideal tweener . . . Also will get the DP (7) but can be run on (5 for 5) . . . Finished red-hot with a 1.04 ERA his last 25 outings . . . Gangly ex-Tennessee basketballer who'll turn up in somebody's pen next season.

DONN PALL

Why in the world would the White Sox get rid of him? . . . Was TPERing 88 for the Sox (right around where he's been three of the last four years) when they dumped him on the Phils where he promptly TPERed 67 . . . Forget waiting for a walk (14 in 76+ IP) . . . Only four steals allowed along with seven HRs . . . Capable of going two, three or four innings if needed . . . So, given his long-running effectiveness and his fine '93, why did the Phils not immediately make him a bellcow of their shaky pen? Is there something wrong with this split-finger specialist the numbers don't show? Or, more likely, do we simply have a pitcher that two different winning teams did not appreciate?

MARK WOHLERS

Once the "closer-of-the-future". Failed in earlier shots at that job and now seems destined as a tweener . . . Began the year at Richmond. . . . Back in early June to post a none-too-exciting 4.50 ERA but an exceptional TPER of 84 . . . Another of the Braves' bevy of live arms boasting a .218 opponent BA and fanning 45 in 48 IP . . . Seems to be gaining control of his 95 mph heater. That's bad news for NL hitters who managed just a pair of dingers off him . . . Just 24 and his name pops up on lots of other teams' "wish lists."

RICKY TRLICEK

Yet another hurler fished out of the Blue Jays' system. LA grabbed him off waivers during spring training and he gave them a terrific 85 TPER pitching in middle relief and spot situations . . . Double tough on RHHs (.184 BA) . . . Only 3 HRs allowed and just 17 unintentional walks in 63 IP. Nice sinking action produced 9 DPs but 6-of-7 stealers made it . . . Just how much of a ground-ball pitcher is he? Got 109 outs on the ground versus just 40 fly outs! . . . His 4.08 ERA's deceiving. Got thumped in a handful of early-season outings. ERA of 2.08 his last 18 games.

MIKE PEREZ

The best TPER on the staff of all the year-long members . . . The Cards would love him to be their closer but he balked at the thought after Lee Smith left, though he did wind up saving 7 in that role eventually . . . Only 4 HRs and 20 BBs in 72 innings make him the perfect candidate to close. Can also get the strikeout as that total of 58 suggests . . . Now has put outstanding TPERs back-to-back (79–87) . . . Cards have groomed him for the pen. He hasn't made a start in seven years . . . Loves Busch Stadium. Went 7–0 there in '93. For his career he's 13–3 with a 2.08 at home.

DAVID WEST

Former star-in-the-wings of the Mets' organization who finally had a solid major league season . . . Repeatedly flunked trials as a starter with NY and Minnesota. The Phils dealt for him, shuffled him to the pen and, voila, a star is born . . . TPERed at 87, easily the best of his career, . . . Control, a lifelong problem, remained so with a horrid (for a bullpener) 51 BBs in 86+ innings . . . But every other number was good including an unbelievable opponent BA of .194. Yikes! With stuff like that how'd this guy get such an ultra-disappointing resume? . . . Too bad the Phils wore him out

with those 76 regular-season appearances leaving him looking very tired in the playoffs and Series.

JOEL JOHNSTON

Began the season in the minors and quickly landed on the DL. When he got healthy he earned a recall . . . Hit the ground running for the Pirates allowing just 3 ER in 17+ innings. Then that effectiveness disappeared and the league touched him for 15 runs in 23+ innings before he refound himself and finished very strong . . . Opposing hitters scratched for just a .203 BA but belted 7 HRs. Just three runners even tried to steal. Add it all up and you've got an attractive TPER of 87 . . . For the first spring training in his career he'll report in '94 with a job waiting for him.

ROGER MASON

How bizarre stats can be! Pitched exceptionally well in 34 games for the Padres (TPERed at a glittering 80), but all that got him was a 0–7 record. The Phils noticed his effectiveness and dealt for him. But in the exact same number of appearances in the City of Brotherly Love, his efficiency declined dramatically (TPER 105). So what happened to his record? In Philly, this much less impressive pitcher posted a far more impressive record of 5–5 . . . Opponents hit one HR in 49 SD innings and 9 HRs in 50 Philly innings . . . Seven franchises have owned him in the last decade.

JOSE BAUTISTA

A season of firsts for him. Recorded his first full winning season in the bigs. Notched his first save. Got his first hit ever. Drove in his first run. Most important, looked like a major league pitcher for the first time ever . . . Once thought of as hot Orioles property. They grabbed him in the minor league draft from the Mets, and had to keep him in the bigs the entire '88 season or risk losing him on a NY reclaim. The O's, then a dismal team, started him 25 times. At 24 he posted an ugly 6–15 mark . . . He never seemed to recover from that negative experience drifting away from the Baltimore organization and through a series of minor league stops before the Cubs signed him as a minor league free agent . . . They struck it rich with him . . . His 92 TPER ranked in the top third of all NL tweeners . . . Had been 10–20 as a major leaguer before putting up a sparkling 10–3 mark with a 2.82 ERA . . . What changed? Control had always been good. Ball stayed in the park (11 HRs in 111+ IP). Only 5 SBs allowed. League hit just .250. No one outstanding improvement leaps off his sheet. But that's what happens sometimes when pitchers "arrive".

LES LANCASTER

Is the right arm of this once versatile and sturdy pitcher starting to rejuvenate? . . . 1992 had been a terrible season in Detroit. He never seemed to have any stuff when he took the mound and his TPER showed it (127). But his 93 TPER of '93 put him in the top third of all NL tweeners . . . Excellent control (15 unintentional walks in 61+ innings). Only 5 HRs and 3 SBs allowed . . . Used as a middle and long man very effectively with just 10 of the 50 first batters he faced reaching base, an outstanding percentage for a pitcher who often arrives with the bases "heavily populated" . . . Arthroscopic elbow surgery interrupted the season but he returned to pitch efficiently down the stretch . . . What might have caused that horrid '92? How about overwork? Check what the Cubs asked him to do the two previous seasons. In '90, between Iowa and Chicago, he worked in 61 games throwing an eye-catching 126.2 innings. In '91 they decided to "really work him." For the Cubs he made 11 starts and 53 relief appearances covering an ungodly (and for a pitcher perhaps "criminal") 156 innings! . . . No wonder he fell apart in '92! . . . We take just a bit of extra space in this thumbnail to point out that middlemen and spot starter types can be among the most abused members of staff. Their versatility and dependability often make them the "oxen" of a team's staff. And the next season it often turns them into an anvil.

NATIONAL LEAGUE IN-BETWEENERS

Middle Third:

Rank	Pitcher	Team	7/1/94 Age	T	TPER Trendline 1990	1991	1992	3 yr Avg.	1993 TPER
18.	Tom Edens	HOU	33	R	98†	(96)†	87	94	93
19.	Mike Maddux	NYM	32	R	*	73	85	78	93
20.	Al Osuna	HOU	28	L	*	96	120	106	(93)
21.	Matt Turner	FLA	27	R	-	-	-	-	94
22.	Blas Minor	PIT	28	R	-	-	*	*	94
23.	Shawn Boskie	CUB	27	R	98	126	128	117	97
24.	Mel Rojas	MTL	27	R	(116)	99	77	91	97
25.	Roger McDowell	LAD	33	R	95	105	113	104	97
26.	Rob Murphy	STL	34	L	156†	110†	102	124	99
27.	Joe Klink	FLA	32	L	(76)	91	DNP	85	(100)
28.	Rich Rodriguez	SDO/FLA	31	L	90	98	80	89	102
29.	Jeff Reardon	CIN	38	R	94†	100†	103†	100	102
30.	Brian Williams	HOU	25	R	-	*	107	107	102
31.	Jeff Shaw	MTL	27	R	162†	87†	*	116	103
32.	Tim Mauser	PHI/SDO	27	R	-	*	-	*	103
33.	Steve Reed	COL	28	R	-	-	*	*	105
34.	Bob Scanlan	CUB	27	R	-	96	85	91	105
35.	Mike Williams	PHI	24	R	-	-	(103)	(103)	105

* Under 100 TBF-not included in average. ( ) 100-199 TBF. † Includes AL TPER, unadjusted to NL.

TOM EDENS

Underrated and almost anonymous middleman who's now strung together four consecutive below-100 TPERs this decade . . . Began the year on the DL with shoulder problems. Struggled in his first few appearances, then had 10 straight scoreless stints. Later had a stretch where he blanked the opposition in 9 of 10 outings . . . Twins converted him to middle relief in '92 with impressive success . . . Sinker got him 7 DPs in just 49 innings. Nice weapon to have at your disposal if you're a manager in a middle-inning jam.

MIKE MADDUX

Underrated middleman put together another solid season though his TPER did move up from the 73 and 85 of the previous two seasons . . . His 3.60 ERA and 93 TPER would have looked a lot more impressive had he not been drilled for seven runs in two short outings early in June. Subtract those two terrible trips to the hill and he'd have had his third consecutive ERA in the twos . . . Good across-the-board numbers with just a .243 opposing BA and but 3 HRs allowed in 75 innings . . . Everyone knows his famous brother Greg and his $5,550,000 salary in '93. How many know that this Maddux brother also made a million?

AL OSUNA

The prototype of a "spot pitcher" making 44 appearances but throwing only 25+ innings . . . Brought in to get lefties out (.222 BA) but did a much better job against righties (+.184) . . . But 13 walks is too many for a cameo pitcher . . . In 27 of his 44 outings he got two outs or less . . . Only 5-of-44 inherited runners scored . . . Might last forever with this workload.

MATT TURNER

This totally unrespected "scuffler" emerged as a solid set-up man with a fine 94 TPER after a career spent trying to convince somebody that he could pitch "up there" . . . Spent 5½ years with the Braves' organization after signing as an undrafted free agent. Shuffled over to Houston where he worked another season and a half at AAA without getting any major league shot. The Marlins inked him to a AAA contract and reaped the dividends . . . His 2.91 ERA trailed only ace-closer Bryan Harvey in the Florida pen . . . Fanned 59 in 68 innings including twice striking out the side so you know he's got some stuff . . . NL hitters managed just a .227 BA though he did toss 7 gopher balls . . . Forget stealing on him (1 for 3) . . . So how'd he fall through the cracks?

BLAS MINOR

Broke the Pirate record for games pitched by a rookie pitcher with 65 . . . Check that eye-popping strikeouts-to-walks ratio (84–26 in 94+ innings) . . . NL hitters "Blas-ted" 8 HRs off him, well within the acceptable range as was his control of stealers (just 5 of 9) . . . Served a five-game suspension for throwing at Chicago's Mark Grace . . . Looks like the Bucs have found a durable, effective (TPER 94) bullpener. Adding him to Cooke, Wagner, Johnston and Dewey means Pittsburgh, in the midst of their '93 downward spiral, may have found five members of their "staff of the near future."

SHAWN BOSKIE

Has been a candidate for and a disappointment to the rotation this entire decade . . . But maybe Chicago stumbled on something making him a long man in '93 . . . After two horrendous TPER years (126 and 128—yuck!), Boskie appeared to be going nowhere again with the Cubs quickly shipping him to Iowa right after the season began. He got his ears pinned back down on the farm but the Cubs still recalled him on June 15 . . . He returned a changed pitcher. Strung together 14 consecutive scoreless pen games starting in early July . . . Posted the first winning season of his career (5–3) . . . Has learned to keep it in the park (7 HRs in 65 IP after 14 in 91+ the year before) . . . Opponent BA dropped 26 points to .258. And he threw 11 DP balls . . . Former first-round draftee of the Cubs went two or more innings in 17 of his appearances . . . Will they leave him in this role? Or might they take a chance at starting him again?

MEL ROJAS

Lots of pitchers have bad numbers. This guy blamed his bad numbers on his number! . . . Had been #51. Switched to #27 and got off to a horrid 1–5 start. In a fit of frustration he cut a #27 jersey into shreds and returned to #51. Almost immediately his effectiveness returned also. (Hey, as they say in the beer commercial, "Why ask why?") . . . Shortly, after the jersey switchback, he began a streak that saw him go 3–2 with an ERA of 1.47 over his final 49 IP . . . That brought his TPER back down to a creditable 97 after his scintillating 77 the year before . . . Only 6 roundtrippers in 88+ innings. Runners succeeded in 8-of-9 steal attempts . . . Has now logged 188 innings of relief work the last two seasons. That's plenty of work so he opted to skip winter ball this off-season. Good thinking.

ROGER McDOWELL

Veteran former star closer now consigned to life "in the middle" . . . ERA looked nice (2.25). TPER looked mediocre (97) and a 102 average for the decade . . . Has become awfully hittable of late. Opponent BA of .306 in '92 and .285 last season . . . More walks than strikeouts (30–27). But a mere two taters . . . No longer the pitcher who won 14 and saved 22 out of the pen of the marvelous Mets in '86. But this guy's business card should read "Have arm will pitch." Made 54 appearances last year. That's almost like taking a season off for him. It's the fewest games he's pitched in his nine-year career. Check out the incredible durability he's displayed. His yearly game totals starting in '85 have been: 62–75–56–62–69–72–71–65–54.

ROB MURPHY

Elastic-armed tweener made 73 appearances, an all-time record for a Cards lefty . . . The league swatted him for a .290 BA and 8 HRs in 64+ innings. But he also got two-for-one 11 times. Given the types of situations he inherits, that's an important ability to possess . . . And speaking of "inherited"—he allowed only 4 of the 31 men other pitchers left on base to score . . . An avid horse-racing fan who's into breeding and racing thoroughbreds. That fits because he's a "horse" himself having pitched in 494 games the last seven seasons.—an amazing 71 a year.

JOE KLINK

The "Colonel" tied closer Harvey for the most Marlin appearances with 59 . . . Used as a spot pitcher (just 37.2 IP in those 59 games) primarily to get LHHs out—limiting them to a .216 BA. But righties bombed him for a .323 BA . . . His TPER finished at an even 100 thanks to his not permitting a single HR . . . If only he had better control (24 BBs and just 22 Ks in that limited action) . . . But his '93 represents a triumph of sorts for this former Oakland pen member who made it all the way back after blowing out his elbow and missing the entire '92 season.

RICH RODRIGUEZ

This anonymous workhorse made 70 appearances in his combined stints with the Padres and Marlins and has now pitched in 195 games over the past three seasons . . . Does anyone realize that his steady and impressive TPER trendline entering '93 read 90–98–80? His '93 TPER jumped to 102 mainly because of a 22-point rise in opponent BA to .251. . . . Weird stat line: Lefties scratched to hit just .190 against him but three of them took him deep and he walked 10 LHHs while fanning only 3.

JEFF REARDON

This former bullpen ace has now put together four average TPER seasons this decade (94–100–103–102). But his last year or two might actually be viewed as an accomplishment considering that many in the game thought he'd lost all usefulness . . . Had the usual incredible control to thank for what success he had (10 BB in 61+ innings) . . . The league managed a decent average (.270) but only four homers and none in his first 40 games . . . He could only induce one DP all season . . . But he led the Reds with 58 appearances and other pitchers adored him as he allowed just one of 28 inherited runners to score . . . Second to Lee Smith all-time in saves (365 to Smith's 401) . . . If you're one of those who believe he's at the end of his road at 38 be careful. He's begun fooling around with a knuckler that looked pretty decent at times. Hey, Charlie Hough's 46 and still throwing "that thing."

BRIAN WILLIAMS

Converted to relief for the first time in his four-year pro career . . . TPER probably won't ever dip well below 100 (107 and 102 in his two seasons) until he gains better control (80 BB in 178 IP over the two years) . . . Opponent BA a respectable .248 . . . Astros keep waiting for signs he'll pitch to the level that made him a first rounder in June of '90. But in five minor league stops over three years only once did his ERA dip below 4.00.

JEFF SHAW

One of the longest shots to make the Expos when camp began. But he forced his way into Expo plans with a spectacular spring (5–0, ERA of 0.77) . . . His 103 TPER's pretty average and made up of pretty average elements. His biggest weakness gopher-ball tendencies (12 in 95+ innings) . . . His biggest plus—decent control and sinking stuff that brought him 10 DPs . . . Got his first major league win since '90 when he was auditioning as an Indians starter . . . Once he made the club he requested #31 in memory of his friend, the late Cleveland reliever Steve Olin.

TIM MAUSER

Another of the hurlers "auditioned" by the Pads in '93 after being acquired from the Phillies . . . A decent 103 TPER. A little wild but holds runners well . . . OK opponent BA of .245 with exactly one HR every nine IP . . . Probably lucky to get out of the Phils' system where he appeared to have little shot at ever emerging . . . Weird: Actually suited up for two teams in the same day. The Phils and Pads finished a game at 4:40 A.M. July 3. Later that day the trade was made sending Roger Mason to Philly and the two swapped uniforms in time for that evening's game.

STEVE REED

When the Rockies selected him from the Giants with a fourth-round pick in the expansion draft, most assumed he'd lead their bullpen. After all, he'd amassed 43 saves in '92, winning the minor league Rolaids Relief Man Award . . . But he, like teammate Holmes, had a dreadful start and took his 10.50 ERA back to the minors in mid-May . . . By the time he returned so had Holmes who'd claimed the closer role and never let it go. So Reed settled in and did solid work as a set-up man, eventually lowering his TPER to a credible 105 . . . Did the park affect him the most? ERA of 6.39 at home and 1.60 on the road. Some wiseguy GM seeing this might want to pry him away from the Rockies.

BOB SCANLAN

Threw in a clunker after two solid seasons (TPER of 96 and 85) . . . His '93 figure of 105 resulted because the league's hitters jumped 39 points in BA from .235 to .274 . . . His career high 4.54 ERA's bad enough without realizing that his second-half figure was 5.23 . . . Had a five-runs-allowed game and a pair of four-runners . . . Saved 14 the season before so the club felt him ideally suited to set up Myers. Had 25 "holds" but too often the other team "got a hold of him" . . . Spends his off-season working on a mechanical engineering degree from UCLA. Wonder if his troubles last season could be a case of "bad mechanics"?

MIKE WILLIAMS

Former 14th-round pick after a career as a Gobbler at Virginia Tech who's now had a couple of brief chances to make a major league impression . . . Normally excellent minor league control betrayed him last year (22 BB in 51 IP) . . . Other numbers acceptable when viewed in a "debut" situation . . . Solid records as a minor league starter. Ben Rivera had best pitch better very quickly or this guy has a shot at taking his rotation spot.

NATIONAL LEAGUE IN-BETWEENERS

Bottom Third:

Rank	Pitcher	Team	7/1/94 Age	I	TPER Trendline 1990	1991	1992	3 yr Avg.	1993 TPER
36.	Trevor Hoffman	FLA/SDO	26	R	-	-	-	-	105
37.	Richie Lewis	FLA	28	R	-	-	*	*	106
38.	Chuck McElroy	CUB	26	L	-	93	115	103	108
39.	Jeff Innis	NYM	31	R	(95)	74	98	87	109
40.	Dave Burba	SFO	27	R	*	(102)	114	110	111
41.	Tim Scott	SDO/MTL	27	R	-	*	(131)	(131)	111
42.	Todd Burns	TEX/STL	30	R	105	*	92	97	112†
43.	Dan Plesac	CUB	32	L	102†	107†	94†	101	116
44.	Denny Neagle	PIT	25	L	-	*	121	121	118
45.	Gary Wayne	COL	31	L	(100)	*	116	109	120
46.	Dave Righetti	SFO	35	L	106†	88	107	100	120
47.	Jeff Parrett	COL	32	R	117	(139)	98	111	121
48.	Bobby Ayala	CIN	24	R	-	-	(109)	(109)	123
49.	Steve Wilson	LAD	29	L	99	*	116	104	(124)
50.	Bobby Thigpen	CWS/PHI	30	R	71†	115†	116†	97	125†
51.	Mark Davis	PHI/SDO	33	L	140†	105†	164†	135	130
52.	Kevin Wickander	CLE/CIN	29	L	*	-	(110)	(110)	(166)

* Under 100 TBF-not included in average. ( ) 100-199 TBF. † Includes AL TPER, unadjusted to NL.

TREVOR HOFFMAN

Many say he's the closer of the future for the Pads . . . Outstanding fastball fanning 79 in 90+ innings . . . Somewhat high walk total of 39 is actually deceiving. One third of those (13) were intentional. Those must be counted against him and helped inflate his TPER to an above-average 105 . . . Opponents hit just .234 against him but took him deep 10 times. But yielded just two over his last 31 appearances . . . Intriguing story in that he began his pro career as a shortstop in the Reds' organization (11th rounder) . . . Couldn't hit so they noticed that laser arm and gave him a shot at relieving . . . The Marlins snapped him up in the expansion draft. San Diego made him the key man in the deal that sent slugging Gary Sheffield to Florida . . . Made 67 appearances and threw 90 innings so you know he's sturdy . . . Keep an eye on this guy for a possible breakthrough soon.

RICHIE LEWIS

His 77+ innings made him the most used member of the Marlin relief corps . . . The Orioles had groomed him as a starter. But Florida immediately put him in the pen with decent though unspectacular results (TPER 106) . . . Walks, which have been a career-long source of concern, continued to plague him (43 in those 77+ innings). And 9 wild pitches? . . . But the league's hitters had real trouble with him (.239 BA) and managed just 7 HRs . . . Seemed to wear down toward the end of the season.

CHUCK MCELROY

Once a key player in the deal that sent Mitch Williams to the Phils in '91, he's seen his TPER slip from a solid debut season with the Cubs to a pair of very poor campaigns (115 and last year's 108) . . . He continues to have control trouble (25 BB in 47+ IP). So, you can't trust him in any situation where a walk might spell disaster. And now he's becoming hittable (.280). That's a nasty combo . . . Did yield only 4 HRs . . . At one point Chicago lost patience and shipped him to Iowa for 3½ weeks . . . But he's young, healthy and left-handed so there'll be a constant string of opportunities. But how long's the string in Chicago?

JEFF INNIS

After three very solid TPER seasons his figure ballooned to 109 last season. Lots of little things accounted for the rise. Walks

increased some. Opponent BA rose 12 points to .278. Stealers succeeded 9-of-12 times . . . But that TPER and the accompanying 4.11 ERA are both poor and deceptive. In four of his appearances he got lathered for 15 earned runs in just 3⅔ innings. In the other 63 games he had a dazzling 2.47 ERA . . . . . . Almost the blue print for a middleman with 212 appearances spanning 249+ innings over the last three seasons.

DAVE BURBA

SF's middleman and good-luck charm. What else would you call a pitcher whose ERA looked mediocre (4.25) and whose TPER looked sad (111) but whose record drew raves (10–3) . . . Ran off an eight-game win streak (longest since Rick "Big Daddy" Reuschel also won that many consecutively in '89) . . . Needs to develop something to help him retire LHH (BA .320) . . . The league could hit him (.265) and take him out (14 HR in 95 IP). They also ran on him (10 for 13). They just couldn't beat him.

TIM SCOTT

Acquired in late June and plugged into a tweener role . . . Cannot hold runners! That's a dangerous deficiency for a reliever who often appears with runners on. Stealers swiped 18 of 20. Hey, when he arrived at the hill the "go" signal went on . . . Managed just 3 DPs in 71+ innings. But, when the guy at first steals second a lot, there goes the DP . . . Walked more than 4 per 9 IP. But those 65 Ks in 71+ IP tells us he's got some heat . . . Adds up to a 111 TPER. Not good. But if someone teaches him to control the running game, his obviously "live arm" might be much more useful.

TODD BURNS

The "Mad Hatter" capped off a perfectly dreadful '93 by being released in St. Louis . . . Got his nickname for his incessant fiddling with his cap between pitches often appearing as if he can't get the darned thing to fit just right . . . He couldn't get anything just right last year. Was doing decent work at Texas (TPER 105) when they shuffled him off to the Cards in a deal for minor leaguer Duff Brumley. Nothing went right in St. Looie. His TPER skyrocketed to 128 during his 24-game stint for the Redbirds as the NL hit .274 against him with 8 long ones in a mere 30 innings . . . Relieved in the first inning August 24 and surrendered four HRs and five runs before getting San Diego out . . . For the year he totaled 41 BBs, just 45 Ks and went 0–8 . . . It all added up to a 112 TPER and no job. But previous seasons contained OK work so you know somebody will give him a new cap and another chance in the spring.

DAN PLESAC

After a string of superb seasons as Milwaukee's closer (86 saves and three straight ERAs in the twos from '87–'89) he's fallen on hard times . . . Starting with a dismal '90 season his TPER rose into triple figures (102) and then stepped up again in '91 (107). That number dropped to 94 in '92 encouraging the Cubs to give him a fat two-year contract. He gave them his worst season ever . . . That 116 TPER consists of some wretched numbers like a .298 opponent BA and 10 HRs in a mere 62+ innings of work . . . By the end of the year the Cubs used him as nothing more than a spot pitcher, brought on to get one or two outs and quickly gotten out of there . . . Maybe that's his limited future as RHHs lit him up for a .321 average . . . Once a pitcher that hitters would hide from. Now his club's trying to find ways of hiding him.

DENNY NEAGLE

The Pirates keep waiting for him after making him a key man in the March of '92 deal that sent superb lefty John Smiley to the Twins. They're still waiting. Has posted consecutive ugly TPERs of 121 and 118 in his two years at Three Rivers . . . With a TPER like that you know he's got some bad-looking numbers so here goes: 10 HRs and 37 BB in 81+ innings. Just 1 DP. Thieves ran at will (16 of 21) . . . But 73 Ks in 81 IP tells you there's some stuff inside those poor performances . . . After a terrible first half the Bucs gave up and shipped him to Buffalo along with his 6.12 ERA. It seemed to help. He returned to throw much better over his final 23 games (ERA 3.38). But while he struggled to find himself, several other Bucco youngsters stepped forward and the days of Pittsburgh keeping a staff spot open for him have ended.

GARY WAYNE

"Stiff-looking" lefty acquired in a minor deal with Minnesota late in spring training who led the Rockies with 65 appearances as a spot pitcher . . . Had that unattractive 116 TPER with Minnesota in '92 and saw it bump up to 120 with the Rocks . . . Every element in his game's a "little high". In 62+ innings his walks (26), HRs (8), BA (.276) all need to come down a notch to get that TPER to acceptable levels. And it can be done as Ruffin, Holmes and Reed all displayed while working out of the Colorado pen . . . Batted for the first time in his career last year and it would be his only at bat of the season. He singled, driving in a pair of runs and helping himself to one of his five victories. If he never hits again he can tell his grandkids "Yeah, they never got your old granddad out in his major league career."

DAVE RIGHETTI

His career's in a downward spiral . . . Lost his closer role in '92 to Beck. Lost everything in '93 . . . TPER skyrocketed to an ugly 120 . . . Batters feasted on him (.305 BA) with an outrageous 11 HRs in a mere 47 innings . . . Lord, what might his TPER have been if he didn't do an excellent job controlling runners? (1-for-5 stealing and 6 DPs) . . . His 46 saves for the Yanks in '86 stood as the major league record for lefties until Myers saved 53 last year . . . Though he's posted only four saves the last two years, he's still #6 on the active list with 252 . . . . . At one time one of the finest closers in the game with 247 saves in just an eight-year period. Now he's 35 with ERAs in the fives the last two years.

JEFF PARRETT

Veteran reliever whose wild roller-coaster ride of TPERs going up and down continues. This decade it's gone from 117 up to 139 then way down to 98 and rocketed back up to 121 last season . . .

His season ended with major reconstructive elbow surgery in August . . . Wildness really hurt him with 45 walks and 11 wild pitches in 73+ innings . . . Despite being 9–1 for the '92 A's, he had to win a Rockies spot as a non-roster spring invitee . . . Has now carved out a respectable career (49–33 with 22 saves and a 3.87 ERA). So why doesn't anybody keep him around more than a year or two? . . . If the doctors did their work well he'll likely show up trying to earn a job again. And he'll probably do so again.

BOBBY AYALA

Great arm—bad TPER (123) . . . Rookie with "high heat" who'd bounced back and forth between starting and relieving in the Reds system before debuting as, well, both last year—9 starts and 34 in relief . . . Had the deadly duo of poor control (which has seemed to come and go in his career) and "long-ball-itis" (a whopping 16 HRs in 98 IP) . . . Seattle manager Lou Pinella, who'd known him from his days as Reds' skipper, dealt for him right after the season. Lou might want to seriously consider making him a full-time reliever off his '93 performances. As a starter: 2–6 and an ERA of 8.41. As a reliever: 5–4 and a 3.61 ERA.

STEVE WILSON

Has gotten his head handed to him two straight seasons with TPERs of 116 and 124. . . . The ball stayed in the park (2 HRs) but that's about the best that can be said . . . 14 BB in 25+ innings. . . . LA gave him two months to take over the lefty job in their pen then shipped him to Albuquerque in late May not recalling him until September. Didn't win a game down there making 12 starts and going 0–3 . . . LA still desperately needs lefty pen help. Will he get yet another chance?

BOBBY THIGPEN

His effectiveness has totally disappeared . . . In 1990 he shattered the all-time record for saves in a season with 57. Since then his save totals dropped to 30 and then 22 and then 1 last year. His ERA's gone from 1.83 to 3.49 to 4.75 to 5.71 with the '93 Sox and 6.05 with the Phils . . . TPERs? Rising from 71 to 115, 116 and finally 125. . . . Both leagues hit over .300 against him in '93 . . . Hey, we could go on forever talking ugly numbers. So, why did the Phils insist on using him out of their playoff bullpen?

MARK DAVIS

The trials, tribulations and travels of this former Cy Young award winner continue . . . What happened to him? Former wizard of the Padres' pen now has this TPER trendline for the decade: 140–105–164–130. How does he still have a job? . . . Did nothing to impress either the Phils or the Pads who picked him up off the street after a July 2 release . . . Saved a game July 15 versus Philly (bet that felt good). It marked Mark's first save in two years and two months! In 1990 he saved 44 for the Pads. He's had 11 since.

KEVIN WICKANDER

A life of terrible adversity . . . He'd once been an emerging prospect with a fine arm before a bout with alcoholism derailed him. Also had to overcome a shattered elbow suffered when his spikes caught in the minors causing him to fall. Just appeared to be getting it all back together in Cleveland when, last spring, that tragic boating accident killed his best friend and fellow Indian reliever Steve Olin. He simply couldn't cope with it. Frequently sat for long periods of time staring into Olin's empty locker. The Indians, to their credit, realized he desperately needed a change of scenery and dealt him to Cincy. Wickander left asking for and receiving permission to take Olin's shower slippers with him. Admits the memories caused him to unravel at times . . . Forget his atrocious numbers (TPER 166—highest in the majors) and hope he's pulled his life together.

NATIONAL LEAGUE DEBUT PITCHERS

Rank	Pitcher	Team	7/1/94 Age	T	GS	GR	IP	ERA	1993 TPER
Starters:									
1.	Kirk Rueter	MTL	23	L	14	0	85.2	2.73	75
2.	Scott Sanders	SDO	25	R	9	0	52.1	4.13	93
3.	Larry Luebbers	CIN	24	R	14	0	77.1	4.54	96
4.	Tim Worrell	SDO	26	R	16	5	100.2	4.92	103
5.	Pat Rapp	FLA	26	R	16	0	94.0	4.02	105
6.	Salomon Torres	SFO	22	R	8	0	44.2	4.03	(106)
7.	Bobby Jones	NYM	24	R	9	0	61.2	3.65	108
8.	Allen Watson	STL	23	L	15	1	86.0	4.60	112
9.	John Roper	CIN	22	R	15	1	80.0	5.63	122
Utility:									
1.	Tom Urbani	STL	26	L	9	9	62.0	4.65	104
2.	Dave Telgheder	NYM	27	R	7	17	75.2	4.76	104
3.	Curt Leskanic	COL	26	R	8	10	57.0	5.37	108
4.	David Weathers	FLA	24	R	6	8	45.2	5.12	114
5.	Kerry Taylor	SDO	24	R	7	29	68.1	6.45	128
Relievers:									
1.	Pedro A. Martinez	SDO	25	L	0	32	37.0	2.43	(71)
2.	Jerry Spradlin	CIN	27	R	0	37	49.0	3.49	(88)
3.	Omar Daal	LAD	22	L	0	47	35.1	5.09	(117)
4.	Robb Nen	TEX/FLA	24	R	4	20	56.0	6.75	137

* Under 100 TBF-not included in average. ( ) 100-199 TBF. † Includes AL TPER, unadjusted to NL.

KIRK RUETER

A spectacular entrance! . . . Began the season with two years of A ball experience and wasn't even invited to the Expos' camp. But he ripped off five straight wins at the AA level and then stepped to AAA and continued to pitch impressively . . . Montreal called in early July and he made a splashy beginning snuffing out the Giants on two hits over 8.1 innings . . . He wouldn't lose a single time in 14 starts and was the Sporting News' NL Rookie-Pitcher-of-the-Year . . . Fantastic control (18 BBs in 85+ innings) . . . Forget running on him (4 of 11) or overpowering him (allowed just 5 HRs) . . . No wonder nobody scored regularly on him as his wonderful 75 TPER and 2.73 ERA attests . . . One extra plus—if you attend his game there's a solid chance you'll get home for the late news. He hurled Montreal's two shortest games (2:05 and 2:06).

SCOTT SANDERS

What a season for a pitcher who figured to spend '93 at AAA . . . Won his major league debut in an emergency start for the injured Wally Whitehurst August 6 . . . Made 9 starts in all allowing just 4 HRs, 4 steals and 23 BBs in 52 innings. It added up to a 93 TPER bettered only on the Padres' staff by rookie reliever Pedro Martinez . . . Former first-round draftee whose life's included stops in some of America's marvelous outposts. Born in Hannibal (Mo.), lives in Thibodaux (La) and pitched for two years in Waterloo (Ia).

LARRY LUEBBERS

One of the season's few pleasant surprises for the injury-racked Reds . . . Debuted in the majors at mid-season with a modest 2–5 record and 4.54 ERA. His decent TPER of 96 has some attractive elements—only 7 HRs in 77 IP and stealers succeeded just 5-of-13 times. Will occasionally get two for one (7 DPs) . . . But that 38 BB to 38 K ratio's a bit discouraging. But then, even his minor league ratios aren't all that appealing . . . His poor-looking record resulted from him being really "lit up" a few times. But overall he limited opponents to three or fewer runs in 10 of his 14 starts.

TIM WORRELL

An encouraging beginning for this brother of Dodger reliever Todd Worrell . . . Used primarily as a starter with moderate numbers across the board in 100+ innings (11 HRs, 43 BB, .269 BA and 10-of-19 stealers) . . . Had never pitched a pro game in relief before this season . . . His 2–7 record should be mostly ignored. Actually had one very good stretch where he posted a 2.05 ERA over five starts but had no wins to show for it . . . Brother Todd's '92 TPER? 103. Tim in '93? 103.

PAT RAPP

The Marlins' fifth pick in the first round of the expansion process . . . Spent the first half of the year in AAA before his July 5 recall. Placed immediately in the rotation and stayed there for 16 starts through the end of the campaign . . . HRs bothered him early surrendering 6 in his first 49 innings. He then settled down to allow just one his last 45 frames . . . The Marlins had only two starters throw nine-inning complete games—him and Ryan Bowen . . . While the league bounced him around a bit (.281 BA) they took no liberties with him on the bases swiping only 3 in 9 attempts . . . A former Giants first-round pick in the '89 June draft. One wonders why SF left him exposed come expansion draft time.

SALOMON TORRES

At 21 years old he got thrown into the crucible of a pennant race as a starter after he'd posted a total of 14 victories moving from Double A to Triple A during the season . . . SF lost only four of their final 18 games. He got charged with all those losses. But the offense should share the blame scoring just five runs in those games . . . Wildness caused his TPER to rise into three figures (106) with 27 BBs in 44+ innings . . . But with only that amount of work he's still eligible for rookie awards next season. . . . But did the Giants simply ask too much of him? Combining all his stops in their system, by year's end he'd thrown 233 innings, more than any pitcher SF had under contract. Don't you think that's a bit much for a 21-year-old who's 5' 11" and 150 pounds?

BOBBY JONES

Former #1 "sandwich pick" at the top of the draft who's sped through the Mets' system leaving some dominated hitters in his wake (ERAs of 1.85 and 1.88 his first two minor league years) . . . Had a league-leading 10 victories at AAA when the Mets summoned him in August . . . TPERed at 108 with no glaring weakness or outstanding strength . . . The Mets probably rushed him a bit last season. But, when he threw *ten* shutout innings at the Cards in late September, he reaffirmed his position as the youngster most likely to step into next season's rotation.

ALLEN WATSON

Zoomed out of the minors and into the Cards' rotation rattling off six straight wins. No Redbird rookie had begun a career in that fashion since Luis Arroyo in 1955 . . . The streak came to a screeching halt when the Padres drove him out in the first inning and then slaughtered reliever Todd Burns on their way to 13 first-inning runs. That started him going the other way and the tumble never ended finishing the year with seven straight losses . . . It all added up to a rather unattractive 112 TPER . . .Yielded 11 HRs in but 86 innings of work. . . . Allowed 11 steals and the league wound up hitting .271 against him . . . So, will the real Allen Watson please take the mound in '94? But which one is it—Allen Watson #1 or Allen Watson #2?

JOHN ROPER

Some say his is the best arm in the organization. You couldn't tell by last season's ugly 122 TPER . . . Got knocked around at a .295 clip with lots of extra-base hits including 10 HRs in 80 IP. Walked 36 and permitted 10 steals in 14 attempts. Appeared to be overmatched at times. That's reasonable. Was just 21 years old and also struggled with injuries that put him on the Reds DL once and their Indianapolis farm team's DL once . . . The master plan had been to let him experience a full season at AAA. That plan went out the window when massive injuries wrecked the Cincy staff . . . Forget those awful numbers. Realize that in his first three pro seasons after being drafted out of high school, managers in all three leagues he pitched in named him that league's best pitching prospect.

TOM URBANI

Rookie rode the shuttle making four trips up to St. Louis from Louisville and eventually making 18 appearances evenly divided between starts and bullpen work . . . His middling 104 TPER helped greatly by his marvelous ability to stop the running game. Stealers succeeded just once in seven tries and he threw 6 DP balls . . . Only permitted 4 HRs but the league didn't seem fooled most of the time putting up a .296 BA. But that's been part of his minor league profile at various stops . . . Maybe all that traveling had some effect and he'll get to spend '94 in one place—the Cards' pen.

DAVE TELGHEDER

Only three of the Mets' 19 pitchers posted winning records last year. John Franco: 4–3. Rookie Ken Greer: 1–0. And this fellow: 6–2 . . . Pretty hittable (.276) with 10 roundtrippers in just 75 innings. But, even given those unimpressive stats, his TPER stayed at 104 because he showed terrific control (21 BB or 2.5 per 9 IP). Displayed an excellent ability to stifle the running game as stealers went just 4 for 9 while inducing 7 DPs . . . Not overpowering and probably still a long shot to ever be a rotation regular. But the Mets love his makeup and feel he's got a solid future as a middleman.

CURTIS LESKANIC

Far-out rookie who sometimes shaved the hair off his pitching arm to make it "more aerodynamic" . . . TPERed a respectable 108 given those "hitter friendly" conditions in his home park . . . Began the season in the minors reached the bigs in late June, splitting time between the rotation and the pen . . . Only a .266 opponent BA gives reason for hope. His minor league career had been marked by occasional struggles with his control and those continued (27 BBs in 57+ innings) . . . 8 wild pitches didn't help either. A raw rookie worthy of further consideration.

DAVID WEATHERS

Made a couple trips to the bigs splitting time between starting (6) and relief (8) . . . TPER of 114 caused simply by virtue of his being easy to hit (.306). Also had trouble stopping stealers who went a perfect 7 for 7 . . . But the rest of his profile has some appeal. Excellent control (13 BB in 45+ innings) and only 3 HRs allowed. If he could just lower that opponent BA. But one warning—his minor league profile with both the Toronto and Florida organizations suggests he's got one weakness—very hittable. Uh-oh.

KERRY TAYLOR

Grabbed out of the Twins' organization in the Rule V draft. That meant San Diego had to keep him in the bigs all year or offer him back to Minnesota. And keep him they did . . . Hadn't ever pitched above Class A before '93 so you know he had to be horribly overmatched at times and his numbers showed it. His 128 TPER made up of a high opponent BA (.277) and awful control (49 BB in 68+ innings) . . . Also had trouble holding major league runners who stole 13 of 16 . . . Simply ignore those stats, allow him to return to AA next year and see what develops.

PEDRO A. MARTINEZ

The "other" Pedro Martinez, also a rookie reliever converted from a starter . . . but this one's a lefty and pitched for the Padres. And like Pedro J. up the coast, pitched extremely well (71 TPER) . . . 32 App., 37 IP, 2.43 ERA . . . mid-season promo from AAA who'll play a major role for the Pads in '94 in the pen or the rotation. Finally made the bigs in his 7th year, but was only 24.

JERRY SPRADLIN

A late bloomer who finally made it to the majors in July after 5½ years in the Reds' system . . . Nice TPER of 88 based primarily on excellent control (walked just 9 in 49 IP) . . . Yielded just 4 HRs and 4 SBs . . . By September he'd really begun to settle into his middleman job (ERA of 1.26 the last five weeks) . . . Had 34 saves at AA in '92 . . . Got his chance because of the Reds' horrible blight of injuries and took full advantage of it.

OMAR DAAL

LA rushed this youngster to the bigs in their desperate search for an LHP in their pen . . . Used almost exclusively in "spots" as he pitched one inning or less in 40 of his 47 outings . . . More walks than Ks (21–19). . . . Froze runners very well with just two attempted steals . . . But add those walks to a .277 opponent BA and you've got the makings of trouble . . . Write off '93 as a year sacrificed to experience and focus on the fact that LA thought enough of him to believe he could do the job at just 21 years old.

ROBB NEN

Sometimes totally out of control, high-velocity pitcher with an incredible history of being fragile . . . Acquired from Texas in the deal that sent set-up man Cris Carpenter to the Rangers . . . Brought with him the same collection of enticing talents and frustrating problems that have marked his career . . . Walked 20 in 33 innings while fanning 27. Blew away 8 Reds in his most memorable start in posting his only victory . . . But the league tattooed him for 5 HRs in that limited action . . . Made his annual stop on the DL with a groin strain. But at least it wasn't an arm-related problem. He made six separate trips to the DL with arm miseries from '90–'92 . . . But he's young and the radar gun goes crazy when it sees him (can hit 97–98 MPH at times) . . . Florida's got the time to wait and see if he develops. Texas got tired of waiting.

THE
TEAMS

TEAM TOPR: THE ULTIMATE SERVICE MANUAL?

One of the problems that fans, analysts and—one suspects—some organizations have faced for years was how to accurately analyze a baseball team: take it apart, examine its components and find some clue as to why it performed as it did. Then, determine what needed to be done to *fix* it. If, indeed, it needed fixing.

The vision of a sleek, expensive sports car dismembered and its parts strewn in uncatalogued heaps around the floor and on the workbenches of a repair garage is not inappropriate. Nor is the picture of the grizzled mechanic, with his oil-stained cap in hand, scratching his head and wishing he had a service manual for this particular one-of-a-kind model.

The problem has always been the profusion of elements involved in determining a team's performance and their quirky, often unfathomable, interrelationships. What is it, exactly, that makes the team's engine *run*? Or, alternatively, what is making it *stall*?

Was it the pitching? Was it the hitting? Was it power or speed? The answers to the "bigger" questions are *usually* obvious. But not always. The "smaller" stuff is nearly always elusive.

TOPR and TPER, by virtue of their quantification of everything that can be quantified, their apparent relationship to actual results and their direct interaction with one another, may well be the "service manual" we're seeking. It works for individuals. What is a baseball team if not a composite of its team members?

Thus, we have Team TOPR and Team TPER. An accounting of everything a team's individual players and pitchers accomplished in the course of a season: the sum of the parts, with the parts in their proper context.

◆ Team TOPR—the team's complete offensive output. The league average team is, as before, an even 100. An above-average Team TOPR (i.e., over 100) indicates an above-average offense. The further above 100, the more offensive. The league crowns in 1993 went to Detroit (113.4) and Philadelphia (112.9) who, not coincidentally, each scored the most runs in their respective leagues.

◆ Team TPER—the team's overall pitching effectiveness. A Team TPER below 100 means the pitching staff is better than the league average. The further below 100, the better. The leagues' best in '93 were the White Sox (89.0) and the Braves (85.8). No surprise here, either.

◆ Now we come to the *differential* between the Team TOPR and Team TPER. This is what determines winners and losers. The White Sox had the widest positive margin in the AL (+13.1), the Braves in the NL (+17.4). OK, it's not perfect for predicting the winner in a best four-out-of-seven series. But don't be dismayed—the world champion Blue Jays (+11.6), the Phillies (+16.0) and the Giants (+15.3) were right there with Chicago and Atlanta. Those were clearly the five best teams in baseball, weren't they? TOPR and TPER agree.

We'll delve into the Team TOPR and TPER rankings in the perspectives preceding each league. Here, though, is how we organized our thoughts on each team.

Team Trendline

First, we'll look at a five-year Team TOPR and TPER trendline. Where they have been and where their Team TOPR and TPER is

headed. To win, a team has to build a positive margin between their Team TOPR and Team TPER. Do you recall the old cliché about "raising the drawbridge" or "lowering the water" so that a boat can pass under the bridge? In this vein, consider a Team's TOPR to be their "bridge" and their TPER to be their "waterline." Either method of improvement—raising the bridge (offense) or lowering the river (pitching)—becomes an acceptable way to avoid being "under water" at season's end.

Expectations

What was generally expected of the team this year? What did we think given access to their prior TOPR and TPER data?

What Actually Happened

A brief season summary describing, as best we can tell, how it went. What were the key events?

The Home Park

How did their home park affect their performance in 1993? Our method of calculating Park TOPR is discussed in the appendix.

The Offense

We've encapsulated the team's line up in a very revealing graphic display not unlike the earlier positional norms. This gives clear evidence of the offense's strengths and weaknesses. The batting order, in some cases, has to be "synthesized" because of injuries, trades, call-ups and platoon maneuvering—but you'll recognize it. We tried to display the eleven hitters of greatest interest and importance, favoring the second half.

The Pitching

Same neat graphic trick using the eleven most interesting/important pitchers. Starters (St) are in descending order by number of starts. Utility pitchers (Ut) were used as both starters and relievers and appear in descending order by number of innings pitched. Relievers (Bp) are in *ascending* order by number of appearances. Closers (Cl) come, fittingly, last.

What Next?

What opportunities does the team have to move up in the standings? How is it positioned to capitalize on them? What's needed and where might it come from? How do their prospects, which are detailed in another section, fit into the picture?

Team TOPR and TPER Capsules

The key players and pitchers, with their conventional and TOPR/TPER stats summarized. The total team line is also juxtaposed against a line for the league's *average* team.

What Does It Take To Win?

That's the burning question, isn't it?

The Team TOPR/TPER concept illuminates this issue with clarity. *It takes about a +10-point TOPR/TPER differential to win a divi-*

sion. It doesn't make any difference whether the differential was achieved by a superior offense or by sterling pitching. It matters only that the team get ten points worth of clearance between its TOPR bridge and TPER waterline. If a team can do this, it's a near certainty that they can float to a divisional championship (unless another team builds an even bigger TOPR/TPER gap, as Atlanta did over San Francisco).

The Winners (1989-1993)

American League

	East	W-L	TOPR	TPER	Diff.	West	W-L	TOPR	TPER	Diff.
1989	Toronto	89-73	103.4	96.3	+7.1	Oakland	99-63	100.7	88.9	+11.8
1990	Boston	88-74	100.3	96.3	+4.0	Oakland	103-59	106.2	89.8	+16.4
1991	Toronto	91-71	102.6	90.6	+12.0	Minnesota	95-67	104.1	97.1	+7.0
1992	Toronto	96-66	108.6	98.9	+9.7	Oakland	96-66	107.2	100.3	+6.9
1993	Toronto	95-67	110.0	98.4	+11.6	Chicago	94-68	102.1	89.0	+13.1

National League

	East	W-L	TOPR	TPER	Diff.	West	W-L	TOPR	TPER	Diff.
1989	Chicago	93-69	104.5	99.3	+5.2	San Francisco	92-70	105.5	96.4	+9.1
1990	Pittsburgh	95-67	107.0	93.7	+13.3	Cincinnati	91-71	103.5	97.4	+6.1
1991	Pittsburgh	98-64	111.6	95.0	+16.6	Atlanta	94-68	107.2	96.5	+10.7
1992	Pittsburgh	96-66	105.8	97.2	+8.6	Atlanta	98-64	105.7	94.0	+11.7
1993	Philadelphia	97-65	112.9	96.9	+16.0	Atlanta	104-58	103.2	85.8	+17.4

See what we mean? The average division champion over the past five years exhibits a TOPR/TPER differential of +10.7. This was worth 95 W's, on average. Some did it with superior pitching. Others did it with crushing offense. Some of the winners were "balanced." The average winner's TOPR was 105.6 with a TPER of 94.9, a "balanced" situation equally reliant on offense and pitching.

To be fair, we should note that two of the winners above did *not* have the best TOPR/TPER differential in their division. We refer to the two "weakest" winners, the Cubs in 1989 and the BoSox in 1990. They sneaked in when the Mets and Blue Jays failed to convert their superior differential (+8.8 and +9.0, respectively) into a corresponding number of wins. If you thought this edition of the Mets was an underachiever, you were right. If you wondered why Toronto G.M. "Stand Pat" Gillick pulled the trigger on that huge 1990/1991 off-season trade with San Diego, now you know.

These five years are snapshots of four "mini-dynasties"—Toronto, Oakland, Pittsburgh and Atlanta. The Braves' trend is particularly intriguing: their offense is declining but their pitching has gotten better faster so that their differential is still expanding. Looks like they'll be around awhile.

AMERICAN LEAGUE PERSPECTIVE

Opposite are the final 1993 American League divisional standings with runs scored and allowed, all set against Team TOPR and TPER. There's also a standing for the league's parks in terms of 1993 Park TOPR. A park rated above 100 favored the offense. Below 100 and it suppressed offense in the pitcher's favor.

The Standings

The TOPR/TPER differential very closely tracks the teams' actual order of finish. There's no discrepancy big enough to even comment upon. The Twins, though, might be said to have "salvaged" what could have been a *really* disastrous season.

Offense and Pitching

Runs scored and TOPR also closely parallel, as they should. But Texas and, to a lesser degree, Cleveland scored a bushel or two more runs than their Team TOPR says they should have.

It's the same with runs allowed and TPER. There is a very close match as lower Team TPERs resulted in fewer runs allowed. There's a hint, though, that the Indians might have done something to slow down the opposing team's offense. They gave up plenty of runs as it was, but it looks like it could have been worse.

The above noted overachievements on offense (runs scored vs. TOPR) and defense (runs allowed vs. TPER) are worth further study and we'll address them in the Manager's section.

Park TOPR

A couple of shockers here, at least in 1993. Kansas City's Ewing Kauffman Stadium, the home park of a pop-gun lineup and a cannon of a pitching staff, is revealed to have actually been a "hitter's park" (which should make the KC hitters feel even worse about their season). The Royal's park has always been considered a "pitcher's park." But the only aspect of offense it suppressed last year was the home run. The league's hitters more than made up the difference in other categories.

Yankee Stadium has heretofore been thought a "hitter's park." But, in '93, TOPR labels it an extreme "pitcher's park," the best in the majors.

Positional and Role Norms

You first saw these in the Player's and Pitcher's section. They're repeated here so you can relate them to the Lineup TOPRs and Staff TPERs for the individual teams.

AL Positional Norms

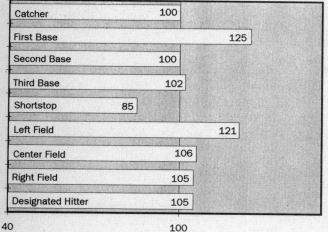

AL Role Norms

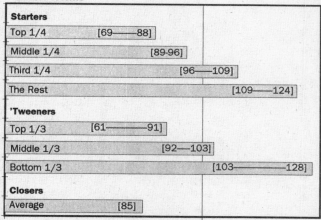

1993
American League Standings

	W-L	TOPR	TPER	*Differential*	Runs ∓
East					
Toronto	95-67	110.0	98.4	*+11.6*	+106
New York	88-74	106.3	100.6	*+5.7*	+60
Detroit	85-77	113.4	106.1	*+7.3*	+62
Baltimore	85-77	102.9	98.0	*+4.9*	+41
Boston	80-82	95.0	93.9	*+1.1*	(12)
Cleveland	76-86	100.3	106.4	*(6.1)*	(23)
Milwaukee	69-93	92.7	103.7	*(11.0)*	(59)
West					
Chicago	94-68	102.1	89.0	*+13.1*	+112
Texas	86-76	102.8	98.7	*+4.1*	+84
Kansas City	84-78	93.0	93.1	*(0.1)*	(19)
Seattle	82-80	100.1	97.0	*+3.1*	+3
California	71-91	93.5	101.5	*(8.0)*	(86)
Minnesota	71-91	90.3	106.5	*(16.2)*	(137)
Oakland	68-94	98.0	107.3	*(9.3)*	(131)
Average Team	*81-81*	*100.0*	*100.0*	*0.0*	*0*

1993 AL Offenses

Team	Runs Scored	TOPR
Detroit	899	113.4
Toronto	847	110.0
Texas	835	102.8
New York	821	106.3
Cleveland	790	100.3
Baltimore	786	102.9
Chicago	776	102.1
Average Team	*728*	*100.0*
Seattle	734	100.1
Milwaukee	733	92.7
Oakland	715	98.0
Minnesota	693	90.3
Boston	686	95.0
California	684	93.5
Kansas City	675	93.0

Note: Runs scored rankings are based on runs per 27 gross outs, not total runs.

1993 AL Pitching

Team	Runs Allowed	TPER
Chicago	664	89.0
Kansas City	694	93.1
Boston	698	95.0
Seattle	731	97.0
Toronto	741	98.4
Baltimore	745	98.0
Texas	751	98.7
New York	761	100.6
Average Team	*762*	*100.0*
California	770	101.5
Milwaukee	792	103.7
Cleveland	813	106.4
Minnesota	830	106.5
Detroit	837	106.1
Oakland	846	107.3

Note: Runs allowed rankings are based on runs per 27 gross outs, not total runs.

1993 AL Park TOPR

Team	Park TOPR
Toronto	110.0
Boston	108.7
Kansas City	106.7
Baltimore	106.3
California	101.7
Chicago	101.4
Minnesota	100.8
Seattle	100.8
Average Park	*100.0*
Milwaukee	97.8
Detroit	97.8
Texas	96.4
Oakland	93.1
Cleveland	93.0
New York	90.0

◄ A ROLLER-COASTER RIDE TO NOWHERE ►
BALTIMORE ORIOLES

On Friday, July 20, Baltimore completed a Herculean task. They'd dug themselves out of a huge hole created by an awful start and actually poked their noses into first place in the AL East. First place! On June 1 that had seemed like nothing more than a distant dream. The Orioles limped past Memorial Day in sixth place ahead of only emotionally-shattered Cleveland. They stood 10 games behind a bevy of pretty sassy-looking contenders in Toronto, Detroit, the Yankees and Boston. But here it was, just 50 days later, and the Birds had flown by all of them. July 20, 1993. Baltimore had ripped off a 47–29 streak to go 10 games over .500 at 52–42. And they'd gotten into first place. Friday, July 20.

How could anyone foresee that that day would be the only one in the entire season the Birds would roost atop the standings. Baltimore spent the entire year alternating between frustrating and fascinating their fans. They'd play horribly, then look like world beaters, then revert to ugliness and just as suddenly begin stretches of beautiful play again. In the end they'd taken their fans and themselves on a wild ride. A ride to nowhere. A ride to the middle of the AL East. In the end they looked like any other team that finishes a few games over .500 and 10 games out of first. During the six months the Birds had been a lot of things—but never dull.

Team Trendline: Baltimore Orioles

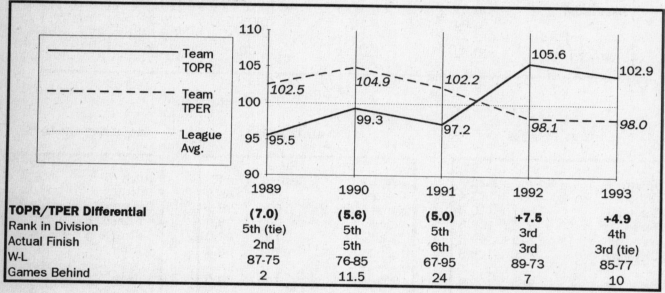

TOPR/TPER Differential	(7.0)	(5.6)	(5.0)	+7.5	+4.9
Rank in Division	5th (tie)	5th	5th	3rd	4th
Actual Finish	2nd	5th	6th	3rd	3rd (tie)
W-L	87-75	76-85	67-95	89-73	85-77
Games Behind	2	11.5	24	7	10

What Was Expected

All of a sudden Bird boosters popped up everywhere entering the '93 campaign. The decade had begun with the Baltimore franchise hitting bottom. Rock bottom. The O's dropped from 87 wins in '89 down to 76 in '90 and all the way to 67 in '91. But the '92 Orioles had risen from the ashes of that horrid previous season to be baseball's surprise team. And they'd done it in a way that encouraged Baltimore fans that only better days lay ahead. The '92 Birds boasted of a flock of young Orioles prospects—Mussina, McDonald, Olson, Hoiles, Anderson, Gomez, Segui. And more like Hammond, Pennington and Rhodes were due to arrive in '93. Blended with a core of vets like Ripken, Baines, Devereaux and

several solid bullpeners, there were those who felt that Baltimore might, just might, give those other birds from Toronto a run for their money. To reinforce their contender status, Baltimore had gone out and signed 2B Harold Reynolds. They'd re-inked injured 1B Glenn Davis, hoping he'd regain the stroke that once made him one of the game's premier power hitters. Just in case some of the younger hurlers stumbled, they'd snatched Jamie Moyer off baseball's junk heap and gave one last chance to former Dodger wunderkind Fernando Valenzuela. Given that the '92 Birds had leaped from 67 victories up to 89, it didn't seem like much more had to be done to make the '93 O's prime contenders.

What Actually Happened

1993 became the Year of the Streak in Baltimore. Never before has an Oriole team run so hot-and-cold. Let us take you on the same roller-coaster ride the Birds took last year.

—The O's fell totally on their face when the bell rang, going 8–13 in April. And they couldn't blame injuries. The Birds experienced their first April ever without placing a single player on the disabled list.

—If as the old cliché suggests, April showers bring May flowers, somebody should have tipped off the Birds. May brought nothing but more misery. And it almost brought history. Had the O's not won on the 31st they'd have lost 17 games in the month, tying their worst month in 35 years. As it was May featured a non-existent offense—a team BA of .237, 21 points lower than any other month of the season.

—June arrived and the Orioles started busting out all over. Segui hit .402 for the month. McDonald's ERA dipped to a microscopic 1.69. Olson's 11 saves led a brilliant bullpen that for the month went 8–0 with 14 saves. The Birds ripped off a 10-game win streak, went 20–7 in June and reentered the pennant race.

—July arrived. The weather turned hot. The Birds pitching got hotter. Valenzuela's 1.56 ERA for the month led the club to its second consecutive month with the best team ERA in the league. The hitters bashed it at a .290 clip, the best month since September of 1973. On July 20 Baltimore surged into first place having won 47 of their last 76 games.

—Another month arrived and more weirdness. On August 2 the O's launched an eight-game win streak followed immediately by an eight-game losing streak. In the eight wins the pitchers yielded just 34 runs. The eight-game skid began with losses to Detroit by the scores of 15–1, 15–5 and 17–11. The next three losses came at New York despite the pitchers allowing only nine runs in the three games. The staff that had been the AL's best in June and July, turned into the worst overnight posting an August ERA of 5.58. Confused? By now, so was everyone else trying to track this bizarre club.

—But just as everyone prepared to attend the Orioles' wake, this corpse came back to life. September began with a win streak that eventually reached eight. Yes, another eight-game streak, their third in a 35-day period from August 2 to September 6. On September 9 the O's perched a half game behind Toronto and the Yanks in what looked like a division headed for a photo finish. Alas, the "other Orioles" showed up again and from that point to the finish the O's flew home on a wing and a prayer going 8–14 eventually winding up 10 back of the Jays and tied for third with the Tigers, the division's other "streaker."

—The Oriole season, which included two eight-game win streaks and one 10-gamer, also had losing streaks of: eight games (once), five games (once), four games (twice) and three games (seven)!

In the end, this Dr. Jekyll and Mr. Hyde wound up looking statistically like what they were—a team that finished barely above .500. Their offense TOPRed at 102.9, slightly above average. They TPERed at 98.0, slightly better than average. But, if you were along for the wild ride of '93, there was nothing "average" about it.

1993 Baltimore Orioles: Month-by-Month

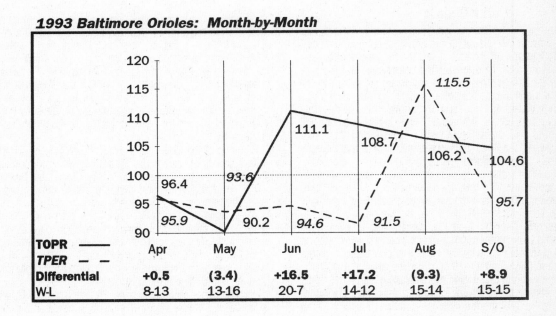

	Apr	May	Jun	Jul	Aug	S/O
TOPR ———	96.4	93.6	111.1	108.7	106.2	104.6
TPER – –	95.9	90.2	94.6	91.5	115.5	95.7
Differential	+0.5	(3.4)	+16.5	+17.2	(9.3)	+8.9
W-L	8-13	13-16	20-7	14-12	15-14	15-15

1993 Orioles Lineup

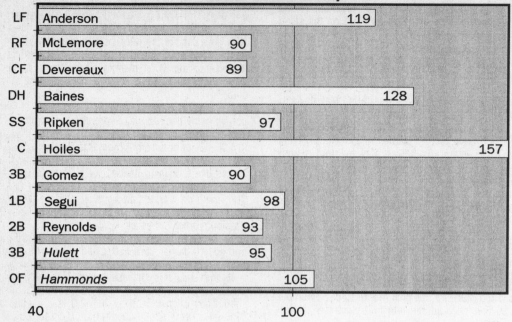

Pos	Player	TOPR
LF	Anderson	119
RF	McLemore	90
CF	Devereaux	89
DH	Baines	128
SS	Ripken	97
C	Hoiles	157
3B	Gomez	90
1B	Segui	98
2B	Reynolds	93
3B	*Hulett*	95
OF	*Hammonds*	105

40   100

The Offense

If, in hindsight, one looks back at the Orioles season trying to find someone or something to blame for the Birds not winning the East, the answer fairly jumps off the stat sheet. Blame the O's offense—at least the first third of the offense. One can reason that the hole Baltimore dug for itself coming out of spring training was, in the end, simply too much to crawl out of, especially against such tough divisional competition. And the primary shovelers who dug that hole had bats in their hands. While the Orioles' pitchers performed gallantly that first pair of months (TPERs of 95.9 and 93.6—far better than average), the Birds' batters wasted much of that pitching with consistently anemic efforts. Through the first two months—50 games—the O's scratched out a meager 3.8 runs per game. In other words, too many "O's"! By then the hole had become huge, eight games under .500. When the bats warmed up to an eventually above average year-long TOPR of 102.9, the victories came with far more frequency. Over the final 112 games Baltimore averaged 5.3 runs a game. But by then some of the pitchers had begun to wear thin trying to make do with the meager support they'd gotten through April and May. That 21–29 start proved to be a Bird killer.

And if one's looking to focus even more clearly on what individual parts of the offense broke down, go no further than the Birds' infield—all of it! None of the four starting positions reached 100 in TOPR, meaning that all four produced like below-average offensive players. That's not good considering that one of those parts is named Ripken, a player famous for the offensive contributions he makes at SS. But Cal, Jr. managed just a 97 TOPR. Yes, that still ranked fourth among those at his position. But that's a far cry from the 141 he TOPRed just two years ago. But he's just one quarter of the infield problem. 1B Segui TOPRed at 98—13th among AL starters. 3B Gomez came in at 90—10th among those in the AL at the hot corner. 2B Reynolds finished at 93—9th in the AL. As a means of comparison, the team Baltimore chased, Toronto, got these TOPRs at 1B, 2B, 3B and SS: 179, 142, 82, 98. Note the huge difference on the right side of the infield. The O's simply didn't get enough infield offense, especially at the corners.

That's not to say this Birds team was without some glittering offensive seasons. Hoiles 157 TOPR made him the major leagues'

best behind the plate. That's a real honor considering the kinds of seasons put together by Daulton, Piazza and Wilkins in the NL and Stanley in the AL. Baines' terrific 128 made him the third best DH, unfortunately behind those of the two teams the Birds fought with all season, Molitor in Toronto and Tartabull in NY. Anderson's 119 ranked only sixth amongst AL LFs. But that's a position populated with some of the "hammers" in the league. The other two OF positions performed far below average with Devereaux's 89 making him the league's worst everyday CF and McLemore's 90 finishing 12th in RF.

Looking at the Birds' "big picture" offensively you see a lineup with a few bright spots but little hope of regularly sustaining big innings or a constant flow of runs. It's a sad but true fact of TOPRism that a club *must* have more than three players TOPRing over 100 to constantly threaten to erupt.

What does the O's "O" need? Let's start with speed. Only the lead-footed Yankees stole fewer bases. Not only didn't Baltimore steal many but they also ran inefficiently getting their meager 73 steals while being thrown out 54 times. In other words, Baltimore would have been better off for the entire year simply forgetting the running game. It cost them runs!

But there's help on the horizon. Rookie Hammonds, who TOPRed at a 105 clip before going down with a herniated disk in his neck, should boost the offense in RF. That would enable the club to move McLemore back to his best position, 2B, where his TOPR isn't nearly as much of a drain offensively as it is when compared to the other RFs in the league.

And before next season begins Baltimore *must* find a way to get rid of a nasty, nasty habit their offense fell into last season—starting slowly. The O's ranked as the worst first and second inning scoring team in the entire league. Baltimore scored just 68 first inning runs, 67 in the second and 76 in the third. Those were their three worst innings for the season. In a game where the team that scores first annually wins from 62% to 67% of all games, that's one fatal flaw. For the season, the O's opponents outscored Baltimore 300–211 over innings 1–2–3. Just like in their season, the Birds tended to dig themselves into early holes.

In retrospect, one wonders what the outcome of the season

might have been had Baltimore been able to pull off a deal they apparently narrowly missed on. Many of baseball's top experts contend the package of prospects the Birds offered San Diego for the rights to slugging first baseman Fred McGriff topped that offered by the Braves. What might have happened over the season's final two months had the "Crime Dog" been hitting cleanup in Baltimore instead of Atlanta? After all, at season's end the O's first sackers had hit only 11 HRs (last in the AL) and had driven in 74 runs (next to last). In just the final couple of months with Atlanta, McGriff belted 19 HRs and drove home 55. What might have been, indeed! Baltimore's roller-coaster ride might have gotten even wilder and it almost certainly wouldn't have wound up in the middle of the AL East had McGriff been "Big Bird" in the middle of the Birds' lineup.

The Pitching

Given the circumstances of the season, with few runs to work with early and major injuries to deal with later, Baltimore must be pretty satisfied with the overall performance of its staff. That 98.0 TPER becomes even more impressive when considered from the standpoint of where they play. Camden Yard has been since its opening a distinctly "hitterish" park. That O's pitchers could, after hurling 81 games there, still be looked upon as an above-average staff speaks well of them.

Even with injuries affecting the Orioles "main men," the entire unit remained fairly stable. Staff ace Mike Mussina, who got injured in one of those silly brawls (June 6 vs. Seattle), never seemed right after that. He kept saying he was OK. He kept pitching like he wasn't. Finally, months later, Mussina conceded his back and neck problems stemmed from that incident. Standout closer Gregg Olson left in early August with a torn elbow ligament and never reappeared. But even with these two staff-crippling injuries, the Birds did not descend into the "Who's-this-week's-rotation" syndrome that others experienced. Nor did they hold weekly "tryouts" for the closer role. Including both injured pitchers, the O's had six men make 160 of their 162 starts. They had six pitchers make 301 of their 355 relief appearances.

But stable or not, Baltimore's days of being the "pitching-rich" Orioles, at least statistically, have passed. Yes, the hitter-friendly

nature of their park certainly has something to do with that. But 1993's team ERA of 4.31, #8 in the AL, represented the 8th time in the last nine years the O's ERA ranged above 4.00. In fact, you could make a very, very, very good case that this Baltimore staff was the "most average" in the AL last season. As proof, we offer a comparison between what an "average" staff and the O's staff did in some key pitching categories:

Staff	ERA	H	BB	K	HR	W	SAV
Orioles	4.32	1476	572	900	153	85	42
AL Average	4.33	1427	579	925	148	81	42

So how, especially in light of playing on a home field that favors hitters, did the O's TPER at a better-than-average 98? Control of runners! O's pitchers allowed 15 fewer steals than the average staff and threw a dozen more DP balls. Tiny but important edges.

The Rotation: For most of the year the Orioles starters looked like three people who desperately wanted to play bridge. Neither could find a "fourth." Even with ace Mussina hurting, the three "M's" of the O's performed splendidly. Moyer (84), McDonald (84) and Mussina (91) all TPERed in the top 18 AL starters. Only the Seattle and White Sox staffs could make that same statement about three members of their rotations. The other three starters—Valenzuela (100), Sutcliffe (124) or Rhodes (127)—could have provided a fifth. But the Birds could never find that fourth man, someone who could join the big three in a consistent rotation.

Moyer's emergence made him one of the, if not THE, biggest pitching surprise in the league. Left for dead on baseball's junk heap, he came to spring as a non-roster invitee, failed to make the team and headed for Rochester where he made life miserable for AAA hitters (6–0, 1.67). Finally, the O's summoned him to the bigs where he allowed more than two runs in just eight of his 25 starts. Offensively we asked where the Orioles might have finished had they acquired McGriff from the Padres. Flip that coin over. To what depths might they have sunk had they not stumbled on Moyer?

McDonald TPERed his best since '90. Mussina TPERed his worst in three major league seasons. But each seems solid for years to come given good health (and no more brawls).

1993 Orioles Staff

St	McDonald	84
St	Valenzuela	100
St	Sutcliffe	124
St	Mussina	91
St	Moyer	84
St	Rhodes	127
Bp	Mills	96
Bp	Williamson	96
Bp	Poole	61
Bp	Frohwirth	90
Cl	Olson	76

50   100

But what of the rest? Other than his dazzling July, Valenzuela generally got hammered. How much did Sutcliffe's knee problem contribute to that ugly 124 TPER, worst of the 54 regular rotation ALers we graded? And he is 38 next season. Will Rhodes ever develop? Two years ago he appeared to be nearing a breakthrough. Last year he seemed at times to be going backward.

The Bullpen: Deep and talented. But what if "The Otter" can't come back? Just how much does Greg "Otter" Olson mean to the O's pen? After 68 games last year the O's pen, with Olson off to a brilliant start, boasted the best ERA in the majors—2.41. For the month of June, Olson saved 11 of 11 allowing four hits and no runs in 12 games. But over the last 94 games of the season, 51 of them without Olson, which coincidentally was when the strain started to show on other pen members, Baltimore's relief corps posted a horrid 4.82 ERA and wound up 13th in the AL for the year. What if rest doesn't cure what's ailing the Otter's elbow?

In front of Olson the Birds line up an impressive group headed by LH spot man Jim Poole, the best TPERing "tweener" in the majors (61). Righties Williamson, Mills and Frohwirth all have solid records of effectiveness and durability with any or all capable of going two or three innings without "losing it."

Rookie Pennington's one of those "teaser" types. He possesses a marvelous arm. Can throw it through a brick wall, as they say. Unfortunately he can't always hit the brick wall. Terrible control. But when he eases up a bit to get the ball over the plate his stuff suffers. But, if he ever gains control of the strike zone, he's got a chance to be downright awesome. His minor league projections though give reason to wonder if that'll ever happen. Is he the next "Wild Thing"?

The Defense

A special note regarding the O's "D." On the final day of '93, Baltimore committed a pair of errors in losing to Toronto. That brought the Orioles' season total to an even 100 and snapped one of the most wonderful defensive streaks in baseball history. Last year marked the first time since 1988 Baltimore had made as many as 100 errors in a year. No other team in baseball history has ever had as many as two back-to-back seasons of under 100 miscues.

Oriole Park at Camden Yards

The Orioles' new showplace had been designed to enhance hitting. In '93, the ballpark built on the site of Ruth's old place delivered (Park TOPR: 106.3). Fortunately, O's hitters benefited more from the park than their pitchers were hurt by it. Check the home/road won-lost record for confirmation.

Batters felt the park's effect pretty much across-the-board, with all elements being enhanced about equally. The oddest result concerned GDPs. With 8% more runners on first base in Baltimore, the O's hit into fewer double-dips (58 at home vs. 73 away). The *opposite* held true for visiting hitters. They grounded into 79 dips in Baltimore vs. 60 when they hosted the O's. Weird!

For most of the season a record-breaking fifth consecutive year under 100 seemed assured. Baltimore made only 56 errors in their first 107 games. Phenomenal fielding! But the defense flubbed 44 times the last 55 games to eventually reach an even 100 and the streak had ended.

What Next?

A championship?

Unlike many other teams, the Orioles off-season plan of attack seemed pretty clear:

A) Find some offensive power, particularly at the "corners" (1B and 3B)
B) Add some badly needed speed
C) Find a fourth for the rotation
D) Pray that Gregg Olson's elbow heals or spend the money to replace him should he not be sound .

The Orioles' new ownership arrived with an aggressive financial attitude. Immediately the club jumped into the free agent market signing Mets lefty Sid Fernandez. If he's well he's a dynamite pitcher. That is IF he's well. He hasn't been two of the last three seasons. He's also fought a continuing battle of the waistline throughout his career. With guaranteed money in his pocket can he keep his hands away from the dinner table? His signing hopefully took care of "C."

Next, the club landed just the kind of player they desperately needed offensively with the signing of Raffy Palmeiro. Insert his 146 TOPR at 1B instead of Segui's 98 and the Orioles' offense becomes far more potent. Plus, Palmeiro adds a base-running element having stolen 22 of 25 last year. Only Anderson stole more for the Birds last year (24) and he got tossed out a dozen times. Palmeiro's arrival helps both "A" and "B."

And if you'll listen closely you can hear the prayers of the Orioles in the distance hoping for "D." If Olson bounces back . . . if CF Devereaux returns to those triple figure TOPRs of '91 and '92 . . . the AL East just might have a bird of a different feather atop the standings in '94.

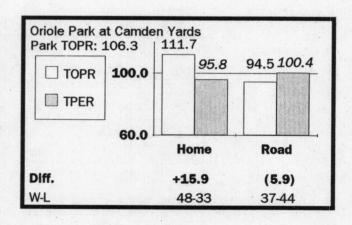

Oriole Park at Camden Yards Park TOPR: 106.3	Home	Road
TOPR	111.7	94.5
TPER	95.8	100.4
Diff.	+15.9	(5.9)
W-L	48-33	37-44

Team TOPR: 1993 Balitimore Orioles

	Bats	BA	OBP	SLG	HR	R	RBI	NBE	GOC	Ratio	TOPR
League Avg. Team	-	.267	.337	.408	148	762	719	2897	4352	.666	100
Baltimore Orioles	-	.267	.346	.413	157	786	744	2965	4328	.685	102.9
Regulars:											
C Chris Hoiles	R	.310	.416	.585	29	80	82	319	306	1.042	157
1B David Segui	B	.273	.351	.400	10	54	60	232	357	.650	98
2B Harold Reynolds	B	.252	.343	.334	4	64	47	244	393	.621	93
3B Leo Gomez	R	.197	.294	.348	10	30	25	122	204	.598	90
Mike Pagliarulo	L	.325	.373	.556	6	24	21	72	81	.889	(133)
SS Cal Ripken	R	.257	.329	.420	24	87	90	326	503	.648	97
LF Brady Anderson	L	.263	.363	.425	13	87	66	350	441	.794	119
CF Mike Devereaux	R	.250	.306	.400	14	72	75	248	417	.595	89
RF Mark McLemore	B	.284	.353	.368	4	81	72	281	469	.599	90
DH Harold Baines	L	.313	.390	.510	20	64	78	262	307	.853	128
Bench (100+ TPA):											
IF Tim Hulett	R	.300	.361	.381	2	40	23	122	192	.635	95
OF Jack Voigt	R	.296	.395	.500	6	32	23	99	110	.900	(135)
1B Glenn Davis	R	.177	.230	.230	1	8	9	33	98	.337	(51)
OF Jeffrey Hammonds	R	.305	.312	.467	3	10	19	55	79	.696	(105)
C Jeff Tackett	R	.172	.277	.207	0	8	9	29	80	.363	(54)

NOTE: Statistics are only for games played with Baltimore. ( ) Under 200 TPA.

Team TPER: 1993 Baltimore Orioles

	Throws	W-L	GS	GR	SV	IP	ERA	NBA	GOE	Ratio	TPER
League Avg. Team	-	81 -81	162	355	42	1444.1	4.33	2897	4352	0.666	100
Baltimore Orioles	-	85 -77	162	329	42	1442.2	4.32	2833	4342	0.652	98.0
The Rotation:											
Ben McDonald	R	13 -14	34	0	0	220.1	3.39	373	664	0.562	84
Fernando Valenzuela	L	8 -10	31	1	0	178.2	4.94	359	540	0.665	100
Rick Sutcliffe	R	10 -10	28	1	0	166	5.75	411	499	0.824	124
Mike Mussina	R	14 -6	25	0	0	167.2	4.46	303	501	0.605	91
Jamie Moyer	L	12 -9	25	0	0	152	3.43	253	451	0.561	84
Arthur Rhodes	L	5 -6	17	0	0	85.2	6.51	218	257	0.848	127
Bullpen:											
Alan Mills	R	5 -4	0	45	4	100.1	3.23	194	302	0.642	96
Todd Frohwirth	R	6 -7	0	70	3	96.1	3.83	176	293	0.601	90
Mark Williamson	R	7 -5	1	47	0	88	4.91	172	269	0.639	96
Jim Poole	L	2 -1	0	55	2	50.1	2.15	62	153	0.405	(61)
Brad Pennington	L	3 -2	0	34	4	33	6.55	92	99	0.929	(140)
Gregg Olson	R	0 -2	0	50	29	45	1.60	69	136	0.507	(76)

NOTE: Statistics are only for games pitched with Baltimore. ( ) Under 200 TBF.

RED SOX COLLAPSE IN THE "4TH QUARTER"
BOSTON RED SOX

Boston played the '93 season as though it were a football game. They played it in "quarters"—four distinct and very separate parts. With most teams in most seasons there's a constant ebb and flow. They experience many ups and many downs and some periods where they just drift along in the standings almost seeming to alternate wins and losses. Not the '93 Sox. Their 162-game package split neatly into four very discernable parts or quarters:

		Record
1Q	Games 1–14	11–3
2Q	Games 15–68	19–35
3Q	Games 69–112	33–11
4Q	Games 113–162	17–33
	Final Score	80–82

Red Sox fans, players and management rode this odd roller coaster upward out of the gate, down to the depths when the Sox on June 20 had lost 35 of 54 to fall 13 games out, wildly back upward with a phenomenal streak that produced 33 victories in a 44-game stretch and actually got them briefly into the lead in the AL East and finally crashing back down from August 11 to the finish with a horrid 17–33 run. Worst of all about that final miserable eight weeks was that most of the collapse happened right in front of the home folks' eyes. A team that had terrorized opponents in Fenway for most of the season (36–19), suddenly could not buy a victory there dropping 23 of their last 30 at home including a last six dismal, season-ending games in a row.

Team Trendline: Boston Red Sox

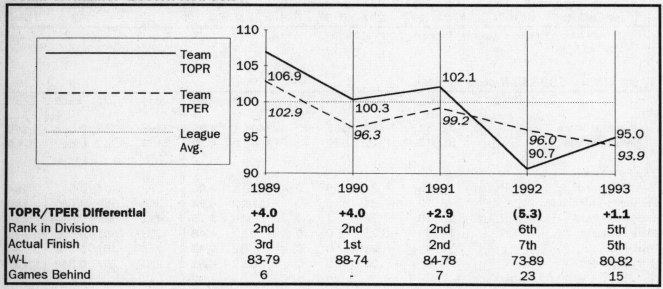

TOPR/TPER Differential	+4.0	+4.0	+2.9	(5.3)	+1.1
Rank in Division	2nd	2nd	2nd	6th	5th
Actual Finish	3rd	1st	2nd	7th	5th
W-L	83-79	88-74	84-78	73-89	80-82
Games Behind	6	-	7	23	15

What Was Expected

The Red Sox had undergone a facelift entering the '93 season. And if ever there'd been a team desperately in need of changing its face it was Boston. The year before the Sox had suddenly become horrible: 73–89. Other franchises have years like that simply as part of the course of a team's up-and-down nature. But not Boston. They hadn't witnessed that kind of a clunker since the '66 Sox embarrassed themselves and the city by going 72–90. In the intervening 25 years Boston had finished beneath .500 just twice and both times by a meager six games. Thus, '92 represented the worst season since LBJ lived in the White House. They had finished dead last. And in perhaps no other baseball city can last feel as dead as in Beantown.

With red faces the Red Sox went busily about the task of immediate major surgery. The face of Wade Boggs, a fixture at 3B, left for free agency and a spot in the lineup of the hated Yankees.

Tom Brunansky, Ellis Burks and Jody Reed, all integral parts of previous Boston contenders, all had gone. Stopper Jeff Reardon had been dealt late in '92. Perennial power prospect Phil Plantier also became part of the purge. Such pitiful play demanded action and during the off-season Boston fans got action.

Realizing their desperate need for outfield pop, the club traded for Ivan Calderon and threw open the club's wallet to ink Andre Dawson, a veteran with an enormously positive on- and off-the-field reputation. Scott Fletcher arrived to plug the 2B hole. Scott Bankhead and Jose Melendez filled bullpen slots. The organization believed 3B Scott Cooper was ready for prime time and fitted him into the gigantic shoes left by Boggs. Finally, unable to land a "quality" stopper, Boston took a chance on free agent Jeff Russell, who'd had some terrific seasons in Texas, but about whom swirled rumors of having a bad arm. Boston gave him a little money up front, lots of incentives and crossed their fingers.

No one questioned whether the Sox had improved. That seemed certain. Just how much remained debatable. Enough to challenge the defending champs of baseball from Toronto? Most thought not. But Boston fans have long and wonderful memories and they couldn't forget that the last hideous edition of the Sox, that disgusting cellar-dweller of a club in '66, had bounced back to win the American League the very next season. Would history repeat?

What Actually Happened

Fenway Park, long famous as the friendliest of hitter's parks, became, in '93, the home of one of the league best pitching staffs. But, alas, the Red Sox, long famous for having a string of offensive machines, produced instead one of the AL's weakest overall attacks. Imagine, if you will, Boston fans sitting in cozy Fenway staring at that inviting wall and realizing the home team, if they were to win, likely would be doing so by 3–2 squeakers, not 10–8 batterings.

In fact, the Boston transformation from a hitting team to a pitching-based club had been underway for years. Check the TOPR-TPER trendlines. In '89 Boston hammered away with a 106.9 TOPR, one of the best in the league. That offense helped cover for a pitching staff that TPERed at a below-average 102.9. The combo produced a second-place finish. But note the remarkable trends since '89. The TOPR trends steadily downward. Boston's attack had become more and more toothless. But the pitching (TPER) got steadily better. Thus, the '93 Sox, with the league's third-best pitching but eleventh best offense, could be viewed as simply a result of trends that had been underway for some time now. But to Sox fans the overall picture still looked odd, especially in light of all the changes that had been made with the express purpose of perking up the run-scoring totals.

Some of the changes worked. Some didn't. In the end, Boston in fact made one too many changes.

From the pitching standpoint, the biggest blessing came from the biggest question mark. Until a late-season ankle injury, closer Russell performed brilliantly. Until injuries struck down Clemens and Viola, the starters formed a solid unit and the middlemen generally gave the Sox dependable, consistent work. Who could have ever imagined that after the year Boston fans would be saying about the pitching: "If only Clemens had given us a good year. . . ." But even with the "Rocket Man" turning in his worst season ever, Boston still had more than enough on the mound to pile up victories.

At the plate they were more often a pile of something else. Calderon proved a disaster and got pink-slipped. Dawson failed to give the club anywhere near the injection of pop they expected. On the flip side, Fletcher and Cooper turned out solid seasons. But the powerless '93 Sox may always look back and wonder what might have been had they not made the San Diego deal that brought reliever Jose Melendez for OF Phil Plantier. Melendez immediately got hurt and never contributed. And, if you analyze the Sox staff, in truth he really wouldn't have been needed anyway for his middle relief specialty. But oh how the Sox could have used Plantier's bat. Somehow he'd gotten crossways with manager Hobson. Communication broke down. Plantier never produced in Boston the kind of sparkling minor league numbers (27 and 33 HR years) that the Sox anticipated. They sent him away and then spent the entire year looking for someone to play right field. Plantier exploded in San Diego (34 HRs and 100 RBIs). The Sox tried Calderon, Quintana and finally dealt for Deer looking for a RF. Those three combined gave them 9 HRs and 53 RBIs in 659 official at bats (197 more official ABs than Plantier had in SD).

Just what might another 20 HRs and 50 RBIs have meant to the Red Sox with their "Odd Couple" combination of rich pitching and poor hitting?

1993 Boston Red Sox: Month-by-Month

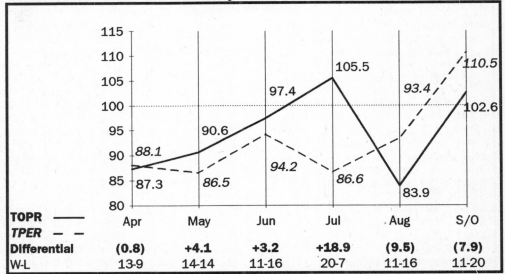

	Apr	May	Jun	Jul	Aug	S/O
TOPR ——						
TPER – –						
Differential	(0.8)	+4.1	+3.2	+18.9	(9.5)	(7.9)
W-L	13-9	14-14	11-16	20-7	11-16	11-20

1993 Red Sox Lineup

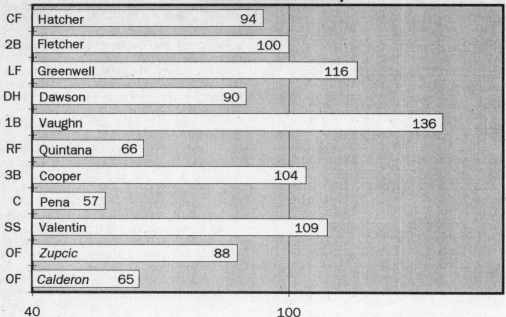

CF	Hatcher	94
2B	Fletcher	100
LF	Greenwell	116
DH	Dawson	90
1B	Vaughn	136
RF	Quintana	66
3B	Cooper	104
C	Pena	57
SS	Valentin	109
OF	*Zupcic*	88
OF	*Calderon*	65

40 ———————————— 100

The Offense

Just as Boston's season broke neatly into four quarters, the offense separated into four distinct parts. The infield performed well. The DH position didn't produce anywhere near acceptable numbers. The outfield, given the "black hole" that existed in right, produced poor overall numbers. Catching was absolutely awful.

As a team the '93 Sox managed just 689 runs, 83 beneath the league average. When you then consider that Fenway continued its reputation as being "Friendly Fenway" for hitters, the team TOPR of 95.0, 11th in the AL, starts to look even more sickly. In a park that rewards power hitters, Boston could boast of having only one, 1B Mo Vaughn. And he hits left-handed, unable to take regular advantage of the short distance to Fenway's left field Green Monster. Vaughn drilled 29 homers. No one else on the "Pink Sox" hit more than 13. Boston finished ahead of only KC in roundtrippers.

But at least the club did have the look of a team "built for Fenway." At home their team TOPR appeared more than respectable—103.9. When they left they obviously did not heed the advice given in the American Express ad for, as far as the Boston offense goes, they DID leave home without it. That wretched 86.6 road TOPR ranked ahead of only KC and Minnesota in the AL. Their huge difference of more than 17 points between home and road TOPRs represents the second highest differential in all of baseball. Only the bizarre Colorado Rockies changed more when leaving home and we've detailed in the book just how the incredible effect of their home park made distorted numbers like theirs happen.

Oh, the Sox did lead the majors in doubles. But when you play in a park that encourages *homers*, doubles represent "half the pie." Fenway also seems to annually have another indirect effect. As the left-field wall beckons, hitters often get less and less selective, leading to low walk totals. Boston finished 10th in overall walks. And 10th is also where the Sox came to rest in overall on-base percentage. Boston teams almost never have much of a speed component and this one certainly wasn't any exception. They managed just 73 steals. Their team total would have barely edged out Cleveland CF Kenny Lofton for the individual title by three steals. So, when you assemble all the pieces we've just reviewed— tied for 13th in HRs, 10th in walks and on-base percentage and

tied for 13th in steals—it's not hard to understand how Boston's attack failed to produce runs.

But let's return to the lineup and that four compartment break-down:

Every one of the Sox infield starters performed at or above the TOPR norm for his position. Vaughn's 136 made him the league's #4 at 1B and behind only the goliaths (Olerud, Thomas and Palmeiro). Fletcher's 100 also brought him in at a surprising (to some) fourth among all 2B regulars. Cooper's 104 placed him slightly above the "average" for a 3B and, importantly for him and the franchise, three points *higher* than Boggs TOPRed in New York. SS John Valentin's a comer. His 109 made him the league's second-best offensive shortstop behind only the venerable Trammell in Detroit. None of the four run well (though Fletcher did lead this lead-footed squad in steals with 16). But that's about the only part of the offensive spectrum that's missing from this foursome.

Greenwell's return to form should encourage the Sox. Though his 116 TOPR's below the AL norm for LF, realize this AL position's got some big bangers (Rickey Henderson, Gonzalez, Raines and Belle) who make it one of the best sources of offense in the AL. Greenie's 116 represented his best effort of the '90s. But it's all downhill from there. CF Hatcher's probably best suited to the fourth outfielder role. His 94 ranked him 10th in the AL, 12 points below the norm for the CF spot. We've already detailed in the season summary what kind of woeful numbers RF produced. The man who played it most, Carlos Quintana, turned in a dismal season. Calderon's total failure truly hurt the most. Deer's arrival came well after the season-closing skid had begun and he failed to contribute much beyond his usual combination of a handful of long balls and bushels of strikeouts.

You must feel for Dawson. For years he dragged his creaky knees onto NL playing fields because, without the DH in that league, if he was to bat he had to play in the field. The DH seemed a perfect way to spend his last few years in the game. And Boston, longing for his career-long combination of power and leadership, seemed the perfect place. But the best laid plans of mice and men went awry again. Arthroscopic knee surgery early and a fractured wrist late limited him to just 121 games. But even when healthy he produced just 13 long ones while contributing a mere 17 walks as opposed to an ugly 18 DPs. That all combined to produce a 90 TOPR. That's 10 points beneath that posted by an "average hitter" and 15 points below the norm for the position. Dawson, projected as one of the league's best DH's, TOPRed 10th best in the end.

We've saved the worst for last. Tony Pena's a wonderful fellow. Has had a terrific career. An outstanding thrower. But '93 suggested it's all over for him as a hitter. His astounding TOPR of 57 made him the worst offensive regular in the major leagues. To give you some idea of just how much Boston "gave away" at this lineup spot offensively, check a comparison of the production of the Boston combination of Pena and light-hitting backup Bob Melvin to that of AL East competitor Baltimore who had the top TOPRing catcher Chris Hoiles.

	AB	BA	OBP	HR	Runs	RBI	BB	TOPR
Boston	480	.196	.248	7	33	42	32	62
Hoiles	419	.310	.416	29	80	82	69	157

Imagine how much extra your other positions must produce just to try to get back to even with the O's offensively. For the season, Baltimore TOPRed, as a team, 7.9 points higher than Boston. Almost all of the difference came from one position—catcher.

The Pitching

Other managers should be as lucky as Boston's Butch Hobson. Once youngster Aaron Sele arrived he could trot out four well above average starters, could call on four well above average set-up men and then turn it over to one of the best closers in the league.

Yes, injuries did wreak some havoc with the group, bothering especially the staff ace Clemens and closer Russell. But the Red Sox staff TPERed with the best of them.

First, foremost and perhaps hardest to believe is the fact that the Sox, playing in a "hitter's park," had the league's hardest-to-hit pitchers. Opponents batted a mere .252. And despite that oh-so-close Green Monster, Sox pitchers surrendered the third fewest HRs. Runners did not take liberties and they threw a league average 127 DPs. This staff, in fact, held the lead in the race for the team

ERA title until the season's closing days when, on September 30, the White Sox inched ahead.

And Boston might have challenged more for the team TPER title except for Hobson's infatuation with intentionally walking opponents. Boston issued 87 such freebies. That's more than an extra half-a-runner per game! Only Detroit employed this tactic more (92). No one else in the league issued more than 59 IBBs.

The Rotation: Clemens wasn't the ace? Wow, that's a chunk to chew on right off the bat. That Boston's staff still performed so splendidly, even with Clemens finally proving he was mortal, underscores even more that solid top-to-bottom ability of the entire group. Darwin stepped forward with his best year ever leading Boston in wins, starts and innings. Viola, who'd never missed a start to injury in his 10 years, had to briefly leave the rotation three times with hurts. The last, and most bothersome, for September elbow surgery. Rookie Sele arrived with a splash, TPERing at the third-best rate on the staff behind only Darwin and closer Russell. Dopson represented the only worse-than-average starter and even his 107 TPER's certainly not all that bad. Our figures show 15 other full-time starters and 16 part-timers arrived at October with worse TPERs than Dopson. But a word of caution here. Of this group, Clemens and Viola are coming off injuries. Uncharacteristic injuries. Each had been among the very sturdiest hurlers in the entire majors. And, of this group, only Sele's under 30 entering next year.

The Bullpen: Not a bummer in the bunch of set-up and utility men. Rookies Ryan and Quantrill made nice debuts. Quantrill, though he TPERed slightly higher, seemed to catch more of the scout's eyes. Ryan's speed can be overpowering. In the upper 90s at times. But his stuff can be "straight as a string." Bankhead's had arm troubles in the past and thus can't be used hard. But, if employed correctly, he's a more than capable long man as that 94 TPER shows. Harris continues to have a rubber arm leading the league with 80 appearances. And they're not simply spot assignments. His workload reached an impressive 112 innings in '93. If you open the dictionary to get the definition of the term "spot lefty," you'll find Tony Fossas' picture next to it. He pitched in 71 games but threw just 40 innings. That's a "spot lefty." But he's

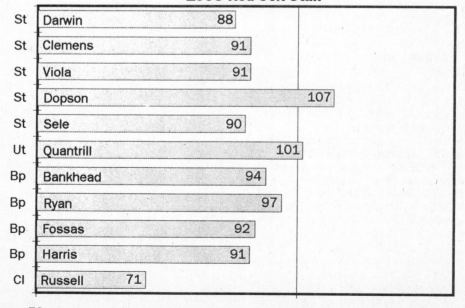

1993 Red Sox Staff

very, very good at his job. Again, a word of caution. Harris, Fossas and injured Joe Hesketh (also part of this tweener group) will all have turned at least 35 by mid '94.

The rest of the baseball world made a horrible misjudgment of Jeff Russell last spring. He'd had some elbow problems late in the season before pitching out of Oakland's pen following the huge Canseco deal that sent him away from Texas. Rumors circulated that spurs in the elbow would require major surgery. So, everyone backed off him in the free agent market. This was the same Jeff Russell who, despite those "major elbow problems," had still saved 30 games in '91 and '92. The same pitcher who's TPERed at 86 and 79 the previous two seasons. Still, other lesser pitchers got huge contracts while Russell's phone didn't ring. Finally, the Sox, desperate for a closer, gave him a small base salary and a contract laden with incentives so that, if and when his elbow exploded, they'd basically owe him very little. Well, as Gomer Pyle used to say "Surprise, surprise, surprise." The elbow never blew out. It was, in fact, an ankle injury that sidelined him the last five weeks. Before then he'd already saved 33, the second best in Boston history. Only Toronto's Duane Ward TPERed better among the league's stoppers (64 to 71).

Just one final rather discouraging note about a staff that otherwise put up encouraging numbers. Why couldn't they cover better when their defense made mistakes? Boston fielded 10th best by percentage in the league. Certainly not great. But also not a disaster. The Sox, however, yielded a whopping 89 unearned runs. Only Detroit, with 95, permitted more in the AL. And the Tigers simply gushed runs, whether they be earned or unearned. Some 12.7% of all runs Boston allowed were unearned. That's one of every eight. That's horrible. And, given the overall quality of the staff, that's also mystifying.

What Next?

The division Boston competes in next year will be smaller (five teams). But the only difference between their new division and last year's AL East will be that the two teams the Red Sox finished ahead of have moved out. Cleveland and Milwaukee ended up in the Central leaving these Sox as the worst of the returning clubs in the AL East.

Boston fans won't accept a third straight below .500 year. Neither will the media. And the pressure's already obvious on the club. Right after the season, manager Hobson fired three coaches—Al Bumbry, Rick Burleson and good friend and pitching coach Rich Gale—even though in the closing weeks Hobson had announced that his staff would all be back. It made for messy headlines in Beantown and indicates there's more than a bit of a power struggle going on inside this organization. Power struggles mean manager pressure. Players can often sense that and it can lead to clubhouse difficulties. But, then, Hobson entered '92 as everyone's candidate for "Most Likely To Be Fired" and yet in mid-August wound up being touted as a possible Manager-of-the-Year candidate.

The Sox moved quickly in the off-season to plug the enormous CF and leadoff hole signing free agent Otis Nixon from Atlanta. But realize he's 35 and coming off a 101 TOPR season that ranked him ninth among all NL CFs and below the norm for the position. And, it's his second consecutive such season. That leaves the giant hole in RF and behind the plate. DH Dawson, signed through '94, simply must bounce back. Boston doesn't have the money or the inclination to try to replace him.

As long as Clemens, Viola and Russell return pain-free, the staff's old but in excellent shape. Especially since youngsters Quantrill, Ryan and prospect Nate Minchey appear to have decent futures. But there's obviously work to be done here. Especially when you're in a division with Toronto, an improved Baltimore, the thumping Tigers and Steinbrenner's Yankees.

And if Boston doesn't "darn some of the holes" in their Sox, the rabid Beantown fans will say a lot more than "Darn those Sox!"

Fenway Park

Recently, Fenway's "park effect" has been the subject of controversy. Once a renowned "hitter's park," a newly constructed press box was thought to have reversed the effect by changing the wind patterns. Somebody even undertook wind tunnel tests with before-and-after models to find out what had happened.

Whatever it was, the Fenway we've known and loved was *back* in '93. The park TOPRed at 108.7, second only to Skydome in its positive effect on offense. The "effect" was effectively disguised, though, by the futility of the Boston offense and the excellence of the BoSox pitching staff. But, on an adjusted basis, the park boosted the Red Sox hitters by +10.6% and opposing hitters by +6.8%. Under the circumstances, this meant 4–3 pitcher's duels (instead of 3–2).

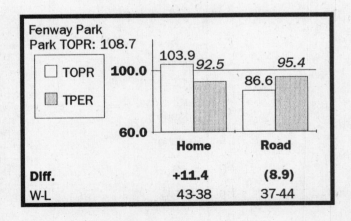

Fenway Park
Park TOPR: 108.7

☐ TOPR
▨ TPER

	Home	Road
	103.9 / 92.5	86.6 / 95.4
Diff.	+11.4	(8.9)
W-L	43-38	37-44

Team TOPR: 1993 Boston Red Sox

	Bats	BA	OBP	SLG	HR	R	RBI	NBE	GOC	Ratio	TOPR
League Avg. Team	-	.267	.337	.408	148	762	719	2897	4352	.666	100
Boston Red Sox	-	.264	.330	.395	114	686	644	2757	4359	.632	95.0
Regulars:											
C Tony Pena	R	.181	.246	.257	4	20	19	107	280	.382	57
1B Mo Vaughn	L	.297	.390	.525	29	86	101	364	403	.903	136
2B Scott Fletcher	R	.285	.341	.402	5	81	45	245	367	.668	100
2B Scott Cooper	L	.279	.354	.397	9	67	63	274	396	.692	104
SS John Valentin	R	.278	.346	.447	11	50	66	270	371	.728	109
LF Mike Greenwell	L	.315	.379	.480	13	77	72	306	396	.773	116
CF Billy Hatcher	R	.287	.336	.400	9	71	57	250	398	.628	94
RF Ivan Calderon	R	.221	.291	.291	1	25	19	79	183	.432	65
Rob Deer	R	.196	.303	.399	7	18	16	79	117	.675	(101)
DH Andre Dawson	R	.273	.313	.425	13	44	67	216	361	.598	90
Bench (100+ TPA):											
I/O Carlos Quintana	R	.244	.317	.271	1	31	19	110	249	.442	66
OF Bob Zupcic	R	.241	.308	.360	2	40	26	139	237	.586	88
C Bob Melvin	R	.222	.251	.313	3	13	23	67	145	.462	(69)
IF Ernest Riles	L	.189	.292	.350	5	15	20	72	127	.567	(85)
IF Luis Rivera	R	.208	.273	.308	1	13	7	52	110	.473	(71)
IF Tim Naehring	R	.331	.377	.433	1	14	17	67	92	.728	(109)

NOTE: Statistics are only for games played with Boston. ( ) Under 200 TPA.

Team TPER: 1993 Boston Red Sox

	Throws	W-L	GS	GR	SV	IP	ERA	NBA	GOE	Ratio	TPER
League Avg. Team	-	81 -81	162	355	42	1444.1	4.33	2897	4352	0.666	100
Boston Red Sox	-	80 -82	162	389	44	1452.1	3.80	2746	4393	0.625	93.9
The Rotation:											
Danny Darwin	R	15 -11	34	0	0	229.1	3.26	403	686	0.587	88
Roger Clemens	R	11 -14	29	0	0	191.2	4.46	349	579	0.603	91
Frank Viola	L	11 -8	29	0	0	183.2	3.14	336	555	0.605	91
John Dopson	R	7 -11	28	6	0	155.2	4.97	333	469	0.710	107
Aaron Sele	R	7 -2	18	0	0	111.2	2.74	202	338	0.598	90
Utility:											
Paul Quantrill	R	6 -12	14	35	1	138	3.91	278	414	0.671	101
Joe Hesketh	L	3 -4	5	23	1	53.1	5.06	115	168	0.685	103
Bullpen:											
Greg Harris	R	6 -7	0	80	8	112.1	3.77	209	344	0.608	91
Scott Bankhead	R	2 -1	0	40	0	64.1	3.50	121	193	0.627	94
Ken Ryan	R	7 -2	0	47	1	50	3.60	99	153	0.647	97
Tony Fossas	L	1 -1	0	71	0	40	5.18	75	123	0.610	(92)
Jeff Russell	R	1 -4	0	51	33	46.2	2.70	67	142	0.472	(71)

NOTE: Statistics are only for games pitched with Boston. ( ) Under 200 TBF.

IF YOU ARE TO GROW WINNERS YOU MUST FIRST PLANT SEEDS
CALIFORNIA ANGELS

Once upon a time baseball's money tree grew in southern California. Angels owner Gene Autry had done everything in life except own a world-champion baseball team. So, as the years passed and the desire to win became more acute, the Angels became more and more active in the free agent market. When California had a hole, they simply reached a bit deeper into "The Cowboy's" saddle bags and threw money at it. Reggie Jackson, Bobby Grich, Fred Lynn, Rod Carew, Don Sutton. Big names all. Big salaries all. But despite their presence over a several year period the Angels could never quite bring "The Cowboy" the title he so coveted. As years passed times gradually changed for this organization. The "money tree" approach to building a team ended. So many players had ridden off into the sunset with their saddle bags packed with the Angels' cash but no championship rings on their fingers that California finally altered their philosophy. Suddenly, players wanting money are leaving California or being encouraged to leave. Wally Joyner, Bryan Harvey and Jim Abbott, all home-grown stars, all gone because the money tree now grows somewhere else besides southern California.

The Angels, in effect, started all over again in '93. They dealt to acquire prospects. They gave playing time to youngsters hoping they'd grow into big-timers. When holes opened in their lineup they looked to their farm system, not the wallet of "The Cowboy." Homegrown pennants do not happen overnight. They take time and patience. California showed that last season and got rewarded with the emergence of what appears to be the makings of a core of a contender. Oh, there's still a lot of growing left to do in southern California. But this organization seems to be committed to switching from being spenders into being farmers. And the first crops are at least encouraging.

Team Trendline: California Angels

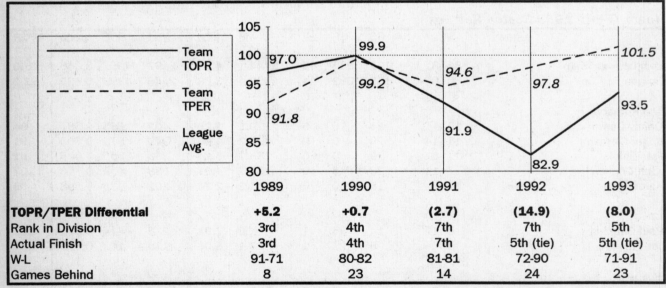

	1989	1990	1991	1992	1993
TOPR/TPER Differential	+5.2	+0.7	(2.7)	(14.9)	(8.0)
Rank in Division	3rd	4th	7th	7th	5th
Actual Finish	3rd	4th	7th	5th (tie)	5th (tie)
W-L	91-71	80-82	81-81	72-90	71-91
Games Behind	8	23	14	24	23

What Was Expected

Coming off back-to-back basement finishes precluded Angel fans from having any preconceived notions about what '93 might hold. In fact, many thought that with the trade of ace lefty Jim Abbott and the exit through the expansion draft of super closer Bryan Harvey, the '93 Angels might in fact be worse than the season before. That is, if there is a place worse than last. No one in preseason chose them anywhere near the top half of the division and the consensus of the experts picking the AL West suggested that, while no one seemed sure who'd win the West, just about everyone agreed who's bringing up the rear—California. The Angels had committed to youth and youth popped up everywhere. Whenever the club had a real choice between a vet or a kid, youth was served. You were free to question the sanity of what the Angels were doing but you couldn't question the fact that they'd definitely throw the entire energy of the organization behind their youth movement. Angel fans, who only a few years ago watched a lineup dotted with aging though still capable stars, now saw a lineup at times filled with "Who's he?"

What Actually Happened

Imagine the shock that Angel fans experienced, indeed, the shock that spread through all of baseball when on the morning of May 31 the standings in their favorite newspaper showed the AL West being led by none other than California—and by a whopping three-game margin. Fueled by fast starts from rookie 1B J. T. Snow and veteran RHP Scott Sanderson, the Angels had bolted from the gate with a 27–20 mark. As the rest of the division struggled to get its act together, the Halos acted like contenders. They'd been especially brilliant in April when their patched-together pitching staff, headed by two superb lefties, Finley and Langston, TPERed along at 88, the best pitching in the entire AL. During April, a baby-faced offense put up average numbers but that proved more than enough given Cal's superb pitching. The Angels ran off a 13–6 mark. Little did anyone know that April would be the pitching staff's best month AND the hitters' best also. But they still hustled along, splitting their first 28 games of May and waking up on May 31 three games ahead.

That's when it all started to come apart. Snow had stopped hitting. Sanderson, 7–2 with a 2.82 ERA on May 31, would lose nine straight decisions (ERA 6.23 in the 11-game stretch) and be released. From that last day of May through the end of the season the Angels would go 44–71. But, while their backslide had begun, their status of contenders certainly didn't end for awhile in a division where absolutely nobody seemed to want to take control. As late as the all-star break Cal still trailed by just two games. But the second half began with a disastrous 1–10 road trip through Cleveland, Boston and New York, and the Halos had said goodbye to the rarified air at the top of the standings. For the season, the Angels, like many young squads, staggered around on the road posting a 27–54 mark, matched in futility only by the equally young Padres.

But, as the club tumbled further and further out of contention, eventually coming to rest tied for fifth (23 games out), fans and club execs had to keep reminding themselves that growth, not contention, had been the original aim of the '93 season. And that goal appears to have been accomplished. By season's end, the facelift that GM Whitey Herzog had embarked on when he arrived late in '91 had been completed. Of the 25-man opening day roster from '92, only six remained active with the club as '93 wound down. The '93 Angels looked at 17 rookies, 11 of them seeing their first major league action ever. Adding them to five second-year men on the roster paints the picture of a team so young that they could have never been more than false contenders at best. But those weeks and months of hanging around the top will provide invaluable experience to the players who wind up being part of Cal's future. And they appear to have uncovered several such future parts. Rookie-of-the-Year Salmon, Curtis, Easley and Disarcina all impressed. Even Snow, shuffled to the minors during his horrendous slump, returned with an encouraging finish. Leftwich and Hathaway got regular rotation work and Grahe got a good feel for the closer job despite having an injury shorten his year. Other keys to the future like Turner, Perez, Springer, Scott, Holzemer, and even the club's #1 pick in the June draft, P Brian Anderson, got their first tastes of major league ball.

In the end, though the contending Angels couldn't keep going, they did keep growing.

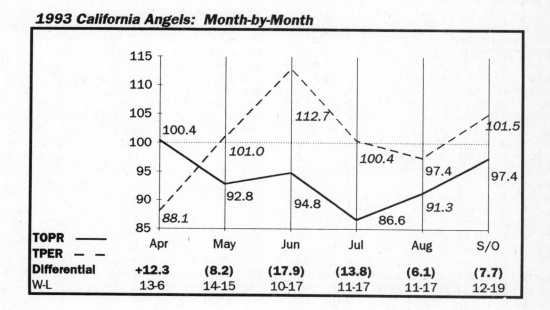

1993 California Angels: Month-by-Month

	Apr	May	Jun	Jul	Aug	S/O
TOPR ——						
TPER – –						
Differential	+12.3	(8.2)	(17.9)	(13.8)	(6.1)	(7.7)
W-L	13-6	14-15	10-17	11-17	11-17	12-19

TOPR values: 100.4, 92.8, 94.8, 86.6, 91.3, 97.4
TPER values: 88.1, 101.0, 112.7, 100.4, 97.4, 101.5

1993 Angels Lineup

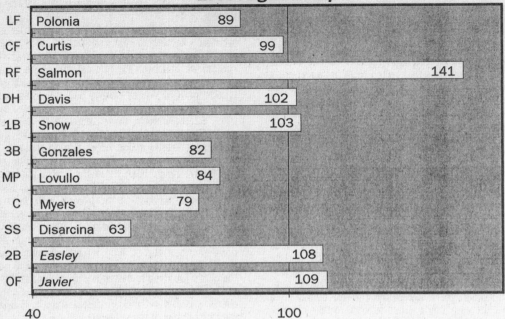

LF	Polonia	89
CF	Curtis	99
RF	Salmon	141
DH	Davis	102
1B	Snow	103
3B	Gonzales	82
MP	Lovullo	84
C	Myers	79
SS	Disarcina	63
2B	*Easley*	108
OF	*Javier*	109

40   100

The Offense

Despite the emergence of some intriguing youngsters, the Angels continued their recent pattern of being a far below average offensive team. Their 93.5 team TOPR placed them ahead of only KC and Milwaukee in the AL. But that's part of a disturbing pattern of late that the organization must address. The Halos must TOPR better.

Just how bad this team was in '92 can be shown by how far they still have to go after a '93 season in which they showed solid improvement. The '93 Angels raised their team BA 17 points to .260. They drilled 26 more HRs, thanks mainly to rookie Salmon's contribution of 31. They drew 148 more walks. And they scored 105 more runs than the Cal team of '92. All that sounds good until you realize that their 114 HRs still tied them for last in the AL. Their 564 walks still didn't get them into the top half of the league in that category. That spiffy .260 BA led only Milwaukee and Oakland. And that huge jump in runs still left them at only 684, 85 short of the league average.

Yes, there's work left to be done offensively. Fortunately there are also some tools already in place.

Just two Angels TOPRed at a rate above the AL norms for their positions. Salmon burst onto the scene with a 141 leading all RFs by a considerable margin. But that had been, to at least some degree, expected. He'd been a heralded minor leaguer whose TOPR projections suggested that just such a boxcar season was well within his reach and, in fact, anticipated. Damien Easley's emergence, however, came as a big surprise. The match-stick thin Easley TOPRed along at 108, fourth best among all AL 2Bs until chronic shin splints ended his season on July 28.

Some other Angels, though not above their positional norms, certainly performed admirably. Young Snow's roller-coaster season ended on an up note and for the year that 103 TOPR looks good, especially when you consider that from May through July he didn't even hit his weight (.188). But he returned from his exile to the minors and plastered pitchers down the stretch (.387 his last 18G) to pull that TOPR into triple figures. Veteran DH Davis had an odd year. TOPR would have been much higher except for his .245 BA, the worst in his last 10 years. Ah, but, he drilled a career-second-best 27 HRs and drove in 112, the best he's ever done by a whopping 19 RBIs. Sparkplug Curtis finished 7th among AL CFs

with his 99 TOPR. But that'll improve substantially as soon as he better learns to pick his spots in the running game. His 24 caught stealings dragged his number down considerably.

But the other TOPRs in the lineup of manager Rodgers didn't wind up in a good neighborhood. None of those who played most often at LF, 3B, C and SS TOPRed as high as the 90s. That's four shaky spots in a nine-man order. That's too many to ever hope to sustain rallies. And that was, in fact, Cal's biggest shortcoming. Their lack of being able to "bat around" caused Rodgers to formulate a strategy based around getting big numbers from the Salmon-Davis duo in the middle and "pecking away" the rest of the time. With a lineup substantially devoid of power, the manager turned to speed. Cal attempted an AL-high 269 steals. They succeeded 169 times. But that inefficient running game cost them an even 100 outs. Just how inefficient? Compare them to Toronto which stole exactly one more base for the year (170) but was thrown out just 48 times. No, the Angels 59% running game, in fact, cost the team. But it remained the only alternative Rodgers had considering that he surely couldn't play "station-to-station" ball with a team whose lineup had, for the course of the entire season, just two people who could be counted on to "clear the stations" every once in a while.

The Angels lineup cried out for more power at various positions. Check out the incredible power outage the Halos suffered at certain stops in their batting order. Here are the '93 homer totals for five of the places in California's lineup:

Leadoff	1
#2	7
#7	7
#8	6
#9	5

Unbelievable! The top two and bottom three spots in the Angels lineup for the entire year combined to provide just 26 HRs. Imagine, then, the relief that an opposing pitcher felt once he'd gotten through the #6 spot. Unless he threw the fattest of fat ones there was almost no chance any one of the next five hitters could take him downtown. He coasts.

Perhaps young 3B Perez will arrive to provide a little more punch toward the bottom. Or maybe they'll strike it rich with a veteran bargain during the off-season. Regardless of where they find it though, Cal must locate more power or somehow become a great deal more proficient in their running game, because even though last season's lineup had some intriguing players, the Halos weren't nearly offensive enough to approach contender status.

The Pitching

Remember the old Braves' staff that got nicknamed "Spahn and Sain and pray for rain" because of its lack of depth. Well, the '93 Angels might correctly be described as "Langston and Finley and then the talent spread thinly."

California could claim the best tandem TPERs in the AL. Adding the top two TPERs of the staff aces in the league produces this table:

Langston–Finley	166
Johnson–Bosio	167
Fernandez–McDowell	167
Moyer–McDonald	168
Key–Abbott	173
Darwin–Clemens	179

The Angels had aces. They just didn't have the rest of the "hand." Cal had always prided itself on being a nasty pitching staff. Hey, even when the Angels were pond scum back in the '70s, they still had Ryan and Tanana atop the rotation. But for the first time in years the Halos finished with a TPER in three figures. A below-average staff in California? That's almost like the passing of a baseball tradition. You have to track back six years to find a team ERA higher than the 4.34 posted in '93. That number qualifies as the third worst team in the club's 33-year history. And that's with Langston and Finley!

Overall the staff suffered from homer-itis. Cal hurlers got touched for 153 long balls, 39 more than their offense belted. And while their teammates' running game struggled, Angel pitchers did a poor job as a group controlling runners. Opposing stealers succeeded at a 70% rate (122 for 174).

The Rotation: Led by Langston and Finley, Cal topped the major leagues in complete games with 26. But beyond their two best, the Angels spent the year searching for stability. The Angels tried and eventually discarded veterans Farrell and Sanderson. They turned to youngsters Leftwich, Hathaway and Springer. Then, late in the year, grabbed vet lefty Magrane who'd been dumped in St. Louis. Of this six-pack only Leftwich could boast of a season-long TPER beneath 100 (a solid 90). Magrane, though, looked much better the last few weeks of the year in Cal and encouraged the Angels enough for them to sign him to a multi-year pact once the season ended.

For the year Langston and Finley combined for a 32–25 record. Those other six were 22–40. But do not confuse the poor record with lack of progress. By season's end Leftwich, Magrane and Hathaway provided a fairly stable look to the 3–5 spots behind Langston and Finley. The minor league numbers of Leftwich (who unfortunately is a righty) are solid across the board. He looks like he fits right in next season. Magrane's intriguing. An 18-game winner four years ago in St. Louis, but dogged by injuries since. If his late season success (3–2 and a 3.94 ERA in just 8 games) indicates he's finally returning to form, the Angels may have stumbled on a real blue light special. Or, he might be a bust. Hathaway's 117 TPER suggests he may need more seasoning. His high walk and low strikeout totals in his Angel stint continue a disturbing trend established as he moved up the minor league ladder. Springer truly disappointed the club. They'd tabbed him as a key acquisition in the Abbott deal and he got his head handed to him in 14 appearances. But he's just 25 with a set of dazzling minor league numbers.

One weird note about the homer-prone Angel starters. They had terrible troubles very, very early in games. In all, the staff allowed 153 taters. But 71 of them, a full 46% of all Angel homers permitted all season, came during the first 30 pitches of the game. Bizarre!

The Bullpen: Critics of the Angels lashed out at them for allowing stud closer Harvey to get away in the expansion draft. And, yes, in retrospect it looks like a horrible mistake especially after he landed in Florida, set an expansion record with an astronomical 45 saves and TPERed at 69, the third-best closer number in all of baseball. Cal had been worried about the health of his arm and the three huge years left on his contract worth more than $10 million total. So they exposed him and the Marlins grabbed him and the whole

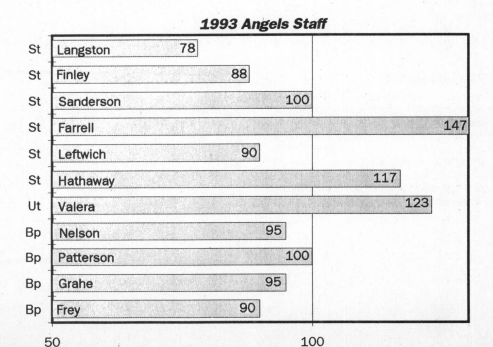

1993 Angels Staff

St	Langston	78
St	Finley	88
St	Sanderson	100
St	Farrell	147
St	Leftwich	90
St	Hathaway	117
Ut	Valera	123
Bp	Nelson	95
Bp	Patterson	100
Bp	Grahe	95
Bp	Frey	90

50   100

world laughed at the Angels. But there really had been a master plan. The Halos thought Grahe looked ready to step into that critical job. And, even if he wasn't, they still had future closer types Troy Percival and Ron Watson climbing the ladder toward the majors. The Angels reasoned they could save some money and retool for the future at the same time. Alas, the best laid plans of mice and men and Angels often go awry. Grahe developed tendinitis which ripped five weeks out of his season and resulted in his being handled ''with kid gloves'' a good part of the rest of the way. Meanwhile, down on the farm, Percival and Watson blew out their arms and have become question marks. So much for the master plan.

Cal wound up with a shared closer situation. Lefty Frey, bothered by control troubles at times, and the tender-armed Grahe split the job. Each TPERed pretty well with Frey in at a career best 90 and Grahe at 95 after posting that glittering 86 the year before which had given Cal so much hope in the first place. But the remainder of the pen struggled. Why Cal dumped effective righty set-up man Gene Nelson still remains a mystery, though. Given the state of the Halos pen, 92 TPERs shouldn't be sent packing. But again, he's into his early 30s and money apparently played a role in his exit. The injury to Valera, which threatens his career, hurt. His 123 TPER for the year belies the fact that when healthy he's one of those spot-starter-go-long-or-close types who could have played a variety of roles on a staff that badly needed such a role player. With their continuing eye to the future, Cal also gave a look-see to minor league relievers Lewis and Scott. Each pitched at the Triple A level in '93 with encouraging numbers, especially those of Lewis who, at least down below, had high strikeout numbers and a low frequency of walks and long balls.

In toto, the staff, like the batting order, used '93 to sort some things out. The shakedown cruise for some of these youngsters probably carries into and perhaps all the way through '94. But, also like their offensive side, the Angels appear to have found some keepers.

What Next?

Patience, patience, patience.

Last year the club found that Salmon, Curtis, Disarcina, Easley, Leftwich and Grahe will play roles in California's return to prominence. Next season becomes a proving ground for Perez, Turner, Hathaway, Springer and a handful of young relievers. Maybe Magrane makes it all the way back, too.

There's a temptation to immediately dismiss '94 as simply the third year in GM Herzog's four- or five-year plan that began in '92. But that may be misjudging this unit. In the realigned AL West they'll have just three other competitors for the crown—a reorganizing Oakland franchise who may, in '94, do what the Angels did in '92, and the Rangers and Mariners, two of the AL's most chronic losers. Each of those latter two teams look much more formidable than Cal on paper. But the truth is, they, like the young Halos, have never done it either.

The future's still probably a year away. But if some offense can be found to even out the lineup, if some of the kiddie pitchers break through, and if Grahe develops into the closer Cal thought he could become, these Angels might hang around even longer than they did last year. And, if the ''growing season'' in Cal continues to be good, it may not be long before Cal starts hanging around all the way to the finish.

Anaheim Stadium

The ''Big A'' produced a series of mixed effects in '93 that balanced out to a slight increase in offense (101.7 Park TOPR). The Angels' offense and pitching both benefited from playing at home (Home TOPR 96.8 vs. 90.3 on the road, Home TPER 99.6 vs. 103.5 away). But neither achieved the full home advantage of around an +8% improvement, which was the league's average home/road differential.

If a team's home park is supposed to be the ''friendly confines,'' you could say the Big A was simply a ''polite host'' to the Angels in '93.

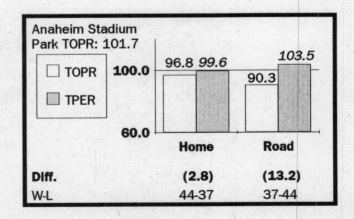

Anaheim Stadium
Park TOPR: 101.7

	TOPR	TPER
	Home	Road
	96.8 / 99.6	90.3 / 103.5
Diff.	(2.8)	(13.2)
W-L	44-37	37-44

Team TOPR: 1993 California Angels

	Bats	BA	OBP	SLG	HR	R	RBI	NBE	GOC	Ratio	TOPR
League Avg. Team	-	.267	.337	.408	148	762	719	2897	4352	.666	100
California Angels	-	.260	.331	.380	114	684	644	2686	4317	.622	93.5
Regulars:											
C Greg Myers	L	.255	.298	.362	7	27	40	122	233	.524	79
1B J.T. Snow	B	.241	.328	.408	16	60	57	234	341	.686	103
2B Damion Easley	R	.313	.392	.413	2	33	22	124	172	.721	108
2B Torey Lovullo	B	.251	.318	.354	6	42	30	165	294	.561	84
3B Rene Gonzales	R	.251	.346	.319	2	34	31	149	272	.548	82
Eduardo Perez	R	.250	.292	.372	4	16	30	76	144	.528	(79)
SS Gary DiSarcina	R	.238	.273	.313	3	44	45	144	345	.417	63
LF Luis Polonia	L	.271	.328	.326	1	75	32	273	462	.591	89
CF Chad Curtis	R	.285	.361	.369	6	94	59	311	471	.660	99
RF Tim Salmon	R	.283	.382	.536	31	93	95	364	389	.936	141
DH Chili Davis	B	.243	.327	.440	27	74	112	309	453	.682	102
Bench (100+ TPA):											
OF Stan Javier	B	.291	.362	.405	3	33	28	131	181	.724	109
IF Rod Correia	R	.266	.319	.305	0	12	9	51	104	.490	(74)
C John Orton	R	.189	.252	.274	1	5	4	34	82	.415	(62)
C Ron Tingley	R	.200	.277	.278	0	7	12	34	82	.415	(62)

NOTE: Statistics are only for games played with California. ( ) Under 200 TPA.

Team TPER: 1993 California Angels

	Throws	W-L	GS	GR	SV	IP	ERA	NBA	GOE	Ratio	TPER
League Avg. Team	-	81 -81	162	355	42	1444.1	4.33	2897	4352	0.666	100
California Angels	-	71 -91	162	320	41	1430.1	4.36	2901	4295	0.675	101.5
The Rotation:											
Mark Langston	L	16 -11	35	0	0	256.1	3.20	400	767	0.522	78
Chuck Finley	L	16 -14	35	0	0	251.1	3.15	446	764	0.584	88
Scott Sanderson	R	7 -11	21	0	0	135.1	4.46	270	406	0.665	100
John Farrell	R	3 -12	17	4	0	90.2	7.35	263	268	0.981	147
Phillip Leftwich	R	4 -6	12	0	0	80.2	3.79	143	240	0.596	90
Hilly Hathaway	L	4 -3	11	0	0	57.1	5.02	128	165	0.776	117
Joe Magrane	L	3 -2	8	0	0	48	3.94	102	148	0.689	104
Utility:											
Russ Springer	R	1 -6	9	5	0	60	7.20	156	178	0.876	132
Julio Valera	R	3 -6	5	14	4	53	6.62	132	161	0.820	123
Bullpen:											
Ken Patterson	L	1 -1	0	46	1	59	4.58	118	177	0.667	100
Joe Grahe	R	4 -1	0	45	11	56.2	2.86	109	172	0.634	95
Gene Nelson	R	0 -5	0	46	4	52.2	3.08	102	161	0.634	95
Mike Butcher	R	1 -0	0	23	8	28.1	2.86	55	87	0.632	(95)
Steve Frey	L	2 -3	0	55	13	48.1	2.98	87	146	0.596	90

NOTE: Statistics are only for games pitched with California. ( ) Under 200 TBF.

AN EMBARRASSMENT OF RICHES
CHICAGO WHITE SOX

Pitching.

Scouts spend their careers looking for it. If only the Tigers had some. Cleveland paid 27 pitchers last season but paid very few effective ones. Texas had so little they went to a *three-man* rotation down the stretch. Even with all of George's money the Yankees couldn't find any to buy. The Brewers thought they had some—they were wrong. Oakland used to have some. So did Minnesota. Even the world-champion Blue Jays had to win with outstanding offense, not pitching.

In a baseball world where teams go mad, mad, mad, mad, mad hunting for pitching, the White Sox at times, seemed like they almost had too much. How else can you explain taking a veteran starter like Kirk McCaskill out of the #5 rotation spot and shuffling him into a bullpen role because he's simply not good enough even though his four-year TPER average makes him one of the league's better starters? Too much pitching?

When the playoffs arrive the Sox' Tim Belcher, who hasn't had a losing season the last six years while making 30 starts a season, got pushed into the pen because his outstanding 92 TPER simply wasn't as good as their other four starters. Too much pitching?

Why in the world would they dump reliever Donnie Pall and his sparkling TPER of 88 (11th best among all AL set-up men) just as the stretch run began? Too much pitching?

Imagine having terrific young prospects like Scott Ruffcorn, James Baldwin, Robert Ellis, Steve Schrenk and Larry Thomas apparently ready in the minors but just leaving them there. Too much pitching?

Eat your hearts out other AL teams. As you scoured waiver wires looking for a few good arms, Chicago spent their season trying to deal with one of its most pressing but delightful "problems"—too much pitching. Lamont had a variety of superb choices when he did have to remove one of his aces. Closer Hernandez ranked third

among all AL "end men" with a fantastic 72 TPER. Set-up men Radinsky (left) and Schwarz (right) finished #7 and #11 among all AL pen-men. Pall would have tied for #11 with his 88 TPER but got sent to the Phillies. Even latecomer DeLeon posted a better than average season. Of the Sox hurlers left at season's end, only McCaskill finished with a worse-than-average TPER (105)—and that's certainly far from "bad."

This staff had no less than five pitchers win at least five straight decisions. Alvarez and Bere (7), McDowell and Radinsky (6) and Fernandez (5). But what ought to scare AL opponents most about this group is not what they did last season, but what they might be doing for seasons to come.

When the Sox started McDowell (27), Fernandez (24), Alvarez (23) and Bere (22) against the Jays in the ALCS they made history. That quartet had become the youngest to ever take the mound in League Championship history—averaging only 24 years old!

They keyed a staff that put up some awful numbers—awful if you're an AL hitter. Chicago allowed only 364 extra-base hits for the season. Every other staff in the league permitted more than 400. Minnesota gave up over 500. The staff ERA of 3.70 led the AL, the first time a Sox team topped the league since the '67 Sox posted that (no one can still believe it) 2.45 ERA. Sox pitchers gave up just 125 HRs, 23 below league average. But perhaps, given their relative youth, the most amazing component of this staff remains their ability to completely stuff the running game. With the help of laser-armed catcher Karkovice, opponents broke even stealing—82 steals and 82 caught stealings. With runners thus frozen at first base, the Sox proceeded to throw 135 DP balls, which put them comfortably above league average.

Impressive numbers like that start with the starters. And the Sox have plenty of 'em. Belcher's departure won't cause even a ripple.

Team Trendline: Chicago White Sox

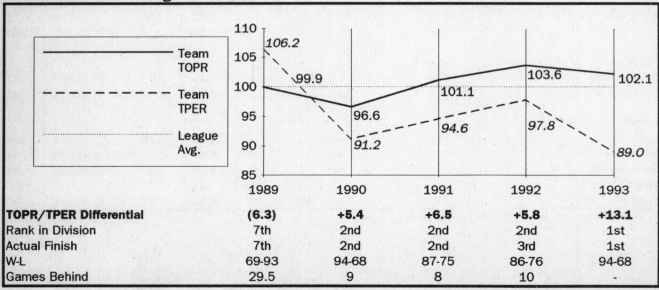

	1989	1990	1991	1992	1993
TOPR/TPER Differential	(6.3)	+5.4	+6.5	+5.8	+13.1
Rank in Division	7th	2nd	2nd	2nd	1st
Actual Finish	7th	2nd	2nd	3rd	1st
W-L	69-93	94-68	87-75	86-76	94-68
Games Behind	29.5	9	8	10	-

Legend: Team TOPR, Team TPER, League Avg.

Chart values — Team TOPR: 106.2 (1989 TPER start), 99.9, 96.6, 101.1, 103.6, 102.1. Team TPER: 106.2, 99.9, 91.2, 94.6, 97.8, 89.0.

What Was Expected

Chicagoans long ago learned never to get their hopes up too much. After all, entering '93 Chicago baseball teams hadn't won a World Series since 1917 when the White Sox took down the Giants in six games. Two years later those "White Sox" had turned into the "Black Sox" and a long period of Windy City frustration had begun. Since 1917 Chicago teams had won eight pennants and three division titles. (New York teams in that interim, for example, had 22 World Series championships, 32 pennants and nine divisional titles.) Forget crowns and rings, hearty Chicago fans simply wished they could see winning baseball with regularity. In the 25 years since 1968 the White Sox and Cubs had each posted winning seasons in the same year just once—1972. But, if fans of constant disappointment like those in Chicago could ever approach a season with quiet confidence, '93 was it. While those on the north side hoped their beloved Cubbies could poke their noses above .500, White Sox backers talked of pennants and, yes, maybe even championships. After all, they'd put up three solid seasons to start the decade finishing a heartbeat or two away from the title for three straight years. Realizing the nearness of such a triumph, management chose to add some playoff-hardened vets. They opted to give former Blue Jays ace Dave Steib a chance to join the rotation. After a long squabble they re-signed White Sox icon and catcher Carlton Fisk. They plugged an obvious OF hole with Ellis Burks and then prayed that his back would hold up. Best of all from a fan's perspective, the right knee of SS Ozzie Guillen had healed and his glove wizardry again made the White Sox left side of the infield a cemetery for ground balls. During the season Chicago would aggressively keep adding to the mix—CF Ivan Calderon, C Mike LaValliere, P Tim Belcher and P Jose DeLeon. Chicago ripped through spring training winning 17 of their last 24. As the season approached, all the pieces appeared to be in place. The experts' consensus said the Sox would win the West for the first time in a decade. Chicago fans smiled broadly—and behind their backs crossed their fingers.

What Actually Happened

The experts were right!

Defending champ Oakland fell apart immediately. Another of the prime contenders, Texas, didn't look ready for prime time. Minnesota lost eight in a row and then lost eight in a row again. Kansas City limped out of the starting gate (So, what else is new?). Seattle suffered numbing injuries. Only California outperformed expectations and everyone expected that ultra-young club to quickly fade. It's as if some White Sox fan had written the script for the season. Oh, that's not to say that everything with the Pale Hose was sugar and spice. Steib simply couldn't pitch anymore. For every one hit he got, Fisk had 100 complaints. Leadoff man and offensive sparkplug Tim Raines headed for the DL almost immediately and wouldn't return for six weeks. DH George Bell had the politically correct last name because every pitcher in the league was "ringing him up." Middle-of-the-lineup heavyweights Frank Thomas and Robin Ventura hit more like middleweights for the first couple of months. The AL West appeared to be sitting there for the White Sox taking. But they weren't taking it. On June 20, the team with obviously the best talent in the division, found itself one game over .500 at 33–32. Luckily for the Sox, the Angels had begun their descent after two heavenly first months and no one else seemed to be able to figure their way out of their current messes, so that disappointing White Sox record still had them in third place, just two games off the pace.

That's when the Sox engine began to purr. They swept a then-disorganized Texas team moving into first place on June 23. They would never move out. From that struggling point on June 20 to the end of the season the Pale Hose won 61 and lost 36. But the last three months were far from a romp. KC got its act together. California hung around much longer than expected. Seattle got pretty healthy and pretty good. Texas got organized and actually crept to within 2½ games of the front-running Sox in mid-September. From the time they moved into first June 23, Chicago never enjoyed more than a five game lead until September 22.

In the end it turned out that all the off-season roster shuffling had been, with the exception of Burks' signing, for naught. The Sox had already had the makings of a titlist in place. All they'd needed and what they got was the sudden maturation of an outstanding group of young pitchers. Chicago hurlers held opponents to three runs or less 60 times! The team TPER of 89 easily gave the White Sox the league's best pitching and second in the majors only to Atlanta's outrageous staff laden with Cy Young winners and Cy Young hopefuls. Alas, in the playoffs, Chicago's own Cy Young winner, McDowell, disintegrated and the Blue Jays better hitting prevailed over the White Sox better pitching. But, at last, White Sox fans again had something real to cheer about. (And, by the way, the Cubs had a winning season too.)

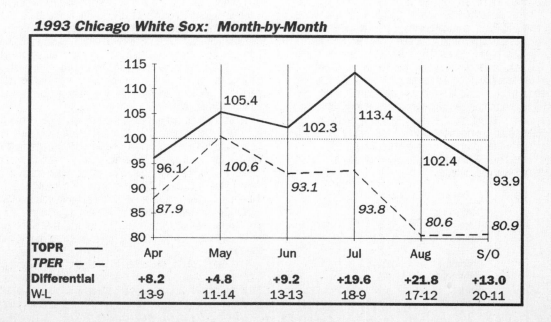

1993 Chicago White Sox: Month-by-Month

	Apr	May	Jun	Jul	Aug	S/O
TOPR ——	96.1	105.4	102.3	113.4	102.4	93.9
TPER – –	87.9	100.6	93.1	93.8	80.6	80.9
Differential	+8.2	+4.8	+9.2	+19.6	+21.8	+13.0
W-L	13-9	11-14	13-13	18-9	17-12	20-11

1993 White Sox Lineup

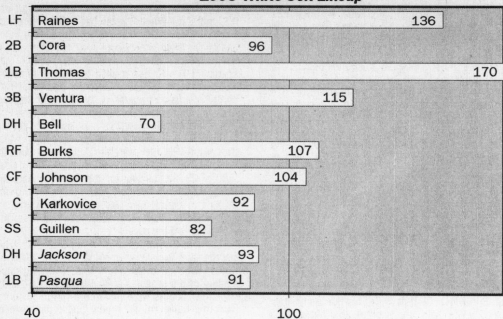

Pos.	Player	Value
LF	Raines	136
2B	Cora	96
1B	Thomas	170
3B	Ventura	115
DH	Bell	70
RF	Burks	107
CF	Johnson	104
C	Karkovice	92
SS	Guillen	82
DH	*Jackson*	93
1B	*Pasqua*	91

40   100

The Offense

Though the Sox attack contained one of the game's true superstars in Thomas, one of the game's most underrated stars in Raines and a handful of solid support players in Burks, Johnson and Ventura, they represented, as a unit, a barely adequate offensive team. In fact, in a year Chicago barely missed a trip to the World Series and a year in which offense rose all around the major leagues, the Pale Hose actually slipped a notch offensively from their performance of the '92 season (TOPR dropped from 103.6 to 102.1). They finished right in the middle of AL teams in runs scored (#7) and oddly led the league in being shutout—an amazing 14 times. (And you didn't think there'd been 14 games Thomas didn't drive in a run!) Even more bizarre was the way the Sox got to their 102.1 TOPR that, as a number, so resembled their performance of '92 (103.6) and '91 (101.1). Chicago actually experienced an enormous power surge in '93. The "Very Pale" Hose of '92 had managed a meager 110 homers. The '93 Sox smashed 52 more! So, how in the world then, did their team TOPR, the measurement of offensive accomplishment, drop? Less noticed areas slipped. The '93 Sox hit 41 fewer doubles, 8 less triples, drew 18 fewer walks and stopped being the Go-Go Sox, stealing 54 fewer bases. In other words, though many of the faces had remained the same, the '93 Sox had actually changed from a running team to a power team.

While their offensive output remained essentially unspectacular, their durability didn't. Other than Raines' exit to injury in the season's first week, manager Lamont enjoyed the luxury of having the steadiest everyday lineup in the league from the season's first pitch to the year's last out. Examine the numbers of games played by the Sox preferred everyday lineup:

Pos.	Player	Games
1B	Thomas	153
2B	Cora	153
SS	Guillen	134
3B	Ventura	157
LF	Raines	115
CF	Johnson	147
RF	Burks	146
C	Karkovice	128

Contrast that, if you will, with the division's defending champion A's who had only three positional players get in more than 107 games. The Sox offense may have been little more than average but at least its members reported to work day after day after day.

What this offense did have though was an extremely odd kind of efficiency and the best kind of odd efficiency to have—it worked early in games. The White Sox led the free world at scoring right away producing a whopping 142 first-inning runs. Given that the team scoring first won 62% of its games in '93 and annually does that well or better, that alone gave the Sox a huge jump toward their winning record. But when added to the remarkable performance of their pitching staff, leaping ahead early for the Sox amounted to a death sentence for the opposition. For the season the Pale Hose outscored their opponents by 112 runs—64 of that edge came in inning #1! As one would expect, with such opening-inning success, the #3 and #4 hitters had early inning explosions. Thomas belted 15 of his 41 HRs in the first and 33 of his 128 RBIs came in that frame. Ventura batted .429 in the first (.262 for the season) and had 31 of his 94 RBIs then. Such early-inning production can be especially important on the road where getting ahead immediately can take the opposing crowd "out of the game" and begins to limit the strategy choices of other managers. Thus, perhaps, we've identified the key reason for the Sox 49 road victories, tops in the AL.

What Chicago did not have though was a DH. They had, instead, a "DO"—designated out! Sox DHs, primarily Bell and Jackson, combined for a woeful .214 BA, 31 points beneath the next worst DH BA in the league (California's .245). The DH reached base a mere 25.2% of the time. No other team had a DH on-base percentage below 30.4%. Chicago DHs coaxed only 33 walks. Boston's finished next worst with 41. What you in effect had was a White Sox lineup that worked like an NL lineup—always working around an almost certain out. In the NL, that's the pitcher's slot. In Chicago it became the hitter designated to bat for the pitcher—the DH.

The Sox would be wise to address the cleanup spot also. Sometimes their DH batted cleanup and we've already touched on their failures to "clean up" anything. But Ventura appears miscast in the role. Oh, yes, he drove in 94. But hitting behind Thomas, who had 286 hits and walks, and Raines, who in just 115 games had 191 H and BB, that's truly a deceiving RBI total. Ventura batted with 248 men in scoring position and knocked in just 57 of them. In all, he batted with 363 men on base and managed to score only 72 of those. (You must subtract the 22 times he drove "himself" in with homers.) Perhaps one signing or trade could accomplish two necessities for Chicago. A big-time DH hitting cleanup would allow Ventura to move to #5 or #6 in the lineup where the harsh glare of expectation wouldn't make his totals look so average at best.

The Sox lineup may have some big names, may boast some big individual numbers. But, in truth, this club rode the backs of its pitchers to a division title. In the end, just how "average" was the Chicago attack? Seven runs. That's how many more scores the Sox had than the average AL offense in '93—seven runs!

The Pitching

Four aces.

A nearly unbeatable hand in poker. A nearly unbeatable staff in baseball.

Many staffs don't even have a single ace. One man who, come baseball hell or high water, steps out there every fourth or fifth day and stops whatever craziness happens to have broken out. White Sox manager Gene Lamont had, from the outset of '93, three aces. Very soon a fourth arrived from the Sox minor league system and joined the rotation. And late, when the Sox made a deal just in case they needed more pitching, one could even make a case for Lamont holding a hand that included *five aces*. No wonder he sat in the dugout night after night with that "poker face" on.

Consider the "aces" Lamont played night after night and their TPERs (and, yes, we realize one of the aces was really a "Black Jack"):

Pitcher	TPER	AL Rank	Record
Fernandez	82	#4	19–9
McDowell	85	#9	22–10
Bere	85	#11	12–5
Alvarez	89	#14	15–8

The Rotation: Imagine the luxury of having four of the best 14 starters in the entire 14-team league. Even the pitching-rich Braves couldn't say that. Their "big four" ranked #2, #5, #17 and #21 among NL starters. Then, as the pennant race heated up, the Sox acquired Belcher who, though his record didn't reflect it, TPERed at a superb 88 for his two-month stay in the Windy City. For the last nine weeks of '93 the Sox rotation consisted of five men TPERing in the 80s. Realize that in all of baseball last year, only 25 starters finished with TPERs of 89 or lower. And for two months the Sox had FIVE such "out-machines."

The quality of Chicago pitching did not, however, end with the rotation. Once the club dumped the unbelievably ineffective Thigpen and, in Chitown this off-season, McCaskill (average TPER for the decade of 97) remains completely capable of filling that #5 slot. But if he fails, the rush of prospects lining up for a place in the rotation might trample pitching coach Jackie Brown. Off their '93 minor league profiles, the Sox appear to have no less than four pitchers who performed at the triple A level last year ready for a shot at the bigs: Ruffcorn, Baldwin, Schrenk and Bolton (who flunked an in-season trial in Chicago last year). Chicago also raves about LH Larry Thomas, though his numbers suggest a hitability and homer problem. Just a step below at Double A sits Robert Ellis, whose profile suggests he might be the best of them all. In reality, that's almost too much pitching. Given that the Sox offense performed barely above average last year and that DH represented the biggest hole in their lineup, wouldn't a pitching-for-hitting swap with the Tigers make sense? Just an idea.

The Bullpen: At first glance, there doesn't seem to be enough bullpenners sitting out there. While other teams' relief corps scramble for seats in those abnormally small bullpen seating areas, Chicago relievers had lots of room. Hey, why carry lots of relievers when you don't need lots of relief? The Sox needed to use their pen just 322 times last season, 33 less than the "average" team. Only two men made more than 41 appearances—Radinsky with 73 and Hernandez with 70. From that point one must tumble all the way down to Schwarz's 41 games on the workload list. White Sox middlemen worked about as much as the Maytag repairman last year. Who needs a middleman when the starter's still always in there in the middle innings? McDowell averaged 7⅔ innings a start.

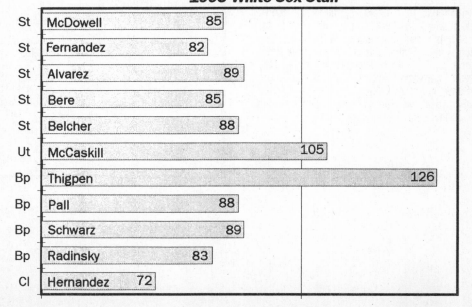

1993 White Sox Staff

St	McDowell	85
St	Fernandez	82
St	Alvarez	89
St	Bere	85
St	Belcher	88
Ut	McCaskill	105
Bp	Thigpen	126
Bp	Pall	88
Bp	Schwarz	89
Bp	Radinsky	83
Cl	Hernandez	72

50   100

Fernandez 7⅓. Alvarez 6⅔. Belcher 6⅓. Bere 6. On any given night, the starter got the Sox at least into the seventh inning and that's Schwarz-Radinsky-Hernandez territory.

Hernandez, though his injury history remains a tiny back-of-the-mind concern, has put up gaudy numbers two years in a row and has just reached "prime time" for a reliever at 29. Radinsky's a horse—68 games a year for every season in the 90s and his TPER's never risen into triple figures. Is Schwarz for real? He spent 11 uneventful years in the minors before bursting onto the scene last year. Might he be a one-year wonder? Or maybe just a late bloomer? DeLeon, picked up late in the year, has always mystified observers of the game. His stuff seems more than capable of making him a big winner. But when the spots get tight, something always seems to happen to him. Maybe the less-pressurized world of middle relief is where he's always belonged.

Unlike the rotation, there do not appear to be any future studs now standing on the Sox' doorstep trying to break down the door to a major league job. But then, unless injury or ineffectiveness suddenly strikes this group, where would the Sox put 'em anyway?

What Next?

What few things the Sox have on their "To Do List" this off-season all revolve around their offense. Chicago must realize that, as good as their pitching looked last season and looks for the future, strange things sometimes befall staffs. The White Sox can not sit idly by accepting a barely-above-average offense and depend on pitching forever. But the tasks are minimal and easily identifiable:
A) Get a DH.
B) Get a RF to replace Burks who left for the money and sheer hitters joy of playing in Colorado.
C) Get LF Raines re-signed.
D) Shop for some bench parts. Or, get a starting 2B and add the pesky-hitting but poor-fielding Cora (19 errors) to the bench.

Other than that, what's to be done on a club that's averaged 90 wins a year in the '90s and joins Toronto as the only two teams in the league who can claim having a winning record every year this decade? And trade proposals to the Sox ought to be plentiful for some time to come. The Sox have a surplus of pitching. That'll keep GM Ron Schueler's phone ringing fairly constantly.

With as little as there appears to be done though, what gets done must be done well. These Sox sit perched on the verge of a World Series championship. They've got so many fine puzzle parts already in place. And those parts are so very young. The right move or two could mean that the 77-year wait in Chicago for a team that will win it all again could end in '94.

New Comiskey Park

New Comiskey favored offense to a slight degree (Park TOPR: 101.4). But, the park seemed to work *against* its occupants. Adjusted for the normal home/road advantage, White Sox hitters suffered a −3.6% decline in offensive output. At the same time, White Sox pitchers were −7.3% less effective at home. New Comiskey didn't act like a "home park" at all. The Sox were more "at home" on the road and their record reflects it.

The internal numbers give us no clue as to the source of this curious effect, so perhaps that's all it is—a curiosity.

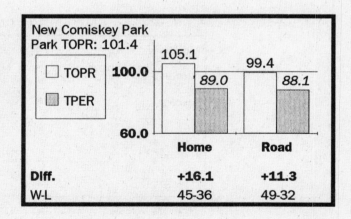

New Comiskey Park Park TOPR: 101.4		
□ TOPR	Home	Road
▨ TPER	105.1 / 89.0	99.4 / 88.1
Diff.	+16.1	+11.3
W-L	45-36	49-32

Team TOPR: 1993 Chicago White Sox

	Bats	BA	OBP	SLG	HR	R	RBI	NBE	GOC	Ratio	TOPR
League Avg. Team	-	.267	.337	.408	148	762	719	2897	4352	.666	100
Chicago White Sox	-	.265	.338	.411	162	776	731	2952	4342	.680	102.1
Regulars:											
C Ron Karkovice	R	.228	.287	.424	20	60	54	209	340	.615	92
1B Frank Thomas	R	.317	.426	.607	41	106	128	452	400	1.130	170
2B Joey Cora	B	.268	.351	.349	2	95	51	299	469	.638	96
3B Robin Ventura	L	.262	.379	.433	22	85	94	335	437	.767	115
SS Ozzie Guillen	L	.280	.292	.374	4	44	50	195	358	.545	82
LF Tim Raines	B	.306	.401	.480	16	75	54	277	306	.905	136
CF Lance Johnson	L	.311	.354	.396	0	75	47	271	392	.691	104
RF Ellis Burks	R	.275	.352	.441	17	75	74	281	393	.715	107
DH George Bell	R	.217	.243	.363	13	36	64	161	345	.467	70
Bench (100+ TPA):											
DH Bo Jackson	R	.232	.289	.433	16	32	45	140	226	.619	93
IF Craig Grebeck	R	.226	.319	.268	1	25	12	74	165	.448	67
I/O Dan Pasqua	L	.205	.302	.358	5	22	20	90	149	.604	91
C Mike LaValliere	L	.258	.282	.278	0	6	8	38	83	.458	(69)

NOTE: Statistics are only for games played with Chicago. ( ) Under 200 TPA.

Team TPER: 1993 Chicago White Sox

	Throws	W-L	GS	GR	SV	IP	ERA	NBA	GOE	Ratio	TPER
League Avg. Team	-	81 -81	162	355	42	1444.1	4.33	2897	4352	0.666	100
Chicago White Sox	-	94 -68	162	322	48	1454	3.72	2600	4386	0.593	89.0
The Rotation:											
Jack McDowell	R	22 -10	34	0	0	256.2	3.37	434	768	0.565	85
Alex Fernandez	R	18 -9	34	0	0	247.1	3.13	405	745	0.544	82
Wilson Alvarez	L	15 -8	31	0	0	207.2	2.95	368	621	0.593	89
Jason Bere	R	12 -5	24	0	0	142.2	3.47	245	432	0.567	85
Tim Belcher	R	3 -5	11	1	0	71.2	4.40	119	216	0.551	83
Rodney Bolton	R	2 -6	8	1	0	42.1	7.44	98	128	0.766	(115)
Utility:											
Kirk McCaskill	R	4 -8	14	16	2	113.2	5.23	239	342	0.699	105
Bullpen:											
Donn Pall	R	2 -3	0	39	1	58.2	3.22	105	180	0.583	88
Scott Radinsky	L	8 -2	0	73	4	54.2	4.28	96	173	0.555	83
Jeff Schwarz	R	2 -2	0	41	0	51	3.71	91	154	0.591	89
Bobby Thigpen	R	0 0	0	25	1	34.2	5.71	89	106	0.840	(126)
Roberto Hernandez	R	3 -4	0	70	38	78.2	2.29	113	235	0.481	72

NOTE: Statistics are only for games pitched with Chicago. ( ) Under 200 TBF.

OF TRAGEDY AND TRIUMPH
CLEVELAND INDIANS

One of the truest "pop" philosophies suggests that: "Life is what happens to you while you're busy making other plans." Cleveland was busy making plans for the fast approaching season when, at dusk on March 22, two of the Indians' pitchers were killed and a third gravely injured when their fishing boat collided with a dock. The tragedy tore the heart out of the pitching staff and ripped the heart out of a young Indians' team thought to be on the verge of becoming respectable and perhaps even more.

The accident claimed the lives of bullpen ace Steven Olin and veteran set-up man Tim Crews and virtually wiped out the season of starter Bob Ojeda. That was the physical cost to the roster. But perhaps just as great were the psychological scars left on surviving team members. Cleveland wandered out of the gate, played ex-tremely poor baseball and fell quickly into the cellar. For some, baseball served only as a reminder of the sadness of what had happened. For others, the games constituted a welcome relief from the grief that gripped the team during the periods of inactivity. For all, April and May became a terrible mixture of constant losing and constant sorrow.

But somewhere, somehow, the Indians managed to pull their lives and their team together. For the last four months they actually played above .500. That they were able to do so speaks volumes about the leadership and motivational abilities of Indians' manager Mike Hargrove and about the character and fortitude of Cleveland's young roster.

Team Trendline: Cleveland Indians

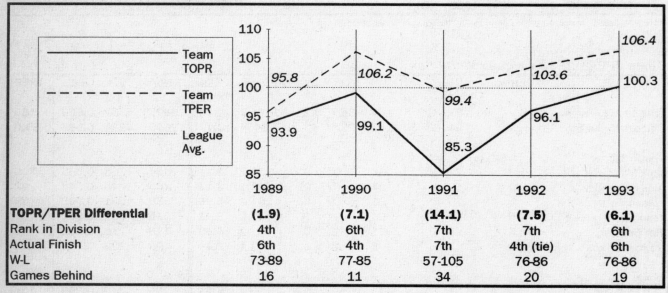

	1989	1990	1991	1992	1993
TOPR/TPER Differential	(1.9)	(7.1)	(14.1)	(7.5)	(6.1)
Rank in Division	4th	6th	7th	7th	6th
Actual Finish	6th	4th	7th	4th (tie)	6th
W-L	73-89	77-85	57-105	76-86	76-86
Games Behind	16	11	34	20	19

What Was Expected

Cleveland arrived at training camp brimming with hope. Oh, not for a pennant or, like AL East bully Toronto, for some shot at being called a dynasty, but for continued improvement. These Indians had been a disgusting 57–105 in '91 but had taken 19 steps up baseball's respectability ladder to 76 wins in '92. The franchise had shown gratitude for the better play by inking the entire core of the club's ultra-young roster to multi-year contracts. Camp in '93 opened with talk of being a better-than-.500 club. And why not? Didn't Cleveland have some of the finest and most exciting young stars in the game in CF Lofton, LF Belle and 2B Baerga? Didn't they already have their ace of the future in place with Nagy? Didn't they already boast of a wonderfully deep bullpen headed by a closer just entering his prime in Olin? And wasn't the Indians' farm system seemingly teeming with prospects? The Tribe had made a commit-ment to youth. But to give the club and especially the staff a touch of stability and leadership, they'd added a trio of veteran pitchers— Ojeda, Crews and Bielecki. Unless something happened '93 ap-peared to be a season for the Tribe to take another important step up that ladder.

Then something happened. Something awful.

What Actually Happened

If only the boating accident that killed Olin and Crews and badly hurt Ojeda had been the only ill-fortune to befall the Tribe. The starting pitching fell totally apart when the tragedy was followed quickly by disabling injuries to Nagy, Alan Embree, Dave Mlicki, Mark Clark and Tommy Kramer. Cleveland had also crossed its fingers that the terrible injury string had ended for catcher Sandy Alomar. But by May 15 he'd again undergone surgery. Super 3B prospect Jim Thome failed miserably and headed back for more Triple A seasoning. Even long after the accident Cleveland continued to look like a textbook example of Murphy's law: Everything that could go wrong, did go wrong.

During a pre-game interview in very early June, manager Hargrove surveyed the grief-filled first two months and attempted to draw a portrait of his team, groped to summarize how helpless he'd felt at times early in the season trying to squeeze something

out of the club that he wasn't even sure was there: "Coming out of spring training after the accident, I had no idea just how empty our emotional tanks were. For the first couple of months, whenever we encountered a hardship, whenever we faced adversity, we just didn't have the emotional reserve to call on. The deaths had drained it all away. Only now do I sense that the life's returning to this team."

Hargrove's insight proved to be right on. Beginning with the first of June, Cleveland perked up. The middle of the order began producing runs regularly. And though the club really never had a "rotation" as such due to continuing injuries and ineffectiveness, the bullpen stabilized and became more than adequate at protecting leads once the offense produced one. That the Indians "managed" to get to 76 victories may qualify as downright miraculous given the staff's season-long state of disarray that had begun at dusk on March 22.

1993 Cleveland Indians: Month-by-Month

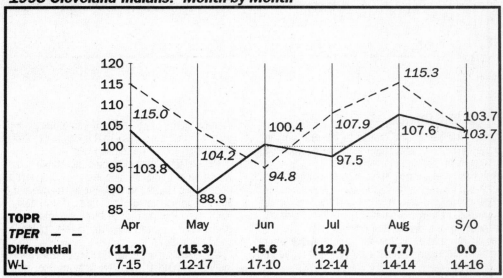

	Apr	May	Jun	Jul	Aug	S/O
TOPR ——	103.8	88.9	100.4	97.5	107.6	103.7
TPER – –	115.0	104.2	94.8	107.9	115.3	103.7
Differential	(11.2)	(15.3)	+5.6	(12.4)	(7.7)	0.0
W-L	7-15	12-17	17-10	12-14	14-14	14-16

Municipal Stadium

In its last year as the Indians' home, the unlamented "Mistake by the Lake" played as a "pitcher's park" (93.0 Park TOPR). This effect, though, traced totally to the Indians' struggling young pitching staff. At home, they *didn't* struggle. They were, in fact, quite effective (95.9 TPER, 3.83 ERA). As a result, Cleveland produced a 46–35 record at home—within four games of the league's best (50–31 by the Yankees and the Rangers).

Once away from familiar surroundings, however, they collapsed. Cleveland's Road TPER skied to 117.3 (5.35 ERA) and their record plummeted to 30–51 (only the Angels were worse, 27–54). This home/road trend seems a hallmark of young staffs, suggesting that with maturity will come improvement.

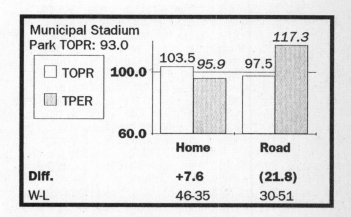

Municipal Stadium
Park TOPR: 93.0

	Home	Road
TOPR	103.5	97.5
TPER	95.9	117.3
Diff.	+7.6	(21.8)
W-L	46-35	30-51

1993 Indians Lineup

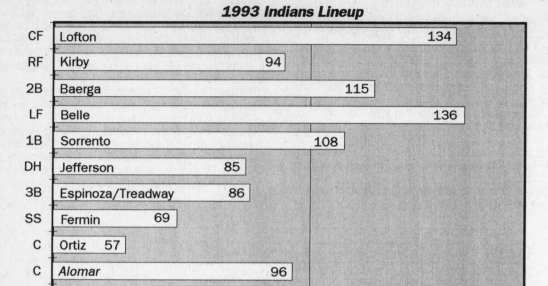

Position	Player	TOPR
CF	Lofton	134
RF	Kirby	94
2B	Baerga	115
LF	Belle	136
1B	Sorrento	108
DH	Jefferson	85
3B	Espinoza/Treadway	86
SS	Fermin	69
C	Ortiz	57
C	Alomar	96
IF	Martinez	78

40   100

The Offense

The Tribe's stars played like stars. And thanks to the outstanding seasons turned in by the heart of the order—Lofton, Baerga and Belle—the Indians became an average offensive team.

Now, that might not seem like much of an accomplishment—to be called "average"—but check the Cleveland Team Trendline. For the first time in five years (and well beyond what our research shows), Cleveland weighed in with a *two* digit TOPR. But in judging the Indians, while focusing one eye on the present, also aim the other down the line at the future, as the Tribe made move after move designed at making themselves better next year and for years to come.

As a team, the '93 Indians' attack had some distinct pluses and minuses. All the pluses center around those same three names—Lofton, Baerga and Belle. Their TOPRs (134, 115 and 136) put each near the very top at his position. The AL had only one CF better than Lofton and that was Seattle's remarkable Griffey, Jr. Only Toronto's Alomar and Detroit's steady Whitaker topped Baerga's 115 at 2B. Belle's 136 ranked behind only Rickey Henderson and Texas' manchild Gonzalez in LF. Prime production from prime players none of whom had, in '93, yet reached the "prime age" of 27. But, other than the best year ever in the career of 1B Sorrento (a 108 TOPR, 9th among AL 1Bs), Cleveland's "Three Bombardiers" got little help from the rest of the lineup.

Some examples: The Tribe stole the third most bases in all the AL (159). But after Lofton's 70, Belle's 23 and Baerga's 15, only RF Kirby had more than four (17). The Tribe bashed 141 homers, good for ninth in the league. But Belle and Baerga accounted for 59 of them. Only Sorrento (18) and Jefferson (10) also managed to get into double figures. After Belle's 129 RBI's and Baerga's 115, you drop to Sorrento at 65. After Lofton's 116 runs comes Baerga at 106, Belle at 93 and down to Sorrento at 75. Now, on the surface, this isn't terribly unusual for a team's best trio to combine to dominate a team's stats. But it does point out how dependent for offense Cleveland becomes on this threesome. And it suggests just how desperate their straits may have become if one or, shudder to think, two had gotten injured. The bottom line here is that, even with this terrific trio, the Tribe could do no better than produce an average team TOPR. That tells you of the extreme need for improvement at other positions. That tells you the Indians' trio needs help. Fortunately help's on the way.

Regardless of whoever joins that troika in the Cleveland lineup, it would be of immense help if they could weedle some walks out of opposing pitchers. As with many, many young players, this Indians' lineup consisted of swingers. They coaxed just 488 walks as a team. Only Kansas City and free-swinging, young Texas drew less. (Once again, by the way, the club's leaders were Lofton with 81 and Belle with 76.)

Cleveland's gaps became obvious from a quick peek at the club's individual TOPRs. The left side of the infield, catcher and DH produced far below league averages for the position.

	Cleveland	AL Norm
3B Espinoza/Treadway	86	102
SS Fermin	69	85
C Ortiz	57	100
DH Jefferson	85	105

The Tribe's three stars gave them major TOPR advantages at their positions. The four positions above eroded that advantage. We purposely avoided RF Kirby, who's an intriguing player. He'd banged around the minors forever. But late in the spring Cleveland traded RF Whiten for pitching help. The Tribe then tried Thomas Howard and Glenallen Hill at times in the spot. Each failed to make any impact. They eventually turned to Kirby recalling him in late April and he gave them more speed and a respectable 94 TOPR along with an outstanding arm in RF (a league leading 19 assists). If, during the off-season, Cleveland moves to acquire a RF and Kirby becomes an IMP (Impact Multi-Position player), he's got a chance to be one of the league's best, given that he plays a variety of spots and can really run. But if he's back in RF in a lineup that can take more advantage of his speed, that's not all that bad either.

But back to the four holes. The imbalance created by having four struggling lineup spots truly dragged the offense down at times. Collectively, the players who started at those spots the most often provided very little power, very little speed and, perhaps most disturbing, very few walks. Jefferson drew 28, Fermin 24, Treadway 14, Ortiz 11 and Espinoza 8. Had this lower part of the order been on base more often when the big boppers' turns came, the Tribe would have become a far above average team offensively.

But let's go to that eye on the future. Catcher Alomar returned for the last eight weeks and looked very good. For the year he TOPRed at 96. But realize that figure included his dismal early-season numbers when he went a dismal 7 for 56 before heading for back surgery. If you break those out of his '93 numbers, upon his return he TOPRed well over 100 and above the catcher's position norm. If he's healthy, that's major improvement #1.

A second could come at 3B. While Thome deeply disappointed the club in the spring, he greatly encouraged everyone over the last seven weeks. After tearing up Triple A pitching, he stepped to the major league level and just kept tearing it up. A TOPR of 134. That, by the way, matches exactly what his minor league TOPR projections suggested he'd do on the big league level. But even, let us say, he drops back 20 points in '94 to a 114, that's a huge improvement over the 86 TOPR that the platoon gave the Tribe at 3B last year.

On to the DH. Cleveland inked veteran 1B Eddie Murray as a free agent. He TOPRed at a 102 rate in the NL. If Murray simply moves into the DH slot and puts up a comparable number, that boosts the TOPR about 20 points at that spot.

All this is to suggest that, while the Tribe's numbers became "average" last year, the near future for this offense certainly doesn't look average.

The Pitching

Where do you start to sort out this jumble?

The '93 Tribe TPER reached its highest level in five years. That's not hard to understand given the turmoil that existed on the staff from day one to day last.

As a group, Cleveland's hurlers gave up too many homers. Way too many homers! Their 182 taters made them the most homer-prone staff in all of baseball. That's right, even more than the Colorado Rockies whose pitchers had the disadvantage of working in the all-time "launching pad" of a home park. If that weren't

enough, Indians' pitchers also walked 591, topped only by the staffs in Toronto, Seattle and Oakland in the AL and the expansion Marlins and Rockies in the NL.

Cleveland's staff, as a group, yielded 41 more homers than their teammates hit and walked 103 more than their mates drew. Those are huge deficits. But then, this was truly one huge group!

The Tribe used a whopping 26 pitchers. They'd have tied the all-time record had they been able to squeeze Calvin Jones into a game late in the season after he reported to the club. If, as a group they didn't pitch particularly well, they must have at least boosted program sales at aging Municipal Stadium because you truly couldn't tell this bunch from one day to the next without a scorecard. In the period of the most intense shuffling, from July 5 through August 7, Cleveland made major league roster moves involving 15 pitchers!

The Rotation: The Indians entered the season with one given among their starters—ace Charles Nagy. The year before he'd broken through with a 76 TPER, one of the league's very best. He'd thrown 252 innings and posted a 17–10 mark for a team that, when he didn't get the decision, was a 17-games-under-.500 club. But Nagy exited soon after the year began, eventually going under the knife June 29 for shoulder repair.

Without Nagy the Tribe had no "rotation." He'd been the guy they "rotated" around. In all, Cleveland would use a mind-boggling 18 different starters. Only Jose Mesa, with 33, would make more than 16 starts. In truth, this club didn't have a rotation—it had tryouts!

Besides Nagy and Ojeda, injuries interrupted the seasons of Clark, Kramer, Mlicki, Embree, Power and Cliff Young. And the injury blight trickled down through the entire organization. At one point, from the top of the Tribe's franchise to its bottom-level rookie league clubs, Cleveland had 18 pitchers on disabled lists.

Veterans Bielecki and Matt Young got bombed and got released. The club gave looks to pitchers like Grimsley, Milacki and Abbott who'd worn out their welcome in other organizations. They took good looks at the faces of their future staff giving trials to Lopez and Tavarez, who were among a group of seven rookies who got starts.

In the end their best TPER belonged to Jose Mesa and that

1993 Indians Staff

Role	Pitcher	TPER
St	Mesa	96
St	Mutis	115
St	Bielecki	121
Ut	Kramer	112
Ut	Clark	98
Ut	M. Young	112
Bp	Wertz	94
Bp	DiPoto	82
Bp	Hernandez	98
Bp	Lilliquist	93
Bp	Plunk	91

50   100

modest 96 made him only the 29th best starter TPER in the AL. But for "Joe Table" it represented the best number of his three full years in the majors. Second, just behind him, came what might be the find of the season. Mark Clark came from St. Louis in the late-spring trade that sent RF Whiten to the Cards. Cleveland really hadn't figured on making such a deal until the boating accident left them in dire need of pitching. They went after Clark. For two months he staggered around putting up terrible numbers, then headed for the minors and eventually the DL (didn't everyone?). But upon his September return, the Tribe's interim pitching coach Dom Chiti noticed something while watching Clark warm up. He asked if he'd ever tried bringing his hands above his head in his motion. Clark explained that that's how he always pitched until the Cards changed him. Chiti suggested he try his old motion. Presto! A new pitcher! In five starts with his "new-old" style, Clark performed brilliantly (38 IP, 26 H, 7 BB, 21 K, ERA 1.91). Did Cleveland find a star?

Kramer, though also bothered by injury, posted the club's best percentage (7–3). But he's walk and homer-prone, a hard combination to live with.

To review all the rest of the names that came in and out of this team's rotation probably becomes fruitless and, in many ways, worthless. For Cleveland spent most of '93 trying to figure out what their '94 staff would look like. If they got some definite answers, either positive or negative, that would be the most productive development expected from last year's star-crossed staff.

The Bullpen: Ah, now here's a very different story. While the Tribe groped for starters, they managed to piece together a very decent bullpen. By year's end, 21 different pitchers had appeared in relief at least once. From them the Tribe assembled a versatile and talented corps.

Note that as a group all six of the relievers we listed TPERed well below 100. All above-average pitchers, in other words. Now, admittedly, the numbers of youngsters Dipoto and Wertz came in partial seasons and Hernandez and Slocumb only arrived by trade on June 1, but the sorting out process among this weighty group went well and produced a solid core approaching '94.

Dipoto's the closer of the future. His strength is the one plus you cherish most among relievers. He keeps it in the park. He threw 56 innings and *never* allowed a homer! But if and when Dipoto either fails or is unavailable, Hargrove can call on a pair of vets coming off solid TPER seasons. Lefty Lilliquist (93) has now put solid seasons back-to-back. Plunk appears to have found new life in Cleveland and now has three seasons out of four in the 90s TPER-wise this decade. Each of these vets joined Dipoto in saving double numbers of games giving the Tribe the look of a team who truly could survive with a "bullpen by committee." Wertz (94), Hernandez (98) and Heathcliff Slocumb (93) gave the Tribe quality depth.

If Cleveland can pull its starting staff together in '94 the world may come to appreciate what in '93 was a vastly underrated pen. No other major league team could boast of having six bullpeners who each made at least 20 appearances and *all* TPERed below 100.

What Next?

While the '93 season became muddled and, at times depressing, the Tribe's task approaching '94 appears crystal clear:

A) They must put more offensive tools around the "Three Bombardiers."
B) They must shore up their rotation.

Work on "A" had begun even before '93 ended. As we detailed in the offensive section, the Tribe's already moved a (hold your breath) healthy Alomar in at backstop. Thome gives every indication of being ready to become a slugging third baseman. Prospect Mark Lewis, who offers far more offense than the incumbent Fermin, conceivably could take over at SS. And the club spent the necessary wampum to bring veteran Murray in to either DH or play 1B (moving Sorrento to DH). Either way, it puts his plus-100 TOPR into the lineup in place of the mediocre DH numbers the Indians put up last year. Cleveland also made some intriguing "minor" moves as '93 wore on, picking up veterans Randy Milligan and Candy Maldonado for depth. Each has impressive career numbers. In the '90s Milligan's TOPR string reads: 143–104–114–136. Maldonado's reads: 109–113–120–82. Those are wonderful numbers to add to a bench, especially when you consider the cheapness of the price to obtain them.

"B," improving the starters, begins with a return to health of the ace, Nagy. Mesa and Clark appear dependable #3 and #4 types. That hole at #2 has been filled by spending $9 million to sign Montreal veteran Dennis Martinez as a free agent. Though his TPER made a worrisome rise in '93 (it's always worrisome when a 38-year-old shows signs of wear and tear), he's still far better than anything else Cleveland could have plugged into that spot. The best and youngest of the starter prospects appears to be Tavarez, though he may need more seasoning. Should somebody from the Indians' fairly large group of younger hurlers step forward, the Tribe could have a pretty interesting rotation to put in front of a deep and talented pen.

But, finally, manager Hargrove, who worked wonders keeping the wheels on this club through all the tragedy and turmoil of '93, might face a different psychological hurdle in '94. While there will be the excitement of moving into their new Gateway Project Stadium and the hope that naturally springs from having a roster dotted with young stars, this team has never won. These players, almost to a man, haven't experienced much winning. This city's grown used to the Indians being an also ran. In fact, Cleveland's gotten used to *all* its teams being limpers. The last major Cleveland pro team to win a championship came in '64 when the Browns defeated Baltimore for the NFL title.

The Indians haven't won a pennant in 40 years. Since 1956 the Tribe's been within 10 games of first place just twice and one of those came in the strike-shortened '81 season. The last time they finished as high as third was 1968. Alvin Dark managed that team. How long ago was that? Hey, the Senators were still in Washington then!

Since 1954, the last time the Indians won the AL, they've finished a total of 812 games out of first place in the intervening 40 seasons!

Yes, Hargrove has more psychological work cut out for him. But a new stadium and new hope fills Cleveland. And, if the gods of baseball are hunting around looking for some team to be nice to, heaven knows the Cleveland Indians are due for some good things to happen to them.

Team TOPR: 1993 Cleveland Indians

	Bats	BA	OBP	SLG	HR	R	RBI	NBE	GOC	Ratio	TOPR
League Avg. Team	-	.267	.337	.408	148	762	719	2897	4352	.666	100
Cleveland Indians	-	.275	.335	.409	141	790	747	2918	4368	.668	100.3
Regulars:											
C Junior Ortiz	R	.221	.267	.273	0	19	20	80	209	.383	57
Sandy Alomar, Jr.	R	.270	.318	.395	6	24	32	106	166	.639	96
1B Paul Sorrento	L	.257	.340	.434	18	75	65	257	359	.716	108
2B Carlos Baerga	B	.321	.355	.486	21	105	114	353	461	.766	115
3B Alvaro Espinoza	R	.278	.298	.380	4	34	27	113	210	.538	81
Jeff Treadway	L	.303	.347	.403	2	25	27	102	164	.622	93
Jim Thome	L	.266	.385	.474	7	28	22	109	122	.893	(134)
SS Felix Fermin	R	.263	.303	.317	2	48	45	173	377	.459	69
LF Albert Belle	R	.290	.370	.552	38	93	129	421	466	.903	136
CF Kenny Lofton	L	.325	.408	.408	1	116	42	368	412	.893	134
RF Wayne Kirby	L	.269	.323	.371	6	71	60	227	361	.629	94
DH Reggie Jefferson	B	.249	.310	.372	10	35	34	164	289	.567	85
Bench (100+ TPA):											
1/3 Carlos Martinez	R	.244	.295	.340	5	26	31	107	207	.517	78
OF Thomas Howard	B	.236	.278	.326	3	26	23	73	146	.500	(75)
OF Glenallen Hill	R	.224	.268	.374	5	19	25	83	146	.568	(85)

NOTE: Statistics are only for games played with Cleveland. ( ) Under 200 TPA.

Team TPER: 1993 Cleveland Indians

	Throws	W-L	GS	GR	SV	IP	ERA	NBA	GOE	Ratio	TPER
League Avg. Team	-	81 -81	162	355	42	1444.1	4.33	2897	4352	0.666	100
Cleveland Indians	-	76 -86	162	410	45	1445.2	4.58	3089	4362	0.708	106.4
The Rotation:											
Jose Mesa	R	10 -12	33	1	0	208.2	4.92	402	628	0.640	96
Jeff Mutis	L	3 -6	13	4	0	81	5.78	187	245	0.763	115
Mike Bielecki	R	4 -5	13	0	0	68.2	5.90	167	208	0.803	121
Charles Nagy	R	2 -6	9	0	0	48.2	6.29	115	150	0.767	115
Bobby Ojeda	L	2 -1	7	2	0	43	4.40	103	130	0.792	(119)
Utility:											
Tom Kramer	R	7 -3	16	23	0	121	4.02	269	362	0.743	112
Mark Clark	R	7 -5	15	11	0	109.1	4.28	215	330	0.652	98
Matt Young	L	1 -6	8	14	0	74.1	5.21	169	227	0.744	112
Cliff Young	L	3 -3	7	14	1	60.1	4.62	131	185	0.708	106
Dennis Cook	L	5 -5	6	19	0	54	5.67	128	163	0.785	118
Bullpen:											
Jeremy Hernandez	R	6 -5	0	49	8	77.1	3.14	150	231	0.649	98
Derek Lilliquist	L	4 -4	2	54	10	64	2.25	118	191	0.618	93
Bill Wertz	R	2 -3	0	34	0	59.2	3.62	111	178	0.624	94
Jerry Dipoto	R	4 -4	0	46	11	56.1	2.40	92	168	0.548	82
Eric Plunk	R	4 -5	0	70	15	71	2.79	133	219	0.607	91

NOTE: Statistics are only for games pitched with Cleveland. ( ) Under 200 TBF.

SAME SONG—FOURTH VERSE
DETROIT TIGERS

You'd think the Detroit franchise and their fans would get tired of marching in place. You'd think that after a certain approach hadn't worked for a few years that there'd be a change in direction. You'd think mediocrity, even as interesting as the Tigers can make things at times, would still be recognized for what it is eventually—mediocrity. That's what you'd think. But that's not what's happened in Detroit this decade. Detroit limped into the '90s off an embarrassing 59–103 season in '89. That disgusting record had been "achieved" by virtue of having a woeful offense and an even more wretched pitching staff. But that's the last season anyone, anywhere, could make disparaging remarks about the Tigers attack being toothless. A pair of big boppers, Cecil Fielder and Travis Fryman, along with superb handyman Tony Phillips arrived in '90. In the space of a few off-season months the sound of the Tiger attack had gone from a meek meow to a roar. And nothing has changed in the years since '90 when the Tigers began bashing opposing pitchers with regularity. Unfortunately, for this team, nothing's different from the state of that dismal pitching staff of 1989. Oh, it's not that Detroit hasn't changed some faces. During the '90s they've inked free agents like Bill Gullickson, Mike Moore, David Wells and Bill Krueger. They've gone for retreads like

Tom Bolton, Eric King and Walt Terrell. They've brought in bullpeners like Les Lancaster, Dave "Magic" Johnson, Mark Leiter, Storm Davis, Joe Boever and Bob MacDonald. They've given chances to an endless string of graduates from their minor league system. The faces change constantly. The results never do. In the '90s Detroit's now been essentially the same kind of club for four consecutive years—tremendous offensively but with terrible pitching. For every year this decade they've TOPRed above 105 topping out at an astounding 113.4 last year when they scored the most runs in the majors since 1953. But during those same four seasons they've TPERed at no better than 106.1—far away from being even an average pitching staff. Same club year after year after year. What's it gotten them? Four middle of the pack finishes. Lots of headlines about the marvelous numbers their attack puts up. But, bottom line, Detroit's gone absolutely nowhere. For the decade of the '90s these always-good-hit, never-good-pitch Tigers stand 323 wins and 325 losses. Never more than 85 victories in a year. Never fewer than 75. Tons of tape-measure homers. But never tons of wins. In other words, incredibly exciting and unpredictable mediocrity.

Team Trendline: Detroit Tigers

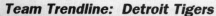

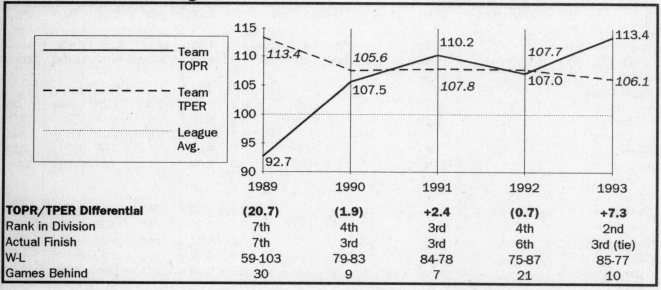

	1989	1990	1991	1992	1993
TOPR/TPER Differential	(20.7)	(1.9)	+2.4	(0.7)	+7.3
Rank in Division	7th	4th	3rd	4th	2nd
Actual Finish	7th	3rd	3rd	6th	3rd (tie)
W-L	59-103	79-83	84-78	75-87	85-77
Games Behind	30	9	7	21	10

What Was Expected

It's not like the Tigers' brass doesn't understand their club's trends. The big cats in the front office realized all too well that Detroit had a championship offense waiting for any kind of pitching to lead them to a title. That's the same formula Detroit had used to win a World Series in '84 and the AL East in '87, along with near misses in '81 and '88. During last year's off-season, Detroit had worked almost non-stop attempting to alter the direction of their disappointing '92 staff. They loosened their purse strings to sign free agents

Mike Moore, Tom Bolton and Bill Krueger. The Tigers allowed Terrell, King, Lancaster and Frank Tanana to leave for free agency. But they paid to keep big winner Bill Gullickson. Just before the season began they inked former Blue Jays lefty David Wells and bought another Toronto portsider, Bob MacDonald. The action certainly had been fast and furious. Just one question remained—had it done any good?

Check out the kind of TPER years Detroit had paid to keep or acquire entering '93:

Pitcher	'92 TPER
Gullickson	106
Moore	105
Krueger	105
Bolton	121
Wells	122
MacDonald	115

What the Tigers had, in effect, done was to ship out a whole bunch of mediocrity and bring in a whole bunch of mediocrity. Oh, it's not that some of these pitchers hadn't had some much better years at times. But off their most recent form none of them even came very close to approaching "average" pitchers. And all of them, except Gullickson, whom they'd retained, now headed for a Detroit home park that, off its history as a hitter's park, figured to inflate their TPERs even more. Offensively they remained one impressive wrecking machine. But had they really done anything to dramatically upgrade their pitching? Most experts thought not and again picked them in the middle of the AL East.

What Actually Happened

For nearly three months Detroit looked like geniuses. The big bats boomed. The new pitching helped stabilize the staff to the point where, shock of shocks, the Tigers actually boasted of an above-average set of hurlers. The combination produced impressive baseball. The Tigers soon ripped off a stretch where they won 11 of 12. They quickly followed that up with a run of 12 out of 16. Just a few days later Detroit took off on another tear again capturing

12 of 16. Detroit zoomed into first place April 23 and 60 days later still camped there. On June 22 the Tigers awoke with a sparkling 43–25 record, a game ahead of a group of AL East challengers setting a frantic pace. Then it all came apart. Not slowly, as some slumps unfold. This descent happened at warp speed. The Tigers lost 10 in a row. Then came another stretch of 9 losses in 11 games and another of 8 defeats in 11. Starting with that game of June 22, Tiger pitchers allowed an outrageous 6.8 runs a game over a 36-game span. At one point they endured a run of 36 games in which the only wins they got came when the offense scored *at least five runs*. By August 9 their tumble had reached epic proportions. They'd lost 32 of 45 and fallen to fifth, eight games out and a game beneath .500. Just as suddenly they turned around again winning 10 of 11. Detroit actually crept back to within 4½ games of first before yet one more dreadful spell of pitching led to a 10-losses-in-14-games slide that sealed their fate. At the end of this remarkable string of peaks and valleys the Tigers wound up looking just like they had the three previous seasons. They'd TOPRed at 113.4, the best offense in the AL. They'd TPERed at 106.1, barely ahead of the league's bottom feeders from Oakland, Minnesota and Cleveland in the race for the dubious distinction of having the league's worst pitching. They'd scored 10 or more runs 18 times! They'd allowed double figures in runs 19 times! At season's end a spent Sparky Anderson, who'd experienced every inch of this incredible roller-coaster ride, summed up his frustration: "Every day, every day, every day, it's the same thing. My God, you don't even dare to go to the john during our games because we'll give away three or four runs before you get back to your seat." Amen, Sparky!

1993 Detroit Tigers: Month-by-Month

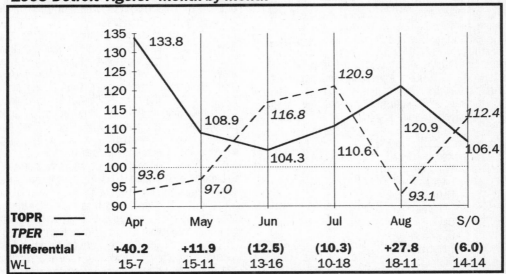

	Apr	May	Jun	Jul	Aug	S/O
TOPR ———	133.8	108.9	104.3	110.6	120.9	106.4
TPER — —	93.6	97.0	116.8	120.9	93.1	112.4
Differential	**+40.2**	**+11.9**	**(12.5)**	**(10.3)**	**+27.8**	**(6.0)**
W-L	15-7	15-11	13-16	10-18	18-11	14-14

1993 Tigers Lineup

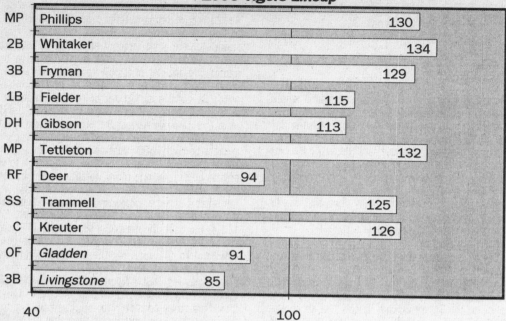

MP	Phillips	130
2B	Whitaker	134
3B	Fryman	129
1B	Fielder	115
DH	Gibson	113
MP	Tettleton	132
RF	Deer	94
SS	Trammell	125
C	Kreuter	126
OF	*Gladden*	91
3B	*Livingstone*	85

40   100

The Offense

There are many offensive styles. Some teams peck away using bunts and hit-and-runs. Some sit back and wait for a big inning. Some try to run their opponents into a frazzle. And Detroit? They're about as subtle as a tire iron across the face. They possess just about every positive offensive ingredient imaginable. The game starts and they begin hammering away. Consider the kind of firepower manager Anderson had by late in the season when the disappointing RF Deer and his 94 TOPR had been dealt away and replaced in the lineup by CF Davis with his 110. If Sparky wanted to use handyman Phillips in LF, put the versatile Tettleton in RF (where he often played) and DH Gibson, here's what the Tigers batting order, complete with TOPRs, looked like (remember, now, any TOPR of 100+ is considered above average):

POS.	Hitter	TOPR
LF	Phillips	130
2B	Whitaker	134
3B	Fryman	129
1B	Fielder	115
RF	Tettleton	132
CF	Davis	110
DH	Gibson	113
SS	Trammell	125
C	Kreuter	126

Unbelievable! Imagine an everyday lineup in which Davis, Gibson and Fielder qualified as the batting order's three WEAKLINGS! Nine far-above-average offensive players. Two of them hit at least 30 homers (Fielder and Tettleton). Two others reached 20 for the year (Fryman and Davis). Gibson, Kreuter and Trammell all hit at least a dozen. The Bengals had three .300 hitters (Phillips, Fryman and Trammell). The lineup had the AL's leading walk man, Phillips (with 132), and Tettleton, who finished fifth with 109. Three of these regulars stole at least a dozen bases (Gibson, Phillips and Trammell). Seven of the nine had at least 23 doubles excepting only Davis and Gibson who finished with 18.

This brigade of bombers produced the most runs of anyone in baseball since the 1953 Dodgers plated 955. The Tigers' 899 scores brought them the major league lead for the second straight year

and the fifth time in the last 13 seasons. The Tigers walked 765 times, 100 more than the next best (Philly had 665). Detroit's .363 on-base percentage also led the majors. Sure they struck out tons of times. But there's a silver lining there also. A "K" is only one out. That so many of these lumbering types fanned a lot kept them out of DPs. The Tigers knocked into only 101 twin killings. Only the fleet-footed Expos had fewer.

But as awesome as this lineup could be, they could also, at times, be handled with surprising ease. The Tigers' attack seemed to run on the "feeding frenzy" theory. Once they began bombing they sometimes never stopped. They seemed to feed off each other. Run totals mushroomed. So did the opponents' team ERAs. But, as with many "big bang" types of approaches, the Tiger offense could suddenly run dry. Yes, they put up 10 runs or more 18 times. But 30 times they tallied two or less. That late-June, 10-game losing streak that dropped them out of first place? In the middle eight games of that downer they managed just 17 runs—2.1 runs a game! Oh, they could be ferocious cats, these Tigers, drubbing Baltimore for an outrageous 47 runs in one three-game series in early August. But in two of the three games before that trio of tramplings and in the two games right after the massacres, Detroit got just one run in each game. Detroit, in fact, sometimes wasted good pitching (what little of it they had). The Tigers lost a total of 15 games in which their beleaguered staff held the opposition to four runs or less. Fans look at the power and potential of this lineup and the huge run totals it produces and they/we sometimes fail to realize the erratic nature of this beast. As awesome as the Tigers attack can be, there remain some stretches when other pitchers have these Tigers by the tail. Perhaps a bit more speed would help tide them over these short periods of the offensive blahs. And that's right where CF Davis comes in. He seems the perfect fit for this club. Detroit quickly re-signed him after the season. With everything else remaining as is, and as ridiculous as the projection may sound, this Tiger attack might actually be a bit *better* in '94.

One final aspect of the Tigers offense bears mentioning—their defense. Why put those two seemingly opposite items together? Because with Detroit, as with many offensively minded teams, one often pays for such an awesome attack by sacrificing a bit defensively. With these Bengals it appears they've sacrificed more than a bit. The Tigers finished 12th in AL fielding leaking 95 unearned runs. Add poor defense to below-par pitching and UER totals often soar. But this one went through the roof. Only those gift-giving Rockies (poor defense plus terrible pitching also) gave away more runs in '93.

Is There a Place in the Hall for "Sweet Lou?"

Three certain Hall of Famers said their goodbyes in '93. A bitter exit from Carlton Fisk. A quick and quiet one from George Brett. A sadly anticlimactic one from Nolan Ryan. Cooperstown also seems certain to keep a slot open for Robin Yount, Dave Winfield and Dennis Eckersley. Mid-career types like Barry Bonds and Ryne Sandberg look like locks right now. And then there's the remarkable set of stars-come-lately like Griffey, Jr., Thomas, Olerud and Gonzalez who've already started generating such talk.

But what about "Sweet Lou?" Much like Toronto's Paul Molitor, Tiger second baseman Lou Whitaker's launched a bid (though somewhat quieter than Molitor's) with a string of terrific seasons as he's reached baseball's "later in life" period. Starting in 1991 at age 34, he's strung together TOPR years of 146–134–134. That's downright sensational. Whitaker's game perfectly fits what an offensive team's trying to do every day. He hits for a high average, hits with power, steals a high percentage, walks a lot and, because he's a fly-ball hitter, hits into very few DPs.

Oh, yes, many will concede he's a good player and at times a very good player. But Hall of Fame material? Check out his credentials. Over the course of 16 full seasons in Detroit, he's posted a .275 career average. His first official AB of '94 will be his 8,000th. He enters '94 with: 2,199 hits, 385 doubles, 218 homers, 1,283 runs, 997 RBIs, 1,125 walks and 137 steals. For his career he's walked 114 times more than he's fanned and made just 173 errors in more than 2,200 games.

Nice numbers, for sure, but certainly not "slugger" credentials. Well, then, let's compare "Sweet Lou" to his own kind—second basemen. In the history of baseball there's been only one other 2B to ever reach 200 HRs and 2,000 hits while playing in more than 2,000 games. That was Joe Morgan. The Hall welcomed him last year. When Whitaker collects three more RBIs he'll reach 1,000. Only eight other 2Bs have ever made it to that plateau: Eddie Collins, Frankie Frisch, Charlie Gehringer, Bobby Doerr, Rogers

Hornsby, Nap Lajoie, Tony Lazzeri and Morgan. All eight have plaques in the Hall.

If Whitaker stopped playing today would there be a spot waiting in Cooperstown? Probably not but who knows? But what if he should put up another banner year in '94? Or two more? Or three? Right now his numbers have reached the point where it's hard to believe the door to the Hall's not at least open a crack already.

The Pitching

Judging Detroit's pitching as a group proves a much easier task than judging them as individuals. As a unit, the staff's populated by a bunch of soft-tossers who aren't likely to either walk or fan many. They're very hittable control pitchers prone to giving up tons of homers. By virtue of being a veteran group, most do more than an adequate job of holding runners.

Together they combined for discouraging numbers:

—Allowed 188 HR, more than Colorado's shell-shocked staff.

—Opponents batted .276. Minnesota and Colorado had the only hurlers in the majors who were easier to hit.

—Their 4.65 ERA marked the highest for a Bengal team since the '53 club (5.25).

—Only the cream-puff staffs of Milwaukee and St. Louis fanned fewer than the Tigers total of 828.

Such numbers make it easy to return an indictment of Tiger pitching. Figuring out who to keep and who to jettison becomes a much harder task because this staff's made up of many very similar pitchers. Things would be much better for the men from Motor City if only these hurlers were more "dissimilar." Most have had some major league success. Many have very respectable resumes. But, as a group, they're simply far less than adequate.

The Rotation: Two in the rotation actually had decent TPERs and four had good records thanks to the cannonading of the offense. Doherty has the look of a comer even though his TPER rose substantially in '93. He still topped the starters with a 90 and with his 14 wins. He's just a kid (27) compared to the remainder of this generally gray-bearded group and, if he becomes a bit less hittable (as he was in '92), he's got the makings of a staff leader. Gullickson and Moore each posted identical 13–9 records with ERAs the size of Lake Michigan (5.37 and 5.22). Gullickson had early season

1993 Tigers Staff

		TPER
St	Moore	112
St	Doherty	90
St	Wells	91
St	Gullickson	119
Ut	Leiter	109
Ut	Bolton	100
Ut	Krueger	97
Bp	Davis	94
Bp	MacDonald	114
Bp	Knudsen	124
Cl	Henneman	92

50   100

injury troubles which may account, at least in part, for his ineffectiveness. But he's TPERed at an average of 109 for the last four years, certainly not an encouraging trendline for a pitcher in his mid-thirties. Moore's virtually at the same point on the calendar with slightly better TPERs. His TPER averages 101 for the decade, and the worst season of his four came in '93. He led the free world in fat pitches surrendering 35 dingers. Gullickson tied for fourth with 28. Wells, as usual, started fast and tailed off. Could it be that his lack of physical conditioning catches up with him in the second halves of seasons? But he's now had three solid years in the '90s and, given what else they had, Detroit simply had to get him re-signed. While they're not eye-popping, that quartet's durable, making 125 of the team's 162 starts. Righty Leiter and lefty Krueger have proven to be useful and durable (at least of late in Leiter's case). Each tends to hang around the 100–104 TPER area. Not world beaters. But you can do much worse. As for possible farm system help, don't hold your breath. That's one of this team's problems. The system's really not produced anyone other than Doherty in years. The Tigers maintain they've got a slew of prospects. But a close inspection of the minor league profiles of names like Gohr, Bergman, Gonzalez, Haas, Thompson, Lira and Lima reveals that all have at least two of the following three negatives: wild, hittable or homer prone. Some have very good arms and do look like possibilities down the road. But as for help in '94, don't count on it.

The Bullpen: Again, you'll have trouble identifying the culprits in the bullpen. Henneman's 92 TPER ranked him just 10th among closers. But he's been extremely steady and ultra-dependable during a Tiger career that now spans seven seasons with between 60 and 69 appearances every year for the last six. Latecomers Boever and Davis arrived after horrid TPERs in Oakland's pitcher-friendly park (106 and 111 respectively) to post glittering figures in Detroit's pitcher-nightmare park (85 for Boever and 94 for Davis). Can those partial seasons be trusted? Which Boever and which Davis might Detroit see next year? Bolton, other than one horrible early season streak, pitched well enough. But the two previous seasons he TPERed terribly (122 and 121). MacDonald pitched so poorly at times the Tigers opted not to pursue re-signing him. Again, the farm system's void of immediate possibilities.

A simple check of the monthly breakdowns from '93, however, gives the perfect picture of what kind of club the Tigers could be with decent pitching. Detroit got above-average work from their staff in three months—April, May and August. The club's combined record in those months was 48–29. In the other three months the pitching soured and with it the won–lost mark: 37–48.

Put yourself in GM Jerry Walker's desk chair. Who would you keep? Who would you dump? The Tiger staff's not simply a bunch of worthless pitchers. Instead, it's a group of hurlers with fair talents. No stars. No bums. But also, probably no chance, as a group, of being the staff of a champion.

What Next?

There may be no team in the majors more in need of doing something *now* than these imbalanced Tigers. They've still got more than enough offense to win. They've still got far too little pitching to ever make a serious run at the brass ring. And their window of opportunity's threatening to close any minute. These Tigers are becoming a collection of "old cats." At the end of '93, here's what the core of the '94 Tigers looked like from the perspective of the "calendar." All ages are as of July 1, 1994.

Hitters	Age		Pitchers	Age
Whitaker	37		Gullickson	35
Trammell	36		Moore	34
Phillips	35		Henneman	31
Fielder	30		Krueger	36
Tettleton	33		Bolton	32
Gibson	37		Davis	32
Davis	31		Boever	33

If something hasn't been done to change the face of this all-offense-no-pitching team, how much longer can the Tigers figure to use these players as a base of contention? Right after the season Detroit again moved to do something about its pitching. But what they did was to keep what they had, giving big money to free agent Wells and decent money to Boever and Storm Davis. That won't cut it unless a number of these aging Tiger staffers suddenly experience "flashbacks" to the best years of their careers. If ever there appeared to be a team in need of dealing offense for pitching and/or defense, it's Detroit. Just how good a pitcher might you be able to get for Tettleton or Fielder or some combination of players involving one or more of this club's big bats? Detroit simply doesn't need another couple of pretty good pitchers. They've got lots of those already. They need a staff leader. In retrospect, they should have put all their financial eggs into one basket and gone for Greg Maddux after the '92 season. Detroit needs a serious injection of "stuff" into a pitching staff that too often gets the "stuffing" beaten out of it. And that injection must come immediately. The '94 Tigers will remain one of the most outrageous and unpredictable offensive wrecking crews in all of baseball when at bat. But unless some real pitching talent's been added, it looks like another year of remarkably exciting mediocrity in the Motor City.

Tiger Stadium

The home of the homer-hittin' Motor City Maulers was a . . . gulp . . . *pitchers park*? Strange but, in '93, true—pitchers received a modest advantage (Park TOPR: 97.8). The park suppressed Tiger and visiting offenses to about the same degree (Tigers −1.5%, visitors −3.1%—park adjusted). Despite this, it was *still* a home-run park—202 combined HR vs. 164 on the road. It turns out Tiger Stadium suppressed singles, not dingers (combined BA .271 at Tiger, .280 on the road).

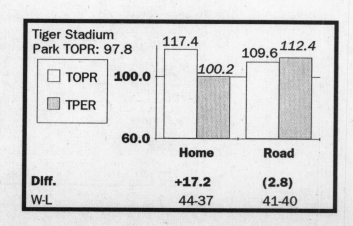

Tiger Stadium
Park TOPR: 97.8

☐ TOPR
▨ TPER

100.0
60.0

	Home	Road
TOPR	117.4	109.6
TPER	100.2	112.4
Diff.	+17.2	(2.8)
W-L	44-37	41-40

Team TOPR: 1993 Detroit Tigers

	Bats	BA	OBP	SLG	HR	R	RBI	NBE	GOC	Ratio	TOPR
League Avg. Team	-	.267	.337	.408	148	762	719	2897	4352	.666	100
Detroit Tigers	-	.275	.362	.434	178	899	853	3263	4323	.755	113.4
Regulars:											
C Chad Kreuter	B	.286	.371	.484	15	59	51	234	278	.842	126
1B Cecil Fielder	R	.267	.368	.464	30	80	117	342	448	.763	115
2B Lou Whitaker	L	.290	.412	.449	9	72	67	260	291	.893	134
3B Travis Fryman	R	.300	.379	.486	22	98	97	380	444	.856	129
SS Alan Trammell	R	.329	.388	.496	12	72	60	242	290	.834	125
CF Milt Cuyler	B	.213	.276	.313	0	46	19	114	205	.556	84
Eric Davis	R	.253	.371	.533	6	14	15	50	62	.806	(121)
RF Rob Deer	R	.217	.302	.381	14	48	39	164	262	.626	94
DH Kirk Gibson	L	.261	.337	.432	13	62	62	232	309	.751	113
MP Tony Phillips	B	.313	.443	.398	7	113	57	360	416	.865	130
Mickey Tettleton	B	.245	.372	.492	32	79	110	363	412	.881	132
Bench (100+ TPA):											
OF Dan Gladden	R	.267	.312	.433	13	52	56	173	286	.605	91
3B Scott Livingstone	L	.293	.328	.359	2	39	39	129	229	.563	85
I/O Skeeter Barnes	R	.281	.318	.381	2	24	27	79	131	.603	(91)
IF Chris Gomez	R	.250	.304	.320	0	11	11	52	103	.505	(76)
OF Gary Thurman	R	.213	.297	.281	0	22	13	43	74	.581	(87)

NOTE: Statistics are only for games played with Detroit. ( ) Under 200 TPA.

Team TPER: 1993 Detroit Tigers

	Throws	W-L	GS	GR	SV	IP	ERA	NBA	GOE	Ratio	TPER
League Avg. Team	-	81 -81	162	355	42	1444.1	4.33	2897	4352	0.666	100
Detroit Tigers	-	85 -77	162	375	36	1436.2	4.70	3072	4348	0.707	106.1
The Rotation:											
Mike Moore	R	13 -9	36	0	0	213.2	5.22	483	647	0.747	112
John Doherty	R	14 -11	31	1	0	184.2	4.44	336	559	0.601	90
David Wells	L	11 -9	30	2	0	187	4.19	345	568	0.607	91
Bill Gullickson	R	13 -9	28	0	0	159.1	5.37	379	477	0.795	119
Sean Bergman	R	1 -4	6	3	0	39.2	5.67	101	122	0.828	(124)
Utility:											
Mark Leiter	R	6 -6	13	14	0	106.2	4.73	233	321	0.726	109
Tom Bolton	L	6 -6	8	35	0	102.2	4.47	207	312	0.663	100
Bill Krueger	L	6 -4	7	25	0	82	3.40	160	247	0.648	97
Bullpen:											
Bob MacDonald	L	3 -3	0	68	3	65.2	5.35	150	198	0.758	114
Kurt Knudsen	R	3 -2	0	30	2	37.2	4.78	95	115	0.826	(124)
Buddy Groom	L	0 -2	3	16	0	36.2	6.14	93	111	0.838	(126)
Storm Davis	R	0 -2	0	24	4	35.1	3.06	66	106	0.623	(94)
Mike Henneman	R	5 -3	0	63	24	71.2	2.64	134	218	0.615	92

NOTE: Statistics are only for games pitched with Detroit. ( ) Under 200 TBF.

A FALSE "TRUTH"
KANSAS CITY ROYALS

"You win with pitching and defense."

Baseball people have said it and baseball fans have believed it a thousand times. Maybe a million. You've heard it preached from baseball pulpits in the Bronx all the way to LA. But don't try to convince Kansas City manager Hal McRae of the truth of this baseball "truism." He might throw something at you.

McRae's Royals boasted the best pitching TPER in the entire league. They played the finest defense in the 25-year history of this proud franchise posting the second best fielding percentage in all of baseball.

So just how much winning did the Royals do with all this fantastic pitching and defense? An 84–78 record, good for a distant third in the AL West. It got them into first place for 25 days in the middle of the season. It got them involved in a mind-boggling 70 one-run games. And it probably started or worsened that many ulcers or more in manager McRae.

KC simply couldn't score. Their offense became one Royal flop. Last in the league in runs. Just how bad were they at the plate? So bad that their on-base percentage placed them dead last in the AL and lower than 11 of the 14 NL teams where the pitcher's part of the batting order! That's not bad. That's putrid.

And about that baseball "truism" that suggests you win with pitching and defense? Replace it with one that's "more true." Even with the most perfect pitching and defense baseball's ever witnessed, you'll still never do better than a 0–0 tie if you can't score.

Team Trendline: Kansas City Royals

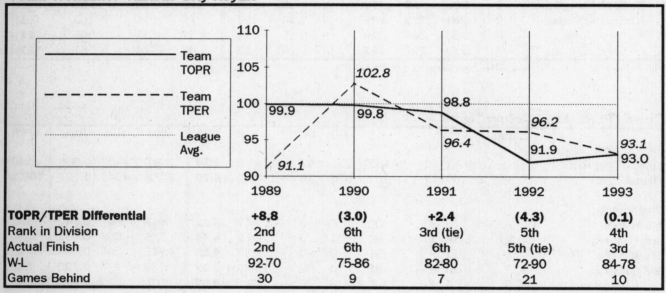

TOPR/TPER Differential	+8.8	(3.0)	+2.4	(4.3)	(0.1)
Rank in Division	2nd	6th	3rd (tie)	5th	4th
Actual Finish	2nd	6th	6th	5th (tie)	3rd
W-L	92-70	75-86	82-80	72-90	84-78
Games Behind	30	9	7	21	10

What Was Expected

The 1992 season sobered Royals fans who'd gotten pretty used to winning over the years. KC had cratered staggering home with a 72–90 record. This from a franchise that had collected six division crowns and seven runner-up finishes in the previous 20 seasons. The Royals hadn't been that far under .500 since the Nixon administration. But even with the specter of that ugly season just months behind them, hope was springing in KC.

The club had again opened its wallets and poured out millions to sign stud right-hander David Cone and unquestionably the finest defensive middle-infield combo in the game—SS Greg Gagne and 2B Jose Lind. They'd acquired the line drive bat of Felix Jose to plug their RF hole.

Like many of their division foes the Royals had some "ifs." If Brian McRae could continue to improve. If P Tom Gordon could refind his once awesome stuff and P Mark Gubicza could refind good health. If 3B Keith Miller could stay healthy. If Kevin McReynolds could, at age 33, halt the downward spiral of his career. If aging George Brett could just tack one more special year onto the end of a special career.

The lack of a dominant team in the West gave KC, as it did everyone else in the division, the hope that "IF" everything broke right there was a possible formula in hand by which KC might rise to the top. And, as it had for the last several seasons, that formula began with pitching and defense.

What Actually Happened

KC lost their first five. Fans started screaming. They'd seen this act before. In fact, they'd seen it the year before when the '92 Royals limped out of the gate with a 1–16 record and buried themselves before the April page had been torn off the monthly calender. Sources close to the organization insist that, if on the first Sunday of the '93 season the Royals had lost thereby dropping to 0–6, McRae would have been fired. But we'll never know if that in fact would have happened. KC won that Sunday.

Many point to McRae's celebrated April 26 post-game tantrum as the point at which the Royals season turned and the club began winning. That's the one where McRae threw everything in sight and ended with a reporter exiting his office bleeding from the face after being struck with something. It's also believed, by the way, that during this explosion the manager easily erased the club record for expletives deleted in a single outburst. But in reality McRae exploded after just one particularly galling loss. KC had, at that point, split its last 14 decisions and had already righted their floundering ship.

The Royals put together a terrific 16–9 May and managed to poke their noses into first place on June 2. They'd hang around that lofty perch until July 6 when the White Sox kicked it into gear and the KC offense didn't. The Royals made one last gasp of a challenge climbing to within five games of the Sox after beating Chicago 9–0 on September 13 behind Appier. But the ChiSox won the next two games of the series and any hopes for some miracle rush disappeared.

Other than the "de-powering" of RF Jose, injuries really didn't play much of a role in the club's season but should be mentioned if only because of the weirdness of some of them. Slipped in among the usual listings of pulled groin muscles and sore shoulders, the Royals saw players lost at various times to disabling injuries like Bell's palsy, foot drop, chicken pox and Morton's neuroma of the foot. Huh? Then, of course, there was that lingering season-long problem of a case of sick bats.

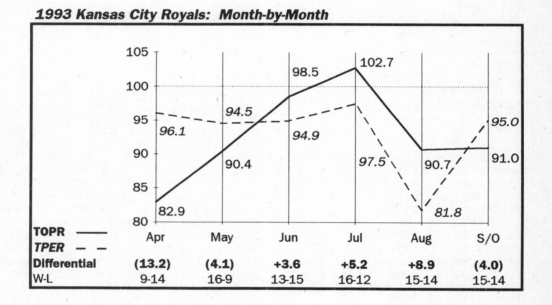

1993 Kansas City Royals: Month-by-Month

	Apr	May	Jun	Jul	Aug	S/O
TOPR ———	82.9	90.4	98.5	102.7	90.7	91.0
TPER – –	96.1	94.5	94.9	97.5	81.8	95.0
Differential	(13.2)	(4.1)	+3.6	+5.2	+8.9	(4.0)
W-L	9-14	16-9	13-15	16-12	15-14	15-14

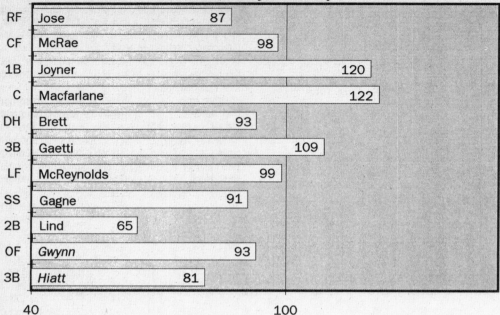

1993 Royals Lineup

Position	Player	Value
RF	Jose	87
CF	McRae	98
1B	Joyner	120
C	Macfarlane	122
DH	Brett	93
3B	Gaetti	109
LF	McReynolds	99
SS	Gagne	91
2B	Lind	65
OF	*Gwynn*	93
3B	*Hiatt*	81

40   100

The Offense

The '93 Royals offense suffered from baseball's "terrible trifecta."
No power.
No speed.
No walks.

When you stop to consider the ways teams score, it really is a fairly limited list. You can be a power team and bludgeon opponents to death. You can have a speed team and steal and pester them into submission. Or you can simply overload the bases so often that runs result from a sheer volume of baserunners.

The Royals could do none of the above.

Of all the AL teams, only the team TOPRs of Minnesota and Milwaukee fell below KC's 93. Even more discouraging was the fact that KC's offense actually was less productive than 11 of the 14 NL teams where the pitcher's feeble batting marks are part of the batting order. Only the miserable Mets, floundering Padres and expansion Marlins rated below them from the NL.

What couldn't the '93 Royals do offensively? In a word—everything!

—Dead last in runs scored in the AL with 675. That total ranked them ahead of only the Mets and Marlins in all of baseball.

—Ninth in the AL in steals with 100 which sounds OK until you figure in the fact that they finished twelfth in being caught stealing—75 times. That's a totally unacceptable 57% efficiency, about 10% below the point at which a running game's considered a plus.

—Tenth in the league in homers.

—Dead last in walks with only 428 free passes. Royals opponents, meanwhile, coaxed 571 freebies out of KC pitchers. That's a whopping difference of 143 baserunners over the course of a year or .88 runners per game. That's an enormous deficit in just this one category.

—Dead last in the AL in on-base percentage. Again, to put this in some kind of perspective, KC, in OBP, finished ahead of only NL bottom feeders Florida, San Diego and the Mets. Yuck!

—Their RBI leader and second-best HR hitter turned 40 during the season and announced his retirement from the game in the closing weeks (George Brett).

A check of the Royals most-used lineup reveals their offensive ineptness even more. Only two of their nine batting order positions performed above the norm for those positions—catcher with MacFarlane and 3B with Gaetti. And the latter's very deceiving. The starter at 3B, Keith Miller went down to injury almost immediately as he always seems to do unfortunately. Rookie replacement Phil Hiatt failed dismally. Curtis Wilkerson broke an ankle. Rico Rossy came down with the chicken pox. David Howard encountered the dual difficulties of Bell's Palsy and a hamstring problem. Only after all these contenders and pretenders for the job had fallen by the wayside did the Royals pick up Gaetti, who'd been jettisoned by the Angels. He did a fine job—for the half season he played. All this becomes part of the explanation that, as a whole, while Gaetti should feel good about his performance, the Royals' entire third base picture for the year certainly wasn't a pretty one and should be considered far below league average. That then means only the catching spot gave KC better-than-average production.

Some excuse should be made for RF Jose. He injured his left shoulder in spring training and it never healed. The pain so bothered him that he quit hitting from the right side and actually faced tough lefties like NY's Jimmy Key hitting left rather than attempt to put pressure on the damaged shoulder. And, while CF Brian McRae still rated below the norm for AL CFs, he did make a substantial 16-point TOPR jump indicating he may soon be a plus offensive performer if that developmental trend continues at age 26.

At 1B Wally Joyner enjoyed his finest TOPR season of the decade (120). But the league's big boppers at the position so distorted the norm for the position that Joyner's totals pale in comparison (Olerud 179, Thomas 170, Palmeiro 146, etc.) In truth, Joyner TOPRed as the fifth best AL 1B and KC will take more of the same from him whenever they can get it. The same goes for SS Greg Gagne. While his 91 TOPR ranks far behind SS leader Alan Trammell, he's still #5 at the position. Given his brilliant play afield, that's more than an acceptable offensive contribution.

But the Royals' biggest problem spots (besides that injury-altered 87 TOPR from RF Jose) remain 2B and LF. Jose Lind's an absolutely brilliant and acrobatic second sacker. But he's horrid as a hitter. He's to an offense what an anvil tied around the neck is to a swimmer. He's an out waiting to happen. Just how long can a player with a 65 TOPR be carried because of his glove? Meanwhile, out in LF, Kevin McReynolds' career continues to deteriorate. His

BA's now dropped five straight years. His HR production's fallen off six years in a row. In '88 with the Mets he put up a .288 BA–27 HR–99 RBI. In '93 his line read: .245–11–42.

When the season had ended, manager McRae surveyed the wreckage left by his struggling and often non-existent offense and summed it up better than anyone else could have saying: "We've got a bow and arrow and the other guy's got a repeater rifle . . . You can fight him off for a while but not for 162 games when he has that much more firepower than you. We've strained offensively all year and it's taken its toll on the players."

Amen, Hal. And native American Indians can tell you very well the long-term chances for survival of a man with a bow and arrow versus one with a repeater rifle. In the end, some awfully good Royals pitchers wound up "getting shot full of holes" by their own attack.

One final thought that might be the scariest of all for Royals fans: check the team TOPR. As impotent as the '93 KC attack was, it actually *improved* over the '92 team!

The Pitching

A handful of aces. Whether you're a poker player or a baseball manager that's a beautiful sight.

That's the hand KC manager Hal McRae found himself holding most of the season. The Royals featured the league's best starter, Kevin Appier, a pair of other "aces" rated among the league's top 24 starters in Cone and Pichardo, the AL's best right-handed utility TPER from Tom "Flash" Gordon and durable Jeff Montgomery, one of the game's most dependable and overlooked closers. The KC staff boasted of strength at the start, in the middle and at the end. Few managers ever get dealt this kind of ace-filled hand.

And McRae played it well. The Royals monthly breakdowns show that KC posted well-above-average TPERs every month of the year.

The Rotation: Workhorse Appier and Cone started 68 games and threw 493 innings, 34% of all KC innings pitched in '93. Appier checked in with an 18–8 record. But that could have been much better. He lost 1–0, 2–1 (twice), 3–1 and 3–2 (three times). Don't blame the voters for not giving him the Cy Young. Blame the Royals' hitters. Had they provided him decent support he could have finished with something outrageous for a record like 23–3,

and Jack McDowell would have been but a distant memory in the balloting. But Cone might have even more reason to complain. At least Appier's record remained outstanding. Cone finished 11–14. In those 14 losses the Royals managed to support him with an almost unthinkable 18 runs!

Quietly, the 24-year-old Pichardo developed into a nice #3 man. Late-season shoulder fatigue landed him on the DL but he'd only made 22 starts through mid-August. Unlike their sometimes rough handling of Cone and Appier, the Royals braintrust seemed to treat this "kid" with "kid gloves." He was allowed to throw more than 115 pitches in a game just four times. A dozen times he left before reaching 100. Cone passed 115 pitches in a game 25 times. Appier did so on 17 occasions. Will such workloads eventually wear away their effectiveness? Check back in a couple seasons.

Normally at this point we'd proceed to the fourth and fifth starters in KC's rotation. But instead, we digress to an important injury. The year before the Royals had grabbed RHP Rusty Meacham and his body that's shaped like a one-iron off of Detroit's junk heap. Immediately Meacham exploded onto the scene as one of the finest middlemen in the game posting a glittering 76 TPER and a 10–4 record. But a month into '93, Meacham headed for the DL with an aching elbow, reappeared briefly a month later and then disappeared for good by mid-June having thrown but 21 ineffective innings. Had he been well that would have freed Tom Gordon to pitch in the rotation and would have given the Royals four terrific starters all year long.

As it was, Gordon didn't exit the pen for a starter's role until late July. He would be 8–4 in the role and finish with an 89 TPER, his best of the decade.

And the Royal's rotation could have used him. After his "big three," McRae groped for effectiveness. Chris Haney got pounded as evidenced by a 107 TPER and an ugly 6.02 ERA. Mark Gardner was even worse. He stood 4–2 on June 3 but never won again, eventually heading for the DL and then Omaha and finally to the unemployment line after the season when KC released him and his 117 TPER and 6.19 ERA. It doesn't take much imagination to understand just how much better the Royals' starters would have been with Gordon's 89 TPER replacing either Haney or Gardner.

The Bullpen: McRae's pen performed admirably. After Gordon

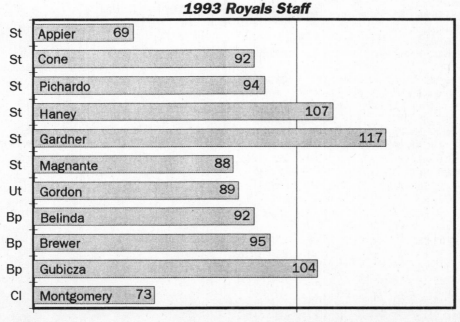

1993 Royals Staff

Pos	Player	TPER
St	Appier	69
St	Cone	92
St	Pichardo	94
St	Haney	107
St	Gardner	117
St	Magnante	88
Ut	Gordon	89
Bp	Belinda	92
Bp	Brewer	95
Bp	Gubicza	104
Cl	Montgomery	73

50   100

came rookie set-up man Billy Brewer (TPER 95) and long-man Mark Gubicza, whose 104 suggests he's still not entirely over the rotator cuff problems that have ruined his entire decade. By August 1 the club had added yet three more serviceable pen parts—lefty Greg Cadaret and righties Stan Belinda and John Habyan.

Which brings us to closer Jeff Montgomery. Why, when baseball people discuss the game's truly great closers, doesn't he get mentioned right away? His TPERs creep downward every year and his save totals keep reaching for the sky. He's gone from 18 saves as a part-time stopper in '89 up to 24, then 33 and 39, and finally to a club record—tying 45 last season. Just what kind of confidence does Montgomery create? The last time the Royals lost a game in which they carried a lead into the ninth inning, Bill Clinton was still considered a long shot to win the Democratic Presidential nomination. It was August 25, 1991. Since then KC's won 128 consecutive games in which they've led into the ninth. During that same period Montgomery's been responsible for more than 90 saves!

In all, this staff allowed the fewest hits and least HRs of any staff in the league. And they'd posted the best KC team TPER of the '90s, the fourth straight year that figure's gotten better. As a group at year's end, Royal pitchers had earned the right to look at the standings and say in unison: "We did our part."

What Next?

As desperate as the Royals' offense made them look at times, that's still probably the easiest part of a team to improve these days. The harder parts, pitching and defense, KC already possesses.

But just how you go about dressing up a Royal attack that's been a royal pain for years (below average TOPRs five consecutive years)

remains their challenge. In previous seasons, even though Kansas City's a small-market team, the franchise had the comforting thought that the team's owner, Ewing Kauffman, seemed to have pockets of almost unlimited depth. Those days are gone. Mr. Kauffman, hailed as one of the game's true sportsmen and gentlemen, passed away August 1 of last season.

The '93 Royals lost an estimated $16 million. That pretty much precludes them being a big player in the free agent market again anytime soon. Besides, the club's still committed to paying Cone, Joyner, Montgomery, McReynolds, Gagne, Lind, Appier and Jose salaries ranging from $5 million down to $1½ million. No, KC can't think of throwing money at their offensive holes.

Brett's bat and leadership must be replaced. The farm system offers few products that seem ready right now though 1B Bob Hamelin did crack 29 HRs at Triple A. OF Kevin Koslofski will get a shot. A healthy Jose's put up TOPRs near 120 in his recent past and would greatly improve the outlook.

But still, no one walks, no one really steals and few go downtown. That means McRae must scratch for runs and for wins as he did last season. In fact, he should get some kind of award. His team got outscored by 19 runs for the year and yet he finished six games above .500. Many say he did it with mirrors. Unless some as yet unforseen force improves the offense dramatically, McRae must keep those managing mirrors perfectly polished.

One final oddball, looking-back thought. In '92 KC had bungled their way to a 72–90 record. San Francisco had exactly the same mark in the NL. What might have happened had the Royals taken all the money they set aside for Cone, Gagne and Lind and had given it to Barry Bonds?

Ewing Kauffman Stadium

The Royals played in a "*hitter's park*" in '93! The third highest Park TOPR in the league (106.7), in fact. As ever, the Kansas City park discouraged HRs (99 total vs. 131 on the road) but *encouraged* every other kind of hit—singles (+9%), doubles (+54%) and triples (+100%).

Despite the much lower number of HRs, the total number of extra bases actually *increased* in Kauffman Stadium (736 vs. 666 on the road, a +10.5% gain).

The Royals' offense was peculiarly well-adapted to the Kansas City carpet. Almost devoid of the speed normally associated with turf clubs, they hit ground balls with abandon. This trait killed the Royals' offense on the road (85.8 TOPR, .244 BA) where their worm-burners didn't skitter through the infield or bounce over the bags into the corners. But, relatively speaking, they thrived at home (100.4 Home TOPR, .283 BA). The Royals' staff, composed of ground ball pitchers, gained no such advantage from the home park—quite the opposite—and are counting the days until the rug's scheduled removal in '95.

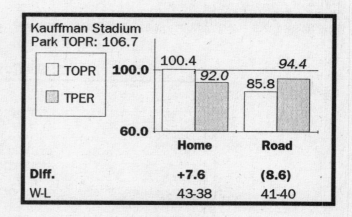

Kauffman Stadium
Park TOPR: 106.7

	Home	Road
TOPR	100.4	85.8
TPER	92.0	94.4
Diff.	+7.6	(8.6)
W-L	43-38	41-40

Team TOPR: 1993 Kansas City Royals

	Bats	BA	OBP	SLG	HR	R	RBI	NBE	GOC	Ratio	TOPR
League Avg. Team	-	.267	.337	.408	148	762	719	2897	4352	.666	100
Kansas City Royals	-	.263	.320	.397	125	675	641	2691	4348	.619	93.0
Regulars:											
C Mike Macfarlane	R	.273	.360	.497	20	55	67	245	302	.811	122
1B Wally Joyner	L	.292	.375	.467	15	83	65	298	374	.797	120
2B Jose Lind	R	.248	.271	.288	0	33	37	151	351	.430	65
3B Phil Hiatt	R	.218	.285	.366	7	30	36	107	199	.538	81
Gary Gaetti	R	.256	.309	.477	14	37	46	161	222	.725	109
SS Greg Gagne	R	.280	.319	.406	10	66	57	251	416	.603	91
LF Kevin McReynolds	R	.245	.316	.425	11	44	42	183	279	.656	99
Chris Gwynn	L	.300	.354	.387	1	36	25	132	213	.620	93
CF Brian McRae	B	.282	.325	.413	12	78	69	318	489	.650	98
RF Felix Jose	B	.253	.303	.349	6	64	43	227	394	.576	87
DH George Brett	L	.266	.312	.434	19	69	75	277	446	.621	93
Bench (100+ TPA):											
C Brent Mayne	L	.254	.317	.337	2	22	22	86	164	.524	79
OF Hubie Brooks	R	.286	.331	.375	1	14	24	70	127	.551	(83)
IF Keith Miller	R	.167	.229	.194	0	9	3	30	95	.316	(47)

NOTE: Statistics are only for games played with Kansas City. ( ) Under 200 TPA.

Team TPER: 1993 Kansas City Royals

	Throws	W-L	GS	GR	SV	IP	ERA	NBA	GOE	Ratio	TPER
League Avg. Team	-	81 -81	162	355	42	1444.1	4.33	2897	4352	0.666	100
Kansas City Royals	-	84 -78	162	303	48	1445.1	4.04	2686	4333	0.620	93.1
The Rotation:											
Kevin Appier	R	18 -8	34	0	0	238.2	2.56	327	714	0.458	69
David Cone	R	11 -14	34	0	0	254	3.33	462	757	0.610	92
Hipolito Pichardo	R	7 -8	25	5	0	165	4.04	313	502	0.624	94
Chris Haney	L	9 -9	23	0	0	124	6.02	265	373	0.710	107
Mark Gardner	R	4 -6	16	1	0	91.2	6.19	211	272	0.776	117
Mike Magnante	L	1 -2	6	1	0	35.1	4.08	61	104	0.587	(88)
Utility:											
Tom Gordon	R	12 -6	14	34	1	155.2	3.58	277	467	0.593	89
Bullpen:											
Mark Gubicza	R	5 -8	6	43	2	104.1	4.66	218	315	0.692	104
Billy Brewer	L	2 -2	0	46	0	39	3.46	73	115	0.635	(95)
Stan Belinda	R	1 -1	0	23	0	27.1	4.28	51	83	0.614	(92)
Jeff Montgomery	R	7 -5	0	69	45	87.1	2.27	126	261	0.483	73

NOTE: Statistics are only for games pitched with Kansas City. ( ) Under 200 TBF.

A COMMITMENT TO MEDIOCRITY
MILWAUKEE BREWERS

The Brewers' team trendline portrays a resolute "average-ness"—except when one side of the TOPR/TPER equation rises above itself (as the pitching did in '92) or another side goes in the tank (as the offense did last year). Otherwise, they've been middle-of-the-pack. Generally respectable, but not threatening.

Team Trendline: Milwaukee Brewers

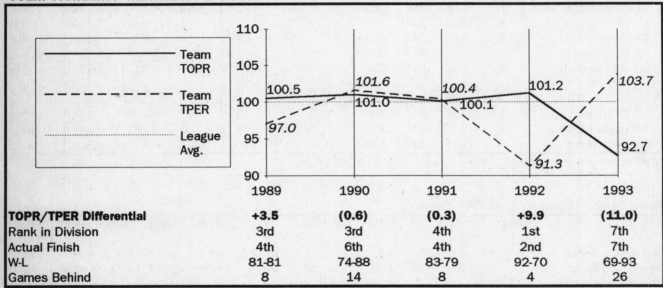

	1989	1990	1991	1992	1993
TOPR/TPER Differential	+3.5	(0.6)	(0.3)	+9.9	(11.0)
Rank in Division	3rd	3rd	4th	1st	7th
Actual Finish	4th	6th	4th	2nd	7th
W-L	81-81	74-88	83-79	92-70	69-93
Games Behind	8	14	8	4	26

Expectations

The Brewers have usually been a hard team to figure. Going into any season, there's a tendency to look at this club and ask "who are these guys?" Then, when the season's over, ask "How did they end up *there*?" As was usual, '93 pre-season predictions were mixed but seemed to come down on the side of a first division finish. After all, they gave Toronto a run for their money in '92, didn't they?

Realistically, they had a shot at .500—maybe—but were most likely destined for a lower status after losing two key cogs, Molitor and Bosio, via free agency.

What Actually Happened

Despite a distressing TOPR/TPER differential, Garner kept the Brewers hanging around .500 for the first two months of the season (22–25 on Memorial Day). In June, the chickens came home to roost. Garner had to acknowledge the loss of Bosio by reverting to a 4-man rotation. Wegman became ineffective and then landed on the DL (sore shoulder). Closer Doug Henry was beyond struggling; he was getting the stuffing beaten out of him is what it was. Offensive sparkplug Listach hit the DL June 1 with a hamstring pull. Dave Nilsson, the catcher-they've-been-waiting-for, was finally off

the DL. Now, the Brewers were waiting for him to hit his weight. DH Kevin Reimer was giving convincing evidence that he was not Paul Molitor.

By the All-Star break Milwaukee had sagged into the cellar (at 37–49) and was, for all intents and purposes, history.

The keys to the season were actually found in the previous off-season, as they so often are. Almost without a fight Molitor and Bosio were lost to free agency. They essentially went unreplaced and the Brewers commitment to mediocrity had been broken. They had become something else, something less. They had joined the fraternity of have-nots.

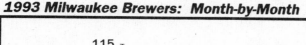

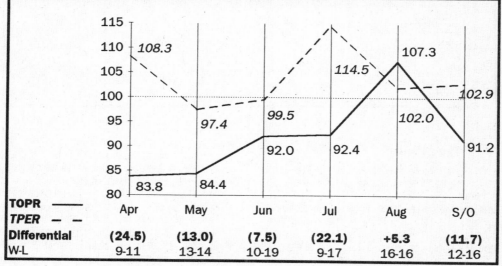

1993 Milwaukee Brewers: Month-by-Month

	Apr	May	Jun	Jul	Aug	S/O
TOPR ——	83.8	84.4	92.0	92.4	107.3	91.2
TPER – –	108.3	97.4	99.5	114.5	102.0	102.9
Differential	**(24.5)**	**(13.0)**	**(7.5)**	**(22.1)**	**+5.3**	**(11.7)**
W-L	9-11	13-14	10-19	9-17	16-16	12-16

County Stadium

The Brewers' home park registered ever-so-slightly as "pitcher-friendly" in '93. This is consistent with the calculations of other analysts. The park, however, has a well-established "hitter's park" image simply because any park that Hank Aaron, Eddie Mathews and "Harvey's Wallbangers" called home would seem to be a hitter's haven. We understand these things better now (we think).

Regardless, the Brewers were a horrid road club—a characteristic generally associated with poor teams.

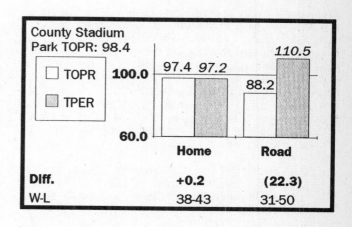

County Stadium
Park TOPR: 98.4

	□ TOPR	▦ TPER
Home	97.4	97.2
Road	88.2	110.5

	Home	Road
Diff.	**+0.2**	**(22.3)**
W-L	38-43	31-50

1993 Brewers Lineup

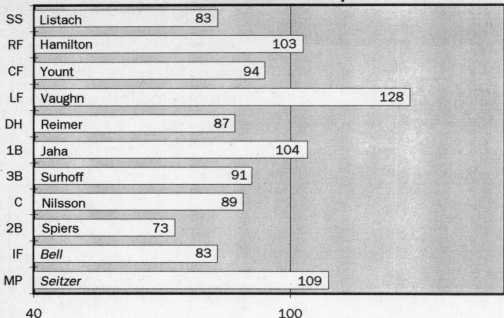

SS	Listach	83
RF	Hamilton	103
CF	Yount	94
LF	Vaughn	128
DH	Reimer	87
1B	Jaha	104
3B	Surhoff	91
C	Nilsson	89
2B	Spiers	73
IF	*Bell*	83
MP	*Seitzer*	109

40   100

The Offense

What can you say about an offense that looks like this? Beyond congratulating Greg Vaughn upon becoming an above-average left fielder, what else is there?

Well, it wasn't the worst offense in the league. That dishonor belonged to Kansas City. OK, they scored a few more runs than they maybe should have. Garner does know how to run a game, even if he didn't have the horses to run this year that he did the year before.

The salient characteristic of '92's otherwise offensively average team had been their ability to run opponents to distraction. The '92 Brewers stole 256 bases, more than any AL team since '76 (Oakland: 341). They employed this weapon to their considerable advantage (69% success ratio). The '93 team, however, stole only 111 bases and with a poorer rate of success (only 64%). Why, then, did Garner seem to change his methods and run less in '93? Easy. He looked at his '93 Opening Day lineup and saw that 100 of those stolen bases were gone (mainly in the persons of Molitor, Bichette, Fletcher and Seitzer). Soon afterward, '92's prime contributor (Listach, with 54) was, quite literally, hamstrung. Garner *had* to change his plan of attack—and he didn't have any other weapons to replace the one that had worked so well but had disappeared.

A quick rundown of the '93 lineup:

◆ Listach—Had to deal with injury problems most of the year. He'll have to get back to his rookie 109 TOPR to be effective because leadoff men with .319 OBP make it awfully hard to crank-up a batting order.

◆ Hamilton—Had a decent year and was satisfactory #2 hitter (.368 OBP, 20 SB). His TOPR profile is a better fit in CF, where he'll probably start next year.

◆ Yount—Will be asked to play a much smaller role next year, if he's back. His 94 TOPR *was* a little marginal. Whoever replaces him will probably play RF and might be better, or might not.

◆ Vaughn—Put together a fine season. As the *only* serious power threat in the order (30 HR, 97 RBI) he could really use some help, like more men on base in front of him, another big bat or two behind him . . . but this is turning into a laundry list of Brewers' needs.

◆ Reimer—A marginal power hitter and a supremely rotten fielder for whom the DH role was created. In '93, however, he was a

sub-standard power hitter (13 HR, .394 SLG). If Yount returns as a DH, where does that leave Reimer with the Brewers?

◆ Jaha—Marvelous minor league numbers which, because of the parks they were accumulated in, probably overstate his potential. He's in his prime years now but he's still adjusting. He *should* be an above-average hitter and at least average for a first baseman. Give him another year to prove it.

◆ Surhoff—On the trading block? Whether as a third baseman, left fielder or a catcher is unknown. He's always TOPRed like a catcher, the strong defensive variety. His '93 year (.274 BA, but only .318 OBP and .391 SLG) was typical.

◆ Nilsson—Has minor league stats like Jaha in the same parks. Had shoulder problems on and off and his weak TOPR should probably be excused temporarily. Swore off switch-hitting to become a full-time LH batter. Seemed almost unaffected, as platoon differential was normal (.272 BA vs. righties, .251 vs. lefties).

◆ Spiers—May be out of a job. They're talking about moving Jose Valentin in at short and Listach to second. Once a solid player until injuries wrecked his career.

◆ Seitzer—Is the reason Surhoff might be expendable. He's a decent player; versatile (filled in at six positions in '93 missing only CF and C), can hit some and run a little. Remember, though, that he's been let go by three clubs in the past two seasons, including *Milwaukee*. Think of him as an IMP (Impact Multiple Position player).

Aside from its feebleness, another feature of the Brewers regular '93 lineup was striking. It's almost 100% homegrown. The only exception is Reimer, who replaced Molitor and *he* was homegrown. These are all players originally signed by the club, brought up through the Brewers' farm system and have called Milwaukee home their entire major league career.

This pattern has been part of the Brewers' master plan, an operational response to the economic facts of "small-market" life. It *should* be less expensive to grow your own talent than to pay top dollar in the free agent market. Baseball owners have claimed this to be true since the specter of free agency first appeared. Why should we doubt them? If it were otherwise, they surely wouldn't have done without free agency for so long.

When free agency time comes around, shouldn't it also be less expensive to re-sign your own? So long as you treat your players with consideration, a modicum of respect and reasonable pay before and during their arbitration eligibility, wouldn't they tend to view a "competitive" contract offer favorably? As most of us can probably attest, moving is a royal pain in the posterior.

The Brewers seem to have followed this exact policy and remained competitive until this past season. What upset the apple cart was a drought in the farm system. The replacement talent that was supposed to be there, wasn't. The Bill Spiers got hurt. The Joey Meyers failed to develop. The Gary Sheffields didn't work out the way they should have. The players who *did* make it, the Surhoffs, Jahas etc., haven't been as good as they were supposed to be. Perhaps the Brewers were misled by their minor league parks which tend to make hitters look better than they are.

For whatever reason, when Molitor and Bosio were legitimately due more money over the off-season, the Brewers couldn't come up with it. They didn't come up with replacements, either.

The Pitching

The starting rotation spent a lot of the summer going out there every fourth day and taking it on the chin. Then, if they left with a lead, the closer didn't close.

It's not a pretty picture, is it?

The Rotation: Contrast the '93 rotation with '92's: Eldred (a remarkable 53 TPER in a half-season's work), Navarro (a solid 85), Bones (an acceptable 104 as a 5th starter), and Wegman (a steady 91, for the full season). With Bosio's 84 in place, the '92 Brewers rotation ranked as the league's best—putting a scrappy, resourceful offense in a position to win with regularity. The rotation was the linchpin of the Brewers' surprising '92 pennant drive. It was both healthy and complete and it was very good.

Subtract only Bosio from this 5-man rotation and what happened? It became a 4-man rotation because there wasn't a "fifth" available. This led to overwork. Eldred made 36 starts, most in the league. That led to deteriorating effectiveness. Overwork may or may not have caused Wegman's residence on the DL. He's had various physical ailments, including a tender arm. But overwork couldn't have helped. It also overexposed Bones, who appeared overmatched at times in 4-man rotation usage.

Apparently, management hoped Teddy Higuera could make his long-awaited comeback. But Teddy last took a regular turn in '90 and his last *really* healthy season was '88. This was a little much to be counting on. No other provision seems to have been made. There was no rest for the weary rotation until Angel Miranda and Rafael Novoa came up in July. By then, though, the damage was done: an effective, but incomplete, rotation had been pitched into the ground.

The Bullpen: The Brewers boast an absolutely glittering middle relief corps—an elusive quantity, the absence of which is now popularly said to have cost teams pennants and world championships. Austin, Fetters, Lloyd and Orosco were clearly THE greatest strength of the Brewers staff but could only account for 212 IP. They were of only marginal value to a team that couldn't score many runs and was without a closer. What's the point of "staying close"?

The closer, Doug Henry, has apparently lost his job to Jesse Orosco, for now. Henry came up in mid-'91 and claimed the job with a spectacular 36 innings in the second half (a parenthetical 57 TPER). This was only his second season in the closer job after four undistinguished years as a starter and middle-reliever in the low minors. His initial performance at Milwaukee thus looked suspiciously out of context, leaving the jury still out. After his first full season as a major league closer in '92 (a worst-in-the-league 103 TPER), the jury came in. But the Brewers had no other choice but to let him continue, while hoping he'd find either a new trick or his old TPER.

The forthcoming move to Orosco also seems borne of desperation. But it may be only temporary. Mike Ignasiak appears ready to contribute at the major league level. An Ignasiak/Orosco co-closing arrangement may emerge and their TPERs suggest it has a good chance of working.

Overall, the Brewers staff isn't in bad shape—just undermanned. Reconstruction will require more than a paint job. It'll take a few new bricks, as well. Fortunately, some bricks are in hand. Miranda is apparently ready for a full year in the rotation; Ignasiak is ready to join the bullpen. Novoa should fit in somewhere. The only questions are whether Bill Wegman will be ready to go and how long Cal Eldred can survive his workload.

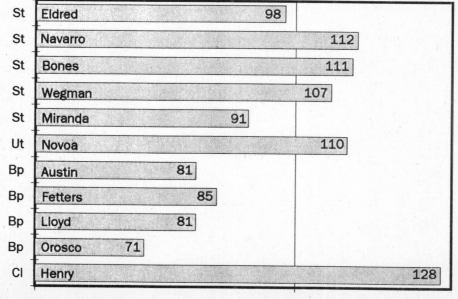

1993 Brewers Staff

St Eldred 98
St Navarro 112
St Bones 111
St Wegman 107
St Miranda 91
Ut Novoa 110
Bp Austin 81
Bp Fetters 85
Bp Lloyd 81
Bp Orosco 71
Cl Henry 128

50   100

What Next?

We can safely assume that Milwaukee will not be the site of any major free agent signings this winter. It's improbable they'll pull off any major trades. But, if they do (and neither Vaughn nor a key pitcher is involved), it's almost certain that they will profit in the exchange. If another club is actively seeking a Brewers player, they are, by our definition, overvaluing the object of their affections.

Any hope of substantive improvement thus lies in the farm system which is not in the greatest shape. At the moment, it's able to provide only replacement troops, not strengthening reinforcements. This places a franchise that has relied on its farm system between a rock and a hard place.

There is, evidently, little money to spend. There is, apparently, no sign of a turn in their talent fortunes. Out of financial necessity, the Brewers' previous commitment to mediocrity must, for a while at least, become a resignation to losing. How long can they survive in Milwaukee under these circumstances with only distant dreams of a new stadium and revenue-sharing among the owners to sustain them? What about the Brewers' fans and *their* dreams?

These aren't pleasant topics, but the situation facing the Brewers isn't a pleasant one, either.

Team TOPR: 1993 Milwaukee Brewers

	Bats	BA	OBP	SLG	HR	R	RBI	NBE	GOC	Ratio	TOPR
League Avg. Team	-	.267	.337	.408	148	762	719	2897	4352	.666	100
Milwaukee Brewers	-	.258	.328	.379	125	733	688	2720	4408	.617	92.7
Regulars:											
C Dave Nilsson	L	.257	.336	.375	7	35	40	143	242	.591	89
1B John Jaha	R	.264	.337	.416	19	78	70	279	402	.694	104
2B Bill Spiers	L	.238	.302	.303	2	43	36	140	290	.483	73
3B B.J. Surhoff	L	.274	.318	.391	7	66	79	259	426	.608	91
SS Pat Listach	R	.244	.319	.317	3	50	30	162	292	.555	83
LF Greg Vaughn	R	.267	.369	.482	30	97	97	369	434	.850	128
CF Robin Yount	R	.258	.326	.379	8	62	51	227	362	.627	94
RF Darryl Hamilton	L	.310	.368	.407	9	74	48	264	386	.684	103
DH Kevin Reimer	L	.249	.303	.394	13	53	60	201	349	.576	87
Bench (100+ TPA):											
IF Juan Bell	R	.234	.321	.322	5	42	29	129	233	.554	83
IF Dickie Thon	R	.269	.324	.331	1	23	33	108	196	.551	83
OF Tom Brunansky	R	.183	.265	.321	6	20	29	92	195	.472	71
C Tom Lampkin	L	.198	.280	.321	4	22	25	80	141	.567	(85)
MP Kevin Seitzer	R	.290	.359	.457	7	21	30	90	124	.726	(109)
C Joe Kmak	R	.218	.317	.264	0	9	7	48	91	.527	(79)

NOTE: Statistics are only for games played with Milwaukee. ( ) Under 200 TPA.

Team TPER: 1993 Milwaukee Brewers

	Throws	W-L	GS	GR	SV	IP	ERA	NBA	GOE	Ratio	TPER
League Avg. Team	-	81 -81	162	355	42	1444.1	4.33	2897	4352	0.666	100
Milwaukee Brewers	-	69 -93	162	353	29	1447	4.47	3010	4361	0.690	103.7
The Rotation:											
Cal Eldred	R	16 -16	36	0	0	258	4.01	506	776	0.652	98
Jaime Navarro	R	11 -12	34	1	0	214.1	5.33	478	642	0.745	112
Ricky Bones	R	11 -11	31	1	0	203.2	4.86	451	611	0.738	111
Bill Wegman	R	4 -14	18	2	0	120.2	4.48	259	363	0.713	107
Angel Miranda	L	4 -5	17	5	0	120	3.30	219	361	0.607	91
Mike Boddicker	R	3 -5	10	0	0	54	5.67	129	160	0.806	121
Teddy Higuera	L	1 -3	8	0	0	30	7.20	96	89	1.079	(162)
Utility:											
Rafael Novoa	L	0 -3	7	8	0	56	4.50	124	169	0.734	110
Bullpen:											
Graeme Lloyd	L	3 -4	0	55	0	63.2	2.83	105	194	0.541	81
Mike Fetters	R	3 -3	0	45	0	59.1	3.34	103	183	0.563	85
Jesse Orosco	L	3 -5	0	57	8	56.2	3.18	82	173	0.474	71
Carlos Maldonado	R	2 -2	0	29	1	37.1	4.58	80	113	0.708	(106)
Mike Ignasiak	R	1 -1	0	27	0	37	3.65	60	113	0.531	(80)
Jim Austin	R	1 -2	0	31	0	33	3.82	53	98	0.541	(81)
Doug Henry	R	4 -4	0	54	17	55	5.56	143	168	0.851	128

NOTE: Statistics are only for games pitched with Milwaukee. ( ) Under 200 TBF.

IT ALL COLLAPSED
MINNESOTA TWINS

I t's the fear of every baseball fan, player, coach, manager and city. What happens to your team when literally everything goes wrong in the same season? When the pitchers can't pitch . . . and the hitters can't hit . . . and the veterans suddenly start looking too old . . . and the young prospects play more like suspects . . . and the stars don't ever star . . . and the injuries never stop . . . and the long-awaited good streak never begins . . . and the season doesn't seem like it'll ever end.

Sort of like what happened to the 1993 Minnesota Twins.

Team Trendline: Minnesota Twins

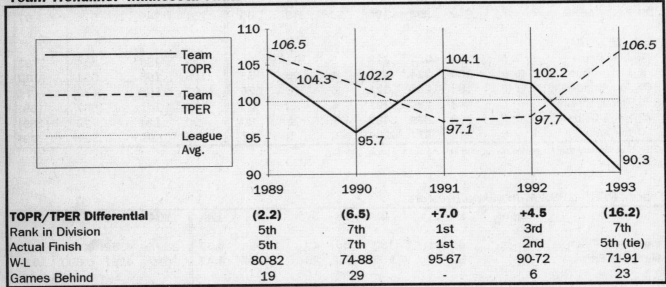

	1989	1990	1991	1992	1993
TOPR/TPER Differential	(2.2)	(6.5)	+7.0	+4.5	(16.2)
Rank in Division	5th	7th	1st	3rd	7th
Actual Finish	5th	7th	1st	2nd	5th (tie)
W-L	80-82	74-88	95-67	90-72	71-91
Games Behind	19	29	-	6	23

What Was Expected

The Twins had never been among baseball's big spenders. But they'd often been among baseball's big winners. And that reputation had become a source of pride in the Twin Cities. The frugal Twins had managed to survive quite nicely, thank you, by keeping one eye on the bottom line and the other eye on the look out for baseball bargains. Twice in the previous six years Minnesota had won it all—the AL West, the pennant, the World Series. The whole shebang. They entered '93 off back-to-back 90-win seasons. Only one other AL team could boast of that distinction—Toronto. And, after all, the Blue Jays, unlike the Twins, had a bajillion bucks to spend every year. Minnesota didn't. They annually made do with one of the lowest payrolls in the game.

And '93 had very much the same look. They hadn't been able to keep long-time shortstop and crowd favorite Greg Gagne from leaving for the lure of big bucks from Kansas City. But they did ink 3B Mike Pagliarulo amid hopes that his career would turn around and that valuable 3B Scott Leius could successfully shuffle over to SS. Free agent lefty John Smiley had headed to Cincy for big, big dollars. So Minnesota opted to sign lefty Jim Deshaies for little, little bucks in hopes he'd experience a career resurgence. Out of the blue, native Minnesotan Dave Winfield called and asked to come home to DH. So Minnesota found the bucks to accommodate him. The Twins still had a solid core of the lineup with Puckett, Hrbek, Harper, Knoblauch and Mack, virtually the same cast of characters who two years ago had been the centerpiece of a world-champion offense. The pitching staff had not one but two young potential aces in Tapani and Erickson, a bullpen headed by one of the game's finest in Aguilera and enough developing youngsters to theoretically cover any possible depth problems.

Yes, the '93 Twins looked like the contending '92 Twins who'd looked like the champion '91 Twins. Little could Minnesota have imagined that they'd wind up playing like the '90 Twins, who'd finished dead last in the West.

What Actually Happened

Where does one begin to describe the season of a team that fell apart? What's the jumping-off point? At the risk of sounding self-serving, perhaps our own TOPR-TPER numbers paint the best portrait of exactly what happened.

Simply comparing the '93 Twins to the contending '92 version brings the scope of the club's tumble into much better focus. The '92 Twins TOPRed at 102.2, an offense slightly better than average. They pitched (TPERed) at 97.7, again slightly better than average. They used these two edges shrewdly in compiling a record of 90–72, good for second place in their division.

The '93 Twins cratered, as they say in football, "on both sides of the ball." Their TOPR dropped like a rock in a vacuum finishing at 90.3. That's an incredible plummet of 11.9 points. Their TPER also went the wrong direction at warp speed leaping to 106.5, a rise of 8.8. Adding the two phases of the game gives you the picture of a team that was more than 20% worse in '93 than they'd been in '92. Just how far had the Twins fallen? That 90.3 TOPR made them the worst offensive team in the AL and ahead of only the expansion Marlins in all of baseball. Their pitching efficiency finished ahead of only Oakland in the AL and the Pirates and Rockies in the senior circuit.

But TOPR and TPER merely begin the string of ugly facts and figures:

—Minnesota recorded eight-game losing streaks in both April and May and a nine-gamer in June. It's the first Twins team in history to have three such eight-game-or-longer downers in a single season.

—A Twins team that had led the majors in team BA the two previous seasons dropped to eighth in the AL and 16th in the majors.

—They posted no winning months.

—Their 36–45 home record, a .444 winning percentage, marked the worst home percentage in the team's 33-year history in Minnesota.

—Their 71 wins ranks third lowest in Twins' history.

Of the nine most used regulars, only Puckett's 110 TOPR ranked him above the offensive norm for this position. Of the five rotation starters, only Jim Deshaies 96 TPER ranked above average and he was dealt late in the year to the pennant-contending Giants. Only the bullpen provided positive numbers. But, generally, by the time they got to work, many of the games had been decided.

Some small allowance must be made for the injuries Minnesota suffered. Ten players wound up on the DL as the club used the hurt list a total of 13 times. Both figures represent club records. SS Leius went down immediately causing the team to rush Meares to the majors at least a year ahead of their schedule for him. Mack's bad shoulder and a variety of Hrbek hurts limited those key players to 128 and 123 games respectively. One of the bullpen's best, and a possible rotation replacement as well, Mark Guthrie encountered serious blood-clotting problems and didn't appear after June 1. But compared to some other teams the Twins' injuries were still no more than moderate and, if accepted as an excuse at all, should be recognized as only a very small one at best.

In truth these Twins should have finished last. The negative difference between their TOPR and TPER of a whopping −16.2 points was easily the largest in the AL. That the Twins not only didn't record the worst mark in the league but actually finished ahead of Milwaukee and Oakland and tied with California can only be credited to the "mirror job" done by manager Tom Kelly whose performance might have been the brightest light in an otherwise dim season in the Twin Cities.

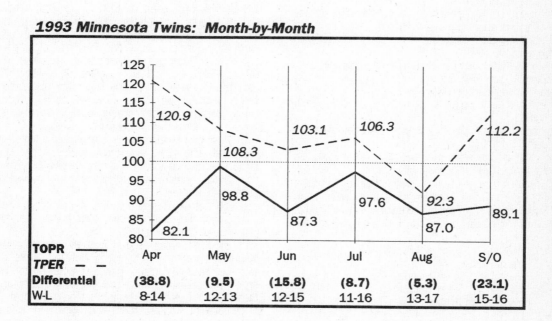

1993 Minnesota Twins: Month-by-Month

	Apr	May	Jun	Jul	Aug	S/O
TOPR ——						
TPER – –						
Differential	**(38.8)**	**(9.5)**	**(15.8)**	**(8.7)**	**(5.3)**	**(23.1)**
W-L	8-14	12-13	12-15	11-16	13-17	15-16

1993 Twins Lineup

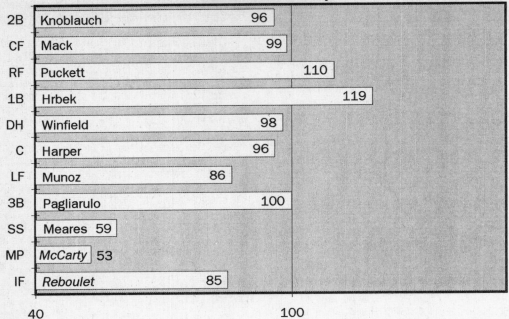

Pos	Player	TOPR
2B	Knoblauch	96
CF	Mack	99
RF	Puckett	110
1B	Hrbek	119
DH	Winfield	98
C	Harper	96
LF	Munoz	86
3B	Pagliarulo	100
SS	Meares	59
MP	*McCarty*	53
IF	*Reboulet*	85

40   100

The Offense

Welcome to TOPR hell.

Every offense depends on its stars to produce. Here's what Minnesota got TOPR-wise from the middle of its lineup:

—RF Puckett's 110 TOPR marked his second worst of the decade and a drop of 16 points from the previous season.

—CF Mack's 99 was easily his worst of the '90s and a huge fall of 35 points from his '92 TOPR.

—DH Winfield's 98? Another decade low and a dip of 36 points from his sparkling '92 year with Toronto.

—C Harper's 96 tied a decade low.

—1B Hrbek's 119 for a partial season tied his second worst TOPR of the '90s.

—2B Knoblauch's 96 represented a three-year career low and a tumble of 21 points from '92.

That leaves us only three other positions and two of them, SS and LF, were the *worst* TOPR positions on the club.

If you're starting to think the bottom dropped out of this team you're right on! Ugly offensive numbers came from everywhere. But none uglier than those produced by the three infield spots other than 1B Hrbek. In all, the Twins played nine men at 2B, SS and 3B:

Meares	Knoblauch
Leius	Pagliarulo
Reboulet	Stahoviak
Hale	Hocking
	Jorgensen

No matter how manager Kelly wrote out his lineup card, every evening three of those names appeared as starters at those three infield spots. (Sometimes four of them when one DHed.) How little Kelly got from those spots literally boggles the mind. Here's the composite season of those nine Twins who filled those three infield positions.

ABs	H	BA	2B	3B	HR	RBI	BB	SB	CS
1890	505	.267	83	12	10	144	164	48	30

For a moment study those figures and what they mean to an offense over a 162-game schedule. Those three spots in the lineup hit well enough. But everything else almost qualifies as astounding. The lack of power is unbelievable—one HR every 16 games out of those three positions combined. (The Twins didn't get a HR from a SS all year!) Barely one walk per game. Well under an RBI a game. Of their 505 hits, 400 were singles! And, not only didn't they provide extra-base pop of any kind, they also contributed very, very little speed. No power, no walks, no RBIs, no steals! Combined, those three spots became like three anvils hung around the neck of an offense that was already drowning.

Of those nine infielders only one reached a triple figure TOPR—Pagliarulo, who by August 15 had been swapped to Baltimore as the Orioles geared up for a run in the AL East. The 100 TOPR represented "Pags" best in years and just missed matching the positional norm for AL 3Bs of 102.

But Minnesota also had offensive shortcomings everywhere else. Even though they increased their team homer total by 17 from the year before, that still only got them up to #12 in the AL. Only cellar-dwellers Oakland and Milwaukee collected fewer extra-base hits. Only Texas, KC and Cleveland drew less walks. Only KC had a worse on-base percentage. Only Baltimore, Boston and the Yanks stole fewer bases and Minnesota got thrown out more than any of those teams. In fact, the Twins' running game basically consisted of two players. Knoblauch (29) and Mack (15), who swiped 44 in 60 attempts. That's solid. But all the rest of the Twins managed 39 steals and were caught 43 times. Ouch! Mix in one last bummer—this team led all of baseball in hitting into DPs with 150—and you have an offense that, overnight, went from one of the better ones in the game to a total mess.

The Pitching

Unlike the offense, which totally disintegrated, only half of the pitching staff self-destructed. The front half. The rotation.

But, as a unit, the Twins posted the second worst team ERA ever. Their 4.71 edged only the 4.77 of the '86 Twins for this ignominious place in club history. That ERA represented a jump of an incredible 1.01 earned runs per game from just the year before! Minnesota's biggest problem as a staff revolved around the most basic element of the pitcher-hitter confrontation. The hitter won far too often! The Twins ranked as the easiest to hit in the entire AL (.283 opponent BA) and second most hittable in the majors behind only the Rockies "rocky" staff.

The lack of effectiveness by the starters showed up especially in early-season games. No one could step up and stop those three long losing streaks Minnesota endured in the first three months. In fact, Twins' starters set a record for consecutive non-complete games going 103 games from opening day until August 4 before Erickson went the distance in a 5–4 loss at Boston. In just the season's first two months, Minnesota allowed the opposition to score in double figures 12 times! That's the same number of double-figure defensive games that the NFL Minnesota Vikings had permitted in the previous season. No, most nights, especially in the first half, watching the Twins pitch was not a pretty sight.

The Rotation: The "aces" in the rotation turned into jokers! Erickson and Tapani, who'd combined to go 36–17 for the '91 championship club and 29–23 for the '92 contending Twins, finished 20–34! In the previous two years neither had had an ERA as high as 4.00. But in '93 Erickson finished at 5.19 and Tapani at 4.43. Their three-year TPERs offer a discouraging trend:

Tapani: 88–99–101
Erickson: 86–95–109

Both trendlines suggest the same direction. From studs down to slightly better than average and then down again to below average over the three years. They ranked as the AL's first and third biggest losers in '93 (Erickson with 19 and Tapani with 15).

But Erickson's difficulties seem the more severe. The velocity and movement on his fastball, that made him one of the league's nastiest pitchers just two years ago, appears to have disappeared. AL hitters had a field day with him, tattooing him to the tune of .305 for the season. That kind of average speaks volumes about a pitcher's stuff or lack of it.

While Erickson's numbers suggest a worrisome "slide," Tapani's look more like a "slump." While the overall numbers did fall off from seasons' past, "Taps" appeared to refind himself after the All-Star break going 9–4 from July 17 on with a terrific 3.12 ERA. But that still couldn't balance out his horrific first half (3–11, 5.79 ERA).

Banks, once the third pick in the first round of the draft, continued to frustrate the Twins. His career had been a collection of minor injuries and erratic performances. Last season was to have been his make or break season. It must have been a "break" because Minnesota dealt him away right after the year ended. He did make 30 starts, but for only 171 innings, less than six innings per start. He didn't complete a single start and begins '94 in a Cubs uniform having never thrown a major league CG in 45 starts.

At mid-season Deshaies qualified as one of the game's biggest surprises. Signed for peanuts, he'd posted a 9–5 record through the end of June despite a hefty ERA in the mid-fours. But that kind of pitching eventually began to catch up to him record-wise. He went 2–8 in the two months following and got swapped to SF for their stretch run.

The club tried the 26-year-old Trombley as a spot starter. His fastball's got some movement at times. But he also looked awfully hittable (.290) with many of those hits going a long, long way (15 HRs in 110 IP). Brummett arrived from SF to post a combined 119 TPER. That's not very impressive but his minor league stats definitely are. He's a possibility. Lefty Guardado got plastered as evidenced by his 133 (Ugh!). But pitching-strapped Minnesota asked him to jump from AA to the majors and he simply wasn't ready. His minor league numbers, like Brummett's, suggest a decent future and he is just 23.

Adding it all up, what did Kelly have to choose from in '93? The starters gave him just two good halves—Deshaies before the break and Tapani after it. Other than them, most nights the starter had the other team's hitters licking their fingers in anticipation.

The Bullpen: The bullpen was the strength of the team. Lefty

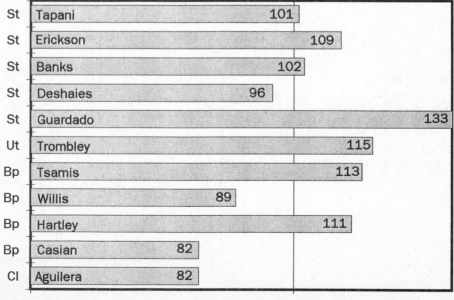

1993 Twins Staff

Pos	Player	TPER
St	Tapani	101
St	Erickson	109
St	Banks	102
St	Deshaies	96
St	Guardado	133
Ut	Trombley	115
Bp	Tsamis	113
Bp	Willis	89
Bp	Hartley	111
Bp	Casian	82
Cl	Aguilera	82

50   100

Casian (82) and righty Willis (89) finished sixth and 12th respectively in the TPER rankings for set-up men. Aguilera's 82 ranked ninth among closers. But one must point out that '93 was an exceptional season for AL closers and it was "Aggie's" fourth consecutive year to TPER at 85 or better and only Henke and Ward can also claim that distinction.

But Kelly's problem obviously centered around getting to this late inning sturdiness with the game still in the balance. The loss of solid middleman Guthrie to injury robbed the club of a versatile, durable 90 TPER pitcher and left that role to various hurlers. None of them made Minnesota forget Guthrie. Hartley, Tsamis and Trombley (when he wasn't starting) all TPERed above 110. If you're Minnesota that makes you long for Guthrie's speedy recovery.

But when, on those occasions the Twins could remain competitive into the late innings, the pen and Kelly's expertise produced solid results. Minnesota finished 10–2 in extra-inning games and 27–19 in games decided by one run. Lord, what might the final record have been had it not been for those positives?

Pitching coach Dick Such made perhaps the most insightful assessment of the staff when, late in the season, he suggested the Twins were "all followers." (He excluded stopper Aguilera from this criticism). What Such longed for was some pitchers to step up and lead his staff. Unless he finds them in '94, the Twins figure to "follow" a lot of teams in the standings.

What Next?

Given that nothing's changed concerning the Twins' status as a small market/small payroll team, nothing will change regarding their approach to putting a team together. Even before the dismal '93 had ended, the entire baseball world knew that Minnesota would not be out there throwing money at the very obvious holes in their lineup.

Offensively they must hope that their stars who faltered so badly as a group last year, will rebound as a group in '94. That core returns intact except for catcher Harper who was allowed to flee to free agency. The club basically faced the financial question of whether to retain Mack or Harper. They chose Mack and that in turn caused them to quickly deal starting pitcher Banks to the Cubs for catching prospect Matt Walbeck to replace Harper. It's a kind of unhappy game these smaller budget teams sometimes get forced into playing as the gap between baseball's rich and baseball's poor grows ever wider. The inability to compete financially creates a hole

that can then only be filled by a deal that creates another hole which in turn must be filled only by making yet another trade, etc . . . etc . . . etc.

Banks' exodus leaves Minnesota even more dependent on the rejuvenation of Tapani and Erickson atop the rotation. Perhaps Brummett, acquired from the Giants, could develop into a #3. But the absence of the two traded starters, Banks and Deshaies, leaves manager Kelly groping to replace the 57 starts they made. Perhaps youngsters Mahomes and or Guardado will emerge. Maybe Trombley's ready to leave his utility role and start every fifth day. Maybe the Twins can, as they have so often, find a bargain veteran or two who'll shore up what looks to be a depth-shy staff. The club's strength remains its pen, that is unless Minnesota feels that some of that strength must be dealt to fill other holes.

And that brings us back to the offense. If Leius returns to good health, at least the Twins will get at least a few homers from the SS position. But 3B and LF remain sore spots unless prospect McCarty has learned to make hitting adjustments over the off-season, something he didn't seem to have the foggiest idea of how to do as his average and TOPR tumbled downward last season.

The system does appear to have a handful of decent positional prospects. But the best of them (OF Becker, SS Hocking, 3B Stahoviak) spent most of '93 at AA and may need at least one more year of seasoning. But somewhere, somehow, Minnesota must find some triple-digit TOPRs or this offense will continue to test the rather sizeable managerial skills of Kelly.

The Twins have always survived on a thin margin for error. This franchise always seemed to have a kiddo or two ready when a lack of dollars or age or injury suddenly opened a gap in their lineup. But '94 might be a difficult transitional year. Several of the key everyday players are reaching ripe-old baseball ages. The prospects appear to need more time to ripen.

But perhaps most disconcerting of all, the money issue seems to be looming larger and larger for such franchises. Of their top 10 picks in last year's amateur draft, the Twins failed to satisfy the contract demands of five of them (#s 1, 4, 5, 7 and 10) who headed for college instead of the Twins' system. That's an ominous sign for a franchise whose organizational bottom line had never before seemed to dramatically affect the team's bottom line performance. Those days for the Twins, and other small-market franchises, may be ending.

Metrodome

The "Humpdome" was no "Homerdome" in '93. The Metrodome acted as the most "offense-neutral" park in the American League—overall (100.8 Park TOPR) and in its effect on home club offense (+0.4%) and opponent offense (+1.1%) after adjustment for normal home/road splits. It was the quintessential "league average park," producing no defining characteristics whatsoever.

Given the way the Twins played in '93, this result seems appropriate.

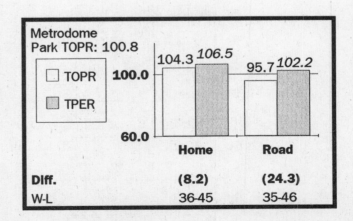

Metrodome Park TOPR: 100.8		
☐ TOPR ▦ TPER	Home	Road
	104.3 / 106.5	95.7 / 102.2
Diff.	(8.2)	(24.3)
W-L	36-45	35-46

Team TOPR: 1993 Minnesota Twins

	Bats	BA	OBP	SLG	HR	R	RBI	NBE	GOC	Ratio	TOPR
League Avg. Team	-	.267	.337	.408	148	762	719	2897	4352	.666	100
Minnesota Twins	-	.264	.327	.385	121	693	642	2641	4393	.601	90.3
Regulars:											
C Brian Harper	R	.304	.347	.425	12	52	73	251	392	.640	96
1B Kent Hrbek	L	.242	.357	.467	25	60	83	252	318	.792	119
2B Chuck Knoblauch	R	.277	.354	.346	2	82	41	298	466	.639	96
3B Mike Pagliarulo	L	.292	.350	.423	3	31	23	128	193	.663	100
SS Pat Meares	R	.251	.266	.309	0	33	33	110	282	.390	59
LF Pedro Munoz	R	.233	.294	.393	13	34	38	148	259	.571	86
Dave McCarty	L	.214	.257	.286	2	36	21	104	295	.353	53
CF Shane Mack	R	.276	.335	.412	10	66	61	254	387	.656	99
RF Kirby Puckett	R	.296	.349	.474	22	89	89	342	465	.735	110
DH Dave Winfield	R	.271	.325	.442	21	72	76	273	419	.652	98
Bench (100+ TPA):											
IF Jeff Reboulet	R	.258	.356	.304	1	33	15	110	195	.564	85
IF Chip Hale	L	.333	.408	.425	3	25	27	104	131	.794	119
I/O Gene Larkin	B	.264	.357	.347	1	17	19	73	118	.619	(93)
IF Terry Jorgensen	R	.224	.270	.289	1	15	12	49	126	.389	(58)
C Lenny Webster	R	.198	.274	.245	1	14	8	37	86	.430	(65)

NOTE: Statistics are only for games played with Minnesota. ( ) Under 200 TPA.

Team TPER: 1993 Minnesota Twins

	Throws	W-L	GS	GR	SV	IP	ERA	NBA	GOE	Ratio	TPER
League Avg. Team	-	81 -81	162	355	42	1444.1	4.33	2897	4352	0.666	100
Minnesota Twins	-	71 -91	162	356	44	1444.1	4.73	3070	4332	0.709	106.5
The Rotation:											
Kevin Tapani	R	12 -15	35	1	0	225.2	4.43	461	684	0.674	101
Scott Erickson	R	8 -19	34	0	0	218.2	5.19	478	659	0.725	109
Willie Banks	R	11 -12	30	1	0	171.1	4.04	347	512	0.678	102
Jim Deshaies	L	11 -13	27	0	0	167.1	4.41	322	503	0.640	96
Eddie Guardado	L	3 -8	16	3	0	94.2	6.18	247	278	0.888	133
Utility:											
Mike Trombley	R	6 -6	10	34	2	114.1	4.88	266	346	0.769	115
Pat Mahomes	R	1 -5	5	7	0	37.1	7.71	110	114	0.965	(145)
Bullpen:											
Mike Hartley	R	1 -2	0	53	1	81	4.00	176	239	0.736	111
George Tsamis	L	1 -2	0	41	1	68.1	6.19	156	207	0.754	113
Carl Willis	R	3 0	0	53	5	58	3.10	101	170	0.594	89
Greg Brummett	R	2 -1	5	0	0	26.2	5.74	60	78	0.769	(116)
Rick Aguilera	R	4 -3	0	65	34	72.1	3.11	119	217	0.548	82

NOTE: Statistics are only for games pitched with Minnesota. ( ) Under 200 TBF.

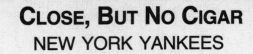

CLOSE, BUT NO CIGAR
NEW YORK YANKEES

ave you ever heard the story of Tantalus from Greek mythology? He'd been received as a guest at the table of the gods, but while among them committed the crime of hubris (foolish pride). The gods sentenced Tantalus to Hades forever. His punishment would be an eternity of thirst and hunger. Tantalus stood in a pool of water but would be forever parched because, when he bent to drink, the water rushed away leaving him standing on dry ground. Just above him hung fruit trees. But when he tried to grab a pear or a pomegranate the winds blew the fruit just out of his reach. From the myth of Tantalus we derive the word "tantalize."

That's what the Yankees did for all of '93—tantalize. From opening day through late September, New York never dropped more than five games behind the tightly packed and frantic AL East. They spent a major league record 93 consecutive days from June 18 through September 18 within three games of first place but never in that time did they ever sit alone in the top spot. The Yanks added a second major league record for tantalization by having a share of first 18 times but never in the entire season having it all to themselves. Seven times the Yankees played a game in which, if they'd have won, they'd have spent that night sleeping in sole possession of first place. All seven times they lost.

As other contenders floated up and down the standings, New York hung right around the top. But they give no awards for being really good at hanging around in baseball. At season's end no one invites you to play in the "hanging around playoffs." In the end, the Yankees and their fans could only commiserate about how close they'd come. Oh, so close. But whenever they'd reached for first, they always found it to be just out of reach.

Team Trendline: New York Yankees

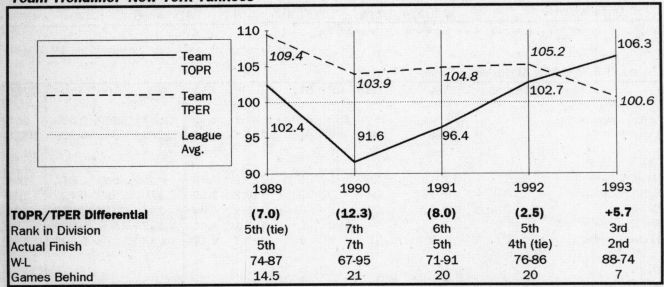

	1989	1990	1991	1992	1993
TOPR/TPER Differential	(7.0)	(12.3)	(8.0)	(2.5)	+5.7
Rank in Division	5th (tie)	7th	6th	5th	3rd
Actual Finish	5th	7th	5th	4th (tie)	2nd
W-L	74-87	67-95	71-91	76-86	88-74
Games Behind	14.5	21	20	20	7

What Was Expected

Yankee fans could hardly wait for '93 to arrive. As the eighties wound down so did the Bronx Bombers. Actually, they'd turned into the "Bronx bummers" with their season records worsening every year for five years bottoming out at a dismal 67–95 in 1990, dead last in the AL East. But Yankee fortunes then began to turn. Their victory total had edged upward to 71 wins in '91 and 76 in '92. The Yanks had made it back to the middle of the pack in that '92 season and '93 dawned with high hopes that they'd challenge for the top spot. New York's upward direction had encouraged Yankee boss George Steinbrenner to return to his old ways of constructing a team—throwing money at whatever holes the club appeared to have. Just one problem these days—lots of people don't want his money. The Yanks shopped furiously during the off-season offering the following contracts to free agents:

OF Barry Bonds	5 years/ $36 M	
P Greg Maddux	5 years/ $35.5 M	
P David Cone	3 years/ $18 M	
P Doug Drabek	4 years/ $21.5 M	
P Jose Guzman	4 years/ $14 M	
C Terry Steinbach	4 years/ $17 M	

All signed somewhere else with three of them taking less money elsewhere (Maddux, Drabek and Steinbach), and two others (Guzman and Cone) signing for virtually the same as the Yanks offered. Undaunted, the Yankees pressed on with their shopping spree. They signed lefty Jimmy Key (4 years/ $17 M) being the only team to offer more than a three-year deal. They inked SS Spike Owen and reliever Steve Howe to contracts worth more than $2 million a year despite the fact that neither had a serious offer from anyone else in baseball. They gave Wade Boggs a three-year deal even though no one else would tender him one of more than two years in length. They swapped CF Roberto Kelly to Cincy to get RF Paul O'Neill. And finally, in what most regarded as a first-rate coup, the Yanks packaged three prospects they didn't need to get outstanding California lefty Jim Abbott in return.

The pace had been extraordinary. And the results looked pretty darn good. In Key and Abbott they'd obtained two of baseball's steadiest and best lefties. Boggs and Owen filled an aching need on the left side of the infield. O'Neill gave them a powerful left-handed bat that seemed perfectly suited to the short RF distance in their stadium. Their bullpen, perhaps the strongest part of the '92 team, looked formidable again with the re-signing of Howe. And with the inking of Key they'd accomplished a second important matter—weakening the staff of the team they had to catch, Toronto.

1993 began with something that hadn't been heard in the Bronx for some time—pennant talk.

What Actually Happened

The Yankees did not win the East in 1993 because their bullpen turned out to be much more "bull" than "pen." They'd entered the season believing their closing combination of Howe-Farr gave them one of the strongest end-of-the-game situations in the majors. But for most of the year what their fans kept asking when either or both of these two entered the game was "How far?"—as in "how far did that one go?" Bullpen long balls killed New York. Between them Howe and Farr yielded 15 shots that caused NY state men to figure "how far" that one had gone. These 15 roundtrippers came in just 97+ innings. (The year before they'd combined to allow 3 HRs in 74 IP). Even worse, these Yankee closers passed the disease of "homeritis" onto the rest of the members of the relief corps. In all, Yankee bullpeners permitted an outrageous 53 homers in 426 innings. Their 4.62 ERA made them the AL's 13th ranked pen. They blew 15 saves. Fifteen games blown in a season where NY spent 93 consecutive days perched near the top of the AL East but never could squeeze into the top spot alone.

Oh, to be sure, the season contained other disappointments. And some of those also involved pitchers, starting pitchers. Abbott looked mediocre. Perez, given a huge contract just before the training camp opened, pitched miserably. And, try as they may, New York simply couldn't talk anyone into dealing them a starter to shore up their rotation as the year unfolded. They tried veterans Mike Witt and (very late) Frank Tanana. They called on youngsters Sterling Hitchcock, Domingo Jean, Jeff Johnson, Mark Hutton and Sam Militello. None appeared ready.

The offense performed better than expected, the best in years in fact. But, as the year wore on, NY kept reaching, reaching for pitching that many nights simply wasn't there.

1993 New York Yankees: Month-by-Month

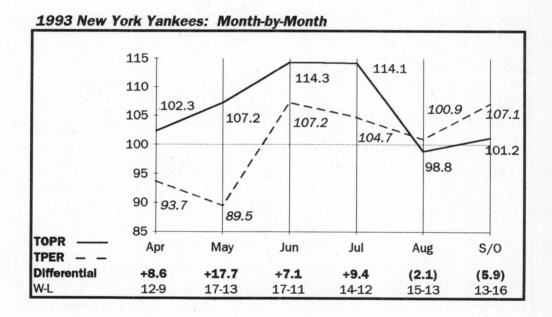

	Apr	May	Jun	Jul	Aug	S/O
TOPR ———						
TPER – – –						
Differential	+8.6	+17.7	+7.1	+9.4	(2.1)	(5.9)
W-L	12-9	17-13	17-11	14-12	15-13	13-16

1993 Yankees Lineup

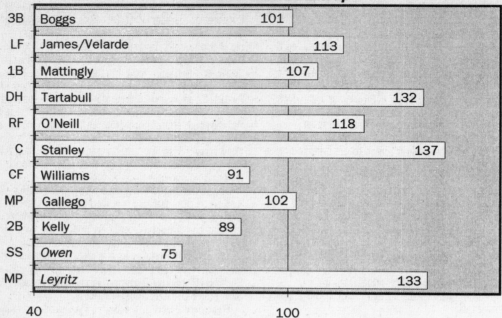

3B	Boggs	101
LF	James/Velarde	113
1B	Mattingly	107
DH	Tartabull	132
RF	O'Neill	118
C	Stanley	137
CF	Williams	91
MP	Gallego	102
2B	Kelly	89
SS	*Owen*	75
MP	*Leyritz*	133

40　　　　　　　　　　100

The Offense

Hooray for the "Goonies!"

During the spring exhibition season, Yankee coach Frank Howard gave the group of Yankee part-timers who always got tabbed to make those long Florida bus trips the nickname of the "Goon Squad." How could Howard have known that in '93, the Yanks would have been goners without the Goonies? All began the year as bench warmers or platooners. Such reserve groups are usually made up of weak hitters or aging pinch hitters or power guys without positions. Then, of course, there's always the obligatory backup catcher who can almost never hit much over his weight. Not these Goonies. Check out the terrific TOPRs of the Yankee Goon Squad.

POS.	Goonie	TOPR
C	Mike Stanley	138
LF	Dion James	121
IMP	Randy Velarde	103
IMP	Jim Leyritz	133
INF	Mike Gallego	102

All five of the Goonies TOPRed in triple figures. Only Gallego failed to bat .300 (he hit a creditable .283). They drilled 64 HRs and drove in 251. Three of the Goonies played so well they weren't Goonies by year's end. Stanley pushed Matt Nokes out of the catching job. Gallego played more SS than Owen. James got most of the playing time in LF. Even Leyritz found himself in the lineup almost every time the opposition started a lefty. Imagine, as a manager, having the luxury, at times, of having five above-average offensive players riding the pine when the game began.

The contributions of the Goonies helped make the Yankees a pretty potent offensive team. Their 106.3 team TOPR put them third in the league behind the thumpers from Detroit and Toronto. But the Bombers deserve a bit more credit than even that considering the hitter's graveyard they play their home games in. For some reason (perhaps that short RF area) many have long regarded Yankee Stadium as a good hitter's park. Au contraire! The stadium depressed offense by exactly 10% in '93. To post a TOPR of 106, that's 6% above average, playing in that "offensive cemetery" ranks as a major achievement.

The '93 Yanks:

—Led the majors in team BA at .279, their highest in 31 years.

—Finished tied for second with 178 homers.

—Topped all of baseball in hits and total bases.

—Had only four hitters TOPR under 100. Unfortunately, all four began the season in the starting lineup (Nokes, Owen, Kelly and B. Williams). Are they future Goonies perhaps?

—Totaled 496 extra-base hits, fourth in the majors behind Toronto, Detroit and Philly.

—Drew 622 walks, fourth in the majors behind Detroit, Philly and Baltimore.

But flip this offensive coin over and you get a handful of very, very discouraging numbers, all of which have to do with this club's aching need—speed! New York qualified as the lead-foots of the free world. What does a lack of speed do to a lineup generating the kind of positive numbers listed above?

—Stole just 39 bases. Five American Leaguers and seven for the NL swiped more. That's not 12 total teams. That's 12 individual players who stole more than the Yanks! It gets worse. They got caught 35 times. Why did the Yanks even bother to *ever* try to run?

—If you can't run you get left on base more. Only Detroit left more men on than the Yanks' 1,247. But Detroit also scored 78 more times.

—Playing station-to-station offense leaves you vulnerable to the double play. The Yanks hit into 149 twin killings—eight Yanks hit into 10 or more DPs. Only one team had more. Appropriately the major league leader in twin killings was the Twins.

The Yanks batting order generally looked about the way you'd expect with the three best TOPRs filling the 4–5–6 spots. Tartabull, though the Yanks don't seem to care for him much (they're always trying to trade him), spent most of the year DHing. NY DHs had the third-best run-producing season in AL history. Only the '82 Royals and '79 Angels DHs drove in more runs over the course of the season than did the '93 Yankees (124). The weaker TOPRs of

Williams, Owen and Kelly nearly always batted in the lowest three spots thereby giving them the fewest chances to hurt the overall offensive effort.

But the pinstripers might want to take a closer look at the top third of their order before '94. Boggs and Mattingly have big names, but not big TOPRs any more. Leadoff man Boggs has TOPRed at 102–101 the last two years. Despite that solid BA he's become an ordinary offensive player. Mattingly's TOPR average for the '90s (96) represents even more reason for concern. Mix in the fact that the excellent 121 TOPR on the usual #2 man in the order, James, will be missing next season (he headed for Japan) and the Yankees have cause for concern about the absence of "table-setters" in front of the booming bats of Tartabull, Stanley, O'Neill.

While the season numbers look very solid, despite the obvious lack of speed, New York must also be concerned with the way this attack faded down the stretch. With the division title hanging in the balance, the Yankees had their two worst TOPR months in August and September. That led to a combined record over the last 57 games of 28–29. There's yet one more evidence of how much "no speed kills." When the bats stopped booming, the Yanks had absolutely no other means of attack at Showalter's disposal. Before next season that gaping speed hole must be filled.

The Pitching

If only the pitching staff had found a few "Goonies." The Yanks desperately needed some of the "role players" on their staff to step up. They needed what the White Sox found lots of—a developing youngster. They needed an alternative to Farr as closer when he mysteriously lost his effectiveness. The Yanks could have also used someone waiting in the wings to replace Perez in the rotation when his shoulder and his ERA each ached.

As a staff, New York actually had its best TPER year in the last five. Since the horror show that the '89 and '90 seasons became, the Yanks have steadily improved their overall performance. But that 100.6 TPER of last season is as deceiving as the offense's 106+ TOPR. Just as the offense truly hit better than that figure suggests, so did the pitchers actually perform far worse than their team figure. And each for the same reason—the nature of their home park. The staff TPER indicates a decent staff. Not good. Not bad. Also, not true. Pitching 81 times in a park that depresses offense as Yankee Stadium does should have produced far, far better TPERs. As evidence, we present the Yankee staff when it left home. When it had to go out on the big, bad road and pitch in stadiums that weren't nearly as friendly to pitchers as their home park. In the Bronx, Yankee pitchers posted a glittering 88.8 TPER. Almost spectacular! But again, with the "pitcher nature" of that field an "average" staff would have posted a 90. But when the Yankees hit the road their pitching reminded everyone of that line from the American Express commercial—they left home without it! Away from home the club TPER shot up to an ugly 112.9. Exactly how bad was that? Worse than the Tigers! Worse than the Colorado Rockies! That's correct—Yankee road pitching effectiveness fell below that of the Tigers and Rockies—baseball's two measuring sticks for bad pitching.

As erratic as these hurlers could be, they also had the capability, at times, of dazzling performances posting a league-high 13 shut-outs. Then, again, 41 times—just over one out of every four games—the opposition tallied seven or more runs. Ladies and gentlemen, we introduce the New York Yankees, the Dr. Jekyll and Mr. Hyde of American League pitching staffs.

The underrated Yankee offense and overrated New York staff did have one thing in common—problems with the running game. New York hitters couldn't steal (just 39 of 74, 53%). New York pitchers had a terrible time stopping the other side's runners. Opposing stealers succeeded in 115-of-162 attempts or almost exactly 71%. When you add the two and get a composite effect of the running game during Yankee contests, it gives the Yankees a minus-64 bases, the biggest negative differential in the league.

The Rotation: What looked like strength at the start of the season certainly didn't wind up that way. Free agent Key performed spectacularly. Had you told the Yanks they'd get an 18–6 record and 80 TPER out of him during spring training, they'd have made plans to print playoff tickets. But their other ace lefty acquisition, Abbott, disappointed. Other than his no-hitter, the year contained few highlights. He proved homer-prone and, though poorly sup-

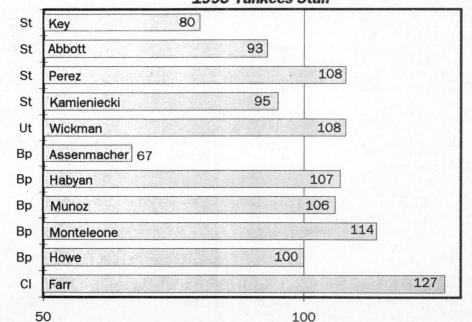

1993 Yankees Staff

St	Key	80
St	Abbott	93
St	Perez	108
St	Kamieniecki	95
Ut	Wickman	108
Bp	Assenmacher	67
Bp	Habyan	107
Bp	Munoz	106
Bp	Monteleone	114
Bp	Howe	100
Cl	Farr	127

50   100

ported at times offensively, really had few complaints or excuses given the level at which he pitched. Perez's dismal season probably hurt the most. After the downward progress of his ERA the four previous seasons (dropping from 5.01 to 4.61 to 3.12 to 2.87), New York figured him to be reaching the staff ace plateau. Instead of ace he became the staff anchor with his hot–cold performances dragging the club down, Kamieniecki qualified as a surprise. New York seemed intent on shoving him out of the picture at times. But, even though he displayed a curious ability to always win at home and always lose on the road, his effectiveness wound up just behind Abbott, a possibility most in the Yankee family would have scoffed at in pre-season. What's more, his TPER's moving in the right direction while Abbott's isn't. The Yankees correctly perceived that Wickman's standout record over the '92–'93 seasons (20–5) had really been achieved more by the good fortune of spectacular support than by his pitching (TPERs of 102 and 108 while working mainly in that "pitcher's park"). Realizing this, New York moved away from him as a rotation option as the year wore on. What may be most disconcerting about the starters could be the failure of anyone from a large group of supposedly terrific minor league prospects to step up to fill voids last season. It's a shame Sam Militello tore up a shoulder because his minor league profile suggested he might have been the most help immediately. But other much-ballyhooed comers like Hitchcock, Hutton and Jean all had shots and came up short. All share something else besides their failure to take advantage of a '93 opportunity—their minor league profiles all suggest control problems. Hutton and Hitchcock also appear to be homer-prone (uh-oh!). Not-yet-ready-for-prime-time super prospect Brien Taylor has a spectacular arm and mammoth control troubles. Jean got sent to Houston in the Hernandez trade. New York may believe they have tons of solid starter prospects. But, off their minor league numbers, that's exactly what they remain at this point—prospects.

The Bullpen: A mess! Farr failed as the closer. Howe failed as Farr's replacement. John Habyan pitched poorly and got traded. Neal Heaton threw miserably and got released. Rich Monteleone never came close to approaching his effectiveness of the previous two seasons. Bobby Munoz appears to be a solid prospect who's almost ready. The Yanks didn't need "almost" last year. They needed NOW! Gibson, Assenmacher and Smith all pitched well after arriving. But they arrived too late. The failings of this bunch have already been detailed in an earlier section of this team summary. But some numbers bear repeating—53 HRs, 4.62 ERA and 15 blown saves! Yuck! Farr left for free agency and after watching him and his 127 TPER last year Yankee fans probably hope he goes "Farr away." Given his history of drug troubles and his mediocre '93, New York may only wish Howe could be sent away. Nope, he's signed through '94 with another $2.1 million due

this year. Smith will test the free agent market carrying with him his worst TPER year ever (112) and a birth certificate that shows he's moved into his later 30s. Monteleone's free too. Assenmacher and Gibson pitched well enough to be kept. Hernandez arrives from Houston with terrific numbers. But can he close? Here's where the most work remains to be done on this Yankee roster. The '93 Yanks suffered from a horrible lack of an "end game" as they say in the NBA. Unless something's done about it, the Yankees again figure to fritter away precious victories after the game's "two-minute warning."

What Next?

Figuring out how to make changes used to be easy in New York. George simply opened his wallet, the money poured out and talent rolled in. Now, this approach didn't always work. In fact, hasn't worked well enough to bring even a division title to the Bronx since the strike season of '81. But at least New York always had a plan—identify a need and throw money at it.

Those days are gone, at least for now. Owner Steinbrenner ordered far more fiscal responsibility this off-season. Before he'd approve more multi-millionaires arriving, he wanted to see a few heading out the door. Unfortunately, the rest of baseball's not happily grabbing at down-on-their-TOPRs-and-TPERs types anymore. The Yanks appear stuck with the likes of Perez, Owen, Howe, Nokes and Tartabull (though it would appear several teams would like to be "stuck" with his numbers). That restricted the type of shopping spree that GM Gene Michael embarked on last year. New York needs a starter (if none of the youngsters steps in). They need speed—desperately. With James gone, a left fielder who can run would fit perfectly. Would Rickey Henderson come back to the Big Apple? Would George tear open his wallet for that much? But the biggest need still appears to be stabilizing a bullpen that imploded last year. Michael moved very early to start that rebuilding, acquiring Xavier Hernandez from the Astros where he posted the third best TPER in the entire NL corps of set-up men (77). One problem. The Yanks talk in terms of making him their closer. He's never done that job in the bigs and, when given chances by Houston last year, did record nine saves. But he also had eight blown saves, second only to the ridiculously ineffective Dibble in the entire NL.

If you'll lean back and look at the Yankees' "big picture," though, you'll find reason for encouragement. Were you at Belmont Park you'd suggest this team had the look of a race horse "coming into form." NY's moved steadily up from that disastrous 1990 season climbing to fifth and then fourth and finally to second last year. Might they sneak their nose in front of this pack at the wire next season? Or, if Michael's trades and George's money don't combine to plug some obvious holes, might '94 simply turn out to be another year in which Yankee fans are tantalized?

Yankee Stadium

TPER presents its 1993 "pitcher's park of the year." With a park TOPR of 90.0, Yankee Stadium was the place to pitch. On a park adjusted basis, the Yankees' offense suffered a −5.1% decline. The Yankees' pitchers, on the other hand, pushed visiting offense down by a whopping −15.1%. At home, then, the Yankee staff looked like a good one. Yankee fans thought differently, though, when they viewed or listened to road games. The differences between the staff's home and road performances are flat shocking:

Yankee Pitching	BA	OBP	SLG	ERA
At Home	.246	.313	.379	3.85
On the Road	.288	.353	.453	4.91

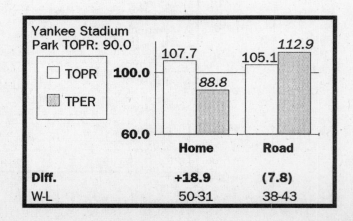

Yankee Stadium
Park TOPR: 90.0

	Home	Road
TOPR	107.7	105.1
TPER	88.8	112.9
Diff.	+18.9	(7.8)
W-L	50-31	38-43

Team TOPR: 1993 New York Yankees

	Bats	BA	OBP	SLG	HR	R	RBI	NBE	GOC	Ratio	TOPR
League Avg. Team	-	.267	.337	.408	148	762	719	2897	4352	.666	100
New York Yankees	-	.279	.353	.435	178	821	793	3045	4301	.708	106.3
Regulars:											
C Mike Stanley	R	.305	.389	.534	26	70	84	284	311	.913	137
1B Don Mattingly	L	.291	.364	.445	17	78	86	283	398	.711	107
2B Pat Kelly	R	.273	.317	.389	7	49	51	197	331	.595	89
3B Wade Boggs	L	.302	.378	.363	2	83	59	276	412	.670	101
SS Mike Gallego	R	.283	.364	.412	10	63	54	213	315	.676	102
Spike Owen	B	.234	.294	.311	2	41	20	133	267	.498	75
LF Dion James	L	.332	.390	.466	7	62	36	190	236	.805	121
Randy Velarde	R	.301	.360	.469	7	28	24	121	177	.684	103
CF Bernie Williams	B	.268	.333	.400	12	67	68	271	445	.609	91
RF Paul O'Neill	L	.311	.367	.504	20	71	75	285	363	.785	118
DH Danny Tartabull	R	.250	.363	.503	31	87	102	348	397	.877	132
Bench (100+ TPA):											
MP Jim Leyritz	R	.309	.410	.525	14	43	53	170	192	.885	133
C Matt Nokes	L	.249	.303	.424	10	25	35	109	170	.641	96
DH Kevin Maas	L	.205	.316	.411	9	20	25	86	124	.694	(104)

NOTE: Statistics are only for games played with New York. ( ) Under 200 TPA.

Team TPER: 1993 New York Yankees

	Throws	W-L	GS	GR	SV	IP	ERA	NBA	GOE	Ratio	TPER
League Avg. Team	-	81 -81	162	355	42	1444.1	4.33	2897	4352	0.666	100
New York Yankees	-	88 -74	162	332	38	1438.1	4.37	2905	4339	0.670	100.6
The Rotation:											
Jimmy Key	L	18 -6	34	0	0	236.2	3.00	383	716	0.535	80
Jim Abbott	L	11 -14	32	0	0	214	4.37	399	644	0.620	93
Melido Perez	R	6 -14	25	0	0	163	5.19	351	490	0.716	108
Scott Kamieniecki	R	10 -7	20	10	1	154.1	4.08	294	466	0.631	95
Mike Witt	R	3 -2	9	0	0	41	5.27	91	122	0.746	(112)
Utility:											
Bob Wickman	R	14 -4	19	22	4	140	4.63	306	426	0.718	108
Domingo Jean	R	1 -1	6	4	0	40.1	4.46	91	120	0.758	(114)
Bullpen:											
Rich Monteleone	R	7 -4	0	42	0	85.2	4.94	194	256	0.758	114
Steve Howe	L	3 -5	0	51	4	50.2	4.97	102	153	0.667	100
Bobby Munoz	R	3 -3	0	38	0	45.2	5.32	95	135	0.704	106
John Habyan	R	2 -1	0	36	1	42.1	4.04	88	124	0.710	(107)
Paul Gibson	L	2 0	0	20	0	35.1	3.06	64	106	0.604	(91)
Steve Farr	R	2 -2	0	49	25	47	4.21	119	141	0.844	127

NOTE: Statistics are only for games pitched with New York. ( ) Under 200 TBF.

FROM THE PENTHOUSE TO THE OUTHOUSE
OAKLAND ATHLETICS

ach season every player and every team harbors dreams of making history. But the '93 A's wanted no part of the history they became part of. Oakland suffered the ignominy of being just the second team this century to fall from first place to sole possession of last place in a single season. Oakland's great, great, great grandfathers, the 1915 Philadelphia A's had experienced such a tumble. But at least that team had a terrific excuse. In 1914 the A's had run roughshod over the AL posting a sparkling 99–53 record. But, under the pressure of a money crunch, Philly sold many of its top players during the off-season and also suffered raids from the upstart Federal League. The '15 A's fell like the

proverbial "lead balloon," dropping all the way to 43–109. The '93 A's also had their excuses including the usual list of injuries and defections and sudden collapses by stars. But who could have ever imagined the kind of tumble Oakland experienced? After all, these were the mighty A's! They'd won the West four of the last five years . . . captured the AL pennant in three of those seasons . . . and only three years before reigned as baseball's champions. From '88–'92 they'd averaged 98 victories a season and had never spent a day beneath .500 in any of those five years. The '93 A's got hit by a speeding train . . . and they never saw it coming.

Team Trendline: Oakland Athletics

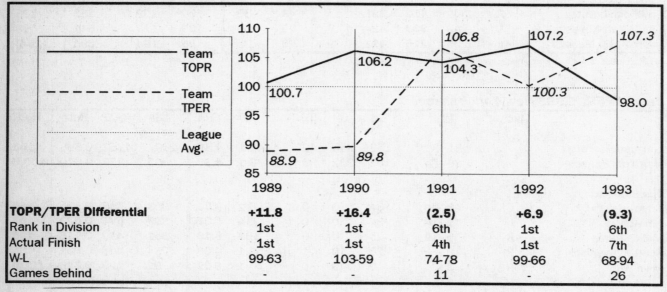

TOPR/TPER Differential	+11.8	+16.4	(2.5)	+6.9	(9.3)
Rank in Division	1st	1st	6th	1st	6th
Actual Finish	1st	1st	4th	1st	7th
W-L	99-63	103-59	74-78	99-66	68-94
Games Behind	-	-	11	-	26

What Was Expected

The build-up prior to the '93 season seemed just like other years. Baseball and, indeed, the A's and their fans, too, had come to expect championship caliber ball from the "other city by the Bay." Oh, there did appear to be more concern for the quality of this Oakland pitching staff than in other years because of the defection to free agency of their ace and emotional leader Dave Stewart and steady, durable vet Mike Moore. But the A's still had genius pitching coach Dave Duncan—the master of rejuvenating the careers of junk heap hurlers. They still had shrewd manager Tony LaRussa, who squeezed blood out of a stone with prior staffs. They'd gone out and signed just the kinds of pitchers Duncan often worked miracles with—Ed Nunez, Joe Boever and Goose Gossage. And they'd re-signed several others at a crossroads in their careers like Ron Darling, Storm Davis, Shawn Hillegas and Kelly Downs. Fans of the green and gold have seen LaRussa and Duncan patch together

staffs before, with less to work with, so pitching didn't seem to present a problem. After all, it never was in Oakland. The attack had also lost its emotional rudder when Carney Lansford retired. Jose Canseco had been traded late the season before. But many regarded this as a "good riddance" move and happily embraced RF Ruben Sierra as their new star. And besides, the rest of the A's awesome offense returned with household names like Rickey Henderson, Steinbach and McGwire and quiet contributors like Bordick, Blankenship and Browne. Journeyman Kevin Seitzer's been picked up to fill Lansford's 3B vacancy. Some intriguing youngsters, especially pitchers, waited in the wings. Oh, sure, the '93 A's had holes. But so had many of their teams in the recent past and someone or something always came along to plug them. And the A's then plugged their fingers into more championship rings. Why should '93 be any different? Oakland and its fans settled back and waited for another exciting run at a world title.

What Actually Happened

The gods of baseball played just about every cruel trick imaginable on the '93 A's.

—April 13. Detroit rakes the proud Oakland staff for 20 runs. Eight come off Storm Davis, who got only seven outs. Eight more come off rookie Mike Mohler, who'd looked ready for the bigs in spring training. Davis would eventually be released taking his 6.18 ERA to Tiger-town.

—April 15. The A's lead 2–1 going to the bottom of the ninth. Here comes Eckersley. Put it in the books. Oh, oh, there goes the win as light-hitting Chad Kreuter doubles in the second of two Tiger runs. It's the first of a single season career-high 10 blown saves for "The Eck." He'll also blow saves his next two outings.

—April 17. The A's lose 6–3 to the Brewers as staff ace Bob Welch gets drilled for all six in the first three innings. Oakland falls to 4–5, the first time the franchise has been under .500 since September 29, 1987.

—April 19. Ultra-valuable handyman Jerry Browne lands on the DL with a fractured wrist. He'll be out nearly two months.

—April 25. Cleveland's Jose Mesa shuts out Oakland dumping the A's into last place.

—May 1. Incredibly Mesa shuts out Oakland AGAIN! The A's stand 7–12 and in the cellar. They'll never rise above sixth again.

—May 14. McGwire's throbbing heel isn't healing. He heads for the DL. It'll be exactly 100 games before he reappears and then only for a September "cameo."

—June 5. CF Dave Henderson's aching groin and legs aren't getting better. It's the DL for Hendu.

—June 12. A's lose for the eighth time in nine games. Witt gets hammered. And he's the *best* of the starters.

—June 15. The best of the relievers, Rick Honeycutt, breaks his wrist. Kiss him goodbye for 39 days.

—July 18. Oakland's tired of watching Seitzer not cut it at 3B. He gets pink-slipped.

—July 19. Welch, Downs, Darling, Davis and just about every other starter besides Witt has been getting his head handed to him. LaRussa announces his "flotation rotation." He has nine pitchers working up to three innings each or 50 pitches (whichever comes first). Other teams giggle. Wags suggested the A's have invented "tag-team pitching." LaRussa, a manager famous for lineup manipulation, finds himself carrying 13 pitchers and just 12 positional players because of the desperate straits of the staff. That means he starts each game with only three bench people. Forget maneuvering. Forget the very stuff that made some think of him as a genius. In fact, forget the season.

—July 31. The A's wave the white flag. They trade Rickey Henderson to Toronto for a couple of prospects. At the time, they're 13½ games out and tied for the basement. It gets worse.

—Aug. 16. Catcher Steinbach breaks his wrist. End of season. On the same day Blankenship also lands on the DL with rotator cuff problems. End of season.

—Aug. 30. Gossage breaks his wrist falling down in the dugout. Yeah, it's been that kind of year.

—Sept. 5. Welch gets drummed again 9–2 by the Orioles. It's the sixth straight Oakland loss. The standings read 52–83, the low point of the season.

—Oct. 3. It mercifully ends, with a loss of course. Oakland's again made history. But for the first time in years it's the wrong kind of history. At 68–94 they've gone from first to worst.

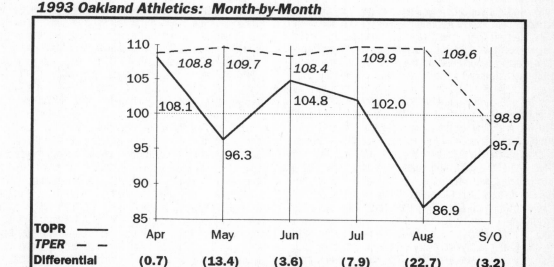

1993 Oakland Athletics: Month-by-Month

	Apr	May	Jun	Jul	Aug	S/O
TOPR ———						
TPER – –						
Differential	(0.7)	(13.4)	(3.6)	(7.9)	(22.7)	(3.2)
W-L	7-11	12-16	12-14	12-17	9-21	16-15

1993 Athletics Lineup

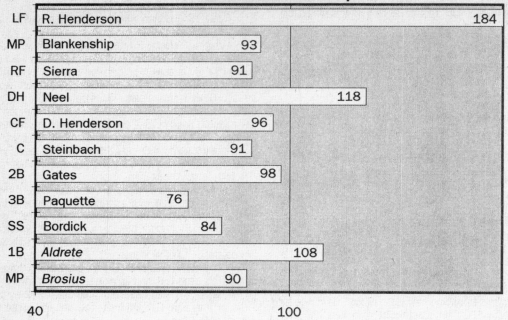

LF	R. Henderson	184
MP	Blankenship	93
RF	Sierra	91
DH	Neel	118
CF	D. Henderson	96
C	Steinbach	91
2B	Gates	98
3B	Paquette	76
SS	Bordick	84
1B	*Aldrete*	108
MP	*Brosius*	90

40   100

The Offense

A team's offense can be compared to a car. It's made up of many parts working together. If some of the parts break or for some reason stop working, it's still a car. It just doesn't run well anymore. It may still look like the shiny set of wheels you invested in, but it simply won't get you where you need to go. That appears to have happened to the Oakland A's offense. For years it had been a Mercedes. Shiny exterior, great engine, plush interior, incredible horsepower, never seemed to go out of style. They went from zero to 100 wins faster than anybody else on the road. Oh, from year to year, the chauffeur, LaRussa had to tune it up occasionally. But season after season the A's kept motoring along being driven to championships by one of the game's "luxury models." You car buyers check out the miles and the tires. We at *Essential Baseball* inspect the TOPRs. And they were classics. Despite playing in one of baseball's most "pitcher friendly" parks the A's offense cruised along driving other pitching staffs over the cliff. The '90, '91 and '92 A's TOPRed well above 100. And again remember, that's in a park that annually *depressed* offense. But in '93, parts of this one-owner, low-mileage beauty began to break. All of a sudden, the A's offense ran like any other clunker. The classic green and gold A's had become a lemon.

The Oakland "O" had always been one of the most dependable attacks in the game. But last year, every time you turned around, off to the shop it went for more repairs. The most serious concerned 1B McGwire's blown-out heel. He'd gotten off to a spectacular start breaking all TOPR limits at 215. But when he left to virtually never return, the A's had lost their drivin' wheel. Sierra, when batting ahead of McGwire, hit .297. With Big Mac in the garage, Sierra's average dipped to a career low .233 and he TPERed like some glove wiz who plays in the middle infield (91). But other key parts broke too. Steinbach, never really much of a TOPR superstar, departed and his replacements couldn't even match his 91. CF Dave Henderson, when in good working order, used to put up 110s and 117s. Not any more. He's a 96 these days. Rickey Henderson remained the sleek racer he'd always been. But by late July the A's had traded him in on a couple of younger models.

Seitzer simply never worked at 3B and his fill-in Paquette never seemed ready for life in the fast lane (TOPR 76). Valuable spare parts Browne and Blankenship wound up with broken body parts and diminished TOPRs. In the end, the A's offense simply crashed.

As a group that steep TOPR tumble can be attributed to a falloff in several areas. Their team BA dropped to a league low of .254. Steals slipped. But you'd expect that when Henderson didn't contribute to the last two months of the running game. Walks fell by 85 from '92. That's slightly over a half-a-runner per game. That's a major decline. None of these in and of themselves may seem like earth shattering stats. But realize again that '93 saw a giant *jump* in offense in the game. That the A's fell while almost everyone stepped up puts their offensive trouble in a better (or maybe worse) light.

The year, as dismal as it unfolded, was not without some bright spots, however. DH Troy Neel TOPRed at 118, the best of any Oakland everyday player and the only one in the regular lineup all year who managed a triple-digit TOPR. Think of that for a minute and what it says about the A's offense of last season. Once McGwire went down and Henderson went away, the "stud" in the lineup was a 27-year-old rookie who'd starred in high school as an El Campo Ricebird (Texas), had gone to Texas A&M on a football scholarship and had been acquired straight up in January of '91 from Cleveland for Larry Arndt in a somewhat less than ballyhooed deal. His major league resume entering '93 consisted of 53 official at bats. Troy Neel had become their TOPR topper and finished #4 among all AL DHs. LaRussa, by the way, employed 16 hitters in the DH slot. Oakland had, with injuries to various middle infielders, also decided to rush 2B Brent Gates to the majors. Wonderful move. His 98 TOPR ranked fifth among all AL second sackers. SS Bordick's 84 can be looked at in two ways. First, it represented an enormous fall from his 103 of '92. But, given his horrendous start, that figure (6th in the AL at SS) reflects the efforts of a player who spent the last three months of the season trying to erase the awful numbers of the first three months. That's about it for the positives.

Can this engine be fixed in time to make another run in '94? Any chance that Oakland's former top-of-the-line TOPR has of returning begins with a return to health of McGwire. With him at cleanup, Sierra's TOPRs in the 115 area should return. Gates appears to be a player on the come and his TOPRs should increase accordingly. But what about the hole left by Rickey's departure? After all, as woeful as the A's offense performed last season (in comparison with other A's teams), it did so *with* four months of exceptional play from Henderson. What happens to the A's without their igniter? Add that hole to offensive gaps at 3B and CF. Bordick must bounce back at SS. Steinbach, even if he's totally healthy, hasn't TOPRed in triple figures this decade. Unless the A's go out and find some new parts, "more gears" if you will, this attack may have the look of just another used car in '94. And that's not the kind of model Oakland fans want to ride with.

The Pitching

Fifteen pitchers made 15 or more appearances for Oakland last season. Of them, only starter Bobby Witt and relievers Rick Honeycutt and Dennis Eckersley TPERed under 102. Let the enormity of that sink in for just a moment. Unless Witt opened or Honey or Eck came on to get the final outs, manager LaRussa had a worse than average pitcher on the mound for the A's! Other than those three the A's played "Go Fish" for pitching with TPERs ranging from Horsman's 102 to Briscoe's 122. The A's, long feared for their devastating staff, had become little more than a "grab bag" group. And even with that "better than average" trio, "ace" Witt ranked just 28th among AL starters and closer Eckersley had the worst season of his Oakland career finishing a shocking 11th of the 14 AL closers.

Just how bad did things get? Bad! Very bad!

—Oakland employed 22 pitchers and 19 of them won at least one game. Together they walked 680 hitters, the highest ever for an Oakland team and the most in the majors since the '87 Texas staff (with the "Wild Thing" in the pen) which free ticketed 780.

—The A's completed just eight games tying the fewest by this franchise in the period stretching from 1901 to the present.

—They barely missed being the most scored on team in Oakland history falling just 14 runs short of the '79 staff's record of 860.

—That ugly 4.90 ERA represented the worst in the AL in six years, the highest since the team moved to Oakland and the most in franchise history since the 1955 A's (5.35).

—Their use of 424 relievers tied the all-time major league record. (But, of course, at the same time Colorado was setting a new one using 453 in the NL.)

—The "Duncan's Dozen" starters ERAed at 5.19. That represented an incredible jump of 1.32 earned runs *per game* over the previous season.

But it must be pointed out that the A's pitching staff had been, for a couple years already, living on a reputation for quality that was not deserved. Oh, yes, Oakland had won the West in '92. But they'd done it *offensively*. Certainly not with pitching. The '92 title A's TPERed at 100.3. That's right at league average. But realize they play in a park that has long had and long deserved the designation of being a fabulous pitcher's park. To be no more than an average staff in a park that represses offense at approximately 7% really doesn't say much for a staff. And track the A's back one more year. In '91, when they finished fourth and six games over .500, they did so due to the expertise of manager LaRussa and again the offense. The staff actually TPERed at a dismal 106.8. That's downright horrible considering the park situation they pitch in 81 times a season. No, '93 did NOT represent a season in which the A's pitching *collapsed*. It simply was a year in which a few more things went wrong thus causing a staff already on the brink to snap and descend to the depths of the AL dragging the rest of the team with them.

The Rotation: What rotation? It started as Welch, Witt and Darling along with some combination of Storm Davis, Downs and Hillegas in the #4 and #5 slots. By mid-season it had turned into "tag team" pitching with nine hurlers in LaRussa's famous "flotation rotation." By season's end Welch, Witt and Darling had been joined by "the future"—Van Poppel, Karsay and Jimenez. It's obvious that initial trio still holds the key to immediate improvement of the starting group. Witt, through the patient handling of Duncan

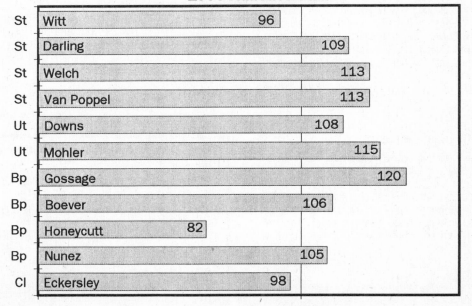

1993 Athletics Staff

St	Witt	96
St	Darling	109
St	Welch	113
St	Van Poppel	113
Ut	Downs	108
Ut	Mohler	115
Bp	Gossage	120
Bp	Boever	106
Bp	Honeycutt	82
Bp	Nunez	105
Cl	Eckersley	98

50   100

and LaRussa, actually made real strides while everything else was collapsing. He dropped his walks-per-9 IP from that ghastly 6.16 in his seven Texas seasons, to 3.73 in Oakland. That's still high for most pitchers. For Witt, it constitutes "fantastic control!" He's now the bellcow. It's the 37-year-old Welch and the 33-year-old Darling (each signed to multi-year, big-bucks contracts) that kept Oakland lying awake on long winter nights. Welch's TPER leaped to 113, 51st among the 54 regular rotation starters in the league. Darling slipped in just ahead of him at 109 and #46. Those are the TPERs and rankings of #5 starters, not #2 and #3. But with Oakland's off-season predicament of basically not having any free agent bucks to throw around and not having any spare stars to trade, the club must cross its fingers and hope last season was a mirage. Maybe for Welch, who'd put together a string of solid TPER seasons before '93. But what of Darling, who's had just one below-100 TPER this decade? And why did Oakland sign him to that contract when he was coming off that one good year?

Karsay, acquired from Toronto for Henderson, supposedly rated as that team's #1 minor league pitching prospect (though many scouts privately prefer RH flame-thrower Jose Silva). But Karsay's a legit prospect, though bothered during his minor league tenure by a tendency to give up the long ball. That wart didn't surface in his eight starts late in the season and his 96 TPER certainly encourages the A's that he might be ready right now. Van Poppel and Jimenez are "homegrown." If either eventually makes it to the majors as a regular rotation type, it'll end a long drought for the A's system. Oakland hasn't produced a major league regular turn-taker since Kevin Tapani, who they selected in the '86 draft. Van Poppel's troubled by terrible wildness (62 BB in 84 IP) leading to his 113 TPER in a half year trial. But he does have a major league arm and, if he can find the plate, could eventually become something special. Jimenez appears a much longer shot. He's got the same awful walks tendency in his minor league profile added to a penchant for yielding the long one. Uh-oh. That's a nasty daily double for a prospect.

The Bullpen: Only Honeycutt performed as advertised. Everything else went south including Eckersley. A 96 TPER might be fine for some guys. But for a future Hall of Famer who spent his career in the rarified TPER air of the 60s and 70s and yes, even a 42 in '90 (do you know how good you have to be to get a 42?), a 98 represents disaster. All of a sudden Eck became hittable (.261) and some of the hits went a long, long way (7 HRs in 67 IP). But after Honeycutt's 82 TPER, LaRussa's choices couldn't exactly be called "appetizing." Davis and Boever (before they left), Mohler, Downs, Gossage, Nunez and Briscoe all TPERed between 106 and 122. Ugh. *You* go to the mound and pick one. LaRussa got tired of doing

it. Lefty spot man Horsman did come in at 102, but pitched only 25 innings in 40 appearances. Somewhere, somehow, this group must be repaired. Unfortunately the best of them, Honeycutt, headed for the free agent market and quickly signed with A's Western Division rival Texas. It appears that everyone else in front of Eckersley must either experience a group revival or a group exit. Expect the A's to do what limited shopping they can this off-season looking for more reclamation projects on which Duncan can hopefully work his magic. But it appears they'll get no help in this area from their system. Starters maybe. Bullpeners—no!

What Next?

Much of Oakland's ability to bounce back to respectability lies in the hands of the gods. Will McGwire and Steinbach come back from injury? Is Sierra's TOPR plummet in '93 proof, as some scouts have contended, that he's bulked up too much and a career decline's already started? Will we ever see the "old Eck" again? Are Welch and Darling aboard baseball's "down elevator"? Oakland has absolutely no choice in this matter, or do they?

Last year having rushed to the bigs almost any kiddo in their organization who could play, there doesn't appear to be any "out-of-nowhere" prospects who'll suddenly take this organization by storm. Henderson's left a gaping hole in left field. But when he exited he also left the door open to his returning if Oakland came up with the bucks (the story of Rickey's life). But should he be gone for good, LF is a black hole and third base is another. The bullpen's a mess. Bobby Witt's suddenly the staff "ace." The rest of the rotation's a set of question marks.

There'll be no predictions of pennant in the "other city by the Bay" approaching '94. But can a franchise used to winning accept that? Might it not have been better for the A's to think "rebuilding" rather than "reloading" for '94? Sometimes teams get so used to thinking of themselves in a certain way (contender, pretender, champion, project) that they can't think straight enough to consider their present situation honestly. We all engage in such practices. It's called self-deception. The plain fact of the matter remains that the team Oakland put on the field last year *deserved* to finish last. Some of that core of "bounce-back types" won't bounce back. Should Oakland have considered tearing the franchise down in the off-season instead of patching holes? It's a decision they must make and only time will judge.

Fortunately, this is a franchise that's become famous for right decisions over the years. The one they make this off-season is critical to what the next few years will look like in Oakland.

Oakland Coliseum

The two Bay Area parks exhibited near-identical Park TOPRs in '93 (Oakland, 93.1; San Francisco, 92.2). In both cases, home hitters got penalized relatively more than the visiting hitters. The park suppressed power more than anything else. But the A's hitters lost 18.3% of their extra-base production when they got off the plane back home in Oakland. Visiting hitters, however, dropped by only −5.2%. The A's pitching staff might have had something to do with that.

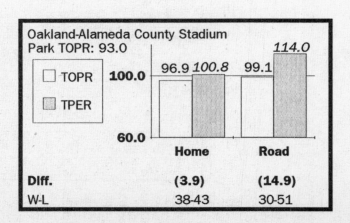

Oakland-Alameda County Stadium
Park TOPR: 93.0

□ TOPR
▨ TPER

	Home	Road
TOPR	96.9	99.1
TPER	100.8	114.0
Diff.	(3.9)	(14.9)
W-L	38-43	30-51

Team TOPR: 1993 Oakland Athletics

	Bats	BA	OBP	SLG	HR	R	RBI	NBE	GOC	Ratio	TOPR
League Avg. Team	-	.267	.337	.408	148	762	719	2897	4352	.666	100
Oakland Athletics	-	.254	.330	.394	158	715	679	2881	4414	.653	98.0
Regulars:											
C Terry Steinbach	R	.285	.331	.416	10	47	43	178	295	.603	91
1B Mark McGwire	R	.333	.467	.726	9	16	24	83	58	1.431	(215)
Mike Aldrete	L	.267	.353	.443	10	40	33	143	198	.722	108
2B Brent Gates	B	.290	.357	.391	7	64	69	270	414	.652	98
3B Craig Paquette	R	.219	.245	.382	12	35	46	161	318	.506	76
SS Mike Bordick	R	.249	.332	.311	3	60	48	248	445	.557	84
LF Rickey Henderson	R	.327	.469	.553	17	77	47	282	230	1.226	184
CF Dave Henderson	R	.220	.275	.427	20	37	53	199	310	.642	96
RF Ruben Sierra	B	.233	.288	.390	22	77	101	311	515	.604	91
DH Troy Neel	L	.290	.367	.473	19	59	63	248	317	.782	118
Bench (100+ TPA):											
MP Lance Blankenship	R	.190	.363	.254	2	43	23	139	225	.618	93
MP Kevin Seitzer	R	.255	.324	.357	4	24	27	115	210	.548	82
MP Jerry Browne	B	.250	.306	.323	2	27	19	105	208	.505	76
C Scott Hemond	R	.256	.353	.414	6	31	26	136	174	.782	117
MP Scott Brosius	R	.249	.296	.390	6	26	25	103	171	.602	90
OF Scott Lydy	R	.225	.288	.333	2	11	7	44	80	.550	(83)

NOTE: Statistics are only for games played with Oakland. ( ) Under 200 TPA.

Team TPER: 1993 Oakland Athletics

	Throws	W-L	GS	GR	SV	IP	ERA	NBA	GOE	Ratio	TPER
League Avg. Team	-	81 -81	162	355	42	1444.1	4.33	2897	4352	0.666	100
Oakland Athletics	-	68 -94	162	424	42	1452.1	4.90	3126	4378	0.714	107.3
The Rotation:											
Bobby Witt	R	14 -13	33	2	0	220	4.21	424	665	0.638	96
Ron Darling	R	5 -9	29	2	0	178	5.16	392	539	0.727	109
Bob Welch	R	9 -11	28	2	0	166.2	5.29	382	506	0.755	113
Todd Van Poppel	R	6 -6	16	0	0	84	5.04	188	251	0.749	113
Steve Karsay	R	3 -3	8	0	0	49	4.04	94	147	0.639	96
Utility:											
Kelly Downs	R	5 -10	12	30	0	119.2	5.64	260	361	0.720	108
Mike Mohler	L	1 -6	9	33	0	64.1	5.60	150	196	0.765	115
Storm Davis	R	2 -6	8	11	0	62.2	6.18	139	188	0.739	111
Shawn Hillegas	R	3 -6	11	7	0	60.2	6.97	159	182	0.874	131
Bullpen:											
Joe Boever	R	4 -2	0	42	0	79.1	3.86	169	240	0.704	106
Edwin Nunez	R	3 -6	0	56	1	75.2	3.81	157	225	0.698	105
Goosse Gossage	R	4 -5	0	39	1	47.2	4.53	113	141	0.801	120
Rick Honeycutt	L	1 -4	0	52	1	41.2	2.81	70	129	0.543	(82)
Dennis Eckersley	R	2 -4	0	64	36	67	4.16	130	199	0.653	98

NOTE: Statistics are only for games pitched with Oakland. ( ) Under 200 TBF.

WHAT MIGHT HAVE BEEN
SEATTLE MARINERS

"For the want of a nail a shoe was lost,
For the want of a shoe a horse was lost . . ."
Benjamin Franklin

"**W**hat if?" Seldom in the Mariners misery-filled histories has a season ended like the '93 year—with the Mariners playing "what if?" What if steady, young lefty Dave Fleming hadn't missed the first two months with an inflamed elbow? What if key free agent signee Chris Bosio hadn't broken his collarbone on April 27 covering first base on a double play and then aggravated the injury during a brawl in Baltimore forcing him to miss a combined 41 games and seven or eight turns in the rotation? What if closer Norm Charlton hadn't blown out his elbow wiping out the last ten-weeks-plus? What if defending batting champ Edgar Martinez hadn't taken that false step in an April 3 exhibition in Vancouver and pulled a hamstring, an injury that would dog him all season long and limit him to a mere 135 at bats? What if first baseman Tino Martinez hadn't torn a knee ligament ending his season on August 10? What if none of this had happened to a team that, despite it all, went on to post an 82–80 record and finish fourth, 12 games back of the division-winning White Sox? What if? What if none of them had been lost?

Team Trendline: Seattle Mariners

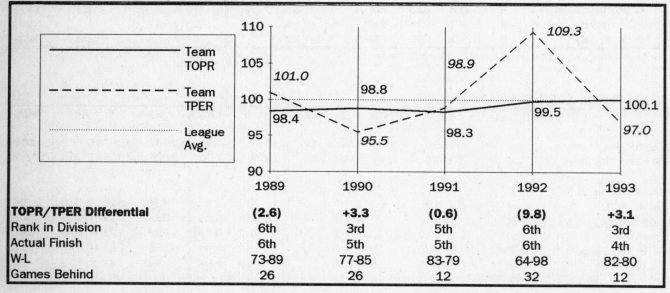

Team TOPR				
Team TPER				
League Avg.				

	1989	1990	1991	1992	1993
TOPR/TPER Differential	(2.6)	+3.3	(0.6)	(9.8)	+3.1
Rank in Division	6th	3rd	5th	6th	3rd
Actual Finish	6th	5th	5th	6th	4th
W-L	73-89	77-85	83-79	64-98	82-80
Games Behind	26	26	12	32	12

TOPR values: 98.4, 98.8, 98.3, 99.5, 100.1
TPER values: 101.0, 95.5, 98.9, 109.3, 97.0

What Was Expected

It's hard to imagine a team that had had just one winning season in 16 years having major hopes. But the Mariners entered '93 looking more than a bit like the cat that had swallowed the canary.

While they had all the historical reasons to be discouraged, they'd quietly gone about putting together the "dark horse" of the AL West. First and foremost they'd hired Lou Pinella, a manager with a Midas touch who'd had winning seasons in his debut years with his two previous franchises. And while "Sweet Lou" did inherit a team with obvious flaws (for one, a pitching staff with an ugly 109.3 TPER from the season before that led to a horrible 34-games-under-.500 finish), Seattle obviously also had some building blocks like Ken Griffey, Jr., batting leader Martinez and a pitching staff that featured holdover standouts in Randy Johnson and Fleming. The M's new ownership had also meant a better financial structure that had enabled them to sign free agent starter Bosio and acquire bullpen stopper and former Cincinnati "Nasty Boy" Charlton. Yes, these were the Mariners who'd posted an ugly 64–98 record the year before. But most observers picked them to be a middle-of-the-pack club with some feeling that if everything broke right they just might contend for the AL West crown. Instead, everything simply broke.

What Actually Happened

The "dark horse" ran well but broke down at key points of the race.

The M's TOPR-TPER numbers have the look of a slightly above average team. An offense that's right at average—100.1. A pitching staff that posted a better-than-expected TPER of 97.0 which represented an enormous improvement from the 109.3 of the season before and the second best TPER of the last five seasons. Combine those two figures and you'd expect to get about what Seattle got— an 82–80 mark. Month by month Seattle gave every indication that they were indeed the classic .500 team basically breaking even every month until stepping up slightly down the September–October stretch.

But one must go inside the numbers to truly grade the Mariners' season. Seattle "managed" to hang around in their division despite the worst injuries imaginable. Seattle used the disabled list 19 times, a club record. Major injuries struck every area of the club ripping middle-of-the-lineup hitters Edgar and Tino Martinez out of Pinella's order. Starters Fleming and Bosio went down for huge chunks of time and closer Charlton exited for good on August 7. In fact, while Seattle title hopes had probably disappeared by then, the August 7–9 stretch drove the final nail in the M's coffin. In consecutive days the club lost Charlton, reliever Brad Holman and 1B Martinez to injury.

The Mariners showed a kind of resilience during the tough times that had seldom marked the team's play historically. Despite the ever changing lineup and hurting staff, the M's still posted the second best record in franchise existence. And during August, when the M's were dropping like flies physically, as previously noted, the club hung in there. Note the TOPR-TPER figures for that month. With the TOPR well below the league average of 100 (M's had a 91.2 for the month) and the pitching staggering to a 107.4, Seattle still somehow scraped together a 14–13 month. But notice that earlier in the season in both April and May, when Seattle's TOPR-TPER numbers were far more positive and thus suggestive of a club that should have been piling up wins, the Mariners finished, in fact, one game beneath .500 combined.

But the final record still left baseball fans in the Great Northwest wondering just what kind of a run the M's might have made had all the club's horses remained healthy.

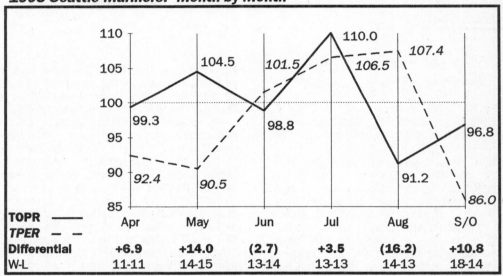

1993 Seattle Mariners: Month-by-Month

	Apr	May	Jun	Jul	Aug	S/O
TOPR ——	99.3	104.5	98.8	110.0	91.2	96.8
TPER – –	92.4	90.5	101.5	106.5	107.4	86.0
Differential	+6.9	+14.0	(2.7)	+3.5	(16.2)	+10.8
W-L	11-11	14-15	13-14	13-13	14-13	18-14

Kingdome

The Mariners' home dome, long thought to be a "hitter's paradise," played as a "neutral" park in '93 (100.8 Park TOPR). There was *no* evidence supporting the contention that the Kingdome was a "homer dome." The M's and their opponents hit only 140 HR there, compared to a total of 156 in away games. In reality, the Kingdome was a better site for a track meet than a hitting contest. The dome had no significant effect on hitting, but its artificial surface enhanced speed, as shown in the below comparison of the Batting and Baserunning Sub-sets for Seattle and their opponents in the dome and away.

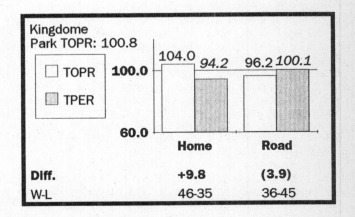

Kingdome
Park TOPR: 100.8

	TOPR	TPER
Home	104.0	94.2
Road	96.2	100.1

	Home	Road
Diff.	+9.8	(3.9)
W-L	46-35	36-45

SEA + Opp. Offense	Batting Sub-set			Baserunner Sub-set		TOPR Ratio
	TBB	TBO	Ratio	BRB	BRO	(NBE/GOC)
At Home	2887	4019	.718	23	298	.674
On the Road	2860	4008	.714	(27)	330	.653

1993 Mariners Lineup

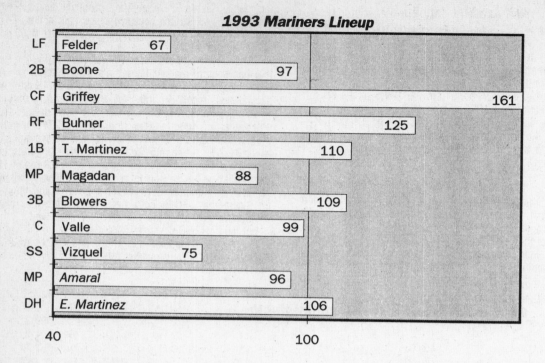

LF	Felder	67
2B	Boone	97
CF	Griffey	161
RF	Buhner	125
1B	T. Martinez	110
MP	Magadan	88
3B	Blowers	109
C	Valle	99
SS	Vizquel	75
MP	*Amaral*	96
DH	*E. Martinez*	106

40   100

The Offense

If you like a solid, consistent lineup you wouldn't have liked the '93 Mariners.

They had the splash and dash of Griffey, Jr.'s 161 TOPR and the breakthrough career year of RF Buhner hitting right behind him in the order (125). But the holes in Pinella's everyday lineup jump out at you: left field and designated hitter.

The positional norm TOPR-wise for AL left-fielders was 121. It was the second most offensive position in the entire league behind first base. But for the M's, LF was the least productive spot in the entire order. Mike Felder, the most frequent to patrol out there, could produce only a measly 67. Henry Cotto failed miserably and was dealt. Rookie Marc Newfield came up and returned quickly to the minors judged to be not ready for prime time. Dann Howitt, Brian Turang, the names came and went and none produced anywhere near what that position was doing for Mariner rivals.

The same could be said for DH, though after Magadan's arrival the position gave the M's a bit more than they'd been getting. Still, Mariner DHs finished ninth in the AL in average (.253), 11th in HRs (19) and 13th in RBIs (77). Here's a club where even George Bell might have looked like an improvement. And here's where the injuries took their toll. Had Edgar Martinez not gotten hurt, sooner or later the club would have probably turned to benchwarmer Mike Blowers to fill that role, even on a part-time basis. As it was, Blowers represented the club's most pleasant offensive surprise. A career .200 hitter, he stepped in for Martinez and gave the M's a 109 TOPR, above the norm for the 3B position in the league. Seldom can any team expect such a happening—that a reserve will replace an injured star and the position will remain above average. But, had Martinez stayed healthy, that Blowers TOPR would have looked mighty good at DH and a healthy Martinez TOPRing around 130 would have made the M's order even more stout.

Boone and Amaral combined to give them a decent 2B. Valle had his best season ever rising to right at the positional norm which, given his catching ability, made the spot an overall plus in the lineup. Vizquel simply must produce more with the bat. His TOPR's 10 points below the norm. Even with his glove work, that's a lot of non-production to accept. And his 14-caught stealings hurt terribly from a player who produced just 18 extra-base hits. Tino Martinez'

TOPR looks fine—110. But the first sackers in this league combined for a positional norm of 125. Hey, there are some big bombers at 1B in the AL! But Tino's emergence (110 is a career high), even though it's below the norm, can be accepted.

What's weird about this uneven lineup is that, even with all the inconsistency, even with the injuries, it should have produced more runs than it did. The M's had a team TOPR right at the league average—100.1. That *should* have resulted in the league average number of runs—769. It didn't. Seattle scored a mere 734 runs, 35 short of what their offense, by all measurements, should have produced. That's significant. But that's been a trait of Pinella-managed teams in the past. Digging back into Pinella's managerial past we find similar happenings in New York and Cincy at times. Take the '93 Indians for comparison. They posted a team TOPR of 100.3, virtually identical to Seattle's. But the Tribe squeezed 790 runs out of that same amount of offensive input. Somewhere Seattle's leaking runs. The leaks must be plugged before '94.

Griffey, Jr.: "Something Extra"

38–3–45. No, this isn't the most unusual set of body measurements in human history. It's Ken Griffey, Jr.'s extra-base-hit line for '93. He accumulated 38 doubles, 3 triples and 45 homers—86 extra basers.

Don't simply pass this total by. Don't let it get lost in all the other magnificent accomplishments for one so young. Extra-base-hit totals this high are usually a combination of talents—exceptional power and outstanding speed. At age 23 Griffey's season thrust him onto a level that's reserved for only the very best. Just what does 86 extra-base hits in a year represent? Perhaps it's best put in perspective by switching from the positive to the negative. Here's a list of players who never had so much as an 80 extra-base-hit season with their single season best total in parentheses.

Lou Brock (66 in '68)
Ralph Kiner (79 in '51)
Brooks Robinson (66 in '64)
Jackie Robinson (64 in '49)

Pete Rose (61 in '78)
Mickey Mantle (79 in '56)
Roberto Clemente (71 in '66)
Carl Yaztrzemski (79 in '67)
Harmon Killebrew (73 in '61)
Ty Cobb (79 in '11)

By the way, those 10 have all made the Hall of Fame. Now let's take that extra step up the ladder. We added the names of players who never topped 85 extras.

Willie McCovey (80 in '70)
Johnny Bench (84 in '70)
Ernie Banks (83 in '57)
George Brett (85 in '79)
Roger Maris (81 in '61)
Ted Williams (85 in '49)
Frank Robinson (85 in '66)

A couple of historical footnotes before we proceed. One very special tip of the hat more than 80 years later to Cobb who managed 79 extra basers in 1911, long before the livelier ball was introduced that so increased the number of homers. Cobb, to get to 79, smacked 47 doubles, 24 triples (both league-leading totals) and eight roundtrippers. And, yes, Maris got only 81 extra-base hits in '61, the year he hit 61 homers. He added just 16 doubles and 4 triples.

"The Kid" and his 86 still fall far short of Babe Ruth's amazing 1921 when he piled up 119 long hits in just a 152-game season. That was one of nine seasons the Babe reached 80. Willie Mays had five 80-or-better years topped by a best of 90 in '62. Lou Gehrig totaled an absolutely amazing 10 seasons of 80+ including 117 in '27. Aaron had only two with 92 in '59 being his best. Joe DiMaggio had three such years with the topper being 96 in 1937. Three players had five such glittering long-hit years where they reached 80: Stan Musial, Rogers Hornsby and Jimmie Foxx while Hank Greenberg had six, with four of them being 96 or better.

But back to Griffey. At 23 what lies ahead? Who knows? But history already places his '93 campaign among the better seasons ever.

Add that to some of his other "youngest" achievements:

—Fifth youngest to ever have three 100 RBI seasons before turning 24 behind Mel Ott, Cobb, WIlliams and DiMaggio (all in the Hall).

—Third most HRs before reaching 24 behind only Ott and Eddie Mathews (both in the Hall).

—Tenth youngest to ever reach 40 HRs in a season behind Ott, Mathews, Bench, DiMaggio, Killebrew, Reggie Jackson, Mays, Aaron (all in the Hall) and Texas wunderkind Juan Gonzalez.

Griffey's now gotten 832 hits before his 24th birthday. At the same point of his career, all-time hit leader Pete Rose was at 309. Junior has 132 homers. At the same stage Aaron had 110. Son-of-Ken already has piled up 453 RBIs. Aaron had 399 at this point.

Only time will determine if Griffey joins the immortals he's now listed with. But his '93 measurements of 38–3–45 already indicate the "shape" of his career.

The Pitching

What would you like first, the good news or the bad news?

The good news—the starters.

The bad news—the bullpen.

Seattle put together a staff that posted an overall 97 TPER, fourth best in the AL behind Chicago, KC and Boston. But the way they went about it gave Pinella ulcers if he didn't already have them.

The Rotation: Actually, we should entitle this sub-segment "What rotation?" The M's started juggling even before the season began (never had their starting five intact until after the All-Star Game, at which point closer Charlton went out for the year).

Crafty young lefty Fleming went down to elbow problems during the spring and would not throw his first pitch until late May. And when he did return, his 101 TPER, though solid enough, looked nothing like the kind of dazzling 88 he'd recorded his rookie campaign.

Bosio put together a very, very nice year. It might have been even better had he not battled the broken collarbone he suffered in a freak injury against Cleveland and had he not reinjured it during a brouhaha against the Orioles. But he put up a stunning 84, sixth best in the league. But then, Bosio'd TPERed at 83–84 the two

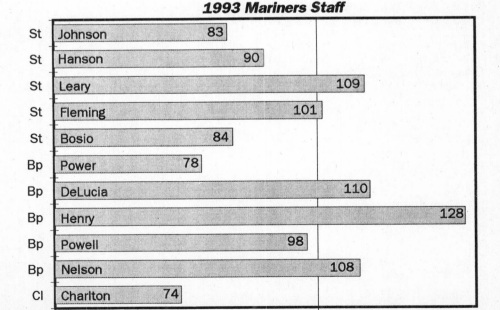

1993 Mariners Staff

St	Johnson	83
St	Hanson	90
St	Leary	109
St	Fleming	101
St	Bosio	84
Bp	Power	78
Bp	DeLucia	110
Bp	Henry	128
Bp	Powell	98
Bp	Nelson	108
Cl	Charlton	74

50   100

previous years, so the M's had spent money wisely for a terrific pitcher and that's what he gave them when well enough to take his turn.

The staff ace, though by just a TPER whisker (83 to 84) over Bosio, was gigantic Randy "The Big Unit" Johnson. After years of being a gaudy though substantially mediocre hurler, the 6'10" former USC basketballer had a superb season. An eight-game win streak and 19 overall victories. People who'd seen his talent in past seasons and could only sigh wondering why he didn't mature, now talked about him being "Cy" as in a Cy Young candidate.

Eric Hanson bounced back from a pair of truly mediocre TPER years (99–101) to give the club the 16th best-rated starter in the AL TOPR-wise. Johnson and Bosio came in at #5 and #6. He was especially effective early, winning his first five decisions and leading our TPER standings through mid-May. He then seemed to lose it dropping a half dozen consecutive decisions before settling in for a decent overall season.

Tim Leary resurrected his career giving the M's a pretty fair #5. He managed 27 starts and 169 innings, important numbers from a #5 on a staff that had injury and middle-relief problems. That 109 TPER won't knock any eyes out. But then, check beneath him on the pitcher TPER standings and you'll find names like Morris, Darling, Navarro, Moore, Welch, Gullickson and Sutcliffe, none of whom represented anything like a #5 starter to their respective staffs.

As a group, M's starters gave Pinella the third best ERA in the league. Even with the injuries they made 141 starts and threw 971 innings—right at seven innings per start. Again, that's significant given the "bad news" part of our equation, the relief corps.

The Bullpen: Actually we'd probably have been better off calling this portion of the club by another word that starts with "bull."

The M's had the worst pen in the AL. A league worst ERA of 4.74. More than 20 blown saves. Charlton (TPER 74) gave the club some end-of-game stability for as long as he remained healthy. But the middle and set-up relief for the season were an overall disaster.

Checking the club rundown you'll see that Ted Power did solid work after being picked off the scrap heap (Cleveland released him). But once you get by his two-month 78 TPER recorded after Charlton went down, you get to the heart of the M's problem. This group might have had a hard time spelling "R-E-L-I-E-F" much less providing it.

Dennis Powell, the best of this corps, TPERed at 98. That made him the 33rd best of the AL in-betweeners. You must then drop all the way to #50 in the league before finding the next best Seattle pen man—Jeff Nelson and his 108.

The club tried everything and everyone. Rich DeLlucia, Bob Ayrault, Dwayne Henry (his 128 TPER ranked him 62nd and dead last on our "tweeners" listings), Mike Hampton, Kevin King, Eric Plantenberg, Russ Swan, Zack Shinall. Well, you get the picture.

Young Brad Holman might have provided more the final month and a half had he not had a baseball lined back off his forehead in Texas on August 8. But by then the die had been cast on this club. The bullpen was nothing but bull.

What Next?

The '94 M's could be extremely dangerous!

Start with starting pitching. Johnson, Bosio and Fleming could all post TPERs in the 80s. So what, you ask? There were only 14 starters in the 80s in the entire league last season and only the White Sox, with an outrageous four of them, had more than two!

Offensively, both Martinezes should be back and healthy—though word is Edgar's hamstring may prevent him from playing in the field. Put them around Griffey and Buhner and you've got a stout middle of the lineup. But if Seattle hasn't plugged its LF and DH black holes, this club will again be doomed to being a sporadic offensive team, producing regular runs only when its studs are on hot streaks like the one Griffey enjoyed last July, homering in eight straight games. Turang and Newfield, a pair of rookies who had look-sees last season, each have the minor league TOPRs to be possibilities though neither looked ready last season. Ideally the solutions in LF and DH would be left-handed hitters so that Seattle could improve on its 47–62 record against RH starters.

Defensively the Mariners led the AL in fielding with a .985 percentage, seventh best in league history.

Faced with the reality that catcher Dave Valle could leave for free agency, the M's dealt Hanson and Bret Boone to Cincy for reliever Bobby Ayala and young backstop Dan Wilson. He's a singles hitter who threw out only 2 of 27 stealers in limited playing time last year in Cincinnati. The Reds staff posted a 5.25 ERA working to Wilson and a 4.39 when anyone else caught. But Pinella's familiar with both the youngsters acquired and the M's system really didn't have a standout catching prospect anywhere near ready.

That brings us to the bullpen. Charlton's gone! The M's released him when it became apparent his major arm injury would wipe out a good deal of the '94 season, his last before free agency. Unless Seattle finds several answers to their late inning problems, this team's in trouble again from the sixth inning on. Perhaps long-time star prospect Roger Salkeld could provide part of the solution. But he's only 23. Isn't that asking a bit much? Maybe youngsters Ayala or King or Plantenberg or Holman or . . . maybe a veteran will step forward like Power or Nelson or. . . .

But when Pinella looks to the Mariner pen he'll not want to see maybes. That's what he saw all last season. Without some definite solutions to their late inning woes "maybe" Seattle can again hang around .500.

But should they solidify the pen, just maybe . . .

Team TOPR: 1993 Seattle Mariners

	Bats	BA	OBP	SLG	HR	R	RBI	NBE	GOC	Ratio	TOPR
League Avg. Team	-	.267	.337	.408	148	762	719	2897	4352	.666	100
Seattle Mariners	-	.260	.339	.406	161	734	681	2917	4379	.666	100.1
Regulars:											
C Dave Valle	R	.258	.354	.395	13	48	63	227	344	.660	99
1B Tino Martinez	L	.265	.343	.456	17	48	60	232	316	.734	110
2B Rich Amaral	R	.290	.348	.367	1	53	44	188	293	.642	96
Bret Boone	R	.251	.301	.443	12	31	38	144	222	.649	97
3B Mike Blowers	R	.280	.357	.475	15	55	57	214	294	.728	109
Dave Magadan	L	.259	.356	.320	1	27	21	107	183	.585	88
SS Omar Vizquel	B	.255	.319	.298	2	68	31	228	454	.502	75
LF Mike Felder	B	.211	.262	.269	1	31	20	128	289	.443	67
CF Ken Griffey, Jr.	L	.309	.408	.617	45	113	109	462	432	1.069	161
RF Jay Buhner	R	.272	.379	.476	27	91	98	365	437	.835	125
DH Pete O'Brien	L	.257	.335	.390	7	30	27	103	167	.617	93
Edgar Martinez	R	.237	.366	.378	4	20	13	77	109	.706	(106)
Bench (100+ TPA):											
OF Mackey Sasser	L	.218	.274	.309	1	18	21	72	158	.456	68
I/O Greg Litton	R	.299	.366	.448	3	25	25	96	135	.711	(107
OF Brian Turang	R	.250	.340	.343	0	22	7	69	111	.622	(93)
C Bill Haselman	R	.255	.316	.423	5	21	16	71	112	.634	(95)
OF Henry Cotto	R	.190	.213	.257	2	10	7	32	90	.356	(53)

NOTE: Statistics are only for games played with Seattle. ( ) Under 200 TPA.

Team TPER: 1993 Seattle Mariners

	Throws	W-L	GS	GR	SV	IP	ERA	NBA	GOE	Ratio	TPER
League Avg. Team	-	81 -81	162	355	42	1444.1	4.33	2897	4352	0.666	100
Seattle Mariners	-	82 -80	162	353	41	1453.2	4.20	2826	4376	0.646	97.0
The Rotation:											
Randy Johnson	L	19 -8	34	1	1	255.1	3.24	424	771	0.550	83
Erik Hanson	R	11 -12	30	1	0	215	3.47	391	650	0.602	90
Tim Leary	R	11 -9	27	6	0	169.1	5.05	369	508	0.726	109
Dave Fleming	L	12 -5	26	0	0	167.1	4.36	338	503	0.672	101
Chris Bosio	R	9 -9	24	5	1	164.1	3.45	277	494	0.561	84
John Cummings	L	0 -6	8	2	0	46.1	6.02	95	141	0.674	101
Bullpen:											
Jeff Nelson	R	5 -3	0	71	1	60	4.35	129	179	0.721	108
Dwayne Henry	R	2 -1	1	30	2	54	6.67	137	161	0.851	128
Dennis Powell	L	0 0	2	31	0	47.2	4.15	93	143	0.650	(98)
Rich DeLucia	R	3 -6	1	29	0	42.2	4.64	94	128	0.734	(110)
Brad Holman	R	1 -3	0	19	3	36.1	3.72	54	109	0.495	(74)
Ted Power	R	2 -2	0	25	13	25.1	3.91	39	75	0.520	(78)
Norm Charlton	L	1 -3	0	34	18	34.2	2.34	53	107	0.495	74

NOTE: Statistics are only for games pitched with Seattle. ( ) Under 200 TBF.

A MOMENT OF TRUTH
TEXAS RANGERS

Friday, June 25. Rain poured down on Arlington Stadium canceling the Rangers game against Oakland. The weather seemed fitting for it appeared that this Ranger team was a sinking ship taking on water at an alarming rate. They'd fallen eight games under .500 after leading the division the first weeks of the year. Texas had lost 21 of 29. Four weeks earlier, rookie manager Kevin Kennedy had foolishly allowed slugger Jose Canseco to throw an inning of relief in Boston and ever since it was Canseco who'd needed relief—from an aching elbow. DH Julio Franco was still limping on a surgically repaired knee. Night after night Canseco or Franco or both would scratch themselves from the middle of the lineup. Locker room grumbling got louder and louder. Nolan Ryan was hurt. Shortstop had become a revolving door. It was at this point on Friday, June 25, that Kennedy, with the support of the team's GM Tom Grieve and President Tom Schieffer, laid down the law in a closed-door meeting. He told Franco to either go full speed or go away. He ordered Canseco onto the DL. Suddenly the dark clouds disappeared. Texas began winning and never stopped posting a 55–37 record for the last three months plus, fifth best in the majors.

Team Trendline: Texas Rangers

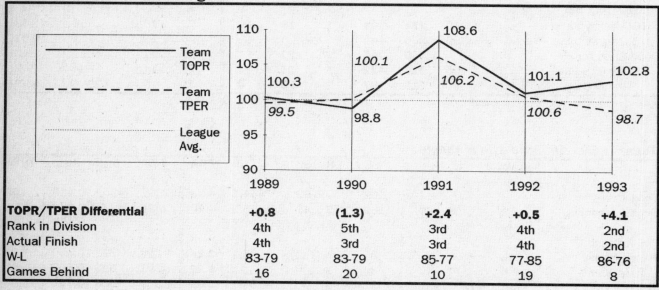

TOPR/TPER Differential	+0.8	(1.3)	+2.4	+0.5	+4.1
Rank in Division	4th	5th	3rd	4th	2nd
Actual Finish	4th	3rd	3rd	4th	2nd
W-L	83-79	83-79	85-77	77-85	86-76
Games Behind	16	20	10	19	8

What Was Expected

Texas fans have learned to live with lowered expectations. This club, which had often featured some of the bright young stars in the game, had managed middle-of-the-pack finishes the previous four years (4–3–3–4). That's generally where most had picked Texas again in '93. Starter Jose Guzman had left to free agency. Bobby Witt had been dealt away late the season before along with bullpen stopper Jeff Russell. The annual hole at shortstop had been plugged by the signing of Manny Lee from Toronto. Veteran lefties Charlie Liebrandt, Craig Lefferts and Bob Patterson had been added to fill staff roles. Tom Henke, one of the finest closers in the game year after year, had cost the team another eight million over two years. They still had that slugging middle with Canseco, Juan Gonzalez, Dean Palmer and Raffy Palmeiro. Mix in baby-faced Pudge Rodriguez behind the plate and Texas had some very attractive puzzle parts. Oh, sure, there were the annual holes in the pitching staff and second base was unsettled. But no one in the jumbled West really frightened anyone. So the Rangers and their fans crossed their fingers that they'd get one more productive season out of Nolan Ryan, that the new vets on the staff would give the club the kind of depth they'd never had in the seven-and-a-half-year Bobby Valentine regime and that the booming bats would carry the club to something Texas had never enjoyed in 21 previous seasons—a September to remember.

What Actually Happened

By mid-season the Rangers' master plan had become a shambles. Ryan and Liebrandt had landed on the shelf. Ryan had one first-half victory. Liebrandt wouldn't win a game after the all-star break. Canseco had had elbow surgery and any discussion about him concerned whether or not he'd be ready for *next* season. Texas had played six shortstops, six center-fielders and was well on its way to using eight right-fielders. In all, the franchise used the disabled list a record 27 times involving 19 different players. Veterans Lefferts and Patterson provided little relief. From the start of spring training games in early March through the end of the season, manager Kennedy would use the regular nine-man lineup he wanted a grand total of 11 times!

With all that turmoil you'd think the club would have finished south of the Mexican League. Wrong! Kenny Rogers and Roger Pavlik came out of nowhere to give Texas a pair of young, sturdy starters. Role players like Mario Diaz, Doug Strange and Gary Redus made major contributions. And the cannonading continued from the middle of the lineup even without Canseco. Gonzalez, Palmeiro and Palmer thumped 116 homers, the sixth most ever from a trio of teammates. Rookie CF David Hulse developed into a contributor. But perhaps most significant, Texas found it had a rookie who could manage in the majors.

Kennedy juggled, platooned and squeezed terrific performances out of some spare parts and kept the wheels on a team that actually drew within two and a half games of Chicago on September 13, the closest a Ranger team had ever been that late in the season.

1993 Texas Rangers: Month-by-Month

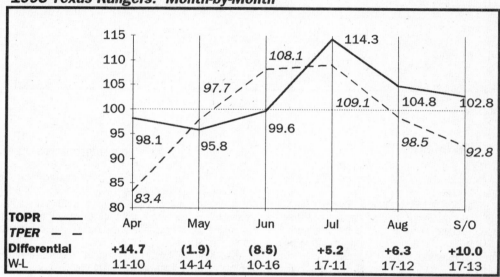

	Apr	May	Jun	Jul	Aug	S/O
TOPR ——	98.1	95.8	99.6	114.3	104.8	102.8
TPER – –	83.4	97.7	108.1	109.1	98.5	92.8
Differential	**+14.7**	**(1.9)**	**(8.5)**	**+5.2**	**+6.3**	**+10.0**
W-L	11-10	14-14	10-16	17-11	17-12	17-13

Arlington Stadium

Arlington remained a modest "pitcher's park" in '93, but in a one-sided way. The Texas pitchers thrived, becoming a staff of "aces" at home (90.7 TPER). They went about it strangely too—suppressing singles and walks but *not* slugging. Opponents' batting average dropped significantly (.251 at home vs. .282 on the road) as did OBP (.317 at home vs. .356 away). But isolated power (extra bases divided by AB) was almost the same (.133 at home, .144 away).

Arlington Stadium will be gone in '94, replaced by The Ballpark in Arlington, a magnificent and elegantly named facility. Like most of the new generation parks. This palace will favor hitters with an inviting RF porch and even more shelter from the Texas winds.

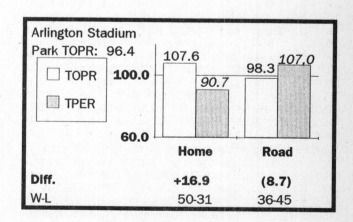

Arlington Stadium Park TOPR: 96.4		
□ TOPR ■ TPER	Home	Road
	107.6 / 90.7	98.3 / 107.0
Diff.	**+16.9**	**(8.7)**
W-L	50-31	36-45

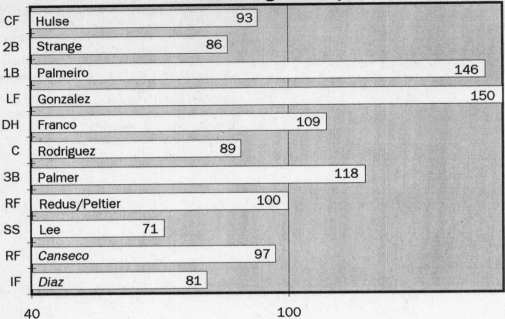

1993 Rangers Lineup

CF	Hulse	93
2B	Strange	86
1B	Palmeiro	146
LF	Gonzalez	150
DH	Franco	109
C	Rodriguez	89
3B	Palmer	118
RF	Redus/Peltier	100
SS	Lee	71
RF	*Canseco*	97
IF	*Diaz*	81

40   100

The Offense

There's a temptation to think of these Rangers, who led the majors in homers with 181, as fencebusters and nothing more. TOPR tells us that would be wrong. So wrong.

In the midst of Texas' barrage of roundtrippers, Kennedy found a way to create far more runs than Texas should have scored. Their team TOPR of 102.8 was fifth best in the AL, just behind Baltimore and right ahead of the White Sox. But notice the kind of scoring the Rangers generated from their offensive input.

	TOPR	Runs
Baltimore	102.9	786
Texas	102.8	835
Chicago	102.1	776

The Rangers and Orioles basically generated the same amount of offense. But Texas somehow (manager?) turned theirs into 49 more runs than the O's and 59 more than the team just below them on the TOPR rankings. In the Seattle team offensive essay, we detailed how the Mariners had "underproduced" given the amount of offensive "pieces" they'd assembled. Texas "overproduced" and that's generally traceable to a manager making wise decisions as to when to play for a single run given the circumstances and likewise when to go for the jugular in an inning. Kennedy gets high marks in this area and part of it may be attributable to his managerial upbringing in an NL system and his understanding the "little inning" theory of managing that we expound on in an essay comparing AL ball to NL ball.

But the ability to manufacture runs is just one element that leaps off the Rangers offensive stat sheet. Another concerns Canseco. Could it be that the Texas offense actually got *better* when he went away? No way, Jose, you say? Think again. Canseco headed for the DL for good in late June. Texas was at that point concluding its third consecutive below-average TOPR month. All of a sudden the Ranger attack exploded for three straight superb TOPR months (July, August and September) leading to three consecutive solid monthly records of 17–11, 17–12 and 17–13. Good baseball.

This is not to blame Canseco for the offense's early failings though he was having a TOPR year (97) far beneath the norm for

his position (105), and even farther below the standards he'd set for himself (a 136 average for the first three seasons of the decade). Rather, the Rangers' outburst must focus on the "Texas two-step" of Franco's resurrection and the incredible months Palmeiro experienced right after Canseco left. Those two, combined with the constant power production of Gonzalez and Palmer, created a Ranger machine that averaged more than six runs per game for the entire month of July.

Had Kennedy gotten more input from the two top spots in his order, heaven knows what kind of scoring Texas might have generated in a year that, as it was, broke the all-time franchise record for runs. Young CF Hulse, who'd played less than 400 professional games before winning the regular job, TOPRed at a 93, 13 points below the norm for a CF, and one of the lower leadoff TOPRs in the league (Milwaukee, Seattle, California and KC finished below Texas in the #1 batting order spot). Second baseman Doug Strange also finished 14 points below the norm for a 2B, but one must remember that he was, at best, the club's fifth choice at that position until injuries wiped out Franco (as a fielder), Billy Ripken, Jeff Huson and Jeff Frye. That Strange 86 may look low. But his steady play was, in fact, a godsend for a Ranger team desperate to find some stability at the position.

Once a pitcher arrived at Texas' #3 spot, he waded into the "deep water." Palmeiro and Gonzalez were the AL's 7th and 6th best TOPR stars. Franco, after a lagging start, weighed in as an above-average DH with his 109 TOPR. Rodriguez, whose lack of walks and extremely high DP count dragged him down, finished well below the average backstop. But Palmer, generally hitting in the seven spot, gave the offense an enormous power potential from that slot. Kennedy got decent mileage out of his corps of RFs after Canseco went down. Lee, out of the lineup a good part of the year and useless offensively until September, dragged down the bottom of the order until suddenly coming to life and hitting over .300 the last five weeks.

As a club, Texas still doesn't walk nearly enough. You'd expect big boppers, like those in the Ranger order, to draw many free passes as pitchers carefully worked around them. Not these Rangers. Just 483 walks. Only KC had less. As a means of comparison, notice that Detroit and New York, who each banged 178 HRs (just three less than the Rangers), drew 765 and 629 walks, hundreds more than Texas. But the walkless problem in the Rangers' lineup doesn't rest with the free swinging big guys as much as it does with the little people. Hulse and Strange at the top of the order and Lee at the bottom combined to draw just 91 walks! Those coming in 1,222 plate appearances. Add this deficiency to the fact that Gonzalez and Rodriguez basically will not take a walk and the Texas offense, outstanding though it is, suffers.

And finally, given the amount of pop in this lineup, will someone please explain how this team went the month of April without ever scoring a first inning run? Just one more weirdism on a team with puzzling offensive patterns but an attractive bottom line.

The Pitching

Lots of things went wrong. Several things went right.

If, before the season, you'd have known that ace Kevin Brown would be incredibly streaky. If you'd have known veterans Nolan Ryan and Charlie Liebrandt would each miss half the year with injuries and total just 14 wins. If you'd have known the middlemen and set-up portion of the pen would crater. If you'd have known all this, you'd have figured Texas would nestle into a cozy spot at the bottom of the AL West standings.

But . . . if you'd have known that rookie Roger Pavlik would return from an April banishment to the minors to go 12–6. If any one could have foreseen former bullpener Kenny Rogers making a spectacular conversion to starter posting a 16–10 mark. If you had known Tom Henke would be at his terminating best setting an all-time Texas record for saves. If you'd have known all these facts before the season, you'd have picked the Rangers to win the division for the first time in club history.

The Rotation: For much of the year, pitching coach Claude Osteen's five-man rotation was at best a four-man and down the stretch just a three-man.

Brown, coming off a 21-win '92, bolted from the gate to go 4–1. Then he struggled through a 1–5 stretch. He rebounded to go 4–1, then slumped through his last five August starts (1–4, ERA 6.00) before a scorching 5–0, 1.74 finish. It all added up to two things: An overall solid 85 TPER and lots of head scratching among the Ranger coaches.

Rogers had had a previously horrible experience as a starter. But in spring training he requested a shot at starting again. For the first three months he struggled. But from July 6 on he rang up an 11–4 record, the most wins by any AL pitcher from that point on.

Pavlik had been the disappointment of the spring. So much so that Texas shipped him off to Oklahoma City, stuck veteran Craig Lefferts in the rotation and forged ahead. But Lefferts got bombed and Ryan got hurt. Pavlik got recalled. And the rest is, as they say, history. Texas compiled a gaudy 19–7 record in his starts, winning the last 10. And realize, this is a team that finished just 10 games over .500. He TPERed at 96, just behind Rogers, giving Texas three of the league's top 30 starters.

You had to feel for Ryan. He so wanted to go out in style in his history-making 27th major league season. Instead, one injury followed another. When able, he gave Texas a 100 TPER. In other words, it took 27 years, but Ryan finally became just an average pitcher.

Liebrandt's shoulder ached but he continued to pitch. His nine victories topped the club at the all-star break. He would win no more. A pitcher who'd spent his career TPERing in the 80s and 90s rose to a 108.

By September Texas' rotation had been reduced to Brown, Rogers and Pavlik. Rookie Steve Dreyer came up to make a couple emergency starts. Ryan and Liebrandt made unsuccessful last gasps. All in all it could have been a lot worse had Rogers and Pavlik not stepped forward. But it could have been something special had Ryan and Liebrandt held together.

The Bullpen: The left-handed side completely cratered. Lefferts, Patterson and Bohanon all put up mediocre-to-ugly TPERs. All were released at season's end. Todd Burns and mid-season acquisition Cris Carpenter fared little better. Only Matt Whiteside, of the middle guys, posted a TPER worth talking about (85). But even his season was a model of inconsistency with him performing brilliantly early and then slumping so badly in mid-year that Texas bought him a plane ticket to Oklahoma City. As a group, the Texas "tweeners" pitched unacceptably. And most paid for their poor performance by losing their jobs during or after the season.

Only Henke stood out. The sixth best closer TPER in the league. But #4 if you figure that Boston's Russell and Seattle's Charlton couldn't hold together physically to finish the year.

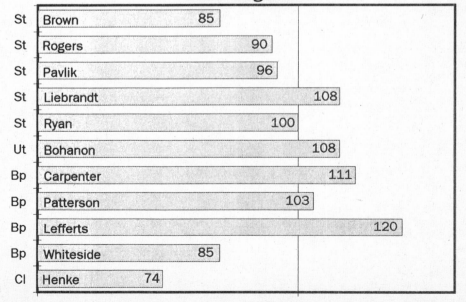

1993 Rangers Staff

		TPER
St	Brown	85
St	Rogers	90
St	Pavlik	96
St	Liebrandt	108
St	Ryan	100
Ut	Bohanon	108
Bp	Carpenter	111
Bp	Patterson	103
Bp	Lefferts	120
Bp	Whiteside	85
Cl	Henke	74

50   100

In total, Texas TPERed at 98.7, their best mark in the last five years. The presence of Osteen resulted in drops in walks and wild pitches and a leap in pickoffs. Tiny things. But all elements of winning baseball.

What Next?

Texas figures to be the pre-season pick to win the realigned four-team AL West. But just because they're favorites doesn't mean there aren't holes.

With Palmeiro and Franco gone to free agency, the Rangers have lost two of the integral parts of their terrific offense over the final half of '93. Free agent signee Will Clark replaces Palmeiro's smoking left-handed hitting bat. But can Canseco make it all the way back to DH? If so, the core of the lineup again will be among the most feared in the league.

The lightweight TOPRs at SS, 2B and CF must be improved. Lee holds down shortstop until super prospect Benji Gil takes over in '95. Hulse, if he learns to walk more, should be more than adequate in CF. With as young as Gonzalez, Palmer and Rodriguez are, their TOPRs figure to continue to rise with Rodriguez having by far the most room for improvement. RF figures to be the most competitive spot in the lineup with a half dozen players having designs on playing time there. But if Canseco should make it *all* the way back and be able to play afield (even though he'd fallen to a below-par fielder before the injury) it opens the DH spot. But the Texas defense, never a strong point (11th in the AL in fielding last year with 132 errors—the fewest since 1988) probably would prefer that Canseco's position be "batter" and someone capable of truly patrolling that spot take over like the late-blooming Rob Ducey or respected veteran Gary Redus.

The club moves into its spectacular new home next year and the millions more in extra revenue enabled Texas to make some early off-season moves. Clark's signing grabbed all the headlines. But maybe just as significant was the inking of Oakland left-handed set-up man Rick Honeycutt. "Honey," after a couple of injury dotted years, regained his place of prominence amongst set-up men in '93 with that excellent 82 TPER. Combined with the underrated Whiteside, late season pickup Gene Nelson (TPER 92) and, hopefully, a bounce back from Carpenter, the Rangers relief corps has a chance to be among the best in the majors should the dependable Henke just keep steaming along at age 36.

The rotation won't have Ryan or Liebrandt. But then, Texas didn't have them much of last season. Brown, Rogers and Pavlik form a solid nucleus IF the seasons of Rogers and Pavlik last year weren't mirages. Superb prospect Rick Helling knocked everyone's eyes out as he reached Triple A last year and appears ready for the #4 spot. Barring a veteran pickup, Dreyer figures to get the first shot at being #5. But there's precious little depth here. They'll be OK if nothing goes wrong with their starters. But that's what lots of teams say heading into new seasons. In fact, that's what Texas said last year.

Team TOPR: 1993 Texas Rangers

		Bats	BA	OBP	SLG	HR	R	RBI	NBE	GOC	Ratio	TOPR
	League Avg. Team	-	.267	.337	.408	148	762	719	2897	4352	.666	100
	Texas Rangers	-	.267	.329	.431	181	835	780	2969	4340	.684	102.8
Regulars:												
C	Ivan Rodriguez	R	.273	.315	.412	10	56	66	226	380	.595	89
1B	Rafael Palmeiro	L	.295	.371	.554	37	124	105	431	443	.973	146
2B	Doug Strange	B	.256	.318	.360	7	58	60	222	388	.572	86
3B	Dean Palmer	R	.245	.321	.503	33	88	96	323	412	.784	118
SS	Manuel Lee	B	.220	.300	.259	1	31	12	83	176	.472	71
	Mario Diaz	R	.273	.297	.361	2	24	24	90	167	.539	81
LF	Juan Gonzalez	R	.310	.368	.632	46	105	118	382	383	.997	150
CF	David Hulse	L	.290	.333	.369	1	71	29	195	314	.621	93
RF	Jose Canseco	R	.255	.308	.455	10	30	46	121	187	.647	97
	Gary Redus	R	.288	.351	.459	6	28	31	125	168	.744	112
	Dan Peltier	L	.269	.352	.344	1	23	17	71	126	.563	(85)
DH	Julio Franco	R	.289	.360	.438	14	85	84	298	409	.729	109
Bench (100+ TPA):												
OF	Butch Davis	R	.245	.273	.415	3	24	20	79	126	.627	(94)
OF	Doug Dascenzo	B	.199	.239	.288	2	20	10	55	122	.451	(68)
C	Geno Petralli	B	.241	.348	.301	1	16	13	60	107	.561	(84)
IF	Billy Ripken	R	.189	.270	.220	0	12	11	42	121	.347	(52)
OF	Rob Ducey	L	.282	.351	.494	2	15	9	54	69	.783	(118)

NOTE: Statistics are only for games played with Texas. ( ) Under 200 TPA.

Team TPER: 1993 Texas Rangers

	Throws	W-L	GS	GR	SV	IP	ERA	NBA	GOE	Ratio	TPER
League Avg. Team	-	81 -81	162	355	42	1444.1	4.33	2897	4352	0.666	100
Texas Rangers	-	86 -76	162	359	45	1438.1	4.28	2848	4336	0.657	98.7
The Rotation:											
Kevin Brown	R	15 -12	34	0	0	233	3.59	401	708	0.566	85
Kenny Rogers	R	16 -10	33	2	0	208.1	4.10	392	623	0.629	95
Roger Pavlik	R	12 -6	26	0	0	166.1	3.41	321	501	0.641	96
Charlie Liebrandt	L	9 -10	26	0	0	150.1	4.55	326	454	0.718	108
Nolan Ryan	R	5 -5	13	0	0	66.1	4.88	135	203	0.665	100
Utility:											
Brian Bohanon	L	4 -4	8	28	0	92.2	4.76	201	280	0.718	108
Steve Dreyer	R	3 -3	6	4	0	41	5.71	95	124	0.766	(115)
Bullpen:											
Craig Lefferts	L	3 -9	8	44	0	83.1	6.05	200	251	0.797	120
Matt Whiteside	R	2 -1	0	60	1	73	4.32	125	220	0.568	85
Todd Burns	R	0 -4	5	20	0	65	4.57	138	198	0.697	105
Bob Patterson	L	2 -4	0	52	1	52.2	4.78	108	157	0.688	103
Cris Carpenter	R	4 -1	0	27	1	32	4.22	69	93	0.742	(111)
Tom Henke	R	5 -5	0	66	40	74.1	2.91	112	226	0.496	74

NOTE: Statistics are only for games pitched with Texas. ( ) Under 200 TBF.

WAMCO
TORONTO BLUE JAYS

Why'd Toronto win it all again in the AL? WAMCO, that's why. The acronym "WAMCO" stands for White, Alomar, Molitor, Carter and Olerud, the top five hitters in the Blue Jays lineup through the first two-thirds of the season. All had TOPRs of 113 or better. Basically what the Blue Jays did was bludgeon opponents into submission. Not that Toronto didn't understand they had a fundamental weakness in their pitching staff. They understood very well and tried mightily to rectify it through trades as the season progressed. But, with no proper deal presenting itself, the Jays decided that they'd have to win it all with offense. Sooooo, WAMCO became HAMCOW with Rickey Hender-son's fat 124 TOPR added to the top of their lineup and White dropped to sixth. Would it not have been even more appropriate if manager Gaston had simply slipped Henderson into the number-two slot in this batting order of bangers thus changing the acronym to "WHAMCO"? WHAMCO indeed! But as if that wasn't enough, along the way they also added an "F" player—star shortstop Tony Fernandez. Opposing AL pitchers looked at that Jays lineup and said several "F words." In '89 Toronto won the East with a solid TOPR-TPER balance. In '91 they were back atop the AL East with a barely-above-average attack but boasting a fantastic pitching staff. In '93 they featured the offense of WAMCO and HAMCOW plus F.

Team Trendline: Toronto Blue Jays

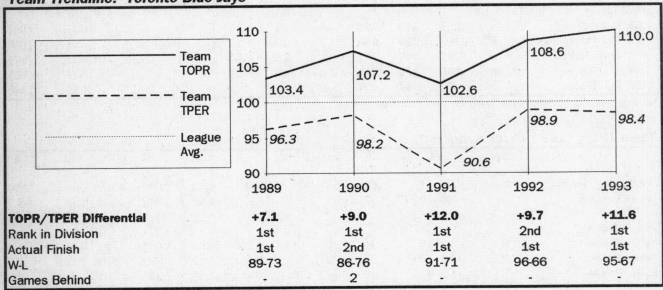

	1989	1990	1991	1992	1993
TOPR/TPER Differential	+7.1	+9.0	+12.0	+9.7	+11.6
Rank in Division	1st	1st	1st	2nd	1st
Actual Finish	1st	2nd	1st	1st	1st
W-L	89-73	86-76	91-71	96-66	95-67
Games Behind	-	2	-	-	-

What Was Expected

Baseball observers have come to expect Toronto in first place. After all, counting '93, in four of the last five years the Blue Jays haven't spent a day in September or October out of first. And remember, this was the defending champion of baseball. Or were they? The Jays entered last season with the lowest percentage of returning innings pitched and at bats of any World Series winner in history. Gone, through trade, free agency, expansion or what have you, were pitching ace David Cone, steady lefty Jimmy Key, stopper Tom Henke, lefty David Wells and long-time Blue Jays star Dave Stieb. And that's just the pitching staff. Veteran DH Dave Winfield had headed for Minnesota. Also absent was the entire left side of the champion's '92 lineup—SS Manny Lee, 3B Kelly Gruber and LF Candy Maldonado. The bench bats of Derek Bell and Pat Tabler had also exited. From mid-spring training '92 through the start of '93 the Jays organization had lost 24 players. But the power-packed offensive core of White, Alomar, Carter and Olerud (then only "WACO") remained. And the Jays busily went about adding to it signing the "M"—Paul Molitor to DH. They plugged Ed Sprague in at 3B and Dick Schofield at SS, signed Oakland bellcow Dave Stewart for the rotation, slotted Danny Cox and Tony Castillo into their bullpen and presto—everyone expected these "new Jays" to be just as fierce as the "old Jays" of 1992.

What Actually Happened

For the first time in anyone's memory the Blue Jays began a season using a term that had been, until then, "foreign" to the ultra-successful Canadian franchise—"budgetary restraint." Oh, they still had one of the game's highest payrolls, right up there with the Yanks, Red Sox and Mets (Ugh!). But Toronto'd decided to fill some holes from within their prospect-heavy farm system instead of simply throwing money at their holes (what few they had). However, by the end of the season the payroll had risen to an all-time baseball single-season high of $48,169,166. They'd opened their coffers to add Henderson and Fernandez. They'd have spent more had a reasonable deal for a high-priced pitcher presented itself. And they rolled merrily along.

Imagine a team winning the pennant without a starter ranked in the top 25 TPERs in the league? That's what Toronto did. In fact, the Jays won it all with only two of their starting five rated as "better than average" by TPER standings. But there are lots of ways to win titles and the Jays have become adept at finding all of them. Last year they combined a thunderous attack with a superb bullpen, blended in two all-stars from later deals and put another 95-win season in the books.

The key to Toronto's success can be found in their monthly TOPR-TPER trendline. Actually, in just the TOPR trends. The Jays played 27 games over .500 in May, June, August and September because of one overriding fact—they pounded the ball. In each of those months Toronto had a Team TOPR of 110 or better topped by that staggering 118.5 down the stretch. If anyone tries to feed you that old baseball cliché that "good pitching always stops good hitting," point to the '93 Jays and proudly say "Not always!"

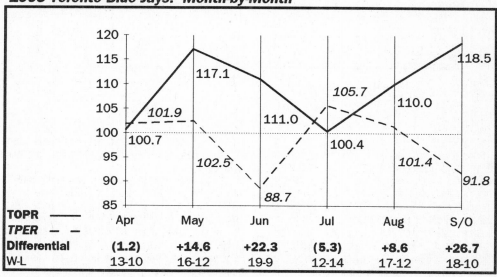

1993 Toronto Blue Jays: Month-by-Month

	Apr	May	Jun	Jul	Aug	S/O
TOPR ———	100.7	117.1	111.0	100.4	110.0	118.5
TPER − −	101.9	102.5	88.7	105.7	101.4	91.8
Differential	(1.2)	+14.6	+22.3	(5.3)	+8.6	+26.7
W-L	13-10	16-12	19-9	12-14	17-12	18-10

Skydome

Recognized as a "hitter's park" since opening in mid-season '89, Skydome favors sluggers capable of the extra-base knock. But, in '93, only the *opponents'* sluggers benefited. The Blue Jays' pitchers got *pasted* at home—posting a league-worst 103.8 home TPER. Away from Skydome they posted a 2nd-best-in-the-league 92.8 road TPER. The latter equals an outstanding "park-adjusted" 88.8 TPER, so the collapse at home is really puzzling—suggesting the Toronto staff is somehow ill-adapted to the park. The Blue Jays' hitters, on the other hand, benefited only to the extent of a normal home/road differential.

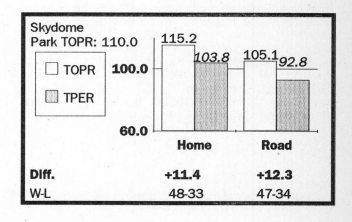

Skydome
Park TOPR: 110.0

	Home	Road
TOPR	115.2	105.1
TPER	103.8	92.8
Diff.	+11.4	+12.3
W-L	48-33	47-34

1993 HAMCOW (formerly WAMCO)

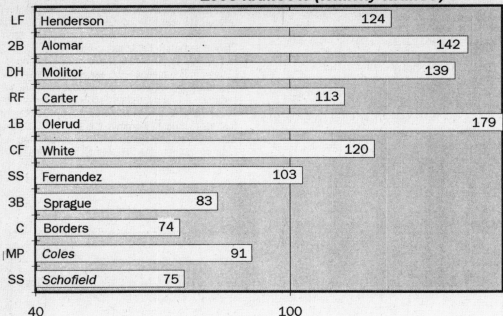

LF	Henderson	124
2B	Alomar	142
DH	Molitor	139
RF	Carter	113
1B	Olerud	179
CF	White	120
SS	Fernandez	103
3B	Sprague	83
C	Borders	74
MP	*Coles*	91
SS	*Schofield*	75

40   100

The Offense

Just how good must a team's attack be when, as it headed down the stretch of another pennant drive, the *weak link* in the order's top six hitters was Joe Carter who's averaged 32 HR, 114RBI and 15 SB a year for the last five seasons?

But "weak" was precisely what Carter's TOPR graded out as amid this bevy of bashers. His 113 ranked sixth best among the top six hitters in the Blue Jays stretch run lineup. All six ranked above the norms for their positions. That's right, six. No other team could boast of such an "offensive" lineup. And that batting order could literally do everything. The .279 team BA's the best in team history. They led the majors with 518 extra-base hits and they had seven players get at least 30 doubles including two who weren't members of "WAMCO"—Sprague and Borders. Five stole at least 21 bases last year. Four finished in the top 10 TOPRs in the league: Olerud (#1), Henderson (#3), Alomar (#8) and Molitor (#10). For the first time in exactly 100 years a team had the top three finishers in the batting race (Olerud, Molitor, Alomar). The 1893 Philadelphia team had been the last to accomplish that with outfielders "Slidin' Billy" Hamilton (.380), Sam Thompson (.370) and Ed Delehanty (.368). (By the way, that team finished *fourth*!)

The accolades go on and on. The club led the AL in slugging percentage (.436); had three 100-RBI men for the first time in franchise history ("weakling" Carter, Molitor and Olerud); broke the team record for runs scored (847); was shutout once (congratulations Fernando Valenzuela!); and had four players score at least 100 runs.

If you look long enough you *can* find some "soft spots" in the lineup. Borders had the worst TOPR of his career and 13th among AL starting catchers. Sprague's 83 brought him in 19 points below the norm for the 3B position in the league. And if you really want to nit-pick, their pinch hitters stunk. Manager Gaston used an all-time low of 27 PH and they produced five hits (a mere .185 BA). But then, when you look up and down this lineup, one overriding question surfaces—who do you pinch-hit for?

All in all, the Jays lineup could remind you of the closing line of the weekly monologue of humorist Garrison Keillor who describes his fictional hometown of Lake Woebegone as being: "Where all the men are strong, all the women are beautiful and all the children are above average." Sounds like the Blue Jays offense.

The lineup had terrific balance with three switch hitters (Alomar, White and Fernandez). It had power scattered everywhere with eight different Jays being in double figures in HRs. Only the shortstop position didn't represent a threat to go deep. And, just for grins, mix in the fact that Alomar and White received Gold Gloves for a Jays team that ranked ninth in the major leagues in fielding percentage.

The Pitching

Can you win it all with average pitching? You bet. In fact, you can do it two years in a row. The proof's just north of the border.

The Jays team TPER of 98.4 made them the AL's sixth best staff, just behind Baltimore and immediately ahead of Texas. It's the second straight season Toronto's staff's finished in the middle-of-the-pack while the club's risen to the top-of-the-heap.

As a staff, Jays pitchers profiled as being: a bit more difficult to hit and score on than the average AL staff, easier to run on, less likely to throw the rally-killing DP ball but also less likely to yield HRs or other types of extra-base hits. One extremely bizarre trait marked Toronto pitchers—they performed far, far better on the road than at Skydome. Note the seasonal breakdown showing them as a below average 103.8 TPER at home, making them the league's worst home-park staff, and a road TPER of 92.8, second best away figure to the White Sox. Why? Well, as they say in the beer commercial "Why ask why?" Ah, baseball can be a mystifying game at times.

But to portray this group as mediocre is unfair. It elevates one-half of the staff (the starters) and denigrates the other half (the relievers).

The Rotation: Would you believe that nine other AL staffs had at least one starter who TPERed better than the Jays ace Juan Guzman? The White Sox had five! That's right, Guzman's 96 would not have made him eligible to crack the Sox starting five of (in order): Fernandez, McDowell, Bere, Alvarez and late-season acquisition Belcher. Baltimore had three starters ranked better than the Toronto leader. So did Boston and Kansas City. The only teams with "aces" rated beneath Guzman were Cleveland, Minnesota, Milwaukee and Oakland and the standings give you ample evidence where these "pitching poor" rotations wound up. Why, for heaven's sake, *three* ex-Jays from the '92 staff TPERed better than Guzman—Key, Wells and Cone!

Guzman had a weird year. Great record, 14–3, the best winning percentage in the AL. But his ERA leaped one-and-one-third runs from his prior season. But his winning continued because of the Jays offensive cannonading. He threw 221 innings, the most on the staff. But the league hit him at a .252 rate. Not bad. But the year before that average had been a microscopic .207! And how many other aces had so few decisions? Only 17 wins and losses to go along with 16 no-decisions.

Pat Hentgen's emergence probably decided the division. He'd never won more than 11 games in a single season anywhere in his seven previous pro seasons. He'd been 5–2 lifetime before bursting through with a staff high 19 wins and a rotation best 3.87 ERA. His 99 TPER rated 32nd among all AL starters.

The very next ranked TPER starter behind Hentgen was Dave Stewart (100). He spent the first six weeks on the DL with an aching elbow and thus made just 26 starts, by far his lowest total

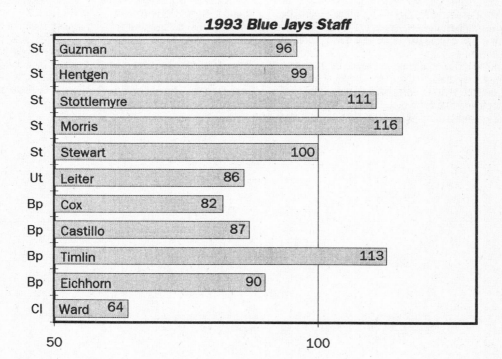

1993 Blue Jays Staff

	Player	TPER
St	Guzman	96
St	Hentgen	99
St	Stottlemyre	111
St	Morris	116
St	Stewart	100
Ut	Leiter	86
Bp	Cox	82
Bp	Castillo	87
Bp	Timlin	113
Bp	Eichhorn	90
Cl	Ward	64

50   100

in seven seasons. When the chips were down, though, this "money pitcher" kicked it in gear. In his last six starts Stew allowed more than one earned run just once, posting four wins and two no-decisions.

But from Stewart down the drop off is dramatic. Todd Stottlemyre and Jack Morris turned in the worst years of their careers with their TPERs zooming up to 111 and 116 respectively. How bad was that? They ranked 48th and 52nd among the 54 starters graded! At least Morris had the excuse of age AND injury. Why Stottlemyre disintegrated at age 28 remains a mystery.

If you simply average the TPERs of these five (and we did use the phrase "simply"), you get a 104. Only the fives of Cleveland, Minnesota, Milwaukee and Oakland had worse figures. Yet, this team won the division, pennant and World Series. Amazing!

The Bullpen: Here's where the Jays staff shined. In fact, behind that explosive offense, the pen's reason #2 why the Jays took it all. Only middleman Mike Timlin had an off year (TPER 113). Closer Duane Ward posted the finest stopper TPER in the AL and second only to the Braves rookie McMichael in all of baseball (and McMichael didn't close the first half or, sadly, in the playoffs.) But Ward, with his 45 save season and microscopic .193 opponent's BA, was just part of the story, albeit a major part.

Al Leiter provided Toronto with as good a spot-starter-middleman as the league had. His 86 TPER would have made him the core of almost any other rotation in the league. And between lefty Leiter and righty stopper Ward, the Jays could use any one of three standout set-up men: RH Danny Cox (82), LH Tony Castillo (86) or RH Mark Eichhorn (90). Respectively, their TPERs made them the fourth, tenth and fourteenth best in-betweeners in the AL. Only the vastly underrated Brewer pen could rave about also having three of the top 14 in the 'tweener role.

In toto, the Jays' bullpen allowed Gaston the flexibility managers crave. And as a group they helped the Jays dominate the late innings of games. Combine that Toronto offense with this relief corps and you get the picture of a team that "owned" the seventh, eighth and ninth innings outscoring their foes over those three innings 261–188. That's a plus 73 runs in the innings that decide so many games. That's nearly half a run per game. That's enormous! And that pen so stifled the opposition that the Jays were able to rally and win 27 times in games they were either tied or trailed entering the seventh inning. That's gigantic!

That's the mark of winners.

What Next?

The Jays will again be favored to take it all. But again there'll be changes. Henderson was allowed to flee to free agency. Fernandez left too. But the club feels it has a star-in-the-wings in 21-year-old SS Alex Gonzalez. Another farm system plum, 22-year-old catcher Carlos Delgado, may also be ready. The first shot at LF probably goes to young native Canadian Rob Butler. But should any or all fail, the Jays can always fall back on their wallets and enter the marketplace offering bucks and prospects in return. Otherwise, the core remains. WAMCO's wonderful. Guzman and Hentgen at the top of the rotation and their terrific bullpen headed by Ward gives the club a solid pitching base. With Jack Morris gone and no pitching prospects immediately banging on the door, the Jays must shop for #4 and #5 starter types. And Toronto might want to spend a bit more time constructing their bench. It appeared to be one of the weakest in all the majors last year and the Jays may have been fortunate that at no point of the season was it needed for long stretches of time as the Jays remained, from an opponent's standpoint, disgustingly healthy afield. History tells us that's not a trend to trust long term.

But a 12th consecutive winning season seems a mere formality. Their current run of 11 straight is easily the best around with the White Sox and their four consecutive over .500 seasons next in line. What may be most interesting about this club will be the way they try to win it all again. They've done it with pitching, done it with balance, done it with pure offense. Is there another way? If there is, be assured the Jays will find it.

Team TOPR: 1993 Toronto Blue Jays

	Bats	BA	OBP	SLG	HR	R	RBI	NBE	GOC	Ratio	TOPR
League Avg. Team	-	.267	.337	.408	148	762	719	2897	4352	.666	100
Toronto Blue Jays	-	.279	.350	.436	159	847	796	3157	4310	.732	110.0
Regulars:											
C Pat Borders	R	.254	.285	.371	9	38	55	195	394	.495	74
1B John Olerud	L	.363	.473	.599	24	109	107	444	372	1.194	179
2B Roberto Alomar	B	.326	.408	.492	17	109	93	411	434	.947	142
3B Ed Sprague	R	.260	.310	.386	12	50	73	239	435	.549	83
SS Tony Fernandez	B	.306	.361	.442	4	45	50	187	272	.688	103
LF Darrin Jackson	R	.216	.250	.347	5	15	19	63	154	.409	(61)
Rickey Henderson	R	.215	.356	.319	4	37	12	111	134	.828	124
CF Devon White	B	.273	.341	.438	15	116	52	359	448	.801	120
RF Joe Carter	R	.254	.312	.489	33	92	121	356	473	.753	113
DH Paul Molitor	R	.332	.402	.509	22	121	111	418	451	.927	139
Bench (100+ TPA):											
OF Darnell Coles	R	.253	.319	.371	4	26	26	92	152	.605	91
OF Turner Ward	B	.192	.287	.311	4	20	28	76	152	.500	(75)
IF Dick Schofield	R	.191	.294	.236	0	11	5	46	92	.500	(75)
C Randy Knorr	R	.248	.309	.436	4	11	20	53	80	.663	(100)
IF Alfredo Griffin	B	.211	.235	.242	0	15	3	27	82	.329	(49)

NOTE: Statistics are only for games played with Toronto. ( ) Under 200 TPA.

Team TPER: 1993 Toronto Blue Jays

	Throws	W-L	GS	GR	SV	IP	ERA	NBA	GOE	Ratio	TPER
League Avg. Team	-	81 -81	162	355	42	1444.1	4.33	2897	4352	0.666	100
Toronto Blue Jays	-	95 -67	162	344	50	1441.1	4.22	2850	4349	0.655	98.4
The Rotation:											
Juan Guzman	R	14 -3	33	0	0	221	3.99	424	666	0.637	96
Pat Hentgen	R	19 -9	32	2	0	216.1	3.87	429	654	0.656	99
Todd Stottlemyre	R	11 -12	28	2	0	176.2	4.84	390	528	0.739	111
Jack Morris	R	7 -12	27	0	0	152.2	6.19	360	465	0.774	116
Dave Stewart	R	12 -8	26	0	0	162	4.44	325	489	0.665	100
Utility:											
Al Leiter	L	9 -6	12	22	2	105	4.11	180	316	0.570	86
Bullpen:											
Danny Cox	R	7 -6	0	44	2	83.2	3.12	138	254	0.543	82
Mark Eichhorn	R	3 -1	0	54	0	72.2	2.72	131	219	0.598	90
Mike Timlin	R	4 -2	0	54	1	55.2	4.69	126	168	0.750	113
Tony Castillo	L	3 -2	0	51	0	50.2	3.38	89	153	0.582	87
Woody Williams	R	3 -1	0	30	0	37	4.38	76	112	0.679	(102)
Duane Ward	R	2 -3	0	71	45	71.2	2.13	91	214	0.425	64

NOTE: Statistics are only for games pitched with Toronto. ( ) Under 200 TBF.

NATIONAL LEAGUE PERSPECTIVE

The final '93 National League divisional standings with runs scored and allowed are compared to Team TOPR and TPER opposite. Plus, we've included a rundown of our TOPR calculation on the league's parks.

The Standings

Team TOPR/TPER tracks the NL standings and runs scored/allowed differentials almost perfectly. Even the two exceptions are consistent with general perceptions of the season: the scope of the Mets' underachievement and the Rockies' overachievement is, thus, quantified.

Their second place finish obscures the truly outstanding season that the San Francisco Giants had. In virtually any other year, in virtually any division, a 107 TOPR with a 91.7 TPER waltzes to a championship. It was a down-to-the-wire horse race between two thoroughbreds, though, and the Braves won by a nose in a photo finish.

Offense and Pitching

You'll see a few discrepancies popping up between runs scored/allowed and TOPR/TPER. With TOPR, these discrepancies indicate the relative efficiency with which a team was able to convert their bases earned into runs scored. With TPER, they indicate the team's relative effectiveness in blocking opponents' conversion of *their* bases into runs.

We'll examine this subject in more detail later. It's plain, though, that Montreal had a relatively inefficient offense—almost average scoring with a 103.4 TOPR. Three teams with a lower TOPR outscored them. Plus, it's clear that Florida's team defense was relatively hard to score against while Philly gave up some runs they shouldn't have.

Park TOPR

NL hitters certainly responded to mountain air, didn't they? It's debatable whether any park in major league history distorted the game like Mile High did in '93. The only possibilities we can think of are LA's Wrigley Field, the bandbox where the expansion Angels played their inaugural season in '61, or the old Baker Bowl, which housed the Phillies until '38.

That Mile High would be a "hitter's park" was expected. That it would be so out of all context was not. By *itself*, Mile High raised the entire National League's TOPR by 2%. The Rockies will move to their new home, Coors Field, in '95. But the implications of Mile High are enormous. We'll address them separately in the Colorado section.

Don't you find Dodger Stadium being ranked neutral in '93 a little surprising? It's supposed to be one of the league's best "pitcher's parks" but it wasn't in '93. Shea Stadium appears to have been more of a "pitcher's park" than usual last year. There's a very interesting twist to this, though, which we'll discuss in the Mets essay.

Positional and Role Norms

We're repeating the data from the Player's and Pitcher's section. These are for comparison to the lineup TOPRs and staff TPERs you'll see with the individual teams.

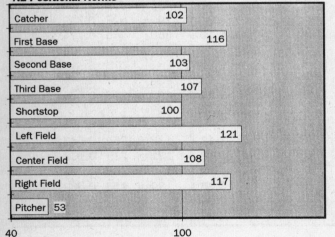

NL Positional Norms

Catcher	102
First Base	116
Second Base	103
Third Base	107
Shortstop	100
Left Field	121
Center Field	108
Right Field	117
Pitcher	53

40   100

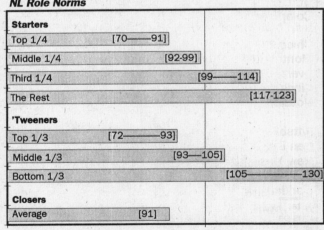

NL Role Norms

Starters	
Top 1/4	[70——91]
Middle 1/4	[92-99]
Third 1/4	[99——114]
The Rest	[117-123]
'Tweeners	
Top 1/3	[72——93]
Middle 1/3	[93—105]
Bottom 1/3	[105——130]
Closers	
Average	[91]

50   100

1993
National League Standings

	W-L	TOPR	TPER	*Differential*	Runs ∓
East					
Philadelphia	97-65	112.9	96.9	*+16.0*	+137
Montreal	94-68	103.4	96.5	*+6.9*	+50
St. Louis	87-75	101.8	100.5	*+1.3*	+14
Chicago	84-78	100.1	101.0	*(0.9)*	(1)
Pittsburgh	75-87	99.0	109.4	*(10.4)*	(99)
Florida	64-98	87.5	102.8	*(15.3)*	(143)
New York	59-103	93.3	100.6	*(7.3)*	(72)
West					
Atlanta	104-58	103.2	85.8	*+17.4*	+208
San Francisco	103-59	107.0	91.7	*+15.3*	+172
Houston	85-77	100.8	91.9	*+8.9*	+86
Los Angeles	81-81	96.2	93.3	*+2.9*	+13
Cincinnati	73-89	99.7	106.3	*(6.6)*	(63)
Colorado	67-95	100.1	119.4	*(19.3)*	(209)
San Diego	61-101	95.3	104.4	*(9.1)*	(93)
Average Team	*81-81*	*100.0*	*100.0*	*0.0*	*0*

1993 NL Offenses

Team	Runs Scored	TOPR
Philadelphia	877	112.9
San Francisco	808	107.0
Atlanta	767	103.2
St. Louis	758	101.8
Colorado	758	100.1
Chicago	738	100.1
Montreal	732	103.4
Average Team	*728*	*100.0*
Cincinnati	722	99.7
Houston	716	100.8
Pittsburgh	707	99.0
San Diego	679	95.3
New York	672	93.3
Los Angeles	675	96.2
Florida	581	87.5

Note: Runs scored rankings are based on runs per 27 gross outs, not total runs.

1993 NL Pitching

Team	Runs Allowed	TPER
Atlanta	559	85.8
San Francisco	636	91.7
Houston	630	91.9
Los Angeles	662	93.3
Montreal	682	96.5
Florida	724	102.8
Average Team	*728*	*100.0*
Philadelphia	740	96.9
St. Louis	744	100.5
Chicago	739	101.0
New York	744	100.6
San Diego	772	104.4
Cincinnati	785	106.3
Pittsburgh	806	109.4
Colorado	967	119.4

Note: Runs allowed rankings are based on runs per 27 gross outs, not total runs.

1993 NL Park TOPR

Team	Park TOPR
Colorado	127.6
Chicago	105.0
Florida	103.9
Los Angeles	100.4
Average Park	*100.0*
Cincinnati	99.8
Atlanta	99.3
Montreal	98.4
Philadelphia	98.1
Pittsburgh	97.6
San Diego	95.6
St. Louis	95.1
Houston	94.5
New York	93.7
San Francisco	92.2

THE "NL GAME"

1993 League TOPR: AL vs. NL Average Team

	H	BB	HP	XB	Batter Sub-set			SH	SF	SB	CS	GDP	Baserunner Sub-set		
					TBB	TBO	Ratio						BRB	BRO	Ratio
AL	1476	572	45	781	2874	4060	.708	50	52	111	-62	-127	23	292	.080
NL	1459	507	41	749	2756	4076	.676	79	50	122	-56	-116	79	302	.261
Player	1408	495	40	737	2680	3787	.708	36	49	122	-56	-111	40	253	.158
Pitcher	51	12	1	12	76	289	.263	43	1	*	*	-5	39	49	.785

* Less than 1/2. NOTE: Individual components may not add up correctly due to rounding.

	NBE	GOC	Ratio	Runs	Base/Run
AL	2897	4352	.666	762	3.80
NL	2835	4378	.647	728	3.89
Player	2719	4039	.673	-	-
Pitcher	115	339	.340	-	-

Is there an "NL Game"? We keep hearing about it. Does it really exist? And, if so, what is it, exactly?

Let's find out. Check out the TOPR lines of the AL and the NL, expressed on an average team basis, with the NL players and pitchers broken out separately. We've reintroduced the Batting Ratio to summarize the Batting Sub-set and the Baserunner Ratio to consolidate the Baserunner Sub-set.

Frankly this past year isn't necessarily the best year to address the subject. The differences between the two leagues have been dampened somewhat, compared to prior years, by a couple of factors. First, expansion into Mile High Stadium brought a massive amount of offense into the National League. Second, there have been some interesting developments in the AL over the past two years, largely tracing to the influx of new managers with an NL background (Garner, Piniella, Lamont, Kennedy, etc.).

Nonetheless, let's examine the comparative line, working our way from left to right:

♦ First, there is a small difference in the hit column. The BAs are virtually the same, .267 in the AL and .264 in the NL. This is despite the "pitcher-as-hitter," who substantially reduces the senior league's BA.
♦ There's a large difference in the walk (BB) column. The average NL team gets 65 fewer walks per season. This is only partially attributable directly to the "pitcher-as-hitter" who hardly walks at all. The balance, though, is probably indirectly attributable to him, since one of the primary jobs of the #8 hitter in the NL is not to walk. The difference in OBP is .337 vs. .327.
♦ Extra bases aren't terribly far apart. Their composition, though, is decidedly different. The NL team hit almost 20 fewer doubles and about eight fewer HRs, but over six more triples. The "pitcher-as-hitter" is at work here again, plus, probably a park effect. Slugging percentages are .408 AL vs. .399 NL.
♦ The total batting sub-set shows a differential between the leagues, then, that is largely made up of walks (over half the total difference of 118 bases). Take away the "pitcher-as-hitter" and the balance of the NL lineup is dead even with the AL (Batter Ratios of .708).
♦ The sac bunt totals are, as is well known, the largest proportional difference between the two leagues. If you take away the "pitcher-as-hitter" again, though, the difference more than vanishes. The remaining NL lineup spots actually bunted less than their AL counterparts—about 4.3 times per lineup slot vs.

5.6 per slot in the AL. The "pitcher-as-hitter" soaks up plate appearances equivalent to 64% of the #9 slot, consequently, the NL has 8.36 slots left to work with (the other 36% of the #9 slot is, of course, pinch hitters or the result of "double switches").
♦ Sac flies are about the same and are no factor in this discussion.
♦ Stolen bases are higher in the NL and their runners are caught less. This difference is not as large in 1993 as it usually is. The pitcher is no factor at all in the running game so the stolen bases per lineup slot even more greatly favors the NL.
♦ Ground ball double plays occur more frequently in the AL than in the NL. As with stolen bases, this margin is also somewhat narrower than has been the case for the previous three years.
♦ As a result of all this activity, the NL holds a giant advantage over the AL in the Baserunner Sub-set. Even after the NL pitchers' sac bunts are washed out, the player-to-player comparison remains strongly in favor of the NL.

The eventual result of this exercise reveals that, while the AL TOPR ratio is superior to the NL, the NL "Position Players Only" TOPR ratio is actually a little higher (.673 vs. .666). Further, it shows that the NL's edge traces solely to the Baserunner Sub-set. Let's look at these particular results on the basis of available lineup slots, to equalize the relationship.

Baserunner Sub-set/Lineup Slot

	BRB	BRO	Ratio
AL (9 lineup slots)	2.6	32.4	.080
NL (8.36 lineup slots)	4.8	30.3	.158

Hmmmm, looks like the NL gets almost twice as much value (net bases) from baserunner utilization while expending fewer outs. And, this was in an "off-year" for the NL in this category.

It may seem that we're arguing about penny-ante stuff here, but a team's accumulation of about 20 more net bases while using 40 fewer outs over the course of a season is not penny-ante. It's roughly the equivalent of 15 runs. Maybe more, given that we're dealing with bases that move runners into scoring position and avoid the erasure of baserunners already in place. In addition, the affect of these baserunner bases on W's is probably increased because these "little" things assume the most importance and tend to occur more frequently in close games.

Falling back and taking a broader perspective, where are we now?

♦ For one thing, we believe we've established that the "NL Game" is not defined by the sac bunt. Instead, this device is only the logical response to the necessity of allocating your #9 hole to futility personified. Sacrificing is the single most productive thing you can do with the "pitcher-as-hitter" when there's a man on first and less than two outs or even a man on second with nobody out. Having him swing away almost certainly will result in an out and very possibly two. The common strikeout can even constitute a blessing. He didn't advance the runner but at least he didn't kill him either.

◆ The "NL Game" is actually characterized by the SB/CS and GDP columns with sac bunts playing only a bit part. The true strategy behind these exercises is actually twofold: to advance the baserunner *and to conserve* him by avoiding the double play. This seems curiously like a TOPR-based strategy and we wonder if we're revealing trade secrets here. In this sense, the stolen base, the hit-and-run, the run-and-hit and all their permutations are less weapons than they are protective mechanisms.

Does the "NL Game" work then? Does it produce runs—more runs than the "AL Game"? On its surface, that's a silly question. The average AL team scored 34 more runs than the average NL club by our own example. Doesn't it, however, strike you that this total is an absurdly small difference between a team with a DH versus a team with a "pitcher-as-hitter"? The run-scoring differential between the leagues has, in fact, recently been as low as 15

runs per team, as in '90 when the NL posted an enormous .373 Baserunner Ratio vs. the AL's .064.

The AL's DHs were a pretty disappointing group this year. But any conventional comparison between them and the NL's #9 hitter (which is 64% "P-as-H" and the balance pinch hitter) is no contest.

League Average	BA	OBP	SLG	HR	Runs	RBI
AL DH	.262	.330	.421	22	83	94
NL #9	.181	.226	.235	4	41	39

How could a difference like this possibly be worth only 34 runs? Of course, we have to concede that the two players above are batting in different places in the batting order, perhaps explaining the disparity in runs and RBI, which are highly dependent on team context. But, as far as input into the total team offense, can a .330 on-base average and .421 slugging only be worth 34 more runs than a .226 and .235 over the course of a full season?

TOPR reveals, shockingly, that it's *not*!

Here's how TOPR views the AL's DH and the NL's #9.

1993 TOPR: AL Designated Hitter vs. NL #9 Hitter

	H	BB	HP	XB	Batter Sub-set TBB	TBQ	SH	SF	SB	CS	GDP	Baserunner Sub-set BRB	BRQ	NBE	GOC
AL DH	164	65	4	100	333	463	1	6	7	-4	-17	-7	28	326	491
NL #9	97	31	1	29	158	440	46	2	2	-1	-10	39	59	197	499

In sum, we find that the difference between our DH and our #9 hitter (who is mostly a "P-as-H," remember) amounts to a total of 129 Net Bases Earned (NBE) in favor of the AL's DH. Both consumed about the same number of outs in the process. The huge margin that the DH ran up in the Batting Sub-set was reduced, substantially, by resourceful employment of the sacrifice bunt to advance existing runners and avoid doubling them up.

As indicated on the earlier league TOPR lines, we know that it took the AL 3.80 Net Bases Earned (NBE) to produce a run, while it took the NL 3.89. We can measure, then what each lineup slot's output contributed toward the team's run manufacturing.

	NBE	League NBE/Run	Equivalent Runs Contributed
AL DH	326	3.80	85.8
NL #9	197	3.89	50.6
Difference	129		35.2

We were looking for the 34 run differential in favor of the AL. It turns out that the DH's advantage amounts to the equivalent of 35 runs for the AL team. That's all the difference a DH makes in the total scheme of things!

What we have here is evidence that the NL managers, as a group, are adept at making the best of a bad thing. Plus, a pretty strong validation of the TOPR concept—i.e., a base is a base and about four of them, no matter how earned, will eventually somehow result in a run.

We also have evidence that, were it *not* for the "P-as-H," the "NL Game" of advancing runners/avoiding outs would produce slightly more runs than the "AL Game" that puts less emphasis on these tactics. It is patently impossible for a NL manager to sustain a sequential offense through the black hole of the #9 slot. They must accept the interruption of an out while getting something in return and go on from there. They have no option. The TOPR edge they have built with their tactics elsewhere in the lineup (remember the .673 TOPR for NL "Players Only" vs. the .666 for the AL and how it was obtained) must be surrendered at the bottom of the order.

Summing up, two vital characteristics define the "NL Game":

1. Relentlessly advancing baserunners while taking steps to avoid additional and *unnecessary* outs.
2. Accepting, and playing for, one run when one run is the only *reasonable* expectation.

Would the "NL Game" work in the AL? The presence of the DH doesn't necessarily preclude its employment, after all. A better question is, "Does it work in the AL?," because it's been tried on quite a few occasions without having necessarily been recognized. When done well, it worked like a charm. Trebelhorn's '90 Brewers, Garner's '92 Brewers and Kennedy's '93 Rangers represent prime examples. All played the "NL Game" and all scored more runs than they otherwise would or should have.

The NL Player vs. the AL Player

Is the NL player better than the AL player? The question arises when we look at their comparative TOPR ratios: .673 vs. .666. We have no way of knowing for sure, but he probably isn't. Their Batter Ratios, for example, are identical (.708). Only their Baserunner Ratios separate them (.158 vs. .080) and that Baserunner Sub-set is largely subject to managerial control. Plus, we don't know whether the NL pitchers are "better" or "worse" than their AL counterparts. We do know, though, that when players or pitchers change leagues they seem to retain about the same level of performance as a group. Moreover, there's the park factor to consider.

The Park Factor

The "NL Game" probably traces its creation to the introduction of turf. The NL was "fastest" with the "mostest," though they should hardly be proud of the distinction. Until this year, the NL was evenly split between turf and grass parks, six apiece. The AL has always favored grass parks with the current count being ten to four. With turf's physical characteristics of enhancing speed and "trueness of hop," as well as increasing injuries, the "NL Game" seems a brilliant adaptation to circumstances.

With turf parks now on the wane, no more being built and some clubs ripping them up (Kansas City's rug goes bye-bye in '95) the impetus for this kind of strategy may tend to subside. It shouldn't, though, because it works just fine on grass, too.

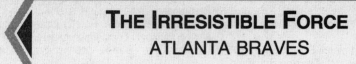

THE IRRESISTIBLE FORCE
ATLANTA BRAVES

Three seasons in a row, the Atlanta Braves have put together second-half pennant drives that have first pressured then eventually humbled their opposition.

	Post All-Star Record			Position in Standings		
	W–L	Pct		Deficit	Eventual Margin	Net Gain
1991	55–28	.663		−9.5G	+1G	+11G
1992	49–27	.645		−2G	+8G	+10G
1993	54–19	.740		−9G	+1G	+10G

None of their victims qualified as undeserving "patsies." Nor did any of them collapse in front of the onrushing Braves. They simply got overhauled in the stretch by superior horsepower. The veteran '91 Dodgers, assembled expressly for the purpose of claiming a championship, went 44–38 over the same period. The injury riddled '92 Reds fought to a still respectable 39–37. The '93 Giants provided an even more worthy adversary than the Braves' earlier victims (44–29).

In the end, though, it made no difference. All found themselves in the path of an irresistible force—the Braves' finely-tuned offense operating in complete harmony with a superior pitching staff.

Team Trendline: Atlanta Braves

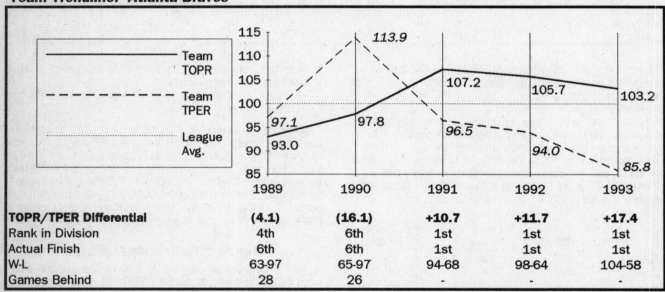

	1989	1990	1991	1992	1993
TOPR/TPER Differential	(4.1)	(16.1)	+10.7	+11.7	+17.4
Rank in Division	4th	6th	1st	1st	1st
Actual Finish	6th	6th	1st	1st	1st
W-L	63-97	65-97	94-68	98-64	104-58
Games Behind	28	26	-	-	-

What Was Expected

This time around, there would be no doubts. The experts and fans believed the Braves would win it. Not just the division or the pennant, but *all* of it. The team thought no less. Twice they had fought their way to the mountain top. Twice they'd been pushed off of it—by the Twins in '91 and the Jays in '92. If the Braves were indeed the "best team in baseball," as many including themselves believed, the time had come to *prove* it.

Going into '93, the Braves' offense had become somewhat suspect as the ravages of age and injury appeared to be creeping up on several key contributors. Otis Nixon, the leadoff catalyst would be 34. Terry Pendleton, with his new-found potency at the plate, would be 32. Sid Bream would also be 32, but his knees were past 50. These players also played key roles in the team's superb defense and its chemistry.

But not to worry. The already fearsome pitching staff had been bolstered by the signing of free agent Greg Maddux, winner of 20 games and the Cy Young in '92. Arguably, the best starting rotation in the league had been joined by the best starter in the league. If the other team couldn't score, the Braves couldn't lose—even if their offense did sputter.

What Actually Happened

Through the first half, all the pre-season predictions proved uncannily accurate. The pitching proved to be everything it was cracked up to be. At the break, Atlanta's 3.21 ERA led the majors. The suspicions about the offense had also come true. It sputtered and was scoring barely four runs a game. A struggling Nixon (.237 BA, only .327 OBP), saw only sporadic use behind an equally struggling Deion Sanders (.256 BA, and worse .295 OBP). Pendleton slumped (.259 BA, just 5 HR) and Bream fared no better (.243 BA, .402 SLG). SS Jeff Blauser carried the club's offense (.311 BA, .416 OBP, .426 SLG) while the rest of the lineup appeared dazed and distracted by their futility. Nonetheless, as planned, the combination had been sufficient to win at a pennant contender's pace (50–39).

There was just one little problem, though. The surprising Giants, setting a much faster pace (59–30), seemed well on their way to spread-eagling the division. If things stayed the way they were the Braves wouldn't catch them.

On July 20, five games after the break, Fred McGriff arrived from San Diego and things changed immediately. McGriff's presence catalyzed the entire lineup. A suddenly supercharged offense started *cruising* past their now overwhelmed opponents.

	W–L	Team TOPR	Team TPER	TOPR/TPER Diff.	Average Runs		
					Scored	Allowed	Diff.
Pre- McGriff	55–41	94.8	86.7	+ 8.1	3.99	3.49	+ .50
Post-McGriff	51–17	115.1	84.2	+30.9	5.76	3.40	+2.36

The change came not a moment too soon. The Braves had just enough time to catch and then squeak by the Giants on the season's final day. The effort expended down the stretch became apparent, though, when the Braves met a fresh and rested Phillies club in the NLCS. The Braves' emotional tanks were empty and they fell in six games. Redemption would have to wait until next year.

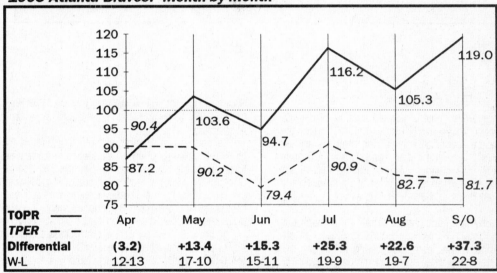

1993 Atlanta Braves: Month-by-Month

	Apr	May	Jun	Jul	Aug	S/O
TOPR ———	90.4	103.6	94.7	116.2	105.3	119.0
TPER – –	87.2	90.2	79.4	90.9	82.7	81.7
Differential	(3.2)	+13.4	+15.3	+25.3	+22.6	+37.3
W-L	12-13	17-10	15-11	19-9	19-7	22-8

Atlanta–Fulton County Stadium

Contrary to all previous analyses, "The Launching Pad" rated as a neutral park in '93 (99.3 Park TOPR). It didn't even act like a "home" park—the Braves had a better record away (53–28) than at home (51–30). This split wasn't a fluke either because the Braves actually were a better team on the road (+20.9 TOPR/TPER diff.) than in Atlanta (+13.9).

True, opposition hitters found the venue hospitable and the Atlanta pitchers slightly more vulnerable in Atlanta than elsewhere. That's to be expected. Oddly, though, Braves hitters weren't reaching the fences as often in their home park. Even though they led the league with 169 HR, they hit the majority (91) on the road.

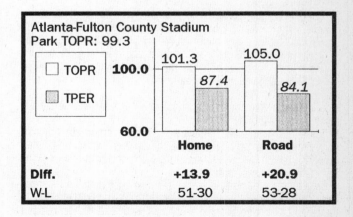

Atlanta-Fulton County Stadium
Park TOPR: 99.3

		Home	Road
□ TOPR		101.3	105.0
▨ TPER		87.4	84.1
Diff.		+13.9	+20.9
W-L		51-30	53-28

1993 Braves Lineup

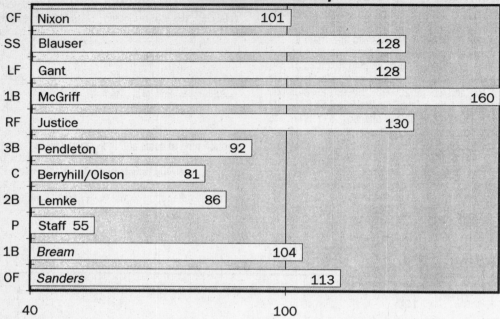

CF	Nixon	101
SS	Blauser	128
LF	Gant	128
1B	McGriff	160
RF	Justice	130
3B	Pendleton	92
C	Berryhill/Olson	81
2B	Lemke	86
P	Staff	55
1B	*Bream*	104
OF	*Sanders*	113

40   100

The Offense

In its final makeup, the Braves' lineup formed a thing of beauty. McGriff, replacing Bream, made a significant contribution to the giant 20-point jump in the Team TOPR occurring after his arrival. But his 160 vs. Bream's 104 netted out to "only" about a 6-point gain in the Team TOPR. The balance came from the rest of the team. His arrival halted the individual struggles of teammates and collectively re-enmeshed them in the offense. It was very much a "team effect."

Atlanta manager Bobby Cox consistently constructs lineups that create a TOPRific symphony. The batting order begins with an on-base obbligato, builds to an orchestral crescendo in the middle, then drops gradually to the pitcher's soft concluding coda. The practical effect is to maximize the productivity of the lineup by:

1. Getting runners on base—so they can score, and give the opposing pitchers something else to worry about.
2. Bringing up the heavy artillery when it can do the most damage—with runners on base and the opposing pitcher distracted.
3. Saving outs at every opportunity—by placing the batters least likely to make outs early in the order and reserving the batters most likely to make outs for the bottom (where they'll make fewer of them because they bat less).

This seems elemental. But, shockingly, not all managers have mastered the concept.

Cox's "orchestration" principle in batting order construction may also explain why the rest of the batters "woke up" when McGriff arrived. And why he wasn't the only factor in this awakening—Otis Nixon was another.

Before July 20, the 3–6 slots—manned by Pendleton, Justice, Gant and Bream—struggled along with the Nixon/Sanders duo in the leadoff slot (who boasted a composite .312 OBP). Deprived of baserunners in front of them, or a meaningful threat behind them, Justice and Gant tried mightily to shoulder the whole load. They hit HRs (21 and 20, respectively) but weren't driving in a lot of runs (61 and 55). They and Blauser, though, were about all the offense Atlanta had.

The addition of McGriff significantly altered the equation. The interrupted 2–4–5 offensive sequence became a seamless 2–3–4–5 as the batting order was restructured to accommodate "Crime Dog" in the cleanup slot. With Nixon's subsequent resurgence in the leadoff spot, the sequence extended five batters deep. With runners now present on the basepaths and the middle of the order prepared to strike, the symphony began to perform.

The preceding Nixon/Sanders conflict had introduced a disturbing discordance to a team that evidently thrives on harmony, both on the field and in the clubhouse. Nixon, with his leadoff skills and superb fielding, had performed a key role in Atlanta's previous two NL championships. Sanders, as the 4th outfielder in '92, had demonstrated his supreme talents as a baseball player, as well as a football player. All he lacked, perhaps, was commitment which an appropriate contract might secure.

On May 21, when the contract (3 years, $11 million) came down on the heels of an AWOL Sanders' 3-week "vacation," stuff hit the fan. Sanders was named the starter in CF, Nixon hit the bench, grousing all the way, and demanded a trade. The Braves tried to accommodate him but couldn't because of "inadequate" offers. In the meantime, Sanders played poorly, Nixon didn't play at all and nobody seemed happy.

Cox worked out a *modus vivendi*, splitting the playing time between an unenthusiastic Sanders and Nixon, both of whom continued to turn in less-than-acceptable performances. The McGriff trade, however, submerged the story and apparently submerged their conflict as well. Both Sanders and Nixon stepped up their play from that point. When Sanders went on the DL with a respiratory ailment on August 18, Nixon took over with a vengeance (.331 BA from there on). The Braves' second half proved once again that a team can be greater than the sum of its parts.

The Pitching

If the Braves as a team were an irresistible force, the engine that drove them all year long was their pitching staff.

The Team TPER of 85.5 led the league by a wide margin, of course. The San Francisco (91.7) and Houston (91.9) staffs came closest but were merely outstanding, not epic.

The Atlanta staff was so strong, and so deep, that the only two pitchers that TPERed "above the line" (Pete Smith at 114 and Mike Stanton with a 109) pitched only 142.2 innings, just 9.8% of the Braves' total. The opposition couldn't exploit a weakness if they never saw it.

The Rotation: The Big 4 rotation performed brilliantly. Two past and two potential Cy Young winners made up the rotation (Greg Maddux and Tom Glavine, plus Steve Avery and John Smoltz). The group didn't miss a single start, making 142 altogether. The rotation members *averaged* 243.1 IP each producing 67% of the club's total innings, and throwing 18 complete games. They combined for a 75–33 record, with a 3.01 ERA. The opposition was thus confronted by an ace-quality starter (85.0 was their *average* TPER) nearly every day. It's well they were for the Braves won only 8 of the 20 games the Big 4 didn't start.

Greg Maddux has clearly established himself as one of the premier pitchers of his time. During his last six years, he *averaged* 35 starts, 254 IP, 18 wins and a 2.99 ERA. In the past two years, he's won a pair of Cy Youngs, 20 games twice, and an ERA crown, posting TPERs of 75 and 74. Greg's durable, reliable and consistently excellent. He's led the league in IP for three years in a row and earns over 800 outs a year. Next season he'll only be 28 and belongs to the Braves at least through 1997. Greg and Barry Bonds were the two biggest bargains of the '92–'93 free agent market, even at their huge signing prices.

Tom Glavine collected his third consecutive 20-win season, going 12–2 the second half to quiet critics who had questioned his stamina. But now there are some new questions. His 22 wins tied John Burkett of SF for the league lead—but he gave up 236 hits along the way, leading the league in this department. Tom's a control pitcher but was 3rd in the league in walks allowed (90) right behind teammate John Smoltz (100)—who's not a control pitcher. He was 8th in ERA (3.20) but his '92 TPER ranked him 17th. Glavine remains, without a doubt, a very good pitcher, but some small signs of slippage have crept into his line. Pitchers tend to work their way from one TPER "plateau" to another. Maddux didn't reach the mid-seventies level until '92, dropping from the mid-eighties. Glavine produced a 79 in '91 followed by an 80 in '92. Is his '93 level (92) going to be his new level? It's something new to worry about.

Some thought John Smoltz slipped some in '93, too. His ERA went up (from 2.85 to 3.62) and, though he won 15 again, the Braves finished only 18–17 in his starts (by far the worst record for any of the Big 4). The Braves' offense, however, provided him little support and scored just 24 runs in his 11 losses. He remained extremely hard to hit (.230 opponent BA, 3rd in the league) but his control worsened slightly. His TPER stayed in the low nineties (94) where it's always been.

If the theory of TPER "plateaus" holds true, Steve Avery found himself on a new one in '93. He had the 5th lowest TPER in the league (81), down from 93 in '91 and 94 in '92. Avery was the youngest of the 53 NL pitchers who made 20 or more starts in '93. At 23 next year, he's still learning and growing as a major league pitcher. Who knows what plateau he'll eventually reach.

The Bullpen: If an opponent found themselves lucky enough to knock out an Atlanta starter and "get into their bullpen," they had an unpleasant surprise waiting for them. They had merely leapt from one frying pan to another.

Four of TPER's top 11 middlemen in the league worked out of the Braves' bullpen—Mark Wohlers (#11), Kent Mercker (#7), Steve Bedrosian (#5), and Jay Howell (#1). On top of that, Greg McMichael, who took over the closer's job at the end of July, finished with a 63 TPER and 19 saves. This earned him the #1 TPER spot among all NL relievers. The Braves found him as they were rummaging through the minor league free agent lists in the '90–'91 off-season. He actually came to camp in '93 as a non-roster invitee. Nice payoff for some patient, meticulous shopping.

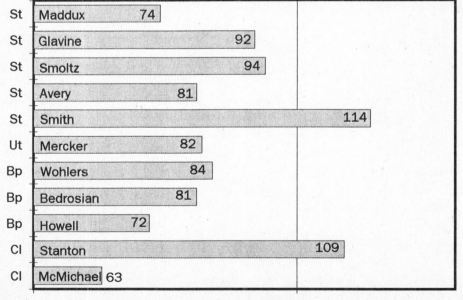

1993 Braves Staff

St	Maddux 74
St	Glavine 92
St	Smoltz 94
St	Avery 81
St	Smith 114
Ut	Mercker 82
Bp	Wohlers 84
Bp	Bedrosian 81
Bp	Howell 72
Cl	Stanton 109
Cl	McMichael 63

50   100

The only chink in the bullpen's armor appeared to be lefty Mike Stanton and his 109 TPER. His 4.67 ERA, 51 hits and 29 walks in 52 IP looks a little scary. But strike his awful July and August, when something obviously wasn't working, and you see a different Stanton: 3.02 ERA, 32 hits and 14 walks in 35.2 IP with 21 saves. In all he gained 27 saves, giving the Braves' bullpen a total of 46 on the season.

The extraordinary effectiveness of the entire Braves staff meant that from the first inning to the last, manager Cox usually had his opponent exactly where he wanted him—trailing or within reach, and always under control.

What Next?

Though the Braves have taken on the imposing look of a dynasty, they remain a relatively young team. Expected roster turnover, therefore, would likely be modest, particularly as no areas of severe underproduction cry out for a solution.

The Atlanta club, though, may have reached a crossroads. They have been to the mountain three times now and have yet to return with the holy grail. A press of young talent at AAA awaits their chance. The payroll has grown with the Braves' success (from $21 million in '91 to $42 million in '93—and it will push past $50 million in '94). There's also this mysterious closer "problem," which never seems to exist in the regular season but pops up only at critical moments in the post-season.

Roster turnover that has already taken place (or will take place) includes Otis Nixon (lost to free agency at *his* option), Greg Olson (the rotation's catcher-of-choice) and Sid Bream (a fan and clubhouse favorite, displaced by McGriff). All three have played important roles in the team's '91–'93 success and, perhaps even more important, in the clubhouse.

Prospects will fill the talent gaps created by the turnover. Javy Lopez has been handed the catcher's job and Tony Tarasco will almost certainly take over as the 4th outfielder. But the key to Atlanta GM John Schuerholz's off-season personnel decisions will be a third prospect—Chipper Jones. The switch-hitting shortstop is the kind of prospect that teams make room for, even if there isn't room. He can hit (.325 BA), hit with power (.500 SLG), walk (.387 OBP) and run (23 SB). Jones is only 22 but he's *ready*.

Atlanta GM John Schuerholz thus confronts a major decision. Does he clear a slot for Jones by moving an established player? If so, which one? Or does he trade Jones to solve the mysterious closer problem? The '94 Braves will be the product of that decision.

Team TOPR: 1993 Atlanta Braves

	Bats	BA	OBP	SLG	HR	R	RBI	NBE	GOC	Ratio	TOPR
League Avg. Team	-	.264	.327	.399	140	728	681	2835	4378	0.647	100
Atlanta Braves	-	.262	.331	.408	169	767	712	2918	4368	0.668	103.2
Regulars:											
C Damon Berryhill	B	.245	.291	.382	8	24	43	149	265	0.562	87
Greg Olson	R	.225	.304	.309	4	23	24	104	217	0.479	74
1B Fred McGriff	L	.310	.392	.612	19	59	55	188	182	1.033	160
2B Mark Lemke	B	.252	.335	.341	7	52	49	223	402	0.555	86
3B Terry Pendleton	B	.272	.311	.408	17	81	84	293	490	0.598	92
SS Jeff Blauser	R	.305	.401	.436	15	110	73	370	446	0.830	128
LF Ron Gant	R	.274	.345	.510	36	113	117	388	470	0.826	128
CF Otis Nixon	R	.269	.351	.315	1	77	24	241	369	0.653	101
RF Dave Justice	L	.270	.357	.515	40	90	120	374	446	0.839	130
Bench (100+ TPA):											
1B Sid Bream	L	.260	.332	.415	9	33	35	145	216	0.671	104
OF Deion Sanders	L	.276	.321	.452	6	42	28	154	210	0.733	113

NOTE: Statistics are only for games played with Atlanta. ( ) Under 200 TPA.

Team TPER: 1993 Atlanta Braves

	Throws	W-L	GS	GR	SV	IP	ERA	NBA	GOE	Ratio	TPER
League Avg. Team	-	81 -81	162	381	43	1449	4.04	2835	4378	0.647	100
Atlanta Braves	-	104 -58	162	353	46	1455	3.14	2441	4393	0.556	85.8
The Rotation:											
Greg Maddux	R	20 -10	36	0	0	267	2.36	387	810	0.478	74
Tom Glavine	L	22 -6	36	0	0	239.1	3.20	425	716	0.594	92
Steve Avery	L	18 -6	35	0	0	223.1	2.94	354	671	0.528	81
John Smoltz	R	15 -11	35	0	0	243.2	3.62	447	736	0.607	94
Pete Smith	R	4 -8	14	6	0	90.2	4.37	203	274	0.741	114
Bullpen:											
Kent Mercker	L	3 -1	6	37	0	66	2.86	106	200	0.530	82
Jay Howell	R	3 -3	0	54	0	58.1	2.31	83	177	0.469	72
Steve Bedrosian	R	5 -2	0	49	0	49.2	1.63	79	151	0.523	81
Mark Wohlers	R	6 -2	0	46	0	48	4.50	78	143	0.545	(84)
Greg McMichael	R	2 -3	0	74	19	91.2	2.06	114	280	0.407	63
Mike Stanton	L	4 -6	0	63	27	52	4.67	112	159	0.704	109

NOTE: Statistics are only for games pitched with Atlanta. ( ) Under 200 TBF.

FEAR'S FICKLE FINGER
CHICAGO CUBS

Three dreadful thoughts chill the bones of baseball people, be they GM or field manager. In many respects, each represents a circumstance beyond their control. All are job-threatening.

1. My star leaves through free agency.
2. My star gets hurt and can't play.
3. My boss has higher expectations for the team than the talent justifies.

Welcome to storied Wrigley, which became a field of fears come true in '93. Greg Maddux, the Cubs' 20-game winner and arguably the league's best pitcher, couldn't (or wouldn't) come to terms and bolted to Atlanta.

Ryne Sandberg, the Cubs' best (and highest-paid) player, broke his hand in the first spring game, could play only sporadically and didn't play up to his usual standard.

Somehow, despite all this and the more-or-less average collection of players who remained, some people still thought the Cubbies should be contending for the pennant. For "some people," read Cubs' GM Larry Himes—which bode ill for manager Jim Lefebvre.

The Cubs nonetheless had their best year since the '89 divisional championship. Their 84 wins represented a six-game improvement over '92. It meant fourth place again. But there really were three better clubs in the division.

All things considered, '93 wasn't a bad year at all. Unless you were Larry Himes or Jim Lefebvre.

Team Trendline: Chicago Cubs

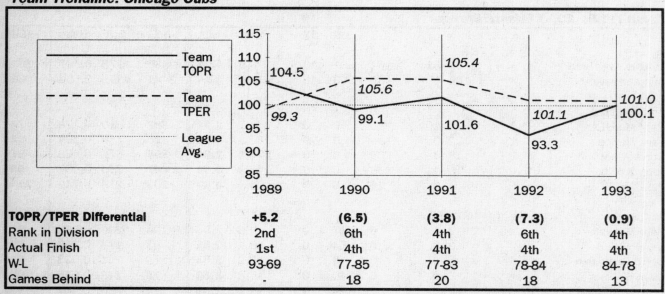

TOPR/TPER Differential	+5.2	(6.5)	(3.8)	(7.3)	(0.9)
Rank in Division	2nd	6th	4th	6th	4th
Actual Finish	1st	4th	4th	4th	4th
W-L	93-69	77-85	77-83	78-84	84-78
Games Behind	-	18	20	18	13

What Was Expected

When Maddux departed, he took the heart out of what had been shaping up as the best Cubs rotation in years. The follow-up signing of free agent Jose Guzman to *occupy* Maddux's spot didn't, by any means, *replace* Maddux.

Other off-season acquisitions included free agent Randy Myers for the vacant closer's job and Greg Hibbard to bring the rotation up to full strength. In addition, 37-year-old Willie Wilson signed on to play CF and bat leadoff. Shawon Dunston's return to SS remained uncertain as his injured back wasn't responding to treatment. Only

Myers offered any hope of radical improvement as the closer problem had reached intolerable proportions in '92. But Myers himself arrived surrounded by questions. With his '91 and '92 performances for Cincinnati and San Diego, he'd lost a lot of luster.

The Cubs gathered at Mesa with an unsettled OF picture, a serviceable but diminished rotation, a new closer (maybe) and no shortstop (probably). Then Sandberg broke his hand. The time had arrived to wonder whether the team could crawl up to .500. Not, as Himes kept suggesting, whether they would win the division.

What Actually Happened

From the outset, the club played .500 ball. Never more than two games below or two games above in April. Never more than six games under nor six games over the rest of the way. Myers turned his career around with an NL record 53 saves, but that was about all the good news an otherwise yeoman pitching staff delivered. Rick Wilkins broke through with a season that Cubs fans hadn't seen from a catcher since Gabby Hartnett (.303 BA with 30 HR). But Sandberg's injury caused him to play in only 117 games and evidently hampered his play all year long. Dunston virtually didn't make it back at all.

A star's departure and a star's injury cost the Cubs a possible shot at contention. In the face of these events, unrealistic expectations cost Lefebvre his job.

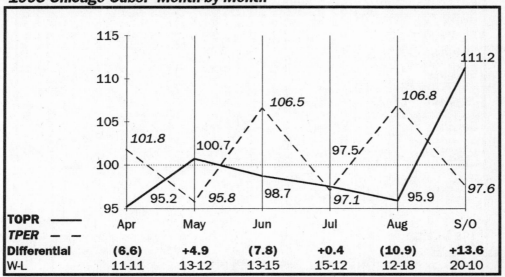

1993 Chicago Cubs: Month-by-Month

	Apr	May	Jun	Jul	Aug	S/O
TOPR ———						
TPER – –						
Differential	**(6.6)**	**+4.9**	**(7.8)**	**+0.4**	**(10.9)**	**+13.6**
W-L	11-11	13-12	13-15	15-12	12-18	20-10

Wrigley Field

Wrigley's still a "hitter's park" (Park TOPR: 105.0). At least, Cubs opponents say it is. Cubs pitchers got pounded for 94 HRs at Wrigley vs. only 59 on the road. Cubs hitters, however, couldn't find the range—76 at home, 85 away. Note that the wind must have blown in from right toward left when the Cubbies batted . . .

Cub Home Runs	At Wrigley	Away
LH batters	26	44
RH batters	44	32
Switch-hitters	6	9

The biggest HR splits: LH Rick Wilkins (10 home, 20 away), RH Sammy Sosa (23 at home, 10 away).

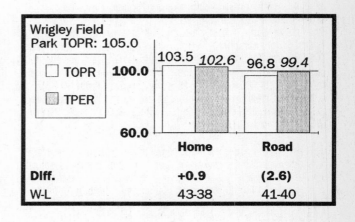

Wrigley Field
Park TOPR: 105.0

	Home	Road
TOPR	103.5	96.8
TPER	102.6	99.4
Diff.	**+0.9**	**(2.6)**
W-L	43-38	41-40

1993 Cubs Lineup

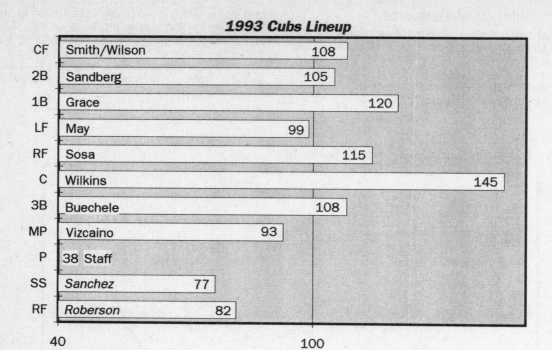

		TOPR
CF	Smith/Wilson	108
2B	Sandberg	105
1B	Grace	120
LF	May	99
RF	Sosa	115
C	Wilkins	145
3B	Buechele	108
MP	Vizcaino	93
P	38 Staff	
SS	Sanchez	77
RF	Roberson	82

40   100

The Offense

The Cubs' offensive assets include:

A. A top-notch leadoff hitter who both hit for average (.325) and walked (71 BB), producing an outstanding .393 OBP. He's not necessarily a base stealer, but he's got some pop (57 extra-base hits) that got him into scoring position regularly. It all added up to a 120 TOPR in '93.
B. One of the game's best all-round hitters, perfect for the #3 slot. Though hampered by injury in '93, his prior three-year TOPRs were 145, 144, 142. In a healthy year, he's got average (around .300), power (around 30 HR), drives in and scores runs (multiple 100+ years). Plus, he can run (about 30 SB).
C. A burly LH cleanup hitter who can empty the sacks and keep the rally going. He emerged in '93 with a .303 average, 30 HR, .561 SLG and 145 TOPR.

The rest of the Cubs' lineup consists of essentially average offensive players, with some power but almost no ability to get on base. They're all #6–#7–#8 types, which presents difficulties when they have to fill the remaining five spots in the batting order.

The trouble with all this, as you've no doubt surmised, is that Mark Grace doesn't bat leadoff, Sandberg isn't the #3 hitter and Wilkins doesn't bat cleanup. The critical leadoff and cleanup slots are left to the #6–#7–#8 types.

The Cubs' problem is further compounded by the fact that their middle-of-the-order type power comes from up-the-middle players—C Wilkins, 2B Sandberg and CF Sammy Sosa. The infield and outfield corners, then, must set the table for them. Only 1B Grace fits this scheme, but that's not the way he's been used.

You might be wondering why TOPR credits Grace with a 120 mark, just slightly above the NL norm for his position (116). Didn't he hit .325 and collect 98 RBI, garnering all-star support with what was considered a breakthrough season? Yes, but TOPR found a fly in Mark's ointment—25 GDP, tieing with Charlie Hayes for the league lead. This affinity for DPs limits his value in the middle of the order, but wouldn't be a factor leading off.

The Cubs wrestled unsuccessfully with their awkward construction. In '93, their efforts created gaping holes at leadoff and cleanup.

The two table-setting spots at the top of the order were most often occupied by erstwhile utility IF Jose Vizcaino (106 games, .340 OBP), platoon OF Dwight Smith (66 games, .354 OBP) and fill-in SS Rey Sanchez (53 games, .316 OBP). Willie Wilson, signed to bat leadoff, only made 30 appearances there and posted an appalling .301 OBP. These performances left the table pretty bare while using up a passel of outs. Interestingly, all were part-time players—and the best of them, Smith, may not be invited back.

Derrick May most frequently hit cleanup. His only qualification for the slot would appear to be that he plays LF—"where cleanup hitters come from." A high average contact hitter without any appreciable power, walks or speed, he supposedly "emerged" this year. A 99 TOPR says he's a below average offensive player for an outfielder, much less a cleanup hitter.

While the whole OF situation for the Cubs remains foggy, Sammy Sosa at least solved ⅓ of the puzzle. His 30/30/30 year (33 HR, 36 SB, 32 unintentional BB) added up to only a 114 TOPR, but that's a plus in CF—where he also displays excellent defensive skills. Himes, who's traded for Sosa twice (for both the White Sox and the Cubs) finally saw his faith rewarded. The Cubs are still looking for a LF and a RF and have a plethora of candidates—May, Kevin Roberson, Glenallen Hill, Karl Rhodes, Eddie Zambrano and, maybe, Dwight Smith.

Only Smith, who's consistently overlooked, and Rhodes appear capable of improving the situation. But in Rhodes' case, you have to believe in his '93 minor league season (.318 BA, .602 SLG, 148 TOPR)—very impressive, but totally out of context with his career. The Cubs seem more fond of May's .295 BA (and 99 TOPR) and Roberson's power potential (and 82 TOPR), though.

A brief note on Sandberg. The hand injury must have severely restricted his offense as well as his playing time (only 117 games). His .309 BA obscured the fact that, for the first time since '86, he actually hit like a 2B (only a 105 TOPR). His power disappeared with a .412 SLG, rather than the .500+ that's been his custom. The Cubs need his 140+ TOPR back.

The Pitching

The Cubs' '93 pitchers ended up a little below average (101.1 TPER). Given Wrigley's "hitter's park" status though (105.0 Park TOPR), the staff actually grades out slightly better than average. Regardless, there was reason to be disappointed—every pitcher on the staff slumped from his prior three-year TPER standard (except Myers and the surprising Shawn Boskie).

The Rotation: Wrigley Field rewards ground-ball pitchers and good control in particular. These traits tend to reduce opposition HRs and their potential cost. Cubs starters all possessed at least one of these characteristics and Cubbie hurlers tied for the league lead in DPs induced (134). Greg Hibbard had both characteristics going for him and got rewarded with a 15–11, 3.96 ERA, 98 TPER season. Mike Morgan, an *extreme* ground-baller, has flourished in the "friendly confines" and has an 18–8 career record in 36 starts at Wrigley with a 2.05 ERA and only 8 HR allowed (one per 33 IP). His overall 10–15 record in '93 belied his 4.03 ERA and fine 92 TPER.

The rest of the starters slipped, though. Jose Guzman, after being out of action for over two seasons, has made an incredible comeback from shoulder surgery. Before going out with shoulder tendinitis in September, he'd made 88 consecutive starts without missing a turn. But, as his arm has gotten stronger, a puzzling thing is occurring. He's getting more Ks, but he's also yielding more HRs—and becoming less effective.

	K/9 IP	IP/HR	TPER
Rangers '91	6.6	17.0	90
Rangers '92	7.2	13.2	98
Cubs '93	7.7	7.6	108

Some of this traces to Wrigley, of course, but surely not all of it. It's a disturbing trend (along with the tendinitis popping up).

Mike Harkey pitched better than his 5.28 ERA, but a 107 TPER's nothing to shout about. Between a cartilage tear in '92, a ruptured patella tendon in '92 and a tendinitis flare-up in '93, Mike's having a hard time getting his career underway.

Lord only knows what happened to Frank Castillo. There's no injury reported, just a record of season-long ineffectiveness. The only fly-ball pitcher on the staff, his K rate is going down while his HR rate is going up—producing a TPER trendline that looks like Guzman's (91, 100, 114). Castillo averaged a little less than 5½ IP per start and went at least 7 in only 9 of 25 tries.

The Cubs' rotation will probably have a different look in '94. Willie Banks came from Minnesota in an off-season deal. He pitches up in the strike zone (often wildly) and doesn't seem to fit the Wrigley Field mold. Steve Trachsel and Turk Wendell, up from AAA, may get their chance. But another 267 IP and 20 wins from Maddux sure would've looked good in the Cubs' rotation, wouldn't it?

The Bullpen: Randy Myers completely changed the Cubs' bullpen, reestablishing himself as a premiere closer. His 84 TPER stood him only seventh in the NL closer rankings, but that's a very strong number and he *was* in Wrigley. The Cubs' closer problem is solved!

At the other end of the pen, longman Jose Bautista finally got it going. Notoriously homer-prone in his two years as a starter for the Orioles in '88–'89 (one HR/6.6 IP), Jose came to Wrigley and miraculously kept it in the park (one HR/10.2 IP). That earned him a glittering 10–3 record and 2.82 ERA in 111.2 IP, with a 92 TPER.

For the previous three years, RHP Shawn Boskie had been the Cubs' "starter-in-waiting" at AAA Iowa. When a starter went down, Boskie got called up, then got lit up ('91–'92 TPERs, 126 and 128). Converted to a relief role in '93, he became effective (3.43 ERA, 97 TPER). Bob Scanlan, the other RH middleman, had some troubles in '93 (4.54 ERA, 105 TPER) after an outstanding '92 (2.89 ERA, 85 TPER). He wore down some in the second half, which might be attributed to his workload.

From the other side, the Cubs somehow felt it necessary to carry four southpaw relievers in '93 (counting Myers). Two of them have since departed (Paul Assenmacher to the Yankees and Chuck McElroy to the Reds), leaving the least effective. Over the entire season, Dan Plesac got beaten up in his NL debut (4.74 ERA, 116 TPER). But, as he adjusted to conditions and got reassigned to spot work, he regained his effectiveness. In the second half, he pitched in 31 games and only gave up one HR in 23 innings. By contrast, in his first ten appearances he gave up 12 earned runs (and 5 HR) in 15 innings.

Overall, the bullpen shapes up as the least of the Cubs' problems—but an effective lefty would be nice.

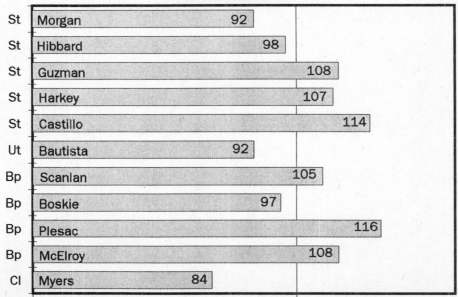

1993 Cubs Staff

		TPER
St	Morgan	92
St	Hibbard	98
St	Guzman	108
St	Harkey	107
St	Castillo	114
Ut	Bautista	92
Bp	Scanlan	105
Bp	Boskie	97
Bp	Plesac	116
Bp	McElroy	108
Cl	Myers	84

50   100

What Next?

New manager Tom Trebelhorn faces many of the same tasks that his predecessor faced: sorting out the Cubs' OF, arranging the batting order in a coherent pattern and making do without a rotation anchor. If Sandberg returns to form, his job becomes a lot easier.

Trebelhorn performed some minor miracles with the Brewers during his five years in Milwaukee (422–397). His seemingly below average teams generally achieved averageness. That's to a manager's credit. In Chicago, he inherits an average team to start with and might boost them above that level.

The composition of the new NL Central provides the Cubs with an opportunity to actually be contenders in '94. Their '93 record of 84–78 would have placed them third (behind St. Louis' 87 wins and Houston's 85). Both Cincinnati and Pittsburgh figure to be improved in '94, so the division could really turn into a dogfight.

Under these circumstances, the Cubs have two choices:

1. Gamble dollars on one player who could make the difference— one more big stick or a #1 starter. Or . . .
2. Stand pat—gambling on a monster comeback by Sandberg and a couple of kids coming through.

If fear remains a motivation, how and how much does one gamble?

Team TOPR: 1993 Chicago Cubs

	Bats	BA	OBP	SLG	HR	R	RBI	NBE	GOC	Ratio	TOPR
League Avg. Team	-	.264	.327	.399	140	728	681	2835	4378	0.647	100
Chicago Cubs	-	.270	.325	.414	161	738	706	2843	4388	0.648	100.1
Regulars:											
C Rick Wilkins	L	.303	.376	.561	30	78	73	299	319	0.937	145
1B Mark Grace	L	.325	.393	.475	14	86	98	343	440	0.780	120
2B Ryne Sandberg	R	.309	.359	.412	9	67	45	230	337	0.682	105
3B Steve Buechele	R	.272	.345	.437	15	53	65	249	355	0.701	108
SS Jose Vizcaino	B	.287	.340	.358	4	74	54	257	428	0.600	93
LF Derrick May	L	.295	.336	.422	10	62	77	226	352	0.642	99
CF Dwight Smith	L	.300	.354	.494	11	51	35	184	230	0.800	124
Willie Wilson	B	.258	.301	.348	1	29	11	96	170	0.565	87
RF Sammy Sosa	R	.261	.309	.485	33	92	93	345	467	0.739	114
Bench (100+ TPA):											
IF Rey Sanchez	R	.282	.316	.326	0	35	28	133	267	0.498	77
OF Kevin Roberson	B	.189	.251	.372	9	23	27	79	149	0.530	(82)
OF Candy Maldonado	R	.186	.260	.286	3	8	15	51	117	0.436	(67)
C Steve Lake	R	.225	.250	.400	5	11	13	46	103	0.447	(69)
IF Eric Yelding	R	.204	.277	.296	1	14	10	45	95	0.474	(73)

NOTE: Statistics are only for games played with Chicago. ( ) Under 200 TPA.

Team TPER: 1993 Chicago Cubs

	Throws	W-L	GS	GR	SV	IP	ERA	NBA	GOE	Ratio	TPER
League Avg. Team	-	81 -81	162	381	43	1449	4.04	2835	4378	0.647	100
Chicago Cubs	-	84 -78	163	423	56	1449.2	4.18	2848	4354	0.654	101.0
The Rotation:											
Mike Morgan	R	10 -15	32	0	0	207.2	4.03	375	627	0.598	92
Greg Hibbard	L	15 -11	31	0	0	191	3.96	363	575	0.631	98
Jose Guzman	R	12 -10	30	0	0	191	4.34	401	574	0.699	108
Mike Harkey	R	10 -10	28	0	0	157.1	5.26	323	466	0.693	107
Frank Castillo	R	5 -8	25	4	0	141.1	4.84	312	422	0.739	114
Bullpen:											
Jose Bautista	R	10 -3	7	52	2	111.2	2.82	197	330	0.597	92
Bob Scanlan	R	4 -5	0	70	0	75.1	4.54	155	228	0.680	105
Shawn Boskie	R	5 -3	2	37	0	65.2	3.43	124	198	0.626	97
Dan Plesac	L	2 -1	0	57	0	62.2	4.74	141	188	0.750	116
Chuck McElroy	L	2 -2	0	49	0	47.1	4.56	101	144	0.701	(108)
Paul Assenmacher	L	2 -1	0	46	0	38.2	3.49	76	115	0.661	(102)
Randy Myers	L	2 -4	0	73	53	75.1	3.11	125	230	0.543	84

NOTE: Statistics are only for games pitched with Chicago. ( ) Under 200 TBF.

MEMORANDUM
CINCINNATI REDS

TO: The Baseball Gods
FROM: Jim Bowden, GM
SUBJECT: UNFAIR TREATMENT

The Cincinnati Reds' organization wishes to file a formal protest over their treatment at your hands the past two years.

The '92 season was quite enough: 14 stays on the disabled list by 12 separate players totaling 395 player games lost due to injury.

But you outdid yourselves in '93! I just saw the final figures and I'm frankly appalled. Twenty trips to the DL this time, by 15 different players (who continue to draw full salary, I remind you). A total of *798 PLAYER GAMES LOST DUE TO INJURY*!!! That's almost five seasons worth, for crying out loud.

Oh, and this time, you *really* hit us where it hurts—the 8-man everyday lineup, the 5-man rotation and the core of the bullpen. On their own, those 15 roster spots produced 14 visits to the list by 10 of these most important players and a *total of 586 games missed*. Five regulars in the everyday lineup played less than 100 games. We were able to put the team we wanted on the field in only four games. That we went 3–1 on these rare days is of no particular solace.

We note with interest that our competitors, the Atlanta Braves, suffered injuries to only four players—a backup catcher and a spare outfielder, the #5 starter and a redundant bullpener. All were adequately backed up. But even our backups fell like flies. We had to use a record 51 players, all told, just to field a team.

Look, I know this whole protest procedure is fruitless and might as well be written on toilet paper. But, give me a break. What do I tell Marge when she gets back, huh?

Team Trendline: Cincinnati Reds

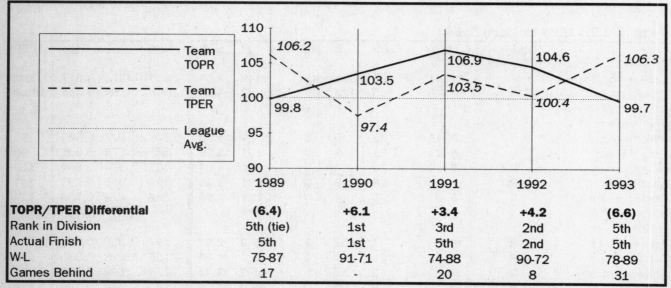

	1989	1990	1991	1992	1993
TOPR/TPER Differential	(6.4)	+6.1	+3.4	+4.2	(6.6)
Rank in Division	5th (tie)	1st	3rd	2nd	5th
Actual Finish	5th	1st	5th	2nd	5th
W-L	75-87	91-71	74-88	90-72	78-89
Games Behind	17	-	20	8	31

What Was Expected

A flurry of off-season moves seemed to recast the star-crossed '92 Reds into perhaps an even stronger contender. The acquisition of Kevin Mitchell introduced a power bat into a lineup that needed one. It cost a closer-quality reliever in Norm Charlton. But the Reds had another and probably better one in Rob Dibble. John Smiley signed to fill out the rotation making Greg Swindell's departure via free agency of no moment. CF Bobby Kelly would add even more speed, while the traded Paul O'Neill would hardly be missed with Reggie Sanders available to play full-time. On paper, the '93 Reds were again a worthy contender—melding a destructive offense with an imposing rotation, though the bullpen looked a little thin. This mirrored the profile of the target Braves. If NL champion Atlanta was to be dethroned, Cincinnati seemed "the team most likely."

What Actually Happened

The '93 Reds, as they appeared on paper, almost never appeared on the field. Accordingly, we've no way of knowing what this team may have accomplished. The Reds fielded their "paper" lineup only on June 15, 16, 18 and 25 (3 wins and a loss).

The troubles began in spring training. The Reds came north with 1B Hal Morris out with a shoulder separation and closer Rob Dibble suffering severe control problems (of a strike zone variety) due to a perforated eardrum. On an April 22 play at the plate, Dibble added a broken arm and sprained ankle to his medical chart, joining Morris on the DL. Both would be out through May.

In May the list grew. Steve Foster, scheduled to play a major role in the bullpen and performing brilliantly (71 TPER), joined the DL with shoulder problems. Mainstay 3B Chris Sabo, still hobbled somewhat by an ankle injury from '92, ruptured a disc. The Reds struggled around .500 (25–26 at the end of May).

June came. Bill Landrum, Foster's backup, went out for the season with elbow inflammation. Foster returned, but for only three days, then was pronounced out for the season. Sabo returned, too, but at something less than his normal productivity. John Roper, a rookie starter taking up some of the slack, traded in his earlier elbow tendinitis for a strained ribcage muscle. As the month ended, the .500 mark remained just beyond the Reds' grasp (38–40).

July arrived and all the previous misfortunes paled in its carnage. Leadoff man Bip Roberts, already troubled by a sore right shoulder (April 12), a sprained right wrist (April 16) and a sprained left thumb (June 11), finally succumbed to the thumb injury on July 2.

Starter John Smiley, strangely ineffective to that time, went out for the season July 3 with a bone spur in his left elbow. Kevin Mitchell, in and out of the lineup because of a broken sesamoid bone in his foot and a shoulder strain, now pulled up lame with a hamstring on July 9. Bobby Kelly, leading the league in hits, separated his shoulder on July 14. Say bye-bye Bobby. In a matter of two weeks, the season had essentially ended for four key players. They would be joined by two more, SS Barry Larkin and starter Tom Browning, in early August.

The Reds nonetheless fought back, reaching the season's high-water mark of 59–55 on August 8. The rest of the season's record (14–34) and its injury lists are of academic importance only, as the Reds' roster became more of a full-time try-out camp.

1993 Cincinnati Reds: Month-by-Month

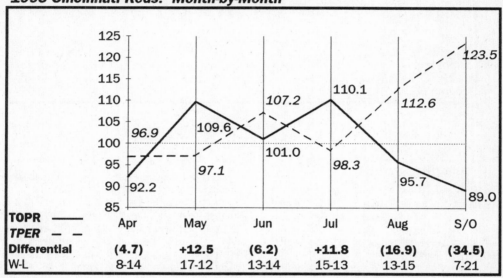

	Apr	May	Jun	Jul	Aug	S/O
TOPR ——						
TPER – –						
Differential	**(4.7)**	**+12.5**	**(6.2)**	**+11.8**	**(16.9)**	**(34.5)**
W-L	8-14	17-12	13-14	15-13	13-15	7-21

Riverfront Stadium

The NL's collection of "cookie-cutter" stadia—Three Rivers, the Vet and Riverfront—effectively defined the league norm in '93. Each produced a Park TOPR of about 100, smack-dab in the middle.

Riverfront's 99.3 Park TOPR exemplified the breed. Nothing more than a normal home advantage was granted the Reds' hitters or their pitchers. Strictly a "park-neutral" effect on offense, perfectly suited to its "neutral" appearance.

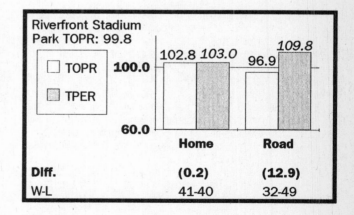

Riverfront Stadium
Park TOPR: 99.8

	Home	Road
TOPR	102.8	96.9
TPER	103.0	109.8
Diff.	**(0.2)**	**(12.9)**
W-L	41-40	32-49

1993 Reds Lineup

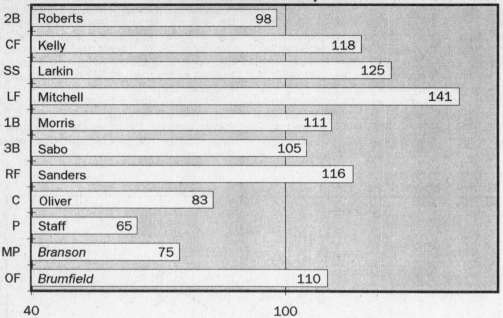

Position	Player	TOPR
2B	Roberts	98
CF	Kelly	118
SS	Larkin	125
LF	Mitchell	141
1B	Morris	111
3B	Sabo	105
RF	Sanders	116
C	Oliver	83
P	Staff	65
MP	*Branson*	75
OF	*Brumfield*	110

40   100

The Offense

The Reds' '93 Team TOPR (99.7) and the lineup graphic above seemingly bear no relationship to each other. The paradox is explained by:

1. Only three of the regulars listed below started as many as 100 games (Sabo, Sanders and Joe Oliver).
2. At that, five of the regulars spent all or a considerable part of their season playing hurt (Roberts, Larkin, Mitchell, Morris and Sabo). Some of their TOPRs showed it.

The impact of these injuries on what figured to be a highly productive offense is an issue worth detailing.

The most grievous of the season's injuries, insofar as its impact on the Reds' offense is concerned, were perhaps those suffered by leadoff man Bip Roberts. In '92, the Bipster had been the NL's best leadoff hitter (.323 BA, .393 OBP with 44 SB and 138 TPER). With a more powerful lineup behind him in '93, a similar performance would have yielded bushels of runs beyond the 92 he scored in '92. But, hampered by hurts, his batting dropped precipitously (.240 BA, .330 OBP, a disappointing 98 TOPR) in only 83 games. His replacement, Juan Samuel, performed even worse than a crippled Bip (.230 BA, .298 OBP, 86 TOPR).

At the time of his injury, CF Bobby Kelly led the NL in hits (102) and ranked among the league leaders in steals (21) and total bases (152 in 78 games). From May 6 on, his BA was a scorching .347. Defensively, he had committed only one error in 202 chances. Bobby's 118 TOPR at the time was replaced by reserve OF Jacob Brumfield, who exhibited almost identical skills but at a slightly lower level (110 TOPR).

Playing hurt in most of his 98 starts, SS Barry Larkin had a sub-standard 125 TOPR year (.315 BA, .394 OBP, .406 SLG). Healthy, he's in 140 territory with a high average, power and speed (MVP material at short). Reserve IF Jeff Branson, who helped cover the injuries at 2B and 3B as well as SS, took his dreadful 75 TOPR to the plate a total of 412 times as a consequence. With a .241 BA, .275 OBP, .310 SLG and only 19 BB vs. 73 Ks, Branson's bat was a mere twig compared to Larkin's lumber.

Kevin Mitchell showed up at Plant City looking like Fat City and limping on a broken foot. Appropriately, he hit a homer in his first spring training AB, avoiding the need to run it out. His season in LF was relatively brief, but cast a giant shadow (.341 BA, .601 SLG, 19 HR with 64 RBI and a TOPR as tall as Kevin was wide, 141). So, while his condition didn't seem to affect his play, it limited his playing time. Mitchell's two stints on the DL covered 33 games missed. But he only started in 86 of the remaining 129. In Mitchell's absence, the Reds used 13 other left fielders. The best of them turned out to be Thomas Howard, who was at least average (100 TOPR with Cincinnati).

After he returned from the DL in June, Hal Morris registered a superficially good year, hitting his customary .317. Unfortunately, BA was about all there was to his TOPR (a below-par 111) as he provided little power (95 singles in his 120 hits). Morris' stand-in, Randy Milligan, actually had a more productive season (121). But nobody noticed and he was traded to Cleveland for Howard.

Chris Sabo wasn't invited back after two sub-standard seasons at 3B. A gamer who plays hurt, "Spuds" didn't help himself with his TOPR numbers (99 in '92 and 105 in '93). The ankle injury he suffered in '92 and its lingering effects, robbed him of his speed (only 10 of 19 on the basepaths the past two years) and ability to turn on the ball ('92–'93 SLG of .433 vs. .491 in '90–'91) as well as his agility in the field.

Only two Reds regulars made it through the year unscathed, second-year RF Sanders and C Oliver. Sanders unaccountably took a step back from his impressive rookie year (TOPR dipping from 132 to 116). He showed virtually no improvement in any aspect of his offensive game. Oliver kept on plugging along at his standard pace (83 TOPR), providing some power (14 HR and 29 2B) at the bottom of the order and little else.

The '93 Reds offense could have been a good one. But injury problems effectively gutted it. It could be a good one in '94 if:

◆ Everybody shows up, and stays healthy. Mitchell is the largest question (in more ways than one).
◆ The new 2B and 3B, Bret Boone and Willie Greene, are as good

as their minor league numbers suggest (i.e., at or above their positional norms).

◆ An effective leadoff hitter can be found. Sanders could be devastating in this role (if he picked up his development pace).

But, in Cincinnati, it's not wise to count on sure things—much less ifs.

The Pitching

The presence of seven starters in the '93 Reds "rotation" gives you an inkling of the problem, doesn't it? Along with the total of 24 pitchers the club used over the year, well, you get the picture.

After Jose Rijo, whom we'll save for later, the staff presented one problem after another—most of them injury related.

Healthy, but plagued by inconsistency, Rookie Tim Pugh's 114 TPER was pure Jekyll and Hyde:

◆ In his 10 wins, he pitched at least seven innings in every one with a 2.02 ERA and only 16 BB in 75.2 IP.
◆ In his 14 losses as a starter, he averaged less than five innings per outing, gave up 35 BB in 65 IP with an ERA of 9.28.

To be effective, Pugh must be "in control." He seemed to be gaining on it toward season's end. If Jekyll wins out, Pugh could be much improved in '94.

Browning's future, though, has been heavily clouded. Injuries have prematurely ended two consecutive horrid seasons. Both would have ranked him among the five least effective rotation starters in the league had he completed them (131 and 117 TPERs). Accordingly, he should *not* be counted upon in '94.

Smiley, signed to replace Swindell in the rotation, gave almost no sign of his previous low-nineties TPER level of effectiveness (112 TPER in '93). Probably it was the bone spur. Probably, surgery on August 2 corrected it. Probably, he'll be 100% for spring training. Probably, he'll be a 20-game winner again in '94.

Rookie John Roper, bounced from Indianapolis to the DL to the Reds' rotation, spending what was left of his year auditioning for a job in '94. He had a few good days and a few more bad ones (122 TPER). Roper went 1–5 with a poor 5.63 ERA (6.15 in his final 11 starts). He may not be ready for the rotation job the Reds would like him to take.

Veteran Tim Belcher and another auditioning rookie, Larry Luebbers, were both traded for badly needed bullpen help. Belcher, who was fading at the All-Star break brought a rich harvest from the White Sox—prospects Johnny Ruffin and Jeff Pierce. Luebbers formed part of a package to the Cubs for LH set-up man Chuck McElroy. Though Luebbers seemed encouraging in his debut (2–5 in 14 starts, 4.54 ERA, 96 TPER), his minor league profile suggests he won't be missed.

The Reds' pen put forth a disgraceful performance in '93 and must be completely rebuilt. The reconstruction will have to start around Dibble, who was either hurt or wild as a sailor's first night in port virtually the entire year. His awful 147 TPER complemented his ugly 6.48 ERA and 42 BB in 41.2 IP. If his troubles, in fact, traced to a perforated eardrum, a broken arm, a sprained ankle and "muscle weakness" in *both* shoulders (which finally ended his season September 22) then it may be that he got everything out of his system at once. Maybe he'll saw his TPER in half next year. The Reds have to hope so.

Other key pieces may already be in place. Jerry Spradlin did a fine job in his major league debut (3.42 ERA, 88 TPER in 49 IP) and warrants a spot. Johnny Ruffin got called up after the Belcher trade and looked strong (3.58 ERA, 36 H, 11 BB, 30 K in 37.2 IP). His 107 TPER showed promise but the long ball betrayed him. Scott Service, now a fugitive from three different organizations, has always looked like an ideal longman. The Reds finally gave him a chance and he came through for them (3.70 ERA, 36 H, 15 BB and 41 K in 41.1 IP, 99 TPER). The addition of McElroy from the Cubs provides a solid southpaw set-up man for the mix. The bullpen starts looking capable. Given Dibble, of course.

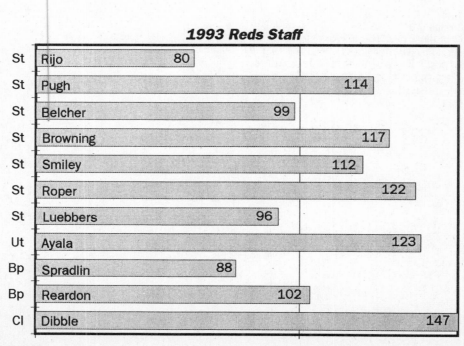

1993 Reds Staff

St	Rijo — 80
St	Pugh — 114
St	Belcher — 99
St	Browning — 117
St	Smiley — 112
St	Roper — 122
St	Luebbers — 96
Ut	Ayala — 123
Bp	Spradlin — 88
Bp	Reardon — 102
Cl	Dibble — 147

50   100

36 Epic Starts

The best we saved for last. Did you notice what Jose Rijo did this year? *Really* notice? He tied for the major league lead in starts (36) and was second in the league in both ERA (2.48) and IP (257.1). Jose led the league in strikeouts (227) and ranked third in opponent BA (.230). He only finished 14–9 because a) five times he left the game in the 9th with a lead that the bullpen didn't hold (only one was a one-run lead, by the way), and b) in his nine losses, the Reds scored a *total* of eight runs. More remarkable, however, is the incredibly high and consistent quality of his 36 starts. Here are the innings pitched and earned runs allowed in each:

Rijo: 36 for the book

IP	ER	Result	IP	ER	Result
April			*July*		
8.0	0	W	7.0	4	L
7.1	1	ND	7.0	3	L
7.0	3	L	8.0	2	ND
5.2	5	ND	8.0	0	W
7.0	0	W	7.0	1	ND
May			8.0	0	W
7.0	4	W	8.0	1	W
6.0	4	W	*August*		
5.0	2	W	7.0	1	W
7.2	1	ND	7.0	2	L
8.0	2	W	7.0	1	L
7.0	2	ND	7.0	1	ND
June			8.0	0	W
7.0	3	ND	6.0	2	W
7.0	5	L	*September*		
6.2	3	ND	7.0	1	W
7.0	3	ND	7.0	1	ND
8.0	4	ND	6.0	2	ND
7.0	0	L	8.0	5	L
			9.0	0	W
			7.0	2	L

More than four earned runs allowed in only three of his 36 starts and 7 IP or more in 31 of them (counting a five-inning complete game rainout on May 12). In his last 17 starts he *allowed more than two earned runs but once!* OK, he went the full nine only once. But the man pitched well enough to win 30 games. Easy! Ironically, '93 marked the first time in Rijo's six years with the Reds that *he* didn't make a trip to the DL.

What Next?

The '94 Reds don't appear as strong, on paper, as the '92 and '93 Reds. But if they make it off the paper and onto the field, they're as likely to win the new NL Central Division as anybody.

Lingering injury questions remain to be answered. Naturally! There's Morris, Larkin, Mitchell, Kelly, Smiley and Dibble. There's even a pair of new ones. Willie Greene, scheduled for 3B in '94, dislocated his thumb in August and took his turn on the DL. Plus Brian Holman, who's evidently counted upon as a staff member, hasn't pitched in two years while recovering from arm surgery.

At this point, there's little else to be done—except checking the reports on the clipboards at the foot of each bed.

Team TOPR: 1993 Cincinnati Reds

	Bats	BA	OBP	SLG	HR	R	RBI	NBE	GOC	Ratio	TOPR
League Avg. Team	-	.264	.327	.399	140	728	681	2835	4378	0.647	100
Cincinnati Reds	-	.264	.324	.396	137	722	669	2810	4352	0.646	99.7
Regulars:											
C Joe Oliver	R	.239	.276	.384	14	40	75	211	391	0.540	83
1B Hal Morris	L	.317	.371	.420	7	48	49	196	272	0.721	111
2B Bip Roberts	B	.240	.330	.295	1	46	18	148	233	0.635	98
3B Chris Sabo	R	.259	.315	.440	21	86	82	294	433	0.679	105
SS Barry Larkin	R	.315	.394	.445	8	57	51	227	281	0.808	125
LF Kevin Mitchell	R	.341	.385	.601	19	56	64	211	231	0.913	141
CF Roberto Kelly	R	.319	.353	.475	9	44	35	180	236	0.763	118
RF Reggie Sanders	R	.274	.343	.444	20	90	83	294	391	0.752	116
Bench (100+ TPA):											
IF Jeff Branson	L	.241	.275	.310	3	40	22	148	306	0.484	75
OF Jacob Brumfield	R	.268	.321	.419	6	40	23	152	213	0.714	110
2B Juan Samuel	R	.230	.298	.345	4	31	26	118	212	0.557	86
1B Randy Milligan	R	.274	.394	.406	6	30	29	138	176	0.784	121
OF Thomas Howard	B	.277	.331	.461	4	22	13	73	113	0.646	(100)
OF Gary Varsho	L	.232	.302	.358	2	8	11	48	78	0.615	(95)
1B Tim Costo	R	.224	.250	.367	3	13	12	41	79	0.519	(80)

NOTE: Statistics are only for games played with Cincinnati. ( ) Under 200 TPA.

Team TPER: 1993 Cincinnati Reds

	Throws	W-L	GS	GR	SV	IP	ERA	NBA	GOE	Ratio	TPER
League Avg. Team	-	81 -81	162	381	43	1449	4.04	2835	4378	0.647	100
Cincinnati Reds	-	73 -89	162	375	37	1434	4.51	2972	4318	0.688	106.3
The Rotation:											
Jose Rijo	R	14 -9	36	0	0	257.1	2.48	400	774	0.517	80
Tim Pugh	R	10 -15	27	4	0	164.1	5.26	363	494	0.735	113
Tim Belcher	R	9 -6	22	0	0	137	4.47	265	413	0.642	99
Tom Browning	L	7 -7	20	1	0	114	4.74	258	341	0.757	117
John Smiley	L	3 -9	18	0	0	105.2	5.62	231	318	0.726	112
John Roper	R	2 -5	15	1	0	80	5.63	190	240	0.792	122
Larry Luebbers	L	2 -5	14	0	0	77.1	4.54	145	234	0.620	96
Bullpen:											
Bobby Ayala	R	7 -10	9	34	3	98	5.60	238	299	0.796	123
Jeff Reardon	R	4 -6	0	58	8	61.2	4.09	124	188	0.660	102
Jerry Spradlin	R	2 -1	0	37	2	49	3.49	84	147	0.571	88
Scott Service	R	2 -2	0	26	2	41.1	3.70	80	125	0.640	(99)
Johnny Ruffin	R	2 -1	0	21	2	37.2	3.58	78	113	0.690	(107)
Greg Cadaret	L	2 -1	0	34	1	32.2	4.96	78	100	0.780	(120)
Rob Dibble	R	1 -4	0	45	19	41.2	6.48	117	123	0.951	147

NOTE: Statistics are only for games pitched with Cincinnati. ( ) Under 200 TBF.

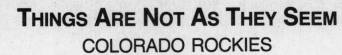

THINGS ARE NOT AS THEY SEEM
COLORADO ROCKIES

If one is to understand the Colorado Rockies and their inaugural '93 season, one must first understand their home park. Mile High Stadium created an effect not unlike the "hall of mirrors" in a sideshow Fun House. One distorted image next to another, equally distorted but different.

From its minor league history in the AAA American Association, Mile High was expected to be a "hitter's park." But major league hitters took advantage of its conditions to produce an inflation in offense that was totally unexpected and without precedent. Further,

there were clearly *two* sources for this inflation—mainly the park's altitude, with its configuration a secondary factor. The implications as they regard hitters and pitchers are thus totally different. As a consequence, any assessment of the Rockies as a team must first deal with the distorted images they present.

Overall, Mile High was responsible for an estimated +27.6% increase in offensive output. And it had a dramatic affect on *every element* of the pitcher-batter confrontation, as shown below.

1993 Park Effect: Mile High Stadium

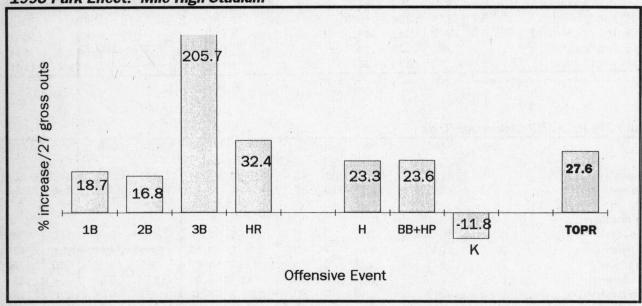

What Was Expected

The '93 Rockies really didn't have expectations. They were, after all, an expansion club. Realism prevailed in all sectors—among the fans, media, front office and other experts. Most analyses instead focused on the relative performance of the two expansion clubs. The race became the Rockies vs. the Marlins. Both got consigned to the cellar in their respective divisions, and the issue was confined to which of the two would win the most games and whether either could escape 100 losses. The contrast in the two teams' draft strategies was an important factor. The Rockies seemed to have gone for "instant credibility" by drafting "proven major league players." The Marlins had gone for the "future" by choosing "prospects." Generally, Colorado figured to come out on top in '93 and would be the most likely to avoid 100 losses. Florida, most reasoned, would be better positioned for the longer term.

The Rockies' home park, Mile High Stadium, aroused interest on its own. The short left field (335' down the line, 375' to the gap) coupled with the high altitude and relatively thin, dry air, had made

Mile High a "hitter's park" in the minors. How major league hitters would respond to it was a subject for the Hot Stove League.

What Actually Happened

In many respects, the first home series of the year set the tone for Colorado's '93 season. The Rockies, having dropped a pair to the Mets, came home to Mile High and a major league record opening day attendance of 80,227 greeted them. The home boys bashed the visiting Expos 11–4 for the club's first-ever win. Another win followed the next day and the Rockies stood at .500 for the first time ever (and the last time in '93). Montreal salvaged the closing game of the series. But a total of 57 runs had been scored in the three games revealing the true nature of the park. It would produce an average of almost 13 runs per game over the course of the season (the other parks in the league averaged less than nine).

Four brutal months followed in which the offense continued to produce runs (but only at home it seemed) and the pitching staff churned constantly in a frantic search for *anybody* who could get *somebody* out. By the end of July, the staff ERA stood at an unsightly 5.98 and the club drifted in the midst of yet another losing streak. Colorado reached its nadir on August 6, dropping a double-dip at San Diego, their 12th and 13th losses in a row. The record stood at a league worst 36–74 and at least 100 losses looked assured.

The fans hadn't given up, though. Home attendance totaled 3¼ million, over 58 thousand per date. The club was a cinch to top 4 million and set an all-time major league single-season attendance record. And the team hadn't given up either. From that point, they won 12 of their next 15, finishing August on an up note. In September, the fans still flocked to Mile High and the Rockies

continued to win, moving past the sinking Padres on the 15th. The all-time attendance record fell on the 17th. They won their 63rd on the 21st leaving the ignominy of 100 losses behind them. The very next night the 1,000th run of the season crossed Mile High's plate.

At season's end, the Rockies had gone 31–21 since August 6, the NL's 3rd best record from that point behind only the Braves and Giants. They had also moved into 6th place and won 67 games in all vs. the Marlins' 64. Pride and hope for the future flourished. Four million fans had poured into Mile High in '93 and watched a total of 1,040 runners cross the plate (489 wearing a Rockies' uniform). It had been an exciting and financially gratifying season.

1993 Colorado Rockies: Month-by-Month

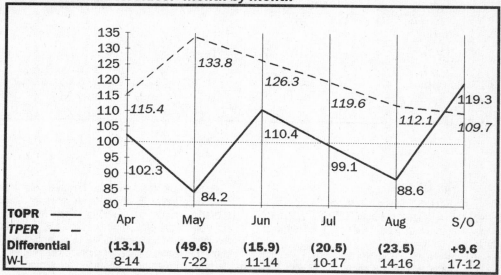

	Apr	May	Jun	Jul	Aug	S/O
TOPR ———						
TPER – –						
Differential	(13.1)	(49.6)	(15.9)	(20.5)	(23.5)	+9.6
W-L	8-14	7-22	11-14	10-17	14-16	17-12

Mile High Stadium

In its inaugural season, Mile High inflated offense an astounding +27.6%. It's doubtful whether *any* major league park has ever so distorted the game or the performance of the team that called it home.

As indicated in the graph opposite, the park profoundly affected *every* aspect of offense. The "park effect" itself appears *secondary*, restricted to the bizarre increase in triples (RF is immense, 370' down the line) and an increment of HRs (left field is short, 335' down the line). Pitchers felt the *primary* effect—atmospheric conditions that caused a pitched ball to behave other than as planned. An "altitude effect," if you will. Understandably, Rockies' pitchers seemed better adapted to these conditions than opposing pitchers. Accordingly, the Rockies' hitters benefited disproportionately.

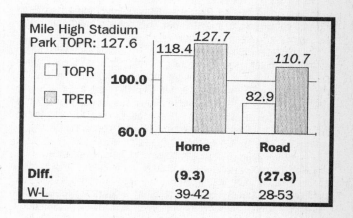

	Home	Road
Diff.	(9.3)	(27.8)
W-L	39-42	28-53

1993 Rockies Lineup

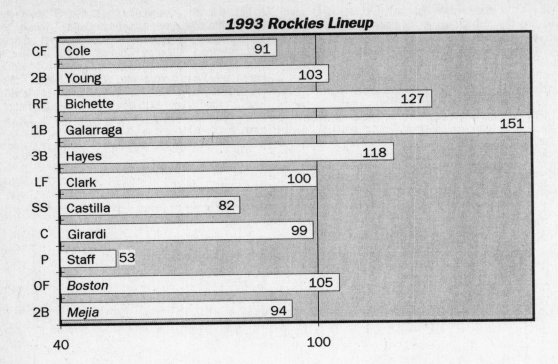

Position	Player	Value
CF	Cole	91
2B	Young	103
RF	Bichette	127
1B	Galarraga	151
3B	Hayes	118
LF	Clark	100
SS	Castilla	82
C	Girardi	99
P	Staff	53
OF	*Boston*	105
2B	*Mejia*	94

40   100

The Offense

On its surface, the '93 Rockies' lineup appeared surprisingly respectable for a first year. A league average TOPR (100.1) produced an above-average number of runs (758). A solid core of hitters seemed to have been gathered.

In reality, nothing was really further from the truth. The Colorado hitters were the major beneficiaries of the complex "effect" that came into play at Mile High Stadium. With the "mountain air" taken out of the Team TOPR, the true level of the offense computes as a puny 86.0. This is slightly *below* a similarly adjusted Florida Team TOPR (86.7). The Rockies' offense, which looked so good and was considered such a strength, was actually no stronger than the weakest offense in the league.

This really shouldn't shock anybody. When Colorado stocked up on "proven major leaguers" at the expansion draft, all these players had "proved" was that they were *mediocre* major league players offensively. In TOPR terms, Dante Bichette had a prior 3-year average of 92 through '92, Charlie Hayes an 85, Joe Girardi a 72. Are we to believe that they were all capable of, and would simultaneously achieve, "breakthrough" years equivalent to a stupendous +34% gain over their established level? Hardly. In fact, they were the same competent players as before—below-average offensive performers whose defense was good enough to earn them a job until something better came along. But in their fantastic new offensive environment, they have taken on a deceiving appearance.

The new NL batting king, Andres Galarraga, had a season good enough to suspect his offensive credentials might be reestablished. If this was the objective that he and his agent had in mind when they signed a one-year pact with Colorado, their gamble paid off. Galarraga's experience may start a new trend the Colorado franchise would be wise to capitalize upon during its formative years. Aging ballplayers in search of career and contract rejuvenation should seek Mile High's refreshing mountain air just as the European royalty of another era journeyed to Baden to take the waters.

Jerald Clark and Alex Cole, however, did themselves no favors. San Diego patiently waited three years for Clark, a RH hitter with sporadic power, to develop. When he didn't, they made him available in the draft. One suspects that if he didn't develop under the ideal conditions prevailing in Colorado—regular playing time, short LF fence, facing pitchers struggling with the altitude—he *never will.* Cole, too, had the job he wanted—regular leadoff hitter. He couldn't hold it, though, with a .256 BA and .339 OBP. And when Alex's bat failed him, his glove wouldn't keep him in the lineup.

Eric Young had a quietly impressive, but strangely contrary, season. He led the team in walks (63), on a team that didn't walk (388, lowest in the majors). He led the team in steals (42, with a high success rate of 69%), on a team that didn't run well but ran often (90 CS, highest in the league, and only a 62% success rate). His .355 OBP made him the only potential tablesetter on the team. But unsteady fielding cost him his job at 2B after the all-star break. He shuffled to the outfield and was being groomed to take over in CF. But the Rockies signed free agent Ellis Burks for the CF job.

Young's replacement at 2B, Roberto Mejia, shot through the minors like a meteor—arriving in Mile High after two and a half seasons. He's got glove problems, too, and neither walks nor runs. But Roberto's supposed to hit homers and he's only 22.

Galarraga became a free agent and then re-signed. Mejia is probably a keeper. The rest of the Colorado cast of regulars and bench personnel should be considered disposable at any time, without advance notice, subject only to the availability of a better player. That's a hard concept to grasp given the numbers some of them amassed. But for the Colorado club to make progress, they must see through the illusions created by Mile High to recognize that beneath this collection of sky-high numbers lies an offense that's actually under water.

The Pitching

The list of Rockies' pitching accomplishments makes for dreary reading: highest ERA in the majors (5.44), most hits allowed (1664), most walks (609), most HRs (181), and the most runs (967). Plus, for the present, an all-time record major league high TPER of 119.4. Now for the good news. Taking into account Mile High's "park effect," they weren't as horrid as they looked.

They were still pretty bad, though. "Park adjustment" lowered their league-worst 119.4 TPER to a league-worst 110.1. At that level, they became comparable to the Pirates' staff. But, relatively speaking, the Rockies' pitching staff appears in better shape than the offense. That will come as a major surprise to many.

It's worth dwelling on Mile High's apparent impact on a pitching staff. The park's immense RF area readily explains the unreal number of triples. The friendly LF wall helps forgive the high HR rate. But when a park's also the scene of 19% more singles and 17% more doubles than the average park, and pitchers are giving up 23.6% more walks to go with 23.3% more hits and getting 11.8% fewer strikeouts, it's clear there's some powerful underlying reason for it. The Mile High altitude seems such a reason. Pitches behave differently in thin air than they do in the denser atmosphere at sea level. These conditions are totally new to major league baseball, the previous high elevation being Atlanta (just over 1,000 ft.). Pitches that don't break or move like they do at lower elevations are more likely to get hit and to cause control problems. And less likely to result in a whiff. To the best of their ability, the pitchers must adjust—and that takes time. The Rockies' staff had more time and, as a consequence, better adjusted to their unique situation than opposing pitchers. Indeed, runs scored in Colorado dropped almost 1½ per game from the league's first go 'round in Mile High to their second visit. The pitchers *did* adjust.

It's questionable whether the Rockies will ever be able to develop a staff with an impressive ERA or a killer TPER. They'll always be better than their somewhat ugly numbers make them look. Even the '93 Atlanta staff, with its 85.8 TPER, might look kind of average

in Mile High (they gave up an uncharacteristic 5.14 runs per game there in '93). The move to the new Coors Stadium in '95 probably won't change anything beyond the secondary "park effects." The "altitude effect" will remain in play.

The Rotation: The experience of Greg W. Harris, acquired in trade from the Padres on July 26, provides ample evidence of the "altitude effect."

	GS	IP	W–L	ERA	HR	TPER
w/San Diego	22	152.0	10–9	3.67	18	101
w/Colorado	13	73.1	1–8	6.50	15	137

Harris relies on a big breaking curve ball. With Colorado, the hook didn't bite and he turned into tater-bait. Certain kinds of pitchers will survive in the Colorado environment. Others are doomed to failure.

The Rockies did find a few pitchers who *could* survive in '93, making some encouraging progress toward building a staff.

Armando Reynoso proved a bigger contributor in '93 than the other pitcher drafted from the Braves' organization, first pick David Nied. Reynoso used good control and ground balls (a very useful combination) to put in a season that could have qualified for "Mile High Cy" Young consideration (12–11, 4.00 ERA, 107 TPER). Nied had difficulty adjusting simultaneously to the big leagues and the park. He'd lost six in a row when he hit the DL on June 3. On his return three months later, better control helped him finish strong in September (total: 5–9, 5.17 ERA, 123 TPER)

The Bullpen: After setting a minor league save record in '92, Steve Reed emerged as a reliable RH set-up man. He also had trouble adjusting initially and spent a month at Colorado Springs to figure things out. Reed took over the set-up job upon his return and was excellent from there on out (9–5 with 4.48 ERA in 64 App, 84.1 IP, 105 TPER). His road ERA of 1.60 perhaps better indicates his effectiveness.

Bruce Ruffin, of all people, produced a 100 TPER and proved a solid left-hander out of the bullpen. He began the year in the

1993 Rockies Staff

		TPER
St	Reynoso	107
St	Nied	123
St	Henry	127
St	Bottenfield	134
St	Harris	137
Ut	Blair	119
Ut	Ruffin	100
Bp	Parrett	121
Bp	Reed	105
Bp	Wayne	120
Cl	Holmes	80

50   100

rotation, making 12 starts, but became a full-time reliever from July 1 on (2.40 ERA in this role). He made the club as a non-roster invitee, after having somehow parlayed one year of major league success in '86 into a 7-year career that had apparently ended after Milwaukee released him in '92. His '93 success was predicated on a strikeout-pitch-from-nowhere (K'ed 126 in 139.2 IP, six years after a previous major league high of 93 in 204.2 IP).

Like Reynoso, Darren Holmes should have earned year-end awards consideration. Under the conditions, as they're now understood, his performance stands out (3–3, 25 SV, 4.05 ERA, 80 TPER). Another one of the Rockies' pitchers who needed time at Colorado Springs to collect himself, Holmes had a 17.19 ERA (not a misprint) through May 5 when he was sent down. Upon his return, he became a top-flight stopper, posting a 2.43 ERA the rest of the way.

What Next?

Where the Rockies go from here should be determined by management's ability to:

1. Perceive the team as it really is, not as it seems to be.
2. Identify the kind of pitchers who can survive in their peculiar environment, then find and develop them.

A premium should be placed on pitchers with good control, who rely on velocity to get Ks or location to get ground balls. Easy to say, tough to find. But pitchers who can survive in Colorado should also prosper on the road. This becomes a job for their scouting and development program because the Rockies aren't going to find pitchers like this on the free agent market. Any pitcher who values his career numbers will avoid a Colorado contract like the plague.

On the other hand, Colorado should hold a special attraction for free agent hitters. The signing of Howard Johnson, late of the Mets, indicates both parties know exactly what they're doing.

The Rockies' farm system also got off to a solid start. Three products of their initial '92 amateur free agent draft seem on the verge of being ready. Jason Bates, a switch-hitting shortstop, and two RH starters, John Burke and Mark Thompson, all made it to AAA in their second pro year and performed very well. All three are bona fide quality major league prospects and should start contributing no later than '95. The numbers they produced at AAA, by the way, require the same type of scrutiny as those produced at Mile High Stadium. The Rockies' AAA affiliate is just down the road at Colorado Springs, in the shadow of Pike's Peak. The Rockies' "laboratory" thus duplicates the "altitude effect" present in Denver. In addition, Jayhawk Owens may develop into a good enough hitter to replace Girardi—if he's good enough behind the plate. And if Eric Wedge *ever* gets healthy, he'll be a good enough hitter to replace just about anybody.

The Rockies seem to be on the right road but it's probably going to be a rough and, ah, rocky one.

Team TOPR: 1993 Colorado Rockies

	Bats	BA	OBP	SLG	HR	R	RBI	NBE	GOC	Ratio	TOPR
League Avg. Team	-	.264	.327	.399	140	728	681	2835	4378	0.647	100
Colorado Rockies	-	.273	.323	.422	142	758	704	2816	4347	0.648	100.1
Regulars:											
C Joe Girardi	R	.290	.346	.397	3	35	31	157	245	0.641	99
1B Andres Galarraga	R	.370	.403	.602	22	71	98	308	315	0.978	151
2B Eric Young	R	.269	.355	.353	3	82	42	262	394	0.665	103
Roberto Mejia	R	.231	.275	.402	5	31	20	112	184	0.609	94
3B Charlie Hayes	R	.305	.355	.522	25	89	98	336	438	0.767	118
SS Vinny Castilla	R	.255	.283	.404	9	36	30	143	271	0.528	82
LF Jerald Clark	R	.282	.324	.444	13	65	67	237	365	0.649	100
CF Alex Cole	L	.256	.339	.305	0	50	24	168	284	0.592	91
RF Dante Bichette	R	.310	.348	.526	21	93	89	325	394	0.825	127
Bench (100+ TPA):											
OF Daryl Boston	L	.261	.325	.464	14	46	40	154	227	0.678	105
C Danny Sheaffer	R	.278	.299	.384	4	26	32	90	176	0.511	79
OF Chris Jones	R	.273	.305	.450	6	29	31	109	168	0.649	100
IF Freddie Benavides	R	.286	.305	.404	3	20	26	93	162	0.574	89
IF Nelson Liriano	B	.305	.376	.424	2	28	15	84	121	0.694	(107)
1/3 Jimmy Tatum	R	.204	.245	.286	1	7	12	36	80	0.450	(70)

NOTE: Statistics are only for games played with Colorado. ( ) Under 200 TPA.

Team TPER: 1993 Colorado Rockies

	Throws	W-L	GS	GR	SV	IP	ERA	NBA	GOE	Ratio	TPER
League Avg. Team	-	81 -81	162	381	43	1449	4.04	2835	4378	0.647	100
Colorado Rockies	-	67 -95	162	453	35	1431.1	5.44	3349	4331	0.773	119.4
The Rotation:											
Armando Reynoso	R	12 -11	30	0	0	189	4.00	400	575	0.696	107
Dave Nied	R	5 -9	16	0	0	87	5.17	209	262	0.798	123
Butch Henry	L	2 -8	15	5	0	84.2	6.59	213	259	0.822	127
Kent Bottenfield	R	3 -5	14	0	0	76.2	6.10	192	221	0.869	134
Greg Harris	R	1 -8	13	0	0	73.1	6.50	198	223	0.888	137
Utility:											
Willie Blair	R	6 -10	18	28	0	146	4.75	345	447	0.772	119
Bruce Ruffin	L	6 -5	12	47	2	139.2	3.87	275	426	0.646	100
Curt Leskanic	R	1 -5	8	10	0	57	5.37	123	176	0.699	108
Andy Ashby	R	0 -4	9	11	1	54	8.50	165	160	1.031	159
Lance Painter	L	2 -2	6	4	0	39	6.00	87	113	0.770	(119)
Mo Sanford	R	1 -2	6	5	0	35.2	5.30	98	106	0.925	(143)
Bullpen:											
Steve Reed	R	9 -5	0	64	3	84.1	4.48	168	248	0.677	105
Jeff Parrett	R	3 -3	6	34	1	73.2	5.38	173	221	0.783	121
Gary Wayne	L	5 -3	0	65	1	62.1	5.05	151	195	0.774	120
Darren Holmes	R	3 -3	0	62	25	66.2	4.05	105	203	0.517	80

NOTE: Statistics are only for games pitched with Baltimore. ( ) Under 200 TBF.

WHAT SHORTAGE OF PITCHING?
FLORIDA MARLINS

 chorus of blues wailers furnished entertainment at the November '92 expansion draft party, topping off their performance with that old favorite, "Got Those Mean Ol' Expansion Pitcher Blues."

Since there already "wasn't enough pitching to go around," the expansion clubs were obviously rummaging through a bare cupboard. The protected lists supposedly held every pitcher who was worth holding on to, along with a lot who weren't.

As a result the expansion Rockies' staff got mauled, of course. A lot of the established clubs struggled with their pitching, too, because the "already thin pitching" had been "diluted" even further.

How, then, did the expansion Florida Marlins end up with a *better* staff than seven of the existing NL clubs? A pitching staff with a park-adjusted TPER *below* the league average?

Exhibit I for the Marlins:

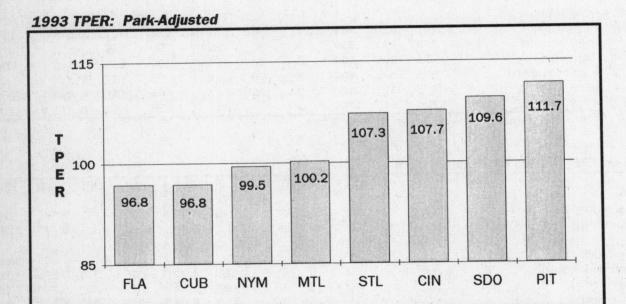

1993 TPER: Park-Adjusted

What Was Expected

As with their expansion mate, Colorado, realism prevailed. A cellar finish was expected—less than 100 losses a hope. If Marlins GM Dave Dombrowski had been asked whether the Marlins' finish was important to his organization, he would have responded that the performance of the Edmonton Trappers concerned him more.

He wouldn't have been kidding, either. Edmonton, their AAA farm club in the Pacific Coast League, was where the Marlins sent their future to grow. From the very outset, the Marlins had focused on the future. In the expansion draft, Florida chose only *two* "proven major leaguers" in their first 18 selections—Bryan Harvey and Greg Hibbard, the latter being immediately traded to the Cubs for two prospects. In contrast, Colorado chose eleven such players in the first 18 picks. Florida selected only six players of this ilk altogether, and the same day traded three of them for a total of six more youngsters.

The Marlins' plan was indeed a plan for the long haul.

What Actually Happened

During the remainder of the off-season and into spring training, the Marlins continued to wheel and deal. They aimed to firm up the major league club but never at the expense of their future. Three major league free agents were signed: Charlie Hough, Dave Magadan and Benito Santiago. Orestes Destrade came from Japan to take over 1B. Two nifty spring training deals, for Chris Hammond (from Cincinnati) and Luis Aquino (from Kansas City) fleshed out the rotation with veteran talent. Now, they were ready for their debut.

After stumbling out of the gate, the Marlins became surprisingly good for a surprisingly long time. On June 13, they beat Pittsburgh at home to move into fourth place and within one game of .500 (30–31). That was as good as they got. The pitching staff started fraying around the edges and the club's record drifted downward to an eventual 64–98 finish. The Marlins first year, which could

have been worse (see the Mets), met expectations at the major league level.

The higher and more important expectations for the minor league system were fulfilled, too.

	League	Level	W–L	Finish
Edmonton	PCL	AAA	72–79	2nd (1st half), 5th (2nd half)
High Desert	CAL	A+	85–52	1st (both halves)
Kane County	MID	A	75–62	3rd (both halves)
Elmira	NYP	A–	31–44	3rd
Marlins	GCL	R	32–28	2nd

The system's composite .536 winning percentage was the fourth best in baseball. And it contained promising prospects at every level.

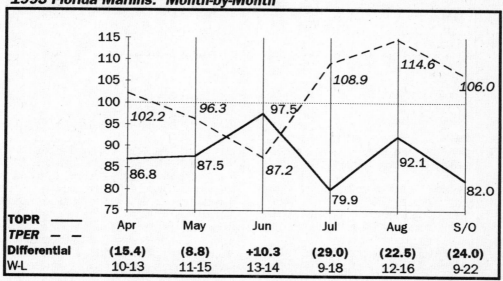

1993 Florida Marlins: Month-by-Month

	Apr	May	Jun	Jul	Aug	S/O
TOPR ——	86.8	87.5	97.5	79.9	92.1	82.0
TPER – –	102.2	96.3	87.2	108.9	114.6	106.0
Differential	(15.4)	(8.8)	+10.3	(29.0)	(22.5)	(24.0)
W-L	10-13	11-15	13-14	9-18	12-16	9-22

Joe Robbie Stadium

In its first year of baseball use, Joe Robbie Stadium slightly favored the offense (Park TOPR: 103.9). It apparently had nothing to do with the park's configuration, which is almost symmetrical, without idiosyncracy and of standard dimensions (335′ LF line, 410′ to center, 345′ RF line). The source was instead found in the Baserunner Sub-set for the Florida pitchers.

FLA Opponents	SH	SF	SB	CS	GDP	BRB	BRO	Ratio
Home	47	31	68	−24	−49	73	151	.483
Road	33	19	50	−28	−55	19	135	.141

They got hurt more at home than on the road in every aspect. Seems like a one-year anomaly to us.

Some concern had been expressed about rain-outs in this venue. It happened only once (a day game on May 31).

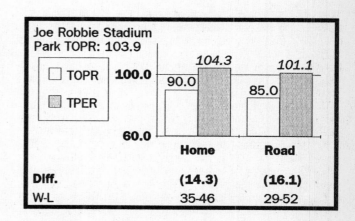

Joe Robbie Stadium
Park TOPR: 103.9

□ TOPR
▦ TPER

	Home	Road
TOPR	90.0	85.0
TPER	104.3	101.1
Diff.	(14.3)	(16.1)
W-L	35-46	29-52

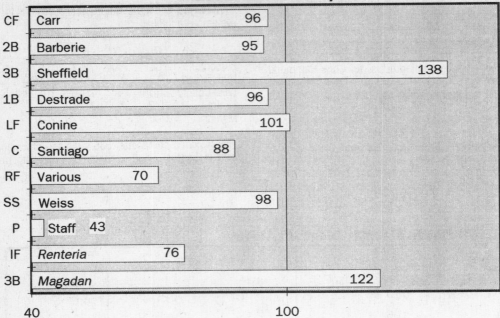

1993 Marlins Lineup

Position	Player	TOPR
CF	Carr	96
2B	Barberie	95
3B	Sheffield	138
1B	Destrade	96
LF	Conine	101
C	Santiago	88
RF	Various	70
SS	Weiss	98
P	Staff	43
IF	*Renteria*	76
3B	*Magadan*	122

40   100

The Offense

The feeblest offense in the league (581 runs, 91 fewer than the Mets). The Marlins sure didn't find many hitters (but, then, neither did the Rockies). The batting order reveals more than a few weaknesses.

The Marlins' Team TOPR of 87.5 trailed the league but, on a park-adjusted basis, matched Colorado's (86.7 vs. the Rockies' 86.0). The Marlins can take satisfaction that their relative youth provides some built-in growth potential, while the Rockies have far less. There remains, however, a lot of work to be done.

The most serious concern would be lack of production in the critical leadoff and cleanup slots. A leadoff hitter who only scores 75 runs and a cleanup man who only drives in 87 identify the chief sources of their scoring deficiencies.

In his rookie year, switch-hitting CF Chuck Carr led the league in stolen bases (58 in 80 tries) but, frankly, disappointed as a leadoff hitter. His stolen base title didn't make up for a .327 OBP. Only the Mets, Pirates and Giants rated lower in this essential department. With a 96 TOPR, he's also below the league norm for his position (108) so he needs to make up some ground somewhere. Drawing walks would be the logical solution, but Carr has *never* developed a taste for them (his 49 BB in '93 was his most ever in eight pro seasons).

The power and strike zone judgment that Orestes Destrade demonstrated in Japan apparently didn't travel well. After averaging 41 HR and 88 BB in 130 games played during the last three years in the Orient, Destrade could produce only 20 homers and 58 BB for the Marlins in '93 (in 153 games). His TOPR of 96 was way below the standards for both cleanup hitters and first basemen. He might show some improvement in '94, but his minor league TOPR at AAA, before he went overseas, was only 116. This suggests a low ceiling.

Gary Sheffield was a mid-season acquisition. A marquee-type player whose relative youth and career potential inspired Dombrowski to surrender some of his treasured prospects at the prostrate Padres estate sale. Sheffield can be a devastating offensive player, as his '92 triple-crown challenge and its 150 TOPR demonstrated. His 3B play can be a little brutal, though, so he'll move to RF in '94—plugging another big drain in the Marlins' offense.

In '94, 3B will again become the property of Dave Magadan. Displaced by Sheffield and then traded to Seattle for reserve OF Henry Cotto and relief prospect Jeff Darwin on June 27, Magadan returned on November 9 in exchange for . . . relief prospect Jeff Darwin. Thus Sheffield's move to the outfield won't create a new hole in the infield.

Two other positions appear to be in capable hands, those of Bret Barberie and Jeff Conine. Second baseman Bret Barberie was the Marlins' third pick in the draft, out of the Expo organization. The Florida braintrust is largely staffed with Montreal alumni, suggesting that their expressed faith in his future is founded on something more than guesswork. Used irregularly at 3B in Montreal, Bret's a natural 2B who led the Southern League in fielding at that spot in '90. In '93 he spent over two months on the DL with two separate injuries (elbow, knee), limiting him to 99 games, and still put up an acceptable 95 TOPR. Bret knows how to walk and has shown some extra-base pop. He'll be a plus in the Florida lineup.

Another draft pick, LF Jeff Conine, appears promising, too. His BA hovered around .300 all year long, finishing at .292. Jeff's approach to this opportunity appears to have been cautious, focusing initially on contact and sacrificing power over the first two months. As a result, 32 of his 39 extra-base hits came after June 2. He's got more power than he showed, so his 101 TOPR could move up significantly next year.

Shortstop Walt Weiss enjoyed his first season without a visit to the DL since his '88 rookie year. It was also his best. His 98 TOPR and excellent glove (only 15 E and 2nd in the league .977 fielding) may not be back though, due to free agency. In that case, SS will probably be occupied by Alex Arias and his adequate 88 TOPR until the farm system produces an heir.

The catcher's spot also lends itself to "the system is the solution" policy. Benito Santiago last exhibited decent offensive production in '90. At the relative young age of 29, both his offensive and defensive skills have deteriorated dangerously. To go with his 88 TOPR, he threw out only 30% of steal attempts, tied for the league lead in errors with 11, and helped the Marlins lead the league in wild pitches (85) and passed balls (29). It wasn't all Charlie Hough's fault. The catcher-of-the-future, Charlie Johnson, passed the test at A ball in '93 and the Marlins will mark time at this position until he's ready.

All in all, despite their weak performance in '93, you have to admit the Marlins' offense is taking on a promising form. For an expansion club going into its second season, a surprising number of the pieces are in place and more are being developed in the system. The vital leadoff and cleanup slots will block any possible "breakthrough" in '94, though.

The Pitching Staff

This should count as the Marlins' proudest accomplishment in their first year: A Portrait of an NL Average Staff.

Dave Dombrowski should hang this graphic on his wall.

Five of these pitchers came in the expansion draft (Armstrong, Bowen, Rapp, Lewis and Harvey), three by trade (Hammond and Aquino for virtually nothing and Rodriguez as a throw-in with Sheffield) and three were free agents (Hough, Turner and Klink) who were initially signed to *minor* league contracts. In other words, the established major league clubs didn't think enough of them to protect them, ask very much for them or even want them around. Their success makes a statement, doesn't it, about the "shortage of pitching"? In addition, the Marlins took six more developmental pitchers in the draft who look like they have a legitimate chance to be major league pitchers.

The Rotation: Due to their off-season dealing, the Marlins were able to enter the season with a mostly veteran 5-man rotation that remained intact and accounted for every single start until July 5. There was nothing particularly outstanding about their performance except their durability, dependability and reliability. This may sound prosaic, but these traits are valuable to any team. And the stability it provided was especially important to an expansion team like the Marlins. That four of them turned out to be of at least average effectiveness (in the 96–104 TPER range) was icing on the cake.

Charlie Hough exemplified the rotation. Ol' Man River never missed a turn (34 starts) and cranked out innings (204.1). He did

the job he was hired for and did it well (9–16, 4.27 ERA, 99 TPER). Having re-signed with Florida, Charlie will do it for them again next year—at age 46, his 22nd full season in the majors.

After what happened to Ryan Bowen in Houston in '92 (9 starts, 8 beatings, a 10.96 ERA with a mushroom cloud 189 TPER), who'd have thought he'd *ever* surface again, much less be a successful rotation starter (8–12, 4.42 ERA, 104 TPER)? The coming season looms important for him. Whether he takes a step forward, improving his control and consistency, or not, will determine his future with the franchise. Selecting him in the draft was a calculated risk that paid off.

Jack Armstrong was another calculated risk, one of the very few veterans that the Marlins bothered with. He wobbled and teetered but hung in there for 33 starts and almost 200 IP (196.1). That helped, but his 117 TPER didn't. The Marlins evidently hoped that he'd rediscover what had made him an All-Star game starter in '90. It kept him from throwing gopher balls—one every 18.4 IP in '90, one every 6.5 IP since. For Jack, "it" is the difference between stardom and the edge of oblivion—where he now stands.

Chris Hammond was available to the Marlins for two minor leaguers of slight promise (3B Gary Scott and P Hector Carrasco) because he was unwelcome in Cincinnati. Hammond took over a spot in the rotation and pitched about as he had for the Reds—which was good enough to earn and keep the job (96 TPER). It also meant that the Marlins didn't have to rush a kid into the rotation.

Another deal brought over Luis Aquino for cash from Kansas City. Luis pitched consistently well over four years for the Royals (21–19 in 107 App., 50 starts, 3.58 ERA, 94 TPER) but seemingly baffled them with his success. Again, Florida benefited from an underevaluation and he saved yet another kid from being rushed into the rotation. Aquino began the year as the 5th starter and pitched well—leading the league in ERA into June. He hit the DL with tendinitis in his right shoulder on July 4, returned on August 3 and took over a relief role. All in all, it was a typical Aquino year (6–8, 38 App., 13 starts, 3.42 ERA and 97 TPER). As a swing man, he adds depth to the Marlins' staff.

When Aquino went down, Pat Rapp was called up from Edmon-

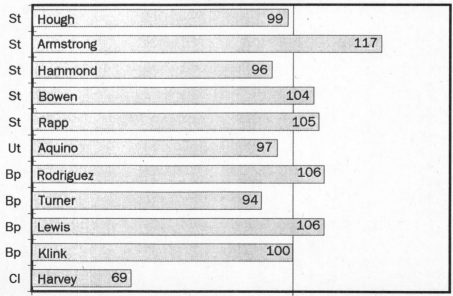

1993 Marlins Staff

St	Hough	99
St	Armstrong	117
St	Hammond	96
St	Bowen	104
St	Rapp	105
Ut	Aquino	97
Bp	Rodriguez	106
Bp	Turner	94
Bp	Lewis	106
Bp	Klink	100
Cl	Harvey	69

50   100

ton. He may not have been ready in the spring, but he was ready now. He went into the rotation on July 5 and never came out. Rapp gave a steady performance (4–6, 4.02 ERA, 105 TPER) and should be expected to pick up the pace in '94.

The Bullpen: The Marlins' bullpen was amazingly sound. The middlemen displayed the same kind of solid reliability that the rotation was producing.

The RH tandem of Richie Lewis (106 TPER) and Matt Turner (94 TPER) was a bit of a surprise. Neither had ever pitched an inning of relief in the majors. Lewis, the long man, had only two starts in the majors while Turner, the set-up man, had spent seven years in the minors and never gotten The Call. Between them they made 112 appearances covering 145.1 innings and yielded only 123 hits. They held the fort.

Lefties Rich Rodriquez and Joe Klink split the work from the other side with the same kind of quiet effectiveness. Rodriguez, an appendage to the Sheffield trade, had an extended history of success in the three years prior to his arrival (average 62 App., 85.1 IP, with a 2.77 ERA and 90 TPER). Perceptions of leftie relievers being as they are, this *should* have made him a very valuable commodity. He didn't seem quite up to par with the Marlins (walk and HR rates up, strikeout rate down) and may have been hurting.

Closer Bryan Harvey became the most valuable of all the players selected in the expansion draft. The NL's premier closer (45 SV, 1.70 ERA, 69 TPER), he assures the Marlins of a bullpen anchor during their development years—if he stays. If the Marlins choose to trade Harvey, he'll bring a high return that would strengthen their future beyond that point. The Marlins will likely opt for the future, but are in a position where they can't lose either way.

It should be noted that the Marlins' staff, unlike their lineup, has limited long-term potential. Only Bowen and Rapp can be considered part of the future. But assembling such a solid staff amounted to a *tour de force,* even if its *primary* purpose was to buy time for the pitching staff of the future—which will assemble next year at Edmonton and Portland (their new AA affiliate in the Eastern League).

What Next?

The Marlins obviously have a plan. It apparently calls for steady, measured progress through the next two years, with a serious and balanced contender taking shape by '96—supported by a pipeline of prospects ready to provide a steady influx of replacement talent. That may seem a trifle deliberate, but it is in fact quite ambitious. Among prior expansion clubs, only Kansas City made such a serious move so quickly (over .500 in their third year and contention by their fifth).

Given the Marlins' history to date, the major league talent on hand, the state of their farm system and the moves they've made, one concludes the plan is a good one. And that it's working. The Marlins are on schedule.

Team TOPR: 1993 Florida Marlins

	Bats	BA	OBP	SLG	HR	R	RBI	NBE	GOC	Ratio	TOPR
League Avg. Team	-	.264	.327	.399	140	728	681	2835	4378	0.647	100
Florida Marlins	-	.248	.314	.346	94	581	542	2489	4395	0.566	87.5
Regulars:											
C Benito Santiago	R	.230	.291	.380	13	49	50	218	381	0.572	88
1B Orestes Destrade	B	.255	.324	.406	20	61	87	280	450	0.622	96
2B Bret Barberie	B	.277	.344	.371	5	45	33	178	290	0.614	95
3B Dave Magadan	L	.286	.400	.392	4	22	29	133	169	0.787	122
Gary Sheffield	R	.292	.378	.479	10	33	37	158	177	0.893	138
SS Walt Weiss	B	.266	.367	.308	1	50	39	244	384	0.635	98
LF Jeff Conine	R	.292	.351	.403	12	75	79	289	443	0.652	101
CF Chuck Carr	B	.267	.327	.330	4	75	41	274	443	0.619	96
RF Junior Felix	B	.238	.276	.397	7	25	22	91	170	0.535	83
Darrell Whitmore	L	.204	.249	.300	4	24	19	86	211	0.408	63
Bench (100+ TPA):											
IF Rich Renteria	R	.255	.314	.327	2	27	30	103	210	0.490	76
IF Alex Arias	R	.269	.344	.321	2	27	20	109	192	0.568	88
OF Greg Briley	L	.194	.250	.282	3	17	12	63	145	0.434	(67)
OF Henry Cotto	R	.296	.312	.415	3	15	14	70	102	0.686	(106)
C Bob Natal	R	.214	.273	.291	1	3	6	44	101	0.436	(67)

NOTE: Statistics are only for games played with Florida. ( ) Under 200 TPA.

Team TPER: 1993 Florida Marlins

	Throws	W-L	GS	GR	SV	IP	ERA	NBA	GOE	Ratio	TPER
League Avg. Team	-	81 -81	162	381	43	1449	4.04	2835	4378	0.647	100
Florida Marlins	-	64 -98	162	409	48	1440.1	4.15	2894	4350	0.665	102.8
The Rotation:											
Charlie Hough	R	9 -16	34	0	0	204.1	4.27	398	621	0.641	99
Jack Armstrong	R	9 -17	33	3	0	196.1	4.49	453	596	0.760	117
Chris Hammond	L	11 -12	32	0	0	191	4.66	361	578	0.625	96
Ryan Bowen	R	8 -12	27	0	0	156.2	4.48	315	469	0.672	104
Pat Rapp	R	4 -6	16	0	0	94	4.02	193	284	0.680	105
Utility:											
Luis Aquino	R	6 -8	13	25	0	110.2	3.42	207	328	0.631	97
Dave Weathers	R	2 -3	6	8	0	45.2	5.12	100	136	0.735	114
Bullpen:											
Richie Lewis	R	6 -3	0	57	0	77.1	3.14	163	237	0.688	106
Matt Turner	R	4 -5	0	55	0	68	2.91	122	201	0.607	94
Rich Rodriguez	L	0 -1	0	36	1	46	4.11	95	139	0.683	(106)
Joe Klink	L	0 -2	0	59	0	37.2	5.02	74	114	0.649	(100)
Cris Carpenter	R	0 -1	0	29	0	37.1	2.89	62	112	0.554	(86)
Trevor Hoffman	R	2 -2	0	28	2	35.2	3.28	67	110	0.609	(94)
Robb Nen	R	1 0	1	14	0	33.1	7.02	88	104	0.846	(131)
Bryan Harvey	R	1 -5	0	59	45	69	1.70	93	208	0.447	69

NOTE: Statistics are only for games pitched with Florida. ( ) Under 200 TBF.

RELAX! IT REALLY WAS PROGRESS
HOUSTON ASTROS

The Houston ownership is said to be upset. Having shelled out several gazillion dollars to add two premiere starters, a pennant didn't automatically follow.

Astros fans are also reportedly perturbed. The '92 club's .500 finish appeared to promise continued improvement. Yet, the rotation's new pitchers along with sharp gains by the rest of the starting cast, only produced a teeny four-game step in the win column. The Astros, perceived as contenders, didn't contend.

Three little oversights produced these disappointments.

First, the new arms, while not producing up to expectations, were a darn sight better than the arms they replaced (Butch Henry and Jimmy Jones). And, if a pennant actually was the objective, half of the club's shortcomings were addressed. Nothing had been done about the offense.

Second, the '92 club's .500 finish proved about as misleading as possible. The '92 TOPR/TPER differential was a *negative* 5.2, so 74–75 wins was really about as good as they were. Ex-manager Art Howe maneuvered the young '92 Astros above their true level, thus fitting himself for the noose in '93. But the staggering +14.1 improvement in the differential from '92 to '93 *was real*, and so were the 85 wins.

Third, if one team in the division runs off and hides—like SF did—it's impossible to play the contender (unless you're the Atlanta Braves, which the Houston Astros weren't). Nobody in the new NL Central should be able to hide from the Astros in '94.

Team Trendline: Houston Astros

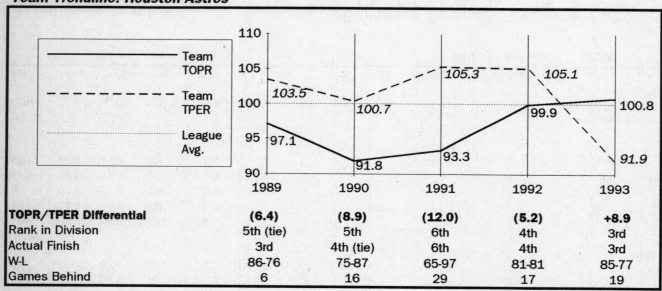

	1989	1990	1991	1992	1993
TOPR/TPER Differential	(6.4)	(8.9)	(12.0)	(5.2)	+8.9
Rank in Division	5th (tie)	5th	6th	4th	3rd
Actual Finish	3rd	4th (tie)	6th	4th	3rd
W-L	86-76	75-87	65-97	81-81	85-77
Games Behind	6	16	29	17	19

What Was Expected
As noted, they were high. Too high.

What Actually Happened

About what should have been expected. The Astros got off to a good start and led the league going into May. There followed a two-month soft spell and they closed June barely above .500 (38–37) and completely out of touch with the division leading Giants (12½ games back).

They approached the rest of their schedule in a workmanlike fashion with three consecutive winning months. By season's end, they stood 85–77, 19 games back of the champion Braves. Despite having a much-improved team, and a contender's record, events denied them either the fans' applause or year-end drama.

The strangest aspect of the Astros' season had to be their dismal record against the expansion Rockies (2–11, dropping all 7 games in Denver). Conversely, the division champion Braves swept all 13 of their games with Colorado. The 9-game swing accounts for almost half the difference between the two teams in the final standings.

Uncharacteristically, the Astros hit 138 HR—a club record. But only stole 103 bases, ninth in the league and their lowest total since '85. Plus, they won on the road (41–40), only the fifth time in history they'd won both home and away.

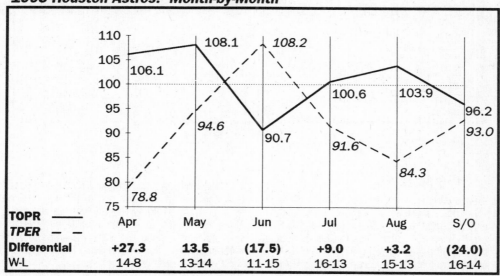

1993 Houston Astros: Month-by-Month

	Apr	May	Jun	Jul	Aug	S/O
TOPR ——	106.1	108.1	90.7	100.6	103.9	96.2
TPER – –	78.8	94.6	108.2	91.6	84.3	93.0
Differential	+27.3	13.5	(17.5)	+9.0	+3.2	(24.0)
W-L	14-8	13-14	11-15	16-13	15-13	16-14

The Astrodome

The home of the 'Stros held no surprises in '93. Of course, it's a "pitcher's park" (Park TOPR: 94.5). It suppressed Houston's offense and the visitors' about equally—a negative 4.6% and 6.5%, respectively, park adjusted.

The primary effect is expressed in terms of power, as measured by slugging percentage.

Slugging %	Houston	Opponents
Astrodome	.406	.351
On the Road	.412	.381

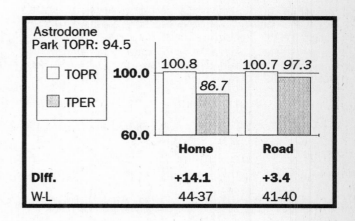

Astrodome
Park TOPR: 94.5

□ TOPR
▨ TPER

	Home	Road
TOPR	100.8	100.7
TPER	86.7	97.3
Diff.	+14.1	+3.4
W-L	44-37	41-40

1993 Astros Lineup

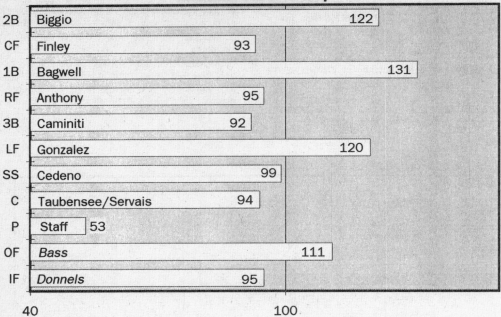

2B	Biggio	122
CF	Finley	93
1B	Bagwell	131
RF	Anthony	95
3B	Caminiti	92
LF	Gonzalez	120
SS	Cedeno	99
C	Taubensee/Servais	94
P	Staff	53
OF	*Bass*	111
IF	*Donnels*	95

40   100

The Offense

In '92, the improving Astros mustered an average offense (99.9 Team TOPR). Between '92 and '93, there was virtually no change in personnel. Eric Anthony became the everyday RF (after platooning with Pete Incaviglia in '92) while Andujar Cedeno took over as the full-time SS (after starting 69 games there in '92). Predictably, the same lineup produced essentially the same result (100.8 Team TOPR). Thus, an average offense went unchanged and, presto, stayed average.

Actually, the Astros' offense has solid potential. With a healthy Steve Finley, the top third of the order ranks among the league's best. The bottom third's probably as good as anybody's. There is, though, this little problem in the middle.

The first three hitters in the Astros' order—Craig Biggio, Steve Finley and Jeff Bagwell—formed an awesome unit in '92. As a group, their line looked like:

	BA	OBP	SLG	SB/CS	R	RBI	TOPR
Biggio '92	.277	.378	.369	38/15	96	39	125
Finley '92	.292	.355	.407	44/9	84	55	125
Bagwell '92	.273	.368	.444	10/6	87	96	129
HOU 1–2–3 '92	.281	.368	.406	92/30	267	190	126

These three guys all hit, got on base and ran. They propelled themselves into scoring position, via an extra-base hit or a stolen base, a combined total of 238 times. Individually, their offensive characteristics fit perfectly with their slots in the order:

In '93, Craig Biggio virtually duplicated his '92 TOPR (122) while adding more power (21 HR, 67 extra-base hits and .474 SLG). But his baserunning decayed seriously (only 15 SB in 32 attempts, a miserable 47% success rate). After the season, rumors circulated that the Astros' signs were an open secret around the league. If that's indeed the case, Biggio's new-found power coupled with a return of his former basepath skills, should make him an extra-potent leadoff hitter.

Finley dropped off sharply in '93 (from 125 to 93 TOPR), probably because of early-season injuries (Bell's palsy, followed by

a broken wrist). As a consequence, he didn't get back on track until mid-May and hit .278 the rest of the way. His walks plummeted, though, from 58 to 28—producing an unsatisfactory .304 OBP. Many thought his '92 season a fluke, but TOPR trends indicate '93 was the fluke instead. An ideal #2 hitter who, in addition to his other offensive skills, can bunt (16 SH in '92).

Bagwell, a prototypical #3, remains an all-around hitter with average (.320 BA in '93) and power (20 HR, .516 SLG) who also gets on base (.388 OBP) and can run (13 SB in 17 attempts). Thus, with the table-setters in front of him, he not only starts what should be an RBI parade, but sets himself up to score as well.

But, with all these pluses, you'd think this trio would have scored more than 267 runs in '92 and only 243 in '93. What happened?

What came up next is what happened. The middle of the Houston order became a swamp where runs went to die. The Astros' cleanup hitter (Eric Anthony) and #5 hitter (Ken Caminiti) combined to drive in a grand total of 141 runs between them—only 18 more than Barry Bonds drove in by himself. They actually *scored* more runs than they drove home (150), but that's a tribute to the quality of the batters behind them. No other team in the majors exhibited this unusual circumstance. But then, no other team in the majors presented a #4–#5 combo that TOPRed *below* their #7–#8 combo.

We hasten to add that Houston's #6 hitter, LF Luis Gonzalez, played no role in the middle-of-the-order's failure. He posted a fine 120 TOPR (.300 BA, .361 OBP, .457 SLG with 15 HR). At 25, he emerged right on TOPRs schedule and can safely move up in the order in '94.

To a degree, Caminiti can be excused due to extenuating circumstances—he was miscast. He's the regular third-sacker because of his defense. He's the #5 hitter because a) as a fielder, he has to bat somewhere in the lineup and b) he had an uncharacteristically good offensive year in '92 (117 TOPR). His 92 TOPR in '93 marks a reversion to form ('91 TOPR was also 92) revealing him as bottom-of-the-order material.

That leaves Anthony—a cleanup hitter who TOPRed at 95, drove in 66 runs and slugged .397. All three counts were the lowest of any cleanup hitter in the league. On his own team, only Biggio, Finley and Cedeno drove in fewer runs. Only Finley and Caminiti (!)

had a lower slugging percentage. Among the league's regular RF, only Willie McGee had a lower TOPR (94). Seemingly encouraged by a 103 TOPR in platoon use in '92, Houston's braintrust counted on further development in '93. It didn't happen and the Astros' whole offensive structure collapsed for want of a middle. Think of last year's lineup as a glazed donut. Tasty around the edges, but with a hole in the middle.

The Astros have since disposed of last year's problem player by shipping Anthony to Seattle. But the problem remains. Until the club comes up with one more big stick in the middle of the lineup, the Astros will remain only contenders—and not winners. A tasty donut, but no brass ring.

The Pitching

Quick, now, one NL team had three rotation starters ranked in the league's top 13. (Hint: it wasn't Atlanta.)

The correct answer is: the Astros with starters Mark Portugal (84 TPER, #7), Pete Harnisch (86, #8) and Darryl Kile (90, #13). Atlanta had to go 17-deep for their #3 TPER starter (Glavine). Moreover, Houston placed *four* starters in the league's top half (Doug Drabek at 94, #22). The only others with this claim were the division champions, Atlanta and Philly.

The Astros' Team TPER (91.9) ranked third in the league—behind only Atlanta (an unreal 85.8) and San Francisco (91.7), the two teams ahead of them in the division standings. The Astros' '93 TPER represented a quantum improvement from their awful '92 (105.3). No question about it—the Astros built a pennant-winning staff for their '93 team!

The Rotation: There shouldn't be any quibble with the rotation's output, only where it came from. The 'Stros had expected more from Drabek and Greg Swindell. Nonetheless, Drabek pitched well, his 94 TPER and 3.79 ERA belying his 9–18 record. He was a victim of non-support, the offense scoring only 30 runs in his 18 losses (they were shut out in three and produced but a single run in six). Drabek also maintained his outstanding record of durability leading the staff in starts (34) and innings pitched (237.2, fifth in the league).

Swindell, however, pitched erratically. It could have been an arm problem. Disabled with a shoulder strain at the break, he was 6–8

with 4.95 ERA at the time. After he returned to the rotation on August 1, he went 6–5 with a 3.06 ERA. On the other hand, it could have been the 'Dome. He was 9–4 with a 3.59 ERA on the road, but only 3–9 at home (4.90 ERA). Given the Astrodome's well-earned reputation as a "pitcher's park," you'll recognize Swindell's home/road split as bass-ackwards. Could it be the Texas native son suffered a little nervousness in front of the home folks?

Both Drabek and Swindell are high-quality pitchers, deservant of top dollar. Really, the only blot on their record had been a certain inconsistency, as revealed by their TPER trendlines:

	1990	1991	1992	1993
Drabek	79	99	79	94
Swindell	102	83	92	106

As staff "aces," both have carried heavy workloads. It could be that, unlike the Madduxes and Clemenses, they're physically over-taxed by the effort involved. Just maybe, they should be allowed to pitch fewer complete games as a means of conserving their strength. At their age (Drabek will be 31, Swindell 29 in '94) there should be lots of fine seasons left in them. It would seem wise for the Astros to protect their investment.

The rest of the rotation was simply brilliant. Pete Harnisch proved "ace" quality himself (16–9, 2.98 ERA, 86 TPER) and delivered over 200 IP for the third consecutive year. Darryl Kile produced a breakthrough of massive proportions, going 15–8 (vs. 12–21 in the previous two years) with a 3.51 ERA and a 90 TPER (vs. 118 and 115 in '91 and '92). His September 8 no-hitter was mere icing on the cake. Mark Portugal seemed to prove he was more than the #5 starter he's always been cast as (18–4, 2.77 ERA, 84 TPER). But, away from the 'Dome he's 33–30 with a 4.59 ERA (in it, he's 30–9, 2.38 ERA).

The Bullpen: Like Swindell's uneven performance in the rotation, the bullpen exhibited only one troubling element. Unfortunately, it was the closer Doug Jones. In his five years in the role, Jones has been the hardest-working closer (based on IP) in his league all five of them. As a result, he suffers spells of ineffectiveness and all of '93 was one of them. Closers who produce only 26 saves, with 8 "blown saves" plus 10 losses, an ERA of 4.54 and a 104 TPER, generally get asked to find new work. Jones, no different from the

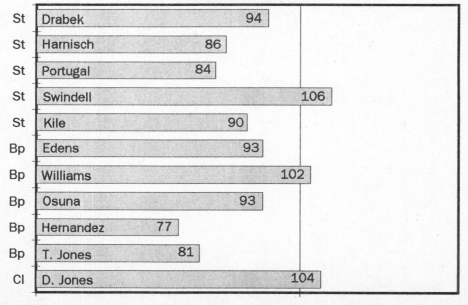

1993 Astros Staff

St	Drabek	94
St	Harnisch	86
St	Portugal	84
St	Swindell	106
St	Kile	90
Bp	Edens	93
Bp	Williams	102
Bp	Osuna	93
Bp	Hernandez	77
Bp	T. Jones	81
Cl	D. Jones	104

50   100

others, was traded to Philly after the season. His replacement? Mitch Williams, who'll produce no fewer cases of heartburn and ulcers than Jones did (but tends to be a little more successful in the process).

After Jones and Xavier Hernandez (whose outstanding 77 TPER also left in trade) reeled off almost half of the bullpen's total appearances (143 of 324) and IP (182 of 392) between them, there wasn't much left for the others to do. Longman Brian Williams (102 TPER), middleman Tom Edens (93 TPER) and LH specialist Al Osuna (93 TPER) all pitched satisfactorily in their roles (which essentially meant backing up Jones and Hernandez). But with the main men both traded—there are a lot of innings to replace. Mitch Williams gets Jones' job, rookie Todd Jones (who debuted with an 81 TPER) probably gets Hernandez's. The Astros need to think hard about their pen over the winter.

What Next?

The '93 Astros, with their championship-level pitching and fourth-place hitting, couldn't contend in the NL West. They got overwhelmed by teams with championship pitching AND championship hitting.

The new NL Central, however, presents them with a God-given opportunity. The 'Stros produced 85 wins in '93, enough to have joined an excruciatingly tight race with the Cards (87) and the Cubs (84). Thus, by maintaining their superb pitching and judiciously adding to their offense, Houston could move to the top.

The transactions to date rate as positive steps toward this goal. With Brian Williams, Shane Reynolds and acquisition Domingo Jean available to replace the departed Portugal, the rotation shouldn't be hurt. Mitch Williams, along with the promising Todd Jones, may keep the bullpen in a stable order (though using "Mitch" and "a stable order" in the same sentence somehow seems a contradiction in terms). Other than removing Anthony from the scene, however, the offensive problem is yet to be addressed.

A power-hitting outfielder seems all that would keep the otherwise '93 Astros from becoming the NL Central's legitimate favorite in '94. But, there is a risk that the '93 Astros won't be around in '94. Reportedly, ownership gave new GM Bob Watson his first order of business: cut the payroll. Inevitably, this would seem to mean giving up pitching for hitting (if hitting is to be acquired at all). Robbing Peter to pay Paul, changing the team without improving it and hoping it still somehow adds up to 85 wins. Which, again, might not be enough.

Team TOPR: 1993 Houston Astros

	Bats	BA	OBP	SLG	HR	R	RBI	NBE	GOC	Ratio	TOPR
League Avg. Team	-	.264	.327	.399	140	728	681	2835	4378	0.647	100
Houston Astros	-	.267	.330	.409	138	716	656	2818	4320	0.652	100.8
Regulars:											
C Eddie Taubensee	L	.250	.299	.389	9	26	42	129	227	0.568	88
Scott Servais	R	.244	.313	.415	11	24	32	134	207	0.647	100
1B Jeff Bagwell	R	.320	.388	.516	20	76	88	338	398	0.849	131
2B Craig Biggio	R	.287	.373	.474	21	98	64	373	471	0.792	122
3B Ken Caminiti	R	.262	.321	.390	13	75	75	253	425	0.595	92
SS Andujar Cedeno	R	.283	.343	.412	11	69	56	253	395	0.641	99
LF Luis Gonzalez	L	.300	.361	.457	15	82	72	319	409	0.780	120
CF Steve Finley	L	.266	.304	.385	8	69	44	255	423	0.603	93
RF Eric Anthony	L	.249	.319	.397	15	70	66	235	381	0.617	95
Bench (100+ TPA):											
OF Kevin Bass	B	.284	.359	.402	3	31	37	123	171	0.719	111
IF Chris Donnels	L	.257	.327	.391	2	18	24	86	140	0.614	(95)
OF Chris James	R	.256	.333	.488	6	19	19	82	101	0.812	(125)
I/O Casey Candaele	B	.240	.298	.331	1	18	7	49	95	0.516	(80)

NOTE: Statistics are only for games played with Houston. ( ) Under 200 TPA.

Team TPER: 1993 Houston Astros

	Throws	W-L	GS	GR	SV	IP	ERA	NBA	GOE	Ratio	TPER
League Avg. Team	-	81 -81	162	381	43	1449	4.04	2835	4378	0.647	100
Houston Astros	-	85 -77	162	324	42	1441.1	3.49	2589	4349	0.595	91.9
The Rotation:											
Doug Drabek	R	9 -18	34	0	0	237.2	3.79	433	711	0.609	94
Pete Harnisch	R	16 -9	33	0	0	217.2	2.98	366	658	0.556	86
Mark Portugal	R	18 -4	33	0	0	208	2.77	340	622	0.547	84
Greg Swindell	L	12 -13	30	1	0	190.1	4.16	399	582	0.686	106
Darryl Kile	R	15 -8	26	6	0	171.2	3.51	301	518	0.581	90
Bullpen:											
Xavier Hernandez	R	4 -5	0	72	9	96.2	2.61	148	295	0.502	77
Brian Williams	R	4 -4	5	37	3	82	4.83	163	247	0.660	102
Tom Edens	R	1 -1	0	38	0	49	3.12	87	145	0.600	93
Todd Jones	R	1 -2	0	27	2	37.1	3.13	59	112	0.527	(81)
Al Osuna	L	1 -1	0	44	2	25.1	3.20	47	78	0.603	(93)
Doug Jones	R	4 -10	0	71	26	85.1	4.54	172	256	0.672	104

NOTE: Statistics are only for games pitched with Houston. ( ) Under 200 TBF.

RIGHT . . . AND WRONG
LOS ANGELES DODGERS

Since their ill-fated pennant push in '92, the Dodgers seem to have correctly identified all their problems. But, more often than not, they seem to have chosen all the wrong solutions.

In the immediate wake of '91's frustrating second-place finish, the Dodgers recognized they had a major decision to make. To reload and take another shot at it? Or to rebuild with the kids their fabled farm system had standing by? At the time, there seemed to be good reasons for doing either.

Strangely, the Dodgers chose to do both. Eddie Murray and Alfredo Griffin were allowed to escape through free agency. Two kids, Eric Karros and Jose Offerman, received promotions. Their two *best* pitchers in '91 (Mike Morgan and Tim Belcher) took free agency and were traded, respectively. But veteran Tom Candiotti was signed to replace Morgan and Belcher was traded, along with pitching prospect John Wetteland, for veteran Eric Davis. Rebuilding or reloading, which was it? Whatever it was, it didn't work (63–99 in '92).

After the horrid '92 season, the Dodgers perceived a problem at both 2B and 3B and the closer spot (Wetteland having been traded). Right, again! They picked up veterans Jody Reed, Tim Wallach and Tim Worrell to solve the problems. Wrong again!

They also tried some more kids—Mike Piazza, Pedro Astacio and Pedro Martinez. A very right idea, as it turned out. But the class of '92 still struggled to find the baseball—Karros with his bat, Offerman with his glove. Now, they have become part of a whole new problem. And while all this tinkering has been going on with the infield and pitching staff, the outfield's fallen apart—with no replacements in sight.

This weary succession of problems unsolved and multiplying puts the Dodgers squarely on a treadmill—running hard, but going no place.

Team Trendline: Los Angeles Dodgers

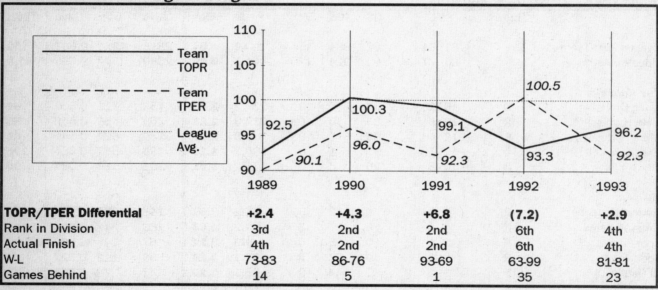

	1989	1990	1991	1992	1993
TOPR/TPER Differential	+2.4	+4.3	+6.8	(7.2)	+2.9
Rank in Division	3rd	2nd	2nd	6th	4th
Actual Finish	4th	2nd	2nd	6th	4th
W-L	73-83	86-76	93-69	63-99	81-81
Games Behind	14	5	1	35	23

(Legend: Team TOPR, Team TPER, League Avg. Values on chart: 92.5, 100.3, 99.1, 100.5, 96.2 (TOPR); 90.1, 96.0, 92.3, 93.3, 92.3 (TPER))

What Was Expected

Strange as it was, the pre-season predictions didn't prominently feature the Dodgers' chances. Coming off a 63–99 season tends to dampen enthusiasm for the immediate future.

Most thought the Dodgers would improve on their sorry '92, though. The pitching, as usual, still looked pretty good. Davis and Darryl Strawberry had only played in 132 games between them. If they could play in that many games apiece, the punch missing in '92 would return. A couple of trades had added Reed and Wallach to the infield. That would help stabilize what had been a league-worst infield defense and, since both had hit in the past, might also add some offense.

There were some interesting kids, too. Astacio looked terrific in his 11 '92 starts. Pedro Martinez and Mike Piazza appeared to be more than pedigreed Dodger-Blue bloods. They actually looked like real players.

What Actually Happened

As the season began, the Dodgers had some trouble getting their engine cranked. One cylinder in particular refused to fire. Darryl Strawberry, sidelined for much of '92, continued to experience lower-back problems and wasn't hitting at all (.152 BA through April).

Nonetheless, he continued to play, but his availability was day to day. Strawberry's failure to produce in the middle of the order and the distraction his troubles seemed to create for the entire team put the club in an offensive "funk." As a consequence, the Dodgers wasted some excellent pitching and stood 14–22 by mid-May.

Finally, on May 14 the Dodgers bit the bullet. Strawberry headed for the DL as the club resolved to make do without him. The new strategy relied on the pitching staff to hold down the score while a makeshift lineup would try to score runs any way it could. In other words, the classic Dodgers formula (their 107 sac bunts led the league).

On May 17, with everything finally settled, the club started on an 11-game winning streak. By the end of the month, they were above .500 (26–23) and stayed right around that level for the rest of the season.

The season's biggest news was that, for the first time in years, the Dodgers got some high-impact performances from their kids. Mike Piazza carried the club offensively, leading the team in BA (.315), HR (35) and RBI (112). His unanimous choice for Rookie-of-the-Year (the Dodgers' 13th in history) surprised nobody. Pedro Astacio demonstrated that his '92 trial was no fluke. He became the Dodgers' best starter and posted the only winning record among them (14–9). Pedro Martinez emerged as the league's best long-reliever (10–5, 2.61 ERA).

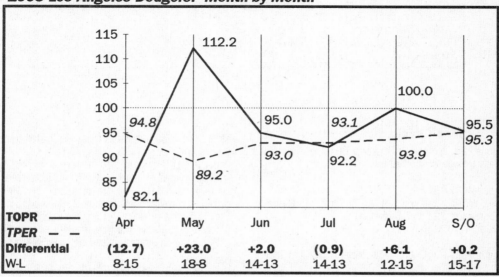

1993 Los Angeles Dodgers: Month-by-Month

	Apr	May	Jun	Jul	Aug	S/O
TOPR ——	82.1	112.2	95.0	93.1	100.0	95.5
TPER – –	94.8	89.2	93.0	92.2	93.9	95.3
Differential	(12.7)	+23.0	+2.0	(0.9)	+6.1	+0.2
W-L	8-15	18-8	14-13	14-13	12-15	15-17

Dodgers Stadium

What's going on here? Could Dodgers Stadium be an "offense neutral park," maybe even a slight "hitter's park"? Yep, in 1993 at least, that's what it looked like.

The 100.4 Park TOPR derives from LA's pitching getting their expected edge at home, coupled with a surprising boost to the Dodger hitters. Thus, the Dodgers show a giant home/road performance split—a pennant winning +12.3 TOPR/TPER differential at home, but a loser's −6.2 on the road. But the Dodgers wound up with identical records home and away, so how could that be? The answer lies in LA's defensive play. At home, they gave up a doubly disgraceful 55 unearned runs, a monstrous 17.3% on the total runs scored by opponents in LA.

If you're confused by all of this, so are the Dodgers. Did somebody *plow* the infield between innings?

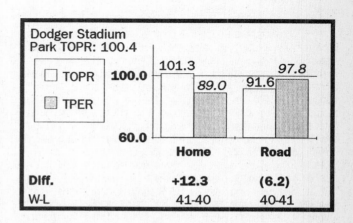

Dodger Stadium
Park TOPR: 100.4

	TOPR	TPER
Home	101.3	89.0
Road	91.6	97.8

	Home	Road
Diff.	+12.3	(6.2)
W-L	41-40	40-41

1993 Dodgers Lineup

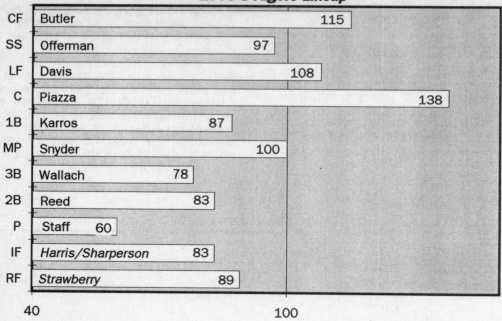

CF	Butler	115
SS	Offerman	97
LF	Davis	108
C	Piazza	138
1B	Karros	87
MP	Snyder	100
3B	Wallach	78
2B	Reed	83
P	Staff	60
IF	*Harris/Sharperson*	83
RF	*Strawberry*	89

40   100

The Offense

With Strawberry gone, the Dodgers' offense turned into a simple three-step affair, easy as a–b–c. It relied on:

a. Butler to reach base (.387 OBP).
b. Working him into scoring position (39 SB for Butler, a league-leading 25 sac bunts for #2 hitter Offerman).
c. Piazza to drive him in (112 RBI).

Then, the Dodgers waited until the order turned over and they could try it again.

The lack of offensive production from the Dodgers' infield was striking. The four regulars (Karros, Reed, Wallach and Offerman) produced the following average offensive line:

BA	OBP	SP	HR	R	RBI	TOPR
.254	.311	.359	9	60	59	88

In other words, the Dodgers' infielders hit about like four Royce Claytons (the SF shortstop, also an 88 TOPR). Now Royce Clayton's a fine SS, but you wouldn't want four of him in your batting order.

Of the four, only Offerman (with a 97 TOPR) displayed adequate offensive production. At that, he was just below the NL norm for the position (100). An "adequate" bat at that position needs to be accompanied by at least "adequate" defense which, of course, Offerman doesn't offer. Nor is his bat so good that you would want to move him to another position to take advantage of it. So, even the infield's *best* hitter in '93 represents a problem.

At 1B, Karros gained Rookie-of-the-Year honors in '92. But he didn't produce enough offense to earn it even then (101 TOPR). In '93, he went backward—his 87 TOPR competing with Pittsburgh's Kevin Young and Montreal's Frank Bolick (since released) for last among NL first-sackers. To mount any kind of offense, the Dodgers must get more from his position.

Essentially, by assuming his contract, the Dodgers paid $10 million cash for Tim Wallach. He was no "$10 million man" at 3B, his 78 TOPR being the lowest-ranked in the league at that position. The infield corners are supposed to be reserved for offense. But

Mike Piazza, by himself, almost duplicated the offensive output of the Dodgers' corners (35 HR, 142 RBI).

Jody Reed's offense also continued its decline and his 83 TOPR was the lowest of any NL 2B. If the Dodgers' thought was to help Offerman's defense by surrounding him with gloves, the price proved high—in both offense and dollars. Acquiring 2B Delino Deshields this off-season from the Expos, however, counts as one problem recognized and one problem *effectively* solved.

While the Dodgers focused on their infield, the outfield went to pot.

RF Darryl Strawberry presents a conundrum. Despite an impressive career, two injury-marred seasons make his future questionable. His on-field and off-field antics have made him anathema to the fans and, apparently, to the management and team. His contract is long-term enormous. He's unwelcome but untradeable—even "unwaiverable," as it turns out. The Dodgers are confronted by a thorny dilemma: release him and eat his contract or pray for a turnaround. Neither course is attractive.

In the meantime, the Eric Davis experiment in LF was written off. After two lackluster seasons (104 and 108 TOPRs), LA shuffled Davis off to Detroit and the LF position became vacant. In CF and the leadoff spot, Brett Butler kept on truckin', enjoying yet another fine season. But, at 37 in '94, how many more of them does he have?

The Dodgers' OF, then, has one hole to fill for sure in '94 (LF). A second one, in RF, may open up as well. The third (CF) may be living on borrowed time. Nobody on the Dodger prospect list appears ready to undertake the task. Raul Mondesi, Henry Rodriguez, Tom Goodwin and Billy Ashley have all had their touts as the outfielders-of-the-future—but, if their '93 TOPRs are any indication, none will hit a lick.

	Class	'93 TOPR	Comment
Ashley	AAA	109	143 K, 35 BB
Goodwin	AAA	90	.329 OBP
Mondesi	AAA	91	85 K, 18 BB
Rodriguez	AAA/Majors	102/95	Also plays 1B

The Pitching

The Dodgers' staff remained the team's tower of strength—fourth best in the league (93.3 Team TPER). A solid and dependable five-man rotation started 160 of 162 games. When needed, the bullpen lent effective support.

The Rotation: No problems here. All TPERed under 100. All will be back next year. And while age creeps up on two key members (Orel Hershiser will be 35, Candiotti 36), Hershiser takes superb care of himself and Candiotti is a knuckle-baller (which means he might only now be entering his prime).

Hershiser has come back from his career-threatening arm troubles to post consecutive TPERs of 89, 99 and, now, 92. He's made 66 starts and pitched 426.1 innings the past two years, with an ERA of 3.53. He seems healthy enough. Since his free agent signing in '92, Candiotti has been equally able (97 and 89 TPERs) and sturdy (62 starts, 417.1 IP, 3.06 ERA).

Ramon Martinez reassumed a regular work schedule in '93 after experiencing arm trouble that curtailed his '92 season. He didn't exhibit his '90 and '91 effectiveness (86 and 89 TPER), but his performance was nonetheless encouraging (98 TPER). At his age (26 in '94), regaining his strength may be only the first step toward regaining his effectiveness. Kevin Gross also gave a steady performance (99 TPER).

The rotation appears to have an "ace-in-waiting." Pedro Astacio followed up his brilliant '92 debut (74 TPER, four shutouts in 11 starts) with a near-repeat performance. He produced the only winning record among the starters (14–9) and the staff's lowest TPER (87). Manager Tom Lasorda resisted the temptation to overuse Astacio, holding him to only 31 starts (least in the rotation) and 186.1 IP (a modest 6.0 IP/start). Having learned his lesson with Ramon Martinez, Tommy took steps to preserve this 23-year-old arm for the future.

The Bullpen: It didn't happen exactly the way the Dodgers planned, but the bullpen gave a stalwart performance in '93.

Recognizing a closer problem after the '92 season (a league-low 29 saves, plus 18 blown saves), the Dodgers hastened to sign free agent Todd Worrell. An effective closer for the Cardinals from '86 to '89, Worrell suffered arm woes and missed two entire seasons in '90 and '91. Upon his return to action in '92, St. Louis handled him with kid gloves. Used to set up Lee Smith, he never appeared before the eighth inning and never pitched more than one inning in any of his 67 outings. His effectiveness apparently restored (2.11 ERA, but with his 103 TPER as a warning signal), the Dodgers pounced on him.

Their investment proved unrewarding. Two stints on the DL (strained right forearm, soreness in right elbow) totaled half the season. The remaining half became a catastrophe (38.2 IP, 6.05 ERA, 127 TPER).

Into this void stepped what had been the Dodgers' best answer all along. Jim Gott, ironically acquired under similar circumstances before the '90 season, proceeded to reestablish his closer credentials. After three years of success in the set-up role (103, 92 and 85 TPERs), Gott delivered the fourth-lowest TPER among NL closers (78).

Ramon Martinez's younger brother, rookie Pedro, took over the long-relief role and made a splashy debut. His performance attracted attention to a job that generally receives little note. In 65 appearances (2 starts) he rolled up 107 IP, restricting the opposition to just 76 hits and registering 119 Ks. His 10–5 record, 2.61 ERA and 82 TPER got enough attention. Enough, in fact, to entice the Expos to give up Delino Deshields to get him.

Ricky Trlicek and Roger McDowell filled the innings between Martinez and Gott capably. But the Dodgers' never-ending quest for a left-hander in their bullpen remains unfulfilled. Rookie Omar Daal reported from Albuquerque in April, but at only 22 and just beginning his second minor league year, Daal offered faint hope and failed to produce (117 TPER).

Overall, the Dodgers can view their pitching situation with satisfaction. Few teams will approach '94 with as proven a five-man rotation and such a solid core in the bullpen. A little touching up around the fringes and they'll be set.

1993 Dodgers Staff

Pos	Pitcher	TPER
St	Hershiser	92
St	Candiotti	89
St	R. Martinez	98
St	Kev. Gross	99
St	Astacio	87
Bp	Worrell	127
Bp	Trlicek	86
Bp	Daal	117
Bp	McDowell	97
Bp	P. Martinez	82
Cl	Gott	78

50   100

What Next?

While the Dodgers will in '94 operate out of the new NL West, a competitively weak division, they shouldn't be confused by pennant dreams. The Giants appear beyond reach, barring a calamity (e.g., Barry Bonds breaks a leg). With their pitching, though, the Dodgers clearly stand as the best of the also-rans—they should get no threat from San Diego or Colorado.

This almost-certain status as a "solid second" in a way, gives LA time. Time to reevaluate their problems, which appear concentrated solely on the offensive side of the ball. Time to assess and, perhaps, reassess their past methods used for problem solving. Maybe they'll find there are other means besides throwing money at holes, which certainly hasn't worked with Wallach, Reed, Davis, Worrell or "The Straw Man." There'll be time to investigate why their famed farm system had been virtually barren until the arrivals recently of Piazza, Astacio and Martinez, their first truly quality crop in more than a decade.

Perhaps, given the time that a '94 season of chasing San Francisco probably affords, the Dodgers will correctly identify both the problem AND the solution better in the future.

Team TOPR: 1993 Los Angeles Dodgers

	Bats	BA	OBP	SLG	HR	R	RBI	NBE	GOC	Ratio	TOPR
League Avg. Team	-	.264	.327	.399	140	728	681	2835	4378	0.647	100
Los Angeles Dodgers	-	.261	.321	.383	130	675	639	2772	4449	0.623	96.2
Regulars:											
C Mike Piazza	R	.318	.370	.561	35	81	112	351	393	0.893	138
1B Eric Karros	R	.247	.287	.409	23	74	80	274	487	0.563	87
2B Jody Reed	R	.276	.333	.346	2	48	31	195	361	0.540	83
3B Tim Wallach	R	.222	.271	.342	12	42	62	197	392	0.503	78
SS Jose Offerman	B	.269	.346	.331	1	77	62	306	489	0.626	97
LF Eric Davis	R	.234	.308	.391	14	57	53	213	305	0.698	108
CF Brett Butler	L	.298	.387	.371	1	80	42	348	469	0.742	115
RF Darryl Strawberry	L	.140	.267	.310	5	12	12	51	89	0.573	(89)
Cory Snyder	R	.266	.331	.397	11	61	56	254	391	0.650	100
Bench (100+ TPA):											
OF Mitch Webster	B	.244	.293	.337	2	26	14	73	146	0.500	(77)
I/O Henry Rodriguez	L	.222	.266	.415	8	20	23	85	139	0.612	(94)
IF Lenny Harris	L	.238	.303	.325	2	20	11	66	128	0.516	(80)
3B Dave Hansen	L	.362	.465	.505	4	13	30	74	69	1.072	(166)
C Carlos Hernandez	R	.253	.267	.364	2	6	7	39	75	0.520	(80)
IF Mike Sharperson	R	.256	.299	.367	2	13	10	40	70	0.571	(88)

NOTE: Statistics are only for games played with Los Angeles. ( ) Under 200 TPA.

Team TPER: 1993 Los Angeles Dodgers

	Throws	W-L	GS	GR	SV	IP	ERA	NBA	GOE	Ratio	TPER
League Avg. Team	-	81 -81	162	381	43	1449	4.04	2835	4378	0.647	100
Los Angeles Dodgers	-	81 -81	162	346	36	1472.2	3.50	2682	4441	0.604	93.3
The Rotation:											
Orel Hershiser	R	12 -14	33	0	0	215.2	3.59	390	653	0.597	92
Tom Candiotti	R	8 -10	32	1	0	213.2	3.12	375	649	0.578	89
Ramon Martinez	R	10 -12	32	0	0	211.2	3.44	404	635	0.636	98
Kevin Gross	R	13 -13	32	1	0	202.1	4.14	391	612	0.639	99
Pedro Astacio	R	14 -9	31	0	0	186.1	3.57	320	569	0.562	87
Bullpen:											
Pedro Martinez	R	10 -5	2	63	2	107	2.61	168	318	0.528	82
Roger McDowell	R	5 -3	0	54	2	68	2.25	128	203	0.631	97
Ricky Trlicek	R	1 -2	0	41	1	64	4.08	108	195	0.554	86
Todd Worrell	R	1 -1	0	35	5	38.2	6.05	95	116	0.819	(126)
Omar Daal	L	2 -3	0	47	0	35.1	5.09	78	103	0.757	(117)
Steve Wilson	L	1 0	0	25	1	25.2	4.56	62	77	0.805	(124)
Jim Gott	R	4 -8	0	62	25	77.2	2.32	118	234	0.504	78

NOTE: Statistics are only for games pitched with Los Angeles. ( ) Under 200 TBF.

Too Many Toys?
MONTREAL EXPOS

After the youthful '92 Expos made their surprising run at the Pirates, closing within three games in mid-September, many thought the club appeared set for a pennant push in '93. Push they did, making a late rush that carried them to three games back of the Phillies at season's end. "Set" they weren't, though.

A total of 48 players played for the '93 Expos, 22 of them pitchers and 14 of them made at least one start. There were a total of 18 rookies—14 position players who accounted for 32.9% of the team's at bats and four pitchers who went 13–10. In addition, 10 non-rookie players with *less* than one year's major league experience saw duty. Young and inexperienced as the '92 Expos were, '93's team inevitably became even younger and more raw.

The rawness showed. The Expos led the league in unearned runs allowed (108, 15.8% of their total). With the third most potent offense in the league (103.4 TOPR), they finished just seventh in runs scored (732, about 40 fewer than they should have had).

It's worth noting that only injury-riddled Cincinnati used more players than the Expos (51). Cleveland's never-ending search for pitching also produced 48 names on the major league roster. Even desperate clubs like San Diego (47) and Colorado (46) used fewer players than the Expos. Injuries and the need to shore up certain spots will always produce some roster movement over a given year. But the Expos' incessant tinkering seemed to be more than that. Finding themselves with a roster full of young talent, a farm system overflowing with more of the same and a practiced skill at picking the pockets of other organizations, they seemingly couldn't resist the temptation to play with their many attractive options. This approach worked well enough to win 94 games. But how many would they have won if they'd resisted the urge to fiddle? And concentrated instead on putting their best "toys" into the game?

Team Trendline: Montreal Expos

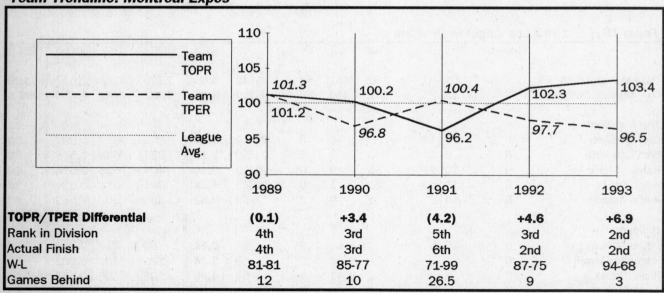

TOPR/TPER Differential	(0.1)	+3.4	(4.2)	+4.6	+6.9
Rank in Division	4th	3rd	5th	3rd	2nd
Actual Finish	4th	3rd	6th	2nd	2nd
W-L	81-81	85-77	71-99	87-75	94-68
Games Behind	12	10	26.5	9	3

What Was Expected?

Predictably, the experts picked Montreal as one of the favorites to win the NL East. Everybody thought well of their chances but many offered reservations regarding the club's youth and its still "unfinished" state—no proven first or third basemen, only three proven starters, etc. Many noted that the organization had taken no palpable action over the winter to improve the team and project it to a pennant level. Instead, Montreal had been content to continue business as is their usual, doing nickel and dime deals, predicated on giving a nickel in hopes of receiving a dime, and sorting through their stable of talent blossoming in the farm system.

What Actually Happened

While the Phillies broke from the gate at a full gallop, the Expos loped lazily through the season—never more than 8 games over .500. After a loss to the Reds on August 20, the Expos stood 64–59 and 14½ games off the pace. Time had come to knock off the pretense and get down to the business of "next year."

Accordingly, on August 25 Montreal's front office cut a deal to send free-agent-to-be Dennis Martinez, their most reliable but aging (37) pitcher, to Atlanta in support of the Braves' desperate drive on the Giants. Coincidentally, this deal would have also kept Martinez out of the clutches of the Giants, who *really* needed him. In mid-game, Martinez bade an emotional farewell to his Montreal teammates and left the dugout—presumably to join a pennant race. The next day, however, Martinez nixed the deal when Atlanta wouldn't guarantee him a spot in their rotation. As a 10–5 man (ten years in the majors with the last five with one team), he was within his rights to do so. As it turned out, the deal never happened. But the pennant race did.

Starting on August 21 the Expos ran up a 30–9 record, gaining 11½ games on the Phillies. Written off in mid-August, they actually weren't eliminated until October 1. The most encouraging aspect of the run, perhaps, was its effect on the Montreal fans. Never much enamored with this *les Jeux partie* stuff, the *Quebecois* flocked to *Le Stade* for a mid-September weekend "showdown" series with the flagging Phillies. Over 136,000 showed up for the proceedings and saw some *le grand balle.* In all three games, the Expos trailed by at least three runs into the 7th inning, yet came back to pick up two 1-run victories (8–7 in 12 and 6–5). They dropped the Saturday game 5–4 after getting the tying run to third with one out in the 9th. The fans were pumped up even further by the appearance of home-boy Denis Boucher, who started the Saturday game (only one other Quebec native has played for the Expos, pitcher Claude Raymond in '69–'71). Baseball was alive and well in Quebec. In September, no less.

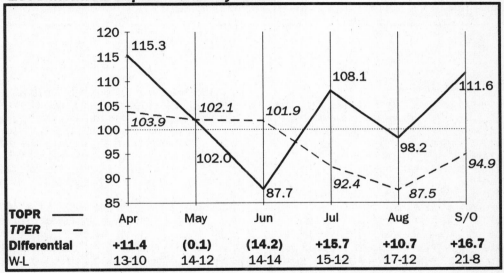

1993 Montreal Expos: Month-by-Month

	Apr	May	Jun	Jul	Aug	S/O
TOPR ———	115.3	102.0	87.7	108.1	98.2	111.6
TPER – –	103.9	102.1	101.9	92.4	87.5	94.9
Differential	**+11.4**	**(0.1)**	**(14.2)**	**+15.7**	**+10.7**	**+16.7**
W-L	13-10	14-12	14-14	15-12	17-12	21-8

Olympic Stadium

Neither a "hitter's park" nor a "pitcher's park" in '93 (Park TOPR: 98.4). Instead, *Le Stade* was a "home park" *par excellence.* No other park in the majors provided so pronounced an advantage to its occupant. On a park-adjusted basis, with the home/road differential washed out of it, the Expos' offense improved by +4.0% and their pitchers' effectiveness stepped up by +7.3% in Montreal. Not surprisingly, this resulted in the best home record in the majors (55–26).

The team's improvement was general, not concentrated in any one aspect of the game. The single biggest difference, though, showed up in the Baserunner Sub-set. The Expos' offense, which ran extremely well everywhere else, ran even better at home. On the other hand, Montreal pitching, which did a poor job of controlling baserunners anywhere, didn't do quite so poorly on their own turf.

Home cooking for the Expos, evidently, has a French-Canadian flavor.

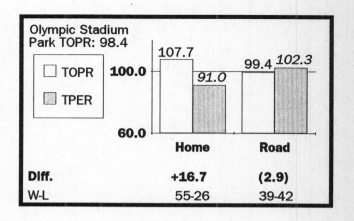

Olympic Stadium
Park TOPR: 98.4

	Home	Road
☐ TOPR	107.7	99.4
▨ TPER	91.0	102.3
Diff.	**+16.7**	**(2.9)**
W-L	55-26	39-42

1993 Expos Lineup

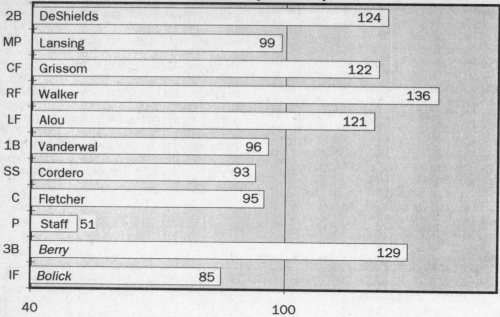

Position	Player	Value
2B	DeShields	124
MP	Lansing	99
CF	Grissom	122
RF	Walker	136
LF	Alou	121
1B	Vanderwal	96
SS	Cordero	93
C	Fletcher	95
P	Staff	51
3B	*Berry*	129
IF	*Bolick*	85

40   100

The Offense

Superficially, the Expos had a sub-par offense. The team BA (.257), OBP (.326) and SLG (.386) all fell below the league norms. Yet their 103.4 TOPR ranked third highest in the league. Why? Speed! The Expos ran at will, swiping 228 bases while being caught only 56 times—an amazing 80.2% success rate (the league averaged 122–56, 68.5%). Speed existed throughout the lineup (8 players were in double-digits).

Yet, the Expos had difficulty translating their speed into runs. They scored a league average total of 732, more than their below-average batting statistics alone would have produced, but not as many as their total offensive production (TOPR) should have yielded. Atlanta, with a slightly lower 103.2 TOPR, scored 35 more. Accordingly, Montreal should have tabled 770. About 40 runs were missing. Where did they go?

They were stranded. Not because of an abnormally high left-on-base figure (732 runs scored equaled 36.6% of earned baserunners H + BB + HP, just above the league average). Instead, it was because the runners were left stranded *in scoring position*. The Expos' league high stolen bases (228) and 3rd highest sacrifices (100) helped push 756 earned baserunners into scoring position or beyond—a league high 37.8% (league average 31.6%). The effort expended getting them there, however, didn't pay off because of a problem with the batting order.

To optimize their run production, the Expos needed either *a)* some power (they hit just 122 HRs, 11th in the league) or *b)* a longer offensive sequence. In either event, more production had to come from 1B or 3B, or both. The problems at both positions surfaced in '92 and Montreal had, in their own way, addressed them.

In a couple of those off-season "nickel and dime" deals late in '92, the Expos had acquired a pair of minor league 3Bs—Sean Berry from Kansas City and Frank Bolick from Seattle. They hoped this pair would provide at least a platoon solution. At 1B, Greg Colbrunn showed some late season power in '92 and, when healthy, had been a potent minor league hitter. Jim Vanderwal had proved a useful LH bat off the bench. Perhaps, another workable and inexpensive platoon could form there. The switch-hitting Bolick could play 1B, too, and more players waited in the high minors. The Expos certainly didn't lack options.

The season soon became more complicated as Delino Deshields contracted chicken pox, allowing one of those options—Mike Lansing—a chance to show his stuff at 2B. And he had some *good* stuff to show, good enough to stay in the lineup when Deshields returned. Lansing moved to 3B, converting that platoon into a crowd. But shortstop was his best position and talk turned to using rookie SS Will Cordero as a third-sacker. Bolick made five errors in his first 40 chances and got shuffled to 1B, easing the 3B crunch a little.

The other corner became a revolving door. Colbrunn got hurt, again, but hadn't hit anyway. Vanderwal, sure enough, proved to be a useful LH bat off the bench. Bolick became hopelessly confused. None qualified as real first basemen anyway (Bolick had been a 3B, Vanderwal an outfielder and Colbrunn a catcher). Defense, predictably became a concern and, altogether, 10 different players took turns at the position. The converted third-sacker Bolick started more than any of them (39).

The lineup graphic reveals that neither Vanderwal nor Bolick provided anything like the production expected from 1B. Colbrunn, Orestes Marrero, Derrick White, Archi Cianfrocco, *et al*, were no better. It also reveals that Sean Berry (remember him?) had a heckuva season. Well, half a season, really. By the time he fought his way through the crowd at the other corner, almost half the year had passed. After the All-Star break, Berry finally became a "Berry, Berry good" everyday player providing more power (14 HR, .465 SLG) to the offensive sequence and helping improve run production by almost ½ a run per game (4.76 vs. 4.27) in the second half.

Would it have taken so long to find Berry had there not been so *many* other options? If there hadn't been so many potential combinations already at hand, or within the reach of a phone call and a plane ticket, would it have taken so long to admit that something major had to be done at 1B? Some teams make decisions and commit to living with them because they have no other real choice in the matter. Sometimes, these teams find gratification by seeing their commitment pay off after an initial period of struggle. But when a team has a cornucopia of choices, they may not feel the need for a real decision much less a commitment. Sometimes all these teams get to see are the initial struggles, a whole series of them.

The Pitching

The Expos pitching was better than average, among the league's best (96.5 TPER, and a 4th ranking 3.44 ERA). The club's bottom line failed to reveal it, though, because of their miserable defense. Montreal allowed a free-world leading 108 unearned runs (⅔ of a run per game). The team committed 159 errors (almost one per game), with only Colorado and San Diego flubbing more chances. Moreover, the "rotation" was a season-long search for five pitchers who would be healthy and effective at the same time. This condition existed for a little less than four weeks during late July and early August when Dennis Martinez, Ken Hill, Jeff Fassero, Kirk Rueter and Chris Nabholz took regular turns. The Expos had 11 pitchers make five or more starts and used 14 different starters in all.

Injuries, to be sure, contributed to the instability of the staff. Closer John Wetteland and set-up man Mel Rojas, two critical members of the bullpen, both had brief stints on the DL. Nabholz exited for 32 days with a strained forearm muscle and also spent 3 weeks in Ottawa taking a refresher course in his craft. Hill, off to an impressive 6–0 start, suffered a groin strain running out a ground ball May 21. He spent only 20 days on the DL but appeared hampered by the injury for the rest of the season.

But, again, we see the same sort of shuffling through the options deck. The Expos had promising young talent like Brian Barnes and Rueter. They effortlessly acquired competent journeymen like Jeff Shaw. Fassero proved he could play most any role. Most of these improvisations worked, so, in a way, the solutions became problems of their own. With so many solutions, which one was really *best?* Finding that solution took even more time and not until All-Star time did the rotation of choice emerge. Nabholz then broke down and more attractive options emerged—Gil Heredia, then Denis Boucher—confusing the picture even further.

The Montreal system has an enviable record of producing promising young pitchers. However, they have been notably less successful in furthering their development at the major league level.

Mark Gardner, Chris Haney and Kent Bottenfield came and went. Brian Barnes and Chris Nabholz first arrived in the '90s with powerful minor league credentials, which were immediately confirmed at the major league level. They've had only sporadic success since and, in '93, both took steps backward. There's no question as to their potential or their "stuff," only their ability to employ it to their advantage. Could the unsettled, highly competitive environment on the Expos' staff have something to do with this? Would they respond better if a "decision" was made then backed by a "commitment"? It's worth thinking about, especially with *wunderkind* control-artist Kirk Rueter climbing into the same boat.

Perhaps the off-season will bring some clarification. Dennis Martinez left for free agency and will help Cleveland pursue its pennant hopes. Hill moves into the role of rotation anchor and, if he's fully recovered, seems well suited to succeed. The rest of the rotation will be filled out by Fassero, Rueter and . . . who? Here we go again, Nabholz (if he's still around), Pedro Martinez (if he adjusts to life outside the Dodger womb), Boucher (the accountants are praying he's for real), Barnes (if he rediscovers his effectiveness), Heredia (if he can step it up a notch) or the next wave of promising young talent (Gabe White, Joey Eischen or Tavo Alvarez joined by Brian Looney or Rod Henderson in mid-season). Add to that the possibility of some new veteran "sleepers" culled off the waiver wire or from the minor league free agent list.

The bullpen's situation starts with Wetteland, a rock-solid closer. But ends with questions. Will the Expos risk arbitration with Rojas? Will they pass the set-up baton to Tim Scott (whose 109 TPER with Montreal, 111 for the season, argues such a move)? Who replaces Fassero's steady contribution from the left side? Who in the farm system, or from one of those "nickel and dime" trades, will catch the Expos' eye and inspire even more restructuring?

Questions are everywhere one turns on this team. And it always seems there are more answers than there are questions. So what's the problem?

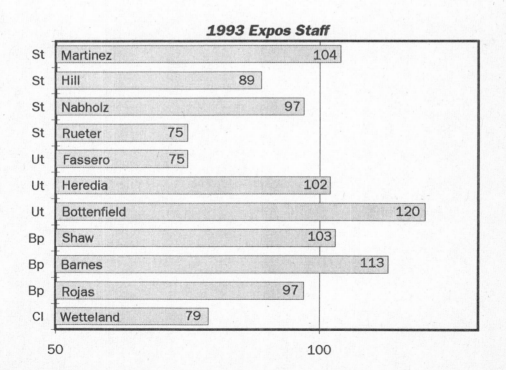

1993 Expos Staff

St	Martinez	104
St	Hill	89
St	Nabholz	97
St	Rueter	75
Ut	Fassero	75
Ut	Heredia	102
Ut	Bottenfield	120
Bp	Shaw	103
Bp	Barnes	113
Bp	Rojas	97
Cl	Wetteland	79

50   100

What Next?

Perhaps the Expos, with eyes fixed upon the future for so long, have lost sight of what stands immediately before them: A chance to win it *all!* A chance to establish a dynasty of their own, based on an assemblage of highly talented young players in a balanced team format. They're strong and deep in both offense and pitching, supported by a productive farm system. This may sound like we're talking about Atlanta, but it applies equally to Montreal. Maybe more so.

Some will say that's "poppycock," the Expos simply can't afford it in their situation. They'll point out that the Braves' payroll is creeping toward $50 million and that the Expos' management wouldn't spring for that even if they *could* afford it. Wait a minute. The Braves' '91 payroll totaled only $21 mil. The Expos can afford that. As to the $50 mil, let's see what happens in *Le Stade* if the Expos make it clear they're going for it, get off to a good start and spend the entire summer engaged in what is almost bound to be a red-hot pennant race. What if it were then capped by a pennant and some post-season action? What would happen, eh, if *les Expos* found themselves facing Toronto in October? It's too good to be true, of course, but "what if," indeed? Down the road we'd wager $50 million could and would be found.

The only apparent difference between the two organizations is Atlanta made their decisions when they needed to make them, stood by them and events proved them correct.

Now it's the Expos' turn to make some decisions and shift their focus to the present. After reviewing their attractive options, settle on a team composition that they believe can successfully challenge Atlanta in the newly restructured NL East. Then, in spring training, concentrate on preparing *that* team for its assigned task—taking care to answer any and all remaining questions *before* heading north. Opening day '94 should mark the end of any continuing major league development program and the beginning of a dead-serious quest for a pennant.

Because, if they just come close again, the payroll is going to skyrocket anyway. Without a big financial season to cushion the blow, the now open "window" will have begun closing.

Team TOPR: 1993 Montreal Expos

	Bats	BA	OBP	SLG	HR	R	RBI	NBE	GOC	Ratio	TOPR
League Avg. Team	-	.264	.327	.399	140	728	681	2835	4378	0.647	100
Montreal Expos	-	.257	.326	.386	122	732	682	2935	4384	0.669	103.4
Regulars:											
C Darrin Fletcher	L	.255	.320	.379	9	33	60	192	311	0.617	95
1B Frank Bolick	B	.211	.298	.329	4	25	24	96	174	0.552	85
Greg Colbrunn	R	.255	.282	.392	4	15	23	72	121	0.595	(92)
John VanderWal	L	.233	.320	.372	5	34	30	108	173	0.624	96
2B Delino DeShields	L	.295	.389	.372	2	75	29	288	360	0.800	124
3B Mike Lansing	R	.287	.352	.369	3	64	45	247	384	0.643	99
Sean Berry	R	.261	.348	.465	14	50	49	197	236	0.835	129
SS Wil Cordero	R	.248	.308	.387	10	56	58	227	377	0.602	93
LF Moises Alou	R	.286	.340	.483	18	70	85	288	369	0.780	121
CF Marquis Grissom	R	.298	.351	.438	19	104	95	372	470	0.791	122
RF Larry Walker	L	.265	.371	.469	22	85	86	336	381	0.882	136
Bench (100+ TPA):											
OF Lou Frazier	B	.286	.340	.349	1	27	16	100	146	0.685	106
IF Randy Ready	R	.254	.367	.351	1	22	10	69	106	0.651	(101)
C Tim Spehr	R	.230	.281	.368	2	14	10	46	72	0.639	(99)
OF Rondell White	R	.260	.321	.411	2	9	15	37	61	0.607	(94)

NOTE: Statistics are only for games played with Montreal. ( ) Under 200 TPA.

Team TPER: 1993 Montreal Expos

	Throws	W-L	GS	GR	SV	IP	ERA	NBA	GOE	Ratio	TPER
League Avg. Team	-	81 -81	162	381	43	1449	4.04	2835	4378	0.647	100
Montreal Expos	-	94 -68	163	385	61	1456.2	3.55	2764	4425	0.625	96.5
The Rotation:											
Dennis Martinez	R	15 -9	34	1	1	224.2	3.85	460	685	0.672	104
Ken Hill	R	9 -7	28	0	0	183.2	3.23	323	561	0.576	89
Chris Nabholz	L	9 -8	21	5	0	116.2	4.09	223	355	0.628	97
Kirk Rueter	L	8 0	14	0	0	85.2	2.73	124	257	0.482	75
Utility:											
Jeff Fassero	L	12 -5	15	41	1	149.2	2.29	223	457	0.488	75
Kent Bottenfield	R	2 -5	11	12	0	83	4.12	197	254	0.776	120
Gil Heredia	R	4 -2	9	11	2	57.1	3.92	112	169	0.663	102
Bullpen:											
Brian Barnes	L	2 -6	8	44	3	100	4.41	218	299	0.729	113
Jeff Shaw	R	2 -7	8	47	0	95.2	4.14	190	286	0.664	103
Mel Rojas	R	5 -8	0	66	10	88.1	2.95	172	274	0.628	97
Tim Scott	R	5 -2	0	32	1	34	3.71	71	101	0.703	(109)
John Wetteland	R	9 -3	0	70	43	85.1	1.37	132	258	0.512	79

NOTE: Statistics are only for games pitched with Montreal. ( ) Under 200 TBF.

FADE TO BLACK
NEW YORK METS

The season just past saw the end of an important era in the New York Mets' history. The reconstruction of the under-achieving '89 team reached completion.

The extensive effort and endless dollars invested produced 103 losses, a dead-last finish behind an expansion team, no less. And all this had been achieved in an atmosphere totally devoid of good humor.

The last three years of this project presented a series of climactic calamities, approaching farce. Now, at last, it is over. The demolition has begun. Once the crater is cleared of debris, reconstruction will begin. The architectural style hasn't been chosen as yet. But two things are certain. The '94 club will bear no resemblance to its predecessor. And it will take more than one year to reverse these appalling trendlines.

Team Trendline: New York Mets

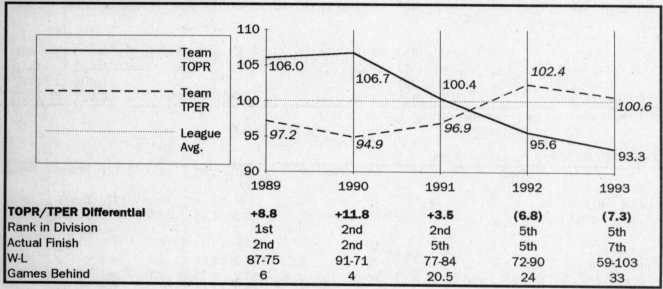

	1989	1990	1991	1992	1993
TOPR/TPER Differential	+8.8	+11.8	+3.5	(6.8)	(7.3)
Rank in Division	1st	2nd	2nd	5th	5th
Actual Finish	2nd	2nd	5th	5th	7th
W-L	87-75	91-71	77-84	72-90	59-103
Games Behind	6	4	20.5	24	33

What Was Expected

The '93 season began, as most Mets seasons begin, with high expectations and a contender's label. It was as if '92 hadn't happened. Nor '91 before that. The excuses: the '92 Mets suffered all those injuries and '91 had been an aberration. Everybody *knew* they were better than that.

It was thought that, given a healthy HoJo and a ready Vince Coleman, the lineup would recover its old ferocity. A full season of Bret Saberhagen and John Franco would bring the pitching back up to its normal standard of excellence and the Mets would then reassume their accustomed place among the leaders.

This rather sanguine approach to analysis overlooked, however, the simple fact that, even with all the pieces in place, the '92 Mets really weren't anywhere near contenders. The rash of injuries had cost them a shot at .500 in '92, not the division championship. Trapped in a free agent web of their own making, the Mets were stuck with a bevy of declining, high-salaried players who were unproductive, untradeable and, at times, downright unsocial.

What Actually Happened

The '93 season opened with a bang. On opening day, Dwight Gooden shut out the expansion Rockies at home and the Mets swept the 2-game series. That was about it, as far as the good news goes. That weekend, the Mets got swept in turn at Shea by the Astros. The season's dreary death march began.

Unable to detect any good news worth reporting, certainly didn't leave the New York media at a loss for words. The fans were able to follow any number of long-running story lines:

◆ The trial and subsequent guillotining of manager Jeff Torborg on May 19. The slumping Mets stood at 13–25 (4–18 in their last 22).
◆ The trial and subsequent resignation of GM Al Harazin concluded June 22 with the record at 21–47.
◆ Anthony Young's pursuit of an 82-year-old major league record, achieved June 27 with his 24th consecutive loss.
◆ The entire team's inability to win even *two* in a row. Finally, they

did it on June 29–30 in Florida breaking a 65-game stretch of futility and shattering the previous league record.

In July, the plot lines changed from soap opera to "True Detective." "Who Fired the Super Soaker?" and "Was It a Fire-cracker, or Was It a Bomb?" became popular themes. In the midst of these publicity travails, the Mets quietly had their best month (12–16).

When August came it was time for courtroom drama. Vince Coleman, aka The Mad Bomber, was on leave-of-absence-with-pay. He faced a California court hearing on his July 24 "playful-act-turned-sour" in the parking lot at Dodger Stadium. Coleman's legal fate unresolved, his professional fate was nonetheless announced August 24. For the first time in memory, a major league ballplayer holding a long-term, big money contract was *fired* (with pay, at least for now). That's the only way to describe it. Coleman got asked to clear out his locker just like a failed corporate executive complete with "golden parachute." It might as well have come over the Dow-Jones wire, "NYM Corp. Fires Starting Left Fielder." The Mets won that night to reach 43–82, but were mathematically eliminated the next day and ceased to be news of any kind.

One got the feeling that the Mets' '93 season had very little to do with baseball. And everything to do with failure and the fate of the failed. A modern-day morality play, so to speak.

1993 New York Mets: Month-by-Month

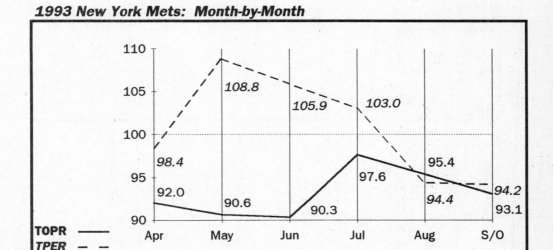

	Apr	May	Jun	Jul	Aug	S/O
TOPR ———	92.0	90.6	90.3	97.6	95.4	93.1
TPER – –	98.4	108.8	105.9	103.0	94.4	94.2
Differential	(6.4)	(18.2)	(15.6)	(5.4)	+1.0	(1.1)
W-L	8-13	9-18	6-21	12-16	11-18	13-17

Shea Stadium

The home of the Mets rated a first-class "pitcher's park" in '93 (93.7 Park TOPR), ranking behind only Candlestick as the least hitter-friendly park in the league.

Intriguingly, the Mets' pitchers enjoyed a normal home/road differential in New York. But the Mets' hitters had a devil of a time in what, for a home team, was supposed to be the "friendly confines." On an adjusted basis, the Mets' offense (what there was of it) declined an alarming *13.8%* when it came back home to Shea.

In fact, every single element of the Mets' offense went in the tank at home: batting average (.245 at Shea vs. .251 on the road), on-base percentage (.297 vs. .313), slugging (.380 vs. .400), HRs (75 vs. 83), walks (196 vs. 252) and TOPRs net baserunner bases (16 vs. 39).

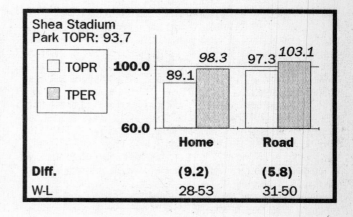

Shea Stadium
Park TOPR: 93.7

	Home	Road
TOPR	89.1	97.3
TPER	98.3	103.1
Diff.	(9.2)	(5.8)
W-L	28-53	31-50

1993 Mets Lineup

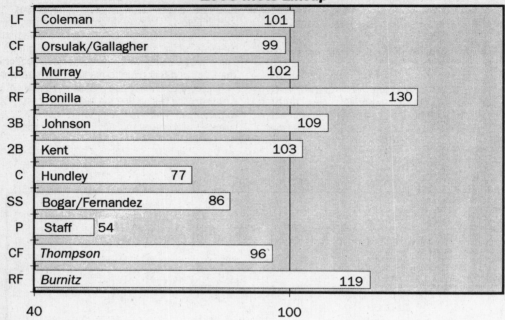

Position	Player	TOPR
LF	Coleman	101
CF	Orsulak/Gallagher	99
1B	Murray	102
RF	Bonilla	130
3B	Johnson	109
2B	Kent	103
C	Hundley	77
SS	Bogar/Fernandez	86
P	Staff	54
CF	*Thompson*	96
RF	*Burnitz*	119

40   100

The Offense

With the exception of Howard Johnson, the most notable aspect of the '93 Mets lineup is that *nobody had a bad year* compared to what might legitimately have been expected of them. That's to say, this edition of the Mets didn't underachieve, at least individually.

If you're surprised by this analysis, take the projected '93 starting lineup from the top:

Vince Coleman, due to injury, had played less than 100 games in both '91 and '92. He made it three straight, but for a very different reason. As a leadoff hitter, his primary qualification was stealing bases. However, it's difficult to steal a lot of them if you can't reach first and Coleman's on-base average finished significantly below average (.316 OBP vs. .327 for the entire league). Prior 3-year TOPR: 112. TOPR expectation: given age (31) and injury history, something less. '93 TOPR: 101.

Tony Fernandez, acquired in the off-season from San Diego, had been a quality shortstop and an above-average hitter for the position. Good trade. Prior 3-year TOPR: 102. TOPR expectation: about the same. '93 TOPR: 98, but, unaccountably, 87 with the Mets before his repackaging and shipment to Toronto where he awakened (moving from the outhouse to the penthouse will often do that to a player).

Eddie Murray seemed, at 37, well into his declining phase from his "Eddie Murray" years. In '91 and '92 he was, at best, an average hitter for an NL first baseman. Prior 3-year TOPR: 119. TOPR expectation: less, probably quite a bit less. '93 TOPR: 102. Don't be fooled by those 27 HRs and 100 RBIs, his *overall* offensive production was league average—not what you want from 1B or in the middle of the order.

Bobby Bonilla had what was perceived as a bad year in '92. It seemed worse than it was due to a bizarre home/road split—he was still Bobby Bo on the road but became Kevin Elster at home. Presumably, he was capable of overcoming this schizoid performance. Prior 3-year TOPR: 129. TOPR expectation: he was still good for the same. '93 TOPR: 130.

Howard Johnson seemed a legitimate candidate to explode, regaining his former stature as a top-notch offensive performer (a league-leading 170 TOPR in '89 and a potent 147 in '91). Purportedly recovered from a '92 season-ending wrist injury and

moving back to his familiar 3B position, the stage had been set for a proper comeback. Prior 3-year TOPR: 127. TOPR expectation: that same area at least. '93 TOPR: 109, duplicating his dreadful '92.

Jeff Kent would experience his first full season as a big league regular. Rookie TOPR: 108. TOPR expectation: about the same or better, depending on how slow he started and how quickly he adjusted. '93 TOPR: 103. Not bad, he'll do better and the Cone trade that brought him will end up looking like a good one.

Ryan Thompson presented credentials akin to every other Toronto OF prospect, one good year at Syracuse after a history of struggling at the lower levels. His reputedly great glove would negate his offensive deficiencies only on a team with more bats than the Mets had. Rookie TOPR: 92. TOPR expectations: about the same which would eventually land him in Norfolk. '93 TOPR: 96, and he spent the summer in Norfolk.

Todd Hundley produced only a 78 TOPR in his first full year in '92, very marginal even for a catcher. His minor league record suggested he might be a little more productive than that. Prior TOPR: 78. TOPR expectations: given his youth and minor league record, modest improvement. '93 TOPR: 77, clouding his future.

The sum total of TOPR's expectations for the '93 Mets, if they dodged the injury bullets, made them a dead-average offense. They didn't avoid the injuries, of course, and ended up well below average (93.3).

Four of the above eight are already gone from the Mets lineup (Coleman, Fernandez, Murray and Johnson) and the team received nothing in return, except a vacant roster spot—which has its merits under the circumstances. In addition, the rumor mill has Bonilla on the block. Hundley's starting job remains in jeopardy. And there are (and probably ought to be) second thoughts about Thompson. On opening day '94, Jeff Kent may be the only survivor. And he might be at a different position.

Of the eight players promoted from the minors to try their luck at plugging holes in the dike, only Jeromy Burnitz capitalized on the opportunity (Rookie TOPR: 119). His power bat will find a place in the '94 lineup for certain. And, if he recaptures the strike zone judgment he showed at AA in '91 (104 BB), the Mets will have found a dandy.

Was It Intimidation?

The Mets really stunk up Shea Stadium last year (28–53). Oh, you already knew that? But did you know they didn't stink up opposing stadiums in '93—any worse, that is, than road teams normally do? Their road record (31–50) doesn't necessarily reflect it, but the Mets' road offense (97.3 Road TOPR) finished right at the league average (97.6). Similarly, the Mets' pitching staff was not only average overall (100.3 TPER) but about average on the road (103.1 Road TPER, 102.5 league average).

Mets' hitters coming home weren't like the swallows at Capistrano, though. Nobody seemed to look forward to it. And, maybe, that's exactly what caused the alarming 13.8% decline in the Mets' offensive production at their "unfriendly confines." The complete home/road TOPR line showed that every element of the Mets' offense at home fell below their road performance. The most striking difference, however, came in their walk column. The Mets took 56 fewer free passes at home (196 vs. 252) while striking out just about as often (5.33/9 vs. 5.47). This one facet of their offense cost them almost half of the total net base deficiency they experienced at home (−1.44 per game). This, in turn, reduced their scoring rate by almost half-a-run per game.

Could this stat, a product of poor patience, betray an anxiety to please the home folks? Or a "get it over with and let's go home" approach to the game in the face of the fans' vocal displeasure? We'll probably never know, will we?

The Pitching

The Mets' '93 staff didn't achieve its past standards of excellence. But at least it achieved a level of average effectiveness (100.3 TPER, 4.05 ERA vs. NL average 4.04) and wasn't nearly as embarrassing as the Mets' offense. In fact, the starting rotation would have ranked as one of the leagues most solid, had much of it not strayed to the DL.

The Rotation: The overriding problem, of course, stemmed from the team's three most effective starters making only 66 starts between them, Dwight Gooden (29), Bret Saberhagen (19) and Sid Fernandez (18). Over 100 starts had been expected from this trio

and, had they made them, the Mets may have gained a little more respect.

Though he ended up on the dark-side of .500 for the second consecutive season, Gooden's year marked his first meaningful improvement since '89. His '91 TPER ranked 14th in the league and marked a significant step in the right direction after his '90–'92 (97, 95, 98). But when he took himself out of a start on August 31, after only four innings, the alarm bells went off. The affliction, last described as a "tired shoulder," followed rotator cuff surgery ('91) and a 3-week stay on the DL with "inflammation" ('92). Uh-oh.

Saberhagen ended his season under the knife, arthroscopic surgery to remove a bone spur in his pitching elbow. Coming on top of knee surgery and an earlier ankle injury, his future effectiveness also becomes subject to question. With a $20 million, 3-year contract extension kicking in for '94, a positive answer to the question is imperative. As always, "The Bleach Boy" pitched very well, when he could pitch at all.

The same song, second verse, applied to Fernandez. A heckuva pitcher, when he pitched. Two knee surgeries in three years, though, and he too finds himself surrounded by question marks. But it's Baltimore who'll find out the answers, not the Mets.

Frank Tanana's gone, too. And his 29 starts tied Gooden for the team lead.

The rest of the starts got meted out to a collection of diverse talent. Eric Hillman, a LH seemingly on his way to becoming a career minor-leaguer, got 22 of them and did surprisingly well (98 TPER). But he also got eight starts in '92 and was pasted (121). If his true level of effectiveness lies somewhere in-between, a reasonable assumption, he could compete for the #5 spot. The same goes in reverse for Pete Schourek (18 starts), who got ripped to shreds in '93 (123 TPER) but was decent in '92 (103). Another LH pitcher, another potential utility guy.

Mets' fans also got to see rookie Bobby Jones in the rotation. He made nine starts and pitched reasonably well (six "quality" starts). His Debut TPER came in at a middling 108, but minor league indications are he'll get better with experience. Has the Mets' farm system actually produced its first rotation starter since Dwight Gooden in '84?

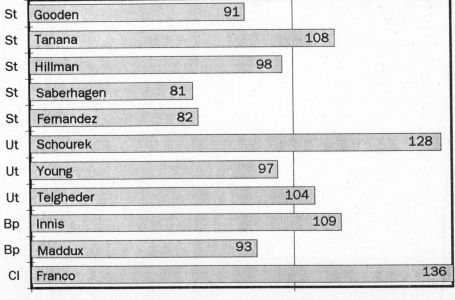

1993 Mets Staff

	Player	TPER
St	Gooden	91
St	Tanana	108
St	Hillman	98
St	Saberhagen	81
St	Fernandez	82
Ut	Schourek	128
Ut	Young	97
Ut	Telgheder	104
Bp	Innis	109
Bp	Maddux	93
Cl	Franco	136

50   100

Surprisingly, it turns out the guy who lost 27 consecutive games actually pitched pretty well. Anthony Young's 97 TPER was better than average and so was his ERA (3.77 vs. the NL average of 4.04). Two circumstances combined to produce the "streak." First, almost every third run he yielded was unearned (20 of the 62 total runs). Second, he suffered from pure bad luck. When he pitched well, which was reasonably often, the Mets didn't score (e.g., no decision in two starts where he left with a 1–0 lead). Actually, a pitcher who loses 27 consecutive games has to be pretty good when you stop and think about it. How else would he have gotten so many opportunities if he weren't? Young's no savior, but he could fill a hole in the rotation for the Mets next year (3.52 ERA in 10 starts, 4.21 in 29 relief appearances).

The Bullpen: Circumstances conspired to limit the Mets' bullpen to the fewest appearances in the league (297 vs. league average 381). With 103 losses, the Mets weren't called upon to pitch in the 9th very often and the regular starters managed to average almost 7 IP per start.

As a result, only the Atlanta bullpen worked fewer innings than the Mets' (373.2 innings). Which was just as well because the Mets' bullpen gave a desultory performance when called upon. The primary middlemen, Mike Maddux and Jeff Innis, got worked hard (125 App., 151.2 IP combined) in what became meaningless roles—with no leads to protect and no closer to set-up. They performed "OK," but they've both been better. The utility crew that shuttled between relieving and starting (Young, Schourek and Dave Telgheder) was "inconsistent," to be gentle. The closer, John Franco, was either hurt, incapable of frequent use or ineffective. A tender pitching elbow, after September '92 surgery, has restricted him to only 69 innings pitched in the past two years, putting this once premier closer's future under a cloud.

Thus, virtually every potentially bright spot in the Mets' pitching picture—starters Gooden, Saberhagen, the rookie Jones and bull-penners Innis, Maddux and Franco—end up haloed with question marks. The team may have a solid core of pitching talent to rely on in '94. But, then again, they may not. Where it all goes from here is anybody's guess.

What Next?

The '93 team has ceased to exist. There were no mourners at its graveside nor did it leave an estate of any sort.

As a consequence, they'll be only one certain returnee in the '94 lineup (Kent). The pitching staff has a few answers and just as many questions. The farm system's cupboard of immediately available talent remains nearly bare (only Burnitz and Jones can be counted upon to make a contribution in '94).

Trades of both Bonilla and Saberhagen have been rumored as a means of expanding the available and prospective talent base. But both finished the season on the DL and both have long-term contracts that are totally out of line with their current market value. Any return they might bring thus becomes subject to discount.

At this stage, '94 shouldn't be an issue. The focus needs to be on '95, '96 and beyond when the farm will yield new and probably better crops. Reality has finally set in. These Mets are a long way from being respectable again, much less contenders. In '94 the Mets will be a totally different team and almost certainly a losing team again. But they may have something the '93 Mets didn't. A future.

Team TOPR: 1993 New York Mets

	Bats	BA	OBP	SLG	HR	R	RBI	NBE	GOC	Ratio	TOPR
League Avg. Team	-	.264	.327	.399	140	728	681	2835	4378	0.647	100
New York Mets	-	.248	.305	.390	158	672	632	2653	4394	0.604	93.3
Regulars:											
C Todd Hundley	B	.228	.269	.357	11	40	53	170	339	0.501	77
1B Eddie Murray	B	.285	.325	.467	27	77	100	310	471	0.658	102
2B Jeff Kent	R	.270	.320	.446	21	65	80	258	387	0.667	103
3B Howard Johnson	B	.238	.354	.379	7	32	26	133	188	0.707	109
SS Tony Fernandez	B	.225	.323	.295	1	20	14	82	145	0.566	87
Tim Bogar	R	.244	.300	.351	3	19	25	88	160	0.550	85
LF Vince Coleman	B	.279	.316	.375	2	64	25	189	289	0.654	101
CF Joe Orsulak	L	.284	.331	.399	8	59	35	190	305	0.623	96
Dave Gallagher	R	.274	.338	.443	6	34	28	110	162	0.679	105
RF Bobby Bonilla	B	.265	.352	.522	34	81	87	330	392	0.842	130
Bench (100+ TPA):											
OF Ryan Thompson	R	.250	.302	.444	11	34	26	146	234	0.624	96
OF Jeromy Burnitz	L	.243	.339	.475	13	49	38	163	211	0.773	119
I/O Chico Walker	B	.225	.270	.338	5	18	19	92	170	0.541	84
C Charlie O'Brien	R	.255	.312	.378	4	15	23	87	149	0.584	90
IF Jeff McKnight	B	.256	.311	.323	2	19	13	69	130	0.531	(82)
IF Kevin Baez	R	.183	.259	.254	0	10	7	48	108	0.444	(69)

NOTE: Statistics are only for games played with New York. ( ) Under 200 TPA.

Team TPER: 1993 New York Mets

	Throws	W-L	GS	GR	SV	IP	ERA	NBA	GOE	Ratio	TPER
League Avg. Team	-	81 -81	162	381	43	1449	4.04	2835	4378	0.647	100
New York Mets	-	59 -103	162	297	22	1438	4.05	2836	4353	0.652	100.6
The Rotation:											
Dwight Gooden	R	12 -15	29	0	0	208.2	3.45	371	631	0.588	91
Frank Tanzania	L	7 -15	29	0	0	183	4.48	386	550	0.702	108
Eric Hilling	L	2 -9	22	5	0	145	3.97	284	448	0.634	98
Brat Saberhagen	R	7 -7	19	0	0	139.1	3.29	219	419	0.523	81
Sid Fernandez	L	5 -6	18	0	0	119.2	2.93	190	358	0.531	82
Bobby Jones	R	2 -4	9	0	0	61.2	3.65	129	185	0.697	108
Utility:											
Pete Schourek	L	5 -12	18	23	0	128.1	5.96	315	380	0.829	128
Anthony Young	R	1 -16	10	29	3	100.1	3.77	198	314	0.631	97
Dave Telgheder	R	6 -2	7	17	0	75.2	4.76	155	230	0.674	104
Bullpen:											
Jeff Innis	R	2 -3	0	67	3	76.2	4.11	164	233	0.704	109
Mike Maddux	R	3 -8	0	58	5	75	3.60	139	231	0.602	93
Mike Draper	R	1 -1	1	28	0	42.1	4.25	94	126	0.746	(115)
John Franco	L	4 -3	0	35	10	36.1	5.20	95	108	0.880	(136)

NOTE: Statistics are only for games pitched with New York. ( ) Under 200 TBF.

THAT'S ENTERTAINMENT
PHILADELPHIA PHILLIES

After six years of rooting for a loser and being buried in the basement three times, just imagine what Philly fans dreamed of in the '92–'93 off-season.

◆ At last, after unending futility, some reason to hope for a turnaround.
◆ Early confirmation of their hopes with a fast start laying waste to the rest of the division.
◆ At least some drama, no pennant race is complete without it. Something, perhaps, that might revive the nightmare of '64. Then, once and for all, dispose of it with final redemption.

◆ A team with "character." One that could win when it had to, sure, but would be quirky and unconventional. Winning dull would be nice, but winning with guys who looked and acted like they were fans, too . . . That would be great.

And, while they were dreaming, why wouldn't they go ahead and dream themselves through the division championship, to the NL pennant and into the Big One where anything could happen?

And what if their dream came true? From phutility, to phantasy, to phantastic. And all of it, every bit of it, was PHUN!

Team Trendline: Philadelphia Phillies

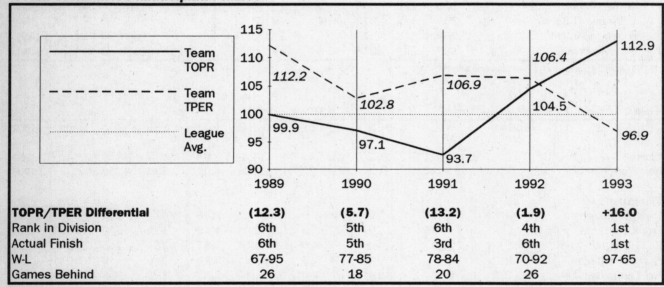

	1989	1990	1991	1992	1993
TOPR/TPER Differential	(12.3)	(5.7)	(13.2)	(1.9)	+16.0
Rank in Division	6th	5th	6th	4th	1st
Actual Finish	6th	5th	3rd	6th	1st
W-L	67-95	77-85	78-84	70-92	97-65
Games Behind	26	18	20	26	-

What Was Expected

The '92 Phillies had been racked by injuries and finished in last place in the NL East. The expected return to health of key personnel like CF Lenny Dykstra and starter Tommie Greene obviously bode well. Coupled with some inspired free agent patchwork by GM Lee Thomas, many perceived that the '93 Phillies actually had a chance.

The rotation, if healthy, seemed respectable. If the bullpen could hold its own, the pitching would be OK. The offense, if it jelled around the enormous production of Dykstra, John Kruk and Darren Daulton, appeared capable of scoring gobs of runs. Yes, there was reason to dream—if the injury bug didn't bite.

What Actually Happened

The '93 Phillies romped through the season. The rotation proved steady. The bullpen turned over, but still held together. Actually, the pitching ended up better than respectable—it was *pretty good*. The offense did jell and scored more than a gob of runs—a league-leading 877, the most in the league since '62 and the most by a Philly club since '30.

As the season progressed, Thomas continued to refine the bullpen—but the late-inning contingent of Larry Andersen, David West and Mitch Williams remained intact and effective. Shortstop, the team's only troublesome "hole," was plugged by Kevin Stock-

er's call up from AAA on July 7. The dread injury bug only nibbled, but didn't bite.

Except for April 9, the Phillies spent every day of the season in first place. Sinking spells by the pitching in July and by the offense in September provided windows of opportunity for challengers. But the Phillies had built a lead too great for either the Cardinals or the Expos to overcome.

The division championship and the NL pennant belonged to the Phillies and their fans (a club record 3,137,674 of them). Joe Carter and the Jays would claim the World Championship. But the '93 Phillies became the team that people will remember.

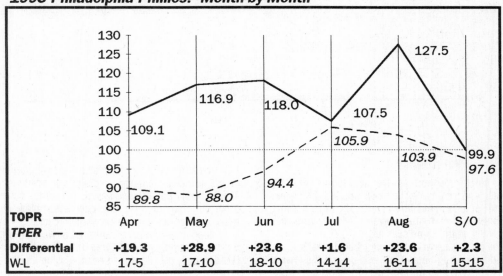

1993 Philadelphia Phillies: Month-by-Month

	Apr	May	Jun	Jul	Aug	S/O
TOPR ———	109.1	116.9	118.0	107.5	127.5	99.9
TPER — —	89.8	88.0	94.4	105.9	103.9	97.6
Differential	**+19.3**	**+28.9**	**+23.6**	**+1.6**	**+23.6**	**+2.3**
W-L	17-5	17-10	18-10	14-14	16-11	15-15

Veterans Stadium

The Vet produced a Park TOPR of 98.1, appropriately in line with Riverfront and Three Rivers. Like its relatives, it was also all-around "neutral." The slight suppression of offense it caused equally affected both Phillies and visiting batters alike (−1.3% and −2.4%, respectively, park adjusted).

In short, nothing remarkable from a stadium with no remarkable features. Only a remarkable team and its fans.

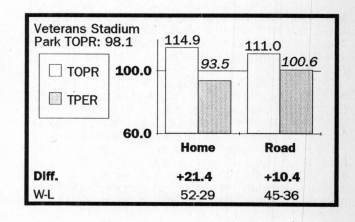

Veterans Stadium
Park TOPR: 98.1

		Home	Road
□ TOPR		114.9	111.0
▦ TPER		93.5	100.6
Diff.		**+21.4**	**+10.4**
W-L		52-29	45-36

1993 Phillies Lineup

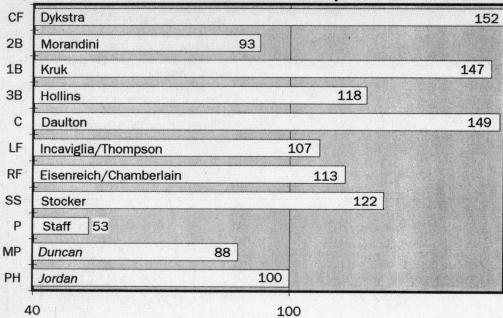

CF	Dykstra	152
2B	Morandini	93
1B	Kruk	147
3B	Hollins	118
C	Daulton	149
LF	Incaviglia/Thompson	107
RF	Eisenreich/Chamberlain	113
SS	Stocker	122
P	Staff	53
MP	Duncan	88
PH	Jordan	100

40   100

The Offense

Walks received prominent mention as the key to the Phillies' awesome '93 offense. And why not? Their 665 BBs led the league by a wide margin and set an all-time club record. The Phils became the first club in NL history to have three players (Dykstra, Kruk and Daulton) reach 100 walks in the same season.

But, to the '93 Phillies, walks were but one tactical means to an apparent strategic end: avoiding outs. They also posted the fewest CS in the league (32, succeeding on fully 75% of their 123 attempts). Their DP count (105) finished among the league's lowest (only speedy "little game" enthusiasts St. Louis, LA and Montreal had fewer). But the Phillies put far more runners on first base than any of these teams—a massive total of 1,758 (via single + BB + HP)—so that they lost only 6.0% of these baserunners via the double play, a lower proportion than any other team in the majors (except the Tigers, who play the exact same type of offensive game).

In '93 the Phillies' steadfast avoidance of outs allowed them to amass 6,527 PAs—248 more than any other team in the league and, in fact, the most in the majors. This gave them almost two more times at bat *per game* than the average NL team. You can do a lot of damage with two extra batters per game—and the Phillies proved it.

The Phillies' Team TOPR (112.9) led the league. Looking back, the '91 Pirates graded out at 111.6 and the '87 Mets at 110.4. Our current historical database doesn't extend far enough to find a higher one. Let's just say that the Phillies were the league's foremost practitioners of TOPRism since "we don't know when."

The Phillies' lineup presented opposing pitchers a near insurmountable problem. It contained three of the top 5 TOPRs in the league—Dykstra (152, #2), Daulton (149, #4) and Kruk (147, #5). In between these relative "Tetons," even the "valleys" were elevated. The lineup offered no soft spots to afford pitchers a moment's relaxation.

Forced to run up immense pitch counts in the face of the Phillies' patience, most starters succumbed early. Phillies' hitters then feasted greedily on the exposed middle of opposition bullpens, scoring in double digits 17 times.

The Philly offense should have come as no surprise. There were no "overachieving" regular Phillies, though nothing in Kevin Stocker's minor league history remotely suggested his 122 major league TOPR. In his flea market way, Lee Thomas constructed a batting order out of spare parts that, once assembled, proved to be those of a bulldozer designed to excavate pitchers.

So long as all the parts remained in working order, the offensive machine should have left a trail of buried pitchers. But for the past two seasons, the 'dozer had been missing its blade.

The Importance of Being Lenny

In his injury-interrupted '91 and '92 seasons, the Phillies stood 76–71 when Lenny played and 72–105 when he didn't. This data suggests that with Lenny Dykstra in the lineup, the Phillies weren't all that "phutile." Could he be *that* important to his team's success?

Certainly, when a TOPR of 149 ('91) or 140 ('92) is missing from a lineup, guys like Von Hayes, John Morris, Stan Javier and Ruben Amaro aren't going to replace it. But there's more to it than that. A hitter, *especially* a leadoff hitter, with a .420 OBP makes his teammates behind him better hitters.

The proof of this lies in the average hitter's performance with a) the bases empty and b) with a runner on. These data for the '92 NL season, for example:

	BA	OBP	SLG	Batting Sub-set		
				TBB	TBO	Ratio	BPR
Bases Empty	.249	.307	.364	17002	28537	.596	95.9
Runner(s) On	.255	.326	.374	13580	20673	.657	105.7
Total	.252	.315	.368	30582	49210	.621	100.0

With a runner on base in front of him, the average hitter hits for higher average, reaches bases himself more often and hits with more power. According to TOPRs Batting Sub-set, he becomes a *+ 10% better hitter!*

Why does this happen? Is it a manifestation of that old chestnut "clutch hitting"? A much more likely explanation is that baserunners force pitchers to work out of the stretch. If pitchers were more effective that way, why would they even bother with a full wind-up?

To this rather profound effect, now add Lenny's base-stealing ability and the additional distraction it creates for the pitcher. But subtract him from the head of the Philly order and not only is his production lost, the entire team suffers from his loss.

We're confronting three important lessons in this exercise.

1. A hitter who exhibits a higher batting average with men on base, despite what the media might tell us, is the *rule* rather than the exception.
2. The supreme importance of the leadoff hitter. Players like Lenny Dykstra and Rickey Henderson are of remarkable value.
3. The best "protection" for a given hitter may well be the hitters in *front* of him, rather than behind.

The Pitching

The year-to-year improvement in the Phillies' offense was mirrored by a sharp gain in the effectiveness of their pitching. It jumped from pathetic in '92 (106.4 TPER) to better than average (96.9). The rotation and the bullpen each contributed to the staff's resurrection.

	NL Avg. ERA	Philly Starters	Philly Relievers
1992	3.50	4.10	4.20
1993	4.04	3.95	4.00

While the rest of the league was going up, the Phillies foxed 'em. Their ERA took the down elevator.

The Rotation: The starting rotation benefited from Tommie Greene's healthy return and Danny Jackson's presence via trade. As a result, the five main men took their turn 152 times in '93 and went 69–40. In '92, the only three regular rotation starters—Terry Mulholland, Curt Schilling and Ben Rivera—made just 72 starts between them (going 34–26). The remaining 90 starts were consigned to 12 different pitchers who ran up a 5.34 ERA on their way to a 14–43 record. You *bet* Greene and Jackson made a difference.

The Phillies found Schilling after the Astros and Orioles had both "lost" him. Two presumably pitching-savvy organizations failed to notice a latent "ace" in their midst, so Lee Thomas picked him up for what amounted to pocket change (once prospect, now suspect

RHP Jason Grimsley). TPERs '92 NL "King of the Hill" (73) provided confirmation with a 16–7, 4.02 ERA and 91 TPER year.

Jackson provided 210.1 valuable innings of quality work (96 TPER) that the Phillies hadn't had in '92. Two low minor league unprovens (LHP Matt Whisenant and Joel Adamson) secured him from the prospect-hungry Marlins after the Pirates failed to protect him in the expansion draft.

Another one of Thomas' ingenious little deals brought Greene to the Phillies. A throw-in with Dale Murphy from Atlanta that had cost Jeff Parrett and two non-prospects, Greene emerged as a solid starter in '92 (96 TPER). Arm trouble set him back in '92, but he returned to the rotation with a vengeance in '93 (16–4, 3.42 ERA, 88 TPER).

A reliever who'd seen better days (Steve Bedrosian) brought Mulholland from the Giants. His last four years of TPERs with the Phillies—89, 89, 85, 83—represent consistent excellence.

Big Ben Rivera, also acquired on the cheap (from Atlanta for prospect RHP Donnie Elliott), slipped badly in '93. His 13–9 record didn't reveal it, but a bloated ERA (5.02) and TPER (114) did. After an impressive debut (100 TPER in 117.1 IP), his TPER expanded along with his girth. Only the Phillies could have afforded a #5 starter with his level of ineffectiveness.

The Bullpen: Thomas indulged in frantic maneuvering to reconstruct his bullpen after '92's debacle. Only Mitch Williams survived the purge. Thomas wasn't satisfied with his handiwork, though, and reconstruction continued into September '93. Only prime setup men (Larry Andersen and David West) and Mitch survived this time. Essentially, what he did was blow out every reliever with a TPER *over* 100 in search of, and keeping, only those with TPERs *below* 100. With one exception: Mitch, again.

'92 Pen (TPER)	'93 Pen (TPER)	
	Start	Finish
M. Williams (126)	(106)	(106)
M. Hartley (119)	L. Andersen (82)	(82)
B. Jones (130)	D. West (87)	(87)
D. Cox (117)	J. DeLeon (103)	R. Mason (92)
C. Brantley (118)	M. Davis (127)	D. Pall (83)
B. Ayrault (94)	Ayrault/Mauser (137)	B. Thigpen (125)

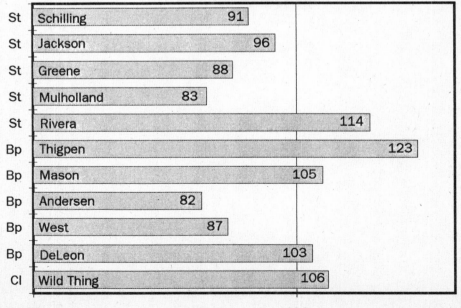

1993 Phillies Staff

		TPER
St	Schilling	91
St	Jackson	96
St	Greene	88
St	Mulholland	83
St	Rivera	114
Bp	Thigpen	123
Bp	Mason	105
Bp	Andersen	82
Bp	West	87
Bp	DeLeon	103
Cl	Wild Thing	106

50   100

One wonders why, in heaven's name, would Thomas be content with a 100+ TPER in the *closer's* role when it wasn't good enough in any other spot? Manager Jim Fregosi has loyally answered the question. To paraphrase: because he's all we had and, somehow, he gets the job done. So true. Mitch garnered 43 saves in 51 opportunities, living dangerously all the while. In his career, he's yet to TPER under 100. Mitch is the exception to the TPER rule—he beats the system.

What Next?

The key cogs in the Phillies' offense remain under contract and, obviously, there's no need to change anything. The same goes for the rotation.

The bullpen, though, will undergo another off-season renovation—including the closer's spot this time. With Mitch and his 106 TPER traded to Houston for nearly as troubling Doug Jones (104), Thomas paid his dues to his manager's dwindling supply of Maalox, the Phillies' fans and, perhaps, to Mitch himself.

The off-season will thus find Thomas beating the bushes for more bargains to restock his bullpen. For the most part, it'll have to be other people's bushes, as the Philly farm system remains relatively barren. It would be wise, too, for all Philly fans to spend a little time on their knees, praying for deliverance from crippling injury. That seemed to work last year.

Team TOPR: *1993 Philadelphia Phillies*

	Bats	BA	OBP	SLG	HR	R	RBI	NBE	GOC	Ratio	TOPR
League Avg. Team	-	.264	.327	.399	140	728	681	2835	4378	0.647	100
Philadelphia Phillies	-	.274	.351	.426	156	877	811	3218	4402	0.731	112.9
Regulars:											
C Darren Daulton	L	.257	.392	.482	24	90	105	376	389	0.967	149
1B John Kruk	L	.316	.430	.475	14	100	85	364	383	0.950	147
2B Mickey Morandini	L	.247	.309	.355	3	57	33	201	334	0.602	93
3B Dave Hollins	B	.273	.372	.442	18	104	93	321	420	0.764	118
SS Kevin Stocker	R	.324	.409	.417	2	46	31	148	188	0.787	122
LF Pete Incaviglia	R	.274	.318	.530	24	60	89	220	284	0.775	120
Milt Thompson	L	.262	.341	.350	4	42	44	163	268	0.608	94
CF Lenny Dykstra	L	.305	.420	.482	19	143	66	460	468	0.983	152
RF Jim Eisenreich	L	.318	.363	.445	7	51	54	192	258	0.744	115
Wes Chamberlain	R	.282	.320	.493	12	34	45	156	216	0.722	112
Bench (100+ TPA):											
IF Mariano Duncan	B	.282	.304	.417	11	68	73	217	380	0.571	88
1B Ricky Jordan	R	.289	.324	.421	5	21	18	76	117	0.650	(100)
IF Kim Batiste	R	.282	.298	.436	5	14	29	69	117	0.590	(91)
C Todd Pratt	R	.287	.330	.529	5	8	13	52	66	0.788	(122)

NOTE: Statistics are only for games played with Philadelphia. ( ) Under 200 TPA.

Team TPER: *1993 Philadelphia Phillies*

	Throws	W-L	GS	GR	SV	IP	ERA	NBA	GOE	Ratio	TPER
League Avg. Team	-	81 -81	162	381	43	1449	4.04	2835	4378	0.647	100
Philadelphia Phillies	-	97 -65	162	350	46	1472.2	3.97	2807	4472	0.628	96.9
The Rotation:											
Curt Schilling	R	16 -7	34	0	0	235.1	4.02	419	711	0.589	91
Danny Jackson	L	12 -11	32	0	0	210.1	3.77	400	643	0.622	96
Tommy Greene	R	16 -4	30	1	0	200	3.42	344	606	0.568	88
Terry Mulholland	L	12 -9	28	1	0	191	3.25	315	583	0.540	83
Ben Rivera	R	13 -9	28	2	0	163	5.02	362	492	0.736	114
Bullpen:											
David West	L	6 -4	0	76	3	86.1	2.92	152	269	0.565	87
Larry Andersen	R	3 -2	0	64	0	61.2	2.92	99	186	0.532	82
Mike Williams	R	1 -3	4	13	0	51	5.29	105	154	0.682	105
Roger Mason	R	5 -5	0	34	0	49.2	4.89	101	149	0.678	105
Jose DeLeon	R	3 0	3	21	0	47	3.26	96	144	0.667	(103)
Mark Davis	L	1 -2	0	25	0	31.1	5.17	80	97	0.825	(127)
Mitch Williams	L	3 -7	0	65	43	62	3.34	128	186	0.688	106

NOTE: Statistics are only for games pitched with Philadelphia. ( ) Under 200 TBF.

PICKING UP THE PIECES
PITTSBURGH PIRATES

The end came in a brief spasm of action. The performers on stage—Stan Belinda, Francisco Cabrera, Barry Bonds, Sid Bream and Mike LaValliere. The focus of their attention was a round, white object tracing a blurred path from Belinda's hand to Cabrera's bat to Bonds' glove and back toward home plate where an anxious LaValliere waited. A desperate, pumping Bream came chugging down the line, racing the ball home. When Sid's foot reached it a millisecond in front of Mike's frantic tag, the curtain fell on a riveting drama. And the saga of the Pittsburgh Pirates was over. You somehow knew that this team, with the best record in baseball the past three years, no longer existed from that precise moment. When spring came, all who could or might be gone, *would* be gone. The NL pennants and world championships that might've been and never were, never would be.

The Pirates' '93 season would be a time for picking up the pieces of a shattered dream and getting on with the rest of their baseball lives.

Team Trendline: Pittsburgh Pirates

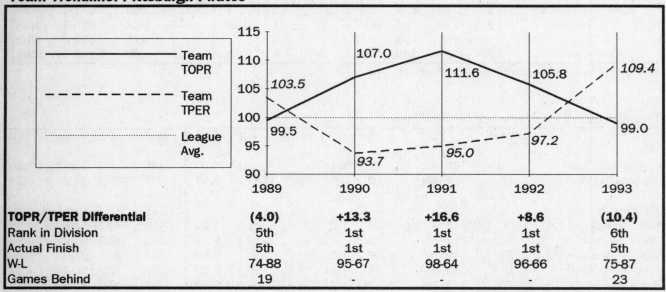

	1989	1990	1991	1992	1993
TOPR/TPER Differential	(4.0)	+13.3	+16.6	+8.6	(10.4)
Rank in Division	5th	1st	1st	1st	6th
Actual Finish	5th	1st	1st	1st	5th
W-L	74-88	95-67	98-64	96-66	75-87
Games Behind	19	-	-	-	23

What Was Expected

Before Christmas '92, everybody knew the '93 Pirates would be only half the team the '92 version had been. That is, only half would return. And it would be the "better half" that had left. The missing would include two everyday regulars (Barry Bonds and Jose Lind), two platoon regulars (Alex Cole and Gary Redus with a third, Mike LaValliere, to follow) and two members of the rotation (Doug Drabek and Danny Jackson) as well as some bench and bullpen turnover.

With the roster turned inside out, expectations were accordingly subdued. Fans had become frustrated by the organization's steadfast refusal to compete for "their own" free agents—epitomized by Bobby Bonilla's exit after '91, the trading of John Smiley prior to his free agent year in '92 and both Bonds' and Drabek's flight after the season just past. All were born-and-bred Bucs. All gone for the want of big money. "Small-market" Pittsburgh simply could not afford to sustain the success the franchise had achieved, or so management claimed. The decision to rebuild, then, was based on logic but was, nonetheless, a bitter pill to swallow.

What Actually Happened

When the '93 Pirates took the field on Opening Day, three rookies dotted the starting lineup. The last time this happened, "I Like Ike" buttons were in vogue. The year was 1952.

1993 Rookies	*1952 Rookies*
2B—Carlos Garcia	2B—Jack Merson
LF—Al Martin	SS—Clem Koshorek
1B—Kevin Young	3B—Dick Hall

Merson soon lost the regular job and lapsed into part-timer status, batting .246 for the year in 111 games. He got another 4 AB with the Pirates in '53 and never appeared in the majors again. "Scooter" Koshorek played an even smaller role—98 games in a utility role with a .261 BA. After only one AB in '53, he too disappeared from the majors. Hall made only five starts at 3B, playing in 26 games all told, before he and his .138 were shipped to the minors. His was by far the longest career, however. Con-

verted to a pitcher in '55, he spent 19 years in the bigs as an effective RH reliever (93–75, 68 SV, 3.32 ERA). The '52 Pirates, by the way, went 42–112, hardly an encouraging omen.

The '93 Pirates rotation, which had a chance to be decent, was dogged by injuries (Zane Smith and Randy Tomlin), ineffectiveness (Tim Wakefield) and resultant overexposure (Bob Walk). The already weak bullpen was thus stretched in two directions—to fill the missing starts and innings from injured and knocked-out starters, and to cover the absence of a true closer (particularly once the erstwhile chairman of the committee, Stan Belinda, was traded at the break). The pitching collapsed, ending up with a 4.77 ERA and a 109.4 TPER, next-to-the-worst in the league (and on a park-adjusted basis, actually a little *worse* than the Rockies' staff).

The offense, full of rookie hitters, started slowly but improved over the course of the season. In the end, it almost reached average (99.0 TOPR). From August the pitching started to stabilize as rookies began to mature in the rotation (Steve Cooke and Paul Wagner) and a reliable corps of young bullpeners began to emerge. After August 2, the Pirates played .500 ball (28–28).

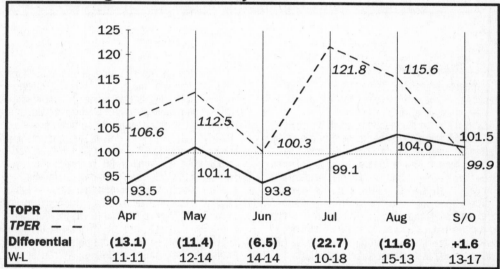

1993 Pittsburgh Pirates: Month-by-Month

	Apr	May	Jun	Jul	Aug	S/O
TOPR ———	93.5	101.1	93.8	99.1	104.0	101.5
TPER – –	106.6	112.5	100.3	121.8	115.6	99.9
Differential	**(13.1)**	**(11.4)**	**(6.5)**	**(22.7)**	**(11.6)**	**+1.6**
W-L	11-11	12-14	14-14	10-18	15-13	13-17

Three Rivers Stadium

Pittsburgh's ballyard was, like its "cookie-cutter" brethren, close to being a league-average park in '93. Its 97.6 Park TOPR indicates it favored the pitchers by a tad. Hard to accept, in view of the brutal performance by the Pirates' staff, but true.

The effect was near equivalent on both the home and visiting pitchers, supporting a conclusion that the effect was totally environmental rather than the product of any particular adaptation.

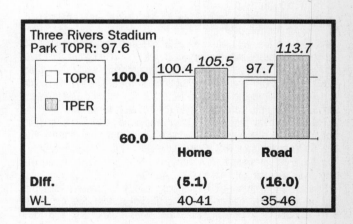

Three Rivers Stadium
Park TOPR: 97.6

	TOPR	TPER
Home	100.4	105.5
Road	97.7	113.7

	Home	Road
Diff.	**(5.1)**	**(16.0)**
W-L	40-41	35-46

1993 Pirates Lineup

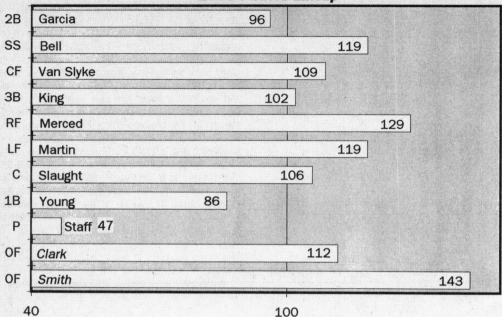

2B	Garcia	96
SS	Bell	119
CF	Van Slyke	109
3B	King	102
RF	Merced	129
LF	Martin	119
C	Slaught	106
1B	Young	86
P	Staff	47
OF	*Clark*	112
OF	*Smith*	143

40   100

The Offense

The Pittsburgh lineup reflects manager Jim Leyland's willingness to gamble on and practice patience with rookies. Opening day's trio were in the lineup to stay, come what may.

At the same time, it's evident that the team's makeup did Leyland no favors. The critical leadoff and cleanup spots were occupied by hitters clearly unsuited to the roles. Garcia's .316 OBP ranked next-to-last among the league's leadoff hitters (tied with Vince Coleman and ahead of only SF's Darren Lewis) and, puzzlingly, next-to-last *on his own team*. Similarly, Jeff King's .406 SLG ranked next-to-last among cleanup hitters (tied with Orestes Destrade and ahead of only Houston's Eric Anthony) and stood only 6th on his own team! However, King's performance serves as another demonstration of how an otherwise average hitter can produce impressive RBI counts in this slot. No particular importance should be attached to his 95 RBI (nor Eddie Murray's 100, for that matter), because there's nothing remarkable about it—except he got the opportunity (and Don Slaught, *e.g.*, didn't).

The most notable aspect of the Pirates' '93 lineup, however, is its potential for improvement.

Aside from his being miscast as a leadoff hitter, Garcia enjoyed a quite satisfactory introductory year. He converted from SS to 2B with apparent ease and offered encouragement with his hitting (.269 BA, 96 TOPR). His forte, though, is power (12 HR his rookie year, .425 SLG in the minors). He's due for further development and would sure put some punch in the 7th slot, for example.

The only proven hitter left in the lineup, Andy Van Slyke, spoiled a good-year-in-progress by breaking his collarbone on June 14. His 122 TOPR at the time was "Van Slyke-like," his 72 TOPR after his August 16 return wasn't. A healthy, full-time Van Slyke in '94 will help give the Bucs' offense a potent middle.

Rookie Al Martin's 119 TOPR looks pretty impressive (second-highest rookie TOPR after Mike Piazza). But consider its composition: 100 before the break, 142 after (with a .376 OBP and .549 SLG). He may be Barry Bonds' replacement, and he's admittedly no Barry Bonds, but Martin might well be a Bobby Bonilla (with speed). The Pirates would settle for that. Another comparison of Martin to Pirates-past: he hit the most homers (18) of any rookie since Ralph Kiner (23 in '46) and broke Kiner's rookie strikeout record (109) with 122.

A third rookie, Kevin Young, found himself engaged in a season-long struggle with the bat. This was surprising since he'd been an excellent hitter in his brief minor league career (133 minor league TOPR, with high average, doubles power and good strike zone judgment). In the majors, he suffered a giant drop in average (to .236 BA) and some loss in K zone judgment (82 Ks but only 36 BBs, compared to 67 apiece at AAA in '92). Perhaps the adjustment to 1B from his familiar 3B bothered him (he led the league in fielding pct. at his new position). Or maybe he tried to deliver the power normally expected of a first-sacker—which he doesn't have. Leyland never lost faith, but he indulged in some platooning the second half (moving Merced to 1B, playing Dave Clark in RF against some RH starters). Into the off-season, the manager continued his support of Young. Wanna bet he's rewarded with a big year from Young in '94? And that Young fills the bill as the leadoff hitter Pittsburgh desperately needs, despite being a 1B (an old Pirate trick, remember the Merced/Redus platoon in '91?).

A couple of recent additions to the bench might also serve to strengthen the Pirates' attack in '94. Brian Hunter, acquired from Atlanta, affords insurance (and competition) for Young as well as for Lloyd McClendon's advancing age (35) and slumping bat (80 TOPR). Career minor-leaguer Jerry Goff, though, could be a key addition at backup catcher. A LH power bat, he complements Don Slaught much better than the RH hitting Tom Prince. Replace Prince's 75 TOPR with Goff's 100-or-so and that's a meaningful improvement. Even more meaningful could be the effect on Slaught, who was forced to bat against RH pitchers much more often in 1993—and his TOPR suffered accordingly.

Don Slaught	'92	'93
AB's vs. RH pitchers	81	257
AB's vs. LH pitchers	174	120
Overall TOPR	132	106

We haven't mentioned the excellent years turned in by SS Jay Bell and RF Orlando Merced. Bell produced a laudable 119 TOPR (third-highest SS in the league) and landed a Gold Glove for his fielding. Merced's year (.313 BA, .414 OBP, .443 SLG) surprised many. But his 129 TOPR was right on schedule—given his age

(26) and prior TOPR history. Plus, he had 11 OF assists in 109 games (84 starts) in RF.

Special mention should be made of the Buc fielders' exquisite defensive contribution in '93. A young club, undergoing considerable turnover, they nonetheless set club records for fielding pct. (.983) and fewest errors (105)—second in the league (to SF) on both counts. But they led the league, by a wide margin, in fewest unearned runs allowed (only 40) and *unearned runs as a percent of total runs* (only 4.96% vs. league average of 10.50%). This performance gave a big boost to a young pitching staff struggling to find itself.

The Pitching

The Bucs' '93 staff needed all the help it could get. The entire rotation was composed of 100+ TPERs and the bullpen ranged from middling to down right messy.

Yet, just like the Pittsburgh offense, there's a gob of encouragement to be found throughout the staff.

The Rotation: Only rookie LH Steve Cooke and yeoman RH Bob Walk took their regular turn in the rotation (32 starts each). Cooke led all major league rookie pitchers in starts, innings pitched (210.2) and strikeouts (132). He gave a steady, poised performance season long (10–10, 3.89 ERA) and surrendered three earned runs or less in 22 of his starts, working into the 6th inning in all but four. He's a very good bet to show improvement from his rookie 104 TPER in '94. Walk, if he's re-signed, may be allowed to move back to a more appropriate "swing" role. Forced into serving as the "staff ace," he responded gamely and gave the club what it needed: starts and innings (187). Never mind that he got pummeled (5.68 ERA, 113 TPER)—he bent, but he kept the rotation from breaking (13–14, the team going 16–16 in his starts).

The flutter-ball phenomenon of '92, Tim Wakefield, became the enigma of '93). He made 15 starts (4–8 with a bloated 6.35 ERA) before being exiled to AA, where he was even worse (3–5, 6.99 ERA). Then he returned to the majors and in his first three starts went 0–3 (7.63 ERA). Then it *happened.* Two complete game shutouts, back-to-back, to close the season.

What are we to make of this? Has the delicate spirit of *le papillon* returned as mysteriously as it departed? And will it continue

inhabiting young Wakefield, long enough so that he might have a career? Let's say it does, if Leyland agrees to never repeat April 27 (10 innings and a total of 172 pitches—the most since Valenzuela's 173 on 8/30/87). Let's say it merely results in a "Charlie Hough season" (say 30+ starts, over 200 IP, a TPER in the 90s). The rotation would get a giant boost.

Both Randy Tomlin (elbow) and Zane Smith (shoulder) spent about half the season on the DL. Both were obviously hurting when they did pitch (112 and 103 TPERs, respectively). If either or both recover their former effectiveness, the Pirate staff could greatly benefit. A healthy Smith could be attractive trade bait, though, and even if the elbow problems forced Tomlin into a relief role the staff would still be improved.

Paul Wagner will work full-time in the rotation and his 98 rookie TPER says he'll be effective. Opening the season in the bullpen, he made his first start June 2. Wagner was much more effective in his 17 starts (6–5, 3.96 ERA) than in relief (2–3, 5.15 ERA).

The Bullpen: Over the course of the season, Leyland finally managed to cobble up a respectable bullpen. Rookie RH Blas Minor stayed solid the entire season (65 App., 94.1 IP, 4.10 ERA, 94 TPER). Joel Johnston came up from Buffalo on July 7 and turned in a strong performance (33 App., 53.1 IP, 3.38 ERA, 87 TPER). He remains a risk as this period represented one of his "spells" of good control (only 19 BB). They tend to come and go (e.g., 25 BB in 31.1 IP at Buffalo before his call up, 7.76 ERA).

The Pirates also gave RH Mark Dewey another chance. The Giants and the Mets had already passed on him—and the 96 and 88 TPERs he gave them. Again, Dewey pitched well (21 App., 7 SV, 26.2 IP, 2.36 ERA, 77 TPER). It's a safe bet Leyland noticed what Roger Craig and Jeff Torborg didn't—Dewey can help a major league bullpen (career: 55 App., 82.2 IP, 73 H, 25 BB, 45 K, 3.27 ERA, 87 TPER—the equivalent of a darned fine season). Maybe Dewey's perception problem has been the Ks. He apparently doesn't have an *arm*. Instead all he's got is the ability to get *outs*.

Then there's Alejandro Pena. The Pirates' one free agent indulgence didn't see action in '93, stymied by a balky elbow. In a surprisingly civilized renegotiation, the Pirates and Pena agreed to extend the contract's term and reduce the '93 payments accordingly. As a full-time closer or as a committeeman, a healthy Pena would work wonders for the '94 bullpen.

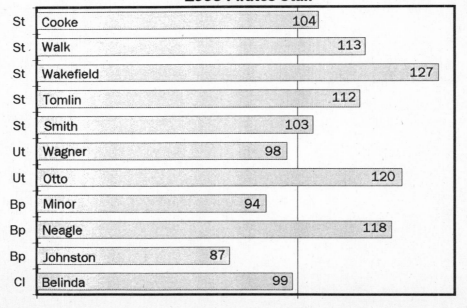

1993 Pirates Staff

St	Cooke	104
St	Walk	113
St	Wakefield	127
St	Tomlin	112
St	Smith	103
Ut	Wagner	98
Ut	Otto	120
Bp	Minor	94
Bp	Neagle	118
Bp	Johnston	87
Cl	Belinda	99

50   100

There's a wild card in the Pirates' deck, too. Danny Neagle came from the Twins in the Smiley trade. The young leftie had a minor league career that stamped him as a potential big winner (53 starts, 32–10 record, 2.54 ERA, 352 K and 103 BB in 354.1 IP). For two years, he toiled in the Bucco pen with an occasional start and has shown very little (7–11, 4.88 ERA, 119 TPER).

But, on July 25, Leyland sentenced Neagle to serve a term in Buffalo. He was "paroled" back to the parent club only nine days later. But he returned a different pitcher.

	IP	H/9	BB/9	K/9	ERA
Before July 25	57.1	10.46	4.53	8.43	6.09
After August 3	24.0	5.63	3.00	7.12	3.38

The "after" line bears a favorable resemblance to the pitcher the Pirates thought they were getting when they traded for him.

Maybe it was a lucky streak. But Neagle knew he had to work on his control and he got the job done. For a while, at least.

As he turns 25, Neagle may be in the process of conquering his control problems and emerging as a potentially dominant pitcher. Leyland and the Pirates have their fingers crossed for him.

What Next?

Buc management can view their rebuilding program with satisfaction. In all likelihood, it bottomed out in its first year. A few finishing touches gleaned from the third tier and the minor league free agent markets should yield a respectable major league club in '94. Perhaps even one that could contend in the competitively compact new division that is the NL Central.

While the '94 team appears potentially competent and solid at every point, the organization still lacks two elements. There are no star-quality players on the roster capable of carrying the team a step beyond, to the preeminence of a true winner. Nor are any such standouts visible in the farm system, which is still a long way from being rebuilt. No particular help should be expected from this quarter for a year or two (though the Belinda and Lonnie Smith trades in '93 helped repopulate it with some decent prospects).

The '94 season, regardless of what it may bring, is still too early to avert the Bucs' focus from their future.

Team TOPR: 1993 Pittsburgh Pirates

	Bats	BA	OBP	SLG	HR	R	RBI	NBE	GOC	Ratio	TOPR
League Avg. Team	-	.264	.327	.399	140	728	681	2835	4378	0.647	100
Pittsburgh Pirates	-	.267	.335	.393	110	707	664	2807	4378	0.641	99.0
Regulars:											
C Don Slaught	R	.300	.356	.440	10	34	55	197	286	0.689	106
1B Kevin Young	R	.236	.300	.343	6	38	47	204	368	0.554	86
2B Carlos Garcia	R	.269	.316	.399	12	77	47	267	430	0.621	96
3B Jeff King	R	.295	.356	.406	9	82	98	305	463	0.659	102
SS Jay Bell	R	.310	.392	.437	9	102	51	351	457	0.768	119
LF Al Martin	L	.281	.338	.481	18	85	64	281	364	0.772	119
CF Andy Van Slyke	L	.310	.356	.449	8	42	50	171	242	0.707	109
RF Orlando Merced	B	.313	.414	.443	8	68	70	269	321	0.838	129
Bench (100+ TPA):											
OF Dave Clark	L	.271	.358	.444	11	43	46	155	214	0.724	112
OF Lonnie Smith	R	.286	.422	.442	6	35	24	143	154	0.929	143
IF Tom Foley	L	.253	.287	.366	3	18	22	84	155	0.542	84
OF Lloyd McClendon	R	.221	.306	.326	2	21	19	78	151	0.517	80
C Tom Prince	R	.196	.272	.307	2	14	24	75	155	0.484	75

NOTE: Statistics are only for games played with Pittsburgh. ( ) Under 200 TPA.

Team TPER: 1993 Pittsburgh Pirates

	Throws	W-L	GS	GR	SV	IP	ERA	NBA	GOE	Ratio	TPER
League Avg. Team	-	81 -81	162	381	43	1449	4.04	2835	4378	0.647	100
Pittsburgh Pirates	-	75 -87	162	384	34	1445.2	4.77	3076	4342	0.708	109.4
The Rotation:											
Steve Cooke	L	10 -10	32	0	0	210.2	3.89	427	632	0.676	104
Bob Walk	R	13 -14	32	0	0	187	5.68	412	563	0.732	113
Tim Wakefield	R	6 -11	20	4	0	128.1	5.61	314	382	0.822	127
Randy Tomlin	L	4 -8	18	0	0	98.1	4.85	213	294	0.724	112
Zane Smith	L	3 -7	14	0	0	83	4.55	166	249	0.667	103
Utility:											
Paul Wagner	R	8 -8	17	27	2	141.1	4.27	271	429	0.632	98
Dave Otto	L	3 -4	8	20	0	68	5.03	160	206	0.777	120
Bullpen:											
Blas Minor	R	8 -6	0	65	2	94.1	4.10	173	284	0.609	94
Denny Neagle	L	3 -5	7	43	1	81.1	5.31	186	244	0.762	118
Jeff Ballard	L	4 -1	5	20	0	53.2	4.86	106	161	0.658	102
Joel Johnston	R	2 -4	0	33	2	53.1	3.38	90	159	0.566	87
Mark Dewey	R	1 -2	0	21	7	26.2	2.36	41	82	0.500	(77)
Stan Belinda	R	3 -1	0	40	19	42.1	3.61	81	127	0.638	99

NOTE: Statistics are only for games pitched with Pittsburgh. ( ) Under 200 TBF.

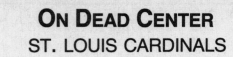

ON DEAD CENTER
ST. LOUIS CARDINALS

Four of the past five years, the Cardinals have won between 83 and 87 games, finishing in 2nd or 3rd place, 7 to 14 games behind the leader. Even in that fifth year ("The Herzog Mutiny" of '90), they strayed from the path only through gross under-achievement. Over the entire period, neither the Team TOPR nor TPER was more than 3.6 points from the league norm.

If "modest success" can be a legitimate goal, the Cardinals have achieved it with admirable consistency.

Team Trendline: St. Louis Cardinals

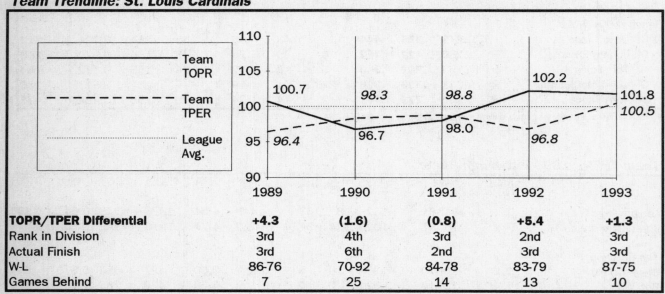

	1989	1990	1991	1992	1993
TOPR/TPER Differential	+4.3	(1.6)	(0.8)	+5.4	+1.3
Rank in Division	3rd	4th	3rd	2nd	3rd
Actual Finish	3rd	6th	2nd	3rd	3rd
W-L	86-76	70-92	84-78	83-79	87-75
Games Behind	7	25	14	13	10

What Was Expected

The fall of the Pirates cleared the way for a new set of contenders in the NL East. Montreal, Philadelphia and St. Louis lined up as the identifiable candidates. But when subjected to the analyst's magnifying glass, some warts appeared. The Expos were young. Perhaps too young. The Phillies had no depth. Injuries might abort their challenge. The Cardinals, however, had no apparent weaknesses and consequently gathered a plurality of support. Their nomination, however, overlooked the fact they also lacked any particular strength that would project them above the pack.

What Actually Happened

The Phillies took immediate charge of the race. The first of June found the Cardinals plugging along at .500 (25–25) as the team's offense couldn't escape the doldrums.

At that point, Gregg Jefferies' bat came alive and the offense surged with him. The Cardinals began winning (20–6 the rest of June) and kept on winning past the All-Star break. The run included taking three out of four from the leading Phillies at home in late June and by July 19 they'd gone 30–12 (55–37 for the season) and moved within three games of the lead. At that point, the Cards' pitching collapsed and the Phillies swept a 3-game series in late July. The Cards gradually drifted back down the hill they had climbed, slipping beneath Montreal into third place, and went 32–38 in the final 70 games. They finished in what has become their accustomed position (87–75, 3rd place, 10 games back).

Along the way, though, they discovered a weakness that Cardinal teams hadn't displayed in years. Suddenly their defense had become one of the league's worst! Only the fumbling Padres and Rockies committed more errors than the Cardinals did (159, almost one per game). In '92 the Cardinals led the NL in fielding, with only 94 errors. The shocking collapse occurred in an experienced and normally adept infield and pitching staff that had combined to commit only 56 E in '92, but nearly doubled their flubs in '93 (103).

1993 St. Louis Cardinals: Month-by-Month

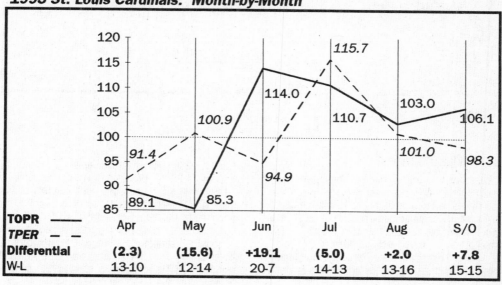

	Apr	May	Jun	Jul	Aug	S/O
TOPR ———						
TPER – –						
Differential	(2.3)	(15.6)	+19.1	(5.0)	+2.0	+7.8
W-L	13-10	12-14	20-7	14-13	13-16	15-15

Busch Stadium

The Cardinals' home park maintained its reputation as a "pitcher's park" in '93 (95.1 Park TOPR). However, it was the St. Louis pitching alone that accounted for the effect.

The Cardinals' staff was extremely effective in Busch, producing a park-adjusted TPER of 93.7. On the road, they were chopped meat (park-adjusted TPER: 107.3). Given that they're ground-ball pitchers working in a turf park, this effect is the reverse of what you'd expect. Contrarily, the Cards' collection of ground-ball hitters worked the turf to their advantage. Puzzling.

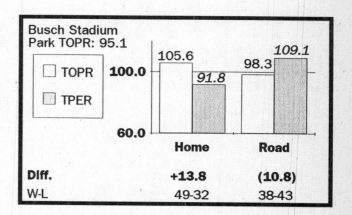

Busch Stadium
Park TOPR: 95.1

	Home	Road
Diff.	+13.8	(10.8)
W-L	49-32	38-43

1993 Cardinals Lineup

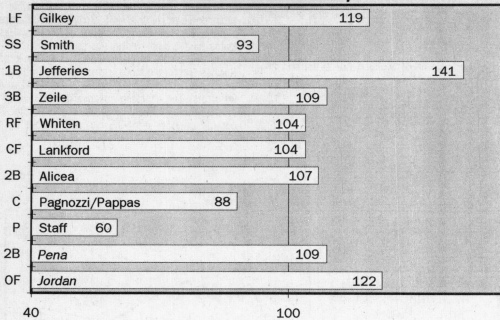

LF	Gilkey	119
SS	Smith	93
1B	Jefferies	141
3B	Zeile	109
RF	Whiten	104
CF	Lankford	104
2B	Alicea	107
C	Pagnozzi/Pappas	88
P	Staff	60
2B	*Pena*	109
OF	*Jordan*	122

40   100

The Offense

The '93 Cardinal offense presents an analogue of the entire team. No gaping weaknesses. But virtually no strengths—only two hitters represented a serious offensive threat and only at 1B did the Cards significantly exceed the league's positional norms. As a result, the Cards remained a barely above average offense (101.8 Team TOPR).

The Cards' offense in '93 revolved around their two "plus" TOPRs, Bernard Gilkey and Gregg Jefferies. The rest of the lineup was mostly concerned with capitalizing on the opportunities these two hitters generated.

Bernard Gilkey established his credentials in '92 (121 TOPR) and gave a repeat performance in '93 (119 TOPR, with .305 BA, .370 OBP, 99 R scored). His TOPR only matched the norm for LF in the NL (121), but as a leadoff hitter he gave the Cards' batting order a rampaging kick-start. That the leadoff hitter would also be #2 on the club in slugging (.481 SLG) and *lead* the team in extra-base hits (61, including 40 2B and 16 HR) rates as a little unusual, though. It says a lot, in fact, about what came behind him in the order. He gave a star performance in the field, too, racking up a league-leading 19 OF assists. Bernard Gilkey has emerged as a very valuable performer.

As noted, when Gregg Jefferies got hot, the team got hot. No wonder. From June 6, he hit .380 to raise his BA from .261 to a fifth in the league .342. He set career highs in HR (16), RBI (83) and SB (46). His 141 TOPR ranked 7th in the league, a far cry from his previous high (110 in '90) and career average (106). We'll pursue this intriguing development further.

After Jefferies, however, the Cardinals batting order actually became quite ordinary. Cleanup man Todd Zeile collected 103 RBI, but produced only a 109 TOPR, down from 117 in a '92 season during which he'd been sent off to Louisville to recapture his stroke. RF Mark Whiten gained raves for his club-leading 25 HR, particularly their distance (13 were measured at over 400'), and 99 RBI. But only 13 2B doubles came with them and a rather un-sluggerly .423 SLG and 104 TOPR.

After a '92 that seemed to promise stardom (131 TOPR), Ray Lankford fell off dramatically to a lackluster 104. His BA collapsed

(.293 to .238), his extra-base power vanished (40 2B, 20 HR, .480 SLG to 17 2B, 7 HR, .346 SLG) and his speed evaporated (42 to 14 SB, with a 50% success rate). Injuries certainly contributed to his ineffectiveness (shoulder strain on April 9, slight separation on August 29 and two weeks on the DL with a wrist problem). A contract hassle during spring training can't have helped, either.

However, Lankford's job appears jeopardized by Brian Jordan's development as a baseball player. The erstwhile Atlanta Falcon teammate of Deion Sanders showed the same level of offensive potential for the Cards in '93 as Sanders has displayed for the Braves. His 122 TOPR combined a high BA (.309) with big-time power (.543 SLG). There's no indication he'll ever walk (only 12 BB in 242 PA) and his relatively high strikeout rate (35) suggests his poor strike zone judgment may consume his hitting numbers in everyday use.

It's strange that a team with the offensive "blahs" would have an excess of offensive talent, but the Cardinals are in this position—both in the OF and at 2B. Their choice is between Luis Alicea, defensively competent and offensively adequate (107 TOPR) and Geronimo Pena who is offensively blessed (TOPRs of 122 and 145 in '91 and '92). But he can be inconsistent, both at bat (109 in '93) and in the field, and seems injury-prone.

Ozzie Smith continued to collect stamps on his Hall of Fame visa. He had another good year with the bat (.288 BA), stole some bases (21) and played his 2,223rd career game (surpassing Larry Bowa's record). He didn't win his 14th consecutive Gold Glove, though, and his TOPR slid from 114 in '92 to 93. Ozzie remains a productive player, but he slipped a full level below the best in '93.

When Tom Pagnozzi went on the DL from May 8 to June 16, the Cards caught a small break. They found a backup catcher who could make a positive contribution, Erik Pappas (94 TOPR).

There are no huge holes that need plugging in the Cardinal offense. But it could sure use another TOPR spike or two. A healthy Lankford, plus Jordan and Pena could provide them but it's a question of getting them all into the lineup—which probably won't happen.

Gregg Jefferies Rediscovers Himself

The Cardinals became the third major league team to try their hand at solving the puzzle that young Jefferies had become. Only 26 and in his fifth full year in the bigs, Gregg's appeal to "baseball people" is obvious: a line-drive hitter with extra-base power who makes consistent contact from either side of the plate. Plus, from the mere age of 17, he established himself as the bluest of blue chip prospects—shredding a couple of minor leagues a year on his way to the majors. His minor league record was indeed fantastic:

Year	Level	BA	OBP	SLG	SB/CS	TOPR
1985	R+/A	.326	.376	.500	28/1	152
1986	A/A+/AA	.353	.412	.549	57/9	156
1987	AA	.367	.423	.598	26/10	152
1988	AAA	.282	.322	.395	32/6	115

Through AA, those are extraordinary stats, comprising a complete offensive package with gold-plated TOPRs. The year at AAA could be considered troubling, but it was still pretty good. And at 20, he was *very* young for such a high level. Moreover, he turned tiger in his September trial with the Mets. The kid was *ready!* But would the NL be ready for him?

Year	Level	BA	OBP	SLG	SB/CS	TOPR
1988	NL	.321	.364	.596	5/1	(197)
1989	NL	.258	.314	.392	21/6	103
1990	NL	.283	.337	.434	11/2	110
1991	NL	.272	.336	.374	26/5	106
1992	AL	.285	.329	.404	19/9	95

Somewhere between AA Jackson and Shea Stadium, the Gregg Jefferies the league was steeling itself against, disappeared. In his place was another Gregg Jefferies, only an average hitter with defensive liabilities. A minor league SS, Jefferies converted to 2B and then to 3B in the interest of damage control. It never worked. Disappointment ran rampant among the fans and the front office.

First in New York, then in Kansas City, a sense of being "gypped" by Jefferies' "unrealized potential" prevailed.

Then St. Louis decided to take a chance. The therapy apparently prescribed was to reduce Gregg's defensive responsibility to a practical minimum—put him at 1B and hope for the best. His bat responded and, along with his base-stealing ability (never lost, but seriously underused by prior managers), the Gregg Jefferies that had been missing since that summer in Jackson magically reappeared (.342 BA, .408 OBP, .485 SLG, 46/10 SB/CS, 141 TOPR).

To be honest, Gregg's still got problems with the leather. His inexperience at 1B doubtless caused many of the increased errors in the Cardinal infield. Assuming that's fixable, the real question before the house is: has Jefferies rediscovered himself *for good?* Both the Cardinals and Gregg himself sure hope so.

The Pitching

Even more than the lineup, the pitching staff reveals the Cardinals' middle-class mentality—a relative absence of weakness, a near-total void of strength.

Another defining characteristic of the staff was its control—leading the league in fewest walks (only 383, 51 fewer than the Mets, their nearest competitor). At the same time, they produced the fewest strikeouts (only 775, 92 fewer than the Mets).

Interestingly, the Cards' ERA (4.09) trailed the Mets (4.05) by a narrow margin and their Team TPERs were near identical (100.5 for St. Louis, 100.6 for the Mets). They gave up exactly the same number of runs (774). Going further, the Mets made 156 E, the Cardinals 159. For all the world, the Cardinals' and Mets' staffs and defenses were interchangeable. Could it be that only a slightly better than average offense separated the Cards from the abyss? Frightening thought.

The Rotation: The supreme corner-painter of them all, of course, was Bob Tewksbury. For much of the season, "Tewks" worked on a parlay of historical proportions—more wins and hits (for himself) than walks allowed. He ended the season with 17 W and 14 H in his batting account, but his control "failed" him. After walking only

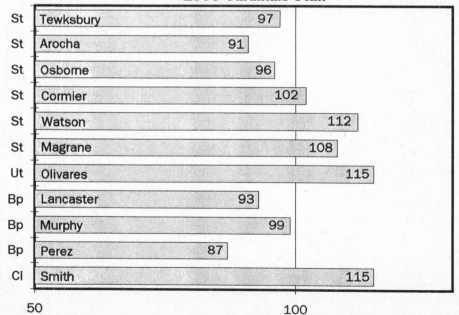

1993 Cardinals Staff

St	Tewksbury	97
St	Arocha	91
St	Osborne	96
St	Cormier	102
St	Watson	112
St	Magrane	108
Ut	Olivares	115
Bp	Lancaster	93
Bp	Murphy	99
Bp	Perez	87
Cl	Smith	115

50   100

7 batters in his first 19 starts (127.2 IP), he passed 13 in his last 14 (86.1 IP). Nonetheless, his 0.84 BB/9 IP led the league. And his 97 K *led the club.* His 97 TPER earned him a 17–10 record and a 3.83 ERA, but ranked as middle-of-the-pack and constituted a disturbing increase from his sterling 77 in '92.

Rene Arocha served as Tewksbury's bookend in the Cardinal rotation. His 1.48 BA/9 IP finished #2 in the league and his 96 Ks were 2nd to Tewksbury on the Cardinals' staff. The 27-year-old rookie produced the rotation's lowest TPER (91), though, while going 11–8 with a 3.78 ERA.

The staff's third control artist, Rheal Cormier (1.67 BB/9 IP), was shuttled between the rotation and the bullpen. One wonders "why?" His three separate tours in the rotation amounted to 21 starts with a 3.92 ERA. In bullpen service, his 17 appearances yielded a 6.46 ERA. Overall, he pieced together a 7–6 season, 4.33 ERA and 102 TPER.

Second-year man Donovan Osborne sat out September with tendinitis. But he improved on his rookie TPER (from 101 to 96) and turned in a 10–7 year (3.76 ERA). True to the pattern, he walked few (47) and struck out only a few more (83 in 155.2 IP).

Rookie LH Allen Watson arrived with great fanfare on July 7 and proceeded to bring the league to its knees, going 6–0 in his first 7 starts. Then he *lost* 7 straight. The long ball did him in, as he allowed only two in his first seven starts (44.2 IP) but nine in his last eight (38.1 IP). In the minors, he'd evidenced vulnerability on this account (a HR rate 42% above the league average).

Watson's 112 rookie TPER is edging toward marginal. Used to overpowering hitters in the minors (305 H in 372 IP, with 326 K) Watson wasn't foolin' 'em in the majors (90 H in 86 IP, with only 49 K). He's got some work to do.

The Bullpen: The Cards' bullpen was almost completely overhauled in the '92–'93 off-season. Only set-up man Mike Perez and closer Lee Smith survived. The new pen never jelled, yielding a scary 4.36 ERA overall. Only Rob Murphy (99) and Mike Perez (87) were effective from beginning to end, while Les Lancaster (93, but on the DL for eight weeks) and Lee Guetterman (83 after his June 30 call-up) contributed while they were around. Nothing else worked. Todd Burns, acquired from the Rangers to replace Lancaster, being a prominent example (128). Omar Olivares, an effective starter in '92, didn't adapt well to life in the long-relief role and spluttered badly (115). In September, Smith was sent packing to the Yankees. The realization had struck that the save count wasn't

necessarily a reliable measure of a closer's effectiveness (his TPER had sagged to 115).

The pitching had been the closest thing the team had to a strength in '92 (96.8 TPER). Its erosion in '93 has to be a cause for concern. Most of the staff probably merits an average or slightly better rating. But, like the lineup, some strengths need to be developed—both in the rotation and the pen.

What Next?

Since Whitey Herzog departed, the Cardinals have become a conservative organization—almost stodgy.

Not that the Cards need a splashy big-budget free agent signing (imagine the result, though, had they anted up for Barry Bonds or Greg Maddux). But those flashes of baseball insight, often appearing whimsical, that helped create their past success don't seem to occur nowadays. No Willie McGees pulled from another team's hornswoggled hat. No sweet-talking a San Diego to convince them that a good-hitting SS (Garry Templeton) would be more desirable than a weak-hitting one (Ozzie Smith). No inspired perception that a lead-footed slugger (Jack Clark) is just what a herd of rabbits needed in their midst.

Instead, the organization makes safe, predictable moves. Like trading Lee Smith once it became obvious to everybody, including Lee, that he didn't have it anymore. Or trying to trade Lankford and Pena, perhaps, when it's widely suspected they're not wanted anymore.

Nonetheless, the needs *are* obvious. Build some strengths—somewhere in the lineup and in the rotation. Rebuild the bullpen. The farm system's full of pitchers, but the starters look to be a year away and, just maybe, a tad overrated. No position players appear ready to move up. The best of them, Dmitri Young, remains at least a full year away and is yet to find a position—and may not have one.

The Cards' '93 record (87–75) was the best among their new NL Central competitors. A repeat performance might well be enough to capture the Division. There's no certainty, though, that the Cards can manage even that record if they don't make some needed changes. A 10-game slippage even could throw them into the cellar of what promises to be an extremely tight grouping of teams.

Their current style of "managed mediocrity" becomes risky when both the penthouse and the outhouse are so close at hand.

Team TOPR: 1993 St. Louis Cardinals

	Bats	BA	OBP	SLG	HR	R	RBI	NBE	GOC	Ratio	TOPR
League Avg. Team	-	.264	.327	.399	140	728	681	2835	4378	0.647	100
St. Louis Cardinals	-	.272	.341	.395	118	758	724	2871	4358	0.659	101.8
Regulars:											
C Tom Pagnozzi	R	.258	.296	.373	7	31	41	142	257	0.553	85
1B Gregg Jefferies	B	.342	.408	.485	16	89	83	353	387	0.912	141
2B Luis Alicea	B	.279	.362	.373	3	50	46	194	280	0.693	107
3B Todd Zeile	R	.277	.352	.433	17	82	103	309	438	0.705	109
SS Ozzie Smith	B	.288	.337	.356	1	75	53	254	421	0.603	93
LF Bernard Gilkey	R	.305	.370	.481	16	99	70	322	418	0.770	119
CF Ray Lankford	L	.238	.366	.346	7	64	45	224	333	0.673	104
RF Mark Whiten	B	.253	.323	.423	25	81	99	298	443	0.673	104
Bench (100+ TPA):											
2B Geronimo Pena	B	.256	.330	.406	5	34	30	143	203	0.704	109
C Erik Pappas	R	.276	.368	.342	1	25	28	107	178	0.601	93
OF Brian Jordan	R	.309	.351	.543	10	33	44	134	169	0.793	122
I/O Rod Brewer	L	.286	.359	.381	2	15	20	74	114	0.649	(100)
1B Gerald Perry	L	.337	.440	.510	4	21	16	64	70	0.914	(141)

NOTE: Statistics are only for games played with St. Louis. ( ) Under 200 TPA.

Team TPER: 1993 St. Louis Cardinals

	Throws	W-L	GS	GR	SV	IP	ERA	NBA	GOE	Ratio	TPER
League Avg. Team	-	81 -81	162	381	43	1449	4.04	2835	4378	0.647	100
St. Louis Cardinals	-	87 -75	162	423	54	1453	4.10	2865	4405	0.650	100.5
The Rotation:											
Bob Tewksbury	R	17 -10	32	0	0	213.2	3.83	403	644	0.626	97
Rene Arocha	R	11 -8	29	3	0	188	3.78	338	573	0.590	91
Donovan Osborne	L	10 -7	26	0	0	155.2	3.76	292	468	0.624	96
Joe Magrane	L	8 -10	20	2	0	116	4.97	246	351	0.701	108
Allen Watson	L	6 -7	15	1	0	86	4.60	190	261	0.728	112
Utility:											
Rheal Cormier	L	7 -6	21	17	0	145.1	4.33	292	443	0.659	102
Tom Urbani	L	1 -3	9	9	0	62	4.65	132	196	0.673	104
Bullpen:											
Omar Olivares	R	5 -3	9	49	1	118.2	4.17	264	356	0.742	115
Mike Perez	R	7 -2	0	65	7	72.2	2.48	123	218	0.564	87
Rob Murphy	L	5 -7	0	73	1	64.2	4.87	126	197	0.640	99
Les Lancaster	R	4 -1	0	50	0	61.1	2.93	112	187	0.599	93
Lee Guetterman	L	3 -3	0	40	1	46	2.93	75	140	0.536	(83)
Lee Smith	R	2 -4	0	55	43	50	4.50	112	151	0.742	115

NOTE: Statistics are only for games pitched with St. Louis. ( ) Under 200 TBF.

LET'S CHANGE THE SUBJECT
SAN DIEGO PADRES

Quoting from the San Diego Padres' '93 Media Guide:

"The ownership of the San Diego Padres is committed to building a strong and cohesive team, a team consisting of strong management and talented players with a desire to win.

"The San Diego Padres' team was purchased during the '90 season by a group of Southern California's most influential business leaders, men who are winners in their respective fields of expertise and are contributors to the community. The 15 partners, led by Chairman and Managing Partner Tom Werner,

are committed to make the San Diego Padres contenders for years to come."[1]

A river of spleen, bile and sarcasm has flowed into San Diego Bay since the '92–'93 off-season because of such statements. We chose not to add to it.

Instead, we'll skip through the past, except where it bears on the future, and focus on the "years to come."

[1]1993 *San Diego Padres Media Guide*, P 4.

Team Trendline: San Diego Padres

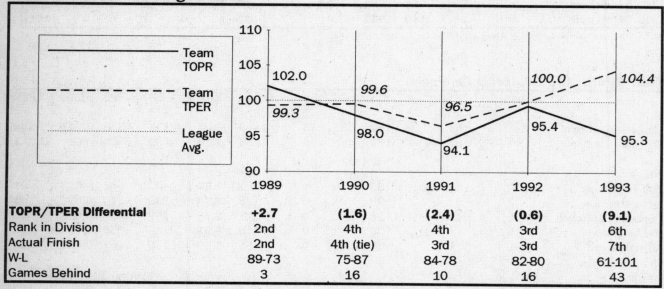

	1989	1990	1991	1992	1993
TOPR/TPER Differential	+2.7	(1.6)	(2.4)	(0.6)	(9.1)
Rank in Division	2nd	4th	4th	3rd	6th
Actual Finish	2nd	4th (tie)	3rd	3rd	7th
W-L	89-73	75-87	84-78	82-80	61-101
Games Behind	3	16	10	16	43

What Was Expected

In sunny San Diego, worried looks were everywhere as the '93 season approached. The fans heard Padre management saying words like, "players who can help us win" and "committed to building a contending team." They saw management doing something else, as the players who fit the description were shipped out in return for prospects who could contribute little to the stated goal.

Worse, rumors abounded that even the team's *best* players were on the block and that management's only "commitment" was to slicing the payroll. The relationship between the fans and Padres management deteriorated. The season began with a forecast seldom heard in Southern California: "partly cloudy with a chance of storms, perhaps locally severe."

What Actually Happened

The forecast was conservative. It should have read "gathering clouds, becoming unsettled toward mid-season, then rapid changes followed by gales of outrage continuing into the off-season."

The storms had started forming late in the '92 season. The transaction list catalogues their outbreak:

Aug. 31 — Craig Lefferts (LH starter) traded to Baltimore for prospects Erik Shullstrom (RHP) and Ricky Gutierrez (INF).

Oct. 26 — Tony Fernandez (starting SS) traded to the Mets for Wally Whitehurst (RH starter/reliever) and prospects D. J. Dozier (OF) and Raul Casanova (C).

Nov. 17 — Jerald Clark (starting LF) to Colorado in expansion draft.

Dec. 9 — Jose Melendez (RH middle reliever) traded to Boston for Phil Plantier (OF).

Winter — Free agents Larry Andersen (RH set-up man), Jim Deshaies (LH starter), Randy Myers (LH closer) and Benito Santiago (starting C) *all* signed with other clubs.

Mar. 30 — Darrin Jackson (starting CF) traded to Toronto for prospect Derek Bell (OF).

Jun. 1 — Jeremy Hernandez (RH middle reliever) traded to Cleveland for prospects Tracy Sanders (OF) and Fernando Hernandez (RHP).

Jun. 23 — Tim Scott (RH middle reliever) traded to Montreal for Archi Cianfrocco (INF).

Jun. 24 — Gary Sheffield (starting 3B) and Rich Rodriguez (LH set-up man) traded to Florida for prospects Trevor Hoffman (RHP) Jose Martinez (RHP) and Andres Berumen (RHP).

Jul. 3 — Roger Mason (RH set-up) traded to Philadelphia for prospect Tim Mauser (RHP).

Jul. 18 — Fred McGriff (starting 1B) traded to Atlanta for prospects Melvin Nieves (OF), Donnie Elliot (RHP) and Vince Moore (OF).

Jul. 26 — Greg W. Harris (RH starter) and Bruce Hurst (LH starter) traded to Colorado for Andy Ashby (RHP) and prospects Brad Ausmus (C) and Doug Bochtler (RHP).

In the meantime, the ball club staggered downhill through the season—finally cratering in September. The bottom line: 61–101, dead last in the division.

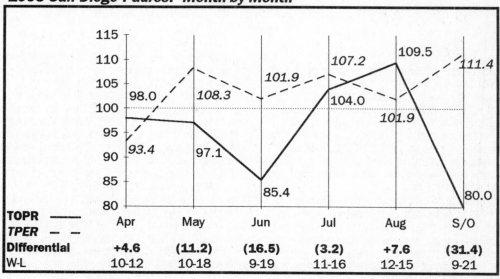

1993 San Diego Padres: Month-by-Month

	Apr	May	Jun	Jul	Aug	S/O
TOPR ———	98.0	97.1	85.4	104.0	109.5	80.0
TPER – –	93.4	108.3	101.9	107.2	101.9	111.4
Differential	+4.6	(11.2)	(16.5)	(3.2)	+7.6	(31.4)
W-L	10-12	10-18	9-19	11-16	12-15	9-21

Jack Murphy Stadium

In '93, "The Murph" favored pitchers (Park TOPR: 95.6). But to benefit, the pitcher had to wear a Padres uniform. Park adjusted, their home TPER was near average (99.6), while they got lit up on the road (109.6). The face-off between the Padres' offense and visiting pitchers revealed only the standard home advantage for the Pads.

The described effect seems suspiciously like a normal characteristic of young pitching staffs. Accordingly, as they mature, some improvement is probable and "The Murph" will gravitate back toward a neutral park.

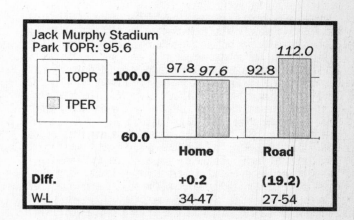

Jack Murphy Stadium
Park TOPR: 95.6

	□ TOPR	▨ TPER	Home	Road
TOPR			97.8	92.8
TPER			97.6	112.0
Diff.			+0.2	(19.2)
W-L			34-47	27-54

1993 Padres Lineup

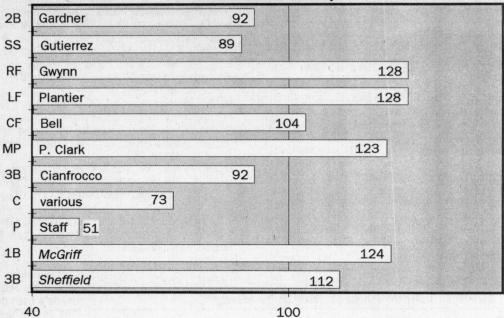

2B	Gardner	92
SS	Gutierrez	89
RF	Gwynn	128
LF	Plantier	128
CF	Bell	104
MP	P. Clark	123
3B	Cianfrocco	92
C	various	73
P	Staff	51
1B	*McGriff*	124
3B	*Sheffield*	112

40   100

The Offense

The Padres' offense TOPRed below average even when it had bangers Gary Sheffield and Fred McGriff in the lineup. Why then did it spurt up so sharply in July and August after they'd gone? For one thing, Gwynn got red-hot—hitting an incredible .448 from July 26 through August 29. For another, Plantier exploded, blasting 8 homers and driving in 15 runs over a 12-game span starting July 29. He then did a repeat the week of August 23–29 (.409, 5 HR, 18 RBI). Gwynn played his last game on September 5 before undergoing arthroscopic surgery. Plantier and a raft of call-ups couldn't keep up the pace in September.

After all's said and done, only Tony Gwynn survived through the off-season and mid-season upheavals in the regular lineup. And when he went on the DL in September, it became an entirely new cast of characters. After all these changes, where do the Padres stand and where might they go from here?

After all the trades and turmoil, the Padres ended up with a decent cadre of *young* players, who can and will improve.

Rickey Gutierrez demonstrated that the Lefferts deal can't be faulted. A marginal, aging pitcher (Lefferts' '92 TPER was 105) for a young, slick-fielding SS who's offensively adequate (89 TOPR, and should improve) makes a lot of sense. As a 23-year-old rookie, Gutierrez became part of the Padres' future.

Tony Gwynn, the untouchable icon of the franchise, passed the 2,000 hit mark in '93. Gwynn, who'll turn 34 in '94, probably won't be around when the Padres mount their next major push. His '93 TOPR (128) marks his highest level since '89. The intervening years were unremarkable (107, 109, 111). The argument *can* be made that, if the present was to be traded for the future, it should have been Tony. His perceived offensive value has been greater than his actual contribution, which is pretty much limited to hits (albeit a lot of them). The mere thought of dealing Capt. Tony is heresy in San Diego, a kind of "last straw" to Padres' fans. But it possesses a certain validity, given all the other moves which have occurred.

Phil Plantier, a steal! A middle-reliever for a 24-year-old LH who can hit 34 HR and slug .509 with a 128 TOPR that's still way beneath his ceiling. Melendez, when he gets well, will be a good middleman for the BoSox (who really didn't need another one). Plantier, as he improves, will become a *star* (and the new-look Padres desperately need one of those).

Derek Bell came in return for Darrin Jackson. In reality, Bell hit about like Jackson did (a 104 TOPR compared to Jackson's 101 average with San Diego), both had a clutch of HRs and little else. But, he's over six years younger (24) and a lot cheaper. This trade produces a positive balance in the Padres' column. But where will he play? Bell doesn't carry Jackson's leather and asked to (had to?) move from CF. A brief trial at 3B eliminated that as a possibility. The OF corners are set, with Gwynn and Plantier. Even if one were moved to 1B (a possibility), there's no guarantee Derek would beat out Melvin Nieves (one of the prospects attained in the McGriff deal) who's probably a better hitter than he is. Looks like CF, the bench eventually or the block.

Phil Clark proved a handy guy to have around. Played some 1B, LF and RF, even a little C and 3B. Another waiver acquisition (from Detroit), Jerald Clark's younger brother proved more valuable to the Padres than Jerald ever did. Only 25, his versatility earns him a job. His 123 TOPR earns him a lot of ABs.

Brad Ausmus, the key to the Harris/Hurst trade with the Rockies, took over the regular catcher's job immediately upon arrival from Colorado Springs, the Rockies' AAA farm club. He carries excellent defensive credentials and proved capable with the bat (92 TOPR). Ausmus hit 5 HRs in just two months of action, after never having hit more than 3 in any one minor league season. At this early stage he remains a high-quality prospect, with strong indications that he'll be a quality major leaguer. If he's adding power to his offensive arsenal, he could be more than that.

The remaining regulars, Jeff Gardner and Archi Cianfrocco, look like stop-gaps. Gardner played as a 29-year-old rookie in '93 and thus doesn't fit the "prospect" mold. His offensive value in the minors was based on his ability to draw walks, but he only garnered 48 in the majors holding his TOPR to a marginal 92. Cianfrocco's acquisition set up the Sheffield trade. He immediately became the regular there, but moved to 1B when Guillermo Velasquez fumbled his chance (69 TOPR) to replace McGriff. Cianfrocco's 92 TOPR proves he's no Sheffield or McGriff, by any stretch, but his versatility could earn him a bench job. Or if he ever added any plate discipline (only 17 BB in 324 PA) to his power (11 HR in what amounts to half a season) he might find a regular job at 3B.

On the offensive side, the moves we can measure so far have been in favor of the Padres. Even the loss of Benito Santiago to free agency should go unlamented. His '93 in Florida gave further indication of his slippage, both offensively and defensively. The Padres are better off with Ausmus right now, much less down the road.

However, all the returns from the Sheffield and McGriff trades, the real key to any analysis, haven't come in yet. Nieves, though, looks like a hitter (137 minor league TOPR) and could break into the Padres lineup in '94. Vince Moore, another ex-Atlanta prospect, remains a few years away. Tracy Sanders, who came from Cleveland in the Jeremy Hernandez deal, may prove to be the best hitting prospect of them all (143 minor league TOPR with excellent power and outstanding strike zone judgment).

The Pitching

Talk about turnover! With the exception of the departed G. W. Harris, only three of the pitchers listed had appeared in a San Diego uniform before '93. And two of them (Doug Brocail and Gene Harris) pitched a combined total of only 35.1 innings for the Padres in '92. Five of them didn't even start the season with the club.

The Padres used 23 pitchers all told, 11 of whom are no longer with the organization. One look at their Team TPER (104.4) tells you why.

What's left doesn't look all that good either, does it? Apparently, the Padres ended up just shuffling the deck.

	IP	W–L	ERA	TPER
The 12 keepers	981.2	43–71	4.25	104.0
The 11 departed	464.0	18–30	4.18	105.4

Of course they hoped to inject more youth into their staff. The average age of the "keepers" was 25.8, compared to 28.1 for the departed, so they succeeded. But did they improve their future outlook?

The Rotation: In '92, it had been Benes, Harris, Hurst, Deshaies and Lefferts. By the end of '93, it was Benes and a whole bunch of new guys.

Andy Benes continued as the staff's bellcow. His '93 TOPR (94) marked no improvement from his established level (also 94). To date, Benes has been a solid pitcher but not the ace he was expected to be. He'll be 26 in '94 and '95 is his free agent year. If he's ever going to "breakthrough," now's the time. It may also be the time to trade him, since he's made it clear he's not inclined to re-sign with the Padres. And because the market still values his as yet unrealized potential, he could bring a truckload of futures now vs. nothing later. Tough call.

After Benes, it's not easy to sort out exactly what remained in a mixed bag of veterans and kids.

Wally Whitehurst can probably provide some help in a #4 starter role. He's quietly established himself as a moderately effective pitcher with useful versatility. Over 139 major league appearances, Wally's moved back and forth from the bullpen to starting (total 50 starts). From '90 through '93, his TPER's read 76, 97, 103 and 97. He seems reliable.

Andy Ashby, of the 53 NL pitchers who made 20 or more starts, ranked dead last (136 TPER, 118 with the Pads). Obtained from Colorado in the Harris/Hurst trade, he's been getting chances for three years now without capitalizing on any of them (prior TPERs of 120 and 143). Andy's at the bar in baseball's "Last Chance Saloon."

Doug Brocail, among the kids, spent the year in the rotation, suffering a painful debut. His 4–13 record, 4.56 ERA and 114 TPER were nothing to write home about. Brocail's got a long way to go and, at 27 in '94, it's getting late.

Two later call-ups, Tim Worrell and Scott Sanders, gave encouraging performances, however. Worrell pitched better than his 2–7 record and 4.92 ERA suggest. His 103 TPER in 16 starts stamps him as a possible contributor. Sanders also impressed in his nine starts (3–3, 4.13 ERA, 93 TPER). There's a risk associated with

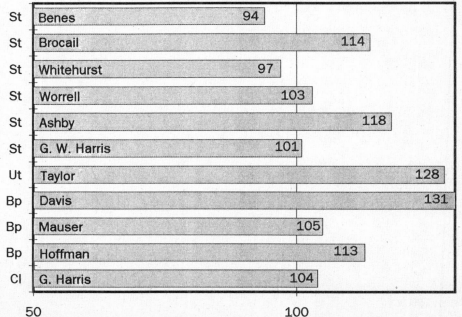

1993 Padres Staff

St	Benes	94
St	Brocail	114
St	Whitehurst	97
St	Worrell	103
St	Ashby	118
St	G. W. Harris	101
Ut	Taylor	128
Bp	Davis	131
Bp	Mauser	105
Bp	Hoffman	113
Cl	G. Harris	104

50   100

both, however. Prone to giving up HRs in the minors, they somehow escaped this scourge in their major league debuts, and thus bear close watching.

The Bullpen: The '92 bullpen consisted of Melendez, Hernandez, Maddux, Rodriguez, Andersen and Myers. Not a solitary sole survived. And, from this total transfusion of talent, only two sure keepers emerged.

The Pads didn't pull the trigger on the Sheffield deal until Trevor Hoffman was included. A 25-year-old with a first-class heater (90 IP, 79 K in '93), he's rated a "can't miss" closer prospect. Hoffman registered a so-so 105 on the TPER gun for his full rookie year (113 with San Diego). A converted SS, this was only his third year on the mound, so he's still a little rough around the edges. Plus he carried a heavy workload in '93 and seemed to wear down toward the finish. The Padres think he could be something special. They might be right.

The strongest rookie performance by a Padre pitcher, though, belonged to 24-year-old, LH Pedro A. Martinez. In 32 appearances out of the bullpen, he hung up a sparkling 71 TPER to go with a 3–1 record and 2.43 ERA. In 37 IP he gave up only 23 H, 13 BB with 32 K. Almost exclusively a starter in his 7-year minor league career, he was stalled at AA Wichita for three of them. Pedro finally got it going in '92 and by mid-season '93 reached the majors. Judging by his debut, he'll make an impact in '94—whether in the pen or in the rotation is the only question.

Then it gets ugly, though. The Padres chose to re-sign Mark Davis after he'd given them a presentable 3.52 ERA in 35 appearances (38.1 IP). But his 131 TPER with the club *wasn't* presentable, nor are any of his TPERs since the Cinderella '89 Cy Young season (140, 105, 164 and 130—56th out of 57 'tweeners in the NL). Ugh! RH Tim Mauser produced a 105 TPER for the Padres which means as an unestablished middle-reliever, he'll hang on until he has two bad outings in a row.

In '93 Gene Harris got his big chance to be a big league closer. His 104 TPER ranked 9th in the league, abreast of Doug Jones, Mitch Williams and Mike Stanton—all of whom were traded or lost their jobs. Why should Harris be any different? Odds are Hoffman gets the closer job in '94.

San Diego fans should view the Padres pitching with some perspective, though. With the exception of Benes the entire staff turned over. The Team TPER rose only 4.4 points (from 100.0 to 104.4). The new staff was considerably less expensive, true, but it was also younger and is *potentially* better. Admittedly, many nights it was hard for Padre fans to watch but, at the same time, it's hard to fault.

What Next?

We'd be remiss if we didn't make this very important point. The fans' hackles started rising with the Lefferts trade on August 31, 1992. It had seemed so tragically shortsighted at the time for a team "in contention" to trade a rotation starter for the cliché "player-to-be-named-later." But were the Padres really "in contention"? That night, Lefferts had started and lost to St. Louis, dropping the Pads 8½ games behind an Atlanta team that showed no sign of impending collapse.

Further, check out the Padres' trendline for their final '92 numbers—99.4 TOPR and a 100.0 TPER, a −0.6 deficiency, a .500 club all around (they finished 82–80). Suitable to contend for 2nd place, perhaps, but *not* the division championship. Did the '92 club have the core that a future champion could be built upon? McGriff, Sheffield, Fernandez and Gwynn provided a formidable base. But the other four positions had become gaping TOPR holes. And the Pads had zilch in their minor league pipeline. The pitching staff seemed competent top to bottom, but was aging and expensive.

What would you have done in this situation? Maybe you'd have gone about it a little differently than the Padres' management did. Been more forthcoming and a little cooler under fire, perhaps. But you'd still probably have bitten the rebuilding bullet. The Padres' management may be stewing in their own PR juices, but the rebuilding effort so far merits a diagnosis of at least "guarded recovery."

Team TOPR: 1993 San Diego Padres

	Bats	BA	OBP	SLG	HR	R	RBI	NBE	GOC	Ratio	TOPR
League Avg. Team	-	.264	.327	.399	140	728	681	2891	4378	0.647	100
San Diego Padres	-	.252	.312	.389	153	679	634	2754	4398	0.617	95.3
Regulars:											
C Kevin Higgins	L	.221	.294	.254	0	17	13	61	150	0.400	62
Brad Ausmus	R	.256	.281	.413	5	18	12	72	121	0.595	(92)
1B Fred McGriff	L	.275	.361	.497	18	52	46	192	235	0.804	124
2B Jeff Gardner	L	.262	.337	.356	1	53	24	191	309	0.599	92
3B Gary Sheffield	R	.295	.344	.473	10	34	36	142	195	0.723	112
SS Ricky Gutierrez	R	.251	.334	.331	5	76	26	199	340	0.576	89
LF Phil Plantier	L	.240	.335	.509	34	67	100	309	366	0.831	128
CF Derek Bell	R	.262	.303	.417	21	73	72	288	420	0.674	104
RF Tony Gwynn	L	.358	.398	.497	7	70	59	284	341	0.830	128
Bench (100+ TPA):											
1/3 Archi Cianfrocco	R	.244	.289	.412	11	27	47	135	227	0.595	92
I/O Phil Clark	R	.313	.345	.496	9	33	33	135	170	0.794	123
IF Craig Shipley	R	.235	.275	.326	4	25	22	99	184	0.522	81
IF Tim Teufel	R	.250	.338	.430	7	26	31	110	165	0.655	101
OF Billy Bean	L	.260	.284	.395	5	19	32	83	146	0.541	(84)
OF Jarvis Brown	R	.233	.335	.331	0	21	8	67	112	0.571	(88)

NOTE: Statistics are only for games played with San Diego. ( ) Under 200 TPA.

Team TPER: 1993 San Diego Padres

	Throws	W-L	GS	GR	SV	IP	ERA	NBA	GOE	Ratio	TPER
League Avg. Team	-	81 -81	162	381	43	1449	4.04	2835	4378	0.647	100
San Diego Padres	-	61 -101	162	397	32	1437.2	4.23	2952	4366	0.676	104.4
The Rotation:											
Andy Benes	R	15 -15	34	0	0	230.2	3.78	425	700	0.607	94
Doug Brocail	R	4 -13	24	0	0	128.1	4.56	289	390	0.741	114
Greg Harris	R	10 -9	22	0	0	152	3.67	299	457	0.654	101
Wally Whitehurst	R	4 -7	19	2	0	105.2	3.83	199	317	0.628	97
Tim Worrell	R	2 -7	16	5	0	100.2	4.92	208	311	0.669	103
Andy Ashby	R	3 -6	12	0	0	69	5.48	159	209	0.761	118
Scott Sanders	R	3 -3	9	0	0	52.1	4.13	97	161	0.602	93
Utility:											
Frank Seminara	R	3 -3	7	11	0	46.1	4.47	110	141	0.780	120
Bullpen:											
Kerry Taylor	R	0 -5	7	29	0	68.1	6.45	172	208	0.827	128
Trevor Hoffman	R	2 -4	0	39	3	54.1	4.31	120	164	0.732	113
Roger Mason	R	0 -7	0	34	0	50	3.24	78	151	0.517	80
Mark Davis	L	0 -3	0	35	4	38.1	3.52	97	114	0.851	(131)
Tim Mauser	R	0 -1	0	28	0	37.2	3.58	78	115	0.678	(105)
Pedro Martinez	L	3 -1	0	32	0	37	2.43	53	115	0.461	(71)
Gene Harris	R	6 -6	0	59	23	59.1	3.03	121	179	0.676	104

NOTE: Statistics are only for games pitched with Baltimore. ( ) Under 200 TBF.

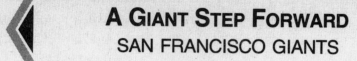

A GIANT STEP FORWARD
SAN FRANCISCO GIANTS

In November '92, the new, but as yet unconfirmed, owners of the beleaguered San Francisco Giants made a significant decision. They budgeted $40 plus million toward improvement of the team's competitive position. A 72–90 record in the prior season had resulted in a dismal fifth place finish. The offense had been pathetic—only one NL team had scored fewer runs. The pitching was in shambles—only three other NL teams had allowed more runs. Where to start? The ownership made a momentous decision. They invested the entire amount in *one* player. They invested in Bonds.

It was a giant investment. And it produced a Giant step forward.

Team Trendline: San Francisco Giants

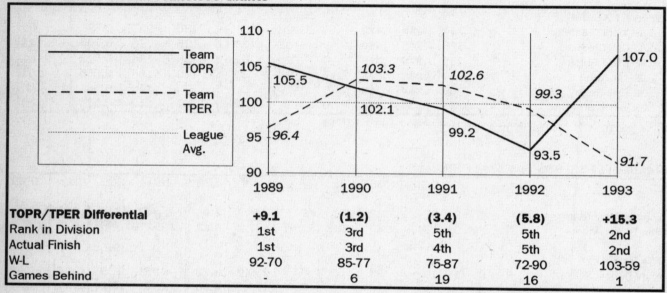

	Team TOPR	Team TPER	League Avg.

	1989	1990	1991	1992	1993
TOPR/TPER Differential	+9.1	(1.2)	(3.4)	(5.8)	+15.3
Rank in Division	1st	3rd	5th	5th	2nd
Actual Finish	1st	3rd	4th	5th	2nd
W-L	92-70	85-77	75-87	72-90	103-59
Games Behind	-	6	19	16	1

What Was Expected

None doubted the Giants were an improved team. But, aside from the Bonds signing, little else had changed on the field. Besides LF, all the other positions would be manned by the same starters who had held those jobs in '92. The pitching staff that had yielded all those runs would be composed of the exact same pitchers, save a rookie left-hander whom it was hoped would shore up the bullpen in this particular specialty.

How much could Bonds, just one player, be worth to the team's performance in the standings? Everyone recognized he was a high-quality player, one of the best in the league, certainly. The predictions of those paid to have an opinion ran the gamut. But the hard fact was that Bonds was only one player, after all, on what had been a bad team. The consensus: around .500 maybe, or a little better if Dusty Baker, the new manager, took a more coherent approach to pitching staff management than his predecessor Roger Craig.

What Actually Happened

The Giants claimed first place on April 15 and, except for two days, held onto it until September 11 when the Braves caught them in the midst of an eight-game SF losing streak. The Giants got off the floor, rallied strongly and won 14 of their last 17 games, catching Atlanta on the 28th with five games to go. The last week of the season saw one of the most exciting pennant chases ever as two thoroughbreds came pounding down the stretch racing for the finish. At the wire, Atlanta kept stride, holding off Colorado 5–3. San Francisco, though, stumbled—losing 12–1 in LA. It was no solace that the Giants had done the self-same thing to the Dodgers in '91 when it had been their historical rival chasing the Braves. It was over. 103 wins but no post-season.

This rousing performance came as a surprise to many. What had happened was that one player had indeed been enough to change the entire team's offensive character and thus their entire direction.

At the same time, the pitching staff had suddenly gotten much better, too. But there was no mystery in this event. The '92 staff had *not* been as bad as all the runs allowed suggested. Their TPER was a slightly better than average 99.3, after all. To some extent, they had been victimized in '92 by their own defense, as the team's best defensive players at three key positions (C, SS and CF) had all started fewer than 100 games. In '93, Kirt Manwaring, Royce Clayton and Darren Lewis all started at least 130 (unearned runs went down from 61 to 49). Moreover, the staff had escaped Roger Craig's whimsical practice of "rotating the rotation" and found themselves assigned to well-defined and conceived roles. Finally, Bill Swift made it through the year without shoulder miseries. And John Burkett, the one pitcher who's role Craig had never tinkered with (and, coincidentally, just about the only pitcher without an injury history), blossomed.

In the end, though, pitching is what cost the Giants. That is, if a team that wins 103 games can be said to have come up short anywhere. From the outset, the plan had been a 4-man rotation (Swift, Burkett, Bud Black and Trevor Wilson) supplemented by a fifth "spot" starter. However, both Black and Wilson made three separate trips to the DL and after July 10 both were effectively out for the season. The ensuing scramble for not one but *three* other starters destabilized the staff just enough to create heartbreak. The Giants continued to win with regularity as you can see below, but at not *quite* the same pace.

1993 San Francisco Giants: Month-by-Month

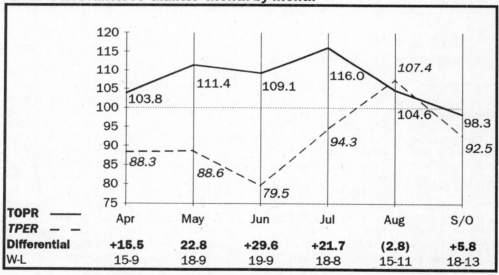

	Apr	May	Jun	Jul	Aug	S/O
Differential	+15.5	22.8	+29.6	+21.7	(2.8)	+5.8
W-L	15-9	18-9	19-9	18-8	15-11	18-13

TOPR ——
TPER – –

Candlestick Park

Thoughts of Candlestick invariably include wind, fog and chill—not to mention earthquakes. The "atmospheric effect" is essentially the opposite of Mile High. "Pitcher's weather" it is and, indeed, it's a "pitcher's park." The best such park in the league in '93 (92.8 Park TOPR). The effect was almost solely confined to the SF Hitters, whose park-adjusted TOPR fell from 114.5 on the road to 99.3 at home (the meat of the order—Clark, Williams and Bonds—are all fly-ball hitters). The Giants' pitchers enjoyed no reciprocal home advantage since they were accomplished ground-ball pitchers who tend to be equally effective in any atmospheric environment (park-adjusted 92.0 TPER on the road, 91.1 at home).

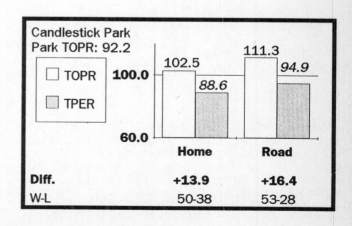

Candlestick Park
Park TOPR: 92.2

□ TOPR
▨ TPER

	Home	Road
Diff.	+13.9	+16.4
W-L	50-38	53-28

1993 Giants Lineup

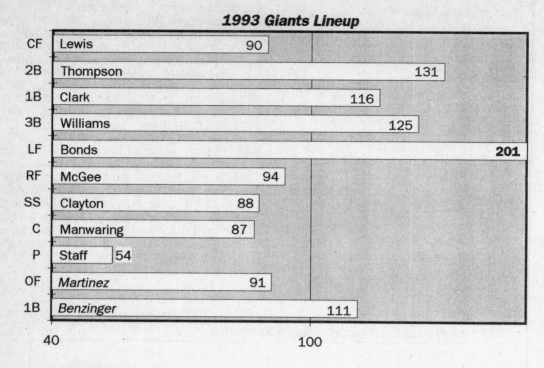

CF	Lewis	90
2B	Thompson	131
1B	Clark	116
3B	Williams	125
LF	Bonds	**201**
RF	McGee	94
SS	Clayton	88
C	Manwaring	87
P	Staff	54
OF	*Martinez*	91
1B	*Benzinger*	111

40   100

The Offense

The TOPR chart for the Giants' offense has a somewhat curious shape.

Uh-huh. Bonds kinda "sticks out," doesn't he?

Overall, the Giants' lineup performed above the NL positional norm at only three positions, 2B (Norm:103), 3B (Norm:107) and LF (Norm:121). Yet, they produced a second-in-the-league 107.0 Team TOPR, up from their next-to-last 93.5 in '92.

That's a +13.5 point rise in one season which is, we assure you, an extreme rarity. Can one player make that much of a difference? Was Bonds alone really responsible?

Yes, almost *solely* responsible. Some other players did better in '93 than in '92 (e.g., Thompson, up from 110). But others had worse years (e.g., Clark, down from 145). On balance, all the other year-to-year fluctuations by individual players just about evened out. Barry Bonds was the man, as demonstrated by a comparison of his '93 numbers to the combination of players he replaced in LF.

Giants' Left Fielders ('93 vs. '92)

	TPA	NBE	GOC	Ratio	TOPR
Kevin Bass '92	285	123	210	.586	98
Chris James '92	267	109	196	.556	93
Mark Leonard '92	148	65	102	.637	106
Total	700	297	508	.585	98
Barry Bonds '93	674	506	388	1.304	201

Between them, Bass, James and Leonard started 130 games in LF for the Giants in '92. Their total plate appearances virtually match Bonds' in '93, so the comparison is a very direct one. In both cases, the TPA amount to about 11% of the team's total.

In replacing the '92 triumvirate in LF, Bonds essentially replaced an average offensive player. He added a total of 103 TOPR points to the position and, since he accounted for 11% of the team's TPA, he thus added a net of 11.3 TOPR points to the Team TOPR. That accounts for nearly all of the +13.5 point differential in the Team

TOPR from '92 to '93. The rest of the hitters contributed a net increase of only +2.2 TOPR points.

There's more. Bonds increased the production from the position by 209 net bases, of course. *And he used 120 fewer outs to produce them.* He returned these 120 outs to the team for the use of other players. That's equally important because his teammates could then do something of their own with them. The rest of the team recorded an out in only 66.6% of its plate appearances, meaning these 120 extra opportunities produced a total of 180 new plate appearances, yielding 60 new baserunners (120 ÷ .666). The Team TOPR ratio of .693 means that the availability of 120 *extra* outs generated an additional 83 net bases (120 × .693). These were also added to the team total—aside from Barry's own total of +209 incremental net bases. In other words, Bonds' presence in the lineup contributed almost 300 *new* net bases to the Giants' offense. That's an immense total.

There's an important lesson here. It has to do with the value of *saving outs.* Every out avoided goes back to the team's "bank," to be reissued to another batter for his own use. When he does something with it, it gets passed along again. And again, and again. The estimated 180 "new" plate appearances resulting from Bonds' presence accounts for almost all of the 201 more TPA the Giants had in '93 vs. '92. They amount to more than one additional plate appearance per game—and how many times have you seen games end when teams were trying to get just one more batter to the plate?

With TOPR, calculating the value of a "pass-along" out becomes simple. One out saved is worth its equivalent in the Team TOPR. In the Giants' case, .693 bases. A walk may not be exciting to fans or satisfying to the player, but *it is a lot better than an out.*

Aside from Bonds' enormous contribution to their offense the Giants have an advantage over most teams in the abnormally high production they enjoy from 2B, courtesy of Robby Thompson. But the production from the outfield, other than Bonds, is seriously sub-standard. CF and RF are problems, especially if they have to cover the leadoff spot (as they do). It's shocking that a team with a 107.0 TOPR and 808 runs scored had a leadoff hitter who only scored 84 times (Lewis).

The Pitching

This display of the Giants' pitching staff can be a little misleading. Only Swift and Burkett stayed in the rotation all year. After them, the starting assignments went to smithereens (Wilson and Black only made 18 and 16 starts, respectively).

As noted, with the exception of Kevin Rogers, this is essentially the same staff that toiled for the Giants in '92. Fact is, if you include Rogers in the '92 group (he made six starts), the two years compare as follows:

	1992	1993
Games Started		
The '93 Staff	134	134
Others	28	28
Relief Appearances		
The '93 Staff	314	396
Others	55	14

Of course, we're counting the 32 starts that Bryan Hickerson (15), Jeff Brantley (12) and Dave Burba (5) had to make in '93 as rotation-fillers. But these three also made 16 starts in '92. The point remains, little changed on this staff from '92 to '93—except for its effectiveness. What was the source of their marked improvement?

Let's start with the fact that the '92 staff wasn't *bad,* merely average (99.3 TPER). So the '93 improvement wasn't "dramatic" as many people thought. Due to both the vagaries of injury and to more rational usage, the better pitchers got to pitch more and the less effective pitchers less. Swift, Burkett and Rogers accounted for 166.2 more IP than they did the year before while Wilson, Black and Righetti threw 158.1 fewer innings. In addition, the supplemental starters in the #5 spot and the replacements who plugged the holes left by Wilson's and Black's injuries were "acceptable" (instead of "atrocious" as such things often turn out). Plus, there were a couple of pleasant surprises—the veteran Burkett and the rookie Rogers.

Bill Swift's incredible effectiveness did *not* come as a surprise to TPER, though. Our '93 NL "King of the Hill" finished '92 behind only Curt Schilling by the narrowest of margins (73.0 TPER vs. 72.7). His contribution to the staff's improvement was measured by 34 starts (instead of 22) and 232.2 IP (instead of 164.2).

John Burkett, though, suddenly became a *pitcher.* After cruising along as a touch-better-than-average pitcher for three years ('90–'92 avg. 98 TPER), he blossomed into an ACE. The improvement was across the board. He was slightly harder to hit (opponents' BA down from .255 to .246), his strikeouts went up a little (from 5.1 per 9 IP to 5.7) and his already sharp control sharpened to pinpoint (from 2.1 per 9 IP to 1.6). But the biggest single difference between the two years concerned how he dealt with baserunners. Here's a comparison of the Baserunner Sub-set from his TPERs.

	SH	SF	SB	CS	GDP	BRB	BRO	Ratio
1992	11	4	17	−7	−13	12	35	.343
1993	8	4	14	−14	−21	(9)	47	(.191)

Obviously, Kirt Manwaring's intimately involved in this improvement, too. But he was there last year as well. What this indicates is that Burkett went from an average pitcher in this respect to a superior one. Maybe he learned a trick or two from Dick Pole, his new pitching coach. Or from teammate Swift who is the master of it (−20 net bases vs. 44 gross outs in '93). Plus his improvement in control allowed him to get the DP ball more often than usual.

The surprise from Kevin Rogers came in the way he was able to master the relief role over one winter. He made six late season starts for the Giants in '92 and produced encouraging results (0–2, 4.24 ERA, 103 TPER in 34 IP). Kevin had made only three relief appearances in the minors during his five-year progression. Yet, the decision was made at season's end to send him to the Arizona Fall League to retool as a reliever. He did the job well enough to grab the #5 spot on TPER's list of the top relievers in the NL.

The conclusions you can draw about the Giants' pitching are:

1. They have an excellent rotation. If it can stay healthy, it's among the best in the league.
2. The "utility" group who did yeoman duty as starters/relievers

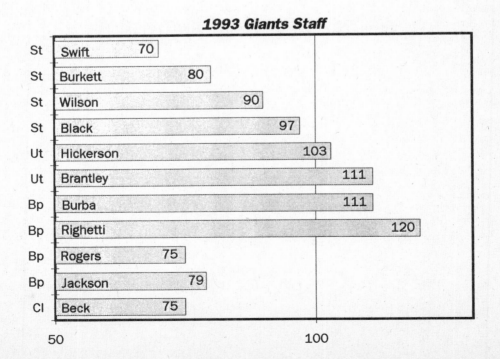

1993 Giants Staff

St	Swift	70
St	Burkett	80
St	Wilson	90
St	Black	97
Ut	Hickerson	103
Ut	Brantley	111
Bp	Burba	111
Bp	Righetti	120
Bp	Rogers	75
Bp	Jackson	79
Cl	Beck	75

50   100

(Hickerson, Brantley and Dave Burba) proved a competent set. Every team should be so lucky.

3. The bullpen was well-nigh bulletproof. The corps of Mike Jackson, Rogers and then Rod Beck can effectively snuff an enemy's rally and then close 'em out.

It was—and is—a much better staff than it got credit for. Plus, there's some rotation help on the way. Salomon Torres got his baptism under fire, taking over a spot in what had become a straight forward "4-man, 4-day" rotation in the final weeks of the race. Torres, in fact, started and lost the only four games the Giants dropped in their last 18. Nonetheless, he had won his previous three starts and debuted with a TPER of 106, so he looks capable. The only question concerns how well five key members of the staff (Swift, Burkett, Jackson, Rogers and Beck) recover from their '93 workload. They were worked awfully hard down the stretch.

What Next?

Just as the roster was little changed from '92 to '93, there will apparently be little change from '93 to '94. But, instead of a magnificent addition, it will be a significant subtraction. Claiming an attack of fiscal reality, the Giants made no particular effort to re-sign their free agent first baseman, Will Clark, so "The Thrill" is gone . . . to Texas.

Giants ownership's decision was complicated by two key players being eligible for free agency, 2B Robby Thompson as well as Clark. Plus a stated need to add a veteran starter for the crippled rotation. A glance at their P&L statement convinced them they could not afford to deal with all three situations and Clark became the odd man out.

Granted, Clark had an off season in '93 (116 TOPR). But, coming at the age of 29 on the heels of a '90–'92 average of 137, it has more the look of an aberration than a trend. Some nagging injuries (knee, wrist) took their toll and he required some rare DL time. Will hit only .218 until May 26, but .318 in the 87 games he played after that date. He was especially strong in the September stretch (.367) and, importantly, the Giants were 87–41 in the games he started and only 16–18 in those he didn't. His oft-mentioned RBI shortage the last two years (73 in both '92 and '93) is revealed to be a "red herring" when you consider his games played (144 and 132, respectively) and the leadoff hitters who didn't get on base in front of him.

The decision to do without Clark and entrust the position to some combination of rookie J. R. Phillips and spare parts Todd Benzinger and Mark Carreon is fraught with risk. It's highly unlikely that this combination can even match the TOPR that a diminished Clark produced in '93, much less contribute what Clark might have in '94. Moreover, Clark's uncharacteristically low TOPR still had a high on-base component (.367 OBP) and a full season would have seen him score 100 runs (he scored 82 in his 132 games). The 1B combine will probably produce nothing like that, nor do the Giants have anybody else who can (save Thompson and Bonds). They're liable to end up with an offense composed of Matt Williams and Bonds driving in Thompson, followed by a long pause for reloading.

In this circumstance, the leadoff spot begs for improvement. CF Darren Lewis' OBP (.302) is flatly unacceptable. If his defense justifies his staying in the lineup, then he ought to be moved down in the order. But the only feasible leadoff replacement is RF Willie McGee, who's neither comfortable nor particularly effective in this role. And no options appear available within the farm system, either. This problem now becomes more serious, and will evidently stay unsolved.

The offensive burden in '93, then, rests even more on Barry Bonds' one-man gang act. Is it wise to *plan* on yet another 200 TOPR?

The '94 pitching staff will see young Torres and free-agent signee Mark Portugal added to the rotation. Thus, the Giants won't have to count on both Wilson and/or Black recovering their former effectiveness.

The '94 pitching staff should maintain a high level of effectiveness. The benefit of the two new starters in the rotation, though, will probably be offset by some erosion elsewhere as the heavy '93 workload exacts its price.

Overall, the Giants figure to suffer an offensive slippage but retain a winning TPER edge. They're probably not going to win 103 games again in '94, but it will be sufficient to handle the weak competition in the restructured NL Western Division. This time, they should make the playoffs—but, oddly, with a weaker team.

Team TOPR: 1993 San Francisco Giants

	Bats	BA	OBP	SLG	HR	R	RBI	NBE	GOC	Ratio	TOPR
League Avg. Team	-	.264	.327	.399	140	728	681	2835	4378	0.647	100
San Francisco Giants	-	.276	.340	.427	168	808	759	3021	4361	0.693	107.0
Regulars:											
C Kirt Manwaring	R	.275	.345	.350	5	48	49	189	337	0.561	87
1B Will Clark	L	.283	.367	.432	14	82	73	278	371	0.749	116
2B Robby Thompson	R	.312	.375	.496	19	85	65	309	364	0.849	131
3B Matt Williams	R	.294	.325	.561	38	105	110	351	433	0.811	125
SS Royce Clayton	R	.282	.331	.372	6	54	70	247	435	0.568	88
LF Barry Bonds	L	.336	.458	.677	46	129	123	506	388	1.304	201
CF Darren Lewis	R	.253	.302	.324	2	84	48	246	422	0.583	90
RF Willie McGee	B	.301	.353	.389	4	53	46	218	358	0.609	94
Bench (100+ TPA):											
OF Dave Martinez	L	.241	.317	.361	5	28	27	112	191	0.586	91
MP Todd Benzinger	B	.288	.332	.452	6	25	26	95	132	0.720	(111)
OF Mark Carreon	R	.327	.373	.540	7	22	33	93	114	0.816	(126)
IF Mike Benjamin	R	.199	.264	.329	4	22	16	64	126	0.508	(78)
C Jeff Reed	L	.261	.346	.437	6	10	12	66	92	0.717	(111)
IF Steve Scarsone	R	.252	.278	.398	2	18	15	49	83	0.590	(91)

NOTE: Statistics are only for games played with San Francisco. ( ) Under 200 TPA.

Team TPER: 1993 San Francisco Giants

	Throws	W-L	GS	GR	SV	IP	ERA	NBA	GOE	Ratio	TPER
League Avg. Team	-	81 -81	162	381	43	1449	4.04	2835	4378	0.647	100
San Francisco Giants	-	103 -59	162	414	50	1456.2	3.63	2609	4395	0.594	91.7
The Rotation:											
Bill Swift	R	21 -8	34	0	0	232.2	2.82	322	710	0.454	70
John Burkett	R	22 -7	34	0	0	231.2	3.65	364	702	0.519	80
Trevor Wilson	L	7 -5	18	4	0	110	3.60	188	322	0.584	90
Bud Black	L	8 -2	16	0	0	93.2	3.56	180	288	0.625	97
Scott Sanderson	R	4 -2	8	3	0	48.2	3.51	101	147	0.687	106
Salomon Torres	R	3 -5	8	0	0	44.2	4.03	94	137	0.686	(106)
Utility:											
Bryan Hickerson	L	7 -5	15	32	0	120.1	4.26	244	365	0.668	103
Jeff Brantley	R	5 -6	12	41	0	113.2	4.28	244	341	0.716	111
Bullpen:											
Dave Burba	R	10 -3	5	49	0	95.1	4.25	202	281	0.719	111
Kevin Rogers	L	2 -2	0	64	0	80.2	2.68	118	242	0.488	75
Mike Jackson	R	6 -6	0	81	1	77.1	3.03	120	235	0.511	79
Dave Righetti	L	1 -1	0	51	1	47.1	5.70	112	144	0.778	120
Rod Beck	R	3 -1	0	76	48	79.1	2.16	117	240	0.488	75

NOTE: Statistics are only for games pitched with San Francisco. ( ) Under 200 TBF.

ON
THE
FARM

TOPR GOES TO THE MINORS

Minor league players are, quite literally, climbing a hill. It's the front of the TOPR curve and it describes their path to the majors. It looks something like this.

The TOPR Curve:

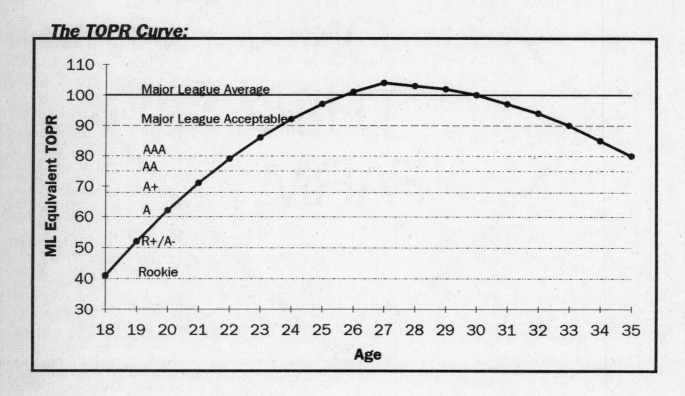

This *theoretical* curve visualizes, in a generalized form, the career path of an *average* offensive player. He signed out of high school spending his first professional year in a Rookie League. There followed a normal progression up the ladder, level by level, year by year, and he was about average at every stop. A college player would have joined this progression at an older age and correspondingly higher level. By the age of 24 or 25, he's achieved acceptable major league ability and his production peaks a few years later at 27 or 28. He stays in that vicinity for a while before he starts sliding and becomes vulnerable to replacement. The right-hand side of the curve may never happen for him. It is conceivable that he never even made the major leagues at all.

Our purpose in presenting this curve is to give us perspective. An *above*-average player will have a curve of *identical* configuration—but above this one. This means that he is much more likely to get to the majors in the first place, get there sooner, stay longer and have a more impressive and more extended peak period. He'll make a lot more money, too.

Similarly, *below*-average players will have a curve of the same shape—but *below* our theoretical average player. Any kind of major league career is a long-odds possibility for this kind of player, unless he's blessed with an extreme skill in one area (fielding, most likely).

Prospect TOPR

We're concerned here with the front of the curve: the players who are working their way up the hill. You'll note we've identified the TOPR level of each minor league classification. The locations are approximated but they are pretty darned close. The AAA line is at .80 in terms of major league equivalency. In essence, here's what that means:

◆ A 23-year-old player producing a 120 TOPR in the International League is performing at the equivalent of a 96 major league TOPR (120 × .80).
◆ If he makes the big club next year, as a regular, he'll probably deliver something like a 102 (120 × .85) as he continues his year-to-year development.

We've arrived at this conclusion by tracking rookie crops, starting with the 1988 vintage, and using their prior 3-year-average minor league TOPR. Every year, about forty rookies stick around long enough to pick up their first 200 TPAs. As a group, these forty players will retreat, in their rookie season, by about 15% from their 3-year minor league TOPR. Still as a group, they will then advance at the rate of about +6% per year. Virtually all of them who stick

Rookie TOPR:

Rookie Year	Minor League TOPR Trend				Major League TOPR Trend				BB:K Frequency	
	R-3	R-2	R-1	3 Yr Avg	R	R+1	R+2	R+3	Last Minor	First Major
1990										
Sandy Alomar, Jr.	90	113	108	**104**	102	(57)	75	96	73:64	58:65
Dave Justice	90	129	126	**117**	148	144	135	130	143:95	162:121
1991										
Chuck Knoblauch	-	136	116	**123**	103	117	96	-	125:37	114:43
Jeff Bagwell	-	123	147	**139**	130	129	131	-	132:64	141:114
1992										
Pat Listach	91	129	104	**108**	109	83	-	-	133:136	104:136
Kenny Lofton	136	148	116	**126**	121	134	-	-	86:108	123:59
Eric Karros	135	151	138	**141**	101	87	-	-	101:99	80:114
Reggie Sanders	136	142	160	**145**	132	116	-	-	113:109	146:145
1993										
Tim Salmon	138	128	190	**152**	141	-	-	-	175:139	152:150
Mike Piazza	90	119	149	**124**	138	-	-	-	97:92	91:93

( ) Less than 200 TPA.

around will at least reproduce their minor league TOPR in the major leagues by their third year.

Individual players do, of course, stray from the group. In general, the rookie year "TOPR discount" ranges from 0% to −30%, with the majority of them clustered around −15%.

There is a *strong* correlation between the degree of "discount" and strike zone judgment. As a rule, the more a player walks, and thus the better his strike zone judgment, the less will be his "discount." Interestingly, strikeouts have much less to do with this phenomenon than you would think. So long as his strikeout rate (relative to the league norm) is *below* his walk rate (relative to the league norm), he'll probably be OK. If it's not, we can almost guarantee you he'll struggle.

It's time for a demonstration. Let's look at the TOPR trendlines for the 1990–1993 Rookies-of-the-Year, their minor league TOPRs coming in and their major league TOPRs since. We'll also show their demonstrated strike zone judgment for their last minor league season and their first major league season. This is expressed as relative BB/K frequency—walks (as a % of TPA) relative to the league norm: strikeouts (as a % of TPA) relative to the league norm. Jeff Bagwell, for example, walked +32% more often and struck out only 64% as often as the average Eastern League player in 1990, his last full year in the minors.

The 1992 list includes Kenny Lofton and Reggie Sanders because they were TOPRs Rookies-of-the-Year.

As you can see, there is a strong resemblance between a player's major league performance and his minor league TOPRs. Further, there is a relationship between his BB/K frequency and his minors-to-majors "TOPR discount."

Some interpretive background is in order, however:

◆ Justice took a big step forward upon entering the majors. This is very rare, but you can sense it coming by his sharp improvement in his R-2 year and his excellent BB/K frequency.
◆ Knoblauch and Bagwell both "skipped" a grade, moving to the majors directly from AA. Normally, this would have involved a higher "discount." But their superb BB/K frequencies indicated they were highly polished prospects.
◆ Listach and Karros both took a hickey on their BB/K frequencies upon entering the majors, and neither had much of a margin to

work with. Also, both came out of minor league "hitter's parks" (Denver and Albuquerque) and into major league "pitcher's parks" (Milwaukee and Los Angeles). These factors worked against them, and both surprised us in their rookie year. Listach was better than we thought he'd be. Karros fell off much more than we expected and now appears to be going backward.
◆ Lofton had some caution signs on him as a rookie. He had an off-year in R-1 and a negative BB/K frequency (the only one on this list, by the way). In his favor, though, he had skipped from A+ to AAA ball in his R-1 year and his BB/K frequency in R-2 had been a much more acceptable 113:80 in the Florida State League. He was temporarily overmatched in AAA but adjusted very quickly at the major league level. Whoever's responsible, Kenny or the Cleveland coaching staff, congratulations on making him a top-flight, lead-off hitter.
◆ Piazza looks like he might have overachieved somewhat but his trendline describes a player undergoing *explosive* development. If it continues, look out!

As should be evident, a minor league player's TOPR is generally translatable to a *probable* major league performance level. Prospect TOPR isn't perfect. But a lot of what used to be "guesswork" can now proceed as "informed judgment."

By now, we've analyzed the performance of well over 200 rookie players and over 80% of them fit the pattern we've described. The remainder reveal other patterns for which we've developed "rules-of-thumb." For example: be wary of Blue Jays outfield prospects whose sole apparent credential is one big year at Syracuse. It's likely to be the only one they'll ever have. There's insufficient space here to list all of these "rules-of-thumb," but we'll be applying them to the Prospect Capsules that follow.

What About Prospect TPER?

Alas, there is no Prospect TPER. Available minor league stats for pitchers don't include stats like total bases allowed or ground ball double plays induced. They simply aren't reported.

Total bases allowed are *critical* to a pitcher's TPER calculations. But the only element reported is HRs allowed. We tried several methods of projecting total bases allowed from home run data but discovered that whatever correlation there may be, if any, is a loose one. Ground ball DPs are extremely important to a particular group of pitchers, the sinker-balling Kevin Browns and Bill Swifts-to-be. Ignoring this data risks overlooking these types altogether.

The traditional means of rating pitching prospects, ERA, hits per inning, strikeout to walk ratio, etc., all have some limitations in the minor league environment. We can all agree, can't we, that a pitcher's W–L record in the minors is essentially meaningless?

The problem with ERA and even its companion, total runs allowed per 9 IP, is that they are both highly dependent on context. In the major leagues, we're used to seeing unearned runs accounting for only 8% to 10% of the total runs. We, therefore, know pretty much what an ERA means in this context. In the minor leagues, though, unearned runs amount to a much higher percentage of the total runs. They range from around 15% in the high minors to over 30% in the low minors. We can also assume that the quality of bullpens might be somewhat uneven in the minors. The percent of inherited runners scoring could, therefore, be all over the lot. Both a pitcher's

ERA and his total runs allowed tend to become less reliable indicators of his actual accomplishments in these varied contexts.

In fact, *any* stat that is innings-based is liable to be distorted by this factor. Minor league pitchers suffer through far more 4-out innings than their counterparts in the majors. That makes it tough.

Thus, the first decision we made about analyzing minor league pitchers was to *base everything on Total Batters Faced (TBF)*. The second decision was to maintain our practice of relating all performance data to the particular league's norm in the particular year in which the pitcher performed. Minor league contexts are widely varied. They vary not only from level to level but between leagues at the same level and from year to year. Finally, we decided to present a set of ''TPER indicators'' which would a) present an idea of *what kind of a pitcher* the prospect might be, and b) provide a clue as to his probable effectiveness in TPER terms. For example, here's the minor league line as developed for the Mets' Bobby Jones. He had an encouraging debut after his call-up and is ticketed for the Mets' '94 rotation.

Prospect Capsule:

						TPER Indicators				
		7/1/94		Period	1993	OB	HR	H	BB	K
Pitcher:	Role	Age	Throws	Profiled	Level	Freq	Freq	Freq	*Freq*	*Freq*
Bobby Jones	Starter	24	R	1993	AAA	87	60	95	57	111

Jones is a right-handed starter and will be 24 for the 1994 season. His data comes from his 1993 season at AAA Norfolk. Compared to the norms for the International League, he allowed only 87% as many runners per batter faced (via hit, walk or hit batsman) and gave up only 60% as many home runs per batter faced. These are excellent ratios. Jones was also better than average in terms of hits per batter faced, and walked far fewer batters (total walks less intentional walks) while striking out a few more than the average. He looks like a competent, all-around pitcher. He gives up some hits but has excellent control and doesn't surrender the long ball. A really good prospect.

How did this performance translate to the majors? Let's look at his comparable major league ''TPER Indicators.''

	OB Freq.	HR Freq.	H Freq.	BB Freq.	K Freq.
Bobby Jones NL 1993	99	101	95	98	86

Not surprisingly, he got hit a little harder in the bigs and his control degenerated. He didn't strike out as many hitters as he had in the minors. It's not a *bad* line, though, in any respect. And it produced a 108 TPER over nine starts. Doubtless, rookie pitchers have the same kind of adjustment period in the majors that rookie position players do. Their ability to adjust is likewise going to be importantly dependent on their control of the strike zone just like rookie hitters. Jones' AAA line indicates he can do this, so the signs are that he'll prove to be a solid starter for the Mets next year (mid-to-high-90s TPER, perhaps).

Sometimes, in the translation to the majors, a pitcher's TPER profile changes very little. This was the case with Kevin Appier, a pitcher we now know quite a bit about. Appier came up in '90. Here's what TPER would have told us about his previous year in the minors and how he actually translated into the majors.

	OB Freq.	HR Freq.	H Freq.	BB Freq.	K Freq.
Kevin Appier 1990 AAA	97	68	101	81	117
Kevin Appier 1991 AL	92	80	98	81	110

Palpably the same pitcher as a big leaguer, even a little better. His HR frequency got bruised a bit but we now know that this almost always happens—so that a homer-prone pitcher in the minors might have ''major'' problems in the majors. Nothing else really changed. He seemed to adjust instantly and delivered an 85 TPER in his rookie season. Appier has gone on from there to become the American League's premier starter.

The Prospect Capsules

We've listed twelve prospects for each club, with the mix of hitters and pitchers varying. We've focused first on the personnel that are most likely to help the big club in 1994, whether anyone else agrees with us or not. Some of these won't be classic ''prospects,'' they may have been around a little. But in some cases, TOPR/TPER causes us to believe they could earn a job if they got a chance. We've also included younger prospects from among the ''highly touted'' list, as long as they spent at least half a season at AA. These are the guys you'll start hearing about in '94, but probably won't see until '95.

For hitters, we've included their position, which side they bat from and, of course, their age. Their TOPR Trendline you should now be familiar with, as well as their past year's BB/K frequency (which, remember, is expressed in terms of BB or K as a % of TPA vs. the league's norm).

For pitchers, the line is as shown for Bobby Jones. Only the most recent year is shown since the format precludes showing data for multiple years. If a '92 line is shown, it means that he was hurt in '93 and spent all or most of the year on the DL.

An advance warning: we still consider the ''TPER indicators'' to be experimental. We'd be a lot more comfortable if we could fully TPER-ize the minors (it would be a lot less work, too). One hint on their interpretation: the OB column is ''heaviest'' of the group, containing three TPER elements (H + BB + HP). Use it as a guide—if it's in the 70s or 80s, get *real* interested—then revise it upward or downward based on what you see from left to right. For example, Kirk Rueter's 79 OB frequency was an omen of a 75 TPER in his debut season. In most cases, though, the resultant ''TPER Estimate'' should be revised upward to reflect the normal rookie adjustment period (just as rookie hitters are ''discounted'').

And, now, we present next year's crop . . .

ATLANTA BRAVES

Prospect Capsule: Atlanta Braves

| | | 7/1/94 | | 1993 | | Minor League TOPR | | | BB | K |
Hitters:	Pos	Age	Bats	Level	1991	1992	1993	3 yr Avg	Freq	Freq
Ramon Caraballo	2B	26	B	AAA	103	98	94	**99**	66	93
Chipper Jones	SS	22	R	AAA	170	136	138	**147**	109	69
Ryan Klesko	1B	23	L	AAA	142	103	131	**125**	138	103
Mike Kelly	OF	24	R	AAA	(143)	125	106	**119**	94	136
Javy Lopez	C	23	R	AAA	93	135	111	**113**	35	78
Jose Oliva	3B	23	R	AAA	110	127	102	**113**	93	176
Tony Tarasco	OF	23	L	AAA	111	110	143	**121**	101	77
Jerry Willard	C	34	L	AAA	133	(116)	143	**134**	179	98

| | | 7/1/94 | | | | TPER Indicators | | | | |
| | | | | | | OB | HR | H | BB | K |
Pitchers:	Role	Age	Throws	Year	Level	Freq	Freq	Freq	Freq	Freq
Brian Bark	Starter	25	L	1993	AAA	101	83	93	122	93
Mike Hostetler	Starter	24	R	1993	AA/AAA	93	91	96	77	106
Pedro Borbon	Reliever	26	L	1993	AAA	102	91	88	122	164
Bill Taylor	Closer	32	R	1993	AAA	91	48	85	86	170

NOTE: Frequency is expressed as a percent of TPA or TBF, relative to league norms. ( ) 100-199 TPA or TBF. * less than 100 TPA or TBF.

The Braves built their renaissance on the farm system. Three consecutive division titles and two NL pennants tell you what a good job they did. The talent continues to flow. As to the apparent thinness of pitchers, they're found in the lower classifications.

Players They Kept . . .

Hitters	Pitchers
Ron Gant ('88)	Steve Bedrosian ('82)
Jeff Glauser ('89)	Tom Glavine ('87)
David Justice ('90)	Steve Avery ('90)
Mark Lemke ('90)	Kent Mercker ('90)
	Mike Stanton ('91)

. . . And Ones That Got Away

Hitters	Pitchers
Brett Butler ('82)	Zane Smith ('85)
Milt Thompson ('85)	Paul Assenmacher ('86)
Vinny Castilla ('93)	Duane Ward ('88)
Al Martin ('93)	Derek Lilliquist ('89)
	Tommie Greene ('90)
	Armando Reynoso ('93)
	Ben Rivera ('92)

Something Else You Should Know

The AAA Richmond roster contained a legitimate prospect at all eight positions (the eighth, Melvin Nieves, was traded to San Diego in the McGriff package). Even a DH, if you counted 33-year-old Jerry Willard (who always has, and still can, hit).

Most Promising Prospects

Position Player: Chipper Jones—covered at length in Braves essay . . . nothing else needs to be said.

Pitcher: Mike Hostetler—went 8–5 with 2.72 ERA at AA Greenville . . . 1–3 and 5.06 ERA at AAA suggests he needs another year away from the brick wall of the parent club's rotation.

Sleeper

Pedro Borbon—only 5–5 with 4.23 ERA at Richmond in relief . . . an off year for him . . . still attractive long-relief prospect.

Most Likely to Disappoint

Javy Lopez—will probably have trouble keeping his numbers (.305 BA, 11 HR, .511 SLG) in the majors . . . impatient hitter (11 unintentional BB).

BALTIMORE ORIOLES

Prospect Capsule: Baltimore Orioles

							Minor League TOPR				
		7/1/94		1993				3 yr	BB	K
Hitters:	Pos	Age	Bats	Level	1991	1992	1993	Avg	Freq	Freq
Manny Alexander	SS	28	R	AAA	129	99	83	102	56	71
Damon Buford	OF	24	R	AAA	124	111	(108)	120	96	90
Paul Carey	1B	26	L	AAA	124	122	149	131	172	137
Jeffrey Hammonds	OF	23	R	AA/AAA	-	-	116	116	64	100
Mark Leonard	OF	29	L	AAA	(108)	(140)	147	142	175	118
Sherman Obando	OF/DH	23	R	Major	(141)	127	*	122	74	97
Mark Smith	OF	24	R	AAA	(87)	114	101	104	81	100
Jack Voight	OF	28	R	AAA	111	122	*	122	137	119

						TPER Indicators				
		7/1/94				OB	HR	H	BB	K
Pitchers:	Role	Age	Throws	Year	Level	Freq	Freq	Freq	Freq	Freq
Brian Dubois	Starter	27	L	1993	A+/AA	94	59	100	86	93
Rick Krivda	Starter	24	L	1993	AA/AAA	94	97	89	118	117
Kevin McGehee	Starter	25	R	1993	AAA	96	105	98	82	99
John O'Donoghue	Starter	25	L	1993	AAA	93	91	96	96	121

NOTE: Frequency is expressed as a percent of TPA or TBF, relative to league norms. ( ) 100-199 TPA or TBF. * less than 100 TPA or TBF.

The O's plan a big push in '94 and expect their farm system to help. They may be disappointed. While the farm system annually produces something of value, there seems a poor fit between need and inventory.

Players They Kept . . .

Hitters	Pitchers
Cal Ripken ('82)	Greg Olson ('89)
Leo Gomez ('91)	Ben McDonald ('90)
David Segui ('91)	Mike Mussina ('91)
	Arthur Rhodes ('92)

. . . And Ones That Got Away

Hitters	Pitchers
Eddie Murray ('77)	Dennis Martinez ('77)
Steve Finley ('89)	Pete Harnisch ('89)
Rickey Gutierrez ('93)	Mark Leiter ('91)

Something Else You Should Know

Note the advancing age of some of their top "prospects." Given Ripken's continued durability, "prospect" Alexander may be 35 before he gets a chance.

Most Promising Prospects

Position Player: Jack Voight—O's are looking for an OF and this guy posted a 135 TOPR in 177 TPA with excellent ratio (25 BB: 33 K) . . . can play 1B/3B/OF, so he's handy to have around.
Pitcher: Rick Krivda—advanced five levels in three years . . . 10–5, 2.83 ERA in '93 . . . has a quality look about him.

Sleeper

Brian Dubois—out two years rehabbing with arm trouble . . . 12–5, 2.71 ERA at three levels in '93.

Most Likely to Disappoint

Jeffrey Hammonds—O's are counting on him after .305 BA in '93 major league trial. TOPR has serious reservations . . . trial also produced 105 TOPR (with one unintentional BB in 110 TPA).

BOSTON RED SOX

Prospect Capsule: Boston Red Sox

		7/1/94		1993	Minor League TOPR			3 yr	BB	K
Hitters:	Pos	Age	Bats	Level	1991	1992	1993	Avg	Freq	Freq
Greg Blosser	OF	23	L	AAA	88	131	108	**108**	124	152
John Flaherty	C	26	R	AAA	90	(57)	90	**82**	79	61
Scott Hatteberg	C	24	L	AAA	105	84	105	**97**	167	88
Jeff McNeely	OF	24	R	AAA	141	83	96	**107**	96	109
Tim Naehring	IF	27	R	AAA	-	*	129	**117**	169	66
Luis Ortiz	3B	24	R	AAA	(148)	112	109	**116**	30	104

		7/1/94				TPER Indicators				
						OB	HR	H	BB	K
Pitchers:	Role	Age	Throws	Year	Level	Freq	Freq	Freq	Freq	Freq
Gar Finnvold	Starter	26	R	1993	AAA	96	162	94	111	131
Nate Minchey	Starter	24	R	1993	AAA	91	121	96	76	82
Frank Rodriguez	Starter	21	R	1993	AA	96	131	89	117	122
Tim Vanegmond	Starter	25	R	1993	AA	92	126	100	62	120
Cory Bailey	Closer	23	R	1993	AAA	93	17	78	135	133
Joe Caruso	Utility	23	R	1993	AAA	116	120	105	154	69

NOTE: Frequency is expressed as a percent of TPA or TBF, relative to league norms. ( ) 100-199 TPA or TBF. * less than 100 TPA or TBF.

Historically, the BoSox haven't been much for building through the system. Purportedly, they're now intent on pursuing this avenue. There's been a recent spate of production but it looks like they're about to hit another thin spot.

Players They Kept . . .

Hitters	Pitchers
Mike Greenwell ('87)	Roger Clemens ('84)
Carlos Quintana ('90)	Paul Quantrill ('93)
Mo Vaughn ('91)	Aaron Sele ('93)
Scott Cooper ('92)	Ken Ryan ('93)
Bob Zupcic ('92)	

. . . And Ones That Got Away

Hitters	Pitchers
Wade Boggs ('82)	Tom Bolton ('87)
Ellis Burks ('87)	Curt Schilling ('89)
Brody Anderson ('88)	
Jody Reed ('88)	
Phil Plantier ('91)	
Jeff Bagwell ('91)	

Something Else You Should Know

The Sox keep listening to offers for former #1 pick Rodriguez. Highly touted. But maybe the Boston people have noticed the combination of being homer-prone and wild.

Most Promising Prospects

Position Player: Tim Naehring—doesn't fit "prospect" definition but he'll be the most help.
Pitcher: Cory Bailey—closer prospect . . . 2.88 ERA at Pawtucket, .211 BA against.

Sleeper

Boston believes Scott Hatteberg's making real strides and feels he's in Beantown by '95.

Most Likely to Disappoint

Greg Blosser—has power, little else . . . .228 BA, 28 HR, .312 OBP, 139 K at Pawtucket '93.

CALIFORNIA ANGELS

Prospect Capsule: California Angels

		7/1/94		1993	Minor League TOPR			3 yr	BB	K
Hitters:	Pos	Age	Bats	Level	1991	1992	1993	Avg	Freq	Freq
Garret Anderson	OF	22	L	AAA	74	87	82	**82**	54	119
Jim Edmonds	OF	24	L	AAA	130	131	113	**124**	109	127
Kevin Flora	2B	25	R	AAA	120	122	(102)	**113**	142	96
Jorge Fabregas	C	24	L	AA	-	75	95	**87**	77	78
P. J. Forbes	2B	26	R	AA	92	117	109	**106**	60	54
Eduardo Perez	3B	24	R	AAA	(117)	105	116	**111**	69	133
Chris Turner	C	25	R	AAA	107	143	102	**119**	163	80
		7/1/94			TPER Indicators				BB	K
					OB	HR	H			
Pitchers:	Role	Age	Throws	Year	Level	Freq	Freq	Freq	Freq	Freq
John Fritz	Starter	25	R	1993	AA/AAA	99	107	101	95	92
Hilly Hathaway	Starter	24	L	1993	AAA	86	90	80	110	96
Mark Holzemer	Starter	24	R	1993	AAA	102	73	96	125	79
Phil Leftwich	Starter	25	R	1993	AAA	95	73	97	94	117
Scott Lewis	Reliever	28	R	1993	AAA	73	34	77	53	154
Darryl Scott	Closer	25	R	1993	AAA	75	102	66	98	175

NOTE: Frequency is expressed as a percent of TPA or TBF, relative to league norms. ( ) 100-199 TPA or TBF. * less than 100 TPA or TBF.

Once infatuated with the idea that a championship lay just beyond the next big check, the Angels have gone almost (but not quite) cold turkey. Now, the club emphasizes the farm system and may have found a surer route to their goal.

Players They Kept . . .

Hitters	Pitchers
Chad Curtis ('92)	Chuck Finley ('86)
Gary DiSarcina ('92)	Joe Grahe ('91)
Damion Easley ('92)	
Tim Salmon ('93)	

. . . And The Ones That Got Away

Hitters	Pitchers
Wally Joyner ('86)	Bryan Harvey ('88)
Mark McLemore ('87)	Jim Abbott ('89)
Devon White ('87)	Mark Fetters ('90)
Dante Bichette ('90)	Roberto Hernandez ('92)
	Alan Mills ('92)

Something Else You Should Know

After being awarded extra picks in the '86 draft because they'd lost several free agents, the Angels wound up with a bonanza—five choices in that first round. None of the five players they selected remain with the club. 1B Lee Stevens appeared with them briefly, disappointed and now struggles in the minors to return with the Toronto organization. P Mike Fetters got dealt to Milwaukee. P Roberto Hernandez, now Chicago's star closer, left in a minor trade. P Daryl Green and OF Terry Carr are out of baseball. Total production: 14 HRs and 3 pitching victories.

Most Promising Prospects

Position Player: Kevin Flora—Left the game last year when his wife was killed in a car accident. If he's regrouped emotionally he has the look of a hitter.
Pitcher: Phil Leftwich—'93 was first impressive minor league season (7–7 at Vancouver, with 4.64 ERA . . . OK in PCL) . . . confirmed by major league trial (3.79 ERA, 90 TOPR in 12 starts).

Sleeper

Daryl Scott—nasty stats look like closer numbers . . . 2.19 ERA in 246.2 IP (171 H, 320 K) in four-year minor league career.

Most Likely to Disappoint

Garret Anderson—impressive .293 BA at Vancouver . . . just 21 and already in AAA . . . BUT no walks (31 BB), no power (.409 SLG), no speed (3 SB in seven tries, 15 GDP) . . . will have to hit like Wade Boggs used to (he's LH).

CHICAGO CUBS

Prospect Capsule: Chicago Cubs

Hitters:	Pos	7/1/94 Age	Bats	1993 Level	Minor League TOPR					
					1991	1992	1993	3 yr Avg	BB Freq	K Freq
Matt Franco	1B/3B	24	L	AA/AAA	87	100	123	106	99	74
Doug Glanville	OF	23	R	A+/AA	(126)	99	104	103	78	68
Richie Grayum	OF	25	L	AA	129	123	128	126	177	134
Karl Rhodes	OF	25	L	AAA	76	113	148	116	112	95
Kevin Roberson	OF	26	B	AAA	117	112	133	116	70	148
Matt Walbeck	C	24	B	AAA	93	111	89	98	50	86
Eddie Zambrano	OF	28	R	AAA	103	125	139	124	100	112

Pitchers:	Role	7/1/94 Age	Throws	Year	Level	TPER Indicators				
						OB Freq	HR Freq	H Freq	BB Freq	K Freq
Lance Dickson	Starter	24	L	1993	AA/AAA	87	144	92	84	142
Kenny Steenstra	Starter	23	R	1993	A+/AA	99	68	105	75	84
Steve Trachsel	Starter	23	R	1993	AAA	95	116	101	80	125
Turk Wendell	Starter	27	R	1993	AAA	95	58	97	92	112
Jesse Hollins	Closer	24	R	1992	AAA	97	84	89	127	139

NOTE: Frequency is expressed as a percent of TPA or TBF, relative to league norms. ( ) 100-199 TPA or TBF. * less than 100 TPA or TBF.

The Cubs' farm system is in better shape than it's been for years. At least, the talent available for promotion presents a pick-and-choose proposition, rather than take-it-or-leave-it.

Players They Kept . . .

Hitters	Pitchers
Mark Grace ('88)	Mike Harkey ('90)
Dwight Smith ('89)	Frank Castillo ('91)
Rick Wilkins ('91)	
Derrick May ('92)	

. . . And Ones That Got Away

Hitters	Pitchers
Scott Fletcher ('83)	Lee Smith ('81)
Joe Carter ('84)	Jamie Moyer ('86)
Billy Hatcher ('85)	Greg Maddux ('87)
Dave Martinez ('87)	
Rafael Palmeiro ('87)	
Damon Berryhill ('88)	
Rich Amaral ('93)	

Something Else You Should Know

During the 25 years from the amateur draft's inception in 1965 through 1989, the Cubs made 27 first-round picks. They were to harvest from these picks only four players who became major league regulars—Roger Metzger ('69: 1,219 major league games), Joe Carter ('81: 1,499 games), Rafael Palmeiro ('85: 1,046) and Shawon Dunston ('82: 925 games). Dunston's still with the club, of course, but the Cubs themselves got a grand total of 282 games out of the other three. How about pitchers you ask? How about Drew Hall? He appeared in 125 major league games—the most of any pitcher on the list (and only 45 of them with the Cubs). The most recent floppolas? Ty Griffin in '88 and Earl Cunningham in '89. Definitely not a pretty picture. Who does their drafting—Stephen King?

Most Promising Prospects

Position Player: Karl "Tubby" Rhodes—Traded by both Houston and KC during the season . . . '93 numbers at AAA were fantastic . . . hit .318 with 30 HR and .602 SLG between Omaha and Iowa . . . led Amer Assoc in runs (112), doubles (43), extra-base hits, total bases and slugging . . . trouble is, he's never before had a season remotely like it (previous career HR high: 4!) . . . sense that Astro organization was trying to make him something he wasn't (ground-ball hitting speed merchant) . . . Cubs may come up smelling like roses on this one.
Pitcher: Nothing looks really noteworthy.

Sleeper

None.

Most Likely to Disappoint

Kevin Roberson—hangs up big power numbers (16 HR in 67 G at Iowa, 9 in 62 G with the Cubs) . . . but does little else . . . 82 TOPR with the big club a product of strike zone judgement (12 BB, 48 K). One time around the league last year and the advance scouts had already found the "holes" in his swing.

CHICAGO WHITE SOX

Prospect Capsule: Chicago White Sox

Hitters:	Pos	7/1/94 Age	Bats	1993 Level	Minor League TOPR 1991	1992	1993	3 yr Avg	BB Freq	K Freq
Ray Durham	2B	22	B	AA	(139)	148	99	116	80	97
Warren Newson	OF	29	L	AAA	(169)	*	148	147	196	113
Mike Robertson	1B	23	L	AA	109	112	107	109	112	96
Brandon Wilson	SS	25	R	AA	138	125	103	121	109	79
Jerry Wolak	OF	23	R	AA	115	113	104	110	50	97

Pitchers:	Role	7/1/94 Age	Throws	Year	Level	TPER Indicators OB Freq	HR Freq	H Freq	BB Freq	K Freq
James Baldwin	Starter	22	R	1993	AA/AAA	87	68	76	124	131
Rodney Bolton	Starter	25	R	1993	AAA	92	84	93	90	100
Robert Ellis	Starter	23	R	1993	A+/AA	84	46	86	80	127
Steve Olsen	Starter	24	R	1993	AA	105	188	109	96	86
Scott Ruffcorn	Starter	24	R	1993	AA/AAA	83	74	81	96	149
Steve Schrenk	Starter	25	R	1993	AA/AAA	83	76	83	84	108
Larry Thomas	Starter	24	L	1993	AAA	100	139	108	80	99

NOTE: Frequency is expressed as a percent of TPA or TBF, relative to league norms. ( ) 100-199 TPA or TBF. * less than 100 TPA or TBF.

Previously moribund, the Sox system has only recently begun to draft and develop quality players. Their recent production and success is proof. The system's excess of pitchers allows trading for the players they need.

Players They Kept . . .

Hitters	Pitchers
Daryl Boston ('85)	Jack McDowell ('88)
Ron Karkovice ('90)	Donn Pall ('89)
Frank Thomas ('90)	Alex Fernandez ('90)
Robin Ventura ('90)	Scott Radinsky ('90)
	Jason Bere ('93)

. . . And Ones That Got Away

Hitters	Pitchers
Harold Baines ('80)	Doug Drabek ('86)
Randy Velarde ('90)	

Something Else You Should Know

Got "lucky" in '85. Picking two spots in front of them, Texas went for a football player taking Texas Tech DB Donald Harris (a bust) and leaving Auburn TE Frank Thomas for the White Sox at #7.

Most Promising Prospects

Position Player: Warren Newson—"The Deacon" would look great in the top of the Sox order . . . career major league .406 OBP in 382 PA . . . walks a *lot* . . . but can hit some and run a little to boot.
Pitcher: James Baldwin and Scott Ruffcorn—pitched extraordinarily at Birmingham and Nashville . . . young "ace" quality pitchers.

Sleeper

None. All the pitchers have gotten their due notice and appear to merit it.

Most Likely to Disappoint

Brandon Wilson—of whom great things were expected . . . looks like he's increasingly overmatched as he moves up the ladder.

CINCINNATI REDS

Prospect Capsule: Cincinnati Reds

Hitters:	Pos	7/1/94 Age	Bats	1993 Level	Minor League TOPR 1991	1992	1993	3 yr Avg	BB Freq	K Freq
Bret Boone	2B	25	R	AAA	114	124	110	**116**	107	119
Tim Costo	1B	25	R	AAA	98	128	123	**115**	67	100
Jamie Dismuke	1B	24	L	AA	104	131	127	**120**	88	61
Steve Gibralter	OF	21	R	AA	92	136	80	**102**	42	122
Willie Greene	SS/3B	22	L	AAA	120	140	126	**130**	155	136
Pokey Reese	SS	21	R	AA	88	110	76	**92**	69	117

Pitchers:	Role	7/1/94 Age	Throws	Year	Level	TPER Indicators OB Freq	HR Freq	H Freq	BB Freq	K Freq
Larry Luebbers	Starter	24	R	1993	AAA	106	75	89	139	87
John Roper	Starter	22	R	1992	AA	95	135	100	82	109
Jeff Pierce	Closer	25	R	1993	AA	77	77	80	65	141
Johnny Ruffin	Reliever	22	R	1993	AAA	79	77	80	61	182
Scott Service	Reliever	22	R	1993	AAA	88	24	71	124	192
Jerry Spradlin	Reliever	27	R	1993	AAA	88	68	101	53	125

NOTE: Frequency is expressed as a percent of TPA or TBF, relative to league norms. ( ) 100-199 TPA or TBF. * less than 100 TPA or TBF.

The organization has benefited in the past from an assembly-line-like progression of both stars and serviceable regulars. This may be changing—only half of the prospects capsulized above were originally signed by the Reds' organization. Most of the rest have come in trade for an established player.

Players They Kept . . .

Hitters	Pitchers
Barry Larkin ('86)	Tom Browning ('85)
Chris Sabo ('88)	Rob Dibble ('88)
Joe Oliver ('88)	Bobby Ayala ('93)
Reggie Sanders ('92)	Tim Pugh ('93)

. . . And Ones That Got Away

Hitters	Pitchers
Gary Redus ('83)	Charlie Leibrandt ('80)
Eric Davis ('84)	Jay Howell ('83)
Danny Tartabull ('86)	Jeff Russell ('83)
Paul O'Neill ('87)	Jack Armstrong ('87)
Eddie Taubensee ('92)	Jeff Montgomery ('88)
Chuck Carr ('93)	Chris Hammond ('91)
Reggie Jefferson ('93)	

Something Else You Should Know

Owner Marge Schott was reportedly once heard to say something like "Who needs scouts? All they ever do is watch baseball games." Oh, yeah, this system figures to bear lots of fruit, eh? Maybe lots of "dogs" instead.

Most Promising Prospects

Position Player: Willie Greene—lefty-hitting 3B prospect with power who walks . . . former lst-round draft pick (Pirates) . . . traded twice in first 3 years, but always for quality (to Expos in Zane Smith package, to Reds in Wetteland package) . . . hit .267 at AAA Indianapolis in '93 with 22 HR and .516 SLG in 98 G.
Pitcher: Johnny Ruffin—RH pitcher acquired from Sox in Belcher trade . . . had '93 ERA of 3.11, with 51 H, 75 K, only 18 BB in 66.2 IP at AAA . . . call-up to Cincy yielded similar line (3.58 ERA, with 36 H, 30 K, only 11 BB in 37.2 IP) . . . major league TPER encouraging, but on high side (107) . . . got hurt by long ball, which indicators say won't happen much . . . worked exclusively set-up role all year . . . but always started in the past . . . could probably close, too.

Sleeper

Scott Service—not established yet . . . but consistent success in 7-year minor league career . . . impressive TPER indicator line above (from '92 at Indianapolis and Nashville) . . . strong '93 major league outing (3.70 ERA in 26 relief App., 41.1 IP) with 99 TPER . . . has all the makings of a quality major league long reliever . . . no big deal (until you need one) . . . deserves a job.

Most Likely to Disappoint

John Roper—presents a decent (but not outstanding) TPER line . . . except for HRs, which could kill him . . . and they did, 15 starts with Reds produced 2–5 record with ugly 5.63 ERA . . . 10 HR in 80 IP . . . still young enough to regroup.

CLEVELAND INDIANS

Prospect Capsule: Cleveland Indians

		7/1/94		1993	Minor League TOPR				BB	K
Hitters:	Pos	Age	Bats	Level	1991	1992	1993	3 yr Avg	Freq	Freq
Mark Lewis	SS	24	R	AAA	102	96	103	**101**	69	81
Manny Ramirez	OF	22	R	AA/AAA	228	135	166	**169**	126	105
Jim Thome	3B	23	L	AAA	125	110	169	**138**	174	112
Omar Ramirez	OF	23	R	AA	122	126	122	**123**	101	49

		7/1/94				TPER Indicators				
						OB	HR	H	BB	K
Pitchers:	Role	Age	Throws	Year	Level	Freq	Freq	Freq	Freq	Freq
Paul Byrd	Starter	23	R	1993	AAA	98	117	95	106	94
Alan Embree	Starter	24	L	1992	A+/AA	91	99	93	94	129
Albie Lopez	Starter	22	R	1993	AA	87	121	76	114	103
Dave Mlicki	Starter	26	R	1992	AA	98	82	89	127	122
Chad Ogea	Starter	23	R	1993	AAA	92	155	96	91	107
Julian Tavarez	Starter	21	R	1993	A+/AA	85	84	91	62	113
Jerry Dipoto	Closer	26	R	1993	AAA	83	51	82	79	147
Bill Wertz	Reliever	27	R	1993	AAA	84	87	87	61	135

NOTE: Frequency is expressed as a percent of TPA or TBF, relative to league norms. ( ) 100-199 TPA or TBF. * less than 100 TPA or TBF.

The Indians have come a long, long, *long* way. This organization was in the pits only a few years ago. Now, they're in such good shape we had to cull out several deserving positional prospects from the list just so we could include the pitchers which are of greater current interest and importance to the big league effort.

Players They Kept . . .

Hitters	Pitchers
Albert Belle ('93)	Charles Nagy ('90)
	Jerry Dipoto ('93)
	Tom Kramer ('93)
	Bill Wertz ('93)

. . . And Ones That Got Away

Hitters	Pitchers
Cory Snyder ('86)	Dennis Eckersley ('75)
Dave Clark ('88)	Larry Andersen ('81)
	Greg Swindell ('86)
	Jeff Shaw ('90)

Something Else You Should Know

Jim Thome and Manny Ramirez both ranked in the top five of all minor league hitters TOPRs in '93 (first and fourth, respectively).

Most Promising Prospects

Position Player: Jim Thome—could take the AL by storm in '94, but the league's been forewarned (134 TOPR in late-season call-up, 192 PA) . . . should hit for average, power and walk, too (.332 BA, 25 HR, 102 RBI, .585 SLG with 76 BB at Charlotte in '93).
Pitcher: Julian Tavarez—got a look-see in '93, but was hit hard (6.57 ERA in 37 IP) . . . never mind, he's very young . . . 13–6, 2.22 ERA at Kinston and Canton, with strong TPER indicators. Means he's only a season or two away. But don't rush him.

Sleeper

None.

Most Likely to Disappoint

None. All expectations for their prospects we're aware of seem to be supportable by TOPR and TPER.

COLORADO ROCKIES

Prospect Capsule: Colorado Rockies

		7/1/94		1993	Minor League TOPR			3 yr	BB	K
Hitters:	Pos	Age	Bats	Level	1991	1992	1993	Avg	Freq	Freq
Jason Bates	SS	23	B	AAA	-	147	94	**111**	95	123
Pedro Castellano	1B/3B	24	R	AAA	127	93	118	**113**	120	112
Nelson Liriano	IF	30	B	AAA	100	122	117	**114**	119	60
Roberto Mejia	2B	22	R	AAA	(112)	121	108	**114**	68	113
Jayhawk Owens	C	25	R	AAA	115	118	123	**120**	104	112
Eric Wedge	C/1B	26	R	AAA	110	130	(112)	**119**	124	106

		7/1/94			TPER Indicators				BB	K
						OB	HR	H		
Pitchers:	Role	Age	Throws	Year	Level	Freq	Freq	Freq	Freq	Freq
John Burke	Starter	24	R	1993	A+/AAA	95	36	87	121	126
Ryan Hawblitzel	Starter	23	R	1993	AAA	101	110	112	76	75
Curt Leskanic	Starter	26	R	1993	AAA	97	81	78	158	123
Dave Nied	Starter	25	R	1992	AAA	87	111	92	74	141
Lance Painter	Starter	26	L	1993	AAA	99	86	105	81	94
Mark Thompson	Starter	22	R	1993	A+/AAA	76	53	76	70	139

NOTE: Frequency is expressed as a percent of TPA or TBF, relative to league norms. ( ) 100-199 TPA or TBF. * less than 100 TPA or TBF.

When the time arrived to create the Colorado Rockies from scratch, management opted for a conservative recipe. Compared to their expansion-mate Florida, Colorado's draft selections were generally older and more experienced. The Rockies left the table on draft day with nine established major league players on their roster, the Marlins with only five. Altogether, over ⅔ of the Rockies' players had some major league experience—compared to barely half of the new Marlins. Essentially, the Rockies chose to give draft priority to the major league team they would field in '93 and then address their future development needs. As a consequence, 15 of their original 36 players formed the core of the Rockies' '93 major league roster. Ten more remain with the organization in the minor league system, the other eleven having been traded or released.

In lieu of a production history, we'll use the draft picks as a "farm system."

Draft Disposition

With Parent Club in '93		Played Elsewhere in '93	
Hitters	Pitchers	Hitters	Pitchers
Majors:			
Joe Girardi	David Nied	Brad Ausmus	Andy Ashby
Charlie Hayes	Darren Holmes		Butch Henry
Eric Young	Willie Blair		
Freddie Benavides	Armando Reynoso		
Roberto Mejia	Steve Reed		
Vinny Castilla			
Jerald Clark			
Alex Cole			
Dante Bichette			
Jim Tatum			
Minors:			
Pedro Castellano	Lance Painter	Braulio Castillo	Scott Aldred
Eric Wedge	Ryan Hawblitzel		Doug Bochtler
Jay Owens	Keith Shepherd		Brett Merriman
	Marcus Moore		Calvin Jones

With Parent Club in '93		Played Elsewhere in '93	
Hitters	Pitchers	Hitters	Pitchers
	Mo Sanford		Denis Boucher
	Curt Leskanic		
	Scott Frederickson		

Most Promising Prospects

Position Player: Jason Bates—from '92 amateur draft . . . switch-hitting SS . . . leap-frogged three levels from short-season A to spend entire '93 season at AAA in 2nd pro year . . . performed credibly under circumstances . . . hit .267 with 13 HR and 62 RBI, scored 76 R . . . BB/K ratio took understandable dip (56 BB: 55 K at Bend, 45:99 at Colorado Springs) . . . could develop into a good-hitting major league SS, with ability to get on base and a little power.

Pitcher: Mark Thompson—also from '92 amateur draft . . . RH jumped from A+ to AAA in mid-season . . . went combined 6–2 with 2.36 ERA in 15 starts . . . only gave up 77 H and 29 BB in 103 IP, striking out 94 . . . has now dominated hitters at three minor league levels . . . unfazed by high-altitude "hitter's park" in AAA Colorado Springs, gave up single HR in 33.1 IP . . . shut down early for precautionary measures . . . arm well worth protecting.

Sleeper

Eric Wedge—expansion draft from Boston . . . various injuries have seriously limited playing time since signing (only 38 G in '93) . . . career to date mostly fragments, few of them healthy . . . but healthy fragments suggest scary potential . . . see 130 TOPR above in '92 half-season at AAA Pawtucket (.299 BA, .389 OBP, .490 SLG) . . . add tantalizing '92 trial at Boston (.250 BA, .500 SLG, with 5 HR in 82 PA, a 147 TOPR) . . . drafting him a gamble, but a good one.

Most Likely to Disappoint

None—We're not aware of any inflated expectations.

DETROIT TIGERS

Prospect Capsule: Detroit Tigers

Hitters:	Pos	7/1/94 Age	Bats	1993 Level	Minor League TOPR 1991	1992	1993	3 yr Avg	BB Freq	K Freq
Danny Bautista	OF	22	R	AA	65	87	101	**87**	76	86
Chris Gomez	SS	23	R	AAA	-	86	82	**84**	94	71
Shawn Hare	OF	27	L	AAA	121	140	110	**120**	72	104
Rich Rowland	C	27	R	AAA	119	106	131	**117**	159	112

Pitchers:	Role	7/1/94 Age	Throws	Year	Level	TPER Indicators OB Freq	HR Freq	H Freq	BB Freq	K Freq
Sean Bergman	Starter	24	R	1993	AAA	112	80	105	134	107
Brian Blomdahl	Starter	23	R	1993	AA/AAA	98	101	99	93	96
Greg Gohr	Starter	26	R	1993	AAA	107	148	112	94	94
Frank Gonzales	Starter	26	R	1993	AAA	103	116	107	99	91
Buddy Groom	Starter	28	L	1993	AAA	94	53	100	87	100
Jose Lima	Starter	21	R	1993	AA	91	142	94	85	108
Felipe Lira	Starter	22	R	1993	AA/AAA	96	145	106	70	110
Justin Thompson	Starter	21	R	1993	A+/AA	107	107	114	99	116

NOTE: <u>Frequency</u> is expressed as a percent of TPA or TBF, relative to league norms. ( ) 100-199 TPA or TBF. * less than 100 TPA or TBF.

The Tigers' farm system continues to struggle. With the major league club already going grey, they're going to need some kids *eventually*. They don't have many. We've focused on pitching because, if the big club is to get over the hump in '94, that's what they'll be needing.

Players They Kept . . .

Hitters	Pitchers
Alan Trammell ('78)	Mark Henneman ('87)
Lou Whitaker ('78)	John Doherty ('90)
Kirk Gibson ('80)	
Travis Fryman ('90)	
Milt Cuyler ('91)	

. . . And Ones That Got Away

Hitters	Pitchers
Howard Johnson ('82)	Jack Morris ('78)
Doug Strange ('89)	Carl Willis ('86)
Chris Hoiles ('91)	Roger Mason ('86)
Torey Lovullo ('93)	John Smoltz ('88)
Phil Clark ('93)	Ken Hill ('89)

Something Else You Should Know

For some reason, all the Tiger pitching prospects look almost alike—average across-the-board, maybe a little HR-prone. During their major league break-in period, that tends to lead to ugly ERAs—especially in Tiger Stadium. If they last long enough, it means they're decent middle-of-the-staff candidates.

Most Promising Prospects

Position Player: Rich Rowland—a C with a power bat (21 HR, .548 SLG at Toledo in '93) and good K zone judgment . . . probably a major league hitter . . . with Kreuter and Tettleton in front of him, we may never know. Somebody get this guy out of Detroit and give him a chance.

Pitcher: Jose Lima—but that's pushing it . . . 8–13, 4.07 ERA at London in '93 . . . young enough to maybe learn to control HR tendency . . . same goes for Felipe Lira (11–6, 3.58 ERA, but even more "hittable" than Lima—.267 BA against vs. Lima's .238).

Sleeper

Danny Bautista. Extremely raw natural athlete. Could be a tease. Could be a real star. Note the steady upward TOPR trend even as he's going up through the minor league classifications.

Most Likely to Disappoint

There's a real risk that *all* the pitchers will.

FLORIDA MARLINS

Prospect Capsule: Florida Marlins

		7/1/94		1993		Minor League TOPR		3 yr	BB	K
Hitters:	Pos	Age	Bats	Level	1991	1992	1993	Avg	Freq	Freq
Steve Decker	C	28	R	D.L.	(113)	90	-	**104**	99	87
Carl Everett	OF	24	B	A+/AAA	114	123	137	**125**	84	165
Monty Fariss	1B/OF	26	R	AAA	125	140	99	**120**	160	155
Rob Natal	C	28	R	Major	128	119	*	**122**	77	69
Scott Pose	OF	27	L	AAA	105	122	82	**103**	103	51
Darrell Whitmore	OF	25	L	AAA	*	117	116	**115**	87	112
Nigel Wilson	OF	24	L	AAA	145	135	119	**133**	52	167

		7/1/94				TPER Indicators				
						OB	HR	H	BB	K
Pitchers:	Role	Age	Throws	Year	Level	Freq	Freq	Freq	Freq	Freq
John Johnstone	Starter	25	R	1993	AAA	102	130	101	104	124
Kurt Miller	Starter	21	R	1993	AA/AAA	106	83	94	153	80
Mike Myers	Starter	25	L	1993	AAA	99	143	103	83	97
David Weathers	Starter	24	R	1993	AAA	92	103	95	87	121
Kip Yaughn	Starter	24	R	1992	AA	85	96	84	84	137

NOTE: <u>Frequency</u> is expressed as a percent of TPA or TBF, relative to league norms. ( ) 100-199 TPA or TBF. * less than 100 TPA or TBF.

After the November '92 expansion draft, the Marlins commenced their major league baseball operation with an inventory of 38 players (draft day trades resulted in a net addition of two players beyond the 36 originally drafted). At the end of the '93 season, only 26 of these players remained in the Marlins' organization—10 had been traded and 2 released. For a new club shaping its roster, the turnover rate isn't particularly surprising. But it's shocking to find that *only ten* of the original 38 played a significant role on the major league club in '93. The other 16 players remaining played their parts in the minors. In effect, the Marlins invested more draft picks in the Edmonton and High Desert rosters than they did in the major league roster. On draft day '92, the Marlins went about drafting their '95 team.

In lieu of a production history, we'll treat the draft as their "farm system."

Draft Disposition

With Parent Club in '93		Played Elsewhere in '93	
Hitters	Pitchers	Hitters	Pitchers
Majors:			
Bret Barberie	Pat Rapp	Chris Donnels	Trevor Hoffman
Jeff Conine	Bryan Harvey		Cris Carpenter
Alex Arias*	Jack Armstrong		
Walt Weiss*	Richie Lewis		
Chuck Carr	Ryan Bowen		
Minors:			
Steve Decker	Kip Yaughn	Gary Scott*	Jose Martinez
Ramon Martinez	David Weathers		Andres Berumen
Nigel Wilson	John Johnstone		Jamie McAndrew
Rob Natal	Robert Person		Jeff Tabaka
Darrel Whitmore	Jim Corsi		Brian Griffiths*

*Acquired in draft day trades

With Parent Club in '93		Played Elsewhere in '93	
Hitters	Pitchers	Hitters	Pitchers
Jesus Tavarez	Joey Adamson*		Hector Carrasco*
Carl Everett	Matt Whisenant*		
Kerwin Moore			
Monty Fariss			

Most Promising Prospects

Position Player: Carl Everett—drafted from Yankee organization . . . young switch-hitter seems to have it all . . . at advanced A (59 G) and AAA (34 G) in '93, he hit for average (.296 BA) . . . added surprising power (16 HR, 51 extra-base hits, .535 SLG) . . . ran like a rabbit (36 SB, 10 triples) . . . and was brilliant in CF (.985 fielding pct. would've led Cal League outfielders, unbelievable 12 OFA in 34 G was 3rd highest in PCL) . . . only fly in ointment is negative BB/K rate.

Pitcher: Kip Yaughn—drafted from O's chain . . . was shut down in late '92 and missed most of '93 with arm troubles . . . in 18 starts at AA Hagerstown in '92, went 7–8 with 3.48 ERA . . . his TPER indicator's much more impressive . . . was only 3rd pro season and has shown steady improvement each year in both control and HR allowed rate . . . if arm is sound, won't take long until he challenges for job in major league rotation.

Sleeper

None

Most Likely to Disappoint

Nigel Wilson—club 1st-draft pick (#2 overall) . . . at AAA Edmonton, hit .292 with 17 HR and 68 RBI in 96 G . . . essentially duplicated his past 3-year performance in every respect . . . which includes striking out once a game and walking once a week . . . only 18 unintentional BB and 108 K in '93 . . . terrible BB/K frequency suggests major league pitchers will cut him to shreds.

HOUSTON ASTROS

Prospect Capsule: Houston Astros

Hitters:	Pos	7/1/94 Age	Bats	1993 Level	Minor League TOPR 1991	1992	1993	3 yr Avg	BB Freq	K Freq
Braulio Castillo	OF	26	R	AAA	123	109	137	**120**	98	141
Chris Hatcher	OF	25	R	AA	106	147	96	**113**	36	151
Orlando Miller	SS	25	R	AAA	93	100	116	**105**	42	101
Jamie Mouton	2B	25	R	AAA	149	161	133	**146**	133	81
Phil Nevin	3B	23	R	AAA	-	-	98	**98**	118	123
Roberto Petagine	1B	23	L	AA	121	151	168	**146**	173	95
Fletcher Thompson	2B	25	L	AA	141	DNP	124	**133**	182	124

Pitchers:	Role	7/1/94 Age	Throws	Year	Level	TPER Indicators OB Freq	HR Freq	H Freq	BB Freq	K Freq
Jeff Juden	Starter	23	R	1993	AAA	97	55	90	119	131
Alvin Morman	Starter	25	L	1993	AA	86	95	84	93	146
Shane Reynolds	Starter	26	R	1993	AAA	83	36	98	43	115
James Dougherty	Closer	26	R	1993	AA	90	77	81	133	151
Todd Jones	Closer	26	R	1993	AAA	103	119	87	156	129

NOTE: Frequency is expressed as a percent of TPA or TBF, relative to league norms. ( ) 100-199 TPA or TBF. * less than 100 TPA or TBF.

The Astros turned over the franchise to youngsters in '91, blowing all the deadwood away. It turned out to be the right decision and the farm system has reinforcements on the way. As yet, the Astros haven't had enough products get away to populate the league, have they?

Players They Kept . . .

Hitters	Pitchers
Ken Caminiti ('87)	Darryl Kile ('91)
Craig Biggio ('89)	Brian Williams ('92)
Eric Anthony ('90)	
Andujar Cedeno ('91)	
Luis Gonzalez ('91)	
Scott Servais ('92)	

. . . And Ones That Got Away

Hitters	Pitchers
Kenny Lofton ('92)	Ryne Bowen ('91)

Something Else You Should Know

The Houston system's yield of only 10 regulars or key role players active in the majors during '93 is the lowest total for any farm system (expansion teams excluded). The Astros won two division titles ('80 and '86) and regularly contended throughout the eighties. But as they reaped they did not sow. A new G.M. took over in '87 and quietly rebuilt the system to its current high level of productivity. That new G.M. is now ex-G.M. Bill Wood.

Most Promising Prospects

Position Player: Jamie Mouton—a big, big year in the PCL . . . hit .315 with 16 HR (plus 42 doubles and 12 triples), 92 RBI and 40 SB . . . scored 126 R in 134 G . . . played 2B like the converted outfielder he is (43 E, .936 fielding pct.) . . . a move back to the OF probable.

Pitcher: Shane Reynolds—went 10–6 with 3.62 ERA at Tucson . . . *very* encouraging TPER indicators.

Sleeper

Jeff Juden—if he loses 50 pounds.

Most Likely to Disappoint

Chris Hatcher—Astros waiting for his power bat . . . only 15 HR and .439 SLG at AA Jackson . . . little concept of strike zone (11 BB in 101 G) . . . it may be a long wait . . . Another Eric Anthony?

KANSAS CITY ROYALS

Prospect Capsule: Kansas City Royals

Hitters:	Pos	7/1/94 Age	Bats	1993 Level	Minor League TOPR 1991	1992	1993	3 yr Avg	BB Freq	K Freq
Bob Hamelin	1B	26	L	AAA	(82)	133	130	**124**	159	106
Shane Halter	SS	24	R	A+/AA	103	114	101	**106**	114	120
Kevin Koslofski	OF	27	L	AAA	136	114	102	**116**	113	106
Les Norman	OF	25	R	AA	(87)	126	127	**122**	100	91
Joe Randa	3B	24	R	AA	163	113	108	**122**	79	75
Terry Shumpert	2B	27	R	AAA	-	65	131	**111**	106	83
Michael Tucker	2B	22	L	A+/AA	-	DNP	144	**144**	157	96
Joe Vitiello	1B	24	R	AA	95	119	129	**117**	135	114

Pitchers:	Role	7/1/94 Age	Throws	Year	Level	TPER Indicators OB Freq	HR Freq	H Freq	BB Freq	K Freq
Brian Bevil	Starter	22	R	1993	A+/AA	87	70	83	102	110
Mark Fyrhie	Starter	24	R	1993	AA	110	100	107	121	59
Dera Clark	Reliever	28	R	1993	AAA	98	184	101	99	97
Chris Limbach	Reliever	26	L	1993	AA	85	69	96	68	124

NOTE: <u>Frequency</u> is expressed as a percent of TPA or TBF, relative to league norms. ( ) 100-199 TPA or TBF. * less than 100 TPA or TBF.

hen the Royals placed strong reliance on their farm system, it helped them build a solid contending club that won championships. For some reason, they got away from it and became major players in the free agent market. Reportedly, the grow-your-own idea is back in vogue. But it doesn't show up in this year's prospect capsule. It took digging to find 12 presentables.

Players They Kept . . .

Hitters	Pitchers
George Brett ('74)	Mark Gubicza ('84)
Mike Macfarlane ('88)	David Cone ('87)
Brian McRae ('90)	Tom Gordon ('89)
	Kevin Appier ('90)
	Hipolito Pichardo ('92)

. . . And Ones That Got Away

Hitters	Pitchers
Don Slaught ('83)	Tom Candiotti ('83)
Cecil Fielder ('87)	Bret Saberhagen ('84)
Bo Jackson ('87)	Danny Jackson ('84)
Kevin Seitzer ('87)	Melido Perez ('88)
Sean Berry ('93)	Greg Hibbard ('89)
	Joel Johnston ('93)

Something Else You Should Know

The Royals had an excellent '91 draft. It's only beginning to show at the AA level. Maybe the times are 'achangin'.

Most Promising Prospects

Position Player: Michael Tucker—from the '92 draft . . . played with Olympic team in '92 . . . .292 BA, .435 SLG (with 15 HR, 79 RBI) and 24 SB in '93 . . . may be in the majors by mid-season (could switch to OF).

Pitcher: Brian Bevel—from aforementioned '91 draft . . . made it through Advanced A unscathed (7–1, 2.30 ERA, .180 BA against) . . . got touched up at AA (3.3, 4.36 ERA, .281 BA against), then shut down . . . work ethic has been questioned.

Sleeper

None.

Most Likely to Disappoint

Joe Randa—was the 3B prospect the Royals were waiting for . . . TOPR trendline is steadily downhill as he progresses upward . . . '93 numbers at Memphis impressive (.295 BA, 11 HR, 72 RBI) but his 109 TOPR isn't.

LOS ANGELES DODGERS

Prospect Capsule: Los Angeles Dodgers

Hitters:	Pos	7/1/94 Age	Bats	1993 Level	Minor League TOPR 1991	1992	1993	3 yr Avg	BB Freq	K Freq
Billy Ashley	OF	23	R	AAA	110	118	118	**117**	77	173
Mike Busch	3B	25	R	AAA	*	108	118	**122**	117	113
Roger Cedeño	OF	19	B	AA	-	143	100	**116**	111	99
Todd Hollandsworth	OF	20	L	AA	113	108	108	**109**	69	111
Raul Mondesi	OF	23	R	AAA	109	117	91	**102**	37	119
Henry Rodriguez	1B/OF	26	L	AAA	83	112	(102)	**110**	71	96

Pitchers:	Role	7/1/94 Age	Throws	Year	Level	TPER Indicators OB Freq	HR Freq	H Freq	BB Freq	K Freq
John DeSilva	Starter	26	R	1993	AAA	93	86	92	109	119
Rich Gorecki	Starter	20	R	1993	AA	95	49	89	120	103
Greg Hansell	Starter	23	R	1993	AAA	115	99	107	146	79
Jose Parra	Starter	21	R	1993	AA	82	118	98	29	109
Ben VanRyn	Starter	22	L	1993	AA/AAA	94	47	95	102	131
Kip Gross	Utility	29	R	1993	AAA	86	70	86	79	117

NOTE: Frequency is expressed as a percent of TPA or TBF, relative to league norms. ( ) 100-199 TPA or TBF. * less than 100 TPA or TBF.

Note the imbalance between hitters and pitchers in LA's production history. The quantity's one thing. The quality's another. Mike Piazza emerges as the first offensive player of well above average quality the system's produced since, good Lord, WHO? Pedro Guerrero? Nope, he originally signed with Cleveland. Sorry, Steve Sax doesn't count. It has to be the Lopes-Cey-Garvey trio from the early seventies. Twenty years between hitters! Without checking, we'd wager no other system has suffered such an extended drought. As a result, the Dodgers have been forced to work overtime developing excess pitching, to be exchanged via trade for every shred of positive offense it can bring. Over reliance on a single crop, we're told, is a dangerous farming practice.

Players They Kept . . .

Hitters	Pitchers
Eric Karros ('92)	Orel Hershiser ('84)
Jose Offerman ('92)	Ramon Martinez ('89)
Mike Piazza ('93)	Pedro Astacio ('92)
	Pedro Martinez ('93)

. . . And Ones That Got Away

Hitters	Pitchers
Mariano Duncan ('85)	Charlie Hough ('73)
Mike Devereaux ('89)	Bob Welch ('78)
Chris Gwynn ('90)	Rick Sutcliffe ('79)
Jose Vizcaino ('91)	Steve Howe ('80)
Darrin Fletcher ('92)	Dave Stewart ('81)
Wayne Kirby ('93)	Fernando Valenzuela ('81)
	John Franco ('84)
	Sid Fernandez ('85)
	John Wetteland ('89)
	Mike Hartley ('90)
	Juan Guzman ('91)
	Darren Holmes ('91)
	Jim Poole ('91)

Something Else You Should Know

Albuquerque, the Dodgers' AAA farm, is a "hitter's park" in the PCL, a "hitter's league." Offensive stats for their hitters are thus inflated. The Dodgers know this, because they aren't afraid of an Albuquerque pitcher's bloated ERA (when he got The Call in mid-season '92, Pedro Astacio's ERA stood at 5.47). But they are afraid, rightly, of big hitting numbers—which could mean anything (e.g., a Karros or a Piazza).

Most Promising Prospects

Position Player: Roger Cedeno—19-year-old switch-hitting CF . . . played his first full professional season at AA San Antonio . . . a good one (.288 BA, 28 SB, decent K zone judgement, 100 TOPR), given he was well beyond his age group . . . tore up rookie-level Pioneer League in '92, probably would have done the same at Class A in '93 . . . but the Dodgers want him ready by '95 (when Butler's contract runs out).

Pitcher: Ben VanRyn—went 14–4 at AA with 2.21 ERA before call-up to Albuquerque (and a brutal lesson) . . . young LH from the Expos' chain with a good-looking TPER line.

Sleeper

Woe to any Dodger publicist who allowed any kid prospect to be labeled a "sleeper." But would you notice Kip Gross' line above. Kip's not a kid any more but remember, he pitched in Albuquerque. Great numbers in a "hitter's heaven." The Rockies need to be on his case.

Most Likely to Disappoint

All of the hitters, except young Cedeno.

MILWAUKEE BREWERS

Prospect Capsule: Milwaukee Brewers

		7/1/94		1993	Minor League TOPR			3 yr	BB	K
Hitters:	Pos	Age	Bats	Level	1991	1992	1993	Avg	Freq	Freq
Jeff Cirillo	2B/3B	24	R	AA/AAA	130	139	126	**132**	130	79
Matt Mieske	OF	26	R	AAA	166	105	97	**125**	111	110
Troy O'Leary	OF	24	L	AAA	104	139	104	**116**	102	89
Duane Singleton	OF	21	L	AA	118	111	79	**101**	89	102
Jose Valentin	SS	24	B	AAA	109	90	102	**100**	122	122
Wes Weger	SS	23	R	AA	-	150	95	**114**	69	48

		7/1/94				TPER Indicators				
						OB	HR	H	BB	K
Pitchers:	Role	Age	Throws	Year	Level	Freq	Freq	Freq	Freq	Freq
Marshall Boze	Starter	23	R	1993	A+/AA	97	67	93	102	81
Mike Farrell	Starter	25	L	1993	AAA	95	141	108	61	64
Mark Kiefer	Starter	25	R	1993	AA/AAA	100	125	93	134	115
Rafael Novoa	Starter	26	L	1993	AAA	98	174	93	93	102
Scott Taylor	Starter	27	R	1993	AA/AAA	98	50	96	93	108
Mike Ignasiak	Closer	27	R	1993	AAA	64	74	49	103	180

NOTE: Frequency is expressed as a percent of TPA or TBF, relative to league norms. ( ) 100-199 TPA or TBF. * less than 100 TPA or TBF.

As remarked in the team essay, homegrown remains the Brewers' way. But the fruit hasn't been particularly sweet of late and next year's crop looks pretty thin. The Brewers have a long way to go.

Players They Kept . . . .

Hitters	Pitchers
Robin Yount ('74)	Bill Wegman ('86)
B. J. Surhoff ('87)	Jaime Mavarro ('89)
Bill Spiers ('89)	Doug Henry ('91)
Darryl Hamilton ('90)	Cal Eldred ('92)
Greg Vaughn ('90)	Angel Miranda ('93)
John Jaha ('92)	
Pat Listach ('92)	
Dave Nilsson ('93)	

. . . And Ones That Got Away

Hitters	Pitchers
Paul Molitor ('78)	Chris Bosio ('87)
Kevin Bass ('83)	Doug Jones ('87)
Mike Felder ('87)	
Gary Sheffield ('89)	

Something Else You Should Know

The home parks for the Brewers' minor league affiliates all qualified as "hitter's parks" (in "hitter's leagues," too) until the '93 season.

The AAA club's move from Denver (and we know all about that park by now) to New Orleans seems to have introduced some realistic deflation into the hitter's numbers.

Most Promising Prospects

Position Player: Jeff Cirillo—looks like a comer . . . combined .319 BA, .476 SLG, 12 HR, 73 RBI at El Paso and New Orleans . . . fell off badly in half-season at AAA (104 TOPR) . . . needs more time at AAA, but with the Brewers' needs may not get it.

Pitcher: Mike Ignasiak—converted from starter to closer role at Denver in '92 . . . *good* move (1.09 ERA, 26 H and 61 K in 57.2 IP at New Orleans '93) . . . 80 TPER in 37 IP in late-season Milwaukee call-up.

Sleeper

Scott Taylor—passed through Seattle and Atlanta systems with only intermittent success . . . really broke through when moved from El Paso to New Orleans in mid-season (5–1, 2.31 ERA, .223 BA against) . . . strong middle-relief candidate at least.

Most Likely to Disappoint

Matt Mieske—was the hope for the Brewers' vacant OF job . . . has struggled since his acquisition from the Padres in Sheffield deal . . . wrist injury a problem in '92 . . . probably affected '93 as well (.260 BA in only 60 G) . . . far from ready.

MINNESOTA TWINS

Prospect Capsule: **Minnesota Twins**

					Minor League TOPR					
		7/1/94		1993				3 yr	BB	K
Hitters:	Pos	Age	Bats	Level	1991	1992	1993	Avg	Freq	Freq
Rich Becker	OF	22	B	AA	134	154	138	**142**	170	109
Marty Cordova	OF	24	R	AA	81	154	117	**126**	123	150
Denny Hocking	SS	24	B	AA	119	132	92	**116**	89	84
Derek Lee	OF	27	L	AAA	141	110	130	**128**	151	71
Derek Parks	C	25	R	AAA	97	102	121	**108**	132	86
Paul Russo	3B/1B	25	R	AAA	145	119	100	**122**	106	135
Scott Stahoviak	3B	24	L	AA	-	133	134	**134**	162	153
						TPER Indicators				
		7/1/94				OB	HR	H	BB	K
Pitchers:	Role	Age	Throws	Year	Level	Freq	Freq	Freq	Freq	Freq
Greg Brummett	Starter	27	R	1993	AAA	89	35	98	62	117
Eddie Guardado	Starter	22	L	1993	AA	77	21	90	46	129
Pat Mahomes	Starter	23	R	1993	AAA	87	123	74	134	127
Oscar Muñoz	Starter	24	R	1993	AA/AAA	95	90	91	112	140
Brett Merriman	Reliever	27	R	1993	AAA	82	-	87	103	89

NOTE: Frequency is expressed as a percent of TPA or TBF, relative to league norms. ( ) 100-199 TPA or TBF. * less than 100 TPA or TBF.

The Twins needed help from their system last year and couldn't find any. Pat Meares and Eddie Guardado were called up and flopped in '93, being rushed far too soon. Dave McCarty was supposed to be ready and, for some reason, wasn't even close. Twins fans should rest easy, though, the talent's there—the timetable just didn't work out.

Players They Kept . . .

Hitters	Pitchers
Kent Hrbek ('82)	Scott Erickson ('90)
Kirby Puckett ('84)	Willie Banks ('92)
Chuck Knoblauch ('91)	Eddie Guardado ('93)
Dave McCarty ('93)	Mike Trombley ('93)
Pat Meares ('93)	

. . . And Ones That Got Away

Hitters	Pitchers
Gary Gaetti ('82)	Frank Viola ('82)
Jay Bell ('88)	Jesse Orosco ('82)
Jim Eisenreich ('88)	Mark Portugal ('86)
	Bryon Hickerson ('91)
	Denny Neagle ('92)

Something Else You Should Know

An incredibly disturbing 1993 draft. For whatever reason the Twins failed to sign their picks in rounds 1, 4, 5, 7 and 10. For a small-market team the amateur draft's the last place to try to save money.

Most Promising Prospects

Position Player: Rich Becker—in '93, he hit (.287 BA), ran (29 SB), walked (94 BB) and added power to his mix (15 HR) . . . we thought him a leadoff candidate, maybe he's more.
Pitcher: Eddie Guardado—only two years separated his contract signing and his big league debut . . . it wasn't enough (134 AL TPER) . . . has excelled at every previous level . . . rookie league (1.86 ERA), A ball (4.37), advanced A (1.64), AA (1.24) . . . a valuable property still.

Sleeper

Derek Parks—had been given up on by many . . . but he's still young and improving . . . gained K zone judgment in '93 and turned into a hitter (.311 BA, .521 SLG, 17 HR at Portland) . . . the Twins have their catcher.

Most Likely to Disappoint

Pat Mahomes—looks like he'll never find the plate . . . until he does, there will be runners on when he has to come in with a fat one. But Minnesota insists he has a rotation spot as '94 spring training opens.

MONTREAL EXPOS

Prospect Capsule: Montreal Expos

Hitters:	Pos	7/1/94 Age	Bats	1993 Level	Minor League TOPR 1991	1992	1993	3 yr Avg	BB Freq	K Freq
Shane Andrews	3B	22	R	AA	111	150	120	**128**	138	135
Cliff Floyd	OF/1B	21	L	AA/AAA	128	151	151	**147**	110	105
Glenn Murray	OF	23	R	AA	106	136	128	**122**	117	120
Curtis Pride	OF	25	L	AA/AAA	130	101	153	**129**	95	114
Tim Spehr	C	27	R	AAA	126	130	(86)	**113**	160	135
Rondell White	OF	22	R	AA/AAA	129	142	150	**140**	66	95

Pitchers:	Role	7/1/94 Age	Throws	Year	Level	TPER Indicators OB Freq	HR Freq	H Freq	BB Freq	K Freq
Tavo Alvarez	Starter	22	R	1993	AAA	107	70	110	106	72
Denis Boucher	Starter	26	L	1993	AAA	105	119	110	85	84
Joey Eischen	Starter	24	L	1993	AA/AAA	102	106	97	126	117
Brian Looney	Starter	24	L	1993	A+/AA	88	46	93	77	172
Kirk Rueter	Starter	23	L	1993	AA/AAA	79	139	101	30	93
Gabe White	Starter	22	L	1993	AA/AAA	84	65	91	72	113

NOTE: Frequency is expressed as a percent of TPA or TBF, relative to league norms. ( ) 100-199 TPA or TBF. * less than 100 TPA or TBF.

Welcome to Fat City! If they wanted to avoid arbitration badly enough, the Expos could jettison the entire major league roster, call up 25 kids and probably have another pennant contender in a couple of years. Yes, the system is that rich! At last report, the scouting and development budgets were being fine-tuned with an axe, though. In view of the big club's restricted funds and imminent opportunity, this decision's probably for the best. The Expos produce more talent than they can feasibly use, anyway.

Players They Kept . . .

Hitters	Pitchers
Delino DeShields ('90)	Chris Nabholz ('90)
Marquis Grissom ('90)	Mel Rojas ('90)
Larry Walker ('90)	Brian Barnes ('91)
John Vanderwal ('92)	Kirk Rueter ('93)
Wil Cordero ('93)	
Mike Lansing ('93)	

. . . And Ones That Got Away

Hitters	Pitchers
Andre Dawson ('77)	Scott Sanderson ('78)
Tim Raines ('81)	Bill Gullickson ('80)
Tim Wallach ('81)	Jeff Parrett ('87)
Tony Phillips ('83)	Norm Charlton ('88)
Andres Galarraga ('86)	John Dopson ('88)
Rene Gonzales ('88)	Gene Harris ('89)
Mike Blowers ('91)	Randy Johnson ('89)
Bret Barberie ('91)	Mark Gardner ('90)
	Chris Haney ('91)

Something Else You Should Know

Our report only covers AA and up. But the club's filthy rich at the lower levels, too.

Most Promising Prospects

Position Player: Cliff Floyd—combined '93 Harrisburg/Ottawa numbers inspire awe . . . hit .303 slugged .535 with 28 HR and 119 RBI in 133 games . . . walked 70 times for .396 OBP, scored 94 R . . . stole 31 bases (caught just 10 times) . . . only 20-years old in second full professional season . . . CF-capable outfielder converting to 1B, where he'll play in Montreal . . . 151 TOPR in '93, with the trendline to support it. Gets first crack at 1B in the spring.

Pitcher: Gabe White—since you already know about Kirk Rueter . . . White's TPER line suggests a highly polished complete pitcher (not unlike Kevin Appier's last minor league season) . . . went combined 9–3 with 2.43 ERA at AA and AAA . . . will be only 22 in '94, but he looks rotation-ready now.

Sleeper

Brian Looney—if forced to choose one from numerous possibilities . . . flat blew away Florida State and Eastern League batters in '93 . . . went 7–8 with 2.81 ERA . . . currently a starter, could make potent LH reliever.

Most Likely to Disappoint

Denis Boucher—whose naming in this particular space will no doubt inflame Gallic tempers . . . minor league TPER line that of long reliever hanging on . . . Expos' '94 pennant hopes won't allow this . . . raised hopes with 5 solid starts down '93 stretch (3–1, 1.91 ERA, only 3 BB in 28.1 IP), totally out-of-context with previous performances at Toronto and Cleveland . . . Montrealers, we hope we're wrong.

NEW YORK METS

Prospect Capsule: New York Mets

Hitters:	Pos	7/1/94 Age	Bats	1993 Level	1991	1992	1993	3 yr Avg	BB Freq	K Freq
						Minor League TOPR				
Jeromy Burnitz	OF	25	L	AAA	156	98	94	120	102	110
Brook Fordyce	C	24	R	AAA	100	110	80	96	65	82
Butch Huskey	3B	22	R	AA	140	112	107	119	88	102
Tito Navarro	SS	23	B	AAA	110	DNP	98	118	129	73
Reggie Otero	OF	22	R	AA	158	146	95	127	74	60
Ryan Thompson	OF	26	R	AAA	89	124	126	104	109	188
Quilvio Veras	2B	23	B	AA	173	161	142	155	188	66

Pitchers:	Role	7/1/94 Age	Throws	Year	Level	OB Freq	HR Freq	H Freq	BB Freq	K Freq
						TPER Indicators				
Jason Jacome	Starter	23	L	1993	A+/AA	99	72	106	87	96
Bobby Jones	Starter	24	R	1993	AAA	87	60	95	57	111
Joe Vitko	Starter	24	R	1992	AA	102	117	104	90	78
Denny Harriger	Utility	24	R	1993	AA	94	62	106	64	73
Tom Wegmann	Reliever	25	R	1993	AAA	88	101	82	93	165

NOTE: Frequency is expressed as a percent of TPA or TBF, relative to league norms. ( ) 100-199 TPA or TBF. * less than 100 TPA or TBF.

We all know what happened to the Mets this year. Catastrophe! We all know what the Mets have to do now. Start over! With what? During the high-spending, pennant-pursuing free agent years just past, the Mets' once-productive farm system fell into decay. It wasn't needed, after all. Given all these circumstances, the system appears in better shape than it has any right to be. A few players—pretty good players, really—will be ready for '94. Maybe a few more in '95. But the talent volume available doesn't approach the parent club's requirements—which is, virtually, a whole new lineup and a brand-new staff. And they need it NOW! Good luck.

Players They Kept . . .

Hitters	Pitchers
Todd Hundley ('92)	Dwight Gooden ('84)
Jeromy Burnitz ('93)	Jeff Innis ('89)
	Pete Schourek ('91)
	Anthony Young ('91)
	Eric Hillman ('92)

. . . And Ones That Got Away

Hitters	Pitchers
Darryl Strawberry ('83)	Nolan Ryan ('68)
Lenny Dykstra ('85)	Jeff Reardon ('80)
Kevin Mitchell ('86)	Greg A. Harris ('81)
Dave Magadan ('87)	Tim Leary ('84)
Gregg Jefferies ('89)	Rick Aguilera ('85)
Randy Milligan ('89)	Roger McDowell ('85)
Jeff Gardner ('93)	Randy Myers ('87)
	Jose Bautista ('88)
	David West ('89)
	Rich Rodriguez ('90)
	Julio Valera ('92)

Something Else You Should Know

In the past, the Mets have tended to follow a rigid policy of step-by-step advancement through the minors—Class A one year, the next at advanced A ball, then a year each at AA and AAA. This policy can probably now be found in File 13.

Most Promising Prospects

Position Players: Quilvio Veras—produced a lead off hitter's line at AA Binghamton that's a knockout . . . hit .306 with 91 BB (.430 OBP), plus 52 SB . . . switch-hitting 2B . . . some signs of defensive problems (23 E, but led the league's 2B in chances) . . . the decay in his trendline is normal for a player of his type (SB rates decline in higher classifications because the pitchers/catchers/infielders are learning how to control baserunners) . . . the Mets have a job for him, soon.

Pitchers: Bobby Jones—looks like he could be big winner . . . that'll be tough to do with the '94 Mets . . . went 12–10 with 3.63 ERA at AAA Norfolk . . . TPER line suggests he's in control of every aspect of his craft . . . produced decent 108 TPER in major league trial (9 starts, 2–4, 3.65 ERA) . . . belongs in Mets rotation (just about anybody's, in fact).

Sleeper

Tom Wegmann—looks like he could be a "force" in long relief or set-up role . . . thankless tasks with '94 Mets . . . went 5–3 with 3.23 ERA at Norfolk . . . four-year career totals: 30–15 with 2.62 ERA, 415 IP with 299 H, 474 K . . . Mets haven't known what to do with him (48 starts, 65 relief app. in career) . . . nor believed in him (out pitch is a change-up) . . . looks like they're coming around. Maybe he'll be in the '94 pen.

Most Likely to Disappoint

Ryan Thompson—major league trials in '92 and '93 have produced consecutive TOPRs of 92 and 96 . . . hits .250 with a little power, but poor K zone (19 BB, 81 K) and baserunning (2 SB in 9 attempts) judgment . . . the strike zone problem just isn't going to let him get much better. Another Toronto "super prospect" they talked someone into taking in a trade.

NEW YORK YANKEES

Prospect Capsule: New York Yankees

Hitters:	Pos	7/1/94 Age	Bats	1993 Level	Minor League TOPR			3 yr Avg	BB Freq	K Freq
					1991	1992	1993			
Russ Davis	3B	24	R	AAA	89	132	119	**113**	102	146
Robert Eenhorn	SS	26	R	AA	(107)	104	96	**102**	67	67
Kevin Jordan	2B	24	R	AA	114	118	115	**116**	81	54
Billy Masse	OF	27	R	AAA	143	111	168	**141**	209	81
Dave Silvestri	SS	26	R	AAA	124	127	125	**125**	151	150
Gerald Williams	OF	27	R	AAA	103	116	110	**110**	66	107

Pitchers:	Role	7/1/94 Age	Throws	Year	Level	TPER Indicators			BB Freq	K Freq
						OB Freq	HR Freq	H Freq		
Ron Frazier	Starter	25	R	1993	A+/AA	88	70	101	62	129
Sterling Hitchcock	Starter	23	L	1993	AAA	104	107	102	106	151
Mark Hutton	Starter	24	R	1993	AAA	90	115	77	124	122
Domingo Jean	Starter	25	R	1993	AA/AAA	93	33	81	124	107
Sam Militello	Starter	24	R	1992	AAA	87	44	79	94	159
Brien Taylor	Starter	22	L	1993	AA	101	55	78	164	123

NOTE: Frequency is expressed as a percent of TPA or TBF, relative to league norms. ( ) 100-199 TPA or TBF. * less than 100 TPA or TBF.

While George busily shelled out big bucks for free agents, popular opinion had it that blue chip after blue chip moldered in the farm system. Now that the Yankee strategy has reportedly changed, it is said the fruitful system will begin paying off. Forgive us for harboring doubts but the prospects that have been harvested haven't been all *that* good. And the ones that remain aren't knocking the socks off TOPR and TPER.

Players They Kept . . .

Hitters	*Pitchers*
Don Mattingly ('83)	Scott Kamieniecki ('91)
Jim Leyritz ('90)	Bob Wickman ('92)
Pat Kelly ('91)	
Bernie Williams ('91)	

. . . And Ones That Got Away

Hitters	*Pitchers*
Willie McGee ('82)	Jose Rijo ('84)
Mike Pagliarulo ('84)	Jim Deshaies ('86)
Greg Gagne ('85)	Eric Plunk ('86)
Otis Nixon ('85)	Al Leiter ('88)
Fred McGriff ('87)	Steve Frey ('90)
Roberto Kelly ('89)	
Hal Morris ('90)	
Deion Sanders ('92)	
J. T. Snow ('93)	

Something Else You Should Know

Brien Taylor, the jewel of the system, has suddenly become the question mark of the system. Injured his pitching shoulder in an off-season fight requiring surgery that'll idle him all of '94.

Most Promising Prospects

Position Player: Billy Masse—popped up with the #2 TOPR in the minors in '93 . . . unfortunately his .316 BA, .438 OBP and .560 SLG (with 19 HR and 91 RBI) probably won't get him any nearer to the bigs than Columbus (the Yanks like Luis Polonia?). Granted, he's getting some age on him . . . but he can *hit*.
Pitcher: Sam Militello—with injury reservations . . . marvelous '92 season at Columbus (12–2, 2.29 ERA) . . . big league debut wasn't bad either (92 TPER). A shoulder problem ruined '93.

Sleeper

There's never, ever, ever such a thing as a "sleeper" in a New York system.

Most Likely to Disappoint

Gerald Williams—all the tools in the world they say . . . except K zone judgment . . . getting past prospect age now, too.

◀ OAKLAND A's ▶

Prospect Capsule: Oakland Athletics

		7/1/94		1993	Minor League TOPR				BB	K
Hitters:	Pos	Age	Bats	Level	1991	1992	1993	3 yr Avg	Freq	Freq
Kurt Abbott	SS	25	R	AAA	93	97	114	102	66	149
Marcos Armas	1B	24	R	AAA	93	125	110	109	84	149
Fausto Cruz	IF	22	R	A+/AAA	87	125	86	101	97	98
Scott Lydy	OF	25	R	AAA	121	134	116	125	140	139
Mike Neill	IF	24	L	A+/AA	150	135	88	126	129	100
George Williams	C	25	B	AA	119	142	134	134	153	73
Ernie Young	OF	24	R	A+/AA	140	130	163	147	181	144

		7/1/94				TPER Indicator			BB	K
						OB	HR	H		
Pitchers:	Role	Age	Throws	Year	Level	Freq	Freq	Freq	Freq	Freq
Miguel Jimenez	Starter	24	R	1993	AAA	100	115	81	163	128
Steve Karsay	Starter	22	R	1993	AA	94	118	98	82	144
Gavin Osteen	Starter	24	L	1993	AA/AAA	92	41	92	97	87
Todd Van Poppel	Starter	22	R	1993	AAA	99	74	73	180	126
Todd Revenig	Closer	24	R	1992	AA	58	204	61	58	120

NOTE: Frequency is expressed as a percent of TPA or TBF, relative to league norms. ( ) 100-199 TPA or TBF. * less than 100 TPA or TBF.

The big club's pitching staff finally imploded in '93. The A's need pitching help badly and may not find much in the system. In the way of most clubs that find themselves in a contending position year after year, they've traded prospects to sustain the challenges. Eventually, that catches up with you.

Players They Kept . . .

Hitters	Pitchers
Rickey Henderson ('79)	Mark Mohler ('93)
Mark McGwire ('87)	
Terry Steinbach ('87)	
Lance Blankenship ('90)	
Mike Bordick ('91)	
Brent Gates ('93)	

. . . And Ones That Got Away

Hitters	Pitchers
Mickey Tettleton ('85)	Mike Morgan ('79)
Jose Canseco ('86)	Bill Krueger ('83)
Luis Polonia ('87)	Tim Belcher ('88)
Mike Gallego ('88)	Kevin Tapani ('90)
Walt Weiss ('88)	Wally Whitehurst ('90)
Felix Jose ('90)	Rod Beck ('91)
Darren Lewis ('91)	

Something Else You Should Know

The A's accumulated blue chips arms—Todd Van Poppel, Don Peters, Kirk Dressendorfer and David Zancanaro—all coming within the first 36 picks of the 1990 draft. Injuries struck and only Van Poppel survives. He's the only one who hasn't undergone major surgery.

Most Promising Prospects

Position Player: George Williams—switch-hitting catcher, played at AA Huntsville in '93 . . . hit .295, 14 HR, 77 RBI and knows K zone . . . also played OF.
Pitcher: Steve Karsay—A's held out for him in Henderson deal with Toronto . . . went 8–4, 3.58 ERA at AA . . . HR tendency disturbing but not out of hand in Oakland . . . turned in 96 TPER in September trial (49 IP).

Sleeper

Gavin Osteen—don't hear much about him . . . strange, under the circumstances . . . combined 14–10, 3.81 ERA at Huntsville and Tacoma . . . TPER profile simulates that of a competent major league pitcher (like his dad, Claude Osteen, pitching coach at Texas). A's apparently don't care much for him. Maybe Texas can get him?

Most Likely to Disappoint

Todd Van Poppel—severe control problems in minors carried over into big league trial in '93 . . . went 6–6 with 5.04 ERA and 113 TPER . . . but 62 BB in 84 IP . . . A's pitching coach Dave Duncan has his work cut out for him. If he masters control, he's got real talent. But right now this is a huge "if."

PHILADELPHIA PHILLIES

Prospect Capsule: Philadelphia Phillies

		7/1/94		1993				Minor League TOPR			
									3 yr	BB	K
Hitters:	Pos	Age	Bats	Level	1991	1992	1993		Avg	Freq	Freq
Mike Lieberthal	C	22	R	AAA	106	89	82		91	64	45
Tony Longmire	OF	25	L	AAA	101	-	119		112	89	84
Jason Moler	C	24	R	A+/AA	-	-	120		120	94	80
Kevin Stocker	SS	24	B	AAA	93	113	87		100	96	93
Phil Geisler	OF	24	L	A+/AA	97	85	128		107	82	129

		7/1/94				TPER Indicators					
						OB	HR	H		BB	K
Pitchers:	Role	Age	Throws	Year	Level	Freq	Freq	Freq		Freq	Freq
Kyle Abbott	Starter	26	L	1993	AAA	97	130	96		109	89
Kevin Foster	Starter	25	R	1993	AA/AAA	95	75	86		122	132
Tyler Green	Starter	24	R	1993	AAA	92	72	88		105	104
Mike Williams	Starter	24	R	1993	AAA	88	81	103		53	82
Toby Borland	Reliever	25	R	1993	AA/AAA	94	86	84		121	166
Ricky Bottalico	Closer	24	R	1993	A+/AA	92	64	94		85	132
Jeff Patterson	Reliever	25	R	1993	AAA	96	35	87		101	103

NOTE: Frequency is expressed as a percent of TPA or TBF, relative to league norms. ( ) 100-199 TPA or TBF. * less than 100 TPA or TBF.

After careful study, one must conclude that the NL pennant-winning Phillies—indeed, the whole franchise—rests on a solid foundation of *air*. Sure, Lee Thomas stole the '93 team's players from other major league clubs. But that leads to another question: What in heaven's name did he steal them *with?* To make a trade, a GM must have a player for shipment in the opposite direction. Thomas, to be sure, at one time had a few—Steve Bedrosian, Jeff Parrett, and the like. But how did he get *them?* Every player has a past in somebody's farm system. But since '84, the Phillies' farm system has been producing hitters with no future. Lee Thomas is running a shell game. And, based on our reading of the Phillies' current prospect capsule, he can't afford to stop just yet. There's very, very, very little down below.

Players They Kept . . .

Hitters	Pitchers
Darren Daulton ('86)	
Kevin Stocker ('93)	

. . . And Ones That Got Away

Hitters	Pitchers
Ryne Sandberg ('82)	Bob Walk ('80)
Julio Franco ('83)	Kevin Gross ('83)
George Bell ('84)	Kelly Downs ('86)
	Mike Maddox ('86)
	Bruce Ruffin ('86)
	Mike Jackson ('87)
	Todd Frohwirth ('89)
	Andy Ashby ('91)
	Chuck McElroy ('91)
	Bob Scanlan ('91)

Something Else You Should Know

The Phils called SS Kevin Stocker to the bigs last year realizing he wouldn't hit but played terrific SS. So what did he do? In a half season he TOPRed 122 with a .324 BA—but committed 14 errors.

Most Promising Prospects

Position Player: Jason Moler—first 97 pro games were at advanced A, next 38 at AA Reading . . . combined .287 BA, 17 HR with 76 RBI . . . TOPRed at 128 in FSL, even 100 in Eastern League . . . RH-hitting catcher, played some 1B . . . nailed 46 of 101 attempted thefts in A+ (46%), but only 12 of 37 (32%) in the higher league . . . said to have defensive shortcomings but, hey, it was his first season.

Pitcher: Tyler Green—made 14 starts, 14 relief appearances at AAA Scranton, total 118.1 IP . . . 6–10 with 3.95 ERA, nothing special . . . but he was 1–4, 5.13 in relief . . . 5–6, 3.62 as a starter . . . consider the relief experiment over and Green committed to the rotation . . . TPER says it'll work, so long as the heretofore tender arm stays in working order.

Sleeper

Mike Williams—got a look in '92 and barely got out alive (5.34 ERA in 5 starts) . . . got another look in '93, with outwardly similar results (5.29 ERA) but a decent 105 TOPR . . . minor league TPER line indicates he can pitch but he needs to learn how to approach major league hitters with his limited stuff . . . he may be learning . . . Also keep an eye on Bottalico. Some believe he's their closer by late '94.

Most Likely to Disappoint

Mike Lieberthal—a former #1 draft choice has spent his minor league career proving he can hit like Steve Lake . . . this still gets him to the bigs eventually, but as a backup.

PITTSBURGH PIRATES

Prospect Capsule: Pittsburgh Pirates

		7/1/94		1993	Minor League TOPR			3 yr	BB	K
Hitters:	Pos	Age	Bats	Level	1991	1992	1993	Avg	Freq	Freq
Rich Aude	1B	22	R	AA/AAA	92	121	143	**121**	126	97
Scott Bullett	OF	25	L	AAA	122	98	92	**104**	107	95
Midre Cummings	OF	22	B	AA/AAA	124	135	110	**122**	74	82
Stanton Cameron	OF	24	R	AA	99	152	146	**138**	195	125
Jerry Goff	C	30	L	AAA	116	105	118	**113**	151	125

		7/1/94				TPER Indicators			BB	K
						OB	HR	H		
Pitchers:	Role	Age	Throws	Year	Level	Freq	Freq	Freq	Freq	Freq
Brett Backlund	Starter	23	R	1993	AA/AAA	102	238	110	82	108
Lee Hancock	Starter	27	L	1993	AA/AAA	92	48	99	78	101
John Hope	Starter	23	R	1993	AA/AAA	102	97	115	57	74
Jon Lieber	Starter	24	R	1993	A+/AA	95	77	118	40	101
Jeff McCurry	Reliever	24	R	1993	A+/AA	94	67	93	94	83
Danny Miceli	Closer	23	R	1993	AA	105	148	87	143	156

NOTE: Frequency is expressed as a percent of TPA or TBF, relative to league norms. ( ) 100-199 TPA or TBF. * less than 100 TPA or TBF.

The Pirates strip-mined their farm system to support their early nineties championship habit. Besides Moises Alou and Wes Chamberlain, also count prospects such as Willie Greene, Tony Longmire, Kurt Miller and Hector Fajardo among the costs incurred during this period. Were these players still in hand, the big club and the farm system both would have a rosier outlook. But, then there may not have been any post-season thrills, either. The Pirate system isn't totally bereft, though, thanks largely to some shrewd dealing during the season just past. Ex-GM Ted Simmons caught the Royals and Orioles in exactly the same position that had cost the Pirates so much talent during their pennant races. He took advantage—plucking prospects Jon Lieber (RH starter) and Danny Miceli (RH closer) from the Royals, plus OF Stanton Cameron and RH starter Terry Farrar from the O's. Three of the four made our prospect list (and the other almost did).

Players They Kept . . .

Hitters	Pitchers
Jeff King ('89)	Randy Tomlin ('90)
Orlando Merced ('91)	Tim Wakefield ('92)
Carlos Garcia ('93)	Steve Cooke ('93)
Kevin Young ('93)	Blas Minor ('93)
	Paul Wagner ('93)

. . . And Ones That Got Away

Hitters	Pitchers
Tony Pena ('81)	Rick Honeycutt ('78)
Joe Orsulak ('85)	Steve Farr ('84)
Barry Bonds ('86)	John Smiley ('87)
Bobby Bonilla ('86)	Stan Belinda ('90)
Bip Roberts ('86)	
Jay Buhner ('88)	
Jose Lind ('88)	
Felix Fermin ('89)	
Wes Chamberlain ('91)	
Moises Alou ('92)	

Something Else You Should Know

The Pirates issued 26 separate calls to the minor leagues during the season, in addition to the six rookies who spent the entire season on the major league roster. Of the total, 15 went to pitchers, 11 went to hitters.

Most Promising Prospects

Position Player: Stanton Cameron—came from Baltimore in the Lonnie Smith trade (the O's drafted him from the Mets in the '91–92 off-season) . . . a low-average power hitter who walks, a potent combination . . . in AA Eastern League, hit career-high .276 with 21 HR (5th in league) and 64 RBI, .516 SLG (4th) . . . add in 84 BB (3rd) for a .408 OBP (6th) . . . years prior to and since '91 injury have all been like this . . . a defensive liability could be holding him back . . . but a lot of guys are worse than 6 E and 11 OFA, and most of them don't hit like he does.
Pitcher: Not this year, thank you. But Cooke, Wagner, Minor and Johnston looked fine in '93.

Sleeper

Jerry Goff—will be useful as platoon backup for Slaught, as covered in Pirates essay . . . hit .251 at AAA with 14 HR, 69 RBI.

Most Likely to Disappoint

Midre Cummings—part of the package that came from the Twins for John Smiley . . . hit combined .286 at AA Carolina and AAA Buffalo, with 15 HR and 46 RBI, plus 69 R scored and 10 SB . . . in '92 hit for higher average (.305) with similar power but more speed (23 SB) . . . looks like one of those frustrating 'tweeners—contact hitter with some average, but no OBP (.337 in '93) some power (.456 SLG) but not a slugger . . . so has no real place in the batting order above 7th . . . the Bucs, we think, expected more.

ST. LOUIS CARDINALS

Prospect Capsule: St. Louis Cardinals

		7/1/94		1993		Minor League TOPR		3 yr	BB	K
Hitters:	Pos	Age	Bats	Level	1991	1992	1993	Avg	Freq	Freq
Dan Cholowsky	2B/3B	23	R	A+/AA	*	149	99	**121**	136	134
Darrel Deak	2B	24	B	AA	173	148	115	**139**	155	120
John Mabry	OF	24	L	AA	146	87	95	**103**	57	68
Dmitri Young	3B/1B	20	R	A+/AA	(126)	133	104	**120**	74	73

		7/1/94				TPER Indicators				
						OB	HR	H	BB	K
Pitchers:	Role	Age	Throws	Year	Level	Freq	Freq	Freq	Freq	Freq
Paul Anderson	Starter	25	R	1993	AA/AAA	89	102	100	59	91
Brian Barber	Starter	20	L	1993	AA/AAA	105	154	104	117	115
Scott Simmons	Starter	23	L	1993	A+/AA	90	22	94	90	85
Tom Urbani	Starter	26	L	1993	AAA	89	43	95	73	112
Allen Watson	Starter	23	L	1993	AAA	85	142	90	76	103
Steve Dixon	Reliever	25	L	1993	AAA	97	112	82	112	136
Bryan Eversgerd	Reliever	25	L	1993	AA	91	60	96	73	143
John Kelly	Closer	26	R	1993	AA	83	87	93	37	93

NOTE: Frequency is expressed as a percent of TPA or TBF, relative to league norms. ( ) 100-199 TPA or TBF. * less than 100 TPA or TBF.

The Cardinals organization bears some very distinct and positive characteristics. They grow their own—13 of the 18 regulars or key role players on the club in '93 were home-grown. They develop a balanced crop—both hitters and pitchers, neither predominating. They raise a surplus—players they can use in trades to plug a shortage elsewhere. Theirs is a quality crop—in fact, there isn't a dud even among their trade-aways (no Vince Coleman jokes now, he has been a valuable player . . . and may be again). All in all, a very estimable operation. The current crop warrants some caution, however—it may not be ready until '95 or later.

Players They Kept . . .

Hitters	Pitchers
Luis Alicea ('88)	Joe Magrane ('87)
Tom Pagnozzi ('88)	Rheal Cormier ('91)
Todd Zeile ('90)	Donovan Osborne ('92)
Bernard Gilkey ('91)	Mike Perez ('92)
Ray Lankford ('91)	Rene Arocha ('93)
Geronimo Pena ('91)	Allen Watson ('93)
Brian Jordan ('92)	

. . . And Ones That Got Away

Hitters	Pitchers
Andy Van Slyke ('83)	Jim Gott ('82)
Terry Pendleton ('84)	Danny Cox ('83)
Vince Coleman ('85)	Cris Carpenter ('88)
Lance Johnson ('89)	Joe Boever ('89)
Alex Cole ('90)	Jeff Fassero ('91)
	Mark Clark ('92)
	Jeremy Hernandez ('92)

Something Else You Should Know

The Cardinals maintain eight minor league affiliates—more than any other club. The usual number is six. The "extra" farms are at the short-season entry level (rookie leagues) and the first full-season level (Class A), where the Cards have a total of five (most have but three). St. Louis has room for—and signs—more kids than any other organization. From this quantitative approach, more quality comes out the top. Just like Branch Rickey said.

Most Promising Prospects

Position Player: None warranting mention at this time. As shown above, some high hopes raised in Class A in '92 came crashing down upon elevation to AA Arkansas in '93.

Pitcher: Allen Watson—but we're not ready to go overboard on him just yet . . . his '93 minor league credentials at AAA Louisville look fine (5–4, 2.91 ERA) . . . everything's in order, except this little HR problem (see above) . . . when he was called up, the problem came with him (11 HR in 86 IP—almost the same relative frequency) . . . he's still got some work to do.

Sleeper

Brian Barber, at 20, has no right to be thought of as arriving by sometime in '94. His profile suggests various problems. But the Cards feel those occurred only because they like him so much they're hurrying him up the ladder.

Most Likely to Disappoint

Uncertain—just as there's no clear hitting prospect, it will take another season for a failure to confirm itself. The crop just looks a year away is all.

SAN DIEGO PADRES

Prospect Capsule: San Diego Padres

		7/1/94		1993	Minor League TOPR			3 yr	BB	K
Hitters:	Pos	Age	Bats	Level	*1991*	*1992*	*1993*	*Avg*	*Freq*	*Freq*
Ray Holbert	SS	23	R	AA	101	117	106	**107**	155	108
Luis Lopez	SS	23	B	AAA	70	63	100	**79**	56	77
Ray McDavid	OF	22	L	AA	161	164	124	**149**	159	112
Melvin Nieves	OF	22	B	AAA	137	165	116	**137**	100	157
Tracy Sanders	OF	24	L	AA	146	135	145	**142**	166	118
		7/1/94			TPER Indicators					
						OB	HR	H	BB	K
Pitchers:	Role	Age	Throws	Year	Level	*Freq*	*Freq*	*Freq*	*Freq*	*Freq*
Andres Berumen	Starter	23	R	1993	A+/AA	98	107	99	86	105
Joey Hamilton	Starter	23	R	1993	AA/AAA	104	26	100	112	79
Donnie Elliott	Starter	25	R	1993	AAA	101	159	100	121	134
Jose Martinez	Starter	23	R	1993	AAA	103	182	111	89	55
Pedro Martinez	Starter	25	L	1993	AAA	100	110	96	112	108
Scott Sanders	Starter	25	R	1993	AAA	98	145	96	103	148
Tim Worrell	Starter	26	R	1993	AAA	96	178	104	78	147

NOTE: Frequency is expressed as a percent of TPA or TBF, relative to league norms. ( ) 100-199 TPA or TBF. * less than 100 TPA or TBF.

The Padre organization's production history is a kibitzer's dream. Out of all the hitters they've developed, only one—Tony Gwynn—remains with the club. A potent lineup could be fashioned from among the missing—a relatively young one, too. The Padres' output of hitters ranks among the best in baseball. The pitchers, though, are quite another story. Up the coast, LA struggles with the opposite problem—a surfeit of pitching, a dearth of hitting. A merger would make sense.

Players They Kept . . .

Hitters	Pitchers
Tony Gwynn ('82)	Andy Benes ('89)
	Greg W. Harris ('89)
	Doug Brocail ('93)
	Scott Sanders ('93)
	Tim Worrell ('93)

. . . And Ones That Got Away

Hitters	Pitchers
Dave Winfield ('74)	Bob Patterson ('86)
Ozzie Smith ('75)	Mitch Williams ('86)
Kevin McReynolds ('84)	Omar Olivares ('90)
Ozzie Guillen ('85)	Ricky Bones ('91)
John Kruk ('86)	
Joey Cora ('87)	
Shane Mack ('87)	
Benito Santiago ('87)	
Roberto Alomar ('88)	
Sandy Alomar, Jr. ('90)	
Carlos Baerga ('90)	
Dave Hollins ('91)	
Jerald Clark ('91)	

Something Else You Should Know

The Padres' AAA affiliate is Las Vegas in the PCL—a "hitter's park" in a "hitter's league." Does this mean the Padres can be relaxed about the high HR frequencies shown above for their pitching prospects? We don't think so. In '93, Las Vegas pitchers gave up a PCL-high 141 homers. But, in '92, the Las Vegas staff yielded only a league-average 81. Looks like the '93 prospects are, in truth, suspects.

Most Promising Prospects

Position Player: Tracy Sanders—obtained from Cleveland in the Jeremy Hernandez deal in mid-season '93 . . . LH power-hitting OF who knows the strike zone . . . hit combined .286 with 18 HR and 67 RBI at AA Canton and Wichita . . . minor league TOPR consistently in 140s . . . LATE FLASH: traded to Mets for OF Randy Curtis . . . who hit .319 with 93 BB (.434 OBP) and 52 SB at St. Lucie in advanced A (166 TOPR) . . . seems fair.

Pitcher: Pedro A. Martinez—numbers at Las Vegas not eye-popping . . . 3–5, 4.72 ERA in 14 starts (87.2 IP) . . . what got our attention was 71 TPER at San Diego (32 relief appearances, 37 IP with 2.43 ERA) . . . 7th year with Padre organization, but only 24 . . . always a starter in the minors, converted to pen in majors . . . looks like he found a home. (How'd the Dodgers miss signing a pitcher named "Martinez"?)

Sleeper

They ALL got chances in '93 in the big leagues.

Most Likely to Disappoint

Uncertain—the HR frequencies for the pitching prospects make us queasy about the lot . . . Joey Hamilton passes this test, but was otherwise unimpressive (7–11, 4.12 ERA, with 150 H, 58 BB and only 83 K in 137.2 IP) . . . we can't read the Las Vegas park effect any better than the Padres can.

SAN FRANCISCO GIANTS

Prospect Capsule: San Francisco Giants

		7/1/94		1993	Minor League TOPR			3 yr	BB	K
Hitters:	Pos	Age	Bats	Level	1991	1992	1993	Avg	Freq	Freq
Joel Chimelis	3B/2B	27	R	AA/AAA	82	107	114	**101**	85	81
Rikkert Faneyte	OF	25	R	AAA	118	120	107	**114**	96	95
Steve Hosey	OF	25	R	AAA	131	100	121	**117**	136	154
Luis Mercedes	OF	26	R	AAA	126	111	94	**112**	149	66
Calvin Murray	OF	22	R	A+/AA	-	-	108	**108**	101	102
John Patterson	2B	27	B	D.L.	109	101	*	**106**	81	77
J. R. Phillips	1B	24	L	AAA	103	101	114	**106**	91	141

		7/1/94				TPER Indicators			BB	K
Pitchers:	Role	Age	Throws	Year	Level	OB Freq	HR Freq	H Freq	Freq	Freq
Dan Carlson	Starter	24	R	1993	AA/AAA	94	155	94	94	107
Chris Hancock	Starter	24	L	1993	AA	104	128	99	120	97
Salomon Torres	Starter	22	R	1993	AA/AAA	83	76	92	63	132
Carl Hanselman	Utility	24	R	1993	AA/AAA	103	100	107	87	77
Kurt Peltzer	Reliever	25	L	1993	A+/AAA	86	76	90	76	106

NOTE: Frequency is expressed as a percent of TPA or TBF, relative to league norms. ( ) 100-199 TPA or TBF. * less than 100 TPA or TBF.

I s this a surprisingly thin organization, or what? Only 13 players produced by the system were regulars or key-role players in the majors during '93. Even the Phillies' system produced more, though not of the same quality. It will be a thin crop again in '94. The Giants' system needs some work.

Players They Kept . . .

Hitters	Pitchers
Will Clark ('86)	Jeff Brantley ('89)
Robby Thompson ('86)	John Burkett ('90)
Matt Williams ('88)	Trevor Wilson ('90)
Kirt Manwaring ('89)	Kevin Rogers ('93)
Royce Clayton ('92)	

. . . And Ones That Got Away

Hitters	Pitchers
Chili Davis ('82)	Terry Mulholland ('86)
Rob Deer ('85)	
Charlie Hayes ('89)	

Something Else You Should Know

To be fair, the system has been dogged by injuries (e.g., RHPs Joe Rosselli and Rick Huisman), bad decisions on draft protection lists, allowing RHP Pat Rapp and LHP Mike Myers to get away, and what appears to be bad luck (C Steve Decker). But bad drafting (OF Adam

Hyzdu) and trading (RHP Johnny Ard in and, separately, RHP Kevin McGehee out) have played their part, too.

Most Promising Prospects

Position Players: Not much to pick from.
Pitchers: Salomon Torres—could, by himself, make the crop a memorable one . . . if his 21-year-old arm held up after 34 starts, 233.1 IP at AA Shreveport, AAA Phoenix and SF . . . posted combined 14–8 in the minors, with 3.15 ERA . . . excellent strikeout rate (166 K in 188.2 IP), exquisite control (39 BB) . . . could win big for a long time . . . we know it was a heated pennant race, but was it wise to work him that hard, that young?

Sleeper

Kurt Peltzer—toured the system in '93 . . . San Jose, Shreveport, Phoenix . . . LH reliever . . . evidently wasn't noticed when posting 2.44 ERA at Clinton (A) and San Jose (A+) in '92 . . . went 8–6 with 6 SV and 3.77 ERA in '93 . . . middleman type . . . but he's a healthy lefty, so he's got a future.

Most Likely to Disappoint

J. R. Phillips—said to be heir-apparent to Will Clark's 1B job . . . waived out of the Angels' system after a 5-year minor league career (.217 BA, 285 OBP., .359 SLG) . . . '93 season at Phoenix (.263 BA, 27 HR, 94 RBI) represents improvement in every area (even BB and K rates) . . . but still a long way from even Clark's off year. Besides, everyone hits in the Pacific Coast League.

SEATTLE MARINERS

Prospect Capsule: Seattle Mariners

		7/1/94		1993	Minor League TOPR			3 yr	BB	K
Hitters:	Pos	Age	Bats	Level	1991	1992	1993	Avg	Freq	Freq
Anthony Manahan	IF	25	R	AAA	113	99	95	102	90	61
Marc Newfield	1B/OF	21	R	AA	116	(94)	129	121	100	54
Greg Pirkl	1B	23	R	AAA	110	99	99	102	30	67
Ruben Santana	2B	24	R	AA	107	103	126	112	66	105
Brian Turang	OF	27	R	AAA	80	108	117	106	95	64
Dan Wilson	C	25	R	AAA	101	79	86	90	105	94

		7/1/94				TPER Indicators				
					OB	HR	H		BB	K
Pitchers:	Role	Age	Throws	Year	Level	Freq	Freq	Freq	Freq	Freq
Jim Converse	Starter	22	R	1993	AAA	106	56	99	132	87
John Cummings	Starter	25	L	1993	AA/AAA	93	78	102	70	99
Mike Hampton	Starter	21	L	1993	AA	92	45	86	106	136
Roger Salkeld	Starter	23	R	1993	AA	95	127	92	99	97
Ron Villone	Starter	24	L	1993	A+/AA	104	93	82	160	137
Brad Holman	Starter	26	R	1993	AAA	102	61	99	116	80

NOTE: Frequency is expressed as a percent of TPA or TBF, relative to league norms. ( ) 100-199 TPA or TBF. * less than 100 TPA or TBF.

With the franchise now in more capable financial hands, the M's aren't faced with trading their best players as soon as their contract is in danger of reflecting their worth. The quality core that's forming at the major league level can hang around for a while. There's more pitching help coming through the system. But they're a little shy on hitters.

Players They Kept . . .

Hitters	Pitchers
Dave Valle ('87)	Erik Hanson ('88)
Ken Griffey, Jr. ('89)	Randy Johnson ('89)
Edgar Martinez ('89)	Dave Fleming ('92)
Omar Vizquel ('89)	
Tino Martinez ('92)	
Bret Boone ('93)	

. . . And Ones That Got Away

Hitters	Pitchers
Dave Henderson ('82)	Bud Black ('82)
Harold Reynolds ('86)	Mike Moore ('82)
	Edwin Nunez ('82)
	Mark Langston ('84)
	Bill Swift ('85)
	Dave Burba ('91)

Something Else You Should Know

Prospective Seattle hitters, you'll note, don't walk. Nor do they strike out. The charge to the scouting and development groups must be: give us contact hitters! Didja ever notice that the M's always seem to have trouble filling the leadoff slot?

Most Promising Prospects

Position Player: Marc Newfield—he's been hurt, he's shown some power, seems to have an eye for the K zone, he's still young . . . '93 performance in AA Jacksonville: .307 BA, 19 HR, .530 SLG in 91 G . . . TOPR tarnished by high GDPs (12) . . . hasn't had a big breakthrough year yet, but he's due one . . . unfortunately, has no position (1B/OF/DH).

Pitcher: Mike Hampton—quality AA TPER line for a 20-year-old . . . got barbecued in early-season emergency use at Seattle (1–3, 9.53 ERA) . . . recovered his poise when returned to Jacksonville . . . went 6–4 with 3.71 ERA.

Sleeper

John Cummings—also subjected to early-season emergency duty . . . went 0–6 with 6.02 ERA, but a satisfactory 101 TPER in 46.1 IP (8 starts) . . . was his first exposure above Class A ball . . . also posted encouraging indicators at Jacksonville and AAA Calgary (5–6 with 3.73 ERA).

Most Likely to Disappoint

Roger Salkeld—made surprisingly fast recovery from arm surgery . . . missed '92 season, wasn't expected back until '94 . . . word has it he's ready after a half-season at Jacksonville . . . M's hoping he takes rotation spot with conversion to closer as an option . . . TPER indicators above are worrisome . . . previous profile showed him to be a dominating pitcher with a high K, low H pattern, the '93 version was just about average all around, with a penchant for taters . . . Roger may be back, but his arm isn't yet.

Anthony Manahan—Seattle wants him to be their everyday 2B in '94. His minor league numbers suggest they should have a "Plan B" ready.

TEXAS RANGERS

Prospect Capsule: Texas Rangers

Hitters:	Pos	7/1/94 Age	Bats	1993 Level	1991	1992	1993	3 yr Avg	BB Freq	K Freq
						Minor League TOPR				
Rob Ducey	OF	29	L	AAA	129	-	133	**124**	126	143
Benji Gil	SS	21	R	AA	(113)	106	117	**111**	111	131
Terrell Lowery	OF	23	R	A+/AA	121	DNP	102	**108**	153	98
Rob Maurer	1B	27	L	AAA	162	118	D.L.	**144**	134	127
Trey McCoy	DH	27	R	AA/AAA	(134)	(194)	166	**157**	159	89
Dan Peltier	1B/OF	26	L	AAA	85	109	126	**104**	119	90

Pitchers:	Role	7/1/94 Age	Throws	Year	Level	OB Freq	HR Freq	H Freq	BB Freq	K Freq
						TPER Indicators				
Duff Brumley	Starter	23	R	1993	A+/AA	77	140	74	80	168
Steve Dreyer	Starter	24	R	1993	AA/AAA	92	68	98	82	94
Rick Helling	Starter	23	R	1993	AA	86	96	87	82	153
Dan Smith	Starter	25	L	1992	DL	83	71	85	78	116
Ritchie Moody	Closer	23	L	1993	AA	100	19	87	146	119
Darren Oliver	Reliever	23	L	1993	AA	98	17	69	150	139

NOTE: Frequency is expressed as a percent of TPA or TBF, relative to league norms. ( ) 100-199 TPA or TBF. * less than 100 TPA or TBF.

The Rangers have quietly put together one of the most productive farm systems in the majors. The '94 crop looks like a winner and there's talent deeper in the system. The organization seems to be in good shape for the long haul.

Players They Kept . . .

Hitters	Pitchers
Juan Gonzalez ('91)	Tom Henke ('85)
Dean Palmer ('91)	Kevin Brown ('89)
Ivan Rodriguez ('91)	Kenny Rogers ('89)
David Hulse ('93)	Brian Bohanon ('91)
	Roger Pavlik ('92)
	Matt Whiteside ('93)

. . . And Ones That Got Away

Hitters	Pitchers
Steve Buechele ('85)	Danny Darwin ('79)
Ruben Sierra ('86)	Gene Nelson ('81)
Mike Stanley ('87)	Ron Darling ('84)
Chad Kreuter ('89)	Jose Guzman ('86)
Sammy Sosa ('89)	Bobby Witt ('86)
Kevin Reimer ('91)	Wilson Alvarez ('91)

Something Else You Should Know

At one point last season, Texas had three catchers they drafted (Stanley, Kreuter and Bill Haselman) and two they'd once owned and gotten rid of (Don Slaught and Mark Parent) all start for other major league teams on the same day.

Most Promising Prospects

Position Player: Benji Gil—penciled in for '95 but if Lee stumbles, he'll get the job in '94 . . . .275 BA, 17 HR, 20 SB at Tulsa '93.
Pitcher: Rick Helling—the Rangers are counting on him in '94 rotation . . . he's ready. Hurls thunderbolts (system record 205 Ks in '93), could be dominant.

Sleeper

Trey McCoy—in top 5 minor league TOPR . . . Frank Thomas-like (.290 BA, .585 SLG, 32 HR, 106 RBI, 70 BB) . . . no position. DH-type.

Most Likely to Disappoint

Nobody. CF Donald Harris didn't even make our list and Robb Nen's been shipped out.

TORONTO BLUE JAYS

Prospect Capsule: Toronto Blue Jays

		7/1/94		1993	Minor League TOPR				BB	K
Hitters:	Pos	Age	Bats	Level	1991	1992	1993	3 yr Avg	Freq	Freq
Howard Battle	3B	22	R	AA	134	120	97	**117**	86	94
William Canate	OF	22	R	Major	90	144	*	**112**	94	57
Rob Butler	OF	24	L	AAA	137	135	90	**124**	71	74
Carlos Delgado	C	22	L	AA	187	178	160	**174**	171	97
Alex Gonzalez	SS	21	R	AA	82	107	116	**108**	72	104
Shawn Green	OF	21	L	AA	-	105	89	**97**	71	104
Robert Perez	OF	25	R	AAA	101	86	94	**93**	53	69

		7/1/94			TPER Indicators				BB	K
Pitchers:	Role	Age	Throws	Year	Level	OB Freq	HR Freq	H Freq	Freq	Freq
Scott Brow	Starter	25	R	1993	AA/AAA	97	149	97	97	77
Jesse Cross	Starter	26	R	1993	AAA	94	92	93	104	119
Paul Menhart	Starter	25	R	1993	AAA	103	111	95	124	99
Paul Spoljaric	Starter	23	L	1993	AA/AAA	104	133	91	154	136
Huck Flener	Utility	25	L	1993	AA	94	85	101	81	118

NOTE: <u>F</u>requency is expressed as a percent of TPA or TBF, relative to league norms. ( ) 100-199 TPA or TBF. * less than 100 TPA or TBF.

The Toronto system is fabled for its vast fields of prospects. But, we wonder. Looking at their homegrown players, the only recent product who stands out is Olerud who never saw the minors. Hentgen's 19 wins were a function of powerful support (99 TPER). Among the players traded out of the system or gone to free agency, only Jimmy Key's a bell-ringer and he dates to '84 (we believe in Jeff Kent's future, though). What are we missing here?

Players They Kept . . .

Hitters	Pitchers
Tony Fernandez ('84)	Mark Eichhorn ('86)
Pat Border ('88)	Todd Stottlemyre ('88)
John Olerud ('90)	Tony Castillo ('90)
Ed Sprague ('91)	Pat Hentgen ('92)

. . . And Ones That Got Away

Hitters	Pitchers
Greg Myers ('90)	Jimmy Key ('84)
Pedro Munoz ('91)	David Wells ('88)
Mark Whiten ('91)	Luis Aquino ('89)
Derek Bell ('92)	Willie Blair ('90)
Jeff Kent ('92)	Xavier Hernandez ('90)
Ryan Thompson ('93)	Jose Mesa ('90)

Something Else You Should Know

There's a funny thing about Toronto OF prospects. They tend to look like nothing special as they advance through the system—low average, some power, few walks with massive K counts. Then, they reach Syracuse and burst forth with a giant year that gets them a can't-miss label. Next comes a trade and they revert to form. Are the Jays "salting the claim" somehow? Pedro Munoz, Glenallen Hill, Mark Whiten, Derek Bell and Ryan Thompson all fit the pattern.

Most Promising Prospects

Position Player: Carlos Delgado—claimed fifth-highest minor league TOPR . . . pounded Southern League pitchers for .303 BA, 25 HR, 102 RBI and drew 102 BB . . . young LH-hitting catcher who could use some more polish (14 E, 16 PB, slightly below league average caught stealing) . . . has torn up every league he's played in . . . big-time major league hitting prospect (he hasn't been to Syracuse yet and he knows how to walk).

Pitcher: Huck Flener—consistently used in a utility role (16 starts in 39 '93 App. at Knoxville) for some reason . . . went 13–6 with 3.30 ERA (with two complete games and four saves, strangely) . . . if Jays move Al Leiter to the rotation, they'll need somebody like him. Appeared briefly last year and the Jays weren't ready for him—he debuted wearing a uniform with the name "Green."

Sleeper

Jesse Cross—doesn't get much attention, but had fifth consecutive solid year in the minors . . . went 8–6, 3.16 ERA at AAA . . . career totals 46–43, 3.29 ERA, 586 H and 649 K in 716.1 IP.

Most Likely to Disappoint

Rob Butler—hit .284 in 55 G before '93 call-up and injury . . . slap-hitter like Brett Butler (no relation), but doesn't walk (only 22 B) or run (7 SB in 12 attempts) like Brett . . . when he hit .358 at Dunedin, he was a prospect . . . when he hits .284, he's not.

AWARDS

DREAMS AND NIGHTMARES

It's every General Manager's dream—to get Hall of Fame performances for bottom of the barrel salaries. You're familiar with all the phrases used to refer to various types of players. You know "aces" and "stoppers" and "big boppers" and guys who can "throw some leather." But GMs know the "109s." That's the minimum salary in the majors—$109,000. And players who produce big numbers for that amount populate the dreams of GMs, be they raw rookies or veterans so down on their luck that they accept the minimum just for a chance at a job in the bigs. Conversely, every GM's nightmare consists of guys making Hall of Fame dough but giving performances as forgettable as Roseanne Barr singing the National Anthem. Oh, later on in this section we'll bring you our TOPR-TPER all-stars and our own post-season awards for the '93 season, but we begin with *Essential Baseball*'s 1993 GM's Dream and Nightmare Teams.

To select such "star" teams there must be rules (unlike, for instance, the choices for Gold Gloves where there often appear to be no rules). To be eligible for a "dream team" nomination a player must have made less than a million dollars, the "less" the better (hey, you've got to think like a GM all the time to pick these squads). A hitter must have TOPRed above 100 and a pitcher had to have TPERed below 100. Obviously the further above or below the better. "Nightmares" must have made somewhere in seven figures and have driven their organizations bananas with their on-field (and sometimes off-field) antics. To be a nightmare you must have TOPRed below 100 if you're a hitter and TPERed at 100 or above if you pitched. In "toss-up" situations with starting pitchers on our nightmare teams, we leaned to those with losing records.

Without further delay, our GM's Dream and Nightmare Teams for 1993!

Comments: Note that Baltimore had the most "dreamers" with three. Even big bucks Toronto managed to be represented on this "little bucks" all-star team. Four teams didn't have a dreamer—KC, Minnesota, Seattle and the Yankees (why does that not surprise anyone?). We realize that pitchers Eldred and Hentgen barely sneaked under our requirement of a below-100 TPER but we thought special designation was in store for a player making just 175 grand who threw the most pitches of any hurler in the majors last year (Eldred), and for another who led the world champions in victories despite being the 11th highest paid pitcher on Toronto's 11-man staff (Hentgen). You could have had our entire dream team by paying the rather measly sum of $3,829,500. That's for all 18 of them! And the question about this team isn't whether they'd have been good enough to beat the champion Blue Jays but rather if Toronto would have been good enough to beat the dreamers.

Enough dreaming. Ready for a nightmare?

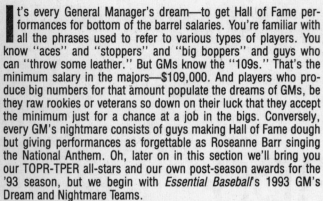

TOPR and TPER Present:
The 1993 American League G.M.'s
"Dream Team"

Pos	Players	TOPR	Salary
C	Chris Hoiles-BAL	157	$350,000
1B	Mo Vaughn-BOS	136	290,000
2B	Damion Easley-CAL	108	112,500
3B	Dean Palmer-TEX	118	275,000
SS	John Valentin-BOS	109	170,000
LF	Juan Gonzalez-TEX	150	525,000
CF	Kenny Lofton-CLE	134	450,000
RF	Tim Salmon-CAL	141	127,500
DH	Troy Neel-OAK	117	130,000
	Pitchers	**TPER**	
St	Jamie Moyer-BAL	84	$200,000
St	Jason Bere-CWS	85	109,000
St	John Doherty-DET	90	170,000
St	Cal Eldred-MIL	98	175,000
St	Pat Hentgen-TOR	99	182,500
Bp	Graeme Lloyd-MIL	81	109,000
Bp	Jim Poole-BAL	61	150,000
Cl	Jerry DiPoto-CLE	82	109,000
Cl	Roberto Hernandez-CWS	72	195,000

TOPR and TPER present:
The 1993 American League G.M.'s
"Nightmare Team"

Pos	Players	TOPR	Salary
C	Tony Peña-BOS	57	$2,200,000
1B	Glenn Davis-BAL	51	3,800,000
2B	Jose Lind-KCR	65	2,400,000
3B	Kelly Gruber-CAL	*	4,333,333
SS	Cal Ripken-BAL	97	5,459,973
LF	Kevin McReynolds-KCR	98	3,666,667
CF	Ruben Sierra-OAK	91	4,200,000
RF	Jose Canseco-TEX	98	4,800,000
DH	George Bell-CWS	70	3,650,000
	Pitchers	**TPER**	
St	Jack Morris-TOR	116	$5,425,000
St	Bob Welch-OAK	113	3,450,000
St	Teddy Higuera-MIL	162	3,250,000
St	Rick Sutcliffe-BAL	124	2,500,000
St	Todd Stottlemyre-TOR	111	2,325,500
Bp	Steve Howe-NYY	100	2,500,000
Bp	Craig Lefferts-TEX	120	1,080,374
Cl	Steve Farr-NYY	127	1,500,000
Cl	Lee Smith-STL/NYY	112	2,691,667

Comments: It should immediately become clear as to why Baltimore and New York couldn't catch the Jays in the AL East. The Orioles had two "nightmares" penciled in as everyday players and another in their starting rotation. One peek at our nightmare team should tell the Yanks where to begin their off-season restructuring. Three of our four nightmare bullpeners ended the year in Yankee pinstripes. About the selection of Ripken for SS. We could have chosen three other millionaire SSs who TOPRed under 100—Texas' Manny Lee, Seattle's Omar Vizquel or the Yankees' Spike Owen. But Ripken made more than those three *combined*! Thus, Cal winds up on the list. Note that we have no TOPR for Gruber. That's because he only appeared at the plate 67 times for his more than $4 mil. We don't even bother to figure TOPRs for such a small sampling. But his last recorded TOPR of 77 in '92 (for the same amount of money) added to his disappearing act in '93 and easily qualified him as a "nightmare". Four teams managed to avoid having any "nightmares"—Minnesota, Seattle and Cleveland (all of whom couldn't afford to have them) and Detroit (some of whose pitchers came awfully close to making the team). In all, these 18 nightmares would have cost you a mere $59,232,514 to gather onto one squad last year. Could this team have edged out the 68–94 A's to avoid being the worst team in the AL?

TOPR and TPER present:
The 1993 National League G.M.'s
"Dream Team"

Pos	Players	TOPR	Salary
C	Rick Wilkins-CUB	145	$212,500
C	Mike Piazza-LAD	138	126,000
1B	Andres Galarraga-COL	151	850,000
2B	Jeff Kent-NYM	103	195.000
3B	Sean Berry-MON	129	121,000
SS	Kevin Stocker-PHI	122	109,000
LF	Al Martin-PIT	119	109,000
CF	Moises Alou-MON	122	210,000
RF	Phil Plantier-SDO	128	245,000
	Pitchers	**TPER**	
St	Kirk Rueter-MON	75	$109,000
St	Rene Arocha-STL	91	109,000
St	Pedro Astacio-LAD	87	136,000
St	Darryl Kile-HOU	90	267,500
St	Steve Avery-ATL	81	560,000
Bp	Kevin Rogers-SFO	75	114,000
Bp	Jeff Fassero-MON	75	187,500
Cl	Gene McMichael-ATL	63	109,000
Cl	Rod Beck-SFO	75	250,000

Comments: The Expos, who've specialized in finding good-and-cheap types, led our NL dream team with four members. The Dodgers finished second with three. Amazingly the Braves, who led the NL in millionaires with 14 (Wow!), also had a pair of dreamers on their pitching staff. Two franchises didn't have one: Cincinnati (you'd have thought they'd have found at least one when they played 53 players) and, would you believe, Florida. But the Marlins, whose team consisted almost entirely of dreamer-types, also just missed with OF Jeff Conine who played all 162 games, TOPRed at 101 and earned just $125,000. You'll also note that we took a catching platoon with Wilkins and Piazza. The absence of the DH in the NL we felt left us some latitude and the sensational seasons produced by those two backstops easily qualified them as "dreamers" in the minds of every GM in the game. You could have gotten this entire set of stellar performers for a mere $4,019,500. About $200,000 more than what the AL dream team would have cost. But

you could have also taken that $4 mil and bought Mets closer John Franco instead. It's your call.

TOPR and TPER present:
The 1993 National League G.M.'s
"Nightmare Team"

Pos	Players	TOPR	Salary
C	Benito Santiago-FLA	88	$3,400,000
1B	Orestes Destrade-FLA	96	2,300,000
2B	Jody Reed-LAD	83	2,500,000
3B	Tim Wallach-LAD	78	3,362,500
SS	Ozzie Smith-STL	93	3,464,458
LF	Darrin Jackson-TOR/NYM	59	2,100,000
CF	Steve Finley-HOU	93	2,900,000
RF	Darryl Strawberry-LAD	89	3,800,000
	Pitchers	**TPER**	
St	Greg Swindell-HOU	106	$3,750,000
St	Jose Guzman-CUB	108	3,500,000
St	Bruce Hurst-SDO/COL	*	3,000,000
St	John Smiley-CIN	112	3,475,000
St	Tom Browning-CIN	117	2,250,000
Bp	Bobby Thigpen-CWS/PHI	125	3,416,667
Bp	Dave Righetti-SFO	120	2,250,000
Cl	John Franco-NYM	136	4,000,000
Cl	Rob Dibble-CIN	147	2,500,000

Comments: Before you go any further check out what might be the ugliest, most overpaid bullpen ever! Anyone still wondering why Cincy fell apart—focus on our "nightmare" pitching staff. Three Reds on there totaling over $8 million in combined salary. Hey, $8 mil just doesn't buy what it used to these days. About the choice of perennial all-star Ozzie Smith at SS. We could have chosen Chicago's Shawon Dunston for batting just 10 times and collecting $3,375,000. But he's been badly injured and has TOPRed above 100 consistently when not hurt. Hmmm, looks like the Dodgers had best do something about their infield, eh? Since there's no DH we again feel the right to take some latitude and name a "Nightmare Team" award of "dishonorable mention" to Mets LF Vince Coleman. Only his TOPRing at 101 kept him off our regular club. But given the misery he caused on and, especially, off the field last season we couldn't let a nightmare team go by without "dishonoring" him. Note that the Marlins had a pair of nightmares despite having only six millionaires on the squad. That's a very high percentage. Four teams can thank their lucky stars their players avoided inclusion on this squad—Pittsburgh, Montreal, San Diego and Atlanta. And, ladies and gentlemen, you too could have owned this very special group of performers last season for the princely sum of "just" $51,968,625. Could this club have beaten the Mets out for distinction as baseball's worst team? Now there's a match considering that the Mets paid nearly as much, in reality, to BE baseball's worst team!

THE ALL-STARS

To save you the trouble of sifting through our individual TOPRs and TPERs to put together a '93 all-star team for each league, we've done it for you. The positional players became an easy job. We simply took the best TOPR at each position from those who played the entire year in the bigs or, in a few cases, almost the entire season. We assembled the pitching staffs by selecting the four rotation starters with the best TPERs and we tossed our "phenom" into the fifth spot. He's the kiddie hurler who appeared and made the most impact with the lowest TPER. We then added a best utility type, a right- and left-hand set-up combo, the best "spot" pitcher and our choice as that league's best long man. In the outfield we went strictly by position resisting, for instance, the temptation to shift LF Juan Gonzalez's 150 TOPR to RF.

Folks, here's the best baseball had to offer in '93:

TOPR and TPER present:
The 1993 American League
ALL-STARS

Pos	Players	TOPR
C	Chris Hoiles-BAL	157
1B	John Olerud-TOR	179
2B	Roberto Alomar-TOR	142
3B	Travis Fryman-DET	129
SS	Alan Trammell-DET	125
LF	Rickey Henderson-TOR	162
CF	Ken Griffey, Jr.-SEA	161
RF	Tim Salmon-CAL	141
DH	Paul Molitor-TOR	139

Pitchers		TPER
St	Kevin Appier-KCR	69
St	Mark Langston-CAL	78
St	Jimmy Key-NYY	80
St	Alex Fernandez-CWS	82
St	Jason Bere-CWS	85
Ut	Al Leiter-TOR	86
Rhs	Danny Cox-TOR	82
Lhs	Jesse Orosco-MIL	71
Spe	Jim Poole-BAL	61
Lng	Graeme Lloyd-MIL	81
Cl	Duane Ward-TOR	64

Comments: Any questions as to why Toronto won it all? Eight members of our all-star team! No other team had more than two chosen. Teams without mention included: Minnesota, Texas (though they barely missed at 3B and LF), Oakland (though they could claim Henderson) and Cleveland (which also barely missed at three positions—CF, 2B and LF). The presence of Salmon and Bere gives you a pretty good idea of who our rookie hitter and rookie

pitcher of the year will be. Note the balance of the staff with five righties and six lefties. And just how good is your offense when Trammell's your "weak link"?

TOPR and TPER present:
The 1993 National League
ALL-STARS

Pos	Players	TOPR
C	Darren Daulton-PHI	149
1B	Andres Galarraga-COL	151
2B	Robby Thompson-SFO	161
3B	Matt Williams-SFO	125
SS	Jeff Blauser-ATL	128
LF	Barry Bonds-SFO	201
CF	Lenny Dykstra-PHI	152
RF	Larry Walker-MON	136

Pitchers		TPER
St	Bill Swift-SFO	70
St	Greg Maddux-ATL	74
St	Jose Rijo-CIN	80
St	John Burkett-SFO	80
St	Kirk Rueter-MON	75
Ut	Jeff Faserro-MON	75
Rhs	Jay Howell-ATL	72
Lhs	Kevin Rogers-SFO	72
Spe	Xavier Hernandez-HOU	77
Lng	Pedro Martinez-LAD	82
Cl	Gene McMichael-ATL	63

Comments: After checking this all-star team you can see why the Giants and Braves clearly established themselves as the league's best regular season teams. Together they had nine of the 19 slots (SF had five). NL East leaders Philadelphia and Montreal accounted for five more with the Expos having three of them. Four clubs weren't represented on our star team: San Diego, Florida, Pittsburgh and the Cubs. The Marlins, though, narrowly missed at closer with Bryan Harvey and at 3B with Gary Sheffield. The Cubs had the runner-up at catcher with Rick Wilkins and the Mets had the #2 RF in Bobby Bonilla. Five members of the 11-man staff earned less than $200,000 last year. Just as with the AL, the lowest TOPR on the team's a 125. But how many would have picked 3B Williams as the "soft touch" in this bunch?

Like all other publications, we've picked the winners of our awards for the '93 season. Like those others, we've picked the best hitters, pitchers, rookies and managers of the year. But unlike those other award givers, we've also chosen the winners (or in some cases "losers") in categories like surprises, bombs, steals and flops for '93.

TOPR and TPER present:
The 1993 Year-End Awards

Hitters	American League	National League
Most Offensive	John Olerud-TOR	Barry Bonds-SFO
Rookie of the Year	Tim Salmon-CAL	Mike Piazza-LAD
Surprise of the Year	Chad Kreuter-DET	Kevin Stocker-PHI
Bomb of the Year	George Bell-CWS	Darrin Jackson-NYM💣*
Free Agent Steal	Paul Molitor-TOR	Barry Bonds-SFO
Free Agent Flop	Ruben Sierra-OAK	Benito Santiago-FLA

Pitchers		
King of the Hill	Kevin Appier-KCR	Bill Swift-SFO
King Closer	Duane Ward-TOR	Gene McMichael-ATL
Rookie of the Year	Jason Bere-CWS	Darryl Kile-HOU
Bomb of the Year	Jack Morris-TOR	Rob Dibble-CIN
Free Agent Steal	Tie: Jimmy Key-NYY	Greg Maddux-ATL
	Jeff Russell-BOS	
Free Agent Flop	Mike Moore-DET	Greg Swindell-HOU

Manager of the Year	Mike Hargrove-CLE	Jim Fregosi-PHI

💣* While stongly tempted to name Vince Coleman the NL "Bomb of the Year", we figured it would be in poor taste.

TOPR and TPER present:
The 1993 American League
MASTER STRATEGIST

Mike Hargrove

Runner Up:
Kevin Kennedy

TOPR and TPER present:
The 1993 National League
MASTER STRATEGIST

Jim Fregosi

Runner Up:
Jim Leyland

THE MANAGER'S JOB

We've dealt with and produced job descriptions for hitters and pitchers at length. What about the manager? How does he fit in the TOPR/TPER scheme?

Recall that we expressed hitters' and pitchers' jobs in terms of bases and outs, reserving responsibility for the production (or prevention) of runs to the team. And *the manager leads the team,* just as a business manager leads a department, division or company. And while a business manager may take a hand in doing the actual jobs in his particular sphere, his *primary* responsibility remains the motivation and direction of his personnel toward a common, defined goal. Since a baseball manager can't perform the actual work (unless he's a player/manager like Pete Rose, Frank Robinson or Lou Boudreau), his *sole* responsibility becomes the motivation and direction of his talent toward their mutual goal.

Their goal, of course, is winning games. Which is accomplished, obviously, by outscoring their opponents. *And the manager can exert a surprising impact on the run-scoring differential.* We estimate, in fact, that managers can be worth as much as 50 to 100 runs by this measure—making the manager *potentially* the most valuable member of his team.

What could a manager possibly contribute that would make him that important to his team's success? First off, let's grant that TOPR and TPER can't measure his vitally important leadership ability and motivational skills any better than you, the press or his boss can. If he gets more performance out of his players than they really had to give, this "intangible" shows up to his credit in the win column as a matter of course.

But certain managerial functions do become "tangible" under TOPR's microscope and their impact on the team's performance can be measured. Considering offense alone, the manager controls two means by which he can powerfully affect the team's conversion of "input" (bases) into "output" (runs).

1. Construction of the batting order—*effective* utilization of resources, so to speak. According to the available TOPR "input"

(bases) and its components (on base, power, speed, etc.) for individual players, he must arrange them to take maximum advantage of their capabilities.

2. Game management—*creative* use of resources. Given the team's actual TOPR "input," he must direct the offense to maximize the opportunities.

The net result of these efforts can be measured in terms of the relative efficiency of the "input" to "output" conversion process: *Net Bases Earned per Run Produced.* And while the average in both leagues was just under four, some teams went about their task more efficiently than others.

Introducing RPER (Ree-per), or Run Production Efficiency Rating—the manager's statistic.

The RPER Curve

Unfortunately, we've got to get a little technical here—because it's not quite so simple as merely dividing each team's Runs Produced into Net Bases Earned, arriving at a result and drawing a conclusion.

You see, as teams generate more "input," their "output" tends to increase even more rapidly, as a matter of course. Thus, teams with massive offensive "input" will tend, by their very nature, to be more efficient than light-hitting teams. You're familiar with the effect. In the absence of any other event in a given inning, how many runs will one single produce? None, obviously. How about two? Still zero. Then three? Four? Five? Six? And so on. As the production of bases increases arithmetically, run production increases at an accelerating rate.

Consequently, measurement of a team's run conversion efficiency must take into account what they had to work with. The standard by which they are measured, then, constantly changes to reflect their level of input and takes the graphic shape of a *curve*—rather than a conveniently straight line.

The RPER Curve

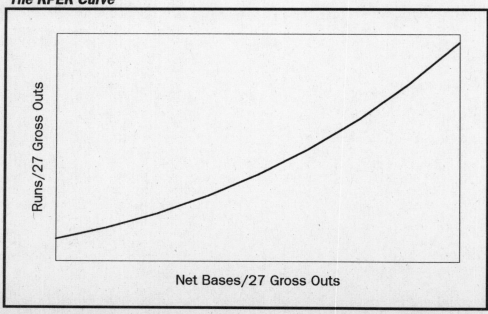

Net Bases/27 Gross Outs

As the NBE/Run result for the 14 teams in each league is plotted, their distribution describes the curved pattern. The individual team's distance, if any, from the "normal" curve then identifies their relative efficiency of run conversion. Above the curve, they produced more runs than they "should have." Below the curve, they made inefficient use of their raw material.

On offense, the manager's job is to place his team *above* the curve!

A Brief Note About Defense

Everything we've said to this point applies equally to defense, as well. Instead of NBE/Run, though, the NBA/Run (Net Bases Allowed) figure for the team is used and plotted against the same curve (the elements of both NBE and NBA are identical, you'll recall). In this case, however, the objective is to get the team *below* the curve.

In a sense, the defensive RPER curve measures "unearned" runs—but it incorporates *more* than errors. It also reflects both defensive "oversights" (missed cutoff men, botched fielder's choices, etc.). Moreover, it catches "turnovers"—potential runs taken away in the form of defensive "coups" (outfield assists, pickoffs, etc.).

The RPER Results

The RPER concept remains in a developmental stage, probably somewhere around class AA at this point, but we believed it deserved a "spot start" here in 1994 *Essential Baseball*. RPER gave us these highlight results in '93.

	Est. "Extra" Runs	Est. Runs "Saved"	Est. Total Positive Run Differential
American League:			
Cleveland	48	29	77
Texas	75	(8)	67
National League:			
Pittsburgh	(3)	31	28

The rest of the teams either ended up "on the curve" or offset a positive performance in one area with a deficiency in another. Only Montreal appeared to be affected with troubles in both, as was discussed in the Expos' essay.

We'll take the concept further in the future but, for now, RPER's given us a slate of nominees for manager-of-the-year.

American League Manager of the Year

At the wire, Cleveland's Mike Hargrove edged the Rangers' Kevin Kennedy in a close ballot.

What separated these two guys from the herd was RPER—no other AL team came anywhere close to outperforming their TOPR and TPER by the margins Hargrove's and Kennedy's did.

In addition, both managers also gave exceptionally strong performances in their leadership roles in '93, as detailed in the Cleveland and Texas team essays. Hargrove, by pulling his team together in the aftermath of their pre-season tragedy and setting the course for their spirited performance from June forward. Kennedy, by forcefully attacking the Rangers' psyche in the midst of their June slump, and converting the roster into a team that believed it was a contender and played like one.

The nod goes to Hargrove . . . barely. Let's examine where the Indians' edges came from:

Offense—Cleveland didn't get runners on base as frequently (.335 OBP vs. .337 league average), but they got them home better (37.9% of earned baserunners scored vs. 36.4% league average). Their power was only average (.409 SLG vs. .408 league average), but they put a high proportion of their runners in a position to score by their aggressive use of TOPR's Baserunner Sub-set.

		Baserunner Sub-set						
	SH	SF	SB	CS	GDP	BRB	BRO	Ratio
Avg. Team	50	52	111	−62	−127	23	292	.080
Cleveland	39	72	159	−54	−131	85	296	.287

The manager exerts a controlling influence on the Baserunner Sub-set by his technique of managing the game and constructing the batting order. Using the same number of outs, Hargrove moved 62 more runners into position to score (SH and SB) or to the plate (SF) than the average team. This factor played a large part in the team's 48 "extra" runs.

Defense—Cleveland's defense led the league in errors (148)! Yet, RPER contends this defense "saved" 29 runs. They were fifth in the league in opposition baserunners erased via GDP or CS (200) and *tops* in the league in outfield assists (44 vs. 25 league average). As a consequence, even though Cleveland pitchers allowed a huge 2,221 baserunners (behind only Oakland), only 37.9% of them scored (just slightly above the league average). Plus, despite the high error count, only 9.6% of the team's runs allowed were unearned (just slightly above the 8.7% league average). The Indians made errors, but they recovered from them, they eliminated opposition baserunners and they appear to have played the game fundamentally well. Hargrove and his staff deserve some of the credit.

National League Manager of the Year

Consideration for the NL Manager-of-the-Year was another close call. The Phillies' Jim Fregosi and the Pirates' Jim Leyland both had a number of things going for them.

The Phils won a pennant, of course. But the Pirates won more games and finished higher in the standings than their TOPR/TPER differential suggests they should have. The Phils evidenced a tremendous team "character" (one hesitates to call it "chemistry") that serves as a tribute to Fregosi's leadership. But the Pirates, a young and inexperienced club, showed a resolute spirit—never giving a sign of collapse in the face of adversity.

So far as RPER's concerned, the Pirates showed an amazing ability to take runs away from their opponents on defense. Conversely, the Phils didn't impress RPER and were, in fact, rather dreadful on the defensive side (an estimated 31 runs "given away").

In the end, though, the issue was decided by high-falutin' philosophical considerations. The whole Phillies' offense, represented an exercise in near perfect TOPRism. Fregosi simply took full advantage of his impressive offensive assets, allowing them to do "their thing," whatever it was, to the best of their ability.

He perfectly aligned the batting order to create scoring opportunities and capitalize on them. Unnecessary outs weren't allowed to happen. The guys who *could* run (Dykstra and Morandini) did. The ones who couldn't, didn't—unless their spot was carefully chosen. The platoon outfielders were given every chance to succeed—e.g., Incaviglia saw lefties and breaking ball pitchers and mashed them. And they were granted little chance to fail—e.g., Chamberlain wasn't asked to deal with pitchers that threw baseballs that featured "mid-course corrections."

The fact that the '93 Phillies scored more runs than any NL team in 31 years is convincing proof that what Fregosi did, worked. What Leyland did also worked. In '93 he simply had a lot less to work with.

FUEL FOR THE HOT STOVE

◀ Fantasy Baseball—GM for a Day ▶

Decades ago, when TVs only came in black and white, a show entitled "Queen For A Day" enjoyed significant popularity. Each week the show's host selected from the audience at random some woman and made her "Queen For A Day." They showered her in gifts. Excused her from the daily humdrum chores of life. Made her feel like royalty.

That's what rotisserie league or so-called fantasy baseball does in a way. It takes the average, everyday fan and lets her or him actually be, for one day, what baseball fans talk about and dream of being the rest of the year—General Manager for a day. For one day a fantasy GM gets to do exactly what a real GM does. He or she has a budget and assembles a team. If the team spends too much on a single star there'll not be enough left over to complete a competent lineup. The rotisserie league GM must have precisely the same skills as a real-life GM. He must be able to anticipate some players diminishing in talent while seeking out others about to step to a higher level. Every baseball GM hunts for a bargain. So do fantasy GMs.

Here's an area where our TOPR-TPER tables might come in the handiest. Trendlines on individual players help ferret out those players whose performances may be about to tumble and, conversely, help identify those whose upward direction may indicate their readiness to perform at a new plateau.

Fantasy GMs want information on the best buys offensively. Or the biggest busts. That's exactly what TOPR does. Fantasy GMs need to know the pitchers who figure to be leaders in wins and/or saves. Our TPER trendlines provide just such advice.

We've broken our fantasy section into American and National Leagues by individual positions. With pitchers we've considered only starters and closers. Tweeners, while they're an incredibly important part of real staffs, generally get few wins or saves and only start piling up such numbers if there's a real emergency on their real staff. But, since they generally accumulate few of the elements most important to fantasy GMs (wins and/or saves), we've eliminated them from our mix except in cases where such a pitcher may figure to play a much more prominent role for his team in '94.

So, if you're ready to be GM for a day, so are we:

American League Hitters

1B—A well-stocked position even before Will Clark switched leagues. The stars jump out at you—Olerud, Thomas and Palmeiro. Be just a tad conscious of the fact that Palmeiro comes off his best season ever and a year in which he headed for free agency. Sometimes players like that slip a notch or two the next season . . . Fielder's fallen off the last couple of years but still carries a big name and probably remains a bit overvalued because of it . . . Mo Vaughn might qualify as a buy. He broke through last year but could, at age 26, take another step upward this year. Don't be afraid to grab him . . . Minnesota's Kent Hrbek might also offer value. Injuries and the serious illness of his child shortened his '93. But "Herbie" TOPRed well and might bounce back. Make sure the price is reasonable . . . Eddie Murray joins this mix in Cleveland. But be very, very careful. Those 27 HRs and 100 RBIs in New York came with him hitting cleanup. In Cleveland that's Albert Belle's job. He might "clean up" so many times there's little left for Eddie. Besides, Murray's recent TOPR decline indicates the end's getting near . . . California's J. T. Snow should appeal to bargain hunters. Despite a world of trouble last season he came on very strongly at

the end. A much bigger '94 might be in store . . . Avoid Don Mattingly. Big name—small numbers . . . The bargain of the year might be Seattle's Tino Martinez. His TOPR's climbed steadily and he's approaching the breakthrough age for young power hitters . . . But perhaps the best buy of all could be Mark McGwire. If he's well again (and he should be) he's a real AND a rotisserie star. Don't be afraid to nab him early.

2B—A position very thin in talent . . . Obviously Alomar's the best. But do not be afraid of Detroit's Lou Whitaker. He's posting terrific numbers but gets so little exposure that other fantasy GMs may have taken little notice . . . Cleveland's Carlos Baerga appears ready to take another step up at age 25. And if he does, it puts him near the superstar and super-TOPR level . . . Scott Fletcher's unbelievably steady but you never know when a team's gonna try to make him a utility player. Boston, for instance, seemed to want to give their 2B job to Tim Naehring at season's end. Avoid Scooter . . . Damion Easley's coming off a terrific TOPR debut. But be forewarned he's almost certain to be a *third baseman* in '94 . . . Chuck Knoblauch and the Twins fell so totally apart that all Minnesota players may have some value come '94 fantasy draft time. He's a gamer and should bounce back with numbers more like those he posted in '92 . . . Pass on the likes of Joey Cora, Harold Reynolds, Bill Spiers, Pat Kelly and Doug Strange. Especially avoid Jose Lind . . . Brent Gates qualifies as our bargain tip. He's a very, very fine young player. Excellent pop in his bat. Will play every day and should move up off an already impressive rookie season . . . Watch out for a California rookie named Kevin Flora. He'll get a shot at the job in the spring. If you want to take a flyer, his minor league numbers suggest there's some sting in his bat.

3B—Not much to choose from here. Fryman and Palmer stand head and shoulders above the rest. Each is only 25 years old and figures to improve. Palmer's the one to really keep an eye on. There's a 40-homer season just waiting in those quick wrists . . . Ventura's produced OK numbers. But realize he'll almost certainly not hit cleanup in '94. That means he's not right behind Thomas in the lineup. That means batting with fewer men on and that means less RBIs . . . Edgar Martinez has reportedly healed pretty nicely. If he's fit (check spring training info) that gaudy 148 TOPR of '92 is only one year old . . . Gary Gaetti's fast finish at KC encouraged the Royals to give him a new contract. "You pays your money and you takes your chances" as they used to say at the sideshow . . . Scott Cooper could be of value. He's a good-looking, line-drive hitter whose numbers might climb as he reaches baseball's prime age . . . Mike Blowers figures as a platoon DH in Seattle with Martinez back. Pass . . . Avoid Wade Boggs. He's become an average offensive player with a big name. That's not what fantasy GMs shop for . . . Our bargain tip? If you're not getting much production out of this position at mid-season try to pick up B. J. Surhoff. He always struggles in the first half and is always good in the second. For a full season, get Jim Thome!

SS—Grab John Valentin! Immediately! He's got real pop in his bat and he's turning 27. Just a guess here, but you might get 20 HRs out of him . . . Trammell's healthy again and with that return to health his numbers came all the way back. Sure he's older. But he's very, very good . . . Ripken's a choice. He's had two down seasons. Is the high-90-TOPR neighborhood where he'll live the rest of his career? Or, as many stars do, will he adjust and turn out another in the 120 area? You make the call . . . Fernandez, if he's still in the league, puts up good numbers. But watch out if he's on a non-competitive team. He looked at times like he didn't care while playing with the Mets and his stats showed it . . . Gagne's coming off his best TOPR season ever—be careful . . . Listach might be the bargain here. If well, his speed should boost that TOPR back into three figures . . . Bordick got off to a miserable start in Oakland dragging his entire '93 season down. Others might not have noticed his fast finish. Tab as a possible steal . . . Guillen, Vizquel, Fermin and Owen offer little hope of respectable numbers . . . Disarcina's a star if it's a fantasy fielding league . . . Watch Minnesota's Scott Leius. He's got some pop and might bounce back to be a decent player. And, having virtually not played in all of '93 you can get him cheap, cheap . . . But maybe cheapest of all could be Manny Lee. Be advised that he had his best season ever in Toronto in the year he approached free agency. His Texas contract's up again at the end of '94. The plain truth of baseball is that some players play harder and don't seem to get hurt nearly as much when their wallet's on the line.

C—A one-star position—Chris Hoiles. Get him! . . . But don't be afraid that Mike Stanley's year might be no more than a "one-year wonder." Stano's always been a much better than average offensive player. The only question about him remains why it took his teams so long to notice that he could do it . . . Mike MacFarlane's put steady figures up the last few years. Has underrated power . . . Maybe the toughest to grade at this position is Detroit's Chad Kreuter. Most of his career he'd been little more than a professional out. But hanging around the rest of those big boppers suddenly transformed him last year. A mirage? Maybe. But maybe not. He plays in a wonderful hitter's yard and will again have all those big bats around him in the lineup. Don't bet against a repeat . . . Dave Valle comes off the best year of his career at age 32 as he neared free agency. Avoid him . . . Brian Harper's got a wonderful batting average but the numbers for a fantasy GM get pretty empty after that . . . Pudge Rodriguez's numbers stepped up last year and, at age 22, might climb again . . . Steinbach's coming off an injury and never TOPRed as well as his reputation suggested he would. Pass . . . Toronto's Pat Borders might lose his job to rookie Carlos Delgado. Pass . . . Ron Karkovice offers some home run power and a steady string of decent seasons before slipping last year. Not a bad middle-of-the-draft choice . . . Our bargain choice leaps out from the Indians roster. Always-injured Sandy Alomar Jr., appeared healthy late last year. Ever better, he looked fit. He'd gotten very heavy during his inactivity of the last couple seasons. Look out—a big year may happen . . . Seattle rookie Dan Wilson has no power and no speed and appeared overmatched at times in the NL last season.

RF—Hook a Salmon! Some might avoid him worrying about the "sophomore jinx." Phooey. His game's very solid. A star is being born . . . Jay Buhner's always been a pretty decent player. With Griffey Jr. always on base in front of him and the two Martinezes healthy again behind him '94 could be a huge year. . . . Paul O'Neill puts up good numbers year after year after year. Good player . . . Joe Carter's TOPR slipped the last couple seasons. He's still a star but be careful. After his World Series heroics he might be overvalued . . . Kirby Puckett seems to be in an up-down-up-down cycle with '94 being an "up" year. Always a good choice . . . This position may offer more bargains than any other this year. Ruben Sierra should be fine if McGwire's fine to hit behind him. Look for a major jump in numbers . . . Felix Jose's had his shoulder repaired. He had a pair of healthy 117–118 TOPRs before getting hurt. Could be a very good value. . . . Maybe the best buy of all could turn out to be Baltimore's rising star Jeffrey Hammonds. An injury cut short '93. But maybe not . . . If you're in a Japanese fantasy league, avoid Rob Deer. All those American homers will drive the bidding up and he'll wind up costing too much yen.

CF—Two stars and at least two real opportunities here . . . Ken Griffey Jr. doesn't need any more written about him . . . Soon, we'll be writing the same about Kenny Lofton whose numbers keep climbing as he reaches 27—the traditional breakthrough age . . .

Devon White's coming off one of his best campaigns. Be careful, he might backslide a bit . . . Realize Darryl Hamilton joins the mix at this position this year. He might be overlooked by other fantasy GMs and has TOPRed above 100 three years in a row . . . Chad Curtis and Brian McRae remain young enough to suggest there's another plateau or two they might step up to. Curtis probably rates a touch better offensively . . . Veteran Mike Devereaux sunk to TOPR depths last year. Avoid him. If he starts slowly the O's could bench him . . . Bernie Williams also slumped. New York's not a patient town . . . David Hulse holds some intrigue. He's played very little pro baseball and appears to still be very much in his learning stage. If he ups his walk total he'll steal a lot more and his value zooms. . . . Lance Johnson's TOPR reached a career high in '93. He doesn't figure to step up any more at age 30 . . . We offer a pair of possible "best buys." Eric Davis seemed to thrive when he arrived in Detroit. This guy once put up huge numbers. He just might again, especially when dropped into this lineup that so often goes on "feeding frenzies" . . . Shane Mack's numbers fell off dramatically last year for a good reason—a very bad shoulder. But, once healed, he snapped right back to the form that's made him one of the best and THE steadiest at this position in the '90s.

LF—A four-star position—Rickey, Gonzalez, Raines and Belle. Henderson just keeps churning out numbers . . . The frightening truth about Texas' "Mr. Juan-derful" is that he's got a chance to improve. And, maybe, improve a lot! . . . Tim Raines gets little notice but puts up big numbers. Exercise a bit of caution here, though. He'll be 34, has a big, new contract and has been nicked a bit recently . . . Albert Belle's a banger sitting on a huge season with new teammate Eddie Murray hitting just behind him. Maybe a monster year ahead? . . . Greg Vaughn leaped to a new level last year. If Milwaukee acquired someone to hit behind him (or in front) he might step up again. Don't be afraid to select him and smile . . . Be careful of Brady Anderson. Oh, he's a nice player. But his value might still be a bit too high off that incredible '92 season . . . The injury plague of Mike Greenwell seems to have ended. The pop's returned and so have the stats. A reasonable choice . . . Seattle's Eric Anthony couldn't produce big figures in Houston hitting behind three superb players. Skip him until he shows more . . . California wants former 3B Eduardo Perez to take a shot at this position. Take care. He's got a future. But he's not "Tony Perez" yet . . . Kevin McReynolds continues to slide. Pass . . . Luis Polonia runs and runs and runs. His BA's solid. The rest of his game's as empty as Elvis' grave.

DH—Some big bangers here . . . The numbers of Paul Molitor, Mickey Tettleton (unless they still list him as a catcher in your league), Tony Phillips and Danny Tartabull make any and all extremely fine picks . . . Hal Baines had a marvelous '93, but has achey-breaky knees and a new contract. You make the call . . . Chili Davis comes off a remarkable power season. But at 34 that may cost you a lot in this year's draft. You may find better value elsewhere . . . Dave Winfield's 42. Andre Dawson's turned 39. Each has a big name with the smallest TOPRs of his career in '93. The same applies to Robin Yount. Control your urge to buy a Hall of Famer . . . Oakland's Troy Neel could offer possibilities. Maybe a late bloomer. Nice power and, given all the "big names" at DH, may go very cheaply . . . Take note of where Cleveland chooses to play Eddie Murray in the spring. Instead of 1B he might settle in at DH. Note our reservations in the 1B notes . . . Wanna pull a "cheap trick" on your fellow league members? Grab Julio Franco. The White Sox signed him to bat behind Frank Thomas. Wow, the numbers he might put up! Got better and better in '93 as his knees stopped aching. You might get a .300 BA, 12 HRs and 90 RBIs. And you might get it all fairly inexpensively . . . Jose Canseco's almost certainly the most puzzling player at this position. He's just 29. If he wants to prove himself, he could put up huge numbers. If he's still there at round four or five, jump on him.

American League Pitchers

Starters—There are almost as many different levels of value in starting pitchers for rotisserie league GMs as there are starters themselves. We've chosen to separate them into six plateaus. Obviously, if a pitcher from a "be careful level" remains on the board after all the more solid pitchers have been selected, he becomes more valuable. So, as with other selections, value remains the key to any choice.

LEVEL 1—Studs. You don't have to be much of a genius to take these guys. They're durable, big-time staff ace types. Lots of innings. Hopefully lots of wins. Kevin Appier, Alex Fernandez, Mark Langston, Randy Johnson, Chris Bosio, Jack McDowell, Chuck Finley, Kevin Brown, Wilson Alvarez, Mike Mussina, Juan Guzman.

LEVEL 2—Possible bargains even though they have big names. Ben McDonald moved to a new plateau last year. Maybe he's Baltimore's ace in '94, not Mussina. Or, maybe they have two . . . Jason Bere may still not be known well enough to command top dollar. He deserves it . . . John Doherty, especially with the kind of run support Detroit gives him, could produce a 20-win season very soon . . . Bobby Witt gained control of his assortment in '93. When Oakland's offense bounces back he stands the best chance to be the number one benefactor . . . Kevin Tapani comes off an awful first half. That's right, not an awful year, but a terrible first half of a year. Too good not to rebound . . . All Seattle's Dave Fleming does is win, win, win . . . Kansas City's Tom Gordon finally appeared to harness his excellent stuff last season. Maybe your fellow fantasy GMs didn't notice. We did . . . Aaron Sele looked like the real deal. Don't shy away from grabbing him as opposed to paying more for a bigger name . . . Roger Pavlik couldn't lose the last two months. He also can't seem to throw a straight pitch. His stuff moves all over the place and his record probably moves up.

LEVEL 3—Be sure to get 'em at the right price . . . Roger Clemens' arm problems were probably minor. But the "Rocket Man" still figures at a premium price and did not have premium control last year . . . Jamie Moyer comes off a spectacular season. But don't overpay for one good year . . . Frank Viola's incredibly steady. But he's reached 34 and encountered the first arm trouble of his career . . . David Cone's incredibly high pitch counts make him a candidate to tumble any season now. And, he's very costly . . . Jim Abbott's strikeouts-to-walks ratio keeps falling and his stuff looked very, very ordinary last year for a pitcher who'll cost "ace dollars" . . . Kenny Rogers made a terrific conversion to starter. Don't get carried away just yet. 1993 was one year . . . Cal Eldred threw more pitches last year than Bob Barker on "The Price Is Right." Be careful. His arm took some heavy abuse in '93 . . . Pat Hentgen won 19 for the Jays and seems to have a glorious future. But his TPER read just 99—very average. Maybe his record looks average in '94? . . . Danny Darwin comes off a terrific season. But he's 38 and how many that age put such seasons back-to-back . . . Tim Belcher posted another solid TPER. He's coming off a free agent year, though, and is reaching an age (32) where high fastball pitchers often go through a period of adjustment.

LEVEL 4—Exercise extreme caution . . . Dennis Martinez arrives in Cleveland with a mediocre TPER but a good record. Those types often drop to .500 or worse . . . Dave Stewart's a major name but with very average pitching efficiency the last few seasons . . . Melido Perez has a bad shoulder and guaranteed money. Uh, oh . . . Ricky Bones TPER keep climbing . . . Bill Wegman comes off tons of physical troubles and a lot of innings in recent seasons . . . Bob Wickman wins lots of games but doesn't pitch consistently well. Those things have a way of evening out . . . Scott Erickson appears headed downhill. You'll still pay a decent amount for him. What if he craters? . . . Ron Darling's had three very poor TPER seasons this decade . . . If Todd Stottlemyre can't win regularly with Toronto's offense behind him, do you want him?

LEVEL 5—No, at almost any cost . . . Fernando Valenzuela, Jack Morris (Whoever thought he'd show up on this list?), Rick Sutcliffe, Ted Higuera or Nolan Ryan. Hey, he's retired. I know you never thought it would happen, but after 27 years he *will not* be back!

LEVEL 6—Possible big-time bargains. For various reasons you may get these hurlers cheaply and they could produce a major hit for you . . . Oakland's Bob Welch had always been a big winner before '93. Might be again if the offense and Eckersley snap back. You should get him at a low cost . . . Mike Moore's a puzzler. But late last year his stuff seemed to be improving. Sturdy enough to make 35 starts. With Detroit's offense that might get you 17–20 wins . . . An even better choice in Tigertown could be Bill Gullickson. Injuries messed up '93. How many would guess he's won 47 games the last three years? . . . Hipolito Pichardo gets absolutely no notice in KC. But he's an improving youngster with a shot at emerging . . . Scott Kamieniecki hung in there to win 10 times last season. If he cures his bizarre problem of not being able to win away from Yankee Stadium, he's a steal . . . Sturdy Jose Mesa might make 35 starts in Cleveland this year. With that Tribe offense who knows how many he could win. And he'll be cheap, cheap . . . Jaime Navarro comes off a horrid season. But he's young, healthy, devalued and won 32 games in '91–'92 . . . If you can get him for almost nothing, Joe Magrane presents an interesting possibility. What if he bounces back and pitches for Whitey Herzog in California like he pitched for him in St. Louis? . . . Charles Nagy's got a chance to be one of the year's best buys. An ace before his injury. There should be no lingering effects. Wins 20 if he's right. And the price may be right because of the arm problem . . . Our best buy we've saved for last—Cleveland's Mark Clark. The Indians found a flaw in his delivery late last season and, when corrected, he became a new pitcher. He'll cost you absolutely nothing.

Shopping tip—Take Tiger lefty David Wells. Get a terrific first half out of him. Then, at the break, pawn him off on some unsuspecting GM who doesn't know Wells' history of second half troubles.

Closers—Just four "sure things" here. Duane Ward, Jeff Montgomery, Roberto Hernandez and Tom Henke qualify as this crop's cream . . . Jeff Russell may become a best buy. He was very underrated last year. Don't be afraid to nab him . . . Rick Aguilera's terrific—if the Twins give him anything to save . . . Mike Henneman keeps piling up an impressive number of wins but has never topped 24 saves . . . Avoid Doug Henry. Milwaukee likely goes to a bullpen by committee . . . You might consider taking a flyer on the Indians' Jerry DiPoto. The Tribe seems intent on shoving him into the closer's role and his minor league profile says nothing but the right things . . . Avoid Gregg Olson. The "Otter" has arm trouble and the O's may go to the "committee approach" with Alan Mills chairing the committee . . . So, what do you do with "The Eck"? Maybe he's actually dropped far enough in value to be a value . . . If you buy Lee Smith you're paying a premium for an aging pitcher off his worst season ever. Pass . . . NY may give their job to Xavier Hernandez. Look out. Houston tried to do that with very mixed results . . . California's Joe Grahe might turn into the "super-sleeper" of the closer set. The Angels babied him a bit while he got over minor arm problems last year. But they seem intent on handing him this job. And remember, he saved 21 in a partial '92 season.

Debut Pitchers—Every year a few come from the minors to make an impact as Bere and Sele did in '93. Phil Leftwich, Todd Van Poppel and Steve Karsay made promising late-season arrivals in '93. But get them cheaply if you want them. Normally we'd have recommended Milwaukee's Angel Miranda, but he injured a leg badly over the winter. Avoid him. Our best "out-of-nowhere" prospect this season is Rick Helling of Texas. The Rangers have opened a rotation spot just for him. He arrives with dazzling numbers and scouts raving. Grab him.

National League Hitters

1B—A position loaded with quality . . . You almost can't make a mistake taking John Kruk, Fred McGriff or Andres Gallaraga now that the "Big Cat's" agreed to stay in "hitters heaven" otherwise known as Colorado. Be just a tad cautious about bidding too much for Gallaraga though. He posted three dismal years to begin the decade. But you'll pay through the nose for him based on last season's stats . . . Jefferies broke new ground with his 146 TOPR last season. But he's only 26 and might live at that level for some time. Solid . . . Jeff Bagwell's incredibly steady. But that may change. He's reaching the age where many sluggers move up to stardom. Could be sitting on a huge year . . . Mark Grace rests on the next level down from those already listed. But an excellent choice . . . That doesn't leave much else at the position. Hal Morris puts up a nice BA but not much else . . . Eric Karros backslid in '93. Not a very strong option . . . Orestes Destrade came on a bit but has reached 32 years old, pretty late to hope a player'll show dramatic improvement from a below par 96 TOPR . . . If you're looking to go cheap, cheap you might try SF's J.R. Phillips. He drilled 27 HRs at Phoenix. Look out, though, he's strikeout prone and hit just .263 . . . Montreal's Cliff Floyd leap-frogged from AA to AAA to the majors last year. A gamble, but a good one.

2B—Several question marks here . . . About the surest thing at this spot probably remains LA's Delino DeShields. Just a toddler by major league age standards but with almost-star offensive capabilities . . . Ryne Sandberg's the traditional choice and ought to bounce back splendidly from his injury-interrupted downer of '93. But he'll cost an arm and a leg and he's 34. Probably an all-star again. But you'll have to pay a heavy price to find out . . . Craig Biggio's numbers slipped in '93 because his running game disappeared. But he added power. If his steals return (Did opponents know Houston's signs?) maybe he's in for a big year . . . The Cards pair of Luis Alicea and Geronimo Pena shared the job last year. If neither's been dealt by the start of the season, avoid each of them figuring they'll again split work time and, thus, split stats . . . We didn't mention Robby Thompson until now despite the fact that he had the league's best TOPR at 2B last year. He's now 32, has a history of back problems, comes off his best season ever and just got a megabucks contract. He'll cost a lot of cash in fantasy ball. Probably worth it because he's a true gamer. But you might find better ways to go with such a top-dollar investment at other positions . . . Jeff Kent's intriguing. He's had a pair of over-100 TOPRs and, given a more settled clubhouse this season, may blossom. A bargain? In New York? . . . Carlos Garcia's in much the same situation as Kent. Same age. Very promising rookie season. Starting to show some power. Expect another step up in '94 . . . Colorado's Eric Young TOPRed in the same vicinity as Kent and Garcia. But he's a multi-position player who could get moved. Might want to avoid . . . If you're into taking flyers on injured players trying to rebound, Bret Barberie's your man. Better than that 95 TOPR of '93. His history suggests you might find the price right and the value attractive . . . Avoid Mark Lemke. He may not have a starting job . . . Pass on Jody Reed. TOPRs have tumbled . . . Mickey Morandini's put two mediocre seasons back-to-back. Look elsewhere . . . Our bargain choice comes from last year's Reds team. Bip Roberts put up outstanding numbers in '90 and '92. Injuries destroyed his '93. In free agency this off-season he wanted only a one-year contract indicating he's willing to play his buns off for a shot at a bigger deal the year after. That's a "buy signal."

3B—Looks like a deep position but really isn't. Gary Sheffield's been moved to the OF. If healthy he puts up wonderful numbers. Because he's done more than his share of complaining he's not a "popular" player and thus sometimes not popular with fantasy GMs. A top level OF you may get for second or third level money. Grab him . . . But, back to the 3Bs. Matt Williams stands above the rest of the field. Right in the "prime time" of his career. But,

one tiny reservation—he's coming off the best year he's ever had. Two in a row? Probably yes . . . Charlie Hayes' numbers zoomed when he arrived in Colorado. If he's still there he's worth a bid . . . Dave Hollins' TOPR slipped a bit. No big deal. But he gets nicked a lot because he plays so hard. A very good player though . . . Todd Zeile and Steve Buechele put up very similar seasons in '93. But Zeile's four years younger and has a history of doing better. Last season was the best ever for "Boo" . . . Jeff King moved up a full notch last year. But TOPR histories suggest he probably won't take another step up in '94 . . . Avoid Terry Pendleton. He's 33, has a big (costly) name and his TOPR points straight downhill. (He looked a bit heavy in '93.) . . . Ken Caminiti has but one good year on his resume—1992. Pass . . . Tim Wallach's once considerable skills appear to have eroded badly. Pass . . . Chris Sabo presents the GM for a day with a real problem. Are his injuries of the last two seasons behind him thus freeing him to return to the hustling "Spuds" Sabo that posted stats with the best of them at 3B? Or have those trips to the DL reduced him to the kind of mediocre offensive player he's been the last two years? You make the call. But you might get him at 10-cents-on-the-dollar compared to his former worth . . . Our bargain basement beauty's Montreal's Sean Berry. His half season last year would have made him the top TOPRing hot sacker. He's right in the usual age window where players break through. You can get him for a song. Start humming some notes.

SS—This position offers three mid-career solid choices and lots of "well, maybe's." Jeff Blauser's moved to the top of this heap with a pair of very good seasons. But super-prospect Chipper Jones looks as ready as he'll ever be to play in the bigs. Might Atlanta make room for him by moving Blauser to 2B? Or, do they wait until Pendleton leaves after '94 and slip him over to 3B? . . . Blauser rules the roost only because Barry Larkin's hurting. Injuries have led to a TOPR deterioration of late. But when healthy he's Hall of Fame material . . . Jay Bell's quietly developed some pop and has moved just in behind our two leaders. He's steady, plays every day and won't cause many second thoughts . . . After this trio you're left with one aging superstar who appears to be in decline (Ozzie Smith), one injured Cub who once seemed ready for stardom (Shawon Dunston) and a veteran Marlin free agent who's healthy again with a respectable TOPR but few bidders for his services (Walt Weiss). We'd recommend a pass on all. If only those three remain, take Weiss . . . Everything else on the SS board consists of early to mid-career shortstops who TOPR under 100, except for Philly rookie Kevin Stocker who debuted with an eye-popping 122. Avoid him! His minor league numbers suggest that he may be last season's biggest mirage . . . The best of the rest is probably a toss-up between Wil Cordero and Andujar Cedeno. Both appear to be emerging offensive talents who may soon join the upper level at this position. Lean to Cordero whose past hints at a bigger future . . . Pass on Vinny Castilla. If you can't TOPR 100 while hitting in Colorado you're in trouble . . . Pass on Jose Offerman. He's never fulfilled the promise LA keeps holding out for him. This might be the year he actually does arrive. But they've been saying that about him for a couple years now . . . Royce Clayton didn't produce much of a figure (88) last year, but he's got a chance to move up as does Ricky Gutierrez. You're guessing when you're down to this level.

C—Get one of the top four! After that you're throwing darts . . . There's not much to choose from between Darren Daulton and Rick Wilkins. Daulton's been at the top but has those pain-filled knees. Wilkins just arrived at this level but looks like he'll settle down here . . . Mike Piazza comes off a spectacular rookie season. He's got all the appearances of a special player. One tiny reservation though. Two years ago Eric Karros of LA won Rookie-of-the-Year and then slipped badly in his sophomore season. But few scouts think there's any real comparison between the two as hitters. A solid choice . . . Don "Sluggo" Slaught just keeps putting consistent numbers up.

If the other three have been taken, make him a priority . . . Then comes an enormous drop-off. None of the other catchers on the NL board has ever TOPRed as high as 100 during the '90s as a regular except for Benito Santiago and his game's headed downhill at warp speed. Pass him . . . If you're still shopping we'll recommend one of four left. Darrin Fletcher turns 27 this year after taking a solid jump up the TOPR ladder last season. An excellent chance to take . . . Joe Girardi plays in Colorado. Enough said . . . Eddie Taubensee hinted he just might be putting things together a bit last year. The problem here concerns what appears to be a Houston plan to platoon him with Scott Servais who got to an even 100 as a part-timer last year . . . Atlanta's Javy Lopez appears ready and the Braves have cleared out this position to make him the starter. Very good minor league credentials . . . Avoid the rest. Think of catcher as NL's "Christmas position." Shop early!

RF—Our best advice in the entire draft might be to get Larry Walker. His TOPR's moved steadily upward this decade as he approaches age 27. He's learned to steal effectively. Look for a step to superstardom . . . Bobby Bonilla's probably moving to 1B. He's unhappily putting up happy numbers in the Big (Rotten) Apple. At first base he joins a crowded, talented group. If he's still in the OF, he and David Justice become natural choices if you've been outbid for Walker . . . Justice, three years younger, keeps putting up fantastic TOPRs. Maybe they'll get even better with McGriff's full-season presence in the middle of the Braves order . . . Give high consideration to Orlando Merced. His TOPR's rising as though filled with helium and he, like Walker, turns 27 this season. If you missed on Walker and want someone cheaper than Bobby Bo or Justice, here's your man . . . Veterans Tony Gwynn and Dante Bichette finished with almost identical TOPRs last season. For Gwynn, his highest this decade. For Bichette (in Colorado) his best ever. Lean to Bichette as long as he hasn't been dealt. If he has, don't touch him! . . . The bargain basement buy we recommend is Cincy's Reggie Sanders. Backslid a bit last season. But in the messy, ever-changing Reds lineup, that's not unexpected. Minor league numbers suggest he's bound for much better things. Might this be the season? He'll come cheap. Very cheap . . . Avoid Philly's platoon at this position and the soap-opera-like saga of Daryl Strawberry . . . Mark Whiten hit a bunch of homers last season but little else. Pass . . . Also pass on the aging Willie McGee . . . Wanna take a chance? The Mets' Jeromy Burnitz may be your guy. Broke in with a bang. But, is he ready? If you've only got a few bucks left and no RF he's worth a shot . . . But one final reminder—Gary Sheffield's either here or in LF and his stats put him right there with the best.

CF—Nail "Nails." Lenny Dykstra's numbers stand head and shoulders above this pack . . . But only one fantasy GM can have this lovable wallbanger . . . The breakthrough candidate here is yet another Expo, Marquis Grissom. Keeps putting positive elements into his game. Stardom may be around this corner . . . Bobby Kelly really seemed to take to the NL before his season-ending injury last year. A word of caution, however: that partial TOPR's his best ever. Is it real? A solid buy if not too expensive . . . Sammy Sosa joined the 30–30 club but still TOPRed at a mere 114 indicating his game still has some pretty major holes in it. On the other hand, he's only 25 and may be on the "UP" elevator. Little to fear here . . . Give special consideration to "overspending" just a bit to get Ellis Burks. He TOPRed 107 for the White Sox. Now goes to a park which inflates offense by 27%. One word of caution, though. Remember his history of back problems . . . Can veteran Brett Butler keep doing it? He's 37 and seemingly in an "up-down" pattern. Don't pay too much . . . Andy Van Slyke's string of outstanding TOPRs ended only due to injury. Very, very solid. Don't pay a premium but be happy if you get him . . . Our shopper's alert in CF centers around a player nicknamed "Prime Time" approaching the age of "prime time." The exit of Otis Nixon opened the door to Deion Sanders playing regularly. Might become a real force. Like Sheffield

there may be some rotisserie GMs who don't like his brashness. Take him and love his numbers . . . Speaking of Nixon, attention AL shoppers: avoid him. TOPRs declining and he simply won't ever drive in any runs . . . Ray Lankford presents the same kind of enigma for fantasy GMs as he does for his real GM in St. Louis. What happened to him? Where'd the supposed superstar go last year? Somebody'll pay pretty handsomely hoping he resurfaces. Pass. He might be a heartbreaker . . . Illness and injury gutted Steve Finley's '93. But he's only had basically one solid season in the majors. Only if he comes cheap . . . If Brian Jordan had a regular job he'd be very worth a flyer. He finally seemed to arrive last season. If the Cards clear a spot for him he'd be a nice addition . . . Derek Bell will hit you a few homers. Chuck Carr'll swipe a bunch of bases. Darren Lewis' glove, not his bat, insures his regular job. If you've reached this point at this position you're bottom feeding.

LF—Invest in Bonds! Simply the best out there. How much you pay's the only question about the best player of this generation . . . If you could know Kevin Mitchell's mind-set, you'd be able to make a legitimate decision on him. When healthy enough to play he destroys pitchers. But that's anybody's guess. Check his waistline when he reports to camp. If it's within 10 inches of his age (32), give him a shot at a moderate price. Then pray . . . Ron Gant's as solid as they come. So why does his name keep coming up in trade talks? . . . Oh, don't you wish you'd have grabbed Phil Plantier last year? You still can. His minor league profile projected him to this level. Figure he goes up . . . What, another possible Expo breakthrough player? That's right. Moises Alou, providing his badly broken ankle's healed, turns 27 with his TOPRs pointing upward. A definite buy . . . Luis Gonzalez, Al Martin and Bernard Gilkey all TOPRed within two points of each other and all are right around baseball's magic age of 27. Gilkey owns the best two previous seasons. Gonzalez' power may give him the best chance to move up a notch . . . Derrick May remains a touted player but the numbers simply don't emerge . . . Given that the Phils again plan to platoon here, you can skip the rest except for our best buy— Howard Johnson. Off a dismal, injury-racked year with the Mutts, he takes his down-on-his-TOPRs career to the place where all dying careers go for resurrection—Colorado. Look what that homer haven did for the likes of Galarraga, Hayes and Bichette. Watch his stats return in full and then some.

National League Pitchers

Starters—As with the AL, we've separated the NL starters into the same seven levels of consideration.

LEVEL 1—Studs. Get all of these you can: Greg Maddux, Jose Rijo, Steve Avery, John Burkett, Pete Harnisch, Pedro Astacio, Ken Hill, Darryl Kile, Curt Schilling and John Smoltz.

LEVEL 2—Big name pitchers who still may for various reasons be possible bargains . . . Doug Drabek, but don't pay "ace" type money to get him (like Houston did) . . . Dwight Gooden's effectiveness seems to be reappearing. If the Mets get better (Can they get worse?) he could give you 15+ victories . . . Rene Arocha debuted in fine style. Excellent control. If the Cards fix their leaky defense and shaky pen situation he moves way up . . . Bret Saberhagen was cooking right along when injuries struck. Nothing that should linger, though. If right, he's one of the best. And last year's "unsavory" season might have cheapened him a great deal . . . Jeff Fassero may have been baseball's most anonymous "ace" last year. Montreal apparently plans on putting him right in the '94 rotation. Good move. Good pick up . . . Tommie Green reached a new TPER low level at age 26. He appears to be the emerging #1 in Philly. But he remains relatively unnoticed in some circles. Grab him, especially with Philly's offense supporting him . . . Andy Benes pitches in San Diego thus may be overlooked. If he gets dealt to some contender jump on him. Even if he's not, he's a solid choice . . . John Smiley's always been a terrific pitcher. Injuries hit him and then everyone hit him. Expect a return to form with the injury depreciating his price to the point where he could have excellent value . . . Nobody seems to appreciate Tom Candiotti for what a fine and sturdy staffer he's become. Always a good pick up.

LEVEL 3—Be sure you get these guys at the right price. All appear to be steady pitchers. But there's something there that might make you hesitate just a bit . . . Bill Swift reigned as the best TPER in the entire league in '93. That'll make him very pricey. But he's got a history of wearing down and that's the last thing you want from a guy you pay top dollar for . . . Terry Mulholland's hip injury late last season and Philly's off-season willingness to shop him around creates real worry. Take care . . . Orel Hershiser's not the same pitcher he once was. But maybe he's almost as good with his new throwing style and repertoire. But he's got a big name and that might drive his price up . . . Ramon Martinez's TPER jumped a full 10 points. Maybe it's nothing more than a glitch in a big offensive year. But he's still viewed as their ace when, in reality, he pitched fourth best of their starters . . . Eric Hanson comes over from Seattle to the Reds carrying a pretty decent TPER but not much of a record. AL pitchers with his particular ability to throw big, sweeping curves to the NL's primarily fastball hitting lineups can sometimes have good initial success . . . Kirk Rueter had a smashing debut and looks like a dynamite pitcher. One worry—many Expo pitchers looked terrific their rookie years and then inexplicably lost it. He probably won't. But that history causes concern.

LEVEL 4—Exercise extreme caution . . . Mark Portugal's coming off the year of his life and leaving the Astrodome where he posted a glittering 30–9 lifetime record. Elsewhere he's barely been a .500 pitcher and now has that huge contract secured . . . Tom Glavine's still regarded as Cy Young material. His TPER, meanwhile, rose suspiciously last year. Be careful. He's undoubtedly a solid pitcher still but not ace type anymore . . . Mike Morgan's 34 and that arm's traveled a lotta miles. His TPER's gone from 76 to 87 to 92 the last three seasons and the Cubs shopped him heavily. Let the buyer beware . . . Danny Jackson's simply never returned to the outstanding form he showed in KC. His barely-better-than-average 96 TPER last season marked his first below-100 effort of the decade. Grab him only if the price becomes very right . . . Bob Tewksbury's effectiveness waned last year. He's 33 and the Cards offered him around a lot. Hmmmmm . . . LA's Kevin Gross went 13–13 last year. That makes it eight years since his last winning season. Pass unless the price gets very low . . . Sid Fernandez, Bud Black and Trevor Wilson. All left-handed. All hurt last year and each hurt a lot lately. All with some decent history, especially El Sid. But these are the types you take and spend the entire season crossing your fingers. Besides, Fernandez now has 25 wins in the '90s, Black's averaged 11 victories a season the last five years and Wilson's had only one season in his career in which he won more than eight . . . Greg Swindell's reputation remains. But his TPER's moved upward two straight years. Besides, he looked a tad heavy last year. Almost certainly overpriced . . . Jose Guzman. Another whose TPERs appear on a worrisome rise. Had shoulder problems years ago and stiffness returned late in the year. Be careful.

LEVEL 5—No, not at any cost . . . Tom Browning still carries a very good name. But his effectiveness has gone through the roof . . . Mike Harkey's running out of time. Something's always keeping his potential from emerging. Guys like this tease GMs and fantasy GMs . . . Greg Harris, Ken Bottenfield, Willie Blair and Bruce Ruffin all pitch in Colorado. Oh, Lord! . . . Only the Phils' outrageous offense saved Ben Rivera. Might lose his rotation spot.

LEVEL 6—Possible big-time bargains. There may be any one of a number of reasons why the following pitchers could come far cheaper than they should. If you can steal a few, do so . . . Donovan Osborne, Chris Hammond, Chris Nabholz and Greg Hibbard are all left-handed, all posted solid TPERs in the mid-90s,

none have a ''huge'' reputation and all remain young enough so that improvement's still possible . . . Yes, Charlie Hough's 46. But he threw 200 innings-plus again last year and, should the Marlins get significantly better, he's on the mound long enough to benefit greatly . . . Marlins youngster Ryan Bowen still has a major league arm and showed real progress last year. Tab for improvement . . . Pirates righty Paul Wagner and lefty Steve Cooke each arrived with attractive performances. Knowing the way Buccos manager Jim Leyland can squeeze out victories, each could be an excellent chance pick, especially Wagner . . . The Mets' Anthony Young can pitch. He just can't win with the Mets. If they've dealt him, grab him for a mere pittance . . . Bruce Hurst missed nearly all of '93 with shoulder problems. He's 36 and many might think he's done for. Look out. This guy's a proven winner with 10 straight double-figure winning seasons prior to '93 and a last losing season in '85. Check the spring box scores. If he looks like he's back, snatch him up . . . Randy Tomlin and Zane Smith each had strung together three exceptional Pirate seasons in the '90s before injury struck. Smith's 33 which causes worry. But Tomlin's only 28. You might get him for virtually nothing . . . We'll recommend only one Colorado starter—Armando Reynoso. Fantasy GMs may simply ignore this staff. Don't skip this guy. His 107 TPER, given that he plays in a horrible park to pitch in, suggests he's a keeper. And also don't forget the incredibly increased offense the Rockies should generate next season with the addition of Burks and Howard Johnson . . . Almost everyone may ignore baby-faced Salomon Torres now that SF's signed Portugal. But he's got an excellent minor league profile and should have benefited from a taste of the pennant race. If Wilson and Black are slow to heal (or don't heal) he gets the #4 spot. In SF that could mean double figure wins.

Closers—Four here merit almost any cost—Bryan Harvey, Rod Beck, Randy Myers and John Wetteland. All have established themselves with multiple solid seasons. All appear healthy. None are over 31. Belly up to the bar and pay the price . . . We'd recommend the same with Gene McMichael except for two reservations—he's had only one-half of one good year and Atlanta seems intent on finding another closer by trade to push him out of that role. Exercise extreme caution . . . Just say no to Mitch Williams and Doug Jones. Each has been a quality stopper but neither comes off a season that encourages confidence. Pass . . . Is Jim Gott for real? Hey, you might get a steal here. He's quietly dropping that TPER through the floor. If there's more to save in LA this year he could put up some big-time numbers . . . Our best buy recommendation goes to Darren Holmes. You'll get him dirt cheap. Hardly anybody knows who the Colorado closer is, for heaven's sake. But once he got his mechanics straightened out in the minors he returned to give the rocky Rockies bullpen a steady hand . . . Gene Harris in San Diego has the arm but never the numbers. Pass . . . Avoid Todd Worrell. LA's fantasy is to just see him pitch . . . Avoid John Franco and Rob Dibble. Big names with big troubles on troubled teams. Not worth the price unless it's very, very, very low . . . And keep one eye on San Diego's Trevor Hoffman who's got the arm to explode. The Padres may force him into the closer role.

Debut Pitchers—There appear to be very, very few NL pitchers who might come from nowhere to impact their clubs immediately. Down the line, reliever Ricky Bottalico might shove his way into Philly's closer picture . . . Pedro A. Martinez might leave middle relief to enter the Padres rotation . . . San Diego does have a pair who came up last season to pitch pretty doggone well in the midst of that sewer that the Padres had become—Tim Worrell and Scott Sanders. Check if either or both have made spring training surges . . . Maybe the best of the long-shot starters to begin '94 could be from the Mets. Bobby Jones, though he TPERed 108, has a decent minor league profile and may get every opportunity to pitch in New York where the Mets regard him as a solid part of their future.

One does not have to be a member of MENSA to draft Frank Thomas or Barry Bonds for one's rotisserie league. The shrewdest and most successful of those who love to be GMs for a day, are the ones who can find bargains. Lemons that turn into lemonade. Ugly ducklings that suddenly become swans. One dollar players who look like a million. We've gathered what we feel may be the top bargains for fantasy GMs in '94. Here's *Essential Baseball*'s "Best Buys."

1994 Fantasy "Best Buys"

AL		NL
Sandy Alomar, Jr.	C	Javy Lopez
Tino Martinez	1B	Jeff Bagwell
Brent Gates	2B	Bip Roberts
Dean Palmer	3B	Sean Berry
John Valentin	SS	Wil Cordero
Greg Vaughn	LF	Howard Johnson
Eric Davis	CF	Deion Sanders
Felix Jose	RF	Larry Walker
Julio Franco	DH	—
Ben McDonald	SP	Steve Avery
John Doherty	SP	Jeff Fassero
Tom Gordon	SP	Bret Saberhagen
Mark Clark	SP	Armando Reynoso
Rick Helling	SP	Bruce Hurst
Joe Grahe	CL	Darren Holmes

BARRY BONDS VS. HISTORY

TOPR Trendline: Barry Bonds' Career

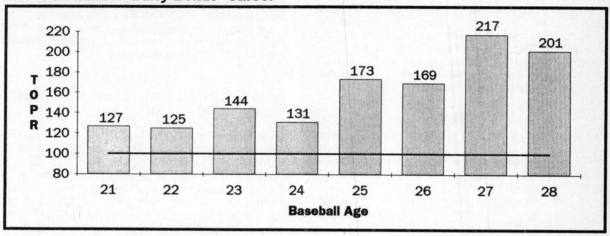

Is there any question that Barry Bonds is the very best player in the game today? No one else really comes close. Here's how TOPR views his career to date.

And, for the record, here are the TOPR ratios (NBE/GOC) for these eight years.

	1986	1987	1988	1989	1990	1991	1992	1993
Net Bases Earned	267	349	343	359	426*	408*	456*	506*
Gross Outs Committed	336	424	402	460	390	395	350	388
NBE/GOC Ratio	.795	.823	.853	.780	1.092*	1.033*	1.303*	1.304*

*League leading totals

Note that total of 506 net bases in '93. It equates to 3.18 net bases for each of the 159 games in which he played, better than a triple a day. File that 506 total for future reference.

His conventional stats for '92 and '93 are equally imposing, embracing excellence in every area of offensive performance.

	BA	OBA	SLG	HR	Run	RBI	SB/CS	BB
1992	.311	.456*	.624*	34	109*	103	39/8	127*
1993	.336	.458*	.677*	46*	129	123*	29/12	126

*League leading totals

Add to this, three MVP awards in the past four years with a 2nd place finish in '91 that could be reasonably debated as unjust (Terry Pendleton's season TOPRed out at 134, far behind Bonds' 169). And realize his new Candlestick home was the least hitter-friendly park in the league in '93. Finally, and most important, his teams have flourished. Division winners in '90–'92 and a surprising second place, one game behind the best record in the majors in '93. But, alas, no pennant to show for it—much less a world championship. That's the only blot on Bonds' ledger and he's gained his own personal demon in the process: the Atlanta Braves. Three years in a row they've edged Bonds' team by the thinnest of baseball margins. He's been one measly game away from playing for it all every time.

How Good Is He?

You could characterize Barry's career to date in the following terms.

◆ He entered the big leagues in '86 as a valuable, highly productive player.
◆ In '88, he advanced his performance to all-star caliber.
◆ In '90, he became MVP timber.
◆ In '92, he became something more than that.

You've doubtless noted that TOPRs around 170 are rare but within the reach of the very finest players. Even among these stars, it usually takes an exceptional year to reach that level. In many years, the league leader fails to post a mark as high as 170. The same can be said for a TOPR ratio (NBE/GOC) of 1.000, which assumes a certain "magic" quality. Any player who delivers one or more net bases for every gross out he commits is doing his job about as well as can be expected of a mere mortal.

But a 200 TOPR? A ratio of 1.300 plus? These last two seasons stick out from our baseball "forest" like two redwoods towering above even the tallest pines. In the brief history of TOPR, they're not only remarkable, they're unprecedented. They beg the question: the best back-to-back seasons since . . . when? We'll use a historical TOPR approach to shed some light on that.

◆ We'll use the TOPR (NBE/GOC) ratio instead of the TOPR number itself. Most historical arguments are couched, rightly or wrongly, in terms of absolute numeric totals, as in "most/biggest," rather than in terms of relativity to league context.
◆ We'll look for players with *consecutive* seasons that are comparable to Bonds' 1.300. It is one thing to have a single super season. Two in a row has a much greater significance.

◆ We'll start with the present, working our way back through players of current memory first.

The Nineties

Rickey Henderson—had a huge season in the AL in '90. Like Bonds, Henderson has the complete offensive package—hits for average (.325 in '90), power (28 HR), has strike zone judgment (97 BB, .439 OBP) and speed (65 SB). The result: a 1.202 ratio (192 TOPR). A remarkable season in its own right, and Henderson's best among his total of *six* 1.000+ ratio seasons (also '83, '85, '87, '92 and '93). Thus, Rickey's career (which is still under construction) exceeds Barry's (who has four such seasons so far). But Henderson's best season only approaches Barry's best because he comes up a bit short in the power department.

The Eighties

Aside from Rickey's string, five other players mounted big seasons in the eighties.

Howard Johnson—a monster '89 with the same kind of components as Barry's seasons—average (.287), power (.559 SLG, 36 HR), strike zone judgment (77 BB) and speed (41 SB). But his numbers fall short of Bonds' in every one of them. His ratio led the league, but it was "only" 1.016 (170 TOPR) and marks the sole 1.000+ season HoJo's had.

Jack Clark—in a big year for offense ('87), Jack had the biggest—a 1.239 ratio (188 TOPR). While he fairly matched Barry in the batting categories, he was no match on the bases. Without comment, we note that Andre Dawson copped the MVP that year with an .836 ratio (127 TOPR).

Mike Schmidt—put up his best TOPR year in the truncated '81 strike season so he never really got full credit for what he accomplished. He produced a ratio of 1.190 in '81 (200 TOPR). His offensive components were very similar to Bonds' but, again, just short of Barry's level. Besides having the first 200 TOPR we've come across, Mike's also the first player since Rickey to produce two consecutive 1.000+ ratios (1.077 in the preceding '80 season). He had four such seasons altogether ('74 and '77, as well) and had seven .900+ seasons.

George Brett—his best season was in '80, of course. The year of the .390 BA also produced a competitive 1.215 ratio (191 TOPR). Competitive with Rickey but not with Barry. His second best year, though, didn't come along until '85 (1.116 ratio, 173 TOPR)—and these were the *only* two 1.000+ years George ever had. Brett is justifiably a mortal lock for the Hall and if you hadn't grasped how good a player has to be to cross the 1.000 ratio line by now, this should convince you.

Reggie Jackson—pumped out his second and last prime year in '80, some 11 years removed from his first and best in '69. His ratios were 1.040 and 1.119, respectively—not really in the same ballpark as Bonds' 1.303 and 1.304. Reggie's another great player whose portfolio includes only two seasons of producing more than one base per out committed. It's a tough standard to match.

The Seventies

The father-son comparison is an inescapable temptation. Father Bobby Bonds had his biggest year in '70. The components were certainly Bonds-like—high average (.302 BA), power (26 HR, .504 SLG), strike zone judgment (77 BB, .374 OBP) and speed (48 SB). But they compute to just a .929 ratio, which could be interpreted to mean that, at his peak, Dad was *70%* of the player his eldest son is. And Bobby was a very, *very* good player.

The other outstanding seasons of the seventies came from:

Hank Aaron—had his best years in Atlanta in '71 and '73. These figured out to ratios of 1.149 and 1.112, respectively. Not as high as Barry's. Nor were they consecutive. With a total of five 1.000+

seasons ('59, '62 and '63 in addition to '71 and '73), Hammerin' Hank is the first player to approach Runnin' Rickey's career mark of six (which says volumes about Henderson). Aaron also totaled seven .900+ seasons, some on the very verge of 1.000, but was held back by a relatively high rate of GDPs, of all things. Somehow, you don't think of the all-time HR king as being a ground ball hitter.

Rod Carew—hit .388 in '77 and achieved a 1.077 ratio. He was boosted to this level by an uncharacteristic (for him) .570 SLG and never challenged the 1.000 mark in any other season.

Joe Morgan—*we have a match!* Such a close one, in fact, as to qualify as uncanny. Here are the comparable TOPR (NBE/GOC) ratios for the consecutive years noted.

	Period	Yr. I	Yr. II	Yr. III	Yr. IV	Yr. V
Bonds	1990–94	1.092	1.033	1.303	1.304	?
Morgan	1973–77	1.007	1.088	1.266	1.323	1.036

See what we mean? Little Joe's best season ('76) could have been a Barry Bonds year—.320 BA, 114 BB (.444 OBP), 27 HR (.576 SLG), 60 SB (caught only nine times), plus 12 sac flies and he hit into only *two* GDPs. Incredible that two men of such dissimilar physical stature would build such similar seasons. Some tie-breaking is in order here. Little Joe didn't quite meet our consecutive 1.300+ ratio criterion. His '76 TOPR ratio topped Barry's best. But Morgan's two years average out less than Bonds'. Guess you'd have to say Barry wins by a strict application of our criteria, but you'd have to respect an argument to the contrary.

Given the striking similarity of their lines through this period, is there a hint that Bonds will follow the same path from here? Morgan's '77 season was his last year of "magic" as he became only above-average in '78 (.752 ratio) and thereafter. There's a major reason to think otherwise though. Morgan was 33 in '77, Bonds will be only 29 in '94.

The Sixties

A curious decade. Star ball players were numerous, but most were players who'd either established their stardom in the fifties or were emerging talents who'd actually peak in the '70s. As a result, only a few players had their prime seasons in the sixties. We've already covered Reggie's '69 and Hank's '62 and '63. Now add:

Frank Robinson—who could be said to have dominated the sixties. His TOPR (NBE/GOC) ratios for the decade:

1960	1.017	1965	.906
1961	.998	1966	1.047
1962	1.093	1967	1.000
1963	.849	1968	.820
1964	.981	1969	.995

To put this performance in perspective, consider:

◆ '63—Spike wound in left arm on September 7 required 30 stitches. It seems safe to assume this may have hampered Robbie's swing somewhat over the last month.

◆ '67—Collision at second base caused concussion and blurred vision. He missed a month but *still* posted a 1.000 ratio.

◆ '68—Vision problems continued. Plus he had the mumps and a sore arm. His *worst* year of the sixties and it would have been a career year for many players.

If you reasonably excuse Frank's '63 and '68 as being unrepresentative due to injuries (most of which didn't keep him from playing), *he averaged a 1.004 ratio for the balance of the entire decade.* Folks, that's playing some serious ball. No two consecutive seasons approached Barry's mark, though.

Other notable seasons in the sixties:

Willie McCovey—knocked the cover off the ball in '69, with a .320 BA, .453 OBP and .656 SLG (with 45 HR). It amounted to a 1.259 TOPR ratio, falling short of Bonds' mark because Willie couldn't run (he didn't even try—not a single SB attempt that year). Stretch posted a 1.177 ratio the following year, completing his total of two 1.000+ seasons.

Carl Yastrzemski—all Bostonians fondly remember his incredible '67. Literally, he picked up the entire BoSox team and carried them and all New England to the World Series. We wish we had his numbers for September alone but the entire year was fabulous enough—.326 BA, .418 OBP, .622 SLG with 44 HR, 112 runs scored and 121 driven in. He led the league in all these categories tieing Harmon Killebrew for the HR crown. His ratio computed to 1.120. Carl had an even better season in '70, producing a 1.140 ratio, but his team refused to go up the hill with him—finishing third, 21 games back of the Orioles. Consequently, we don't remember Yaz's '70 with the same clarity with which we recall '67.

Harmon Killebrew—produced his only two 1.000+ seasons in '67 and '69 (1.019 and 1.104 ratios). The Killer is another Hall-of-Famer with but two such seasons.

Norm Cash—if you recall him at all, you'll remember he "had a pretty good year sometime in the sixties." In '61 he batted .361, hit 41 HR (.662 SLG), drew 124 BB (.487 OBP), drove in 132 runs and scored 119. A *fantastic* year is what it was. It produced a 1.311 ratio (*better* than Bonds'), but it was only *one* year. He never again topped 1.000 in his 17-year career. And all it got him was fourth in the MVP voting, well behind the man who caught the Babe . . .

Roger Maris—whose 61 HR in '61 earned him both an MVP award and an ugly asterisk in the record books. But it didn't earn a 1.000 ratio, only a "mere" .996. Would you believe he only hit 16 doubles that year?

If you're wondering when we'll get to *Roberto Clemente*, we won't. He never had a 1.000 year, his best being .986 late in his career during an injury-riddled '70. An extraordinary player, deserving Hall-of-Famer, but never a 1.000 player. Not enough walks and, thus, too many outs. We told you 1.000 was tough.

The Fifties

Who else to commence this decade's comparisons but:

Willie Mays—the toast of San Francisco in his own time and outfield mate and mentor of Barry's dad. We'll tell you right off that Willie never had a season approaching a 1.300+ ratio, much less two. But their careers to this point are otherwise comparable. We'll start the comparison with '54, Willie's first big year (and the year that the current standards for statistical recording and reporting were first adopted). Willie was 23 that season, so we'll match his '54 with Bonds' '88 (when he was also 23) and carry the TOPR (NBE/GOC) ratios through Bonds' '93, age (28).

	Period	Yr. I	Yr. II	Yr. III	Yr. IV	Yr. V	Yr. VI	6 yr. Avg.
Bonds	1988–93	.853	.780	1.092	1.033	1.303	1.304	1.047
Mays	1954–59	1.124	1.148	.936	1.034	1.082	1.010	1.054
(Age)		(23)	(24)	(25)	(26)	(27)	(28)	

Over the entire six-year period, the two are very close, but the trend clearly favors Barry. The Say Hey Kid would collect four more 1.000+ seasons ('62, '64, '65 and '71). But his two career bests are the seasons that start this comparison. Willie's total of nine "One Grand" seasons, it should be noted, means that Rickey Henderson's collection of six "golden TOPRs" has finally been topped.

Nobody else has shown up with two "platinums," as we now think a 1.300 ratio should be rated. Until we come to . . .

Mickey Mantle—had some 1.300+ seasons. In fact, he had not one, but *two pairs* of back-to-back 1.300+ seasons. The Mick stretched the envelope of baseball productivity even further than Barry has. His first 1.000+ season was in '54 and, along with the 10 seasons that followed, produced TOPR ratios like this:

Year	Age	Ratio	Year	Age	Ratio
1954	22	1.034	1960	28	1.025
1955	23	1.192	1961	29	1.372
1956	24	1.408	1962	30	1.366
1957	25	1.513	1963	31	1.152
1958	26	1.177	1964	32	1.094
1959	27	.970			
			18-year career		1.073

For the record, Mick's "career" 1957 season was composed of: .365 BA (2nd in the league), .512 OBP (2nd), .665 SLG (2nd), with 34 HR (3rd), 146 BB (1st), 121 runs scored (1st), but only 94 RBI (tops on the Yankees). It won him an MVP.

Thus we have the answer to our initial question: Barry Bonds' '92 and '93 seasons are the best back-to-back seasons since . . . Mickey Mantle's '61 and '62.

But we appear to have developed another question along the way. How did Mantle produce a gargantuan 1.513 ratio in '57 and yet *not* lead the league in BA, OBP and SLG? The answer, of course, is . . .

Ted Williams—led the league with a .388 BA, .536 OBP and .731 SLG. Consequently, The Splinter's ratio of 1.554 topped The Mick's 1.513. Of course, this wasn't even Teddy's *best*. He was 38 after all. Williams peaked in '41 when, as a 22-year-old lad, he hit .406 with a ratio of 1.653. What went on before, after and in between these two seasons was a remarkable career. Check out this string of TOPR ratios:

Year	Ratio	Year	Ratio	Year	Ratio
1939	1.135	1946	1.397	1954	1.425
1940	1.088	1947	1.362	1955	1.404
1941	1.653	1948	1.317	1956	1.207
1942	1.360	1949	1.291	1957	1.554
		1950	1.204	1958	1.084
		1951	1.150	1959	.772
				1960	1.230

During the two gaps, '43–'45 and '52–'53, Williams served his country as a Marine fighter pilot. Judging by the before-and-after, "Teddy Ballgame" didn't lose a thing while he was chasing Zeroes over the Pacific and MiGs in Korea. Mantle's career is breathtaking, to say the least. But Williams' career should be held in awe. His *career* TOPR ratio was 1.279, almost as good as Barry's best season. 20 years of uninterrupted excellence, if you count his five years in the USMC (and we're sure the Corps would have no objections to our doing so).

It's worth noting, too, that "The Splendid Splinter" is the only player we've encountered besides Jack Clark and Willie McCovey who didn't run. Mike Schmidt, George Brett, Carl Yastrzemski, all could run a little. Even Norm Cash was 11 of 16 on the bases in '61. But Williams almost never ran (24 SB for 41 lifetime). He did it all *at the plate* (and he didn't hurt himself with GDPs).

Incidentally, Williams accumulated 510 net bases in '49. Remember the 506 net bases Bonds collected in '93? Ted's the first player to exceed that total (Mantle mounted the only other challenge, an even 500 in '56).

So, Bonds' '92–'93 represented the best TOPR ratios in the majors since Mantle's '61–'62 and his 506 net bases in '93 was the most since Williams' 510 in '49. But *we still haven't found anybody in the NL who's topped him*. Let's keep looking. If Aaron or Mays couldn't do it, we'll obviously have to look beyond '54 (Duke Snider and Eddie Mathews didn't do it either, we checked).

A Quick Look Backward

Prior to '54, the scoring system we use today wasn't in force. Some statistical categories weren't recorded and others were interpreted differently. Nor was there the stability in the system that we've come to expect today. The two leagues didn't necessarily keep the same records or maintain identical interpretations. The stats primarily affected by these gyrations were sac flies, caught stealing and double plays. To TOPR, some of these variations are mere nuisances. But some are potentially of major concern (GDPs in particular).

We won't burden you with all the details, but for the purpose of this quick study we'll adopt the policy of adjusting Bonds' ratio to the statistical standards in force at the time of comparison. To do otherwise, to somehow project or estimate the player he's being compared to, would be guessing. With this disclaimer in mind, we find that:

Stan Musial—the contemporary of Ted Williams and the obvious NL comparison doesn't match up with Bonds' numbers. Musial had nine 1.000+ seasons from '44 through '57 but his peak year of '48 produced a 1.253 TOPR ratio (Bonds' '93 line would translate to 1.385 using the '48 NL scoring standard). Stan The Man hit .376 that year, with 39 HR (46 doubles and 18 triples), .450 OBP, .702 SLG, 135 runs scored and 131 runs driven in. But it *wasn't* a Barry Bonds season because he only had 79 BB and 7 SB.

Ralph Kiner—another fine (and very underrated) player of this same era didn't make it either (1.221 in '49).

Proceeding further, into the pre-war years, presents real problems on two fronts: the statistical comparability, as previously mentioned, and what is a different league context. The twenties and thirties, as all fans should know, belonged to the hitters. Overall league batting averages consistently pushed .300 and once exceeded it. The entire NL hit .303 in '30. This circumstance makes a .300 hitter . . . what? An *average* hitter is what it makes him.

Significantly, though, hitters capable of producing 1.000+ seasons remain a rarity—even in this "hit-crazy" environment. But such hitters produced these boxcar years more often in their careers and at higher levels. The 1.300+ seasons we're looking for thus become a bit more frequent, but they're still scarce as hen's teeth (where they had been scarce as hen's tusks before).

For example, Mel Ott probably ranked as the NL's premiere hitter during the thirties. He had a career total of ten 1.000+ seasons by the standards of the time. But the only one that came within spitting distance of Barry's mark was a 1.279 ratio in '29 and Bonds' equivalent ratio (no CS, no GDP) would have been 1.449.

Surprisingly, we have to go all the way back to *Rogers Hornsby's* '24–'25 to find a TOPR performance superior to Barry Bonds' '92–'93. With Barry's TOPR ratio adjusted to Hornsby's standards (no GDPs), here's how they stack up:

	Period	Yr. I	Yr. II
Hornsby	1924–25	1.407	1.513
Bonds	1992–93	1.364	1.371

Plus, in '22 The Rajah amassed 536 net bases topping Barry's peak production (which would have been 517 net bases, since they didn't count GDPs then). All told, chalk up a win for Hornsby vs. Bonds. But one must admit that it's relatively close. Their ages are comparable, too. Hornsby was 29 in '25, the same age Bonds will be in '94.

Over in the AL, a lot of hitters were running up some big stats in the offensive climate that prevailed. But, again, comparisons to Barry remain few. *Jimmie Foxx* had consecutive seasons in '31–'32 that match up. The first graded out better than either of Barry's but the reverse was true for '32. *Lou Gehrig* topped Bonds in four seasons ('27, '30, '34 and '36) but they weren't consecutive.

All comparisons end with the Babe, of course. He towers above them all. Even Ted Williams. How does his 1.784 ratio in '20 strike you (Barry's comparable ratio would be 1.371). All told, he had 10 seasons that would have topped Barry's best (but only three better than Williams' best).

We're starting to lose focus, hampered severely by a lack of context. We don't know precisely how all these hitters compared to their contemporaries. We know that Barry is twice as productive as the average player of his era. Where do Ruth, Hornsby, Foxx and, for that matter, Williams and Mantle stand on this scale? How about that for a subject next year, if we can get the material together?

Summing Up

The question before the house has been resolved.

◆ Barry Bonds is the best offensive player in the major leagues today and the most productive since Mickey Mantle. The arguments of Joe Morgan's supporters are hereby heard with respect and duly noted.

◆ Further, in his time, Mickey Mantle ranked as the best offensive player in the majors . . . once Ted Williams retired.

◆ The NL hasn't contained a player to match Bonds' offensive contribution since Rogers Hornsby. That's nearly *seven decades* ago.

We have on the scene today a player who can be compared favorably to every player, save three, who've played the game. A guy on the same platform as Little Joe, The Iron Horse, Double XX and The Rajah. Right now, he need look up only to The Mick, The Splinter and The Babe. Barry's pretty good, isn't he? He also deserves a proper nickname, don't you think?

Will Barry gain more historical ground in '94? Don't bet against it.

◀ WHO WILL BE THE NEXT BARRY BONDS? ▶

Barry Bonds vs. the Future

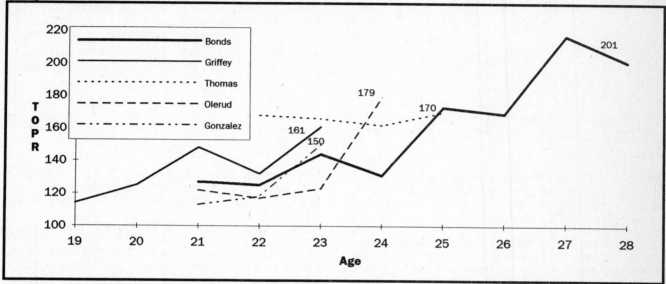

Is it too soon to start considering Bonds in a "mythic" sense? No, not based on the data in the previous essay. We are privileged to watch playing today, before our very eyes, someone who *will* reach legendary status sometime in the future. That legends necessarily require the benefit of hindsight shouldn't diminish our present-day perception of a player who will become one.

In the same sense, is it too soon to start considering who will follow or, perhaps, join him on the stage? Ordinarily, the very idea would be presumptuous. Players like Bonds obviously are few and far between . . . "not since Rogers Hornsby in '24 and '25," etc. But the early '90s seem to have produced a constellation of emerging young stars with unusually high "mythic" potential.

There is, for example, "The Kid" in Seattle who's been very, very good at a very, very young age and who in '93 exhibited the extraordinary extra-base line characteristic of superstardom. There's "The Big Hurt" in Chicago who arrived on the scene in '90 as an already accomplished professional hitter of high order. The quiet young first baseman in Toronto who never played a minor league game and challenged the .400 mark and the league doubles record in '93. And young "Mr. Juan-derful" from Texas who, at the tender age of 23, already owns a pair of home run titles. These players all have the look of "something special," certainly enough to warrant a look-see.

The most meaningful comparison, of course, is how they stand relative to Bonds at the same age. Bonds reached the majors at the age of 21, as did Olerud and Gonzalez. The precocious Griffey arrived at 19 and Thomas at 22. Here's how they match up so far.

At this early stage, Thomas has the most impressive career. Since he broke in he's been so consistent that you could almost fault him for "failing to develop." But, pray tell, *how* is he to develop? By adding base stealing to his repertoire? We think not. And the lack of this one skill puts a ceiling on his TOPR potential. In other words, he'll have to settle for being "merely" long-term fantastic. Like Mel Ott, say.

At this point, Olerud remains a one-year phenomenon. Every aspect of his hitting improved sharply in '93—higher average, more power, better strike zone judgment. Can he can hold this level? He's limited, just like Thomas, by a lack of speed. Ted Williams overrode this lacking with enormous power, but the spray-hitting, line-driving Olerud probably won't develop that kind of power.

This brings up Gonzalez, who *has* that kind of power. Maybe more. In fact, his first two years' TOPRs were constructed almost entirely on this single component. In '93 he added a batting average leap to it and jumped to another level. He has yet to add strike zone judgment, with its resultant addition of positive walks and deletion of negative outs, to his TOPR profile. Should he master this dimension, as Thomas and Olerud have, Gonzalez' awesome power component could carry him beyond 200 TOPRs into Ted Williams territory. That may not happen, but a 60 HR year is *not* an impossibility.

That leaves Griffey. "The Kid" was ahead of Bonds in *all three* years that are directly comparable (ages 21 to 23). At the age of 23 (Griffey in '93, Bonds in '88), they stack up conventionally like this:

	BA	OBP	SLG	HR	R	RBI	BB	SB	CS
Bonds '88	.283	.368	.491	24	97	58	72	17	−11
Griffey '93	.309	.408	.617	45	113	109	96	17	−9

Bonds hit lead-off for the Pirates at the time, remember. That explains his low RBI count. In any prior comparison of Griffey and Bonds, it has been fashionable to point out how Griffey a) didn't hit with Bonds' power, b) didn't walk like Bonds and c) didn't run like Bonds. But, in '93 Griffey *did* do all those things—and he did them better than Bonds did at the same age.

So, will Ken Griffey, Jr. be the "next Barry Bonds"? Lord, he *could* be the "first Ken Griffey, Jr."!

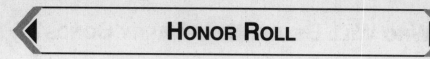

HONOR ROLL

1990-1993 TOPR: Honor Roll

	1990	1991	1992	1993
AL:	R. Henderson 1.202(192)	F. Thomas 1.059(166)	R. Henderson 1.046(167)	J.Olerud 1.194(179)
		D. Tartabull 1.017(159)	F. Thomas 1.017(162)	F. Thomas 1.130(170)
			M. McGwire 1.011(161)	R. Henderson 1.080(162)
				K. Griffey, Jr. 1.069(161)
				C. Hoiles 1.042(157)
NL:	B. Bonds 1.092(171)	B. Bonds 1.033(169)	B. Bonds 1.303(217)	B. Bonds 1.304(201)

502 Minimum Plate Appearances. (TOPR)

There seems to be more than a close connection between a 1.000 TOPR ratio and eventual residence in Cooperstown. This being the case, let's examine who's been assembling their credentials in the '90s.

Rickey Henderson ranks as the active leader with six such seasons (others in '83, '85 and '87). Bonds has had four to date. Frank Thomas has had the three above and also cleared the 1.000 hurdle in his rookie year ('90, 1.051) when he had only 240 plate appearances. Mark McGwire has had a prior 1.000+ year, posted in his rookie season ('87).

Heading into '94, only sixteen active players will have "One Grand" TOPR seasons in their account. In addition to the above eight, the list includes:

Tim Raines ('85, '86, '87)   Daryl Strawberry ('87)
Wade Boggs ('87)   Howard Johnson ('89)
Eric Davis ('86, '87)   Kevin Mitchell ('89)
Paul Molitor ('87)   Lonnie Smith ('89)

Dave Winfield, Robin Yount, Eddie Murray, Ryne Sandberg, Cal Ripken, Jose Canseco—all came perilously close to 1.000 at one time or another. But they haven't done it yet and odds are now they won't.

The "clusters" of 1.000+ TOPR ratios, which appeared in '87 and again in '93, are the subject of the next essay. While the American League appears to dominate the TOPRs of the '90s, you can see in the above "active" list that the NL has had their share, too. It's probably just a cyclical thing.

Everybody who's ever posted a 1.000 ratio isn't in the Hall of Fame, of course. Nor do all the players in the Hall have one in their record. But it's clearly an important milepost along the way and, perhaps, we should start subjecting the sixteen above named players to the closest scrutiny. Especially the ones with multiple "One Grand TOPR" seasons.

◀ THAT "PHENOMENAL" '93 SEASON ▶

"**P**henomenal!'' That's what they called baseball's '93 offensive explosion. Truly it was, but in a much different sense than intended.

As scoring, home runs and other offensive totals mounted, so did the number of explanations. The most prevalent theory suggested, "It's because of all the bad pitching in the majors due to expansion." Since this had been widely speculated prior to the season, it seemed to carry the weight of a self-fulfilling prophecy. Then, of course, came that old standby, "The powers-that-be ordered the ball juiced up again." When no other explanation surfaces, as with '87's fabled offensive extravaganza, this rationale acquires a certain credibility and then the bandwagon effect takes over. During this off-season, the deep thinkers will no doubt chime in with their own reasoned analyses which will point to "expansion park effects, just like every previous expansion."

Well, do you know what it *really* was? The weather! That's right. The weather—with an assist from Colorado's Mile High Stadium—created the explosion. One phenomenon begot another. Expansion, so far as its widely supposed "dilution of pitching," or the clandestine injection of rabbit DNA into the ol' horsehide, had nary a thing to do with it.

It's important to understand this. It means certain hitters who *appeared* to have breakthrough years, probably didn't. It means that some pitchers who *seemed* washed up, may not be. It means that certain managers and pitching coaches who lost their jobs, maybe shouldn't have. It also suggests that the renowned "shortage" of pitching may not be anything more than an "uneven allocation" of pitching.

We owe you some proof of this contention, don't we?

First, let's quantify the increase in offensive output during '93. TOPR, with its Net Bases Earned/Gross Outs Committed (NBE/GOC) ratio, provides an excellent tool for this kind of investigation because it consolidates all of the many offensive variables into a single number. To be sure, both league ratios went off like rockets in '93.

	Net Bases Earned/Gross Outs Committed		
	1992	*1993*	*% Change*
American League	.628	.666	+6.0%
National League	.599	.647	+8.0

As you'll recall from the Colorado essay, Mile High Stadium inflated offense by an astonishing +27.6%. As one of fourteen NL parks, this means that Mile High was, by itself, responsible for a +2.0% rise in the NL's ratio. The Florida park, Joe Robbie, was a "hitter's park" too. But with a Park TOPR of only 103.9 it would have contributed a mere smidgen to the NL's total increase.

Subtracting the Mile High effect from the NL means that *both* leagues experienced an identical increase in offensive output of +6.0%.

What could have caused this kind of significant increase in offense? Was it:

A. "Expansion pitchers"?
B. "Supercharging the ball"?, or
C. "Something else"?

The "Expansion Pitcher" Myth

Let's deal with the "expansion pitcher" myth first. Because that's all it is, a myth. Pure *bunk*. The "expansion pitcher" has been blamed for every offensive outburst that happened to coincide with expansion since the very first one in '61. That was the year, remember, when Roger Maris "feasted on expansion pitchers" to earn an infamous asterisk next to his home run record.

As has now been firmly established, expansion *parks* and not the expansion pitchers caused HR totals to soar in '61. The expansion Angels were initially housed in LA's Wrigley Field, a minor league park of extremely modest dimensions. Major League hitters tapped it for 248 homers. The *old* Washington Senators, displaced by the *new* Washington Senators, moved to Minnesota and became the Twins. Their new park, Metropolitan Stadium, added another home run heaven, yielding 181 taters in its first year. More meaningful, perhaps, is what happened that year to "established pitchers" (those who pitched 150 or more innings in both '60 and '61) as opposed to "expansion pitchers." The American League's ERA rose from 3.87 to 4.02 and fully ⅔ of the "established pitchers" experienced a rise in their ERA, too. And remember, they had the advantage of facing "expansion hitters."

The same pattern occurred in '93. The "expansion park effect" reappeared. But this time it doesn't come close to accounting for the entire increase in just the NL—let alone the AL, which *didn't* expand and had no new parks.

"Expansion pitcher" theorists (or mythologists, if you wish) will reason that the expansion draft drew almost equally from both leagues. Therefore, the quality of pitching was "diluted" almost equally and the offensive increase in both leagues is thereby "explained." It's a bit hard to swallow, though, that the removal of the Kevin Ritzes, Scott Aldreds and Jack Armstrongs from their league is what actually unleashed AL hitters.

Moreover, "established pitchers" once again stumbled just as in '61. League ERAs shot up—in concert with the increased offense, of course—from 3.50 to 4.04 in the NL and from 3.94 to 4.33 in the AL. If we examine the majors' 30 best pitchers in '92, the top 15 on the ERA qualifier list in each league, we get this stunning result: Of the 22 who were injury-free in '93, *all but one experienced an increase in their ERA*—despite the presumed benefit of facing "expansion hitters." Only Frank Viola escaped the trend and saw his ERA shrink.

Considering that expansion brought proportionally as many "expansion hitters" into the majors as "expansion pitchers," the "expansion pitcher" theorist is now trapped in an embarrassing corollary. Since it is obvious that "established pitchers" were also taking a beating, these theorists are forced to argue that "there is *more* than enough hitting to go around" even as they are claiming "there's not enough pitching."

This is, to say the least, a fatuous argument. Let's dismiss it, once and for all. Please!

The "Juiced-up Ball" Theory

You have to grant that maybe, just maybe, this has happened in the past—by design or by accident. Different suppliers have been used. Production locations have been changed (from stateside to Haiti, e.g.). The stitches, cover and core have all been tinkered with from time to time. But you can't blame it on the ball in '93.

We can demonstrate this by examining the minor leagues. It's not generally known, but the minors don't use the same ball as the big boys. Moreover, the minor leagues themselves don't all use the same supplier or necessarily have the same specifications. This *could* be part of the reason why the various minor leagues show distinctly different characteristics—the Pacific Coast League is a "hitter's league," the Eastern League is a "pitcher's league," etc.

At any rate, we develop minor league TOPRs as a matter of course in the process of producing our Prospect TOPR. This time around, we noted that minor league TOPRs seemed to be running higher than usual. We dug deeper and here's what we discovered about the 17 minor leagues in the National Association:

1. *All 17 of these leagues had higher offensive ratios in '93 than in '92.* From the rookie level Arizona League in the Southwest to the AAA International League in the Northeast, each and every league experienced an increase in offensive output.
2. *The overall increase in minor league offensive output was +5.3%.* From the alpine Pioneer "hitter's league" to the sea-level Gulf Coast "pitcher's league"—all were up. And the increase was just about the same as in the major leagues.

This finding throws a whole new light on things. If one buys the "juicing the ball" theory, one has to expand the conspiracy to include 17 more leagues and 167 more clubs and their owners. Plus, more manufacturers. It's patently implausible to credit the powers-that-be for this one. No, juicy as the "juicing" theory was, it must be discarded, too.

At the same time, the "expansion pitcher" theory now becomes total trash. Unless its diehard supporters want to assign to it a "ripple effect" that extended all the way to entry-level rookie ball. Nope. It simply doesn't wash.

The Search for "Something Else"

Now we have a problem composed of the following elements:

1. Offensive output was up +6.0% in both major leagues. Both "expansion pitchers" and the "juiced-up baseball" have proven invalid as explanations. The "expansion park effect" has been accounted for and determined to be responsible for only part of the increase in one league.
2. Offensive output in all 17 minor leagues also increased by a strikingly similar amount (+5.3%). The classification level, the geographic location and prior offensive characteristics of these leagues made no difference as to the end result. All rose.

Conclusion: it had to be "something else"—some kind of nationwide phenomenon that occurred throughout baseball wherever and however it was played in '93.

So, what was it?

TOPR's flexibility allowed us to address this question from two directions. First, was any one element of offense more affected by this phenomenon? Second, was the offensive increase associated with any particular time frame?

For purposes of demonstration, we'll confine ourselves to the AL. For the inquisitive, though, we'll assure you that the NL (after being corrected for the Mile High "park effect") and the minor leagues reveal *exactly* the same patterns.

First, what element of offense was most affected by the phenomenon? Let's look at a TOPR line of the average AL "game" of '93 vs. '92—a 27 Gross Out slice of the two seasons.

On average, each AL "game" produced one more Net Base Earned (NBE) for each side in '93 than in '92. That may seem a piddly amount until you consider that this one additional base was responsible for almost half-a-run (average scoring per game was

up from 4.32 to 4.71 runs per game). That's the nature of incremental bases—they're *highly* leveraged in terms of runs scored.

The additional base, obviously, was the result of more robust hitting. Our average "game" showed both more hits and, in particular, more extra bases. Interestingly, we found *virtually no increase in the number of singles* (from 6.28 to 6.34 per "game"). Nearly every "new" hit, then, was for extra bases. Here's what happened to the relative frequency of various types of hits.

	All Hits	Singles	Doubles	Triples	HR
	Frequency Per 27 GOC				
AL 1992	8.82	6.28	1.59	.17	.78
AL 1993	9.16	6.34	1.71	.19	.92
% Difference	+3.9%	+1.0%	+7.5%	+11.8%	+17.9%

In other words, the "longer" the hit, the greater the increase in its frequency last season. Or, put another way, the more likely the hit was to be in the *air* (rather than on the ground), the greater its increase in frequency. Let's file this fact for future reference.

What about the time-frame question? Could the '93 offensive outburst be traced to any particular time of the year?

You bet! And this is the finding that told us we were heading in the right direction. Look at the NBE/GOC ratio for the combined major leagues by month during the '93 season (opposite).

Wouldn't you agree that there's an obvious pattern here? There seems to be a clear seasonality to offense. It starts slowly in the spring, peaks in mid-summer and trends back down in autumn. The crescendo, incidentally, came right around the All Star break. The AL hung up a .696 and a .697 in the weeks on either side of the break (weeks ending July 12 and July 19). The NL peaked a week earlier, a slugging .709 and .693 in the weeks ending July 5 and July 12 (the Rockies, who had been at home during this period, then went on the road and the league's TOPR went with them).

Consider, as well, how the relationship between sunset and game time changes as the season progresses. Early-season games start after several hours of darkness and chilling. Mid-summer games start before the heat of the day has dissipated.

We seem to have our answer, don't we? The '93 offensive surge was tied to some function of summer weather—atmospheric conditions, air temperature and/or humidity—that caused balls hit in the air to travel farther but wouldn't have any discernible effect on ground balls. Regrettably, we don't have month-by-month TOPRs for prior seasons. But it seems a safe assumption that *every* season follows this pattern.

Everybody who follows baseball *instinctively* knows this. Consider how long we've been reporting, hearing and observing that "coming out of spring training, hitters are behind pitchers." Think about how many years we've reported, heard and observed that "in the post-season, good pitching dominates good hitting." Realize how this latter point has been even more prominently made (and has become even more true) as the post-season has shifted to a cooler night-game format played later and later in October.

It seems, then, that we've *always* known this. Yet, we've *never* connected it with the year-to-year ebb and flow of the offensive tides. Until now.

Remember how the spring of '92 was? We complained of the

Average AL "Game": 1993 vs. 1992

	H	BB	HP	XB	*TBB*	*TBO*	SH	SF	SB	CS	GDP	*BRB*	*BRO*	NBE	GOC
1992	8.82	3.40	.26	4.27	*16.75*	*25.19*	.30	.33	.75	-.38	-.80	*.21*	*1.81*	16.96	27.00
1993	9.16	3.55	.28	4.85	*17.83*	*25.19*	.31	.32	.69	-.39	-.79	*.14*	*1.81*	17.97	27.00
Diff.	+.34	+0.15	+.02	+.58	*+1.08*	*—*	+.01	-.01	-.06	-.01	+.01	*-.07*	*—*	+1.01	*—*

NOTE: Individual elements may not add to totals due to rounding.

1993 Major League: Month-by-Month

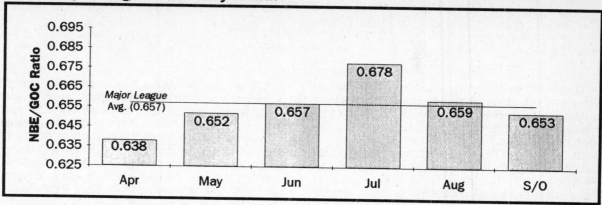

Major League Avg. (0.657)

Apr	May	Jun	Jul	Aug	S/O
0.638	0.652	0.657	0.678	0.659	0.653

NBE/GOC Ratio

unseasonably cool weather, its chill dankness. Winter stayed too long, we said, and the *real* spring weather came behind the calendar. Summer, on the other hand, was remarkably pleasant. "Heat waves" were virtually absent. We also complained loud, and long, about how our favorite team "couldn't get their offense untracked." The '92 season was "Pitcher's Weather."

Now, recall '93? Spring came early, when we were ready for it. Hot summer, too, wasn't it? Occasionally oppressive even. And we were asking, "Lord, why can't our pitchers get *anybody* out?" That's "Hitter's Weather."

And here's the final proof. The offensive trend of the major leagues and the minor leagues, by year since '85, compared to the estimated average daily temperatures for each season. The temperature changes seem absurdly small. But remember the environmental hue and cry about a "new Ice Age" or, alternatively, a "new Jurassic Era" if the mean temperature of the Earth changed by a degree or two. If atmospheric conditions affected the flight of a baseball by even 1%, what would happen? Baseball is "a game of inches," and if you add 48 of those inches to a 400-foot drive caught at the wall, it would then be *off* the wall, or even *over* it. And it would arrive a millisecond sooner.

Yes, a perfect match. Even '87. When temperatures go up, TOPR goes up with them. Any further questions?

TOPR Trendline: Major Leagues vs. Minor Leagues

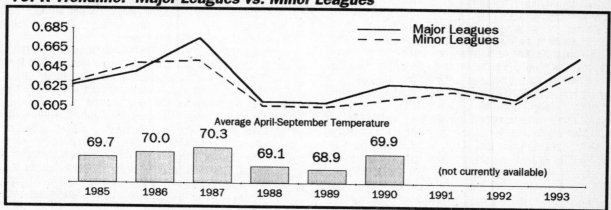

— Major Leagues
- - - Minor Leagues

Average April-September Temperature

1985	1986	1987	1988	1989	1990	1991	1992	1993
69.7	70.0	70.3	69.1	68.9	69.9			

(not currently available)

What It All Means

If you now believe, as we do, that the weather plays an important, even profound, role in baseball's offensive equation, here's what you need to be ready for in '94:

◆ Offense will, almost certainly, decline—perhaps sharply, as in '88. The cyclical patterns of national weather almost demand it.
◆ Many hitters who enjoyed "surprisingly hot" seasons in '93 will "cool off," returning to their old form in '94.
◆ Many pitchers who seemed to stumble in '93 will suddenly "find it" again in '94.
◆ At least one organization will complain that their pitching staff "turned it around" and they'd have won the pennant—if only the hitting hadn't "gone sour."
◆ Finally, if you find yourself playing the outfield in a softball game at the company picnic next July, and it's a particularly hot day, play a little deeper.

It boils down to this: you won't find the best available prediction of major league home run and offensive totals for this coming summer in the *Sporting News, Baseball Weekly, Sports Illustrated* or any other baseball guide. Rather, the very best predictor of the possible rise or fall in the offensive tides will probably be found in your '94 *Farmer's Almanac*.

THE CRYSTAL BALL

e all know the '93 standings will undergo a great deal of change in the upcoming season. How might they change? At this point, you know as much about it as we do. More, actually, because you're reading this in the spring and it's still winter where we sit. A lot will have happened in the interim.

We've cast the TOPR and TPER "bones" in the preceding pages and indicated how we "see" them. That's all we've got to go on. But, taking our cue from the TOPR and TPER Trendlines, we thought it might be possible to make an informed projection of the '94 standings.

In mid-winter, we've made some guesses on final roster composition and who would be in what role. "Who" and "how much," essentially.

We next projected a Team TOPR and TPER for every club, by projecting the individual player's and pitcher's number from his prior three-year trendline. The resultant totals were weighted for each individual's estimated TPA or IP.

In this projection, we made no provision for either "slumps," "breakthroughs" or "injuries." We simply continued the apparent trend, judgmentally accelerating or decelerating it to reflect a given player's age.

Our thought was that *real* "slumps" and "breakthroughs," when they occur, do so on a more-or-less random, individual basis. As such, the context of the entire team would tend to dampen the impact and, just as likely, provide an offsetting "slump" or "breakthrough." Which is to say, the team *as a whole* is more projectable than any of its individual parts.

As to injuries, we made only minor calibrations for old injuries which were thought to have a lingering effect. New injuries, well, how *could* we predict them? Accordingly, we assumed they'd occur randomly, too. The thing about serious, long-term DL-type injuries, though, is that they almost never get offset. The injured player is *gone* and his replacement, if the injury knocked out a key contributor, can seriously degrade the Team TOPR or TPER.

Therefore, all our projections bear the warning "barring injury."

We may have discovered the actual quantitative effect of injuries in the projection process, though. When we totaled up the Team TOPRs and TPERs for both leagues, we came up with the following league totals:

	Projection TOPR	Projection TPER
1993 American League	104.4	96.3
1993 National League	103.1	95.9

Obviously, this could not be. Then, we realized what it was. It was a quantification of probable injuries. We had projected every-

body to be reasonably healthy, thus we had projected the offenses to be more robust than they would actually prove to be once the inevitable injuries struck. Same for the pitching staffs, nothing but strong arms when many would in fact be replaced by weaker ones.

The league-wide "injury effect," then, appears to be worth about four TOPR and TPER points. It could be more, or less, for any specific team, depending on who the injury bug bit or broke.

At the same time, this finding yields insight as to why so many clubs (and their fans) wax positive about their chances in the spring. Note that, as calculated above, the *average* team in the league has a TOPR/TPER differential of around +8. As we know from our review of past winners, a +8 differential makes for at least a contender, sometimes a division winner.

So, the next time a perennial .500 club starts talking pennant in March, take them seriously. If they stay injury-free, they could well do it. Hope springs eternal every spring because it has *reason* to.

Upon determining the probable cause of our seemingly inflated TOPRs and overly sharp TPERs, we decided to treat these levels as "optimums." They would represent what each club was *capable* of—if nobody got hurt.

We then proceeded to "normalize" the projected Team TOPRs and TPERs to return each league to its proper 100.0 average. A differential was then calculated from these "normalized" figures and translated into a theoretical W–L record.

Presto! We had the projected '93 standings which appear on the next page—again barring injury and in-season trades.

OK, we only "picked" one of the four division winners. But you'd have to agree that, overall, these projected standings relate very closely to the actual year-end standings.

For example, TOPR and TPER took teams like Detroit, Texas, Seattle, Philadelphia and San Francisco seriously when few others did. They also sharply discounted the chances of Kansas City, Minnesota, St. Louis and the Mets when these teams were enjoying some heavy popularity in the pre-season polls.

As to the ones that TOPR and TPER missed badly (Cincinnati, Milwaukee and Oakland), well, check their entries on the DL.

Twelve of the 28 teams finished within three games of their projected win total. Since they're mostly clubs that finished around .500, we suspect that our "normalization" technique or our rather roughshod translation of TOPR/TPER differential to W–L may have been to blame. The projected spectrum of wins, top-to-bottom, had looked a little too closely packed to us at the time.

At any rate, we're highly encouraged by the results and will pursue TOPR/TPER projections further. You can bet we'll have a '94 update in our hands by Opening Day.

1993 AL: Pre-Season Projection

East	W-L	GB	Projected TOPR/TPER Differential Optimum	Normalized	Actual
1. New York	89-73	-	+15.6	+7.5	+5.7
2. Baltimore	88-74	1	+15.3	+7.1	+4.9
3. Toronto	84-78	5	+11.6	+3.0	+11.6
4. Detroit	83-79	6	+11.0	+2.5	+7.3
5. Milwaukee	81-81	8	+8.1	+0.5	(11.0)
6. Boston	79-83	10	+5.5	(2.1)	+1.1
7. Cleveland	78-84	11	+4.5	(3.6)	(6.1)
West					
1. Chicago	83-79	-	+10.5	+2.4	+13.1
2. Texas	81-81	2	+7.7	(0.3)	+4.1
3. Oakland	81-81	2	+7.8	(0.5)	(9.3)
4. Seattle	81-81	2	+7.5	(0.5)	+3.1
5. Minnesota	79-83	4	+6.4	(1.7)	(16.2)
6. Kansas City	76-86	7	+2.3	(5.4)	(0.1)
7. California	71-91	12	(1.5)	(9.3)	(8.0)

1993 NL: Pre-Season Projection

East	W-L	GB	Projected TOPR/TPER Differential Optimum	Normalized	Actual
1. Montreal	89-73	-	+14.0	+7.0	+6.9
2. Philadelphia	86-76	3	+12.7	+5.4	+16.0
3. Chicago	83-79	6	+8.4	+1.3	(0.9)
4. Pittsburgh	79-83	10	+5.2	(1.9)	(10.4)
5. St. Louis	78-84	11	+4.9	(2.4)	+1.3
6. New York	77-85	12	+3.1	(4.0)	(7.3)
7. Florida	72-90	17	(1.7)	(8.9)	(15.3)
West					
1. Cincinnati	93-69	-	+18.5	+11.2	(6.6)
2. Atlanta	92-70	1	+17.4	+10.4	+17.4
3. San Francisco	85-77	8	+11.3	+4.1	+15.3
4. Houston	81-81	12	+7.0	0.0	+8.9
5. Los Angeles	78-84	15	+3.1	(3.1)	+2.9
6. San Diego	77-85	16	+4.2	(4.2)	(9.1)
7. Colorado	64-98	29	(9.8)	(16.7)	(19.3)

APPENDIX

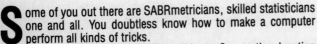

TECHNICAL TALK

Some of you out there are SABRmetricians, skilled statisticians one and all. You doubtless know how to make a computer perform all kinds of tricks.

Fact is, we can do none of these things. Our math education ended well shy of Statistics 323 and our knowledge of computers ends immediately beyond the on/off switch (if we can find it). We can't cite, for example, the "level of confidence" our 200 TPA base reflects, nor do we have the foggiest notion of how our TOPR/TPER standings would relate to the "Spearman coefficient." It's left to us, however, to address some of the questions we know you'll have about TOPR, TPER and their offspring. We'll do the best we can, though many of you might find the technical gruel a little thin.

Giving Credit Where Credit Is Due

There are some folks who, without knowing it, contributed greatly to the TOPR/TPER concept.

First among them is the quintessential First Man of SABRmetrics, Bill James. His *Baseball Abstract* plowed new ground and no baseball fan worth his salt could avoid the nuggets in the newly turned furrows. Indeed, one particular *Abstract* broached an "investment theory" concerning outs. As our concept developed, we took proper note of this, along with a certain satisfaction that our thinking was proceeding on a parallel course.

The philosophy behind TOPR and TPER is, therefore, not unlike the philosophy behind Bill's Runs Created Formula (RCF). There are only slight differences in the player rankings that result from RCF and TOPR. Which is "better"? We're not in a position to make that argument. But the differences hardly seem worth making one anyway. Personally, we're just more comfortable with the factual statement of bases and outs in TOPR than we would be with the necessarily abstract estimate of runs in RCF.

Credit should also be directed toward the First Writer of Baseball, Thomas Boswell of *The Washington Post*. At one point, well after we'd resolved the TOPR/TPER formula, we ran across Tom's Total Average computation. This formula, as modified by Barry Codell, and as we saw it in *The 1990 Baseball Annual*, reads:

$$\frac{\text{Total Bases} + \text{Walks} + \text{HBP}}{\text{At Bats} - \text{Hits} + \text{Caught Stealing} - \text{GIDP}}$$

The theory, and the method, are the same as TOPR—bases earned divided by outs committed. TOPR, though, is a much more complete compilation of the damage a hitter can do (both to the defense and to his own cause). So, Tom, you were there digging before we were. We just dug the hole a little deeper and, we think, found some more of the pay dirt you were looking for.

We will take credit, though, for turning TOPR "around" and applying it to pitchers as TPER.

The TOPR/TPER Formula's Elements

There are ten elements in the TOPR/TPER formula. Before committing to them, we carefully examined each one on its own merits. Overall, though, we were guided by this philosophy:

* * *

A base is a *base*. An out is an *out*.

In the final accounting that's what you start with to develop a serious, applicable definition of the hitter's job. You *can't* start making value judgments on the relative worth of an individual base or an isolated out. Certainly, there are specific games when a home run (4 bases) would yield a bigger run dividend than two singles and two stolen bases (also 4 bases). There are also specific times when a single would be more welcome than a walk. But, *over the course of an entire season,* Team TOPR and TPER tell us that the eventual yield will be essentially the same. How could this be? The answer is that, just as often, the accumulation of a walk, a stolen base and a single—only *three* seemingly inconsequential bases—can also result in a run.

Seemingly, the "Baseball Gods" reward everything . . . and forgive nothing. This game is an incredibly well-constructed scheme.

To review our considerations of each element in this light:

- ◆ Hits—certainly no argument here.
- ◆ Walks—the obvious quibble is with the intentional walk (IW), which TOPR counts as an earned base like any other. But it *is* a base, nonetheless. Plus a free pass constitutes tacit respect for the hitter's talent which is another way of saying he "earned it."
- ◆ HBP—if a hitter gets plunked in the ribs by Randy Johnson's heater, who's going to say he didn't earn it?
- ◆ Extra Bases—we separated Total Bases into Hits + Extra Bases so as to facilitate separation of the Batter Sub-set into separate On Base and Power Components.
- ◆ AB-H—equals Total Batter Outs. How else would you do it?
- ◆ SH & SF—will arouse some disagreements, we know. But what are they other than "one base earned, one out committed"? Getting the bunt down, when it's called for, *is* a positive accomplishment, particularly when measured against the capability of some hitters and pitchers we've seen. Getting the ball in the air to the outfield, when the situation is ripe, also represents an accomplishment (and, if you'll check the individual stats, some are far better at it than others).
- ◆ SB & CS—some have a tendency to discount the stolen base as an offensive weapon as if the steal were somehow a "lesser base." This is, we think, a mistake. If a value judgment is to be applied then it should also take into account the situation. For example, a stolen base in the bottom of the 9th in a tie game should earn a *bonus*. TOPR and TPER record these events as they actually impact the base/out situation and makes no such judgment.
- ◆ GDP—TOPR's and TPER's treatment of the double play illuminates, we think, the severe price it extracts from an offense. The net cost, in TOPR/TPER terms, is one base lost and two outs consumed (one in the AB-H column, one in the GDP column)—which is exactly what happened. Realize that a single DP represents about 7½% of the outs a team has to work with in a game. If you're a football fan, equate a DP to a "turnover," a possession lost. A GDP is deadly to an offense's TOPR precisely because it is deadly to an offense.

The inclusion of stolen bases/caught stealing and GDP in the formula, it should be noted, works strongly in the favor of certain pitchers. As with all else in TOPR and TPERdom, this is as it should be. Pitchers like Bill Swift, John Doherty, Terry Mulholland, *et al,* actually use baserunners as a source of outs. TPER has a special affinity for ground-ball pitchers like these and identifies the source of their peculiar effectiveness.

The Missing Elements

Basically, we wanted TOPR and TPER to be identical in every respect. This would make it possible to directly oppose them in every context, be it Team Trendlines over a five-year period or face-to-face in the 9th inning on Sunday afternoon.

But offensive statistics that fit nicely in a hitter's TOPR line can't be assigned to any pitcher. Advanced Extra Base (AXB), as in going from first to third on a single, for example. This information is available for hitters, if you know where to dig and are willing to dig deep enough. But there's *no* record of the pitcher involved. Nor, of course, did he have anything to do with it.

The same is true for some pitching statistics like wild pitches. The record is readily available, but we don't know who the baserunner was (the batter, of course, is immaterial).

The most regrettable of the missing elements is pickoffs. They would fit in the Baserunner Sub-set, but, while we can get the data for pitchers, tracking down the runner who got caught with his attention out-to-lunch is a different matter altogether.

We decided to treat pickoffs, then, as a completely defensive event within our experimental defensive ratio. This is an equally appropriate location because it also includes the cost of the errors stemming from overthrows on pickoff attempts.

The Scheduling Bias

Comparisons to one unchanging League TOPR standard assumes that every team played the same schedule. And, of course, they didn't. Even though both leagues played a "balanced" schedule in '93, each team played 13 games against each of its division opponents and only 12 against teams in the other division. This means Philadelphia didn't have as many games to fatten up their TOPR against Colorado as San Francisco did. And San Francisco got more chances to shoot the moon in Mile High (7 games) than Los Angeles did (who got the odd game of their Colorado season series at home).

It would be possible to eliminate this bias, of course, by creating a customized "Opponents TOPR/TPER" for each team. But we judged the effect on the final results to be so picayune as to not warrant wasting our time doing it (or yours reading it and trying to understand it).

The Hierarchy of Outs

One thing we observed during our TOPR and TPER exercise was that there appears to be a hierarchy of outs. From an offensive standpoint, some outs are capable of producing positive results (the fly-ball out), some outs are capable of accentuating the negative (the ground-ball out) and others are simply neutral (the strikeout). On defense, of course, the reverse becomes true. Ground balls represent potentially "positive" outs, fly balls potentially "negative" outs and strikeouts remain neutral.

It's not a "big thing," of course, since actual TOPR and TPER results take precedence. But, all other things being equal, you'd prefer your lineup to be full of fly-ball hitters and your pitching staff to be stocked with ground-ball pitchers (with a "K-man" in reserve for special occasions).

It's funny. Turns out strikeouts are of no particular moment in gauging a hitter, but walks are absolutely crucial to his effectiveness. And a pitcher's strikeouts, aside from their diagnostic value, become just another (and more tedious) way to get an out.

Park TOPR

We hadn't really planned to do much with Park TOPR in this initial volume. Our enthusiasm for "park effects" was tempered by:

◆ The fact they've always tended to fall within a relatively narrow range across the league (say, plus or minus 5%).
◆ "Park effects" fluctuate from year to year (Fenway was a "hitter's park," then it was a "pitcher's park," now it belongs to the hitters again, etc.).
◆ There's no legitimate way to apply "park effect," in any *specific* way, to an individual hitter or pitcher. Every park affects every hitter and every pitcher differently, every year.

The returns from Colorado, however, changed our mind and made it an issue.

Here's our procedure for calculating Park TOPR, the objective being to isolate the particular park's effect on *total* offense—both the home team's and the visitor's. We'll use Mile High as our example.

In order to isolate the "park effect," the first thing we have to do is identify the values of the *other* variables involved. These variables are, in this case, the Colorado offense and the Colorado pitching staff. How they perform on the road compared to the other 13 teams in the league, *also on the road*, in the other 13 parks should allow a reliable evaluation. So the first step is to quantify how these other 13 teams did under these conditions.

1993 Park TOPR: Mile High Stadium

Step 1

	Road TOPR			Road TPER		
	NBE	GOC	Ratio	NBE	GOC	Ratio
League Totals	19915	31509	.632	19769	29785	.664
Deduct COL:						
Road TOPR/TPER	(1204)	(2244)		(1504)	(2106)	
Home TPER/TOPR	(1840)	(2225)		(1612)	(2103)	
Equals: other 13 teams on road in other 13 parks	16871	27040	.624	16648	25576	.651

Note that the league's Road TOPR is *below* the Road TPER. That's because Road TPER is also, in fact, Home TOPR. This may cause some momentary confusion but, once you get comfortable with this "mirror-image" characteristic of TOPR and TPER you'll see it actually simplifies the whole exercise. Just keep in mind that TPER is measuring "opponent's offense" as well as "pitching effectiveness."

That's why we deducted the Rockies' Road TOPR and *Home* TPER from the league's Road TOPR (vice versa under the Road TPER column). For the purpose of this calculation, we have to take out not only what the Rockies' offense did on the road, but what their opponents' offenses did in Mile High as well. The Rockies' offense, their pitching and their park are now *all* absent from the above totals. This total becomes our basic value for all subsequent calculations. It is assigned a "TOPR" and a "TPER" of 100.0.

The next step is to compare Colorado's performance on the road against this value. This will establish the *true* level of the Rockies' offense and pitching, as they are being compared to teams competing under the exact same, equally adverse, circumstances—on the road, at 13 different locations.

Step 2

	Road TOPR				Road TPER			
	NBE	GOC	Ratio	"TOPR"	NBE	GOC	Ratio	"TPER"
Other 13 teams on road in other 13 parks: Road TOPR/TPER	16781	27040	.624	**100.0**	16648	25576	.651	**100.0**
Compare COL on road: Road TOPR/TPER	1204	2244	.537	**86.0**	1509	2106	.717	**110.1**

Now, this is *interesting*. We find that the Colorado offense, which was perceived as being "pretty good," is actually quite feeble. Remember that, while it's their Road "TOPR," that *isn't* an excuse for the poor performance. The other 13 teams they're being compared against are on the road, too. At the same time, the Colorado pitching, thought to be "in shambles," is revealed to be merely "in disrepair." Call it their "park adjusted" TOPR and TPER if you will, but the above was the Rockies' true level of ability in '93.

Now that we've identified the value of the Colorado team, it's time to put them back in their home park and calculate the "park effect" in terms of how it reacts with these known quantities.

In the next step, the comparison will again be the Rockies against the other 13 teams. It'll be composed of the Rockies' Home TOPR vs. their opponents' established Road TPERs (and the Rockies' Home TPER vs. the opposition's established Road TOPRs).

Step 3

	Road TOPR				Road TPER			
	NBE	GOC	Ratio	"TOPR"	NBE	GOC	Ratio	"TPER"
Other 13 teams on road in other 13 parks: Road TPER/TOPR	16648	25576	.651	**100.0**	16871	27040	.624	**100.0**
Compare COL at home: Home TOPR/TPER	1612	2103	.767	**117.8**	1840	2225	.827	**132.5**

Boom! Colorado's formerly lamblike lineup becomes a pride of lions at home. The already shaky staff, though, allows the opposing hitters to become even bigger, meaner lions. Mile High Stadium's "park effect" is, to say the least, dramatic.

The final step is to quantify that effect and determine just how "dramatic" it actually was. We do this by comparing the *combined* offensive values of Colorado and their opponents on the road and at Mile High. In this calculation, remember:

1. Colorado's "TPER" is actually their opponents' offense.
2. Both "TOPR" and "TPER" are *corrected* values that take into account the home and road environments. Which is to say, the normal home/road differential is accommodated in "TOPR" and "TPER" and has no effect on the end result.

Step 4

	"TOPR"	"TPER"	Total
COL:			
on road	86.0	110.1	196.1
at home	117.8	132.5	250.3
Est. 1993 Park Effect	**+37.0%**	**+20.3%**	**+27.6%**

The Mile High "park effect" benefited the Rockies' offense by a staggering +37.0%. Opposition hitters benefited too, but by "only" +20.3%. Strange as it may seem, this suggests that the Rockies' pitchers were rather better adapted to the park than the opposition pitchers. On balance, combined offense was up +27.6%, yielding a Park TOPR for Mile High Stadium of 127.6.

There's probably a simpler way to go through all these mathematical exercises and to explain them, but darned if we know what it is.

"Baseball People" and "Conventional Wisdom"

One last tip of the TOPR and TPER hat. "Baseball people" and their "conventional wisdom" take an awful lot of guff from the media and analysts like us. *Sometimes* they deserve it. But, Lord, we all make mistakes. And we've all had our runs of bad luck, foxing us out of "what shoulddabeen."

What impressed us, though, was that as we followed TOPR and TPER into the game's "statistical forest," we kept seeing instances of how "baseball people" reacted to the subtlest of changes. When offensive output started creeping up in '93, the counterreactions appeared immediately. Stolen base attempts slid a little and intentional walks edged up. Almost imperceptibly, managers tightened their reins on some parts of the game and loosened them on others. Amazing!

Or take the red-hot prospect with the big numbers, who didn't seem to get a "fair shot," stymied by a "mystifying" trade or just shuffled off into the oblivion of the bench or another organization. When TOPR gets around to looking at him, sure enough, the warts appear. Perhaps his power would be "warning track" power in a major league park, his base stealing speed would be canceled by misjudgment, or he has a killing walk-to-strike-out ratio, etc. Usually, there is *something* to be worried about, perhaps seriously worried.

The Devil Is in the Details

From here, the most perspicacious of you will be treated to a complete 1993 TOPR and TPER line on everybody who appeared in the Show, including even Jose Canseco's TPER (300.4).

Fantasy Leaguers will find nourishment in the excruciating detail, as well as the adjacent summary of positions played.

Complete team lines also appear and are juxtaposed with the league-average team to allow direct comparison.

If you're just browsing, maybe looking to get a handle on something, pay some attention to the Baserunner Sub-set for the hitters, the pitchers and the teams. You'll find the keys to a lot of seasons and careers in this sector of the TOPR/TPER line.

It's been fun. Hope to see ya around next year.

Norm and Dave

BALTIMORE ORIOLES

1993 Baltimore Orioles Team TOPR

	TPA	Batter Sub-set						Baserunner Sub-set							Total Offense				Positions Played								
		H	BB	HP	XB	TBB	TBQ	SH	SF	SB	CS	GDP	BRB	BRO	NBE	GOC	Ratio	TOPR	C	1B	2B	3B	SS	LF	CF	RF	DH
Avg. AL Team	6256	1476	572	45	781	2874	4060	50	52	111	-62	-127	23	292	2897	4352	0.666	100.0									
Baltimore Orioles	6310	1470	655	41	806	2972	4038	49	56	73	-54	-131	-7	290	2965	4328	0.685	102.9						125	18	3	2
Anderson, Brady	664	147	82	10	91	330	413	6	6	24	-12	-4	20	28	350	441	0.794	119	-	-	-	-	-	-	125	-	116
Baines, Harold	480	130	57	0	82	269	286	1	6	0	-0	-14	-7	21	262	307	0.853	128									17
Buford, Damon	90	18	9	1	11	39	61	1	0	2	-2	-1	0	4	39	65	0.600	90	-	-	-	-	-	5	24	1	5
Carey, Paul	52	10	5	0	1	16	37	0	0	0	-0	-4	-4	4	12	41	0.293	44	-	9	-	-	-	-	-	-	7
Davis, Glenn	123	20	7	1	6	34	93	1	1	0	-1	-2	-1	5	33	98	0.337	51	-	22	-	-	-	-	-	-	
Devereaux, Mike	577	132	43	1	79	255	395	2	4	3	-3	-13	-7	22	248	417	0.595	89	-	-	-	-	-	-	130	-	-
Gomez, Leo	285	48	32	-3	37	120	196	3	2	0	-1	-2	2	8	122	204	0.598	90	-	-	-	70	-	-	-	-	1
Hammonds, Jeffrey	110	32	2	0	17	51	73	1	2	4	-0	-3	4	6	55	79	0.696	105	-	-	-	-	-	14	-	10	8
Hoiles, Chris	503	130	69	9	115	323	289	3	3	1	-1	-10	-4	17	319	306	1.042	157	124	-	-	-	-	-	-	-	2
Hulett, Tim	289	78	23	3	21	125	182	1	2	1	-2	-5	-3	10	122	192	0.635	95	-	-	4	75	8	-	-	-	2
Leonard, Mark	21	1	3	0	1	5	14	0	3	0	-0	-0	3	3	8	17	0.471	71	-	-	-	-	-	4	-	-	3
Martinez, Chito	19	0	4	0	0	4	15	0	0	0	-0	-0	0	0	4	15	0.267	40	-	-	-	-	-	-	-	5	2
McLemore, Mark	663	165	64	1	49	279	416	11	6	21	-15	-21	2	53	281	469	0.599	90	-	-	25	4	-	-	-	124	-
Mercedes, Luis **	30	7	5	0	2	14	17	1	0	1	-1	-1	-1	3	14	20	0.700	105	-	-	-	-	-	-	-	8	2
Obando, Sherman	97	25	4	1	11	41	67	0	0	0	-0	-1	-1	1	40	68	0.588	88	-	-	-	-	-	1	-	7	21
Pagliarulo, Mike *	126	38	8	1	27	74	79	0	0	0	-0	-2	-2	2	72	81	0.889	134	-	4	-	28	-	-	-	-	1
Parent, Mark	61	14	3	0	14	31	40	3	1	0	-0	-1	3	5	34	45	0.756	113	21	-	-	-	-	-	-	-	1
Reynolds, Harold	570	122	66	4	40	232	363	10	5	12	-11	-4	12	30	244	393	0.621	93	-	-	141	-	-	-	-	-	1
Ripken, Cal	718	165	65	6	104	340	476	0	6	1	-4	-17	-14	27	326	503	0.648	97	-	-	-	-	162	-	-	-	
Segui, David	519	123	58	0	57	238	327	3	8	2	-1	-18	-6	30	232	357	0.650	98	-	144	-	-	-	-	-	-	1
Smith, Lonnie **	32	5	8	0	7	20	19	0	0	0	-0	-0	0	0	20	19	1.053	158	-	-	-	-	-	4	-	-	5
Tackett, Jeff	103	15	13	0	3	31	72	2	1	0	-0	-5	-2	8	29	80	0.363	54	38	-	-	-	-	-	-	-	-
Voigt, Jack	177	45	25	0	31	101	107	0	0	1	-0	-3	-2	3	99	110	0.900	135	-	5	-	3	-	22	-	23	9
STAFF	1	0	0	0	0	0	1	0	0	0	-0	-0	0	0	0	1	0.000	0									

NOTE: Statistics are for games played with Baltimore . * Also played for another AL team. ** Also played for an NL team

1993 Baltimore Orioles Team TPER

	W-L	GS	GR	SV	IP	ERA	Batter Sub-set						Baserunner Sub-set							Total Pitching			
							H	BB	HB	XB	TBB	TBQ	SH	SF	SB	CS	GDP	BRB	BRO	NBA	GOE	Ratio	TPER
Avg. AL Team	81 - 81	162	355	42	1444.1	4.33	1476	572	45	781	2874	4060	50	52	111	-62	-127	23	292	2897	4352	0.666	100.0
Baltimore Orioles	85 - 77	162	329	42	1442.2	4.32	1427	579	38	803	2847	4046	51	42	96	-64	-139	-14	296	2833	4342	0.652	98.0
Cook, Mike	0 - 0	0	2	0	3.0	0.00	1	2	0	0	3	10	0	0	0	-0	-0	0	0	3	10	0.300	45
Frohwirth, Todd	6 - 7	0	70	3	96.1	3.83	91	44	3	33	171	264	7	2	16	-4	-16	5	29	176	293	0.601	90
McDonald, Ben	13 - 14	34	0	0	220.1	3.39	185	86	5	93	369	627	7	4	19	-11	-15	4	37	373	664	0.562	84
McGehee, Kevin	0 - 0	0	5	0	16.2	5.94	18	7	2	22	49	46	1	1	2	-0	-1	3	3	52	49	1.061	159
Mills, Alan	5 - 4	0	45	4	100.1	3.23	80	51	4	59	194	276	4	6	6	-3	-13	0	26	194	302	0.642	96
Moyer, Jamie	12 - 9	25	0	0	152.0	3.43	154	38	6	65	263	428	3	1	5	-6	-13	-10	23	253	451	0.561	84
Mussina, Mike	14 - 6	25	0	0	167.2	4.46	163	44	3	98	308	473	6	4	3	-6	-12	-5	28	303	501	0.605	91
O'Donoghue, John	0 - 1	1	10	0	19.2	4.58	22	10	1	19	52	57	0	0	3	-0	-3	0	3	52	60	0.867	130
Olson, Gregg	0 - 2	0	50	29	45.0	1.60	37	18	0	12	67	129	2	2	1	-1	-2	2	7	69	136	0.507	76
Oquist, Mike	0 - 0	0	5	0	11.2	3.86	12	4	0	3	19	34	0	0	0	-1	-0	-1	1	18	35	0.514	77
Pennington, Brad	3 - 2	0	34	4	33.0	6.55	34	25	2	27	88	94	2	1	3	-1	-1	4	5	92	99	0.929	140
Poole, Jim	2 - 1	0	55	2	50.1	2.15	30	21	0	11	62	141	3	2	2	-1	-6	0	12	62	153	0.405	61
Rhodes, Arthur	5 - 6	17	0	0	85.2	6.51	91	49	1	78	219	241	2	3	5	-4	-7	-1	16	218	257	0.848	127
Sutcliffe, Rick	10 - 10	28	1	0	166.0	5.75	212	74	6	123	415	464	4	3	17	-8	-20	-4	35	411	499	0.824	124
Telford, Anthony	0 - 0	0	3	0	7.1	9.82	11	1	1	10	23	21	0	0	1	-0	-0	1	0	24	21	1.143	172
Valenzuela, Fernando	8 - 10	31	1	0	178.2	4.94	179	79	4	110	372	495	4	7	10	-14	-20	-13	45	359	540	0.665	100
Williamson, Mark	7 - 5	1	47	0	88.0	4.91	106	25	0	40	171	243	6	6	3	-4	-10	1	26	172	269	0.639	96
Tackett, Jeff	0 - 0	0	1	0	1.0	0.00	1	1	0	0	2	3	0	0	0	-0	-0	0	0	2	3	0.667	100

NOTE: Statistics are for games played with Baltimore. * Also played for another AL team. ** Also played for an NL team.

1993 Boston Red Sox Team TOPR

	TPA	H	BB	HP	XB	TBB	TBO	SH	SF	SB	CS	GDP	BRB	BRO	NBE	GOC	Ratio	TOPR	C	1B	2B	3B	SS	LF	CF	RF	DH
		Batter Sub-set						**Baserunner Sub-set**							**Total Offense**				**Positions Played**								
Avg. AL Team	6256	1476	572	45	781	2874	4060	50	52	111	-62	-127	23	292	2897	4352	0.666	100.0									
Boston Red Sox	6196	1451	508	62	719	2740	4045	80	49	73	-38	-147	17	314	2757	4359	0.632	95.0									
Blosser, Greg	30	2	2	0	1	5	26	0	0	1	-0	-0	1	0	6	26	0.231	35						9			8
Byrd, Jim	0	0	0	0	0	0	0	0	0	0	-0	-0	0	0	0	0	-	-									2
Calderon, Ivan *	239	47	21	1	15	84	166	2	2	4	-2	-11	-5	17	79	183	0.432	65						9	2	39	19
Cooper, Scott	597	147	58	5	62	272	379	4	3	5	-2	-8	2	17	274	396	0.692	104		2		154					
Dawson, Andre	498	126	17	13	70	226	335	0	7	2	-1	-18	-10	26	216	361	0.598	90								20	87
Deer, Rob *	165	28	20	2	29	79	115	0	0	2	-0	-2	0	2	79	117	0.675	101								36	2
Flaherty, John	29	3	2	1	2	8	22	1	0	0	-0	-0	1	1	9	23	0.391	59	13								
Fletcher, Scott	531	137	37	5	56	235	343	6	3	16	-3	-12	10	24	245	367	0.668	100			116	1	2				1
Greenwell, Mike	603	170	54	4	89	317	370	2	3	5	-4	-17	-11	26	306	396	0.773	116						134			10
Hatcher, Billy	562	146	28	11	57	242	362	11	4	14	-7	-14	8	36	250	398	0.628	94			2				129		2
Lyons, Steve	25	3	2	0	1	6	20	0	0	1	-2	-0	-1	2	5	22	0.227	34	1	1	9	1			6	4	3
McNeely, Jeff	44	11	7	0	3	21	26	0	0	6	-0	-0	6	0	27	26	1.038	156							13		3
Melvin, Bob	190	39	7	1	16	63	137	3	3	0	-0	-2	4	8	67	145	0.462	69	76	1							
Naehring, Tim	141	42	10	0	13	65	85	3	1	1	-0	-3	2	7	67	92	0.728	109			15	9	4				10
Ortiz, Luis	12	3	0	0	0	3	9	0	0	0	-0	-0	0	0	3	9	0.333	50				5					3
Pena, Tony	347	55	25	2	23	105	249	13	3	1	-3	-12	2	31	107	280	0.382	57	125								1
Quintana, Carlos	343	74	31	2	8	115	229	5	2	1	-0	-13	-5	20	110	249	0.442	66		53				1		50	
Richardson, Jeff	27	5	1	0	2	8	19	2	0	0	-0	-0	2	2	10	21	0.476	72			8	1					2
Riles, Ernest	170	27	20	2	23	72	116	2	3	1	-3	-3	0	11	72	127	0.567	85		1	20	11					15
Rivera, Luis	145	27	11	1	13	52	103	2	1	1	-2	-2	0	7	52	110	0.473	71			27	2	27				7
Valentin, John	539	130	49	2	79	260	338	16	4	3	-4	-9	10	33	270	371	0.728	109					144				
Vaughn, Mo	633	160	79	8	123	370	379	0	7	4	-3	-14	-6	24	364	403	0.903	136		131							19
Zupcic, Bob	326	69	27	2	34	132	217	8	3	5	-2	-7	7	20	139	237	0.586	88						48	37	54	5

NOTE: Statistics are for games played with Boston. * Also played for another AL team. ** Also played for an NL team.

1993 Boston Red Sox Team TPER

	W-L	GS	GR	SV	IP	ERA	H	BB	HB	XB	TBB	TBO	SH	SF	SB	CS	GDP	BRB	BRO	NBA	GOE	Ratio	TPER
							Batter Sub-set						**Baserunner Sub-set**							**Total Pitching**			
Avg. AL Team	81 – 81	162	355	42	1444.1	4.33	1476	572	45	781	2874	4060	50	52	111	-62	-127	23	292	2897	4352	0.666	100.0
Boston Red Sox	80 – 82	162	389	44	1452.1	3.80	1379	552	48	728	2707	4104	58	60	92	-44	-127	39	289	2746	4393	0.625	93.9
Bailey, Cory	0 – 1	0	11	0	15.2	3.45	12	12	0	3	27	40	1	1	3	-2	-3	0	7	27	47	0.574	86
Bankhead, Scott	2 – 1	0	40	0	64.1	3.50	59	29	0	32	120	177	3	4	3	-2	-7	1	16	121	193	0.627	94
Clemens, Roger	11 – 14	29	0	0	191.2	4.46	175	67	11	92	345	543	5	7	16	-7	-17	4	36	349	579	0.603	91
Darwin, Danny	15 – 11	34	0	0	229.1	3.26	196	49	3	144	392	656	6	9	11	-5	-10	11	30	403	686	0.587	88
Dopson, John	7 – 11	28	6	0	155.2	4.97	170	59	2	94	325	434	8	8	11	-5	-14	8	35	333	469	0.710	107
Fossas, Tony	1 – 1	0	71	0	40.0	5.18	38	15	2	19	74	119	0	1	3	-0	-3	1	4	75	123	0.610	92
Harris, Greg	6 – 7	0	80	8	112.1	3.77	95	60	10	40	205	315	10	4	5	-4	-11	4	29	209	344	0.608	91
Hesketh, Joe	3 – 4	5	23	1	53.1	5.06	62	29	0	27	118	149	4	2	4	-2	-11	-3	19	115	168	0.685	103
Melendez, Jose	2 – 1	0	9	0	16.0	2.25	10	5	0	12	27	46	0	2	0	-0	-0	2	2	29	48	0.604	91
Minchey, Nate	1 – 2	5	0	0	33.0	3.55	35	8	0	25	68	97	1	0	1	-1	-3	-2	5	66	102	0.647	97
Quantrill, Paul	6 – 12	14	35	1	138.0	3.91	151	44	2	80	277	391	4	2	12	-1	-16	1	23	278	414	0.671	101
Russell, Jeff	1 – 4	0	51	33	46.2	2.70	39	14	1	14	68	130	1	4	1	-1	-6	-1	12	67	142	0.472	71
Ryan, Ken	7 – 2	0	47	1	50.0	3.60	43	29	3	18	93	140	4	4	3	-2	-3	6	13	99	153	0.647	97
Sele, Aaron	7 – 2	18	0	0	111.2	2.74	100	48	7	41	196	322	2	5	8	-1	-8	6	16	202	338	0.598	90
Taylor, Scott	0 – 1	0	16	0	11.0	8.18	14	12	1	9	36	31	1	0	0	-0	-0	1	1	37	32	1.156	174
Viola, Frank	11 – 8	29	0	0	183.2	3.14	180	72	6	78	336	514	8	7	11	-11	-15	0	41	336	555	0.605	91

NOTE: Statistics are for games played with Boston. * Also played for another AL team. ** Also played for an NL team.

1993 California Angels Team TOPR

	TPA	H	BB	HP	XB	TBB	TBQ	SH	SF	SB	CS	GDP	BRB	BRO	NBE	GQC	Ratio	TOPR	C	1B	2B	3B	SS	LF	CF	RF	DH
Avg. AL Team	6256	1476	572	45	781	2874	4060	50	52	111	-62	-127	23	292	2897	4352	0.666	100.0									
California Angels	6089	1399	564	38	649	2650	3992	50	46	169	-100	-129	36	325	2686	4317	0.622	93.5									
Correia, Rod	143	34	6	4	5	49	94	5	0	2	-4	-1	2	10	51	104	0.490	74	-	-	11	3	40	-	-	-	6
Curtis, Chad	671	166	70	4	49	289	417	7	7	48	-24	-16	22	54	311	471	0.660	99	-	-	3	-	-	-	151	-	-
Davis, Chili	645	139	71	1	113	324	434	0	0	4	-1	-18	-15	19	309	453	0.682	102	-	-	-	-	-	-	-	-	150
DiSarcina, Gary	445	99	15	6	31	151	317	5	3	5	-7	-13	-7	28	144	345	0.417	63	-	-	-	-	126	-	-	-	-
Easley, Damion	264	72	28	3	23	126	158	1	2	6	-6	-5	-2	14	124	172	0.721	108	-	-	54	14	-	-	-	-	1
Edmonds, Jim	63	15	2	0	6	23	46	0	0	0	-2	-1	-3	3	20	49	0.408	61	-	-	-	-	-	1	1	15	-
Gaetti, Gary *	56	9	5	0	2	16	41	0	1	1	-0	-3	-1	4	15	45	0.333	50	-	6	-	7	-	-	-	-	-
Gonzales, Larry	3	1	1	0	0	2	1	0	0	0	-0	-0	0	0	2	1	2.000	300	2	-	-	-	-	-	-	-	-
Gonzales, Rene	389	84	49	1	23	157	251	2	2	5	-5	-12	-8	21	149	272	0.548	82	-	31	4	79	5	-	-	-	-
Gruber, Kelly	70	18	2	1	12	33	47	2	0	0	-0	-2	0	4	33	51	0.647	97	-	-	-	17	1	-	-	-	1
Javier, Stan	269	69	27	1	27	124	168	1	3	12	-2	-7	7	13	131	181	0.724	109	-	12	2	-	-	36	16	16	1
Lovullo, Torey	409	92	36	1	38	167	275	3	2	7	-6	-8	-2	19	165	294	0.561	84	-	1	91	14	9	-	-	2	1
Myers, Greg	315	74	17	2	31	124	216	3	3	3	-3	-8	-2	17	122	233	0.524	79	97	-	-	-	-	-	-	-	2
Orton, John	105	18	7	1	8	34	77	2	0	1	-2	-1	0	9	34	82	0.415	62	35	-	-	-	-	-	-	-	-
Perez, Eduardo	192	45	9	2	22	78	135	0	1	5	-4	-4	-2	9	76	144	0.528	79	-	-	-	45	-	-	-	-	3
Polonia, Luis	637	156	48	2	32	238	420	8	3	55	-24	-7	35	42	273	462	0.591	89	-	-	-	-	-	-	141	-	4
Salmon, Tim	610	146	82	5	130	363	369	0	8	5	-6	-6	1	20	364	389	0.936	141	-	-	-	-	-	-	1	140	1
Snow, J.T.	489	101	55	2	70	228	318	7	6	3	-0	-10	6	23	234	341	0.686	103	-	129	-	-	-	-	-	-	-
Stillwell, Kurt **	68	16	4	0	6	26	45	1	2	2	-0	-2	3	5	29	50	0.580	87	-	-	18	7	-	-	-	-	-
Tingley, Ron	104	18	9	1	7	35	72	3	1	1	-2	-4	-1	10	34	82	0.415	62	58	-	-	-	-	-	-	-	-
Turner, Chris	86	21	9	1	8	39	54	0	1	1	-1	-1	0	3	39	57	0.684	103	25	-	-	-	-	-	-	-	-
Van Burkleo, Ty	39	5	6	0	6	17	28	0	0	1	-0	-0	1	0	18	28	0.643	97	-	12	-	-	-	-	-	-	-
Walewander, Jim	14	1	5	0	1	6	7	0	1	1	-1	-0	1	2	7	9	0.778	117	-	-	2	6	-	-	-	-	3
Walton, Jerome	3	0	1	0	0	1	2	0	0	1	-0	-0	1	0	2	2	1.000	150	-	-	-	-	-	-	-	1	4

NOTE: Statistics are for games played with California. * Also played for another AL team. ** Also played for an NL team

1993 California Angels Team TPER

	W-L	GS	GR	SV	IP	ERA	H	BB	HB	XB	TBB	TBQ	SH	SF	SB	CS	GDP	BRB	BRO	NBA	GQE	Ratio	TPER
Avg. AL Team	81 – 81	162	355	42	1444.1	4.33	1476	572	45	781	2874	4060	50	52	111	-62	-127	23	292	2897	4352	0.666	100.0
California Angels	71 – 91	162	320	41	1430.1	4.36	1482	550	51	757	2840	4006	53	61	122	-52	-123	61	289	2901	4295	0.675	101.5
Anderson, Brian	0 - 0	1	3	0	11.1	3.97	11	2	0	8	21	32	0	0	1	-0	-2	-1	2	20	34	0.588	88
Butcher, Mike	1 - 0	0	23	8	28.1	2.86	21	15	2	10	48	82	1	3	4	-0	-1	7	5	55	87	0.632	95
Crim, Chuck	2 - 2	0	11	0	15.1	5.87	17	5	2	8	32	40	2	1	3	-0	-2	4	5	36	45	0.800	120
Farrell, John	3 - 12	17	4	0	90.2	7.35	110	44	7	93	254	255	2	2	14	-3	-6	9	13	263	268	0.981	147
Finley, Chuck	16 - 14	35	0	0	251.1	3.15	243	82	6	106	437	716	11	7	21	-9	-21	9	48	446	764	0.584	88
Frey, Steve	2 - 3	0	55	13	48.1	2.98	41	26	3	13	83	137	4	1	3	-1	-3	4	9	87	146	0.596	90
Grahe, Joe	4 - 1	0	45	11	56.2	2.86	54	25	2	25	106	161	2	3	4	-0	-6	3	11	109	172	0.634	95
Hathaway, Hilly	4 - 3	11	0	0	57.1	5.02	71	26	5	29	131	147	1	3	7	-3	-11	-3	18	128	165	0.776	117
Holzemer, Mark	0 - 3	4	1	0	23.1	8.87	34	13	3	14	64	66	1	0	2	-1	-0	2	2	66	68	0.971	146
Langston, Mark	16 - 11	35	0	0	256.1	3.20	220	85	1	107	413	722	3	8	10	-12	-22	-13	45	400	767	0.522	78
Leftwich, Phillip	4 - 6	12	0	0	80.2	3.79	81	27	3	32	143	228	3	1	4	-4	-4	0	12	143	240	0.596	90
Lewis, Scott	1 - 2	4	11	0	32.0	4.22	37	12	2	16	67	82	2	7	1	-1	-3	6	13	73	95	0.768	115
Linton, Doug *	2 - 0	0	19	0	25.2	7.71	35	14	0	31	80	73	0	1	3	-2	-1	1	4	81	77	1.052	158
Magrane, Joe **	3 - 2	8	0	0	48.0	3.94	48	21	0	25	94	133	4	3	9	-6	-2	8	15	102	148	0.689	104
Nelson, Gene *	0 - 5	0	46	4	52.2	3.08	50	23	2	22	97	149	3	4	3	-1	-4	5	12	102	161	0.634	95
Nielsen, Jerry	0 - 0	0	10	0	12.1	8.03	18	4	1	5	28	35	1	3	1	-0	-0	5	4	33	39	0.846	127
Patterson, Ken	1 - 1	0	46	1	59.0	4.58	54	35	0	30	119	163	2	1	7	-3	-8	-1	14	118	177	0.667	100
Sanderson, Scott *	7 - 11	21	0	0	135.1	4.46	153	27	5	81	266	377	6	8	5	-4	-11	4	29	270	406	0.665	100
Scott, Darryl	1 - 2	0	16	0	20.0	5.85	19	11	1	9	40	57	0	2	4	-0	-0	6	2	46	59	0.780	117
Springer, Russ	1 - 6	9	5	0	60.0	7.20	73	32	3	43	151	168	1	1	11	-1	-7	5	10	156	178	0.876	132
Swingle, Paul	0 - 1	0	9	0	9.2	8.38	15	6	0	10	31	27	0	1	3	-0	-1	3	2	34	29	1.172	176
Valera, Julio	3 - 6	5	14	4	53.0	6.62	77	15	2	40	134	147	4	1	2	-1	-8	-2	14	132	161	0.820	123
Davis, Chili	0 - 0	0	1	0	2.0	0.00	0	0	0	0	0	6	0	0	0	-0	-0	0	0	1	6	0.167	25
Gonzales, Rene	0 - 0	0	1	0	1.0	0.00	0	0	0	0	0	3	0	0	0	-0	-0	0	0	0	3	0.000	0

NOTE: Statistics are for games played with California. * Also played for another AL team. ** Also played for an NL team.

1993 Chicago White Sox Team TOPR

	TPA	Batter Sub-set H	BB	HP	XB	TBB	TBO	Baserunner Sub-set SH	SF	SB	CS	GDP	BRB	BRO	Total Offense NBE	GOC	Ratio	TOPR	Positions Played C	1B	2B	3B	SS	LF	CF	RF	DH
Avg. AL Team	6256	1476	572	45	781	2874	4060	50	52	111	-62	-127	23	292	2897	4352	0.666	100.0									
Chicago White Sox	6253	1454	604	33	802	2893	4029	72	61	106	-57	-123	59	313	2952	4342	0.680	102.1									
Bell, George	436	89	13	4	60	166	321	0	9	1	-1	-14	-5	24	161	345	0.467	70									102
Burks, Ellis	574	137	60	4	83	284	362	3	8	6	-9	-11	-3	31	281	393	0.715	107							21	132	
Calderon, Ivan *	26	3	0	0	2	5	23	0	0	0	-0	-2	-2	2	3	25	0.120	18									6
Cora, Joey	678	155	67	9	47	278	424	19	4	20	-8	-14	21	45	299	469	0.638	96			151	3					
Denson, Drew	5	1	0	0	0	1	4	0	0	0	-0	-0	0	0	1	4	0.250	38		3							
Fisk, Carlton	58	10	2	1	3	16	43	1	1	0	-1	-0	1	3	17	46	0.370	56	25								
Grebeck, Craig	223	43	26	0	8	77	147	7	0	1	-2	-9	-3	18	74	165	0.448	67			16	14	46				
Guillen, Ozzie	486	128	10	0	43	181	329	13	6	5	-4	-6	14	29	195	358	0.545	82					133				
Huff, Mike	57	8	9	1	5	23	36	1	2	1	-0	-0	4	3	27	39	0.692	104						31	8	7	
Jackson, Bo	308	66	23	0	57	146	218	0	1	0	-2	-5	-6	8	140	226	0.619	93							28	19	36
Johnson, Lance	579	168	36	0	46	250	372	3	0	35	-7	-10	21	20	271	392	0.691	104							146		
Karkovice, Ron	453	92	29	6	79	206	311	11	4	2	-2	-12	3	29	209	340	0.615	92	127								
LaValliere, Mike **	110	25	4	0	2	31	72	7	2	0	-1	-1	7	11	38	83	0.458	69	37								
Lindsey, Doug **	1	0	0	0	0	0	1	0	0	0	-0	-0	0	0	0	1	0.000	0	2								
Martin, Norberto	15	5	1	0	0	6	9	0	0	0	-0	-0	0	0	6	9	0.667	100			5						
Merullo, Matt	21	1	0	0	0	1	19	1	0	0	-0	-1	0	2	1	21	0.048	7									6
Newson, Warren	49	12	9	0	6	27	28	0	0	0	-0	-2	-2	2	25	30	0.833	125						2		3	10
Pasqua, Dan	206	36	26	0	27	89	140	1	3	2	-2	-3	1	9	90	149	0.604	91		32				11		26	6
Raines, Tim	486	127	64	3	72	266	288	2	2	21	-7	-7	11	18	277	306	0.905	136						112			
Sax, Steve	129	28	8	0	8	44	91	2	0	7	-3	-1	5	6	49	97	0.505	76			1			26		6	21
Thomas, Frank	676	174	112	2	159	447	375	0	13	4	-2	-10	5	25	452	400	1.130	170		150							4
Ventura, Robin	669	145	105	3	95	348	409	1	6	1	-6	-15	-13	28	335	437	0.767	115		4		155					
Wrona, Rick	8	1	0	0	0	1	7	0	0	0	-0	-0	0	0	1	7	0.143	21	4								

NOTE: Statistics are for games played with Chicago. * Also played for another AL team. ** Also played for an NL team.

1993 Chicago White Sox Team TPER

	W-L	GS	GR	SV	IP	ERA	Batter Sub-set H	BB	HB	XB	TBB	TBO	Baserunner Sub-set SH	SF	SB	CS	GDP	BRB	BRO	Total Pitching NBA	GOE	Ratio	TPER
Avg. AL Team	81 – 81	162	355	42	1444.1	4.33	1476	572	45	781	2874	4060	50	52	111	-62	-127	23	292	2897	4352	0.666	100.0
Chicago White Sox	94 – 68	162	322	48	1454.0	3.72	1398	566	40	636	2640	4074	54	41	82	-82	-135	-40	312	2600	4386	0.593	89.0
Alvarez, Wilson	15 – 8	31	0	0	207.2	2.95	168	122	7	72	369	561	13	6	21	-17	-24	-1	60	368	621	0.593	89
Belcher, Tim **	3 – 5	11	1	0	71.2	4.40	64	27	1	36	128	201	2	1	0	-5	-7	-9	15	119	216	0.551	83
Bere, Jason	12 – 5	24	0	0	142.2	3.47	109	81	5	52	247	409	4	2	9	-8	-9	-2	23	245	432	0.567	85
Bolton, Rodney	2 – 6	8	1	0	42.1	7.44	55	16	1	22	94	120	1	4	2	-0	-3	4	8	98	128	0.766	115
Cary, Chuck	1 – 0	0	16	0	20.2	5.23	22	11	3	11	47	55	1	4	0	-2	-0	3	7	50	62	0.806	121
DeLeon, Jose **	0 – 0	0	11	0	10.1	1.74	5	3	1	6	15	28	0	0	0	-0	-3	-3	3	12	31	0.387	58
Drahman, Brian	0 – 0	0	5	1	5.1	0.00	7	2	0	1	10	14	0	0	0	-0	-2	-2	2	8	16	0.500	75
Fernandez, Alex	18 – 9	34	0	0	247.1	3.13	221	67	6	129	423	698	9	3	5	-11	-24	-18	47	405	745	0.544	82
Hernandez, Roberto	3 – 4	0	70	38	78.2	2.29	66	20	0	28	114	224	2	2	2	-4	-3	-1	11	113	235	0.481	72
Howard, Chris	1 – 0	0	3	0	2.1	0.00	2	3	0	0	5	5	0	0	0	-1	-1	-2	2	3	7	0.429	64
Jones, Barry	0 – 1	0	6	0	7.1	8.59	14	3	0	7	24	20	1	0	1	-1	-1	0	3	24	23	1.043	157
Leach, Terry	0 – 0	0	14	1	16.0	2.81	15	2	1	3	21	45	0	1	0	-0	-2	-1	3	20	48	0.417	63
McCaskill, Kirk	4 – 8	14	16	2	113.2	5.23	144	36	1	66	247	316	2	3	8	-9	-12	-8	26	239	342	0.699	105
McDowell, Jack	22 – 10	34	0	0	256.2	3.37	261	69	3	111	444	720	8	6	10	-15	-19	-10	48	434	768	0.565	85
Pall, Donn **	2 – 3	0	39	1	58.2	3.22	62	11	2	23	98	169	6	1	4	-0	-4	7	11	105	180	0.583	88
Radinsky, Scott	8 – 2	0	73	4	54.2	4.28	61	19	1	15	96	167	2	0	2	-0	-4	0	6	96	173	0.555	83
Ruffcorn, Scott	0 – 2	2	1	0	10.0	8.10	9	10	0	8	27	25	1	1	5	-0	-2	5	4	32	29	1.103	166
Schwarz, Jeff	2 – 2	0	41	0	51.0	3.71	35	38	3	16	92	139	0	3	8	-5	-7	-1	15	91	154	0.591	89
Stieb, Dave	1 – 3	4	0	0	22.1	6.04	27	14	0	6	47	63	2	1	3	-1	-3	2	7	49	70	0.700	105
Thigpen, Bobby **	0 – 0	0	25	1	34.2	5.71	51	12	5	24	92	95	0	3	2	-3	-5	-3	11	89	106	0.840	126

NOTE: Statistics are for games played with Chicago. * Also played for another AL team. ** Also played for an NL team.

1993 Cleveland Indians Team TOPR

		Batter Sub-set						Baserunner Sub-set							Total Offense				Positions Played								
	TPA	H	BB	HP	XB	TBB	TBO	SH	SF	SB	CS	GDP	BRB	BRO	NBE	GOC	Ratio	TOPR	C	1B	2B	3B	SS	LF	CF	RF	DH
Avg. AL Team	6256	1476	572	45	781	2874	4060	50	52	111	-62	-127	23	292	2897	4352	0.666	100.0									
Cleveland Indians	6267	1547	488	49	749	2833	4072	39	72	159	-54	-131	85	296	2918	4368	0.668	100.3									
Alomar, Sandy Jr.	237	58	11	6	27	102	157	1	4	3	-1	-3	4	9	106	166	0.639	96	64								
Baerga, Carlos	680	200	34	6	103	343	424	3	13	15	-4	-17	10	37	353	461	0.766	115			150						4
Belle, Albert	693	172	76	8	156	412	422	1	14	23	-11	-18	9	44	421	466	0.903	136						150			9
Espinoza, Alvaro	283	73	8	1	27	109	190	8	3	2	-2	-7	4	9	113	210	0.538	81				2	99	35			
Fermin, Felix	514	126	24	4	26	180	354	5	1	4	-5	-12	-7	23	173	377	0.459	69					140				
Hill, Glenallen **	191	39	11	1	26	77	135	1	4	7	-3	-3	6	11	83	146	0.568	85						9		30	18
Horn, Sam	36	15	1	1	13	30	18	0	1	0	-0	-1	0	2	30	20	1.500	225									11
Howard, Thomas **	194	42	12	0	16	70	136	0	4	5	-1	-5	3	10	73	146	0.500	75						9	11	28	7
Jefferson, Reggie	403	91	28	5	45	169	275	1	3	1	-3	-7	-5	14	164	289	0.567	85		15							88
Kirby, Wayne	511	123	37	3	47	210	335	7	6	17	-5	-8	17	26	227	361	0.629	94					2	15		113	5
Levis, Jesse	67	11	2	0	2	15	52	1	1	0	-0	-0	2	2	17	54	0.315	47	29								
Lewis, Mark	53	13	0	0	5	18	39	1	0	3	-0	-1	3	2	21	41	0.512	77					13				
Lofton, Kenny	657	185	81	1	47	314	384	2	4	70	-14	-8	54	28	368	412	0.893	134							146		2
Maldonado, Candy **	94	20	11	0	17	48	61	1	1	0	-1	-2	-1	5	47	66	0.712	107						2		25	2
Martinez, Carlos	285	64	20	0	25	109	198	0	3	1	-1	-5	-2	9	107	207	0.517	78		22		25					19
Milligan, Randy **	61	20	14	0	7	41	27	0	0	0	-0	-0	0	0	41	27	1.519	228		18							1
Ortiz, Junior	270	55	11	5	13	84	194	4	1	1	-0	-10	-4	15	80	209	0.383	57	95								
Parrish, Lance	24	4	4	0	4	12	16	0	0	1	-0	-2	-1	2	11	18	0.611	92	10								
Ramirez, Manny	55	9	2	0	7	18	44	0	0	0	-0	-3	-3	3	15	47	0.319	48								1	21
Sorrento, Paul	527	119	58	2	82	261	344	0	4	3	-1	-10	-4	15	257	359	0.716	108		144						3	1
Thome, Jim	192	41	29	4	32	106	113	0	5	2	-1	-3	3	9	109	122	0.893	134				47					
Treadway, Jeff	240	67	14	2	22	105	154	1	2	1	-1	-6	-3	10	102	164	0.622	93			19	42					4

NOTE: Statistics are for games played with Cleveland. * Also played for another AL team. ** Also played for an NL team

1993 Cleveland Indians Team TPER

	W-L	GS	GR	SV	IP	ERA	Batter Sub-set						Baserunner Sub-set							Total Pitching			
							H	BB	HB	XB	TBB	TBO	SH	SF	SB	CS	GDP	BRB	BRO	NBA	GOE	Ratio	TPER
Avg. AL Team	81 – 81	162	355	42	1444.1	4.33	1476	572	45	781	2874	4060	50	52	111	-62	-127	23	292	2897	4352	0.666	100.0
Cleveland Indians	76 – 86	162	410	45	1445.2	4.58	1591	591	39	866	3087	4073	48	41	113	-68	-132	2	289	3089	4362	0.708	106.4
Abbott, Paul	0 – 1	5	0	0	18.1	6.38	19	11	0	22	52	54	0	0	3	-0	-1	2	1	54	55	0.982	147
Bielecki, Mike	4 – 5	13	0	0	68.2	5.90	90	23	2	42	157	200	0	2	14	-1	-5	10	8	167	208	0.803	121
Christopher, Mike	0 – 0	0	9	0	11.2	3.86	14	2	0	10	26	35	0	0	1	-0	-0	1	0	27	35	0.771	116
Clark, Mark	7 – 5	15	11	0	109.1	4.28	119	25	1	81	226	307	1	1	8	-10	-11	-11	23	215	330	0.652	98
Cook, Dennis	5 – 5	6	19	0	54.0	5.67	62	16	2	52	132	148	3	2	1	-5	-5	-4	15	128	163	0.785	118
Dipoto, Jerry	4 – 4	0	46	11	56.1	2.40	57	30	1	7	95	154	3	2	1	-0	-9	-3	14	92	168	0.548	82
Grimsley, Jason	3 – 4	6	4	0	42.1	5.31	52	20	1	15	88	120	1	0	7	-1	-7	0	9	88	129	0.682	102
Hernandez, Jeremy **	6 – 5	0	49	8	77.1	3.14	75	27	0	50	152	212	2	5	3	-4	-8	-2	19	150	231	0.649	98
Kramer, Tom	7 – 3	16	23	0	121.0	4.02	126	59	2	85	272	343	3	2	6	-7	-7	-3	19	269	362	0.743	112
Lilliquist, Derek	4 – 4	2	54	10	64.0	2.25	64	19	1	29	113	178	6	2	2	-0	-5	5	13	118	191	0.618	93
Lopez, Albie	3 – 1	9	0	0	49.2	5.98	49	32	1	28	110	138	1	1	5	-3	-5	-1	10	109	148	0.736	111
Mesa, Jose	10 – 12	33	1	0	208.2	4.92	232	62	7	103	404	578	9	9	12	-14	-18	-2	50	402	628	0.640	96
Milacki, Bob	1 – 1	2	3	0	16.0	3.38	19	11	0	13	43	44	0	0	1	-0	-2	-1	2	42	46	0.913	137
Mlicki, Dave	0 – 0	3	0	0	13.1	3.38	11	6	2	9	28	39	0	0	2	-0	-0	0	2	28	41	0.683	103
Mutis, Jeff	3 – 6	13	4	0	81.0	5.78	93	33	7	60	193	229	0	2	6	-3	-11	-6	16	187	245	0.763	115
Nagy, Charles	2 – 6	9	0	0	48.2	6.29	66	13	2	29	110	139	2	1	10	-2	-6	5	11	115	150	0.767	115
Ojeda, Bobby	2 – 1	7	2	0	43.0	4.40	48	21	0	30	99	118	4	3	2	-1	-4	4	12	103	130	0.792	119
Plunk, Eric	4 – 5	0	70	15	71.0	2.79	61	30	0	34	125	209	4	2	6	-1	-3	8	10	133	219	0.607	91
Power, Ted *	0 – 2	0	20	0	20.0	7.20	30	8	0	15	53	60	2	1	1	-0	-1	3	4	56	64	0.875	131
Scudder, Scott	0 – 1	1	1	0	4.0	9.00	5	4	1	3	13	10	0	0	2	-1	-0	1	1	14	11	1.273	191
Slocumb, Heathcliff *	3 – 1	0	20	0	27.1	4.28	28	16	0	11	55	75	1	2	2	-0	-3	2	6	57	81	0.704	106
Tavarez, Julian	2 – 2	7	1	0	37.0	6.57	53	13	2	29	97	103	0	1	2	-2	-5	-4	8	93	111	0.838	126
Wertz, Bill	2 – 3	0	34	0	59.2	3.62	54	32	1	24	111	173	1	1	1	-0	-3	0	5	111	178	0.624	94
Wickander, Kevin **	0 – 0	0	11	0	8.2	4.15	15	3	0	11	29	26	0	0	2	-0	-0	2	0	31	26	1.192	179
Young, Cliff	3 – 3	7	14	1	60.1	4.62	74	18	3	39	134	174	1	1	4	-4	-5	-3	11	131	185	0.708	106
Young, Matt	1 – 6	8	14	0	74.1	5.21	75	57	3	35	170	207	4	1	9	-7	-8	-1	20	169	227	0.744	112

NOTE: Statistics are for games played with Cleveland. * Also played for another AL team. ** Also played for an NL team.

1993 Detroit Tigers Team TOPR

	TPA	Batter Sub-set						Baserunner Sub-set							Total Offense				Positions Played								
		H	BB	HP	XB	TBB	TBO	SH	SF	SB	CS	GDP	BRB	BRO	NBE	GOC	Ratio	TOPR	C	1B	2B	3B	SS	LF	CF	RF	DH
Avg. AL Team	6256	1476	572	45	781	2874	4060	50	52	111	-62	-127	23	292	2897	4352	0.666	100.0									
Detroit Tigers	6505	1546	765	35	892	3238	4074	33	52	104	-63	-101	25	249	3263	4323	0.755	113.4									
Barnes, Skeeter	180	45	11	0	16	72	115	4	5	5	-5	-2	7	16	79	131	0.603	91		27	10	13	2	12		6	13
Bautista, Daniel	63	19	1	0	6	26	42	0	1	3	-1	-1	2	3	28	45	0.622	93							9	8	1
Cuyler, Milt	276	53	19	3	25	100	196	4	1	13	-2	-2	14	9	114	205	0.556	84							80		1
Davis, Eric **	89	19	14	0	21	54	56	0	0	2	-2	-4	-4	6	50	62	0.806	121						18			5
Deer, Rob *	367	70	38	3	53	164	253	0	3	3	-2	-4	0	9	164	262	0.626	94							2	84	5
Fielder, Cecil	672	153	90	4	113	360	420	0	5	0	-1	-22	-18	28	342	448	0.763	115		119							36
Fryman, Travis	695	182	77	4	113	376	425	1	6	9	-4	-8	4	19	380	444	0.856	129				69	81				
Gibson, Kirk	454	105	44	4	69	222	298	0	3	15	-6	-2	10	11	232	309	0.751	113						2	30		76
Gladden, Dan	386	95	21	3	59	178	261	4	2	8	-5	-14	-5	25	173	286	0.605	91						69	18		5
Gomez, Chris	141	32	9	1	9	51	96	3	0	2	-2	-2	1	7	52	103	0.505	76			17		29				1
Kreuter, Chad	431	107	49	3	74	233	267	2	3	2	-1	-5	1	11	234	278	0.842	126	112	1							2
Livingstone, Scott	330	89	19	0	20	128	215	1	6	1	-3	-4	1	14	129	229	0.563	85				62					2
Phillips, Tony	707	177	132	4	48	361	389	1	4	16	-11	-11	-1	27	360	416	0.865	130			51	1		70	9	34	4
Rowland, Rich	52	10	5	0	3	18	36	1	0	0	-0	-1	0	2	18	38	0.474	71	17								3
Tettleton, Mickey	637	128	109	0	129	366	394	0	6	3	-7	-5	-3	18	363	412	0.881	132	56	59				18		39	4
Thurman, Gary	102	19	11	0	6	36	70	1	1	7	-0	-2	7	4	43	74	0.581	87						17	21	15	8
Trammell, Alan	447	132	38	2	67	239	269	4	2	12	-8	-7	3	21	242	290	0.834	125				35	63	4	4		6
Whitaker, Lou	476	111	78	4	61	254	272	7	4	3	-3	-5	6	19	260	291	0.893	134			110						6

NOTE: Statistics are for games played with Detroit. * Also played for another AL team. ** Also played for an NL team.

1993 Detroit Tigers Team TPER

	W-L	GS	GR	SV	IP	ERA	Batter Sub-set						Baserunner Sub-set							Total Pitching			
							H	BB	HB	XB	TBB	TBO	SH	SF	SB	CS	GDP	BRB	BRO	NBA	GOE	Ratio	TPER
Avg. AL Team	81 – 81	162	355	42	1444.1	4.33	1476	572	45	781	2874	4060	50	52	111	-62	-127	23	292	2897	4352	0.666	100.0
Detroit Tigers	85 – 77	162	375	36	1436.2	4.70	1547	542	48	897	3034	4058	56	57	102	-57	-120	38	290	3072	4348	0.707	106.1
Bergman, Sean	1 – 4	6	3	0	39.2	5.67	47	23	1	25	96	113	3	2	4	-0	-4	5	9	101	122	0.828	124
Boever, Joe *	2 – 1	0	19	3	23.0	2.74	14	11	0	8	33	64	3	4	0	-0	-0	7	7	40	71	0.563	85
Bolton, Tom	6 – 6	8	35	0	102.2	4.47	113	45	7	41	206	288	7	2	7	-5	-10	1	24	207	312	0.663	100
Davis, Storm *	0 – 2	0	24	4	35.1	3.06	25	15	1	22	63	101	1	1	4	-1	-2	3	5	66	106	0.623	94
DeSilva, John **	0 – 0	0	1	0	1.0	9.00	2	0	0	1	3	1	0	1	0	-0	-1	0	2	3	3	1.000	150
Doherty, John	14 – 11	31	1	0	184.2	4.44	205	48	5	99	357	513	5	4	7	-12	-25	-21	46	336	559	0.601	90
Gardiner, Mike *	0 – 0	0	10	0	11.1	3.97	12	7	0	3	22	31	1	0	1	-0	-1	1	2	23	33	0.697	105
Gohr, Greg	0 – 0	0	16	0	22.2	5.96	26	14	2	11	53	64	1	1	1	-0	-1	2	3	55	67	0.821	123
Grater, Mark	0 – 0	0	6	0	5.0	5.40	6	4	0	0	10	15	0	0	0	-0	-0	0	0	10	15	0.667	100
Groom, Buddy	0 – 2	3	16	0	36.2	6.14	48	13	2	24	87	101	2	4	4	-2	-2	6	10	93	111	0.838	126
Gullickson, Bill	13 – 9	28	0	0	159.1	5.37	186	44	3	131	364	453	6	7	13	-5	-6	15	24	379	477	0.795	119
Haas, Dave	1 – 2	0	20	0	28.0	6.11	45	8	0	31	84	75	2	1	1	-0	-7	-3	10	81	85	0.953	143
Henneman, Mike	5 – 3	0	63	24	71.2	2.64	69	32	2	29	132	206	5	2	0	-0	-5	2	12	134	218	0.615	92
Johnson, Dave	1 – 1	0	6	0	8.1	12.96	13	5	2	10	30	25	0	1	0	-0	-1	0	2	30	27	1.111	167
Kiely, John	0 – 2	0	8	0	11.2	7.71	13	13	1	9	36	31	1	0	0	-0	-1	-3	5	33	36	0.917	138
Knudsen, Kurt	3 – 2	0	30	2	37.2	4.78	41	16	4	32	93	105	2	3	2	-3	-2	2	10	95	115	0.826	124
Krueger, Bill	6 – 4	7	25	0	82.0	3.40	90	30	4	34	158	226	3	3	11	-4	-11	2	21	160	247	0.648	97
Leiter, Mark	6 – 6	13	14	0	106.2	4.73	111	44	3	67	225	305	3	5	8	-4	-4	8	16	233	321	0.726	109
MacDonald, Bob	3 – 3	0	68	3	65.2	5.35	67	33	1	44	145	183	4	5	2	-3	-3	5	15	150	198	0.758	114
Moore, Mike	13 – 9	36	0	0	213.2	5.22	227	89	3	153	472	611	4	8	23	-8	-16	11	36	483	647	0.747	112
Munoz, Mike **	0 – 1	0	8	0	3.0	6.00	4	6	0	6	16	9	0	0	0	-0	-1	-1	1	15	10	1.500	225
Wells, David	11 – 9	30	2	0	187.0	4.19	183	42	7	117	349	538	3	3	14	-10	-14	-4	30	345	568	0.607	91

NOTE: Statistics are for games played with Detroit. * Also played for another AL team. ** Also played for an NL team.

KANSAS CITY ROYALS

1993 Kansas City Royals Team TOPR

		Batter Sub-set						Baserunner Sub-set							Total Offense				Positions Played								
	TPA	H	BB	HP	XB	TBB	TBO	SH	SF	SB	CS	GDP	BRB	BRO	NBE	GOC	Ratio	TOPR	C	1B	2B	3B	SS	LF	CF	RF	DH
Avg. AL Team	6256	1476	572	45	781	2874	4060	50	52	111	-62	-127	23	292	2897	4352	0.666	100.0									
Kansas City Royals	6101	1455	428	52	739	2674	4067	48	51	100	-75	-107	17	281	2691	4348	0.619	93.0									
Brett, George	612	149	39	3	94	285	411	0	10	7	-5	-20	-8	35	277	446	0.621	93									140
Brooks, Hubie	181	48	11	1	15	75	120	0	1	0	-1	-5	-5	7	70	127	0.551	83							6	34	9
Gaetti, Gary *	313	72	16	8	62	158	209	2	6	0	-3	-2	3	13	161	222	0.725	109		18		72					1
Gagne, Greg	581	151	33	0	68	252	389	4	4	10	-12	-7	-1	27	251	416	0.603	91					159				
Gwynn, Chris	316	86	24	1	25	136	201	2	2	0	-1	-7	-4	12	132	213	0.620	93						66		19	5
Hamelin, Bob	55	11	6	0	9	26	38	0	0	0	-0	-2	-2	2	24	40	0.600	90		15							9
Hiatt, Phil	263	52	16	7	35	110	186	0	2	6	-3	-8	-3	13	107	199	0.538	81				70					
Howard, Dave	29	8	2	0	2	12	16	2	1	1	-0	-0	4	3	16	19	0.842	126			7	2	3			1	
Jose, Felix	539	126	36	1	48	211	373	1	2	31	-13	-5	16	21	227	394	0.576	87							10	136	1
Joyner, Wally	573	145	66	3	87	301	352	2	5	5	-9	-6	-3	22	298	374	0.797	120		140							
Koslofski, Kevin	32	7	4	1	3	15	19	1	0	0	-1	-1	-1	3	14	22	0.636	96						3	4	7	1
Lind, Jose	464	107	13	2	17	139	324	13	5	3	-2	-7	12	27	151	351	0.430	65			136						
Macfarlane, Mike	451	106	40	16	87	249	282	1	6	2	-5	-8	-4	20	245	302	0.811	122	114								1
Mayne, Brent	227	52	18	1	17	88	153	3	0	3	-2	-6	-2	11	86	164	0.524	79	68								
McRae, Brian	685	177	37	4	82	300	450	14	3	23	-14	-8	18	39	318	489	0.650	98							104		1
McReynolds, Kevin	393	86	37	1	63	187	265	1	3	2	-2	-8	-4	14	183	279	0.656	99						104	4		6
Miller, Keith	118	18	8	1	3	30	90	0	1	3	-1	-3	0	5	30	95	0.316	47				3	21		12	16	
Pulliam, Harvey	65	18	6	2	1	27	46	0	0	0	-0	-3	-3	3	24	49	0.490	74				24	16	11			
Rossy, Rico	97	19	9	1	10	39	67	1	0	0	-0	-0	1	1	40	68	0.588	88			8						
Santovenia, Nelson	9	1	1	0	0	2	7	0	0	0	-0	-0	0	0	2	7	0.286	43	4								
Shumpert, Terry	12	1	2	0	0	3	9	0	0	1	-0	-0	1	0	4	9	0.444	67			8						
Wilkerson, Curt	29	4	1	0	0	5	24	0	0	2	-0	-1	1	1	6	25	0.240	36			10		4				
Wilson, Craig	57	13	7	0	4	24	36	1	0	1	-1	-0	1	2	25	38	0.658	99			1			15		1	

NOTE: Statistics are for games played with Kansas City. * Also played for another AL team. ** Also played for an NL team.

1993 Kansas City Royals Team TPER

	W-L	GS	GR	SV	IP	ERA	Batter Sub-set						Baserunner Sub-set							Total Pitching			
							H	BB	HB	XB	TBB	TBO	SH	SF	SB	CS	GDP	BRB	BRO	NBA	GOE	Ratio	TPER
Avg. AL Team	81 – 81	162	355	42	1444.1	4.33	1476	572	45	781	2874	4060	50	52	111	-62	-127	23	292	2897	4352	0.666	100.0
Kansas City Royals	84 – 78	162	303	48	1445.1	4.04	1379	571	44	663	2657	4057	41	52	119	-71	-112	29	276	2686	4333	0.620	93.1
Appier, Kevin	18 – 8	34	0	0	238.2	2.56	183	81	1	69	334	680	3	5	11	-8	-18	-7	34	327	714	0.458	69
Belinda, Stan **	1 – 1	0	23	0	27.1	4.28	30	6	1	12	49	77	2	0	4	-2	-2	2	6	51	83	0.614	92
Brewer, Billy	2 – 2	0	46	0	39.0	3.46	31	20	0	24	75	104	1	1	5	-2	-7	-2	11	73	115	0.635	95
Burgos, Enrique	0 – 1	0	5	0	5.0	9.00	5	6	1	2	14	16	0	0	1	-0	-0	0	0	14	16	0.875	131
Cadaret, Greg **	1 – 1	0	13	0	15.1	2.93	14	7	1	2	24	39	1	0	1	-2	-1	-1	4	23	43	0.535	80
Cone, David	11 – 14	34	0	0	254.0	3.33	205	114	10	111	440	715	7	9	32	-13	-13	22	42	462	757	0.610	92
DiPino, Frank	1 – 1	0	11	0	15.2	6.89	21	6	2	16	45	43	0	2	0	-0	-2	0	4	45	47	0.957	144
Gardner, Mark	4 – 6	16	1	0	91.2	6.19	92	36	4	81	213	246	1	7	8	-11	-7	-2	26	211	272	0.776	117
Gordon, Tom	12 – 6	14	34	1	155.2	3.58	125	77	1	66	269	436	6	6	15	-9	-10	8	31	277	467	0.593	89
Granger, Jeff	0 – 0	0	1	0	1.0	27.00	3	2	0	0	5	3	0	0	0	-0	-0	0	0	5	3	1.667	250
Gubicza, Mark	5 – 8	6	43	2	104.1	4.66	128	43	2	36	209	289	6	6	11	-2	-12	9	26	218	315	0.692	104
Habyan, John *	0 – 0	0	12	0	14.0	4.50	14	4	0	8	26	40	0	0	3	-0	-2	1	2	27	42	0.643	97
Haney, Chris	9 – 9	23	0	0	124.0	6.02	141	53	3	68	265	352	3	4	7	-4	-10	0	21	265	373	0.710	107
Magnante, Mike	1 – 1	6	1	0	35.1	4.08	37	11	1	18	67	94	1	1	0	-4	-4	-6	10	61	104	0.587	88
Meacham, Rusty	2 – 2	0	15	0	21.0	5.57	31	5	3	14	53	64	0	1	1	-0	-1	1	2	54	66	0.818	123
Montgomery, Jeff	7 – 5	0	69	45	87.1	2.27	65	23	2	27	117	251	5	1	7	-1	-3	9	10	126	261	0.483	73
Pichardo, Hipolito	7 – 8	25	5	0	165.0	4.04	183	53	6	76	318	467	3	8	8	-7	-17	-5	35	313	502	0.624	94
Rasmussen, Dennis	1 – 2	4	5	0	29.0	7.45	40	14	1	23	78	82	0	1	0	-4	-1	-3	6	75	88	0.852	128
Reed, Rick *	0 – 0	0	1	0	3.2	9.82	6	1	1	3	11	10	0	0	0	-0	-0	0	0	11	10	1.100	165
Sampen, Bill	2 – 2	0	18	0	18.1	5.89	25	9	4	8	46	49	2	0	4	-2	-2	2	6	48	55	0.873	131

NOTE: Statistics are for games played with Kansas City. * Also played for another AL team. ** Also played for an NL team.

1993 Milwaukee Brewers Team TOPR

		Batter Sub-set						Baserunner Sub-set							Total Offense				Positions Played									
	TPA	H	BB	HP	XB	TBB	TBO	SH	SF	SB	CS	GDP	BRB	BRO	NBE	GOC	Ratio	TOPR	C	1B	2B	3B	SS	LF	CF	RF	DH
Avg. AL Team	6256	1476	572	45	781	2874	4060	50	52	111	-62	-127	23	292	2897	4352	0.666	100.0									
Milwaukee Brewers	6222	1426	555	40	665	2686	4098	58	45	138	-93	-114	34	310	2720	4408	0.617	92.7									
Bell, Juan **	327	67	36	1	25	129	219	3	1	6	-6	-4	0	14	129	233	0.554	83	-	-	47	-	40	-	1	2	2
Brunansky, Tom	251	41	25	0	31	97	183	2	0	3	-4	-6	-5	12	92	195	0.472	71	-	-	-	-	-	-	-	71	6
Diaz, Alex	72	22	0	0	2	24	47	3	0	5	-3	-3	2	9	26	56	0.464	70	-	-	-	-	-	4	12	13	1
Doran, Billy	67	13	6	0	4	23	47	0	1	1	-0	-3	-1	4	22	51	0.431	65	-	4	17	-	-	-	-	-	-
Hamilton, Darryl	573	161	45	3	50	259	358	5	1	21	-13	-9	5	28	264	386	0.684	103	-	-	-	-	-	31	49	70	1
Jaha, John	582	136	51	8	78	273	379	4	4	13	-9	-6	6	23	279	402	0.694	104	-	150	1	1	-	-	-	-	-
Kmak, Joe	127	24	14	2	5	45	86	1	0	6	-2	-2	3	5	48	91	0.527	79	50	-	-	-	-	-	-	-	-
Lampkin, Tom	188	32	20	0	20	72	130	2	4	7	-3	-2	8	11	80	141	0.567	85	60	-	-	-	-	-	-	-	-
Listach, Pat	403	87	37	3	26	153	269	5	2	18	-9	-7	9	23	162	292	0.555	83	-	-	-	-	95	-	6	-	-
Mieske, Matt	63	14	4	0	9	27	44	1	0	0	-2	-2	-3	5	24	49	0.490	74	-	-	-	-	-	1	9	12	-
Nilsson, Dave	340	76	37	0	35	148	220	4	3	3	-6	-9	-5	22	143	242	0.591	89	91	4	-	-	-	-	-	-	4
O'Leary, Troy	49	12	5	0	3	20	29	3	0	0	-0	-1	2	4	22	33	0.667	100	-	-	-	-	-	15	-	5	-
Reimer, Kevin	477	109	30	5	63	207	328	1	4	5	-4	-12	-6	21	201	349	0.576	87	-	-	-	-	-	28	-	10	83
Seitzer, Kevin *	182	47	17	1	27	92	115	1	1	3	-0	-7	-2	9	90	124	0.726	109	-	-	7	1	33	-	-	1	3
Spiers, Bill	386	81	29	4	22	136	259	9	4	9	-8	-10	4	31	140	290	0.483	73	-	-	104	4	-	2	2	4	1
Suero, William	15	4	1	0	0	5	10	0	0	0	-1	-1	-2	2	3	12	0.250	38	-	-	8	1	-	-	-	-	-
Surhoff, B.J.	599	151	36	2	65	254	401	4	5	12	-9	-7	5	25	259	426	0.608	91	3	8	-	121	-	12	-	14	1
Thon, Dickie	275	66	22	0	15	103	179	3	5	6	-5	-4	5	17	108	196	0.551	83	-	-	22	25	28	-	-	-	14
Valentin, Jose	63	13	7	1	8	29	40	2	0	1	-0	-1	2	3	31	43	0.721	108	-	-	-	19	-	-	-	-	-
Vaughn, Greg	667	152	89	5	122	368	417	0	4	10	-7	-6	1	17	369	434	0.850	128	-	-	-	-	-	94	-	-	58
Yount, Robin	514	117	44	5	55	221	337	5	6	9	-2	-12	6	25	227	362	0.627	94	-	7	-	-	-	-	114	-	6
STAFF	2	1	0	0	0	1	1	0	0	0	-0	-0	0	0	1	1	1.000	150	-	-	-	-	-	-	-	-	-

NOTE: Statistics are for games played with Milwaukee. * Also played for another AL team. ** Also played for an NL team

1993 Milwaukee Brewers Team TPER

							Batter Sub-set						Baserunner Sub-set							Total Pitching			
	W-L	GS	GR	SV	IP	ERA	H	BB	HB	XB	TBB	TBO	SH	SF	SB	CS	GDP	BRB	BRO	NBA	GOE	Ratio	TPER
Avg. AL Team	81 - 81	162	355	42	1444.1	4.33	1476	572	45	781	2874	4060	50	52	111	-62	-127	23	292	2897	4352	0.666	100.0
Milwaukee Brewers	69 - 93	162	353	29	1447.0	4.47	1511	522	60	845	2938	4066	50	76	115	-50	-119	72	295	3010	4361	0.690	103.7
Austin, Jim	1 - 2	0	31	0	33.0	3.82	28	13	1	13	55	94	1	0	0	-1	-2	-2	4	53	98	0.541	81
Boddicker, Mike	3 - 5	10	0	0	54.0	5.67	77	15	4	32	128	151	1	1	6	-3	-4	1	9	129	160	0.806	121
Bones, Ricky	11 - 11	31	1	0	203.2	4.86	222	63	8	147	440	578	5	7	20	-5	-16	11	33	451	611	0.738	111
Eldred, Cal	16 - 16	36	0	0	258.0	4.01	232	91	10	157	490	737	5	12	21	-9	-13	16	39	506	776	0.652	98
Fetters, Mike	3 - 3	0	45	0	59.1	3.34	59	22	2	24	107	153	5	5	6	-7	-13	-4	30	103	183	0.563	85
Henry, Doug	4 - 4	0	54	17	55.0	5.56	67	25	3	38	133	156	5	4	4	-0	-3	10	12	143	168	0.851	128
Higuera, Teddy	1 - 3	8	0	0	30.0	7.20	43	16	1	32	92	86	1	1	3	-1	-0	4	3	96	89	1.079	162
Ignasiak, Mike	1 - 1	0	27	0	37.0	3.65	32	21	2	12	67	101	1	1	1	-3	-7	-7	12	60	113	0.531	80
Kiefer, Mark	0 - 0	0	6	1	9.1	0.00	3	5	1	0	9	28	0	0	1	-0	-0	1	0	10	28	0.357	54
Lloyd, Graeme	3 - 4	0	55	0	63.2	2.83	64	13	3	25	105	186	1	2	2	-0	-5	0	8	105	194	0.541	81
Maldonado, Carlos	2 - 2	0	29	1	37.1	4.58	40	17	0	16	73	102	4	4	2	-0	-3	7	11	80	113	0.708	106
Manzanillo, Josias **	1 - 1	1	9	1	17.0	9.53	22	10	2	12	46	48	2	2	1	-0	-1	4	5	50	53	0.943	142
Maysey, Matt	1 - 2	0	23	1	22.0	5.73	28	13	1	17	59	59	2	2	3	-0	-4	3	8	62	67	0.925	139
Miranda, Angel	4 - 5	17	5	0	120.0	3.30	100	52	2	65	219	342	3	3	7	-3	-10	0	19	219	361	0.607	91
Navarro, Jaime	11 - 12	34	1	0	214.1	5.33	254	73	11	119	457	594	6	17	23	-6	-19	21	48	478	642	0.745	112
Novoa, Rafael	0 - 3	7	8	0	56.0	4.50	58	22	4	35	119	159	4	2	3	-1	-3	5	10	124	169	0.734	110
Orosco, Jesse	3 - 5	0	57	8	56.2	3.18	47	17	3	17	84	163	1	2	2	-4	-3	-2	10	82	173	0.474	71
Wegman, Bill	4 - 14	18	2	0	120.2	4.48	135	34	2	84	255	329	3	11	10	-7	-13	4	34	259	363	0.713	107

NOTE: Statistics are for games played with Milwaukee. * Also played for another AL team. ** Also played for an NL team.

1993 Minnesota Twins Team TOPR

	TPA	H	BB	HP	XB	TBB	TBO	SH	SF	SB	CS	GDP	BRB	BRO	NBE	GOC	Ratio	TOPR	C	1B	2B	3B	SS	LF	CF	RF	DH
Avg. AL Team	6256	1476	572	45	781	2874	4060	50	52	111	-62	-127	23	292	2897	4352	0.666	100.0									
Minnesota Twins	6209	1480	493	51	678	2702	4121	27	37	83	-59	-149	-61	272	2641	4393	0.601	90.3									
Becker, Rich	12	2	5	0	2	9	5	0	0	1	-1	-0	0	1	9	6	1.500	225	-	-	-	-	-	-	3	-	-
Brito, Bernardo	55	13	1	0	14	28	41	0	0	0	-0	-1	-1	1	27	42	0.643	97	-	-	-	-	-	10	-	-	7
Bruett, J.T.	22	5	1	1	2	9	15	0	0	0	-0	-0	0	0	9	15	0.600	90	-	-	-	-	-	-	2	4	8
Bush, Randy	52	7	7	0	2	16	38	0	0	0	-0	-3	-3	3	13	41	0.317	48	-	4	-	-	-	-	-	1	5
Hale, Chip	213	62	18	6	17	103	124	2	1	2	-1	-3	1	7	104	131	0.794	119	-	1	21	19	1	-	-	-	19
Harper, Brian	573	161	29	9	64	263	369	0	5	1	-3	-15	-12	23	251	392	0.640	96	134	-	-	-	-	-	-	-	7
Hocking, Denny	42	5	6	0	1	12	31	0	0	1	-0	-1	0	1	12	32	0.375	56	-	-	1	-	12	-	-	-	-
Hrbek, Kent	471	95	71	1	88	255	297	3	4	4	-2	-12	-3	21	252	318	0.792	119	-	115	-	-	-	-	-	-	2
Jorgensen, Terry	163	34	10	0	10	54	118	0	1	1	-0	-7	-5	8	49	126	0.389	58	-	9	-	45	6	-	-	-	-
Knoblauch, Chuck	685	167	65	9	41	282	435	4	5	29	-11	-11	16	31	298	466	0.639	96	-	-	148	6	-	-	1	-	-
Larkin, Gene	173	38	21	2	12	73	106	2	4	0	-1	-5	0	12	73	118	0.619	93	-	18	-	2	-	4	-	25	3
Lee, Derek	34	5	1	0	1	7	28	0	0	0	-0	-0	0	0	7	28	0.250	38	-	-	-	-	-	9	-	4	-
Leius, Scott	22	3	2	0	0	5	15	0	2	0	-0	-1	1	3	6	18	0.333	50	-	-	-	-	9	-	-	-	-
Mack, Shane	553	139	41	4	68	252	364	3	2	15	-5	-13	2	23	254	387	0.656	99	-	-	-	-	-	-	64	67	2
Maksudian, Mike	17	2	4	0	1	7	10	0	1	0	-0	-2	-1	3	6	13	0.462	69	-	4	-	1	-	-	-	-	-
McCarty, Dave	371	75	19	1	25	120	275	1	0	2	-6	-13	-16	20	104	295	0.353	53	-	36	-	-	-	38	2	34	2
Meares, Pat	361	87	7	1	20	115	259	4	3	4	-5	-11	-5	23	110	282	0.390	59	-	-	-	-	111	-	-	-	-
Munoz, Pedro	354	76	25	3	52	156	250	0	0	1	-2	-7	-8	9	148	259	0.571	86	-	-	-	-	-	64	-	41	-
Pagliarulo, Mike *	279	74	18	5	33	130	179	2	1	6	-6	-5	-2	14	128	193	0.663	100	-	-	-	79	-	-	-	-	-
Parks, Derek	21	4	1	0	0	5	16	0	0	0	-0	-0	0	0	5	16	0.313	47	7	-	-	-	-	-	-	-	-
Puckett, Kirby	682	184	47	7	111	349	438	1	5	8	-6	-15	-7	27	342	465	0.735	110	-	-	-	-	-	1	95	47	17
Reboulet, Jeff	283	62	35	2	11	110	178	5	1	5	-5	-6	0	17	110	195	0.564	85	-	-	11	35	62	1	2	-	1
Stahoviak, Scott	60	11	3	0	4	18	46	0	0	0	-2	-2	-4	4	14	50	0.280	42	-	-	-	19	-	-	-	-	-
Webster, Lenny	117	21	11	0	5	37	85	0	0	1	-0	-1	0	1	37	86	0.430	65	45	-	-	-	-	-	-	-	1
Winfield, Dave	594	148	45	0	94	287	399	0	2	2	-3	-15	-14	20	273	419	0.652	98	-	5	-	-	-	-	-	31	105

NOTE: Statistics are for games played with Minnesota. * Also played for another AL team. ** Also played for an NL team

1993 Minnesota Twins Team TPER

	W-L	GS	GR	SV	IP	ERA	H	BB	HB	XB	TBB	TBO	SH	SF	SB	CS	GDP	BRB	BRO	NBA	GOE	Ratio	TPER
Avg. AL Team	81 – 81	162	355	42	1444.1	4.33	1476	572	45	781	2874	4060	50	52	111	-62	-127	23	292	2897	4352	0.666	100.0
Minnesota Twins	71 – 91	162	356	44	1444.1	4.73	1591	514	45	871	3021	4026	43	66	137	-66	-131	49	306	3070	4332	0.709	106.5
Aguilera, Rick	4 – 3	0	65	34	72.1	3.11	60	14	1	42	117	209	2	1	4	-0	-5	2	8	119	217	0.548	82
Banks, Willie	11 – 12	30	1	0	171.1	4.04	186	78	3	91	358	479	4	4	6	-6	-19	-11	33	347	512	0.678	102
Brummett, Greg **	2 – 1	5	0	0	26.2	5.74	29	15	0	15	59	68	0	3	5	-1	-6	1	10	60	78	0.769	116
Casian, Larry	5 – 3	0	54	1	56.2	3.02	59	14	1	15	89	161	3	3	1	-0	-3	4	9	93	170	0.547	82
Deshaies, Jim **	11 – 13	27	0	0	167.1	4.41	159	51	6	112	328	465	5	7	8	-15	-11	-6	38	322	503	0.640	96
Erickson, Scott	8 – 19	34	0	0	218.2	5.19	266	71	10	110	457	606	10	13	28	-4	-26	21	53	478	659	0.725	109
Garces, Rich	0 – 0	0	3	0	4.0	0.00	4	2	0	0	6	12	0	0	0	-0	-1	1	1	5	13	0.385	58
Guardado, Eddie	3 – 8	16	3	0	94.2	6.18	123	36	1	83	243	262	1	3	12	-5	-7	4	16	247	278	0.888	133
Guthrie, Mark	2 – 1	0	22	0	21.0	4.71	20	16	0	10	46	55	1	2	4	-3	-1	3	7	49	62	0.790	119
Hartley, Mike	1 – 2	0	53	1	81.0	4.00	86	36	7	35	164	220	4	6	11	-4	-5	12	19	176	239	0.736	111
Mahomes, Pat	1 – 5	5	7	0	37.1	7.71	47	16	1	42	106	105	1	3	5	-3	-2	4	9	110	114	0.965	145
Merriman, Brett	1 – 1	0	19	0	27.0	9.67	36	23	3	21	83	69	2	2	0	-1	-6	-3	11	80	80	1.000	150
Tapani, Kevin	12 – 15	35	1	0	225.2	4.43	243	57	6	131	437	650	3	5	42	-13	-13	24	34	461	684	0.674	101
Trombley, Mike	6 – 6	10	34	2	114.1	4.88	131	41	3	90	265	320	3	7	7	-6	-10	1	26	266	346	0.769	115
Tsamis, George	1 – 2	0	41	1	68.1	6.19	86	27	3	46	162	185	2	6	0	-4	-10	-6	22	156	207	0.754	113
Willis, Carl	3 – 0	0	53	5	58.0	3.10	56	17	0	28	101	160	2	1	4	-1	-6	0	10	101	170	0.594	89

NOTE: Statistics are for games played with Minnesota. * Also played for another AL team. ** Also played for an NL team.

1993 New York Yankees Team TOPR

	TPA	H	BB	HP	XB	TBB	TBO	SH	SF	SB	CS	GDP	BRB	BRO	NBE	GOC	Ratio	TOPR	C	1B	2B	3B	SS	LF	CF	RF	DH
Avg. AL Team	6256	1476	572	45	781	2874	4060	50	52	111	-62	-127	23	292	2897	4352	0.666	100.0									
New York Yankees	6359	1568	629	43	876	3116	4047	22	50	39	-35	-147	-71	254	3045	4301	0.708	106.3									
Boggs, Wade	644	169	74	0	34	277	391	1	9	0	-1	-10	-1	21	276	412	0.670	101	-	-	-	134	-	-	-	-	8
Gallego, Mike	465	114	50	4	52	220	289	3	5	3	-2	-16	-7	26	213	315	0.676	102	-	-	52	27	55	-	-	-	1
Humphreys, Mike	40	6	4	0	7	17	29	0	1	2	-1	-0	2	2	19	31	0.613	92	-	-	-	-	-	11	5	7	3
James, Dion	378	114	31	2	46	193	229	1	1	0	-0	-5	-3	7	190	236	0.805	121	-	1	-	-	-	91	14	1	1
Kelly, Pat	451	111	24	5	47	187	295	10	6	14	-11	-9	10	36	197	331	0.595	89	-	-	125	-	-	-	-	-	-
Leyritz, Jim	305	80	37	8	56	181	179	0	1	0	-0	-12	-11	13	170	192	0.885	133	12	29	-	-	-	6	-	23	21
Maas, Kevin	177	31	24	1	31	87	120	0	1	1	-1	-2	-1	4	86	124	0.694	104	-	17	-	-	-	-	-	-	31
Mattingly, Don	596	154	61	2	82	299	376	0	3	0	-0	-19	-16	22	283	398	0.711	107	-	130	-	-	-	-	-	-	5
Meulens, Hensley	61	9	8	0	9	26	44	0	0	0	-1	-2	-3	3	23	47	0.489	74	-	3	-	1	-	22	-	1	-
Nokes, Matt	238	54	16	2	38	110	163	0	3	0	-0	-4	-1	7	109	170	0.641	96	56	-	-	-	-	-	-	-	11
O'Neill, Paul	547	155	44	2	96	297	343	0	3	2	-4	-13	-12	20	285	363	0.785	118	-	-	-	-	-	46	-	103	2
Owen, Spike	367	78	29	0	26	133	256	3	1	3	-2	-5	0	11	133	267	0.498	75	-	-	-	-	96	-	-	-	2
Silvestri, Dave	26	6	5	0	4	15	15	0	0	0	-0	-1	-1	1	14	16	0.875	131	-	-	-	3	4	-	-	-	2
Stankiewicz, Andy	10	0	1	0	0	1	9	0	0	0	-0	-0	0	0	1	9	0.111	17	-	-	6	4	1	-	-	-	1
Stanley, Mike	491	129	57	5	97	288	294	0	6	1	-1	-10	-4	17	284	311	0.913	137	122	-	-	-	-	-	-	-	2
Tartabull, Danny	611	128	92	2	130	352	385	0	4	0	-0	-8	-4	12	348	397	0.877	132	-	-	-	-	-	-	-	50	88
Velarde, Randy	253	68	18	4	38	128	158	3	2	2	-2	-12	-7	19	121	177	0.684	103	-	-	-	16	26	48	2	-	1
Williams, Bernie	628	152	53	4	75	284	415	1	3	9	-9	-17	-13	30	271	445	0.609	91	-	-	-	-	-	-	139	-	1
Williams, Gerald	71	10	1	2	8	21	57	0	1	2	-0	-2	1	3	22	60	0.367	55	-	-	-	-	-	10	17	12	1

NOTE: Statistics are for games played with New York. * Also played for another AL team. ** Also played for an NL team.

1993 New York Yankees Team TPER

	W-L	GS	GR	SV	IP	ERA	H	BB	HB	XB	TBB	TBO	SH	SF	SB	CS	GDP	BRB	BRO	NBA	GOE	Ratio	TPER
Avg. AL Team	81 - 81	162	355	42	1444.1	4.33	1476	572	45	781	2874	4060	50	52	111	-62	-127	23	292	2897	4352	0.666	100.0
New York Yankees	88 - 74	162	332	38	1438.1	4.37	1467	552	29	832	2880	4055	50	47	115	-47	-140	25	284	2905	4339	0.670	100.6
Abbott, Jim	11 - 14	32	0	0	214.0	4.37	221	73	3	105	402	593	12	4	16	-6	-29	-3	51	399	644	0.620	93
Assenmacher, Paul *	2 - 2	0	26	0	17.1	3.12	10	9	1	2	22	47	4	0	1	-0	-3	2	7	24	54	0.444	67
Cook, Andy	0 - 1	0	4	0	5.1	5.06	4	7	0	4	15	16	1	0	0	-0	-0	1	1	16	17	0.941	141
Farr, Steve	2 - 2	0	49	25	47.0	4.21	44	28	2	38	112	130	3	4	4	-1	-3	7	11	119	141	0.844	127
Gibson, Paul **	2 - 0	0	20	0	35.1	3.06	31	9	0	20	60	99	0	3	5	-0	-4	4	7	64	106	0.604	91
Habyan, John *	2 - 1	0	36	1	42.1	4.04	45	16	0	26	87	118	0	2	3	-0	-4	1	6	88	124	0.710	107
Heaton, Neal	1 - 0	0	18	0	27.0	6.00	34	11	3	23	71	79	0	1	2	-0	-3	-0	4	71	83	0.855	128
Hitchcock, Sterling	1 - 2	6	0	0	31.0	4.65	32	14	1	19	66	86	0	2	3	-2	-5	-2	9	64	95	0.674	101
Howe, Steve	3 - 5	0	51	4	50.2	4.97	58	10	3	32	103	137	5	2	1	-1	-8	-1	16	102	153	0.667	100
Hutton, Mark	1 - 1	4	3	0	22.0	5.73	24	17	1	11	53	58	2	2	4	-1	-5	2	10	55	68	0.809	121
Jean, Domingo	1 - 1	6	4	0	40.1	4.46	37	19	0	32	88	119	0	1	2	-0	-0	3	1	91	120	0.758	114
Johnson, Jeff	0 - 2	2	0	0	2.2	30.38	12	2	0	6	20	8	0	0	1	-1	-0	0	1	20	9	2.222	334
Kamieniecki, Scott	10 - 7	20	10	1	154.1	4.08	163	59	3	86	311	426	3	5	7	-10	-22	-17	40	294	466	0.631	95
Key, Jimmy	18 - 6	34	0	0	236.2	3.00	219	43	1	121	384	670	6	9	15	-6	-25	-1	46	383	716	0.535	80
Militello, Sam	1 - 1	2	1	0	9.1	6.75	10	7	2	6	25	27	0	0	1	-0	-0	1	0	26	27	0.963	145
Monteleone, Rich	7 - 4	0	42	0	85.2	4.94	85	35	0	67	187	240	4	5	5	-1	-6	7	16	194	256	0.758	114
Munoz, Bobby	3 - 3	0	38	0	45.2	5.32	48	26	0	12	86	130	1	3	6	-0	-1	9	5	95	135	0.704	106
Perez, Melido	6 - 14	25	0	0	163.0	5.19	173	64	1	106	344	474	4	2	11	-6	-4	7	16	351	490	0.716	108
Smith, Lee **	0 - 0	0	8	3	8.0	0.00	4	5	0	1	10	23	0	1	4	-0	-0	5	1	15	24	0.625	94
Tanana, Frank **	0 - 2	3	0	0	19.2	3.20	18	7	0	11	36	63	0	0	1	-0	-0	1	0	37	63	0.587	88
Wickman, Bob	14 - 4	19	22	4	140.0	4.63	156	69	5	78	308	394	4	1	20	-9	-18	-2	32	306	426	0.718	108
Witt, Mike	3 - 2	9	0	0	41.0	5.27	39	22	3	26	90	118	1	0	3	-3	-0	1	4	91	122	0.746	112

NOTE: Statistics are for games played with New York. * Also played for another AL team. ** Also played for an NL team.

1993 Oakland Athletics Team TOPR

Columns — Batter Sub-set: H, BB, HP, XB, TBB, TBO · Baserunner Sub-set: SH, SF, SB, CS, GDP, BRB, BRO · Total Offense: NBE, GOC, Ratio, TOPR · Positions Played: C, 1B, 2B, 3B, SS, LF, CF, RF, DH

Player	TPA	H	BB	HP	XB	TBB	TBO	SH	SF	SB	CS	GDP	BRB	BRO	NBE	GOC	Ratio	TOPR	C	1B	2B	3B	SS	LF	CF	RF	DH
Avg. AL Team	6256	1476	572	45	781	2874	4060	50	52	111	-62	-127	23	292	2897	4352	0.666	100.0									
Oakland Athletics	6295	1408	622	33	776	2839	4135	46	49	131	-59	-125	42	279	2881	4414	0.653	98.0									
Abbott, Kurt	67	15	3	0	10	28	46	3	0	2	-0	-3	2	6	30	52	0.577	87	-	-	2	-	6	13	-	-	-
Aldrete, Mike	292	68	34	0	45	147	187	3	0	1	-1	-7	-4	11	143	198	0.722	108	-	59	-	-	-	-	-	17	-
Armas, Marcos	33	6	1	1	5	13	25	0	0	1	-0	-0	1	0	14	25	0.560	84	-	6	-	-	-	-	-	2	5
Blankenship, Lance	328	48	67	2	16	133	204	6	1	13	-5	-9	6	21	139	225	0.618	93	-	-	19	-	-	17	49	-	-
Bordick, Mike	633	136	60	11	34	241	410	10	6	10	-10	-9	7	35	248	445	0.557	84	-	-	-	-	159	-	-	-	-
Brosius, Scott	233	53	14	1	30	98	160	3	2	6	-0	-6	5	11	103	171	0.602	90	-	2	3	13	-	30	26	4	-
Browne, Jerry	286	65	22	0	19	106	195	2	2	4	-0	-9	-1	13	105	208	0.505	76	-	-	-	-	-	5	18	3	2
Fox, Eric	61	8	2	0	4	14	48	3	0	0	-2	-0	1	5	15	53	0.283	43	-	-	139	-	-	-	-	-	-
Gates, Brent	609	155	56	4	54	269	380	6	8	7	-3	-17	1	34	270	414	0.652	98	-	-	139	-	-	-	-	-	-
Helfand, Eric	13	3	0	0	0	3	10	0	0	0	-0	-0	0	0	3	10	0.300	45	5	-	-	-	-	-	-	-	-
Hemond, Scott	255	55	32	1	34	122	160	6	1	14	-5	-2	14	14	136	174	0.782	117	75	1	1	-	-	4	1	1	3
Henderson, Dave	422	84	32	0	79	195	298	0	8	0	-3	-1	4	12	199	310	0.642	96	-	-	-	-	-	2	60	14	28
Henderson, Rickey *	407	104	85	2	72	263	214	0	2	31	-6	-8	19	16	282	230	1.226	184	-	-	-	-	-	74	-	-	2
Lydy, Scott	111	23	8	1	11	43	79	0	0	2	-0	-1	1	1	44	80	0.550	83	-	-	-	-	-	17	5	16	2
McGwire, Mark	107	28	21	1	33	83	56	0	1	0	-1	-0	0	2	83	58	1.431	215	-	25	-	-	-	-	-	-	1
Mercedes, Henry	50	10	2	1	2	15	37	0	0	1	-1	-0	0	1	15	38	0.395	59	18	-	-	-	-	-	-	-	85
Neel, Troy	482	124	49	4	78	255	303	0	2	3	-5	-7	-7	14	248	317	0.782	118	-	34	-	-	-	-	-	-	1
Paquette, Craig	409	86	14	0	64	164	307	1	1	4	-2	-7	-3	11	161	318	0.506	76	-	-	-	104	1	3	-	-	3
Seitzer, Kevin *	289	65	27	1	26	119	190	2	4	4	-7	-7	-4	20	115	210	0.548	82	-	24	2	46	1	3	-	-	3
Sierra, Ruben	692	147	52	0	99	298	483	0	10	25	-5	-17	13	32	311	515	0.604	91	-	-	-	-	-	-	-	133	25
Steinbach, Terry	420	111	25	3	51	190	278	0	1	3	-3	-13	-12	17	178	295	0.603	91	86	15	-	-	-	-	-	-	6
Sveum, Dale	96	14	16	0	10	40	65	1	0	0	-0	-2	-1	3	39	68	0.574	86	-	14	4	7	1	1	-	-	2

NOTE: Statistics are for games played with Oakland. * Also played for another AL team. ** Also played for an NL team.

1993 Oakland Athletics Team TPER

Columns — Batter Sub-set: H, BB, HB, XB, TBB, TBO · Baserunner Sub-set: SH, SF, SB, CS, GDP, BRB, BRO · Total Pitching: NBA, GOE, Ratio, TPER

Player	W-L	GS	GR	SV	IP	ERA	H	BB	HB	XB	TBB	TBO	SH	SF	SB	CS	GDP	BRB	BRO	NBA	GOE	Ratio	TPER
Avg. AL Team	81 - 81	162	355	42	1444.1	4.33	1476	572	45	781	2874	4060	50	52	111	-62	-127	23	292	2897	4352	0.666	100.0
Oakland Athletics	68 - 94	162	424	42	1452.1	4.90	1551	680	49	824	3104	4072	57	47	120	-71	-131	22	306	3126	4378	0.714	107.3
Boever, Joe *	4 - 2	0	42	0	79.1	3.86	87	33	4	47	171	224	2	3	4	-3	-8	-2	16	169	240	0.704	106
Briscoe, John	1 - 0	0	17	0	24.2	8.03	26	26	0	12	64	68	0	2	0	-2	-3	-3	7	61	75	0.813	122
Campbell, Kevin	0 - 0	0	11	0	16.0	7.31	20	11	1	8	40	44	0	1	0	-2	-0	-1	3	39	47	0.830	125
Darling, Ron	5 - 9	29	2	0	178.0	5.16	198	72	5	113	388	507	5	6	14	-11	-10	4	32	392	539	0.727	109
Davis, Storm *	2 - 6	8	11	0	62.2	6.18	68	33	2	29	132	178	1	2	11	-2	-5	7	10	139	184	0.739	111
Downs, Kelly	5 - 10	12	30	0	119.2	5.64	135	60	2	62	259	335	3	4	13	-4	-15	1	26	260	361	0.720	108
Eckersley, Dennis	2 - 4	0	64	36	67.0	4.16	67	13	2	37	119	190	2	2	12	-2	-3	11	9	130	199	0.653	98
Gossage, Goose	4 - 5	0	39	1	47.2	4.53	49	26	1	33	109	135	3	2	2	-4	-3	4	6	113	141	0.801	120
Hillegas, Shawn	3 - 6	11	7	0	60.2	6.97	78	33	4	46	161	168	3	2	2	-3	-3	-2	14	159	182	0.874	131
Honeycutt, Rick	1 - 4	0	52	1	41.2	2.81	30	20	1	12	63	112	7	4	2	-3	-3	7	17	70	129	0.543	82
Horsman, Vince	2 - 0	0	40	0	25.0	5.40	25	15	3	8	51	73	0	0	2	-1	-1	0	2	51	75	0.680	102
Jimenez, Miguel	1 - 0	4	1	0	27.0	4.00	27	16	1	19	63	76	0	0	1	-1	-3	-3	4	60	80	0.750	113
Karsay, Steve	3 - 3	8	0	0	49.0	4.04	49	16	2	24	91	141	0	2	5	-2	-2	3	6	94	147	0.639	96
Mohler, Mike	1 - 6	9	33	0	64.1	5.60	57	44	2	41	144	180	5	2	8	-3	-5	6	16	150	196	0.765	115
Nunez, Edwin	3 - 6	0	56	1	75.2	3.81	89	29	6	29	153	210	5	2	5	-2	-5	4	15	157	225	0.698	105
Slusarski, Joe	0 - 0	1	1	0	8.2	5.19	9	11	0	4	24	21	2	0	0	-0	-3	-1	5	23	26	0.885	133
Smithberg, Roger	1 - 2	0	13	3	19.2	2.75	13	7	1	9	30	53	2	0	1	-0	-5	-2	7	28	60	0.467	70
Van Poppel, Todd	6 - 6	16	0	0	84.0	5.04	76	62	2	51	191	237	1	2	5	-5	-6	-3	14	188	251	0.749	113
Welch, Bob	9 - 11	28	2	0	166.2	5.29	208	56	7	121	392	462	10	3	8	-12	-19	-10	44	382	506	0.755	113
Witt, Bobby	14 - 13	33	2	0	220.0	4.21	226	91	3	103	423	613	9	8	19	-9	-26	1	52	424	665	0.638	96
Young, Curt	1 - 1	3	0	0	14.2	4.30	14	6	0	16	36	44	0	0	2	-1	-0	1	1	37	45	0.822	124
Seitzer, Kevin	0 - 0	0	1	0	0.1	0.00	0	0	0	0	0	1	0	0	0	-0	-0	0	0	1	0	0.000	0

NOTE: Statistics are for games played with Oakland. * Also played for another AL team. ** Also played for an NL team.

1993 Seattle Mariners Team TOPR

	TPA	H	BB	HP	XB	TBB	TBO	SH	SF	SB	CS	GDP	BRB	BRO	NBE	GOC	Ratio	TOPR	C	1B	2B	3B	SS	LF	CF	RF	DH
																					Batter Sub-set			Baserunner Sub-set		Total Offense	Positions Played
Avg. AL Team	6256	1476	572	45	781	2874	4060	50	52	111	-62	-127	23	292	2897	4352	0.666	100.0									
Seattle Mariners	6288	1429	624	56	803	2912	4065	63	51	91	-68	-132	5	314	2917	4379	0.666	100.1									
Amaral, Rich	421	108	33	3	29	173	265	7	5	19	-11	-5	15	28	188	293	0.642	96	-	3	77	19	14	-	-	-	9
Backman, Wally	31	4	1	0	0	5	25	1	0	0	-0	-0	1	1	6	26	0.231	35	-	-	1	9	-	-	-	-	-
Blowers, Mike	429	106	44	2	74	226	273	3	1	1	-5	-12	-12	21	214	294	0.728	109	1	1	-	117	-	1	-	1	3
Boone, Bret	302	68	17	4	52	141	203	6	4	2	-3	-6	3	19	144	222	0.649	97	-	-	74	-	-	-	-	-	1
Buhner, Jay	675	153	100	2	115	370	410	2	8	2	-5	-12	-5	27	365	437	0.835	125	-	-	-	-	-	-	-	148	10
Cotto, Henry **	109	20	2	1	7	30	85	1	0	5	-4	-0	2	5	32	90	0.356	53	-	-	-	-	-	23	9	4	15
Felder, Mike	374	72	22	2	20	116	270	7	1	15	-9	-2	12	19	128	289	0.443	67	-	-	-	2	-	89	7	-	6
Griffey, Ken Jr.	691	180	96	6	179	461	402	0	7	17	-9	-14	1	30	462	432	1.069	161	-	1	-	-	-	-	139	-	19
Haselman, Bill	154	35	12	1	23	71	102	2	2	2	-1	-5	0	10	71	112	0.634	95	49	-	-	-	-	-	-	2	4
Howard, Chris	1	0	0	0	0	0	1	0	0	0	-0	-0	0	0	0	1	0.000	0	4	-	-	-	-	-	-	-	-
Howitt, Dann	80	16	4	0	11	31	60	0	0	0	-0	-0	0	0	31	60	0.517	78	-	-	-	-	-	16	6	12	2
Litton, Greg	199	52	18	1	26	97	122	5	1	0	-1	-6	-1	13	96	135	0.711	107	-	13	17	7	5	21	-	2	12
Magadan, Dave **	269	59	36	0	14	109	169	2	3	2	-0	-9	-2	14	107	183	0.585	88	-	41	-	27	-	-	-	-	2
Martinez, Edgar	165	32	28	0	19	79	103	1	1	0	-0	-4	-2	6	77	109	0.706	106	-	-	-	16	-	-	-	-	24
Martinez, Tino	464	108	45	5	78	236	300	3	3	0	-3	-7	-4	16	232	316	0.734	110	-	103	-	-	-	-	-	-	6
Newfield, Marc	70	15	2	1	6	24	51	0	1	0	-1	-2	-2	4	22	55	0.400	60	-	-	-	-	-	5	-	-	15
O'Brien, Pete	239	54	26	0	28	108	156	0	3	0	-0	-8	-5	11	103	167	0.617	93	-	9	-	-	-	1	-	-	52
Pirkl, Greg	23	4	0	0	3	7	19	0	0	0	-0	-2	-2	2	5	21	0.238	36	-	5	-	-	-	-	-	-	2
Sasser, Mackey	208	41	15	1	17	74	147	0	4	1	-0	-7	-2	11	72	158	0.456	68	4	1	-	-	-	26	-	11	19
Sheets, Larry	20	2	2	1	1	6	15	0	0	0	-0	-2	-2	2	4	17	0.235	35	-	-	-	-	-	-	-	1	5
Tinsley, Lee	21	3	2	0	4	9	16	0	0	0	-0	-1	-1	1	8	17	0.471	71	-	-	-	-	-	5	1	1	2
Turang, Brian	160	35	17	2	13	67	105	1	0	6	-2	-3	2	6	69	111	0.622	93	-	-	1	2	-	26	14	1	1
Valle, Dave	500	109	48	17	58	232	314	8	4	1	-0	-18	-5	30	227	344	0.660	99	135	-	-	-	-	-	-	-	-
Vina, Fernando	53	10	4	3	2	19	35	1	0	6	-0	-0	7	1	26	36	0.722	108	-	-	16	-	4	-	-	-	2
Vizquel, Omar	630	143	50	4	24	221	417	13	3	12	-14	-7	7	37	228	454	0.502	75	-	-	-	-	155	-	-	-	2

NOTE: Statistics are for games played with Seattle. * Also played for another AL team. ** Also played for an NL team.

1993 Seattle Mariners Team TPER

	W-L	GS	GR	SV	IP	ERA	H	BB	HB	XB	TBB	TBO	SH	SF	SB	CS	GDP	BRB	BRO	NBA	GOE	Ratio	TPER
									Batter Sub-set						Baserunner Sub-set					Total Pitching		
Avg. AL Team	81 - 81	162	355	42	1444.1	4.33	1476	572	45	781	2874	4060	50	52	111	-62	-127	23	292	2897	4352	0.666	100.0
Seattle Marniners	82 - 80	162	353	41	1453.2	4.20	1421	605	66	743	2835	4062	55	45	105	-68	-146	-9	314	2826	4376	0.646	97.0
Ayrault, Bob **	1 - 1	0	14	0	19.2	3.20	18	6	0	10	34	53	1	2	0	-0	-2	1	5	35	58	0.603	91
Bosio, Chris	9 - 9	24	5	1	164.1	3.45	138	59	6	74	277	464	7	4	8	-6	-13	0	30	277	494	0.561	84
Charlton, Norm	1 - 3	0	34	18	34.2	2.34	22	17	0	15	54	101	0	1	3	-0	-5	-1	6	53	107	0.495	74
Converse, Jim	1 - 3	4	0	0	20.1	5.31	23	14	0	7	44	55	0	1	2	-2	-1	-0	4	44	59	0.746	112
Cummings, John	0 - 6	8	2	0	46.1	6.02	59	16	2	25	102	128	0	2	2	-4	-7	-7	13	95	141	0.674	101
DeLucia, Rich	3 - 6	1	29	0	42.2	4.64	46	23	1	23	93	123	1	1	2	-2	-1	1	5	94	128	0.734	110
Fleming, Dave	12 - 5	26	0	0	167.1	4.36	189	67	6	84	346	463	4	8	8	-12	-16	-8	40	338	503	0.672	101
Hampton, Mike	1 - 3	3	10	1	17.0	9.53	28	17	0	17	62	48	1	1	4	-0	-2	4	4	66	52	1.269	191
Hanson, Erik	11 - 12	30	1	0	215.0	3.47	215	60	5	114	394	604	10	4	15	-13	-19	-3	46	391	650	0.602	90
Henry, Dwayne **	2 - 1	1	30	2	54.0	6.67	56	35	2	39	132	149	3	4	3	-2	-5	5	12	137	161	0.851	128
Holman, Brad	1 - 3	0	19	3	36.1	3.72	27	16	5	9	57	103	1	0	1	-0	-5	-3	6	54	109	0.495	74
Johnson, Randy	19 - 8	34	1	1	255.1	3.24	185	99	16	109	409	728	8	7	28	-12	-16	15	43	424	771	0.550	83
King, Kevin	0 - 1	0	13	0	11.2	6.17	9	4	1	12	26	30	3	2	1	-0	-1	5	6	31	36	0.861	129
Leary, Tim	11 - 9	27	6	0	169.1	5.05	202	58	8	115	383	472	5	1	10	-9	-21	-14	36	369	508	0.726	109
Nelson, Jeff	5 - 3	0	71	1	60.0	4.35	57	34	8	23	122	164	2	4	10	-1	-8	7	15	129	179	0.721	108
Ontiveros, Steve	0 - 2	0	14	0	18.0	1.00	18	6	0	4	28	47	1	0	1	-0	-6	-4	7	24	54	0.444	67
Plantenberg, Erik	0 - 0	0	20	1	9.2	6.52	11	12	1	2	26	28	1	0	0	-0	-0	1	1	27	29	0.931	140
Powell, Dennis	0 - 0	2	31	0	47.2	4.15	42	24	1	28	95	123	5	2	4	-3	-10	-2	20	93	143	0.650	98
Power, Ted *	2 - 2	0	25	13	25.1	3.91	27	9	0	7	43	67	1	1	0	-1	-5	-4	8	39	75	0.520	78
Salkeld, Roger	0 - 0	2	1	0	14.1	2.51	13	4	1	7	25	43	0	0	0	-0	-2	-2	2	23	45	0.511	77
Shinall, Zak	0 - 0	0	1	0	2.2	3.38	4	2	0	6	12	8	0	0	0	-0	-0	0	0	12	8	1.500	225
Swan, Russ	3 - 3	0	23	0	19.2	9.15	25	18	2	9	54	54	1	0	1	-1	-3	-2	5	52	59	0.881	132
Wainhouse, David	0 - 0	0	3	0	2.1	27.00	7	5	1	4	17	7	0	0	2	-0	-0	2	0	19	7	2.714	408

NOTE: Statistics are for games played with Seattle. * Also played for another AL team. ** Also played for an NL team.

1993 Texas Rangers Team TOPR

	TPA	H	BB	HP	XB	TBB	TBQ	SH	SF	SB	CS	GDP	BRB	BRO	NBE	GOC	Ratio	TOPR	C	1B	2B	3B	SS	LF	CF	RF	DH
Avg. AL Team	6256	1476	572	45	781	2874	4060	50	52	111	-62	-127	23	292	2897	4352	0.666	100.0									
Texas Rangers	6166	1472	483	48	905	2908	4038	69	56	113	-67	-110	61	302	2969	4340	0.684	102.8									
Balboni, Steve	5	3	0	0	0	3	2	0	0	0	-0	-0	0	0	3	2	1.500	225									2
Canseco, Jose	253	59	16	3	46	124	172	0	3	6	-6	-6	-3	15	121	187	0.647	97								49	9
Dascenzo, Doug	158	29	8	0	13	50	117	3	1	2	-0	-1	5	5	55	122	0.451	68						16	35	25	2
Davis, Butch	170	39	5	1	27	72	120	5	0	3	-1	-0	7	6	79	126	0.627	94						23	10	17	11
Diaz, Mario	226	56	8	1	18	83	149	7	5	1	-0	-6	7	18	90	167	0.539	81		1		12	57				
Ducey, Rob	99	24	10	0	18	52	61	2	2	2	-3	-1	2	8	54	69	0.783	118						1	14	13	
Franco, Julio	607	154	62	1	79	296	378	5	7	9	-3	-16	2	31	298	409	0.729	109									140
Gil, Benji	66	7	5	0	0	12	50	4	0	1	-2	-0	3	6	15	56	0.268	40					22				
Gonzalez, Juan	587	166	37	13	173	389	370	0	1	4	-1	-11	-7	13	382	383	1.000	150							129		10
Harris, Donald	86	15	5	1	5	26	61	3	1	0	-1	-0	3	5	29	66	0.439	66						1	27	11	3
Hulse, David	441	118	26	1	32	177	289	5	2	29	-9	-9	18	25	195	314	0.621	93							112		2
Huson, Jeff	46	6	0	0	3	9	39	1	0	0	-0	-0	1	1	10	40	0.250	38			5	2	12				
James, Chris **	34	11	3	0	10	24	20	0	0	0	-0	-0	0	0	24	20	1.200	180						4		4	
Lee, Manuel	239	45	22	2	8	77	160	9	1	2	-4	-2	6	16	83	176	0.472	71					72				1
Palmeiro, Rafael	686	176	73	5	155	409	421	2	9	22	-3	-8	22	22	431	443	0.973	146		160							
Palmer, Dean	585	127	53	8	134	322	392	0	5	11	-10	-5	1	20	323	412	0.784	118				148	1				
Peltier, Dan	183	43	20	1	12	76	117	1	1	0	-4	-3	-5	9	71	126	0.563	85		5				2		54	
Petralli, Geno	156	32	22	0	8	62	101	1	0	2	-0	-5	-2	6	60	107	0.561	84	39		1	1					2
Redus, Gary	248	64	23	0	38	125	158	0	3	4	-4	-3	0	10	125	168	0.744	112		5	1			5	17	46	1
Ripken, Billy	153	25	11	4	4	44	107	5	1	0	-2	-6	-2	14	42	121	0.347	52			34	9	18				
Rodriguez, Pudge	519	129	29	4	66	228	344	5	8	8	-7	-16	-2	36	226	380	0.595	89	134								1
Russell, John	24	5	2	0	4	11	17	0	0	0	-0	-0	0	0	11	17	0.647	97	11	1		1		1			
Shave, Jon	52	15	0	0	2	17	32	3	2	1	-3	-0	3	8	20	40	0.500	75			8		9				
Strange, Doug	542	124	43	3	50	220	360	8	4	6	-4	-12	2	28	222	388	0.572	86			135	9	1				
STAFF	1	0	0	0	0	0	1	0	0	0	-0	-0	0	0	0	1	0.000	0									

NOTE: Statistics are for games played with Texas. * Also played for another AL team. ** Also played for an NL team.

1993 Texas Rangers Team TPER

	W-L	GS	GR	SV	IP	ERA	H	BB	HB	XB	TBB	TBO	SH	SF	SB	CS	GDP	BRB	BRO	NBA	GOE	Ratio	TPER
Avg. AL Team	81 – 81	162	355	42	1444.1	4.33	1476	572	45	781	2874	4060	50	52	111	-62	-127	23	292	2897	4352	0.666	100.0
Texas Rangers	86 – 76	162	359	45	1438.1	4.28	1476	562	44	768	2850	4059	48	42	95	-67	-120	-2	277	2848	4336	0.657	98.7
Bohanon, Brian	4 – 4	8	28	0	92.2	4.76	107	46	4	48	205	254	2	5	8	-7	-12	-4	26	201	280	0.718	108
Bronkey, Jeff	1 – 1	0	21	1	36.0	4.00	39	11	1	20	71	98	1	2	0	-1	-7	-5	11	66	109	0.606	91
Brown, Kevin	15 – 12	34	0	0	233.0	3.59	228	74	15	91	408	675	5	3	10	-10	-15	-7	33	401	708	0.566	85
Burns, Todd **	0 – 4	5	20	0	65.0	4.57	63	32	2	40	137	186	2	3	3	-2	-5	1	12	138	198	0.697	105
Carpenter, Cris **	4 – 1	0	27	1	32.0	4.22	35	12	2	19	68	86	1	3	0	-1	-2	1	7	69	93	0.742	111
Dreyer, Steve	3 – 3	6	4	0	41.0	5.71	48	20	1	31	100	117	0	0	2	-2	-5	-5	7	95	124	0.766	115
Fajardo, Hector	0 - 0	0	1	0	0.2	0.00	0	0	0	0	0	2	0	0	0	-0	-0	0	0	0	2	0.000	0
Henke, Tom	5 – 5	0	66	40	74.1	2.91	55	27	1	27	110	213	3	3	3	-2	-5	2	13	112	226	0.496	74
Lefferts, Craig	3 – 9	8	44	0	83.1	6.05	102	28	1	65	196	233	6	3	4	-4	-5	4	18	200	251	0.797	120
Leibrandt, Charlie	9 – 10	26	0	0	150.1	4.55	169	45	4	93	311	426	8	4	19	-5	-11	15	28	326	454	0.718	108
Nelson, Gene *	0 - 0	0	6	1	8.0	3.38	10	1	0	1	12	23	0	0	0	-0	-1	-1	1	11	24	0.458	69
Nen, Robb **	1 – 1	3	6	0	22.2	6.35	28	26	0	12	66	58	0	1	1	-2	-3	-3	6	63	64	0.984	148
Oliver, Darren	0 - 0	0	2	0	3.1	2.70	2	1	0	3	6	11	0	0	1	-0	-0	1	0	7	11	0.636	96
Patterson, Bob	2 – 4	0	52	1	52.2	4.78	59	11	1	35	106	150	1	2	3	-2	-2	2	7	108	157	0.688	103
Pavlik, Roger	12 – 6	26	0	0	166.1	3.41	151	80	5	85	321	466	6	4	15	-6	-19	0	35	321	501	0.641	96
Reed, Rick *	1 – 0	0	2	0	4.0	2.25	6	1	1	3	11	10	0	0	0	-1	-1	-2	2	9	12	0.750	113
Rogers, Kenny	16 – 10	33	2	0	208.1	4.10	210	71	4	114	399	588	7	5	4	-11	-12	-7	35	392	623	0.629	95
Ryan, Nolan	5 – 5	13	0	0	66.1	4.88	54	40	1	30	125	192	2	2	13	-4	-3	10	11	135	203	0.665	100
Schooler, Mike	3 – 0	0	17	0	24.1	5.55	30	10	0	18	58	69	2	0	5	-1	-1	5	4	63	73	0.863	130
Whiteside, Matt	2 – 1	0	60	1	73.0	4.32	78	23	1	33	135	200	2	1	4	-6	-11	-10	20	125	220	0.568	85
Canseco, Jose	0 - 0	0	1	0	1.0	27.00	2	3	0	0	5	2	0	1	0	-0	-0	1	1	6	3	2.000	300

NOTE: Statistics are for games played with Texas. * Also played for another AL team. ** Also played for an NL team.

1993 Toronto Blue Jays Team TOPR

	TPA	H	BB	HP	XB	TBB	TBO	SH	SF	SB	CS	GDP	BRB	BRO	NBE	GOC	Ratio	TOPR	C	1B	2B	3B	SS	LF	CF	RF	DH
Avg. AL Team	6256	1476	572	45	781	2874	4060	50	52	111	-62	-127	23	292	2897	4352	0.666	100.0									
Toronto Blue Jays	6319	1556	588	52	878	3074	4023	46	54	170	-49	-138	83	287	3157	4310	0.732	110.0									
Alomar, Roberto	683	192	80	5	98	375	397	4	5	55	-15	-13	36	37	411	434	0.947	142	-	-	150	-	-	-	-	-	-
Borders, Pat	520	124	20	2	57	203	364	7	3	2	-2	-18	-8	30	195	394	0.495	74	138	-	-	-	-	-	-	-	-
Butler, Rob	56	13	7	1	4	25	35	0	0	2	-2	-0	0	2	25	37	0.676	101	-	-	-	-	-	15	1	-	-
Canate, Willie	57	10	6	1	3	20	37	2	1	1	-1	-2	1	6	21	43	0.488	73	-	-	-	-	-	17	6	9	1
Carter, Joe	669	153	47	9	142	351	450	0	10	8	-3	-10	5	23	356	473	0.753	113	-	-	-	-	-	55	-	96	3
Cedeno, Domingo	50	8	1	0	0	9	38	2	1	1	-0	-2	2	5	11	43	0.256	38	-	-	5	-	10	-	-	-	-
Coles, Darnell	217	49	16	4	23	92	145	1	2	1	-1	-3	0	7	92	152	0.605	31	-	1	-	16	-	31	-	13	1
Delgado, Carlos	2	0	1	0	0	1	1	0	0	0	-0	-0	0	0	1	1	1.000	150	1	-	-	-	-	-	-	-	1
Fernandez, Tony **	390	108	31	0	48	187	245	5	1	15	-8	-13	0	27	187	272	0.688	103	-	-	-	-	94	-	-	-	-
Green, Shawn	6	0	0	0	0	0	6	0	0	0	-0	-0	0	0	0	6	0.000	0	-	-	-	-	-	-	-	2	1
Griffin, Alfredo	102	20	3	0	3	26	75	4	0	0	-0	-3	1	7	27	82	0.329	49	-	-	11	6	20	-	-	-	-
Henderson, Rickey *	203	35	35	2	17	89	128	1	2	22	-2	-1	22	6	111	134	0.828	124	-	-	-	-	-	44	-	-	-
Jackson, Darrin **	189	38	8	0	23	69	138	5	0	0	-2	-9	-6	16	63	154	0.409	61	-	-	-	-	-	-	10	37	-
Knorr, Randy	112	25	9	0	19	53	76	2	0	0	-0	-2	0	4	53	80	0.663	100	39	-	-	-	-	-	-	-	-
Martinez, Domingo	15	4	1	0	3	8	10	0	0	0	-0	-0	0	0	8	10	0.800	120	-	7	-	1	-	-	-	-	-
Molitor, Paul	725	211	77	3	113	404	425	1	8	22	-4	-13	14	26	418	451	0.927	139	-	23	-	-	-	-	-	-	137
Olerud, John	679	200	114	7	130	451	351	0	7	0	-2	-12	-7	21	444	372	1.194	179	-	137	-	-	-	-	-	-	20
Schofield, Dick	128	21	16	0	5	42	89	2	0	3	-0	-1	4	3	46	92	0.500	75	-	-	-	-	36	-	-	-	-
Sojo, Luis	54	8	4	0	2	14	39	2	1	0	-0	-3	0	6	14	45	0.311	47	-	-	8	3	8	-	-	-	-
Sprague, Ed	596	142	32	10	69	253	404	2	6	1	-0	-23	-14	31	239	435	0.549	83	-	-	-	150	-	-	-	-	-
Ward, Turner	198	32	23	1	20	76	135	3	4	3	-3	-7	0	17	76	152	0.500	75	-	1	-	-	-	33	10	22	-
White, Devon	668	163	57	7	99	326	435	3	3	34	-4	-3	33	13	359	448	0.801	120	-	-	-	-	-	-	145	-	-

NOTE: Statistics are for games played with Toronto. * Also played for another AL team. ** Also played for an NL team.

1993 Toronto Blue Jays Team TPER

	W-L	GS	GR	SV	IP	ERA	H	BB	HB	XB	TBB	TBO	SH	SF	SB	CS	GDP	BRB	BRO	NBA	GOE	Ratio	TPER
Avg. AL Team	81 - 81	162	355	42	1444.1	4.33	1476	572	45	781	2874	4060	50	52	111	-62	-127	23	292	2897	4352	0.666	100.0
Toronto Blue Jays	95 - 67	162	344	50	1441.1	4.22	1441	620	32	704	2797	4086	38	52	136	-64	-109	53	263	2850	4349	0.655	98.4
Brow, Scott	1 - 1	3	3	0	18.0	6.00	19	10	1	8	38	50	1	2	2	-0	-2	3	5	41	55	0.745	112
Castillo, Tony	3 - 2	0	51	0	50.2	3.38	44	22	0	20	86	138	5	2	4	-1	-7	3	15	89	153	0.582	87
Cox, Danny	7 - 6	0	44	2	83.2	3.12	73	29	0	36	138	245	0	1	7	-3	-5	0	9	138	254	0.543	82
Dayley, Ken	0 - 0	0	2	0	0.2	0.00	1	4	0	1	6	2	0	0	0	-0	-0	0	0	6	2	3.000	451
Eichhorn, Mark	3 - 1	0	54	0	72.2	2.72	76	22	3	28	129	203	3	2	8	-3	-8	2	16	131	219	0.598	90
Flener, Huck	0 - 0	0	6	0	6.2	4.05	7	4	0	4	15	19	0	0	1	-0	-1	0	1	15	20	0.750	113
Guzman, Juan	14 - 3	33	0	0	221.0	3.99	211	110	3	88	412	625	5	9	25	-17	-10	12	41	424	666	0.637	96
Hentgen, Pat	19 - 9	32	2	0	216.1	3.87	215	74	7	130	426	619	6	5	16	-6	-18	3	35	429	654	0.656	99
Leiter, Al	9 - 6	12	22	2	105.0	4.11	93	56	4	29	182	295	3	3	7	-5	-10	-2	21	180	316	0.570	86
Linton, Doug *	0 - 1	1	3	0	11.0	6.55	11	9	1	6	27	32	0	2	0	-0	-0	2	2	29	34	0.853	128
Morris, Jack	7 - 12	27	0	0	152.2	6.19	189	65	3	97	354	436	4	5	17	-10	-10	6	29	360	465	0.774	116
Stewart, Dave	12 - 8	26	0	0	162.0	4.44	146	72	4	107	329	458	3	4	13	-12	-12	-4	31	325	489	0.665	100
Stottlemyre, Todd	11 - 12	28	2	0	176.2	4.84	204	69	3	92	368	494	5	11	24	-7	-11	22	34	390	528	0.739	111
Timlin, Mike	4 - 2	0	54	1	55.2	4.69	63	27	1	27	118	159	1	3	9	-0	-5	8	9	126	168	0.750	113
Ward, Duane	2 - 3	0	71	45	71.2	2.13	49	25	1	18	93	205	0	2	3	-0	-7	-2	9	91	214	0.425	64
Williams, Woody	3 - 1	0	30	0	37.0	4.38	40	22	1	13	76	106	2	1	0	-0	-3	0	6	76	112	0.679	102

NOTE: Statistics are for games played with Toronto. * Also played for another AL team. ** Also played for an NL team.

1993 Pitchers with 2 Teams-Same League

		W-L	GS	GR	SV	IP	ERA	Batter Sub-set						Baserunner Sub-set							Total Pitching			
								H	BB	HB	XB	TBB	TBQ	SH	SF	SB	CS	GDP	BRB	BRO	NBA	GOE	Ratio	TPER
Pitched with 2 AL Teams																								
Boever, Joe	OAK/DET	6 - 3	0	61	3	102.1	3.61	101	44	4	55	204	288	5	7	4	-3	-8	5	23	209	311	0.672	101
Davis, Storm	OAK/DET	2 - 8	8	35	4	98.0	5.05	93	48	3	51	195	279	2	3	15	-3	-7	10	15	205	294	0.697	105
Habyan, John	NYY/KCR	2 - 1	0	48	1	56.1	4.15	59	20	0	34	113	158	0	2	6	-0	-6	2	8	115	166	0.692	104
Linton, Doug	TOR/CAL	2 - 1	1	22	0	36.2	7.36	46	23	1	37	107	105	0	3	3	-2	-1	3	6	110	111	0.991	149
Nelson, Gene	CAL/TEX	0 - 5	0	52	5	60.2	3.12	60	24	2	23	109	172	3	4	3	-1	-5	4	13	113	185	0.611	92
Power, Ted	CLE/SEA	2 - 4	0	45	13	45.1	5.36	57	17	0	22	96	127	3	2	1	-1	-6	-1	12	95	139	0.683	103
Reed, Rick	KCR/TEX	1 - 0	0	3	0	7.2	4.69	12	2	2	6	22	20	0	0	0	-1	-1	-2	2	20	22	0.909	136
Pitched with 2 NL Teams																								
Aldred, Scott	COL/MON	1 - 0	0	8	0	12.0	9.00	19	10	1	11	41	33	2	0	2	-1	-1	2	4	43	37	1.162	180
Ashby, Andy	COL/SDO	3 - 10	21	11	1	123.0	6.80	168	56	4	92	320	336	6	7	11	-1	-19	4	33	324	369	0.878	136
Bottenfield, Kent	MON/COL	5 - 10	25	12	0	159.2	5.07	179	71	6	113	367	429	21	4	16	-6	-15	20	46	389	475	0.819	126
Davis, Mark	PHI/SDO	1 - 5	0	60	4	69.2	4.26	79	44	1	48	172	198	4	1	8	-2	-6	5	13	177	211	0.839	130
Grant, Mark	HOU/COL	0 - 1	0	20	1	25.1	7.46	34	11	0	20	65	67	0	2	1	-1	-6	-4	9	61	76	0.803	124
Harris, Greg	SDO/COL	11 - 17	35	0	0	225.1	4.59	239	69	7	162	477	642	14	4	22	-10	-10	20	38	497	680	0.731	113
Henry, Butch	COL/MON	3 - 9	16	14	0	103.0	6.12	135	28	1	74	238	291	6	6	9	-4	-9	8	25	246	316	0.778	120
Hoffman, Trevor	FLA/SDO	4 - 6	0	67	5	90.0	3.90	80	39	1	54	174	262	4	5	7	-1	-2	13	12	187	274	0.682	105
Hurst, Bruce	SDO/COL	0 - 2	5	0	0	13.0	7.62	15	6	0	4	25	38	1	0	3	-1	-1	2	3	27	41	0.659	102
Kaiser, Jeff	CIN/NYM	0 - 0	0	9	0	8.0	7.88	10	5	0	7	22	21	0	1	4	-1	-1	3	3	25	24	1.042	161
Mason, Roger	SDO/PHI	5 - 12	0	68	0	99.2	4.06	90	34	2	45	171	279	7	5	5	-5	-4	8	21	179	300	0.597	92
Masuer, Tim	PHI/SDO	0 - 1	0	36	0	54.0	4.00	51	24	1	31	107	157	1	1	4	-3	-1	2	6	109	163	0.669	103
Rodriguez, Rich	SDO/FLA	2 - 4	0	70	3	76.0	3.79	73	33	2	42	150	218	5	0	5	-2	-6	2	13	152	231	0.658	102
Scott, Tim	SDO/MON	7 - 2	0	56	1	71.2	3.01	69	34	4	29	136	204	3	2	18	-2	-3	18	10	154	214	0.720	111
Service, Scott	COL/CIN	2 - 2	0	29	2	46.0	4.30	44	16	2	33	95	129	2	4	2	-1	-3	4	10	99	139	0.712	110

1993 Pitchers with 2 Teams-Different League

		W-L	GS	GR	SV	IP	ERA	Batter Sub-set						Baserunner Sub-set							Total Pitching			
								H	BB	HB	XB	TBB	TBQ	SH	SF	SB	CS	GDP	BRB	BRO	NBA	GOE	Ratio	TPER
Assenmacher, Paul	CUB/NYY	4 - 3	0	72	0	56.0	3.38	54	22	1	24	101	156	4	0	4	-1	-8	-1	13	100	169	0.592	91
Ayrault, Bob	PHI/SEA	3 - 1	0	24	0	30.0	5.40	36	16	1	17	70	83	1	2	4	-0	-3	4	6	74	89	0.831	126
Belcher, Tim	CIN/CWS	12 - 11	33	1	0	208.2	4.44	198	74	8	104	384	594	8	4	11	-8	-15	0	35	384	629	0.610	93
Belinda, Stan	PIT/KCR	4 - 2	0	63	19	69.2	3.88	65	17	2	33	117	198	3	2	17	-2	-5	15	12	132	210	0.629	96
Brummett, Greg	SFO/MIN	4 - 4	13	0	0	72.2	5.08	82	28	0	49	159	194	1	5	12	-1	-11	6	18	165	212	0.778	119
Burns, Todd	TEX/STL	0 - 8	5	44	0	95.2	5.08	95	41	2	72	210	271	5	5	3	-3	-6	4	19	214	290	0.738	112
Cadaret, Greg	CIN/KCR	3 - 2	0	47	1	48.0	4.31	54	30	2	17	103	130	4	0	3	-3	-6	-2	13	101	143	0.706	108
Carpenter, Cris	FLA/TEX	4 - 2	0	56	1	69.1	3.50	64	25	4	32	125	194	2	4	5	-1	-4	6	11	131	205	0.639	97
DeLeon, Jose	PHI/CWS	3 - 0	3	32	0	57.1	2.98	44	30	6	30	110	158	3	2	5	-8	-4	-2	17	108	175	0.617	95
Deshaies, Jim	MIN/SFO	13 - 15	31	1	0	184.1	4.39	183	57	7	125	372	510	6	7	8	-18	-14	-11	45	361	555	0.650	101
DeSilva, John	DET/LAD	0 - 0	0	4	0	6.1	7.11	8	1	0	3	12	17	0	1	0	-0	-1	0	2	12	19	0.632	97
Gardiner, Mike	MON/DET	2 - 3	2	32	0	49.1	4.93	52	26	1	23	102	140	2	3	4	-2	-4	3	11	105	151	0.695	107
Gibson, Paul	NYM/NYY	3 - 1	0	28	0	44.0	3.48	45	11	0	26	82	125	0	3	5	-0	-4	4	7	86	132	0.652	98
Henry, Dwayne	CIN/SEA	2 - 2	1	33	2	58.2	6.44	62	39	2	42	145	165	3	4	3	-2	-3	5	12	150	177	0.847	128
Hernandez, Jeremy	SDO/CLE	6 - 7	0	70	8	111.2	3.63	116	34	0	65	215	307	4	6	4	-6	-10	-2	26	213	333	0.640	97
Magrane, Joe	STL/CAL	11 - 12	28	2	0	164.0	4.66	175	58	5	97	335	450	10	10	22	-13	-16	13	49	348	499	0.697	107
Manzanillo, Josias	MIL/NYM	1 - 1	1	15	1	29.0	6.83	30	19	2	16	67	83	3	3	2	-0	-1	7	7	74	90	0.822	125
Munoz, Mike	DET/COL	2 - 2	0	29	0	21.0	4.71	25	15	0	16	56	56	3	2	1	-1	-4	1	10	57	66	0.864	133
Nen, Robb	TEX/FLA	2 - 1	4	20	0	56.0	6.75	63	46	0	39	148	160	1	2	5	-2	-3	3	8	151	168	0.899	137
Pall, Donn	CWS/PHI	3 - 3	0	47	1	76.1	3.07	77	14	2	29	122	219	7	1	4	-0	-6	6	14	128	233	0.549	83
Sanderson, Scott	CAL/SFO	11 - 13	29	3	0	184.0	4.21	201	34	6	121	362	517	9	10	7	-6	-11	9	36	371	553	0.671	102
Slocumb, Heathcliff	CLE/CUB	4 - 1	0	30	0	38.0	4.03	35	20	0	12	67	105	1	3	4	-0	-5	3	9	70	114	0.614	93
Smith, Lee	STL/NYY	2 - 4	0	63	46	58.0	3.88	53	14	0	48	115	169	0	3	12	-2	-1	12	6	127	175	0.726	112
Tanana, Frank	NYM/NYY	7 - 17	32	0	0	202.2	4.35	216	55	9	133	413	576	12	4	15	-6	-15	10	37	423	613	0.690	106
Thigpen, Bobby	CWS/PHI	3 - 1	0	42	1	54.0	5.83	74	21	6	35	136	147	2	4	4	-4	-7	-1	17	135	164	0.823	125
Wickander, Kevin	CLE/CIN	1 - 0	0	44	0	34.0	6.09	47	22	2	34	105	98	1	0	3	-1	-0	3	2	108	100	1.080	166

1993 Players with 2 Teams-Same League

	TPA	H	BB	HP	XB	TBB	TBO	SH	SF	SB	CS	GDP	BRB	BRO	NBE	GOC	Ratio	TOPR	C	1B	2B	3B	SS	LF	CF	RF	DH
Played with 2 AL Teams																											
Calderon, Ivan	265	50	21	1	17	89	189	2	2	4	-2	-13	-7	19	82	208	0.394	**59**	-	-	-	-	-	9	2	39	25
Deer Rob	532	98	58	5	82	243	368	0	3	5	-2	-6	0	11	243	369	0.659	**99**	-	-	-	-	-	-	2	120	6
Gaetti, Gary	369	81	21	8	64	174	250	2	7	1	-3	-5	2	17	176	267	0.659	**99**	-	24	-	79	-	-	-	-	6
Henderson, Rickey	610	139	120	4	89	352	342	1	4	53	-8	-9	41	22	393	364	1.080	**162**	-	-	-	-	-	118	-	-	16
Pagliarulo, Mike	405	112	26	6	60	204	258	2	1	6	-6	-7	-4	16	200	274	0.730	**110**	-	4	-	107	-	-	-	-	-
Seitzer, Kevin	471	112	44	2	53	211	305	3	5	7	-7	-14	-6	29	205	334	0.614	**92**	-	31	3	79	1	3	-	1	6
Played with 2 NL Teams																											
Cianfrocco, Archi	324	72	17	3	51	143	224	2	5	2	-0	-9	0	16	143	240	0.596	**92**	-	42	-	64	-	-	-	-	-
Daugherty, Jack	74	14	11	0	8	33	48	0	1	0	-0	-0	1	1	34	49	0.694	**107**	-	3	-	-	-	11	-	6	-
McGriff, Fred	640	162	76	2	144	384	395	0	5	5	-3	-14	-7	-22	377	417	0.904	**140**	-	149	-	-	-	-	-	-	-
Rhodes, Karl	65	15	11	0	13	39	39	0	0	2	-0	-0	2	0	41	39	1.051	**162**	-	-	-	-	-	7	16	2	-
Sheffield, Gary	557	145	47	9	90	291	349	0	7	17	-5	-11	8	23	299	372	0.804	**124**	-	-	-	133	-	-	-	-	-

1993 Played with 2 Teams-Different League

	TPA	H	BB	HP	XB	TBB	TBO	SH	SF	SB	CS	GDP	BRB	BRO	NBE	GOC	Ratio	TOPR	C	1B	2B	3B	SS	LF	CF	RF	DH
Bell, Juan	400	80	41	2	33	156	271	5	1	6	-7	-4	1	17	157	288	0.545	**82**	-	-	47	-	66	-	1	2	2
Cotto, Henry	251	60	5	2	23	90	180	2	2	16	-5	-3	12	12	102	192	0.531	**81**	-	-	-	-	-	36	24	25	15
Davis, Eric	511	107	55	1	80	243	344	0	4	35	-7	-12	20	23	263	367	0.717	**110**	-	-	-	-	-	101	18	-	5
Fernandez, Tony	594	147	56	1	60	264	379	8	3	21	-10	-17	5	38	269	417	0.645	**98**	-	-	-	-	142	-	-	-	18
Hill, Glenallen	284	69	17	1	63	150	192	1	4	8	-3	-4	6	12	156	204	0.765	**116**	-	-	-	-	-	27	4	30	18
Howard, Thomas	348	81	24	0	42	147	238	0	5	10	-7	-9	-1	21	146	259	0.564	**87**	-	-	-	-	-	36	23	28	7
Jackson, Darren	280	55	10	0	27	91	208	6	1	0	-2	-9	-4	18	87	226	0.389	**60**	-	-	-	-	-	-	10	37	-
James, Chris	182	44	18	1	40	103	116	1	2	2	-0	-2	3	5	106	121	0.876	**135**	-	-	-	-	-	20	-	22	-
LaValliere, Mike	115	26	4	0	2	32	76	7	2	0	-1	-1	7	11	39	87	0.448	**67**	38	-	-	-	-	-	-	-	-
Lindsey, Doug	3	1	0	0	0	1	2	0	0	0	-0	-0	0	0	1	2	0.500	**76**	4	-	-	-	-	-	-	-	-
Magadan, Dave	544	124	80	1	38	243	331	2	6	2	-1	-12	-3	21	240	352	0.682	**104**	-	43	-	100	-	-	-	-	2
Maldonado, Candy	248	46	24	1	31	102	175	1	1	0	-1	-5	-4	8	98	183	0.536	**82**	-	-	-	-	-	31	-	39	2
Mercedes, Luis	59	11	6	2	4	23	38	2	0	1	-2	-1	0	5	23	43	0.535	**82**	-	-	-	-	-	1	3	9	2
Milligan, Randy	343	84	60	1	38	183	197	0	1	0	-2	-3	-4	6	179	203	0.882	**136**	-	79	-	-	-	9	-	-	1
Smith, Lonnie	284	62	51	5	38	156	161	3	2	9	-4	-3	7	12	163	173	0.942	**145**	-	-	-	-	-	62	3	-	5
Stillwell, Kurt	203	42	15	1	13	71	140	3	2	6	-3	-4	4	12	75	152	0.493	**80**	-	-	18	10	30	-	-	-	-

1993 Atlanta Braves Team TOPR

	TPA	H	BB	HP	XB	TBB	TBO	SH	SF	SB	CS	GDP	BRB	BRO	NBE	GOC	Ratio	TOPR	C	1B	2B	3B	SS	LF	CF	RF	P
Avg. NL Team	6213	1459	507	41	749	2756	4076	79	50	122	-56	-117	79	302	2835	4378	0.647	100.0									
Atlanta Braves	6234	1444	560	36	804	2844	4071	73	50	125	-48	-126	74	297	2918	4368	0.668	103.2									
Belliard, Rafael	89	18	4	3	5	30	61	3	0	0	-0	-1	2	4	32	65	0.492	76	-	-	24	58	-	-	-	-	-
Berryhill, Damon	363	82	21	2	46	151	253	2	3	0	-0	-7	-2	12	149	265	0.562	87	105	-	-	-	-	-	-	-	-
Blauser, Jeff	710	182	85	16	78	361	415	5	7	16	-6	-13	9	31	370	446	0.830	128	-	-	-	-	161	-	-	-	-
Bream, Sid	311	72	31	0	43	146	205	1	2	4	-2	-6	-1	11	145	216	0.671	104	-	90	-	-	-	-	-	-	-
Cabrera, Francisco	91	20	8	0	15	43	63	0	0	0	-0	-2	-2	2	41	65	0.631	97	2	12	-	-	-	-	-	-	-
Gant, Ron	682	166	67	2	143	378	440	0	7	26	-9	-14	10	30	388	470	0.826	128	-	-	-	-	-	155	-	-	-
Hunter, Brian	85	11	2	0	5	18	69	0	3	0	-0	-1	2	4	20	73	0.274	42	-	29	-	-	-	-	-	2	-
Jones, Chipper	4	2	1	0	1	4	1	0	0	0	-0	-0	0	0	4	1	4.000	618	-	-	-	-	3	-	-	-	-
Justice, Dave	670	158	78	3	143	382	427	0	4	3	-5	-10	-8	19	374	446	0.839	130	-	-	-	-	-	-	-	157	-
Klesko, Ryan	20	6	3	0	7	16	11	0	0	0	-0	-0	0	0	16	11	1.455	225	-	3	-	-	2	-	-	-	-
Lemke, Mark	569	124	65	0	44	233	369	5	6	1	-2	-20	-10	33	223	402	0.555	86	-	-	150	-	-	-	-	-	-
Lopez, Javy	17	6	0	1	6	13	10	0	0	0	-0	-0	0	0	13	10	1.300	201	7	-	-	-	-	-	-	-	-
McGriff, Fred *	291	79	34	1	77	191	176	0	1	1	-0	-5	-3	6	188	182	1.033	160	-	149	-	-	-	-	-	-	-
Nixon, Otis	532	124	61	0	21	206	337	5	5	47	-13	-9	35	32	241	369	0.653	101	-	-	-	-	-	-	115	2	-
Olson, Greg	295	59	29	1	22	111	203	2	1	1	-0	-11	-7	14	104	217	0.479	74	81	-	-	-	-	-	-	-	-
Pecota, Bill	65	20	2	0	4	26	42	1	0	1	-1	-0	1	2	27	44	0.614	95	-	-	4	23	-	-	-	-	1
Pendleton, Terry	682	172	36	3	86	297	461	3	7	5	-1	-18	-4	29	293	490	0.598	92	-	-	-	161	-	-	-	-	-
Sanders, Deion	294	75	16	3	48	142	197	1	2	19	-7	-3	12	13	154	210	0.733	113	-	-	-	-	-	5	55	-	-
Tarasco, Tony	37	8	0	1	2	11	27	0	1	0	-1	-1	-1	3	10	30	0.333	51	-	-	-	-	-	4	8	-	-
STAFF	427	60	17	0	8	85	304	45	1	1	-1	-5	41	52	126	356	0.357	55									

NOTE: Statistics are for games played with Atlanta. * Also played for another NL team. ** Also played for an AL team

1993 Atlanta Braves Team TPER

	W-L	GS	GR	SV	IP	ERA	H	BB	HB	XB	TBB	TBO	SH	SF	SB	CS	GDP	BRB	BRO	NBA	GOE	Ratio	TPER
Avg. NL Team	81 – 81	162	381	43	1449.0	4.04	1459	507	41	749	2756	4076	79	50	122	-56	-117	79	302	2835	4378	0.647	100.0
Atlanta Braves	104 – 58	162	353	46	1455.0	3.14	1297	480	22	585	2384	4097	77	39	121	-53	-127	57	296	2441	4393	0.556	85.8
Avery, Steve	18 – 6	35	0	0	223.1	2.94	216	43	0	83	342	611	12	8	32	-14	-26	12	60	354	671	0.528	81
Bedrosian, Steve	5 – 2	0	49	0	49.2	1.63	34	14	2	19	69	141	3	4	6	-2	-1	10	10	79	151	0.523	81
Borbon, Pedro	0 – 0	0	3	0	1.2	21.60	3	3	0	1	7	4	1	0	0	-0	-0	1	1	8	5	1.600	247
Freeman, Marvin	2 – 0	0	21	0	23.2	6.08	24	10	1	10	45	68	0	0	3	-3	-0	0	3	45	71	0.634	98
Glavine, Tom	22 – 6	36	0	0	239.1	3.20	236	90	2	106	434	674	10	2	9	-5	-25	-9	42	425	716	0.594	92
Howell, Jay	3 – 3	0	54	0	58.1	2.31	48	16	0	15	79	162	3	4	5	-5	-3	4	15	83	177	0.469	72
Maddux, Greg	20 – 10	36	0	0	267.0	2.36	228	52	6	84	370	756	15	7	27	-6	-26	17	54	387	810	0.478	74
McMichael, Greg	2 – 3	0	74	19	91.2	2.06	68	29	0	18	115	262	4	2	5	-2	-10	-1	18	114	280	0.407	63
Mercker, Kent	3 – 1	6	37	0	66.0	2.86	52	36	2	19	109	191	0	0	6	-2	-7	-3	9	106	200	0.530	82
Smith, Pete	4 – 8	14	6	0	90.2	4.37	92	36	2	68	198	249	6	5	8	-8	-6	5	25	203	274	0.741	114
Smoltz, John	15 – 11	35	0	0	243.2	3.62	208	100	6	126	440	697	13	4	12	-5	-17	7	39	447	736	0.607	94
Stanton, Mike	4 – 6	0	63	27	52.0	4.67	51	29	0	23	103	149	5	2	5	-1	-2	9	10	112	159	0.704	109
Wohlers, Mark	6 – 2	0	46	0	48.0	4.50	37	22	1	13	73	133	5	1	3	-0	-4	5	10	78	143	0.545	84

NOTE: Statistics are for games played with Atlanta. * Also played for another NL team. ** Also played for an AL team.

1993 Chicago Cubs Team TOPR

		Batter Sub-set						Baserunner Sub-set							Total Offense				Positions Played								
	TPA	H	BB	HP	XB	TBB	TBO	SH	SF	SB	CS	GDP	BRB	BRO	NBE	GOC	Ratio	TOPR	C	1B	2B	3B	SS	LF	CF	RF	P
Avg. NL Team	6213	1459	507	41	749	2756	4076	79	50	122	-56	-117	79	302	2835	4378	0.647	100.0									
Chicago Cubs	6217	1521	446	34	806	2807	4106	67	42	100	-43	-130	36	282	2843	4388	0.648	100.1									
Buechele, Steve	520	125	48	5	76	254	335	4	3	1	-1	-12	-5	20	249	355	0.701	108		6		129					
Dunston, Shawon	10	4	0	0	2	6	6	0	0	0	-0	-0	0	0	6	6	1.000	154					2				
Grace, Mark	676	193	71	1	89	354	401	1	9	8	-4	-25	-11	39	343	440	0.780	120		154							
Hill, Glenallen **	93	30	6	0	37	73	57	0	0	1	-0	-1	0	1	73	58	1.259	194						18	4		
Jennings, Doug	57	13	3	2	11	29	39	0	0	0	-0	-0	0	0	29	39	0.744	115		10							
Lake, Steve	126	27	4	0	21	52	93	2	0	0	-0	-8	-6	10	46	103	0.447	69	41								
Maldonado, Candy **	154	26	13	1	14	54	114	0	0	0	-0	-3	-3	3	51	117	0.436	67						29		14	
May, Derrick	503	137	31	1	59	228	328	0	6	10	-3	-15	-2	24	226	352	0.642	99						121		2	
Rhodes, Karl *	63	15	11	0	13	39	37	0	0	2	-0	-0	2	0	41	37	1.108	171						7	14	2	
Roberson, Kevin	195	34	12	3	33	82	146	0	0	0	-1	-2	-3	3	79	149	0.530	82						14		42	
Sanchez, Rey	373	97	15	3	15	130	247	9	2	1	-1	-8	3	20	133	267	0.498	77					98				
Sandberg, Ryne	503	141	37	2	47	227	315	2	6	9	-2	-12	3	22	230	337	0.682	105			115						
Shields, Tommy	36	6	2	0	1	9	28	0	0	0	-0	-1	-1	1	8	29	0.276	43		1	7	7		1			
Smith, Dwight	343	93	25	3	60	181	217	1	3	8	-6	-3	3	13	184	230	0.800	124						14	53	28	
Sosa, Sammy	641	156	38	4	134	332	442	0	1	36	-11	-13	13	25	345	467	0.739	114							70	114	
Vizcaino, Jose	617	158	46	3	39	246	393	8	9	12	-9	-9	11	35	257	428	0.600	93			34	44	81				
Walbeck, Matt	31	6	1	0	5	12	24	0	0	0	-0	-0	0	0	12	24	0.500	71	11								
Wilkins, Rick	500	135	50	3	115	303	311	0	1	2	-1	-6	-4	8	299	319	0.937	145	133								
Wilson, Willie	237	57	11	3	20	91	164	1	1	7	-2	-2	5	6	96	170	0.565	87							82		
Yelding, Eric	123	22	11	0	10	43	86	4	0	3	-2	-3	2	9	45	95	0.474	73			32	7	1		1		
Zambrano, Eddie	18	5	1	0	0	6	12	0	0	0	-0	-1	-1	1	5	13	0.385	59		2					1		3
STAFF	398	41	10	0	5	56	311	35	1	0	-0	-6	30	42	86	353	0.244	38									

NOTE: Statistics are for games played with Chicago. * Also played for another NL team. ** Also played for an AL team.

1993 Chicago Cubs Team TPER

							Batter Sub-set						Baserunner Sub-set							Total Pitching			
	W-L	GS	GR	SV	IP	ERA	H	BB	HB	XB	TBB	TBO	SH	SF	SB	CS	GDP	BRB	BRO	NBA	GOE	Ratio	TPER
Avg. NL Team	81 – 81	162	381	43	1449.0	4.04	1459	507	41	749	2756	4076	79	50	122	-56	-117	79	302	2835	4378	0.647	100.0
Chicago Cubs	84 – 78	163	423	56	1449.2	4.18	1514	470	43	820	2847	4031	69	51	84	-69	-134	1	323	2848	4354	0.654	101.0
Assenmacher, Paul *	2 – 1	0	46	0	38.2	3.49	44	13	0	22	79	109	0	0	3	-1	-5	-3	6	76	115	0.661	102
Bautista, Jose	10 – 3	7	52	2	111.2	2.82	105	27	5	56	193	315	4	3	5	-2	-6	4	15	197	330	0.597	92
Boskie, Shawn	5 – 3	2	37	0	65.2	3.43	63	21	7	36	127	181	4	1	4	-1	-11	-3	17	124	198	0.626	97
Brennan, Bill	2 – 1	1	7	0	15.0	4.20	18	8	1	8	33	39	0	1	1	-3	-2	-3	6	30	45	0.667	103
Bullinger, Jim	1 – 0	0	15	1	16.2	4.32	18	9	0	10	37	47	0	1	1	-1	-2	-1	4	36	51	0.706	109
Castillo, Frank	5 – 8	25	4	0	141.1	4.84	162	39	9	100	310	391	10	3	7	-12	-6	2	31	312	422	0.739	114
Guzman, Jose	12 – 10	30	0	0	191.0	4.34	188	74	3	124	389	541	8	5	19	-10	-10	12	33	401	574	0.699	108
Harkey, Mike	10 – 10	28	0	0	157.1	5.26	187	43	3	90	323	427	8	8	7	-6	-17	0	39	323	466	0.693	107
Hibbard, Greg	15 – 11	31	0	0	191.0	3.96	209	47	3	117	376	522	9	10	2	-10	-24	-13	53	363	575	0.631	98
McElroy, Chuck	2 – 2	0	49	0	47.1	4.56	51	25	1	21	98	131	5	1	4	-2	-5	3	13	101	144	0.701	108
Morgan, Mike	10 – 15	32	0	0	207.2	4.03	206	74	7	86	373	580	11	5	17	-14	-17	2	47	375	627	0.598	92
Myers, Randy	2 – 4	0	73	53	75.1	3.11	65	26	1	38	130	218	1	2	1	-1	-8	-5	12	125	230	0.543	84
Plesac, Dan	2 – 1	0	57	0	62.2	4.74	74	21	0	43	138	174	4	3	3	-2	-5	3	14	141	188	0.750	116
Scanlan, Bob	4 – 5	0	70	0	75.1	4.54	79	28	3	47	157	205	2	6	5	-4	-11	-2	23	155	228	0.680	105
Slocumb, Heathcliff *	1 – 0	0	10	0	10.2	3.38	7	4	0	1	12	30	0	1	2	-0	-2	1	3	13	33	0.394	61
Trachsel, Steve	0 – 2	3	0	0	19.2	4.58	16	3	0	17	36	57	1	1	2	-0	-1	1	3	39	60	0.650	100
Wendell, Turk	1 – 2	4	3	0	22.2	4.37	24	8	0	4	36	64	2	0	1	-0	-2	1	4	37	68	0.544	84

NOTE: Statistics are for games played with Chicago. * Also played for another NL team. ** Also played for an AL team.

1993 Cincinnati Reds Team TOPR

	TPA	H	BB	HP	XB	TBB	TBQ	SH	SF	SB	CS	GDP	BRB	BRO	NBE	GOC	Ratio	TOPR	C	1B	2B	3B	SS	LF	CF	RF	P
Avg. NL Team	6213	1459	507	41	749	2756	4076	79	50	122	-56	-117	79	302	2835	4378	0.647	100.0									
Cincinnati Reds	6164	1457	485	32	728	2702	4060	63	66	142	-59	-104	108	292	2810	4352	0.646	99.7									
Branson, Jeff	412	92	19	0	26	137	289	8	4	4	-1	-4	11	17	148	306	0.484	75	-	1	45	14	59	-	-	-	-
Brumfield, Jacob	299	73	21	1	41	136	199	3	2	20	-8	-1	16	14	152	213	0.714	110	-	-	4	-	-	24	68	5	-
Costo, Tim	104	22	4	0	14	40	76	0	2	0	-0	-1	1	3	41	79	0.519	80	-	2	-	2	-	11	-	16	-
Daugherty, Jack *	71	13	11	0	8	32	46	0	1	0	-0	-0	1	1	33	47	0.702	108	-	2	-	-	-	11	-	5	-
Dorsett, Brian	66	16	3	0	10	29	47	0	0	0	-0	-1	-1	1	28	48	0.583	90	18	3	-	-	-	-	-	-	-
Espy, Cecil	76	14	14	0	2	30	46	0	2	2	-2	-2	0	6	30	52	0.577	89	-	-	-	-	-	18	-	1	-
Gordon, Keith	6	1	0	0	0	1	5	0	0	0	-0	-0	0	0	1	5	0.200	31	-	-	-	-	-	2	-	-	-
Greene, Willie	53	8	2	0	9	19	42	0	1	0	-0	-1	0	2	19	44	0.432	67	-	-	-	5	10	-	-	-	-
Gregg, Tommy	13	2	0	0	2	2	10	0	1	0	-0	-0	1	1	3	11	0.273	42	-	-	-	-	-	3	-	1	-
Hernandez, Cesar	26	2	1	0	0	3	22	1	0	1	-2	-0	0	3	3	25	0.120	19	-	-	-	-	-	17	7	-	-
Howard, Thomas **	154	39	12	0	26	77	102	0	1	5	-6	-4	-4	11	73	113	0.646	100	-	-	-	-	-	27	12	-	-
Hughes, Keith	4	0	0	0	0	0	4	0	0	0	-0	-0	0	0	0	4	0.000	0	-	-	-	-	-	2	-	-	-
Kelly, Bobby	343	102	17	2	50	171	218	0	3	21	-5	-10	9	18	180	236	0.763	118	-	-	-	-	-	-	77	-	-
Kessinger, Keith	32	7	4	0	4	15	20	0	1	0	-0	-1	0	2	15	22	0.682	105	-	-	-	-	11	-	-	-	-
Koelling, Brian	16	1	0	1	0	2	14	0	0	0	-0	-0	0	0	2	14	0.143	22	-	-	3	-	2	-	-	-	-
Larkin, Barry	440	121	51	1	50	223	263	1	3	14	-1	-13	4	18	227	281	0.808	125	-	-	-	-	99	-	-	-	-
Milligan, Randy **	282	64	46	1	31	142	170	0	1	0	-2	-3	-4	6	138	176	0.784	121	-	61	-	-	-	9	-	-	-
Mitchell, Kevin	353	110	25	1	84	220	213	0	4	1	-0	-14	-9	18	211	231	0.913	141	-	-	-	-	-	85	2	-	-
Morris, Hal	421	120	34	2	39	195	259	0	6	2	-2	-5	1	13	196	272	0.721	111	-	98	-	-	-	-	-	-	-
Oliver, Joe	521	115	27	1	70	213	367	2	9	0	-0	-13	-2	24	211	391	0.540	83	133	12	-	-	-	-	-	-	-
Roberts, Bip	336	70	38	3	16	127	222	0	3	26	-6	-2	21	11	148	233	0.635	98	-	-	64	3	1	11	1	-	-
Sabo, Chris	611	143	43	6	100	292	409	2	8	6	-4	-10	2	24	294	433	0.679	105	-	-	-	148	-	-	-	-	-
Samuel, Juan	289	60	23	3	30	116	201	0	2	9	-7	-2	2	11	118	212	0.557	86	-	6	70	4	1	2	1	-	-
Sanders, Reggie	563	136	51	5	84	276	360	3	8	27	-10	-10	18	31	294	391	0.752	116	-	-	-	-	-	-	4	135	-
Tubbs, Greg	74	11	14	1	3	29	48	0	0	3	-1	-0	2	1	31	49	0.633	98	-	-	-	-	-	11	14	2	-
Varsho, Gary	109	22	9	1	12	44	73	3	1	1	-0	-1	4	5	48	78	0.615	95	-	-	-	-	-	13	-	9	-
Wilson, Dan	88	17	9	0	3	29	59	2	1	0	-0	-2	1	5	30	64	0.469	72	35	-	-	-	-	-	-	-	-
STAFF	401	75	7	3	16	101	276	38	2	0	-2	-4	34	46	135	322	0.425	66									

NOTE: Statistics are for games played with Cincinnati. * Also played for another NL team. ** Also played for an AL team.

1993 Cincinnati Reds Team TPER

	W-L	GS	GR	SV	IP	ERA	H	BB	HB	XB	TBB	TBO	SH	SF	SB	CS	GDP	BRB	BRO	NBA	GOE	Ratio	TPER
Avg. NL Team	81 - 81	162	381	43	1449.0	4.04	1459	507	41	749	2756	4076	79	50	122	-56	-117	79	302	2835	4378	0.647	100.0
Cincinnati Reds	73 - 89	162	375	37	1434.0	4.51	1510	508	44	821	2883	4039	77	40	134	-56	-106	89	279	2972	4318	0.688	106.3
Anderson, Mike	0 - 0	0	3	0	5.1	18.56	12	3	0	9	24	15	0	0	0	-0	-1	-1	1	23	16	1.438	222
Ayala, Bobby	7 - 10	9	34	3	98.0	5.60	106	45	7	67	225	281	9	2	9	-1	-6	13	18	238	299	0.796	123
Belcher, Tim **	9 - 6	22	0	0	137.0	4.47	134	47	7	68	256	393	6	3	11	-3	-8	9	20	265	413	0.642	99
Browning, Tom	7 - 7	20	1	0	114.0	4.74	159	20	1	83	263	319	4	2	5	-7	-9	-5	22	258	341	0.757	117
Bushing, Chris	0 - 0	0	6	0	4.1	12.46	9	4	0	8	21	11	0	1	0	-0	-2	-1	3	20	14	1.429	221
Cadaret, Greg *	2 - 1	0	34	1	32.2	4.96	40	23	1	15	79	91	3	0	2	-1	-5	-1	9	78	100	0.780	120
Dibble, Rob	1 - 4	0	45	19	41.2	6.48	34	42	2	30	108	117	1	0	13	-2	-3	9	6	117	123	0.951	147
Foster, Steve	2 - 2	0	17	0	25.2	1.75	23	5	1	8	37	75	1	0	0	-0	-2	-1	3	36	78	0.462	71
Henry, Dwayne **	0 - 1	0	3	0	4.2	3.86	6	4	0	3	13	16	0	0	0	-0	-0	0	0	13	16	0.813	125
Hill, Milt	3 - 0	0	19	0	28.2	5.65	34	9	0	24	67	79	0	3	2	-2	-1	2	6	69	85	0.812	125
Kaiser, Jeff *	0 - 0	0	3	0	3.1	2.70	4	2	0	2	8	10	0	0	0	-0	-0	0	0	8	10	0.800	124
Landrum, Bill	0 - 2	0	18	0	21.2	3.74	18	6	0	11	35	60	2	0	4	-1	-1	4	4	39	64	0.609	94
Luebbers, Larry	2 - 5	14	0	0	77.1	4.54	74	38	1	33	146	210	2	4	5	-8	-7	-1	24	145	234	0.620	96
Powell, Ross	0 - 3	1	8	0	16.1	4.41	13	6	0	6	25	45	2	0	2	-1	-1	2	4	27	49	0.551	85
Pugh, Tim	10 - 15	27	4	0	164.1	5.26	200	59	7	89	355	461	6	5	19	-7	-15	8	33	363	494	0.735	113
Reardon, Jeff	4 - 6	0	58	8	61.2	4.09	66	10	5	31	112	178	4	4	6	-1	-1	12	10	124	188	0.660	102
Rijo, Jose	14 - 9	36	0	0	257.1	2.48	218	62	2	107	389	731	13	3	22	-10	-17	11	43	400	774	0.517	80
Roper, John	2 - 5	15	1	0	80.0	5.63	92	36	4	52	184	220	5	3	10	-4	-8	6	20	190	240	0.792	122
Ruffin, Johnny	2 - 1	0	21	2	37.2	3.58	36	11	1	27	75	110	1	0	4	-0	-2	3	3	78	113	0.690	107
Ruskin, Scott	0 - 0	0	4	0	1.0	18.00	3	2	0	4	9	3	0	0	0	-0	-0	0	0	9	3	3.000	463
Service, Scott *	2 - 2	0	26	2	41.1	3.70	36	15	1	26	78	117	2	2	2	-1	-3	2	8	80	125	0.640	99
Smiley, John	3 - 9	18	0	0	105.2	5.62	117	31	2	68	218	292	10	3	13	-4	-9	13	26	231	318	0.726	112
Spradlin, Jerry	2 - 1	0	37	2	49.0	3.49	44	9	0	27	80	133	3	4	4	-2	-5	4	14	84	147	0.571	88
Wickander, Kevin **	1 - 0	0	33	0	25.1	6.75	32	19	2	23	76	72	1	0	1	-1	-0	1	2	77	74	1.041	161

NOTE: Statistics are for games played with Cincinnati. * Also played for another NL team. ** Also played for an AL team.

1993 Colorado Rockies Team TOPR

	TPA	H	BB	HP	XB	TBB	TBO	SH	SF	SB	CS	GDP	BRB	BRO	NBE	GOC	Ratio	TOPR	C	1B	2B	3B	SS	LF	CF	RF	P
						Batter Sub-set					Baserunner Sub-set					Total Offense							Positions Played				
Avg. NL Team	6213	1459	507	41	749	2756	4076	79	50	122	-56	-117	79	302	2835	4378	0.647	100.0									
Colorado Rockies	6073	1507	388	46	822	2763	4010	70	52	146	-90	-125	53	337	2816	4347	0.648	100.1									
Benavides, Freddie	223	61	6	0	25	92	152	3	1	3	-2	-4	1	10	93	162	0.574	89	-	1	19	5	48	-	-	-	-
Bichette, Dante	581	167	28	7	116	318	371	0	8	14	-8	-7	7	23	325	394	0.825	127	-	-	-	-	-	-	9	134	-
Boston, Daryl	320	76	26	2	59	163	215	0	1	1	-6	-5	-9	12	154	227	0.678	105	-	-	-	-	-	41	31	9	-
Castellano, Pedro	79	13	8	0	11	32	58	0	0	1	-1	-1	-1	2	31	60	0.517	80	-	10	4	13	5	-	-	-	-
Castilla, Vinny	357	86	13	2	50	151	251	0	5	2	-5	-10	-8	20	143	271	0.528	82	-	-	-	-	104	-	-	-	-
Clark, Jerald	512	135	20	10	77	242	343	3	1	9	-6	-12	-5	22	237	365	0.649	100	-	37	-	-	-	80	-	17	-
Cole, Alex	399	89	43	2	17	151	259	4	2	30	-13	-6	17	25	168	284	0.592	91	-	-	-	-	-	-	93	-	-
Gainer, Jay	45	7	4	0	9	20	34	0	0	1	-1	-0	0	1	20	35	0.571	88	-	7	-	-	-	-	-	-	-
Galarraga, Andres	506	174	24	6	109	313	296	0	6	2	-4	-9	-5	19	308	315	0.978	151	-	119	-	-	-	-	-	-	-
Girardi, Joe	350	90	24	3	33	150	220	12	1	6	-6	-6	7	25	157	245	0.641	99	84	-	-	-	-	-	-	-	-
Hayes, Charlie	630	175	43	5	124	347	398	1	8	11	-6	-25	-11	40	336	438	0.767	118	-	-	-	154	1	-	-	-	-
Jones, Chris	225	57	10	0	37	104	152	5	1	9	-4	-6	5	16	109	168	0.649	100	-	-	-	-	-	16	52	4	-
Liriano, Nelson	175	46	18	0	18	82	105	5	1	6	-4	-6	2	16	84	121	0.694	107	-	-	16	1	35	-	-	-	-
Mejia, Roberto	248	53	13	1	39	106	176	4	1	4	-1	-2	6	8	112	184	0.609	94	-	-	65	-	-	-	-	-	-
Murphy, Dale	49	6	5	0	1	12	36	0	2	0	-0	-5	-3	7	9	43	0.209	32	-	-	-	-	-	2	-	11	-
Owens, Jayhawk	94	18	6	2	14	40	68	0	0	1	-0	-1	0	1	40	69	0.580	90	32	-	-	-	-	-	-	-	-
Sheaffer, Danny	233	60	8	1	23	92	156	2	6	2	-3	-9	-2	20	90	176	0.511	79	65	7	-	1	-	2	-	-	-
Tatum, Jimmy	106	20	5	1	8	34	78	0	2	0	-0	-0	2	2	36	80	0.450	70	-	12	-	6	-	2	-	1	-
Wedge, Eric	11	2	0	0	0	2	9	0	0	0	-0	-0	0	0	2	9	0.222	34	1	-	-	-	-	-	-	-	-
Young, Eric	565	132	63	4	41	240	358	4	4	42	-19	-9	22	36	262	394	0.665	103	-	-	79	-	-	46	10	-	-
Young, Gerald	23	1	4	0	0	5	18	0	0	0	-1	-2	-3	3	2	21	0.095	15	-	-	-	-	-	4	3	5	-
STAFF	341	38	17	0	11	66	257	27	2	2	-0	-0	31	29	97	286	0.339	52									

NOTE: Statistics are for games played with . * Also played for another NL team. ** Also player for an AL team

1993 Colorado Rockies Team TPER

	W-L	GS	GR	SV	IP	ERA	H	BB	HB	XB	TBB	TBO	SH	SF	SB	CS	GDP	BRB	BRO	NBA	GOE	Ratio	TPER
							Batter Sub-set						Baserunner Sub-set							Total Pitching			
Avg. NL Team	81 – 81	162	381	43	1449.0	4.04	1459	507	41	749	2756	4076	79	50	122	-56	-117	79	302	2835	4378	0.647	100.0
Colorado Rockies	67 – 95	162	453	35	1431.1	5.44	1664	609	41	931	3245	3996	82	78	119	-56	-119	104	335	3349	4331	0.773	119.4
Aldred, Scott *	0 - 0	0	5	0	6.2	10.80	10	9	1	6	26	18	2	0	1	-0	-1	2	3	28	21	1.333	206
Ashby, Andy *	0 - 4	9	11	1	54.0	8.50	89	32	3	35	159	147	3	3	7	-0	-7	6	13	165	160	1.031	159
Blair, Willie	6 - 10	18	28	0	146.0	4.75	184	42	3	102	331	417	10	8	8	-4	-8	14	30	345	447	0.772	119
Bottenfield, Kent *	3 - 5	14	0	0	76.2	6.10	86	38	1	56	181	199	10	3	7	-5	-4	11	22	192	221	0.869	134
Fredrickson, Scott	0 - 1	0	25	0	29.0	6.21	33	17	1	15	66	82	2	2	1	-2	-0	0	9	66	91	0.725	112
Grant, Mark *	0 - 1	0	14	1	14.1	12.56	23	6	0	16	45	38	0	1	0	-0	-2	-1	3	44	41	1.073	166
Harris, Greg *	1 - 8	13	0	0	73.1	6.50	88	30	4	72	194	206	6	2	5	-4	-5	4	17	198	223	0.888	137
Henry, Butch *	2 - 8	15	5	0	84.2	6.59	117	24	1	64	206	237	6	5	7	-3	-8	7	22	213	259	0.822	127
Holmes, Darren	3 - 3	0	62	25	66.2	4.05	56	20	2	31	109	196	0	0	3	-2	-5	-4	7	105	203	0.517	80
Hurst, Bruce *	0 - 1	3	0	0	8.2	5.19	6	3	0	3	12	25	0	0	0	-0	-0	0	0	12	25	0.480	74
Knudson, Mark	0 - 0	0	4	0	5.2	22.24	16	5	0	15	36	18	0	0	0	-0	-0	0	0	36	18	2.000	309
Leskanic, Curt	1 - 5	8	10	0	57.0	5.37	59	27	2	30	118	163	5	4	0	-1	-3	5	13	123	176	0.699	108
Moore, Marcus	3 - 1	0	27	0	26.1	6.84	30	20	1	21	72	73	0	4	2	-0	-4	2	8	74	81	0.914	141
Munoz, Mike **	2 - 1	0	21	0	18.0	4.50	21	9	0	10	40	47	3	2	1	-1	-3	2	9	42	56	0.750	116
Nied, Dave	5 - 9	16	0	0	87.0	5.17	99	42	1	45	187	236	9	7	16	-2	-8	22	26	209	262	0.798	123
Painter, Lance	2 - 2	6	4	0	39.0	6.00	52	9	0	31	92	104	1	0	2	-4	-4	-5	9	87	113	0.770	119
Parrett, Jeff	3 - 3	6	34	1	73.2	5.38	78	45	2	33	158	207	4	5	11	-2	-3	15	14	173	221	0.783	121
Reed, Steve	9 - 5	0	64	3	84.1	4.48	80	30	3	56	169	229	2	3	8	-7	-7	2	19	168	248	0.677	105
Reynoso, Armando	12 - 11	30	0	0	189.0	4.00	206	63	9	121	399	539	5	8	11	-5	-18	1	36	400	575	0.696	107
Ruffin, Bruce	6 - 5	12	47	2	139.2	3.87	145	69	1	60	275	394	4	5	14	-9	-14	0	32	275	426	0.646	100
Sanford, Mo	1 - 2	6	5	0	35.2	5.30	37	27	0	24	88	96	4	2	8	-1	-3	10	10	98	106	0.925	143
Service, Scott *	0 - 0	0	3	0	4.2	9.64	8	1	1	7	17	12	0	2	0	-0	-0	2	2	19	14	1.357	210
Shepherd, Keith	1 - 3	1	13	1	19.1	6.98	26	4	1	16	47	52	1	1	0	-2	-3	-3	7	44	59	0.746	115
Smith, Bryn	2 - 4	5	6	0	29.2	8.49	47	11	3	12	73	83	2	4	4	-1	-0	9	7	82	90	0.911	141
Wayne, Gary	5 - 3	0	65	1	62.1	5.05	68	26	1	50	145	178	3	7	3	-1	-6	6	17	151	195	0.774	120

NOTE: Statistics are for games played with Colorado. * Also played for another NL team. ** Also player for an AL team.

FLORIDA MARLINS

1993 Florida Marlins Team TOPR

	TPA	Batter Sub-set						Baserunner Sub-set							Total Offense				Positions Played								
		H	BB	HP	XB	TBB	TBO	SH	SF	SB	CS	GDP	BRB	BRO	NBE	GOC	Ratio	TOPR	C	1B	2B	3B	SS	LF	CF	RF	P
Avg. NL Team	6213	1459	507	41	749	2756	4076	79	50	122	-56	-117	79	302	2835	4378	0.647	100.0									
Florida Marlins	6127	1356	498	51	541	2446	4119	58	43	117	-56	-119	43	276	2489	4395	0.566	87.5									
Arias, Alex	283	67	27	3	13	110	182	1	3	1	-1	-5	-1	10	109	192	0.568	88	-	-	30	22	18	-	-	-	-
Barberie, Bret	424	104	33	7	35	179	271	5	3	2	-4	-7	-1	19	178	290	0.614	95	-	-	97	-	-	-	-	-	-
Berroa, Geronimo	36	4	2	0	1	7	30	0	0	0	-0	-2	-2	2	5	32	0.156	24	-	-	-	-	-	1	-	-	8
Briley, Greg	185	33	12	1	15	61	137	1	1	6	-2	-4	2	8	63	145	0.434	67	-	-	-	-	-	32	1	36	-
Carr, Chuck	613	147	49	2	35	233	404	7	4	58	-22	-6	41	39	274	443	0.619	96	-	-	-	-	-	-	139	-	-
Carrillo, Matias	58	14	1	1	6	22	41	1	0	0	-0	-5	-4	6	18	47	0.383	59	-	-	-	-	-	4	5	9	-
Conine, Jeff	658	174	52	5	66	297	421	0	6	2	-2	-14	-8	22	289	443	0.652	101	-	43	-	-	-	147	-	-	-
Cotto, Henry **	142	40	3	1	16	60	95	1	2	11	-1	-3	10	7	70	102	0.686	106	-	-	-	-	-	13	15	21	-
Decker, Steve	19	0	3	0	0	3	15	0	1	0	-0	-2	-1	3	2	18	0.111	17	5	-	-	-	-	-	-	-	-
Destrade, Orestes	637	145	58	3	86	292	424	1	6	0	-2	-17	-12	26	280	450	0.622	96	-	152	-	-	-	-	-	-	-
Everett, Carl	20	2	1	0	0	3	17	0	0	1	-0	-0	1	0	4	17	0.235	36	-	-	-	-	-	-	8	-	-
Fariss, Monty	34	5	5	0	4	14	24	0	0	0	-0	-2	-2	2	12	26	0.462	71	-	-	-	-	-	1	-	7	-
Felix, Junior	225	51	10	1	34	96	163	0	0	2	-1	-6	-5	7	91	170	0.535	83	-	-	-	-	-	-	-	3	50
Lyden, Mitch	10	3	0	0	3	6	7	0	0	0	-0	-0	0	0	6	7	0.857	132	2	-	-	-	-	-	-	-	-
Magadan, Dave **	275	65	44	1	24	134	162	0	3	0	-1	-3	-1	7	133	169	0.787	122	-	2	-	63	-	-	-	-	-
McGriff, Terry	8	0	1	0	0	1	7	0	0	0	-0	-0	0	0	1	7	0.143	22	3	-	-	-	-	-	-	-	-
Natal, Bob	131	25	6	4	9	44	92	3	1	1	-0	-5	-0	9	44	101	0.436	67	38	-	-	-	-	-	-	-	-
Polidor, Gus	6	1	0	0	1	2	5	0	0	0	-0	-0	0	0	2	5	0.400	62	-	-	1	1	-	-	-	-	-
Pose, Scott	43	8	2	0	2	12	33	0	0	0	-2	-0	-2	2	10	35	0.286	44	-	-	-	-	-	-	6	8	-
Renteria, Rich	290	67	21	2	19	109	196	3	1	0	-2	-8	-6	14	103	210	0.490	76	-	-	-	45	25	-	1	-	-
Santiago, Benito	516	108	37	5	70	220	361	0	4	10	-7	-9	-2	20	218	381	0.572	88	136	-	-	-	-	1	-	-	-
Sheffield, Gary *	275	69	29	6	44	148	167	0	4	12	-4	-2	10	10	158	177	0.893	138	-	-	-	66	-	-	-	-	-
Weiss, Walt	591	133	79	3	21	236	367	5	4	7	-3	-5	8	17	244	384	0.635	98	-	-	-	-	153	-	-	-	-
Whitmore, Darrell	267	51	10	5	24	90	199	2	0	4	-2	-8	-4	12	86	211	0.408	63	-	-	-	-	-	1	-	69	-
Wilson, Nigel	16	0	0	0	0	0	16	0	0	0	-0	-0	0	0	0	16	0.000	0	-	-	-	-	-	-	3	-	-
STAFF	365	40	13	1	13	67	283	28	0	0	-0	-6	22	34	89	317	0.281	42									

NOTE: Statistics are for games played with . * Also played for another NL team. ** Also player for an AL team.

1993 Florida Marlins Team TPER

	W-L	GS	GR	SV	IP	ERA	Batter Sub-set						Baserunner Sub-set							Total Pitching			
							H	BB	HB	XB	TBB	TBO	SH	SF	SB	CS	GDP	BRB	BRO	NBA	GOE	Ratio	TPER
Avg. NL Team	81 - 81	162	381	43	1449.0	4.04	1459	507	41	749	2756	4076	79	50	122	-56	-117	79	302	2835	4378	0.647	100.0
Florida Marlins	64 - 98	162	409	48	1440.1	4.15	1437	598	32	735	2802	4064	80	50	118	-52	-104	92	286	2894	4350	0.665	102.8
Aquino, Luis	6 - 8	13	25	0	110.2	3.42	115	40	5	45	205	302	7	2	10	-6	-11	2	26	207	328	0.631	97
Armstrong, Jack	9 - 17	33	3	0	196.1	4.49	210	78	7	134	429	566	8	10	18	-3	-9	24	30	453	596	0.760	117
Bowen, Ryan	8 - 12	27	0	0	156.2	4.48	156	87	3	67	313	438	5	4	15	-7	-15	2	31	315	469	0.672	104
Carpenter, Cris **	0 - 1	0	29	0	37.1	2.89	29	13	2	13	57	108	1	1	5	-0	-2	5	4	62	112	0.554	86
Corsi, Jim	0 - 2	0	15	0	20.1	6.64	28	10	0	7	45	55	3	1	2	-0	-2	4	6	49	61	0.803	124
Hammond, Chris	11 - 12	32	0	0	191.0	4.66	207	66	1	96	370	540	10	2	5	-6	-20	-9	38	361	578	0.625	96
Harvey, Bryan	1 - 5	0	59	45	69.0	1.70	45	13	0	13	71	197	3	6	15	-0	-2	22	11	93	208	0.447	69
Hoffman, Trevor *	2 - 2	0	28	2	35.2	3.28	24	19	0	21	64	106	2	1	1	-0	-1	3	4	67	110	0.609	94
Hough, Charlie	9 - 16	34	0	0	204.1	4.27	202	71	8	106	387	577	11	7	19	-14	-12	11	44	398	621	0.641	99
Johnstone, John	0 - 2	0	7	0	10.2	5.91	16	7	0	7	30	31	0	0	1	-0	-1	0	1	30	32	0.938	145
Klink, Joe	0 - 2	0	59	0	37.2	5.02	37	24	0	10	71	102	2	3	5	-3	-4	3	12	74	114	0.649	100
Lewis, Richie	6 - 3	0	57	0	77.1	3.14	68	43	1	42	154	217	8	4	5	-3	-5	9	20	163	237	0.688	106
McClure, Bob	1 - 1	0	14	0	6.1	7.11	13	5	0	8	26	18	0	0	0	-2	-0	-2	2	24	20	1.200	185
Nen, Robb **	1 - 0	0	14	0	33.1	7.02	35	20	0	27	82	102	1	1	4	-0	-0	6	2	88	104	0.846	131
Rapp, Pat	4 - 6	16	0	0	94.0	4.02	101	39	2	50	192	258	8	4	3	-6	-8	1	26	193	284	0.680	105
Rodriguez, Rich *	0 - 1	0	36	1	46.0	4.11	39	24	1	31	95	131	3	0	2	-0	-5	0	8	95	139	0.683	106
Turner, Matt	4 - 5	0	55	0	68.0	2.91	55	26	1	33	115	187	6	4	1	-2	-2	7	14	122	201	0.607	94
Weathers, Dave	2 - 3	6	8	0	45.2	5.12	57	13	1	25	96	129	2	0	7	-0	-5	4	7	100	136	0.735	114

NOTE: Statistics are for games played with Florida. * Also played for another NL team. ** Also played for an AL team.

1993 Houston Astros Team TOPR

	TPA	H	BB	HP	XB	TBB	TBO	SH	SF	SB	CS	GDP	BRB	BRO	NBE	GOC	Ratio	TOPR	C	1B	2B	3B	SS	LF	CF	RF	P
Avg. NL Team	6213	1459	507	41	749	2756	4076	79	50	122	-56	-117	79	302	2835	4378	0.647	100.0									
Houston Astros	6136	1459	497	40	776	2772	4005	82	47	103	-60	-126	46	315	2818	4320	0.652	100.8									
Anthony, Eric	540	121	49	2	72	244	365	0	2	3	-5	-9	-9	16	235	381	0.617	95							23	121	
Bagwell, Jeff	609	171	62	3	105	341	364	0	9	13	-4	-21	-3	34	338	398	0.849	131		140							
Bass, Kevin	258	65	26	1	27	119	164	2	0	7	-1	-4	4	7	123	171	0.719	111						12	2	51	
Biggio, Craig	707	175	77	10	114	376	435	4	5	15	-17	-10	-3	36	373	471	0.792	122			155						
Brumley, Mike	11	3	1	0	0	4	7	0	0	0	-1	-0	-1	1	3	8	0.375	58				1	1	1		1	
Caminiti, Ken	596	142	49	0	70	261	401	1	3	8	-5	-15	-8	24	253	425	0.595	92				143					
Candaele, Casey	131	29	10	0	11	50	92	0	0	2	-3	-0	-1	3	49	95	0.516	80			19	4	14	4	12	2	
Cedeno, Andujar	569	143	48	3	65	259	362	4	5	9	-7	-17	-6	33	253	395	0.641	99				1	139				
Daugherty, Jack *	3	1	0	0	0	1	2	0	0	0	-0	-0	0	0	1	2	0.500	77		1						1	
Donnels, Chris	199	46	19	0	24	89	133	0	1	2	-0	-6	-3	7	86	140	0.614	95		23	1	31					
Finley, Steve	585	145	28	3	65	241	400	6	3	19	-6	-8	14	23	255	423	0.603	93							140		
Gonzalez, Luis	610	162	47	10	85	304	378	3	10	20	-9	-9	15	31	319	409	0.780	120						149			
James, Chris **	148	33	15	1	30	79	96	1	2	2	-0	-2	3	5	82	101	0.812	125						16		18	
Lindeman, Jim	23	8	0	0	3	11	15	0	0	0	-0	-0	0	0	11	15	0.733	113		9							
Parker, Rick	49	15	3	0	3	21	30	1	0	1	-2	-2	-2	5	19	35	0.543	84				1	1	3	13	1	
Rhodes, Karl *	2	0	0	0	0	0	2	0	0	0	-0	-0	0	0	0	2	0.000	0							2		
Servais, Scott	291	63	22	5	44	134	195	3	3	0	-0	-6	0	12	134	207	0.647	100	82								
Taubensee, Eddie	312	72	21	0	40	133	216	1	2	1	-0	-8	-4	11	129	227	0.568	88	90								
Tucker, Scooter	28	5	2	0	1	8	21	0	0	0	-0	-0	0	0	8	21	0.381	59	8								
Uribe, Jose	66	13	8	1	1	23	40	4	0	1	-0	-1	4	5	27	45	0.600	93					41				
STAFF	399	47	10	1	16	74	287	52	2	0	-0	-8	46	62	120	349	0.344	53									

NOTE: Statistics are for games played with Houston. * Also played for another NL team. ** Also played for an AL team.

1993 Houston Astros Team TPER

	W-L	GS	GR	SV	IP	ERA	H	BB	HB	XB	TBB	TBO	SH	SF	SB	CS	GDP	BRB	BRO	NBA	GOE	Ratio	TPER
Avg. NL Team	81 - 81	162	381	43	1449.0	4.04	1459	507	41	749	2756	4076	79	50	122	-56	-117	79	302	2835	4378	0.647	100.0
Houston Astros	85 - 77	162	324	42	1441.1	3.49	1363	476	41	627	2507	4077	79	43	110	-42	-108	82	272	2589	4349	0.595	91.9
Agosto, Juan	0 - 0	0	6	0	6.0	6.00	8	0	0	4	12	18	0	0	1	-0	-0	1	0	13	18	0.722	112
Bell, Eric	0 - 1	0	10	0	7.1	6.14	10	2	0	1	13	22	0	0	2	-0	-0	2	0	15	22	0.682	105
Drabek, Doug	9 - 18	34	0	0	237.2	3.79	242	60	3	103	408	664	14	8	28	-7	-18	25	47	433	711	0.609	94
Edens, Tom	1 - 1	0	38	0	49.0	3.12	47	19	0	20	86	132	4	1	4	-1	-7	1	13	87	145	0.600	93
Grant, Mark *	0 - 0	0	6	0	11.0	0.82	11	5	0	4	20	29	0	1	1	-1	-4	-3	6	17	35	0.486	75
Harnisch, Pete	16 - 9	33	0	0	217.2	2.98	171	79	6	100	356	627	9	4	15	-6	-12	10	31	366	658	0.556	86
Hernandez, Xavier	4 - 5	0	72	9	96.2	2.61	75	28	1	39	143	279	3	3	9	-2	-8	5	16	148	295	0.502	77
Jones, Doug	4 - 10	0	71	26	85.1	4.54	102	21	5	32	160	240	9	4	2	-0	-3	12	16	172	256	0.672	104
Jones, Todd	1 - 2	0	27	2	37.1	3.13	28	15	1	16	60	103	2	1	2	-3	-3	-1	9	59	112	0.527	81
Juden, Jeff	0 - 1	0	2	0	5.0	5.40	4	4	0	4	12	14	0	1	1	-0	-0	2	1	14	15	0.933	144
Kile, Darryl	15 - 8	26	6	0	171.2	3.51	152	69	15	65	301	485	5	7	9	-5	-16	0	33	301	518	0.581	90
Osuna, Al	1 - 1	0	44	2	25.1	3.20	17	13	1	10	41	68	4	4	0	-0	-2	6	10	47	78	0.603	93
Portugal, Mark	18 - 4	33	0	0	208.0	2.77	194	77	4	58	333	587	11	3	14	-4	-17	7	35	340	622	0.547	84
Reynolds, Shane	0 - 0	1	4	0	11.0	0.82	11	6	0	1	18	32	0	0	0	-0	-3	-3	3	15	35	0.429	66
Swindell, Greg	12 - 13	30	1	0	190.1	4.16	215	40	1	131	387	546	13	3	16	-11	-9	12	36	399	582	0.686	106
Williams, Brian	4 - 4	5	37	3	82.0	4.83	76	38	4	39	157	231	5	3	6	-2	-6	6	16	163	247	0.660	102

NOTE: Statistics are for games played with Houston. * Also played for another NL team. ** Also played for an AL team.

1993 Los Angeles Dodgers Team TOPR

	TPA	Batter Sub-set						Baserunner Sub-set							Total Offense				Positions Played								
		H	BB	HP	XB	TBB	TBO	SH	SF	SB	CS	GDP	BRB	BRO	NBE	GOC	Ratio	TOPR	C	1B	2B	3B	SS	LF	CF	RF	P
Avg. NL Team	6213	1459	507	41	749	2756	4076	79	50	122	-56	-117	79	302	2835	4378	0.647	100.0									
Los Angeles Dodgers	6261	1458	492	27	680	2657	4130	107	47	126	-61	-104	115	319	2772	4449	0.623	96.2									
Ashley, Billy	39	9	2	0	0	11	28	0	0	0	-0	-0	0	0	11	28	0.393	61	-	-	-	-	-	11	-	-	-
Bournigal, Rafael	18	9	0	0	1	10	9	0	0	0	-0	-0	0	0	10	9	1.111	172	-	-	4	-	6	-	-	-	-
Brooks, Jerry	9	2	0	0	4	6	7	0	0	0	-0	-0	0	0	6	7	0.857	132	-	-	-	-	-	-	-	2	-
Butler, Brett	716	181	86	5	44	316	426	14	4	39	-19	-6	32	43	348	469	0.742	115	-	-	-	-	-	-	155	-	-
Davis, Eric **	422	88	41	1	59	189	288	0	4	33	-5	-8	24	17	213	305	0.698	108	-	-	-	-	-	101	-	-	-
Goodwin, Tom	18	5	1	0	1	7	12	0	0	1	-2	-1	-2	3	5	15	0.333	51	-	-	-	-	-	6	4	2	-
Hansen, Dave	127	38	21	0	15	74	67	0	1	0	-1	-0	0	2	66	69	1.072	166	-	-	-	18	-	-	-	-	-
Harris, Lenny	176	38	15	0	14	67	122	1	0	3	-1	-4	-1	6	66	128	0.516	80	-	-	35	17	3	-	-	2	-
Hernandez, Carlos	102	25	2	0	11	38	74	1	0	0	-0	-0	1	1	39	75	0.520	80	43	-	-	-	-	-	-	-	-
Karros, Eric	658	153	34	2	100	289	466	0	3	0	-1	-17	-15	21	274	487	0.563	87	-	157	-	-	-	-	-	-	-
Mondesi, Raul	91	25	4	0	17	46	61	1	0	4	-1	-1	3	3	49	64	0.766	118	-	-	-	-	-	20	6	17	-
Offerman, Jose	696	159	71	2	36	268	431	25	8	30	-13	-12	38	58	306	489	0.626	97	-	-	-	-	158	-	-	-	-
Piazza, Mike	602	174	46	3	133	356	373	0	6	3	-4	-10	-5	20	351	393	0.893	138	146	1	-	-	-	-	-	-	-
Reed, Jody	504	123	38	1	31	193	322	17	3	1	-3	-16	2	39	195	361	0.540	83	-	-	132	-	-	-	-	-	-
Rodriguez, Henry	188	39	11	0	34	84	137	0	1	1	-0	-1	1	2	85	139	0.612	94	-	13	-	-	-	-	26	23	-
Sharperson, Mike	97	23	5	1	10	39	67	0	1	2	-0	-2	1	3	40	70	0.571	88	-	1	17	6	3	-	-	-	1
Snyder, Cory	570	137	47	4	68	256	379	2	1	4	-1	-8	-2	12	254	391	0.650	100	-	12	-	23	2	2	1	113	-
Strawberry, Darryl	120	14	16	2	17	49	86	0	2	1	-0	-1	2	3	51	89	0.573	89	-	-	-	-	-	-	4	25	-
Wallach, Tim	522	106	32	3	57	198	371	1	9	0	-2	-9	-1	21	197	392	0.503	78	-	1	-	130	-	-	-	-	-
Webster, Mitch	192	42	11	2	16	71	130	4	3	4	-6	-3	2	16	73	146	0.500	77	-	-	-	-	-	32	2	27	-
STAFF	393	68	8	1	12	89	274	41	1	0	-2	-5	35	49	124	323	0.390	60									

NOTE: Statistics are for games played with Los Angeles. * Also played for another NL team. ** Also played for an AL team

1993 Los Angeles Dodgers Team TPER

	W-L	GS	GR	SV	IP	ERA	Batter Sub-set						Baserunner Sub-set							Total Pitching			
							H	BB	HB	XB	TBB	TBO	SH	SF	SB	CS	GDP	BRB	BRO	NBA	GOE	Ratio	TPER
Avg. NL Team	81 - 81	162	381	43	1449.0	4.04	1459	507	41	749	2756	4076	79	50	122	-56	-117	79	302	2835	4378	0.647	100.0
Los Angeles Dodgers	81 - 81	162	346	36	1472.2	3.50	1406	567	37	598	2608	4138	76	48	129	-66	-113	74	303	2682	4441	0.604	93.3
Astacio, Pedro	14 - 9	31	0	0	186.1	3.57	165	68	5	78	316	524	7	8	19	-12	-18	4	45	320	569	0.562	87
Candiotti, Tom	8 - 10	32	1	0	213.2	3.12	192	71	6	77	346	605	15	9	25	-6	-14	29	44	375	649	0.578	89
Daal, Omar	2 - 3	0	47	0	35.1	5.09	36	21	0	21	78	94	2	2	1	-1	-4	0	9	78	103	0.757	117
DeSilva, John **	0 - 0	0	3	0	5.1	6.75	6	1	0	2	9	16	0	0	0	-0	-0	0	0	9	16	0.563	87
Gott, Jim	4 - 8	0	62	25	77.2	2.32	71	17	1	26	115	215	7	2	4	-2	-8	3	19	118	234	0.504	78
Gross, Kevin	13 - 13	32	1	0	202.1	4.14	224	74	5	77	380	571	11	6	18	-10	-14	11	41	391	612	0.639	99
Gross, Kip	0 - 0	0	10	0	15.0	0.60	13	4	0	2	19	42	0	0	2	-1	-0	1	1	20	43	0.465	72
Hershiser, Orel	12 - 14	33	0	0	215.2	3.59	201	72	7	105	385	616	12	4	10	-10	-11	5	37	390	653	0.597	92
Martinez, Pedro	10 - 5	2	63	2	107.0	2.61	76	57	4	31	168	302	0	5	6	-4	-7	0	16	168	318	0.528	82
Martinez, Ramon	10 - 12	32	0	0	211.2	3.44	202	104	4	88	398	591	12	5	16	-11	-16	6	44	404	635	0.636	98
McDowell, Roger	5 - 3	0	54	2	68.0	2.25	76	30	2	19	127	188	3	1	8	-6	-5	1	15	128	203	0.631	97
Nichols, Rod	0 - 1	0	4	0	6.1	5.68	9	2	0	5	16	16	1	0	0	-0	-1	0	2	16	18	0.889	137
Trlicek, Ricky	1 - 2	0	41	0	64.0	4.08	59	21	2	28	110	183	2	0	6	-1	-9	-2	12	108	195	0.554	86
Wilson, Steve	1 - 0	0	25	1	25.2	4.56	30	14	1	13	58	74	1	0	5	-1	-1	4	3	62	77	0.805	124
Worrell, Todd	1 - 1	0	35	5	38.2	6.05	46	11	0	26	83	101	3	6	9	-1	-5	12	15	95	116	0.819	126

NOTE: Statistics are for games played with Los Angeles. * Also played for another NL team. ** Also played for an AL team.

1993 Montreal Expos Team TOPR

	TPA	Batter Sub-set						Baserunner Sub-set							Total Offense				Positions Played									
		H	BB	HP	XB	TBB	TBO	SH	SF	SB	CS	GDP	BRB	BRO	NBE	GOC	Ratio	TOPR	C	1B	2B	3B	SS	LF	CF	RF	P
Avg. NL Team	6213	1459	507	41	749	2756	4076	79	50	122	-56	-117	79	302	2835	4378	0.647	100.0									
Montreal Expos	6233	1410	542	48	708	2708	4083	100	50	228	-56	-95	227	301	2935	4384	0.669	103.4									
Alou, Moises	535	138	38	5	95	276	344	3	7	17	-6	-9	12	25	288	369	0.780	121				-	-		102	12	34	-
Berry, Sean	351	78	41	2	61	182	221	3	6	12	-2	-4	15	15	197	236	0.835	129				96					
Bolick, Frank	242	45	23	4	25	97	168	0	2	1	-0	-4	-1	6	96	174	0.552	85		51		24					-
Cianfrocco, Archi *	17	4	0	0	4	8	13	0	0	0	-0	-0	0	0	8	13	0.615	95	-	3				-			
Colbrunn, Gregg	164	39	6	1	21	67	114	1	3	4	-2	-1	5	7	72	121	0.595	92	-	61				-			-
Cordero, Wil	521	118	34	7	66	225	357	4	1	12	-3	-12	2	20	227	377	0.602	93				2	134				
DeShields, Delino	562	142	72	3	37	254	339	4	2	43	-10	-5	34	21	288	360	0.800	124			123						
Fletcher, Darrin	445	101	34	6	49	190	295	5	4	0	-0	-7	2	16	192	311	0.617	95	127								
Floyd, Cliff	31	7	0	0	3	10	24	0	0	0	-0	-0	0	0	10	24	0.417	64	-	10				-			
Frazier, Lou	211	54	16	0	12	82	135	5	1	17	-2	-3	18	11	100	146	0.685	106	-	8	1	-	-	52	7	2	
Grissom, Marquis	693	188	52	3	88	331	442	0	8	53	-10	-10	41	28	372	470	0.791	122				-	-		157		-
Laker, Tim	93	17	2	1	4	24	69	3	1	2	-0	-2	4	6	28	75	0.373	58	43								
Lansing, Mike	555	141	46	5	40	232	350	10	3	23	-5	-16	15	34	247	384	0.643	99	-		25	81	51				
Marrero, Oreste	95	17	14	0	10	41	64	0	0	1	-3	-0	-2	3	39	67	0.582	90	-	32			-				
McIntosh, Tim	21	2	0	0	1	3	19	0	0	0	-0	-0	0	0	3	19	0.158	24	5				-	2	-	6	
Montoyo, Charlie	5	2	0	0	1	3	3	0	0	0	-0	-0	0	0	3	3	1.000	154		-	3			-			
Pride, Curtis	9	4	0	0	6	10	5	0	0	1	-0	-0	1	0	11	5	2.200	340				-	-	2	-		
Ready, Randy	159	34	23	1	13	71	100	1	0	2	-1	-4	-2	6	69	106	0.651	101	-	13	28	3		-			
Siddall, Joe	21	2	1	0	1	4	18	0	0	0	-0	-0	0	0	4	18	0.222	34	15	1		-		1			
Spehr, Tim	99	20	6	1	12	39	67	3	2	2	-0	-0	7	5	46	72	0.639	99	49								
Stairs, Matt	8	3	0	0	1	4	5	0	0	0	-0	-1	-1	1	3	6	0.500	77		-		-	-	1	-		
VanderWal, John	244	50	27	1	30	108	165	0	1	6	-3	-4	0	8	108	173	0.624	96	-	42		-		27	2	10	-
White, Derrick	52	11	2	1	9	23	38	0	0	2	-0	-1	1	1	24	39	0.615	95	-	4				-		132	-
White, Rondell	83	19	7	0	11	37	54	2	1	1	-2	-2	0	7	37	61	0.607	94		-		-	-		19	5	-
Wood, Ted	32	5	3	0	1	9	21	3	0	0	-0	-0	3	3	12	24	0.500	77		-		-	-		8	-	1
STAFF	403	39	15	1	7	62	293	53	2	0	-0	-2	53	57	115	350	0.329	51									

NOTE: Statistics are for games played with Montreal. * Also played for another NL team. ** Also played for an AL team

1993 Montreal Expos Team TPER

	W-L	GS	GR	SV	IP	ERA	Batter Sub-set						Baserunner Sub-set							Total Pitching			
							H	BB	HB	XB	TBB	TBO	SH	SF	SB	CS	GDP	BRB	BRO	NBA	GOE	Ratio	TPER
Avg. NL Team	81-81	162	381	43	1449.0	4.04	1459	507	41	749	2756	4076	79	50	122	-56	-117	79	302	2835	4378	0.647	100.0
Montreal Expos	94-68	163	385	61	1456.2	3.55	1369	521	47	704	2641	4132	82	40	172	-51	-120	123	293	2764	4425	0.625	96.5
Aldred, Scott	1-0	0	3	0	5.1	6.75	9	1	0	5	15	15	0	0	1	-1	-0	0	1	15	16	0.938	145
Barnes, Brian	2-6	8	44	3	100.0	4.41	105	48	0	56	209	278	8	3	8	-3	-7	9	21	218	299	0.729	113
Bottenfield, Kent *	2-5	11	12	0	83.0	4.12	93	33	5	57	188	230	11	1	9	-1	-11	9	24	197	254	0.776	120
Boucher, Denis	3-1	5	0	0	28.1	1.91	24	3	0	11	38	81	0	3	1	-2	-1	1	6	39	87	0.448	69
Fassero, Jeff	12-5	15	41	1	149.2	2.29	119	54	0	41	214	432	7	4	12	-4	-10	9	25	223	457	0.488	75
Gardiner, Mike **	2-3	2	22	0	38.0	5.21	40	19	1	20	80	109	1	3	3	-2	-3	2	9	82	118	0.695	107
Henry, Butch *	1-1	1	9	0	18.1	3.93	18	4	0	10	32	54	0	1	2	-1	-1	1	3	33	57	0.579	89
Heredia, Gil	4-2	9	11	2	57.1	3.92	66	14	2	23	105	159	4	1	7	-0	-5	7	10	112	169	0.663	102
Hill, Ken	9-7	28	0	0	183.2	3.23	163	74	6	67	310	521	9	7	21	-8	-16	13	40	323	561	0.576	89
Jones, Jimmy	4-1	6	6	0	39.2	6.35	47	9	0	30	86	118	1	0	5	-0	-1	5	2	91	120	0.758	117
Looney, Brian	0-0	1	2	0	6.0	3.00	8	2	0	2	12	18	0	0	0	-0	-0	0	0	12	18	0.667	103
Martinez, Dennis	15-9	34	1	1	224.2	3.85	211	64	11	137	423	645	10	4	49	-6	-20	37	40	460	685	0.672	104
Nabholz, Chris	9-8	21	5	0	116.2	4.09	100	63	8	47	218	323	7	4	15	-9	-12	5	32	223	355	0.628	97
Risley, Bill	0-0	0	2	0	3.0	6.00	2	1	1	3	8	8	1	0	0	-0	-0	1	1	9	9	1.000	154
Rojas, Mel	5-8	0	66	10	88.1	2.95	80	30	4	46	160	250	8	6	8	-1	-9	12	24	172	274	0.628	97
Rueter, Kirk	8-0	14	0	0	85.2	2.73	85	18	0	35	138	237	1	0	4	-7	-12	-14	20	124	257	0.482	75
Scott, Tim *	5-2	0	32	1	34.0	3.71	31	19	0	15	65	97	1	0	8	-1	-2	6	4	71	101	0.703	109
Shaw, Jeff	2-7	8	47	0	95.2	4.14	91	32	7	60	190	267	5	2	5	-2	-10	0	19	190	286	0.664	103
Valdez, Sergio	0-0	0	4	0	3.0	9.00	4	1	0	4	9	9	0	0	1	-1	-0	0	1	9	10	0.900	139
Walton, Bruce	0-0	0	4	0	5.2	9.53	11	3	0	4	18	16	2	0	0	-0	-0	2	2	20	18	1.111	172
Wetteland, John	9-3	0	70	43	85.1	1.37	58	28	2	27	115	250	5	1	13	-2	-0	17	8	132	258	0.512	79
Young, Pete	1-0	0	4	0	5.1	3.38	4	0	0	4	8	15	1	0	0	-0	-0	1	1	9	16	0.563	87

NOTE: Statistics are for games played with Montreal. * Also played for another NL team. ** Also played for an AL team.

NEW YORK METS

1993 New York Mets Team TOPR

	TPA	H	BB	HP	XB	TBB	TBQ	SH	SF	SB	CS	GDP	BRB	BRO	NBE	GOC	Ratio	TOPR	C	1B	2B	3B	SS	LF	CF	RF	P
Avg. NL Team	6213	1459	507	41	749	2756	4076	79	50	122	-56	-117	79	302	2835	4378	0.647	100.0									
New York Mets	6057	1350	448	24	776	2598	4098	89	47	79	-51	-109	55	296	2653	4394	0.604	93.3									
Baez, Kevin	143	23	13	0	9	45	103	4	0	0	-0	-1	3	5	48	108	0.444	69	-	-	-	-	52	-	-	-	-
Bogar, Tim	224	50	14	3	22	89	155	1	1	0	-1	-2	-1	5	88	160	0.550	85	-	-	6	7	66	-	-	-	-
Bonilla, Bobby	582	133	72	0	129	334	369	0	8	3	-3	-12	-4	23	330	392	0.842	130	-	5	-	52	-	-	-	85	-
Burnitz, Jeromy	306	64	38	1	61	164	199	2	2	3	-6	-2	-1	12	163	211	0.773	119	-	-	-	-	-	-	20	61	-
Coleman, Vince	399	104	21	0	36	161	269	3	2	38	-13	-2	28	20	189	289	0.654	101	-	-	-	-	-	90	-	-	-
Fernandez, Tony **	204	39	25	1	12	77	134	3	2	6	-2	-4	5	11	82	145	0.566	87	-	-	-	-	48	-	-	-	-
Gallagher, Dave	229	55	20	0	34	109	146	7	1	1	-1	-7	1	16	110	162	0.679	105	-	9	-	-	-	19	39	20	-
Housie, Wayne	17	3	1	0	1	5	13	0	0	0	-0	-0	0	0	5	13	0.385	59	-	-	-	-	-	-	-	2	-
Hundley, Todd	448	95	23	2	54	174	322	2	4	1	-1	-10	-4	17	170	339	0.501	77	123	-	-	-	-	-	-	-	-
Huskey, Butch	44	6	1	0	1	8	35	0	2	0	-0	-0	2	2	10	37	0.270	42	-	-	-	13	-	-	-	-	-
Jackson, Darrin **	91	17	2	0	4	23	70	1	1	0	-0	-0	2	2	25	72	0.347	54	-	-	-	-	-	-	10	16	-
Johnson, Howard	280	56	43	0	33	132	179	0	2	6	-4	-3	1	9	133	188	0.707	109	-	-	-	67	-	-	-	-	-
Kent, Jeff	544	134	30	8	87	259	362	6	4	4	-4	-11	-1	25	258	387	0.667	103	-	-	127	12	2	-	-	-	-
Landrum, Ced	20	5	0	0	1	6	14	1	0	0	-0	-0	1	1	7	15	0.467	72	-	-	-	-	-	3	-	-	-
McKnight, Jeff	183	42	13	1	11	67	122	3	2	0	-0	-3	2	8	69	130	0.531	82	1	10	15	9	29	-	-	-	-
Murray, Eddie	659	174	40	0	111	325	436	0	9	2	-2	-24	-15	35	310	471	0.658	102	-	154	-	-	-	-	-	-	-
Navarro, Tito	18	1	0	0	0	1	16	1	0	0	-0	-1	0	2	. 1	18	0.056	9	-	-	-	2	-	-	-	-	-
O'Brien, Charlie	208	48	14	2	23	87	140	3	1	1	-1	-4	0	9	87	149	0.584	90	65	-	-	-	-	-	-	-	-
Orsulak, Joe	441	116	28	2	47	193	293	0	2	5	-4	-6	-3	12	190	305	0.623	96	-	4	-	-	-	66	40	23	-
Saunders, Doug	73	14	3	0	2	19	53	3	0	0	-0	-2	1	5	20	58	0.345	53	-	-	22	4	-	-	-	-	-
Thompson, Ryan	316	72	19	3	56	150	216	5	1	2	-7	-5	-4	18	146	234	0.624	96	-	-	-	-	-	-	76	-	-
Walker, Chico	230	48	14	0	24	86	165	0	2	7	-0	-3	6	5	92	170	0.541	84	-	-	24	23	-	15	-	1	-
STAFF	398	51	14	1	18	84	287	44	1	0	-2	-7	36	54	120	341	0.358	55									

NOTE: Statistics are for games played with New York. * Also played for another NL team. ** Also played for an AL team

1993 New York Mets Team TPER

	W-L	GS	GR	SV	IP	ERA	H	BB	HB	XB	TBB	TBQ	SH	SF	SB	CS	GDP	BRB	BRO	NBA	GOE	Ratio	TPER
Avg. NL Team	81 - 81	162	381	43	1449.0	4.04	1459	507	41	749	2756	4076	79	50	122	-56	-117	79	302	2835	4378	0.647	100.0
New York Mets	59 - 103	162	297	22	1438.0	4.05	1483	434	50	750	2717	4039	87	58	143	-56	-113	119	314	2836	4353	0.652	100.6
Draper, Mike	1 - 1	1	28	0	42.1	4.25	53	14	0	21	88	109	3	5	7	-1	-8	6	17	94	126	0.746	115
Fernandez, Sid	5 - 6	18	0	0	119.2	2.93	82	36	3	62	183	344	3	1	13	-4	-6	7	14	190	358	0.531	82
Franco, John	4 - 3	0	35	10	36.1	5.20	46	19	1	22	88	101	4	1	4	-0	-2	7	7	95	108	0.880	136
Gibson, Paul **	1 - 1	0	8	0	8.2	5.19	14	2	0	6	22	26	0	0	0	-0	-0	0	0	22	26	0.846	131
Gooden, Dwight	12 - 15	29	0	0	208.2	3.45	188	61	9	90	348	590	11	7	28	-10	-13	23	41	371	631	0.588	91
Gozzo, Mauro	0 - 1	0	10	1	14.0	2.57	11	5	0	4	20	41	0	0	1	-0	-2	-1	2	19	43	0.442	68
Greer, Ken	1 - 0	0	1	0	1.0	0.00	0	0	0	0	0	3	0	0	0	-0	-0	0	0	0	3	0.000	0
Hillman, Eric	2 - 9	22	5	0	145.0	3.97	173	24	4	74	275	406	10	10	11	-8	-14	9	42	284	448	0.634	98
Innis, Jeff	2 - 3	0	67	3	76.2	4.11	81	38	6	33	158	210	9	1	9	-3	-10	6	23	164	233	0.704	109
Jones, Bobby	2 - 4	9	0	0	61.2	3.65	61	22	2	38	123	172	5	3	3	-2	-3	6	13	129	185	0.697	108
Kaiser, Jeff *	0 - 0	0	6	0	4.2	11.57	6	3	0	5	14	11	0	1	4	-1	-1	3	3	17	14	1.214	188
Maddux, Mike	3 - 8	0	58	5	75.0	3.60	67	27	4	28	126	209	7	6	9	-3	-6	13	22	139	231	0.602	93
Manzanillo, Josias **	0 - 0	0	6	0	12.0	3.00	8	9	0	4	21	35	1	1	1	-0	-0	3	2	24	37	0.649	100
Saberhagen, Bret	7 - 7	19	0	0	139.1	3.29	131	17	3	61	212	393	6	6	9	-7	-7	7	26	219	419	0.523	81
Schourek, Pete	5 - 12	18	23	0	128.1	5.96	168	45	3	88	304	359	3	8	10	-4	-6	11	21	315	380	0.829	128
Tanana, Frank **	7 - 15	29	0	0	183.0	4.48	198	48	9	122	377	513	12	4	14	-6	-15	9	37	386	550	0.702	108
Telgheder, Dave	6 - 2	7	17	0	75.2	4.76	82	21	4	53	160	215	2	1	4	-5	-7	-5	15	155	230	0.674	104
Weston, Mickey	0 - 0	0	4	0	5.2	7.94	11	1	1	1	14	17	0	0	1	-0	-0	1	0	15	17	0.882	136
Young, Anthony	1 - 16	10	29	3	100.1	3.77	103	42	1	38	184	285	11	3	15	-2	-13	14	29	198	314	0.631	97

NOTE: Statistics are for games played with New York. * Also played for another NL team. ** Also played for an AL team.

1993 Philadelphia Phillies Team TOPR

	TPA	H	BB	HP	XB	TBB	TBO	SH	SF	SB	CS	GDP	BRB	BRO	NBE	GOC	Ratio	TOPR	C	1B	2B	3B	SS	LF	CF	RF	P
Avg. NL Team	6213	1459	507	41	749	2756	4076	79	50	122	-56	-117	79	302	2835	4378	0.647	100.0									
Philadelphia Phillies	6527	1555	665	42	867	3129	4130	84	51	91	-32	-105	89	272	3218	4402	0.731	112.9									
Amaro, Ruben	58	16	6	0	9	31	32	3	1	0	-0	-1	3	5	34	37	0.919	142	-	-	-	-	-	3	8	6	-
Batiste, Kim	161	44	3	1	24	72	112	0	1	0	-1	-3	-3	5	69	117	0.590	91	-	-	-	58	24	-	-	-	-
Bell, Juan **	73	13	5	1	8	27	52	2	0	0	-1	-0	1	3	28	55	0.509	79	-	-	-	-	22	-	-	-	-
Chamberlain, Wes	306	80	17	1	60	158	204	0	4	2	-1	-7	-2	12	156	216	0.722	112	-	-	-	-	-	-	-	76	-
Daulton, Darren	637	131	117	2	115	365	379	0	8	5	-0	-2	11	10	376	389	0.967	149	146	-	-	-	-	-	-	-	-
Duncan, Mariano	518	140	12	4	67	223	356	4	2	6	-5	-13	-6	24	217	380	0.571	88	-	-	65	-	59	-	-	-	-
Dykstra, Lenny	773	194	129	2	113	438	443	0	5	37	-12	-8	22	25	460	468	0.983	152	-	-	-	-	-	-	160	-	-
Eisenreich, Jim	394	115	26	1	46	188	247	3	2	5	-0	-6	4	11	192	258	0.744	115	-	1	-	-	-	1	3	133	-
Hollins, Dave	640	148	85	5	92	330	395	0	7	2	-3	-15	-9	25	321	420	0.764	118	-	-	-	143	-	-	-	-	-
Incaviglia, Pete	402	101	21	6	94	222	267	0	7	1	-1	-9	-2	17	220	284	0.775	120	-	-	-	-	-	89	-	8	-
Jordan, Ricky	170	46	8	1	21	76	113	0	2	0	-0	-2	0	4	76	117	0.650	100	-	33	-	-	-	-	-	-	-
Kruk, John	651	169	111	0	85	365	366	0	5	6	-2	-10	-1	17	364	383	0.950	147	-	144	-	-	-	-	-	-	-
Lindsey, Doug **	2	1	0	0	0	1	1	0	0	0	-0	-0	0	0	1	1	1.000	154	2	-	-	-	-	-	-	-	-
Longmire, Tony	13	3	0	0	0	3	10	0	0	0	-0	-0	0	0	3	10	0.300	46	-	-	-	-	-	-	2	-	-
Manto, Jeff	19	1	0	1	0	2	17	0	0	0	-0	-0	0	0	2	17	0.118	18	-	-	-	6	1	-	-	-	-
Millette, Joe	14	2	1	0	0	3	8	3	0	0	-0	-1	2	4	5	12	0.417	64	-	-	-	3	7	-	-	-	-
Morandini, Mickey	470	105	34	5	46	190	320	4	2	13	-2	-6	11	14	201	334	0.602	93	-	-	111	-	-	-	-	-	-
Pratt, Todd	95	25	5	1	21	52	62	1	1	0	-0	-2	0	4	52	66	0.788	122	26	-	-	-	-	-	-	-	-
Stocker, Kevin	302	84	30	8	24	146	175	4	1	5	-0	-8	2	13	148	188	0.787	122	-	-	-	-	70	-	-	-	-
Thompson, Milt	387	89	40	2	30	161	251	3	2	9	-4	-8	2	17	163	268	0.608	94	-	-	-	-	-	102	4	-	-
STAFF	440	46	15	1	12	74	320	57	1	0	-0	-4	54	62	128	382	0.335	52									

NOTE: Statistics are for games played with Philadelphia. * Also played for another NL team. ** Also played for an AL team

1993 Philadelphia Phillies Team TPER

	W-L	GS	GR	SV	IP	ERA	H	BB	HB	XB	TBB	TBO	SH	SF	SB	CS	GDP	BRB	BRO	NBA	GOE	Ratio	TPER
Avg. NL Team	81 - 81	162	381	43	1449.0	4.04	1459	507	41	749	2756	4076	79	50	122	-56	-117	79	302	2835	4378	0.647	100.0
Philadelphia Phillies	97 - 65	162	350	46	1472.2	3.97	1419	573	37	712	2741	4223	65	42	101	-49	-93	66	249	2807	4472	0.628	96.9
Andersen, Larry	3 - 2	0	64	0	61.2	2.92	54	21	1	23	99	178	2	0	4	-1	-5	0	8	99	186	0.532	82
Ayrault, Bob **	2 - 0	0	10	0	10.1	9.58	18	10	1	7	36	30	0	0	4	-0	-1	3	1	39	31	1.258	194
Brink, Brad	0 - 0	0	2	0	6.0	3.00	3	3	0	4	10	18	0	0	0	-0	-0	0	0	10	18	0.556	86
Davis, Mark *	1 - 2	0	25	0	31.1	5.17	35	24	1	21	81	93	1	0	1	-0	-3	-1	4	80	97	0.825	127
DeLeon, Jose **	3 - 0	3	21	0	47.0	3.26	39	27	5	24	95	130	3	2	5	-8	-1	1	14	96	144	0.667	103
Fletcher, Paul	0 - 0	0	1	0	0.1	0.00	0	0	0	0	0	1	0	0	0	-0	-0	0	0	0	1	0.000	0
Foster, Kevin	0 - 1	1	1	0	6.2	14.85	13	7	0	12	32	20	0	0	2	-0	-0	2	0	34	20	1.700	263
Green, Tyler	0 - 0	2	1	0	7.1	7.36	16	5	0	5	26	20	0	0	0	-1	-2	3	3	23	23	1.000	154
Greene, Tommy	16 - 4	30	1	0	200.0	3.42	175	62	3	80	320	576	9	9	18	-5	-7	24	30	344	606	0.568	88
Jackson, Danny	12 - 11	32	0	0	210.1	3.77	214	80	4	87	385	599	14	8	15	-7	-15	15	44	400	643	0.622	96
Mason, Roger *	5 - 5	0	34	0	49.2	4.89	47	16	0	35	98	144	1	2	2	-1	-1	3	5	101	149	0.678	105
Mauser, Tim	0 - 0	0	8	0	16.1	4.96	15	7	1	7	30	48	0	0	1	-0	-0	1	0	31	48	0.646	100
Mulholland, Terry	12 - 9	28	1	0	191.0	3.25	177	40	3	102	322	557	5	4	1	-5	-12	-7	26	315	583	0.540	83
Pall, Donn **	1 - 0	0	8	0	17.2	2.55	15	3	0	6	24	50	1	0	0	-0	-2	-1	3	23	53	0.434	67
Rivera, Ben	13 - 9	28	2	0	163.0	5.02	175	85	6	87	353	466	5	5	15	-3	-13	9	26	362	492	0.736	114
Schilling, Curt	16 - 7	34	0	0	235.1	4.02	234	57	4	121	416	671	9	7	11	-11	-13	3	40	419	711	0.589	91
Thigpen, Bobby **	3 - 1	0	17	0	19.1	6.05	23	9	1	11	44	52	2	1	2	-1	-2	2	6	46	58	0.793	122
West, David	6 - 4	0	76	0	86.1	2.92	60	51	5	31	147	249	8	2	5	-3	-7	5	20	152	269	0.565	87
Williams, Mike	1 - 3	4	13	0	51.0	5.29	50	22	0	31	103	148	1	0	6	-3	-2	2	6	105	154	0.682	105
Williams, Mitch	3 - 7	0	65	43	62.0	3.34	56	44	2	18	120	173	4	2	9	-0	-7	8	13	128	186	0.688	106

NOTE: Statistics are for games played with Philadelphia. * Also played for another NL team. ** Also played for an AL team.

PITTSBURGH PIRATES

1993 Pittsburgh Pirates Team TOPR

		Batter Sub-set							Baserunner Sub-set							Total Offense				Positions Played								
	TPA	H	BB	HP	XB	TBB	TBO	SH	SF	SB	CS	GDP	BRB	BRO	NBE	GOC	Ratio	TOPR	C	1B	2B	3B	SS	LF	CF	RF	P
Avg. NL Team	6213	1459	507	41	749	2756	4076	79	50	122	-56	-117	79	302	2835	4378	0.647	100.0									
Pittsburgh Pirates	6269	1482	536	55	697	2770	4067	76	52	92	-55	-128	37	311	2807	4378	0.641	99.0									
Aude, Rich	27	3	1	0	1	5	23	0	0	0	-0	-0	0	0	5	23	0.217	34		7				1			
Bell, Jay	701	187	77	6	77	347	417	13	1	16	-10	-16	4	40	351	457	0.768	119					154				
Bullett, Scott	59	11	3	0	4	18	44	0	1	3	-2	-1	1	4	19	48	0.396	61							18	1	
Clark, Dave	318	75	38	1	48	162	202	0	2	1	-0	-10	-7	12	155	214	0.724	112							40	53	
Cummings, Midre	41	4	4	0	1	9	32	0	1	0	-0	-1	0	2	9	34	0.265	41						5	5	1	
Foley, Tom	211	49	11	0	22	82	145	2	4	0	-0	-4	2	10	84	155	0.542	84		12	35	7	6				
Garcia, Carlos	597	147	31	9	71	258	399	6	5	18	-11	-9	9	31	267	430	0.621	96			140		3				
Goff, Jerry	46	11	8	0	8	27	26	1	0	0	-0	-0	1	1	28	27	1.037	160	14								
King, Jeff	683	180	59	4	68	311	431	1	8	8	-6	-17	-6	32	305	463	0.659	102			2	156	2				
LaValliere, Mike **	5	1	0	0	0	1	4	0	0	0	-0	-0	0	0	1	4	0.250	39	1								
Martin, Al	528	135	42	1	96	274	345	2	3	16	-9	-5	7	19	281	364	0.772	119						81	63	6	
McClendon, Lloyd	207	40	23	0	19	82	141	1	2	0	-3	-4	-4	10	78	151	0.517	80		6					21	47	
Merced, Orlando	527	140	77	1	58	276	307	0	2	3	-3	-9	-7	14	269	321	0.838	129		42						109	
Pennyfeather, William	34	7	0	0	1	8	27	0	0	0	-0	-1	-2	2	6	29	0.207	32						1	15	2	
Prince, Tom	204	35	13	7	20	75	144	2	3	1	-1	-5	0	11	75	155	0.484	75	59								
Shelton, Ben	27	6	3	0	7	16	18	0	0	0	-0	-2	-2	2	14	20	0.700	108		2				6			
Slaught, Don	420	113	29	6	53	201	264	4	4	2	-1	-13	-4	22	197	286	0.689	106	105								
Smith, Lonnie **	252	57	43	5	31	136	142	3	2	9	-4	-3	7	12	143	154	0.929	143						58	3		
Tomberlin, Andy	45	12	2	1	5	20	30	0	0	0	-0	-0	0	0	20	30	0.667	103						6		1	
Van Slyke, Andy	354	100	24	2	45	171	223	0	4	11	-2	-13	0	19	171	242	0.707	109							78		
Wehner, John	43	5	6	0	0	11	30	2	0	0	-0	-0	2	2	13	32	0.406	63				3	3		4	8	2
Wilson, Glenn	15	2	0	0	0	2	12	1	0	0	-0	-0	1	1	3	13	0.231	36								3	2
Womack, Tony	28	2	3	0	0	5	22	1	0	2	-0	-0	3	1	8	23	0.348	54					6				
Young, Kevin	508	106	36	9	48	199	343	5	9	2	-2	-9	5	25	204	368	0.554	86		135		6					
STAFF	388	54	2	3	14	73	296	32	1	0	-0	-6	27	39	100	335	0.299	46									

NOTE: Statistics are for games played with Pittsburgh. * Also played for another NL team. ** Also played for an AL team

1993 Pittsburgh Pirates Team TPER

							Batter Sub-set						Baserunner Sub-set							Total Pitching			
	W-L	GS	GR	SV	IP	ERA	H	BB	HB	XB	TBB	TBO	SH	SF	SB	CS	GDP	BRB	BRO	NBA	GOE	Ratio	TPER
Avg. NL Team	81 - 81	162	381	43	1449.0	4.04	1459	507	41	749	2756	4076	79	50	122	-56	-117	79	302	2835	4378	0.647	100.0
Pittsburgh Pirates	75 - 87	162	384	34	1445.2	4.77	1557	485	46	876	2964	4010	93	55	148	-51	-133	112	332	3076	4342	0.708	109.4
Ballard, Jeff	4 - 1	5	20	0	53.2	4.86	70	15	2	25	112	141	5	1	2	-1	-13	-6	20	106	161	0.658	102
Belinda, Stan **	3 - 1	0	40	19	42.1	3.61	35	11	1	21	68	121	1	2	13	-0	-3	13	6	81	127	0.638	99
Candelaria, John	0 - 3	0	24	1	19.2	8.24	25	9	1	15	50	55	1	1	1	-1	-1	1	4	51	59	0.864	134
Cooke, Steve	10 - 10	32	0	0	210.2	3.89	207	59	3	136	405	594	13	6	22	-9	-10	22	38	427	632	0.676	104
Dewey, Mark	1 - 2	0	21	7	26.2	2.36	14	10	3	7	34	75	3	3	2	-0	-1	7	7	41	82	0.500	77
Hope, John	0 - 2	7	0	0	38.0	4.03	47	8	2	21	78	103	5	1	3	-2	-4	3	12	90	115	0.704	109
Johnston, Joel	2 - 4	0	33	2	53.1	3.38	38	19	0	33	90	149	4	0	2	-1	-5	0	10	90	159	0.566	87
Menendez, Tony	2 - 0	0	14	0	21.0	3.00	20	4	1	16	41	58	1	1	0	-1	-1	0	4	41	62	0.661	102
Miceli, Danny	0 - 0	0	9	0	5.1	5.06	6	3	0	2	11	16	0	0	2	-0	-0	2	0	13	16	0.813	125
Miller, Paul	0 - 0	2	1	0	10.0	5.40	15	2	0	9	26	28	2	0	1	-0	-0	3	2	29	30	0.967	149
Minor, Blas	8 - 6	0	65	2	94.1	4.10	94	26	4	44	168	264	6	4	5	-4	-6	5	20	173	284	0.609	94
Moeller, Dennis	1 - 0	0	10	0	16.1	9.92	26	7	1	10	44	47	1	0	2	-1	-1	1	3	45	50	0.900	139
Neagle, Denny	3 - 5	7	43	1	81.1	5.31	82	37	3	52	174	236	1	1	16	-5	-1	12	8	186	244	0.762	118
Otto, Dave	3 - 4	8	20	0	68.0	5.03	85	28	3	45	161	183	6	1	8	-2	-14	-1	23	160	206	0.777	120
Petkovsek, Mark	3 - 0	0	26	0	32.1	6.96	43	9	0	36	88	88	4	1	7	-0	-2	10	7	98	95	1.032	159
Robertson, Rich	0 - 1	0	9	0	9.0	6.00	15	4	0	3	22	24	1	0	1	-0	-2	0	3	22	27	0.815	126
Shouse, Brian	0 - 0	0	6	0	4.0	9.00	7	2	0	4	13	12	0	1	0	-0	-0	1	1	14	13	1.077	166
Smith, Zane	3 - 7	14	0	0	83.0	4.55	97	22	0	49	168	228	6	0	7	-2	-13	-2	21	166	249	0.667	103
Toliver, Fred	1 - 0	0	12	0	21.2	3.74	20	8	2	8	38	55	2	3	2	-0	-3	4	8	42	63	0.667	103
Tomlin, Randy	4 - 8	18	0	0	98.1	4.85	109	15	5	73	202	266	8	8	7	-4	-8	11	28	213	294	0.724	112
Wagner, Paul	8 - 8	17	27	2	141.1	4.27	143	42	1	70	256	400	6	7	18	-7	-9	15	29	271	429	0.632	98
Wakefield, Tim	6 - 11	20	4	0	128.1	5.61	145	75	9	82	311	353	7	5	8	-5	-12	3	29	314	382	0.822	127
Walk, Bob	13 - 14	32	0	0	187.0	5.68	214	70	5	115	404	514	10	9	19	-6	-24	8	49	412	563	0.732	113

NOTE: Statistics are for games played with Pittsburgh. * Also played for another NL team. ** Also played for an AL team.

1993 St. Louis Cardinals Team TOPR

	TPA	H	BB	HP	XB	TBB	TBO	SH	SF	SB	CS	GDP	BRB	BRO	NBE	GOC	Ratio	TOPR	C	1B	2B	3B	SS	LF	CF	RF	P
Avg. NL Team	6213	1459	507	41	749	2756	4076	79	50	122	-56	-117	79	302	2835	4378	0.647	100.0									
St. Louis Cardinals	6279	1508	588	27	684	2807	4043	59	54	153	-73	-129	64	315	2871	4358	0.659	101.8									
Alicea, Luis	421	101	47	4	34	186	261	1	7	11	-1	-10	8	19	194	280	0.693	107	-	-	96	1	-	4	-	-	-
Brewer, Rod	169	42	17	1	14	74	105	2	2	1	-0	-5	0	9	74	114	0.649	100	-	32	-	-	-	15	-	19	1
Canseco, Ozzie	18	3	1	0	0	4	14	0	0	0	-0	-0	0	0	4	14	0.286	44	-	-	-	-	-	15	-	19	1
Cromer, Tripp	24	2	1	0	0	3	21	0	0	0	-0	-0	0	0	3	21	0.143	22	-	-	-	-	5	-	-	-	-
Gilkey, Bernard	622	170	56	4	98	328	387	0	5	15	-10	-16	-6	31	322	418	0.770	119	-	3	-	-	-	133	-	2	-
Jefferies, Gregg	612	186	62	2	78	328	358	0	4	46	-10	-15	25	29	353	387	0.912	141	-	140	1	-	-	-	-	-	-
Jones, Tim	73	16	9	1	6	32	45	2	0	2	-2	-0	2	4	34	49	0.694	107	-	-	7	-	21	-	-	-	-
Jordan, Brian	242	69	12	4	52	137	154	0	3	6	-6	-6	-3	15	134	169	0.793	122	-	-	-	-	-	23	37	12	-
Lankford, Ray	495	97	81	3	44	225	310	1	3	14	-14	-5	-1	23	224	333	0.673	104	-	-	-	-	-	-	121	-	-
Maclin, Lonnie	14	1	0	0	0	1	12	0	1	1	-0	-0	2	1	3	13	0.231	36	-	-	-	-	-	5	-	-	-
Oquendo, Jose	89	15	12	0	0	27	58	3	1	0	-0	-5	-1	9	26	67	0.388	60	-	-	16	-	22	-	-	-	-
Pagnozzi, Tom	355	85	19	1	38	143	245	0	5	1	-0	-7	-1	12	142	257	0.553	85	92	-	-	-	-	-	-	-	-
Pappas, Erik	266	63	35	0	15	113	165	0	3	1	-3	-7	-6	13	107	178	0.601	93	63	2	-	-	-	1	-	15	-
Pena, Geronimo	289	65	25	4	38	132	189	4	2	13	-5	-3	11	14	143	203	0.704	109	-	-	64	-	-	-	-	-	-
Perry, Gerald	116	33	18	0	17	68	65	0	0	1	-1	-4	-4	5	64	70	0.914	141	-	15	-	-	-	-	-	1	-
Ronan, Marc	12	1	0	0	0	1	11	0	0	0	-0	-0	0	0	1	11	0.091	14	6	-	-	-	-	-	-	-	-
Royer, Stan	48	14	2	0	5	21	32	0	0	0	-1	-2	-3	3	18	35	0.514	79	-	2	-	10	-	-	-	-	-
Smith, Ozzie	603	157	43	1	37	238	388	7	7	21	-8	-11	16	33	254	421	0.603	93	-	-	-	-	134	-	-	-	-
Villanueva, Hector	59	8	4	0	10	22	47	0	0	0	-0	-3	-3	3	19	50	0.380	59	17	-	-	-	-	-	-	-	-
Whiten, Mark	626	142	58	2	96	298	420	0	4	15	-8	-11	0	23	298	443	0.673	104	-	-	-	-	-	-	-	22	138
Woodson, Tracy	79	16	1	0	2	19	61	0	1	0	-0	-1	0	2	19	63	0.302	47	-	11	-	28	-	-	-	-	-
Zeile, Todd	647	158	70	0	89	317	413	0	6	5	-4	-15	-8	25	309	438	0.705	109	-	-	-	153	-	-	-	-	-
STAFF	400	64	15	0	11	90	282	39	0	0	-0	-3	36	42	126	324	0.389	60									

NOTE: Statistics are for games played with St. Louis. * Also played for another NL team. ** Also played for an AL team

1993 St. Louis Cardinals Team TPER

	W-L	GS	GR	SV	IP	ERA	H	BB	HB	XB	TBB	TBO	SH	SF	SB	CS	GDP	BRB	BRO	NBA	GOE	Ratio	TPER
Avg. NL Team	81 - 81	162	381	43	1449.0	4.04	1459	507	41	749	2756	4076	79	50	122	-56	-117	79	302	2835	4378	0.647	100.0
St. Louis Cardinals	87 - 75	162	423	54	1453.0	4.10	1553	383	43	826	2805	4079	80	57	112	-55	-134	60	326	2865	4405	0.650	100.5
Arocha, Rene	11 - 8	29	3	0	188.0	3.78	197	31	3	110	341	530	8	5	14	-9	-21	3	43	338	573	0.590	91
Batchelor, Richard	0 - 0	0	9	0	10.0	8.10	14	3	0	5	22	25	1	2	2	-0	-1	4	4	26	29	0.897	138
Burns, Todd **	0 - 4	0	24	0	30.2	6.16	32	9	0	32	73	85	3	2	0	-1	-1	3	7	76	92	0.826	128
Cormier, Rheal	7 - 6	21	17	0	145.1	4.33	163	27	4	99	293	411	10	4	3	-2	-16	-1	32	292	443	0.659	102
Dixon, Steve	0 - 0	0	4	0	2.2	33.75	7	5	0	5	17	6	2	0	0	-0	-1	1	3	18	9	2.000	309
Guetterman, Lee	3 - 3	0	40	1	46.0	2.93	41	16	2	15	74	130	1	2	5	-0	-7	1	10	75	140	0.536	83
Kilgus, Paul	1 - 0	1	21	1	28.2	0.63	18	8	1	6	33	82	0	0	4	-2	-3	-1	5	32	87	0.368	57
Lancaster, Les	4 - 1	0	50	0	61.1	2.93	56	21	1	31	109	175	5	1	3	-3	-3	3	12	112	187	0.599	93
Magrane, Joe **	8 - 10	20	2	0	116.0	4.97	127	37	5	72	241	317	6	7	13	-7	-14	5	34	246	351	0.701	108
Murphy, Rob	5 - 7	0	73	1	64.2	4.87	73	20	1	35	129	179	4	2	3	-1	-11	-3	18	126	197	0.640	99
Olivares, Omar	5 - 3	9	49	1	118.2	4.17	134	54	9	63	260	332	4	4	12	-5	-11	4	24	264	356	0.742	115
Osborne, Donovan	10 - 7	26	0	0	155.2	3.76	153	47	7	91	298	442	6	2	4	-5	-13	-6	26	292	468	0.624	96
Perez, Mike	7 - 2	0	65	7	72.2	2.48	65	20	1	26	112	201	5	5	8	-2	-5	11	17	123	218	0.564	87
Smith, Lee	2 - 4	0	55	43	50.0	4.50	49	9	0	47	105	146	0	2	8	-2	-1	7	5	112	151	0.742	115
Tewksbury, Bob	17 - 10	32	0	0	213.2	3.83	258	20	6	95	379	599	15	9	21	-6	-15	24	45	403	644	0.626	97
Urbani, Tom	1 - 3	9	9	0	62.0	4.65	73	26	0	34	133	174	4	6	1	-6	-6	-1	22	132	196	0.673	104
Watson, Allen	6 - 7	15	1	0	86.0	4.60	90	28	3	57	178	242	6	4	11	-4	-5	12	19	190	261	0.728	112
Brewer, Rod	0 - 0	0	1	0	1.0	45.00	3	2	0	3	8	3	0	0	0	-0	-0	0	0	8	3	2.667	412

NOTE: Statistics are for games played with St. Louis. * Also played for another NL team. ** Also played for an AL team.

SAN DIEGO PADRES

1993 San Diego Padres Team TOPR

	TPA	H	BB	HP	XB	TBB	TBO	SH	SF	SB	CS	GDP	BRB	BRO	NBE	GOC	Ratio	TOPR	C	1B	2B	3B	SS	LF	CF	RF	P
		Batter Sub-set						**Baserunner Sub-set**							**Total Offense**				**Positions Played**								
Avg. NL Team	6213	1459	507	41	749	2756	4076	79	50	122	-56	-117	79	302	2891	4378	0.647	100.0									
San Diego Padres	6137	1386	443	59	754	2642	4117	80	50	92	-41	-110	71	281	2754	4398	0.617	95.3									
Ausmus, Brad	167	41	6	0	25	72	119	0	0	2	-0	-2	0	2	72	121	0.595	92	49								
Bean, Billy	192	46	6	2	24	78	131	2	5	2	-4	-4	1	15	83	146	0.541	84		12				11	17	32	
Bell, Derek	585	142	23	12	84	261	400	0	8	26	-5	-7	22	20	288	420	0.674	104				19		1	119	6	
Brown, Jarvis	157	31	15	6	13	65	102	2	1	3	-3	-4	-1	10	67	112	0.571	88						5	40		
Cianfrocco, Archi *	307	68	17	3	47	135	211	2	5	2	-0	-9	0	16	135	227	0.595	92		39		64					
Clark, Phil	256	75	8	5	44	132	165	1	2	2	-0	-2	3	5	135	170	0.794	123	11	24		5	1	22		15	
Gardner, Jeff	452	106	45	1	38	190	298	1	1	2	-6	-3	-5	11	191	309	0.599	92			133	1	1				
Geren, Bob	162	31	13	0	15	59	114	4	0	0	-0	-4	0	8	59	122	0.484	75	49	1		1					
Gutierrez, Ricky	495	110	50	5	35	200	328	1	1	4	-3	-7	-4	12	199	341	0.576	89			6	4	117	3		2	
Gwynn, Tony	534	175	36	1	68	280	314	1	7	14	-1	-18	3	27	284	341	0.830	128							4	121	
Higgins, Kevin	202	40	16	3	6	65	141	1	1	0	-1	-6	-5	9	61	150	0.400	62	59	3	1	4		1		2	
Lopez, Luis	44	5	0	0	1	6	38	0	1	0	-0	-0	1	1	7	39	0.179	28			15						
McGriff, Fred *	349	83	42	1	67	193	219	0	4	4	-3	-9	-4	16	192	235	0.804	124		83							
Nieves, Melvin	51	9	3	1	6	19	38	0	0	0	-0	-0	0	0	19	38	0.500	77								15	
Plantier, Phil	536	111	61	7	124	303	351	1	5	4	-5	-4	1	15	309	366	0.831	128						134			
Sheffield, Gary *	282	76	18	3	46	143	182	0	3	5	-1	-9	-2	13	142	195	0.723	112				67					
Sherman, Darrell	74	14	6	3	1	24	49	1	1	2	-1	-0	3	3	28	52	0.519	80						24	6	1	
Shipley, Craig	245	54	10	3	21	88	176	1	1	12	-3	-3	8	8	99	184	0.522	81			12	37	38	2	3		
Staton, Dave	46	11	3	1	18	33	31	0	0	0	-0	-2	-2	2	31	33	0.939	145		12							
Stillwell, Kurt *	135	26	11	1	7	45	95	2	0	4	-3	-2	1	7	49	102	0.451	70				3	30				
Teufel, Tim	231	50	27	0	36	113	150	3	1	2	-2	-9	-5	15	110	165	0.655	101		8	52	9					
Velasquez, Guillermo	157	30	13	0	11	54	113	0	1	0	-0	-3	-2	4	52	117	0.444	69		38				4		2	
Walters, Dan	102	19	7	0	6	32	75	0	1	0	-0	-2	-1	3	31	78	0.397	61	26								
STAFF	376	33	7	1	11	52	277	57	1	2	-0	-1	59	59	111	336	0.330	51									

NOTE: Statistics are for games played with San Diego. * Also played for another NL team. ** Also played for an AL team.

1993 San Diego Padres Team TPER

	W-L	GS	GR	SV	IP	ERA	H	BB	HB	XB	TBB	TBO	SH	SF	SB	CS	GDP	BRB	BRO	NBA	GOE	Ratio	TPER
							Batter Sub-set						**Baserunner Sub-set**							**Total Pitching**			
Avg. NL Team	81 – 81	162	381	43	1449.0	4.04	1459	507	41	749	2756	4076	79	50	122	-56	-117	79	302	2835	4378	0.647	100.0
San Diego Padres	61 – 101	162	397	32	1437.2	4.23	1470	558	34	762	2824	4050	89	62	142	-68	-97	128	316	2952	4366	0.676	104.4
Ashby, Andy *	3 – 6	12	0	0	69.0	5.48	79	24	1	57	161	189	3	4	4	-1	-12	-2	20	159	209	0.761	118
Benes, Andy	15 – 15	34	0	0	230.2	3.78	200	86	4	120	410	662	10	6	21	-7	-15	15	38	425	700	0.607	94
Brocail, Doug	4 – 13	24	0	0	128.1	4.56	143	42	4	81	270	363	10	8	10	-4	-5	19	27	289	390	0.741	114
Davis, Mark *	0 – 3	0	35	4	38.1	3.52	44	20	0	27	91	105	3	1	7	-2	-3	6	9	97	114	0.851	131
Eiland, Dave	0 – 3	9	1	0	48.1	5.21	58	17	1	26	102	137	2	2	8	-3	-7	2	14	104	151	0.689	106
Ettles, Mark	1 – 0	0	14	0	18.0	6.50	23	4	0	15	42	52	0	2	0	-0	-1	1	3	43	55	0.782	121
Gomez, Pat	1 – 2	1	26	0	31.2	5.12	35	19	0	14	68	84	1	4	0	-3	-2	0	10	68	94	0.723	112
Harris, Gene	6 – 6	0	59	23	59.1	3.03	57	37	1	15	110	166	5	2	10	-0	-6	11	13	121	179	0.676	104
Harris, Greg *	10 – 9	22	0	0	152.0	3.67	151	39	3	90	283	436	8	2	17	-6	-5	16	21	299	457	0.654	101
Hernandez, Jeremy **	0 – 2	0	21	0	34.1	4.72	41	7	0	15	63	95	2	1	1	-2	-2	0	7	63	102	0.618	95
Hoffman, Trevor *	2 – 4	0	39	3	54.1	4.31	56	20	1	33	110	156	2	4	6	-1	-1	10	8	120	164	0.732	113
Hurst, Bruce *	0 – 1	2	0	0	4.1	12.46	9	3	0	1	13	13	1	0	3	-1	-1	2	3	15	16	0.938	145
Martinez, Pedro	3 – 1	0	32	0	37.0	2.43	23	13	1	17	54	111	0	0	3	-2	-2	-1	4	53	115	0.461	71
Mason, Roger *	0 – 7	0	34	0	50.0	3.24	43	18	2	10	73	135	6	3	3	-4	-3	5	16	78	151	0.517	80
Mauser, Tim *	0 – 1	0	28	0	37.2	3.58	36	17	0	24	77	109	1	1	3	-3	-1	1	6	78	115	0.678	105
Rodriguez, Rich *	2 – 3	0	34	2	30.0	3.30	34	9	1	11	55	87	2	0	3	-2	-1	2	5	57	92	0.620	96
Sanders, Scott	3 – 3	9	0	0	52.1	4.13	54	23	1	20	98	150	1	2	4	-4	-4	-1	11	97	161	0.602	93
Scott, Tim *	2 – 0	0	24	0	37.2	2.39	38	15	4	14	71	107	2	2	10	-1	-1	12	6	83	113	0.735	113
Seanez, Rudy	0 – 0	0	3	0	3.1	13.50	8	2	0	4	14	9	1	0	0	-0	-1	0	2	14	11	1.273	197
Seminara, Frank	3 – 3	7	11	0	46.1	4.47	53	21	3	28	105	127	6	2	3	-3	-3	5	14	110	141	0.780	120
Taylor, Kerry	0 – 5	7	29	0	68.1	6.45	72	49	4	28	153	188	10	3	13	-3	-4	19	20	172	208	0.827	128
Whitehurst, Wally	4 – 7	19	2	0	105.2	3.83	109	30	3	59	201	286	5	8	3	-7	-11	-2	31	199	317	0.628	97
Worrell, Tim	2 – 7	16	5	0	100.2	4.92	104	43	0	53	200	283	8	5	10	-9	-6	8	28	208	311	0.669	103

NOTE: Statistics are for games played with San Diego. * Also played for another NL team. ** Also played for an AL team.

1993 San Francisco Giants Team TOPR

	TPA	Batter Sub-set H	BB	HP	XB	TBB	TBO	Baserunner Sub-set SH	SF	SB	CS	GDP	BRB	BRO	Total Offense NBE	GOC	Ratio	TOPR	Positions Played C	1B	2B	3B	SS	LF	CF	RF	P
Avg. NL Team	6213	1459	507	41	749	2756	4076	79	50	122	-56	-117	79	302	2835	4378	0.647	100.0									
San Francisco Giants	6271	1534	516	46	839	2935	4023	102	50	120	-65	-121	86	338	3021	4361	0.693	107.0									
Allanson, Andy	26	4	1	0	1	6	20	1	0	0	-0	-1	0	2	6	22	0.273	42	8	2							
Benjamin, Mike	165	29	9	4	19	61	117	6	0	0	-0	-3	3	9	64	126	0.508	78			23	16	23				
Benzinger, Todd	194	51	13	0	29	93	126	1	3	0	-0	-2	2	6	95	132	0.720	111		40		1		7			
Bonds, Barry	674	181	126	2	184	493	358	0	7	29	-12	-11	13	30	506	388	1.304	201						157			
Carreon, Mark	169	49	13	1	32	95	101	0	5	1	-0	-8	-2	13	93	114	0.816	126		3				9	5	30	
Clark, Will	567	139	63	6	73	281	352	1	6	2	-2	-10	-3	19	278	371	0.749	116		129							
Clayton, Royce	607	155	38	5	49	247	394	8	7	11	-10	-16	0	41	247	435	0.568	88					153				
Colbert, Craig	40	6	3	0	5	14	31	0	0	0	-0	-0	0	0	14	31	0.452	70	10		2	1					
Faneyte, Rikkert	17	2	2	0	0	4	13	0	0	0	-0	-0	0	0	4	13	0.308	48							1	5	
Faries, Paul	39	8	1		4	13	28	1	1	2	-0	-1	3	3	16	31	0.516	80				7	1	4			
Hosey, Steve	3	1	1	0	1	3	1	0	0	0	-0	-0	0	0	3	1	3.000	463								1	
Johnson, Erik	5	2	0	0	2	4	3	0	0	0	-0	-0	0	0	4	3	1.333	206			2	1	1				
Lewis, Darren	572	132	30	7	37	206	390	12	1	46	-15	-4	40	32	246	422	0.583	90							131		
Manwaring, Kirt	486	119	41	6	32	198	313	5	2	1	-3	-14	-9	24	189	337	0.561	87	130								
Martinez, Dave	268	58	27	0	29	114	183	0	0	6	-3	-5	-2	8	112	191	0.586	91						3	43	34	
McGee, Willie	519	143	38	1	42	224	332	3	2	10	-9	-12	-6	26	218	358	0.609	94								126	
McNamara, Jim	7	1	0	0	0	1	6	0	0	0	-0	-0	0	0	1	6	0.167	26	4								
Mercedes, Luis **	29	4	1	2	2	9	21	1	0	0	-1	-0	0	2	9	23	0.391	60						1	3	1	
Patterson, John	16	3	0	0	3	6	13	0	0	0	-0	-0	-1	1	5	14	0.357	55									
Phillips, J.R.	16	5	0	0	6	11	11	0	0	0	-0	-0	0	0	11	11	1.000	154		5							
Reed, Jeff	136	31	16	0	21	68	88	0	1	0	-1	-2	-2	4	66	92	0.717	111	37								
Scarsone, Steve	112	26	4	0	15	45	77	4	1	0	-1	-0	4	6	49	83	0.590	91		6	20	8					
Thompson, Robby	559	154	45	7	91	297	340	9	4	10	-4	-7	12	24	309	364	0.849	131			128						
Williams, Matt	619	170	27	4	155	356	409	0	9	1	-3	-12	-5	24	351	433	0.811	125				144					
STAFF	425	60	17	1	7	85	296	50	1	1	-0	-13	39	64	124	360	0.344	53									

NOTE: Statistics are for games played with San Francisco. * Also played for another NL team. ** Also played for an AL team

1993 San Francisco Giants Team TPER

	W-L	GS	GR	SV	IP	ERA	Batter Sub-set H	BB	HB	XB	TBB	TBO	Baserunner Sub-set SH	SF	SB	CS	GDP	BRB	BRO	Total Pitching NBA	GOE	Ratio	TPER
Avg. NL Team	81 – 81	162	381	43	1449.0	4.04	1459	507	41	749	2756	4076	79	50	122	-56	-117	79	302	2835	4378	0.647	100.0
San Francisco Giants	103 – 59	162	414	50	1456.2	3.63	1385	442	50	735	2612	4087	74	38	81	-66	-130	-3	308	2609	4395	0.594	91.7
Beck, Rod	3 – 1	0	76	48	79.1	2.16	57	13	3	38	111	227	6	3	1	-0	-4	6	13	117	240	0.488	75
Black, Bud	8 – 2	16	0	0	93.2	3.56	89	33	2	53	177	258	8	4	9	-8	-10	3	30	180	288	0.625	97
Brantley, Jeff	5 – 6	12	41	0	113.2	4.28	112	46	7	78	243	321	5	5	1	-5	-5	1	20	244	341	0.716	111
Bross, Terry	0 – 0	0	2	0	2.0	9.00	3	1	0	3	7	6	0	0	0	-0	-0	0	0	7	6	1.167	180
Brummett, Greg **	2 – 3	8	0	0	46.0	4.70	53	13	0	34	100	126	1	2	7	-0	-5	5	8	105	134	0.784	121
Burba, Dave	10 – 3	5	49	0	95.1	4.25	95	37	3	56	191	264	6	3	10	-3	-5	11	17	202	281	0.719	111
Burkett, John	22 – 7	34	0	0	231.2	3.65	224	40	11	98	373	655	8	4	14	-14	-21	-9	47	364	702	0.519	80
Deshaies, Jim **	2 – 2	4	1	0	17.0	4.24	24	6	1	13	44	45	1	0	0	-3	-3	-5	7	39	52	0.750	116
Hickerson, Bryan	7 – 5	15	32	0	120.1	4.26	137	39	1	65	242	333	11	4	4	-6	-11	2	32	244	365	0.668	103
Jackson, Mike	6 – 6	0	81	1	77.1	3.03	58	24	3	31	116	226	4	2	1	-1	-2	4	9	120	235	0.511	79
Layana, Tim	0 – 0	0	1	0	2.0	22.50	7	1	0	5	13	6	1	0	2	-0	-0	3	1	16	7	2.286	353
Minutelli, Gino	0 – 1	0	9	0	14.1	3.77	7	15	0	9	31	39	1	2	2	-0	-0	5	3	36	42	0.857	132
Righetti, Dave	1 – 1	0	51	1	47.1	5.70	58	17	1	43	119	132	2	0	1	-4	-6	-7	12	112	144	0.778	120
Rogers, Kevin	2 – 2	0	64	0	80.2	2.68	71	28	4	19	122	230	0	1	6	-2	-9	-4	12	118	242	0.488	75
Sanderson, Scott **	4 – 2	8	3	0	48.2	3.51	48	7	1	40	96	140	3	2	2	-2	-0	5	7	101	147	0.687	106
Swift, Bill	21 – 8	34	0	0	232.2	2.82	195	55	6	86	342	666	4	2	12	-11	-27	-20	44	322	710	0.454	70
Torres, Salomon	3 – 5	8	0	0	44.2	4.03	37	27	1	22	87	123	7	1	5	-3	-3	7	14	94	137	0.686	106
Wilson, Trevor	7 – 5	18	4	0	110.0	3.60	110	40	6	42	198	290	6	3	4	-4	-19	-10	32	188	322	0.584	90

NOTE: Statistics are for games played with San Francisco. * Also played for another NL team. ** Also played for an AL team.